7 1 0 BOOK STORE
Top CASH For BOOKS Anytime
"YOURS — FOR LOWER COSTS
OF HIGHER EDUCATION "

WILDLIFE MANAGEMENT TECHNIQUES MANUAL

FOURTH EDITION: REVISED

Edited by: SANFORD D. SCHEMNITZ
Professor, Department Head
New Mexico State University

Illustrated by: LARRY TOSCHIK
Phoenix, Arizona

THE WILDLIFE SOCIETY
WASHINGTON, D.C.

1980

Wildlife Management Techniques Manual

Printed in the United States of America for The Wildlife Society

Mention of trade names does not imply endorsement of the product.

This book is the fourth in a series on wildlife techniques published by the Wildlife Society

Editor, Henry S. Mosby
Manual of Game Investigational Techniques
(1) First Edition—May 1960
Second Printing—February 1961
Wildlife Investigational Techniques
(2) Second Edition—May 1963
Second Printing (Revised)—March 1965
Third through Sixth Printing—March 1966 to September 1968

Editor, Robert H. Giles, Jr.
Wildlife Management Techniques
(3) Third Edition—June 1969
Second Printing (Revised)—January 1971
Third Printing—May 1972

Editor, Sanford D. Schemnitz
Wildlife Management Techniques Manual
(4) Fourth Edition—September 1980

ISBN 0-933564-08-2

Library of Congress Cataloging in Publication Data

Main entry under title:

Wildlife management techniques manual.

Third ed., prepared by the Wildlife Society's Wildlife Techniques Manual Committee, published under title: Wildlife management techniques.
Bibliography: p.
Includes index.
1. Wildlife managment--Technique.
I. Schemnitz, Sanford D. II. Wildlife Society. Wildlife Techniques Manual Committee. Wildlife management techniques. III. Title.
SK353.W59 639.9 80-19970
ISBN 0-933564-08-2

FOREWORD

Through information and timely publications, The Wildlife Society seeks to encourage improved management of wildlife on a sound biological basis and maintain high professional standards. This volume is evidence of professional wildlifers' pledge to help ensure that wildlife, along with other natural resources, continue to have a prominent place in our culture.

Meeting that goal hinges on the reliability of techniques used to assess wildlife populations and habitats, as well as citizen attitudes and demands. Wildlife biologists and managers always have sought precision for their methods, data and reports through colleague consultations. In addition, since 1 January 1970, when the National Environmental Policy Act became effective, court challenges and reviews have expanded demands for accuracy.

This volume culminates a half-century (1930–1980) of response to demands for a useful reference of reliable methods to generate information required to carry out resource management on a sound basis. Use of any of the techniques described here, adapted to fit local and regional situations, should help improve the quality of data.

Completion of this fourth edition, as well as its predecessors, is the result of generous contributions of dozens of authors, editors, and reviewers that volunteered their time and talents. The Wildlife Society is grateful for their dedicated services.

It is a distinct privilege to release this fourth edition for use by students, educators, biologists, resource managers and others. We believe it deserves a prominent place in any library.

Laurence R. Jahn

PREFACE

The *Wildlife Management Techniques Manual*, fourth edition, is an updating and enlargement of the third edition. The latter, ably edited by Robert H. Giles, Jr., has been well received, as evidenced by it being the best-selling publication of The Wildlife Society.

As editor, one of my main dilemmas has been how to maintain key information from past editions, add new material, and yet keep the size and cost of the manual within reach of students and wildlifers in the field. As a result, some readers—particularly veteran researchers—will find that this edition, like previous ones, lacks the in-depth treatment they may desire. Nevertheless, readers should find an introduction to key literature on each subject. Literature references cited usually are those that describe a technique in greatest detail. I directly converted English to metric units wherever feasible. Many of these conversions resulted in decimal fractions which should not imply undue accuracy to the reader.

Responses by members of The Wildlife Society to an invitation to offer suggestions for building this manual have been gratifying. Many members, too numerous to mention individually, submitted relevant proposals for revision and expansion. Past editors Mosby and Giles provided encouragement and sage advice. All of these contributions are most appreciated.

My role as editor, at best, was only to serve as a catalyst. Success of the volume rests with the quality and acceptance of the individual chapters. Most authors accepted the vigorous job of writing with enthusiasm, meeting deadlines promptly and accepting editorial suggestions graciously. It has been a distinct pleasure to work with all of them.

We anticipate the fourth edition will stimulate development of new and improved research-management techniques, as did the past three editions. Eleven new chapters in this volume, on subjects touched on lightly or not at all in previous editions, emphasize the remarkable progress in wildlife management in the past 10 years.

Editorial assistance of a number of people was enlisted to cover the broad spectrum of wildlife management techniques. I gratefully acknowledge editorial suggestions and assistance of the following individuals: A. W. Alldredge, E. D. Bailey, C. F. Banasiak, C. E. Braun, C. J. Brink, J. W. Caslick, J. R. Cooley, H. N. Coulombe, R. D. Crawford, C. A. Davis, D. J. Decker, R. L. Downing, R. J. Ellis, D. L. Gilbert, J. Ghiselin, J. G. Gleich, R. J. Greenwood, G. W. Gullion, S. L. Hatch, V. W. Howard, Jr., L. J. Hunt, J. F. Keefe, A. L. Kolz, R. A. Lange, M. S. Lenarz, A. S. Leopold, J. B. Madson, R. L. Marchinton, R. E. Marsh, W. W. Mautz, J. F. McInroy, K. A. Nagy, V. F. Nettles, R. D. Owens, H. D. Parker, D. Peck, R. E. Pieper, J. E. Pinder III, E. E. Provost, H. D. Saastamoinen, M. Schamberger, H. L. Short, G. S. Smith, G. M. Southward, R. St. Ores, F. J. Svoboda, T. W. Taylor, R. E. Tomlinson, D. O. Trainer, Jr., D. A. Wade, J. P. Weigand, L. E. Williams, Jr.

Presidents of The Wildlife Society, B. T. Crawford, R. A. McCabe, J. W. Thomas, W. L. Pengelly and L. R. Jahn, and members of The Wildlife Society Council have supported my efforts. Former Executive Director F. G. Evenden and former Field Director M. D. Zagata deserve thanks for their help in expediting manuscript completion. Current Executive Director R. N. Denney and Field Director H. E. Hodgdon have provided counsel and assistance in final stages of preparing the manuscript for publication.

Four wildlife students at New Mexico State University, M. Johnson, C. Mitchell, S. Van Velsor, and M. Wisdom in particular, made substantial voluntary contributions. Their editorial comments, verification of literature accuracy and numerous other essential tasks were most helpful.

Encouragement of my wife Mary is acknowledged sincerely. She has been a key supporter, proofreader and inspiration to complete this fourth edition.

Editor Mosby defined the second edition audience as practicing field biologists, wildlife administrators and college instructors of wildlife management courses. To this list, I add upperclass and graduate students in wildlife.

All of these users and others are invited to identify errors and oversights in this volume. Constructive suggestions are welcomed and will be passed on to the next editor. They will help ensure reaching the common goal of improving the science and art of wildlife research and management.

Sanford D. Schemnitz
Editor

Contents

Chapter One

Planning Wildlife Management Investigations and Projects

THOMAS H. RIPLEY
Manager, Office of Natural Resources
Tennessee Valley Authority
Norris, Tennessee

Those who study and manage wildlife populations and habitats are involved in the processes of solving problems to develop knowledge or to achieve some managerial objectives. Whether deciding the seeding mixture for renewal of a food patch or testing a hypothesis about density-stress, the root process is intellectual; i.e., planning.

This chapter, and indeed much of this volume, is concerned with planning the investigation or management project.[1] The chapter outlines how the study is selected and described, how alternatives for approaches are identified, and how the prospectus and the investigational plan are prepared. The interrelationships of the prospectus and plan are discussed since these are the commonly used documents in research program development. A parallel discussion for management plans emphasizes the management problem solution. Other chapters in this book treat the tools and techniques available for conducting investigations and achieving management objectives. Knowledge of them is essential for effective planning. Such knowledge allows choice between alternatives, establishes realistic constraints, allows plans to be more "practical," and speeds the development of efficient research methodology.

[1]In this chapter, a *project* will be considered as a work unit (organizationally) which exists to solve some problem or accomplish some managerial goal. The term *investigational* will be synonymous with *study* and construed to mean any unit of inquiry, however small or large, developed to assemble or acquire knowledge or develop methods, techniques, and procedures.

PROGRAM DEVELOPMENT

A conservation objective, or set of objectives, is achieved only through a program that identifies and removes obstacles in an orderly and efficient manner. This attainment requires the development of a logical sequence for programming work. Thus, effective program development and planning are inseparable.

The common root of all investigations is a deficiency of knowledge: (a) There is a problem to solve or (b) someone is curious. Few wildlife workers are privileged to pursue a research effort out of sheer curiosity. Usually, there are one or more problems to solve in order to accomplish some conservation or resource-management objective. The solution may involve a major project effort with numerous investigations or studies, or it may be a brief, direct question for which a single investigation will fully satisfy the deficiency.

The probability of solving wildlife research and management problems increases with good planning. The problems vary widely in magnitude, clarity, importance to total programs, relation to similar problems, and ease of solution. *Ease* of solution is controlled by time, labor, equipment, finance requirements, accessibility, and technological advancement. Because of these differences, wildlifers must be keenly aware of the need for assigning priorities to work and investigation.

One of the most fundamental needs in assigning priorities is acceptance of the concept of working sequentially through problems toward major goals. This concept is contrasted to the "brush-fire" and "stop-gap" types of research and management action, but should provide for innovative diversions and creative new paths of study.

It is a difficult and intriguing problem to determine how much relative effort to put into basic and applied research. Some insight into this problem is given by Sherwin and Isenson (1967), who found that a very high percentage of technological advance in weapons, at least for a short run, came from "directed" science. On a longer time scale, however, the need for "undirected" or basic study is undeniable. The problem is real for those who must secure as much benefit as possible from the research dollar. The researcher often can and should make some effort to conduct a cost-and-benefit ratio study for applied studies. Such studies are very unlikely for basic research. Therefore, the administrator-researcher must recognize the need to provide funds, either directly or indirectly, to basic study. At the present state of wildlife management, it is difficult to specify a desirable ratio between basic and applied study.

If the benefits of research or management can be measured in comparable terms such as dollars, it may be desirable to determine priorities by some optimizing procedure. The dangers of using common terms to compare benefits accruing differently have been noted by many. The question of optimizing returns from expenditures has received considerable attention in recent years. It is not within the scope of this chapter to deal with the question of optimizing knowledge output or achieving degrees of problem solutions. It is important, however, to recognize that such optimization is becoming a well-known and widely considered step in research program planning and will soon find its way into wildlife research. The investigator who may wish to review the subject as it relates to a natural resources research question should study Bethune (1967). An excellent treatment of the general subject is given by Ackoff (1962).

Collectively, the important considerations in setting priorities are: (1) Probability of solution, (2) ease of solution, (3) budgetary constraints, (4) prediction of future research needs, (5) predictions of future goals and objectives, (6) predictions of availability of funds, and (7) predictions of administrative support for (a) long-term vs. short-term research management programs, (b) similar or diverse research, and (c) supportive personnel and facilities.

PROBLEM STATEMENT

The development of a clear problem statement is one of the most important steps of planning. Reduction of problems to the lowest common denominator, to the most precise question, or to the simplest hypothesis is not easy. However, no time spent on this effort will be wasted. If the problem can be stated, it can be solved—or the reasons given for why it cannot.

Problem statements vary according to research or management program needs, but all specify one or more obstacles which must be overcome. If the problem is large, or complex, it should be broken into meaningful interrelated segments so that results from segments can be synthesized toward solution. The following example constitutes a general problem statement for wildlife habitat research; it is one of several problems identified for analysis and study by the U.S. Forest Service, Wildlife Habitat Research Project at Blacksburg, Virginia.[2]

Problem—Determination of the Need and Opportunity to Supplement Forest Wildlife Habitat in the Mountains of the Southeast

Attempts by game managers to correct habitat deficiencies through supplemental measures are legion, and most of this work involves the use of untested measures—such as clearings planted to improved forage species. Questions can appropriately be raised whether these measures are necessary since there is little evidence in support of their widespread use. On the other hand, there is little evidence to suggest that they are not of benefit, and many techniques are very popular with the public in general.

This problem probably has a most direct bearing on poor site ridge and valley lands, but it will involve considerations for supplementation on all forests in the Southeastern mountains. There appears to be a consensus that forage supplementation may be useful on lands with limited disturbance from timber operations. On better site commercial hardwood lands, it appears that wildlife production objectives may be met by skillful coordination of timber management activities to maximize and stabilize production of important habitat elements. Thus, the question of supplementation and its role as a wildlife habitat management might be best investigated initially on poor site, mixed oak-pine mountain lands.

Actually, we have given considerable attention to this problem, and the long-term cooperative compartment studies which have been undertaken with the Virginia Unit in Broad Run may shed some light on the contribution of supplemental habitat measures and this work should be reviewed closely. Current studies that bear on this problem will be continued, but the problem is of lower priority generally, and new research will not be programmed until work on other and more vital problems has been fully implemented. Note: A thorough analysis of this problem has been made (Larson 1966), and studies have been programmed for its solution in keeping with the priority consideration indicated above.

STATE OF KNOWLEDGE

The first and most absolute requirement of investigative action or any planning effort is to examine objectively the "state of knowledge" to determine the real nature of the problem. After priorities have been established, and a top priority problem decided upon, the question of why it yet exists should be answered. Two possibilities are: it exists because information has not yet been compiled (or published); or because existing

[2]Unpublished Problem Selection Document (1966). USDA, Forest Service, Southeastern Forest Experiment Station. Project SE-1801. *Improved Management of Wildlife Habitat in the Southeast.*

information or solutions have not yet been studied or discovered. Failure to recognize this distinction has probably wasted more energy, money, and time in redundant or duplicate effort than has been spent advancing knowledge. Some workers wonder at lack of interest in their efforts even though they are working on "old hat" projects only slightly different from past or current work. Not much is gained by working on problems that, in one sense, no longer exist; they have been solved. Very early in the consideration of a problem the literature must be searched. By determining the state of man's knowledge of the problem, a major step will have been made toward its solution, perhaps the final step.

THE PLANNING PROCESS

Usually, the researcher works between the *synthesis* of the known into a solution and the *probe* beyond the fringes of knowledge. Investigations, therefore, normally require both critical literature review and a program of observation and experimentation. It is necessary to develop at this point, either formally or informally, an analytical process and plan of study. Whether such a plan will be formalized and a research prospectus developed, or only a few mental notes made, will be determined by the scope and complexity of the selected problem.

The manager is equally concerned with the planning process. Planning is a continuous process, of alternative seeking, which leads to a decision on actions. He must specify how he will overcome a managerial obstacle (solve his problem). If the problem is complex, long term, or of major consequence, it may require a formal set of plans and specifications; if not, it may be only a mental noting of how some job will be done.

Once several approaches to the solution of the selected problem have been imagined, the need arises to determine which approach, within the constraints of funds, manpower, etc., offers the highest yield of benefits.

In research, selection of the approach will indicate the general literature review requirements and the amount and type of field and laboratory work required. The planner must refocus on the purpose of the work to seek an approach to the problem that will avoid "oversolving" or, perhaps more importantly, avoid an inadequate or unrealistic attack on the problem.

The same general considerations go into the selection of the approach as in the selection of a problem. It is unlikely that sophisticated cost-benefit analyses will be practical since alternatives are usually sharp and their relative merits rather obvious. When working with a large problem of a number of parts, stepwise or simultaneous solutions should be considered, and if necessary, a phasing schedule should be set.

One of the most effective tools available to the research and management planner is the use of simulation. At its lowest level, it is like playing a game of "what if?" The planner who regularly uses this technique will simulate or mentally create possible problems or chains of events. By solving these hypothetical problems, he can develop alternative approaches, evaluate his techniques, and study the practicality of his research design, and the possibility of solving the problems.

Early in research planning, hypotheses should be developed concerning results, conditions, or outcomes, Both null and alternate hypotheses should be stated if classical methods of experimentation are to be used. Even though not stated specifically, hypotheses should be implied within or intrinsic to statements of research objectives. The hypothesis of each research or management objective should be accorded 3 general possibilities of treatment after study: acceptance, rejection, or inconclusive.

The Prospectus

The results of the prestudy or preplanning activities just discussed should be documented for all major research and management efforts in some type of prospectus. A prospectus outlines early thinking on a problem, describes problem analysis, establishes tentative objectives, states what will not be studied, suggests approaches and techniques of solution, and estimates needs. Prospectuses vary widely in form, depending on the situation, author, and audience. For example, they may be lengthy letters, several pages of narrative, or brief outlines. Their purpose is to record past thought, to solicit advice and assistance, and to communicate current interests, awareness, and ideas. They may, in the case of a complex problem, detail a group of studies with separate objectives and establish priority and schedules. Responses to prospectuses prevent researchers from duplicating past work, from missing significant ideas, from pursuing unprofitable or impossible objectives, or from establishing faulty study priorities.

The prospectus may later become a preamble to a report in documentation of the reasoning and selection mechanics for both problem and approaches.

The Investigational Plan

The following discussion is obviously relevant to the outline for reports (Chapter 5). The investigational plan is a complete "blueprint" for a research effort to meet and answer one, or often more specific questions. There are no alternative courses open at this level of planning. The plan describes *the* selected course of action which tells what, when, where, how, and by whom the work is to be done. The investigational plan is not only a desirable document; it is absolutely essential. Investigational plans may be scant or detailed, simple or complex, depending upon the problem and research requirements. As much time as possible should be spent in careful preparation of the plan.

An expanded outline (checklist) of the components of an investigational plan follows. This is a typical case and would have to be altered for specific study needs:

I. *Title*—A meaningful group of approximately 10 key words that clearly indicates the essential consideration of the study. This title is usually more inclusive than the final report title or titles for publications.

II. *Problem Definition and Selection*

   A. Scope—A brief statement of the problem and the context in which it exists. Specify related areas or approaches that will not be explored. A total project "abstract" often is useful in this position of the paper.

B. Objective—A precise statement of goals and purposes of the study.

C. Hypotheses—Major hypotheses compatible with the objectives should be stated.

D. Source—The origin, cause, or stimulus of the idea.

E. Justification—the needs, suitability, implications, potential benefits, and values of the work. List the inferences which may be expected and some alternatives, consequences, and applications of these hypothetical results. Often "future outlook" is included in this category.

III. *Study Approach and Situation*

A. Past Work—A literature review and summary of work in progress, past experiences, and present knowledge of the problem and possible solutions.

B. Descriptions

1. Study area or laboratory descriptions and general suitability for achieving objectives.
2. Population (habitat or animal) descriptions and characteristics pertinent to sampling and observations to be made. Statistical variances and expected difference of means of populations to be observed should be denoted here as reported or estimated.

IV. *Solution Procedures*

A. Study resources—briefly state the kinds of people, facilities, and materials, to be applied to the study.

B. Assumptions—List the major assumptions necessary for meaningful sampling, observation, and analyses or results.

C. Analyses

1. Define the elements, components, and subtopics to be studied.
2. State the research procedures, designs, and sampling plans to be used on each element of the problem.
3. Specify the kind and amount of data needed and to be sought.
4. Describe in detail how all data are to be obtained including details of instrumentation, equipment, and development needs.
5. Describe how the data are to be treated, including specifying what statistics are to be calculated, what models will be used, what tests of data will be used, what mathematical procedures and consultants will be employed, what electronic data processing or computer facilities will be employed, what existing machine programs will be used, and what programs must be developed.
6. List checks and balances, especially those to prevent observations of "things that are not there" including replications, backup instruments, and accuracy checks of personnel and equipment. Consider here the effect of the research procedure on the objects and systems under study.

V. *Timing*

A. Proposed date of initiation.

B. Duration.

C. Other time considerations like report deadlines, environmental or land-use changes, and time-related budgetary constraints.

VI. *Costs*

(Prepare detailed budgets in categories such as)

A. Capital outlay—equipment and construction of facilities (laboratories, pens, etc.).

B. Salaries—permanent and part-time employees and consultants.

C. Expendable supplies.

D. Rented equipment and depreciation costs.

E. Travel—local and scientific conferences.

F. Publication costs.

G. Overhead, insurance, compensations, and administrative costs.

H. Contingency—5 to 10% of total.

The entire plan should be evaluated to be sure all sections are consistent and directed toward the accomplishment of the stated objectives. The plan must be prepared so that any other scientist in a related field can understand and criticize the entire plan. Such plans, no matter how difficult to prepare, are essential to efficient, successful studies. Many past failures in wildlife management research can be directly attributed to inadequate or faulty planning, lack of documents to maintain continuity when personnel move, and lack of documented planning to allow past errors to be avoided.

The Management or Development Plan

Very similar to the investigational plan, the wildlife management plan is a description of the objectives and goals which will be met by the manipulation of habitat, populations, and people, and the ways these objectives will be reached. Helpful publications for this planning are Anon. (1955), Davis (1966), and the vast literature of forest and agricultural management.

Desirable management plans like research plans are objective oriented. They specify units of desired output for various goals like man-hours of hunting, or numbers of harvestable animals. Such plans also emphasize land development for "target game species," although usually they will attempt to optimize the total production of desired benefits from several major species on an area.

Plans dealing with relatively small programs in small areas or concerning a single species or management technique are informal and require only limited documentation. Examples would be a series of forest clearings, trails, and waterholes for the Wardensville Wildlife Management Area, Hardy County, West Virginia; a dike building and repair operation on an Ohio public waterfowl hunting area. The use of systemic insecticides in a grove of high mast-producing trees in an eastern forest.

Such plans normally include:

1. A letter of transmittal (e.g., to farmer, supervisor, granting agency).
2. A cover page stating title, location, date, author, and affiliation of author.
3. An abstract.
4. Location of area or facilities and general descriptions.

5. Statement of objectives.
6. Justification, including past experiences, expected benefits and values, wildlife use, estimated human accessibility, and expected use over time.
7. Description of procedures, operations, construction, repairs, and management activity, including maps, sketches, and flow-diagrams.
8. Cost estimates and summary.
9. Sources of funds (where appropriate).
10. Provisions for evaluation.
11. Literature cited.

Another type of plan is the one for large land areas. One published work, suggestive of the level of sophistication and type of study and planning needed is *Focus on the Hudson* (USDI 1966).

Major land-use plans integrating wildlife management objectives or special-use plans are needed as land values and demands for, and pressures on, wildlife increase. The following outline provides the essential considerations for a wildlife management plan for a farm, refuge, ranger district, or park. It is far more detailed than needed for most situations, but it can serve as a checklist and be fitted to the situation. The cost of such a plan in man-hours of study and preparation are great, but it is essential for coordinated best use of land and wildlife populations. Such plans steer the activities and establish duties, provide for personnel changes, protect past management investments, and on public lands establish policy necessary for continued wise management under changing economic, political, and social conditions.

I. *Letter of Transmittal*—The purpose of this letter is to introduce the report to the landowner or reader. It should include: (1) A reference to the original order or request for the plan, (2) a brief statement of the purpose of the report and any fundamental premises which have been assumed, (3) the scope or what main considerations have been included and excluded, and (4) brief acknowledgments to technical personnel engaged in the planning and reviewing of the plan. It also serves the purpose of dating the plan and indicating the present employment status of the author.

II. *Title, Author, and Date*

III. *Table of Contents*

IV. *Acknowledgments*—Courteous acknowledgment with specific services rendered by personnel or agencies involved in the plan.

V. *Purpose of Plan*—A general statement potentially the same for all such plans. Specifics should also be included such as, "This plan also attempts to meet the recreational needs and hunting pressure being exerted by the rapidly expanding (1961) suburban community of Ridgevale."

VI. *General Management Objectives and Goals*

VII. *Description of Area*
   - A. General—Include a map of the area showing boundaries and working units, and a location map showing the area in relation to well-known landmarks.
   - B. Past conditions—an ecological history
   - C. Topography
   - D. Geology
   - E. Nature of soils
   - F. Water and climate
   - G. Land-use types
   - H. Vegetative cover
   - I. Flood, fire, and other calamity history

VIII. *Wildlife Population Status*—Using every index available, from conversations with older residents, statewide records, and detailed research, make some estimate or expression of wildlife occurrence and abundance as a basis for species management and as a datum for management effects.
   - A. Fish
   - B. Big game
   - C. Small game
   - D. Furbearers
   - E. Game birds
   - F. Songbirds and other animals

IX. *Needs of the Human Population Using the Area*
   - A. Employment and social strata of adjoining areas and communities
   - B. Economic status of adjoining human populations
   - C. Percentages of resident and nonresident hunters using the area for hunting, fishing, or wildlife recreation
   - D. Pertinent interests, customs, and prejudices of the groups using the area
   - E. Directives for management deduced from appraisal of user-needs and desires functioning in a democracy

X. *Coordinating Measures and Broad Management Objectives*—Write measures that must be used to provide multiple-use of resources, adjustments needed to insure the fulfillment of the definition of conservation, and special considerations for "tying in" wildlife management with other land uses including:
   - A. Range and cropland management
   - B. Timber management
   - C. Watershed management
   - D. Recreation

XI. *Area Wildlife Management Practices*—Make a general statement about priorities of practices and needs for integrating practices.
   - A. Habitat improvements
     - 1. Fish
       - a. Construction of ponds, riffles, use of gabions, etc., including diagrams.
       - b. Stocking and feeding—including schedule.
       - c. Shoreline improvement—including materials, species, labor, and costs.
       - d. Others, including, for example, fencing to exclude livestock or fences to allow wildlife passage.
     - 2. Game and furbearers
       - a. List each practice. State the primary or "target" species of the practice and list with total costs all seed, planting stock, materials, equipment, labor, time, and

annual maintenance time required. Include acreages and sketch on a map or map overlay the recommended locations and types of all suggested improvements. Indicate existing desirable food and cover that should be maintained or slightly modified for increased benefit. Show improvements in relation to other wildlife needs such as water and distance from dwelling. Make waterfowl recommendations for resting, feeding, or nesting sites.

b. Include provisions for protection of practices from fire, grazing, insects, and disease.

c. Include a reasonable schedule for establishment of recommended practices. A 10-year general plan is recommended with a specific 2-year plan of action an essential.

B. Regulation of the harvest
1. General principles and bases for legislative recommendations.
2. Suggestions for landowner and his staff on how to influence state and national game regulations affecting his lands.
3. Recommendations for posting and limiting hunting areas.
4. Maximum harvest limits for game species to insure continued resource use.
5. Sharing of costs by users of the area, including licensing; fees; sharing portions of the kill; contributions of time, equipment, or materials for habitat improvement; hunting lodge construction with guaranteed use only within seasons; leasing of quality game habitat; etc.
6. Permit systems and regulation of numbers of hunters on all or portions of the area where kill is to be encouraged or discouraged.
7. Law enforcement
   a. Purposes.
   b. State and federal coordination.
   c. Additional needs, including provisions for transportation or outside help such as specialists or laboratory work.

C. Access
1. Principle of providing access for hunting, fishing, or research.
2. Road construction needs, including map and estimated costs of construction and maintenance.
3. Foot trail construction needs, including maps and estimated costs of construction, marking, and maintenance.
4. Boat or bridge access needs, including landing costs, boat and operation costs, bridge costs, and maintenance.
5. Guides to road, trail, or bridge, gating or closure.
6. Road, trail, and bridge standards and sketches of needed work.

D. Refuges and closed areas
1. Principles and needs of refuges.
2. Recommendations for establishment, including costs of posting, fencing, advertising, and enforcement.
3. Equate benefits with costs.

E. Predator control
1. Principles of use.
2. Recommendations, including costs of traps, poison, gas, fencing, repellent, labor, and effective periods of use.
3. Equate benefits with costs.
4. Specify disposition of predators; e.g., pelts and carcasses.
5. Special considerations for free-running dogs and other feral animals.

F. Other practices; e.g., salting, feeding, and stocking.

XII. *Surveys and Inventories*

A. Disease and parasite surveys that should be made with recommendations for preservation of specimens and their transfer to competent authorities.

B. Field records of observations with system described and plans for its use stating by whom, when, and why certain observations will be summarized and used.

C. Provisions for records on all habitat improvement practices including description of practice, initial costs, maintenance, fertilizer, etc. Also include provisions for future use of such records for improvement of management practices.

D. Inventory
1. General observations with record system.
2. Specific studies; e.g., pellet counts, live-trapping, seining.
3. Bag and creel checks.
4. Required reporting of game or fish taken off area.

XIII. *Measures for Testing the Effectiveness of the Plan in Action*

XIV. *Provisions for Compliance Checks. Periodic Review of Plan and Revisions*

XV. *Special Equipment Needed*

XVI. *Budget*

A. Estimated annual and total costs.
B. Estimated benefits and profits.
C. Financial source or aid.

XVII. *Amendments*

SUMMARY

An effective program of research or management results from critical planning and documentation to solve a definable problem or to overcome knowledge or environmental obstacles. The documentation must include complete display of the approaches and methods that will be used in assembling and utilizing information. Planning documents must be prepared so that any competent professional can understand and criticize any or all of the essential steps. A big order? Not at all! Well-prepared plans provide for direct and effective development of new knowledge and effective wildlife management.

Chapter Two

Wildlife Management Literature*

JULIE L. MOORE
Bibliographer
Biological Information Service
Riverside, California

PURPOSE AND SCOPE OF THIS GUIDE

This chapter is addressed to both the consumers and producers of the professional literature in wildlife management, with the hope that they may more effectively use their literature and become more knowledgeable about the fields of research by utilizing the prior experience of others.

The purpose of this chapter is to introduce the reader to some of the standard library source materials in the field of wildlife management, to show how and under what circumstances they are best used, and finally, to point out some of the more important bibliographic sources for disciplines closely related to wildlife management. Following the practice adopted in previous editions of this manual, greatest emphasis has been placed on the literature covering Mammalia and Aves, including those species which are hunted or preserved for economic reasons or on a legal basis. Every effort has been made to include only publications which are easily available. This approach has ruled out many important publications with a limited distribution, such as processed material, in-house reports, open-file reports, agency publications listed as "Not for publication," and papers presented orally at meetings.

A library, like any other investigational tool, will produce good or poor results depending upon how it is used. The library user faces complex and far-reaching problems which can delay or even destroy the credence of his research. Indeed, bibliographic research must be regarded as a tool of importance equal to those used in the laboratory or field. Proper use of library sources is made only when the investigator clearly understands why he is using the literature, the range of sources available to him, and what is the proper function of each source.

Mosby (1963b), in an earlier edition of this manual, noted that one of the most common errors made by the North American wildlife worker engaged in a bibliographic problem was his failure to make use of foreign literature. For this reason, many sources published outside the U.S. have been included in this section in a deliberate attempt to bring them to the attention of the investigator.

This chapter is written as a guide to a representative collection of library sources important to the wildlife biologist. It is not a list of the best books for the field, nor is it a list of recommended items for a working library, although it does provide the basic titles for both these

*Revised from the 1969 chapter by Robert W. Burns

purposes. The reader will discover that many items have been omitted. No guide can include everything and probably should not try. To do so would only overwhelm the reader with more material than he could assimilate successfully.

In the sense in which it is used in this chapter, the word "literature" refers to the total body of printed as well as nonprinted materials which the scholar uses in his work—the recorded word, as opposed to private correspondence. The literature of a subject field will include books, journals, serials, reports, memorandums, newsletters, newspapers, patents, theses, tables, translations, in-house and open file reports, pamphlets, films, microtext, tapes and drawings, both published and unpublished.

Since this chapter is limited to the literature of interest to the wildlife biologist, it is important that the characteristics of this body of literature be identified. They are as follows:

1. The literature is not well defined or compact in scope. The wildlife biologist might use zoology or biology journals one day and mathematics books the next. It is a composite discipline, and any discussion of its parameters must take this characteristic into account.
2. The literature is international and will appear in many languages, some not understood by the scientist who must use it.
3. Each scientific discipline, including wildlife, has terms which have meaning only for the individual trained in that particular jargon. This difficulty must be recognized by the wildlife biologist who uses the specialized literature. Further complications will occur when a term changes meaning from discipline to discipline, e.g., population.
4. Important papers will be published in obscure journals. This means that no library will be able to supply everything required by a wildlife researcher in his work. Other sources must be used.
5. Serial literature will be a large share of the bibliographic source material, due to the necessity for currency in research results. The journal is of primary importance to the work of the wildlife biologist.
6. A large part of the wildlife literature published will be regional in coverage and, therefore, of limited use to the biologist in another location. There are many local museums, conservation societies, academies of science and naturalist groups publishing this type of material.
7. Much of the wildlife literature is free or inexpensive, but it must be identified and requested by the investigator. A few agencies keep mailing lists and will send new titles upon publication. However, this method of acquisition is not to be relied upon since most agencies are understaffed for nonagency personnel requests. An annual request for new titles from an agency will usually produce either copies, or lists of most new material published.

These characteristics should not be taken to imply that the problems facing the wildlife manager are unique to his field. Many of these are the same problems faced by other scientists who must make effective use of the literature in their respective disciplines. The volume, diversity of publication media, numerous languages of publication, together with the inability of any single library to contain everything on a subject, all contribute to a situation which is becoming more and more difficult to manage.

THE LITERATURE OF SCIENCE WITH SPECIAL EMPHASIS ON WILDLIFE MANAGEMENT

Serial Literature

Serials are defined as publications issued in successive parts bearing numerical or chronological designations and intended to be continued indefinitely (American National Standards Institute 1970). Cagle (1960) has estimated the number of biological serials at between 15,000 and 25,000, while the National Academy of Sciences (1970) estimated approximately 13,000 in the life sciences. Porter (1964) placed the number of journals in pure biology at 7,000 which would exclude part of the 13,000 the NAS includes as medical/life sciences journals. Keeping these figures in mind, it is interesting to note that *Biological Abstracts* indexed 8,580 serial titles published in 113 countries in 1979 (Biosis 1979). *Wildlife Review* screens slightly more than 2,000 serials. *Zoological Record* scanned 6,000 in 1970 (Zoological Society of London 1971). Table 2.1 is a list of important serials in the field of wildlife management, based upon frequency counts of the Biological Information Service's files. It is not intended to be complete, but to point out a few of the more prominent titles and to indicate their relative coverage by the abstract/index (A/I) services. No attempt was made to determine whether indexing was on a comprehensive or selective basis for the individual titles.

No one knows the extent of the serial literature necessary to the wildlife worker. Nevertheless, some idea as to how many titles exist, to what extent they are used, in what languages they appear, in what countries they are published, and the extent of their coverage, are appropriate topics for research by wildlife biologists. The article by Hein (1967) is an example of the type of study proposed. Similar investigations have been conducted for other disciplines. Numata (1958) prepared a list of Japanese publications in plant and animal ecology; while Dagg (1972) prepared one on Canadian mammals. The techniques of citation counting and/or frequency counts in secondary literature have been used to investigate the periodical literature of ecology (Anderson 1966), mammalogy (Anderson and Van Gelder 1970), biology and its core literature (Reddin and Feinberg 1973) as well as in biochemical literature (Sengupta 1973). Several articles on the need for identifying and controlling the biological periodicals, with appropriate standards of data definition, were published by National Academy of Sciences (1970), Foote (1972), Douglass (1976), and Kennedy (1976). The future of bibliographic control on biology was aptly and theoretically discussed by Simon (1974). More analytical work of this type is necessary if intelligent decisions are to be made regarding what materials best meet our need to communicate with one another, and what types of material are to be placed in libraries. Fortunately, the increasing use of computers to perform the necessary statistical work has made these types of studies easier for the informed re-

Table 2.1. Important serials in the field of wildlife management and where they are indexed.

	Wildlife Review	Biological Abstracts	Zool. Record	Biblio. of Agric.	Forestry Abstracts
American Midland Naturalist	x	x	x		x
American Naturalist	x	x	x		x
Animal Behaviour	x	x	x		
Animal Kingdom	x	x	x		
Audubon	x	x	x		
Auk	x	x	x		
Australian Wildlife Research	x	x	x		
Avian Diseases	x	x	x		
Behavioral Biology	x	x			
Bird-Banding	x	x	x		
British Birds	x	x	x		
California Fish & Game	x	x	x		
Canadian Field-Naturalist	x	x	x		
Canadian Journal of Zoology	x	x		x	
Canadian Wildlife Service. Occas. papers, Report series	2x	2x			
Condor	x	x	x		
Conservationist (New York)	x	x			
Danish Review of Game Biology	x	x			
East African Wildlife Journal	x	x	x		x
Ecological Monographs	x	x	x		x
Ecology	x	x	x	x	x
Florida Naturalist	x	x			
Ibis	x	x			
IUCN Bulletin, Publications	2x	2x			
Illinois Nat. Hist. Survey. Biol. Notes, Bull. & Circulars	3x	3x			
Internatl. Assoc. of Game, Fish & Conserv. Comm. Proceedings	x				
Journal of Animal Ecology	x	x	x		x
Journal of Applied Ecology	x	x	x		x
Journal of Ecology	x	x	x		x
Journal of Mammalogy	x	x	x		x
Journal of Range Management	x	x			x
Journal of Wildlife Diseases	x	x			
Journal of Wildlife Management	x	x	x		
Koedoe	x	x			
Natural History	x	x			
Naturaliste Canadien	x	x	x		
New York Fish & Game Journal	x	x			
North American Fauna	x	x			
North American Wildlife Conf. Trans.	x		x		
Northeast Sect. Wildlife Society Proc.	x				
Oryx	x	x	x		
Pennsylvania Game News	x				
Puku	x	x	x		
Riistatieteellisia Julkaisuja	x	x			
Saeugetierkundliche Mitteilungen	x	x	x		
Southeastern Assoc. Game & Fish Comm. Proc. of Annual Conference	x	x			
Southwestern Naturalist	x	x			
Suomen Riista	x	x	x		
Terre et la Vie	x	x	x		
U.S. Fish & Wildlife Service Spec. Scientific Reports: Wildlife	x	x			
U.S. Fish & Wildlife Service Research Reports	x		x		

Table 2.1 *Continued*

	Wildlife Review	Biological Abstracts	Zool. Record	Biblio. of Agric.	Forestry Abstracts
U.S. Fish & Wildlife Service Resource Publications	x	x			
U.S. National Museum Bulletin	x	x			
U.S. National Museum Proceedings		x			
Univ. of Kansas. Museum of Nat. Hist. Misc. Publ., Occ. Papers, Publ.	3x	3x	3x		
Viltrevy	x	x	x		
Wildlife Diseases	x	x	x		
Wildlife Monographs	x	x	x		
Wilson Bulletin	x	x	x		
Zeit. fuer Jagdwissenschaft	x	x	x		x
Zeit. fuer Saeugetierkunde	x	x	x		
Zoologicheskii Zhurnal	x	x	x		

searcher to compile and analyze. It is hoped that the future will see more data studies performed in this area of periodical literature.

Lists of serials, especially union lists, are helpful in determining the location of journals, their recommended abbreviation, price, publisher, language, country of origin, holdings, etc. The *Union List of Serials in Libraries of the United States and Canada*, 3rd Edition, (1965) is the fundamental reference work for determining the location of a journal in the U.S. and Canada. In addition to listing libraries which own part or complete holdings of a particular serial, the *Union List* will indicate the bibliographic history of a journal showing the former titles, deaths, mergers, supplements, etc. It is kept up to date by a serial publication from the Library of Congress called *New Serial Titles*. There is a 20-year cumulation of this publication (1950–1970) which acts as the successor to the *Union List*, but its holdings records are not complete. The NST *(New Serial Titles)* is issued monthly, and cumulated quarterly and annually. A separate section in the back of each issue gives the births, deaths, and mergers for the month (quarter, year). *Ulrich's International Periodicals Directory* and its companion volume, *Irregular Serials and Annuals*, have been a valuable aid in locating the prices, publishers, editors, and pertinent bibliographic information about the more prevalent journals in all disciplines. However, many titles are not listed in these 2 annual publications, particularly the more ephemeral titles or newsletters and societies. The *World List of Scientific Periodicals, 1900–1960* (Brown and Stratton 1963), published by Butterworths is more inclusive. The 4th edition of this work is kept up to date by annual supplements. The British Museum (Natural History)'s Dept. of Zoology and the Library of the Zoological Society of London have each prepared lists of their serial holdings. In the United States, the Center for Research Libraries (formerly called the Midwest Interlibrary Center) has published a list of its serial holdings covering many of the more obscure journals indexed in *Biological Abstracts* and *Zoological Record*. These journals are made available to other libraries via interlibrary loan. In addition to the national union lists of serials, many of the larger university and research libraries have their own serial lists, such as the University of California, Los Angeles, and the University of Chicago. These are issued irregularly, depending upon the library administration. Some geographic areas or networks have union lists, such as the *Union List of Serials in the Libraries of the Consortium of Universities of the Metropolitan Washington Area* and the *Southwestern Union List of Serials*. A check with the local library will reveal the existence of these union lists and their availability. Most are for sale by the issuing institution and could be ordered for personal use.

When serial literature is cited, it is usually cited in abbreviated form rather than spelled out in full. These title abbreviations may cause confusion to the unfamiliar users, and must be translated into complete form for interlibrary loan or library searching. Many of the problems and sources for identification are listed in Kinney (1967). Lists published by *Biological Abstracts* (BIOSIS List of Serials) and CODEN may identify the titles by abbreviation, and then give the full title entry. Although there are standards for the abbreviation of periodical titles (American National Standards Institute 1970), the practice of abbreviating periodical titles seems dependent upon the individual journal editorial staff rather than any established list. In wildlife, the BIOSIS lists seem to be the most standard source consulted by the individual author. The *CBE Style Manual* (1978) may provide supplemental information for an author trying to create an abbreviation for a journal.

Monographic Literature

Keeping aware of new books and the new editions of old titles as they are published, as well as determining what books are in print within one's field, are not difficult problems for books in the English language. Many journals, including *Biological Abstracts*, *Journal of Wildlife Management*, *BioScience*, *Auk* and the *Journal of Mammalogy*, have sections listing new books. Some of these journals also include critical book reviews as well as new titles. Later in this section, some examples of indexes will be given to guide the reader to these sources.

It is possible to determine the most recent domestic books published in one's field by querying *Subject*

Guide to Books in Print, Subject Guide to Forthcoming Books, American Book Publishing Record, or the *Publishers' Weekly,* all publications of the Bowker Corporation in New York. In addition to the above irregular serial titles, there is the *Weekly Record* which lists the books on all subjects, alphabetically by author, issued during the prior week. However, its entries are compiled into the *American Book Publishing Record* monthly, and the entries are then arranged by Dewey Decimal Numbers, which facilitates subject browsing. *The American Book Publishing Record Cumulative 1950–1977* contains the last 20 years of publishing records, arranged by the Dewey Decimal Numbers, just like the monthly journal. A separate subject index is arranged by Library of Congress headings. In addition to the above sources, Bowker also publishes a companion serial called *Technical and Scientific Books in Print.* This serial is issued annually, derived from the *Subject Guide to Books in Print,* with an author, title and subject index for the volumes. The *Cumulative Book Index,* a monthly publication of the H. W. Wilson Co., is a world index to current books in the English language, regardless of country of publication. However, emphasis is on American, Canadian and British publishers, with only a few titles listed from other publishing countries. It is cumulated both quarterly and annually. The *National Union Catalog* and its companion publication, the *Library of Congress Catalog: Books: Subjects* act as guides to a large share of the world's monographic publications. Many state and foreign publications which would otherwise be difficult to locate can be found by using these tools. In addition to being indexes to monographic literature, they also act as union lists by including a limited number of locations where books may be found and used in various libraries of the United States, Canada and Puerto Rico.

The out-of-print market for books and journals has become increasingly important during recent years, due to the needs of many more researchers and new libraries. One result of this increasing demand has been the brisk trade by OP book dealers, especially in the fields of science and natural history. *The American Book Trade Directory,* a biannual serial published by Bowker, lists publishers, booksellers, wholesalers, etc. in the United States, Canada, and other countries. Specialty OP dealers are listed in sections 1 and 6.

In addition to acquiring the original OP book or journal, a collector may also purchase a reprint or microform of the original work. Some publishers list catalogs and titles available. *Guide to Reprints* and *Announced Reprints,* quarterly journals both issued by Microcard Editions in Washington, D.C., list most reprinted titles, regardless of publisher. Another source of titles is the annual publication, *Catalog of Reprints in Series,* published by the Scarecrow Press, Metuchen, N.J. If the hardbound edition is not available, University Microfilms, Ann Arbor, may have some titles available. *Guide to Microforms in Print, Subject Guide to Microforms in Print,* and *International Microforms in Print,* all list microforms available, some microcards, and microfiche sets by individual title. Most microforms materials are journals, not individual books. Occasionally books are published simultaneously in microform and hard copy.

Book Reviewing Media

Sarton (1960) stated that the purpose of book reviewing is to communicate to the public the results of one's analysis. His article includes many pertinent remarks on the ingredients of a good book review and how to prepare one. There are several types of review articles, including analytical, descriptive, and synthesis, but most users prefer the analytical. For those users interested in the synthesis of several titles in a review article, Maizell et al. (1971) listed the elements of a good article in their Chapter 4, while discussing abstracting. The table of contents, preface, and bibliography all play an important part in the evaluation of a scientific book or monograph and must be included as part of the review article.

The reader can find detailed, critical reviews of the scientific literature in many journals, *American Scientist, Auk, Bioscience, Canadian Field-Naturalist, Canadian Journal of Zoology, Endeavor, Journal of Ecology, Journal of Mammalogy, Journal of Wildlife Management, Natural History, Science,* and *Scientific American,* as well as shorter notes on the listing of new books. The *Quarterly Review of Biology* and *Biologisches Zentralblatt* list some titles that are not ordinarily reviewed by the major biological journals. If a review of a particular title is needed, the *Book Review Digest* and the *Book Review Index,* both serial publications, may provide one or more review notices published in the scientific journals. However, both are rather selective in the coverage of nonfiction books and are of limited value in wildlife research.

Nature, Science, and *Natural History* prepare annual surveys of science books which are helpful to anyone wishing to survey the major new works in science for the year. Critical annotations, which are usually shorter than the conventional book review, appear in 2 journals, *Choice* and *Science Books.* These journals list many more titles in science than the *Book Review Index* or the *Book Review Digest* and aim towards the university and college audience. *Science Books* also lists items to supplement titles in the secondary grades and junior colleges, as part of their book review sections.

Some Examples of Books Important to the Wildlife Biologist

All scientific disciplines rely heavily upon the monograph, whether it be a textbook, manual, or handbook. Indeed, many disciplines have standard manuals or handbooks which are essential to its workers. Many of these will be of help to the game biologist, including prior editions of the *Wildlife Techniques Manual* (Mosby 1963a, Burns 1969). However, frequently these books are known only by the name of the original author which makes them quite difficult to locate. Most are landmarks in their respective fields, and are considered essential to anyone working in that area. Some examples of these basic guides are Hitchcock (1951) on grasses; Hotchkiss (1967) on aquatic plants; Ward and Whipple (Edmondson 1959) on freshwater biology; Gray's (Fernald 1950) manual on flowering plants and ferns of the Central and Northeastern United States, supplemented by Rickett (1966–1973) for the entire United States; the Merck veterinary manual (Siegmund 1979); Society of

American Foresters' handbook (Forbes and Meyer 1955); the 4 biological handbooks from the American Societies for Experimental Biology covering general biological data (Altman and Dittmer 1972–1974), growth (Altman and Dittmer 1962), blood and other body fluids (Altman and Dittmer 1961) and environmental biology (Altman and Dittmer 1966); the Chemical Rubber Co. mathematical tables (Selby 1975); and Fisher and Yates (1963) statistical tables for biologists. Barron (1976) listed the 7 "most-cited" statistical texts used by fish and wildlife personnel. The wildlife manager should have at least a speaking acquaintance with these general reference sources. In addition, there are a number of texts more closely related to the field of wildlife research which should be of interest to the user. Although it is not possible to list all of them here, some mention should be made of a few of the more important titles. The reader will find many others throughout this and other chapters. Any wildlife manager will have several favorites of his own, no doubt, which are not included, but this list is intended to serve only as a partial reference list and for suggestions. Each researcher or manager will wish to develop his own lists and collections of titles in this field as his knowledge expands.

The fiction and nonfiction of Ernest Thompson Seton will always rank near the top on any list of books covering wildlife. Although now somewhat dated, his *Lives of Game Animals* (1937) is a wildlife classic. Other titles of importance are Beebe (1926), McAtee (1945), Allen (1956), and Delacour (1977) on the pheasant; Elliott (1897), Edminster (1954), and Johnsgard (1975a) on North American game birds; Stoddard (1931 reprinted in 1978) on bobwhite quail; Leopold (1977) on California quail; Schorger (1966a) and Hewitt (1967) on wild turkey; Johnsgard (1973) on grouse and quails of North America; Delacour (1954–1964), Johnsgard (1975b, 1978), and Bellrose (1976) on waterfowl; Hancock and Elliott (1978) on herons; Ripley (1977) on rails; Tuck (1972) on snipe and Sheldon (1967) on woodcock; Goodwin (1977) on pigeons and doves; Sanderson (1977) on migratory shore and upland game birds; Errington (1963) on the muskrat; Schmidt and Gilbert (1978) on big game; Einarsen (1948) on the pronghorn antelope; Murie (1951) on North American elk; Peterson (1955) on North American moose; Lydekker (1898) on deer; Taylor (1956) on North American deer; Millais (1897), Darling (1937), and Whitehead (1964) on deer of the British Isles, and Whitlock (1974) on deer of the world; Roe (1951), McHugh (1972), Meagher (1973), and Dary (1974) on the American buffalo; Geist and Walther (1974) on ungulate behavior; Ewer (1973) on carnivores; Murie (1944), Young and Goldman (1944 reprinted 1978), Mech (1970), and Klinghammer (1979) on wolves; Young and Jackson (1951) and Bekoff (1978) on the coyote; Fox (1975) on wild canids; Young and Goldman (1946) on the puma; Young (1958 reprinted 1978) on the bobcat; and Leyhausen (1979) on domestic and wild cats. Wildlife conservation and game management are covered by Leopold (1933), Gabrielson (1941), Trippensee (1948–1953), Burger (1973), Bailey et al. (1974), Giles (1978) and, in Europe, by Dagg (1977); zoogeography by Darlington (1957) and the AAAS Symposium (Hubbs 1958); food habits by Martin et al. (1951); trophy records by Nesbitt and Parker (1977) for North America, Best (1971) for Africa, and Fitz (1963) on how to measure and score trophies. Rare, endangered and extinct species are listed in the American Committee for International Wild Life Protection's *Special Publications nos.* 11, 12, and 13 (reprinted by Dover Publications in 1967); the International Union for the Conservation of Nature and Natural Resources' *Red Data Books;* and the U.S. Fish and Wildlife Service's Resource Publication no. 114: *Threatened Wildlife of the United States* (1973).

Bibliographic Sources

ABSTRACTING AND INDEXING SERVICES

Basic to any literature search or review is a thorough knowledge of the indexing and abstracting services available for that particular field. Of these two, the abstracting service is more satisfactory when locating and identifying references because it tells something of the nature of the material, whereas the indexing services include only titles and bibliographic information. Both types can serve as alerting or current-awareness services. However, special tools for this particular function will be discussed later with several examples.

The choice of an abstracting or indexing serial for literature searching depends upon the characteristics of each serial or service, and upon the understanding of its function and purpose. In addition, the choice must also consider the type of literature search to be conducted—current-awareness searching, retrospective searching, or topical (subject) searching. The characteristic which distinguishes an abstract or index to be used as a retrospective-searching tool from one to be used for current-awareness purposes is the presence of a cumulated internal index enabling the user to move through the serial without having to consult each individual issue.

There are only a dozen or so services which the wildlife biologist must know well. Apart from this group of serials, there are specialized services which cover a limited subject in more detail or cover a chronological period which has no abstract or indexing services. Of the latter type of material, the wildlife manager needs only a speaking acquaintance and the knowledge that such tools exist. (The section on 'Guides to the Literature' later in this chapter will list the most common sources of more information.)

Included in this core of essential abstracting and indexing services for the English-speaking wildlife manager are *Biological Abstracts*, and its supplementary serial, *BioResearch Index; Wildlife Review* and its cumulations *Wildlife Abstracts; Zoological Record,* especially the *Aves, Insecta,* and *Mammalia* sections; *Bibliography of Agriculture; Biological and Agricultural Index* and its predecessor, the *Agricultural Index; Applied Ecology Abstracts; Forestry Abstracts;* and *Chemical Abstracts.* The wildlife biologist will not necessarily use each of these serials every time he performs a literature search. However, this group is capable of meeting most of his needs and covers most of the wildlife literature.

The best use of this basic group will be made when the searcher has a thorough knowledge of the characteristics of each title. Table 2.2 illustrates how these serials overlap in coverage of selected journal titles. This knowledge will be of assistance in helping to select the abstracting or indexing journal which is most efficient for the purpose of the search.

In addition to the core group of Abstract/Index serials, there are also 2 regular sources available for current-awareness searches; the "Recent Literature of Mammalogy" supplement of the *Journal of Mammalogy*, which is compiled by the American Society of Mammalogists' Bibliography Committee, and the "Current Literature" section published at the back of each issue of *Auk*. Both of these bibliographic sections are extensive and have been compiled on a regular basis. The overlap of the serials is not consistent, and a judgment of the effectiveness of each A/I serial must be made by the searcher.

Outside of this basic group of A/I serials, there is a large group of specialized subject-oriented services sponsored by governmental agencies, societies, private publishing houses, foundations, and information groups. A guide to abstracting services was developed by the International Federation for Documentation (1969) and another for bibliographic services for 1965–1969 by Avicenne (1972). Some of these services are maintained for in-house use only, most are published as a journal or serial, and many have a computer data base available, as well as the printed version. For computer systems and computer data bases, Kruzas (1974) listed many organizations and agencies, with details of available services.

Published Versions

• Biological Abstracts

Biological Abstracts (BA), published by the Biosciences Information Service (BIOSIS), is an outstanding index to the world's published biological research literature, both monographic and serial. Since 1926, when its coverage began, BA has published over 3.5 million abstracts in its 2 publications, *Biological Abstracts* and *BioResearch Index* (Steere 1976). It was created by the merger of *Botanical Abstracts* with *Abstracts of Bacteriology* in 1925, and enlarged its coverage to include all zoological literature as well. From 1927 to 1959 the coverage, although more comprehensive than any other service, was based upon selected periodicals. In 1959 an effort to include most of the world's literature resulted in a quantum jump of coverage to nearly 140,012 abstracts in 1975 (Anon. 1976) from 8,312 journals of 116 different countries (Biosis 1979). A list of the serials indexed and abstracted is issued as a separate publication from the BA volumes. In the earlier volumes, some unpublished reports and papers were included, but this practice ceased in 1964 (Anon. 1964).

There are 4 indexes published to the abstracts of BA and BIORI (BioResearch Index). These are author (both personal and corporate), biosystematic, keyword or subject index, and CROSS (Computer Rearrangement of Subject Specialties). The latter index is a special type of subject index with assigned codes for a topical approach to the literature. In addition, most of the recent issues and the earlier issues (but not the 1960's) have a geographic index. BASIC (Biological Abstracts Subjects in Context) was the original subject index of keyword-in-titles, and was issued separately from the abstract issue. However, this series has been discontinued. Each of the 4 indexes, as well as the geographic when present, is cumulated at the end of each volume. Some years also contain a genera index, but it was not comprehensive for the years covered.

Steere (1976) is an excellent source on the history of BA and all its publications. In addition to the basic serials, a computer data base back to 1959 is present and commercially available (See the section on computer data bases for more information). A microform copy of *Biological Abstracts* is also available, but limited to subscribers who already order the printed edition. Cumulative 5-year indexes are available on microform from BIOSIS. Should a searcher wish to see the complete text of a reference, he may write to John Crerar Library, 86 East Randolph Street, Chicago, Ill., where many of the journals are deposited after they have been indexed.

• BioResearch Index

BioResearch Index (prior to January 1967 it was called *BioResearch Titles)* is an international title listing of ma-

Table 2.2. Abstract/Index services which include selected material from other services.

Biological Services	Dissertation Abstracts	Bibliography of Agriculture	Biological Abstracts	Chemical Abstracts	Forestry Abstracts	Wildlife Review	Zoological Record
*Biological Abstracts		x	x	x		x	x
*Chemical Abstracts		x	x	x	x		
Forestry Abstracts	x	x	x	x	x		
Wildlife Review	x	x	x	x		x	
*Bibliography of Agriculture	x	x			x		
Recent Literature of Mammalogy	x		x				x
Zoological Record	x		x				x
Current Literature *(Auk)*	x		x			x	x

*Computer data base also.

terials not included in BA. It serves as a supplementary journal to BA, and lists literature considered as "less important." Many conference titles are listed in this serial, as well as annual reviews, books formed by a compilation of authors, popular journals in biology, some report literature, etc. Since wildlife materials are often found in this type of literature, *BioResearch Index* is an important source to be searched as well as BA. It has all the same indexes as BA and is also available on a computer data base since its inception in September 1965. It should be noted that no abstracts are included in BIORI—titles are only listed. As an example, in the early years of coverage, *Journal of Wildlife Management* was listed in *BioResearch Titles* since wildlife journals had a rather limited audience. As the field grew and more original research was published, the *Journal of Wildlife Management* was assigned to be indexed, abstracted, and published in BA. Many of the new environmental journals are also listed in BIORI before being assigned for abstracting as their coverage and audience expands.

• Zoological Record

The *Zoological Record* (ZR) has been a bulwark of zoological bibliography since 1864 and is one of the oldest index services in continuous operation in the field. It indexes both monographs and journals, including some annual review papers and conference proceedings. Neave (1950a) described it as a unique example of scientific bibliography; it is particularly important for the systematist seeking to locate the original citations for new genera and species. Its coverage overlaps somewhat with BA, especially in the later years, but its coverage of local and regional natural history societies in the British Isles is especially important. ZR is composed of 20 separate sections, with 1 section title "List of New Genera and Subgenera," another "Comprehensive Zoology," and 18 additional sections based on a phylogenetic group, i.e., "Aves," "Mammalia," "Insecta," etc. Each section of ZR may be purchased separately, both in the printed version, and in a microform format (microfiche) for the years 1864–1948. Reprints of the 1948–1972 years are available from Johnson Reprints, New York.

Each section of ZR is arranged by author with citation information, a geographic index, subject index, and systematic index for the year. The chief difficulty encountered in using ZR is that a publication is often 2 to 4 years behind coverage. In 1970 a separate supplement listing serials indexed was issued (Zoological Society of London 1971).

• Wildlife Review

Wildlife Review (WR) began in 1935 as an irregular publication of the U.S. Dept. of Agriculture's Bureau of Biological Survey. Today it is a quarterly publication issued by the U.S. Fish and Wildlife Service, monitoring more than 2,000 journals as well as monographs from the world's wildlife literature (Kenneth Chiavetta, pers. comm. 1977). Despite its lack of cumulative indexes, it serves as a useful tool by acting as a current-awareness service to alert the wildlife manager to publications which might be of interest. Both WR and its cumulations, *Wildlife Abstracts*, are available in many depository libraries and most biological research centers. Four cumulations were issued between 1951 and 1977; they are 1935–1951; 1952–1955; 1956–1960; 1961–1970. Despite the title, these cumulative volumes do not contain abstracts, but refer the user back to the original WR entry. The cumulations offer a subject index which are not available in *Wildlife Review*.

WR has been querying BA for citations since 1957 (Anon. 1957). In the 1950's and 1960's an exchange program was established, but current policy of BA seems to have dropped the formal exchange of citations. Nonetheless, cooperation between the 2 abstracting services still exists and citations are often found in both journals. Citations are also taken from "Recent Literature of Mammalogy" sections, the American Society of Mammalogists for selected entries. A discussion of the coverage of WR for the 1950's appears in *Wildlife Review No. 75* (1954).

• Key-Word-Index of Wildlife Research

The *Key-Word-Index of Wildlife Research* is an annual publication of the Swiss Wildlife Information Service, Zurich, Switzerland. It began in 1974 to identify published sources of European wildlife, with some significant non-European sources in wildlife management. There are 2 parts to each issue. Part 1 contains the title keyword-index and the author-title index. Part 2 is a list of keywords (called a Thesaurus although it is merely a guide to cross references) and a list of geographic and veterinary keywords. Also included are alphabetical and systematic species lists, a list of periodicals and the copying services available through the Swiss Wildlife Information Service. The current editor is Rolf Anderegg. This is a published source of wildlife literature, similar in selection to the *Wildlife Review*. Coverage of some of the more obscure European journals are included in this source, as well as the significant government documents of the various national game agencies.

• Bibliography of Agriculture

The *Bibliography of Agriculture* (BoA) is an index to all important monographs and serials received by the National Agricultural Library, in Beltsville, Maryland, covering agriculture and its related disciplines, including some forestry and farm game wildlife. This service was started in 1942 and is issued once a month, with cumulated subject, personal and organizational indexes annually. Coverage has changed during the years of existence in this journal. During the 1950's and 1960's, agriculture was interpreted rather broadly and subsequently included much material of value to the wildlife biologists. The inclusion of various agricultural and forest experiment station reports and bulletins has also varied throughout the years. A list of journals indexed is printed in the front of each issue; any searcher using this tool should be aware of what journals were covered when. A short introduction discussing the BoA's coverage and language limitations is also included on the first page of each issue. During the 1970's, major policy revisions have occurred in this journal.

BoA includes several journals also indexed by other A/I services, such as BA and *Forestry Abstracts*, but no direct exchange relation or agreement is in effect (in 1979). Some selected references from the Commonwealth Agricultural Bureaux's magnetic tapes are included. See Table 2.2 for an example of coverage overlap between BoA and other services.

• Biological and Agricultural Index

The *Biological and Agricultural Index*, formerly called the *Agricultural Index*, started in 1919 and goes back to 1916 in its coverage. This monthly publication is a subject index to a very limited group of English-language periodicals, all of which are indexed more comprehensively by other abstracting and indexing services. It covered state agricultural experiment station publications, up to September, 1964. The advantages of this index are the ease with which it is handled, and the high quality of the periodicals covered. Moreover, its distribution by the Wilson Co. (publishers of *Reader's Guide)* has made this index title more available in smaller libraries and research centers who do not subscribe to the BoA or BA. However, it is not a good substitute for the purposes of the wildlife searcher.

• Forestry Abstracts

Forestry Abstracts (FA) is a monthly publication of the Commonwealth Forestry Bureaux. Starting in 1939, with coverage back to 1937, it is an index journal to the world's forestry literature appearing in monographic or serial form. Its primary emphasis is on forestry, but it also includes numerous articles on entomology, soils and some on wildlife species. Like BoA, the policy of coverage has varied during the years, with the 1955–1968 years as the best coverage of wildlife literature. A special feature of some of the issues of this index journal is the review article on some aspect of forestry, with extensive bibliographies. There is an annual author, subject, and geographical index to the recent volumes. FA also appears 4 times a month on cards by special subscription, which offers the reader a ready-made, current-awareness service.

• Chemical Abstracts

Chemical Abstracts (CA) is one of the largest, if not the largest, abstracting services in the world. It started in 1907, appears weekly, and indexes 14,000 serials annually. It covers many subjects becoming more and more important to wildlife research including pesticides, drugs and their physiological effects, mammalian biochemistry, etc. In areas of biochemical coverage, a project of co-ordinated indexing is being studied by BA and CA (Steere 1976). Both systems utilize automated data processing techniques and hope to coordinate selected references from journals relevant to both fields.

CA has 5 internal indices—author (personal and corporate), subject, patent, formula and ring. In addition, there are decennial and a quinquennial cumulative indexes. An index of Ring Systems began in the 1967 issues. In 1971 CA issued a separate listing of its journals as the *Chemical Abstracts Services Source Index*, formerly called *Access* issued in 1969. The listing gives complete bibliographic information locations of libraries receiving titles, and proper abbreviation for chemical journals.

Like BA and the BoA, CA has a data base of its tapes for computer searching. Details of the data base will be covered in a later section of this chapter.

Some Services for Related Disciplines

Outside the nucleus of essential abstracting and indexing services discussed in the preceding paragraphs is a multitude of special purpose indexing services. Their use is determined partly by their availability, partly by the needs of the searcher for specialized coverage, and partly by the knowledge of the searcher regarding their existence. The International Federation for Documentation (1969) lists most of the current ones, but new ones are being developed every year.

Two other national services worth mentioning are published in France and Russia. The French national service is called *Bulletin Signaletique* (formerly *Bulletin analytique*) and appears in 18 *Sections mensuelles.* Section 12: *Biophysique, Biochimie, Chimie analogique* and Section 16: *Biologie et physiologie animale* are the 2 most important sections for wildlife biologists. The Russian publication is called *Referativyni Zhurnal* (RZ) and appears in approximately 50 sections. The *Biologiia* section (n. 4) is composed of many parts, but is the primary section for zoological and wildlife literature. Few titles indexed in RZ are indexed anywhere else in the world. The best source for overlapping coverage is BA, but RZ naturally contains references to many of the more obscure Russian journals which BA does not index. Many sections were indirectly available to the western scientist during the early 1960's due to the international cooperation between BA, CA and RZ. After 1970, BA began receiving and indexing the original Russian journals instead of translating abstracts of RZ.

The following serials are also worthy of the wildlife manager's attention. However, their use is limited and care should be exercised in their selection, keeping in mind the special areas they cover:

• Index Veterinarius

Index Veterinarius started in 1933 as a publication of the Commonwealth Bureaux of Animal Health, which is now part of the Commonwealth Agricultural Bureaux. Emphasis is on diseases and their incidence or prevention in domestic animals, but it covers much material that is of interest to wildlife biologists. Subject and author indexes are provided with each issue.

• Index-Catalogue of Medical and Veterinary Zoology

This journal is a publication of the U.S. Dept. of Agriculture's Bureau of Animal Industry, dating back to 1902. It is a source covering the world's literature on trematodes, cestodes, roundworms, and similar parasites. Some duplication of entries overlap with the *Index Veterinarius* but there also is enough unique material to justify using it.

• Soils and Fertilizers

Published monthly by the Commonwealth Agricultural Bureaux, this journal indexes the world's literature on soil and fertilizer sciences. Two sections, one on soil chemistry, and one on techniques and analysis, are of importance to the wildlife biologist. Another section on forest soils is of interest to those biologists working with forest species. SAF has been collected into 4-year cumulations under the title *Bibliography of Soil Science, Fertilizers and General Agronomy*, from 1934 (1931–34) to 1962 (1959–62). No new cumulations have been issued since 1963. Indexes to current issues are available each year

• Pesticides Documentation Bulletin

This title is the same name for 2 different journals, both issued by the National Agricultural Library. The first journal was issued from 1965 to 1969; the second was issued in 6 numbers through 1970. Both journals were designed to serve as an index to the world's literature on diseases of biochemical origin, some nematodes and parasites affecting plants, animals and man. However, the National Agriculture Library changed its policy in regard to coverage in this journal and subsequently ceased to publish. Current articles in pesticide and pollutant literature are indexed in the NAL's *Bibliography of Agriculture; Pesticide Abstracts* or several other specialized publications on plant and livestock diseases, such as the *Index-Catalogue of Medical and Veterinary Zoology.*

• Pesticides Abstracts

This journal was issued in 1968 by the U.S Public Health Service as *Health Aspects of Pesticides*. In 1974 its title was changed to *Pesticides Abstracts* and is issued monthly by the Environmental Protection Agency. Its coverage was enlarged to include all pesticides, relevant to man and insect, plant, or non-target species, including wildlife species. In 1975, pollution literature was also reviewed in addition to pesticide effects. Much material on effects of pesticides and pesticides monitoring is included in this index. Annual author and subject indexes are also issued since 1968.

• Meteorological and Geoastrophysical Abstracts

The American Meteorological Society published this journal since 1950. Originally this journal was entitled *Meteorological Abstracts and Bibliography* (1950–1960). Annotated bibliographies have been compiled for some of the issues, including articles on forest micrometeorology, dew, frost, radiation levels, bioclimatology, etc. Each issue has author, subject, and geographic indexes, plus annual cumulated indexes. G. K. Hall, Inc. (Boston, Mass.) has issued a cumulated index for 1950–1969 titled: *American Meteorological Society. Cumulated Bibliography and Index to Meteorological and Geoastrophysical Abstracts, 1950–1969; Classified Subject and Author Arrangements.*

• Indices Covering the Nineteenth and Early Twentieth Centuries

Quite often the investigator will need to trace a literature reference or carry his search for material back into the nineteenth century. There are very few sources for material published during this period. The *Zoological Record* offers the searcher an author or subject approach to the literature of the second half of the nineteenth century. A similar source is a card index-file called *Concilium Bibliographicum*, published in Zurich, Switzerland (1896–1940). The most recent years were issued in monographic format instead of cards. There is little overlap between ZR and the *Concilium Bibliographicum* for the early twentieth century literature. Both files index journal articles. *The Catalogue of Scientific Papers of the Royal Society of London is an author* index to the contents of 1,555 periodicals from learned societies and academies of Europe, including Russia, published during the nineteenth century. As might be expected, comprehensive bibliographies can be of great help in locating materials published during the nineteenth century. Meisel (1924–1929), Phillips (1930), Altsheler (1940), Gill and Coues (1974) and Smit (1974) will support this type of literature searching as will many of the more specialized subject bibliographies.

There is only 1 broad-based source covering the first decade of the twentieth century. This is the *International Catalog of Scientific Literature* issued annually in 17 sections from 1901 to 1914. Sections of special interest to the wildlife biologist are 'L' which covers general biology, 'M' covers botany and 'N' covers zoology.

Computer Data Bases

In addition to the published sources of Abstract/Indexing materials, there are a number of computer data bases which can be searched, either for current material, or for retrospective material. Most of these data bases are limited to the literature of the 1970's, although a few do go back into the early part of the century. Most also are merely the machine-readable format of the printed versions and are subject to the same index limitations as the printed indexes. Table 2.3 lists some of the more important and accessible ones for the wildlife biologist.

The recent development of on-line systems accessing these data bases has allowed a number of commercial services to provide searches at nominal costs, by demand of the user. The 3 largest sources for on-line data bases are Systems Development Corporation (SDC) in Santa Monica, Lockheed Information Services in Palo Alto, California, and Bibliographic Retrieval Services, New York. These commercial vendors have developed programs and supportive computer hardware to allow multiple users to search on-line. Various lease arrangements are made with the producers of the data base (such as *Biological Abstracts)* and the user may utilize any terminal source available to him. There are also a number of private data bases developed for special purposes which may be accessed through SDC, BRS, or Lockheed, but only with permission of the producer. Finally, there are several individual data bases available but must be searched by the developer with the consultation of the user. At this time, the state of on-line searching is still evolving and only generalizations for these sources will be contained in this section.

Some of the parameters of the data bases, such as BA Previews, Agricola, Chemical Abstracts, Index Veterinarius, Helminthological Abstracts, and Soils and Fertilizers have already been discussed under the section on 'Printed Versions'. This section will discuss the parameters of those data bases with no printed versions, or special features which pertain only to the computer searching capabilities.

Table 2.3. Some computer data bases important to wildlife studies.

Name	Published Version	Dates of Coverage	On-line Vendors
BA Previews	Biological Abstracts & BioResearch Index	1959–date	1971–date
Agricola*	Bibliography of Agriculture &	1970–date	1970–date
	Pesticides Documentation Bulletin	1968–1969	1968–1969
Chemical Abstracts (CA)	Chemical Abstracts	1971–date	1971–date
CAB Abstracts	Index Veterinarius &	1972–date	1973–date
	Helminthological Abstracts &	1973–date	1973–date
	Soils and Fertilizers	1973–date	1973–date
Fish and Wildlife Reference Service	None	1934–date	none
HERMAN (Biological Info Service)	None	1934–date	none
WESTFORNET**	None	1971–date	none
Toxicology Information (Oak Ridge Natl. Lab.)	None	1970–1972	none
Enviroline	Environment Abstracts	1971–date	1971–date
Envirobib	Environmental Periodicals Bibliography	1972–date	1972–date
NTIS	Government Reports Announcements	1964–date	1972–date
CDI	Dissertation Abstracts & Americal Doctoral Dissertations	1861–date	1861–date
Pollution Abstracts	Pollution Abstracts	1970–date	1970–date
Meteorological Abstracts	Meteorological Abstracts	1972–date	1972–date
Toxline (Natl. Library of Medicine)	none	1967–date	none
Sci Search	Science Citation Index	1974–date	1974–date
ASCA	Current Contents	1974–date	current only
SWIS (U.S. Corp. of Engineers)	None	1900–date	none

*Former data base name: CAIN
**Former data base name: PACFORNET

• HERMAN (Hierarchical Environmental Retrieval for Management and Networking)

This is a commercially-developed data base designed for wildlife bibliographic entries, especially printed and published sources. Some dissertations and theses are included. The wildlife species are North American or Holarctic species; foreign literature is included for the Holarctic species. Both retrospective and current-awareness searches can be made through its owners, the Biological Information Service, Riverside and Los Angeles, California.

• SWIS (Sensitive Wildlife Information System)

This is an information system developed by the U.S. Army Engineer's Waterways Experiment Station, Vicksburg, to monitor information on endangered and/or threatened species. At the present time (1979) it does not contain all species legally (federally) defined as endangered, but the birds and mammals are being added as priority items. Output consists of a computer summary of brief biological information, with bibliography attached. This data base is available, currently free of charge, for researchers and consultants dealing in endangered species. This is an on-line system, but query must be made through Vicksburg, Mississippi.

• Fish and Wildlife Reference Service, Denver

This data base is composed of the Pittman-Robertson and Dingell-Johnson unpublished reports from the Federal Aid in Wildlife Restoration projects, since its inception in 1934. This is a federal-contract data base, primarily available to cooperators in the Federal Aid program; however, for a fee, any wildlife biologist may have a retrospective search performed. Xerox copies of the unpublished reports can also be ordered. The present contracting organization for this data base is Denver Public Library, Fish and Wildlife Reference Service staff. Some theses and unpublished reports from non-P-R projects are also available through this service but do not form part of the data base.

• WESTFORNET (Western Forestry Information Network)

This information retrieval system became operational under this name in May 1978 to provide services to U.S. Forest Service employees and other authorized users. It contains its own data base on forestry and utilizes other commercially-available data bases, such as BA Previews and Agricola. Both retrospective searches (back to 1971) and current awareness services are available. Each month, a publication, *Monthly Alert*, is issued for selected items from the data bases. There is a special section for wildlife.

• Toxicology Information

This is an in-house data base developed for the Oak Ridge National Laboratories personnel. It collected material on all chemical toxicants, including pollutants and pesticides. Retrospective searches only are available through the Oak Ridge National Laboratories, Toxicology Information Center. Current material is not available through this data base.

• Toxline (Toxicology Information On-Line)

This is a publicly-available data base developed by the National Library of Medicine, covering the biological effect of chemicals, drugs and pollutants. Pesticides are included as part of the chemical and pollutant sections. Sources of bibliographic entries are taken from *Chemical-Biological Activities* (part of the Chemical Abstracts data base), *Abstracts of Health Effects of Environmental Pollutants* (part of the BA Previews data base), *Toxicity Bibliography* (part of Medline data base), *Pesticides Abstracts* and *International Pharmaceutical Abstracts*. Retrospective searches are currently available, with plans to implement current-awareness searches. All requests must be accessed through the National Library of Medicine system.

• Enviroline

This is another commercially-available data base, developed by the Environment Information Center, Inc., New York. Its emphasis is the environment (earth, water, oil, timber, etc.) with a section on wildlife publications. Most of the data can be obtained from other wildlife sources, but those aspects dealing with social determinants, land use, and economic evaluation are indexed for this data base. A journal is published every month, called *Environment Abstracts*. Some newspaper and popular journal articles on wildlife are present in this data base as well. A scan through any issue of *Environment Abstracts* would indicate the type of journal coverage for the data base.

• Envirobib

Like Enviroline, this commercially-available data base emphasizes the environmental aspects, especially in social and economic studies. Only a very small portion of the data base deals with wildlife articles, again mostly available in other sources, especially BA Previews. A journal, *Environmental Periodicals Bibliography*, is issued by the Environmental Studies Institute, Santa Barbara, bimonthly. This is a listing of the articles in the various issues of the new journals, by the journal and issue title, similar to *Current-Contents* in arrangement. No abstracts are provided, but a subject index, composed of added descriptors is included for each published issue of the EPB, plus a cumulated annual index.

• NTIS (National Technical Information Service)

This is a national, federally-sponsored data base of unpublished reports, mainly emanating from federally-funded studies, but also some private or foundation-funded projects. Not all federal reports are in this system, only those deposited at the discretion of the agency. All subjects including wildlife and biological reports, are listed in this data base which is available to any member of the public. New report titles are listed in several published journals: *Government Reports Announcements* lists most titles entered into the data base; *Weekly Governmental Abstracts: Natural Resources* and *WGA: Medicine and Biology* are selected listings of GRA entries for a limited audience. There are several *Weekly* series covering various types of subjects; since these are compiled during a year. Wildlife titles may be included in several *Weekly* journals, or be contained primarily in the *Natural Resources* or *Medicine and Biology* ones. The NTIS is located in Springfield, Virginia.

• CDI or Comprehensive Dissertation Index

This is the name of the data base forming bibliographic entries of the unpublished Ph.D, D.D.S. and Ed.D. dissertations, especially in the United States and Canada. Theses from other countries are included, but not as comprehensively as the North American ones. All subjects are represented, but wildlife searches must be performed by using all keywords that may occur in the title of the dissertation. Only retrospective searches can be made, either through the terminal or directly through the developer University Microfilms, Inc. Ann Arbor, MI.

• Pollution Abstracts

This data base covers technical literature on air and

water pollution, solid wastes, noise, pesticides and radiation. Wildlife biologists will need to search on keywords to obtain subject information. The published journal, *Pollution Abstracts* does not have a separate section of environmental pollutants *per se.* However, most of the material is available through other data bases, such as Enviroline and Chemical Abstracts (CA). Although *Pollution Abstracts* is described as using a special thesaurus, the terms do not apply well to the wildlife aspects of pollution, pesticides and environmental radiation. Keywords should be used.

• Sci Search

This data base is composed of entries and their connectors from the *Science Citation Index.* The published version began in 1964, issued by the Institute of Scientific Information, Philadelphia, covering the 1961 literature. It is the only scientific, commercially-available data base using the theory of citation-referencing; that is, if a good paper on a subject is produced, it will be cited by both the contemporary researchers and subsequent ones. If cited frequently enough, an idea and its development may be traced to only the most relevant literature. The *Science Citation Index* has received both praise (Garfield 1964) and criticism (Steinbach 1964) from its users. Most users must make their own decision regarding its usefulness, since it differs from most data bases and journals in that the searcher must move forward in time rather than backward. The user begins with the name of an author who wrote a landmark or fundamental paper, and then moves to other papers which have cited the original paper.

This data base also provides subject searching, since the current entries are made from the titles produced in *Current Contents,* a current-awareness journal. However, so few titles in the wildlife field are contained in this data base, compared to *Biological Abstracts,* that most searchers of subject retrospective material in wildlife should utilize other data bases. The uniqueness of Sci Search lies in its citation-referencing capabilities.

Current-Awareness Searching

There are a number of different ways for the wildlife biologist to keep aware of what is currently being published in his own field and in the fields closely related to his specialty. A very common method is to use the "Current Literature," "Schriftenschau," or "Referate" sections in the professional journals. Of direct interest to wildlife biologists are the supplement to the *Journal of Mammalogy,* the section in *Auk, Zeitschrift fuer Jagdwissenschaft, Animal Behaviour, Science, Nature* and *Bioscience.* Each discipline has a major journal, which frequently lists or reviews new books; botany, *Bulletin of the Torrey Botanical Club,* herpetology, *Herpetological Review;* ecology, *Ecology, Journal of Animal Ecology* and *La Terre et La Vie;* systematics, *Systematic Zoology,* etc.

Another method of keeping alert is to use the journal *Current Contents: Life Sciences* and *Current Contents: Agricultural, Biological* and *Environmental Sciences* which list all title pages, with contents, for journals selected as important in the life sciences. This is a weekly journal and provides easy scanning of titles listed. In the back of each issue is an alphabetical index to first authors with a complete mailing address, so that reprints may be requested from the author. In addition to the printed version, there is also a data base (ASCA) which can be queried weekly for new items. Some subject profiles are available bi-weekly from ISI on a subscription basis.

Each of the data bases that has been mentioned as having printed versions also provides a subject index to the printed version. A searcher can scan the indexes, or may query directly to the data base on a regular basis. Some, such as BA, provide a special service for current-awareness profiles (a profile is the list of terms or descriptors to be searched each time). Table 2.4 lists those with this service. The HERMAN data base offers a choice of standard profiles rather than the user establishing one, but at this time it cannot be varied to fit the user's needs. The U.S. Forest Service's data base (WESTFORNET) and systems also have a current-awareness feature, with individual profile capabilities. Although it is currently limited to USFS, it may become available to other federal agencies in the near future. The query of a data base on a regular basis, or the scanning of the indexes printed for the data base provides a third way of keeping up with the literature.

Table 2.4. Computer data bases important for current-awareness in wildlife.

Name	Program Name	Frequency	Output Format
BA Previews	C.L.A.S.S.	3 times per mo.	5" x 8" cards 8" x 11.5" paper
HERMAN	SDI Wildlife	2 times per mo.	3" x 5" cards
Chemical Abstracts		2–4 times per mo.	8" x 11" paper
Current Contents	ASCA	4–5 times per mo.	6" x 8" paper
WESTFORNET	None	1 time per mo.	8" x 11" paper

SUBJECT BIBLIOGRAPHIES

Subject bibliographies can be extremely valuable when used as source materials to survey the literature of a particular field. Indeed, as Page (1965) pointed out, bibliographies serve a number of useful purposes by keeping an orderly record of the knowledge in a field, helping to prevent needless repetition, keeping arguments about priority reasonably accurate, and aiding the library user in his search for material. One need only point to the bibliographies of Strong (1939–1959), Yeager (1941), Makepeace (1956), Crispens (1960), Godin (1964), Karstad (1964), Kirsch and Greer (1968) or Todd and Kenyon (1972) in order to better appreciate their potential for literature research. As a service to wildlife biologists, the U.S. Dept. of the Interior's Library has issued a number of specialized bibliographies on topics of interest since 1967. The U.S. Bureau of Land Management has also issued a series of bibliographies on endangered species as part of its *Technical Notes* series.

In a sense, guides to the literature, as well as the abstracting and indexing services, are subject bibliographies. Both are treated in other sections of this chapter, however, and this section has been limited to the nonrecurring bibliography listing references on a particular subject (Roberts-Pichette 1972), region (McKinley 1960) or state (Dalke 1973, Jones and Homan 1976), period (Phillips 1930), individual (Schorger 1966b), or taxon (Clark et al. 1978). Continuing subject bibliographies are covered in the appropriate sections of the abstracting and indexing services. Most of them also contain a separate section for nonrecurring bibliographies and new books as well.

Bibliographies are published in a variety of ways. They are normally used to document article and books of a research nature. Sometimes they are published independently, in book or journal form, and occasionally as supplements to both. The third volume of Walker et al. (1964) is an excellent classified bibliography on mammals of the world and will give the literature searcher a good starting point for work in mammalogy. Unfortunately it was not updated or re-issued when the second and third editions of Walker et al. were published. The bibliographies at the back of these editions are reprints of the partial contents of the 1964 edition. UNESCO (1963) published a review book on the soils, flora, and fauna of Africa, which contains extensive bibliographies. Both the Utah Cooperative Wildlife Research Unit and the Colorado Division of Wildlife (formerly Dept. of Game, Fish and Parks) have published literature reviews. From the latter, examples are reviews on the sage grouse (Gill 1966), pronghorn behavior (Prenzlow 1965) and cottontail rabbits (de Calesta 1971). Other places to look are in the terminal bibliographies accompanying review articles in serials with the titles *Annual Review of . . . , Fortschritte der . . . , Advances in . . . , Progress in . . . , etc.*

Because they are scattered through the literature, the searcher must expect to look in several places to determine if a bibliography exists. The logical place to begin such a search is at the library card catalog. Here he can expect to find bibliographies noted as parts of books by a statement on the individual cards, as well as under the subject heading 'Bibliography' or as a subject heading modifier under the topic being searched, i.e., 'Rabbits-Bibliography.' It should be pointed out, however, that individual cataloging practices vary from library to library. After the card catalog a search can be made through the *Bibliographic Index*, a cumulated quarterly journal, the volumes of Besterman (1966) or his cumulation in the *Biological Sciences* (Besterman 1971), and into the indexing services such as the *Monthly Checklist of State Publications, Monthly Catalog of United States Government Publications, Government Reports Announcements, Biological Abstracts, Zoological Record,* or *Wildlife Abstracts* where one can find bibliographies listed under the index heading 'Bibliographies' and/or under the subject. Several examples of these bibliographies have been identified under the Abstracting and Indexing Services section in this chapter.

It is a fairly common practice to include extensive bibliographies in general textbooks and field guides on natural history. These terminal bibliographies may be of tremendous value to the reader by enabling him to work deeper into the literature, or to pursue an interesting topic outside his immediate interest. Examples of such bibliographies occur in Peterson (1961), Bourliere (1964), Dasmann (1964), Southern (1964), Ingles (1965), Benton and Werner (1974), and at the end of this book.

Another approach which can be used in the search for material on a particular subject is to use the lists of publications which accompany many of the biographies of outstanding scientists. Illustrations of this occur in the lists of publications by Elliott Coues (Allen 1909), C. H. Merriam (Osgood 1947 and Sterling 1974), as well as current scientists' writings in special bibliographies (Egler 1973). Equally useful are the bibliographies given in the *Biographical Memoirs of Fellows of the Royal Society*. One should keep in mind the bibliographies which often accompany obituaries. Excellent examples of J. F. Dymond (Scott 1965), William Rowan (Salt 1958), Rudolph M. Anderson (Soper 1962) and Paul L. Errington (Schorger 1966b) have appeared in this way.

Still another location for bibliographies are the journals themselves where special extensive bibliographies are occasionally printed, such as the one on wildlife diseases (Halloran 1955). Both *Wildlife Diseases* and *Bioscience* have issued a number of such bibliographies. *Bioscience* has published extensive bibliographies on amphibians (Highton 1965), biotelemetry (Adams 1965), mammalogy (Musser and Hooper 1966), entomology (Downey 1966), embryology (Coulombre 1966), animal ecology (Seidenberg 1966) and organic evolution (Ehrle and Birx 1970–1971), to mention only a few.

A number of government and professional organizations will prepare bibliographies under special circumstances. The National Library of Medicine and the National Agriculture Library used to prepare a publication series on topical interests, but the new data base manipulations are superseding the programs of publications. The Wildlife Disease Association and The Wildlife Society both have 'Bibliography Committees' whose members compile various listings, and evaluate manuscript bibliographies for publication.

Another important group of subject bibliographies is

that of the large, multivolume sets devoted to a single broad subject area. Recently, there have been several publications, chiefly from the press of G. K. Hall, Inc. These are, for the most part duplications of library, museum, or herbaria card catalogs. They represent a substantial addition to the literature of a subject, and are especially useful for retrospective searching. Examples of these book catalogs have been produced for the Yale Forestry Library (1962), Conservation Library, Denver Public Library (1974), U.S. Dept. of the Interior Library Center (1969), Blacker-Wood Library of Zoology and Ornithology, McGill University (1966), Museum of Comparative Zoology Library, Harvard University (1969), and the U.S. Geological Survey Library (1964).

Reference Sources—Location and Function

In addition to specialized sources available to wildlife biologists, there are a number of types of literature listed in various reference sources, whose value may not be immediately obvious to the wildlife searcher. This section will discuss some of the types of reference sources dealing with various types of literature, and their function in performing a literature search.

GOVERNMENTAL PUBLICATIONS

Government publications are of major importance to the wildlife biologist. Federal, state, provincial, dominion, etc. governments have many agencies whose publications relate directly to the work of the wildlife biologists. In 1958 the National Science Foundation began a series, now defunct, called Scientific Information Activities of Federal Agencies, which outlined their policies and procedures relative to the various aspects of scientific information. Of special interest is no. 1, covering the U.S. Dept. of Agriculture; no. 6, the National Science Foundation; no. 12, the Dept. of the Interior, which also includes the U.S. Fish and Wildlife Service publications; and no. 30, the National Agricultural Library. Much of this information is dated, but still of interest since the basic policies are consistent.

Of special importance to the wildlife manager in the field is a system of depository libraries for U.S. Government documents. Under this program, many, but not all, federal publications are automatically sent by the Superintendent of Documents to selected libraries over the United States to be kept *in perpetuum*. Unfortunately, many of the U.S. Fish and Wildlife Service publications did not fall under this program in its early years (1930–1965). Those publications deposited under this program are designated by a large round dot next to their entry in the *Monthly Catalog of the United States Government Publications* (hereafter referred to as the *Monthly Catalog).* Many libraries choose to keep their documents separate from the library's main collection and do not list them in the central card catalog. Depository collections are to be found in some public libraries, all state or territorial libraries, most large university libraries, and a few specially designated institutions. A list of depository libraries is given in the appendix of Schmeckebier and Eastin (1969).

It is possible to locate government documents by using private abstracting and indexing services, including data base searches. Some of these include CIS (Congress Information Service) which covers all congressional publications indexed by committee and subject, and the Federal Index, which is an index to the published *Congressional Record, Federal Register, Commerce Business Daily, Code of Federal Regulations, United States Code* and various presidential documents. Unfortunately the latter data base only goes back to January 1977 and is, at the present time, of limited value.

The best place to begin looking for a recent federal (U.S.) document is in the *Monthly Catalog.* This index is sent free to all depository libraries. If a subject search is desired, a privately published set of volumes, *Cumulated Subject Index to the Monthly Catalog of United States Government Publications, 1900–1971,* provides a good starting place. For early documents, the *Checklist of United States Public Documents, 1789–1909,* published in 1911 and reprinted in 1962, is the best source. However, since the *Checklist* is arranged by issuing agency, and has no subject index, its value is limited in the initial steps of a subject search. The coverage of the *Checklist* is carried through 1940 by the *Catalog of Public Documents of the 53rd to 76th Congress and All Departments of the United States for the Period March 4, 1892 to December 31, 1940,* an author-subject-title index in 25 volumes, more commonly known as the *Document Catalog.* Although the *Monthly Catalog* has been published since 1895, its indexes were published erratically during its early years; nor were the congressional papers included as they are in the *Document Catalog.*

It is also possible to locate Federal documents in several other ways. The U.S. Government regularly issues price lists of its publications in special subjects through the Government Printing Office. Often individual departments will issue lists of their publications. Such lists are also found in the *Monthly Catalog* or can be obtained by writing to the department directly.

Several very important documents have been issued by the various departments, such as Arthur Cleveland Bent's series: *Bent's Life Histories of North American Birds.* The first volume of this series first appeared in 1919 as the National Museum's *Bulletin no. 107,* continuing an earlier series begun by Major Charles E. Bendire under the Smithsonian Institution's *Special Bulletins nos. 1 and 3,* 1892 and 1895 respectively. These *Life Histories* are a major foundation of ornithological literature now, and have proven so popular that they have been reprinted by the Dover Publishing Company, New York. Bulletins of special interest to the game biologist are Bent's *North American Diving Birds* (no. 107), *North American Wild Fowl* (nos. 126 and 130), *North American Marsh Birds* (no. 135), *Gallinaceous Birds* (no. 162), and *Birds of Prey* (nos. 167 and 170). Another series of special interest to the game biologist is the *Fauna of the National Parks of the United States,* starting in 1933 under the U.S. National Park Service. This monographic series deals exclusively with the vertebrate fauna of our National Parks, including such classics as Murie's *The Wolves of Mount McKinley,* the Welles' *The Bighorn of Death Valley*, Mech's *The Wolves of Isle Royale* and others. This series should not be confused with the older and more general series called *North American Fauna* begun in 1889 by the Bureau of Biological Survey under the Dept. of Agriculture, now under the Fish and Wildlife Service, Dept. of the Interior. This later series includes systematic synopses and regional studies covering birds as well as land and ocean mammals. All 3 series are excellent examples of federal documents relevant to the wildlife biologist.

State (U.S.) publications follow a pattern similar to that of the federal documents in their indexing, but lack the comprehensiveness and facility available at the federal level. There is no system of depository libraries, except for the various State Library Systems within each individual state. The *Monthly Checklist of State Publications*, issued by the U.S. Library of Congress since 1910, is a list of the publications emanating from state agencies. However, it includes only those state documents received by the Library of Congress and should be thought of as a checklist rather than as an index to state publications. Many states issue their own checklists and must be contacted directly for specific information. In many instances, a state natural resource, or game and fish agency may have its own library. Their catalogs and lists provide materials by request. Most allow the public to use their library at certain times or by appointment. Again, the various State Library Systems may be able to guide the user to the appropriate journals and state agencies. Another source for the identification of state agencies and their publications, particularly journals, is the *Conservation Directory*, an annual directory published by the National Wildlife Federation. This directory lists the state fish and game agencies, conservation organizations, and wildlife serial publications, with addresses and publishers. The earlier state literature (prior to 1941) is best covered by searching in *Wildlife Abstracts*, or Corbin (1965). For the early part of the nineteenth century, Meisel (1924–1929) is useful. The book catalogs of the Conservation Library, Denver Public Library, and of the U.S. Dept. of the Interior Library are both sources for state documents of the 1930–1950 decades in the field of wildlife biology.

Canadian federal documents are difficult to identify and locate, particularly in the early part of the century. *Monthly Catalogue of Canadian Government Publications* is issued by the Canadian Information Canada agency, similar to the (U.S.) *Monthly Catalog*. Annual cumulations are issued for 1971 to date. This is a bilingual catalog, in English and French. The series has been cumulated from 1953–1969 into 17 annual volumes, issued by the Canada Dept. of Public Printing and Stationery. This series is the single source of material for Canadian federal documents. Bhatia (1971) is a bibliography listing other sources of materials for provincial documents, each province tending to issue its own checklist or compilations through the years. The best source for provincial or federal (Canadian) documents is to write to the various agencies, listed in the *Conservation Directory*.

THESES AND DISSERTATIONS

The location of a scientific thesis can be one of the most challenging bibliographic problems faced by a literature searcher. Coverage by the abstracting and indexing services is uneven at best and has often lacked sufficient depth in its subject approach. Currently, few services include theses as part of their coverage, relying upon the *Dissertation Abstracts International* journal to cover all relevant doctoral theses. Coverage of masters' theses, as well as most non-U.S.A. or non-Canadian doctoral theses, is difficult to find. Acquisition of all theses remains difficult, and in many cases even interlibrary loan is complex.

For the wildlife searcher, Moore (1970) remains the best source for both masters and doctoral theses in the United States and Canada. Other subject bibliographies include lists published once a year in *Forest Science* for forestry theses, special issues of *Wildlife Review* (nos. 59, 63, and 98) as well as other issues containing a large number of theses, the list of Canadian theses on forestry (*Forestry Chronicle*, Smith 1962), an ornithological list from *Auk* (Wolfson et al. 1954), and range management list (*Journal of Range Management*, Box 1966).

For a more systematic search of doctoral theses, there are several sources. The U.S. Library of Congress (1913–1940) produced a series for doctoral theses published in the United States since 1912. For earlier titles, *Science* carried an annual listing for 1898–1915. No attempt was made to index either of these series for subject searches. The current index to doctoral dissertations prepared in the U.S. and Canada is called *Dissertation Abstracts International* (DAI), published in 2 sections, A and B. Section B covers "Sciences and Engineering" including wildlife and agriculture. Some entries from *Dissertation Abstracts* may be listed in *Wildlife Review;* few other abstracting and indexing services pick up selected titles. A companion volume is *American Doctoral Dissertations*, an annual volume which lists all titles and authors for all the universities in the U.S. DAI does not cover all dissertations, relying for its information upon the volunteer efforts of the various universities. Some major universities, such as Columbia and Chicago have not participated in the program. Moore (1972a, b) gives an analysis of coverage in the early years of *Dissertation Abstract's* program. In 1973, University Microfilms, the publishers of DAI, issued a 37-volume set of doctoral titles called *Comprehensive Dissertation Index, 1861–1972*, which in effect superseded the Library of Congress lists, the early years of *American Doctoral Dissertations* volumes, and added those theses not listed in its own volumes of *Dissertation Abstracts*. The entries are composed of an author-thesis title-degree granting university, and date, with DA entry number when available. The arrangement is classified, with the title keywords forming subject index to each classed set, i.e., v. 11–13 form "Biological Sciences" with appropriate subject (keyword) index. In addition, this set also superseded University Microfilm's 1970 *Retrospective Index to Dissertation Abstracts International, v. 1–29*.

Foreign dissertations are listed in *Dissertation Abstracts International*, but are limited. Those foreign theses held by the Library of Congress are listed in the Library of Congress *Author Catalog* and its companion volumes of *Books: Subjects*. Bishop (1959) has suggested a number of tools which can aid the searcher in locating a thesis prepared in the United Kingdom,

France, Germany, or the United States, as well as sources to write to obtain copies. Unfortunately, many of the depositories for theses established in the late 1950's to early 1960's have ceased to actively collect theses, especially U.S. and Canadian titles. The Center for Research Libraries, Chicago, has a number of theses from France and Germany but has no separate listing (they are given to *Dissertation Abstracts International* for inclusion). French theses are listed in the *Catalogue des thèses de doctorat soutenues devant les universités francaises,* an annual series published by the Direction des Bibliothèques de France, Paris. German theses are listed in *Jahresverzeichnis der Deutschen Hochschulschriften,* an irregular journal published by the VEB Verlag fuer Buch- und Bibliothekswesen, Leipzig. In Great Britain, the library association Aslib publishes an annual serial: *Index to Theses Accepted for Higher Degrees in the Universities of Great Britain and Ireland.* For Russian titles, the Publichnaia Biblioteka publishes a quarterly list titled *Katalog kandidatskikh i doktorskikh dissertatsii, postupivshikh v Biblioteku imeni V. I. Lenina i Gosudarstvennuiu Tsentral'nuiu Nauchuiu Meditsinskuiu Biblioteku.* Most countries have lists of theses at the doctoral level, but acquisition of a specific title is difficult. Canada is the basic exception. The National Library of Canada acquires and copies all Canadian dissertations, listing them in their annual publication *Canadian Theses/Thèses canadiennes* since 1960, and also in *Dissertation Abstracts International* for selected titles. Hence, microfilm copies can be obtained from the National Library of Canada, Ottawa, relatively easily. Earlier titles, if identified, can be obtained from the degree-granting school by interlibrary loan.

Masters' theses are not under good bibliographic control. Moore (1970) listed most of the masters' theses from schools specializing in wildlife in the United States and Canada, but none in forestry and range management. The quarterly journal, *Masters Abstracts,* from University Microfilms, Inc. does not list many theses at all with exceedingly few in wildlife studies. Black (1965) has compiled a guide of various means to identify masters' theses through the university publications and published sources. Bledsoe (1954) prepared a single volume for masters' theses, but it did not cover topics of wildlife. In 1957, Plenum Press began a series called *Masters Theses in Pure and Applied Sciences,* but the life sciences were excluded. Some biochemical and bioengineering theses are included under the chemistry and engineering sections. Subject indexing was discontinued after 1960. *Wildlife Review* continues to list many wildlife theses as they come to the attention of the editors. Moore continues to collect titles of masters' theses, but they have not been published outside of the Biological Information Service's data base.

Many schools publish lists of the theses accepted as part of their degree requirements. These lists can also serve as aids to help locate theses of interest to the wildlife researcher. Both Black (1965) and Moore (1970) included lists arranged by school as part of their bibliographies.

Most schools will loan their masters' theses through interlibrary loan. The usual procedure is to request that your local library borrow the thesis and then loan it to the requestor. Doctoral theses are available through University Microfilms as either microfilm or hardcopy (Xerox) by purchase. Those universities not participating in the University Microfilm program usually make copies for individuals by request.

TRANSLATIONS

Many publications concerning wildlife management have been written in languages other than English. Wood (1966) found less than 25% of the papers in *Biological Abstracts* (1965) were not in English; Kosin (1972) found 39% of BA (1969) papers were not in English; Reddin and Feinberg (1973) found the bulk of BA papers came from a small number of countries, with the United States and the United Kingdom leading, followed closely by USSR, Germany, France and Japan. Feinberg (1973) stated that the BIOSIS *List of Serials* indicated that the USA and UK produced only 27.58% of the biological literature. Wood (1966) also said that less than half of the papers in *Index Medicus* were in English; the current percentage is closer to *Biological Abstract's* 75%. This means that many major papers in wildlife will be found in foreign languages, especially Russian and German. However, the true monolinguist will find English summaries or abstracts in most important foreign journals.

Russian is one of the most important foreign languages in the scientific literature. Abelson (1965) and Kosin (1972) both demonstrate that it is the second language of science, yet few scientists are able to read Russian. For this reason, this section is concerned principally with the identification and location of scientific material translated from the Russian.

Several good introductions to the problem of translations and translation services have been written. Martin (1960) and the Special Libraries Association (1976) gave good guidelines for obtaining translations. The American Translators Association (1976) provided a list of translators and their specialties. Parker (1959), Kaiser (1965), Millard (1968), Himmelsbach and Brociner (1972) and British Library, Lending Division (1977) listed specific sources of translation materials. The British Library, Lending Division and Himmelsbach and Brociner both dealt with cover-to-cover translations of journals, primarily Russian titles, while the others dealt with sources and translation services available. Although dated, Kaiser is still the most useful of the 3 translators' guides. Martin deals primarily with Russian literature translation problems and, although now out of date, still gives a good theoretical discussion to the translation in scientific literature problems.

There are also journals listing translations available. In the United States, the *Translations Register-Index,* issued monthly by the John Crerar Library, Chicago, lists available translations in natural, physical, medical and social sciences. This library is the National Translations Center depository, and includes translations from the National Technical Information Service (NTIS) (formerly the Clearinghouse for Federal Scientific and Technical Information). As such, the *Translations Register-Index* superseded the NTIS's publication,

Technical Translations (1959–1967). Moreover, it superseded the *Translation Monthly* (1955–1958) issued by the Special Libraries Association and the *Bibliography of Translations from the Russian Scientific and Technical Literature* (1953–1956) issued by the Library of Congress. For Russian literature prior to the *Bibliography of Translations,* the Library of Congress issued the *Monthly Index of Russian Accessions* (1948–1969), which listed titles from the Russian, rather than a list of translations. However, many of the titles were translated by various agencies of the U.S. Government and deposited in the NTIS data base or the John Crerar Library. There is little overlap between the *Monthly Index of Russian Accessions* and *Technical Translations/Bibliography of Translations/Translations Register-Index.* The *East European Accessions List,* issued by the Library of Congress from 1951–1960 is similar to the *Monthly Index of Russian Accessions* for the 10 East European countries (Poland, Hungary, Czechoslovakia, Bulgaria, Rumania, Latvia, Lithuania, Estonia, Yugoslavia and Albania). These tools are very satisfactorily used as sources of identification for translation, but the lack of indexes makes them difficult to use as a retrospective searching source. During the early 1960's a number of items concerned with biology were indexed also in *Biological Abstracts,* but this is no longer true. All these sources list both monographic (book) literature and individual journal articles. Those items listed in *Technical Translations* are also supposed to be listed in the current NTIS data base; however, care should be exercised when doing a subject search. The older records and documents of the NTIS data base are currently difficult to locate in the NTIS files.

Another journal, issued by the United Nations Educational, Scientific and Cultural Organization (UNESCO), is called *Index Translationum.* Early issues from 1932 to 1940 were quarterly; then in 1948 it was re-issued as an annual journal. G. K. Hall published the *Cumulated Index to English Translations of the Index Translationum, 1948–1968* in 1973. This cumulated index provides a valuable tool for searching by subject. The *Index Translationum* and its cumulated index are arranged by Dewey Decimal Number (500 for biology) and can be easily scanned for translations. Currently over 75 countries are represented in these volumes. There is no central depository for these items, but many are available through the national libraries of the countries performing the translation, such as the Science Museum Library in Great Britain or the Library of Congress in the United States.

Several governmental agencies also issue lists of translations done by their staffs. Examples of these are the U.S. National Marine Fisheries Service's monthly journals, *Received or Planned Current Fishery and Oceanic Bibliography,* which lists translations from the NMFS and other agencies, and *Translated Tables of Contents of Current Foreign Fishery and Oceanography Publications.* The Canadian Fisheries and Marine Service also publishes a *List of Translations,* primarily of Russian and Japanese articles which have been translated by the staff, and are available through the Canadian Fisheries and Marine Service. From 1957–1960, the Canadian Wildlife Service (CWS) issued 7 volumes of a series called *Translations of Russian Game Reports,* a partial translation of *Voprosy Biologii Pushnykh Zverei.* This series is now discontinued, but the various translation activities of the Canadian Wildlife Service are still available to members of the CWS. Their translations are not listed in any of the translation journals mentioned earlier and must be requested by a user.

The Special Foreign Currency Science Information Program, also known as the P.L. 480 project, was a governmental program administered by the National Science Foundation, which resulted in a number of translations being produced in Israel, Poland, and Yugoslavia. This program is still active under the U.S. government agencies and includes titles from India as well as the East European countries. The translations performed under this program are listed in the *Translations Register-Index,* and frequently are available through the National Technical Information Service, Springfield, Va. Some of the more important titles produced under this program are the series *Mammals of the USSR and Adjacent Countries* by S. I. Ognev (1962–1966), several parts of the series *Fauna USSR* notably Novikov (1962) on carnivorous mammals, Flerov (1960) on musk deer and deer, and Isakov (1961) studies on terrestrial vertebrate resources. All of the above titles were issued by the Israel Program for Scientific Translation, in Jerusalem. In addition, a recent catalog for their translations would list many other special articles of interest to the wildlife researcher. Most, but not all are also listed in the *Translations Register-Index.* The U.S. Forest Service, Division of Forest Management Research, issued a series of translations of forestry titles from 1934–1940. *Wildlife Review* (nos. 76, 81, 84, 99) also has sections listing translations made from Russian literature, but most translations were discontinued in the middle 1960's. A special issue of *Wildlife Review* (no. 164) listed the complete proceedings of the International Union of Game Biologists' Congress, 1st (1954) through 11th (1973) by title, translated title, and brief annotation. Many of these papers are in non-English languages with English summaries. Copies of the papers are available from the Library at the Colorado State University, Fort Collins, Colorado. A separate list of titles, in Russian, for the 13th Congress is appended to the *Wildlife Review* issue.

The commercial field of translations services has developed recently, and many publishers issue regular translated journals and series. The cover-to-cover journal translations listed by Himmelsbach and Brociner (1972) included the major publishers as well: The most prominent are Scripta Technica, Plenum Press, Academic Press, Interscience (Wiley & Sons, Inc.), Gordon & Beach, Pergamon Press, and Macmillan. Special catalogs are available from each of these firms. The professional societies, including the American Institute of Biological Sciences, the Academy of Natural Sciences of Philadelphia, and the Federation of American Societies for Experimental Biology (FASEB) also issue translations on an irregular basis, and must be queried for particulars.

THE CRITICAL REVIEW

The critical review is that portion of the scientific literature intended to survey, evaluate, summarize and synthesize the work in a particular field, or a special aspect of that field. A review is not part of original research work, although a good review contains original intellectual material. The section on 'Book Reviewing Media' lists some sources for critical reviews. The most comprehensive critical reviews are found in annual publications established for the purpose of summarizing the literature. They are usually titled *Annual Review of . . .* , *Advances in . . .* , or *Progress on . . . .* A firm in Palo Alto, California, Annual Reviews, Inc., is a nonprofit corporation publishing only annual reviews. Pergamon Press, Plenum Press, Interscience (Wiley & Sons), Butterworths, and the American Institute of Biological Sciences have all published series of reviews. Some series are discontinued as the field progresses and splinters into sub-fields; others have been issued for years. Some have begun only recently. However, some publishers will issue proceedings, transactions or symposia of international meetings with the titles "Advances" or "Reviews" which are not summations or critiques of the literature. These titles should not be confused with the critical review series. Some titles of current interest to the biologist looking for reviews are: *Quarterly Review of Biology, Advances in Ecological Research, Advances in Parasitology, Annual Review of Ecology and Systematics, Annual Review of Physiology, Annual Review of Entomology, Advances in Botanical Research, Advances in Behavioral Biology, Biological Reviews* of the Cambridge Philosophical Society, *International Review of Forestry Research, Fortschritte der Zoologie* and *International Review of General and Experimental Zoology* (now ceased publication). Some of these titles have multiyear indexes by subject which are valuable for summations of the field under review at that particular time.

MICROMATERIALS

This is a storage technique in which the printed or typewritten page is reduced in size and photographed for storage on sheets or rolls of film. Sometimes, the sheet of film is reproduced as a positive and pasted onto the back of cardstock, opaque to a special reading machine. Collectively, micromaterials (or microforms) is a term which covers microfilm, microfiche, microprints, microcard, etc. For the most part, these are reprints of publications which initially appeared as hardcopy—newspapers, theses, journals, books, and unpublished conference papers. One journal, *Wildlife Diseases,* issued by the Wildlife Disease Association, is composed of original material. At first the journal was published on microcards (the opaque medium of micromaterials) in 1959, but in 1965 it was issued in the transparent medium known as microfiche due to the continuous popularity of microfiche over microcard format, based upon the economics of producing microcards, and the improvement of reading equipment for the transparencies. Now there are hand-models of microfiche/film readers which further the use of microform copy.

Some idea of the tremendous amount of micromaterials available can be gained by looking through the annual publications *Guide to Microforms in Print* and *Subject Guide to Microforms in Print* issued by the Microcard Editions, Inc. in Washington, D.C. These publications list most of the commercially available microforms with the exception of theses and dissertations and technical reports. In addition, there is an annual called *International Microforms in Print,* issued by Microform Review, Inc., Weston, Conn., for non-U.S.A. and Canadian producers. For older microforms, Tilton (1964) is a good source, while *Microform Review,* issued quarterly from Weston, Conn., is a good source of current materials in microforms. In addition to articles on microform projects and developments, there is a large section devoted to critical review and evaluation of various microform series.

Since these materials are unreadable to the human eye, viewing equipment is necessary. Although *Microform Review* has some articles and advertisements about new equipment in this field, there is no single place to search for specifics. The National Microfilm Association (NMA) has an annual publication, *Buyer's Guide to Microfilm Equipment, Products and Services,* which is a directory of members of NMA by product and service. Ballou (1968) has a guide and directory of models and manufacturers of various types of equipment produced in the United States, entitled *Guide to Microreproduction Equipment.* A companion volume, *International Directory of Micrographic Equipment* (Rubin 1967), was issued for non-U.S.A. producers. Veaner (1971) produced an evaluation handbook of the technical aspects of micropublications with a detailed evaluation checklist for new micromaterials.

PUBLICATIONS OF SOCIETIES, NATIONAL AND STATE ACADEMIES OF SCIENCE, MUSEUMS, ZOOS, AND GEOLOGICAL SURVEYS

These agencies are prolific publishers of annual reports, bulletins, journals, proceedings, occasional papers, and monographs. Many of them publish guides to regional fauna, description of collections, flora, keys, descriptions of specimens and expeditions, technique manuals, and lists of type specimens. In addition, they publish directories of the names of staff or officers, with addresses, but this type of publication will be discussed later in this chapter. This section will discuss only the publications of these agencies.

Clapp (1962) has prepared a detailed bibliography of the various publications issued by museums, zoological gardens, and aquariums. It is arranged by subject and covers both the monographic and serial publications. Clapp (part 2) dealt with the publications in biology and earth sciences. Walker et al. (1964) has a short list of museum publications on page 737, v. 3, a list of publications from or about zoos on page 766, and a list of annual reports from zoological societies on page 678. *The Official Museum Directory,* an annual publication, lists the serial publications of museums, zoological gardens, and arboretums. Skallerup (1957) discussed the American state academies of science publications with a list of their publications arranged by series—proceedings, newsletters, transactions, bulletins, etc.—without giving the titles of numbers within each series. However, for the wildlife biologist, this listing is very important in regional work. Within the annual *Conservation Directory* (National Wildlife Federation), many publications of state and local institutions are listed under the institution's entry. The biennial *Naturalists' Directory* has a section of publications or periodicals in the natural sciences, many of which are local or regional for the United States. Regular publications issued by societies are listed in Gray and Langord (1961) and Murra (1962) for both U.S. and foreign societies, while a directory sponsored by the National Academy of Sciences (1971) listed publications of societies in the U.S. For eighteenth and nineteenth centuries, Meisel (1924–1929) listed the natural history publications of nearly 90 scientific societies, 25 journals, 15 natural history museums and botanic gardens, 36 state geological and natural history surveys, and over 70 Federal (U.S.) exploring expeditions spanning the period 1769 to 1865. Corbin (1965) has compiled a bibliography of State Geological Survey publications, excluding Hawaii and Alaska, arranged by author, subject, series title and series number. This bibliography is especially important because of the many publications from State Geological and Natural History Surveys (often combined) of interest to the wildlife biologist. Clapp (1962) also covered some of this material, but Corbin was intended to supplement her work.

MEETINGS AND PROCEEDINGS

Papers presented at meetings, symposia, congresses, etc. are frequently published 6 months to 2 years after the event. Moreover, it is often necessary to know what meetings are forthcoming in order to present papers or learn of new developments in the field. Three journal publications list meetings to be held: *Scientific Meetings* issued 3 times a year by Special Libraries Association; *World Meetings: United States and Canada* and *World Meetings: Outside United States and Canada*, 2 quarterly journals published by Macmillan Information, Inc. These journals have indexes by keyword of the meeting title, a schedule of meeting dates, sponsors and any item of general information, and who is in charge of arrangements. A note is also given as to whether the proceedings are expected to be published. *Directory of Published Proceedings*, published monthly by InterDok Corp., in New York, is a directory of preprints and scientific published proceedings available. It is arranged chronologically by the date of the meeting or conference, and has keyword indexes. *Proceedings in Print* is a bimonthly journal of all published proceedings still available, primarily through commercial or society publishers. Each issue is in 2 parts, 1 containing entries for publication during the prior 2 years, the other listing older entries still in print. A single index covers corporate authors (institutions, societies, etc.) and subject entries. In addition to these sources, *BioScience* and publications of the Wildlife Society also have sections listing the forthcoming conferences, and frequently mention available proceedings of earlier conferences.

ABBREVIATIONS, ACRONYMS, SIGNS, SYMBOLS AND CODEN

It is hard for many people to appreciate fully how easily abbreviations and acronyms can be misunderstood. This problem is especially relevant when abbreviations are used for the names of scientific journals; i.e., "Z" can stand for Zeitschrift, Zentralblatt, or Zhurnal. The American National Standards Institute (formerly Association) has helped standardize abbreviations with their list of recommendations (American National Standards Institute 1970). In addition, the Biosis *List of Serials,* issued by the Biological Abstracts, will also identify abbreviated journal titles. Most of the A/I services publish lists of journals they index, but Biosis is probably the single best source for wildlife titles. *Wildlife Abstracts, 1961–1970,* is also another good source for identification. Coden is still another source of journal titles with a unique 5-letter code for each journal published in the world. Currently, a directory of Coden codes and journal titles is published by the Franklin Institute, Philadelphia, under the title *Coden for Periodical Titles,* 3rd Edition, 1970. Two supplements of new titles have been issued, with the fourth edition being planned. The best source of European journals, including many obscure and local titles, is the *World List* (Brown and Stratton 1963) with its supplements.

For unpublished report literature, the *Dictionary of Report Series Codes* (Godfrey and Redman 1973) will identify the issuing agency for federal reports. All wildlife biologists should be familiar with the P-R designation, which stands for 'Pittman-Robertson' reports, filed at the Library Reference Service, Federal Aid to Wildlife Restoration, Denver, Colorado. Most of the other federal documents are filed in the National Technical Information Service, Springfield, Virginia, and can be obtained using the report series code.

Acronyms, abbreviations for words, and signs or symbols have a number of special dictionaries for interpretation. The Council of Biology Editors (1978) provides the basic style manual for the biological sciences, but there are others also in use: Chicago University Press (1969), GPO (U.S. Government Printing Office 1973), Nicholson (1967). All have the standard proofer's marks illustrated. Kenneth (1963) and Gray (1970) include lists of commonly used abbreviations, signs and symbols. There are also dictionaries of acronyms: Pugh (1970) Crowley and Thomas (1973); abbreviations—Schwartz (1955), Buttress (1966), Paxton (1974), and De Sola (1978). The latter dictionary also includes a list of proofer's marks as well as the Russian, Hebrew, German and Greek alphabets.

DICTIONARIES, GLOSSARIES AND SINGLE-VOLUME ENCYCLOPEDIAS

This section includes those source materials for a paragraph or page-length discussion of a topic, for a 1- to 2-line definition of a term, or to locate a corresponding term in another language. The single-volume dictionary is the best example of this type of material, although occasionally glossaries are encountered in the scientific journals. Walker et al. (1964, v. 3, p. 692) gave a short list of dictionaries for the biologist.

Van Nostrand's Scientific Encyclopedia, now in its fourth edition, is a single-volume compilation of scientific terms, and is considered one of the best examples of an all-purpose scientific encyclopedia. The *Harper Encyclopedia of Science* (1967) is another good 1-volume source. The *McGraw-Hill Encyclopedia of Science and Technology*, in 15 volumes, also has a number of good articles for the wildlife biologist, but the index is necessary to access information scattered in various articles. In the biological sciences, Gray (1970) has compiled a single-volume encyclopedia; in ornithology, Thomson (1964); in microscopy, Clark (1961) and Gray (1973); in microbiology, Jacobs et al. (1957). In addition, a hunter's and outdoorsman's encyclopedia by Trefethen and Miracle (1966) provides a good source of wildlife information.

A single-volume dictionary of great importance to the biologist is Henderson and Henderson (Kenneth 1963). Three other dictionaries of biology are Steen (1971), Abercrombie et al. (1973), and Lapedes (1977) which contain some of the newer terms created for the biological sciences. In addition to the 1- or 2-line definitions, Henderson and Henderson included the pronunciation and derivation of terms. In this respect it resembles 2 books by Jaeger, a sourcebook (1955) which included definitions, and the other a pronunciation handbook (1960) without definitions.

For the more specialized needs of the wildlife biologist, there are individual, specialized dictionaries, several of which may help the wildlife manager. The following list contains several of the more important titles: wildlife terms (Krumholz 1957); range management (Huss 1974); ecology (Carpenter 1938, Hanson 1962); wildlands (Schwarz et al. 1976); botanical terms used in range management (Dayton 1950); economic plants (Uphof 1959, McVaugh et al. 1968); forest terminology (Society of American Foresters, Committee on Terminology 1958); botany (Usher 1966, Swartz 1971); entomology (Foote 1977); zoology (Pennak 1964, Leftwich 1973); ornithology (Newton 1893–1896); water terminology (Veatch and Humphrys 1966); geology (Gary et al. 1972); weather (Thiessen 1946); soil and water conservation (Soil Conservation Society of America 1952). In addition, there are various checklists of names, both common and vulgar, of organisms. Jeffrey (1977) gave a good discussion of scientific names, with explanation of various taxonomic designates.

For foreign terms and phrases, there are a number of special-language dictionaries. Some are multilingual; Haensch and Haberkamp (1976) in biology with German/English/French/Spanish terms cross indexed; Weck (1966) in forestry with German/English/French/Spanish/Russian; Haensch and Haberkamp (1966) in agriculture with German/English/French/Spanish; and Heymer (1978) in ethology with German/English/French. The DeVries dictionaries rank at the top of the list for those supplying English equivalents of general scientific terms in German (1978) or French (1976). Carpovich (1960) has compiled a Russian-English dictionary with emphasis on the medical sciences; Dumbleton (1964) published a Russian-English dictionary for biological sciences; Ricker (1973) for fisheries and aquatic biology. MacLennan (1958) has prepared a useful Russian-English glossary for ornithologists, covering 712 of the bird species found in the Soviet Union, while Kuroda (1971) compiled a list of the family Anatidae (waterfowl) with the Latin and Japanese equivalent names. Choate (1973) provided a list of common American names, scientific names and an English/Latin glossary for ornithologists. Grzimek (1974–1977) listed common names of various species for each of the European languages, with the scientific name at the back of each volume. A seven-language source of common names (Latin, German, English, French, Hungarian, Spanish and Russian) is provided by Gozmany et al. (1979) for European animals (invertebrates to mammals). In addition, Gotch (1979) lists all the mammalian names in Latin with an explanation and their place in animal classification.

DIRECTORIES

The reader will find international organizations, agencies, associations, and research institutes listed in several sources: *Research Centers Directory*, issued every 2 years by Gale Research Co.; the Minerva handbooks of *Wissenschaftlich Gesellschaften* and *Forschungsintitute*, both published by Walter de Gruyter in 1972; *World of Learning*, issued annually by Europa Publications; *Index Generalis* (1919–1939, (1953–1955); and several directories issued by the Library of Congress National Referral Center in biological sciences (1972), physical sciences and engineering (1971), water (1966) and toxicology (1969). Other sources will be found in Gray and Langord (1961), Murra (1962), and UNESCO's directory (1965). These are international directories for research institutes, universities and scientific societies.

Other specialized directories have been issued for collections of zoological specimens in tropical institutes (UNESCO 1962); institutions engaged in arid-zone research (UNESCO 1953); biological field stations (Jack 1945); national wildlife refuges in the United States (U.S. Fish and Wildlife Service 1975, Riley and Riley 1979); bird clubs and ornithological societies (Rickert 1978); agriculture and biology in the United States (National Agricultural Library 1971); conservation organizations (*Conservation Directory* and Anon. 1961–1966), natural history collections (Sherborn 1940); environment (Halstead 1972, Thibeau 1972 and Paulson 1974); museums (Hudson and Nicholls 1975); inland biological field stations (Arvey and Riemer 1966); marine, freshwater, mountain, desert and special laboratories (Vernberg 1963); zoos and aquariums (Hoff 1966); national parks (IUCN 1971–1977); National Park System (U.S. National Park Service 1976); mammal collections (Anderson et al. 1963) and arctic research (Stanka 1958).

Specialized directories are also available for research institutes and agencies in other countries, by country or function: Great Britain (Anon. 1884–1976), Germany (Domay 1964), Eastern Europe (National Academy of Sciences 1963, Little 1967), U.S.S.R. (Battelle Memorial Institute 1963), Latin America (UNESCO 1949+); United States (Bates 1965, National Academy of Sciences 1971 and prior issues). A special functional geographic directory by Lysaght (1959) listed natural history societies in Great Britain.

Another type of specialized directory is an equipment directory, or catalogue. The U.S. Fish and Wildlife Service *Wildlife Leaflet* series contains several directory issues, listing manufacturers of animal traps (no. 263, 1962), rodenticides (no. 465, 1964), chemical animal repellents (no. 464, 1964) and bird control devices (no. 409, 1964). *Science* issues an annual supplement called "Guide to Scientific Instruments"; *Instruments and Control Systems* and *Chemical Week* each publish an annual "Buyer's Guide." These special issues include a directory of equipment manufacturers, laboratory supply houses, and new developments in the field of scientific accessories. *Chemical Week* also lists chemicals and services for sale as well as equipment. Another source for locating the names of dealers handling the more common chemicals, raw materials, equipment, etc. is *Thomas' Register of American Manufacturers*, issued annually. This is published in several volumes and includes the names of dealers handling such items as animal traps, telemetry devices, testing equipment, etc. Once a manufacturer is found, a letter can be written to ask for their catalogs. Most manufacturers are quite willing to supply further information about their supplies and services.

BIOGRAPHICAL INFORMATION

The traditional sources of biographic information include biographical directories, who's who type publications, membership lists, newspaper reports, and journal articles in memoria or honoria. Typical of the information available in these sources are titles, addresses, positions held, degrees, occasionally lists of publications, together with general information regarding family, membership in social or professional groups, and awards and honors. For many years the H. W. Wilson Co. has published a continuing index to this type of information, called the *Biography Index*. This monthly publication lists all biographical articles and newspaper reports of any individual, referring to the original citation. A single volume is cumulated at the end of the year within this series, and then into 3-year volumes. Both living and dead individuals are indexed, but the emphasis is on the living or books about the historical.

A number of single-volume biographical directories for scientists, both living and deceased have been compiled. The most useful of these is Ireland (1962); although Kuznetsov (1961–1965), Asimov (1972), and Williams (1974) are also of value. The last one, being in Russian, has limited value for the most American users. In addition to these scientific biographic directories, there are 2 general dictionary-type publications which list 1 to 2 lines about famous scientists: *Chamber's Biographical Dictionary*, published in 1969, and *Webster's Biographical Dictionary*, published in 1943 and 1972.

The who's who type of publications are numerous: They tend to supply limited information of a current nature on individuals still alive. A single source for American and Canadian biographies is the index work *Biographical Dictionaries Master Index*, 1975–1976 (LaBeau and Tarbert 1976) which provided references to many of the individual who's who publications. However, it must be used in conjunction with the who's who originally published. One of the best sources for scientists in the United States or Canada is still the *American Men and Women of Science* (1979) in its fourteenth edition. Similar types of publications have been prepared for Britain in 1963–1967 as *Directory of British Scientists*, and in 1970 and 1972 as *Who's Who of British Scientists*. In the U.S.S.R. the *Biografischeskii slovar' deiatelei estestvoznaniia i tekhniki*, published in 1958–1959 provided similar information. From its 4,500 entries, nearly 1,000 were selected and translated, with editing by Telberg (1964) to provide an English-language source of Russian scientists. Turkevich (1963) provided another listing of Russian scientists; Turkevich and Turkevich (1968) provided one for European scientists. The *Who's Who in Publishing*, issued by the Institute for Scientific Information annually, is not a typical who's who publication. It provides addresses for published scientists during the prior year with no other biographic information provided.

Specialized directories are available for many fields. Soviet zoologists are covered by Strelkov and Yur'yev (1962); Polish ones by the Polska Akademia Nauk, Komitet Zoologiczny (1962). Specialists in plant taxonomy (De Roon 1958), zoological taxonomists (Blackwelder and Blackwelder 1961), ecology (Special Reports, Inc. 1973), British and Irish botanists (Britten and Boulger 1931) are some further examples of specialized directories. The *Index de Zoologists*, published in Paris by the Union Internationale des Sciences Biologiques in 1953, and the *Naturalists' Directory*, a biennial publication, list only addresses with the specialty research interests of their listees. The entries of the *Naturalists' Directory* and *Who's Who in Publishing* have little overlap. The former lists many amateur naturalists while the latter takes its entries from research journals in this field.

GUIDES TO THE LITERATURE AND CHECKLISTS OF RECOMMENDED BOOKS

Guides or literature manuals have as their purpose the double function of guiding the research worker through the literature of his discipline and introducing the novice to some of the tools of his trade. These are much more than subject bibliographies, for they usually include more bibliographic detail, contents notes, and a list of the important sources with a discussion on how to make the best use of them. (This chapter is a literature guide.) In general, they give the reader a better concept of the extent of the literature of his field. It is unfortunate that there are no literature guides available for the wildlife biologist comparable to the manuals which have been prepared for the chemist, mathematician, physicist or geologist. In fact, only a handful have been published covering even the related disciplines.

A literature guide can be very short, such as the one by Ficken and Ficken (1966) to the literature of avian field ethology, or it can be a monograph like the early study made by Wood (1931) of the zoological literature. This study by Wood covers vertebrate zoology and is important due to its historical treatment of the literature. The recent books by Bottle and Wyatt (1971) and Kirk (1978) provide a good guide into the current biological literature, including those fields needed by the wildlife biologist. Smith and Reid (1972) also provided an outline guide to the zoological literature by topic and annotated title lists. Although coverage has been enlarged to include other life sciences, its primary emphasis is still on zoological literature. Used in conjunction with Bottle and Wyatt (1971), the overview of the wildlife literature is covered. Several good guides are found in chapters of Bonn (1973), especially the ones by Sarah Thomas, James Kollegger, and Gerald Zimmerman for those wildlife biologists involved in using the environmental literature.

Several specialized literature guides have relevance to wildlife studies, notably Adomaitis et al. (1967) for the chemical and related technical literature in wildlife conservation; Sharma (1977) for planning and land use in wildlife conservation; Stone (1933) for a historical summary of American ornithological literature published from 1883–1933; Vaurie (1964, 1966) for Russian ornithological literature, which also updated the earlier work of Johansen (1952); Blackwelder (1972) for taxonomic literature of vertebrates, including fauna guides, and Blackwelder (1963a) for a more general zoological guide to books.

Hickey (1943), Southern (1964), Mosby (1963b) and Benton and Werner (1974) have also included chapters discussing the literature of their fields, as part of a general book. The appendix in Benton and Werner lists books and journals of interest to the field biologists covering lower plants, wildflowers, trees and shrubs, invertebrates and vertebrates. Olson (1958) has discussed the Russian literature for the natural sciences in his review of history, scope, patterns, style, and use. Much of his discussion on procurement is now outdated but of value in identifying the problems involved. Eakin (1958) has published a checklist for a forestry library, which includes a section on wildlife literature. Like Smith and Reid, its value is limited to titles rather than a true guide to the literature.

Indeed, the entire question of bibliographic guides and literature handling has assumed a new importance in today's information-minded world. Although communication among scientists has always been a goal, recently there has been a concentrated effort to have library networks, national governments, international agencies and other multi-institutional organizations provide a formal and comprehensive information transfer network. utilizing both published materials and unpublished reports, memos, and position papers. In 1962, a translation of the bibliographic problems in the natural sciences was compiled by Kibrick (1962) with an emphasis on Russian biological bibliographies. The Council on Biological Sciences Information (1970), part of the National Research Council, produced a functional analysis of the types of information media and their access and storage problems. In 1971, the U.S. House of Representatives issued a report to provide for a national environmental data system, which was not funded *per se*, but provided a background into those problems, also faced by the wildlife communities. Edwards et al. (1971) also issued a series of lectures on the problems of biological information and its storage and access. The section by Dadd (1971) on the *Zoological Record* described basic criteria of selection and acquisition especially relevant to wildlife users. The latest comprehensive effort at biological literature problems and its attendant proposed solutions can be found in the National Academy of Sciences report for 1970. All of these sources provide specific information on the various problems of bibliographic control in the biological sciences, and will give specific information to the wildlife user who is interested in the magnitude of the problems and possible solutions.

THE SYSTEMATIC LITERATURE

The systematic literature of biology is voluminous and complex. Only a few of the basic publications will be discussed here. The reader who needs additional information should review the chapter in Smith and Reid (1972) and use the sections in Blackwelder (1972). The manual by Jeffrey (1977) is a good basic introduction to taxonomic nomenclature, sponsored by the Systematics Association. Further readings in Simpson (1945), Mayr et al. (1953) and Crowson (1970) will enable the wildlife biologist to acquire an understanding of the fundamentals of taxonomy and systematics. Simpson (1961) is a more general book on classification than Crowson (1970), but the beginning taxonomist will find Crowson easier to understand.

For a general reference work in classification, Clark and Panchen (1971) and Blackwelder (1963b) provided a synopsis of animal classification; Lord Rothschild (1965) has issued a list of most of the animal orders, phyla, subphyla, classes and genera of extant species. The basic volume is arranged in systematic order, with scientific name and a vulgar name index. Burton (1962) has written a systematic dictionary, covering the more common species of mammals with their general characteristics, food, breeding, habit and range. Anderson and Jones (1967) have written a taxonomic synopsis of the families of extant (living) mammals, which includes description, distribution, biological characteristics, and the recent genera and range maps of each family. Corbet (1978) has written a taxonomic review of all the mammals of the Palaearctic region, including prior names, keys to the species, and distribution notes. For the United States, Blair et al. (1968) have prepared keys to the vertebrates, including fishes, amphibians, reptiles, birds and mammals to the species level. A very limited set of taxonomic keys to the more common animals (excluding birds) of the North Central states has been prepared by Eddy and Hodson (1961). Ingles (1965) has a number of keys scattered through his book, including a general key to the orders and an artificial generic skull key for animals.

The International Commission on Zoological Nomenclature (1964) is responsible for making recommendations for amendments or additions to the International Code of Zoological Nomenclature; rendering opinions on questions of zoological nomenclature; compiling official lists of the family, generic and specific names in zoology, and resolving various questions of taxonomic groupings. The *Bulletin of Zoological Nomenclature* is the official organ of this Commission. In addition to its other work, the Commission publishes official lists of invalid and rejected names at the generic and species levels. Frequently these changes are noted in the *Bulletin of Zoological Nomenclature* before the Commission makes final rulings upon their status. The *Zoological Record* publishes a "List of New Genera and Subgenera" as a separate section, no. 20. Within the Aves and Mammalia sections, the index also contains the list of relevant new genera or subgenera names. Ali opinions of the Commission are listed also in the annual compilations of the *Zoological Record.*

In tracing the origin of a particular zoological name, the wildlife biologists will find the work of Neave (1939–1940) and its supplements (Neave 1950a, Edwards and Hopwood 1966) of particular value. *Zoological Record, Biological Abstracts* and various fauna guides, checklists, and catalogues supplement Neave's work. Neave's *Nomenclator Zoologicus* is a list of the names of genera and subgenera used in the literature from Linneaus' 10th ed., 1758 to the end of 1935 with bibliographic information for the original citation and descriptions. Neave's (1950b) supplement brings the list from 1935 to 1945. Edwards and Hopwood (1966) brings it up to 1955.

Catalogs listing type specimens of recent mammals available in their collections have been issued by the American Museum of Natural History (Goodwin 1953), the Chicago Natural History Museum (Sanborn 1947), the Carnegie Museum for birds (Todd 1928), the United States National Museum for birds (Deignan 1961) and mammals (Poole and Schantz 1942). There are a number of specimen lists, most of which can be found in Blackwelder (1972) or by writing the museum directly.

For the wildlife biologist seeking to determine correct nomenclature, phylogenetic relationships, or to locate the original description of a mammal, 3 basic sources to be consulted are Miller and Kellogg (1955), Hall and Kelson (1959), and Hall (1979). All of these books update an earlier work by Anderson (1946) for Canadian mammals and cover the North American (Nearctic) species. Miller and Kellogg summarized the results of taxonomic studies of North American mammals and indicated the specimens represented in the collections of the United States National Museum up to Jan. 1, 1953. The work by Hall brings this synopsis up to 1979, and in many ways, replaces the earlier works of Anderson, Miller and Kellogg, and Banfield (1974). For similar problems relating to birds, the reader is directed to the *Checklist of Birds of the World* by Peters (1931–1970), a parallel publication from the British Ornithologists' Union (1952), Wetmore's (1960) systematic classification for birds of the world, Mayr and Amadon's (1951) classification of recent birds, Clements' (1974) and Edwards' (1974) true checklists of the birds of the world. The last 2 checklists have a complete systematic list, with Latin and English names; Clements (1974) included the faunal regions of distribution; Edwards used a coded set for distribution. The American Ornithologists' Union provides the authoritative checklist of names and distribution for North American species (AOU 1957). Updates to the list are published in *Auk*, usually annually.

FIELD GUIDES, REGIONAL FAUNAS AND CHECKLISTS

The wildlife biologist will find field guides, manuals, handbooks, and regional faunas of great assistance in his work. Field guides are especially useful, and range in subject matter from algae and astronomy to seashore life, bird watching (Hickey 1943), wildflowers, mushrooms (Lange and Hora 1963, Smith 1963) mammals, and birds. They can be used to identify specimens, tracks, scat or habitat. One of the best-known writers and editors of field guides is Roger Tory Peterson, who has been compiling field guides since 1934. His books on birds are indispensable to the field observer. Houghton Mifflin has issued a series of field guides he has edited, known popularly as the Peterson Field Guide series. These include books on amphibians, animal tracks, birds, butterflies, mammals, reptiles, rocks, and shells. Most are oriented towards North America, but some include mammals of West Africa, birds and mammals of Britain and Europe, etc. A recent biography (Devlin and Naismith 1977) lists the various titles he has edited, written and compiled, including the field guides. In addition, Putnam, Doubleday, Golden Press (edited by Herbert Zim), the University of California Press (Berkeley), the American Museum of Natural History, the National Audubon Society (Washington, D.C.), and the Canadian National Museum also have issued field guides.

In England, Warne publishes the Wayside and Woodland series while Collins publishes the New Naturalist series. Both these British series are oriented towards the United Kingdom and western Europe. In addition, the Mammal Society of the British Isles started publishing a series called Field Guide to British Mammals. The first book (Page 1959) was an excellent guide to deer. Although there are many field guides, each will include special features of interest, such as bird songs (Robbins et al. 1966) animals in winter (Morgan 1939), pictures of skulls (Palmer 1957, Burt and Grossenheider 1976), flight silhouettes (Booth 1950, Perkins 1954, Collins 1959, Peterson 1961, Ingles 1965, Robbins et al. 1966, Peterson et al. 1977), illustrations in color (Anthony 1928, Collins 1959, Peterson 1961, Robbins et al. 1966, Burt and Grossenheider 1976, Peterson et al. 1977, Pettingill 1977), drawings of tracks (Murie 1954, Perkins 1954, Palmer 1957, Seton 1958, Rollins 1959, Page 1959, Ingles 1965, Burt and Grossenheider 1976), or scat (Murie 1954, Palmer 1957, Seton 1958, Ingels 1965), picture keys (Booth 1950), color keys (Chapman 1912), and coverage of both domestic as well as wild animals (Palmer 1957). There are wide variations in the coverage and quality of these manuals, and the reader should exercise great care in their selection.

Most of the field guides contain distribution maps and include bibliographies, which though often short, can lead the reader into more specialized publications. Palmer (1957), Peterson (1961), Peterson et al. (1977) and Pettingill (1956, 1977) include short bibliographies. Anthony (1928), Pettingill (1956) and Burt and Grossenheider (1976) have arranged their bibliographies to show publications for various localities. In addition, Anthony has prepared a short bibliography to serve as a point of departure for a literature search involving the life zones, Insectivora, Rodentia, Carnivora, Artiodactyla, etc.

Supplementing these general field guides are the numerous state, provincial, and regional guides to birds and mammals published by local clubs, museums academies of science, societies, governmental agencies, natural history surveys, university and private publishing houses. Blackwelder (1972) has several good sections under Reptilia, Aves, and Mammalia which list many of the available field guides or checklists. The reader should also note the section on systematic literature in this chapter, and check the bibliography of Walker et al. (1964) for further guides to regional literature.

Although there is no comprehensive bibliography of faunas comparable to the guide prepared for the world's floras by Blake and Atwood (1942, 1961) or Terres' (1961) bibliography of regional checklists for birds of the United States, Canada and the West Indies, Blackwelder's (1972) provides a good starting list of guides. F. M. Chapman's (1912) *Faunal Bibliography* on birds is still useful although now outdated. Morris (1965) has compiled a short list of regional faunas followed by a critical discussion of the principal regional authorities. Malclés (1958), Walker et al. (1964), the *Zoological Record, Wildlife Abstracts,* and the *Wildlife Review* all have sections listing regional fauna guides as they are published. The North American Fauna series also contains a number of systematic synopses for recent mammals, as does the University of Kansas Museum of Natural History series. Miller (1978) has prepared a bibliography of unpublished reports of the Canadian Wildlife Service concerning the National Parks of Canada. The work by Smart and Taylor (1953) listed a major selection of available guides to the fauna and flora of the British Isles.

The following are a few examples of regional guides: mammals of Arizona (Cockrum 1960, Lowe 1964), Colorado (Warren 1942, Armstrong 1972), Kansas (Cockrum 1952, Hall 1955), Kentucky (Barbour and Davis 1974), Louisiana (Lowery 1974a), Michigan (Burt 1954), Minnesota (Gunderson and Beer 1953), Missouri (Schwartz and Schwartz 1959), Montana (Hoffman and Pattie 1968), Nebraska (Jones 1964), New Mexico (Findley et al. 1975), New England (Godin 1977), Nevada (Hall 1946), Rhode Island (Cronan and Brooks 1968), South Carolina (Golley 1966), Wisconsin (Jackson 1961), Wyoming (Long 1965), Great Lakes region (Burt 1957), the Sierra Nevada (Sumner and Dixon 1953), the Pacific States (Ingles 1965), eastern United States (Hamilton and Whitaker 1979), eastern Canada (Peterson 1966), Canada (Anderson 1946, Banfield 1974), Ontario (Dagg 1974), New Brunswick (Squires 1968), Manitoba (Soper 1961), Great Britian (Southern 1964, Lawrence and Brown 1973), western Europe (Corbet 1966), Mexico (Leopold 1959), palearctic and Indian mammals (Ellerman and Morrison-Scott 1966), West African carnivores (Rosevear 1974), a popular guide to mammals of South Africa (Roberts 1951), and the older checklist of Allen (1939); on birds of Alabama (Imhof 1976), Alaska (Gabrielson and Lincoln 1959), Arizona (Phillips et al. 1964), California (Dawson 1923, Small 1974), Canada (Taverner 1953, Godfrey 1966), Colorado (Bailey and Niedrach 1965), Florida (Sprunt 1954), Georgia (Burleigh 1958), Idaho (Burleigh 1972), Kentucky (Barbour et al. 1973), Louisiana (Lowery 1974b), Massachusetts (Forbush 1925–1929), Minnesota (Green and Janssen 1975), Nevada (Linsdale 1936), New Jersey (Leck 1975), North Dakota (Stewart 1975), Oklahoma (Sutton 1967), Oregon (Gabrielson and Jewett 1940, 1970), Texas (Peterson 1960, Oberholser and Kincaid 1974), Washington (Jewett et al. 1953), Wisconsin (Gromme 1963), Labrador (Todd 1963), British Isles (Witherby et al. 1943), east and central Africa (Williams 1963), west central and western Africa (Mackworth-Praed and Grant 1973), eastern and northeastern Africa (Mackworth-Praed and Grant 1957), South Africa (Roberts 1940) and Central America (Blake 1977). To aid in the identification of introduced species, particularly in the United States, Laycock (1966) provided a history of introductions and current distribution.

WILDLIFE TECHNIQUES AND THEIR LOCATION IN THE LITERATURE

The location and selection of the best technique for the solution of a problem, be it field, laboratory, or statistical problem, is a critical undertaking. The reader can expect to find field and laboratory techniques scattered throughout the literature, with discussions ranging in complexity from the simple "cookbook" type descriptions to detailed discussions of complex instruments and statistical techniques. For additional bibliographic material, the reader should study the other chapters of this book and look at the section on "Methods (taxonomic)" in Blackwelder (1972). These sections deal not only with taxonomic techniques, but also with various statistical approaches.

A few of the sources for articles describing techniques useful to the wildlife biologist can be found in the *Journal of Wildlife Management, Nature, Laboratory Investigation, Laboratory Practice, Journal of Mammalogy, Biometrics, Science, BioScience, Curator, Journal of Wildlife Diseases, Stain Technology,* and *Quarterly Journal of Microscopical Science,* as well as the house organs from several of the scientific supply houses. A more systematic approach to look for articles on techniques would be to utilize one or more of the indexing and information services available. Specialized techniques are indexed in *Biological Abstracts* under the name of the technique, the name of its originator, or the name of the instrument. Moreover, several of the individual sections, i.e., "Bones, Joints, Fasciae . . ." and "Blood, Blood-forming Organs and Body Fluids" have separate subsections on "Methods," which can be easily browsed. *Wildlife Review* and *Wildlife Abstracts* have sections listing techniques under the main heading of "Wildlife," "Birds," and "Mammals." The *Zoological Record: Mammalia* has a subsection on techniques, available through the subject index. The *Journal of Wildlife Management* has its own index, with a separate heading for techniques.

There are a number of bibliographies which list publications covering techniques. Mosby (1963a) has included a 33-page bibliography arranged by author. Vol. 3 of Walker et al. (1964) has a 2-page bibliography on techniques and methods. Anderson (1965) and Southwood (1966) both have useful bibliographies scattered through their texts; Knudsen (1966) provided a short bibliography on the collecting techniques for each of the major groups of plants and animals; Morris (1967) has compiled a bibliography of statistical methods for grassland research; Humason (1972) wrote a 26-page bibliography on animal tissue techniques; and Will and Patric (1972) have a bibliography on wildlife telemetry and radio tracking. Schultz's (1961) bibliography on statistics in ecological research and Tepper's (1967) bibliography on statistical methods for population estimation provide lists of the major sources and methods in this field.

As far as texts available, Mosby (1963a), Anderson (1965), Wyoming Game and Fish Dept. (1977), Lehner (1979) and the chapters in the *Wildlife Techniques Manual* probably come closest to answering the immediate needs of the wildlife biologist. Their work can be supplemented by the Atlantic Waterfowl Council's (1972) handbook on waterfowl techniques, the earlier work of Wight (1938) on field techniques, Flood et al. (1977) on habitat evaluation techniques, the interim suggestions of Ansell (1965) on the standardization of field data taken from mammals, including such things as measurements (see also Smithers 1973a), apparatus, and standards of accuracy, Mahoney (1966) and Emmel and Cowdry (1964) on laboratory techniques supplemented by Atkins (1960) and Oster (1955–1964) for specialized techniques of biological research, or Friend (1967, 1968) for the eye lens technique, Moyer (1953) on taxidermy, the short chapters in Hall and Kelson (1959) and Ingles (1965), as well as Hall (1962) and Smithers (1973b), on the collection and preparation of specimens for study, and the suggestions of Blake (1949) and Van Tyne (1952) on collecting and preserving bird specimens for taxonomic work. Southwood's (1966) manual on ecological methods, although principally concerned with insects and large populations, will be of assistance in the selection of statistical sampling techniques involving measurement and sampling, supplemented by the critical review of Sokal (1965) on statistical methods in systematics. Hower's (1967) work on the freeze-dry preservation of specimens also should be reviewed in work involving the accurate measurement of organs. These in turn can be augmented by the more detailed publications describing an instrument, a research technique or methods for collecting, skinning, preserving and mounting the specimen. Such manuals have been prepared for invertebrates (Wagstaffe and Fidler 1955), birds (Chapin 1946, Blake 1949, Harrison 1978), mammals (Dice 1932, Anthony 1950) and agricultural specimens (Fessenden 1949). Recent works on handling live specimens for marking and behavioral study include Fowler (1978) and Markowitz and Stevens (1978). In addition, the reader will find the reference manual by Hale (1965) of immense value in the laboratory and field. This pocket-size manual contains a wealth of information on such things as pH buffers, staining, standard deviation, decalcifying fluids, twistdrill gauges, etc.

Many museums publish descriptive manuals on the preservation, preparation, and collection of natural history specimens. The Smithsonian Institution and the U.S. National Museum have issued collectors' manuals covering birds, birds' eggs, rough skeletons, and study specimens of small mammals in Bulletin no. 39, and in the Smithsonian Institution's Publication no. 3766: ***Field Collector's Manual in Natural History***. The British Museum (Natural History) publishes a series called "Instructions for Collectors." Handbooks of interest to the wildlife biologist in this series have been published for mammals, birds, and bird eggs; reptiles, amphibians, and fishes; insects; worms; invertebrates (animals other than insects); plants, and alcohol and alcoholmeters. The University of Kansas Museum of Natural History has also issued several publications on collecting and preserving specimens, such as Hall (1962), while the Chicago Field Museum of Natural History has a numbered series of pamphlets illustrating various museum techniques called *Fieldiana: Techniques*. The American Museum of Natural History (Chapin 1946, Anthony 1950, Lucas 1950), the National Museum of Canada (Anderson 1965), and the Cleveland Museum of Natural History (Bole 1939) have all published material on the preparation of biological specimens of interest to the wildlife biologist. Blackwelder (1972) has various sections listing articles on collecting techniques under the subheadings of "Methods" within each of his groups of vertebrates. The magazine *Curator* will occasionally include articles on this topic. Many examples from the journal are noted in the Borhegyi and Dodson (1961) bibliography.

Some examples of the more specialized publications are those covering staining (Gurr 1971, Conn 1977), microtechniques (Lee 1950, Gray 1954, 1964), limnological methods (Welch 1948), analysis of rodent populations (Davis 1956, Eberhardt 1969), cutting of thin sections (Steedman 1960), sexing and aging techniques (Thompson 1958, Godin 1960), techniques for measuring understory vegetation (Cain and Castro 1959, U.S. Forest Service 1959), study and preparation of animal tissue (Humason 1972), telemetry (Slater 1963, Southern 1963, Mech 1967), nature photography (Winkler and Adams 1968, Kinne 1971, Turner-Ettlinger 1976), aerial photography (Gilbert and Hahn 1959, Colwell 1960, Murtha 1964), and techniques of biological illustration (Zweifel 1961).

In addition to the single-volume handbooks, there are a number of series covering techniques which begin with the words *Methods in . . . .* These exist for cell physiology, virology, soil analysis, serological research, vitamin assay, cancer, immunology, membrane biology, and enzymology. They serve a useful function by bringing the latest research techniques to the reader's attention.

The reader should also be aware of the various ancillary manuals for range research. The Joint Committee of the American Society of Range Management and the Agricultural Board (1962) have prepared a standard textbook for advanced students on the problems and techniques of range research. Other manuals of methodology have been prepared by the U.S. Forest Service (1963); the Grassland Research Institute (1961); and the Joint Committee of the American Society of Agronomy, American Dairy Science Association, American Society of Animal Production, and the American Society of Range Management (1962). The latter manual emphasizes pasture and range research involving livestock.

ENCYCLOPEDIAS, HANDBOOKS AND TRAITÉ SETS

When a wildlife biologist finds himself in need of a lengthy, detailed discussion of a scientific topic or of a particular animal or group of animals, there are several sources to which reference can be made. The broad-based *McGraw-Hill Encyclopedia of Science and Technology* is the most common place to look. When an animal, or taxonomic group of animals, is under investigation, *Grzimek's Animal Life Encyclopedia* provides lengthy, detailed articles, especially in v. 7–9 (Birds I–III) and v. 10–13 (Mammals I–IV). For other types of information, the multivolume sets similar to the German *Handbucher* or French *Traité* series may be necessary. These are usually cooperative works, prepared by many contributors, each of whom is considered an expert in his own segment of the broad field. Such contributions offer the reader an introduction to his topic, and are often the best summaries of what is known about a particular subject or organism. Many of the titles mentioned here are still being published; moreover, it is characteristic of this type of publication that volumes or parts may appear out of sequence. Examples of these multivolume sets which should be familiar to the wildlife biologist are H. G. Bronn's *Klassen und Ordnugen des Tierreichs,* founded in 1859 and still being published (many of the earlier volumes of this set are now out of print and being reissued by Johnson Reprints, Inc.); *Handbuch der Zoologie* by Kuckenthal; *Traité de Zoologie* by Pierre-P. Grassé; *Das Tierreich* by Franz Schulze; and 2 older works: *Treatise on Zoology* by Sir Ray Lankester and the *Cambridge Natural History* by S. F. Harmer and A. E. Shipley. *Handbook of North American Birds* by R. S. Palmer and *Manual of Neotropical Birds* by E. R. Blake are examples of this type of publication prepared for the ornithologist. Another example of the knowledge in a special field being systematically organized and presented is the American Physiological Society's *Handbook of Physiology*, covering both vertebrates and invertebrates.

LAWS, REGULATIONS AND INTERNATIONAL TREATIES

In the United States, Title 16: *Conservation* and Title 43: *Public Lands* of the *United States Code* will provide the wildlife biologist with statements of appropriate Federal law governing these 2 areas. Recently, a compilation called *Index to U.S. Federal Wildlife Regulations* (Berger and Phillips 1977) has been issued to provide copies of all the laws and regulations applicable to wildlife biology. It includes sections of the *U.S. Code,* as well as the *Code of Federal Regulations: Title 50* which covers such things as the hunting and possession of wildlife, the national wildlife refuge system, management of wildlife research areas, and federal aid to states in fish and wildlife restoration. The U.S. Fish and Wildlife Service frequently reprints sections of *Title 50* as its series: *Hunting Regulations.* The U.S. Fish and Wildlife Service publishes an annual leaflet describing migratory bird hunting regulations for each of the 4 waterfowl flyways (Atlantic, Mississippi, Central, Pacific). It is called *Summary of Federal Hunting Regulations* (1979) and is available from the Migratory Bird Program, U.S. Fish Wildlife Service, Laurel, Maryland. The *Index to U.S. Federal Wildlife Regulations* also contains the text of treaties and international conventions which deal with wildlife, such as the "Migratory Bird Convention with Japan."

New laws appear separately as slip laws (bearing P.L. numbers) until they can be incorporated into the *United States Code.* New administrative regulations appear in the *Federal Register,* a periodical appearing 5 times a week, until they can become a part of the *Code of Federal Regulations.* In 1977, the House of Representative's Committee on Merchant Marine and Fisheries ordered *A Compilation of Federal Laws Relating to Conservation and Development of Our Nation's Fish and Wildlife Resources, Environmental Quality, and Oceanography* which was compiled by the Congressional Research Service, Library of Congress. It updated the 1973 and 1975 committee prints on the same topic, as well as earlier editions. This volume includes the summary of Federal laws relating to fish and wildlife from the *U.S. Code* and *U.S. Statutes at Large.* It includes such things as the Dingell-Johnson Act, Pittman-Robertson Act, Bald Eagle Protection Act, National Bison Range Act. An index list for the popular and statutory names of these acts is given in the front of this volume. The number of the item for the *United States Code* is also indicated, or the Executive Order number, etc. should the reader wish to refer to the original legal statute. A recent publication describing the history of federal wildlife laws is *The Evolution of National Wildlife Law,* by Bean (1977). A similar publication containing the texts of international treaties is also available from the U.S. Senate's Committee on Commerce, entitled *Treaties and Other International Agreements on Fisheries, Oceanographic Resources and Wildlife to which the United States is a Party,* now in its 3rd edition (1974). It covers multilateral treaties, bilateral treaties and agreements which were not yet in force in the United States as of January 1975.

A bibliography of State and Territorial laws for the United States, with the Provincial laws for Canada was given in Phillips (1930). It also included a list of Executive Orders and Proclamations, United States Statutes and Supreme Court decisions which have affected wildlife. Although dated, this bibliography will be of help in locating early state and provincial laws. The Dept. of Agriculture issued a series of game laws for the various states and Canadian provinces from 1917 through 1936 as part of the *Farmers' Bulletins.* In addition, they issued laws relating to furbearers and trapping as part of this same series from 1917 through 1931. After that the series was taken over by the U.S. Biological Survey and then by the Fish and Wildlife Service as part of *Wildlife Leaflets.* Hayden (1942) has written a history of international treaties for the protection of the world's wildlife. Unfortunately, no attempt has been made to update his work, although Bean (1977) has prepared a history of the development of wildlife laws in the United States. Matthiessen's (1959) *Chronology of Representative Legislation Affecting North American Wildlife* from 1616 through the 1950's will give the reader some historical perspective into this type of legislation. An earlier chronology by Palmer (1912) is more detailed, but stops with 1911. A newsletter service, published by Bethune Jones, called *From the State Capitols,* has a section called "Fish and Game Reports" which summarizes the state laws and issues for fish and wildlife agencies on a monthly basis. The journal *Defenders of Wildlife* (now *Defenders)* and several other conservation journals from popular organizations, such as the Sierra Club, have special sections of current legislative activity in wildlife and wilderness areas. In May 1976, the American Society of Mammalogists published a summary and reprinted the statutes dealing with "Federal Regulations Pertaining to Collection, Import, Export and Transport of Scientific Specimens of Animals" as a supplement to the *Journal of Mammalogy.* The U.S. Fish and Wildlife Service also publishes several separate items in regard to laws and regulations relevant to wildlife, such as its December 1976, publication on "Selected List of Federal Laws and Treaties Relating to Sport Fish and Wildlife," its *Fishery Leaflet* no. 403 with the fish and wildlife regulations for the District of Columbia (1960) and *Wildlife Leaflet* nos. 475, 486 listing birds protected by Federal law (1967, 1969). Endangered species are listed in the U.S. Fish and Wildlife Service's *Resource Publication No.* 114 and the *Federal Register* notices. The monthly newsletter *Endangered Species Technical Bulletin* issued by the U.S. Fish and Wildlife Service, lists current legal status and changes of endangered species in the United States, with the appropriate *Federal Register* citations. International endangered species are listed in the International Union for the Conservation of Nature and Nature Resource's *Red Data Book,* a looseleaf publication. Worrall (1964) has a short chapter on the laws relating to game animals in Great Britain. Mexican wildlife laws are listed by the U.S. Fish and Wildlife Service (1977a).

For the problems of wildlife law enforcement, Isaacson (1963) and Sigler (1972) have written manuals, outlining the role for the enforcement of conservation regulations, the presentation of testimony and other legal aspects. Both include a list of fish and game cases which will give the game officer some precedent on which to work. For questions involving environmental problems as opposed to game laws, Schwartz (1977) has compiled an annotated bibliography on environmental law. A microfiche collection of all the environmental laws up to 1976 is available from the Environmental Information Center, New York, but most of them do not have direct applicability to the wildlife biologist. However, for the biologist who has to prepare an environmental impact statement or report, the federal guidelines are reprinted in Warden and Dagodag (1976). Each state also has guidelines, but this volume reprints those of California, whose are among the more detailed and specific. Specific laws and regulations must be requested from the states. The microfiche collection of EIC has a number of them, but new laws are constantly being enacted.

RESEARCH IN PROGRESS

Successful planning of a research project demands not only that one become aware of the literature concerning his problem, but that he also determine what related work is currently in progress. For many years, the lack of knowledge about work in progress has constituted a major gap in our research effort and has resulted in duplication of research. To help an investigator keep himself informed about the research of others, the Smithsonian Institution established the Science Information Exchange (SSIE) to provide information between investigators with similar interests and to prevent the duplication of research. As part of their function, a computer data base was created to record investigators, title of project in progress, objectives of research, and any results of studies in progress. The abstracts subsequently created were filed on microfilm, and can be retrieved upon demand. Unfortunately, much of the research being performed is not sent to the SSIE so their searches must, consequently, be incomplete. The SSIE is now a semi-independent data service and provides commercial search services for any investigator in the United States and Canada.

Another way to keep aware of current research projects is to study the annual reports issued by governmental or private agencies interested in wildlife management and related areas. The Patuxent Wildlife Research Center, Wildlife Research Center in Denver, and the Northern Prairie Research Center all issue agency reports or lists of publications, as well as the various U.S. Forest and Range Experiment Stations, the Canadian Wildlife Service, all state and provincial agencies, the Wildfowl Trust, the British Museum (Natural History), and the various conservation organizations. Usually annual reports are mailed to any wildlife biologist who requests them. However, not all annual reports contain research in progress notes, but may contain only a general statement as to projects the agency is interested in and has staff working upon.

For many years current progress reports concerning research in the United States on wildlife restoration under the Federal Aid in Wildlife Restoration Act were reported in the *Pittman-Robertson Quarterly.* In 1955, the *Quarterly* was replaced by annual numbers in the series of U.S. Fish and Wildlife Service *Circulars* under the title 'Survey of Pittman-Robertson Activities' (see *Circular* nos. 38, 47, 52, 56, 82). For information since 1959, a computer search can be made through the Fish and Wildlife Reference Service, Denver Public Library, Denver, Colorado. Although completed reports are listed, and not abstracts of research in progress like SSIE, most of the P-R activities continue from year to year, and hence the prior year's work in a subject is probably still under investigation by the state agency involved. The activities of the Division of Wildlife Research of the U.S. Fish and Wildlife Service have been reported annually since 1960 in series of publications (*Circulars* 104, 146, 166, 188, 220 and *Resource Publications* 23, 43, 74, 85, 94, 104, 111) and as a separate series (1972–1978) titled: *Sport Fishery and Wildlife Research.* In addition to the Division of Wildlife Research, the U.S. Fish and Wildlife Service also issues its own annual report since 1974–75 titled *Conserving Our Fish and Wildlife Heritage* which includes research in progress notes. Both series of annual reports were formerly included as part of the U.S. Dept. of the Interior's *Annual Report.*

The U.S. Fish and Wildlife Service has undertaken to report research projects operating under the Pittman-Robertson and Dingell-Johnson Acts in a publication (published periodically by the Wildlife Management Institute and the Sport Fishing Institute) entitled *Federal Aid in Fish and Wildlife Restoration.* Many of these are also reported at the state level in progress reports and annual reports.

Although the research in progress under the auspices of the Office of Water Resources Research and the Public Health Service may not be of direct interest to the work of the wildlife biologist, he should at least be aware of what is being done in these agencies. The SSIE lists many of the projects currently being performed in these agencies, but the U.S Public Health Service also publishes an annual series called *Research Grants Index* for the purpose of disseminating information about current activities supported by research grants from the P.H.S. The data base comprising information used to publish the *Research Grants Index* can be queried through the National Institutes of Health by any qualified user.

Many journals regularly issue short notes on research in progress or brief communiques summarizing preliminary conclusions. These may take the form of research briefs, short communications, notes of research grants, or letters to the editor. Examples of these can be found in the *Bulletin* of the Wildlife Society, *Journal of Range Management, BioScience, Journal of Mammalogy, Science,* and *Nature.* In addition to these short notices, a journal will sometimes devote an entire article to describing the current and historical research efforts in a particular subject or area, such as Sladen (1965) did for ornithological research in the Antarctic, Jewell (1963) and Talbot (1965) on wildlife research in East Africa, and Scott (1958) for wildlife research in Illinois.

LITERATURE SEARCHES

Literature searches are performed by computer through data bases, or by manual methods, in which an individual makes use of the library and reference tools in order to locate information. At the present time, most computer literature searches are performed by expert bibliographers and librarians who know both the techniques of literature searching and the data base, as well as the computer configurations. However, most manual searches are performed by individuals interested in the subject under investigation. The following discussion will be limited to manual searching, with occasional reference to the section on computer data bases.

In manual searching, the decisions necessary to select the most appropriate library tool for a given situation and the most efficient use of that tool involve a clear knowledge of the objectives of the search. The following paragraphs will outline some of the problems encountered in literature searching, some solutions to these problems, and a method of approach—a means of organizing and conducting an effective and efficient literature search.

The key to success in any literature search is to organize the search in such a way that each step follows in a logical sequence. Wilson (1952), Parke (1958: 35–67), Bottle and Wyatt (1971) and Kirk (1978) all contain excellent chapters on beginning a literature search. Although the first two are primarily concerned with searching the physical sciences, many of the principles and ideas they expound are valid for the biological sciences. Lolley (1974) provided a self-study guide for the beginner, whereas Jahoda (1970) has written a technical monograph of what to do with the information once identified. The last may sound self-evident, but the organization of the information collected, at the point of collection, is necessary for efficient retrieval of such information when needed. Mosby's chapter in this volume provides more detail upon this topic.

Voigt (1961) has suggested that use of information by the scientist arises from 3 identifiable needs: (1) the need to keep up to date with the current progress in one's field, or the current approach, (2) the need for specific information relating to one's work, or everyday approach, and (3) the need for everything locatable on a subject, or the exhaustive approach. Voigt is careful to point out that what he suggests is an oversimplification, since these approaches often overlap. However, these ideas are useful when considering the problems in literature searching, for they help categorize the methods used. For purposes of this discussion, the types of literature searches are current awareness, everyday, and retrospective (exhaustive). Of these, the most difficult is usually the retrospective search since it involves the location and identification of everything pertinent to the subject. Because the retrospective search involves the same techniques and tools used in the other 2 types, but in greater degree, the discussion which follows will be concerned primarily with this type of literature search. However, a discussion of library tools in this context should not be taken to imply that retrospective searching is their only function; current-awareness searches are also possible in many of the same library sources, especially in the periodical literature sources. (The reader will wish to refer to the section of this chapter on the A/I services when considering a current-awareness search methodology.)

A literature search begins with a problem and works toward a solution. The first step is to put the problem into the concrete form of a statement, even writing it down if necessary. It is also important that the problem be clearly understood, and that all terms be defined in such a way that another qualified individual could understand and perform the search equally well if called upon to do so. Completion of this first step may entail some preliminary reading, but from this reading, related subjects under which the topic is indexed, may be determined as well as the related terms to be used as key words. A list of such terms should be prepared as a preliminary step to the formal literature search. As the literature search progresses, other individuals who have worked upon the problem or similar subjects will be identified. Some of the more prominent ones might be added on the preliminary keyword list, since some sources also can be used for author searches, such as *Science Citation Index.*

Next, clear boundary lines must be drawn and plans made to work within them. The hypothesis should be written down, or at least verbalized. It is often possible in the sciences to establish very explicit boundaries for a literature search by not going beyond a certain date, or excluding specific peripheral aspects of the subject, or by limiting the search to selected authors, journals, indexes or books. Deciding what function the information is to serve will also help crystallize the problem. Material needed for a popular journal article will be searched differently than if it were for a comprehensive, detailed research report. Essentially, the initial steps consist of (1) thinking and talking about the project with one's colleagues and a reference librarian, (2) setting up objectives, and (3) establishing boundaries for the search. Library tools, should they be needed at this point, will consist of the basic dictionaries, handbooks, manuals, reviews, and encyclopedias. The wildlife biologist should be especially alert for a subject bibliography, since this will enable him to profit from the efforts of others in his area. Many people well versed in the techniques of literature searching no longer make a conscious effort to perform each of these steps. The processes have simply become part of the entire research effort and are no longer thought of as belonging just to the performance of a literature search.

The logical place to begin the search proper, especially if the topic is ill-defined, is the card file in the library. It is at this point or while using the A/I serials that the searcher usually encounters the most critical factor in any literature search—the access point or keyword needed. These are the terms under which the information has been indexed. They are called subject headings in a library file, or descriptors, index terms or keywords in an A/I file. For standardized tools, such as a library card catalog, there are usually published, or at least printed, lists of index terms. The *Subject Headings* list of the Library of Congress (now in its 8th edition), the National Agricultural Library, the National Library of Medicine, and the staff of the *Biological Abstracts* Biosciences Information Service have all published lists which can be obtained through any large library. In 1969, the Conservation Library Center staff (Denver) published a *Thesaurus of Sport Fish and Wildlife Descriptors* under contract from the Dept. of the Interior. This thesaurus has been kept up to date, and re-issued by the Fish and Wildlife Reference Service (Denver). It consists of 2 volumes, 1 alphabetical and 1 classified, of terms the wildlife biologist uses in this work. It is used as the standard for indexing and searching the computer data bases of the Fish and Wildlife Reference Service and the wildlife data base of the Biological Information Service. Other sources of terms are Yeager's (1940) short list, the thesaurus of the U.S. Office of Water Resources Research (1971), nutrition terminology (Todhunter 1970), wildlands (Schwarz et al. 1976), and forestry (U.S. Forest Service 1976).

Just how difficult the task of choosing the keyword can be is better understood when one considers the large number of synonyms, homonyms, and the hierarchies of related terms present in the English language. The literature searcher must be constantly aware of the generic and specific relationships between terms, of ambiguous, invalid, or rejected names, of variations in the spelling of a given term, of superseded formulas, as well as the various trade names of materials or drugs. The biologist searching for publications on an organism must decide whether to look for his material under the class, order, family, genus or species to which that organism belongs. The literature searcher must also take into consideration the large number of perfectly acceptable scientific terms which mean one thing for discipline A, and something quite different when used in discipline B; i.e., plasma, energy, manifold, and radiation in biology and biophysical sources. Indeed, not only the words but the order in which these words appear can change the entire meaning of a sentence. Consider the classic example of 'blind Venetians' and 'Venetian blinds'. Since there is agreement that subject-matter indexes are no better than the choice of words used by the indexer and the searcher, the problems of selecting and using the appropriate keywords or descriptors becomes a critical one. The searcher must use every related keyword he can think of, unless the index clearly does not accept a particular term. Thesauri and lists of subject headings will be invaluable in establishing "authorized" keywords and their related terms. However, at the present time, the individual's most important tools will be thoroughness and imagination combined with his knowledge of the literature to be covered.

That part of the search strategy concerned with establishing the validity of a keyword for a particular search begins by testing the most specific keyword known against the file or index. If no heading is found under a term, then a move to a synonym should be made. If there are still no results, the next higher generic term should be searched, continuing in this fashion until the necessary connections are made within a desired citation. The reason for proceeding from the specific to the generic level is that the more specific the search term, the more accurate the citations found are to the search topic, the less irrelevant references or "garbage" will be encountered with a hit. This rule is particularly important in searching the A/I services' serials. The general terms usually have more citations to be scanned while a specific term enables the searcher to move directly to his objective. However, synonyms should be considered as valid specific terms if the index is a true KWIC one (Keyword-In-Context). Many authors are not consistent with terminology, using specifically the one the searcher has in mind. An interesting variation on the role of specific-to-general is the CROSS topical index of *Biological Abstracts*. This internal index to BA allows the searcher to select a general term and a specific term, and then to seek the common reference number by comparing the item numbers under each term for a match. The common number found then will lead the searcher to the desired reference.

As soon as pertinent references are located, a personal card file should be started, always noting complete bibliographic information for each item. This information should be transcribed the first time in exactly the style prescribed by the professional style manuals (especially CBE) or journals wherein the searcher hopes to publish. Any details of publication noted, which might cause problems in the final entry, should be written on the card. This will save time since the problem was noted and dealt with when the reference was in hand.

The last problem encountered in a literature search will be deciding when to stop. Here the limits established at the beginning of the search will help. However, stopping at the point where results no longer justify the effort required (point of diminishing returns) requires the judgment which only practice can give. Moreover, the purpose of the literature search will also determine when to stop—if information is sought for a specific purpose and that purpose is met, it is inefficient to search all the possible literature sources.

It is impossible to obtain an adequate appreciation of literature searching by simply talking about it, or utilizing the results some other person has developed. Indeed, literature searching is considered by many to be an art, and one of the most important prerequisites for success is the feeling or intuitive appreciation for the literature of one's field which comes only with intellectual practice in the use of that literature, computer searches notwithstanding.

ORGANIZATION AND PREPARATION OF THE RESEARCH PAPER

Communicating the results of research should rank in importance close to, if not on an equal level with, the actual conducting of the research itself. For if one is inept at communicating his results to others, the time, effort, money and results themselves are lost to the field. It is important that sufficient attention be given to the organization, preparation and final publication of the research. Every experiment should be written up at least once a year, not only to refresh one's memory, but to bring out gaps or weak points in the work. This section, along with the chapter by Scott and Ayars, is intended to suggest some aids which can assist the writer in his task. It does not treat the role of the hypothesis, experimentation, observation, intuition or any of the other facets involved in research before the ideas crystallize in the mind of the investigator. The primary concern here is with the transfer of results from a state of mental understanding to their concrete form in the research paper. Brief mention will be made of 1 or 2 books on the philosophy of research and, because of their everyday usefulness, some examples of the better usage manuals of the English language.

There is an abundance of good material written on the preparation of the research paper. It can be found in many places ranging from the brief style guides of Mosby (1963c), Pugh (1963), Campbell (1969), Scott and Ayars (1969), Allen (1973), and Turabian (1973) to the book-length manuals of Sanford (1958), Nagel (1960), Hillway (1964), Rathbone (1966), Woodford (1968), Trelease (1975), and Jones (1976), which have been written specifically for scientific writers. In particular, Woodford (1968) was written under the auspices of the Council of Biology Editors for graduate students in biology. Each of the above sources has useful ideas to contribute on the planning and writing of a scientific paper or report; however, their style and treatment differ. For this reason, attention will be given to some of the more salient features of these guides.

Campbell, Turabian, Trelease, Allen and Woodford are strong on the mechanics and form which a good research paper or dissertation must follow. Moreover, Campbell and Turabian also include a section on using the library. Trelease has included a section on photographs, drawings, tables, graphs and slides which should be helpful. The *CBE Style Manual* (1978) also has a section on illustrative material for journal publication. The material in Pugh is very elementary and provides a good manual of style. Campbell is the best guide, although Allen is a good substitute when writing a thesis or dissertation.

Quite often the journals themselves will provide suggestions and instructions for their prospective authors. These suggestions appear either as part of the journals, usually on the reverse of the cover pages, or as separate items. In the latter form, they are often published as a society-sponsored booklet. Many societies follow this practice, including the American Institute of Biological Sciences who published the 1st, 2nd, 3rd, and 4th editions of what is now the *CBE Style Manual*. All prospective biologists should read and be familiar with this particular style manual since almost 100 journals now use its format and style suggestions. A careful reading will often prevent a literature searcher from making mistakes or omitting data needed to prepare a correct bibliographic citation entry while performing the search.

Hillway (1964) covers the basic topics important to an understanding of research in an easy, informal style. There are many helpful ideas scattered through his book on using the library, preparing the research paper, gathering a bibliography and note taking. His ideas on research are fundamental and will be of interest to both the beginner and the experienced investigator. Jones (1976) also discussed the simple problems in scientific exposition and provided common solutions in organization and logical sequence. Rathbone (1966) is more concerned with the principles of communication, especially in writing and oral information transfer. His imaginative explanations of the principles of information transfer will appeal more to the advanced student than the beginner. Beveridge (1957) offers the reader a sophisticated treatment of the entire topic of research methodology. Although he includes little on the actual preparation of the scientific paper, his discussion of the research process is erudite and well worth the attention of the mature scientist. His outline of how a research problem in biology may be tackled is thought-provoking; and although some will not agree with him, here at least is a point of departure for a good discussion on research methodology.

One final source for guidance in the preparation of a research paper is a usage manual. There are several which merit attention and any prospective author should own one along with a dictionary and Roget's *Thesaurus*. Because individual styles and tastes differ, it would be wise to examine several before making a purchase. For many years Fowler (1965) has been the standard guide to correct usage although he stresses British as opposed to American usage. Follett (1966) is more appropriate for authors in the United States, although some will prefer Bryant (1962) or Copperud (1970), or even the more informal Strunk and White (1979). A shorter version of Fowler, oriented towards American usage is Nicholson (1957). No matter what the choice, authors should carefully select a usage manual and develop the habit of consulting it.

Since the early 1930's wildlife researchers have heard that "we have a tremendous quantity of accurately assembled statistics at our disposal, most of which we have not learned to use." In many other situations, a conventional wisdom has been espoused that adds up to: We need more generalists; we need more synthesizers; we need to study and use the information we have before trying for the new. Such 'wisdom' is irrelevant in the rapidly growing field of wildlife biology and environmental concern. New information is constantly being discovered, written and/or published for dissemination.

It is passé to argue whether a literature search should be performed before a research study or after. In fact, most are performed near the end of the research design and preliminary results. The probabilities that reading the work of others will channel the thinking of a good wildlife scientist are insignificant to the probabilities of avoiding duplication, gaining insight and direction, and progressively building on the work of others. Every investigation, program, employment of a technique, or speech should begin with literature study. Experience is a good teacher, but there is not enough time, and resources are too critical for every wildlife biologist to make his own mistakes. Moreover, not any one person can know all there is to know about any given topic. The experiences of others are the best teachers, and they are available in the literature of wildlife management.

Sandpipers

Chapter Three

Developing and Maintaining a Small Personal Reprint Library

HENRY S. MOSBY
Professor, Wildlife Management
Department of Fishery and Wildlife Sciences
Virginia Polytechnic Institute and State University
Blacksburg, Virginia

ROBERT W. BURNS Jr.
Librarian for Research and Development
Colorado State University
Fort Collins, Colorado

NEEDS

A part of the continuing education of a successful wildlife manager is the development and use of a personal library. This library, besides its intangible values, can become a powerful working tool when systematically collected, adequately indexed, and consistently used. Personal libraries assembled by small groups of wildlifers who specialize but share materials, become even more useful because of the breadth added by the groups' interest. These literature pools of active wildlife managers and scientists, often spanning several continents, can provide additional motivation to keep up to date and can provide for each other current information.

A personal collection of books is rarely large enough to require indexing, but reprints, bulletins, booklets, tear-sheets, pamphlets, manuscripts, typed reports, and other similar materials require regular, systematic filing and indexing. After the collection of the first several hundred items if not so catalogued, they will not be used effectively, if used at all. For convenience, all of these materials will be called "reprints" in this chapter.

The reprint library is usually thought of as that ubiquitous collection of papers on the bottom shelf, in the file cabinet, or on the floor in the office corner. It never seems to stop growing. The organization and indexing of this material varies from the complex edge-notched or internally punched peek-a-boo card to a miscellaneous collection of materials jammed in between alphabetic separators in a file drawer. Some individuals prefer to keep the actual reprints while others keep microfilms in envelopes. Some keep cards with only the citation and a 3- or 4-line annotation, or extensive abstracts on cards. Some workers keep only a file of references, a bibliographic index, for the literature in their area of interest. In any event, the so-called "reprint" file is a highly individualistic affair with little uniformity in its preparation, use, or maintenance. At least 1 study has been made of the reprint file (Jahoda et al. 1966) and *Biological Abstracts* (Anon. 1966) completed a survey of the personal literature files kept by its users.

Many investigators who attempt to develop a reprint-filing system soon abandon the effort because they find the system which they selected too involved or complicated to maintain. Organization and indexing are, therefore, the most challenging aspects of maintaining and using the reprint collection.

Some individuals prefer a simple author arrangement for their file with little or no indexing. Others prefer subject categories in numerical or alphabetical order. Others develop complicated systems of their own by separating types of publications and combining the above categories.

Yeager's (1940) list of subject categories is still useful and is adaptable to many filing schemes. Some wildlifers simply use the table of contents of *Wildlife Review* as their subject index.

Numerical order of filing reprints is least expensive of storage file boxes and space. As the number of boxes grows with the collection there is never more than 1 partially empty box. An alphabetical order may require few or no file boxes at first but a moderate number will be required as the collection increases. Subject classification requires many file boxes, the number depending upon the extensiveness of the subjects listed. Each system has its advantages and disadvantages. Two systems which have been used very successfully by wildlifers are presented here.

THE MOSBY 3-CARD SYSTEM

Reprints are numbered serially, irrespective of subject, as they are acquired. Either 3, bond-paper 3-inch x 5-inch "cards," or a templet to mark 3-inch x 5-inch cards on sheets of 8 ½-inch x 11-inch paper are used. In either case, 3 copies of each bibliographic reference are made by typewriter or ball-point pen—1 original and 2 carbons. Different colored paper may be used to good advantage for each carbon. The reference to each reprint is typed or written on the card (Fig. 3.1A). The serial number is in the upper right and a complete citation follows. When template and pages are used the first 2 copies are cut to 3-inch x 5-inch cards and the third left intact. The original card is filed alphabetically by author, the second copy filed by primary subject, and the third copy filed numerically. If the third copy is on a card, it is filed with occasional numerical tabs: if a sheet of 8 ½-inch x 11-inch, then it is placed in a loose-leaf binder to give a complete record of the serial numbering of all reprints.

The filing of the author card is easy since it is filed alphabetically. Subject filing is and will continue to be a problem. This card is placed behind the most appropriate classification tab card. Cross-referencing can be done by writing the serial number of the reprint on the front of the tab card of other subjects (Fig. 3.1B).

Using this 3-card system, the investigator can locate the desired reprint either by author, subject, or by number. Since the reprints are filed serially, it is easy to find the reprint and just as easy to replace it after use. This latter characteristic is one of the best features of the 3-card system. From numerical cards or the notebook (third copy), missing items can be identified, errors corrected, and the sequence of receipt determined. While these cards are the least used of the 3, they are of equal value. This system has been widely used, extensively tested for small and moderate size (up to 6,500 reprints) research libraries (e.g., S. E. Forest Experiment Station, Asheville, North Carolina and several Cooperative Wildlife Research Units), and has many devotees.

MARGINAL NOTCHED CARDS

The marginal- or edge-notched card is admirably suited for indexing the small (up to 10,000 cards) personal library.

While discussing the use of such cards, it is appropriate that mention be made of their capabilities for the organization of field or laboratory data (Van Gelder and Anderson 1967) as well as the preparation of keys. It is possible that either marginal-notched or cards of the Mosby system can be integrated with other similar types of record keeping on cards. Uniformity in card size and method have some advantages which should not be overlooked. Extensive bibliographies describing the many applications of marginal-notched cards are to be found in both Casey et al. (1958) and Scheele (1961). The advantages of using the edge-notched card for a personal file are (1) a single card can contain many indexing points, (2) when a card is lifted from the deck it does not have to be returned to the same alphabetical position, and (3) the file can be rearranged in any way the owner wishes with a minimum of effort. The disadvantages of edge-notched cards are (1) the size of the file which can be searched with 1 pass of the needle is limited, (2) the initial preparation of the classification scheme is extremely difficult, (3) the file is expensive in both direct and indirect costs, (4) each time a search is made the entire file must be handled, and (5) the size of a file which can be used efficiently is limited.

Books by Casey et al. (1958) and Scheele (1961) and an article by Bryan (1966) will provide the reader with a basic understanding of coding systems, files, edge-notched cards and how they may be designed and used to best advantage. Also worthy of special mention are articles by Adams on a file for use with small samples (1950) and on the creation of a file for vertebrate ecologists (1955); Schwabe and Davis (1954) on a file used for references in veterinary research; Levine (1955) on a file for parasitologists; Hill and Himwich (1957) on the preparation of a file for material on the central nervous system; and finally, an article by Milne and Milne (1959) giving "after-thoughts" on the preparation of an edge-notched card file. The latter article offers a number of useful hints and should be read by anyone contemplating the preparation of such a file. Although the experience of Milne and Milne is with a file involving literature covering vision in invertebrates, the mistakes they made are almost universal and a careful reading of their article will save the novice many wasted hours and cards.

OTHER SYSTEMS

Individuals well versed in computer science and having ready access to computer services have used this powerful tool in filing and retrieving literature. Reports by Conley and Tipton (1975) and Sterner and Breidenstein (1976) described computer-oriented techniques for filing and retrieving the rapidly expanding wildlife literature.

The number of ways to organize one's personal file is subject only to the limits of the individual's ingenuity, available materials, and special interests. Hellmers (1964) has discussed what he calls a modified coordinate system. There are direct coding systems using a notch (Aldous 1947) or marginal dot (Larimore 1957), a peek-a-boo or see-thru system (Fowler 1965), uniterm coordinate indexing (Weil 1954), and even a code system based upon the phonetics of a word (Thoma 1962). Each of these can be adopted for individual use. However, great care should be exercised in selecting a filing system for one's personal library. Systems such as those described here should be rejected only after they have been carefully explored. Experience has often shown that more problems arise later in indexing and cross-referencing than were ever imagined possible and that

A

2718

Forney, J. L. 1957. Raising bait fish and crayfish in New York ponds. Cornell Ext. Bull. 986. Ithaca.

2719

Hamilton, Max. 1957. Weights of wild bobwhites in central Missouri. Bird Banding, v. 28.

2720

Weller, M. W. 1957. An automatic nest-trap for waterfowl. J. Wildl. Mgmt., 21: 456-458.

Fig. 3.1A. An example of a 3-inch x 5-inch templet-marked, letter-sized page with 3 serially numbered reprints cited.

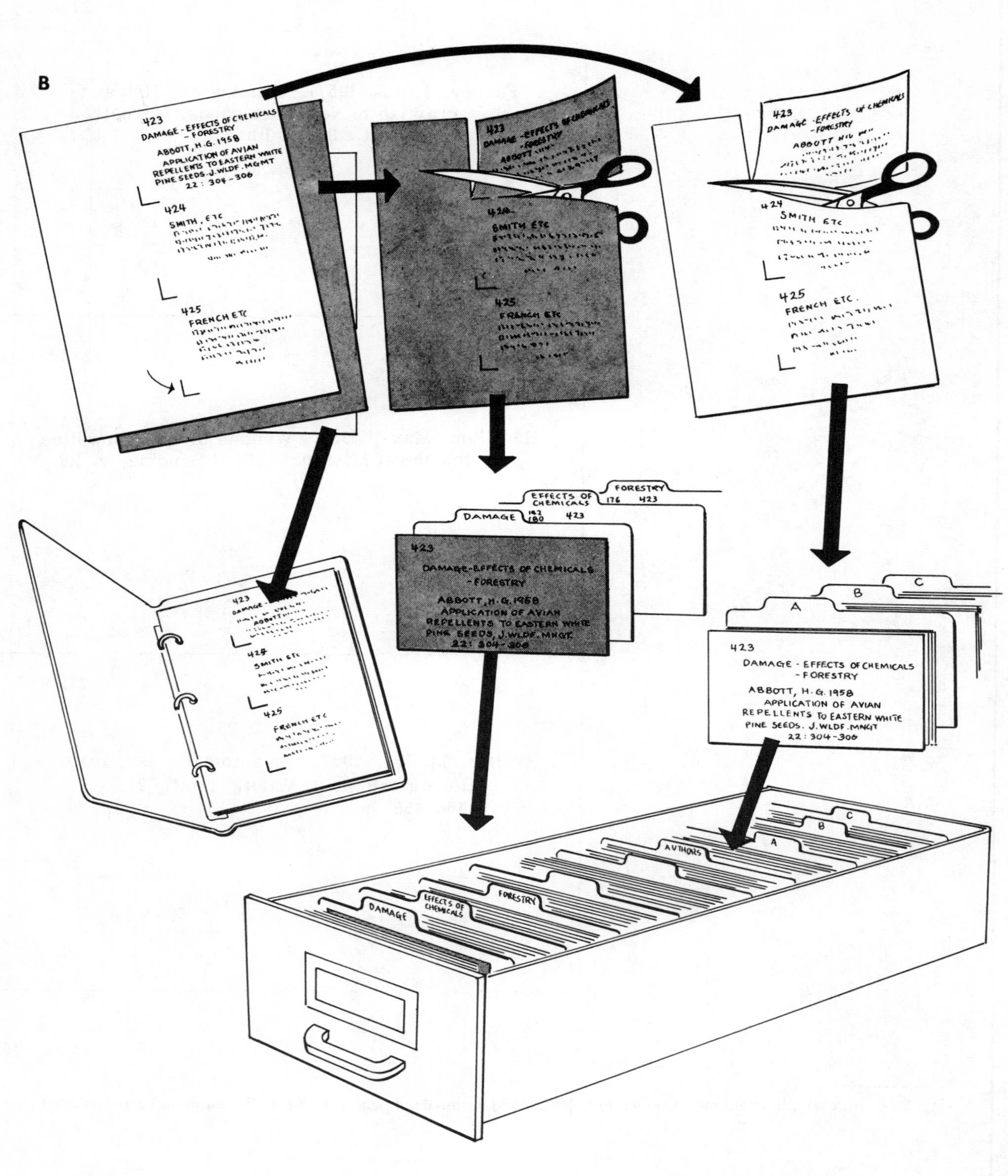

Fig. 3.1B. Examples of author and subject cards as filed for the Mosby 3-card system.

all too often the feeling of the user is: "I have the wrong filing system, but I've gone too far to start all over now."

SECURING REPRINTS

Many wildlifers use printed postcards for requesting reprints of journal articles and other reprint material. Often authors will purchase reprints of their articles which they will supply free, as a courtesy which should not be abused by indiscriminate requestors. Studying the literature, using *Current Contents, Wildlife Review* and literature sections in current journals as well as browsing in the collections of others will also provide titles for requests.

Studying the journals as recommended in Chapter 2 provides titles and addresses for desired reprints. U.S. Government Printing Office publications, for which there are minimal costs, are also a large part of most personal libraries. Some state agencies have mailing lists and most organizations and agencies will supply lists of available publications, many of which are free or have a nominal cost. Many articles not otherwise available can now be reproduced readily on a copy machine. Many materials in this category are not retained by even large libraries since they are "ephemeral." The personal reprint library, then, is essential for having close at hand the pertinent, local, specialized information necessary for successful performance by many wildlife managers.

Chapter Four

Making Observations and Records

HENRY S. MOSBY

Professor, Wildlife Management
Department of Fishery and Wildlife Sciences
Virginia Polytechnic Institute
Blacksburg, Virginia

It has been stated that "The strongest mind is weaker than the palest ink." Those facts which are left to memory are usually questionable; if a written or photographic record is made, this record when properly filed becomes of permanent value. The wildlife investigator should develop the habit of making accurate observations, recording his field and laboratory data in written or photographic form, and classifying and filing these records in such a manner that they may be efficiently consulted.

FIELD NOTES

Nothing will force all individuals to observe accurately the same event and report this event in the same precise detail and manner. Various techniques have been used to train an individual to observe events accurately and to interpret correctly what is seen. The power to observe may be developed by constant and diligent practice. Further, the observational ability may be developed by reducing to writing the events observed. For example, should an observer be in an automobile travelling parallel to a flying duck he might observe in a general way that the duck was flying at a rather high rate of speed. Such an observation would hardly be worth recording. However, if he had developed the habit of making a written record of all such events, he undoubtedly would record the species of duck, note the speed of the automobile from the speedometer, observe if there was a tail or head wind, and determine if the duck was being pursued. Thus, making recordings of such observations increases the precision of the observation.

Distinguishing what is worth recording is a major problem. No hard and fast rule may be stated. Usually, the more detail, the better. The keen observation of what appears to be a trivial event in the field may direct attention at some later date to some phase of a problem that has been completely overlooked. For example, it has been noted that ring-necked pheasants "crow" in response to any sudden noise such as firecrackers, banging a piece of metal, or blowing a car horn. As a result of this observation, which may have appeared trivial at the time, further investigations were made to determine if this method of locating male pheasants could be utilized in estimating pheasant populations.

Predation, dead or diseased animals, and similar events are observed in the field only at rare intervals. They should be recorded in as great a detail as possible, preferably with measurements of distances, notes on weather conditions (depth of snow, time since last rain, and related data), marks on the animals observed, location of these marks, and all other data. Such events usually shout for careful observations and recording, but less spectacular happenings are more frequently observed in the field and often are of equal or greater importance.

It is quite impossible to keep notes on everything; when discoveries are being made, the full meaning of each event may not be realized until the observer has been exposed to his subject for a long time. If there is a skeleton of basic facts in the notes, a framework for understanding is present.

Taking Field Notes

The mechanics of taking field notes has considerable bearing on their systematic indexing and filing. Any method of recording field data that suits the personal preferences of the game investigator is satisfactory so long as it is simple enough to be convenient and workable in the field and permits easy indexing, filing, and recovery of all types of field records. Personal preferences vary widely on the type of paper, size of paper, type of field-form holder, the amount of printed matter on the field form, and type of pencil or ink used. Some investigators prefer 8½- by 11-inch paper, with a printed form for recording all types of field data. Others use slightly smaller sized, permanently-bound printed forms. Still others make good use of detachable-sheeted, pocket-size notebooks. For certain types of field investigations, marginal-notched and IBM-type cards are used. Whatever the personal preference, the mechanics of how and upon what the observer records field data is not important. The important consideration is getting the data recorded and then indexed and filed in such a manner that these records are easily available for future reference.

Both continuous and discrete field data, such as tagging records, kill information, field-plot data (Overton and Sincock 1956, Sincock and Powell 1957), and similar measurements, may be recorded efficiently on edge-punched (key-sort) or mark-sense (machine sort) cards (Casey 1958). Edge-punched cards are used frequently for recording and filing literature abstracts and references (Hood et al. 1953, Adams 1955).

Edge-punched cards (Fig. 4.1A) are available in single- to 4-holed form and in a variety of sizes. A hand punch is used in coding and a needle sorter is employed to hand-sort and select the desired cards by rejection. For example, a hand-operated punch may be employed to punch out a "V" at the proper hole(s), thus recording the data on key-sort cards. A needle sorter is inserted through a stack of cards and all cards with the hole(s) punched out are rejected and the cards with intact holes are removed. Standard printed cards, such as literature abstract cards, are available in any practical size from 3 by 5 inch to 8 by 10½ inch. See Casey et al. (1958: 30 ff.) for a description of the various types and manufacturers of edge-punched cards and accessories.

If the field investigator has access to a Mark Sensing Reproducer and other electronic data-processing equipment, the use of mark-sense cards offers an ideal way of recording a large quantity of data with a minimum of effort. This method of recording field data offers maximum flexibility since the data may be electronically punched, tabulated, and analysed. Mark-sense cards are marked, in the appropriate code block, using a special electrographic pencil (Fig. 4.1B). The special pencil lays down a heavy graphite coating which is detected electronically by 3 brushes of the Mark Sensing Reproducer and, after detection, the marked area is punched on a key-punch machine. Cards coded (Fig. 4.1C) in this manner or by means of the Porta-punch (Rogers and Fleming 1963) may be tabulated in a variety of ways by electronic processing machines (IBM and Remington Rand). Any investigator who anticipates collecting a large quantity of either continuous count or discrete data should examine the possibility of using either hand-sort or machine-sorted punch cards as these techniques offer efficient ways of recording, tabulating, and analyzing information.

Loveless et al. (1966) describe the use of a standard 8½ x 11 - inch Page Reader sheet having 800 marking positions on which to record data. These forms are read electronically by an IBM Optical Mark Page Reader and can be punched directly onto cards. Page "reading" progresses at a maximum of 2000 pages per hour. Rubber-styrene overlay templates on the standard form held on a wooden clipboard indicate the proper position to make marks. One sheet is marked for each series of observations, then inserted beneath the stack of 30–40 sheets on the clipboard. Extra sheets can be carried. The Page Reader has a maximum capacity of 1000 mark positions, the Mark-sense card has 540 (employing both front and back of card), and the Porta-punch has 480.

Loveless et al. (1966:522) make the point that field-note collections should avoid as much as possible copying, editing, grouping, and translation. These operations are tedious, expensive, time-consuming, and often introduce errors into the data. Use of Optical Mark Page Readers provides for data to be directly converted to machine language for tabulation and analysis.

Stelfox et al. (1977) reported the use of computer-compatible wildlife data forms used by the Warden Force of the Canadian National Parks. They found these forms to be of value in the collection of extensive, year-long, wildlife information by the warden force. Output data were generated by a Mark IV file management system capable of handling a large number of cards. Several workshops with members of the Warden Force were necessary to produce uniform recording by the large number of wardens collecting data in the 14 parks and 6 faunal life zones.

AN EXAMPLE

One method of taking, indexing, and filing written field notes is outlined below. It is preferred by the writer after much testing and study of alternate methods.

Field notes are recorded on 4- by 6-inch cards. This size field-note form was selected as it is about as large as can be carried conveniently in the pocket, and still afford a reasonable amount of writing space. Such forms can be carried in a metal datum holder; this holder will preserve them from bending and will keep the field records in good condition. A form is printed on the top of the card for recording the minimum amount of information necessary for all types of observations. An example of this field-note form, with field note #1254, is shown in Fig. 4.2. Lengthy observations are continued on the back side of the card. If needed, a second card may be used, with the second form being assigned the same

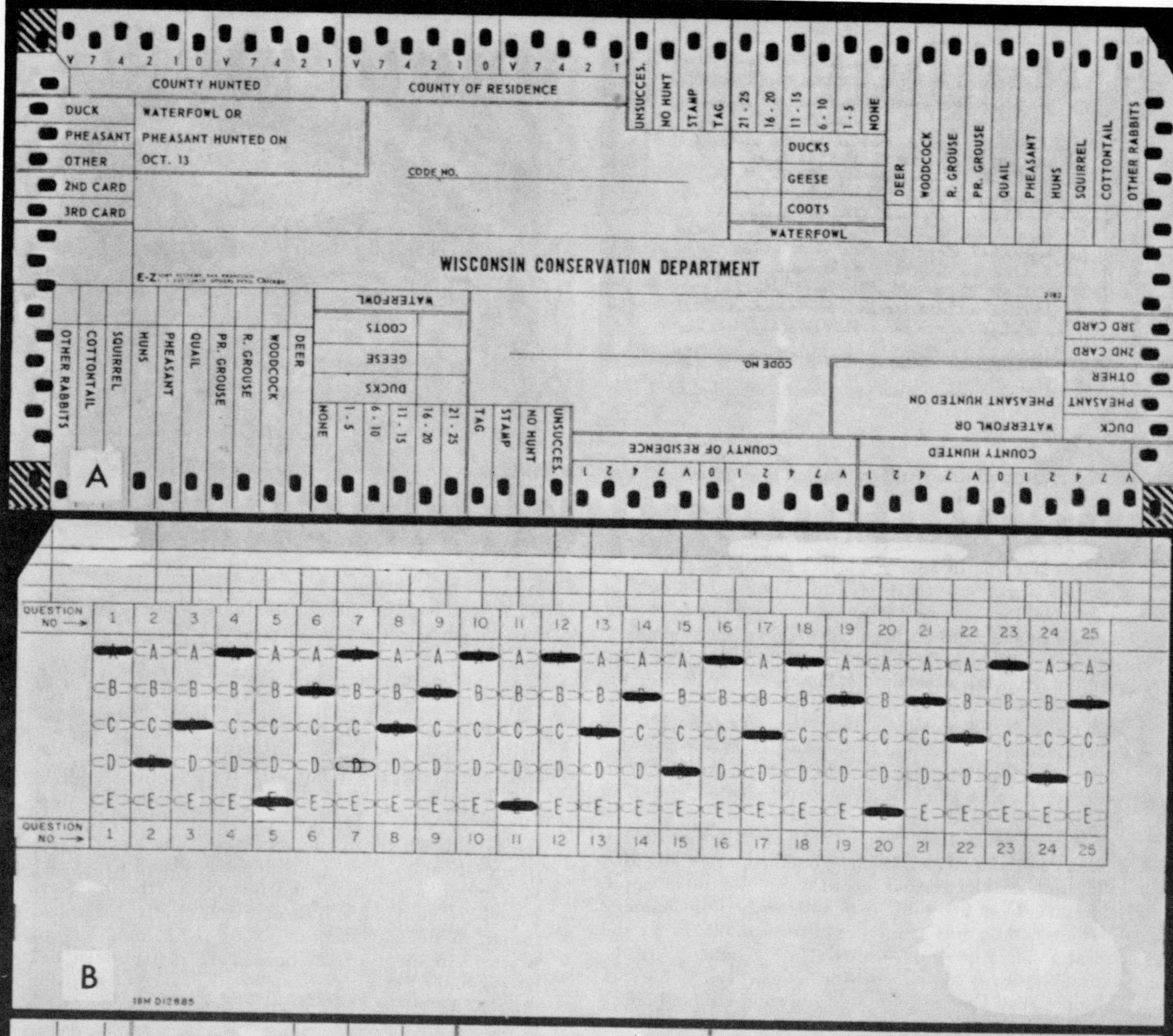

Fig. 4.1. Edge-punched (hand- or key-sort) cards (*A*) are available in a variety of sizes and code combinations. Mark-sense (machine-sort) cards (*B*) are code-marked by means of special electrographic pencils. The marked areas are punched by electronic machines. The Porta-punch (IBM) card (*C*) is punched by means of a portable hand-operated machine which is transported into the field and data punched on specially-printed cards as collected.

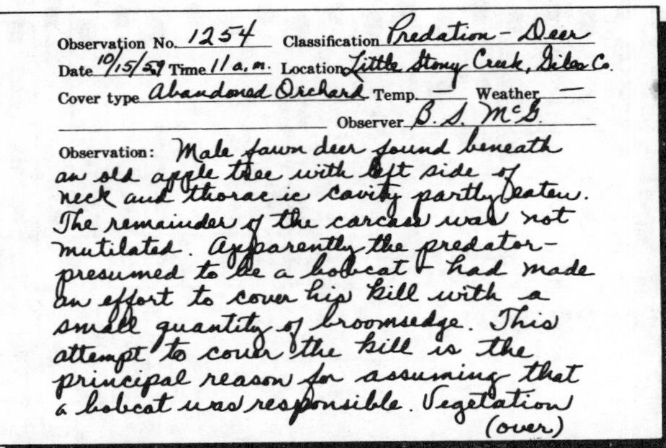

Observation No. 1254 Classification Predation - Deer
Date 10/15/59 Time 11 a.m. Location Little Stony Creek, Giles Co.
Cover type Abandoned Orchard Temp. — Weather —
Observer B. S. McG.

Observation: Male fawn deer found beneath an old apple tree with left side of neck and thoracic cavity partly eaten. The remainder of the carcass was not mutilated. Apparently the predator—presumed to be a bobcat—had made an effort to cover his kill with a small quantity of broomsedge. This attempt to cover the kill is the principal reason for assuming that a bobcat was responsible. Vegetation (over)

Fig. 4.2. Field note observation card and recorded field note.

Fig. 4.3. Battery-operated recorders are especially useful for collecting a large quantity of descriptive or mathematical information in a short period.

observation number. When filed, the original and second card are stapled together.

All field notes are typed as soon as possible after returning from the field. The original notes are typed on letter-size paper (8½ x 11 inch), making at least 2 copies of the letter-size records. The cards should be arranged in the numerical sequence in which they were taken in the field (that is, by observation numbers as assigned to each field-note card) prior to typing. The original typed copy of the field notes should be filed in a fire-proof file and the carbon copy should be filed in some other fire-proof container. Thus, if one copy is lost or damaged, the second copy is available for use. After the data on the original field-note cards have been typed, each original field-note card is filed under the appropriate heading.

A practical alternative personal field note method is to make 1 field card (4 x 6 inches, bond paper) in ink, file it in numerical order, and record its number on an appropriate subject file-guide card as described in Chapter 3. There is then only 1 card per observation filed in order, and a set of file-guide cards. The advantages are that time is saved by not copying cards, each guide card "topic" can be easily divided (or grouped), and all observations on a topic can be pulled for use, and refiling can be accurately done by anyone. The system is more flexible than marginal-notched cards in that it can be easily modified as interests change, certain subject areas are expanded, and as whole groups of cards are discarded. Index words in the upper right corner of each observation card allow secretarial aid in filing and in maintaining the file-guide card cross index.

When a large number of field observations must be recorded in a short period of time, portable recorders have proven of considerable value (Crissey 1953, Bartlett 1954, Miller et al. 1965). Battery-operated recorders (Fig. 4.3) are available in a variety of models, makes, and sizes; they range in price from about $30.00 to $250.00. Observations recorded on tapes or wire may be transcribed, typed, and filed. The tape or wire may be filed or reused as the investigator desires. Many workers now use this technique for almost all field survey work, even in place of the Porta-punch or Optical Mark Page Reader sheets. Secretarial or recording facilities in combination with telephone, radio, or intercom systems should not be overlooked, especially with animal behavior studies.

Field notes on which data are recorded should be planned for rapid key punching onto data cards. Brotzman and Giles (1966) present 1 example. Planning considerations should be for ease of placing each number, letter, or "bit" into each numbered column of the card, (each card contains 80 columns); ease of sequentially and rapidly punching each data line; clarity of numbers and letters; and recognition that the keypunch operator will do little or no interpretive, organizational, or decision-making as to "what numbers go where." Engineers of data-processing companies should be consulted early in research and management planning for the greatest efficiency in data collection as well as processing.

Filing Field Notes

Two methods of filing the field notes have been outlined above. The classification under the most appropriate file heading, the filing, and the cross-referencing of the field notes are all as important as the taking of field notes. An accurate and detailed field note which is lost in the file is of little or no value.

A general outline of file headings which may be used in classifying "general" field observations (including laboratory and literature data if desired) is shown in Fig. 4.4 or the Content page of *Wildlife Review* may be used for the file categories. The index of this book also can be used as a guide. It will be noted that these file headings are very general; each sub-heading could be expanded considerably. When the available data warrant, any section of the file can be subdivided further by the addition of other appropriate file headings. Also see Anderson (1966) and Needy (1966).

Field Note File Classification

Antelope

Bats
Bear
Bibliography—Wildlife
Big Game—General
Birds—General

Chicken—Prairie
Conservation—Wildlife
Control—Wildlife
Coyote

Damage—Wildlife
Disease—Wildlife
Dogs
Dove
Deer

Ecology
Economics—Wildlife

Fish—General
Fish Ponds
Feed and Cover—General
Foods—Food Habits
Forestry—General
Fox

Furbearers—General
Fur Farming

Goat—Mountain
Grouse

Hawks and Owls
History—Wildlife

Insects

Laws—Wildlife
Livestock—Wildlife

Mammals—General
Management—Farm Game
Management—Forest Game
Management—Land
Mink
Muskrat

Opossum

Partridges
Pheasant
Plants—General
Predation
Propagation

Quail

Rabbit
Refuges—Wildlife
Research—Wildlife
Restocking
Rodents

Sheep—Mountain
Skunk
Snakes
Soils
Squirrel

Techniques—Wildlife
Trapping
Turkey—Wild

Utilization—Wildlife

Waterfowl
Weather
Woodchuck
Woodcock

Fig. 4.4. General file classifications used in filing field notes. This simplified filing system can be expanded for any subject when sufficient data are at hand to warrant such an expansion.

When the wildlifer is concerned with a specific topic, species, or project, he should prepare a detailed outline of the classifications, or file categories, under which he wishes to collect data. The investigational plan outline shown in Chapter 1 and the outline in Chapter 5 are useful major headings for some types of filing. Such a detailed outline, if prepared at the beginning of the investigation, will serve to direct the investigator's attention to the topics for which data are required. The simpler the file outline, the more workable it will be; if a complicated file system is attempted, it probably will not be maintained unless the wildlifer has competent office assistance.

It is not necessary to assign the observation number and file classification when the data are recorded on the field-note form in the field. This can be done when the field notes are typed in the office. An observation may refer to more than 1 file heading (classification) and cross-referencing may be necessary. In cross-referencing, the original field-note card is filed under the most appropriate heading and the observation number is listed on the front of the file guide card(s) (see Fig. 4.4) of the other subject(s) to which it may refer. If this is done, and if the field notes are typed in numerical sequence, it is easy to obtain access to all field data bearing on any file subject. In the example shown in Fig. 4.5, the majority of the field note data on predation will be found on the original field cards filed directly behind the "Predation" file guide; observation numbers 216, 219, 328, 451, 682 etc. also refer to predation in some form. These latter observations can be consulted by referring to the typed file notes.

Many beginning filers are overly ambitious in setting up their filing system. If a system is too complicated, the

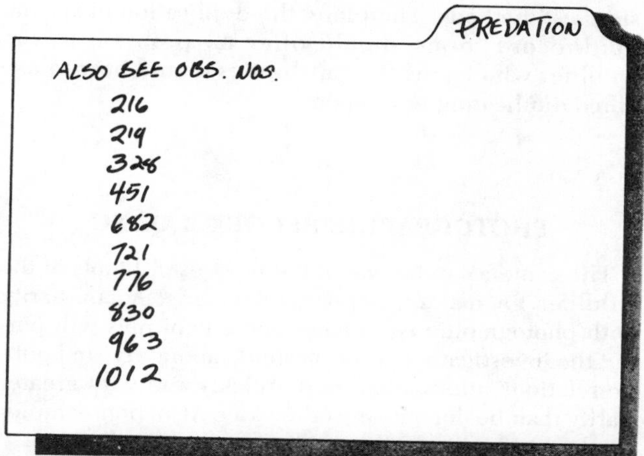

Fig. 4.5. File-guide card for the classification "Predation." All original field notes classified "Predation" are filed behind this file guide card. The observation numbers of other field notes which refer to predation filed elsewhere are recorded on the front of the file-guide card.

wildlifer is prone to put off filing his data and eventually he is convinced that it is a hopeless task. When this is the case, all types of data are filed under "Miscellaneous." Bitter experience has demonstrated that the category "Miscellaneous" should not appear in any filing system, even the very simple one outlined here.

Daily Journal

Every serious game investigator should maintain a field journal in which he records his general field activities. Most investigators prefer a bound journal, usually 8½ by 11 inches, in which to record a condensed "diary-type" entry of each day's activities. These summary records are permanent and are most helpful in preparing monthly, quarterly, and annual project reports; they also are useful in many other ways. The utility of such records has to be experienced to be fully appreciated. It should be emphasized that journal entries should be made *daily*—not periodically.

Special Field Forms

The wildlifer usually has need for special forms upon which to record specific types of data. Examples of such special forms are: trap-record forms, vegetative-survey forms, food-habits forms, form maps (see Chapter 17), and hunting pressure forms. Such special forms, if carefully prepared, facilitate the recording of data and, perhaps more importantly, they assure that complete and uniform data are collected. They can also simplify coding for data processing.

These special forms may be printed, if required in quantity (Loveless et al. 1966). Offset equipment for duplicating forms is usually available to most game investigators, as is mimeograph equipment; both of these types of equipment may be used for quantity duplication. For the duplication of small quantities of forms on 4- by 6-inch cards, the hand-operated Multistamp set (which operates on the mimeograph principle) is very convenient. If the special forms are not exposed to damp conditions, ditto duplication is one of the quickest and simplest methods. Therefore, the duplication of special field-record forms should offer no problem to the wildlifer who learns the capabilities of and how to use office duplicating equipment.

PHOTOGRAPHIC RECORD TAKING

The camera can be one of the most useful tools of the wildlifer for making permanent records. A familiarity with photographic equipment and techniques will permit the investigator to present field, laboratory, and public relations information more quickly and with greater clarity than be done in any other way. Also, photography can be utilized to facilitate office record duplication.

Both still and motion pictures can be utilized to excellent advantage but the still camera has the greater utility for the wildlife worker under most circumstances. Therefore, the following discussion will be concerned only with the general tecuniques of using still cameras. No effort will be made to list all of the various types of equipment, procedures and techniques that may be used by the wildlife investigator. The following elementary discussion will be confined to outlining some of the more obvious uses of the camera in the field of wildlife management.

Photography is mastered only by first-hand experience. Perhaps the best way for the beginner to learn how to use the camera as a field tool is to: (1) review a general publication on photography; (2) get a camera, take photos, develop the negatives, make prints; and then (3) critically examine each print for errors in picture taking, developing, and printing. There is a considerable amount of literature available (much of it free) on all phases of photography but the beginner should start with a general treatment of photography (e.g. Mess 1951, Baines 1958, Olson and Schmidt 1974) before advancing to the more specialized publications (e.g. Miller 1942, Sprungman 1951). Current photography publications (Popular Photography, Modern Photography, etc.) usually contain in each issue a number of articles of value both to the beginning and the advanced photographer. Each photographer has to develop his own preferences for photographic equipment and technique by trial and error. The job of taking good photographs is made simpler if the photographer decides what specific equipment suits his purpose best and then concentrates on as few types of films, chemicals, cameras, and gadgets as possible.

Fox (1959), after conferring with several magazine editors, listed their consensus of what makes a good picture. These attributes of a good story-telling print refer primarily to public-relations photographs but they are equally applicable to technical photographs. The main points listed by Fox are:

1. Plan each picture carefully.
2. Get people or animals into the picture.
3. Avoid stiff, posed, photographs.
4. Make the photograph illustrate the point you have in mind.
5. Take pictures from several angles; film is the cheapest part of photo-taking costs.
6. Avoid long-range, panoramic shots; include close-ups, preferably within 6 to 8 ft.
7. To show scale, use a person or animal; avoid lifeless objects to show size.
8. Watch the background; remove such articles as cars, equipment, and other movable objects.
9. Use fill-in flash when natural light won't reveal the detail you desire.
10. Crop the picture to remove unwanted objects or harsh lighting effects.

Types of Cameras

The number of cameras and camera attachments are bewildering in their variety. However, the general types of cameras are: (1) fixed focus (box), (2) manual focusing (distance estimated and set manually), (3) coupled range finder focusing including (a) roll film or (b) pack-cut film, (4) twin lens reflex and (5) single lens reflex. Examples of several of the various types of cameras are illustrated in Fig. 4.6.

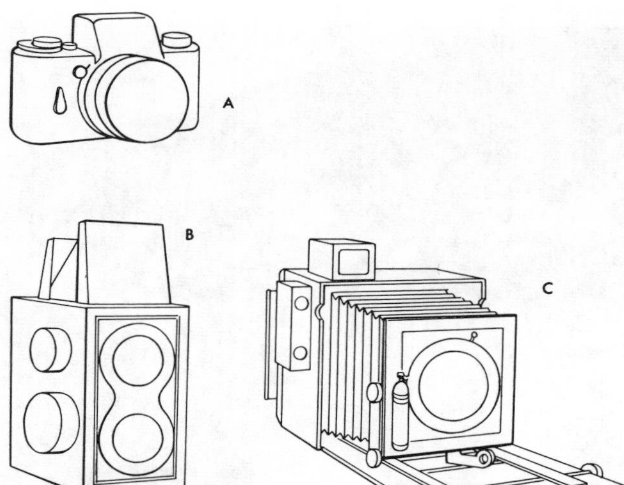

Fig. 4.6. Types of cameras: (A) single lens 35 mm.; (B) twin lens 2¼ x 2¼ reflex; and (C) press type, coupled rangefinder—ground glass focus 4 x 5.

As emphasized previously, the choice of cameras and related equipment is based on personal preference. It should be obvious that each type of camera has certain advantages and disadvantages and *no single type of camera will perform all functions equally well.*

Listed below are my personal camera preferences:

For color slides:
 35 mm single lens reflex
For general field use:
 Twin lens reflex, 2¼ x 2¼, roll film
For field use, copying, and general record taking:
 Coupled rangefinder-ground glass, press type;
 4 x 5, roll or cut film

If only 1 field camera had to be selected, my preference would be a twin lens reflex (with parallax correcting portrait lenses) as it can be used to perform all of the above functions, but with definite limitations. Again, it is emphasized that no single camera will serve all photographic purposes just as no single type of firearm may be used successfully for taking all forms of game.

Field Records

In the hands of a reasonably competent photographer, field events can be recorded photographically with considerable clarity. In many instances, a good photograph is the only satisfactory way in which such events can be recorded in an easily used and permanent manner. For example, the general description of an area is easily depicted photographically (Fig. 4.7A) and ecological succession can be shown in a manner difficult to accomplish with equal clarity by any other technique (see recording habitat improvement practice (Fig. 4.7E), habitat changes (Fig. 4.7C and D), specimens (Fig. 4.7B), cover density changes, field techniques or equipment, field structure, animals (Shaub 1951) and their homes, food (Greenewalt and Jones 1955), signs (Gysel and Davis 1956), animal damage, legal evidence (Rollman 1962), and many other field and laboratory phenomena.

The good field photographer often is stimulated by his camera to be a closer observer and a better recorder. The greater the familiarity of the field worker with the technique of making both written and photographic records, the better field investigator he is likely to be.

Laboratory Records

The camera is equally as useful in the laboratory as in the field. Records of biological specimens (Fig. 4.7B), laboratory equipment, laboratory techniques, biological events and reactions, growth of organisms and related matters are recorded with permanence and clarity by means of the camera. Often a procedure or technique can be shown photographically step by step, with practically no written explanation being required (Fig. 4.8). The use of the camera in the laboratory often extends over the field of "regular" photography, microphotography, and macrophotography. Micro- and macrophotography, are rather specialized aspects of photography that normally require special equipment and critical attention to lighting, depth of field, and related matters. It is recommended, therefore, that the techniques of "regular" photography be mastered before venturing too far into specialized photography.

Office and Public Relations Photography

The availability in many offices of electrostatic copy machines makes "contact" copying of records up to 8½ x 14 inches quite simple. Commercial copy centers using this principle of reproduction often offer pass-through size reductions of 50% or more of oversized records. A word of caution: when a reduction of 25% or more is used, care must be exercised that the reduced copy is legible.

The use of a camera often is a satisfactory way of enlarging or reducing maps (see Chapter 17), or, in fact, any similar records for report purposes.

The camera is an indispensable tool in public-relations work. Most state conservation magazines and similar avenues of publication will not give serious consideration to a paper for publication unless it has photographic illustrations. In many instances, a series of photographs may be used to tell a rather complete story (see Schwartz 1944) or explain a procedure (Fig. 4.8). Such photographic "essays" are highly sought after in public-relations periodicals. Likewise, color slides (usually 35 mm but larger sizes are rapidly becoming more universally used) permit the explanation to public gatherings of reseach and management programs in a manner that is difficult to accomplish in any other way. Such slides should be taken with the presentation of the full topic in mind. A miscellaneous collection of slides seldom, if ever, will include all of the illustrative material necessary to present a logical sequence. For this reason, it is recommended that the topic be outlined and that each slide necessary to present the various aspects of the problem be stated. Then, the photographer must go out and secure all of the photos necessary to present the topic in a full and orderly manner. Some of the "shots" may be in the file, but in most instances it will

Fig. 4.7. The camera may be used to record (A) general habitat conditions; (B) biological specimens; (C and D) cover density changes; (E) habitat improvement practices and (F) other field phenomena.

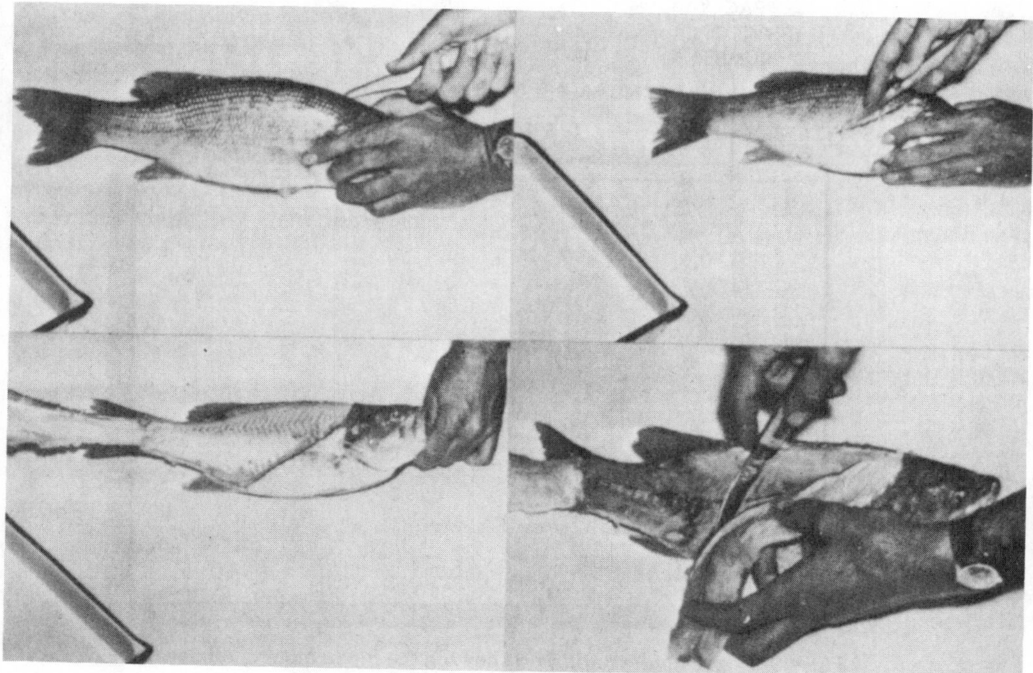

Fig. 4.8. The camera can be used to present a "step-by-step" procedure with a minimum of written explanation.

be necessary to take additional slides on specific aspects of the subject to complete the series in a logical manner. (See Haugen 1964.)

Filing Negatives and Prints

The filing of slides, negatives, and prints often presents quite a problem. Elaborate techniques of filing photographic records are available. Experience indicates, however, that the simpler the filing system, the greater is the probability that it will be used and maintained. The following simple system has proven fairly satisfactory for individual use or for use in an office with a moderate number of slides, negatives, and prints on records.

SLIDES

Slides may be 35 mm or larger. Each size slide has its own file numbering system under the method outlined here. These numbers are arranged in numberical sequence, with a prefix numeral to designate their size classification. For example, the 35 mm slides would be numbered 35-1, 35-2, 35-3, etc., the 2¼ x 2¼ slides as 22-1, 22-2, 22-3, etc., the 3¼ x 4¼ slides as 34-1, 34-2, 34-3, etc. The slides in each size classification are numbered without regard to subject and in the order in which they were taken. A card is prepared on each slide, giving the file number, date, subject, and any other pertinent data. These cards are then filed by subject, with the slide number recorded on the front of the file-guide card of any additional subjects to which cross-referencing is desired (see Fig. 4.5 for the method by which this may be done). Thus, when assembling slides on a given subject, all slides can be located by number by consulting the file cards.

The slide itself is then ready for filing. The slides are filed by the serial slide number. Write on the slide itself the major subject (under which it is filed in the slide card file). Any additional data should be written on the slide in as great detail as space will permit. Of course, it is the usual practice to indicate (by a dot, punch, or other means) the upper right hand corner of the slide as it would be inserted in the projector.

The above system works satisfactorily for small slide collections, (500–2,000). The slides in each size classification are numbered without regard to subject and in the order in which they are to be filed. A 4- x 6-inch card is prepared for each slide, giving the file number, date, subject, other pertinent data, and key words for filing. These cards are filed numerically. A number is written on the slide mounting with any additional information desired. The upper right-hand corner of the slide as it would be inserted into the projector should be indicated by a dot or punch. The slide number is listed on a file-guide card just as for filing field notes and cross-referencing reprint citations (Fig. 4.5). Thus when assembling slides on a given subject, all slides can be located by number for inspection for appropriateness. Since all slides are filed numerically, there are no waste spaces for subject areas not yet filled, re-filing is simple, and the cards provide data on slides not possible to write on the mounting. In addition these cards identify missing slides and provide a device for noting borrrowed slides or slides in current use. When infrequently used by others, their name and date can be penciled on the card; otherwise a borrow-slip can be clipped to each card. The clips showing in the file indicate at a glance the slides that are out and provide a measure of use. This system works satisfactorily for collections of up to several thousand slides. Smaller collections may be filed by

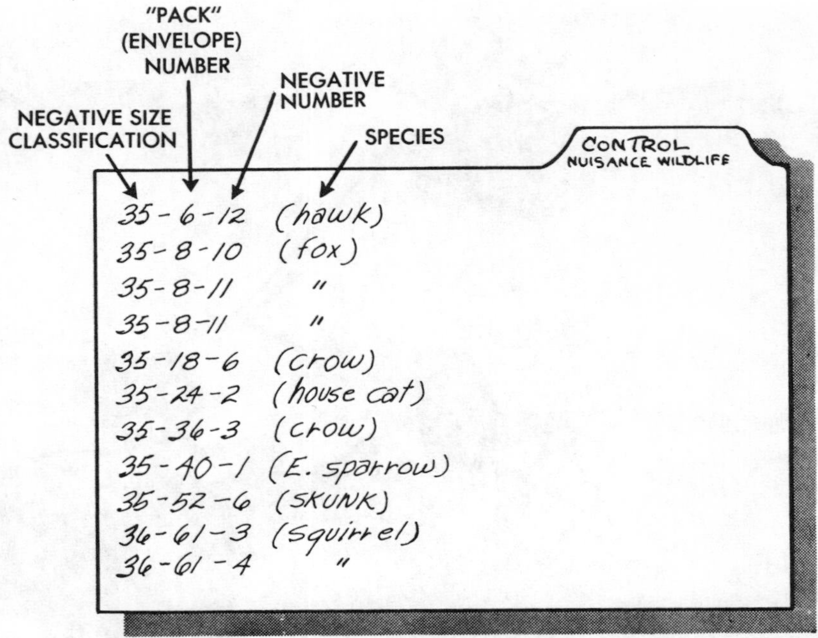

Fig. 4.9. Negative file-guide card showing the file number of all negatives relating to the control of nuisance wildlife.

subject only, with no card file, and large collections may require a more complex filing system.

Other indexing systems such as marginal notch, should not be overlooked. The compatibility of the field note, reprint, and slide filing systems described in this book should be noted as an advantage. Advantages are in similar filing cases, forms, and ease of learning the system.

NEGATIVES

Negatives (irrespective of size) may be filed by "packs," irrespective of subject. This may be done by collecting a convenient number of negatives (from 10 to 20 negatives), assigning a pack number and a sequence number to each negative, and writing this pack-sequence number on each negative in ink. The pertinent data are typed, in 2 copies, on regular 8½- by 11-inch paper, 1 copy of which is cut and pasted on the envelope containing the pack of negatives and the second typed copy is filed. For example, suppose that a group of 14 negatives of various subjects are ready for filing. Assume that the next "pack" number is 86. Thus, the negatives would have the number 86-1, 86-2, 86-3, etc., written on each respective negative in ink. Detailed, typed data on each negative would appear on the front of the envelope containing this pack of negatives. Likewise, each print would have the corresponding negative number recorded on it as will be explained later. A subject file card is prepared and the number of each negative referring to this subject is recorded on the front of this file card (Fig. 4.9). Each negative can be cross-referred to as many subjects as desired. If this is done, all the negatives on a given subject may be located (and the data on each determined) by consulting the subject file card and noting the number of each negative filed under this subject.

PRINTS

Each print is stamped on the back (using a rubber-stamp form). Required data, including the exact number of the negative from which the print was made, is entered in the proper spaces (Fig. 4.10). The print is then filed under the most appropriate subject heading. If it is desired to file prints under more than 1 subject heading, it will be necessary to prepare a print for each file heading. Griffith (1969) described an improved method for filing black and white photographs from each roll of film in a clear plastic protector and then inserting them in a loose-leaf binder.

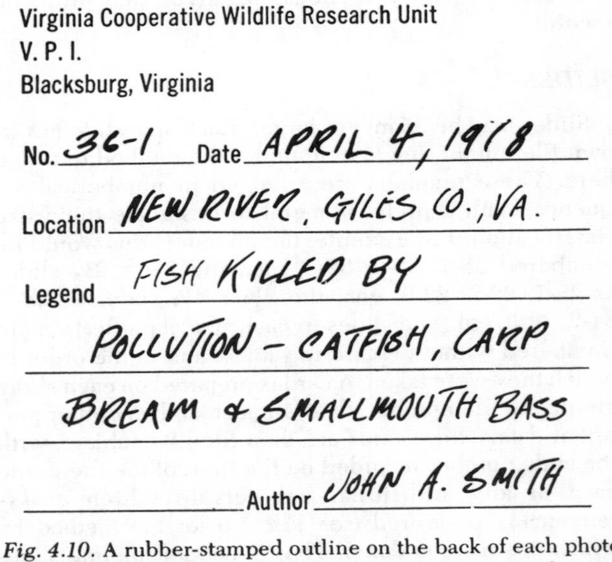

Virginia Cooperative Wildlife Research Unit
V. P. I.
Blacksburg, Virginia

No. 36-1 Date APRIL 4, 1978

Location NEW RIVER, GILES CO., VA.

Legend FISH KILLED BY
POLLUTION – CATFISH, CARP
BREAM & SMALLMOUTH BASS

Author JOHN A. SMITH

Fig. 4.10. A rubber-stamped outline on the back of each photographic print insures that all necessary data relating to the print are recorded.

Chapter Five

Writing the Scientific Report

THOMAS G. SCOTT

Senior Scientist
U.S. Fish and Wildlife Service
Fort Collins, Colorado

JAMES S. AYARS

Head, Section of Publications and Public Relations
Illinois Natural History Survey, Emeritus
Urbana, Illinois

An essential part of the research process is publication of the findings. Unpublished research is incomplete research. Each scientist bears a responsibility for making the results of his research available to other scientists. This responsibility is accomplished most effectively by those who are willing to work hard enough to become proficient writers. Accurate, clear, and concise writing provides a highly rewarding personal experience.

The scientist as an effective writer may be largely self-trained. Courses in rhetoric are helpful; so are useful references on writing. Beyond these, the scientist is largely on his own. The degree of effectiveness he attains will depend largely upon his intelligence and diligence.

BASIC REFERENCES

The scientist-writer will find the following references indispensable:

1. A good style manual. Examples: *Council of Biology Editors Style Manual*, Fourth Edition (Huth et al. 1978); and *Words into Type*, Third Edition (Skillin et al. 1974).
2. A good dictionary. We recommend Webster's *Third New International Dictionary*, unabridged.
3. A handbook of English rhetoric. We suggest *The Elements of Style* (Strunk and White 1979).
4. Thesaurus. We suggest *The New Roget's Thesaurus of the English Language in Dictionary Form* (Lewis 1978) or one similar to it.

THE AUTHOR'S PROCEDURE

Let us assume that an investigation has been terminated and that the results must be prepared for publication. What is the most effective procedure? Many scientists have adopted the following plan, or one fairly close to it.

The First Step (Preparing Outline)

The first step in the preparation of a manuscript is the formulation of a working outline. The outline helps to insure fidelity to the assignment and to give unity to the paper. Trelease's (1975:36) advice is appropriate: "A scientific paper should be a unit, treating a single definite subject. . . . Include only what is necessary to an understanding of the main ideas, but omit nothing that is essential."

The task of preparing an outline has been simplified for scientists because most investigational reports fit a standard format. Some papers may be too short to justify format headings, but the preparatory outline will still follow the format sequence.

The standard format leads the reader from an understandable description of the subject, or a clear statement of purpose, through the investigational techniques used, to the results of the study and an objective discussion of the findings. The parts of the standard format provide a framework for the author's working outline.

In the order of their physical arrangement, the principal divisions of the standard format are:

1. Title
2. By-line
3. Abstract
4. Introductory Statement
5. Acknowledgments (usually included with the introductory remarks)
6. Study Area (used only when a detailed description of the study area is an essential part of the report)
7. Materials and Methods
8. Results (sometimes called "Findings")
9. Discussion (sometimes combined with Results)
10. Literature Cited

Title.—The title, which serves as an index to the content of the paper, should include key words that facilitate machine processing and retrieval. It should be short, specific, and accurate. A 10-word limit is a guide to length. Where appropriate, include the nature of the study, the principal species involved, and the geographic location. Instructions for contributors to *The Journal of Wildlife Management* and to some other journals ask that scientific names be avoided in titles.

By-line.—The by-line identifies the author(s) and the institution(s) where the investigation was made. The relationship of the author and institution is best understood where the author's name is followed by that of the institution. The author should be consistent in the form of his name.

Abstract.—The abstract should be written to stand alone as a condensed report of a paper's contents. It should not be longer than 3% of the paper's length.

Introductory Statement.—The introductory statement should be used to state the objective or purpose of the investigation or paper. It may include a review of the literature pertinent to the investigation.

Materials and Methods.—This section should be detailed enough to allow other scientists to check on the authenticity of the work or to duplicate the procedures used. When *Materials* are not pertinent enough to be listed, the heading becomes *Methods.*

Results.—The observations and data resulting from the investigation are described here. Great latitude is possible in this section. In some papers *Results* and *Discussion* can be combined.

Discussion.—This section is a possibility, not a necessity. It relates the results to the pertinent findings of other scientists and attempts to evaluate the meaning of the findings. It should not be a convenient depository for afterthoughts nor a mere rehash of results. The section may conveniently be used for broadly interpreting the facts presented in the paper and relating them to the findings of other scientists, taking a fresh look at the width and depth of the problems involved, and projecting whatever thinking may be induced by the paper at least a little way into the future.

Literature Cited.—This section lists only the literature that has been cited in the text. It documents the author's interpretations of the literature and provides the reader with a means of evaluating these interpretations.

The Second Step (Planning Tables and Illustrations)

Tables essential for presentation of data must be carefully planned. Carelessness in early tabulations can result in errors that may not be found until it is too late to correct them except in an errata sheet. Errors in tables may result in errors in the text and in the conclusions.

Graphs, charts, maps, and photographs essential to presentation of the findings should be available for reference during the writing stage. At this stage, graphs may be in rough form but with all points accurately plotted.

The Third Step (Assembling References to Literature)

Consultation of pertinent literature is a continuous process throughout the investigation. The results of this will be available for ready reference if you have maintained a file of cards, all the same size (4 × 6 inches or 3 × 5 inches), on which you have accurately copied pertinent ideas and data from the literature and have indicated their sources. If you have limited each card to a single item, you will be able to assign any card you use to a part of your outline and can arrange the cards in the order in which you will refer to them. Some writers follow the practice of writing their first drafts from cards; they write their own ideas and data, as well as those of other authors, on cards and arrange the cards in the order dictated by the outline.

The Fourth Step (Writing)

When you are ready to begin writing try to determine the time of day in which you do your clearest thinking, for this will be the best time for you to write. For many people this time comes early in the day.

Prepare your first draft section by section. Your outline should be detailed enough so that at least one section can be written at a sitting. Many authors find it far better to write a little every day than to write the entire paper at one or a few sittings. Prepare the abstract last.

In the preparation of the first draft, concentrate on the subject matter. Do not allow yourself to be stopped by mental blocks over such things as the right word or phrase. If nothing more, leave a space and continue writing down your ideas as rapidly as possible. In subsequent drafts, you can refine the phraseology and select the right words to convey your meaning precisely.

After preparation of the first draft, examine it section by section and paragraph by paragraph to determine whether the information presented is in the right section and in a logical sequence. A common shortcoming in science writing is the inclusion of information on *Materials and Methods* in the *Results* and *Discussion* sections. Examine the draft also for topical sentences introducing ideas to be discussed, and for transitional sentences or paragraphs between major parts of the manuscript; if well constructed, these contribute to ease of reading and readiness of comprehension.

Study each sentence to determine whether it conveys the correct meaning, whether it can be shortened, and whether it can be omitted. Go about this with the same attitude that you might expect from your severest critic or professional competitor.

After you have revised the manuscript several times and have reached the point where you are no longer effective in making improvements, invite the criticism of a colleague who is a good writer and is knowledgeable in your field. A rest from intensive work on a paper will clear your vision for mistakes that you overlooked earlier.

PREPARATION OF COPY

When your manuscript is nearing completion, read or reread the "Instruction to Contributors" in the journal to which you plan to submit your work. Your manuscript will be ready for its final typing only after it conforms to those instructions. Any of the following suggestions that are not in disagreement with the style of your chosen journal may prove useful in the preparation of your copy.

Paper and Typing

Type all copy—text, footnotes, legends, tables, and table headings—doublespaced on one side of good quality white paper, 16- or 20-pound for ribbon copy, 13- or 16-pound for the 2 or more carbon or Xerox copies.

The ribbon copy and 1 carbon or Xerox copy are for the editor of the journal. Your institution may want 1 or more carbon or Xerox copies. Retain 1 copy for yourself.

The copies should be kept identical, changes in one being made in the others.

Leave margins of at least 1 to 1 ½ inches on each page, the left margin slightly larger than the others.

Type copy in each of these categories—text, tables, legends, and literature cited—on separate sheets, as copy for each may be set on a different machine or at a different time. Whenever possible, avoid the use of footnotes. If you use them, type them on the proper text page, indicating clearly the material to which they apply and that they are footnotes.

Number pages of the final typescript consecutively. If you wish to insert a page give it a number and a letter. Then on the pages immediately preceding and following indicate the position of the page. For example, if you insert a page between pages 10 and 11, number the new page "10A." Indicate at the bottom of page 10 that "Page 10A follows" and at the top of page 11 that "Page 10A precedes."

Headings

Use headings and subheadings descriptive of the text matter to which they apply. If possible, make each short enough to be set in 1 line of type. Most articles of journal length need heads of no more than 3 categories or levels of importance. Indicate for each head the level to which it belongs. For example, use capital letters for a main (No. 1) head; initial caps and lower case letters for a secondary (No. 2) head; and initial caps and lowercase for a tertiary run-in (No. 3) head. The editor may indicate italic or boldface for some of the heads.

> STUDY AREA
> Phenology
> *Early Spring.*—

Follow the head style of the journal to which you intend to submit your paper.

Numbers

Unless you are familiar with the editorial policy for the journal in which you plan to publish your paper, follow the style explained below.

Use numerals for all measurements, including measurements of time: 1 mg, 3 days, 5 months.

In expressing large numbers ending in zeros, combine words and numerals.

> $7 million.

Otherwise, spell numbers one through nine and use numerals for others. In a category (as seeds, birds, insects) containing some numbers under 10 and others over, use numerals for all.

> Of the 35 prairie chickens, 5 were eating seeds.

In sentences containing some categories with numbers below 10 and other categories with some numbers above nine, spell out the numbers in a category having all numbers under 10 and use numerals throughout a category having some numbers above nine.

> Of the seven prairie chickens, three ate 7 seeds each and four ate 33 seeds each.

The editorial policy of *The Journal of Wildlife Management* is to use numerals for all numbers except at the beginning of a sentence.

Citations and Quotations

Use the date system in citing published works. If you wish to be especially helpful to readers and editors, include with the date the page number or numbers on which the cited material can be found. This system is explained on pages 9 and 153 of the *CBE Style Manual*, Third Edition (Ayars et al. 1972.)

> Schoolcraft 1822:67–69 reported prairie chickens in Illinois.
>
> Prairie chickens were reported in Illinois more than a century ago (Schoolcraft 1822:67–69).

Page numbers should always be given for direct quotations and are desirable for easy location of paraphrased material. (Be kind to editors and serious readers.)

In citing a paper by 2 authors, name both: Brown and Black (1967:28). In citing a paper by more than 2 authors, name only the first and add et al. For example, instead of Brown, Black, Green, White, and Goodhue (1935:67), write Brown et al. (1935:67). Alternatives for citing several references on 1 topic follow: (1) Brown (1963), Black (1964), and Green (1965) have contributed to refinement of the concept of plant succession; (2) From 1962 to 1965, 3 Americans (Brown 1962, Black 1964, and Green 1965) made important contributions to our concept of plant succession; (3) In recent years, the concept of plant succession has been expanded (Brown 1963, 1964a, 1964b; Black 1962, 1963; Green 1966); (4) Rabid bats can transmit rabies by biting (Reagan et al. 1957, Tierkel and Arnstein 1958, Bell 1959). Whether the author's name is placed outside or inside parentheses depends upon the construction of the sentence.

Place double quotation marks before and after quoted materials. In quoting material consisting of more than 1 paragraph, use double quotation marks at the beginning of each paragraph and at the end of the last. Use single quotation marks to indicate quotations within quotations.

Place commas and periods inside closing quotation marks even if they are not part of the quotation.

> As used here, "territory" is considered synonymous with "home range." (Period.)
>
> In assessment of "population health," an effective aging technique is needed. (Comma.)

Place semicolons and colons outside the quotation marks unless they are part of the quotation.

> The lens of the eye in the cottontail grows "throughout life"; the data supporting this have been reviewed. (Semicolon.)
>
> There are 2 basic needs for effective evaluation of "food habits": knowledge of the ecology of the study area and information on the relative availability of prey animals. (Colon.)

If you omit 1 or more words from quoted material, indicate the omission by ellipsis marks (3 spaced periods with spaces before and after them). If you omit words from the beginning of a quoted sentence that follows the period ending a preceded quoted sentence, place the ellipsis marks after the period. If you omit words at the end of a sentence, place the ellipsis marks ahead of period. Do not use ellipsis marks for words omitted from the beginning of a sentence quoted, or for single words or phrases lifted from a sentence.

> "Sexual maturity is attained by both sexes at 1 year of age. . . . an occasional early-born doe may be capable of breeding during the mating season the first fall after birth." (The missing words are: "There is reason to believe. . . ." Note the lowercase *a* on "an occasional.")

If you omit words at the end of a quoted sentence but quote the beginning of a following sentence, place the ellipsis marks before the period.

> "The research will continue until a solution is found . . . . The prospects for a solution are good." (The missing words are: "or until all funds are withdrawn." Note the capital *T* on "The prospects and the space after "found.")

Enclose in brackets any changes you make in words or spelling of quoted matter. Otherwise, quote exactly, including errors. You may use [*sic*] following an error to indicate that you know it is an error.

Tables

Because tabular matter is expensive, use tables only when the cost can be justified. Make each table (with its heading) complete. Do not depend upon the text to tell what, when, and where.

Study the style of tables in the journal of your choice and, as far as possible, make your tables conform to that style.

Do not submit a table larger than a page of the journal will accommodate, unless you have persuaded the editor to run your table across facing pages. Break long tables into 2 or more smaller tables, each complete in itself.

Do not repeat in the text the material shown in your tables, except to interpret or to call attention to unusual data.

Photographs

Submit only those photographs that will contribute to an understanding of your paper.

Photographs should be of medium contrast, on glossy finish paper, and slightly larger than they will appear in the journal. Matte finish paper is unacceptable.

If you have photographs made, tell the photographer what you wish them to show. By lighting and other devices, he may be able to emphasize the features you most want your readers to see.

Do not include too much in a single photograph. Learn when to use macro- and when to use microphotographs.

Do not expect black and white photographs to do the work of colored ones.

Graphs and Maps

Submit only those graphs and maps that contribute significantly to the reader's rapid orientation to the problem you have presented and to the results of your work. They should be an integral part of the paper. Do not repeat in graphs material already in the tables you are submitting; some tables have graphic qualities.

Use imagination and judgment in your selection of types of graphs. Bar graphs are sometimes used when line, pie, 3-dimensional, or other types would be more useful.

Submit graphs and maps on good quality white paper or drawing board. They should be about one and a half times the size you expect them to appear in the journal.

Lines, dots, circles, Zip-a-Tone, and lettering should be large enough to take the necessary reduction. A reducing lens is helpful for these determinations.

Letters and numerals should not be freehand, and, to remain legible, they should be at least 1/16 inch tall when reduced for printing. Those carefully made with mechanical lettering devices usually are satisfactory.

Literature Cited

In the Literature Cited section, list only works cited in your paper. Do not list unpublished works, except those that are available in one or more libraries.

Arrange cited works alphabetically by family names of authors, or of senior authors (in cases of joint authorship). Arrange cited works by the same author (or authors) chronologically.

Invert the family name and given names or initials of the author of a paper, but only of the senior author in a paper with joint authorship.

List elements of a journal citation in the following order: author or authors, date of publication, title of article, name of journal, volume number, issue number, and page or pages. Although some journals omit the issue number (except when the pages of the journal are numbered by issue), we prefer always to include the issue number as a convenience to the reader.

Hiller, E. J., and R. Brown. 1948. Influence of some carbon compounds on growth of plant tissues. Anat. Rec. 70(5):68–75.

Abbreviate the titles of periodicals as recommended in the *Council of Biology Editors Style Manual*, Fourth Edition.

List elements of a book citation as follows: author or authors, date of publication, title of book, publisher, place of publication, number of pages.

Menzel, D. H., H. M. Jones, and L. G. Boyd. 1961. Writing a technical paper. McGraw-Hill Book Co., New York. ix + 132 p.

Type citations with hanging indentations, as shown above.

Final Examination

Many authors make the mistake of not examining the final draft, relying on the accuracy of the typist. It is advisable for the author to check the final work for typographical errors and to verify the correctness of technical terms and names of persons. Names of persons are sometimes carelessly used in acknowledgments. Check the Literature Cited section against original sources for accuracy; at the same time, verify the accuracy of quotations. Make certain that the dates used with citations in the text agree with those listed in the Literature Cited section. Determine that the correct abbreviations have been used in the references. Finally, check the numerical data in the tables for typographical errors.

Make certain that you have cleared the manuscript for submission to an editor. Failure to obtain administrative approval for publication can prove extremely embarrassing to everyone concerned. This is true especially where a thesis is involved, and particularly when the thesis has not yet been accepted by the educational institution for which it is written.

PROOF

When you receive galley proof from the printer, read it carefully against your original copy. Read it again for meaning and accuracy. Correct inaccuracies, both yours and the printer's, but do not make "second thought" changes that should have been made in the copy. You may be charged for the cost of making changes that do not involve errors of the printer.

Indicate corrections on the *margins* of the proof sheets. Most printers pay little attention to corrections within lines unless the desired changes are also written on the *margins*. Use printer's symbols if you know them. (Every style manual lists them.) If you do not, write notes to the printer that leave no doubt of your meaning. Draw a line through each word you want omitted and use a caret (∧) to indicate where you want a word or words inserted. In each case, *do not fail to make appropriate marks in the margin.*

Mail the proof promptly to the place to which you are directed to send it.

EDITORIAL LIFE HISTORY OF A MANUSCRIPT

An understanding of the editorial process and of the responsibilities of the editorial staff will be helpful to the writer-scientist.

The editor supervises the editorial process, and a good editor is more than the custodian of a collection station for manuscripts. His job is demanding and complex. He must work on an exacting time schedule with overlapping deadlines. He must possess skill in several technical fields and be constantly sensitive to details. He must be staunch in his adherence to excellence in scientific and editorial standards. He cannot afford indecisiveness. He is the final judge in accepting or rejecting a manuscript.

The following is a list of the steps in the editorial life history of a manuscript.

1. The manuscript is submitted by the author.
2. The editor acknowledges receipt of the manuscript.
3. The manuscript, with a covering letter, is sent by the editor to a number of referees. This procedure is for the author's protection as well as that of the readers and the editor. The referees are qualified by training and experience in the subject area of the manuscript.
4. The referees make comments and suggestions and return the manuscript to the editor. The referees are concerned with scientific accuracy and the value of the contribution made.
5. The editor reads the manuscript and the comments of the referees. He makes the decision to accept or reject the manuscript.
6. If the manuscript is found acceptable, an editorial assistant, or the editor, checks the manuscript for rhetorical irregularities, for errors of syntax, spelling, grammar, consistency in mechanics of style, clarity of thought and expression, orderly arrangement of material, and logical presentation of data in the text and in the tables and figures. Sentences are recast, revisions are made or are suggested, and errors are corrected. The editor or copy editor recasts sentences, makes or suggests revisions, corrects errors and checks every citation against the original reference, if available.
7. The manuscript is sent to the author with a covering letter of suggestions and comments from the editor, and with the referees' reviews of the article.
8. With suggested changes, corrections, and comments in mind, the author revises his manuscript.
9. The manuscript is retyped and returned to the editor.
10. An editorial assistant and the editor check the revised version for possible errors of omission or commission.
11. If necessary, the manuscript is returned to the author for further work and again returned to the editor.
12. The manuscript is marked for the printer and sent to him.
13. Proofs are forwarded to the author for reading and marking and are then returned to the editor.

14. The editor and assistants read and mark the proof sheets and send them to the printer for corrections.

15. The printer sends revised proof sheets to the editor, who, with his assistants, checks and returns them to the printer for publication.

SUGGESTIONS FOR EFFECTIVE SCIENCE WRITING

Application of the following simple guidelines should improve upon the effectiveness of your writing:

1. Feel free to use personal subjects such as "I," "we," "Jones."
2. Avoid too many polysyllabic words.
3. Avoid the use of long and involved sentences.
4. Use the active voice unless the passive voice is clearly preferable.
5. Avoid the excessive use of nouns as adjectives.
6. Avoid excessive hedging.
7. Avoid the use of Latin abbreviations, especially "etc."
8. Avoid using scientific nomenclature throughout a paper if suitable common names are available.

Some common faults in scientific papers are:

1. Illogical grouping of ideas. (A good working outline will minimize this shortcoming.)
2. Omission of vital facts or steps in procedure, interpretation, or conclusion.
3. Needless repetition of facts.
4. Inaccurate paraphrasing of passages or copying of quotations from references.
5. Inaccuracies in the Literature Cited section.
6. Inaccuracy in making computations.
7. Imprecise use of words. Use of words in senses peculiar to the members of only a small group. *Use of words for the sake of the use of words.*
8. Use of obscure or doubtful antecedents for pronouns.
9. Inclusion of data favorable to a desired conclusion, and exclusion of equally valuable data unfavorable to the conclusion.
10. Drawing conclusions unsupported by the facts presented.
11. Failure of authors to read their manuscripts with thoughtfulness, thoroughness, objectivity, and patience.

Chapter Six

Capturing and Marking Wild Animals

GERALD I. DAY

Research Biologist
Arizona Game and Fish Department
Tucson, Arizona

SANFORD D. SCHEMNITZ

Professor and Head
Department of Fishery and Wildlife Sciences
New Mexico State University
Las Cruces, New Mexico

RICHARD D. TABER

Professor
College of Forest Resources
University of Washington
Seattle, Washington

Students of wildlife are living at a time of tremendous advancement in all areas of the wildlife management field. Since the 1969 publication of *Wildlife Management Techniques,* there have been many advancements in capturing and marking animals. Many research and management projects concerned with animal transplants and population studies are dependent upon safe, reliable capture and marking techniques. Improved capture and marking equipment is being developed and marketed to assist wildlife workers in these demands. However, many field technicians are still designing and constructing capture equipment to help reduce costs, improve the devices, and to supply special needs. This chapter will describe and discuss some of the important capturing and marking techniques that have been used effectively by wildlife managers.

CAPTURING WILD ANIMALS

The art of capturing animals for food is as old as human existence on earth. However, few animals are captured solely for food today. Most wild animals are captured to implement various management and research studies. Recent advances, especially in the use of new drug compounds for capturing free-ranging animals, have increased the success of programs initiated by agencies responsible for wildlife management. Successful capture programs do not just happen; they result from the efforts of experienced wildlife managers who have planned, studied, and tested various techniques before beginning any new program.

Trap Baits, Lures and Scents

The success of most animal trapping operations depends on a suitable bait or lure to attract animals into traps. Numerous native foods, commercial foods, artificial lures, and prepared scents have been used as attractants. Unfortunately, there is no universal attractant that works successfully on all species. Consequently, wildlife managers may have to conduct tests with several baits, lures, or scents before ones are found to attract different species in their geographical areas.

BAITS

Livestock or domestic foods are probably the most common baits used in big game trapping. Prebaiting with these foods is an important prerequisite to any trapping program. Howard and Engelking (1974) tested different baits for trapping mule deer in New Mexico. They found apples and pears the most preferred, alfalfa hay and cottonseed cubes moderately to heavily used, and salt and corn only lightly used. Although salt and corn were only lightly used by mule deer in New Mexico, these 2 baits have been widely used to trap white-tailed deer (Hawkins et al. 1967a, Ramsey 1968, Mattfeld et al. 1972).

In the arid climate of the Southwest even water has been an effective bait to trap desert bighorns (Papez and Tsukamoto 1970). Native browse plants are not used as frequently as in the past because of the time and effort required in gathering them. However, Mattfeld et al. (1972) trapped deer effectively with browse plants in the winter and with salt in the summer.

Carnivores are sometimes attracted to snares and traps by meat "stink" baits which are prepared from either fish, poultry, or beef. For example, holes can be punched in cans of fish or meat to make a long-lasting, smelly bait.

Various grains such as corn, milo, wheat, and oats are used extensively to attract game birds. Gullion (1961) found that corn dyed orange, red, blue, or purple was more accepted by grouse than undyed, yellow shelled corn. He soaked the dyed corn in water that caused it to swell and to look like wild fruit.

A mixture of peanut butter and oatmeal has been used as a rodent bait for many years. Anderson and Ohmart (1977) used peanut butter and oats at a ratio of 1:4 and 1:1. They added dimethylphthalate to the bait to discourage ants from taking it. Getz and Prather (1975) used a short fiber cotton with peanut butter which was heated to about 65°C. This bait provided odor and taste of peanut butter, but the cotton made it difficult for insects to remove. Most rodent baits are applied to the trap by hand, but Johnson (1969) used a caulking gun to dispense bait more rapidly in live traps.

SCENTS

For many years fur trappers have used secret passion and curiosity scents to attract furbearing mammals into traps. Basically the major ingredients in scent mixtures are similar except for minor variations. Dobie (1961) reported the important items in coyote scent are coyote urine, anal glands from coyote, fish oil and glycerine as a preservative. Scents composed of rotten eggs, decomposed meat and fish oil also have been used for coyote trapping. Other items such as seal oil, Siberian musk oil, beaver castor and skunk musk are widely used in scents.

Some plant extractions are added to scents. The root of the Asiatic plant asafetida *(Ferula)* imparts a strong persistent odor to scents. The oils from the herbs anise *(Pimpinella)* and valerian *(Valeriana)* also have been added to scent mixtures. Some trappers like to add small amounts of cheap commercial perfumes to their scents.

Scent stations containing 1 g of fermented egg attractant are being used to determine the relative abundance of coyotes in 17 western states (Linhart and Knowlton 1975). The fermented egg attracts coyotes to a circle of sifted earth or sand, 0.9 m in diameter, in which tracks can be clearly detected. Lindzey et al. (1977) used similar scent stations to attract black bears for determining relative numbers.

Scents are used primarily to attract carnivores, but other mammals are attracted to them. Pedersen (1977) successfully trapped elk in the summer with anise oil and salt.

Vole odor left on dirty live traps effectively captured more voles than clean traps (Boonstra and Krebs 1976).

DECOY AND ENTICEMENT LURES

Various live animals and devices have been used successfully to lure animals for capture. Probably the most successful technique is the "bal-chatri" traps for capturing raptors in banding studies (Berger and Mueller 1959). This trap is a chicken wire cage that holds a bird or rodent as a lure. The top of the trap consists of numerous monofilament nooses that can snag the talons of hawks which attack the caged animals. Berger and Hamerstrom (1962) used these traps to protect game bird trapping stations from feeding hawks. Meng (1971) described the Swedish goshawk trap which is baited with live pigeons. Hamerstrom (1963) and Phillips (1978) described a vertical mesh net trap, a dho-gaza, used to capture hawks and baited with a live, tethered horned owl.

Stuffed taxidermy mounts successfully lured sandhill cranes to a site for rocket net capture (Wheeler and Lewis 1972). Male greater prairie chickens responded to hen decoys and were captured with bownets or noose carpets (Anderson and Hamerstrom 1967).

A live female duck decoy was used during the breeding season by Rogers (1964) to entice male ducks into a funnel trap. Blohm and Ward (1979) used a live female gadwall surrounded by 3 funnel entrances to capture male gadwalls. Mirrors have been used to lure drumming ruffed grouse into traps by Tanner and Bowers (1948) and Dorney and Mattison (1956).

Tapes and reed calls have been used effectively to attract different animals. Diem (1954) found a deer call useful in locating deer fawns for capture. Rabbit distress calls have been used to lure predators (Morse and Balser 1961). Taped female grouse calls (Stirling and Bendell 1966) and quail calls (Levy et al. 1966) have enticed responses from breeding males for censusing. Silvy and Robel (1967) used recordings to lure male greater prairie chickens in front of cannon nets for capture. Artmann (1971) captured sharp-tailed grouse hens by using taped chick distress calls. Tape recorded songs in combination with decoys and mist nets have been successful in capturing warblers (Murray and Gill 1976).

Smuts et al. (1977) lured over 600 lions to game carcasses with tape recordings of lions and spotted hyaena calls. They captured 488 of the lions by darting techniques.

Capturing Mammals

Field biologists have a number of new techniques available to capture small rodents and large herbivores. Some techniques are either improved or modified versions of old capture methods. Animals are captured by hand, a mechanical device, remote injection of drugs, or drugs administered orally in baits. In recent years the greatest advancement has occurred in the use of drugs to capture free-ranging animals. New drug compounds, improved delivery systems, and increased knowledge in this field have made drugs a highly successful capture technique. Major emphasis in this chapter will be on the equipment and drugs used for capture; however, the old reliable traps and new mechanical devices also will be included.

STEEL AND SNAP TRAPS

For many years fur trappers and predator control agents have used various commercial steel traps to capture animals. Palmisano and Dupuie (1975) compared leg-hold and conibear steel traps for taking animals in Louisiana. They found long spring leg-hold traps more effective in taking nutria and raccoon while the conibear appeared superior to leg-holds on muskrats. Leg-hold traps with offset and padded jaws have also been used to capture carnivores safely for marking and radio instrumentation. Jonkel and Cowan (1971) used modified Newhouse 150 steel traps to capture black bears for marking. Wolves were captured for study with #4 Newhouse steel traps (Ballenberghe et al. 1975). Storm et al. (1976) captured foxes at dens with #1 and #2 steel traps. However, Nellis (1968) found steel traps unacceptable for live coyote capture because of foot injuries.

The Bailey and Hancock live traps or modified versions are used primarily to capture beaver. However, Northcott and Slade (1976) modified the Hancock trap to capture river otters along slides and pathways.

Commercial snap traps (Victor and Museum Specials) are used to capture and sample small mammal populations. Museum Specials are reported to be more effective than other snap traps because they have a more sensitive trigger mechanism (Smith et al. 1971, Wiener and Smith 1972).

BOX TRAPS

One of the most widely used techniques to capture deer is the "Stephenson" box trap. This trap was developed by J. H. Stephenson of the Michigan Department of Conservation. Bartlett (1938) first reported the use of the Stephenson-type live trap to capture white-tailed deer. The basic design of the trap has remained unchanged except for improvements in construction and tripping devices. The trap is constructed of wood or metal and measures about 1.2 m × 1.2 m × 3.7 m with drop gates at both ends. Trap gates can be tripped by a string or wire, but Webb (1943) used a steel trap as the release device. Runge (1972) described an improved tripping device that uses monofilament fish line and steel rods. Masters (1978) described a simple trigger assembly which used a gate hook, band of iron, and monofilament line.

Large box traps made of corrugated steel culverts have been used to capture bears (Erickson 1957, Black 1958, Troyer et al. 1962). Bear traps can be made of steel plates or 14-gauge culvert sections 1.8–2.4 m long and 1.2 m wide with a steel drop gate at one or both ends. The weight of these traps restricts their use to sites along roads. Most culvert traps are mounted on trailer frames to make them more portable. These traps are useful in capturing nuisance bears which can be hauled within the trap to a new release site.

Apparatuses that resemble box traps have been constructed to restrain captive animals for blood collecting and drugging. Sauer et al. (1969) used a plywood restraint chute with folding doors to control and handle mule deer. A similar device modified with movable padded side panels and a padded plunger successfully restrained white-tailed deer (Mautz et al. 1974). Masters (1978) used a padded, plywood holding box to restrain captured deer for weighing and marking. Deer captured in box traps were forced into the smaller holding box where their necks were held between movable catch bars on the front of the box.

Smaller mammals also can be captured by a variety of commercial "boxlike" traps, such as Havahart, Longworth, National, Sherman and Victor. However, many field workers design and construct their own traps out of either wood, metal, wire, or plastic. A wooden box trap (Figs. 6.1, 6.2) designed by Mosby (1955) was improved to increase catches and reduce escapes of woodchucks by Ludwig and Davis (1975). They increased the trap length from 51 cm to 61 cm, added a transom latch to secure the door, lined the door with metal to discourage chewing, and used a wooden post for a trigger instead of wire. Cushwa and Burnham (1974) designed an inexpensive live trap for snowshoe hares. This trap consisted of #2 hardware cloth (1.3 cm × 1.3 cm) for the

Fig. 6.1. **Small mammal live trap, showing construction details.** ***A.*** **Trap with side removed.** ***B.*** **Trap with top removed.** ***C.*** **Parts of trap, numbered as diagrammed in Fig. 6.2 (from Mosby 1955).**

body and back and plywood sheeting (0.64 cm thick) for the door and treadle. The door frame was reinforced with #8 gauge steel wire around the edge and #2 wire mesh on the inside. Piano wire was used for the trigger mechanism.

Buech (1974) made small mammal traps out of 28-gauge galvanized sheet metal which measured 16.5 cm × 16.5 cm × 10.0 cm. Each trap included a door, treadle, entrance passage, and a nest box containing cotton and food to maintain trapped animals and reduce mortality. Ground squirrels were live captured in simple galvanized wire traps (7.5 × 7.5 × 50 cm) inserted in burrow entrances (Wobeser and Leighton 1979).

Artificial wooden box shelters (2.0 cm thick) were attached on trees to capture flying squirrels (Sonenshine et al. 1973). Trap dimensions were 13.8 cm × 13.8 cm × 36.3 cm inside; the top and bottom measured 17.8 cm × 17.8 cm and the overall height 42.0 cm. A 3.1-cm entrance hole was drilled in the side close to the tree and could easily be blocked when a squirrel used the shelter. Trapped squirrels were removed through a hinged door on the front of the trap.

Small cylinder-shaped live traps have been made out of plastic water pipe and wire or 2 cans and a mouse trap (Fig. 6.3). These traps are reported to be inexpensive, lightweight and successful. Brown et al. (1969) made small traps out of a combination of aluminum tubing (3.8 cm × 3.8 cm), plastic pipe (3.8 cm × 23 cm), and stainless steel strips (2.5 cm × 7.6 cm). A simple pocket gopher trap was made of hardware cloth (0.6 cm) with a diameter of 7.5 and 35.0 cm long (Hart 1973). Hart fashioned a door out of 28-gauge galvanized sheet metal with a spring at the top to assist closing. A trigger loop was made out of spring steel or clothes hanger 18–23 cm long. A small tin can was used to close the open end of the trap.

Wooden shelters have been used effectively to protect live traps from snow or sun (Iverson and Turner 1969, Buech 1974). Getz and Batzli (1974) used wire cages to prevent disturbance by raccoons to small mammals in live traps. Cages consisted of redwood frames and bottoms with 2.5-cm wire mesh on sides and 1.3-cm wire mesh on tops.

Wire cones, fitted with a block to crowd the animal to the end are widely used to handle mammals of medium size. A cone with cloth adapter for traps is shown (Fig. 6.4) for use with animals the size of chipmunks to weasels.

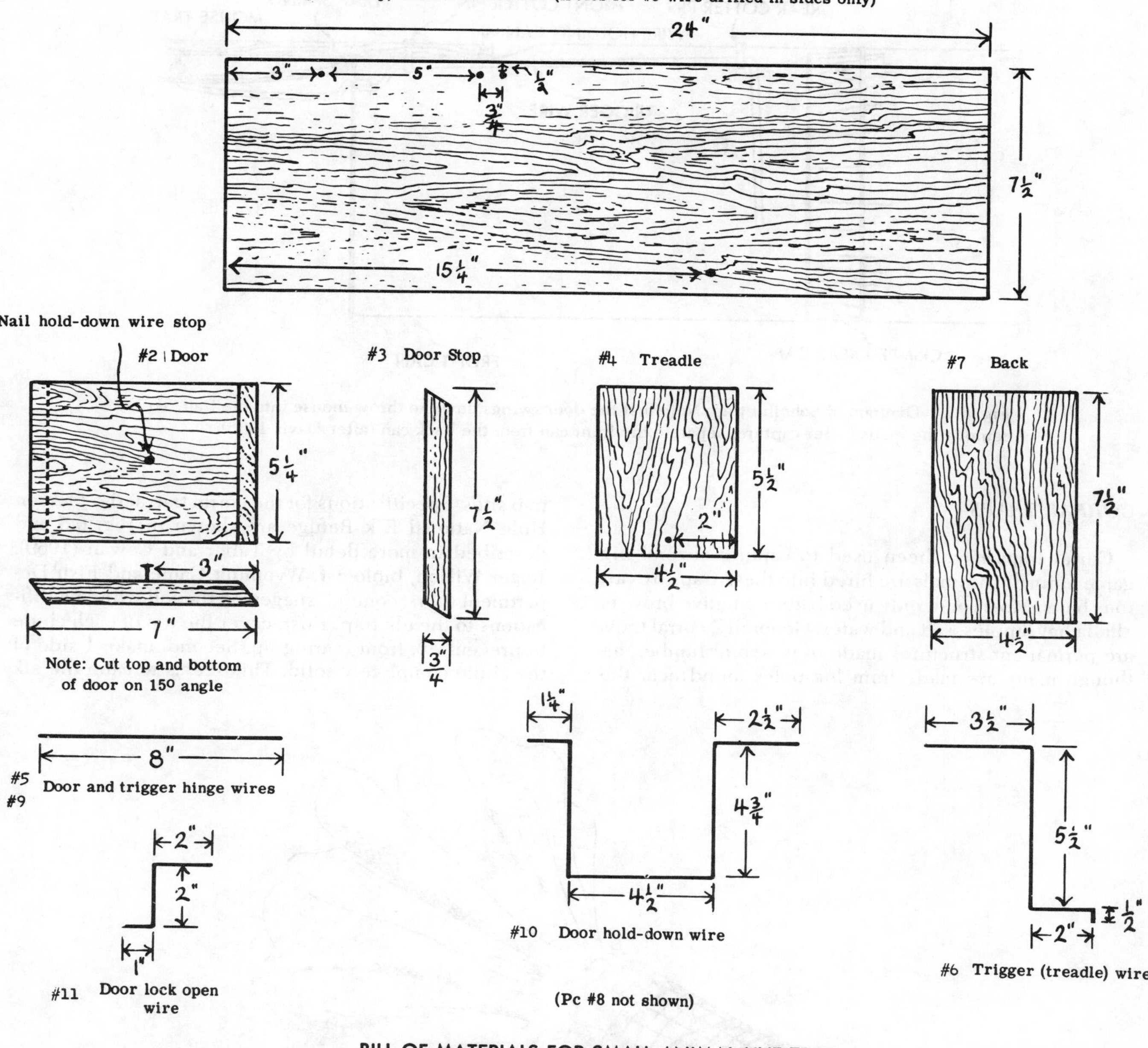

BILL OF MATERIALS FOR SMALL ANIMAL LIVE TRAP

No. Pieces	Dimensions	Part Name	Part No. (See Figs. 1 & 2)
ONE INCH DRESSED WOOD			
4 pcs.	7½" x 24"	Bottom, top sides	#1
1 pc.	5¼" x 7"	Door	#2
2 pcs.	1" x 7½"	Door stops	#3
1 pc.	4½" x 5½"	Trigger Treadle	#4
1 pc.	4½" x 7½"	Back of trap	#7
HARDWARE CLOTH OR WELDED WIRE			
1 pc.	7½" x 9"	Back of trap	#8

No. Pieces	Dimensions	Part Name	Part No.
FROM 9 GAUGE SMOOTH WIRE			
2 pcs.	8"	Door and treadle hinges	#5, #9
1 pc.	11"	Treadle Trigger	#6
1 pc.	17 3/4"	Door hold down wire	#10
1 pc.	5"	Door lock wire	#11

HARDWARE

18 - 6d box nails; 4 - 214 eye screws;
12 - 3/4" staples; 5 - 2d box nails

Fig. 6.2. Parts diagram and bill of materials for small mammal live trap (from Mosby 1955).

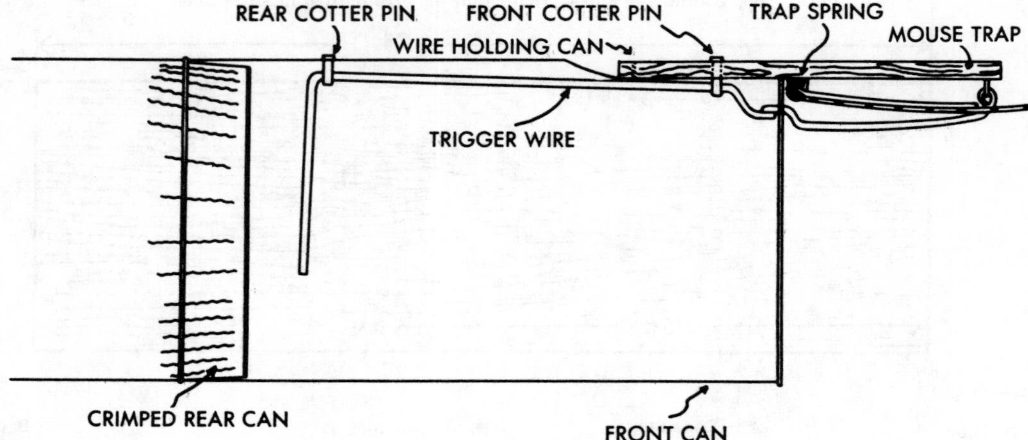

Fig. 6.3. Diagram of Scheffer trap. Note that the door swings down to throw mouse into the trap. To remove the mouse after capture, separate the front can from the back can (after Davis 1956).

CORRAL TRAPS

Corral traps have been used to capture several big game animals. Animals are lured into these traps by various baits. Most commonly used baits are native browse, alfalfa hay, apples, salt and water. Generally, corral traps are permanent structures made of wire and lumber, although many are made from log poles found near the trap sites. Specifications for the corral trap at the Jackson Hole National Elk Refuge are shown in Fig. 6.5 and described in more detail by Taber and Cowan (1969). Roger Wilson, biologist, Wyoming Game and Fish Department (pers. comm.), suggested the following modifications to the elk trap. First, cover the top of each chute to prevent elk from rearing up. Second, make 1 side of the chute completely solid. This seems to calm the elk

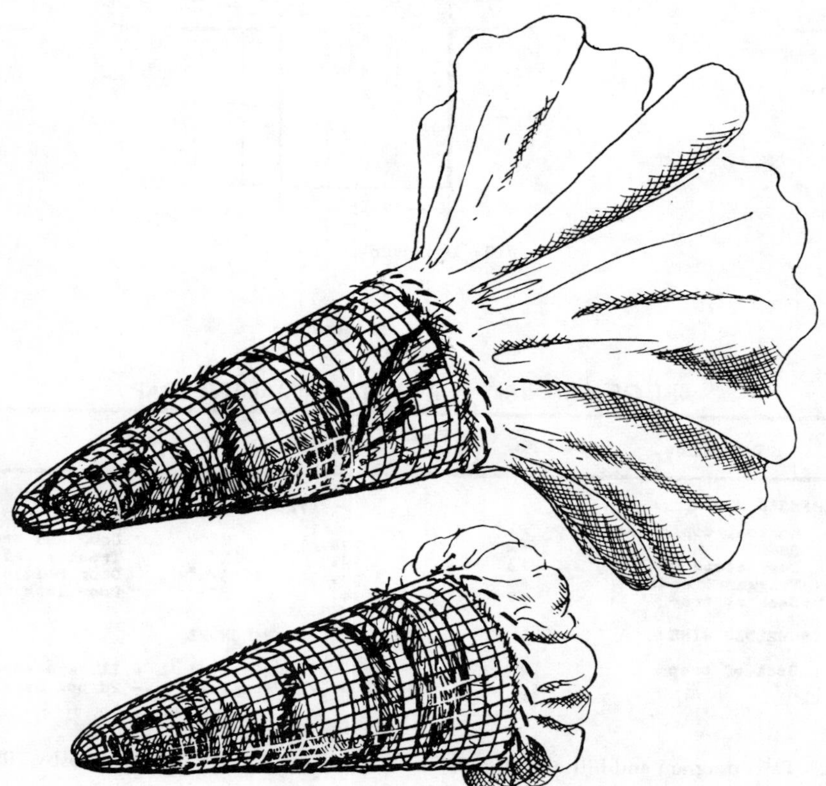

Fig. 6.4. An animal holding device can be made from a cone of hardware cloth or chicken wire attached to a dark-colored cloth adapter. The end of a live trap is enclosed with the adapter, the door or gate opened and the animal will usually run into the cone. They will escape once the cloth has been withdrawn.

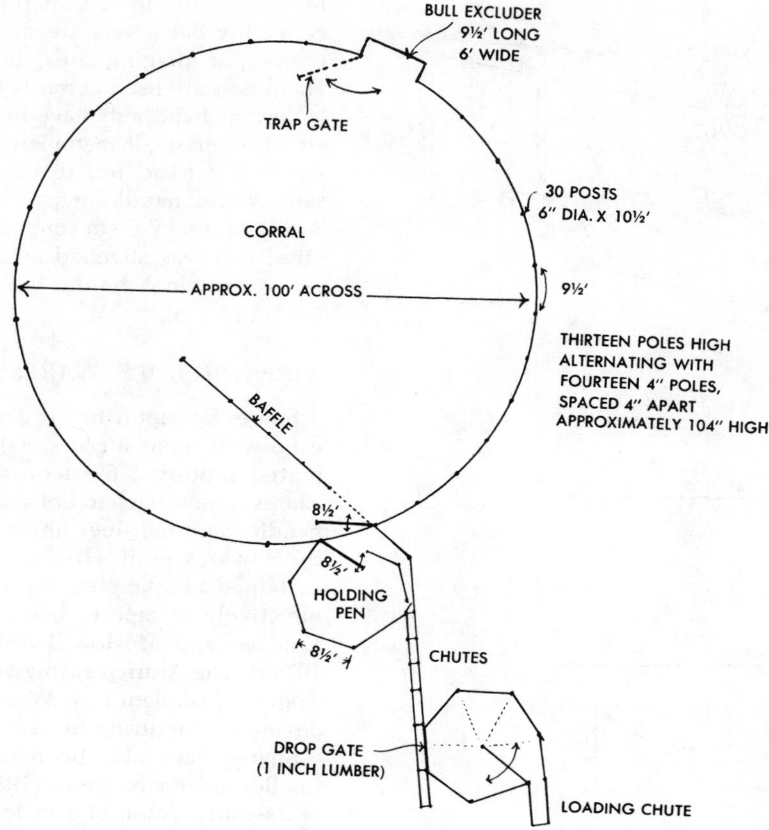

Fig. 6.5. **Diagram of an elk trap at the National Elk Refuge, Jackson, Wyoming (courtesy James Yorgason, Wyoming Game and Fish Commission, Jackson).**

and force them to the open side where tags and collars can be affixed.

A portable corral trap was used to capture Roosevelt elk (Mace 1971). This trap could be assembled by 3 men in less than a day. It was made from 6 wooden panels 3.7 m × 2.4 m that were fastened together by metal bands. Two posts held the 2.4-m × 2.4-m plywood gate, a crowding chute and loading chute.

Rempel and Bertram (1975) used a corral trap with 7 panels (2.4 m × 2.4 m) to capture deer at a salt lick. The corral trap was modified to accommodate 2 Clover traps (Clover 1956). These Clover traps captured the deer as they attempted to escape from the corral which greatly reduced the injuries associated with corral traps.

Sugden (1956) designed a technique to close gates on big game live traps by remote control. Two blasting caps were detonated at 548 m to sever ropes holding trap gates.

NET TRAPS

A portable net trap to capture deer was designed by Clover (1954). He constructed the trap frame out of black pipe or aluminum tubing and then stretched netting over the frame (Fig. 6.6). A drop gate was activated by a trip cord and rat trap. Trapped deer were forced from the trap into a catch-net for handling. Sparrowe and Springer (1970) modified the Clover trap so that the sides would fold over the deer for safe handling by 1 man. This folding technique was improved by McCullough (1975). He designed the trap to fold at the ends when 2 guy lines were unsnapped. The deer were marked within the trap and released when the trap was lifted to the upright position for resetting. Roper et al. (1971) attached additional bars along the bottom of the Clover trap to allow rabbits and porcupines to enter and leave without chewing holes in the netting.

Cannon nets are used primarily to capture birds, but they have been used successfully for larger mammals. Hawkins et al. (1968) used 3 recoilless cannons to project an 18-m × 12-m knotless nylon net with 10-cm square mesh to capture white-tailed deer. The net was fired manually from a blind or by an automatic triggering switch.

Ramsey (1968) used a nylon drop-net 21 m × 21 m with 9-cm square mesh to capture over 300 deer. Five poles supported the net that was released by an explosive triggering device.

Large herds of antelope and other animals have been captured in drive, drift, or funnellike net traps. These traps usually consist of long wings of wire fencing which are shaped like a funnel to guide animals into a net corral. Pienaar (1975b) described the use of plastic material instead of wire for the funnel wings and also for covering the netting around the corral. Oelofse (1970) also used woven plastic material (3 m wide) for the wings and corral of a drive trap. His crew successfully captured 3500 animals in 4 months in South Africa. He

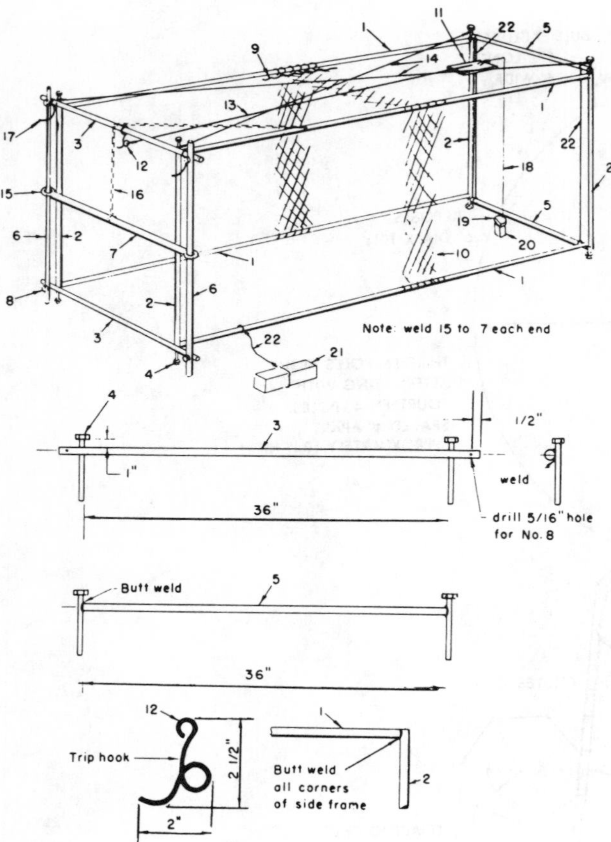

Fig. 6.6. **The Clover single-gate deer trap (from Clover 1956).**

loaded them directly into vehicles without handling. Antelope trap innovations reported by Spillett and ZoBell (1967) utilized burlap panels on the sides of the trap to quiet animals and reduce injuries. Animals are herded into these traps by aircraft, truck or by men afoot.

Hesselton (1970) used tangle nets along trails in deep snow to capture deer. Deer were driven by a large capture crew into the nets. A similar technique was used to capture caribou, but animals were herded and driven by 2 ski-equipped aircraft (DesMeules et al. 1971). They installed nets along forest edges on major trails leading to large lakes. Once the aircraft had the animals moving toward the nets they landed on the frozen, snow-covered lakes and continued to haze the animals on the ground. A crew of 4 to 6 was concealed at the ends of the net wings to capture and fetter tangled caribou. Personnel of the New Mexico Department of Game and Fish successfully captured deer and elk with a 2-m × 305-m net (Fig. 6.7). They used a helicopter to haze deer and elk into the net which was stretched across possible escape routes (Beasom et al. 1980). A portable nylon net 4.3 × 15.2 m with 17.8-cm mesh was used to capture 158 Florida Key deer (Silvy et al. 1975). They captured deer at night along escape routes next to canals. Keith et al. (1968) captured snowshoe hares in the winter with a drive net (0.9 m × 46 m or 91 m). Hares were driven into nets by human beaters on foot who were spaced about 15 m apart.

Bats are frequently captured by hand nets and mist nets. According to Tuttle (1976), black mist nets, used for small bird capture, are the most versatile devices for collecting bats. Nets are more effective near roost entrances, at foraging sites, along trails, and over water. Hand nets are used at roosts by flushing bats into them.

Various hand nets have been used to capture and restrain other small mammals. Jacobson et al. (1970) developed a hand net to capture free-ranging striped skunks and handle trapped animals. They welded a 3-m-long steel 2.5-cm conduit to a shovel handle. At the other end was attached a 1.3-cm conduit hoop (79-cm diameter) which held a bag made out of chicken wire mesh (5.1 cm).

WIRE AND ROPE SNARES

Snares for capturing big game animals alive have been used with some success. Ashcraft and Reese (1957) reported capturing 62 deer without any injury in rope snares. They attached bells to snares in order to hear and handle captured deer immediately. Snares were tested by Hawkins et al. (1967), and the only deer captured sustained a broken leg. Wire foot snares have been used effectively to capture black bears. (Troyer et al. 1962, Lindzey and Meslow 1976) and polar bears (Larsen 1971a). The Aldrich spring-activated foot snare (Aldrich Trap Co., Clallam Bay, Wash.) is the most widely used device for capturing bears.

Snares have also been used effectively to capture smaller mammals. Nellis (1968) made a coyote snare out of 24-gauge cable (1.4 m long) with the addition of a swivel and lock nut to reduce injury. A spring 0.6 m long attached to a rotating base was developed for smaller predator capture (Lensing and Roux 1975). They threaded a 49-strand steel cable through a hollow fishing rod and formed a noose. The rod-snare was bent to a trigger set that consisted of a coyote getter head and release pin. Animals were snared around the thorax behind the shoulder blades, and their movements were reduced by the rod and cable tension. Brocke (1972) used a simple stainless steel wire snare to capture trap-shy snowshoe hares. Ground squirrels were captured at burrow entrances with a cotton cord snare (Lishak 1976). Lishak used a clove hitch noose over the burrow and attached 1 end of the cord to a long rubber band and stake while the other cord end was held by the operator. Squirrels were snared when their heads protruded above the noose.

MISCELLANEOUS TRAPS AND DEVICES

Nellis et al. (1974) found conical pitfall traps for small mammals easier to set and handle than the cylindrical pitfall traps. They welded or riveted 26-gauge galvanized sheet metal into a cone 25 cm long with a 15-cm-diameter top and a 0.6-cm bottom. Traps were inserted into the ground with the aid of a pick and wooden plug which fit into the cone traps.

Tuttle (1974) described a new trap for capturing bats along flight paths from roost areas. The trap consisted of 2 rectangular frames of aluminum tubes (OD-32 mm) measuring 182.9 cm × 157.5 cm and set parallel about 7.5 cm apart. The frames were strung with stainless steel wires (0.20 mm), spaced 2.5 cm apart, and equipped with threaded rods to adjust wire tension. A canvas bag

Fig. 6.7. Nylon drive net for capturing deer and elk (Photo by Larry Temple).

was hung between adjustable legs at the bottom of the trap to hold captured bats. The tautness of the wires should be proportional to the speed of the bats (Tuttle 1976).

Live ferrets were used by Linduska (1947) to drive rabbits from dens for capture. Storm and Dauphin (1965) and Storm et al. (1976) used a mechanical ferret to flush carnivores from dens. This device consisted of 4-mm spring steel wire 6.7 m long. One end was bent into a L-shaped handle; the other end was wound into a coiled spring 30 cm long and 3.7 cm in diameter. A round wooden plug was stapled to the end of the coil.

Carpenter and Martin (1969) captured prairie dogs from dens by flushing them out with a stream of water from a fertilizer applicator tank. Prairie dogs also were forced from dens with the combination of cold water and high-sudsing detergent (Elias et al. 1974). According to the authors this sudsing technique utilized less water and was very effective.

Jackrabbits were captured with hand nets at night by blinding them with powerful 100-w, 13-v aircraft landing lights (Griffith and Evans 1970). Light-blinded rabbits were surrounded by a capture crew. When rabbits tried to escape, the crew began yelling and whistling which caused them to run in circles and be more vulnerable to capture.

Shepherd et al. (1978) found manual capture the most successful technique for collecting large numbers of rabbits at night. They used a person to operate the pursuit vehicle, another to use a spotlight, and a third as a catcher. The catcher usually had to fire a .22 calibre rifle shot near rabbits' heads to make them squat so they could be hand captured.

Tim Wallis recently developed a net-firing gun projected from a helicopter at close range to capture red deer in New Zealand (Dave Beaty, pers. comm.).

USE OF INJECTED DRUGS

Using drugs to capture free-ranging animals or to restrain captive animals has evolved from primitive poison darts to modern projectile syringes. For years primitive tribes such as the Tecuna and Java Indians in South America concocted a paste with the drug curare and used it on the tips of their hunting arrows (Krukoff and Smith 1937). In the 1950's, the early pioneers in the field of drug capture began to test various drug compounds and delivery systems. Hall et al. (1953) conducted tests with the drugs curare and the synthetic compound Flaxedil in a glucose paste and applied it to grooved darts that were fired from a modified air rifle. Other researchers in Georgia began to test these darts in a gun powered by stout rubber tubing (Jenkins et al. 1955). They also tested a modified air gun and a dart made out of a drill bit shank with a cord skirt. They filled the drill bit grooves with a paste of powdered nicotine salicylate and honey (Crockford et al. 1957, Hayes et al. 1957). Soon after, they developed an automatic projectile syringe that expelled liquid drugs by gas pressure. This pressure was formed by the combination of water, sodium bicarbonate and citric acid. Projectile syringes were fired from a CO_2 rifle called a CAP-CHUR gun (Crockford et al. 1958).

Equipment to Administer Drugs

Wildlife workers have a variety of commercial equipment available for injecting drugs into animals. There are also a number of techniques developed that have been published in order to improve capture methods and to reduce costs. It is important for all workers to learn the basic skills and limitations involved before using any of this equipment.

CAP-CHUR Equipment: This was the first remote injection system to be manufactured for animal capture. The projectile syringes and projectors are used widely in the wildlife field. The projectile syringe has been improved from the slow injection of the soda-acid tablet to the rapid, more reliable powder charge. If the projectile syringe hits an animal solidly the powder charge explodes; it produces an instantaneous injection. Occasionally, the pressure from the exploding charge forces the syringe to bounce out of the animal and spray drug on the animal's hide.

CAP-CHUR guns are powered by CO_2 or powder charges (Table 6.1). Gas operated guns are affected by air temperature that affects the velocity and trajectory of syringes. Before using such guns they should always be sighted-in at different temperature extremes to become familiar with this problem. Gas leaks in the CO_2 guns can be a problem but are not difficult to correct. The most common gas leak occurs at the knurled cap on the CO_2 cylinder chamber. A new "O" ring will stop this leak, but it can sometimes be temporarily repaired by reversing the "O" ring and applying some silicone grease. Gas leaks from the internal valve chamber are more difficult to correct. Sometimes rapidly firing the gun will properly seat the valve. Another method is to place a few drops of lightweight oil in the gas port and wait a few hours before testing again (Day 1969). A new valve seat is needed if leaking persists.

The long range powder charge guns use .22 blank loads to fire syringes. These .22 loads are similar to those used in powder actuated tools that set nails in concrete. Frequent cleaning to remove dirt, powder, and wads is essential to keep these guns working efficiently.

Paxarms Equipment: This equipment, manufactured in New Zealand, includes a complete line of capture guns and accessories for animal capture. The Paxarms pistol and rifle are powered by cartridges similar to .22 blanks. New gun models have interchangeable barrels with different bore sizes. This allows the use of syringes holding 1 ml to 25 ml of drug. All of the guns have velocity control gauges that determine impact, range, and trajectory of the projectile syringes (Table 6.1).

Paxarms syringes are made of molded high-tensile plastics. Only the needle shaft is metal and can be removed and replaced if damaged. Syringes are loaded with a special syringe adapter that fits over the needle. Some drug remains in the adapter when loading, and extra drug is needed to compensate for this loss. Another method of loading is to remove the needle shaft and insert the exact dosage into the barrel of the syringe. A plastic collar is used to seal the hole on the side of the needle point. Then a special syringe is used to pump air through the tail valve to pressurize the piston chamber behind the drug. When the collar on the needle is forced back, the drug is expelled by the air pressure and piston. According to the Paxarms Company, loaded syringes may be stored for some time if unpressurized. Cleaning the fired syringes is inconvenient because they do not completely dismantle.

Pneu-Dart Equipment: The Pneu-Dart Company has a complete line of guns and darts for animal capture. Their major innovations are darts containing premeasured powdered drugs rather than liquid. Liscinsky et al. (1969) reported on the development and design of these darts. The powdered drug succinylcholine chloride is measured and loaded into a cavity behind the needle tip in the small capacity darts. The sleeve covering the cavity is forced back on impact depositing the drug in the animal. Larger darts used for long range and larger animals also contain drug in powder form. However, to use the darts the drug is put into solution by injecting sterile water into the drug cavity. When the dart hits an animal, a lead ball compresses a spring and detonates a small explosive cap which injects the drug. Use of these darts eliminates the need to handle or measure drugs, and they can be stored safely at room temperatures for several months if protected from moisture.

Pneu-Dart currently has 3 models of guns available: a short-range .50 caliber air pump gun with a smooth bore, a long-range .50 caliber rifled gun which is operated by .22 blank loads, and a CO_2-powered rifle (Table 6.1).

Blowguns or Blowpipes: This primitive technique of blowguns has been used to capture free-ranging primates at a range of 15 m (Brockelman and Kobayashi 1971). Such blowguns were made out of steel tubes 1–2 m long and with a bore size of 13 mm. A modified 1 cc syringe was used that held a moving brass rod to inject the drug on impact.

Blowguns have been constructed out of aluminum or steel conduit with a bore size of about 16 mm or large enough to hold the CAP-CHUR syringe. Roney (1971) used this equipment effectively on caged animals.

Haigh and Hopf (1976) described a simple projectile dart to use in blowguns for veterinary work. These darts are made out of disposable syringes and use butane to inject the drug from the syringe once it enters the animal.

Pole Syringes or Jab-Sticks: Pole syringes are nothing more than hand syringes that allow the operator to remain a safe distance from the animal while administering drug injections. Most of these devices are made out of wooden or nylon dowels which act as plungers in the syringes. Sturdier ones can be made out of metal tubing with modified syringes at the ends (Ling et al. 1967, White 1967). One commercial pole syringe is constructed of lightweight aluminum tubing with extension lengths (Table 6.1).

Extension syringes are primarily used on caged or trapped animals (Seal et al. 1970, Bailey 1971). Ling et al. (1967) and Cline et al. (1969) used this method suc-

Table 6.1. Commercial equipment used to inject drugs into animals.

Manufacturer	Name	Propellent	Optimum Range (m)	Features
Palmer Chemical Equipment Co., Douglasville, GA	*CAP-CHUR*			
	Extra long-range rifle	.22 blank	70	4 powder loads
	Long-range rifle	CO_2	23	2 CO_2 cylinders
	Short-range pistol	CO_2	14	1 CO_2 cylinder
	Projectile syringe	Drug injected by powder charge	—	Sizes: 1–15 ml (aluminum)
Paxarms Ltd, Timaru, New Zealand. U.S. Dist—Quinn Zool. Assoc., Beverly Hills, CA	*Paxarms*			
	Mark 21 rifle	.22 blank	80	Velocity control, 4 barrel sizes
	Mark 15 pistol	.22 blank	25	Velocity control, 4 barrel sizes
	Projectile syringe	Drug injected by compressed air	—	4 calibers: sizes 1 ml–20 ml (plastic)
Pneu-Dart, Inc. Williamsport, PA	*Pneu-Dart*			
	Model 175–close range	Compressed air pump gun	4–36	3–8 pumps
	Model 170, 171 long range	.22 blank	91	Power control valve & slide lever action
	Model # unknown; being revised	CO_2	?	
	P & C darts	Drug deposited in powder form		Succinylcholine loads, 1–32 mg
	CL & PL darts	Drug injected by explosive cap		Succinylcholine loads, 1–200 mg
Ideal Instrument, Chicago, IL	*Simmons*			
	Pole syringe	Manual	1–3	Aluminum poles, 2 lengths. Uses disp. syringes

cessfully to inject free-ranging seals in their tails. Swimming polar bear cubs were injected by syringes attached to bamboo poles (Larsen 1971a).

Miscellaneous Injection Systems: The longbow and the special arrow syringe were used to capture deer by Anderson (1961). Hawkins et al. (1967a) tested several deer capture methods and experienced high mortality with the longbow and arrow but better accuracy and success with the crossbow. In Africa, Pienaar et al. (1966) reported that a crossbow was accurate at all ranges up to 110 m when used with a quality range finder. A Stevans crossbow (Huntsville, Ark.) was used to deliver a 10-ml syringe accurately into adult bull bison at 32 m (Haugen et al. 1976).

Sowls and Schweinsburg (1967) used an adapter on a .38 caliber revolver and shotshell primers to fire projectile syringes into captive or trapped animals.

A medicated bullet containing powdered drugs was reported by C. Williams et al. (1969). They used a tablet machine to punch out drug loads that could be fired in a Sheridan air rifle up to 27 m range.

An inexpensive syringe made of brass tubing was designed by Shryer (1971). He fired these syringes up to 23 m with a BB cap powder load in a .22 caliber rifle. Hawkins et al. (1970) drilled cavities in .22 BB caps and filled them with drug dosages. These bullet loads were fired from a .22 rifle and successfully captured deer up to 46 m.

A patent was obtained by a Russian inventor (Marks and Clerk 1971) who designed a hollowed-out lead bullet for 5.6-mm bore rifles (.22 caliber). Cavities in the bullets were filled with drug and sealed with glucose and ballistic shaped heads. Large animals have been immobilized at a distance of 70–80 m, but lead fragments from the bullets remain in the animals. Baldwin (1971) shortened .22 caliber short cartridge bullets and attached bullet-shaped projectiles containing various drug compounds.

Lovett and Hill (1977) designed a transmitter (150 MHz) which attaches to a projectile syringe to assist in locating immobilized deer.

Drugs Used in Animal Capture

During the past 10 years several new drugs and combinations of drugs have been developed. These new drug compounds have made the drug capture techniques more predictable and more reliable. The major drugs and combinations currently being used will be discussed in this section. Anyone desiring information on some of the earlier drugs should refer to Taber and Cowan (1969). Hebert and Fetridge (1979) present an up-to-date summary of drug dosages for North American game mammal capture.

Etorphine hydrochloride (M-99, D M Pharmaceuticals): Etorphine is a thebain derivative chemically related to morphine. The drug has the analgesic properties of morphine but with fewer side effects (Bently and Hardy 1963). This narcotic has been reported to have a potency 2,000 to 10,000 times that of morphine (Bently 1964, M. Williams et al. 1969).

The drug M-99 has a wide safety margin, and overdosage is no danger according to Woolf et al. (1973). This report stated that it is better to overdose than underdose, because underdosing produces longer induction time and results in greater excitement. Tranquilizers are not needed when high dosages of M-99 are used to immobilize captive and free-ranging animals (Woolf et al. 1973, Alford et al. 1974). However, Harthoorn (1976) stated that the efficiency of etorphine is greatly increased with the combination of tranquilizing compounds. Neuroleptic tranquilizers added to etorphine display a marked synergistic effect on the action of the analgesic drug (Pienaar 1975a). Many different drug combinations are being used safely and routinely in Africa and other countries (Table 6.2).

The effects of etorphine are rapidly reversed with the antagonist diprenorphine (M 50-50). The antagonist can be administered intravenously or intramuscularly at a rate of 2 times the etorphine dosage (Alford et al. 1974).

Potentially important advantages of M-99 over other immobilizing drugs are its wider safety margin, improved reactions when used with tranquilizers, a minimum of side reactions, and quick reversal by an antagonist. Major disadvantages with M-99 are that it is more expensive than other drugs, is available only in low concentration (1 mg/cc), is a potent narcotic, is dangerous to handle, and is subject to strict government control. Furthermore, the drug cannot be used on animals which may later be used as meat. Both M-99 and M 50-50 have been placed under extreme controls by the Drug Enforcement Administration. Unfortunately the strict controls needed to prevent abuse of these narcotics also will curtail their use in animal restraint programs.

Succinylcholine chloride (Anectine, Burroughs Wellcome & Sucostrin, Squibb): This drug is an ultra short-acting, depolarizing type of skeletal muscle relaxant. It is not a true anesthetic and does not impair the sensory organs. The drug paralyzes muscles by inhibiting the action of actylcholinesterase, thereby permitting acetylcholine to accumulate at the myoneural junction, and thus causing depolarization of the junction (Pistey and Wright 1961). Major advantages of this drug are: fast acting, no excitement stage, and rapid recovery. Critical disadvantages include: narrow tolerance range in most species, wide variation in dosages between species, no effective antidote, and dosages required according to weight, age, sex, and physical condition (Talbot and Lamprey 1961). Jacobsen et al. (1976) also stated that an evaluation of seasonal dosage levels can be more important than accurate weight estimates.

Use of this muscle relaxant can be hazardous because an overdose will paralyze the diaphragm muscles. Emergency resuscitation can be provided effectively with oxygen bottle and plastic bag held over an animal's nose (Dodge and Campbell 1965) or with an Ambu resuscitator and endotracheal tubes (Day et al. 1965).

Succinylcholine is still being widely used by wildlife workers even though mortality may range anywhere from 2–25%. Continued use of this drug instead of some safer compound seems to be influenced by the following: it is nonnarcotic and less restricted in use; it is readily available and can be mixed in various strengths; and meat of animals immobilized can be safely consumed.

Phencyclidine hydrochloride (Sernylan, Bio-Ceutic Lab. or Philips Roxane, Inc.): Sernylan is an immobilizing agent marketed for primates only, but has been used effectively in other species. The drug is an analgesic, cataleptic, immobilizer and anesthetic, depending on the dosage and species. It acts principally on the central nervous system either by stimulation or by depression (Chen et al. 1959). Sernylan is very stable and is not degraded by temperatures used in cooking or freezing. Meat of treated animals contains drug residues and should not be used for human consumption (Beck 1972). The drug should be administered by intramuscular injection. Such injections take effect in 3–10 minutes, but the reaction may last several hours. Disorientation and salivation may occur in many of the species. Some investigators have combined tranquilizers with Sernylan to improve reactions and reduce side effects (Cline et al. 1969, Seal et al. 1972). Serynlan is not a preferred drug for ruminants, but has been used successfully on deer by Dean et al. (1973) and on bighorn sheep by Stelfox and Robertson (1976). Table 6.2 presents some drug dosages used on different species.

In 1978 Sernylan was reclassified by the Drug Enforcement Administration to a Schedule II Controlled Substance, which is the same as the narcotic M-99. Philips Roxane is not presently registered with the DEA to handle Schedule II drugs, and the management of this company has elected to discontinue compounding and marketing all forms of phencyclidine. It is unfortunate that phencyclidine or so called "angel dust" has become a seriously and dangerously abused drug. This illegal use evidently has caused the loss of an important drug for legitimate capture and restraint programs by wildlife workers.

Ketamine hydrochloride (Vetalar, Parke-Davis): Ketamine is an analogue of phencyclidine, possessing about one-fifth to one-sixth of the potency of the parent compound (Beck 1972). It is a fast-acting general anesthetic with a wide margin of safety. The excitement and convulsive problems associated with phencyclidine are greatly reduced in ketamine. Any convulsions can be controlled with small amounts of barbiturates or phenothiazine tranquilizers. Salivation is a common side effect but can be controlled with 0.05 mg/kg of atropine (Beck 1976). Use of ketamine is limited primarily to small sized animals. Large animals over 100 kg take a large quantity of drug that is difficult to inject remotely.

Tiletamine hydrochloride and CI-716 (CI-744 or Tilazol, Parke-Davis): Tiletamine is another analogue of phencyclidine with about one-half the potency of the parent compound and 2 to 3 times as potent as ketamine (Beck 1972). Use of tiletamine alone was discontinued because it produced convulsions in canines and felines.

Table 6.2. Drugs and dosages used for capturing and handling mammals.

Genus	Common Name	Dosages	Remarks	References
		Etorphine hydrochloride (M-99)		
Ursus	Black bear	1.6mg/100g	Used on 80 bears	Beeman et al. 1974
Loxodonta	African Elephant	9.0 mg	Adult	Alford et al. 1974
Dama	Fallow deer	2mg/100kg	Add 30mg Xylazine/ 100kg	Harrington & Wilson 1974
Cervus	Elk	7mg (Ad.cows) 4–5mg (Y1.cows) 5mg (Y1.bulls)	Combined with 20 mg Vesprin	Coggins 1975
Odocoileus	White-tailed deer	2mg/deer	Added 20-30mg Azaperone	Day 1974
		5–6mg	Used alone	Woolf 1970
Alces	Moose	4–5mg/moose	Used alone	Roussel & Patenaude 1975
Aepyeros	Impala	0.5mg (♂) 0.4mg (♀)	85mg Xylazine 65mg Xylazine	Pienaar 1975a
Taurotragus	Eland	4–6.5mg (adult) 3–4mg (juvenile)	400–600mg Xylazine 200–300mg Xylazine	Pienaar 1975a
Ovis	Desert bighorn	2–2.5mg/bighorn	Added 15mg Haloanisone or 20mg Azaperone	Wilson et al. 1973
		2.5–3.75mg (♀)	3–5mg Acetylpromazine or 20–25mg Xylazine	Thorne 1977 (pers. comm.)
		3.5–3.75mg (♂)	5–8mg Acetylpromazine or 30–50mg Xylazine	Thorne 1977 (pers. comm.)
		Succinylcholine Chloride (Anectine and Sucostrin)		
Cervus	Elk	27.0mg/Ad. (♂) 24.4mg/Ad. (♀)	Immobilization 9–12 min. 24% mortality	Varland 1976
		26.4mg/elk	Powder form-latency period 7 min.	Pedersen & Thomas 1975
Odocoileus	White-tailed deer	0.07–0.10mg/kg	Reaction: 5.1 min.	Allen 1970
		0.05–0.09mg/kg	Hyaluronidase added; reaction 2–3 min.	Allen 1970
		0.08–0.26mg/kg	Powder form-mortality 9% adult, 14% fawns	Wesson et al. 1974
	Black-tailed deer	0.15–0.31mg/kg	10% mortality	Miller 1968
Antilocapra	Pronghorn antelope	0.13–2.20mg/kg	Captive—no deaths	Beale & Smith 1967
Alces	Moose	15–17mg/adult 12–14mg/subadult 9–11mg/calf	Dosages for late spring and mid-winter. Dosages reduced 20–30% late winter and early spring	Houston 1969
Ovis	Bighorn sheep	0.44–1.45mg/kg	Lower dose late winter	Stelfox & Robertson 1976
Mirounga	Elephant seal	2.5mg/kg	Apnea periods 4–9 min.	Ling et al. 1967

Table 6.2. Drugs and dosages used for capturing and handling mammals. (cont.)

Genus	Common Name	Dosages	Remarks	References
		Phencyclidine hydrochloride (Sernylan)		
Pan	Chimpanzee	0.5–0.7mg/kg 0.8–1.1mg/kg	Reduced response, catalepsis	Bio-Ceutic Lab 1969
Ursus	Polar bear	3.6mg/kg 3.3mg/kg	Cubs and yearling Adult and subadult	Larsen 1971a
	Black & Grizzly	1.32–1.98mg/kg	2.5mg/kg not lethal	Pearson et al. 1968
Taxidea	Badger	3.5mg/kg	Trapped animals	Fitzgerald 1973
Felis	Mountain lion	1.1mg/kg 1.86–1.96mg/kg	Adults Juveniles	Hornocker & Wiles 1972
Lynx	Bobcat	2.2mg/kg	Trapped animals	Bailey 1971
Lobodon	Crabeater seal	1.0mg/kg	Added Sparine	Cline et al. 1969
Dicotyles	Peccary (Javelina)	60–75mg 25–35mg	Free-ranging Captive	Day 1969
Odocoileus	White-tailed deer	1.5mg/kg	Added Sparine 0.5mg/kg	Seal et al. 1972
	Mule/Black-tailed deer	0.5–1.5mg/kg	Wild and captive deer	Dean et al. 1973
Ovis	Bighorn sheep	2.35mg/kg (♂) 1.89mg/kg (♀)	Added Sparine or Anatran	Stelfox & Robertson 1976
		Ketamine hydrochloride (Vetalar)		
Pan	Chimpanzee	5.0–7.5mg/kg 10.0–15.0mg/kg	Chemical restraint Surgical anest.	Beck & Dresner 1972
Macaca	Rhesus monkey	5.0–10.0mg/kg 20.0–25.0mg/kg	Chemical restraint Surgical anest.	Beck & Dresner 1972
Procyon	Raccoon	8–10mg/kg	Collapsed in 2–5 min.	Bigler & Hoff 1974
Lynx	Bobcat	11mg/kg	Restraint dosage	Bristol Lab 1972
Mirounga	Elephant seal	1.4–6.9mg/kg		Briggs et al. 1975
		Tiletamine hydrochloride (CI-744)		
Ursus	Black bear	4.0mg/kg	Free-ranging	Stewart et al. 1977
Panthera	Tiger	4.7mg/kg	Captive	Seidensticker et al. 1974
Odocoileus	White-tailed deer	9.9mg/kg	Captive (749 tests)	Kitchen et al. 1974
		Xylazine hydrochloride (Rompun)		
Panthera	Lion	0.89–3.30mg/kg	10 captive	York & Huggins 1972
Loxodonta	African Elephant	0.07–1.65mg/kg	Captive	York & Huggins 1972
Cervus	Elk	0.55mg/kg	Captive	Thurmon et al. 1972
		180mg/elk	Added 65mg Ketamine	Wentges 1975
Odocoileus	White-tailed deer	0.89–8.00mg/kg	Used alone, captive (68)	Roughton 1975
Antilocapra	Pronghorn antelope	30mg/antelope	Added 20mg Ketamine	Wentges 1975
Bison	Bison	125mg/bison	Added 100mg Ketamine	Wentges 1975
Ammotragus	Aoudad	0.46mg/kg	Added 1.6mg/kg Ketamine	Boever & Paluch 1974

The tranquilizer CI-716 (arylcycloalkylamine) is a central nervous system depressant with anticonvulsant and antianxiety activity (Gray et al. 1974). Parke-Davis combined CI-716 with tiletamine at a ratio of 1:1 to form CI-744, or Tilazol. The drug combination Tilazol has been submitted to the Food and Drug Administration for approval. If approved it will be marketed for use in dogs and cats. However, experimental tests with this drug have shown it to be useful in the immobilization of wild animals (Table 6.2).

Xyalazine hydrochloride (Rompun, Chemagro Corp.): Rompun is a nonnarcotic compound sold for use in horses only. The drug acts as a sedative and analgesic as well as a muscle relaxant. Intramuscular injections produce a reaction within 10–15 minutes; and analgesia lasts from 15–30 minutes, while a sleeplike state is usually maintained for 1–2 hours (Anon. 1972). York and Huggins (1972) stated that at low dosages an animal is easily awakened and will struggle to regain its feet when handled. Literature with Rompun states that animals can be aroused by noise or other stimuli, and this may increase the risk of injury (Anon. 1972).

Little published information is available on the use of this drug to capture free-ranging animals. Undesirable features of Rompun, such as long interval between injection and deep sedation, long recovery phase, and lack of an antidote, limit its use in animal capture. According to Thurmon et al. (1972) the drug Rompun is better suited for use in domestic and confined wild animals than those in the wild state. The major use of this drug compound is in combination with other drugs. Pienaar (1975a) found that this drug has excellent synergistic and tranquilizing effects when combined with the potent analgesic drug etorphine (Table 6.2).

Stalking and Darting Free-Ranging Animals

Stalking and safely injecting drugs into animals with the available delivery systems is not an easy task. Wildlife investigators should not attempt to use remote injection equipment without being properly trained and prepared for the job.

Many methods have been used to stalk free-ranging animals. Probably the most successful has been done from a vehicle during the daylight or at night with spotlights. Hawkins et al. (1967a) hunted deer from a vehicle at all seasons of the year while testing capture methods.

Helicopters have been used effectively to locate animals and to get gunners within dart gun range of selected animals (Denney 1966, Nielson and Shaw 1967, Wilson et al. 1973, Baer et al. 1978). Tim Wallis recently developed an electric dart fired at close range from a helicopter to capture red deer in New Zealand (Dave Beaty, pers. comm.).

Stalking animals on foot is the most difficult method to use on free-ranging animals. Houston (1969) stalked moose and shot them at about 14-37 m. Roughton (1976) stalked deer on foot at night, but he designed a bright flashing 3-celled flashlight for the job.

Other methods that have been used successfully to approach animals include the use of boats to capture polar bears (Larsen 1971a), use of blinds at waterholes for bighorn sheep (Logsdon 1967), and use of trail dogs and horses to locate mountain lions (Hornocker and Wiles 1972).

The safest injection sites for projectile syringes are in the deep muscle areas of the rear legs of animals. No injections should be made in the chest cavity or stomach region. Hits in these areas usually puncture the lungs or stomachs which may kill the animals. Harthoorn (1976) reported suitable injection sites in the neck and shoulders of larger animals.

Proper Care and Treatment of Drugged Animals

Proper care of drugged animals is extremely important, because it can prevent injuries and reduce losses. Handling procedures differ some with each drug compound. The basic steps in handling captured animals are as follows:

1. Check vital signs such as respiration and heart rate and treat accordingly.
2. Attach blindfold to protect eyes and to calm animal.
3. Place animal in comfortable position—most on brisket, a few on sides.
4. Control head and neck, keep it elevated, but allow for drainage of saliva and stomach fluids.
5. Maintain a clear breathing passage.
6. Keep noise and movements around animal to a minimum.
7. Control leg thrashing or convulsions; may need additional sedation or restraining device.
8. Clean and treat dart wounds with antibiotic and fly repellent if needed.
9. Administer combiotic to combat infections.
10. Protect from predators and adverse weather conditions during recovery.
11. Allow animals to recover quietly and undisturbed.
12. Release fully recovered animals with as little disturbance as possible.

USE OF ORAL DRUGS

Oral drugs for animal capture and restraint should have the following qualities to be effective: the drug should be readily taken in food or water; have a wide safety margin because of the difficulty of controlling the amount ingested; must be fast acting so drugged animals will not be able to move out of view; and should not be injurious to other animals consuming the bait (Day 1971). Unfortunately, there are no drugs on the market that fit all of these requirements; consequently, reliable capture of animals with oral drugs remains largely in the future.

Marlow (1956) used chloral hydrate in water to capture 26 kangaroos, but 3 died. Chloral hydrate is extremely bitter in water which may explain its lack of use by other workers. However, a sugar compound of chloral hydrate called alpha-chloralose has been used more extensively. Austin and Peoples (1967) captured feral swine with this drug. They mixed 2 grams of drug in 1 cup of shelled corn. Stafford and Williams (1968) captured 9 of 17 black bears that ate bait containing alpha-chloralose.

Diazepam (Tranimul or Valium) has been mixed with grain to capture deer successfully (Murry 1965, Montgomery and Hawkins 1967, Thomas et al. 1967). However, according to Hoffman-La Roche Inc., diazepam and other benzodiazepines are currently not available for use in the capture of wildlife.

Youngson and Mitchell (1967) used dosages of M-99 mixed with the spreading agent DMSO (dimethylsulphoxide) to capture red deer. The drug was administered in thin glass capsules. Potatoes were used to hold the capsules which crushed when eaten.

Capturing Birds

The *Manual for Bird Banders* (Lincoln and Baldwin 1929, U.S. Fish and Wildlife Service 1961) and *Guide to Waterfowl Banding* (Addy 1956) contain much more useful detail on trap design than can be presented in this chapter. Also, Wilbur (1967) and Reeves et al. (1968) are excellent sources on capture of upland game birds. These publications are recommended to readers who desire more information.

Various regional bird-banding associations (Eastern, Inland, Western) publish journals, hold annual meetings and workshops, and exchange knowledge and experience among members. These groups provide an excellent source of information on bird capture techniques. Wilbur (1967) listed some important considerations to facilitate bird trapping:

1. The method must take into account the species to be trapped, its habits, food preferences, population size, and wariness. Each species varies greatly in its "catchability" with different traps and different baits. Best results are usually obtained by building the trap for the birds rather than trying to mold the birds to fit the trap.
2. The terrain at the trap site is often limiting. Ease of access to the trap site and degree of trap portability must be considered.
3. The season of year will affect the number of birds in an area, their food preferences, flocking habits, and wariness. Seasonal weather conditions affect the mechanics of some traps, making them unusable.
4. Traps differ in the number of birds they can capture at one time. If many birds are needed, a trap that takes 50 at a time will be better suited to the project than one working equally well but taking only 1 bird at a time.
5. The time allotted for the trapping project will determine the speed with which the birds must be caught, as well as determine the general trap construction.
6. In a few cases, the number of workers available may be limiting. For example, some drive-trapping techniques require a large crew.
7. The funds available will limit the materials used, the number of trappers employed, and the length of the operation.
8. Both federal and state regulations apply to trapping and marking game species. Special permits are required, and certain techniques may be prohibited. Anyone anticipating a trapping program should have full knowledge of the pertinent regulations.

BAITED BOX OR EXCLOSURE TRAPS

Many species of birds, especially the gregarious seed-eaters, can be captured in these traps. Traps differ, aside from size and shape, mainly in the type of entrance. The simplest trap, often used for small birds, consists merely of a mesh box, supported on 1 end by a stick. When the birds feed underneath the box, the hidden operator pulls a string attached to the stick and the box falls, imprisoning the birds. This principle has been used for capturing band-tailed pigeons by Wooten (1955), who used a 4.8-m square wooden frame, tightly covered with 3.8-cm mesh net, supported on 1 side by a 2.1-m pole. A pull-wire ran from the pole to a blind. Weiland (1964) described the use of a solenoid for instantaneous springing of such traps. Braun (1976) described a baited drop trap for band-tailed pigeons which consisted of a pull cord which resulted in the trap falling off 4 wooden blocks onto the ground.

In the funnel-trap, the wide portion of the funnel entrance is flush with the outer side of the trap with the narrow inner opening projecting well into the interior of the trap (Fig. 6.8). Birds that enter seek a way out around the inner face of the box and usually overlook the funnel. Usually, horizontal wires are left to form a fringe around the inner entrance of the funnel to discourage use of the funnel as an exit. Where traps are set on a fluctuating body of water, such as tidal marshes, the funnel is constructed tall enough to accommodate a bird at any level. The funnel entrance is most commonly used on waterfowl traps, being suitable for almost all species. If a trap is constructed of weak metal mesh, or fish-net, the funnel should be constructed of stout wire so that it will hold its shape.

The *swinging-wire* or *bob* entrance is often used in traps designed for taking birds such as pheasants which are accustomed to walking through heavy vegetation. The principle is illustrated in Fig. 6.8.

The *tip-top* entrance is a door in the upper surface of the trap (which may be buried in the ground). The door is balanced with a light spring, so that the weight of the bird will cause it to open. When the bird drops off within the trap, the door springs shut (Fig. 6.8). This trap is not widely used, but has been used successfully for prairie grouse.

The *swinging* or *sliding door* entrance is most often used in songbird traps. The door is supported by a device which is sprung when the weight of the bird depresses a bar or pan. This door is best used on a trap that is intended to catch only 1 bird at a time.

If the body of the trap is large, a smaller catch-box usually is added. The birds are driven into this box and may then be removed through a door in the box. Trapped birds are vulnerable to crowding, exposure, and predation. The best protection against trap mortality is prompt attention to the traps.

Waterfowl trapping is treated in detail in the *Guide to Waterfowl Banding* mentioned previously. However, some methods and considerations will be given here. If possible, traps set in water should be set on a firm bottom, so that the bait will not sink in the mud and so that trapped birds will not churn the bottom into a soupy mud which will mat their feathers. A swift current of

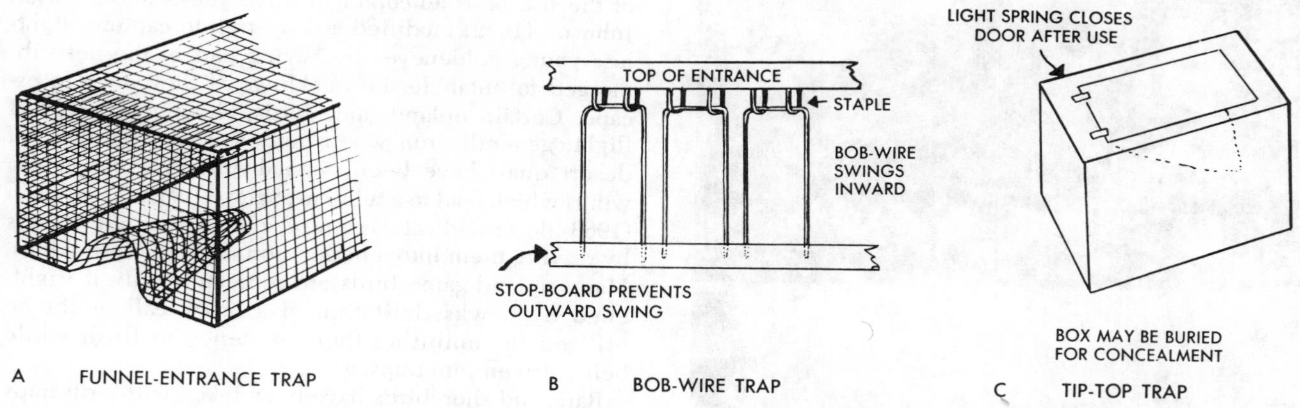

Fig. 6.8. Types of entrances for game-bird traps. *A.* Funnel entrance. *B.* Swinging or bob entrance. *C.* Tip-Top entrance.

water through the trap will carry away bait, while a lack of current will permit the water to freeze readily. Usually, vegetation should be removed from the vicinity of the entrance to waterfowl traps.

Szymczak and Corey (1976) modified materials used in the construction of the Salt Plains duck trap, effective for dabbling ducks, and described by Addy (1956). A large permanent site waterfowl trap with a concrete foundation was presented by Arthur and Kennedy (1972).

A "lily-lead" portable trap useful for diving ducks where water levels fluctuate daily was described by Hunt and Dahlka (1953). A portable, rectangular trap with metal bait-pans and an improved gathering box (McCall 1954) has been used for dabbling ducks. Floating raft traps readily capture waterfowl (Sugden and Poston 1970, Thornsberry and Cowardin 1971).

For upland birds, a variety of traps have been described, including (among other) the description by Aldous (1936) for white-necked raven; Schultz (1950) for the bobwhite; Chambers and English (1958), Edwards (1961), and Gullion (1961) for the ruffed grouse; and Wilbur (1967) for various upland game birds.

Trap size usually is a compromise between efficiency and portability. If the trapped birds are drawn from a population which is migrating through the area, so that new individuals are constantly being caught, the trap may be large and permanent. Often, however, a trap must be moved frequently in order to catch birds previously uncaught. In trap construction, it is desirable to make the top of some soft material, such as fish-net, so that birds jumping or flying upward will not be injured.

BAITED NET TRAPS

For birds, such as the eastern wild turkey, that are too wary to enter an enclosure readily, a baited net trap may be used. A trap made of net and with a tubular metal frame may be suspended over the baiting place, concealed by overhanging foliage and dropped manually when the birds are underneath (Baldwin 1947, Ellis 1961).

The cannon or rocket trap is used widely for wild turkey and waterfowl. It consists of a large, light net which is carried over the baited birds by mortar projectiles or rockets (Fig. 6.9). This is an especially good trap for geese, which are otherwise difficult to trap except during their flightless period (Dill and Thornsberry 1950, Salyer 1955) and also has been used successfully on sandhill cranes (Wheeler and Lewis 1972). Although this method is still being modified and perfected, the following descriptions and comments may be made (from Addy 1956). Net sizes vary with the situation, with nets 9.1 × 18.2 m up to 14.9 × 12.2 m in use. Mesh cotton or nylon nets, 3.2 to 4.4 cm in size, have been used for geese. Cotton (#12 twine) nets should be treated to avoid damage by rodents and moisture; a mixture of gasoline and asphalt serves this purpose. The trailing edge of the net should be attached to stout rubber bands (cut from inner tubes) every 4.6 m and staked securely. Stakes are set securely at the outer edge of the net's flight to lock it in place so that the birds cannot escape. One projectile per 15.2 m usually is used. Each cannon is aimed about 20° from the horizontal, and the corner cannons also are aimed outward at about 45° from the edge of the net and set 5 or 6 m in from the end of the net. Cannons of various types have been tried. The propellant usually is FFG or FFFG black powder, loaded in a 12-gauge shell. A range of 120 to 170 grains of powder per load has been found satisfactory for nets of medium size. The cannon is loaded by inserting the projectile in the barrel, after coating the neoprene projectile-seal with powdered graphite. When the projectile has been rammed firmly against the breech, the shell is inserted in the breech, with electric squib wires (which act as a primer) extending up opposite sides of the barrel. The barrel is then inserted in the tube holder. Firing is accomplished by use of regular electric cable and a blasting machine or by radio (Grieb and Sheldon 1956) or by a 12-volt battery. Two-way radio units may generate sufficient static electricity to cause accidental discharge of electric blasting caps. Blasting machines may fail to operate on cold days and should be warmed before use. The blind should be built first to accustom the birds to it and usually is located 46 to 91 m from the

Fig. 6.9. Projection or cannon net trap. *A.* Net and cannon ready for projection. *B.* Cannons fired and net being thrown; note that cannon in lower right portion of the photo has not fired.

net with a line of vision parallel to the folded net. The area under the net should be free of debris, and inconspicuous markers should be placed to show the location of the leading edge when the net is extended. Before firing, the edges of the net should be lapped under or staked. If the net is shot over water, net and birds should be pulled ashore before birds are removed. With geese, up to 2 weeks may elapse before birds can again be brought into trapping position.

Miller (1957) described a type of cannon in which the propellant was bulk smokeless powder. Marquardt (1960a,b) modified the Miller assembly for more powerful charges, so that larger nets could be propelled. He calculated muzzle velocities for different powder charges when used in the cannon. Arnold and Coon (1972) modified the Dill-type cannon by substituting recoilless rockets and monofilament netting for less weight to capture flocks of cowbirds. Lacher and Lacher (1964) described a cannon net trap mounted on the front of a jeep. Schlatterer (1960) fired 2 nets toward each other to capture sage grouse. A portable, net-firing gun (Mechlin and Shaiffer 1979) was developed to capture individual ducks and offers potential for use with other avian species.

DRIVE AND DRIFT TRAPS

Waterfowl molt all flight feathers at once during the summer, and while flightless they may be driven into traps. Currently, a fyke-net is used in the pothole country for trapping flightless ducks and their half-grown young. Flightless geese may be taken, with care by herding, in a corral trap (Cooch 1953). Heyland (1970) and Timm and Bromley (1976) described the advantages of the use of a helicopter to drive geese into a corral. Johnson (1972) modified a drive-trap to capture flightless young goldeneyes by having part of the net submerged to entangle the ducklings as they dove to escape. Certain upland-game birds, although capable of flight, generally run when herded. Large numbers of desert quail have been taken by herding them into wings which lead to a tubular-enclosed cage. Tomlinson (1963) described catching blue grouse hens and broods by driving them into a highly portable trap with wings. Many upland-game birds are reluctant to fly if frightened by hawks; imitation of a hawk call might be utilized in inhibiting their tendency to flush while being driven into traps.

Rails and shorebirds have been taken with drift traps which consist of long chicken-wire leads directed into funnellike openings. The leads cross the feeding areas, so that walking birds encounter them and are guided into the funnels. These funnels face in both directions and lead into the box of the trap (Low 1935, Stewart 1951, Serventy et al. 1962). Drift traps also have been used successfully on sage grouse by placing traps at access points used by birds feeding in alfalfa fields (Pyrah, pers. comm.).

MIST NETS

Mist netting, long practiced in Asia and the Mediterranean to catch birds for the market, was introduced in the United States in the 1950's as a method of taking birds alive. McClure (1956) described the effective methods used in Japan. As described by Low (1957), the mist net itself is a fine black silk or nylon net, usually from 0.9 to 2.1 m wide and 9.0 to 11.6 m long. Mesh size determines which birds can be caught. A combination of 30 and 36 mm mesh sizes is best for capturing land birds weighing from 5 to 100 g (Heimerdinger and Leberman 1966), while larger mesh is necessary to hold ducks, hawks, or ring-necked pheasants. A taut frame of stout twine crossed by horizontal braces called "shelfstrings," is used in conjunction with the mist net. The net and shelfstrings are supported together by poles at the ends, the shelfstrings being tight, while the net is loose. The excess netting is arranged in a loose bag or pocket 7.6 or 10.2 cm deep below each shelfstring except the topmost one. A bird striking the net from either side carries the net beyond the shelfstring and hangs in the pocket of the net. A net properly hung, with 4 shelves, is about 1.8 m high. Karr (1979) developed a system to allow operation of nets up to 12 m above ground in forested situations. Karr used pulleys and guy lines to erect poles and nets.

In using nets, it is helpful to have a dark background. Wind interferes with netting. Capture rates generally peak at mid-morning (0800–0930) and again in late afternoon (1600–1730) (Ralph 1976). Birds should not be left in the net over 1 hour. Nets should be closed immediately if rain begins. Jewell (1978) devised a simple battery-operated microswitch device connected by wire to a bulb which lighted when a bird hit the net.

Phalaropes have been taken with a weighted mist net suspended horizontally over the water and dropped when they were underneath (Johns 1963). Dorio et al. (1978) captured incubating upland sandpipers and Wilson's phalaropes by lowering a mist net over the bird as it flushed.

Frequently 1 or more people can successfully drive birds, such as snipe, into a series of mist nets set in a group (Fogarty 1969). Blue grouse can be driven into a single net (Schladweiler and Mussehl 1969).

Mist netting is particularly useful for those species that will not come to bait. It is also useful as a sampling device, taking all species in proportion to their abundance. Use of mist nets for the mourning dove is described by Harris and Morse (1958). Waterfowl have been readily captured at night with mist nets (Briggs 1977). In the United States special permission to use mist nets must be obtained from the U.S. Fish and Wildlife Service.

USE OF NETS AND LIGHTS AT NIGHT

Large ground-roosting birds, such as the ring-necked pheasant and sage grouse, can be taken at night on relatively flat terrain. An automobile, equipped with a strong searchlight and seats on the front for the netters, frequently is used. When the birds are "fixed" in the light, the netters can pick them up with long-handled nets and swing them backward to the bed of the vehicle, where they are removed and placed in crates. This method is more effective if a rather steady, loud vehicle and generator noise is maintained throughout the operation. It can be used on waterfowl as well as ground-roosting birds. Labisky (1959, 1968) reported greatest success after birds had been roosting for 3 to 4 hours; he caught ring-necked pheasants (primarily) and also sora rails, Virginia rails, barn owls, screech owls, common coturnix, bobwhite quail, and greater prairie chickens. Drewien et al. (1967) described a portable backpack unit for night-lighting upland game and waterfowl. This combination of light and a loud, steady noise has been applied successfully for capturing water birds by net from a boat at night (Cummings and Hewitt 1964). Brown (1975) was aided by a pointing dog in the night capture of ground-roosting Mearn's quail (see Chapt. 31 for details).

Mitchell (1963) described a successful floodlight trap for capturing large numbers of blackbirds and starlings at roosts.

NEST TRAPS

Ground-nesting birds, such as most waterfowl, may be caught on the nest with a manually-operated drop-net (Sowls 1955). A bow-net is a semicircular frame, hinged at the ends, which flips over the sitting bird by a jerk on the pull-cord, carrying the net with it. Doty and Lee (1974) used a similar system to capture mallards incubating on nesting baskets. Coulter (1958) developed a trap consisting of a circular frame staked to the ground around the nest. A cylindrical net was fastened to the frame and the open end of the net laced with cord to form a purse-net closure when the cord was pulled. The cord led upward to a stake or limb and then to the blind. When the trap was open, the net was concealed around the frame; a pull of the cord raised and closed the net simultaneously. Guide rods prevented the hen from disarranging the net while nest-building and also insured that the net would not close until it passed over the hen.

Miller (1962) used a nest trap with an automatic thermal activating mechanism. An alarm clock also has been used with the turning key on the alarm used to spring a mousetrap which releases a rubber cord. The clock has the advantage that it springs the trap at a set time, and the operator can promptly check to reduce possible harm to bird or nest. This trap has been used successfully on various species of dabbling, diving, and sea ducks (M. Coulter, pers. comm.). Shaiffer and Krapu (1978) further refined the nest-trap triggering device, using a telemetered remote control system. An iron frame, covered with 2.5-cm mesh netting, can be propped over the nest with a stick. Lead weights fastened to the front bar insure a good fall when the trap is tripped by means of a long string.

A circular throw-net has béen used successfully in capturing laying and incubating females. Also, a lightweight cotton net, 2.4 m × 2.4 m, stretched between 2 poles (3.6 m) has been thrown over a previously marked nest. This "clap-net" requires 2 men for its operation. A blanket-net trap, measuring 3.6 × 3.6 m with 2.5-cm mesh, can be suspended over the vegetation around a nest. The edges are brought down loosely and attached. After the set has been left half a day, 2 persons approach from opposite sides and rush the nest. The hen usually flies straight up and hits the net (Addy 1956). Incubating diving ducks can be caught by setting a 1-entrance funnel trap over the nest, with the entrance pointing along the path the female uses in coming to the nest (Addy 1956). Kagarise (1978) readily captured nesting Wilson's phalaropes by placing a long-handled fisherman's landing net over the nest. The net was propped up 8 cm on vegetation to allow the bird to crawl under. This flush-net procedure also has been used by Martin (1969) and Weaver and Kadlec (1970). Gartshore (1978) placed several fine monofilament slip nooses attached to a wire ring over the nests of ground-nesting birds to catch incubating adults.

Mourning doves, nesting in trees, have been caught on the nest (Fig. 6.10) by manually-operated traps (Swank 1952) and with automatic traps (Stewart 1954). Nolan (1961) used a small hoop net to catch birds at open nests in trees and shrubs.

Various methods for capturing birds nesting in tree cavities (Fischer 1944, Jackson 1977, Bull and Pederson 1978) and nest boxes (DeHaven and Guarino 1969, Kibler 1969, Dhondt and van Outreyve 1971, Stewart 1971, Klimkiewicz and Jung 1977) involve boards or nets and mousetrap and rattrap triggering devices.

MISCELLANEOUS METHODS

Newly hatched chicks of ground-nesting species with precocious young may be caught by hand if a low wire fence is placed around the nest before hatching.

Raptorial birds which perch on poles can be taken in steel traps with padded jaws set on top of poles. So that injury will be minimized, the trap should slide to the foot of the pole with the captured bird.

Brownlee and Brown (pers. comm.) dropped a weighted nylon net, approximatley 2.4 m square with

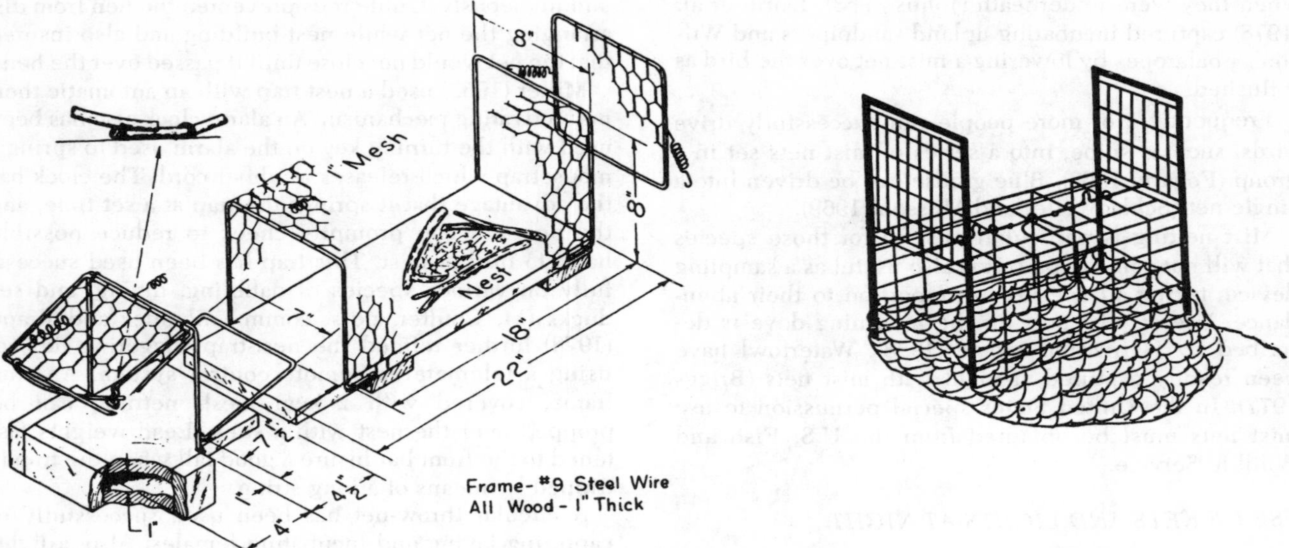

Fig. 6.10. **Dove nest traps. *Left:* Stewart (1954) substrate and nest trap. The central portion is set up as a nest site. If this substrate is used the doors are added to trap the dove on the nest. *Right:* Swank (1952) nest-trap. This trap is assembled around an occupied nest and is sprung manually when the dove returns to the nest.**

2.5-cm mesh attached to a frame, from a helicopter to capture Attwater's prairie chickens.

Fischer (1974) devised a novel lift net trap for capturing male ruffed grouse on drumming logs.

A snare mounted on a long, hand-held pole has proven useful in capturing blue grouse (Zwickel and Bendell 1967b). Hoglund (1968) developed a foot snare set in gaps in vegetative fences to capture willow ptarmigan.

Ellis (1975) found that golden eagles on the ground crouched when approached by a helicopter. A worker on the ground could rush and grab the bird before it took flight.

DRUGS USED TO CAPTURE AND HANDLE BIRDS

Oral drugs are particularly useful in capturing large, wary flocking birds such as wild turkeys (Fig. 6.11) and sandhill cranes (Williams and Phillips 1973). Care must be exercised to prepare the proper dosage to avoid mortality. To prevent overdosing, Williams (1966) made a small incision in the crops of wild turkeys to wash out and remove excess drugs. Other workers have used a turkey baster or large syringe to wash out and remove excess drug from the crop. Cline and Greenwood (1972) tested several anesthetic agents on captive mallard ducks and reported that alpha-chloralose was poisonous at high doses and had a long induction time. They considered tribromoethanol the most satisfactory drug tested. Crider et al. (1968) mixed diazepam and alpha-chloralose and reduced capture time of waterfowl by one-third of that required with alpha-chloralose alone.

Smith (1967) used tribromoethanol to capture seabirds. He put the drug in glycerine capsules that were inserted in fish and seal meat. Captured birds were forced to regurgitate drugged bait to reduce mortality losses. This was done by giving 1.5 l of warm water to each bird and then shaking it for 20–30 seconds while holding its legs and bill. Tribromoethanol has been tested on a variety of birds, but the major limitation is the inability to prevent partially narcotized birds from leaving the bait site (Williams and Phillips 1972, Evans et al. 1975, Krapu 1976, Table 6.3).

Methoxymol administered on bait produced narcosis of wild turkeys in 3 minutes (Williams 1967), in contrast to 1–3 hours required with alpha-chloralose. Unfortunately, methoxymol is distasteful to turkeys and treated bait is not readily consumed.

Captive waterfowl can be anesthetized with intramuscular injections of ketamine (Vetalar) at a rate of 15–20 mg/kg of body weight (Borzio 1973). Davies (1973) used 5–8 mg/kg of Metomidate (Janssen Pharm.) as an intramuscular narcotic for birds.

MARKING ANIMALS FOR IDENTIFICATION

Most captured animals today are marked in some fashion for future identification to aid in various population studies. Proper application of marking devices by wildlife workers is essential for good results. Markers poorly designed or those not attached properly may produce irritations, changes in behavior, or cripples and possible mortality. For example, it is difficult and embarrassing to have to explain to people how a deer caught a foot in a neck collar. Often this can be prevented with the correct collar size properly attached. Many of these situations can be avoided by careful testing of markers on penned animals prior to use on free-ranging animals. Training personnel in suitable procedures and techniques for marking animals is important to the success of any population study.

Markers for Mammals

Marking devices can be divided into 3 main types: permanent, semipermanent, and temporary. Brands and tattoos are examples of permanent markers. Ear tags and neck collars are considered semipermanent but may re-

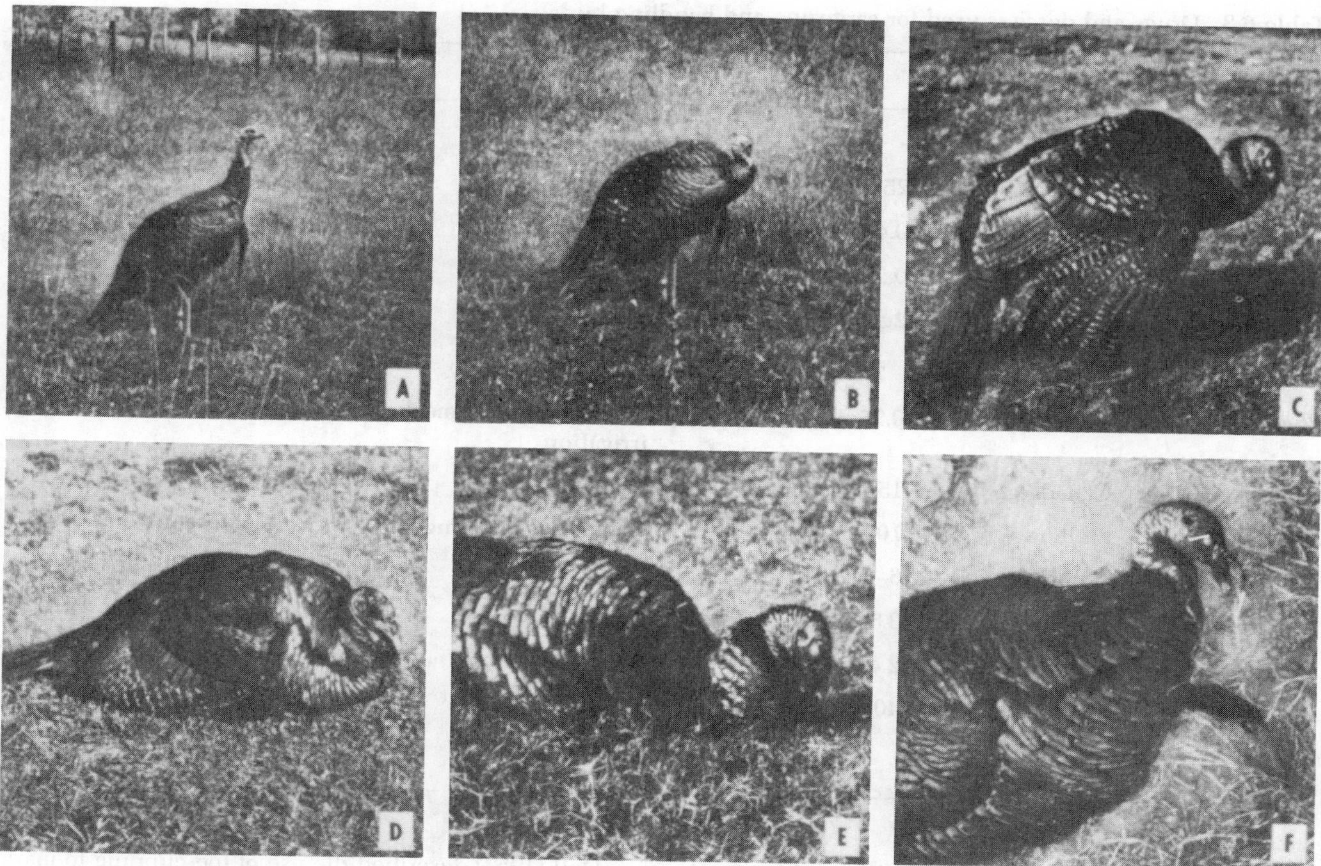

Fig. 6.11. Wild turkeys at various times after beginning to take treated bait. A. After 30–40 minutes. B. After 30–50 minutes. C. After 40–80 minutes. D. After 40–80 minutes. E. After 40–80 minutes. F. General anesthesia 2–3 hours. (Williams 1966).

main attached for the life of the animal. Temporary markers include hair dyes and ear streamers.

PERMANENT MARKERS

For many years hot brands have been used to permanently mark domestic livestock. Limited use of this technique has been reported by wildlife workers. Aldous and Craighead (1958) used hot irons to brand numbers on the horns of bighorn sheep. An explosive branding device was developed to mark 4 species of seals by Homestead et al. (1972). A spear gun was modified to trigger a percussion detonator. Brands were made by using lead-coated instantaneous fuses that were held in a template and ignited by the detonator.

Cryo-branding or freeze branding probably is more acceptable for wildlife than hot branding, because if done correctly there is virtually no chance of infection. This technique was developed for livestock identification by Farrell (1966). Cryo-branding involves the use of copper irons that are supercooled in a mixture of dry ice and alcohol. The cooled irons kill the melanocytes in pigmented hair but not the hair follicles; therefore, new hair comes in white. White hairs begin to appear in about 1 to 2 months after branding. Some scarring or partial hair loss may occur at the brand site if the iron is applied too long.

According to Hadow (1972), freeze branding is the only technique that produces permanent marks for identification of small mammals at a distance. He fashioned small branding irons out of copper rod and copper bar stock. The cold irons were applied for 20–40 seconds to achieve identifying marks. Newsom and Sullivan (1968) freeze-branded white-tailed deer on top of the animals' backs with 10-cm high numbers for 20–25 seconds for the best results (Fig. 6.12). They found these white brands to be permanent and visible from a helicopter.

Tattoos also have been used to permanently identify game animals. Clear and legible tattoos may be made only on a clean body site free of hair by properly applying the tattooing pliers and rubbing adequate dye into the puncture wounds. The most legible tattoos are made on animals with light colored skin. Tattooed numbers poorly applied can be difficult to locate and decipher. Thompson and Armour (1954) identified individual cottontail rabbits, and Keith et al. (1968) identified snowshoe hares by tattooed numbers in the ears. Polar bears were tattooed on the upper lip and groin area by Lentfer (1968). Downing and McGinnes (1969) tattooed white-tailed deer fawns on the ends of the ears with green dye.

Toe-clipping, tail-docking, ear-cropping, hole-punching, fur-clipping, and branding are all forms of mutilation open to the criticism that they maim the animal to some extent and so possibly affect its behavior or survival. Also, the marks applied by the investigator may be confused with those incurred by the animal in some other way. The main advantages of mutilation are

Table 6.3. Drugs and dosages used for capturing and handling birds.

Genus	Common Name	Dosages	Remarks	References
		Alpha-chloralose (used orally)		
Leptotilos	Marabou stork	250mg/bird	Added DMSO	Pomeroy & Woodford 1976
Grus	Sandhill crane	0.45–0.50/cup bait	14% loss	Williams & Phillips 1973
Branta	Canada goose	0.25g/cup bait	2.6% loss	Crider & McDaniel 1967
Meleagris	Turkey	2g/cup bait	9% loss	Williams 1966
		Tribromoethanol-Avertin (used orally)		
Phalacrocorax	Cormorant	0.25g/kg	Effective w/o stomach irrigation	Smith 1967
Branta	Canada goose	150mg/kg		Krapu 1976
Anas	Mallard	100mg/kg	Lethal dose 400 mg/kg	Cline & Greenwood 1972
Colinus	Bobwhite	6–7g/cup bait	Sedated 20 min.	Williams & Phillips 1972
Zenaida	Mourning dove	3.5–6.0g/cup bait	4 min. narcosis	Williams & Phillips 1972
Meleagris	Wild turkey	2.4g/40g bait	20 min. narcosis	Evans et al. 1975
Phasianus	Ring-necked pheasant	40g/kg corn	40 min. narcosis	Fredrickson & Trautman 1978

that marks may be readily applied with a minimum of equipment and the marks, in some cases, may be read at a distance. A standard system for marking small mammals by toe-clipping (Fig. 6.13) and ear-punching has been described by Blair (1941).

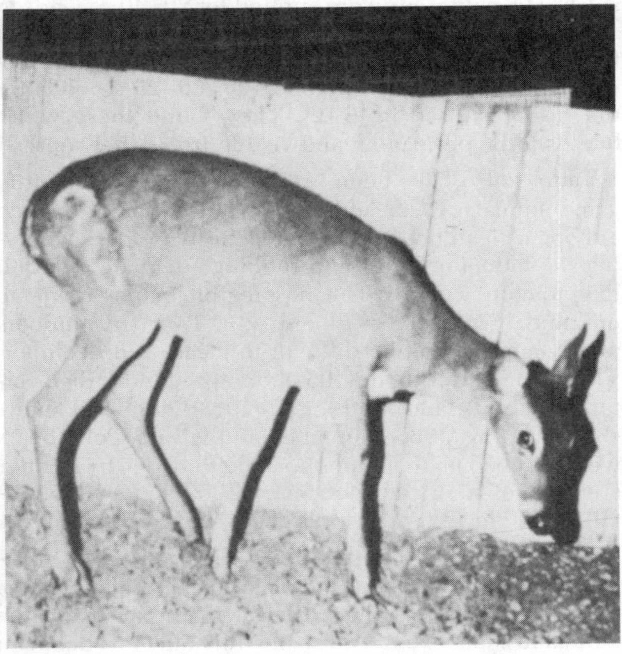

Fig. 6.12. Freeze-branded white-tailed deer (John Newsom, Louisiana Cooperative Wildlife Research Unit).

Dell (1957) described the use of toe-clipping to mark varying hares for track identification. He recommends drawing back all the loose skin from the toe to be amputated and cutting at the joint separating metatarsal and phalange. Only toes from the hind feet were taken, permitting a series of 24 if no more than 1 toe was removed from either foot. He found that tracks of marked snoeshow hares could be identified easily in the snow.

SEMIPERMANENT MARKERS

Numerous plastic, aluminum, and plated steel tags are available from commercial livestock sources. Tags come in a variety of sizes, colors, and identifying symbols or numbers. A few tags can be ordered with notification addresses or other printed matter.

The Tamp-R-Pruf seal (LISCO) was found to be the most reliable ear tag for medium to large animals (Day 1973). This tag comes in 3 sizes and is sealed when a hollow rivet is flattened by the sealer pliers. The tag is considered superior to the interlocking or self-locking tags because it cannot be pried apart easily if the rivet is flattened properly. Ear tags should be affixed to the upper or front edge and as near the base of the ear as possible. In this location the cartilage is thicker and tags are not likely to be pulled out. Both ears should be tagged to minimize the chance of losing the identity of the animals should 1 tag be lost.

Smaller animals such as snowshoe hares have been tagged successfully with #1 self-piercing fingerling tags (National Band and Tag Co., Newport, Kentucky) that were attached to both hind feet behind the prominent intercapitular ligaments (Keith et al. 1968). Evans et al.

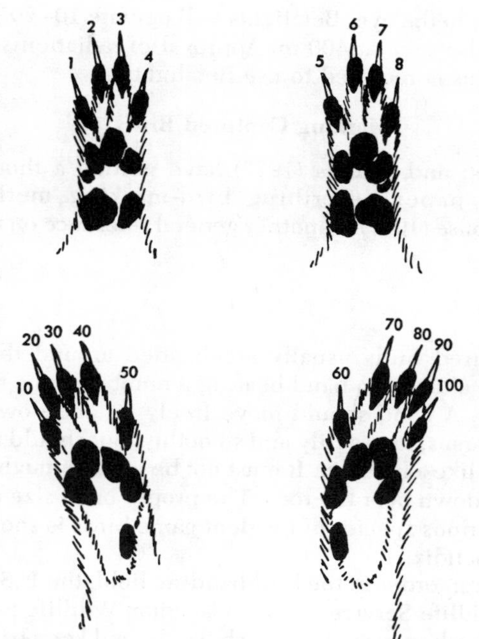

Fig. 6.13. A numbering system used in toe-clipping squirrels (from Baumgartner 1940 and Melchior and Iwen 1965). A. Using only "2" clips, 1 toe per foot, numbers up to 108 can be obtained for marking 98 animals. By considering hyphenated numbers, e.g., 30-90, an additional 106 animals can be marked with the 2-toe constraint. B. Using a constraint of clipping no more than "2" toes per foot the 1247 code, familiar to users of marginal-notched cards (upper left = units; upper right = digits; lower left = hundreds; lower right = thousands and thus 1 + 2 = 3, 7 + 2 = 9, etc.) has additional expansiveness.

(1971) tagged nutria with a #3 self-piercing monel tag inserted through the web of hind foot.

A tattoo punch set was used to put numbers in wing membranes of bats as an alternative to banding (Bonaccorso and Smythe 1972). The punched holes healed in 10 days and left white scar tissue in the form of numbers. However, a more recent article (Bonaccorso et al. 1976) reported tattoo punch marks remained only about 5 months. They recommended soft aluminum bands for small bats less than 10 g in weight, plastic bands for normal size bats up to 50 g in weight, and anodized-hardened aluminum or steel bands for bats over 50 g in size. In an effort to reduce band injury, they made a 10 mm slit on the leading edge of wings. Bands were passed through the slits before clamping them together. LaVal et al. (1977) banded bats with numbered, colored celluloid rings supplied by A. C. Hughes, Hampton Hill, England. They reported few band injuries after 18 months.

Feral goats in New Zealand were marked with epoxy resin horn cones that were slipped over the animals' horns and attached with pop-rivets (Rudge and Joblin 1976). The horn cones included 3 bands of pigmented colors 2.5 cm wide for color coding individual animals. Cones were visible at 20 m with naked eye and 150–200 m with binoculars.

Neck collars or neck bands are probably the most common marking devices for field identification of free-ranging animals. Progulske (1957) used an adjustable leather collar to mark white-tailed deer. Fashingbauer (1962) designed aluminum collars that slipped over the heads of does. He also developed expandable plastic collars for bucks. Collars about 10 cm wide were constructed out of vinyl plastic or plastic impregnated nylon and used successfully on elk, deer, and moose (Knight 1966, Hawkins et al. 1967b, Phillips and Nicholls 1970). Harper and Lightfoot (1966) made collars for elk out of polyethylene rope and attached numbered or lettered flaps of vinyl fabric. Polyethylene rope (96 cm × 1.3 cm) also was used on elk by Craighead et al. (1969). They threaded various colors of vinyl-coated nylon flags through a rope, attached a pendant tag at the bottom, adjusted the rope collars on the animals and secured them with hog rings. By varying flag colors and neck ropes, 1,500 individual combinations were possible each year.

An automatic collaring device was used along deer trails by Verme (1962) and improved by Siglin (1966). This device incorporated a polyethylene rope collar (46 cm × 0.7 cm) with a snap and ring locking mechanism. Beale (1966) made a self-collaring unit out of rubber for antelope. These rubber collars were stretched on a wooden frame over a water trough. When animals placed their heads through the frame for a drink they tripped the collaring device.

Bells have been used frequently to mark individual animals so that they can be relocated (Harper and Lightfoot 1966, Ellisor 1969, Schneegas and Franklin 1972). Ellisor and Harwell (1969) used bells successfully on peccary to determine size of home ranges. Bells were attached to the necks of animals with leather straps, polyethylene braided rope or to marking collars. A potential problem with belled animals is the possibility the bell may attract predators (Day 1973).

Collars equipped with 4 battery-operated neon lights were used by Carpenter et al. (1977) to make night observations of mule deer. They used light intensity and/or flash sequences to identify individual deer. These collars were 35.6 cm wide and weighed 690 g. Blinking units ran for 6–8 months while constant light lasted only 6 days or less. Brooks and Dodge (1978) used a neck collar with flashing light-emitting diodes for nocturnal identification of beavers.

Fluorescent marking of bones and teeth with tetracycline have been tested on coyotes and rodents. Linhart and Kennelly (1967) administered dimethylchlortetracycline (DMCT) orally to captive coyotes at 10 mg/kg of body weight and found it effective in long-term labeling. Oral doses of 50 mg/kg of body weight of DMCT to white laboratory rats labeled lower jaws and teeth for at least 6 months (Crier 1970). He feels this technique is a promising marker for field studies of rodents.

Pelton and Marcum (1975) injected radioisotopes into captured black bears and labeled the animals' feces. They used the tagged radioactive feces to estimate bear populations.

TEMPORARY MARKERS

Several investigators have used dyes to color the hairs of big game species but with limited success. Clover (1954) designed treadle-type spray devices for dyeing deer along game trails. Hansen (1964) and Simmons and

Phillips (1966) dyed bighorn sheep at waterholes with compressed air spray tanks that were activated from blinds. Crump (1961) sprayed antelope from a Super Cub with Nyanzol (D) black powder. Dall sheep were sprayed with clothing dye from a Super Cub rigged with a crop spraying device (Simmons 1971). Red and orange aniline dyes were used successfully to color body hairs of peccary (Day 1973). The dyed peccaries were easier to locate and remained visible for 2 to 3 months. Nyanzol A and D dyes produced the best color retention on hairs of ground squirrels (Melchior and Iwen 1965). Numbers were applied with a paint brush to the body hairs on both sides of squirrels. Keith et al. (1968) used picric acid (yellow) and Rhodamine B (pink) to color-mark snowshoe hares. Rhodamine B solution also was used as a fluorescent tracer and marker in jackrabbits (Evans and Griffith 1973). When jackrabbits ate dyed baits and foliage, their gut, feces, and urine were fluoresced under UV light. Their pelages were marked with direct application of dye. Brady and Pelton (1976) tested Nyanzol D, Rhodamine B, and picric acid dyes on cottontail rabbits. They found all the dyes satisfactory but picric acid was still clearly visible after 7 months.

The Nelson Paint Company (Iron Mountain, Mich.) markets a pistol to mark animals with different paint colors. The gun is operated by CO_2 and propels paint pellets to a distance of 15 m. Also, Paxarms and CAP-CHUR equipment have syringes available for marking captive or free-ranging animals with paint or dyes.

Colored ear streamers and ear swatches have been used as temporary markers for large mammals (Aldous and Craighead 1958, Harper and Lightfoot 1966, Miller and Robertson 1967, Downing and McGinnes 1969). Streamers were attached through slits in the animals' ears or attached with metal tags to the ears. Different materials have been used for streamers but the most durable are the vinyl-coated nylon fabrics. Brady and Pelton (1976) used 2 pieces of vinyl, 1 on the inside of the ear and 1 on the outside. The 2 vinyl swatches were held in place by a self-piercing monel metal tag.

Queal and Hlavachick (1968) attached nylon streamers through a vertical cut made in the hind leg anterior to achilles tendon. Streamers were visible at about 274 m and remained intact for at least 9 months on deer and antelope.

Colored plastic adhesive tape was found to be a simple temporary marker on the horns of bighorn sheep (Day 1973). The tape is tough, durable, fades slowly, and can be wrapped quickly around the horns.

A chemiluminescent tag was used to track bats in flight at night (Buchler 1976). The energy light source Cyalume (American Cyanamid Co.) was injected into hollow glass spheres 6–7 mm in size which were blown from soft glass tubes. These filled spheres were cemented to mid-ventral fur of bats and produced 2–3 hours of light. LaVal et al. (1977) also used the Cyalume light source to track bats at night from a helicopter.

Betalights (Saunders-Roe Developments Inc., Winston-Salem, North Carolina) are another light source that may be useful for marking small mammals. These lights are sealed glass capsules coated with phosphor and filled with tritium gas. They can produce any color within the visible spectrum, but green appears the brightest to the eye. Betalights will operate 10–20 years and can be seen at 400 m. Approval of radiation safety authorities is required to use Betalights.

Marking Captured Birds

Marion and Shamis (1977) have written a thorough review paper describing bird-marking methods. Stonehouse (1977) is another general reference on marking.

BANDS

Captured birds usually are banded around the leg with an aluminum band bearing a number and a return address. A band should move freely up and down the bird's tarsus, turn easily and smoothly, but should not fit loosely like a bracelet. It must not be loose enough to be pulled down over the toes. The proper band size to use with various species of resident game birds is shown in the appendix.

To keep order in the bird-banding field, the U.S. Fish and Wildlife Service and the Canadian Wildlife Service issue banding permits, furnish bands, and keep banding records (at Bird Banding Laboratory, Office of Migratory Bird Management, Laurel, Maryland) for all migratory birds. This standardization requires that banders follow a uniform nomenclature and procedure for keeping records for all migratory birds.

New birds are newly banded; *returns* are recaptures at the original banding station 90 or more days from the time of banding or last date of recapture; *recoveries* are captures of birds trapped by someone else at another location; *repeats* are recaptures of birds banded or trapped at the same station less than 90 days before and includes "repeat" birds originally banded at a different station; *experimentals* are birds held for more than a few hours after removal from the trap, released other than in the immediate vicinity of capture, wing-clipped or pinioned, dyed, neck-banded, painted or subjected to anything more than being immediately leg-banded (numbered and/or colored) and immediately released at the point of capture; *hand-reared* birds are those reared from eggs hatched in an incubator or under a setting hen, reared from domestic stock, or reared at any stage in captivity or from parents which are held, clipped, or pinioned; *sick* or *injured* birds are those not in good normal condition when obtained for banding and includes birds banded after recovery from sickness—such as botulism; *wild* birds are normal healthy birds raised in the wild, *L* or *local* birds are young, incapable of sustained flight; *HY* (hatching year) is a bird capable of sustained flight and known to have hatched during the calendar year in which it was banded; *AHY* (after hatching year) is a bird known to have hatched before the calendar year of banding with the year of hatch otherwise unknown; *SY* (second year) is a bird known to have hatched in the calendar year preceding the year of banding and in its second calendar year of life; *ASY* (after second year) is a bird known to have hatched earlier than the calendar year preceding the year of banding but with the year of hatch otherwise unknown; *TY* (third year) is a bird known to have hatched in the calendar year preceding the year before the year of banding, and now in the third calendar year of life; *ATY* (after third year) is a bird in at least its fourth calendar year of life.

States are required to use their own bands for resident game birds.

Bands are usually strung in numerical order in units of 100. Bands must be opened to be placed on the leg and then closed so that the ends are flush and tight against each other. Bands should be kept round and not squeezed to become ovate to avoid uneven wear on the ends of the oval. Needle-nosed pliers may be used for both these operations; although where many birds must be banded, various devices for holding bands and opening them increase the ease of banding (Addy 1956). Special banding pliers with bored-out circular holes to accommodate various sized bands are available from R. N. MacDonald, Lynnfield, Massachusetts. These pliers facilitate flush, tight closing of the band around a bird's leg.

Colored aluminum or plastic bands have been used to identify prairie grouse, geese, and other birds at a distance. Balham and Elder (1953) used "plexiglas," which was molded in place while hot. Lumsden et al. (1977) perfected a molding tool to preform lightweight plastic numbered leg bands. Ogilvie (1972) used a letter and number code which he engraved on large, plastic leg bands to allow individual recognition of mute swans. Fankhauser (1964) reported that colored, plastic adhesive tape, wrapped twice around the leg, lasted a year or more on caged birds. Johnson (1971) attached Scotch brand pressure sensitive tape around the tarsus. The same tape, placed over ordinary aluminum bands on free-living ruffed grouse, lasted at least 2 years (Gullion 1965).

A combination leg-marker and band has been described by Campbell (1960). A strip of plastic is held parallel to the tarsus by the conventional leg band, which passes through a slot in the plastic and around the tarsus. More durable leg streamers were made of colored polyvinyl chloride plastic (Guarino 1968) and have been secured with brass eyelets (Arnold and Coon 1971). Colored leg streamers have been used successfully on birds ranging in size from hummingbirds to wild turkeys. Grice and Rogers (1965) marked young wood duck ducklings, too small for leg bands, with numbered web tags. Alliston (1975) successfully attached web tags to unhatched duckling toes within pipped eggs.

DYES AND PAINTS

For birds that regularly conceal their legs in herbaceous vegetation, some marker higher on the body is necessary. Borrowing a technique from medieval falconers, brightly colored feathers may be "imped" to the wing or tail (Wright 1939). The imping process is illustrated in Fig. 6.14.

Similarly, colored feathers or a plastic marker may be wired or glued to the tail feathers (Trippensee 1941). The feathers themselves may be painted or sprayed with quick-drying lacquer or "airplane dope" (Swank 1952).

The feathers may be dyed instead of painted. Dye penetrates better and does not cause matting like paint, but dyes are not bright unless applied to white feathers. Ross's and snow geese have been dyed in entirety as an aid in tracing migration routes. Ellis and Ellis (1975) found human hair dyes applied to golden eagles to be durable, easy to apply, and not disruptive of normal behavior. Some methods are summarized in Table 6.4.

An ingenious method has been developed for dyeing duck embryos in the egg, so that they hatch with colored down. The dye, in a concentration of 5–15 g per 100 ml of water, is injected through the egg shell about 2 to 8 days prior to hatching. Care must be taken to seal the opening and to maintain sterile conditions. Two dyes used in the field were Ponceau SC (scarlet) and Fast Green FCF (bright green). Optimum dosages were found to vary according to the size of the egg and amounted to about 0.01 ml per 2.4 g of egg weight (Evans 1951).

BACK TAGS

More permanent color markers are of several kinds. One type consists of 2 tags joined by a silver-plated safety pin, surgical clip, or monel wire. This is fastened to, or through, the loose skin of the back at the base of the neck (Taber 1949, Wint 1951, Nelson 1955, Westfall and Weeden 1956).

These permanent-type color markers have proven successful for upland game birds but not for waterfowl. For coots, it was found necessary to enclose the colored tag in hard, waterproof plastic and to fasten the marker high on the neck (Gullion 1951).

Another permanent back-marker consists of a single tag held in place by a loop around the base of each wing.

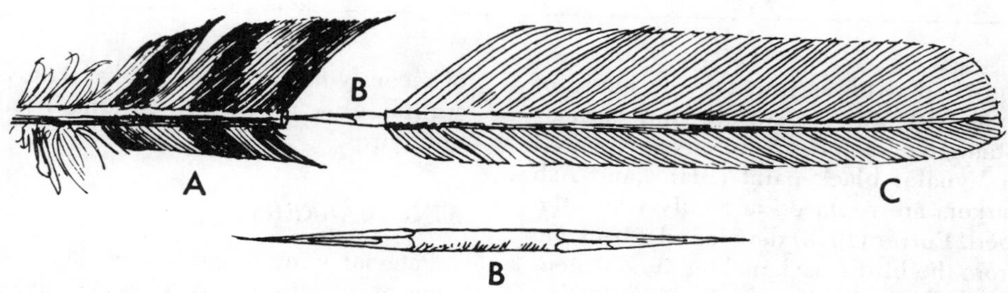

Fig. 6.14. The process of imping (from Wright 1939). The feather of the capture bird *A* is clipped, and a feather of contrasting color *C* is attached to it by means of a double-pointed needle *B*.

Table 6.4. Methods for coloring the plumage of birds.

Species	Coloring Agent	Special Techniques	Duration of Color	Authority
Waterfowl (in egg)	Amaranth, Brilliant Blue FCF, Croceine Scarlet MOO, Fast Green FCF, Patent Blue, Ponceau SX: 5–15 grams per 100 ml water	Inject 0.1 ml per 2.4 grams egg wt. 2–8 days before hatching, under sterile conditions	Field obs.: 23–32 days. Hand: up to 7 wks.	Evans 1951
Waterfowl	Picric acid: saturated solution in water	On undertail coverts	Field obs.: 2–3 weeks	Helm 1955
Snow and Ross' Goose	Rhodamine B, Malachite Green and picric acid in alcohol	Dipped wings and tails in dye.	Field obs.: 3–6 months	Kozlik et al. 1959
Pheasant	Malachite Green, Brilliant Green, Rhodamine B extra, Purple Batik: in 33% alcohol—66% water solution	Applied w/spray gun. Wetting agents useful with some dyes	Field obs.: 2+ mo. on ground; 4–6 mo. flushed	Wadkins 1948
Waterfowl; Mourning Dove	"Airplane Dope": white, yellow and red	On tail and outer half of primaries. Apply thin coat and hold feathers spread until dry to avoid sticking.	Field obs.: about 2 months when flushed	Sowls 1955 Swank 1952
Sage Grouse	Aniline dyes in mixture of equal parts water and 95% grain alcohol	Applied with remote-control spray	Not observed	Moffitt 1942
Ruffed Grouse	Rhodamine B, Auramine, Methyl Violet, Victoria Green, in saturation in 95% ethanol	Dipped tails of adults and rolled young in shallow pan, or sprayed w/atomizer	Field obs.: (shed feathers) and Hand: up to 8 months	Gullion et al. 1961
Mourning Dove; Scaup	Aniline dyes in water, grain alcohol, and acetic acid	Birds dipped and held for drying	Over three months	Winston 1954
Golden Eagle	Human hair dyes	Rinse excess dye	21 months or more	Ellis and Ellis 1975

As used on English partridges, the tape is made of polyvinyl chloride with the cross-piece and harness loops of chrome-tanned horsehide. Numbers are painted on the tag with Vynafor black paint (Blank and Ash 1956). These markers are replaced annually when the birds are retrapped. Furrer (1979) developed a back tag that protruded from the bird's back making it conspicuous and easily read. Retention was better than for leg streamers (Guarino 1968). Cuthbert and Southern (1975) glued a circular numbered tag to the synsacrum region of recently hatched gull chicks. Baltosser (1978) used a similar glue procedure to attach back-tags to hummingbirds.

WING MARKERS

Patagial wing streamers made of various materials, such as plastic-coated SAFLAG nylon flagging, have been used widely (Anderson 1963, Hester 1963, Knowlton et al. 1964, Southern 1971, Weeks 1972, Nes-

Fig. 6.15. Canada geese marked with neck collars (U.S. Fish and Wildlife Service).

bitt 1976, Morgenweck and Marshall 1977) on waterfowl, upland, and passerine birds. Some concern has been expressed about impeding flight. Boag et al. (1975) found that patagial streamers did not adversely influence the survival of red grouse chicks. A major advantage of patagial tags is that the markers are usually more conspicuous than leg markers or back tags (Marion and Shamis 1977).

NECK MARKERS

Markers hung around the neck have been used with considerable success on geese. These may be held in place by staples (Helm 1955) or the jess knot (Craighead and Stockstad 1956). Jess-markers have not proven satisfactory for ducks, as ducks tend to get their bills caught under the marker. Neck collars have been used successfully on geese (Fig. 6.15) but not ducks. Ice may accumulate on collars and cause mortality under certain conditions (Greenwood and Bair 1974). MacInnes et al. (1969) described an aluminum neck collar for Canada geese that apparently eliminated the icing problem. This collar had flanged ends to avoid feather wear. Ankney (1975) suggested that neck bands contributed to starvation of female snow geese. Chabreck and Shroer (1975), however, believed that neck collars did not interfere with reproduction of snow geese. Lensink (1968) showed that neck bands interfered with black brant reproduction. Maltby (1977) designed a neck-collar that did not seem to interfere with brant reproduction. Another type of neck marker is a poncho made of Herculite and used by Pyrah (1970) on sage grouse.

NASAL MARKERS

Nasal saddles and discs (Fig. 6.16) are the most commonly used bill marker. Attachment methods include plastic filament or steel pins (Lee 1960). Nasal saddles (Sugden and Poston 1968) are less hazardous for diving ducks than the discs described by Bartonek and Dane (1964). Doty and Greenwood (1974) improved the technique for applying identifying numbers to polyvinyl choride nasal-saddle markers (Fig. 6.17). Preformed urethane plastic saddles with nylon attachment pins were a further improvement (Greenwood 1977).

Sladen (1973) adapted a system of symbols to be used on markers using only dissimilar letters and symbols to avoid duplication.

MISCELLANEOUS MARKING PROCEDURES

Burger et al. (1970) successfully marked waterfowl ducklings less than 1 day old by removing the alula with small scissors.

Greenwood (1975) attempted to freeze-brand feather tracts of mallard ducklings with negligible success. Freeze-branding of the premaxillae was successful.

Ricklefs (1973) tattooed nestling starlings on the abdomen with black India Ink.

Yellow markers on the heads of mourning doves have been shown to cause disruption of the pair bond, although markers of other colors or locations did not (Goforth and Baskett 1965). Kessler (1964) reported that more pheasants bearing yellow markers were killed by avian predators than those with other colors.

An indirect type of marker has been described by Devine and Peterle (1968), Hanson and Jones (1968), Kelsall and Calaprice (1972), and Kelsall et al. (1975) using the chemical content of primary feathers as biological tracers to determine the breeding grounds of wild geese and ducks.

Marking Birds Without Capture

Several of the devices listed under the marking of mammals without capture could be adapted to marking birds; the snare-marker (Romanov 1956) has been used on grouse in the USSR. Heusmann et al. (1978) developed a self-marking collar which he attached to wood duck boxes to capture nesting hens.

Fig. 6.16. Mallard duckling with nasal discs attached to bill with stainless steel pin and washers (U.S. Fish and Wildlife Service).

Canadian workers have colored ruffed grouse at a short distance by throwing a blown hen's egg, filled with printer's ink dissolved in xylene or carbon tetrachloride. They also placed aluminum and bronze dust in dusting places and found it later in shed feathers (Bendell and Fowle 1950). Birds have also been marked at close range by squirting ink on them with a large syringe (Pearson and Pearson 1955) or by splattering paint (Miller, pers. comm.). An automatic spray device was developed for the sage grouse (Moffitt 1942). This consisted of a cylinder half filled with aniline dye in a 50:50 water and 95% grain alcohol solution. The solution was put under air pressure. A pipe capped with a spray head and equipped with a valve led upward. The valve could be operated manually from a distance. The cylinder was buried on the dancing ground so that only the pipe protruded. Moseley and Mueller (1975) buried a bottle of dye 30 cm from least tern nests and extended rubber tubing 30 m to a blind. They projected a stream of dye 1 m by blowing air through the rubber tubing.

Mossman (1960) applied 2 to 3 cc of "thief detection powder" to a set of eggs of the glaucous-winged gull and found that the parent birds were brilliantly colored with purple. The eggs, also, were colored but the birds did not desert them.

The use of any sort of marking, like banding, on migratory birds is now under the supervision of the U.S. Fish and Wildlife Service and the Canadian Wildlife Service, so that sightings may be recorded systematically and duplications avoided.

Suitability and availability of materials for use in marking continually change with technological advance. Though principles of marker attachment and evaluation of marker effects on behavior and survival most likely will remain unaffected by material substitution, procurement of materials reported in literature often can be difficult. Trade-name materials, especially, are a problem; it is wise to purchase materials by generic name to be sure the product you obtain is what you want. Many materials are not universally compatible and marker failure may result from use of such combinations.

Fig. 6.17 Mallard duckling with nasal saddle attached to bill with stainless steel pin and washers (U.S. Fish and Wildlife Service).

Capturing and Handling Reptiles

Reptiles are captured by a variety of devices, many of which are similar to those used for mammal capture. Balgooyen (1977) reviewed collecting methods used on small reptiles. These methods include: box traps, funnel traps, snap traps, pitfall traps, hand snares, pole nooses and rubber band guns.

Jones (1965) described 3 methods to capture alligators in Florida. He used a long handle dip net to capture small animals and a snare pole for those 1 to 2 m in length. The most effective method was a harpoon made out of a #8/0 fish hook embedded in a 10-cm length of tubing. About 0.6 cm of the hook shaft extended below the barb. A ring was fastened to the tube which held a nylon cord 7.6 m long. A gallon plastic bottle was attached to the cord as a float. The harpoon was delivered into the neck of the animals by 3.7-m wooden pole.

A baited snare trap was used for capturing alligators by Murphy and Fendley (1973). This trap consisted of 2, 1-m by 30-m plywood boards and anchor stakes. The boards were placed in a V-shape and perpendicular to the shore line. The boards guided the animals to baits which triggered a flexible pole snare. The snare was made out of 0.6-m nylon rope which was attached to a tree on shore.

Webb and Messel (1977) reviewed several techniques used to capture crocodiles in Australia. They preferred tongs, harpoons, and rope traps for these animals.

ANESTHETICS FOR HANDLING REPTILES

The new anesthetic ketamine hydrochloride has been used successfully on numerous reptiles (Beck 1976). Glenn et al. (1972) administered the drug intramuscular at 22–66 mg/kg to snakes 1 kg or less in weight. For heavier snakes they gave 88–110 mg/kg and recommended that resuscitation equipment be available for doses greater than 110 mg/kg. Stunkard and Miller (1974) reported that preferred drugs for reptiles included Sernylan at 2.5–5 mg/kg intramuscular, MS-222 (Fisher Scientific Co.) at an IM dose of 40–88 mg/kg, and pentabarbital orally at 44 mg/kg and 24–33 mg/kg intraperitoneal. Refer to Taber and Cowan (1969) for additional anesthetics used on reptiles.

Chapter Seven

Post-Mortem Examination

GARY A. WOBESER

Department of Veterinary Pathology
Western College of Veterinary Medicine
University of Saskatchewan
Saskatoon, Saskatchewan, Canada

TERRY R. SPRAKER

Veterinary Diagnostic Laboratory
School of Veterinary Medicine
Colorado State University
Fort Collins, Colorado

GENERAL CONSIDERATIONS

Pathology is a science that deals with the nature of disease, and one of the basic techniques used is the post-mortem examination or necropsy (*Gr. viewing death*). A necropsy involves the systematic examination of all body organs and tissues and the careful recording of observations. To perform this task, the prosector (person doing the necropsy), must have knowledge of the anatomy and diseases of the species being examined.

In most instances, the biologist will profit by requesting aid with necropsies from a professional veterinary pathologist. In addition to his experience, the pathologist has access to diagnostic facilities such as microbiology, toxicology and parasitology laboratories which generally are not available to the biologist.

The basic reason for doing a necropsy is to collect information, and the results will depend upon the thoroughness of the examination. Necropsies may be performed (1) to determine the cause of death or sickness in an individual or group of animals; (2) to determine the health status of a group of animals; (3) to determine the effect of some natural or experimental factor upon the animal or; (4) to collect specimens for research.

When and Where To Do a Necropsy

Disease in free-living animals is often likened to an iceberg, in that only a small "tip" ever becomes evident. Predators and scavengers quickly dispose of sick and dead animals in the field. Thus, even a single carcass should be regarded as a valuable specimen that merits careful examination. The wildlife biologist should also take advantage of specimens which become available for other reasons. The ubiquitous "road-kill" or animals collected during research can provide invaluable experience in the recognition of normal tissues as well as baseline data on the occurrence and prevalence of lesions and parasites.

Necropsies can be performed either in the field or in the laboratory. Whenever possible, intact specimens should be transported to a laboratory where complete facilities and equipment are available. Occasionally, this may be impractical because of the size of the specimen or the delay in getting specimens to the laboratory. In such cases a necropsy should be performed in the field and selected tissues preserved for later examination in the laboratory.

Why Use a Standard Necropsy Technique?

A good necropsy technique is designed to allow the study of each organ and the functional and anatomical relationships of that organ to all other systems. The general procedure is systematically to identify and examine each organ, and to open all hollow organs.

It is very useful to prepare an outline of the technique which can be followed step-by-step at the time of necropsy. The less experience a prosector has, the more rigidly he should adhere to a standard technique, to ensure that all systems are examined thoroughly. If the prosector uses a standard technique in which all body systems are examined carefully at each necropsy, he will be thoroughly familiar with the *normal* appearance of organs and thus can easily recognize abnormalities.

Zoonotic Diseases

Many of the infectious diseases of wildlife are transmissible to humans, and no necropsy should be undertaken without adequate protection for the prosector. In most cases this consists of wearing protective outer clothing such as coveralls or laboratory coat, a rubber apron and rubber gloves. In certain instances, for example when animals are found showing evidence of central nervous system disease, further precautions are necessary. Two pair of new gloves worn one-inside-the-other will minimize skin contamination if the outer glove is punctured, and a face mask and goggles will prevent nasal or conjunctival inoculation by flying droplets in such cases. Anyone performing necropsies on wild animals should consult his physician concerning immunization for those diseases prevalent in the area.

Where to Find Professional Help

The ideal combination for investigations involving necropsy of wild animals is through a team approach involving a biologist who provides expertise regarding biology and field experience and a pathologist who can perform detailed examinations and has access to ancillary laboratories. The interpretation of the significance of findings often requires input from both scientists.

Few game agencies have specific pathology or disease-oriented laboratories within their organizations, so the wildlife biologist must often seek aid elsewhere.

The U.S. Fish and Wildlife Service and the Canadian Wildlife Service have disease specialists who may be contacted for assistance, particularly in the case of migratory or endangered species. Veterinary pathologists are available in regional, state or provincial veterinary diagnostic laboratories, in Veterinary Colleges and in Departments of Veterinary Science at other universities. Many colleges and universities have faculty members with special interests in microbiology and parasitology, and aid with toxicologic problems may be found in laboratories operated by departments dealing with environmental quality and/or public health.

Animal Collection

The ideal specimen in most instances is a live animal with well-developed clinical signs of illness. This animal may be thoroughly examined, and specimens collected for tests such as serology and hematology prior to euthanasia. If live, sick animals are unavailable, freshly dead specimens should be collected. These animals may be preserved by refrigeration or ice packs for several hours during transport prior to necropsy without serious deterioration.

Freezing of entire specimens should be avoided since freezing produces numerous artifacts, particularly if histopathology is required. In those instances where specimens must be retained for long periods of time, a necropsy should be performed immediately and individual organs or tissues preserved for further study.

In the case of large die-offs where many specimens are available, a sample which is representative of the entire group should be collected and processed.

Whenever possible, the person who will do the necropsy should be consulted in advance with regard to the preferred method of collection. Every specimen should be accompanied by a history sheet on which are recorded the details of the individual (species, sex, age, physical condition, weight), together with information on the location where it was found, the numbers and type of other animals present in the area, clinical signs of disease observed, as well as any other information likely to be helpful in diagnosis or interpretation of the case. This information should be retained and filed with the results of the necropsy.

Record Keeping

The individual necropsy should be regarded as a single scientific observation, and an understanding of any disease or problem is likely to be obtained only when the results of many necropsies can be reviewed, compared and correlated with other factors. For this to be possible, records must be maintained which are sufficiently detailed to allow meaningful retrospective study.

There are many methods for maintaining records (see Chapter 4), and the choice of system is up to the individual. The minimum information which should be recorded for each necropsy includes:

1. history of the case (collected prior to necropsy)
2. the gross necropsy findings
3. the results of all ancillary tests (microbiology, toxicology, etc.)
4. final diagnosis

All specimens which were collected or prepared from the case, i.e., photographs, histologic slides, parasites, etc., should be filed in a way that they can be recovered. The simplest method to link all of these components of a case is to assign a number to each case at the time of necropsy and to use this number on all materials and records relating to the case. In general, a prosector can only remember the results of 1 necropsy at a time, so if a number of animals are being examined the results should be recorded after each individual case.

A camera should be a standard part of the necropsy equipment for the permanent recording of lesions. In most situations, a 35 mm single lens reflex camera with a built-in light meter is suitable, particularly if equipped with interchangeable lenses or with a "macro" lens for close-up photography.

EQUIPMENT

The instruments shown in Fig. 7.1 are adequate for the necropsy of most species of mammals and birds. The choice of instruments from within this group will depend upon the size of the animal being examined. The "lopping shears," originally intended for pruning trees, are highly satisfactory for cutting ribs even in very large species.

A selection can be made from this equipment for field use, the amount to depend upon the method of transportation available. In addition to the instruments, the following equipment should also be available:

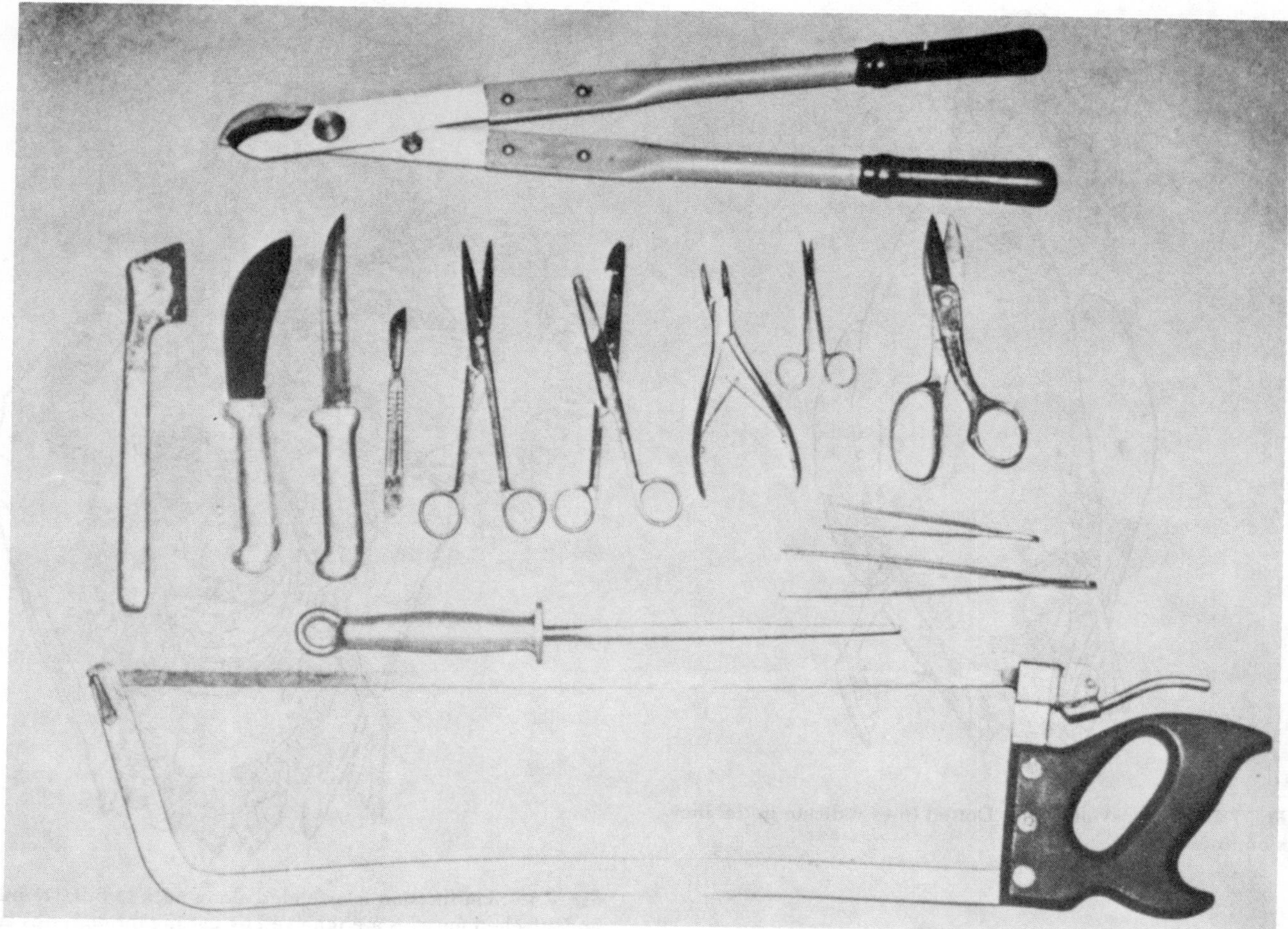

Fig. 7.1. Instruments suitable for performing a necropsy on virtually any mammal or bird. Top: pruning shears. Center from left: rachiotome, curved blade knife, straight blade knife, scalpel with replaceable blades, 25.4 cm straight blade scissors, enterotome, Cleveland bone scissors, 12.7 cm straight blade scissors, serrated blade poultry shears. Bottom: 15.2 cm and 20.3 cm toothed thumb forceps, steel for sharpening knives, butcher's saw, (a hack saw or coping saw works well for small species).

—protective clothing—coveralls, rubber apron, rubber gloves
—tape measure and accurate spring scale
—camera and film
—labeling supplies (tags, string, masking tape, etc.)
—glass microscopic slides for smears and wet mounts
—containers for specimens (plastic bags, plastic petri plates, aluminum foil)
—syringes, needles and tubes for blood and other body fluids
—fixatives (the most generally useful fixative is 10% neutral buffered formalin; a large volume may be taken into the field in a plastic jug and dispensed as needed into leakproof plastic bottles or bags, other fixatives may be used as required for special studies).
—insulated cooler chests containing wet or dry ice for preservation of specimens in warm weather.

NECROPSY OF BIRDS

Each necropsy should begin after consideration of the available history. This should include the species, number, sex and age of affected and unaffected birds in the area, a description of any clinical signs observed, together with as much information as possible on the environment and habits of the affected birds. This is followed by examination of the external surfaces with particular attention to the body orifices and any discharge therefrom. The limbs are manipulated to check for fractures, and the visible joints examined for evidence of swelling. The bird is placed on its back, and an incision is made through the skin between the legs and the body; a transverse incision is then made across the body linking the 2 prior cuts (Fig. 7.2). The resulting skin flaps are reflected exposing the pectoral muscles and abdomen, and 1 of the lateral incisions is extended with scissors along the neck to the base of the bill, exposing the structures of the neck. The abdomen is entered by an incision posterior to the sternum, the sternum is lifted and the abdominal air sacs are inspected. The sternum and pectoral muscles are removed by cutting through the ribs and coracoid with heavy scissors or poultry shears (Fig. 7.3 and 7.4). As the sternum is removed the thoracic air sacs and pericardium are inspected. Because of the anatomical arrangement of the thoracic viscera, it is convenient to remove the heart at this point by sectioning the great vessels as far as possi-

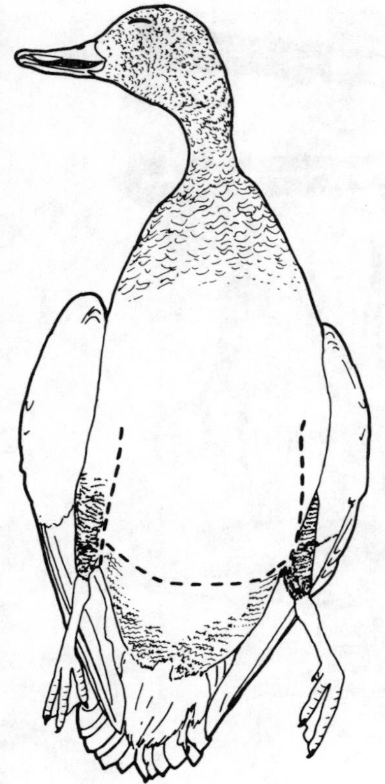

Fig. 7.2. Necropsy of a bird. Dotted lines indicate initial incision lines.

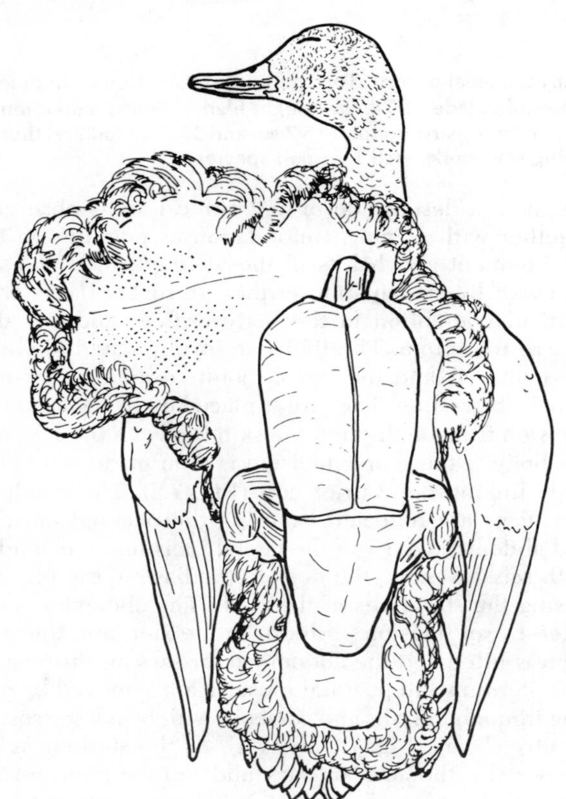

Fig. 7.3. The skin flaps are reflected exposing pectoral muscles and abdomen.

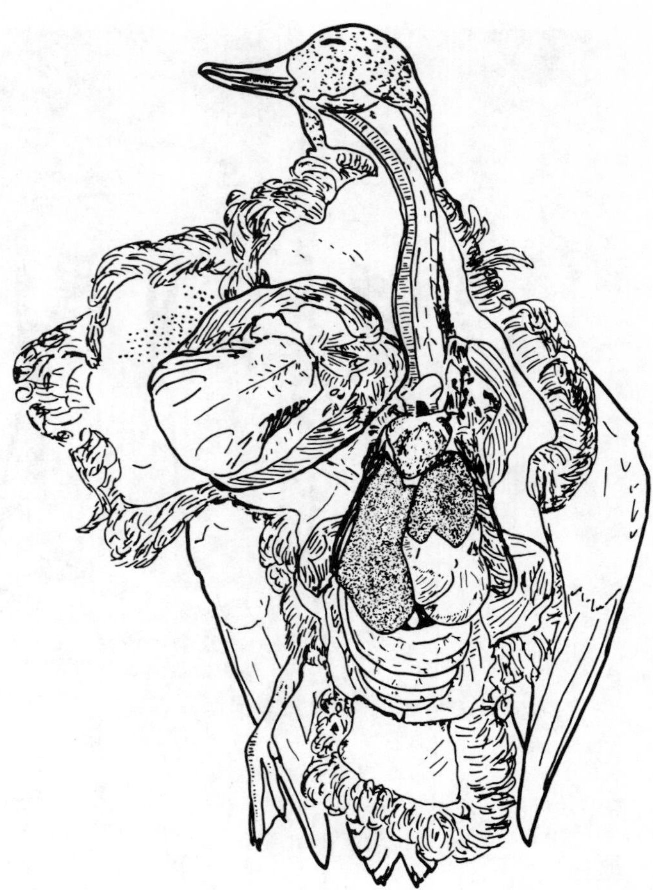

Fig. 7.4. Skin incision is extended along neck to bill, sternum and attached muscles are removed by cutting through ribs and coracoid, exposing the viscera.

ble from the heart. Each body system can now be examined in turn.

Digestive

The oral cavity is opened and a cut is made through the left lateral commisure of the mouth and the mandible into the esophagus. The esophagus and crop are opened longitudinally to the thoracic inlet where it is divided transversely. The distal end of the esophagus together with the proventriculus, gizzard, intestine, pancreas, liver and spleen can now be removed as a unit. A few centimeters of the distal colon are left in the body. The spleen is removed and set aside for later examination. The liver is inspected and freed from the gizzard, the gall bladder and bile duct are opened, and several sections are made to inspect the parenchyma of the liver. The intestine is straightened by gentle traction and limited cutting of the mesentery and the entire digestive tract is opened longitudinally with scissors. The ingesta and mucosa in each compartment is examined. The stump of colon left in the body cavity is opened to the cloaca, taking care to preserve the bursa of Fabricius, ureters, and genital system for later examination.

Respiratory

The abdominal and thoracic air sacs and external nares were examined earlier, the internal nares are examined and the rostrum is sectioned transversely to expose the nasal cavity and the infra-orbital sinuses. The trachea is opened longitudinally to the syrinx with scissors. The lungs are removed and sectioned transversely to expose the parenchyma. The medullary air sacs are exposed later when the bones are examined.

Cardiovascular

The external surface of the heart is inspected and the general outline of the heart is assessed. The heart chambers are opened by following the blood flow, as will be outlined in the section on mammalian necropsy. The aorta is opened longitudinally with scissors.

Urogenital

The extent of examination of the genital system will vary with the sex of the bird and time of year. Usually only an external examination is necessary, but in the laying female the oviduct should be opened.

The kidneys and ureters may be removed from the body by transecting the ureter at the cloaca and then exerting gentle traction on the ureter while freeing the dorsal aspect of each kidney with a scalpel (Fig. 7.5). After removal, the kidney is sectioned and examined.

Hematopoietic and Lymphoid

The spleen is examined and sectioned to expose the parenchyma. Birds have few or no distinct lymph nodes; however, the submucosal lymphoid aggregations in the intestine should be identified as that organ is opened and the bursa of Fabricius is examined. The bone marrow will be exposed when bones are sectioned.

Endocrine

The primary endocrine organs are the pituitary which is exposed as the brain is removed, the adrenal glands located at the anterior pole of each kidney, and the thyroid and parathyroid located near the thoracic inlet. All are examined as exposed.

Nervous

The brachial plexus, vagus and sciatic nerves should be identified and examined. The brain should be examined routinely by removing the calvarium with a fine bone saw or bone forceps (Fig. 7.6). To remove the spinal cord, the dorsal arches of the vertebral bodies are cut away with bone shears, thereby exposing the cord. An alternative is to free the spinal column of as much muscle as possible and then fix the entire column in formalin. After fixation, the bones may be decalcified and histologic sections cut of the cord.

Special Senses

The eyes and external ear openings are examined during the initial inspection. If abnormalities are suspected, the eyes should be carefully removed and fixed. It is difficult to adequately expose the internal ear structures by dissection, and the portion of bone containing these structures may be fixed, decalcified and then cut to expose these organs.

Musculo-Skeletal

The musculature is assessed as the bird is opened. A metatarsal bone should be broken as a subjective meas-

Fig. 7.5. The kidneys are removed by sectioning the ureter at the cloaca and exerting gentle traction on the ureter while freeing the dorsal attachments of the kidney.

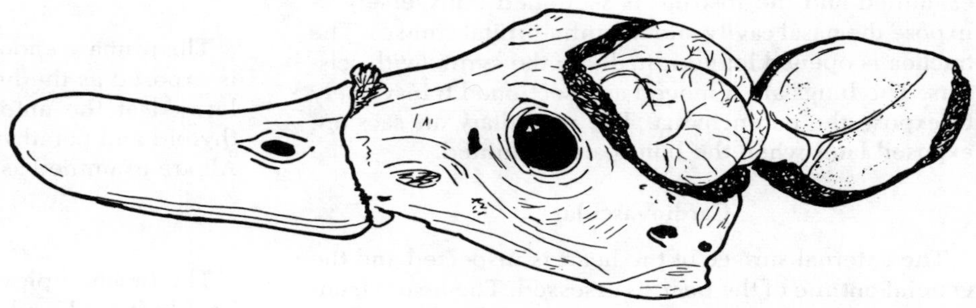

Fig. 7.6. **The brain is exposed by a circular saw cut around the calvarium, beginning at the foramen magnum. Care must be used so that the brain is not cut.**

ure of bone strength. The bone should break with a distinct "snap"; failure to do so, or a bone which bends without breaking suggests poor bone mineralization.

The femoro-tibial and tibio-metatarsal joints and the tendon sheaths on the back of the legs should be opened and examined. The proximal tibia should be sectioned longitudinally to expose the epiphyseal line and the medullary bone marrow. In young birds this can be done by slicing the lateral aspect of the bone with a knife, but in mature birds the bone must be cut with a saw.

NECROPSY OF MAMMALS

Mammals are a very diverse group and techniques must be modified somewhat for different types; particularly with regard to the positioning of the body and removal and examination of the alimentary system. A basic technique for large monogastric animals and modifications for ruminants and small mammals will be described.

The animal should be weighed and body measurements taken prior to necropsy. The external surface, body orifices and mucus membranes are examined and samples of ectoparasites collected. If abnormalities are suspected in the eyes, the entire eye should be carefully removed and fixed intact.

Opening and Removal of Viscera: Monogastrics

The animal is placed in right lateral recumbency, with the legs facing the prosector and the head to the prosector's left. The initial skin incision passes from the lips along the ventral midline to the perineum. The incision should pass to the left of the penis and scrotum in the male and either between, or to the left of the mammary glands in the female. The skin is reflected, the left foreleg is raised and the axillary muscles are cut so that the leg may be reflected dorsally. The hind leg is raised, the muscles are cut along the pelvis and the hip joint is severed (Fig. 7.7). Muscles, fat, superficial lymph nodes, and the flesh side of the skin should be carefully examined. (Bullet wounds are found most easily by skinning the animal and examining the inner surface of the hide). The mammary glands are palpated, and the glands and the draining lymph nodes are incised to inspect the parenchyma.

The abdomen is opened by cutting the body wall along the ventral midline from pelvis to sternum, and then by a second cut which follows the last rib on the left side. The resulting flap is reflected, exposing the abdominal viscera. The left thoracic wall is removed by cutting the ribs near the sternum and vertebral column, respectively, with shears (Fig. 7.8). The thoracic viscera are examined and the condition of the pleural membranes noted. If there is an accumulation of fluid within the pleural or pericardial cavities, a sample should be taken.

The tongue, larynx, thyroids, parathyroids, trachea, esophagus, lungs, heart, and thymus are removed from the body by cutting between lateral margins of the tongue and the mandible, freeing the tongue, and then by a process of traction and cutting, freeing the larynx and other structures. The aorta, posterior vena cava, and esophagus are transected at the diaphragm. (If the stomach is full, the esophagus should be tied prior to cutting). The retropharyngeal and cervical lymph nodes, salivary glands, thyroid, and parathyroid glands are identified and inspected at this time.

The liver, spleen and digestive system are removed as a block by severing the esophagus caudal to the diaphragm; dissecting the liver free from the kidneys by blunt dissection, and severing the mesentery. The colon is transected at the pelvic brim, (if the feces are fluid the colon is tied). The adrenal glands are identified at the anterior pole of the kidneys and removed. The urogenital system is removed from the body as a unit, by splitting the pelvis at the *symphysis pubis* in young animals, or by removing the ventral portion of the pelvis in adults. All abdominal lymph nodes are identified and incised.

Examination of the Thoracic Viscera

The tongue, tonsils, and pharyngeal area are inspected and the esophagus is opened longitudinally with scissors. The external surfaces of the lungs are thoroughly inspected and any lobular differences in color, inflation, and firmness are noted. The presence and size of the thymus is noted. The larynx and trachea are opened by a dorsal longitudinal incision with scissors which should continue within the major bronchi to the tip of the diaphragmatic portion of the lungs (Fig. 7.9). The nature and consistency of any exudate in the airways are noted. Several transverse sections are made through the pulmonary parenchyma, and the bronchial lymph nodes are incised. The pericardial sac is opened and the fluid therein noted. The heart and great vessels are examined while attached to the lungs. (This permits easy reorientation if some anomalous condition of the vessels exists). The epicardial surface of the heart is inspected, and the size and contour of the heart is noted. The heart is usually opened by following the normal path of blood flow beginning in the right atrium.

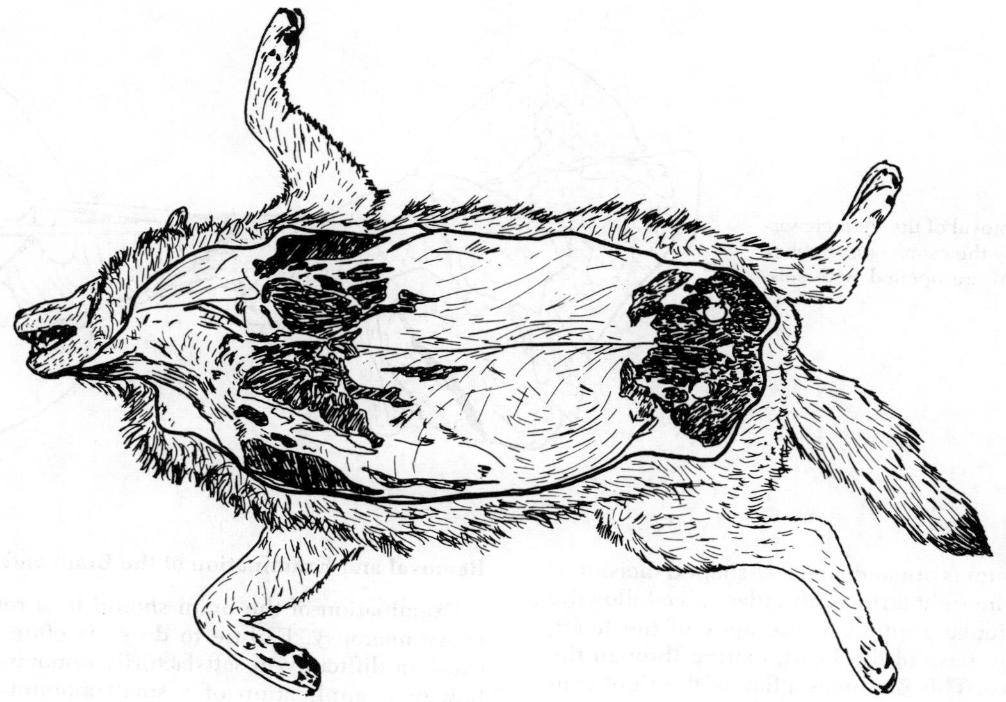

Fig. 7.7. **Necropsy of a wolf. The initial skin incision passes from lips to perineum. This is then extended to separate the left fore and hind limbs from the trunk.**

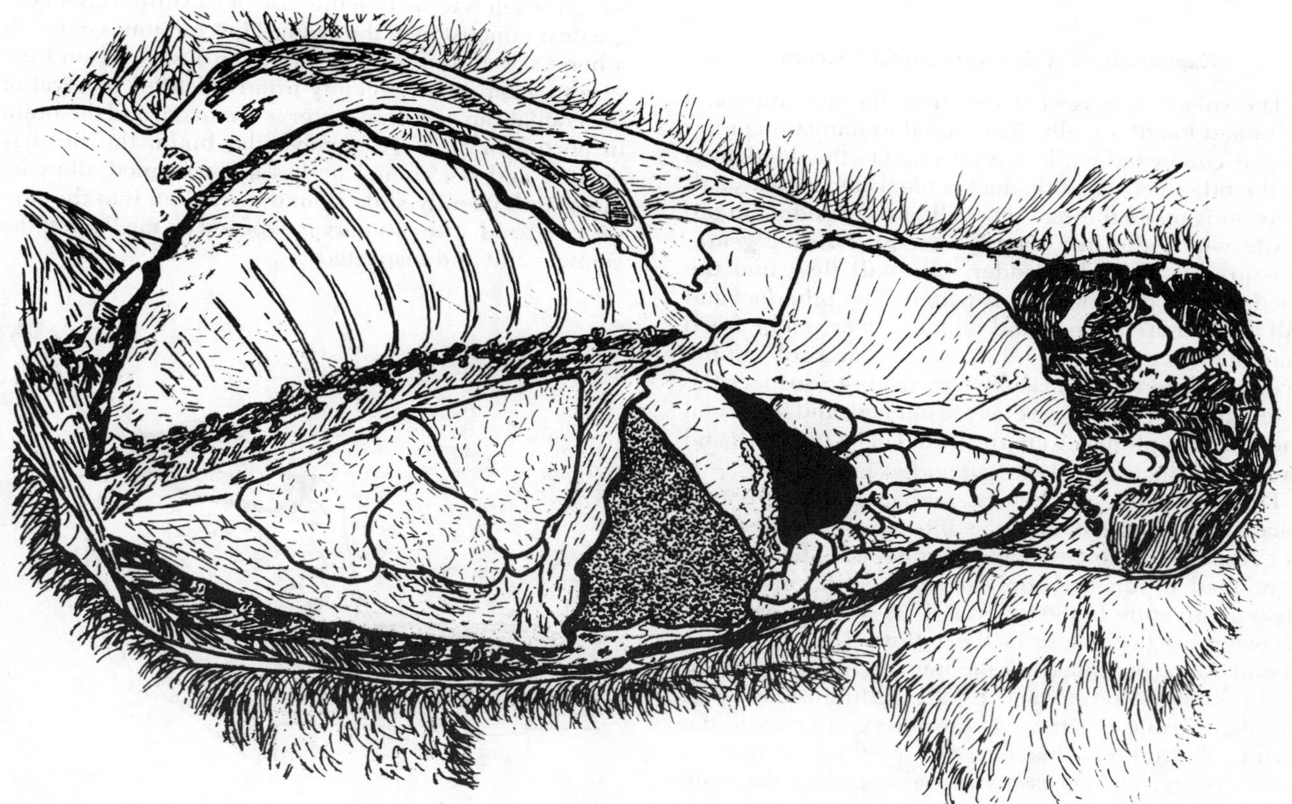

Fig. 7.8. The abdomen and thorax are opened and the flaps reflected to expose the viscera. (The ribs are cut at their sternal and vertebral ends with bone shears).

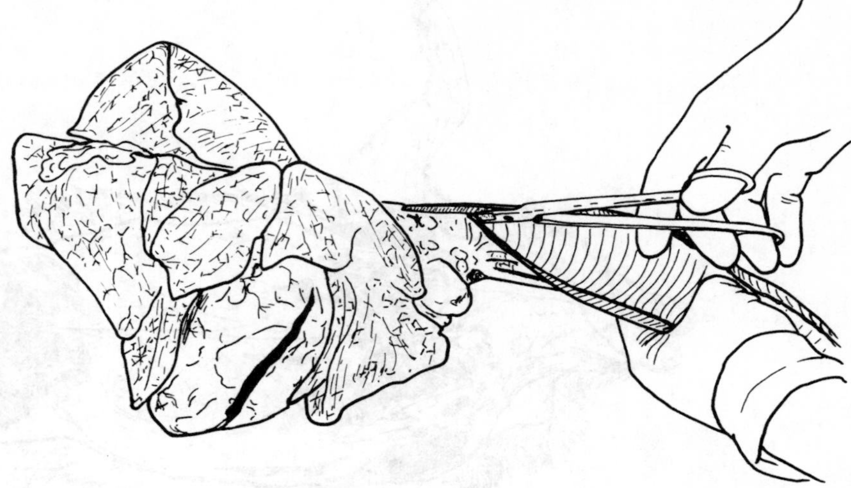

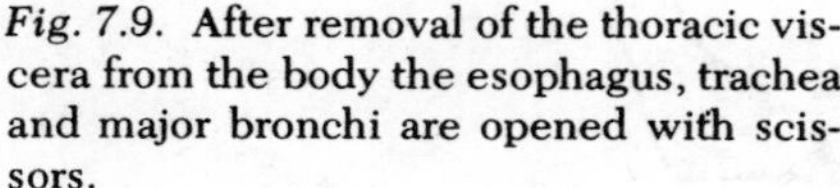

Fig. 7.9. After removal of the thoracic viscera from the body the esophagus, trachea and major bronchi are opened with scissors.

The right atrium is opened, and a U-shaped incision is made through the right atrio-ventricular valve following the inter-ventricular septum to the apex of the heart, then back to the base of the heart, exiting through the pulmonary valve. This produces a flap of the right ventricular wall which can be lifted and rotated to expose the ventricle and the valves. The left side of the heart is opened in a similar manner, the incision beginning in the left atrium, passing through the atrio-ventricular valve to the apex and then back through the aortic valve into the aorta. The pulmonary arteries and thoracic aorta are opened with scissors.

Examination of the Abdominal Viscera

The spleen is dissected free from the omentum and sectioned longitudinally. The initial examination of the liver is conducted while it is attached to the duodenum by the bile duct. The bile duct is identified, and a small incision is made through the wall of the duodenum opposite where the bile duct enters. By exerting *gentle* pressure on the gall bladder, bile will flow into the duodenum if the bile duct is patent. The bile duct and gall bladder are opened and then the liver can be freed from the other viscera. The shape, size, and color of the liver are noted and incisions are made to inspect the parenchyma. The major veins are opened, and the portal and hilar lymph nodes are inspected. The pancreas and pancreatic ducts are identified and examined.

The omentum, mesentery, and mesenteric lymph nodes are examined, and the intestines are dissected free from the mesentery and straightened. The stomach is opened by an incision from the cardia along the greater curvature to the pylorus. This incision can then be extended the length of the intestine. Contents are examined for parasites and the mucosa is inspected.

The kidneys are opened by a longitudinal incision, and the capsule is stripped with forceps to expose the cortex. The ureters, bladder, and urethra are opened with scissors. The accessory sexual organs in the male and the uterus in the female are opened and inspected. The gonads are identified and incised. The amount of perirenal and omental fat should be noted.

Removal and Examination of the Brain and Spinal Cord

Examination of the brain should be a routine part of every necropsy. Failure to do so is often justified because of difficulty in satisfactorily removing this organ; however, application of a small amount of care and common sense make the procedure simple and rapid.

The head is removed from the body by sectioning through the atlanto-occipital joint, the dorsal portion of the cranium is skinned and muscle tissue is removed. When approaching removal of the brain it is well to think of the problem as one of removing a spherical object from a rigid, closely-fitting spherical case. The logical approach is to section the case or calvarium about the greatest dimension of the brain. The cranium is cut with a bone saw in the manner shown in Fig. 7.10, and the resulting cap may be gently pried off. After removal of the cranial cap, the dura mater is removed, and the brain inspected *in situ*. To remove the brain, the head is everted and the cranial nerves are sectioned allowing the brain to gently slide from the cranium into the prosector's hand. The pituitary is exposed on the floor of the cranial vault and inspected.

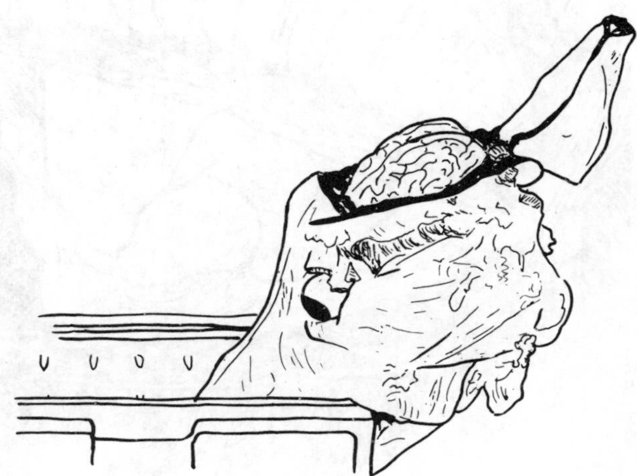

Fig. 7.10. The calvarium is cut in a circular manner beginning at the foramen magnum, and the resulting "cap" is pried off exposing the brain.

The spinal cord should be examined whenever possible; by removal of the dorsal vertebral arches using appropriate sized bone shears (Fig. 7.11) (in large animals one may have to resort to a saw to cut the heavy bone arches).

Examination of the Musculo-Skeletal System

Several components of the musculo-skeletal system have been examined; however, major muscle groups should be incised, and limb joints opened to inspect the synovial fluid, membranes and articular surfaces. At least one long bone, usually the femur, is sectioned longitudinally to allow inspection of epiphyseal plates and medullary bone marrow.

Technique for Ruminants

The procedure for opening the body is the same as used for monogastrics. It is convenient to necropsy ruminants in lateral recumbency with the right side up because of the size of the forestomachs located on the left. The esophagus should be tied routinely prior to sectioning to prevent spillage of fluid rumen content. The alimentary system is removed from the body *en masse* and after examination and removal of the spleen and liver, the forestomachs are separated from the intestine. The forestomachs are spread out in single plane by separating adhesions between the various organs. The rumen is opened by 2 incisions beginning at the cardia and passing to the posterior blind sacs, and the resulting flap is reflected (Fig. 7.12). The other forestomachs can then be opened by a continuous longitudinal incision. The contents are removed, and the mucosa should be rinsed to clear ingesta. The intestinal tract of ruminants is much longer and has a thinner wall than that of carnivores but is handled in the same manner.

Removal of the brain is facilitated in antlered or horned animals if these appendages are removed flush with the skull prior to attempting entry into the cranium.

Small Mammals

Animals the size of rabbits or larger can be conveniently handled by the method outlined previously, but smaller animals such as squirrels and mice are necropsied more easily if some method of immobilization is used. Special devices are available for use with laboratory rodents, but a soft board or sheet of cardboard and 4 stout pins or used hypodermic needles serve equally well (Fig. 7.13). The only other departure is that both sides of the rib cage are severed, and the sternum and attached ribs are removed as a unit.

The collection and preservation of specimens at necropsy is considered in Chapter 32.

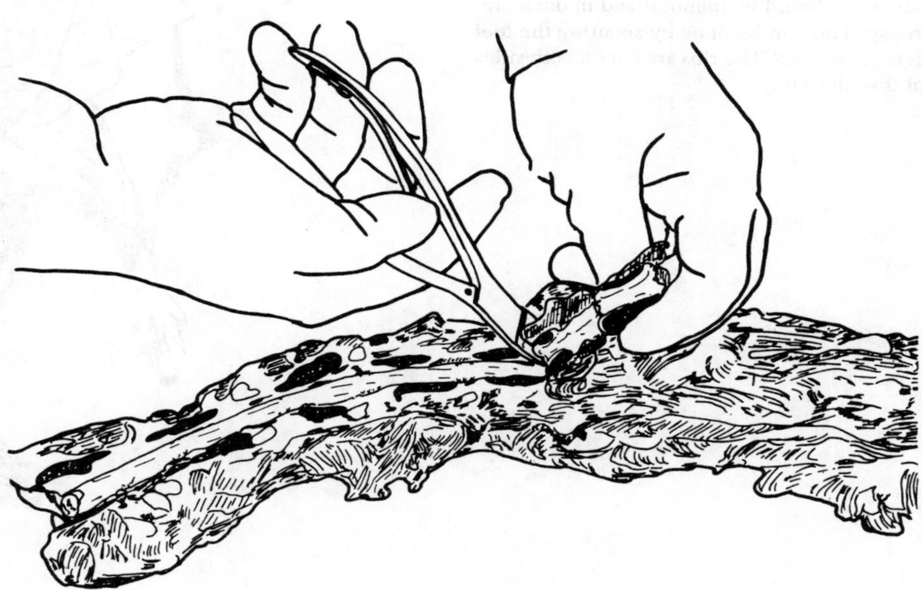

Fig. 7.11. The dorsal arches of the vertebrae are removed with bone shears, exposing the spinal cord for removal.

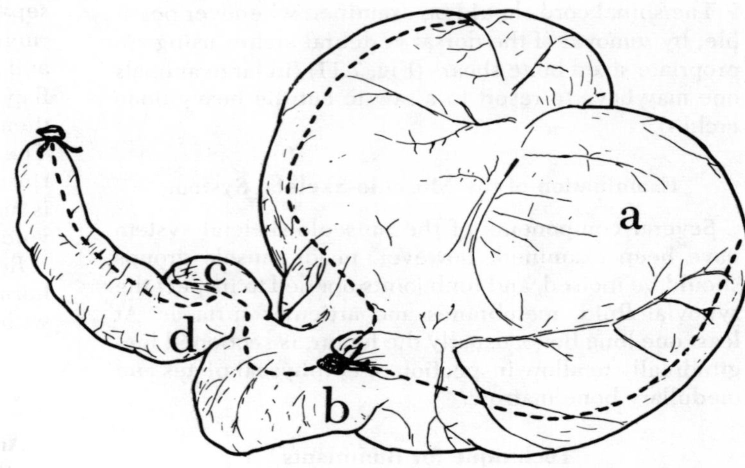

Fig. 7.12. **Method for opening the fore-stomachs of ruminants. The stomachs are separated and laid out flat and incisions are made following the dotted line. (a - rumen, b- reticulum, c - omasum, d- abomasum)**

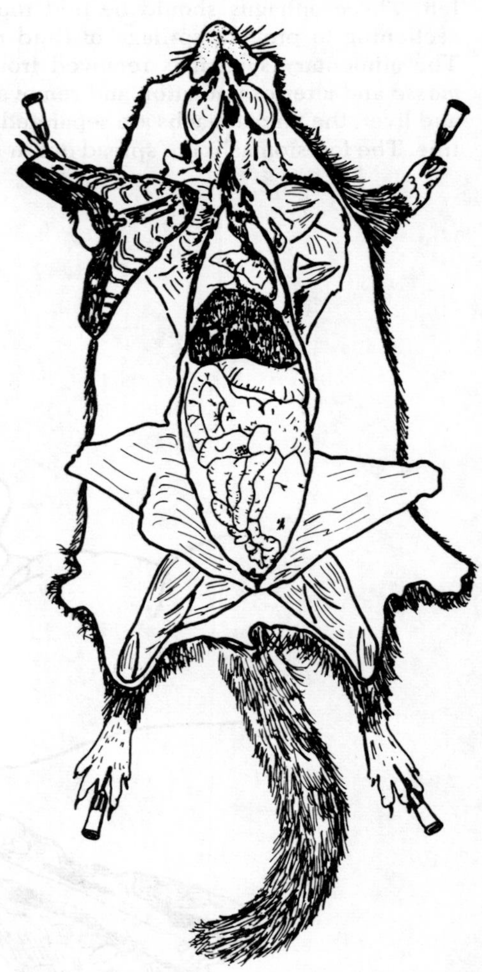

Fig. 7.13. **Small mammals should be immobilized in dorsal recumbency for necropsy. This can be done by securing the feet with pins or hypodermic needles. The ribs are cut on both sides to allow removal of the rib cage.**

Chapter Eight

Physiological Indices in Wildlife Management

ROY L. KIRKPATRICK

Professor of Wildlife Science
Department of Fisheries and Wildlife Sciences
Virginia Polytechnic Institute and State University
Blacksburg, Virginia

INTRODUCTION

It is generally agreed that wildlife management will of necessity become more intensive in the future. As man continues to encroach upon, pollute, and disturb wildlife habitats, it is imperative that we as wildlife scientists and managers "fine tune" our techniques for evaluating the health, condition, and productivity of wildlife populations and habitats. It is no longer sufficient to simply monitor animal numbers as indicators of population and habitat conditions. We need indicators of health, nutritional status, and productivity which alert us to the status of populations and habitats long before detrimental environmental influences become apparent in terms of decreased population size (Kirkpatrick 1975). Only by using these indicators or indices as "predictors" of habitat or environmental suitability, can we truly manage habitats and populations by altering environmental conditions or population size in time to prevent drastic and undesired declines (or increases) in populations.

In the future we will need to know the adequacy or inadequacy of habitats on a seasonal, monthly, or even a weekly basis. Increasingly, research is showing that wildlife population sizes may be directly regulated by environmental conditions at "key" periods of the year. Only by fine tuning our research and basic techniques can we hope to determine what these key periods are and how to monitor them in order to improve management.

Improvements in technology in the industrialized sector of our society will continue at a rapid rate. In many instances this technology will be detrimental rather than beneficial to wildlife habitats and populations. If we, as wildlife managers and scientists, do not improve our technology at an equally rapid rate, then the future of wildlife throughout the world looks bleak indeed.

This chapter attempts to describe and evaluate physiological indices of use or of potential use to wildlife scientists and managers for determining reproductive rates, nutritional condition, and the degree of stress in various wildlife species. Many of these indices are in developmental stages at present and more data (usually of a controlled nature) are needed to assess their applicability and reliability in specific situations. It is recommended that, before using any of the techniques described in this chapter, the reader become thoroughly familiar with their past uses and potential limitations by reading the original papers dealing with that technique. These papers are included in the literature cited.

PHYSIOLOGICAL INDICES OF REPRODUCTION

A fundamental requirement for understanding the population dynamics of a wild species is a knowledge of natality or number of young produced in a given time. This information can be obtained in some instances by livetrapping animals, aging them, and calculating birth dates to determine birth rates at specific times. However, in many instances it is difficult to get good estimates of the number of young entering a population in this manner because mortality of newborn young is often high and the younger age groups are difficult to census or sample. Consequently, estimates of reproductive capacity or attainment in a population are often obtained by examining female reproductive tracts and inferring from structures found there the numbers of young produced, length of breeding seasons, etc. Counts of placental scars, fetuses, and luteal glands (corpora lutea, corpora albicantia, corpora rubra—see Fig. 8.1) can be used to estimate numbers of mammalian young produced.

In both birds and mammals, ovarian follicle counts and measurements can be used to determine if a female is in reproductive condition. In mammals, examination of mammae for milk also is a good "all or none" indicator of reproductive activity, as is crop gland development for birds of the family Columbidae (pigeons, doves).

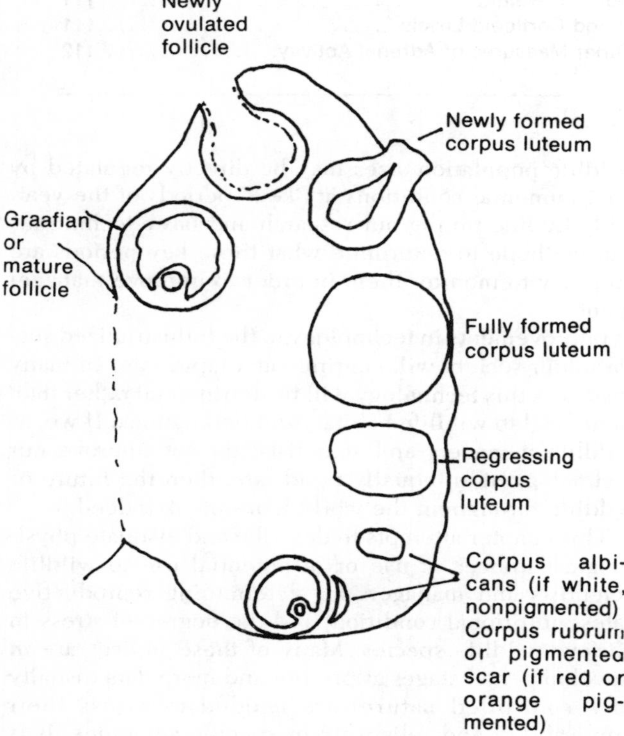

Fig. 8.1. Schematic diagram of an ovary showing the progression of a mature follicle to a corpus luteum to a corpus albicans or corpus rubrum (clockwise).

Measures of male fertility and reproductive development have not received abundant attention in either wild birds or wild mammals. Until recently, weights or sizes of testes and accessory sex organs were our best estimates of male reproductive activity. Spermatozoan counts now offer a more quantitative measure of male reproductive ability.

Methods of determining sex steroid (estrogen, progesterone, and testosterone) levels in the blood also are now available for both sexes of wild birds and mammals. By using one or more of the above physiological indices of reproductive activity, it is now possible to accurately determine breeding seasons, to estimate litter sizes, number of litters produced per female, and to determine what proportion of a population is reproductively active at a given time.

The following pages describe some of the modern physiological techniques for estimating various reproductive characteristics of wild animals.

Luteal Glands

One of the best known and most widely used reproductive indices is that of luteal gland counts. Although they are commonly known as corpora lutea, corpora albicantia, corpora rubra, or "pigmented scars," Mossman and Duke (1973:46) believed that these structures should be called luteal glands since the above names simply refer to various stages of development and regression of the structure formed from the ruptured follicle after ovulation in mammals. The stages of this development and regression are shown diagramatically in Fig. 8.1. The commonly used names of the various stages will be used in this paper for the sake of simplicity and clarity. As seen in Fig. 8.1, a mature ovarian follicle ovulates (i.e., ruptures and releases the ovum) and is transformed into a corpus luteum. The corpus luteum usually is maintained (as a secretory organ producing progesterone) for most of an estrous cycle if the female does not become pregnant or throughout pregnancy if the female does become pregnant. After the estrous cycle or pregnancy is completed the corpus luteum ceases to function and regresses to a corpus albicans or a corpus rubrum (pigmented scar). These latter structures are discernible for varying amounts of time after parturition, depending upon the species.

In general, luteal glands give a rather exact count of the number of ova shed but only an estimate of the number of fetuses or young produced. All luteal glands formed at a given time tend to persist for the same length of time. All formed at the same time behave in the same manner regardless of whether or not the ovum arising from the follicle from which an individual luteal gland was formed is fertilized or not. Thus, if the fertilization rate in a given species is low, or if embryonic or fetal losses are great, luteal gland counts will overestimate the number of young produced.

Luteal gland counts can be made either microscopically or macroscopically. For mammals, the size of cottontail rabbits and larger, macroscopic counts are usually preferred because little preparation of material is required. Cheatum (1949a) first described the macroscopic method for the white-tailed deer, and his paper still stands as a classic in this area. A summarized version of his method follows:

Ovaries are placed in 10% formalin (4% formaldehyde) for preservation and hardening. After at least 24 hours in formalin, they are washed in tapwater and sliced into 1 mm sections along the long axis. The cuts should be made from the side of the ovary furthest from the mesovarium (the ligament holding the ovary *in situ*) towards the mesovarium (Fig. 8.2). If one is careful, the cut can be stopped just before reaching the point of mesovarium attachment to the ovary, and the sliced ovary will remain together with the sections hinged like pages in a book. This is especially useful if the ovary is to be examined again at a later date.

The 2 structures of interest in ovaries of Cervids are the corpora lutea (plural of corpus luteum) of a current pregnancy and the "pigmented scars" or corpora rubra of a previous pregnancy. The corpora lutea are useful for determining the number of ova shed during the estrus at which pregnancy occurred, and usually the number corresponds to the number of fetuses present in the uterus. This is true because fertilization rate is normally quite high and embryonic mortality quite low for the Cervids. For most other mammalian species, only the corpora lutea of pregnancy are of use since the corpora lutea do not leave highly visible "scars" when they regress. Corpora lutea counts have advantages over fetal counts in that they can be made in the early stages of pregnancy whereas fetal counts can be made only during approximately the last two-thirds to three-fourths of pregnancy. Corpora lutea are spherical structures which may or may not be partially hollow. They have a solid, creamy white texture in the deer. Their color varies from yellowish to gray in other species.

Pigmented scars, on the other hand, seem to be reliable estimates of the number of ova shed during the previous pregnancy and persist for approximately 8 months or longer after parturition in deer (Cheatum 1949a). These corpora rubra usually range in color from light yellow to deep brownish orange. They are sometimes grayish in color and often are compressed into triangular and crescent shapes by surrounding follicles and/or new corpora lutea as the latter structures grow.

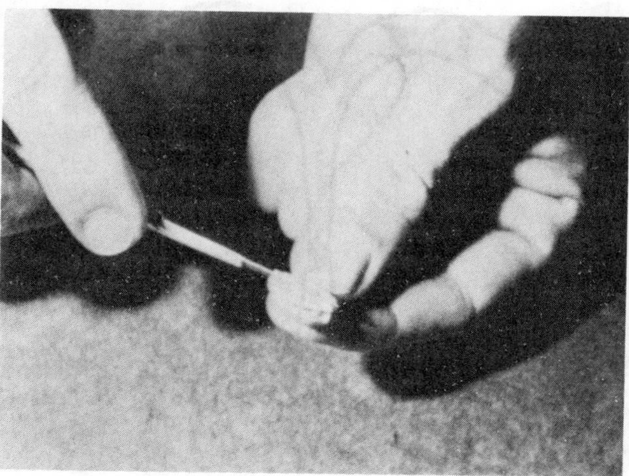

Fig. 8.2. Ovaries are sliced longitudinally into 1 mm sections for counting luteal glands and follicles.

In examining the sliced ovaries for the above structures one must examine both cut surfaces of each slice carefully and "follow" large corpora lutea through the several slices in order to avoid counting the same structure more than once.

Cheatum (1949a) pointed out that errors are possible in making counts because some unruptured follicles also become luteinized (i.e., form corpora lutea). However, he felt that these could be distinguished from corpora lutea of ovulated follicles because of their smaller size and thinner walls. The pigmented scars arising from these luteinized follicles are also much smaller than those arising from corpora lutea of pregnancy.

Further sources of error and possible methods of avoiding these were discussed by Golley (1957). Gibson (1957), Simkin (1965), Teer et al. (1965), Trauger and Haugen (1965), and Mansell (1971) also have commented on the reliability of luteal structures and described methods of differentiating between corpora lutea of estrus and pregnancy and accessory corpora lutea. I strongly recommend that before using this technique, the papers by Cheatum (1949a) and Golley (1957) be read carefully as they take a more conservative approach than the more recent papers in interpreting ovarian structures. In general, I agree with Cheatum's (1949a) original suggestion that "pigmented scar counts" not be made on material collected 8 months beyond parturition in deer.

Corpora lutea counts are reported in the literature for numerous mammalian species. These include beaver (Provost 1962), moose (Simkin 1965), fisher (Wright and Coulter 1967), white-tailed jackrabbit (James and Seabloom 1969), red fox (Oleyar and McGinnes 1974), and cottontail rabbits (Zepp and Kirkpatrick 1976). Provost (1962) also gave an evaluation of ovarian analysis and suggested the use of a new parameter, "parturition frequency," to relate counts of ovarian structures to actual numbers of viable young produced.

Follicle Counts

Although ruptured follicles do not develop into corpora lutea in birds as they do in mammals, the ruptured follicles themselves can be counted and used as an estimate of clutch size. Kabat et al. (1948) described this technique in ring-necked pheasants.

Unruptured ovarian follicle counts can also contribute information on reproductive activity of various wildlife species, especially with respect to determining reproductive status of animals of different ages or at different seasons of the year. Follicle counts can be made macroscopically for birds and the larger mammals but must be made microscopically for the smaller mammals. Techniques for counting tertiary follicles (those with an antrum or fluid-filled cavity) in large mammals are very similar to that described for corpora lutea earlier. If a measure of follicular size is desired, measurements are usually taken at the greatest diameter (Fig. 8.3). Tertiary follicle counts also have been used as measures of reproductive activity in several avian and mammalian species, including band-tailed pigeons (March and Sadleir 1970), mourning doves (Guynn and Scanlon 1973), gray squirrels (Cowles et al. 1977), and white-tailed deer (Kirkpatrick 1974).

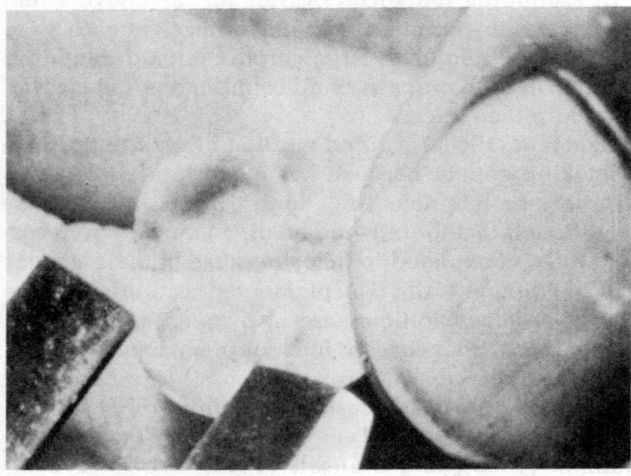

Fig. 8.3. Ovarian follicles and luteal structures are usually measured at their largest diameter and at a right angle to the largest diameter. The 2 diameters are then averaged.

Fetal Counts

Fetal counts or numbers of uterine swellings (Fig. 8.4) are undoubtedly one of the best indices of number of young produced for most mammals. In general, once implantation and organ development in the conceptus occur, there is relatively little *in utero* mortality in most mammals. Also, the mortality which does occur usually takes place early in pregnancy. Fetuses or uterine swellings are visible during only the last two-thirds to three-fourths of pregnancy, however, and this limits their usefulness to that period.

Uterine swelling and large corpora lutea also can be counted in live animals as well as dead by use of the surgical technique of laparotomy. Casida (1960) described the technique in detail for domestic animals, and several wildlife researchers have used it for examining reproductive organs in wild species (small birds, Risser 1971; elk, Follis et al. 1972; cottontail rabbits, Murphy et al. 1973; gray squirrels, Mellace et al. 1973; deer, Scanlon and Lenker 1973). Before conducting laparotomies, it is recommended that a veterinarian be consulted regarding aseptic techniques and current federal and state laws dealing with surgery on experimental animals.

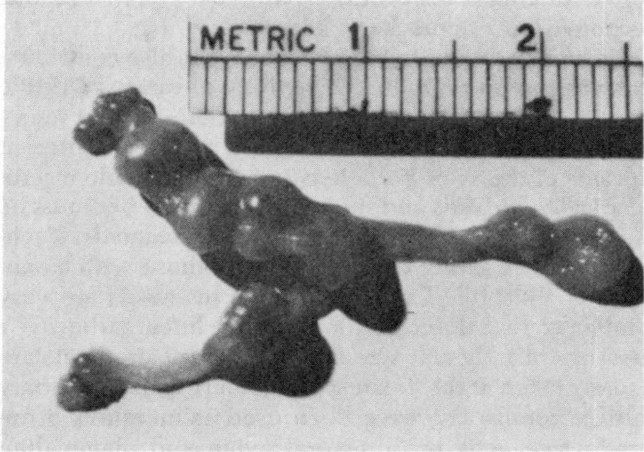

Fig. 8.4. Uterine swellings (fetuses and associated membranes) of a pregnant white-footed mouse. Five swellings are visible in this uterus.

Placental Scars

Placental scars (Fig. 8.5) are pigmented areas of uterine tissue marking sites of previous placental attachment. Their formation has been described by Deno (1937) and Martin et al. (1976).

Placental scars are most prominent in those mammalian species which have an endotheliochorial, hemochorial, or hemoendothelial placenta. In each of these types of placentation there is an erosion of tissue layers of the uterus, and the developing fetus and associated membranes have a more intimate relation to the maternal blood supply than in other types (Gunderson 1976). At parturition the fetus and associated membranes are expelled from the uterus, exposing the underlying layers of tissue. As the new uterine endometrium grows over this wound, stagnant pools of blood apparently become trapped. The hemoglobin in the red blood cells is then degraded to hemosiderin (an iron-containing pigment) by macrophages. The entrapped hemosiderin is visible for a long period as a placental scar.

Placentae of the above types also can be classified as zonary or discoid—referring to the shape of the placenta. Species having these types of placentation belong primarily to the orders Carnivora, Rodentia, Lagomorpha, Insectivora, and Chiroptera.

Placental scars are also most useful in monestrous mammals or those which have only 2 or 3 litters/year and no immediate postpartum estrus. In the smaller rodents which have several litters in rapid succession, often

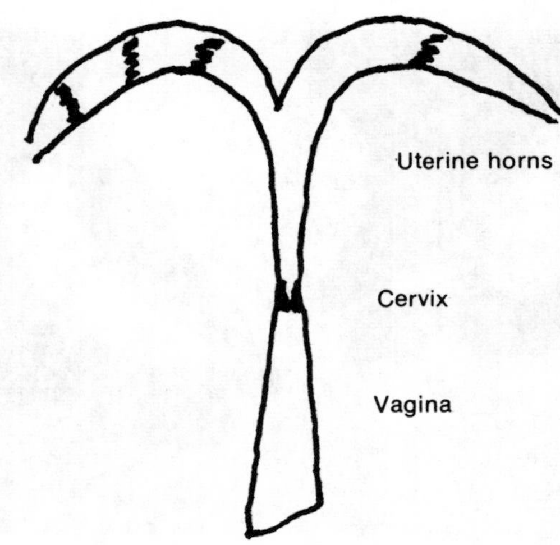

Fig. 8.5. Placental scars appear as darkened bands across uterine wall.

there are problems of separating "sets" of scars (Davis and Emlen 1948, Martin et al. 1976).

In many species, placental scars can be seen easily in fresh or preserved tissue without special treatment. In others they are less distinct and special staining or clearing procedures can make them more visible. The accompanying table (Table 8.1) summarizes information on placental scar counts for several wild species.

In those species in which scars are distinct without special treatment, they usually stand out as darkened spots in the uterus (Fig. 8.5). If the uteri are obtained early enough after parturition there will still be swollen areas about the scars. With increasing time after parturition, however, the scars fade, and it becomes necessary to open the uterine horns longitudinally by inserting one side of a scissors into the uterine lumen and cutting

Table 8.1. Selected references to the use of placental scars as a reproductive index in rodents and carnivores.

Species	Reference	Special techniques	Remarks
ORDER CARNIVORA			
Brown bear	Hensel et al. 1969	—	—
Coyote	Gier 1968	—	—
Red fox	Sheldon 1949	—	—
Gray fox	Oleyar & McGinnes 1974	—	—
Raccoon	Sanderson 1950	—	—
Mink	Elder 1952	—	Scars not visible
Badger	Wright 1966	Cleared in anilin oil, methylsalicylate or benzyl benzoate	Visibility of scars good in cleared tracts; variable in uncleared tracts
Fisher	Wright & Coulter 1967	Cleared in wintergreen oil	Scars disappeared after clearing
Wolverine	Wright & Rausch 1955	Bleached in hydrogen peroxide, dehydrated and cleared in methylsalicylate	Scars not visible in uncleared tracts
ORDER RODENTIA			
Beaver	Henry & Bookhout 1969	Clearing by Orsini's (1962) method	—
	Leege & Williams 1967	—	—
Woodchuck	Ruckel et al. 1976	—	—
Muskrat	Sooter 1946	—	—
Gray squirrel	Nixon et al. 1975	Prussian blue reaction of Humason (1972)	Persist for 1 yr. or less; reliable; could differentiate between 2 breeding periods
	Kirkpatrick et al. 1976a	—	—
Norway rat	Davis & Emlen 1948	—	Counts not reliable valid only as a measure of parity
	Conaway 1955	—	—
Voles	Martin et al. 1976	Examined fresh, fixed and and cleared	Can't separate "sets"; most visible first few weeks in fresh tissue; later on fixing and clearing made scars stand out better
	Rolan & Gier 1967	Stretched uterus on white index card and held to light	Scars believed to persist for 3 mo.; could see up to 3 "sets"

along the length of each horn. The scars then usually appear as darkened, raised bands or discs (depending on the species) in the uterine lumen.

The 2 most common techniques for making placental scars more visible are the "clearing" technique (Orsini 1962, Henry and Bookhout 1969) and the Prussian Blue Reaction (Humason 1972, Nixon et al. 1975) or some variation of these. Since these techniques are quite complex, the reader is referred to the original papers for detailed procedures.

As with all indices, placental scars are only an approximation of the number of young produced. They are, however, a relatively close approximation for most species in which their reliability has been checked. The main source of error arises from the fact that resorptions of fetuses also leave placental scars which are usually indistinguishable from those left by fetuses developing to term (Conaway 1955).

Crop Gland Development

Crop gland development (Fig. 8.6) is a useful index of reproductive activity only in doves and pigeons (family Columbidae). Members of this family nourish their young with a curdlike substance called "crop-milk." This milklike substance is produced by the hypertrophy of the 2 lateral lobes of the crops of both sexes during incubation and the subsequent post-hatching period. The crop-milk is produced by desquamation of the proliferating epithelium of the crop wall (Levi 1969). The crop glands of most pigeons and doves studied show some enlargement between the 9th day of incubation and the 14th day post-hatching (Levi 1969, Mirarchi 1978). The various stages in crop gland development (both macroscopic and microscopic) have been described by March and Sadleir (1970) for the band-tailed pigeon. Their description of macroscopic changes is as follows:

> "Phase I (inactive)—Macroscopically the gland is almost indistinguishable from the general epithelium lining the crop cavity.
>
> Phase II (growth)—Macroscopically the gland is seen as a slightly convoluted ovoid disk about 2 cm in diameter and about 1 cm thick. It is vascular with visible surface blood vessels.
>
> Phase III (active)—During this phase, macroscopic appearance and thickness of the gland are highly variable although the diameter remains the same as in phase II. The surface is extremely convoluted and may appear tesselated. Its color when fresh ranges from pink to pale cream depending on the stage of lipid accumulation. Loose segments of curd may be seen adhering to the surface of the gland or free in the crop lumen. This stage is easily detectable by palpation from the exterior.
>
> Phase IV (lag)—During its decline in activity, the gland's appearance is somewhat difficult to distinguish from the later stages of phase III as loose pieces of curd may still be present. However, it is in a state of attrition and is much redder, less convoluted, and thinner."

If a more objective measure of crop gland development is desired, the weight of the entire crop can be obtained. Guynn and Scanlon (1973) found statistically significant differences in weights of inactive, active and regressing crops in mourning doves, although some overlap in weights was found. The use of crop gland activity has proven quite helpful in determining the proportion of birds which are incubating or rearing young during early fall hunting seasons.

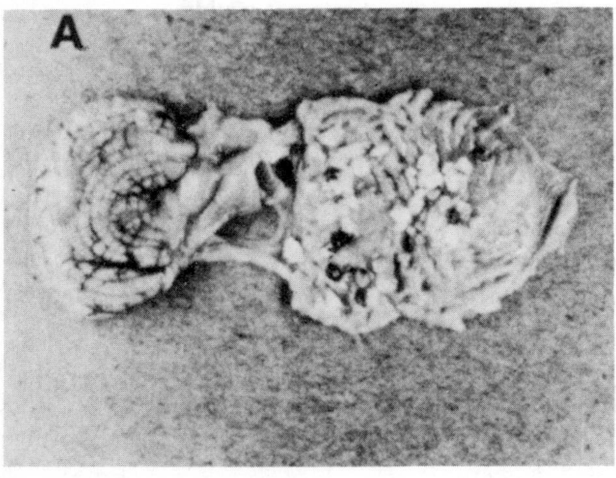

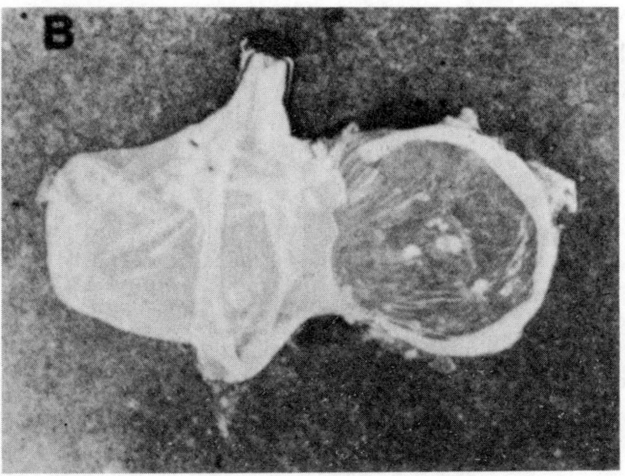

Fig. 8.6. An active (A) and an inactive (B) crop gland from the mourning dove. (Photos by Mirarchi)

Spermatozoan Counts

Spermatozoa in the testes and epididymides are good indicators of reproductive condition and ability in males. Some past studies (James and Seabloom 1969, Kibbe and Kirkpatrick 1971) involved simply cutting the tail of the epididymis, making a sperm smear on a slide and examining the smear under a microscope for presence or absence of motile sperm. However, a relatively rapid technique for estimating total testicular and epididymal spermatozoan reserves has been developed (Amann and Almquist 1961, Amann and Lambiase 1969, Sullivan and Scanlon 1976). Testes or epididymides are homogenized (using a Waring blender or hand held, ground-glass tissue homogenizer) in a physiological saline solution containing 0.01 to 0.05% by volume of Triton X-100 (J. T. Baker Chemical Co., Phillipsburg, N.J.) at a concentration of 1cc/10mg testes weight or 1cc/2mg epididymis weight. Homogenization for 1 minute is usually sufficient if large testes and epididymides (from woodchucks, deer, etc.) are first thoroughly cut into smaller pieces using scissors or scalpel. After homogenization an aliquot is drawn off and a drop is added to both chambers of a standard hemacytometer. After letting the homogenate settle for 2 to 3 minutes, the spermatozoan heads present in the 5 diagonal squares of the 25 medium-sized squares within the large central square are counted. For greater accuracy, 4 counts (2 on each of 2 hemacytometers) are usually made. The concentration of sperm in the homogenate and the testes can then be calculated using the appropriate dilution factors. Counts can be made on either fresh or frozen tissue. Tissue to be frozen should be frozen in a known volume of physiological saline containing Triton X-100. Triton X-100 is a surfactant that prevents foaming of the homogenate during homogenization and allows more accurate counting.

Spermatozoan counts have been used to determine differences in male reproductive activity due to season (Ruckel et al. 1976, Mirarchi et al. 1977a), social stress (Sullivan and Scanlon 1976) and exposure to environmental contaminants (Sanders and Kirkpatrick 1975).

Hormone Levels

The use of sex hormone levels in the blood as reproductive indices is relatively new but may have much future potential. The female sex steroids are progesterone and estrogen. Blood estrogen levels are of quite limited use as an index of reproductive activity for most species since they are high for only a short period of time around estrus.

Progesterone levels have been used by Abler et al. (1976) as indicators of ovulation and puberty in white-tailed deer fawns. Any animal having a blood progestin level of greater then 1 ng/ml was considered to have an active corpus luteum (i.e., to have ovulated). Levels of progestins during the estrous cycle of deer indicated that this was a safe assumption (Kirkpatrick et al. 1976b). Subsequent work (Vogelsang et al. 1977) has shown that progestin levels in deer may also be useful in determining ovulation and fawning rates. Does carrying twin fetuses had approximately twice the blood concentration of progestins throughout pregnancy as those carrying single fawns. Nonpregnant does had progesterone levels which were much lower than those of pregnant does. Harder and Peterle (1974) have also used blood progestins as a measure of corpus luteum function in deer. An element of danger is present in this technique. Wesson et al. (1979b) found relatively high progestin levels in wild female deer immobilized with succinylcholine chloride (a muscle relaxant) during the summer when no corpus luteum was present. It appears from this work that under severe stress (such as immobilization with the muscle relaxant) the adrenal cortex can also secrete large quantities of progesterone. This secretion of progesterone by the adrenal cortex during stress has been shown previously in domestic rats by Butcher (1977). More work on progestins is needed before they can be used with confidence as an index of ovulation or number of young *in utero*.

Blood testosterone levels are another index of gonadal activity in males. Seasonal cycles in testosterone levels have recently been published for several of the Cervidae (McMillin et al. 1974, West and Nordan 1976, Mirarchi et al. 1977b) and the eastern wild turkey (Lisano and Kennamer 1977).

Blood levels of most of these hormones are determined by competitive protein binding assays or radio immunoassays (Diczfalusy 1970). It is beyond the scope of this chapter to describe these techniques in detail. Due to the technical expertise needed to conduct these assays, only those wildlife scientists experienced in this research area should attempt blood hormone determinations. However, those wishing to use this index who do not have the required expertise should probably contract the determinations to laboratories which routinely conduct these assays.

Vaginal Smears

Vaginal smears have limited use in wildlife science and management because they are good indicators of the stage of the estrous cycle for only a few species. The use of vaginal smears as an indicator of stage of the estrous cycle was first described for domestic guinea pigs, rats and mice (Zarrow et al. 1964) and later expanded to dogs and cats (Stabenfeldt and Shille 1977) and several wild species.

The principle involved relies upon changes in the cells in the vaginal epithelium and lumen brought about by changing levels of circulating estrogens and progestins during the estrous cycle. In animals in estrus, the epithelium of the vaginal wall cornifies and sloughs into the uterine lumen. During other phases of the cycle the vaginal smear consists of mixtures of nucleated epithelial cells (from the vaginal wall) and leucocytes. Since the cell types and patterns during the estrous cycle are quite different in different species no attempt will be made to categorize them further here. Vaginal smears can be obtained in several ways. One common method is by vaginal flushing using a medicine dropper and a few drops of water. Other methods involve use of a cotton swab or a thin wire loop for extracting cells from the vagina. Whatever method is used, the cells are spread on a microscope slide and can be examined either in a fresh state or after staining (Zarrow et al. 1964:36). Vaginal smears have been examined with varying degrees of success in deer mice (Clark 1936), pine voles (Kirkpatrick and Valentine 1970), coyotes (Kennelly and Johns 1976), beaver (Doboszynska 1976), and white-footed mice (Sanders and Kirkpatrick 1977) as well as several other wild species. In general, vaginal smears seem to be most reliable in the small spontaneously ovulating rodents and the Canidae.

INDICES OF NUTRITIONAL STATUS

That wildlife population sizes are a function of habitat adequacy is commonly accepted in wildlife management. In a majority of cases it would appear that habitats are important primarily from the standpoint of nutrition. As wildlife management becomes more intense, good measures or indices of nutritional status will be needed to evaluate the adequacy of habitats in supporting a given number of wild animals.

Most of the past work in this area has been on the family Cervidae although limited studies have been conducted in other species. There is much variability in the form and accuracy of indices presently in use. Some can be obtained from the animal only after death (femur fat, kidney fat, etc.) while others can be obtained only from living animals (blood characteristics). Still others can be obtained from either live or dead animals (antler measurements, body measurements, and weights).

Desirable characteristics of a good index of nutritional status have been suggested by both Riney (1955) and LeResche et al. (1974). These can be summarized as follows:

1. It should be sensitive to slight changes in nutritional status.
2. It should be specific in its indications; i.e., capable of indicating energy, mineral, protein, balance, etc.
3. It should involve collection of tissues or measurements easily obtained from both live and dead animals by relatively unskilled personnel.
4. It should measure condition of different age groups and sexes at different times of the year and be little affected by the stress of collection.
5. It should be objective and reproducible.

Fat Stores

Many of the indices of nutritional status (more specifically digestible energy intake) utilize measurements of the various fat stores of the body. Harris (1945) and Riney (1955) have described the order of fat catabolism in animals on a declining nutritional plane as follows: (1) subcutaneous fat over the rump and saddle disappears; (2) abdominal cavity fat is used; and (3) bone marrow fat stores decline. As fat stores are replenished, the opposite order is followed.

FEMUR MARROW FAT

Probably the most widely known and used index of nutritional status is bone marrow fat level. This technique was first described by Cheatum (1949b) and was used to determine if dead white-tailed deer found in the spring in the northern U.S. succumbed to malnutrition. Its use has since been extended to most of the Cervidae as well as several other mammalian species under a variety of conditions. Since marrow fat is believed to be the last fat source depleted in a poorly nourished animal, a low bone marrow fat is indicative of poor nutrition over a relatively long period of time.

Traditionally, the middle third of the femur marrow is used (Fig. 8.7), and the percent fat is determined chemically or estimated visually. Cheatum (1949b) originally suggested rankings of femur marrow based on color and consistency as shown in Table 8.2. Bischoff (1954) suggested reducing the number of marrow color and consistency classes to 4 (white and non-white; solid and gelatinous) and felt that the consistency rating alone would indicate the relative amount of fat present in femur marrow. He believed that a gelatinous marrow alone (regardless of color) indicated poor condition with a high degree of accuracy, whereas no definite conclusion could be made regarding deer condition from a solid marrow. Riney (1955) used still a different criterion (Table 8.2) for red deer in New Zealand.

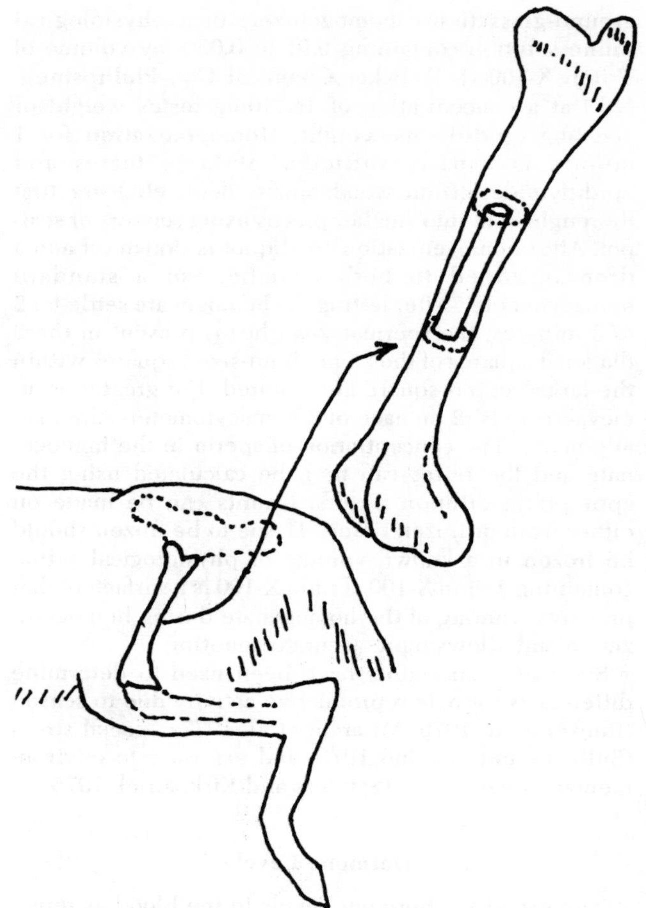

Fig. 8.7. Section of femur marrow normally taken for femur marrow fat analysis. (From Cheatum 1949b)

While useful at one time, all of the above rating schemes are extremely subjective and probably should not be used in modern wildlife management since more objective techniques of determining marrow fat levels are available. The most accurate of these techniques is actual extraction of fat from the marrow by use of a Soxhlet apparatus. Procedures for determination of crude fat have been outlined by Harris (1970:2301), Cullison (1975:16) and Warren and Kirkpatrick (1978). This is a relatively simple procedure which can be conducted easily in most laboratories, or the work can be contracted to a university or other research group.

Two other methods of estimating the amount of fat in marrow have been reported and appear to be fairly objective and accurate. These are the ovendrying method described by Neiland (1970) and the reagent dry technique of Verme and Holland (1973). Neiland (1970) pointed out that bone marrow in caribou

Table 8.2. Subjective rating schemes for bone marrow fat levels.

Author	Category	%Fat[a]	Description
Cheatum (1949b)	1	90	White solid
	2	85	Spotted pink solid
	3	70	Dark pink solid
	4	55	Yellow solid
	5	50	Red solid
	6	1.5	Red gelatinous
	7	1.5	Yellow gelatinous
	Color Rating		
Riney (1955)[b]	0		Reddish or brownish in color
	1		Intermediate between 0 and 2
	2		Light, but with faint wash of color
	3		White, or white streaked with small red vessels
	Texture Rating		
	0		Gelatinous or watery
	1		Slightly greasy
	2		Soft and thickly greasy but not waxy
	3		Firm and waxy

[a]Determined chemically.

[b]Color and texture ratings are added together for an overall score of 0-6.

is a 3-component system comprised of water, fat, and nonfat residue. He felt that the nonfat residue was relatively insignificant in comparison to the proportions of water and fat. He obtained wet weight of a marrow sample and then dried it in an oven at 60–65 C until no further weight loss occurred and reweighed it. The dry weight divided by the wet weight × 100 gives a reliable estimate of percent fat. If maximum accuracy is desired, Neiland (1970) suggested determining nonfat residue levels corresponding to a given dry weight and subtracting this value from that dry weight value to give the corrected percentage of fat.

Verme and Holland (1973) reported an alternative method for obtaining dried weight of the marrow which does not require an oven. In their method, a 2- to 3-g plug of marrow from the middle third of the femur is weighed, macerated to a puttylike consistency, and mixed with 10 ml of a 2:1 solution of chloroform and methanol (Bloor's Reagent). The mixture then is put aside (preferably near a radiator or light bulb or other low heat source) until the chemicals and water contained in the marrow evaporate. The marrow fat dissolves in the chloroform and the water in the methanol. This procedure permits rapid evaporation of the water without spoilage of the marrow sample. The dry weight obtained contains both the fat and nonfat residues. If greater accuracy is desired, a method for correction of the value for nonfat residue similar to that described by Neiland (1970) could be developed.

One more proposed method of estimating femur fat level should be mentioned here, although it appears to be much more subjective than those just described. Greer (1968) used a compressibility test (really another measure of consistency) to estimate femur marrow fat of elk. He took a 7.6 cm section of femur marrow, measured the specimen lying horizontally, and then stood it on end in a specially constructed "jig" and measured its length again. The amount of compression (expressed as a percent) under its own weight was found to be inversely related to the percent fat.

MANDIBULAR CAVITY MARROW FAT

Recently, the use of marrow fat in the mandibular cavity of deer has been proposed as an index of the nutritional status of white-tailed deer (Baker and Lueth 1966, Nichols and Pelton 1972, 1974). The principle is similar to that of femur marrow fat. However, the mandible is much easier to collect from hunter-killed deer (Marshall et al. 1964) than is the femur and often is routinely collected for aging purposes. Baker and Lueth (1966) and Nichols and Pelton (1974) reported that mandibular cavity fat separates into more distinguishable condition classes than does fat from the femur marrow tissues. The portion of the mandible used by Nichols and Pelton (1974) is shown in Fig. 8.8. The reports on mandibular cavity fat have all used percentage fat of the *dry* marrow tissue; however, most investigators measuring femur marrow fat have reported percentage fat of the *wet* marrow tissue. Limited comparisons of the 2 methods of reporting percentage fat have been made, and some papers do not clarify whether wet or dry weight was used. Nichols and Pelton's (1972) report is one of the few which gives percentage fat on both a wet and dry weight basis along with standard deviations of both. If one calculates the coefficient of variations for these data, it appears that much less variability, in relation to size of the mean, is found in samples when they are expressed on a dry weight basis. In essence, then, expressing percentage fat on a dry weight basis may be preferable to expressing it on a wet weight basis. The increased spread between values, when given on a wet weight basis, seems to be more than offset by the increased variability. Although the source of the great variability of wet weight samples is unknown, a major portion probably arises because of dehydration of samples prior to or during initial weighing. If sample values are to be expressed on a wet weight basis, *extreme* caution should be taken to minimize water loss of marrow by sealing samples in small airtight containers immediately upon collection and obtaining wet weights as rapidly as possible after opening.

Although marrow fat levels have been used primarily in large ruminants, recent work indicates that they may be equally useful for evaluating condition in smaller mammals as well. Pelton (1968) and Jacobson et al.

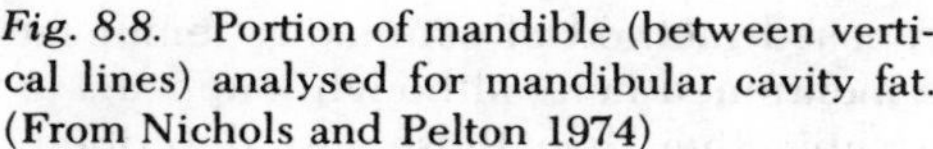

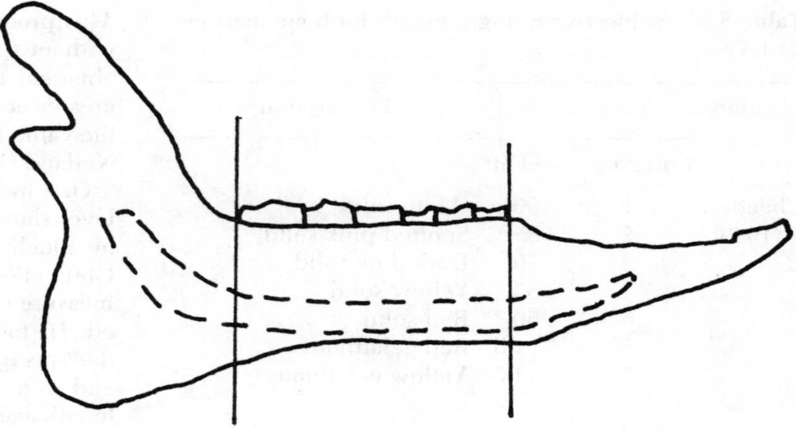

Fig. 8.8. Portion of mandible (between vertical lines) analysed for mandibular cavity fat. (From Nichols and Pelton 1974)

(1978b) have reported differences in percentage fat of femurs and tibias of wild cottontail rabbits as affected by season and sex. Warren and Kirkpatrick (1978) also showed a close relationship between percentage fat of these bones (expressed on a dry weight basis) and known nutritional intake in cottontails.

Bamford (1970) reported that femur marrow fat (expressed on a percentage dry weight basis) was a good indicator of total fat reserves in the brush-tailed possum when fat reserves were low.

KIDNEY FAT INDEX

Another fat index commonly used is the kidney fat index (KFI) developed by Riney (1955) in red deer. The kidney fat index is obtained by removing the kidney and its surrounding fat from the abdominal cavity. The fat is cut at both ends of the kidney perpendicular to the main kidney axis (Fig. 8.9), and the tissue which does not remain affixed to the kidney is discarded. The ratio of the weight of the remaining fat to the weight of the kidney is the kidney fat index. Riney (1955) believed that the KFI was the most satisfactory index of several techniques tested in New Zealand red deer. He believed KFI measured the nutritional status in all seasons, enabled different sized animals to be compared on a uniform basis, and permitted valid measurements over a wide range of environmental conditions. However, Batcheler and Clarke (1970) and Dauphine (1975) reported that kidney weights of red deer and caribou fluctuated seasonally; and, thus, KFI distorts the true seasonal changes in fatness by displacing the measure of maximum fatness from late autumn–early winter towards mid-winter. Flux (1971) did not agree with Batcheler and Clarke's interpretation and felt that KFI was a valid measure of fat reserves in both red deer and hares. Dauphine (1975) suggested that there is little justification for using KFI in place of perirenal fat (perirenal fat being that portion of fat left with the kidney in the KFI) if animals can be grouped by ages for comparison. He felt that grouping by age effectively corrected for gross differences in body size (in caribou, at least) without risk of introducing a seasonal variable.

Without doubt, the kidney fat index or the measured perirenal fat alone measures condition over a wide range since the amount of fat found attached to the kidney area is relatively large and is used during intermediate stages of condition as opposed to marrow fat which is used last or in the poorer stages of condition.

Ransom (1965) suggested using a combination of the kidney fat index and femur marrow fat to measure condition over a very wide range in white-tailed deer. His data indicate that it is best to use KFI down to a value of 30 and then shift to femur marrow fat since marrow fat seemed to begin to decline at this level of KFI.

Smith (1970) reported that KFI was the most satisfactory index of several techniques he tested for appraising condition of several East African ungulates. However, Bamford (1970) found that the perirenal fat was not discrete in the brush-tailed possum; and, therefore, KFI

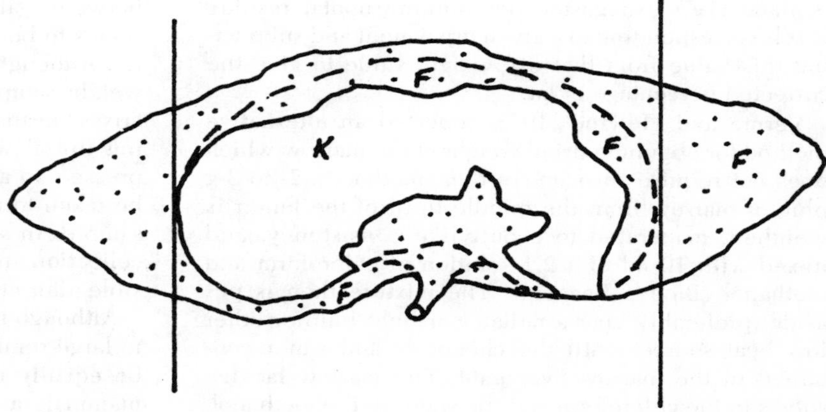

Fig. 8.9. Diagram showing position of cuts (vertical lines) for obtaining kidney fat index. (Clear = kidney tissue, K; dotted = fatty tissue, F.) (From Riney 1955)

was not a suitable index in that species. In cottontail rabbits, Jacobson et al. (1978b) indicated that both KFI and total loin fat (the total fat store surrounding the kidney) were suitable indices for determining condition on a seasonal basis.

In summary, the kidney fat store seems to be a good measure of nutritional status over a relatively wide range of conditions. The exact method of utilizing this store as an index (KFI, perirenal fat, total loin fat) should depend upon the species being studied and the environmental variables of interest. It appears that KFI may not be suitable for evaluating seasonal changes in fat stores because of the seasonal changes in kidney weights in some species.

OTHER FAT INDICES

Several other fat stores have been used as indices of nutritional status or condition, but most either lack objectivity or require elaborate equipment and/or large amounts of time. Riney (1955) used an abdominal fat rating scheme in which the amount of fat was given a score of 0 to 3 on each of the following 3 organs: stomach, intestines, and kidneys. The scores were then added for each animal to give the final abdominal fat rating. Riney (1955) considered this to be a good index but not as good as KFI. He felt that KFI was more objective and applicable over a wider range.

Bear (1971) actually weighed total visceral fat (including mesenteric and kidney fat) in pronghorns and obtained a visceral fat index by dividing the visceral fat weight (grams) by the eviscerated carcass weight (kilograms). This index showed similar seasonal trends to the KFI. Smith (1970) reported that a visual estimate of abdominal fat was an adequate index of condition of East African ungulates also. Bamford (1970), in estimating fat reserves in the brush-tailed possum, found that the mesogastric fat (fat deposited in the mesentary suspending the stomach and spleen) depot was more discrete than that of the kidney. He felt that a mesogastric fat index ($1000 \times$ wt. of mesogastric fat $\div$ body length $^{2.8}$) was the best and most objective measure of fat reserves in this species.

Woodall (1978) reported the amount of fat deposited in the greater omentum of red-billed teal correlated well with total body fat and was a good index of condition in that species.

Other fat indices which have been used on a limited basis in ungulates are backfat depth (Riney 1955, Bear 1971, Dauphine 1971, Anderson et al. 1972), thoracic or brisket fat depth (Bear 1971), and percent leg fat (Smith 1970). These indices seem to measure condition only in the upper ranges and are fairly subjective. Anderson et al. (1972) also used carcass density and percentage carcass fat (which required determination of carcass density for calculation) in estimating fat reserves in mule deer. They felt that carcass density was a good index but that percentage carcass fat (as calculated in their study) was too variable.

Whole body fat has been used as an index of condition of nutritional status primarily in small mammals (Batzli and Pitelka 1971, Fleharty et al. 1973, Cengel et al. 1978) and small birds (Odum and Connell 1956, West and Meng 1968). In most of these studies stomach and intestines are removed, the mesenteric fat is stripped and returned to the body cavity; and the carcasses are minced, dried (either in an oven or freeze dryer), and analyzed for total fat using the Soxhlet apparatus as described earlier in this chapter. Differences between sexes, seasons, and areas have been demonstrated in small mammals and between various stages of migration in birds.

Skeletal Measurements and Weights

Various skeletal measurements, body weights, and their associated ratios have been used by several investigators as indices of growth, condition, and nutritional status, again primarily in the Cervidae. Bandy et al. (1956) predicted body weights from both heart girth measurements and hind foot length and then compared the ratio of the 2 to estimate recent nutritional status of Columbian black-tailed deer. They reasoned that hind foot length, once attained, is not affected as much as is heart girth by nutritional levels. If the ratio of body weight estimated from heart girth to body weight estimated from hind foot length was less than 1, the animal was supposedly in poor condition; if greater than 1, in very good condition. Klein (1964) used femur/hind foot ratio to compare long-term nutritional status of 2 populations of Sitka black-tailed deer. This index is based on the fact that the growth of the metatarsals (which comprise most of the length of the hind foot) is relatively more complete at birth than that of the femur. Thus, the ratio of the 2 in an adult deer can indicate the amount of skeletal growth occurring over the lifetime of an animal and hence the relative long-term nutritional regime of the animal. A low femur/hind foot ratio would be indicative of poor nutrition, whereas a high ratio would be expected in animals on better diets. McEwan and Wood (1966), comparing captive and wild-reared caribou, suggested that body weight/hind foot ratio was a good index of growth rate and long-term nutritional status in this species. Bailey (1968a) calculated the following formula for computing an index to physical condition in cottontail rabbits based on weight and length relationships in Illinois.

$$CI = (W\text{-}16)L^3$$

where CI = condition index,
W = weight in grams
L = length in decimeters

Any animal having a CI greater than 5.48 in his study was heavier than average for its length class.

Body weight and heart girth measurements in red deer were evaluated by Riney (1955). He reported high correlations between body weight and heart girth as have others (Smart et al. 1973, Urbston et al. 1976). He concluded from his work and from a review of the literature that both of these measures were only gross indicators of total fat reserves. Anderson et al. (1972), however, concluded that eviscerated carcass weight (whole body weight minus all fat within the body cavity and all viscera except the esophagus and trachea) was a good index of condition in female mule deer but not in males.

Antler beam diameters also are often used as indices to habitat conditions (Severinghaus et al. 1950, Riney 1955). Since antlers are growing primarily from spring through summer for most Cervidae, this index is most useful in evaluating spring and summer range conditions. Antler beam diameters can be affected by many nutritional factors, thus making differences between areas difficult to interpret. Minerals such as calcium and phosphorus have a marked effect on antler growth as do both energy and protein intake (Magruder et al. 1957). Antler measurements are not a very satisfactory index of nutritional status because they can be influenced by so many different factors, are present only on males of most Cervidae, and are seasonally limited in their indications.

Blood Characteristics

Numerous blood characteristics have been investigated and used as indices of the current nutritional status of wild animals. These have been recently reviewed in some detail by LeResche et al. (1974) and Seal (1977). Only those which show the most promise for applicability at present will be described here.

Blood urea nitrogen (BUN) is undoubtedly one of the most promising indices of nutritional status tested thus far (LeResche et al. 1974). BUN is relatively unaffected by the stress of handling or immobilization with drugs in the Cervidae (Franzmann 1972, Seal et al. 1972, Wesson et al. 1979a). BUN levels are a good indicator of protein intake, being directly related to protein ingested so long as energy intake is constant and above maintenance level (Kirkpatrick et al. 1975). However, high dietary energy levels depress BUN in white-tailed deer (Kirkpatrick et al. 1975) and domestic steers (Preston et al. 1961). This has been attributed to a more efficient utilization of protein by rumen microbes, with a subsequent reduction in ammonia production and urea formation when energy intake is high. Also, when energy levels drop below maintenance levels, BUN may rise as a result of tissue catabolism; and this, too, complicates the use of this indicator. It is likely that some index of energy intake will be needed along with BUN in order to assure proper interpretation to all instances.

Although several blood indices of energy nutrition have been studied, none seems to have the reliability that BUN has for protein nutrition. Serum cholesterol levels show some promise as an index to energy intake. The greatest problem with cholesterol is that it is influenced by stress of handling, etc. (Franzmann 1972). However, Coblentz (1975) showed seasonal changes in cholesterol levels in white-tailed deer which he believed were related to nutritional status. Vogelsang (1977) has demonstrated differences in blood cholesterol levels due to differences in energy intake in both captive and wild white-tailed deer. Serum nonesterified fatty acids were found by Seal (1977) to be negatively related to energy intake and may also be a good candidate for an energy nutrition index. More details of studies described by Seal (1977) can be found in Seal and Hoskinson (1978) and Seal et al. (1978a,b).

BUN and cholesterol have also been tested as nutritional indices in cottontail rabbits. Warren and Kirkpatrick (1978) found no difference in cholesterol levels in rabbits maintained on 2 nutritional levels. BUN, however, was higher in animals on restricted diets. They attributed this to tissue catabolism since the animals on these diets were losing weight rapidly. It also appears the BUN may be affected more by stressors in cottontails than in ruminants. Jacobson et al. (1978a) found significantly higher BUN levels in rabbits confined in box traps than in shot rabbits. Jacobson et al. (1978b), however, also demonstrated distinct seasonal differences in BUN's of shot cottontails which were believed to be related to either differences in parasite load or nutritional intake.

A major problem in using blood characteristics as indices of nutritional status has been the influence of stress of collection. Most blood characteristics are influenced markedly by all types of stressors; and, hence, changes in these characteristics due to handling, immobilization with drugs, shooting, etc. (while not fully understood at present) often override the influence of nutrition. The effects of the above variables on several blood characteristics have been studied and discussed by Wesson et al. (1979a,b,c).

A word of caution is in order for those wishing to use blood characteristics as indices. Many blood characteristics have daily rhythms which are not well understood and most can be influenced by methods of collection. Hence, it is extremely important that all blood samples be taken and handled as uniformly as possible. This includes making collections at approximately the same time of day and collecting and storing samples on ice as quickly as possible after an animal is shot or restrained.

Gastro-intestinal Tract Analysis

Chemical composition of rumen contents of ungulates is another method of habitat assessment. Proximate analysis (determination of crude fiber, crude fat, crude protein, ash, water, and nitrogen-free extract; Cullison 1975) of rumen contents has been used to evaluate range conditions by Klein (1962), Kirkpatrick et al. (1969), and Skeen (1974). Although foodstuffs do undergo changes in the rumen and protein content of rumen material is higher than that of the forages consumed (due to presence of microbial protein and nitrogen recycling), these workers showed that proximate analysis could reflect changes in habitat between areas, seasons, and years. Brüggemann et al. (1968) discussed the uses and limitations of various types of rumen content analyses for assessing nutritional status in ungulates. Besides proximate analysis, these include the Van Soest method of partitioning cell contents and cell wall constituents (Cullison 1975) and determination of molar proportions of rumen volatile fatty acids (Short et al. 1966).

Brüggemann et al. (1968) also suggested that analyses of digesta from different parts of the digestive tract could be used to determine digestibility of foodstuffs. Lignin, which is relatively indigestible (10–15%) in ruminants, less in monogastric species), can be used as a tracer substance for equating a given amount of dry matter in the stomach to a given amount of dry matter in the feces. Gross energies are determined for the equivalent amounts of dry matter in the stomach and in the feces and the difference between the 2 is an estimate of digestible energy. Noffsinger (1976) used this technique successfully for determining digestible energy content of foods consumed by pine voles in different seasons and habitats. This technique may have future potential for use in detailed studies on digestibility of wild animals in natural habitats.

Other Nutritional Indices

Several other measurements have been used or suggested as indices of nutritional status and habitat condition in wild animals. These include sulfur content of hair, ovulation rate, fawning rate, etc.

Sulfur content of hair has been cursorily investigated by Sanders (1971) as an index of habitat quality but results were inconclusive. The use of reproductive rates to evaluate habitat, like whole body weight, lacks desired sensitivity and accuracy and also requires a large sample size. Added to this is the unknown influence of early nutritional history on reproduction in later life.

The Southeastern Cooperative Wildlife Disease Study at the University of Georgia has recently developed an index relating deer populations to carrying capacity by use of abomasal parasite counts (Eve and Kellogg 1977). The basis for this index is that abomasal parasite counts increase as the deer population approaches carrying capacity.

Ozoga and Verme (1978) presented evidence that thymus gland weights may be useful as a nutritional status indicator in deer.

The use of physiological indices in evaluation of nutritional status will undoubtedly increase as wild animals are managed more intensively in selected areas. Emphasis thus far has centered on use of only 1 characteristic at a time as an indicator. In the final analysis it will probably be necessary to measure several characteristics simultaneously in order to delineate nutritional conditions accurately. More research is warranted in this area.

INDICES OF STRESS

Considerable attention has been given in recent years to the concept that "stress" plays an important role in regulating many wildlife populations. *Stress*, according to Selye (1976:15), is the nonspecific response of the body to any demand. A slightly expanded definition is those nonspecific changes in an organism caused by emotional or physical disturbance. The nonspecific changes most often associated with stress are increased adrenal activity (increased epinephrine and corticoid secretion). However, there are many more associated changes. A *stressor* is any stimulus which elicits stress. Typical stressors are pain, fear, cold, blood loss, anoxia, exposure to a foreign substance (chemical), or foreign material (bacteria, etc.), emotional tension, and a variety of additional alarming stimuli. Stressors most often of concern in wildlife populations are those of intraspecific competition and exposure to environmental contaminants.

A good review of the role of the adrenal in the stress response and various indices of stress has been presented by Christian (1963). The reader is referred to this paper for a more complete explanation of stress and adrenal physiology which is beyond the scope of this chapter. Only a few of the most used indices of stress will be discussed here.

Adrenal Weight

Adrenal gland weight (usually paired weight) is probably the most used index of stress. The adrenal is really 2 glands in 1 being made up of an inner medulla (which is neural tissue and secretes epinephrine and norepinephrine) and an outer cortex (which secretes several corticosteroid hormones). The increase in adrenal weight which occurs in many species after a *prolonged* period of exposure to a stressor is due primarily to an enlargement of the adrenal cortex. Short-term exposure to stressors usually does not increase adrenal weights.

Good correlation between adrenal weight and secretory activity has been shown by Bronson and Eleftheriou (1964) and Adams and Hane (1972). Adrenal weights can be obtained easily in both laboratory and field studies and on animals of all sizes. Weights may be taken on fresh or fixed material (after thorough removal of adhering tissues). It is preferable to use fixed materials when dealing with animals the size of mice due to problems in cleaning and rapid dehydration with the very small adrenals.

For data analysis, animals should be grouped by age, sex, and reproductive status if at all possible. Relative weights (mg adrenal weight/100g body weight) are often used, but probably can and should be avoided if animals are grouped as above. Christian (1963) has correctly pointed out that this procedure is arbitrary and usually overcorrects for lighter and undercorrects for heavier animals. A covariance analysis is a more appropriate way to adjust adrenal weights for body weight or length.

It is unwise to make *any* adjustment if the dependent variable (body weight or length in the above example) is affected by experimental treatment (Steel and Torrie 1960:308). The primary function of adjusting an independent variable for a dependent variable is to reduce the error variance. If the dependent variable is influenced by experimental treatment and one adjusts for it, one takes the risk of improperly interpreting the results. For example, if adrenal weights are adjusted for body weights, either by covariance analysis or by a simple adrenal wt/100g body wt ratio, and body weights are affected by experimental treatment, then one can show a difference in relative or adjusted adrenal weights when there was no change in adrenal weight and activity but rather only a change in body weight. This statistical axiom has unfortunately been ignored in many papers and many have presented erroneous pictures of adrenal changes. I suggest that a statistician be consulted if it is believed that adjustments for body weight or size are needed.

Blood Corticoid Levels

Determination of adrenocorticoid levels in the blood is also a good index of adrenal secretory function and, hence, stress. However, blood samples must be taken quickly or corticoid levels will reflect the stress due to handling rather than that due to other causes. Adrenocorticoids (like other steroid hormones) can be determined by competitive protein binding assays (Murphy 1964, 1967). These assays have been used to determine the influence of environmental contaminants

(Sanders and Kirkpatrick 1975), season (Whatley et al. 1977, Jacobson et al. 1978b) and immobilizing drugs (Wesson 1979c) on adrenal activity of wild species.

Other Measures of Adrenal Activity

Numerous other indices of adrenal activity were described by Christian (1963). Adrenal ascorbic acid and adrenal cholesterol levels are both inversely related to adrenal secretory activity. Histological sectioning of the adrenal cortex and measurement of the various cortical zones is also often used in conjunction with adrenal weight. Lymphatic organ involution is also a characteristic of high adrenal secretory activity as is a depression of eosinophil levels.

Chapter Nine

Procedures for Food-Habits Analyses

LEROY J. KORSCHGEN[1]

Senior Wildlife Research Biologist
Wildlife Research Section
Missouri Department of Conservation
Columbia, Missouri

GENERAL PRINCIPLES

History and Importance

The exact beginning of wildlife food-habits studies is obscure, but it is likely that prehistoric hunters employed a knowledge of the feeding habits of wild animals as an aid in capturing their daily sustenance. The scientific study of wildlife foods and feeding habits, however, is of comparatively recent origin. Field observations of what animals fed upon, where, and when, have been recorded and reported through the centuries and evolved into our present-day knowledge of food habits with its associated field and laboratory methods.

Kalmbach (1934) reviewed the early history of stomach analysis and credited Prof. S. A. Forbes as the founder of modern food-habits study because of his 1880 publication on the food of Illinois birds. Federal recognition of food-habits studies occurred in 1885 when Congress authorized the Section of Economic Ornithology in the Division of Entomology, U.S. Department of Agriculture, "for the promotion of economic ornithology, or the study of interrelation of birds and agriculture, an investigation of the food, habits, and migration in relation to both insects and plants and publishing reports thereon" (McAtee 1933).

Many meaningful food-habits analyses were performed by professional biologists prior to official recognition of the subject. Results appeared in reports by Warren (1890), Fisher (1894), Beal (1895, 1897), and Beal and Judd (1898). Additional pioneering data were published by Judd (1903, 1905a, 1905b), Oberholser (1906), McAtee (1908, 1911), and Beal (1911). Results often were derived by both field and laboratory methods.

Early studies were exclusively of birds, largely nongame birds, and particularly of the economic importance of their feeding habits upon agricultural crops, poultry and livestock. Later emphasis was placed on food studies of game species, particularly waterfowl and upland game birds, but included fur, game, and predatory mammals. Greatest activity in food-habits research occurred during the decade from the early 1930's to early 1940's. Technicians were trained or self-taught by experience, techniques were developed, reference collections expanded, and the quality and quantity of wildlife foods information was greatly improved. Kalmbach (1934) emphasized the importance of stomach analysis for directly solving certain practical problems in wildlife management.

Improved facilities and equipment became available with the opening in 1940 of the Food Habits Laboratory at the Patuxent Wildlife Research Refuge, Laurel, Maryland. The new laboratory shared the work load with a western counterpart at Denver, Colorado. Sufficient funds were provided for many significant studies destined to affect wildlife management across the nation.

[1]The extensive use of reference materials presented by Martin (1949 and 1960) are gratefully acknowledged.

It is regrettable that in 1942 the caustic comment was made in Congress that "every small boy knows what a robin eats; it eats angleworms." This illogical remark was advanced as a reason for the termination of formal food-habits studies by the Fish and Wildlife Service (Kalmbach 1954). Legislators have failed for more than 3 decades to appropriate funds for this important phase of wildlife management. These facts are not generally known by many persons who look to the Fish and Wildlife Service as a source of factual information on the foods and economics of wildlife. Fortunately, the 1942 budgetary restrictions of Congress did not totally eliminate food-habits research and thus its contribution to the management of game and other wildlife. Some of the early work of the Service is summarized in Martin et al. (1951). Many state conservation departments and educational institutions have continued studies of wildlife foods, often with less well-equipped and staffed laboratories than were previously available.

Wildlife food-habits investigations have lost none of their significance within the scope of wildlife research, but rather have become more important through new applications. Information needed for modern wildlife management often is obtained only through properly designed and carefully executed food-habits studies. Programs of the Northern Prairie Wildlife Research Center, Jamestown, North Dakota, have recognized the importance of this subject in studies of waterfowl and predator ecology since its opening in 1964.

Purposes and Types of Study

The primary purpose of food-habits investigations is to learn which foods are utilized by wild animals, and how, when, and where such foods are obtained. Depending upon objectives and methods, these investigations are classified basically as either "natural history" or "management" studies.

Natural history food-habits investigations are conducted to determine the foods and feeding habits of all kinds of animals. These studies are time-consuming and investigators require a considerable amount of technical information to identify properly the many biological organisms. Analyses must be meticulously performed to produce complete lists of all foods, irrespective of quantities present. Counts of specific food items, percentage of each in the sample, and other measurements normally are taken. In the results are revealed the important foods of an animal species by bulk and frequency of occurrence, and also the number or bulk of items taken for a single meal. Most of the early food-habits studies were natural-history investigations to determine beneficial or harmful feeding habits of a species, the impact of birds upon insect populations, or predator-prey relationships.

Management food-habits studies provide practical and immediately useful information for management of a particular species and occasionally provide aids to law enforcement. Management studies include obtaining information on the principal or preferred foods of game birds and mammals, assessing damage to crops by wildlife, observing predation upon managed species, observing wildlife selection for and utilization of food-plot plants, and the detection of baiting practices to lure animals for hunting. Recently, management-oriented studies have provided bases for more sophisticated investigations of seasonal variability and availability of important foods, incidence of disease as related to food supplies, population dynamics as related to nutritional factors such as nutritive quality of foods, dietary influences upon reproduction and growth, and establishment or maintenance of game populations. Studies of metabolism, energetics, and pesticide-wildlife relationships are served by results from food-habits examinations.

Food habits analyses techniques vary with objectives. Rough management-oriented food-habits studies often may be simplified by the practical short cuts suggested by Davison (1940) for quail and doves, by Sperry (1941) for field examination of coyote stomachs, and by Korschgen (1962a) for laboratory examination of deer stomach contents. The foods present in greatest quantity seem to be of greatest significance to management. All foods should be identified during analyses, however, and complete listing kept in files of original data.

Food-habits studies include coordinated field and laboratory work. Precise, long-term knowledge of the ecology of a study area is desirable and survey-type information on relative food supplies provides a basis for laboratory analyses. Results from laboratory studies cannot be adequately interpreted without correlating them with field conditions (Kalmbach 1934, Cottam 1936, Davison and Hamor 1960). Knowledge of the availability of a food is essential in order to rate properly the importance of that food. It also aids in evaluation of the effects of one animal population upon another, and of the economics of wildlife feeding as related to other interests of man.

Sampling

The quality of food-habits data is dependent upon quantity and quality of the sample. Precision in the techniques of analysis has little meaning unless an adequate number of samples are collected to show local, seasonal, or annual changes in diets. Adequate sampling is just as important for studies with limited objectives. Inadequate samples often prompt misleading conclusions (Errington 1932:77, Hartley 1948:365–366).

Sample size requirements will vary with different species of wildlife, scope and objectives of study, diversity in habitat, and kind of material available for analyses. Statistical consideration normal to most other situations apply (Cochran 1977). As an example, because of greater variability a greater number of samples will usually be needed to show year-round versus seasonally important foods, state-wide versus regional wildlife feeding habits, or foods of far-ranging versus sedentary species. Generally the number of stomach samples from big game will be fewer than the number needed for game birds, predatory mammals, or birds of prey.

Sampling needs are difficult to establish prior to the investigation, but must be determined by noting the extent of changes that occur when additional units are analyzed and added during the study. Three criteria have been used to judge the extent of these changes with increased samples: (1) uniformity of volumetric percentages, (2) the rate of appearance of important new food items, and (3) uniform occurrence percentages of individual food items. The sample size is large enough when new samples add no significant new information to that obtained from previous samples.

Davison (1940) showed that 100 crops can serve as an adequate sample for bobwhite quail in a county-sized area of similar plant composition. Results from a smaller number of crops showed wide divergence in proportions of food, while those from a much larger number were substantially the same as information from the first 100 crops.

Korschgen (1948:50) arrived at similar conclusions by a different method. He considered a sample as adequate when the cumulative total of crops showed little difference in important foods. Thus, 50 samples from a several-county region contained the important bobwhite quail foods that comprised 92.8% of the volume in 1,200 crops; 100 contained 97.1%; 200 contained 98.8%; and 300 contained the foods that comprised 99.5%. It was concluded that 100 samples (bird crops) obtained from a region of similar plant growth were representative, while 200 or more were preferable. Occurrence of food items proved an unsatisfactory measure for determining sample size.

A statistical method for determining the number of samples required to estimate the food habits of a population was reported by Hanson and Graybill (1956). The method was based on the variance of data for the single most important food in a series.

The span of sampling time often is more important than the number of samples to show the principal or most representative foods of a species. Only rarely can the principal foods be determined by analyses of samples collected during a single season or year. Food desirability, availability, and use vary with food production, quality, abundance, and other factors. Many plant species do not set seed or fruit heavily each year, and populations of prey species often fluctuate annually. Samples should be collected over a minimum period of 2 years to show the most representative foods for any wildlife species. Unfortunately, the food-habits literature abounds with studies based upon inadequate sample sizes or an inadequate number of collection periods.

Equipment

Equipment needed for performing food-habits investigations varies considerably and depends in part on where the primary analyses are made and the objectives of the studies. Field studies for determining relative amounts of foods for management purposes require a minimum of simple equipment: a hand lens, graduated cylinders, screen sieves, forceps, scalpel or knife, tray or heavy paper squares, pencil and tablet or cards for record keeping. Field examination of predator stomachs requires even less equipment, since food amounts are usually estimated.

Greater accuracy can be attained by laboratory analyses, and equipment needs are proportionately greater. Laboratory space equipped with a sink and washing facilities are basic requirements. Good microscopes are essential. The best type for low magnification work is the wide-field, parfocal dissecting binocular with good quality lenses. A useful adaptation for examination of large quantities of material in pans, as in studies on deer or large game birds, is a microscope mounted on a horizontal, swinging arm and supported on a heavy base. Compound binocular microscopes are essential for high magnification examination of hair and feathers and for histological studies.

Other useful equipment includes: pans or trays of various sizes, petri dishes, small forceps, scalpels, dissecting needles, sieves of several screen sizes from approximately 4.7 to 15.75 meshes per cm, glass measuring graduates, metal scoops, and tamping rods to fit various sized graduates (Fig. 9.1). A 15.2-cm section of wood dowel, square-cut on 1 end and sharpened to scalpel form on the other, provides an excellent tool for sorting and tamping items such as seeds and gravel. A small spoon is useful for removing items segregated from a sample for measurement. Funnels covered with bolting cloth may be used to strain off fine materials. A drying oven and squares of blotting paper are useful for drying large wet samples before examination or storage. Scales or balances suitable for ascertaining weights of foods are necessary for gravimetric measurements, such as are required in nutritional studies. A moisture-determination balance is useful for evaluating succulent foods in bird crop samples. Reference texts, photographs, and collections are essential for both the beginning and the experienced food-habits investigator.

Reference Collections

Small, personally developed reference collections are useful for local investigations, but usually are too limited for broader studies. Materials included in reference collections must be correctly identified to be useful and accurate. Plant parts, such as seeds, should be collected from correctly identified whole plants.

Extensive reference collections are needed for more intensive studies requiring identification of both major and minor items. Seed, fruit, plant, mammal, bird, insect, and other invertebrate collections and photographs of these are essential for complete investigations.

The cost of collecting and curating extensive reference materials is very great, and includes the expense of cabinets, boxes, vials, or other containers. Large collections often represent the work of many people over several generations. Universities and research stations often have large reference collections and are staffed with specialists who can identify plant and animal items; these are logical centers for food-habits studies.

Personnel Qualifications

Attitudes and work habits of the investigator have great bearing on achievements from food-habits studies. A successful investigator must commit to memory the detailed characteristics of many kinds of specimen materials. He must be thorough, patient, and persevering at routine work. There is no substitute for experience and hard work; and, as pointed out by Latham (1951), good food-habits technicians are made, not born. The technician must be a taxonomist, anatomist, botanist, mam-

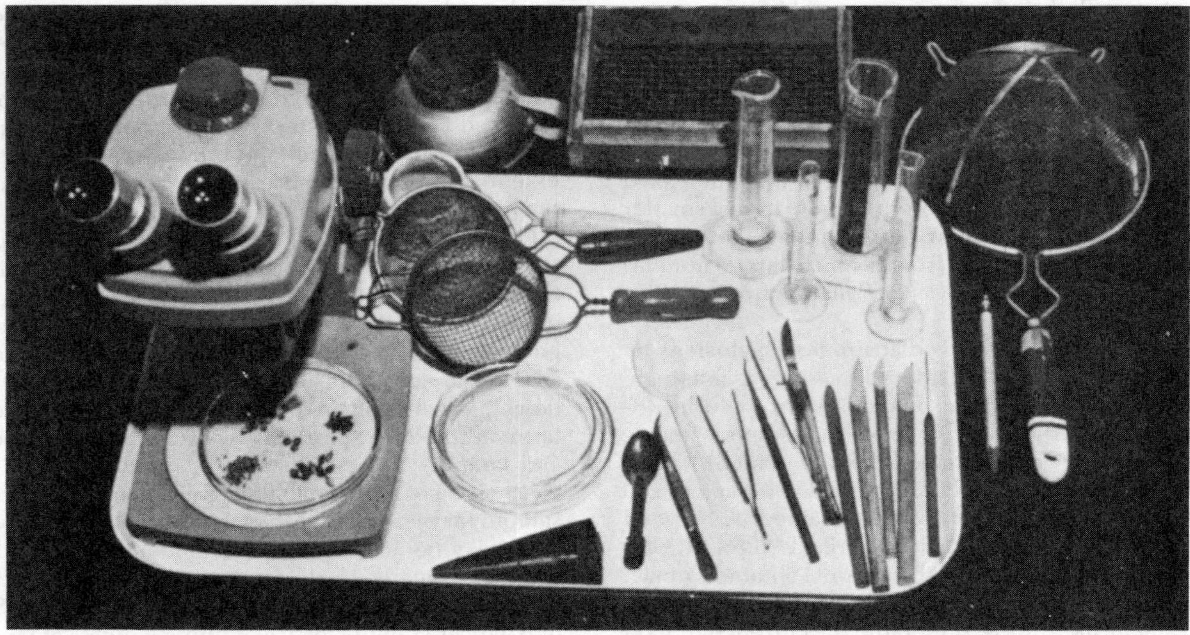

Fig. 9.1. Some equipment used in food-habits analyses: dissecting microscope, enamel tray, petri dishes, glass graduates, screen sieves, forceps, scalpel, dissecting needle, scoop, spoon, and tamping rods.

malogist, ornithologist, entomologist, and herpetologist to recognize plant, mammal, bird, insect, reptile, and amphibian remains. Full accomplishment in all these disciplines is virtually impossible to attain in a lifetime. Therefore, the assistance of subject specialists often is required during food-habits investigations.

MATERIALS AND METHODS

Kinds of Study Materials

Many kinds of materials serve for food-habits study. Specimens commonly are obtained from 3 sources: animals killed during hunting seasons, accidental kills, and samples collected specifically for study. Commonly used study materials from birds are crops, gizzards, and droppings. Crops are always preferable to gizzards or droppings because of the comparative ease and reliability in identifying and measuring foods in proportion to amounts consumed. A flushing tube, as described by Vogtman (1945), may be used for obtaining crop contents without killing the birds. MacGregor (1958) also made effective use of this apparatus to extract food from the crops of nestling mourning doves. Wrazen and Svendsen (1979) extracted stomach contents from eastern chipmunks using an intubation procedure. Use of an emetic to obtain food samples was employed by Moody (1970), Prys-Jones et al. (1974), Radke and Frydendall (1974), Tomback (1975), Zach and Falls (1976), and Lederer and Crane (1978).

Studies of gizzard contents may be used to supplement data from crops, or to determine the kind and quantity of grit, occurrence of lead shot, or retention of hard seeds. Stomach (gizzard) contents traditionally have been used as source material from waterfowl, crows, and other birds which lack a true crop. Waterfowl gullets occasionally contain a sufficient quantity of food for satisfactory analyses. Swanson and Bartonek (1970) recommended use of esophageal contents and the exclusion of gizzard contents for waterfowl food analyses to reduce bias from rapid digestion of soft foods and retention of hard seeds. The method appears to be most applicable to studies conducted in summer on waterfowl breeding areas where birds can be collected while feeding and the food items can be preserved immediately. Problems of obtaining an adequate sample of gullets with food from hunter-killed or migrating birds is nearly unsurmountable in other areas, as noted by Sincock (1962) and the writer, who found only a few cc's of food in esophagi of 300 Canada geese taken by hunters during a fall season. Age of birds, location, purpose of study, food types available and utilized, and practical methods for obtaining samples all have a bearing on procedures for these kinds of investigations.

Droppings of birds can be used successfully as sources of food-habits information, as shown by Dalke (1935) for ring-necked pheasants; Swanson (1940) for sharp-tailed grouse; Dalke et al. (1942) for wild turkeys; Wilson and Vaughn (1944) for bobwhite quail; Korschgen (1962b, 1966) for prairie chickens and ruffed grouse; and Korschgen and Chambers (1970) for Reeves pheasants. This method requires a greater degree of skill in identification, but it is particularly useful when stomachs or crops are unavailable, such as for rare, depleted, or introduced species. Some workers think that only frequency-of-occurrence observations should be taken with droppings; however, principal foods can be determined by ocular estimates of volume for all periods of the year. In a controlled feeding test on bobwhite quail, Jensen and Korschgen (1947:43) found that droppings were equal to stomachs in reliability, but crops were superior for study.

Stomachs are preferred for food studies of predatory birds which consume animal foods, but they are difficult to obtain in sufficient numbers. Regurgitated pellets of undigested food have been used extensively. Errington (1930) concluded that pellets from owls are faithful representations of the birds' diets. Pellets also can supplement stomach analyses, observation, or nest studies of hawks. Problems arise because bony materials are eaten less by hawks than by owls, they do not survive digestion, and pellets are widely scattered. Because of these factors, hawk pellets are more difficult to obtain and analyze than owl pellets. Errington (1932:78–79) found that food of nestling hawks was temporarily retained in the esophagus, and by squeezing their gullets he prompted regurgitation and obtained undigested food for analysis.

Food studies of small and medium-sized mammals are dependent largely upon stomach contents. The large intestine sometimes contains more food than the stomach, especially in trapped animals. Use of both may result in obtaining data from more than a single meal.

Mammal scats may be used as primary or supplemental sources of information. Scott (1941) found a close correlation between food fed to captive foxes and residual evidence in the scats. Murie (1946) showed that the number of rabbit-sized animals can be judged from scats, but mouse-sized animals may be considerably underestimated. Fitch (1948:74–75) assumed 1 average-sized adult of the species in question for each occurrence in coyote scats. Floyd et al. (1978) used weight of undigested remains in scats to estimate the weight and numbers of prey consumed by wolves.

Special knowledge is required for positive scat identification. The field guide by Murie (1954) contains many clues for identification of spoor, including scats. Careful consideration of size, conformation, and composition of scats, along with related evidence such as location and tracks, usually will establish identity of the animal concerned. Odor of a dampened specimen may be distinctive for a species and can be an important aid in identification of some predator scats, especially those of the red fox. If the identity of a scat is questionable, it must not be included in any food-habits investigation. Clues to the identity of droppings from rodent and rabbits were reported by Webb (1940). Reference collections of correctly identified scats may be useful.

Time of day and activity of the animal at time of collection should be considered and recorded. Stevenson (1933) pointed out that passerines feed more or less throughout the daylight hours. Vestjens and Carrick (1974) stated that moths and grasshoppers are easily taken by black-backed magpies in Australia in early morning when these insects are less active. Pinowski et al. (1973) noted that in cage tests tree sparrows in Poland took *Amaranthus retroflexus* seeds intensively only towards evening. Robel (1969) found time of collection affected average volumes of quail crop contents. Each week, Hintz and Dyer (1970) shot 6 to 10 redwings on an hourly schedule and found the mean caloric value of food was significantly higher before noon among males and there were certain hourly peaks for both sexes. Among British rooks (Holyoak 1972), the proportion with empty gizzards showed a slight variation in time of day, the highest percentage being empty in late morning.

Stomach (rumen) contents primarily serve for food studies of deer, elk, and other ruminants, but fecal pellets also have been used. Methods for obtaining rumen samples from living animals were described by Follis and Spillett (1972) and Wilson et al. (1977).

Additional sources of food habits information are available for certain species of wildlife. They include food caches and cheek pouches of rodents and den debris of carnivores. Feeding platforms of muskrats have been used (Takos 1947: 334–335).

Data for Collection

The accumulated data from laboratory analyses may be affected greatly by methods used during collection, handling, and storage of specimen materials. While the highly variable types of materials require different treatments, a few basic rules apply for all.

Accurate information should accompany all samples intended for laboratory examination. Pertinent information includes: species, time (date) and place (locality) of collection, sex of animal, collector's name, and collector's number or acquisition number when a large series of specimens is anticipated.

Additional information often is helpful during laboratory examinations, such as the age of animal, hour of capture, method of capture, kind of bait used, etc. Information on abundance and kinds of food available, cover conditions, and associated plant species will help the investigator interpret the findings from food-habits examinations.

Primariy collection data should be recorded at the time study materials are obtained and attached to each sample (Fig. 9.2). Labels of vulcanized-fiber paper withstand preservatives well. The starchy covering on some paper or cloth tags disintegrates and reduces or destroys the legibility of recorded data. Medium-hard lead pencils or carbon ink (not India ink) should be used to record data on tags to be placed in preservative solutions. Labels may be glued to the outside of large, single sample containers that are protected in carrying cases. Supplementary information may be recorded chronologically in a notebook or on a check sheet for ready reference.

Preservation

The container best suited for holding a sample depends largely on the moisture content of the sample and whether moist conditions must be maintained. Small envelopes, paper bags, plastic bags, shell vials, screw-top glass bottles, or fruit jars of 1/2 pint to 1/2 gallon have proven satisfactory for collecting and transporting food-habits samples. The method of preservation will indicate the kind of container needed.

Three methods commonly are used to preserve study materials in usable condition: wet, dry, and frozen. Materials to be examined within 24 hr after collection generally do not require preservation. Usually examinations require a much longer time, so preservation of samples is necessary. The most practical, reliable, and econom-

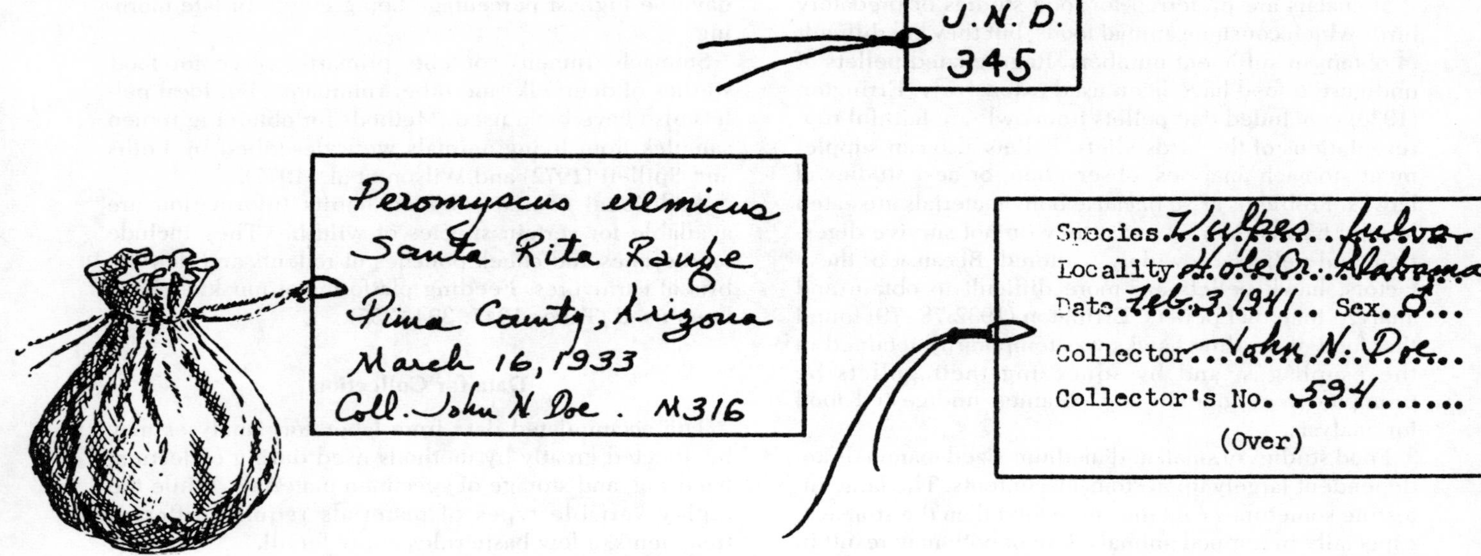

Fig. 9.2. Tags for labeling materials in food-habitats studies.

ical preservative for samples containing flesh is a formalin solution prepared by diluting commercial formaldehyde with tap water. Small to medium-sized stomachs can be preserved adequately with a 5% solution of formalin (1 part commercial formaldehyde in 19 parts of water). A 10% solution is recommended for large specimens. Bear- or deer-sized stomachs preserved intact should be injected with, and then submerged in, formalin solution. Small slits cut through the walls will insure penetration of the preservative. Entire stomach contents of large herbivores rarely are preserved for study. Instead, a quart-sized sample is collected after thoroughly mixing the stomach contents. This material also may be preserved in a 5% formalin solution. Some workers find ruminant stomach samples much more pleasant and easy to work on if the samples are washed on a fine screen soon after collection and then dried in the sun. About 5 gallons of water are needed for each quart of sample.

Alcohol (70%) is satisfactory for small samples of flesh, but alcohol (which extracts chlorophyll) should not be used if green plant material is present.

Special precautions are recommended to prevent spillage and mixing of food contents when a number of stomach samples are preserved in a single large container. The severed ends of the esophagus and intestine should be tied to prevent loss of contents. The entire unit should be wrapped in cheesecloth or muslin and a label attached to each sample.

Material collected for shipment should be kept in the preservative solution for at least 5 days, after which it can be removed, drained, and shipped in moist packing. When preserved in permanent containers, such as sealed glass jars, specimens may be stored indefinitely.

Caution: Formaldehyde gas is irritating to the eyes and respiratory tract. Formalin solutions tend to dry and shrivel the skin. When removing specimens from formalin solution, use forceps or rubber gloves.

Specimens preserved in formalin can be handled safely after deformalizing for 3 to 5 min. in solution prepared as follows:

One gallon of tap water
252 g of sodium bisulfite ($NaHSO_3$)
168 g of sodium sulfite (Na_2SO_3)

Dry preservation has proven satisfactory for a variety of materials. All predatory mammal scats, regurgitated pellets from birds of prey, and droppings from birds are suited to air-dry storage in paper or plastic bags. Samples should be thoroughly dried before containers are tied or sealed. Oven drying should be done at 80–85°C for several hours or a time appropriate to the size of the sample. Moist samples tend to mold, especially in plastic containers. Stomach or crop contents consisting largely of dry seeds, fruits, leaves, and insects may be stored dry for years without harm. Material from large herbivore stomachs also may be held satisfactorily in dry storage, provided it is washed thoroughly to remove digestive juices and completely dried before it is packaged. In all cases of dry storage, materials should be checked and fumigated periodically. If stored in tight containers with PDB (paradichlorobenzene) flakes or similar chemicals, insect damage is prevented.

Quick freezing of samples is a practical and convenient method of preservation, but few laboratories are equipped to handle large quantities of material in this manner for extended periods. Freezing has the special advantage of not seriously impairing either color or texture of materials.

ANALYTICAL PROCEDURES

The best analytical procedure for any particular food-habits study depends upon the animal being studied, the dietary components, and the source of material available for study. Basically, complete examination includes (1) preparation of sample, (2) segregation of contents, (3) identification of food items, (4) recording of data, and (5) appraisal of results. Medin (1970) provided an excellent general reference on stomach content analyses.

Preparation

Preparation of materials for analysis often is guided by previous handling and storage. Dry samples usually need little preparation. Washing may be omitted when contents of crops or stomachs consist mainly of seeds or other plant parts. Dry stored pellets of predatory birds and scats of mammals also require no preparation unless the analyst so desires. The material can be broken apart by hand or picked apart with forceps. Some analysts prefer to wash pellets and scats to remove mucus and to partially clean hair, bones, teeth, and other diagnostic parts. Washing has the disadvantage of mixing food remains when several kinds may form nearly distinct portions of the original sample.

Bird droppings can be examined dry after crumbling them. Washing of droppings in a 40-mesh sieve under the tap and then drying the sample is recommended for removing uric acid and fine particles not useful for identification.

Stomach contents from carnivores and predatory birds usually require thorough washing with hot water through a 12 to 20 mesh sieve to remove grease. The amount of grease removed by this process may be estimated and added to final measurements, or omitted when all samples are prepared in the same manner. Draining or squeezing the wet sample eliminates excess water and hastens drying on blotting paper.

Whole organs preserved in formalin, or alcohol, should be thoroughly washed or placed in deformalizing solution before the contents are removed. Removal of an organ's contents can be facilitated by washing them into screen sieves with tap water under heavy pressure. This wash further eliminates the objectionable formalin from the samples before analysis. The screens should be of proper mesh to retain food particles useful for identification.

Segregation

Objectives of the study, time required, ability of the investigator, and type of study material all affect the feasibility of item separation (Fig. 9.3). Some kinds of materials, such as stomach contents of waterfowl and

gizzards of gallinaceous birds, do not lend themselves to complete separation of food items because some are broken or finely ground. Seeds, insects, and other items in crops can be separated with fair accuracy, and experience teaches many practical shortcuts in foods analyses.

When seeds are in the study material, partial separations often can be accomplished by use of various mesh-sized sieves. Sorting time for seed samples also can be materially reduced by use of a wooden scalpel rather than a forceps. The principal component of a sample is judged by ocular comparison and then drawn with the scalpel to the near edge of the dish. The sorted item then is removed for measurement, and the process repeated until complete analysis is achieved. Screening and scalpel work often can be combined for more rapid results. Mixtures of seeds, animal matter, and gravel, as found in waterfowl stomachs, often appear formidable to the analyst. Many food items in such samples can be segregated by decanting or floating off materials of lowest specific gravity. A simple procedure for removing gravel is to place the sample in a beaker of carbon tetrachloride, trichloroethylene, or other cleaning solution. Vigorous stirring, or swirling, will cause the lighter plant and animal foods to float so they can be decanted into a fine mesh sieve held over a second beaker. Two or 3 such decantations will completely segregate the gravel from food materials. The latter can then be sorted after a few minutes of drying time.

A less effective method involves gently blowing food particles to the top of a tilted dish while gently tapping the container. Gravel and heavy food items will settle to the lower portion for a partial separation. Swanson and Thornsberry (1972) reported a device useful for counting food items in waterfowl samples.

Samples from animals which grind or masticate their food often contain portions that are impractical to separate. The amount of this unsegregated part is determined by volume or weight and the proportions of its constituent items are estimated visually.

The volume of finely masticated wet materials may be accurately measured by centrifuging in calibrated centrifuge tubes. Green vegetation, even though finely masticated and thoroughly mixed with other food materials, can be easily separated out. For example, green vegetation can be separated from nut meat by mixing the sample thoroughly in a beaker of water and then directing a strong, fine stream of water from a wash bottle into the mixture. The fine bubbles of air carried into the mixture by the jet of water will stick to the vegetation and cause it to float to the top (Dudderar pers. comm.).

Segregation of food items in pellets, scats, and stomachs which contain hair, bones, or feathers can be accomplished best with the aid of forceps to remove diagnostic portions. Complete separation of items seldom is practical and a partial measure by visual estimate becomes necessary. Visual estimates of proportions also are commonly used in analysis of bird droppings and fecal pellets of both small and large mammals. Other methods of quantitative analysis may be used. Arata (1959) described a method for gross determinations of muskrat foods by differential sedimentation.

Screens of various sizes commonly are used for partial separation of materials when analyzing stomach contents of large herbivores. One method is to screen-sort and measure the larger, easily identified items, check the remainder for additional foods, and apportion the finer residues on the basis of all larger items identified (Korschgen 1962b). Some investigators visually estimate all proportions; others identify, weigh, or measure the coarser items and leave the mass of finer items unidentified (Harlow and Hooper 1971). If visual estimates are utilized, it is best to compare results with estimates made by a colleague. Dirschl (1962), McCaffery et al. (1974b), Owaga (1978) and Puglisi et al. (1978) recommended analysis of only that portion of the rumen contents retained by a screen or screens of selected size. Adams (1957) and Adams et al. (1962) used only diagnostic "recognition items" identified from fecal pellet analyses to appraise quantities of food consumed. Chamrad and Box (1964) described a method for rumen analysis based on a point frequency method in a large tray. Scotter (1966, 1967) utilized standard sieves of 3 mesh sizes to partially segregate caribou rumen samples for analysis by weight. Robel and Watt (1970) compared accuracy of the volumetric and point-analysis methods.

The choice of segregating material in a dry, moist, or wet condition is largely one to be determined by the investigator. The dry state is definitely advantageous for the analysis of most food-habits samples, but it may be necessary to work with moist materials when soft-bodied insects, spiders, crustaceans, or green vegetation are involved. The common practice of measuring dry food materials in graduated cylinders or beakers is satisfactory if uniform procedures are followed. Air space should be reduced by firmly tamping the material with a wood rod. Air space around irregularly shaped items may be reduced by filling the voids with measured amounts of small lead shot and subtracting the shot volume from final readings, or by water displacement. Inglis and Barstow (1960) described a device adapted to measurement by water displacement, or a known volume of water can be added to the cylinder with a pipette. In water displacement, dry foods should first be moistened or accurate readings cannot be made.

Sorting materials from a liquid medium entails tedious effort with forceps because food materials tend to adhere to each other. Movement of floating materials and refraction of light from the liquid create additional problems.

Whatever the method used, uniformity of procedure is important. Results may be affected by sampling procedures, methods of analysis, standards of measurement, and comparison with data from coordinated field investigations.

Samples which contain only minor amounts of food often are omitted from tabulated results, while items that comprise less than 0.1% of total food contents are listed as "trace" amounts.

Identification

The identification of items found in food-habits analyses becomes easier with experience, properly identified reference materials, pictorial references, field notes from the sampling areas, skin and skeleton materials of vertebrates, and whole specimens of invertebrates. Working with a specialist is the most rapid route to progress with identification of unknown items.

The simple process is best during the initial stages of an investigation. Instead of spending a lot of time trying to identify unknown items or fragments found in the first samples, it is advisable to number or label them and put them aside until more and better specimens are found. Important items will occur repeatedly in a series of examinations and provide additional characteristics for identification. When gross analyses are completed, effort can be concentrated on items of unknown identity.

Accuracy of identification is particularly important. Total lack of recognition is better than reporting misidentified items. Limited amounts of unidentified materials in food lists need not reflect adversely on the analyst, for as Latham (1951: 8) pointed out, a technician who presents a food habits table showing no unidentified materials is either exceedingly skilled, is working with a very simple diet, or is dishonest.

Reference materials should be consulted frequently, and important items that defy recognition should be referred to specialists. Generally, the comparison of several characteristics will lead to positive identification of the specimen. Important aids to the identification of seeds used by wildlife include: *The Seed Identification Manual* (Martin and Barkely 1961); the 15-plate set of photographs of common "weed" seeds that occur on agricultural lands published by the Division of Photography, Office of Information, U.S. Dept. of Agriculture, Washington, D.C.; *The Comparative Internal Morphology of Seeds* (Martin 1946); *Identification of Crop and Weed Seeds* (Musil 1963); and *Seeds of Woody Plants of the United States* (U.S. Forest Service 1974). Other plant parts often can be recognized to genera or species by outline, texture, margins, midrib, venation, or pubescence of leaves using local or regional botanical texts. Final identification should be made from a reference collection, and, if possible, spot-checked by a specialist. Identification of fleshy fungi eaten by wildlife will be aided by the work of Miller and Halls (1969) who provide additional references on the subject.

The identification of small mammal bones will be aided by keys and descriptions published by Brainerd (1939), Driver (1949), Brown (1952), Stains (1959), and Glass (1973). Hildebrand (1955) described the skeletal differences between deer, sheep, and goats. Conformation, muscle attachment ridges, and density are of greater importance than proportions or size for identifying bones. Surfaces of immature bones deteriorate rapidly from weathering or digestion, and show rough surfaces. Immature skulls often have milk dentition. Fish bones may be distinguished from mammal bones by their thin, folded structure. They often have radiating ridges or reticulations, and lack a smooth or rounded appearance. Amphibian limb bones are hollow, very light in weight and structure, and smooth. Bird bones are extremely light, but have a hard, highly polished surface. They often are thin walled, with the interior hollow or filled with a delicately reticulated mesh of bony material. Keys by Eddy and Hodson (1961) will help to accurately identify many biological specimens.

Identification of hairs usually requires high-powered microscopic examination (10x oculars, 40x objectives). Guard hairs are preferable to underfur for showing diagnostic characteristics. Although many hairs can be identified from banding patterns and general appearance under low magnification, others require special preparation.

Hausman (1920), Williams (1938), and Spence (1963) described the structural and identifying characteristics of hairs. Mathiak (1938a,b), Williams (1938), Dearborn (1939), Williamson (1951), Mayer (1952), Stains (1958), Adorjan and Kolenosky (1969), and Moore et al. (1974) provided keys and aids to hair identification.

Williams (1934), Mathiak (1938a), and Coman and Brunner (1971) described methods for cross-sectioning hairs. Permanent reference slides which show scale pattern, medulla, and cross-sections of hairs can be most helpful. Hardy and Plitt (1940) and Koonz and Strandine (1945) described methods for showing the cuticular patterns. Temporary mounts that show scale type and arrangment can be prepared rapidly by partially embedding hairs cleaned in carbon tetrachloride, in clear fingernail polish, clarite, stencil correction fluid, or similar substance. Medullae and internal characteristics show well when clean hairs are immersed in cedar oil under a cover slip on a microscope slide. Procedure for making a semipermanent cast of cuticular scales of mammal hair (Spence 1963) is as follows: The medium is a 3% solution of glycerine jelly which is a gel when cool and fluid when warm. Glycerine, 3 cc, is mixed with 94 cc of warm water, and 3 g of gelatin is added. After stirring, 0.1 g of merthiolate or carbolic acid is added as a preservative. Repeated heating of the gel or heating at too high temperatures may prevent the medium from jelling. Heating the jar with the medium in a pan of water prevents overheating. The medium and slides can be stored in a refrigerator indefinitely.

The procedure for the slides is as follows:

1. Rinse the hair in carbon tetrachloride for 10 to 15 min and let it dry.
2. Place 2 to 3 drops of the medium on a clean slide. With another slide, spread the medium evenly over the center third of the first slide.
3. Before the medium has begun to gel, place the clean hairs vertical to the long axis of the slide. Have 1 end of the hair projecting over the edge of the slide so it can be easily grasped for removal.
4. Let the slide set for 1 to 1½ hr. The time depends on the condition of the medium and the temperature.
5. When the medium has become fairly solid, using forceps remove the hair with a fast jerk to prevent the hair from sticking to the solution. If the hair has stuck tightly to the medium, the cast will appear under the microscope to be an almost exact duplicate of the scales of the hair. If the medium was not completely set, or the hair not well imbedded, the cast will appear smudged or no scales will be visible.

Resins have also been used in a manner similar to gelatin and provide permanent mounts. Gelva V7 (Monsanto Co., St. Louis, Mo.) and Bakelite AYAF (Union Carbide Corp., N.Y.) are clear vinyl acetate polymers soluble in acetone, 95% ethyl alcohol, and 99% isopropyl alcohol. Gelva has a slightly faster dissolving rate, but there seem to be no differences in the quality of slides prepared with either.

A resin solution is prepared and a thin film is spread over one-half of a slide. Allow to dry (40 min. or less). Place the hairs across the hardened resin and cover with another slide. Insert in a press as shown by Williamson (1951) (Fig. 9.4) or apply an even pressure, release, and quickly pull the hairs away with forceps. Cover with a cover slip for a permanent collection. Typical results from this technique appeared in the reports of Adorjan and Kolenosky (1969) and Moore et al. (1974).

The identification of feathers and other small bird remains is difficult without a good reference collection of study skins and skeletal parts, particularly feet and bills. Feathers of the Anatidae were pictured in Broley's article (1950). Chandler (1916) described microscopic techniques for examination of feathers.

Histological techniques are useful in food-habits studies of rabbits, squirrels and other rodents, and some large herbivores that finely masticate their foods. Lay (1965) identified fruits from seed fragments. The microtechniques of Baumgartner and Martin (1939) for squirrels was later employed by Dusi (1949, 1952), Klimstra and Corder (1957) and Sagar (1962) for rabbit food studies. The important work by Metcalfe and Chalk (1950) provided anatomical nomenclature for the histological characteristics of broad-leaved plants, while Metcalfe (1960) reported the characteristics of grasses. Meanwhile, other contributions to the histological microtechnique were made by Martin (1955) in Scotland, on features of plant cuticles, Adams (1957) on recognition characters of plants, Croker (1959) and Hercus (1960), in New Zealand, on determining the diets of sheep and grazing animals. Storr (1961), in Australia, reported a chemical technique for removing plant epidermis and concluded that both qualitative and quantitative data might be obtained because there is little or no digestion of epidermis that is enclosed in cutin, tissues are identifiable to species, and relationships between surface area and dry weight of foliage are determinable. Bacterial maceration to remove plant cuticle was used by Luow et al. (1949), Skoss (1955), and Rogerson et al. (1976). A comparison of bacterial degradation and chemical maceration techniques was made by Fitzgerald and Waddington (1979).

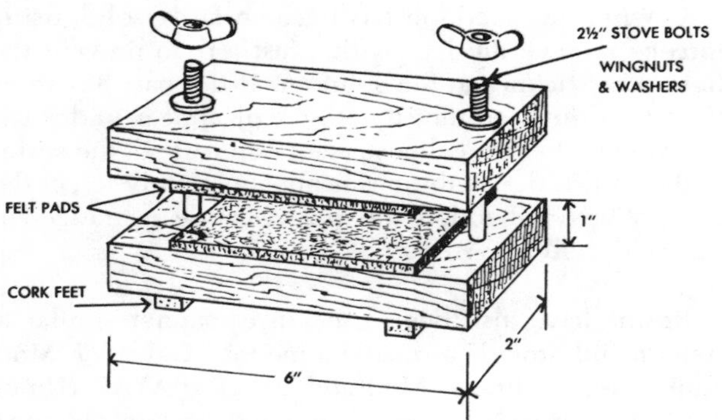

Fig. 9.4. A press for making hair impressions on microscope slides.

Greater use of the microtechnique was made in the U.S. after the 1960's. Food habits studies were reported for pocket gophers (Ward and Keith 1962, Myers and Vaughn 1964), microtines (Williams 1962), deer (Adams et al. 1962, Zyznar and Urness 1969), cattle, sheep and rabbits (Williams 1969). Comprehensive studies for identification of grasses, analyses of feces, and study of wild ungulate food preferences in Africa, were reported by Stewart (1965, 1967, 1970) and Stewart and Stewart (1970). A summary of food studies by Ward (1970) based upon use of the histological microtechnique related primarily to fecal sample analyses for both wild and domestic animals. Various aspects of competition for food, food preferences, and forage use were reported by Galt et al. (1968, 1969), Free et al. (1970), Hansen et al. (1973) and Griffiths et al. (1974). Studies to verify or improve techniques for making qualitative or quantitative estimates of food were reported by Sparks and Malechek (1968) for forage samples, Owen and Kerbes (1971) and Owen (1975b) for waterfowl, Voth and Black (1973) for mountain beaver, Todd and Hansen (1973) for bighorn sheep, Anthony and Smith (1974) for mule deer, Dearden et al. (1975) for reindeer, cattle and bison, and Westoby et al. (1976) for jackrabbits.

The histological microtechnique has been adequately confirmed as a basic method for determining food use for animals that finely masticate their foods. Stomach contents or fecal samples may serve as study materials.

Epidermal fragments for reference collections usually have been obtained by acid treatment, scraping, or stripping from plant parts, and then stained. Squirrel stomach contents prepared for analyses by Nixon et al. (1968) were ovendried, finely ground, and stained before microscopic examination. Korschgen (1973), in preparation for study of cottontail stomach contents, removed epidermal sections for most grasses and broad-leaved plants with a thin razor blade and mounted them, unstained, in high viscosity, water miscible, CMCP-10 mounting medium (Turtox-Cambosco, MacMillan Science Co., Inc., Chicago, Ill.) on microscope slides for reference use. The same procedure was used for study of spring and summer deer food samples (Korschgen et al. 1976). Histological characteristics were readily discernible for most species. Zyznar and Urness (1969), Todd and Hansen (1973) and Owen (1975b) also omitted staining procedures in their studies of deer, bighorn sheep and waterfowl samples, respectively.

Apparently few attempts have been made to prepare taxonomic keys for the epidermal characters of plants. Stewart (1965) listed key characteristics of East African plains grasses, but not in couplet form. Anatomical keys based upon diagnostic characters of 50 grass genera were presented by Liversidge (1970). Most users of the microtechnique rely upon slide and photomicrograph reference collections prepared for plants commonly found on their study areas. Cataloging and collection of plants and preparation of local reference materials are recommended and nearly essential for successful investigations by histological methods (Fig. 9.6).

Data Records

Data from each food-habits investigation should become a matter of permanent record. Initial data from

Odocoileus virginianus — Sex: M — No.: M42909
State: North Carolina — Co.: Pender — Loc.: Wallace Deer Club
Date: 11-16-66 — Hr.: 10:30 A — Collector: W. D. Robbins — Coll. No.: 7
Stom. ______ cc. Crop ______ cc. Anim. ______ % Veg. 100 % Grit ______ cc. ______ %
Examined by: John N. Doe — Date: 3-24-67

Cyrilla racemiflora	85%
Pinus sp.	10%
Ilex sp.	5%

Myrica cerifera
Vaccinium crassifolium
Smilax laurifolia

U. S. GOVERNMENT PRINTING OFFICE 16—15791 — 3-174a—(4-40)

Colinus virginianus — Sex: Male — No.: 550
State: Missouri — Co.: Boone — Loc.: Ashland
Date: 11-15-50 — Hr.: ______ — Collector: John Lewis — Coll. No.: 5
Stom. ______ cc. Crop 6.0 cc. Anim. tr % Veg. 100 % Grit tr cc. tr %
Examined by: L. J. Korschgen — Date: 1-10-51

Lespedeza stipulacea	3.25 cc.
Rhus glabra	2.40
Strophostyles helvola	.25
Vitis sp.	.05
Rhus radicans	.05
Desmodium sp.	trace
Lespedeza striata	trace
Rosa sp.	trace
Acrididae	trace
Gravel	trace

9 — MISSOURI CONSERVATION COMMISSION

Fig. 9.5. Recommended type of food-habits record card.

individual samples may be kept in temporary files. Record cards such as those used by the U.S. Fish and Wildlife Service are recommended for permanent files (Fig. 9.5). The record for each sample examined should contain pertinent collection data and a list of all identified foods recorded by the chosen unit of measurement: number, percentage, volume, or weight. Records of this kind are convenient for tabulating data from a particular study and for permanent reference. Marginal-notched cards or computer-oriented file systems seldom are used for food-habits record keeping because of the great number of items that often are involved and because they ordinarily are tabulated only once in a master list of foods. Data from the cards may be tabulated by month or season and then combined for all-season lists. The single use made of the permanent record usually does not merit the time required for establishing the punch-card or marginal-notched card systems.

Appraisal and Preparation

Appraisal of data necessarily is guided by the unit of measurement chosen by the investigator. Many methods have been used to express results obtained from food-habits analyses. Numbers, frequency of occurrence, volume, and weight are the common denominators employed to show food use or importance. All of these methods, sometimes in combinations, were employed in early studies (McAtee 1912, 1933) and there was little agreement on the best procedure. A single criterion usually is inadequate to provide meaningful results from a series of analyses. Numbers of prey eaten by a predator or seeds eaten by a game bird are of interest, but additional information on how often the item occurred and in what amount is more meaningful. Swanson (1940:433) suggested that the ideal method was to present 2 or more expressions of quantitative data (numbers, volume, occurrence) because each denoted a distinct and significant aspect of the findings.

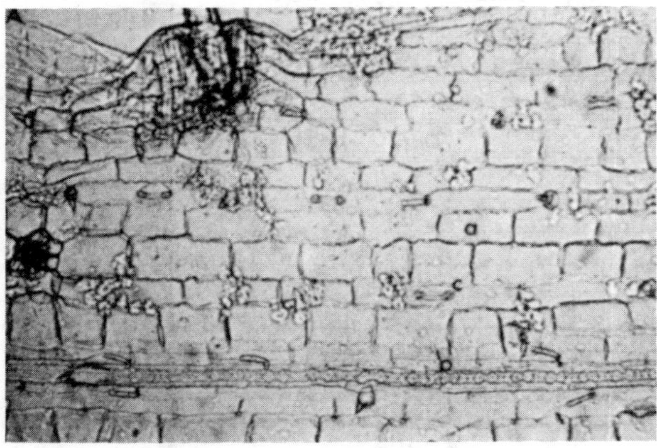

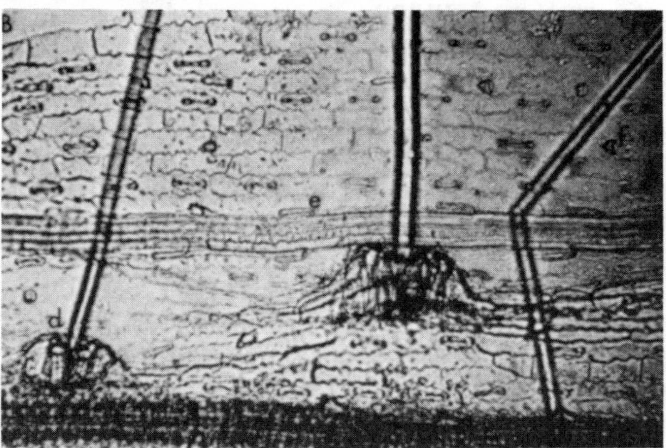

Fig. 9.6. Photomicrograph of upper (A) and lower (B) epidermis from leaf of common crabgrass. A. (a) long-cell. (b) silica-body in vein. (c) stoma. B. (d) macro-hair. (e) micro-hair. (f) hook or prickle hair (Photos by the author).

Numbers of items eaten often are of little more than academic interest because size of food items is not taken into account. Measurements of frequency show that the item was eaten but fail to show a relationship to sustaining values in the diet. A single food item identified in a sample receives the same frequency rating as a full crop or stomach of the 1 item. However, frequency of occurrence becomes meaningful when used with volume or weight expressed as a percentage of the sample. High frequency and high volume indicate a food of high quality or preference. A high rating by 1 standard and low for the other may be reason to suspect sampling biases when making an appraisal of food values.

Frequency data are derived from the number of samples in which a particular food occurred. Volume determinations are derived by various means. Originally, visual estimates of food volumes were recorded as percentages of the sample, but volumetric measurements are preferable. Martin et al. (1946) discussed 2 basic methods for volumetric appraisal of data; the aggregate percentage method and the aggregate volume method. In the first, percentages in a sample series are aggregated and averaged for each food. (See precautionary article by Davis and Zippin [1954].) The method was credited by McAtee (1912) to Dr. S. D. Judd in 1901. More recently, Swanson et al. (1974) recommended this method of appraisal for waterfowl food habits data. The aggregate percentage method serves best when sample contents differ greatly in size, when samples are limited in number, or when samples are unevenly distributed throughout the study period. In long-term studies, it is good practice to compute monthly averages of data based upon samples collected during each month. Yearly averages are then based upon the monthly percentages of principal items. This method may give more accurate yearly averages than when data are based upon the total number of samples collected for the year, especially if uneven monthly distribution of samples occurs.

The aggregate volume method involves summing all volumes for each item in a series before calculating the percentages based upon the total food volume. This method now is standard procedure for routine food-habits summaries. Particular advantages are savings in time and labor for medium to large series of samples, data can be assembled in unaltered form, and each sample has its full influence on final results.

Gravimetric measurements may be substituted for volumetric data when sample contents are subject to complete segregation. Weight data are essential when studying nutrition or food energetics, but weight is often an impractical parameter to obtain for small items.

There is no ideal method of food analysis for all species or groups of animals (Hartley 1948). It is most desirable, however, that published records and summaries be in such form that they can be readily understood and combined with the results from other investigations. The many methods used in reporting data have resulted in chaos in the food-habits literature, and prevented the collation of results from many food studies on species of widespread distribution. For this reason it is recommended that the standard procedure for reporting food-habits data be by frequency of occurrence and volume, or weight. It also is recommended that the most important food items be shown at the beginning of tabular lists arranged in order of decreasing importance by a standard measurement. The total volume or weight of food contents and the number of samples examined should be considered as essential data for any report (Table 9.1). These data enable other investigators to convert from percentages to original amounts for the purpose of combining them with information from similar studies.

Less precise methods have been used to appraise utilization of wildlife foods. Rankings of very high, high, medium, and low were used by Dalke et al. (1942). Wilson and Vaughn (1944) used percentages ranges from rough estimates of volume to designate food use as trace, scant, medium, or abundant. Martin et al. (1951) used a star system based upon percentage groups, while Clark (1957) employed a similar method using 6 percentage groups to estimate volumetric contents. Broad categories of choice, less desirable, and extrėmely minor were used by Davison and Graetz (1957) to express quality and acceptance of wildlife foods. This method was further refined by Davison and Hamor (1960), Davison and Grizzell (1961a, 1961b) and Davison (1962, 1963, 1964), who showed that preferences indicated by stomach analyses were related primarily to availability and taste rather than color, shape, size, or texture of foods.

Weather conditions may affect food habits studies in other ways. Temperature affects amount of food consumed, with less consumed on hot days (Stevenson 1933). Baldwin and Handley (1946), Bookhout (1958), Korschgen (1960), Bishop and Hungerford (1965), Shields and Duncan (1966), and Crook and Ward (1968) make reference to the effects of drought on food habits.

Index formulae methods of appraisal have been suggested to ascertain food importance, palatability, or

Table 9.1. Principal fall foods of ruffed grouse in Missouri, 1961–1964, in percentages by volume, from dropping analyses.

Foods	Months	Sept.	Oct.	Nov.	Season
	Samples	550	550	550	1,650
Wild grapes (*Vitis* spp.)		23.7	19.8	34.3	26.1
Acorns (*Quercus* spp.)		18.4	26.0	18.8	21.1
Tick trefoils (*Desmodium* spp.)		20.0	24.5	13.3	19.2
Green plant materials		15.6	5.7	2.8	7.9
Korean lespedeza (*Lespedeza stipulacea*)		9.8	0.6	—	3.4
Hophornbeam (*Ostrya virginiana*)		1.3	0.9	6.8	3.0
Bush clovers (*Lespedeza* spp.)		0.2	5.8	2.6	2.9
Japanese rose (*Rosa multiflora*)		—	0.3	6.5	2.4
Flowering dogwood (*Cornus florida*)		1.3	3.8	1.3	2.1
Ladies' tobacco (*Antennaria* spp.)		—	0.5	4.2	1.6
Bittersweet (*Celastrus scandens*)		—	1.2	1.6	1.0
White avens (*Geum canadense*)		0.3	0.2	1.4	0.6
Galls		1.4	0.2	Tr.	0.5
Grasshoppers (*Acrididae*)		2.1	1.6	1.5	1.7
Walking sticks (*Phasmidae*)		0.6	2.5	0.5	1.2
Total Foods Examined (cc)		280.4	280.7	296.3	857.4
Percentage of Total Foods		97.4	93.6	95.6	94.7

animal preferences by correlating amounts found in samples with amounts available (Glading et al. 1940, Bellrose and Anderson 1943, Beck 1952, Hungerford 1957, Bartlett 1958, Dwyer 1961, Van Dyne and Heady 1965).

Correction factors can be developed for digestion rates of prey. Custer and Pitelka (1975) described such factors for the snow bunting and compared the results with those of similar studies in the literature. Dirschl (1969) used the Sorenson similarity coefficient to express the degree of similarity of diets in a numerical fashion:

$$\frac{2c}{a + b} \times 100 = \% \text{ similarity (Greig-Smith 1964:137).}$$

a = no. of items on one list
b = no. of items on second list
c = no. of items in common

Related aspects of yield and availability of wildlife foods were studied by Davison et al. (1955), Haugen and Fitch (1955), Korschgen (1960), and Ripley and Perkins (1965). Keeping quality of foods was reported by Neely (1956).

FIELD STUDIES OF FOOD-HABITS

Besides the direct study of samples of food taken from animals, knowledge of food-habits can be obtained indirectly in the field.

Large Herbivores

Many of the techniques for evaluating the food eaten by the large herbivores are described in Chapter 19. The amounts and species of plants eaten are determined by (1) direct observation of feeding, (2) evidence of feeding on plants, and (3) subtraction of remaining quantities from previous quantities to obtain the amount eaten.

Dixon (1934), Hahn (1945), and Wallmo et al. (1973) studied feeding by mule deer and white-tailed deer using a "deer-minutes" technique. Observations were made through binoculars and the time spent by deer feeding upon particular plants was recorded. Feeding observations were followed by on-site inspection of the utilized plants to verify identification. Buechner (1950: 321–322) discussed the merits and shortcomings of this procedure for the study of antelope feeding habits.

When ranges are inhabited by only one or a few species of herbivores, plants eaten can be observed, counted, and weighed; and amounts eaten by each animal in the population can be estimated. Amounts of feeding are also estimated by pellet-group counts as an index to the amount of feeding in a specific habitat type.

Utilization of browse plants has been described by many workers. Reports have been made on clipping studies on paired plots (Dalke 1941), twig length measurements (Shafer 1963), indicator species reflecting amount of range use, indices of occurrence and degree of use (Aldous 1944), and before-and-after animal-introduction comparisons within fenced enclosures (Davenport et al. 1944). Large and small exclosures (Robertson 1954) have been used to restrict the feeding of big game and demonstrate their effects upon native vegetation (Ostrom 1937, 1942; Hough 1949, Webb 1957), to show the differences between rodent, big game, and livestock feeding (Young 1955), and to ascertain the conditions of key browse plants within general range areas (Cole 1959, Hiehle 1964, Schuster 1965, Stickney 1966).

Small Game and Other Wildlife

Certain methods for studying large herbivores in the field have been adapted for use with smaller wildlife species. The feeding habits of cottontail rabbits have been determined by direct observation, inspection of pellets in feeding areas, examination of vegetation near tracks in snow, and by analysis of stomach contents (Dalke 1942:47). Scarcity of a species or the need for food habits information during all seasons may necessitate use of nonlaboratory methods for obtaining data. For example, the hourly and daily feeding activities of bobwhite quail may be observed with binoculars from an elevated blind (Wilson and Vaughn 1944:108). Diligent and conscientious field observations often provide information on the economic aspects of feeding by flocking birds, or to appraise the impact of birds upon insect populations such as spruce budworm in Maine (George and Mitchell 1948, Dowden et al. 1953). Counts of predatory birds have been correlated with rodent caches to determine the nature of rodent distribution over a selected range (Neronov 1962).

Gibb and Hartley (1957) provided an excellent summary of observational methods for investigating the feeding habits of various kinds of birds. They indicated how to ascertain the time and duration of meals, how to determine quantities of food eaten, and how to record mechanically the visits of parent birds to nests. They also described an artificial nestling, perfected by Betts (1954, 1956), whose mouth opens automatically when a bird alights on the nest box perch. Food dropped into the gaping mouth falls down into a receptacle that contains preservative.

RELATED ACTIVITIES

The food-habits specialist, because of his experience with laboratory techniques, often is called upon to make specific identification of meats or bloods by laboratory methods. Such an identification may be needed for food habits information or, more likely, for law enforcement purposes. The precipitin test, using immune sera, has proved a useful technique (Brohn and Korschgen 1950).

Identifying values of hemoglobin crystals were reported by Winter and Honess (1952), while Pinto (1961) reported a modified precipitin technique for the identification of closely related species.

The paper chromatography methods were employed by Jackson (1958, 1962) and Brunetti (1965) to identify meats and bloods. Later attempts to identify meats of game animals by starch-gel electrophoresis showed that electrophoretic patterns were genera specific (Dilworth and McKenzie 1970).

Tempelis and Rodrick (1973) used chemically purified antigens to obtain high titer antibody production and described a method that might be adapted to the identification of blood stains and meat. Munday et al. (1974) identified muscle tissue from mammals by electrophoresis in polyacrilamide gel. The immunoelectrophoresis technique was reported by Oates et al. (1974) and Oates and Weigel (1976) for the same purpose. Bunch et al. (1976) reviewed previously used methods and reported a technique of analytical polyacrylamide gel isoelectric focusing for identification of hemoglobins of wild and domestic animals. Oates et al. (1979) distinguished between mule and white-tailed deer by isoelectric focusing.

Chapter Ten

Wildlife Nutrition

JULIUS G. NAGY

Professor, Dept. of Fishery and Wildlife Biology
Colorado State University
Fort Collins, Colorado

JONATHAN B. HAUFLER[1]

Dept. of Fishery and Wildlife Biology
Colorado State University
Fort Collins, Colorado

INTRODUCTION

N*utrition* is the study of processes by which organic and inorganic substances, ingested by living organisms, are converted to various needs for life processes such as promoting growth, replacing worn and injured tissues and to perpetuate life. *Wildlife nutrition,* in addition to this, is concerned with the supply and quality of foods in an animal's environment. The basic requirements of all wildlife are food, water, and cover. Wildlife nutrition deals mainly with the first 2 of these requirements. Good and adequate cover, however, is important not only for escape and rest but also to secure undisturbed feeding and to conserve energy during temperature extremes.

There are many examples in the literature which illustrate the importance of nutrition for wildlife. In general, animals with adequate food supply grow larger, produce more young, are more vigorous and healthy, produce better trophies, and are more resistant to many forms of mortality than those affected by malnutrition. During failure of mast crops in 1940, reproductive success of Michigan fox squirrels declined (Allen 1954). The reproductive success of white-tailed deer on ranges providing good nutrition was higher than on poor nutritional ranges (Cheatum and Severinghaus 1950). Weights of deer were also higher on ranges providing good nutrition than on ranges providing poor nutrition (Severinghaus 1955, Dahlberg and Guettinger 1956, Taber 1956a, Teer et al. 1965).

During the last decade, wildlife managers and biologists have become increasingly aware of the fact that a knowledge of physiology and nutrition are basic areas to the understanding of wildlife ecology. Most of the advances in the field of wildlife nutrition, as shown by the citations in this chapter, have occurred during the past 10–15 years.

The authors of this chapter realized that many of the techniques used in wildlife nutrition today have been developed in the field of domestic animal nutrition, and have been modified by wildlife biologists to suit the wild species under investigation. Hence, this chapter does not follow the traditional approach of detailed descriptions of methodology. Instead it attempts to present an overview of the subject with discussions of the major techniques, including references to important articles. Space limitations prevented the inclusion of detailed descriptions of standard techniques used by domestic animal nutritionists. The use of numerous references on domestic and wild animal nutrition should supply the reader with ample information to satisfy his needs or curiosity.

---

[1]Present address: Assistant Professor, Dept. of Fisheries and Wildlife, Michigan State University, East Lansing, Michigan.

Finally, the reader will realize that much of our discussion concerns wild ungulates, especially cervids. The reason for this is that the bulk of the research on wildlife nutrition has dealt with these species. Hopefully, the lack of nutritional information on other types of wildlife will motivate both scientists and students to pursue these areas of research and fill major gaps in current knowledge of wildlife nutrition.

NUTRIENT CONTENT OF FOODS

A *nutrient* is any food or feed[1] constituent or a group of constituents that is normally consumed by the animal and is a source of energy or is essential for normal function of the animal. Generally plants and animals contain similar types of chemical substances, and these can be grouped into classes according to their nutrient constitution or function. The main components of foods are:

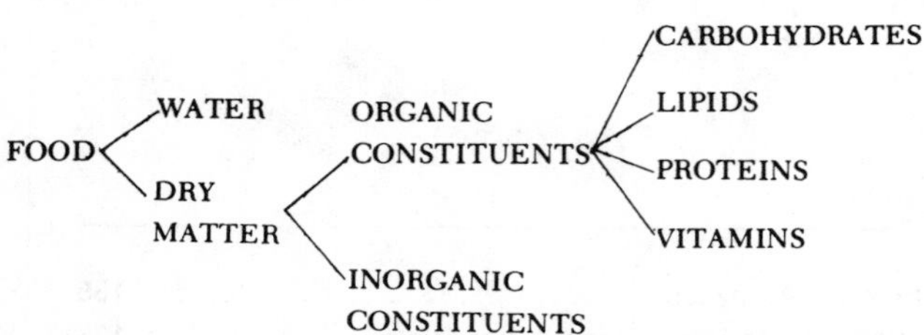

Water

Water is vital to the life of all organisms. It is necessary for digestion, metabolism, cooling, lubrication, and other life processes. Wild vertebrates may obtain water from 3 sources: free water (e.g., lakes, streams, dew on vegetation), water from food consumed, or metabolic water which is produced during the breakdown processes of proteins, carbohydrates, and fats. Numerous studies have examined mechanisms of birds and mammals for maintaining water balance (Schmidt-Nielsen and Schmidt-Nielsen 1952, Chew 1961, Bartholomew and Cade 1963, Nagy et al. 1978).

The *dry matter* of an animal or plant tissue includes everything except water. Most studies investigating the nutrient content of foods report values on a dry matter basis.

Organic Constituents

For a detailed discussion on carbohydrates, proteins, lipids and vitamins the reader is referred to a number of nutrition books dealing with human and animal nutrition as well as chemistry books discussing the specific groups in even more detail (Maynard and Loosli 1969, McDonald et al. 1973, Lehninger 1975).

The term *carbohydrates* is applied to certain nutrient compounds containing only carbon, hydrogen and oxygen. Carbohydrates are the source of energy used in all cellular functions. They form about three-fourths of all the dry matter in plants and are the chief source of energy in the foods of herbivores and many omnivores. Because of their abundance and variety in nature, there are no requirements of the animal body for any specific carbohydrate in the diet.

Carbohydrates are divided into sugars (glucose, lactose, etc.) and non-sugars (cellulose, starch, hemicellulose, etc.). Sugars are easily digested by animals, while digestion of non-sugars is a longer process. Cellulose, one of the most abundant carbohydrates, cannot be digested by higher animals. Only bacteria, fungi, and possibly some protozoa possess the enzyme cellulase necessary to break down the cellulose compounds into simple digestible sugars. Many animals have developed symbiotic relationships with bacteria to enable them to utilize cellulose as a nutrient (see Comparative Anatomy).

Lignin, a phenyl-propyl derivative, is not a carbohydrate but is usually discussed with carbohydrates because of its influence on the digestibility of cellulose and hemicellulose. Lignin forms a complex structure with cellulose and hemicellulose, reducing the digestibility of these compounds.

Lipids are found in both plant and animal tissues and include fats and a number of closely related or associated compounds such as phospholipids and glycolipids which play important roles in the physiological processes of an animal. Lipids are insoluble in water but soluble in common organic solvents such as ether, benzene and chloroform. Because fats contain a high proportion of carbon and hydrogen, they supply 2.25 times as much heat or energy per kilogram as do carbohydrates.

Fats are not specifically required in the diet except as a source of essential fatty acids that free ranging animals receive in sufficient amounts under normal circumstances. Dietary fats, however, are important during the absorption process of fat soluble vitamins (A, D, E, K, and carotene). Many animals store fat which becomes an important energy-reserve during certain stressful periods of their life cycle (see Body Composition).

Proteins are high molecular weight, large colloidal molecules comprised of amino acids. Proteins are the building blocks of every cell. Their importance in the diet is that of supplying various amino acids for the body. Numerous amino acids are required by simple stomached animals and are termed essential amino acids. Ruminants do not require specific amino acids in their diet (see Comparative Anatomy).

Vitamins are organic compounds required by animals in minute quantities. Vitamins are divided into fat soluble vitamins (A, D, E, K) and water soluble vitamins (B complex and ascorbic acid). Although most animals have similar vitamin requirements, the required levels in their diets can vary considerably.

Inorganic Constituents

Various minerals are required by animals for growth or other physiological needs. These minerals are divided into macro-elements (Ca, P, K, S, Na, Cl, Mg) and trace elements (Fe, Mn, Cu, I, Mo, Zn, etc.). Wild ani-

[1]In wildlife literature food is usually referred to as substances eaten by the animal under natural conditions; feed is reserved usually to processed substances, e.g., a pelleted diet consisting of a mixture of seeds, etc.

mals obtain their required minerals through food, water, and ingestion of soils or grit. In addition to a required minimum level, the ratio of intake of various elements is also important. For example, Ca and P should generally occur in the diet in a ratio of between 2:1 and 1:2.

Fifteen trace elements have been identified to date which are required in small amounts by animals. They are termed the essential trace elements. If absent from the diet, metabolic disturbances will occur. Some essential trace elements, and other nonessential trace elements, have toxic effects if ingested in larger amounts. Underwood (1977) is an excellent reference on trace element requirements and toxicities for domestic livestock, but such levels have generally not been established for most wildlife species.

Some examples of the importance of minerals to wild animals are Ca for egg production in pheasants and waterfowl, and Ca and P for antler growth in deer. Several researchers (Dale 1955, Sadler 1961, Kopischke 1966) have found that hen pheasants select grit containing high levels of Ca. Distribution of pheasant populations may be related to soil Ca levels (Dale 1954) or soil levels of Ca and other minerals (Jones et al. 1968). Reduced egg hatchability has been linked to Ca deficiencies in pintail hens (Krapu and Swanson 1975). Nutrient requirements for antler growth in white-tailed deer were investigated by French et al. (1956). They found that Ca or P deficient rations limited antler growth, but felt that P was the most likely to be limiting under natural conditions.

BODY COMPOSITION

A knowledge of the body composition of various wildlife species can be important for several reasons. Fat content can be used as a general indicator of animal condition. Body compositions of prey species are important to investigations of wildlife food chains in order to determine amounts of energy and protein available at higher trophic levels. Game species are often used for human consumption; thus a knowledge of their body compositions is important in evaluating the contribution of hunting to human nutrition.

Animal tissues are composed of water, proteins, fats, minerals, and carbohydrates. Water content is high in newborn animals, approximately 80%, but decreases to between 45–60% in mature animals, depending upon fat content. Carbohydrate content of animals is very low, less than 1%. Mineral content of animals varies between 2–5%, depending upon skeletal size, and protein content is usually between 15–20%.

The fat content of wild animals can vary considerably. This variability influences the relative percentages of the other chemical constituents because the higher the fat content the lower the relative percentages of the other substances. For this reason, body compositions are sometimes presented on a fat-free basis. Fat serves several important functions. It is the primary mechanism of energy storage. This is important for most temperate species, allowing them to either avoid or survive stressful periods, such as winter, when food availability and nutritive quality are low. Birds depend on fat deposits for migration to avoid harsh conditions. Hibernators depend on fat supplies to allow dormancy during the unfavorable season. Considerable weight loss has been observed in hibernating animals (Kayser 1961). Brown fat, a specialized fat deposit, is important to both hibernators and other species requiring non-shivering thermogenesis (Miller 1977). Other species, such as deer, utilize fat as an insulator and to supply energy during the winter. Mautz (1978) discussed the importance of fat reserves to wintering white-tailed deer. Other investigators have examined the deposition and use of body fat by deer (Taber et al. 1959, Trout and Thiessen 1968, Anderson et al. 1972). Deer can lose up to 30% of their body weight during winter (Davenport 1939, deCalesta et al. 1975). The role of fat levels to individual species and in community relationships remains one of the most fascinating research areas in wildlife nutrition and energetics.

COMPARATIVE ANATOMY

Based upon food habits, wildlife species can be categorized into 3 groups: carnivores, omnivores, and herbivores. In addition, the categories of insectivore and granivore are occasionally used. In response to the type of food consumed by each group, characteristic digestive systems have evolved. While a basic digestive system is common in both birds and mammals, various specializations or modifications of digestive organs have developed, especially in herbivores. In this discussion the nutritional implications of these specializations will be stressed, rather than detailed descriptions of anatomical or physiological differences.

Carnivores have evolved the most simple digestive systems because their food is easily digested. In mammals, the simple digestive tract consists of the esophagus, stomach, small intestine, and large intestine. In birds, the basic digestive tract consists of the esophagus, crop, proventriculus, gizzard, small intestine, and large intestine. Complete descriptions of mammal digestive systems are included in numerous anatomy texts (Frandson 1974, Dukes 1977), as are descriptions of bird digestive systems (Bradley and Grahame 1960, Marshall 1960, McLeod et al. 1964, Pettingill 1970).

In birds, 3 types of crops have evolved in response to different dietary selections. Carnivorous birds, including insectivores, typically have only a temporary expansion of the esophagus as a crop. A few carnivores and most leaf-eating birds have a false crop, which is small and poorly developed. Granivorous birds have a true crop or permanent diverticulum. This allows for storage of rapidly gathered food, during which some softening of the seeds by saliva occurs.

An apparent anomaly in the evolution of vertebrates has been the failure to develop enzymes capable of breaking down cellulose. Cellulose is one of the major chemical constituents of plants, and is one of the largest potential sources of energy for animals. As a result, some species of animals have evolved specialized digestive organs which allow for a symbiotic relationship between the animals and microorganisms.

Many species of herbivorous birds, including some granivores, have developed a pair of caeca, located at the junction of the small and large intestine. Each caecum contains microorganisms which continue the breakdown of carbohydrates and proteins remaining after digestion in the proventriculus, gizzard, and small intestine. The microorganisms digest cellulose and other carbohydrates, producing volatile fatty acids which are absorbed through the walls of the caeca and aid in the bird's energy supply.

The occurrence of cellulolytic activity in the caeca of herbivorous birds has been known for many years (Leopold 1953). These birds have a high rate of passage of food through the digestive tract, and although food particles may stay in the caeca for several hours, it is doubtful that cellulose digestion can appreciably add to the energy budget of the birds. During critical periods when food supplies are low, however, even slight energy gains could be beneficial.

As in birds, some mammals have also developed a large caecum and somewhat enlarged large intestine, allowing microbial digestion. Among these are some rodents, lagomorphs, and equines. The caecum allows synthesis of bacterial protein (Kulwich et al. 1953) and vitamins. Caecal contents are high in volatile fatty acids (Alexander and Chowdhury 1958) and a number of amino acids (Yoshida and Kundatsu 1964). The caecum absorbs water, nonprotein nitrogen and vitamins. Bailey and McBee (1964) estimated that about 4–12% of the energy requirement of rabbits is supplied by caecal fermentation.

Some smaller animals, such as lagomorphs, use coprophagy as a means of increasing digestive efficiency. The contents of the caecum, covered by a mucous material, are defecated and immediately reingested and digested in the stomach. This increases the amount of amino acids and vitamins available to the host.

Other rodents such as the hamster rat and golden hamster have developed a primitive type of forestomach. This cardiac portion of the stomach harbors microorganisms that allow some microbial digestion to occur prior to chemical and enzymatic digestion (Moir 1965).

Undoubtedly the most complex digestive system was evolved by the ruminants. Texts providing a detailed discussion of ruminant digestion include Dougherty et al. (1965), Hungate (1966), Phillipson (1970), Frandson (1974), McDonald and Warner (1975), and Dukes (1977).

The stomach complex of ruminants consists of the *rumen, reticulum, omasum,* and *abomasum.* The rumen can be compared to a fermentation vat. As soon as the poorly masticated food enters the rumen it is attacked by billions of microorganisms, and is exposed to a continuous churning process due to the regular contractions of rumen pillars. Due to this mechanical action and the attack of microorganisms, the food is reduced in size while plant sugars and other easily digestible nutrients are converted to microbial and protozoal protein. Fibrous materials (e.g., cellulose, hemicellulose) are slow to digest and may remain in the rumen for several days. The end product of microbial fermentation, volatile fatty acids (VFA), are absorbed through the rumen wall. In ruminants, food protein is broken down first to ammonia which is largely used to build microbial protein. The small, partially digested food particles and microorganisms are washed slowly to the reticulum and enter the omasum. The omasum acts as a filter, returning larger particles back to the rumen, while allowing smaller particles to pass to the abomasum.

Upon entering the abomasum, the food is subjected to acid and peptic digestion. Microorganisms are lysed and their cell contents are made available for the host in the small intestine. One advantage of ruminant digestion is that microorganisms can utilize low grade protein, and by doing so, upgrade the biological value of the protein for the ruminant. Because of this microbial action, ruminants do not require any specific essential amino acids in their diet. The small and large intestines function the same way in ruminants as in monogastrics. There is a caecum at the junction of the small and large intestine, but very little is known about the importance of caecal digestion in ruminants.

Some animals have developed the ability to utilize fibrous plant foods through evolution by the development of various anatomical adaptations. These specialized adaptations and their corresponding influence on an animal's ability to utilize plant nutrients must be considered in both wildlife nutritional investigations and in the management of particular wildlife species.

This brief comparison of digestive strategies of animals reveals the complexity of herbivore foods. Animal tissue, as food for carnivorous species, varies relatively little in terms of digestibility and quality in comparison to the plant foods of herbivores. For this reason, the main emphasis of the remainder of this chapter will be on herbivores and on plants as a food source. Discussion of carnivorous species will be included only in several sections where appropriate.

FEEDING STRATEGIES

The foregoing discussion very briefly covered the major differences in animal anatomy. It should be emphasized that there are many additional differences which influence an animal's habitat and diet selection. For example, wild ruminants differ considerably in size and rumen anatomy; in turn, these differences influence the animal's metabolic rate and nutritional requirements (see Energy Partitioning). Differences in the nutritive quality of grouse diets during winter and summer as well as differences in the nutritive quality of the diets of male and female grouse during spring have been observed (Korschgen 1966, King 1968, Schladweiler 1968). The identification of such differences and their corresponding influence on diet selection has led to the investigation of wildlife feeding strategies.

The investigation of wildlife feeding strategies involves the identification of the selected diet of a species or group of animals, the nutritional basis and significance of this selection, and the effect of the selection on intraspecific and interspecific relationships. Feeding strategies have been investigated for various groups of wildlife including large herbivores, several groups of birds (Cody 1968, Murton 1971, Krebs et al. 1974, Smith and Sweatman 1974, Hespenheide 1975), and small mammals (Rosenzweig and Sterner 1970, Baker 1971, Brown 1975, Mares and Williams 1977).

Some of the best examples of investigations on feeding strategies of wildlife species have been conducted by researchers working with African ungulates (Vesey-Fitzgerald 1960, Lamprey 1963, Talbot and Talbot 1963, Gwynne and Bell 1968, Bell 1971, Jarman 1974, Hirst 1975). Bell (1971) studied the feeding strategies of the zebra, a nonruminant, and 2 ruminants, the wildebeest and Thomson's gazelle. Although zebras have no rumen, they do have an enlarged caecum. Microbial action in this organ improves the nutritive quality of the ingesta, although the caecum, because of its location, is not as efficient in supplying nutrients from fibrous foods as the rumen. In ruminants, the opening between the reticulum and the omasum (reticulo-omasal orifice) restricts passage of larger fibrous food particles. Before these materials can travel to the omasum, microorganisms and the churning action of the rumen must reduce ingested materials to small fragments. Therefore, the rate of passage of the ingesta in a ruminant is influenced by the fiber content of the food. No such restrictions are imposed on the digestive tract of monogastrics, such as the zebra. The zebra, therefore, is able to take large amounts of poor quality fibrous foods, obtain easily digestible nutrients from this food, upgrade some of it in its large caecum, and excrete the fibrous portion. Large amounts of food passing through the digestive tract compensate for low nutritive quality.

The wildebeest is a large ruminant and has a larger rumen, in relation to body size, than does the smaller Thomson's gazelle. Because of its large body size, the wildebeest also has a lower metabolic rate than the gazelle, resulting in lower energy requirements per unit body weight. Thus the wildebeest can utilize a poorer quality forage than the Thomson's gazelle. Consequently, the Thomson's gazelle is more selective in its feeding habits. These differences have resulted in different, complementary forage selections by the 3 species. The zebra is the first species to leave the shortgrass prairie because of food shortages. They move into less preferred lowland areas and feed on large quantities of the coarser parts of grasses, and move to new areas as the quantity of forage available is reduced. The wildebeests utilize lowland areas vacated by zebras by eating the more nutritious lower plant parts exposed by the foraging of the zebras. Finally, the Thomson's gazelles utilize the area, selecting the most nutritious forbs exposed through the foraging of the other 2 species. In this way, competition for food is not only minimized between the 3 species, it is actually complementary. The importance of the study of feeding strategies is exemplified in this relationship. If the population of 1 of these 3 species is seriously impacted by some factor or disturbance, it could have a severe impact on the other 2 species as well. Similar studies conducted on the Pawnee National Grasslands in Colorado have demonstrated divergent grazing strategies between pronghorn and bison in both botanical composition (Schwartz and Nagy 1976) and chemical composition (Schwartz et al. 1977) of the diet.

PLANT CHEMICAL COMPOSITION AND SAMPLING CONSIDERATIONS

Plant Chemical Composition

Plants and animals contain similar types of chemical substances, the primary difference being the relative amounts of these substances in their compositions. Water is a major constituent of plants although its proportion varies considerably, from 5 to 90% (e.g., seeds vs. tubers). Because of this variability, the other plant constituents are usually expressed as a percentage of plant dry weight.

Carbohydrates comprise the majority of plant dry matter. The amount and type of carbohydrates in a plant are major determinants of plant digestibility. Plant matter is often divided into 2 groups: cell contents and cell walls. Carbohydrates contained in the cell contents consist primarily of sugars, starches, and soluble carbohydrates. These are almost completely digestible by animals and are a major source of energy. Cell walls are largely composed of the carbohydrates, cellulose and hemicellulose, along with varying amounts of lignin and cutin. The relative amounts of cellulose, hemicellulose, and lignin influence the digestibility of a plant. Lignin forms a complex compound with cellulose and hemicellulose, reducing the digestibility of these constituents by wildlife, including ruminants. The higher the lignin levels, the less digestible are the cellulose and hemicellulose constituents. Many factors affect the relative amounts of these carbohydrates, such as plant age, season, and plant part, as discussed below.

Plant lipids occur in the cell contents, and consist almost exclusively of fats. Plant fat content is generally low because energy is stored in the form of sugars and starches. Certain plant parts, however, (e.g., seeds and some fruits), do contain higher levels of fats.

Plant proteins also occur primarily in the cell contents. Amino acids and nonprotein nitrogen (NPN) are often considered along with protein in plant chemical analysis. Protein levels of plants are generally low (less than 10%), although considerable variation can occur. Plants are able to synthesize all of their required vitamins, which are present in the cell contents.

The mineral (or ash) content of plants, as in animals, is a small percentage of dry weight. Plants require various macro and trace elements, and can also accumulate some in very high concentrations. High levels of some elements in plants, such as selenium, can pose a hazard to herbivorous animals.

Factors Affecting Plant Composition

Various factors can influence the composition of a plant, which in turn affect its nutritive quality. A brief summary of some of the causative factors affecting plant chemical compositions follows.

PLANT SPECIES

The factor having the greatest influence on plant composition has been found to be plant species (Dietz et al. 1962, Short et al. 1966). Numerous studies have investigated the chemical compositions of various plant species. A compilation of some of these findings for selected plant species is included in the Chemical Analyses section of this chapter.

SEASONAL AND PHENOLOGICAL EFFECTS

Plants vary seasonally in chemical composition. Dietz et al. (1962) and Short et al. (1966) found seasonal variations to be nearly as important as species differences. Seasonal variations are primarily caused by differences in plant phenology (Blair et al. 1977, Hanley and Brady 1977). For this reason, seasonal variations and phenological variations will be considered together.

Crude protein is highest during the growing season (Swank 1956, Dietz et al. 1962, Short et al. 1966, Johnston et al. 1968, Hickman 1975, Blair et al. 1977, Hanley and Brady 1977). Phosphorus levels also are highest during the growing season, decreasing with plant maturity (Swank 1956, Dietz et al. 1962, Short et al. 1966, Johnston et al. 1968, Blair et al. 1977, Hanley and Brady 1977). Other nutrients found at high levels during the growing season are moisture (Swank 1956, Short et al. 1966, Hickman 1975), and carotene (Short et al. 1966, Hanley and Brady 1977). Ash content is highest in late spring and summer according to Dietz et al. (1962), Hickman (1975), and Short et al. (1966). Dietz et al. (1962) measured high calcium levels in the fall while Short et al. (1966) and Hickman (1975) found variable calcium levels between seasons.

As a plant matures, its cellulose content increases (Johnston et al. 1968, Torgerson and Pfander 1971). Other researchers have reported that crude fiber (of which cellulose is a primary constituent, see Chemical Analyses) increases with plant maturity (Dietz et al. 1962, Hickman 1975, Blair et al. 1977). Lignin content of plants also increases with plant maturity (Blair et al. 1977). The increase in these constituents decreases plant digestibility. Seasonal differences in digestibility corresponding to these increases have been reported by a number of researchers including Johnston et al. (1968), Torgerson and Pfander (1971), and Blair et al. (1977).

SITE EFFECTS

Short et al. (1966) and Gibbs (1978) found minor variations in plant compositions caused by site effects. Various researchers have examined the effects of specific site factors on plant compositions, as discussed below. It should be noted, however, that the study of site effects is a very complex subject and that changes in plant chemical composition are usually the result of many factors acting together so that single factor effects are hard to determine or explain (Laycock and Price 1970).

Temperature. Crude protein levels of various herbage species increase with temperature (Deinum et al. 1968, Smith 1970). Temperature also was found to increase ash content of plants (Deinum et al. 1968, Smith 1970). Smith (1970) reported that plant phosphorus levels increased with temperature. Cell wall constituents also increased with temperature (Deinum et al. 1968) as did plant lignin content (Deinum et al. 1968). Bowman and Law (1964), however, found that cellulose and lignin content of grasses was greater at lower temperatures. Plant digestibility has been found to decrease with increasing temperature (Deinum et al. 1968, Smith 1970). Discrepancies in these findings are probably the result of interactions of temperature with other site factors. Additional research is needed on the influence of temperature on plant chemical constituents before conclusions can be drawn.

Moisture. Moisture can influence plant composition in 2 ways, as soil moisture or as precipitation. While these are closely related, the effects of each can be described separately.

The influence of soil moisture on plant composition is difficult to determine because its primary effect is on altering growth rates or phenological stages (Laycock and Price 1970). Soil moisture levels will influence the moisture content of plants (Willard and Schuster 1973). Increases in soil moisture levels have been reported to both increase (Greenhill and Page 1931) and decrease (Browne 1938) crude protein levels.

Precipitation, in addition to altering soil moisture levels, will influence plant compositions by leaching of certain nutrients from the plants. Tukey (1966) listed specific nutrients which can be leached from plants. Leaching of dry herbaceous plants can reduce levels of protein, phosphorus, ash, and carotene (Laycock and Price 1970).

Insolation. Insolation appears to influence plant compositions although these effects often are indirect because shaded areas generally have higher levels of soil moisture (Laycock and Price 1970). For example, shaded plants appear to be more succulent (Dealy 1966), but this may be due to higher soil moisture (Laycock and Price 1970). McEwen and Dietz (1965) found shaded plants to be higher in protein, but this also may be influenced by soil moisture (Laycock and Price 1970) and by somewhat retarded growth caused by the reduced solar radiation. Shaded plants were shown to be lower in nitrogen free extract and sugars than plants growing in sunlight (McEwen and Dietz 1965). However, Deinum et al. (1968) reported that plant digestibility was positively influenced by increased amounts of sunlight.

Soil. The type of soil and level of nutrients in the soil influence plant compositions. Gibbs (1978) felt that soil nutrients had a greater effect on plant compositions than other site factors. Crude protein levels were influenced by soil nutrient levels (Stoddart 1941, Hundley 1959, McEwen and Dietz 1965). More specifically, protein content in plants has been found to be influenced by soil nitrogen levels (Bailey 1968b, Deinum et al. 1968, Bayoumi and Smith 1976). Ash content of plants can be influenced by soil nutrient levels (Stoddart 1941, McEwen and Dietz 1965). Phosphorus levels in plants were correlated with soil phosphorus levels (Daniel and Harper 1934, Browne 1938, Stoddart 1941). Laycock and Price (1970) pointed out that interrelated factors can modify soil nutrient effects.

Plant Palatability and Animal Preference

Palatability can be defined as plant characteristics that stimulate a selective feeding response by animals. Preference is the selection of a plant by an animal. Several plant chemical constituents which appear to influence palatability have been identified. Cook (1959) reported plant protein levels to be positively correlated with palatability. Dietz (1958) felt that plants with high ash content were more palatable than plants with lower ash levels. Swift (1948) supported this finding in relation to calcium levels, and Swift (1948) and Swank (1956) found it to be true for phosphorus. Plant palatability also was positively correlated with moisture content (Reynolds 1967, Radwan and Crouch 1974), and with digestibility (Longhurst et al. 1968). One should keep in mind that palatability and preference are complex subjects, as many factors influence both. Additional research is needed in these areas.

Sampling Considerations

Many factors should be considered in designing sampling procedures to investigate plant nutritive quality. Some of the more important considerations are discussed below.

SELECTION OF STUDY AREAS

The selection of study areas will depend upon the objectives of the investigation. Specific objectives are necessary to determine which characteristics are important to consider in the site selection. For example, if the objectives of the investigation are to determine the influence of 1 or more site factors on the nutritive quality of certain plant species, then study areas should be selected on the basis of differences in the site factors of interest, while minimizing other differences between areas. The objectives of many investigations are to determine the nutritional quality of a range for a specific wildlife species. Seasonal variations in habitat use by the species must be recognized and study areas which are representative of important seasonal habitats on the range should be selected. For example, an investigation of mule deer winter forage quality should be conducted on key wintering areas. For many western ranges, this would mean selecting study areas on open, south-facing slopes within deer winter range, as these slopes appear to receive the greatest use, especially for feeding. Sampling forage quality from other areas could produce biased results due to influences of site effects or differing grazing pressures.

SELECTION OF PLANT SPECIES

The selection of plant species to be investigated is usually based upon a knowledge of the food habits of the wildlife species of interest. Food habits information must be applicable to the season of interest, and from similar habitat types to those under investigation. If adequate food habits information is lacking, a food habits investigation may be required prior to the investigation of plant nutritive quality. Korschgen (Chap. 9) discussed techniques for use in food habits investigations. It should be noted that each determination of wildlife food habits has advantages and disadvantages, including biases in results, which must be considered in interpreting the information.

SAMPLING METHODOLOGY

Wildlife are selective in their choice of foods, not only by the selection of plant species, but also by the selection of particular plants and plant parts. Research has shown that plant parts vary in nutritive quality. As with entire plants, early phenological stages are of higher nutritive value than mature plants. Buds are of high nutritive quality. The nutritive quality of a plant decreases with increasing distance down a stem from the bud (Aldous 1945, Bailey 1967, Blair and Epps 1967, Short and Harrell 1969, Cowan et al. 1970, Short et al. 1972). Wildlife are sensitive to these differences and generally select plant parts of high nutritive value.

While it may not be possible to actually duplicate the diet selection of a wild-ranging animal, every effort should be made to closely approximate it. Clipping of plants for the collection of plant samples should simulate the feeding activities of the wildlife species of interest. This approach to collecting plants for analysis has been utilized by Regelin et al. (1974) and Schwartz (1977), who observed the feeding of tame or wild animals and collected the plant parts observed to be eaten.

The following methods of sampling plants are frequently used to determine the productivity of an area. Grasses and forbs are usually collected by clipping the entire plant at a height of 1 cm above ground. As many animals are seed eaters, it is often desirable to make a separate collection of seed from these plants. Fungi, such as mushrooms, can be collected by clipping at ground level. Browse species require more involved collection methods. Generally, the current annual growth is collected from browse species. Often a maximum diameter of 0.64 cm (¼") or a maximum length of 7.5 cm (3") is used in collecting browse samples. The methods of plant collection to be used must be determined in sufficient detail to assure uniformity among all personnel.

An estimate of the sample size needed to meet the objectives of the investigation is important. Usually this requires preliminary sampling to obtain an estimate of the variance.

Handling of the sample after collection should be planned prior to collection. If a measure of moisture content is desired, then the sample should be placed in plastic bags and frozen until ready for analysis. If moisture content is not important, then most samples, unless of very high water content, can be placed in paper bags and kept in a dry location.

CHEMICAL ANALYSES

The more common methods of food analysis and nutritive value determination will be briefly reviewed. Greater details are available in many textbooks on animal nutrition such as Crampton and Harris (1969).

Proximate Analysis

The most widely used method to estimate the nutritive value of plants is the proximate analysis, also called the Weende method. This method has been used world-wide on many species of plants for more than a century. The main advantage of the method is its wide acceptance and the ability to compare results with past research. The method is standard (AOAC 1975), inexpensive, and relatively simple so that most laboratories are able to perform it.

Proximate analysis determines the moisture, ash, ether extract, crude protein, crude fiber and nitrogen free extract (NFE) fractions of foods. The method of determining each of these fractions will be briefly described along with some of the associated problems.

Moisture is determined by weighing a sample, then drying it at 105°C, or under a vacuum at 60°C, and weighing again. During drying some volatile substances, such as short chain fatty acids and volatile oils, may evaporate.

Ash is determined by burning a sample in a furnace at approximately 600°C. The ash content of a food provides no information about specific elements present. Of special interest are the amounts of essential elements such as calcium, phosphorus, potassium, their ratios, and the amounts of nonessential elements such as aluminum and silicates. Single or multielement techniques must be used to determine the level of each element of interest in the ash fraction.

Ether extract (crude fat) is determined by extracting the sample with ether, then evaporating the ether. Ether extract includes not only fatty acids but all ether soluble materials such as plant pigments (i.e., chlorophyll and carotene), waxes, essential oils and fat soluble vitamins. Because animals cannot metabolize all of these constituents equally, the ether extract fraction often will not supply to the animal 9.0 Kcal of energy which is frequently attributed to fats.

The presence of volatile or essential oils can greatly inflate the ether extract content. A number of plants, such as sagebrush and juniper, contain considerable amounts (2–4%, dry matter basis) of these terpene components which show up in the ether extract portion but are not metabolized by animals. In fact, a number of studies have shown that they have inhibitory effects on rumen microorganisms (Nagy et al. 1964, Longhurst et al. 1968, Nagy and Tengerdy 1968, Oh et al. 1968). Since ruminants depend on their rumen microorganisms for proper digestion, these adverse effects of volatile oils can reduce the nutrient and energy supply for the host.

The test for crude protein is not a true protein determination, but rather a nitrogen determination using the Kjeldahl method (AOAC 1975). This method involves digesting a sample with concentrated sulfuric acid, converting nitrogen in the sample to ammonia. The ammonia is then released to a gaseous state by the addition of sodium hydroxide. The ammonia is distilled and collected in an acid. The amount is determined by titration. The amount of nitrogen found in a sample is converted to percent crude protein by multiplying the amount by 6.25, as the average protein contains 16% nitrogen. Actual protein levels may be lower or higher, depending upon the amount of non-protein nitrogen (NPN) in the food. Crude protein by the Kjeldahl method also provides no information on the amino acid content and distribution of the crude protein fraction.

The crude fiber determination involves boiling the sample first with dilute acid (H_2SO_4) followed by boiling with dilute alkali (NaOH). The procedure is designed to imitate the acid and the alkaline digestion of the digestive tract. The insoluble residue remaining is called the crude fiber, the theoretically indigestible fraction of the food. However, the chemical constituents remaining after this treatment are cellulose and hemicellulose. These constituents can be partially digested by many animals. Most of the lignin, which is indigestible by animals, is dissolved by the treatment, and is not included in the crude fiber fraction. It should be noted that this method is largely replaced by the Van Soest method which will be discussed later.

The nitrogen-free extract (NFE) is determined mathematically by subtracting the weights or percentages of the other fractions from that of the total sample. In other words, NFE is determined indirectly, based on the other chemical analyses. Thus, errors occurring in the determination of any of the other analyses will also cause an error in the NFE fraction. Theoretically, the NFE is the easily digestible carbohydrate portion of the sample such as sugars and starches. While the chemical constituents included in the NFE are easily digested, the problem with the interpretation of NFE results is the discrepancy between actual and determined NFE percentages caused by the indirect methodology.

As mentioned, proximate analysis has been used in many previous studies. Table 10.1 lists the chemical constituents of various selected plant species as determined by proximate analysis. While general comparisons of foods can be made from proximate analyses, the many inherent problems with this technique limit the usefulness of the results.

Van Soest Method

While various modifications of the proximate analysis can be used to overcome some of the problems associated with its use, the determination of the crude fiber fraction fails to provide adequate information on the fibrous portion of a forage. This portion consists primarily of cellulose and hemicellulose which are digestible to varying degrees by cellulolytic microorganisms. The crude fiber fraction does not include lignin, which is indigestible, because it is soluble in alkali solutions. Thus the lignin content of a forage appears in the NFE fraction, which is supposedly highly digestible. Because of these problems, new methods of forage analysis have been developed to provide more valuable information on the chemical constituents of forages, especially those containing appreciable amounts of fiber. The most noteworthy of these new methods of analysis is the one developed by Van Soest (1967).

The Van Soest method is outlined in Fig. 10.1. This method involves first separating the sample into cell contents (CC) and cell wall constituents (CWC). This is accomplished through the use of a neutral detergent which disrupts the cell wall, releasing the cell contents without dissolving the cell wall constituents. The cell contents are approximately 98% digestible, being composed primarily of soluble carbohydrates, proteins, and lipids.

The second step in the Van Soest method involves the determination of the chemical constituents of the cell

Table 10.1. Proximate analyses of selected plant species on a dry matter basis.

Species	% Crude protein	% Ether extract	% Crude fiber	% N.F.E.	% Ash	Part analyzed	Season	State	Source
Abies balsamea	7.9	10.7	26.2	49.9	4.0	C.A.G.[1]	Winter	Michigan	Ullrey et al. 1968
Balsam fir	8.8	11.8	21.7	54.4		C.A.G.	Winter	New Hampshire	Mautz et al. 1976
Acer rubrum	4.3	4.3	30.2	58.7	2.4	C.A.G.	Winter	Virginia	Hundley 1959
Red maple	6.6	2.6	38.7	49.5		C.A.G.	Winter	New Hampshire	Mautz et al. 1976
	5.7	3.7	37.0	51.3			Winter	Pennsylvania	Hellmers 1940
	4.6	4.7	31.2	48.3	3.1	C.A.G. (twigs)	Winter	Missouri	Torgerson and Pfander 1971
	5.6	2.4	32.3	57.1	2.6	C.A.G.	Winter	New Hampshire	Walski and Mautz 1977
Artemisia tridentata	11.0	12.9	19.9	52.5		C.A.G.	Winter	Utah	Smith 1950
Big sagebrush	12.0	12.9	18.1	52.9	4.2		Winter	Colorado	Dietz et al. 1962
	10.3	9.84	17.35	49.84	6.06	Foliage	Winter	Wyoming	Hamilton 1958
	6.23	3.78	38.92	40.75	4.81	C.A.G.	Winter	Wyoming	Hamilton 1958
Cercocarpus montanus	8.4	3.9	27.8	56.9	2.9		Winter	Colorado	Dietz et al. 1962
Mountain mahogany	7.2	4.5	34.7	52.1		C.A.G.	Winter	Utah	Smith 1957
	9.48	6.06	24.69	51.52	2.43	C.A.G.	Winter	Wyoming	Hamilton 1958
Cornus florida	4.7	4.2	25.9	60.5	4.7	C.A.G.	Winter	Virginia	Hundley 1959
Flowering dogwood	6.49	18.75	25.13	38.44	6.01		Winter	Mississippi	Billingsley and Arner 1970
	6.62	11.50	31.79	35.01	5.09	Fruit	Winter	Connecticut	Spinner and Bishop 1950
	8.44	23.95	13.93	43.12	4.73	Pulp	Winter	Connecticut	Spinner and Bishop 1950
	4.5	2.91	41.95	40.22	4.06	Seed	Winter	Connecticut	Spinner and Bishop 1950
Populus tremuloides	9.3	8.7	27.5	51.2	3.4	C.A.G.	Winter	New Hampshire	Walski and Mautz 1977
Quaking aspen	7.9	9.8	28.2	51.1			Winter	Pennsylvania	Hellmers 1940
	8.47	15.46	21.71	44.74	4.07	C.A.G.	Winter	Wyoming	Hamilton 1958
Purshia tridentata Bitterbrush	7.4	5.4	30.6	53.6		C.A.G. & foliage	Winter	Utah	Smith 1952
	9.1	5.7	24.2	58.2	3.1		Winter	Colorado	Dietz et al. 1962
	8.92	6.94	23.4	58.52	2.88	C.A.G. & foliage	Winter	Nevada	Aldous 1945
	7.86	6.14	28.11	49.11	3.11	C.A.G.	Winter	Wyoming	Hamilton 1958
Symphoricarpos	8.5	6.27	21.40	59.78	4.24	Fruit	Winter	Maryland	King and McClure 1944
orbiculatus	6.13	3.36	18.34	67.83	3.89	Fruit	Winter	Connecticut	Spinner and Bishop 1950
Snowberry	4.8	2.2	39.8	44.2	3.0	C.A.G.	Winter	Missouri	Torgerson and Pfander 1971
	5.8	6.9	21.0	56.8	3.6	Fruit	Winter	Missouri	Torgerson and Pfander 1971
Thuja occidentalis	7.2	9.5	27.3	53.2	4.3	C.A.G.	Winter	Michigan	Ullrey et al. 1968
Northern white	6.3	6.8	36.4	46.7	4.8	C.A.G.	Winter	Michigan	Ullrey et al. 1967
cedar	8.5	9.2	26.5	50.4	5.4	C.A.G.	Winter	New Hampshire	Walski and Mautz 1977
Trifolium arvense	20.69	2.77	26.12	46.39	4.38	Seeds	Summer	Maryland	King and McClure 1944
Trifolium repens	24.8	4.6	14.1	47.1			Summer	Kentucky	Forbes and Garrigus 1950
Clover									
Agropyron smithii									
Wheatgrass	14.05	4.51	27.54	43.39	10.51	Top	Winter	Wyoming	Honess and Frost 1942
	8.64	3.13	30.8		9.93		Summer	Alberta	Johnston and Bezeau 1962
Agrostis alba	20.26	7.03	10.34	55.57	6.98	Seeds		Maryland	King and McClure 1944
Bentgrass									
Deschampsia	6.76	1.94	31.16		10.62		Winter	Alberta	Johnston and Bezeau 1962
caespitosa	16.0	2.0	29.0	47.0	6.0		Spring	Colorado	Dietz et al. 1962
Hairgrass									

[1]C.A.G. = Current Annual Growth

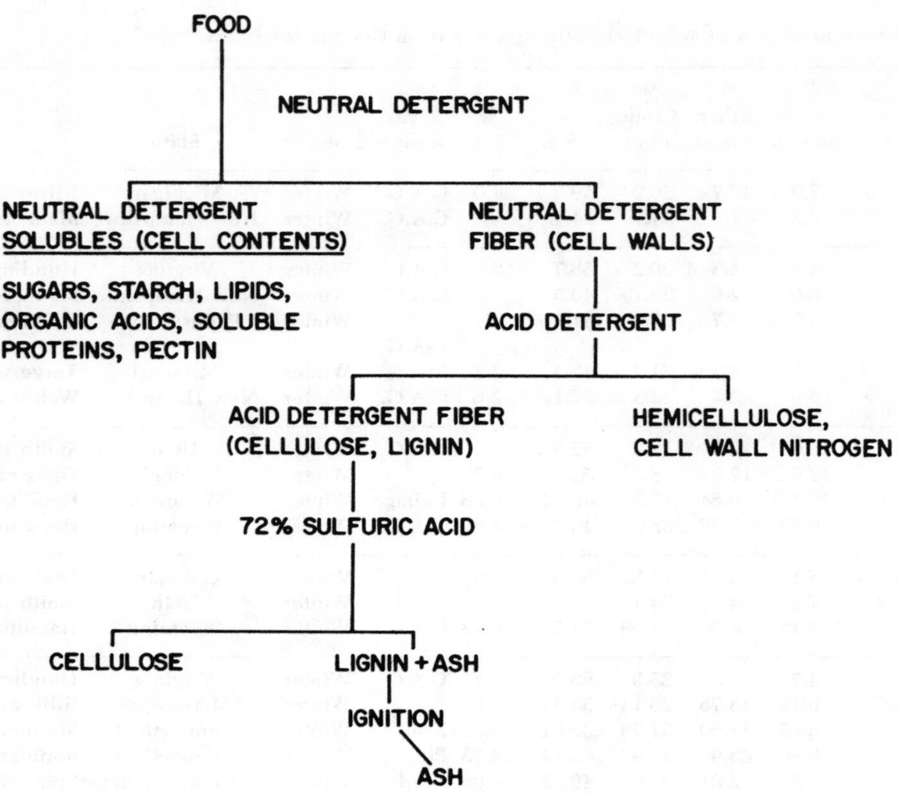

Fig. 10.1. Van Soest method for the determination of forage nutritive quality.

walls, from which the digestibility of the sample can be estimated. First, the sample is placed in an acid detergent which dissolves the hemicellulose and cell wall nitrogen. The remaining fraction, the acid detergent fiber (ADF), is then placed in 72% sulfuric acid, which dissolves the cellulose. The remaining fraction consists of lignin and ash, from which the lignin content can be determined.

The Van Soest method has proved to be very useful in comparing ruminant forages because it provides information on the amounts of cellulose, hemicellulose, and lignin. Van Soest (1967) has determined regression equations for determining forage digestibility based on chemical constituents. A number of forage species, especially grasses, have been tested by this method, and results are comparable with results obtained by actual ruminant digestion trials. More recently researchers have begun to examine important wildlife foods using the Van Soest method (Segelquist et al. 1972, Short et al. 1974, Smith and Malechek 1974, Robbins et al. 1975).

IN VIVO AND *IN VITRO* DIGESTIBILITY TRIALS

In animal nutrition *in vivo* refers to experiments conducted within an animal, while *in vitro* means simulating certain reactions outside of the animal. Although valuable information is gained through chemical analyses, digestion trials are necessary to obtain information on the actual dietary value of foods.

In vivo digestion trials have been used extensively in connection with proximate analysis. Animals are confined in cages and are fed known amounts of a diet. There should be a pre-trial period, approximately 10–14 days in the case of ruminants, to acclimatize the animal for the diet which usually consists of a ground and pelleted ration. Feces are collected and the food and the feces are subjected to proximate analysis. Knowing the differences between the chemical content of the feces and the diet, one can calculate digestibility coefficients and total digestible nutrients (TDN) of the diet, and measure apparent digestibilities of the food. It is almost a prerequisite for such trials that the animals be trained to accept confinement. Even then, confinement can adversely affect results (Dietz et al. 1962, Ullrey et al. 1964, Mautz 1971, Ammann et al. 1973). An additional problem involved with *in vivo* digestion trials on wild animals is that of food intake. For example, deer refused to eat more than token amounts of sagebrush and bitterbrush when these were offered as the sole source of diet (Dietz et al. 1962). This problem could be overcome by running separate feeding trials on, e.g., alfalfa hay, and then mixing the item in question with alfalfa and conducting a second trial. Such digestion trials utilizing differences, however, have a number of inherent problems, such as possible differences in food digestibility caused by the interaction of foods. A number of *in vivo* digestion trials have been conducted on deer (Forbes et al. 1941, Smith 1952, Hagen 1953, Bissell et al. 1955, Dietz et al. 1962, Robbins and Moen 1975, Robbins et al. 1975, Blair et al. 1977). While more detailed digestion trials have been conducted on additional species (see Energy Partitioning), simple *in vivo* digestion trials have not been reported.

A meaningful digestion trial requires several animals and considerable space and equipment. In addition, especially in the case of large wild ruminants such as pronghorn, deer, and elk, it can be difficult to collect adequate amounts of plant material for feeding trials. Using rumen fistulated animals, forage digestion in the rumen can be simulated by placing a number of nylon bags containing different forage items directly in the rumen through the fistula. Johnson (1966) described many of the techniques and procedures used in *in vivo* digestion trials in connection with domestic animals. Peden et al. (1974) used the nylon bag technique with trained buffalo. This method, however, has limited application with wild ruminants due to difficulties encountered with rumen fistulation of these species.

In vitro digestion trials, while only simulating true digestive processes, have several advantages over *in vivo* digestion trials. Such experiments require only a rumen fluid donor, using much less space and equipment than true digestion trials involving many animals. In addition, many forage samples can be run simultaneously. The basic technique involves mixing rumen fluid and a buffer solution with the forage and incubating it for a certain length of time. A good technique is the 2-stage *in vitro* method which simulates rumen microbial as well as chemical digestion (Tilley and Terry 1963). Good reviews of these techniques were published by Johnson (1966) and Pearson (1970). It should be emphasized that the rumen fluid donor should be on a diet which closely resembles the forage to be tested, and the rumen fluid should be brought to the laboratory as soon as possible (Schwartz and Nagy 1972).

In vitro techniques have been used extensively to evaluate forages for domestic ruminants, and there is a large volume of literature correlating *in vitro* and *in vivo* techniques. Information on this topic has been published by Robbins et al. (1975), Palmer et al. (1976), Ruggiero and Whelan (1976), and Milchunas et al. (1978). *In vitro* digestion trials have been conducted on deer (Snider and Asplund 1974, Robbins and Moen 1975, Urness et al. 1975, Dressler and Wood 1976, Blair et al. 1977), moose (Oldemeyer et al. 1977), elk (Ward 1971), and pronghorn (Schwartz et al. 1977). This technique is valuable in comparing digestibilities between different plant species. However, more information is needed on this subject before it will be possible to make digestibility predictions based only on *in vitro* digestibility trials.

ENERGY PARTITIONING

While *in vivo* digestion trials can supply valuable information on the digestibility of a food, often more detailed information is desired, especially on the energy content of foods. *In vivo* digestion trials can be modified to obtain information on the digestible energy of a food. However, measures of digestible energy only indicate the potential energy of a food. This includes energy which is lost to an animal through production of methane, urine, and heat of digestion or heat increment. Digestion trials which determine the losses of energy to each of these factors are therefore often desirable. The determination of these energy losses is called energy partitioning. Various publications provide comprehensive descriptions of energy partitioning (Brody 1945, Swift 1957, Kleiber 1961, Blaxter 1962, 1965, Dougherty et al. 1965, Crampton and Harris 1969).

Figure 10.2 depicts the basic energy partitioning of foods. The major difference between monogastric animals and ruminants in terms of energy partitioning is that ruminants produce considerable amounts of methane gas during digestion, while monogastrics produce little. The energy contained in methane is lost to the animal, and represents a considerable loss to the ruminant. Methane is formed in the rumen by the reduction of carbon dioxide with hydrogen from formic acid (Hungate 1966). Although there is some cecal production of methane by microorganisms, it is probably produced in minute quantities.

Gross energy is the total energy content of a food. This is determined by combusting a sample of the food in a

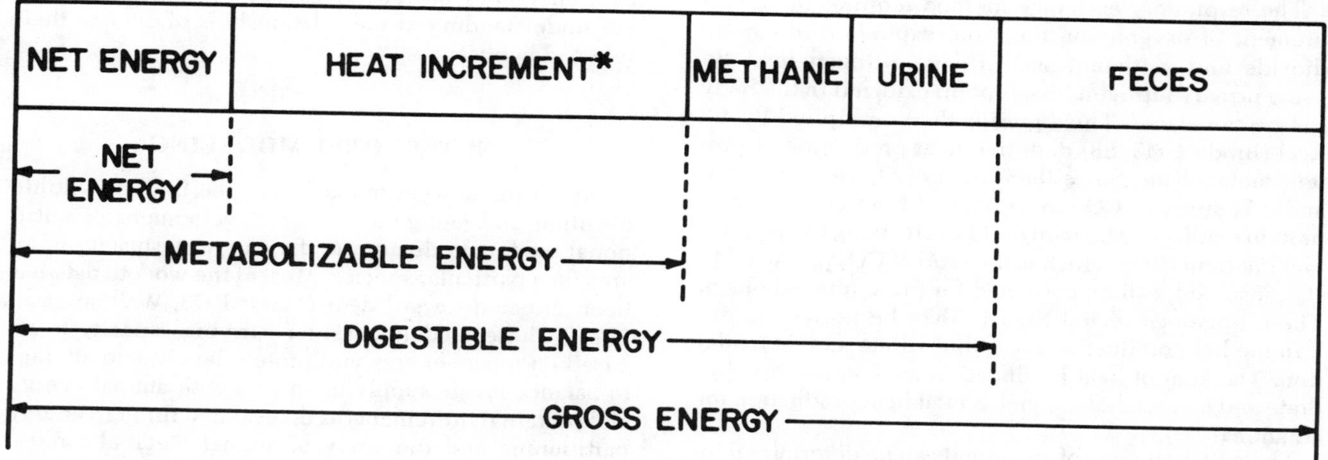

*Heat increment may be net energy if the animal is in an environment with a temperature below its thermal neutral zone.

Fig. 10.2. Energy partitioning of foods, example of a ruminant.

bomb calorimeter, and measuring the heat given off. Fats, carbohydrates, and proteins give off different amounts of energy when combusted, due to their different chemical structure. Fats, for example, have approximately twice the gross energy of carbohydrates.

Digestible energy is determined by subtracting the energy contained in the feces from the gross energy of the food. When the energy lost in the gaseous products of digestion (primarily methane) and in urinary energy are deducted from the digestible energy, *metabolizable energy* is determined. This is the portion of total energy that is actually available for maintenance, production, activity and heat increment (Maynard and Loosli 1969).

Net energy of a food is that portion available to an animal for body maintenance, and various forms of production and activity (Maynard and Loosli 1969). It is quantitatively derived by subtracting the heat increment of a food from its metabolizable portion.

Heat increment has been defined as the increase in heat production due to the consumption of food when an animal is in a thermoneutral environment (Crampton and Harris 1969). The effect of temperature is important because heat increment is wasted energy except when the temperature of the environment is below the critical temperature of the animal (Kleiber 1961). When the environmental temperature is below the critical temperature of the animal, heat produced is used to maintain body temperature and thus becomes part of the net energy for maintenance. Heat increment is calculated by subtracting the heat production of the fasting animal from heat production of the fed animal.

Animal heat production can be measured directly and indirectly. In direct calorimetry, heat produced by the animal is measured through the increase in temperature of a surrounding medium. This method was introduced by Lavosier and Laplace in Blaxter (1962) and modified by Benzinger and Kitzinger (1949). Indirect methods to measure heat production include carbon-nitrogen balance, comparative slaughter, and respiration exchange procedure. The first 2 methods are procedures for measuring production and were reviewed by Garrett et al. (1959), Blaxter (1962), Lofgreen (1965), and Maynard and Loosli (1969).

The respiratory exchange method requires the measurement of oxygen consumption, expiration of carbon dioxide and methane, and urinary nitrogen loss. By using urinary nitrogen loss, protein oxidized in the body can be calculated. This figure is then multiplied by 4.3 Kcal (Brody 1945: 28) to derive heat production of protein metabolism. Since 0.96 liters of O_2 are consumed and 0.77 liters of CO_2 are produced from each gram of protein oxidized (Maynard and Loosli 1969), the respiratory quotient (RQ), which is the ratio of CO_2 produced to O_2 consumed, can be corrected for protein metabolism. The nitrogen-corrected RQ can then be utilized to determine heat production for carbohydrate and fat oxidation. The sum of heat produced from protein, carbohydrate and fat metabolism yields total heat production for an animal.

The metabolic rate of an animal can be determined by the measure of heat production. Metabolic rates are generally expressed as either basal metabolic rate (BMR) or as fasting metabolic rate (FMR). Basal metabolic rate is the heat production of a fasting animal at rest in a thermoneutral environment (Brody 1945). Criteria for its determination are that the animal be resting and in a post-absorptive state. Because of the rumen microbial activity, a post-absorptive state is very difficult to achieve for ruminants. It is also very difficult to relax an animal so that it is at rest both physically and mentally. Therefore, FMR is used routinely.

Energy partitioning of deer has been investigated by Ullrey et al. (1969, 1970) and Mautz et al. (1975, 1976). Energy partitioning has also been investigated for sharp-tailed grouse (Evans and Dietz 1974), fox squirrel (Husband 1976), red fox (Litvaitis and Mautz 1976), and snowshoe hare (Walski and Mautz 1977). Research has been conducted on the metabolic rates of a number of wildlife species including the cardinal (Dawson 1958), snowy owl (Gessaman 1972), grasshopper mouse (Whitford and Conley 1971), gray squirrel (Ludwick et al. 1969), cottontail rabbit (Rose 1973), and mink (Farrell and Wood 1968). Silver et al. (1969) determined fasting metabolic rates for white-tailed deer in both summer and winter, and found the winter rate to be much lower. Other factors have also been found to influence metabolic rates of wildlife species including sex (Nordan et al. 1970) and age (McEwan 1970, Wesley et al. 1973).

Metabolic rates provide information on minimum energy requirements of an animal. Based on these, and also on a knowledge of food utilization by a species determined through digestion trials, a minimum food requirement can be determined for a species. This information can then be used in the determination of a carrying capacity of an area, although this involves the consideration of many additional factors (see Nutritional Modeling).

The study of thermoregulation is a topic of considerable importance in wildlife nutrition and energetics. Homeotherms have a thermal neutral zone, bounded on either end by critical temperatures, above or below which the animal must expend energy to maintain its desired temperature. Moen (1968a,b; 1973, 1976) has conducted considerable research on deer thermoregulation. His findings as well as the results of other work on deer energetics, such as Mattfeld (1973), are increasing our understanding of the relationships of deer to their selected habitat.

NUTRITIONAL MODELING

One of the newer approaches in the field of wildlife nutrition and energetics is the development of nutritional models to determine the carrying capacity of an area for a particular species. Most of the work to date has been directed toward deer (Moen 1973, Wallmo et al. 1977). These models consider carrying capacity to be based on forage energy and protein levels, and attempt to balance forage supply in an area with animal energy and protein requirements as determined through energy partitioning and the study of animal metabolic rates. Figure 10.3 is an example of a model of ruminant energy and nitrogen balance to be used as an aid in determining carrying capacity.

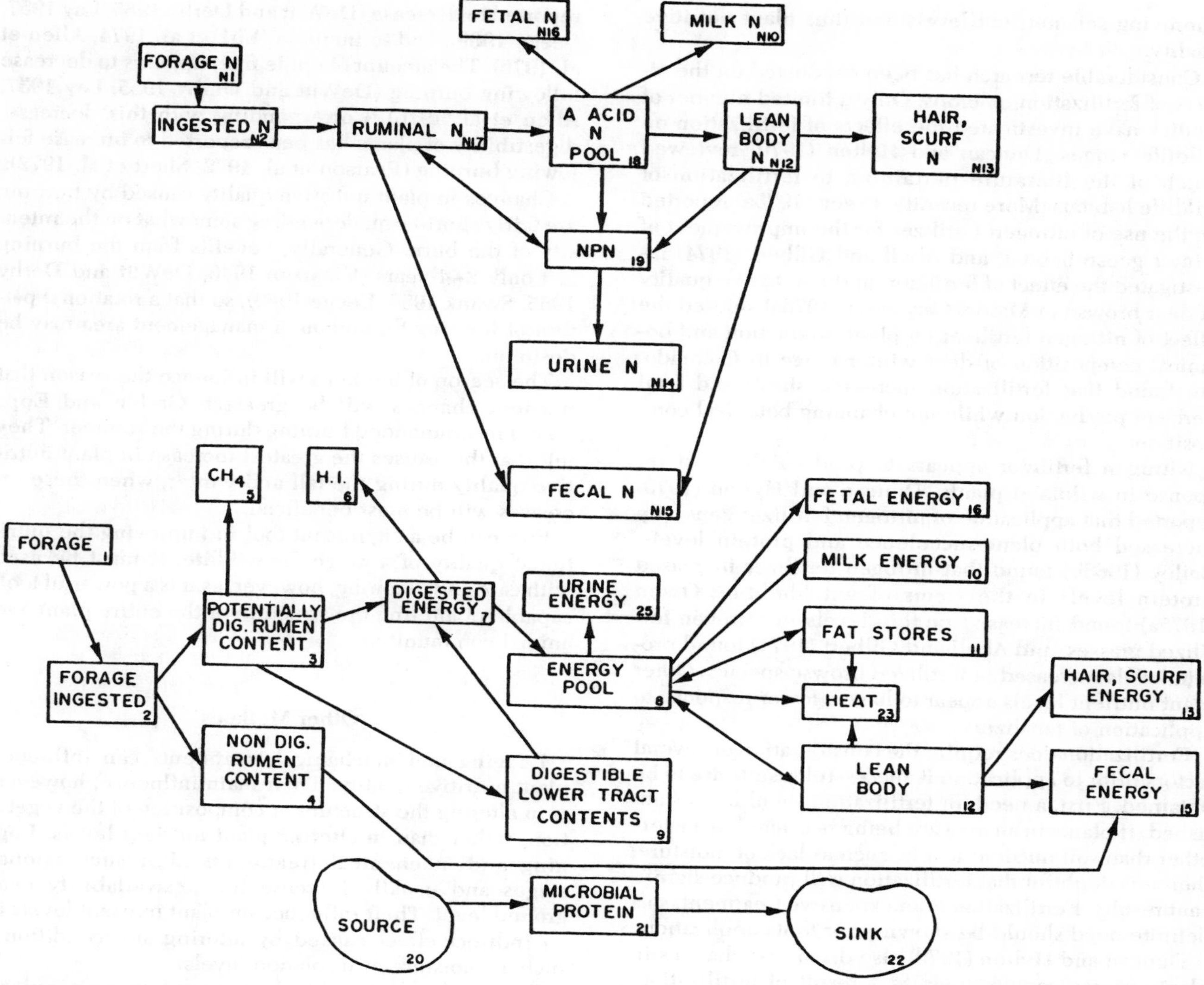

Fig. 10.3. Flow chart of a ruminant energy and nitrogen balance model used as an aid in determining carrying capacity (Swift et al. 1979).

Carrying capacity models have several merits. They are an attempt to obtain more quantitatively and scientifically based estimates of carrying capacity than previously used methods. This is advantageous in that it allows the basis for an estimate to be shown, and the scientific method employed should consistently produce more accurate estimates. Also, a major contribution of modeling is that it reveals gaps in our knowledge and thus shows where additional research is needed.

As with most new approaches, nutritional models of carrying capacity do have some problems. The major problems of most of the models presently being developed are inadequate information on several aspects of the models, and an oversimplification of the energetic and nutritional relationships involved. As additional research adds to the information available for the models and as the complexity of the models is increased allowing for the inclusion of additional variables, the models will greatly enhance the ability to manage wildlife species. Until then, the estimates determined by carrying capacity models should be used only as rough indicators of the carrying capacity of an area.

METHODS OF IMPROVING NUTRITIVE QUALITY

The nutritive quality of an area for carnivorous species is largely dependent upon the abundance of prey. Any manipulations of the habitat which result in an increase in prey abundance or diversity will improve the nutritive quality of an area for carnivores.

Using the techniques described in this chapter, a nutritional evaluation of the plants in an area can be made. Based on such an evaluation, it may be deemed desirable to improve the nutritive quality of plants in the area. Depending upon the vegetation type of interest, a number of methods are available to accomplish this, including fertilization, burning, logging, mechanical treatment, and seeding.

Fertilization

The nutritional quality of a plant can be influenced by the levels of nutrients in the soil. Poor quality sites can restrict plant growth, causing earlier lignification and thus reduce digestibility. Fertilization is a method of improving soil nutrient levels and thus plant nutritive quality.

Considerable research has been conducted on the effects of fertilization on crops. Only a limited number of studies have investigated the effects of fertilization on wildlife ranges. Duncan and Hylton (1970) reviewed much of the literature pertaining to fertilization of wildlife habitats. More recently, Owen (1975a) reported on the use of nitrogen fertilizer for the improvement of winter goose habitat, and Abell and Gilbert (1974) investigated the effect of fertilizer on the nutritive quality of deer browse in Maine. Carpenter (1976a) studied the effect of nitrogen fertilizer on plant production and botanical composition of deer winter range in Colorado. He found that fertilization increased shrub and total herbage production while not changing botanical composition.

Nitrogen fertilizer appears to produce the best response in wildland plants. Duncan and Hylton (1970) reported that application of nitrogen fertilizer generally increased both plant succulence and protein levels. Bailey (1968b) found that nitrogen fertilizer increased protein levels in the stems of witchhobble. Owen (1975a) found increased protein levels in nitrogen fertilized grasses, and Abell and Gilbert (1974) found protein levels increased in fertilized browse species. Other plant nutrient levels appear to have a lower response to application of fertilizers.

Fertilization does require the consideration of several factors prior to application if successful results are to be obtained. First, a need for fertilization should be established. If plants in an area are being restricted by factors other than soil nutrient levels, such as lack of moisture, then it is doubtful that fertilization will produce significant results. Fertilization is an expensive treatment, so a definite need should be shown prior to its application.

Duncan and Hylton (1970) also discussed changes in plant species compositions as a result of fertilization. The possibility of such a change occurring should be evaluated prior to fertilization, and the desirability and effect of such changes should be carefully considered.

Burning

Fire has been used to manipulate wildlife habitat in a number of ways. Its role in altering successional stages has been recognized and utilized for many years. Only recently has the ability of fire to alter plant nutritive quality been recognized.

Burning, like fertilization, produces the greatest change in plant nutritive quality by increasing crude protein levels. Increases in crude protein levels in plants following burning have been reported by many researchers including Einarsen (1946), DeWitt and Derby (1955), Swank (1956), Lay (1957), Biswell (1961), Kirk et al. (1974), and Hallisey and Wood (1976).

Changes in other plant nutrient levels following burning are less dramatic. Ether extract levels have been reported to decrease (DeWitt and Derby 1955, Lay 1957, Leege 1969), and to increase (Kirk et al. 1974, Allen et al. 1976). The amount of crude fiber appears to decrease following burning (DeWitt and Derby 1955, Lay 1957, Allen et al. 1976). Corresponding with this decrease, digestibility of plants has been reported to increase following burning (Pearson et al. 1972, Short et al. 1972).

Changes in plant nutritive quality caused by burning are fairly short-term, depending somewhat on the intensity of the burn. Generally, benefits from the burning last only 2–4 years (Einarsen 1946, DeWitt and Derby 1955, Swank 1956, Leege 1969), so that a rotational pattern of burning throughout a management area may be desirable.

The season of the burn will influence the season that nutrient changes will be greatest. Grelen and Epps (1967) recommended burning during the summer. They felt that this causes the greatest increase in plant nutritive quality during the fall and winter, when these increases will be most beneficial.

Fire can be a significant tool in improving the nutritional quality of a range for wildlife. It must be used with care and planning, however, as it is a powerful tool, capable of altering the structure of the entire plant and animal community.

Other Methods

Logging and mechanical treatments can influence plant nutritive quality. Their main influence, however, is in altering the structure or composition of the vegetation, rather than in altering plant nutrient levels. Logging and mechanical treatments alter successional stages and usually increase forage availability near ground level. Their influence on plant nutrient levels is an indirect effect caused by altering site conditions, such as moisture or insolation levels.

Herbicides have also been used to manipulate wildlife habitat. Plant species compositions can be dramatically altered through herbicide use. As with logging and mechanical treatments, changes in plant nutritive quality as a result of the use of herbicides are primarily caused by the alteration of site conditions and plant species compositions.

Seeding can also change the nutritional quality of a range by changing plant species compositions to include more favorable species. Seeding is usually conducted in conjunction with other treatments, such as logging or mechanical treatments. Seeding without prior alteration of a site usually produces poor results. Selection of species to be seeded on an area is difficult. Plants that will contribute to the quality of an area for wildlife should be selected. Plants, especially exotics, which could spread as noxious weeds, should be avoided. Plant species which green-up early in the spring may be especially beneficial, as animal energy reserves are usually lowest during this period.

Chapter Eleven

Criteria of Sex and Age

JOSEPH S. LARSON

Professor, Department of Forestry and Wildlife Management
University of Massachusetts
Amherst, Massachusetts

RICHARD D. TABER

Professor, School of Forest Resources
University of Washington
Seattle, Washington

"How old is it?" and "Is it a male or a female?" are among the questions the public most often asks of wildlife biologists about wild animals. Biologists also have the same questions in mind but not because of an exclusive interest in the animal at hand. They need to be able to determine the sex and age of a large sample of each species under study or management because this is an important basis for determining the current condition of an animal population and predicting the fate of that population in the near future. The age and sex composition of an animal population and changes in age and sex ratios often are indices of habitat, health factors or of behavioral conditions which directly affect the future size of populations. A life insurance agent, knowing the age and sex of an individual, can estimate the chances of his or her survival to a certain age and thus determine the cost of that person's insurance policy. The wildlife biologist uses sex and age information from a sample of a population of animals to estimate future declines or increases in numbers of that population and recommend appropriate management. The role of aging in wildlife management is clearly introduced in Alexander's (1958) excellent paper. Madsen (1967) has prepared an extensive bibliography on age determination, Wood (1969) has published a bird-bander's guide to age and sex of selected avian species, and a comprehensive review of mammalian age determination principles is found in Morris (1972). *The North American Bird Banding Manual*, Vol. II (U.S. Fish and Wildlife Service and Canadian Wildlife Service 1977) is a basic reference to age and sex criteria.

Many techniques are employed to determine age and sex in animals. Some are simple and employed easily by almost anyone without special training, but for some species sophisticated techniques are required. The criteria for ideal sex or age determination technique focus on the following:

1. Independence from irregular nutritional and physiological variations
2. Clear separations into age classes or year classes without subjective judgement
3. Suitability for living animals of all ages
4. Ease of application by semiskilled technicians

Some standard techniques meet these criteria, but most do not. In most species, one or more of the ideal criteria must be compromised in order to obtain the information needed. The compromises which can be accepted usually depend on the 'degree of accuracy required and on the number of animals that can be obtained reasonably to get the information. Biologists working with rare or endangered species or with very small segments of populations sometimes are prevented from monitoring critical sex and age ratios simply because the only accurate techniques involve an unacceptable risk or sacrifice of too many individuals.

The degree of accuracy required often is a matter of determining the consequences of being wrong. If a small error can shift management recommendations so as to cause significant irreversible impacts on a population or habitat, the techniques and data must be precise and accurate. If, however, the risks are not great, less accurate and usually less expensive techniques may be acceptable.

For some types of research, such as social behavior, errors in sex or age determination are unacceptable. For species that have relatively long lives and take a year or more to attain breeding condition, one usually determines age in annual increments or year classes. For those that breed at less than 1 year of age and rarely exceed 3 years of age, year class accuracy is not necessary, and it usually is sufficient to identify age as either breeding or nonbreeding (age classes).

In the 11 years since this chapter was last revised, many new techniques for determining age and sex (especially those involving age of mammals) have been developed. Where once one could compile a species-by-species description of these techniques, the numbers of species for which techniques have been developed is so numerous as to exceed the space available in this manual. For this reason sex and age criteria, as discussed here, focus on basic principles. These are illustrated with descriptions of classic examples from selected species. Following are accounts of birds and mammals for which the principles have been shown to be valid, and we reference recent publications for specific details. This approach has advantages for those first encountering this subject and at the same time suggests means for developing new techniques for those who have an opportunity to develop age and sex techniques for additional species. The unavoidable disadvantage is that this chapter cannot describe in detail and illustrate all techniques for determining age and sex of all North American species.

DEFINITIONS

Prenatal age—age of egg embryos and fetuses, usually expressed in days.

Postnatal age—follows birth or hatching and involves:

- *Year-class*—actual chronological age in years or
- *Age-class*—Breeding condition of the individual:
  - *Immature or juvenile*—too young to breed but distinguishable from adults by external characteristics (but see below)
  - *Subadult*—has not bred, but externally resembles adult
  - *Adult*—an animal which has bred. ✳

In addition, the following terms are also encountered:

yearling—over 1 but under 2 years of age
two-year-old—over 2 but under 3 years of age
Population turn-over—length of time required for 1 year class to disappear from the population.

Among birds, the following terms have specific meanings:

juvenal—name of plumage following natal down
juvenile—a bird after the downy stage and before sexual maturity
immature—from the post-juvenal molt to full adult plumage via postnuptual molt

AGE DETERMINATION

Embryonic Development

The stage of incubation in eggs or of development of the fetus is indicative of the prenatal age, in days, of many animals.

Candling has long been used as a practical means of determining (1) whether the eggs of domestic birds contain living embryos and (2) the stage (age) of incubation. Commercial candling devices may be used successfully even with eggs that have opaque shells. Weller (1956) described a simple field candler for waterfowl eggs. Westerskov (1950) described the flotation method of determining the age of eggs. Figure 11.1 shows the stages of development in the bobwhite quail (Roseberry and Klimstra 1965) and the ring-necked pheasant (Fant 1957).

The degree of fetal development is indicative of the age in days of prenatal mammals. This may involve both description of the development of certain physical characters of the fetus and measurements such as crown-rump, forehead-rump, and hind leg lengths. Table 11.1 illustrates this technique as applied to white-tailed deer in New York and mule deer in Montana (Armstrong 1950, Hudson and Browman 1959). Salwasser and Holl (1979) found hindfoot length to be the best parameter for aging late term mule deer in California. Development and measurements can be expected to vary among subspecies and among individuals at different intake levels so data should be obtained for different populations of mammals.

While aging techniques based on embryonic development are rather accurate and have been worked out for representative birds and mammals, there still is a need to do this for many more species and subspecies.

Continuous Morphological Development

Techniques in this category are based on animal body parts that progressively change from birth to death and provide a permanent record of attained age. Ridges in horns, changes in physical properties of the crystalline lens of the eye, and annuli in teeth and bones are among the most common techniques in this category.

Horns of wild sheep and mountain goats (Fig. 11.2) display an alternation of smooth areas separated by ridges or checks. The smooth areas represent periods of rapid horn growth and checks represent periods of slow growth. These are related to seasonal changes in nutrition level or breeding activity and therefore checks represent winter periods. The first winter check usually is difficult to detect. The first obvious one forms at about

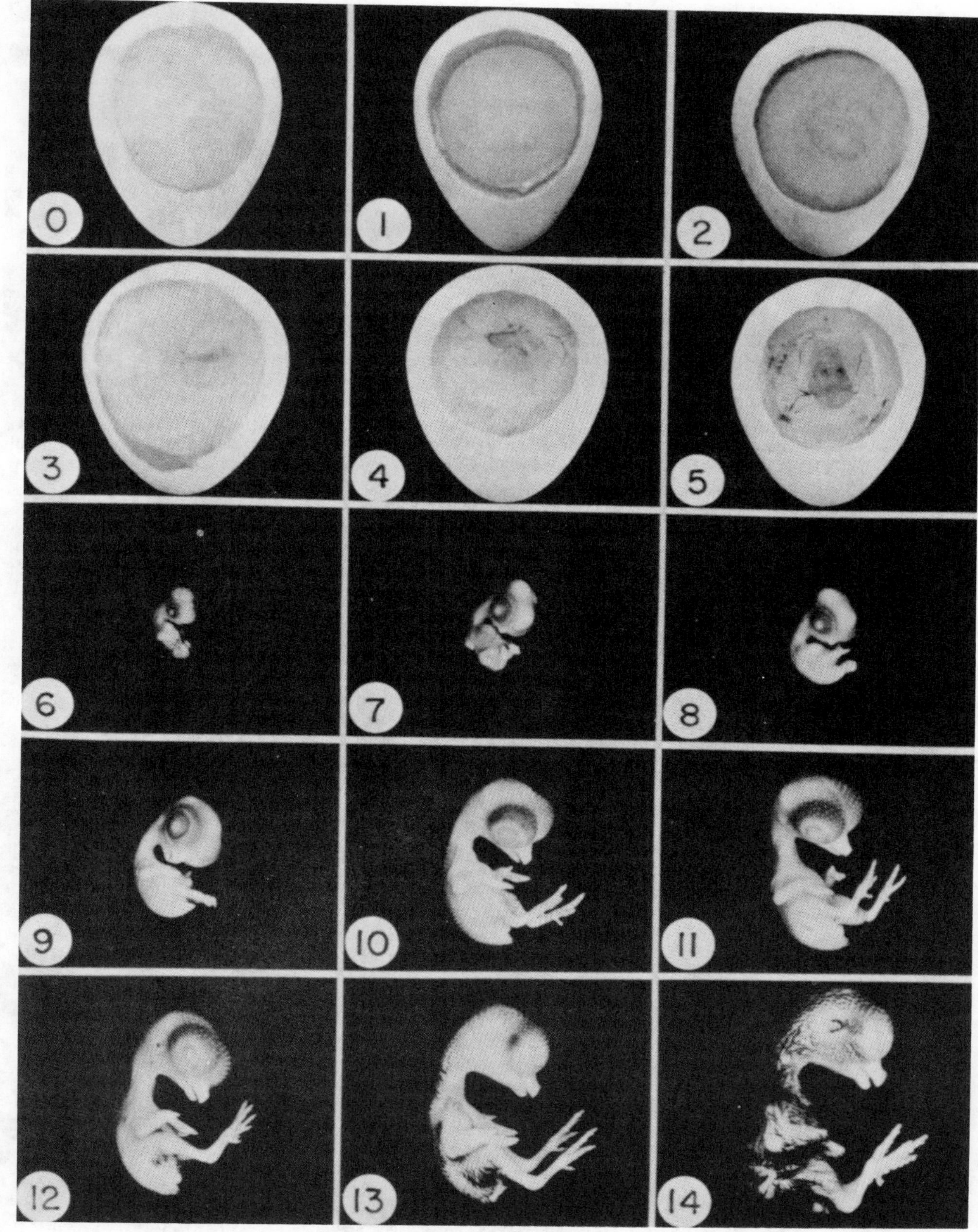

Fig. 11.1. Development of bobwhite quail *A* and ring-necked pheasant *B* during incubation (from Roseberry and Klimstra 1965, and Fant 1957, respectively).

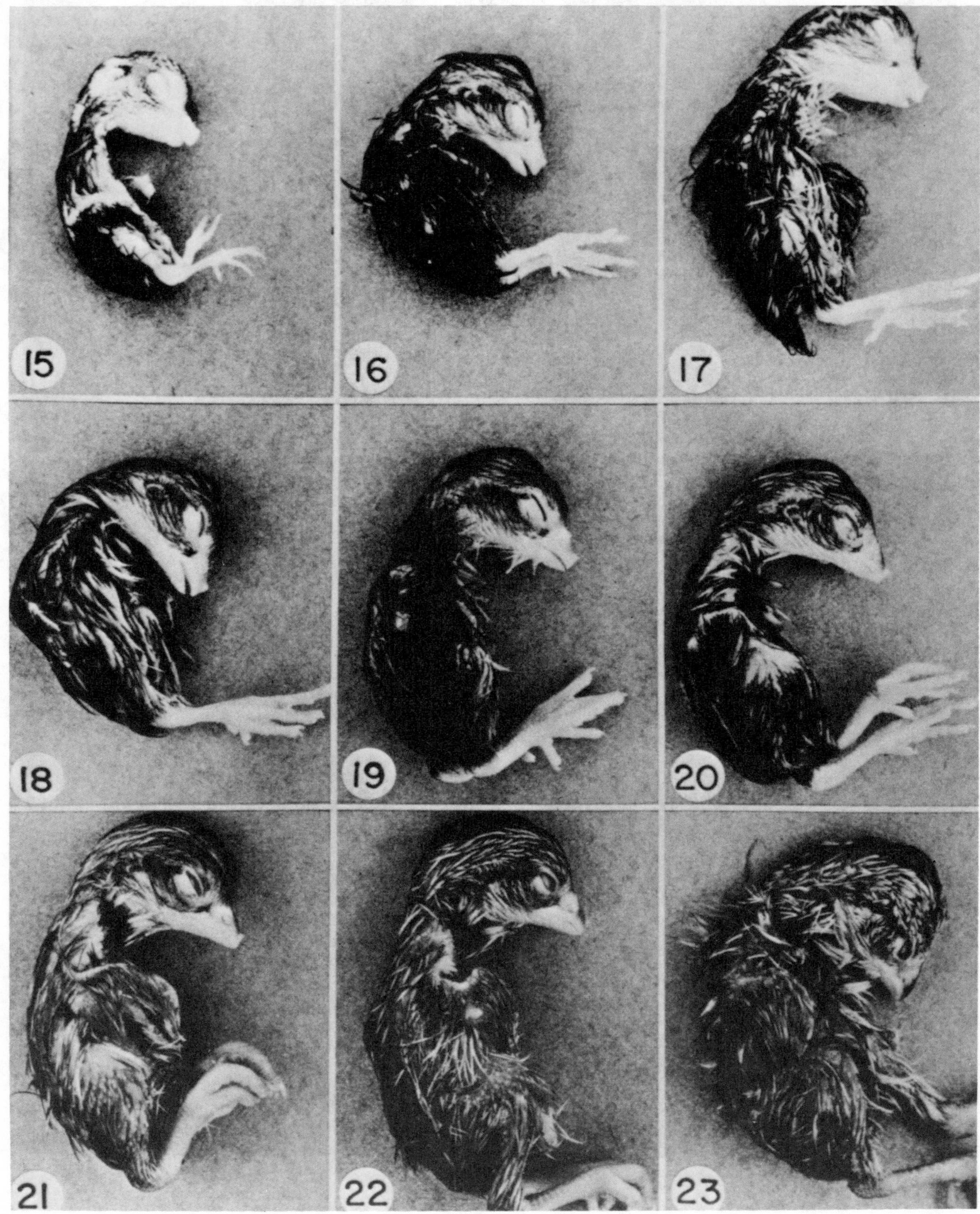

Fig. 11.1. Continued.

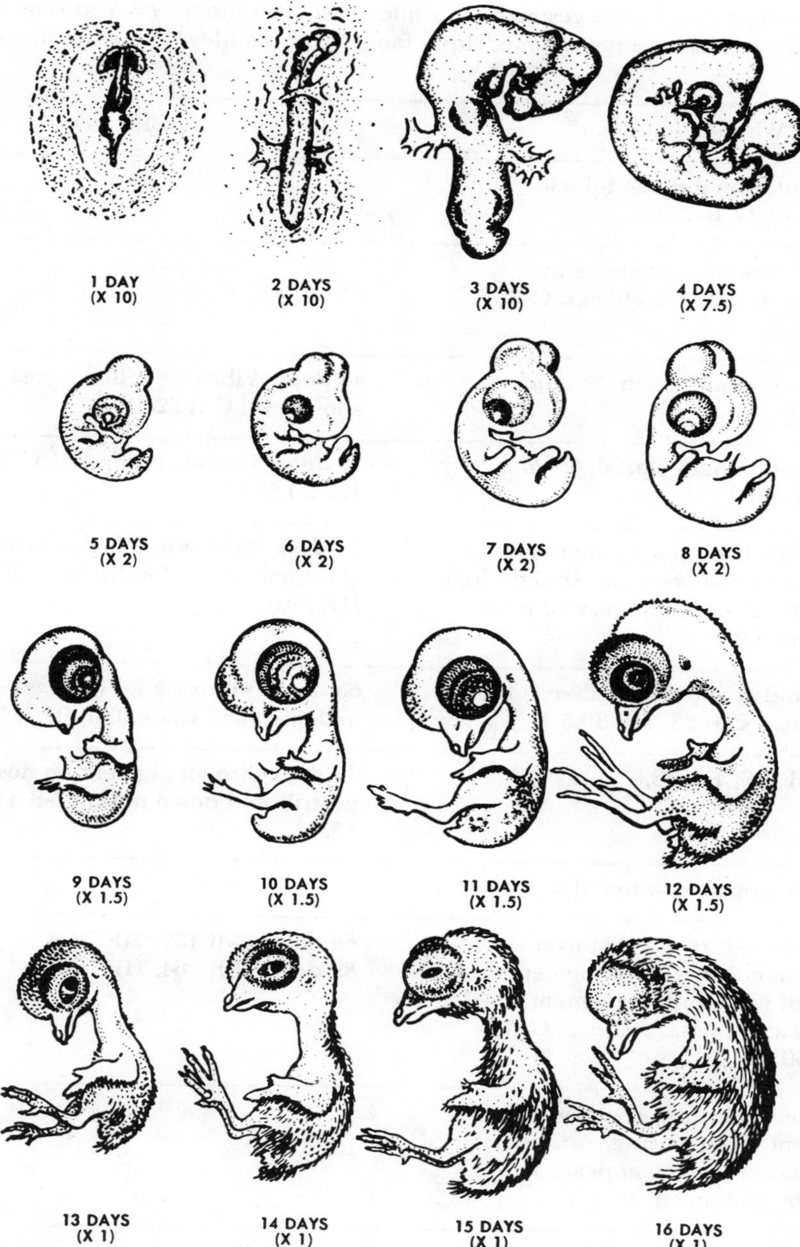

Fig. 11.1. Continued.

1½ years and each year thereafter. This pattern may slow among older animals so that after 5½ years the evidence may become more difficult to read and so slight among the oldest animals that checks may be indistinguishable. Wear or splintering of the horn tips in older animals may destroy the record. This is an example of an aging technique which meets nearly all the ideal criteria outlined above.

The crystalline eye lens of vertebrates grows throughout the life of the animal and is the only organ which does not shed cells (Bloemendal 1977). These special features make it an indicator of age in many bird and mammal species. This technique requires special preservation, drying and weighing of the lens. Freezing adversely affects the lens and in general the degree of error is greater with lenses of small animals. The lens in mammals grows measurably following sexual maturity, but among birds growth is reduced so as to make the technique impractical. Even so, variation in lens weights in mammals is high among adults of the same species. Eye lens weights probably are most useful in separating juveniles from adults and not practical indicators of year-class in adults. Friend (1967) presented a complete review of the technique and the entire July 1967 issue of the *New York Fish and Game Journal*, where his review paper appears, was devoted to critical papers on this technique. This technique can be applied only to freshly killed specimens. Another characteristic of the eye lens may be a more important means of determining age. Tyrosine, an insoluble protein, accumulates in the lens throughout life and affords an accurate age estimation technique for small mammals (Dapson

Table 11.1. Stages in fetal development (days of gestation) in white-tailed deer (from New York) and mule deer (from Montana), showing physical characteristics, crown-rump,* hind-foot,** and hind-leg*** measurements (in millimeters).

Age in days	White-tailed Deer#	Mule Deer##
37–40	Eyelids absent; no vibrissae follicles noticeable. C-R 17.1–27.0	
41–44	Vibrissae follicles present above eye, under eye, on muzzle, on cheeks. C-R 27.7–29.6	
45–52	Eyelids absent; mouth open. *48 days:* C-R 37.8	*48 days:* Vibrissae follicles just present above eye. C-R 32.4
53–60	Eyelids formed; mouth closed. *60 days:* C-R 62.7; HL 20.7	*57 days:* Eyelids cover eye. C-R 59.2; HF 20.5
61–65	Fetus loses fish-hook shape; angle formed between long axis of body and straight line drawn from muzzle through ear equal to or greater than 90.	*61 days;* Vibrissae follicles visible on chest and upper forelimbs. C-R 74.3; HF 29.0
66–68	Pre-orbital fold at anterior median side of eye. *66 days:* C-R 83; HL 30.5	*68 days:* Vibrissae follicles appear on abdomen and trunk. C-R 94.7; HF 37.2
73–75	*75 days:* C-R 113; HL 43.6	*73 days:* Brown pigment on nose between nostrils and down to lip. C-R 110.7; HF 45.7
76–85	Gray pigment appears on top of nose.	
86–90	Vibrissae broken through skin over eye, on muzzle, on cheeks; black pigment on dorsal area of nose; brown pigment on anterior surface of nose. *90 days:* C-R 167.3; HL 69.8	*86 days:* C-R 155; HF 73.9 *89 days:* C-R 164; HF 77.0
91–95	Brown pigment on surface of lower lip; black pigment along closing surface of eyelids; metatarsal gland appears as oblong white spot on tarsus.	
96–105	Hooves black-pigmented. *98 days:* C-R 197.2; HL 98.8	
106–110	Nostrils open. *107 days:* C-R 224.2; HF 114.5. *110 days:* C-R 233.2; HL 124	
111–120	Incomplete hair covering; light pigment spots on trunk; eyelashes grown; dark spots (both sexes) at position of antler-bud. *115 days:* C-R 252; HL 127	*111 days:* Nostrils open; legs and hooves brownish black; hair on muzzle. C-R 232; HF 127. *117 days:* Hair appears on legs. C-R 252; HF 143
121–132	Hair present on anterior and posterior surfaces of skin covering proximal ends of femur and humerus; tarsal glands present.	

Table 11.1. *Continued*

Age in days	White-tailed Deer#	Mule Deer##
133–150	Appearance of hair on legs; row of stiff bristles around top of hoof. *135 days:* C-R 318.5; HL 192	*137 days:* Hair margins metatarsal and covers tarsal gland. C-R 311; HF 185. *144 days:* Short hair present just above hooves; teeth still covered with membrane. C-R 327; HF 193
151–180	Hair covering as in adult; incisors still covered by membrane; black pigment covers nose; metatarsal gland with complete hair covering. *159 days:* C-R 396; HL 251	*161 days:* Tips of incisors and canines exposed. C-R 397; HF 262 *174 days:* Hair covering as in newborn fawn. C-R 443; HF 278
181–200	Incisors erupted; tarsal gland with complete hair covering. *181 days:* C-R 445; HL 304 *192 days:* C-R 459; HL 314	

*C-R is the crown-rump or forehead-rump measurement.
**HF is the measurement of hind feet from the tip of the hoof to the angle of hock.
***HL is the measurement of the hind leg from the tip of the hoof to the tubercle of the tibio-fibula.
#From Armstrong 1950.
##From Hudson and Browman 1959.

and Irland 1972, Otero and Dapson 1972, Birney et al. 1975). Ludwig and Dapson (1977) have shown its use to be effective in white-tailed deer. Freezing affects the lens adversely and because processing large numbers of fresh specimens is impractical, the technique has certain limitations. Where fresh specimens are available it is superior to tooth-wear procedures and is less costly and time consuming than the cementum annuli techniques described below.

In mammals, layers in the cementum of teeth and in the periosteal zone of bones are highly accurate indicators of year class (Klevezal and Kleinenberg 1967). Cementum is deposited on the roots of teeth each year in light (summer) and dark (winter) bands so that the bands close to the dentine are from the earlier years and the layers of the current year lie on the exterior of the root. The exact nature of the process which gives rise to the layers is not known. Klevezal and Mina (1973) reported that the pattern of layers is not affected by sex or a change of physiological state associated with rut or pregnancy. Nor could it be attributed to specific conditions of the year when the layers are formed. They have observed that variability of the pattern is least in populations in a continental climate and is greatest among those in slightly-continental and sea climates. But, they occur in virtually all mammals and the technique is likely to be effective in any mammal if the equipment and skills to expose the layers are available. In a few species, e.g., beaver, the teeth and layers are sufficiently large and distinct so that simple grinding and polishing a saggital section will show the layers well under a dissecting microscope (Van Nostrand and Stephenson 1964, Larson and Van Nostrand 1968). For most species and all small teeth, it is necessary to decalcify the tooth, cut thin histological sections with either a microtome or cryostat (Child 1973), stain, and read the layers under higher magnification. While all teeth have layers, the tooth of choice varies among species and collecting conditions. Some teeth, such as incisors and premolars, are easier to extract and may even be removed from live animals without adverse effect in later life. In trophy specimens, the tooth extracted may be influenced by the requirements of the taxidermist. Decalcification techniques vary among species, and the original literature must be consulted for details on the process. Hematoxylin and eosin stains are widely used; but Stone et al. (1975) and Thomas (1977) reported that stains of the Romanowsky family (Giemsa, Maximow, Field and Metachromatic stains [toluidine blue, thiomin, crystal violet]) are equally or more effective, easier to use, and cheaper. Bourque et al. (1978) have developed a technique for determining age and season of death for mammalian teeth uncovered at archeological sites. Their procedure avoids the decalcification process and uses solid sections.

Layers similar to those in cementum are deposited in the periosteal layer of the bones of many, perhaps all, mammals (Klevesal and Kleinenberg 1967); but because it is easier to obtain teeth, this indicator of age has not been commonly employed by wildlife biologists.

While morphological development has produced very accurate techniques for determining year-classes among mammals, the same has not been developed, as yet, for birds; and there are no techniques developed for determining year-class once a bird has reached sexual maturity. Van Soest and Van Utrecht (1971) have suggested that the layered structure of bird bones may be an indicator of age. However, Nelson (1976) has found that while periosteal adhesion lines are present in decalcified wing and foot bones of Canada geese, they are variable; and age estimates based on this technique were inaccurate.

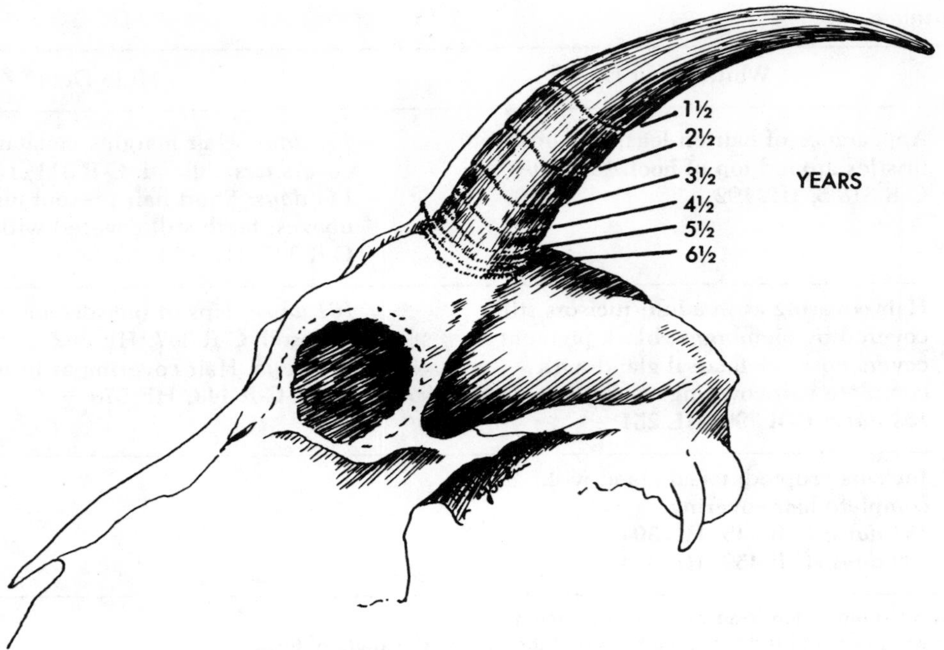

Fig. 11.2. Annual rings on the horn of the mountain goat (after Brandborg 1955).

Growth Maturation

During the period of growth from birth to sexual maturity certain bones of some mammals may be used to estimate the relative stages in this period.

As a mammal grows, its long bones lengthen from the tips. Each long bone has, while it is growing, a cartilaginous zone at each end covered by a bony cap, the epiphysis. Bone is deposited at the inner side of the cartilaginous zone, pushing the cap further out as the bone grows. When growth is complete the cartilage is replaced by solid bone, so that the cap and shaft are fused firmly together. The presence of the cartilaginous zone, a line representing its recent presence, or its complete absence, are criteria of use in aging many mammals (Figs. 11.3, 11.4).

In some species, notably the bears and the members of the dog and weasel families, males have a bone (the baculum) in the penis. The baculum changes with age and is an age indicator in some species (Fig. 11.5 and 11.6).

Both epiphyseal closure and changes in the baculum are very subjective techniques. Use of a reference set of bones from, or based on, known age animals of similar geographic distribution may reduce subjectivity, but usually these techniques are limited to relative indices of age-class.

Wear and Replacement

A number of aging techniques are based on the fact that certain body parts, e.g., teeth and feathers, are replaced in a predictable age-related sequence. Often these parts, or others, become worn over time and the degree of wear is an index to the age of the animal. Replacement techniques usually are limited to estimating age-class or the age of juveniles. Wear techniques are applied, depending on the species, to the entire range of ages.

Replacement of deciduous or milk teeth and subsequent wear of permanent teeth has been a widely used technique and is well illustrated by its use on deer (Fig. 11.7, Tables 11.2 and 11.3 and Fig. 11.8). These are selected examples; and since there is significant geographic variation, the original research from different geographic regions must be consulted (see below in species listings).

Changes in pelage is another index to mammalian age. The spotted fawns of white-tailed deer and the pattern of primeness in the skin side of stretched muskrat pelts (Fig. 11.9) are common examples.

In young birds, there is a rapid succession of molts as the natal down is lost. The juvenal plumage appears and then is replaced by winter plumage. Thus, there is change in both size and appearance as the young mature. Gollop and Marshall (1954) used this fact in devising a system for the age classification of pen-raised wild ducklings.

In gallinaceous birds, a rather accurate method of aging juveniles is based on the replacement and growth of primaries and secondaries—the remiges or main flight-feathers of the wing. In ring-necked pheasant, bobwhite, mourning doves, and Hungarian partridge, for example, the post-juvenal molt of the primaries begins at 4 weeks of age and continues in a regular pattern until about 16 weeks, permitting aging to the nearest week within that span.

The primaries are numbered consecutively from 1 to 10, commencing with the innermost. This numbering follows the sequence in which the primaries are molted, the outer ones being shed and replaced last. The willow ptarmigan, ruffed grouse, Hungarian partridge, and quail molt only through primary #8 in their first fall,

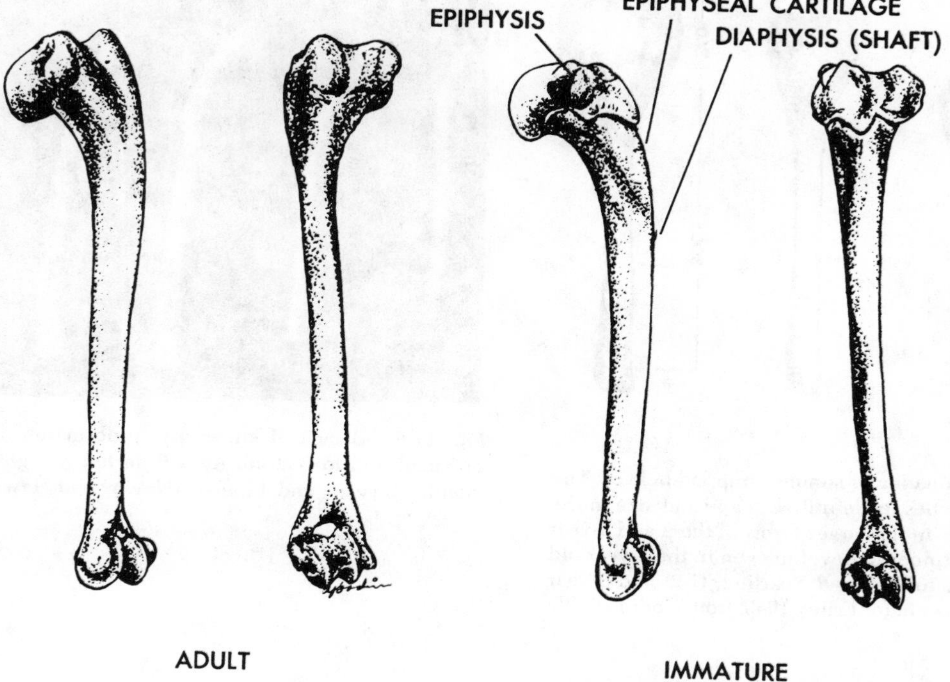

Fig. 11.3. Lateral and posterior view of humerus of cottontail. Note epiphyseal cartilage between epiphysis and diaphysis in immature and its absence in the adult (from Hale 1949, after Godin 1960).

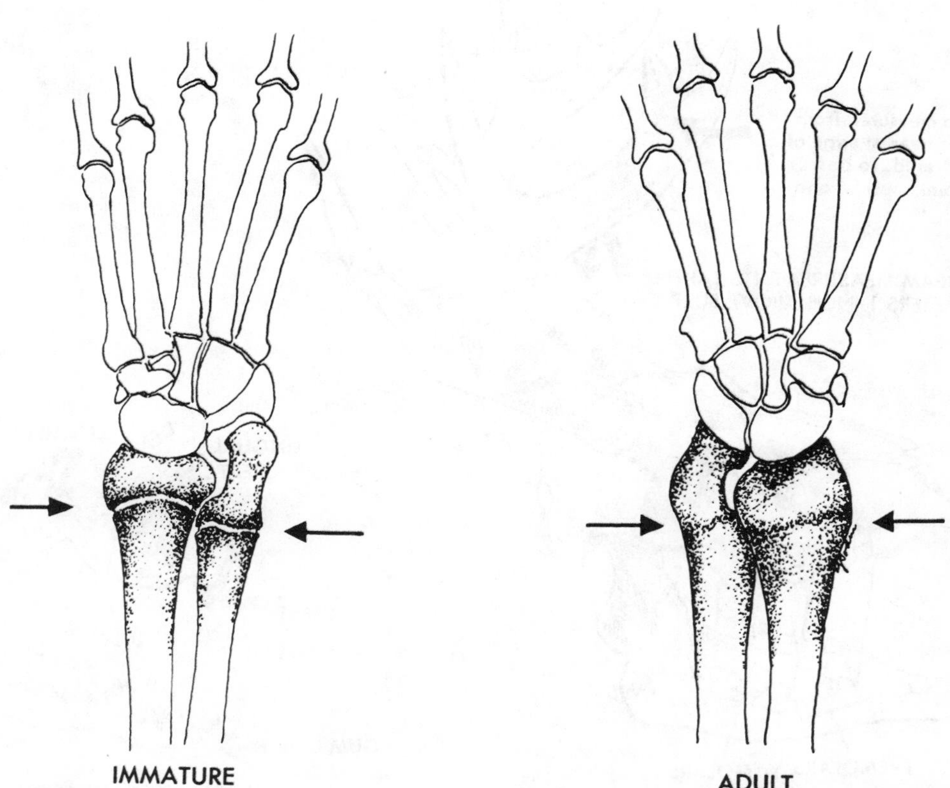

Fig. 11.4. Drawing made from X-ray photograph of radii and ulnae of raccoon showing open (immature) and closed (adult) epiphyses (after Sanderson 1961a, from Godin 1960).

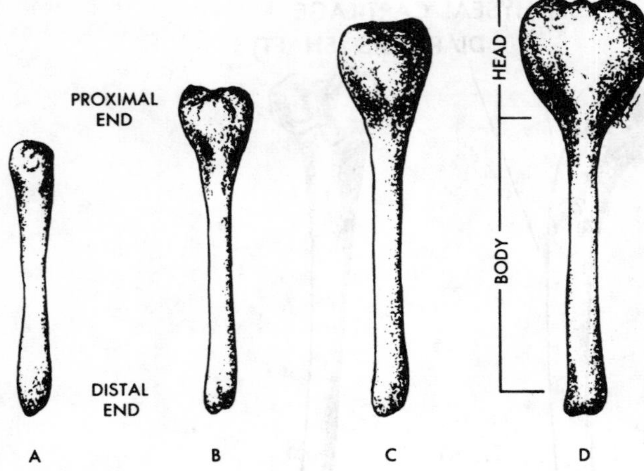

Fig. 11.5. Age determination of summer-trapped beaver. The tail of the baculum reaches its definitive shape and size in the yearling class, the body in the larger forms of the 2 and 3-year olds, and the head continues to develop even in the 4-year old and over class. *A* Immature (kit); *B* Yearling; *C* 2- and 3-year old; *D* 4-year old and over (after Friley 1949, from Godin 1960).

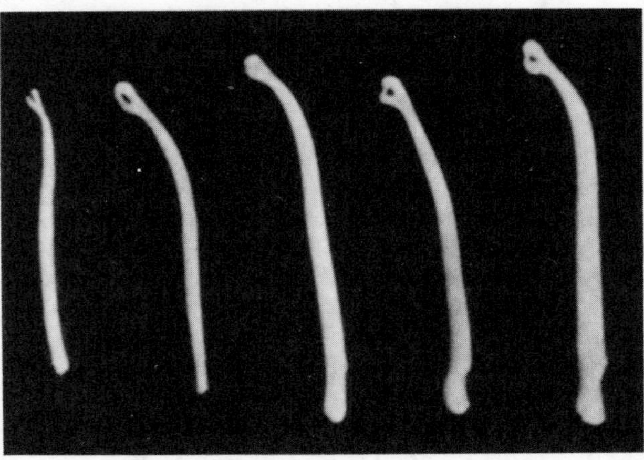

Fig. 11.6. **Bacula of known-age pine marten arranged with proximal end to bottom. Ages from left to right: 5 months, 9 months, 3 years, and 14 years (Newby and Hawley 1954).**

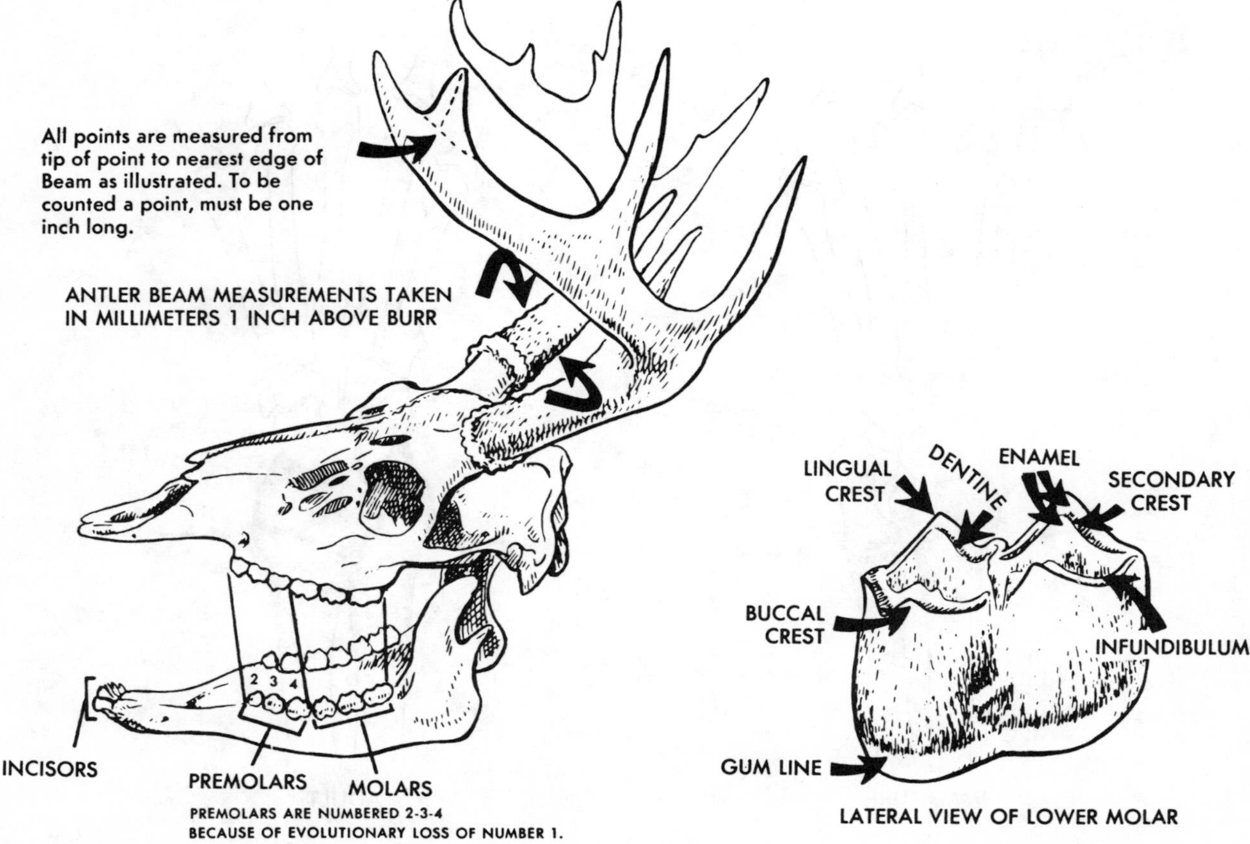

Fig. 11.7. Nomenclature of ungulate teeth and antler measurement criteria (from Riney 1951, by Godin 1960).

Table 11.2. Tooth eruption in the lower jaw of the mule deer (from Cowan 1936 and Taber and Dasmann 1958). Milk or deciduous tooth—D; adult or permanent tooth—P. Parentheses indicate that the tooth is in the process of eruption at that particular time.

Age	Incisors 1	Incisors 2	Incisors 3	Canine 1	Premolars 2	Premolars 3	Premolars 4	Molars 1	Molars 2	Molars 3
1 to 3 weeks	D	D	D	D	D	D	D	—	—	—
2 to 3 months	D	D	D	D	D	D	D	(P)	—	—
6 months	D	D	D	D	D	D	D	(P)	(P)	—
12 months	P*	D P	D	D	D	D	D	P	(P)	—
18 months	P	P	P	D	D	D	D	P	P	(P)
24 months	P	P	P	P	(P)	(P)	(P)	P	P	(P)
30 months	P	P	P	P	P	P	P	P	P	P

*Replacement and eruption are taking place at this time.

Table 11.3. Tooth eruption in the New York white-tailed deer (after Severinghaus 1949). Milk or deciduous tooth—D; permanent tooth—P; parentheses indicate that tooth is in process of erupting at that particular time.

Age	Incisors 1	Incisors 2	Incisors 3	Canine 1	Premolars 2	Premolars 3	Premolars 4	Molars 1	Molars 2	Molars 3
1 to 3 weeks	(D)	(D)	(D)	(D)	(D)	(D)	(D)			
2 to 3 months	D	D	D	D	D	D	D	(P)		
6 months	P	D	D	D	D	D	D	(P)		
12 months	P	P	P	P	D	D	(P)	P	(P)	
18 months	P	P	P	P	P	(P)	P	P	P	P
24 months	P	P	P	P	P	P	P	P	P	P

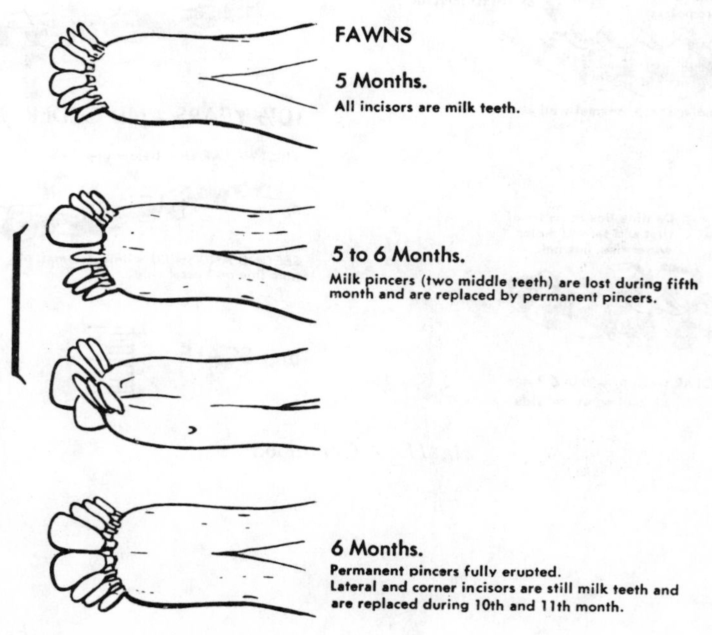

Fig. 11.8. Sequence of eruption and wear for white-tailed deer of New York.

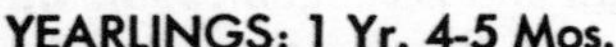

YEARLINGS: 1 Yr. 4-5 Mos.

Milk premolars moderate to heavily worn.

FOURTH MILK PREMOLAR IS THREE CUSPED.

Permanent premolars.

Third molar not fully erupted.

PREMOLARS ARE NUMBERED 2-3-4 BECAUSE OF EVOLUTIONARY LOSS OF NUMBER 1.

YEARLINGS: 1 Yr. 6 Mos.

LOSS OF MILK PREMOLARS AND PARTIALLY ERUPTED PERMANENT PREMOLARS.

FOURTH PERMANENT PREMOLAR TWO CUSPED.

Molars sharp.

Third molar not fully erupted.

YEARLINGS: 1 Yr. 7 Mos.

PERMANENT PREMOLARS usually fully erupted slight wear occasionally showing on grinding surfaces. Slight wear but no dentine line showing on crests of last (third molar).

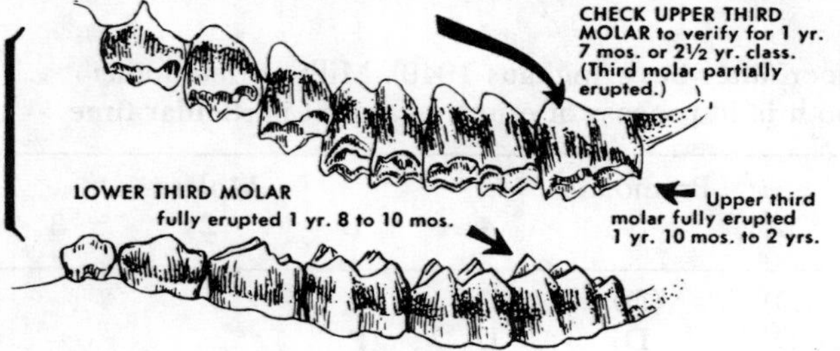

CHECK UPPER THIRD MOLAR to verify for 1 yr. 7 mos. or 2½ yr. class. (Third molar partially erupted.)

LOWER THIRD MOLAR fully erupted 1 yr. 8 to 10 mos.

Upper third molar fully erupted 1 yr. 10 mos. to 2 yrs.

2½ YEARS: Permanent Premolars and Molars

UPPER THIRD MOLAR fully erupted, slight wear.

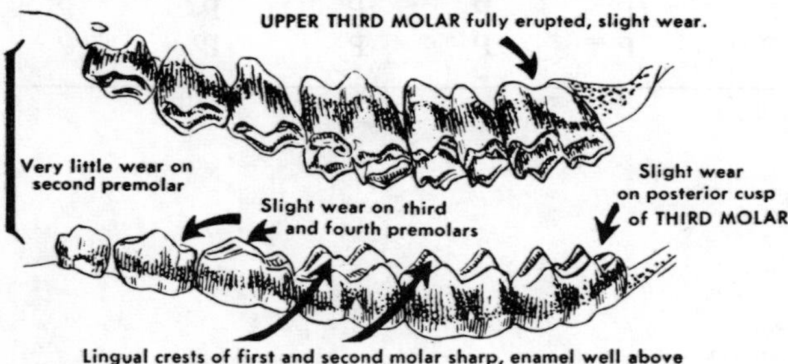

Very little wear on second premolar

Slight wear on third and fourth premolars

Slight wear on posterior cusp of THIRD MOLAR

Lingual crests of first and second molar sharp, enamel well above narrow dentine of the crest.

3½ YEARS: Molars

LINGUAL CRESTS OF FIRST MOLAR blunt, SECONDARY CRESTS prominent and blunt.

Dentine line in crests of first and second molar wider than enamel.

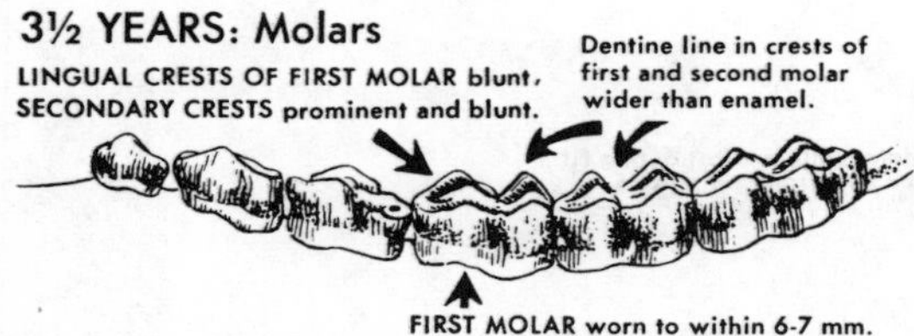

FIRST MOLAR worn to within 6-7 mm. of gum on buccal side.

4½ YEARS: Molars

LINGUAL CRESTS ON FIRST MOLAR ALMOST WORN AWAY. Secondary crests visible.

First molar worn to within 5-6 mm. of gum on buccal side.

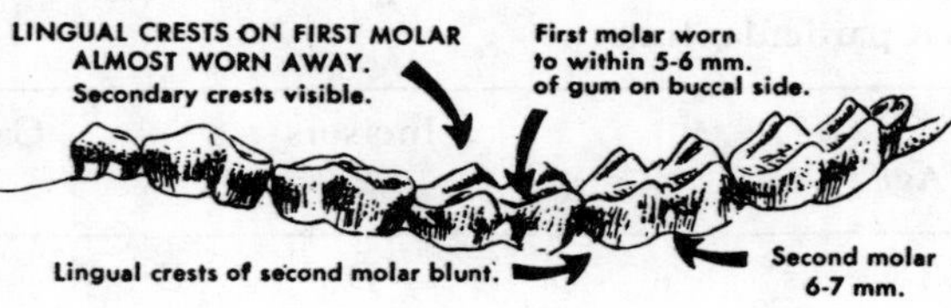

Lingual crests of second molar blunt.

Second molar 6-7 mm.

5½ YEARS: Molars

Original lingual crests of first molar worn away, SIMULATED LINGUAL CRESTS APPEAR. Secondary crests worn away. First molar worn to within 4-5 mm. of gum on buccal side.

Second molar 5-6 mm.

Dentine crests on all molars much broader than enamel.

6½ YEARS: Molars

NO LINGUAL CRESTS ON FIRST MOLAR and worn to within 3-4 mm. of gum on buccal side.

Second molar 4-5 mm.

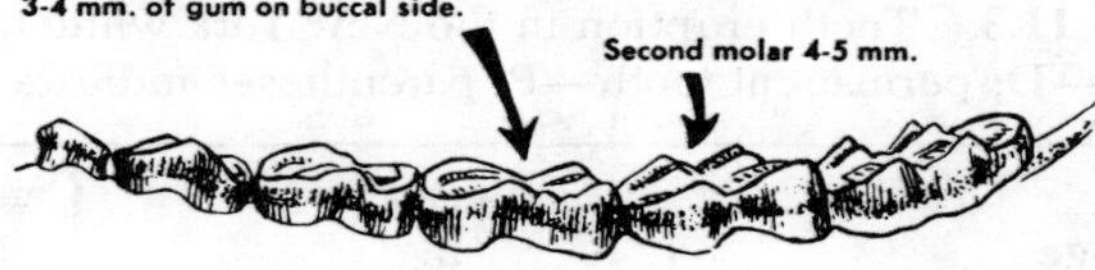

7½ YEARS: Molars

FIRST MOLAR WORN TO WITHIN 2-3 MM. ON BUCCAL SIDE.

Second molar 3-4 mm.

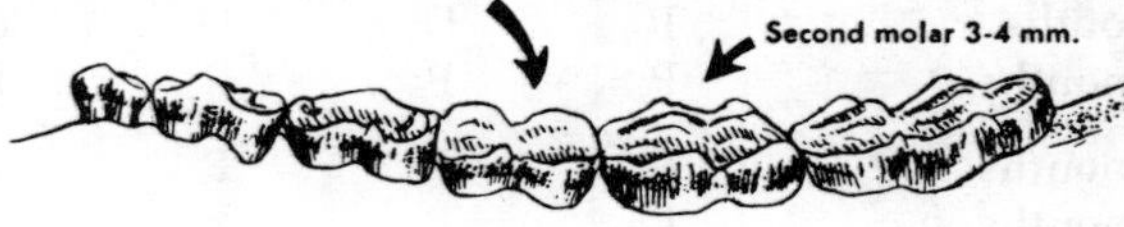

8½-9½ YEARS: Molars

ALL MOLARS WORN TO WITHIN 2-3 MM. OF GUM ON BUCCAL SIDE.

10½ YEARS AND OLDER: Molars

FIRST MOLAR at or below gum line.

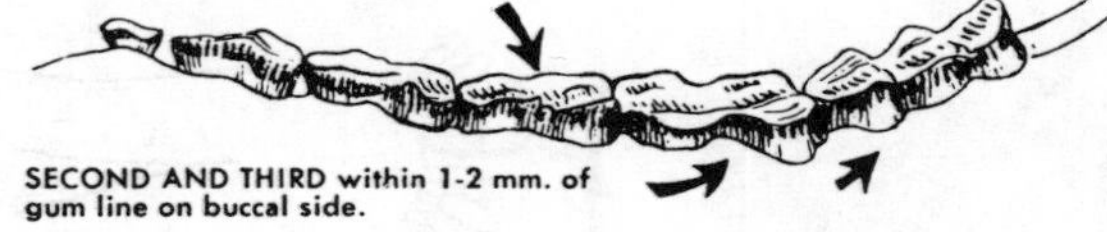

SECOND AND THIRD within 1-2 mm. of gum line on buccal side.

mm SCALE 0 5

Fig. 11.8. Continued.

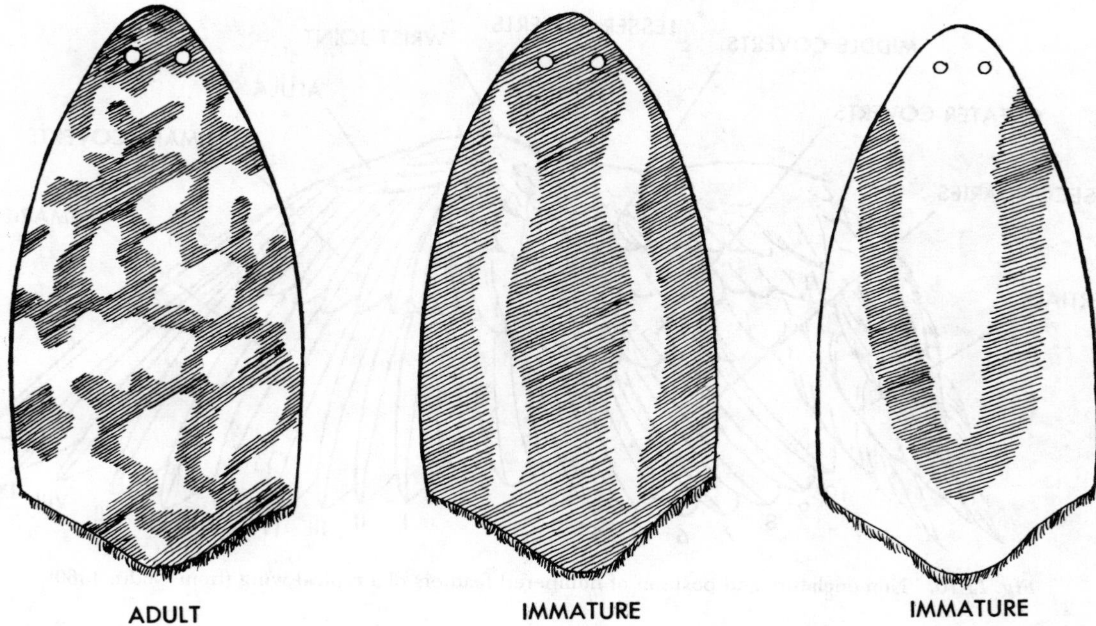

Fig. 11.9. The appearance of stretched muskrat pelts (skin side) showing dark and light color patterns related to age class. White areas denote primed section of hide; shaded areas are unprime (after Dozier 1942, from Godin 1960).

during the post-juvenal molt. In determining the number of the latest-shed primary, indicated by a gap or a growing replacement feather that is blue at the base, it usually is safer to count backwards from 10, the outermost primary, since confusion sometimes arises as to where the secondaries end and primaries begin. Fig. 11.10 shows the location and numbering of the feathers.

Chesness (1966) provided a visual colored guide for aging young ring-necked pheasants. It is available from Full Color Co., 279 Riverwood Drive, Burnsville, Minnesota 55378.

Generally the feathers of the young bird differ in some respects from those of the old. In many species, when the bird enters its first breeding season, it retains some juvenal feathers, especially wing coverts. These feathers thus provide an indication of age. Such diagnostic primary coverts are found in bobwhite and other quail. In the Hungarian partridge, the scapulars are diagnostic of age.

Gallinaceous birds molt their wing and tail feathers in sequence, rather than all at once, as in waterfowl. As it approaches adult size in the fall, the young bird grows wing feathers of adult size during the post-juvenal molt. However, in most species, except the ring-necked pheasant, the 2 outer primaries of the immature bird are not replaced during this molt. They are replaced 1 year later, during the first postnuptial molt, and annually thereafter. The 2 outer juvenal primaries differ in shape (Fig. 11.11) from the adult primaries, being more pointed at the tip, and in some species narrower.

In birds that mature more slowly, such as herring gulls, swans, and geese, there is less difficulty in distinguishing young-of-the-year in fall. Areas that are white in the adult tend to be gray or mottled in the young; areas that are pure black in the adult tend to be dull or brownish black in the young.

During the fall hunting season, a distinction can be made between young-of-the-year and older waterfowl by the appearance of the tips of the rectrices or large tail feathers. In the juvenile tail, there is a notch at the tip caused by the breaking-off of a short section of the shaft. This break is caused by the loss of the down, which precedes the regular tail feather in emergence from the feather follicle in the very young bird. The condition in the young is illustrated in Fig. 11.12. This technique must be used with caution because some individuals molt the tail feathers before or during the hunting season.

General Development

When an animal population has been thoroughly investigated, it usually is possible to establish criteria of weight or measurement that will serve to indicate age, up to the point when rapid growth is finished. Different populations, however, often require different criteria. Weights and body measurements are so influenced by nutrition, health, and genetic inheritance that they are usually only gross indicators of dubious reliability. Popular literature, and early scientific papers on animals are replete with weight and dimension indices of age, but conclusions based on these criteria should be examined closely prior to acceptance.

Among birds, some general development characteristics are useful for age-class determinations. In gallinaceous birds, as a rough rule of thumb, the strength of the lower jaw separates the immatures from the adults in fall. If a dead bird is supported by the lower jaw alone and shaken, and the jaw breaks, it is generally a young bird; if the jaw does not break it is generally older.

A similar test is based on the flexibility of the breastbone. In a young bird the tip of the breastbone

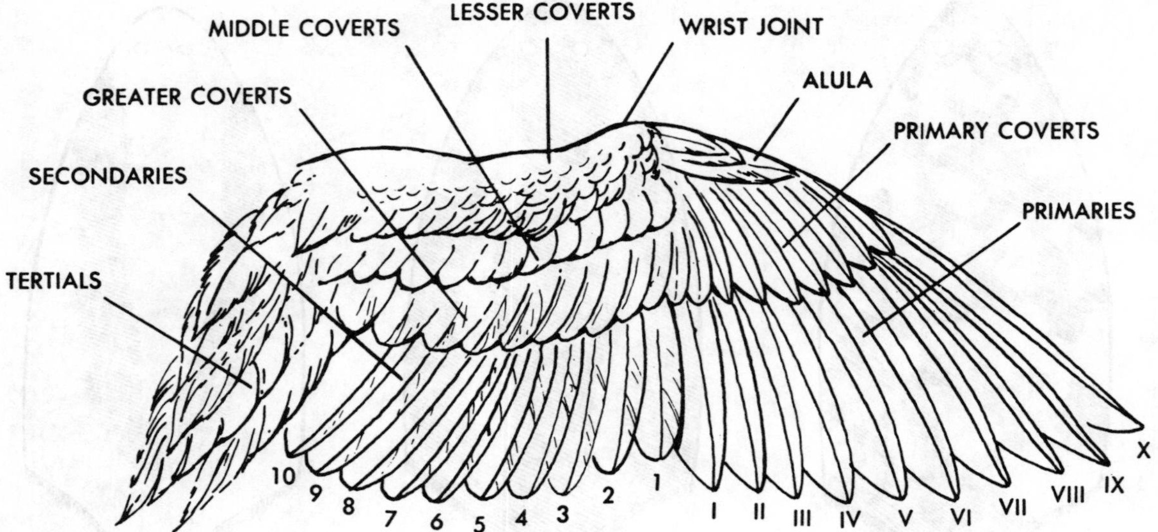

Fig. 11.10. Nomenclature and position of numbered feathers of a typical wing (from Godin 1960).

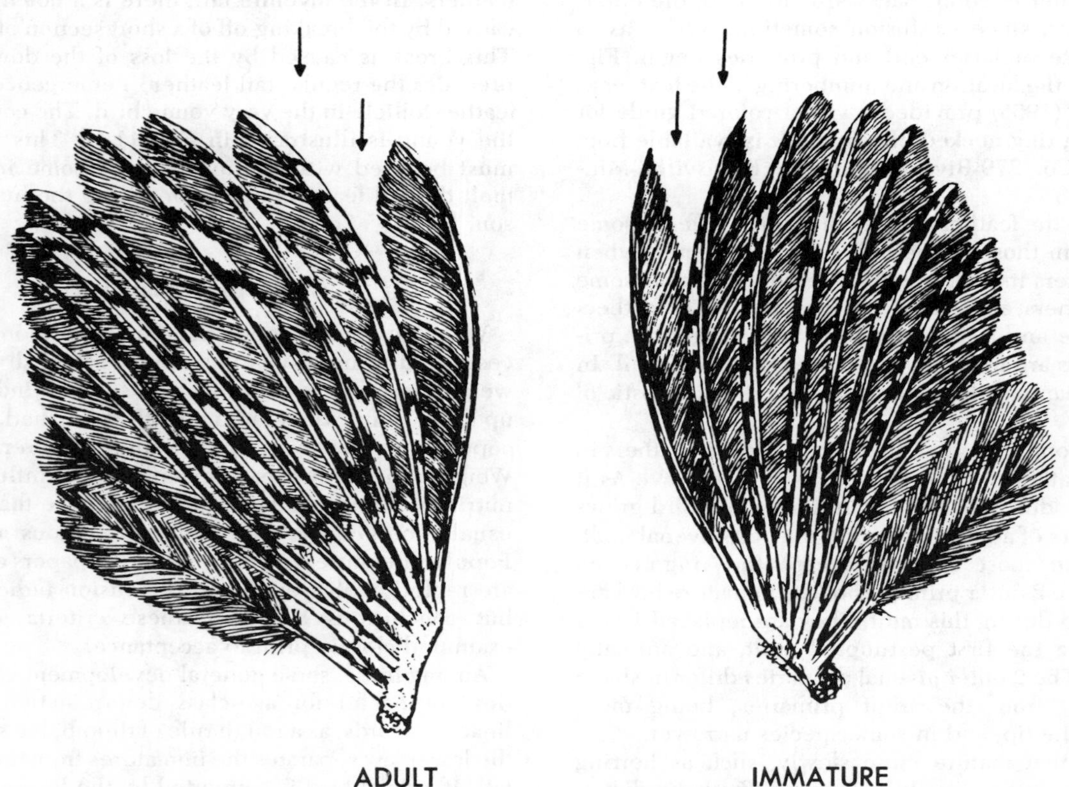

Fig. 11.11. The two outer primaries in immature gallinaceous birds (except the ring-necked pheasant) are retained through the first winter. The immature No. 9 and No. 10 primaries are pointed *Right* as compared to the rounded tips of these feathers in adults *Left*, as shown in the wings of the ruffed grouse (from Godin 1960).

Fig. 11.12. Tail feathers as age criteria in waterfowl. *Left:* Juvenile tail with down attached at tip of shaft. *Center:* Juvenile tail with characteristic "V" notch. *Right:* Adult tail with pointed tip (from Godin 1960).

may be easily bent with one finger; in an older one it is rigid.

A general criterion of age in fall, that has been used for white-tailed ptarmigan (Westerskov 1956) and might be useful for other grouse as well, is the "cranium test." The bird's head is held between the index and middle fingers and the thumb is pressed on the forehead. In young birds the cranium will break, whereas it is not possible to press in the brain case of an adult ptarmigan held in this manner.

A technique well known to bird banders is "skulling" or determination of the degree of ossification of the bird skull to separate juveniles from adults. With experience this condition can be detected in live birds by viewing through the wetted skin of the skull. Adult skulls are whitish and finely speckled while the immature skull is uniformly pink (Wood 1969). Feather barb spacing, color of the mouth, gape, iris, eye ring, feet and legs and degree of gape swelling are other age criteria that may separate juvenile from adult birds (Wood 1969).

Sexual Maturation

As indicated above, sexual maturation is closely related to many indices of age; and therefore, the development of primary and secondary sexual organs themselves are indices of age-class.

Fig. 11.13 shows the generalized sex apparatus of male and female birds. The testes of the male lie on the roof of the body cavity, along the backbone and just forward of the kidneys. In general, the left testis is larger than the right one and both are functional (Wing 1956). The testes appear smooth, compared to the ovary, which is pebbled, or speckled. The testes may be light or dark in color. Testis size is measured by length, width, and weight or volume.

The sex organs of the female bird begin in early life as paired ovaries, but the right fails to develop so that only the left ovary becomes functional. In some members of the Falconiformes (perhaps one-half or more of all individuals) the right ovary persists, but it usually is not functional. The same occurs also in some ducks, a few other species, and perhaps 5% of common birds have a vestige of the right ovary. Ordinarily the right oviduct, like the right ovary, is not functional (Wing 1956). White or yellowish in the nonbreeding season, the ovary grows larger and more orange as the breeding season approaches, due to the growth of the egg follicles and their protrusion. During the laying season, the ovary looks something like a cluster of grapes, the individual follicles exceeding the body of the ovary in size.

The shed ovum (and the yolk of the egg) becomes surrounded by the white albumen and encased in a shell as it travels down the oviduct to the cloaca. As the egg passes down the oviduct, the oviduct walls are stretched. The oviduct of a bird that has laid eggs remains larger than the oviduct of one that has not yet laid eggs. In early spring especially, this may be a useful criterion for distinguishing young females from old.

In adult females also, the opening of the oviduct may be seen (especially in large birds) as a conspicuous slit in the left cloacal wall. In immature females the oviduct is blocked by a membrane, so the left cloacal wall is unbroken (Fig. 11.14).

The cloaca of a bird is the common outlet both for reproduction and for elimination of waste. In many species its appearance and that of related structures is an accurate guide to age-class.

As described by Hochbaum (1942) and illustrated in Fig. 11.14, the penis of the male is located on the wall of the cloaca, on the anterior side in young birds and on the left side in adults. In females, the oviduct opens on the

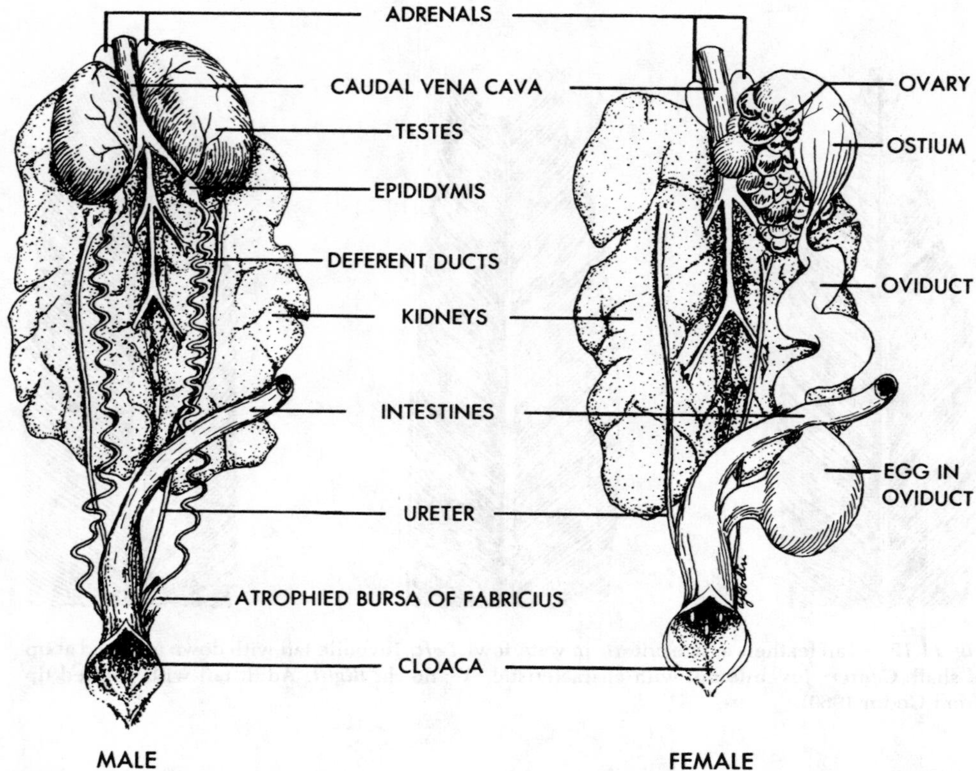

Fig. 11.13. Excised urogenital system of typical breeding birds. *Left:* Male has paired testes (the left is generally the larger) whereas the female, *Right* has a single irregular shaped ovary and convoluted swollen oviduct on the left side (from Godin 1960).

left side of the cloaca but in young birds this opening is usually covered by a membrane. The bursa of Fabricius opens (when it is not covered by a membrane) posterior to the opening of the digestive tract.

The presence and appearance of these structures are indications of sex and age. Their use has been most widespread in waterfowl, where size is large and other criteria are often not reliable.

Since the appearance of the various cloacal organs is closely related to sexual maturity, it is important to know beforehand the age at which sexual maturity is reached in the species in question. Thus, waterfowl may be divided into 2 groups: those which breed at 1 year of age and those which breed later. In the first group are mallard, gadwall, American wigeon, teals, northern shoveler, pintail, redhead, canvasback, lesser scaup, and wood duck; while the second group includes geese, swans, goldeneyes, bufflehead, harlequin duck, scoters, and eiders.

In examining the sex organs of a living duck, the bird is held belly up, tail away, with the outer fingers of each hand holding the wings and legs (Fig. 11.14A). The vent is located with the forefingers. As the vent is located, the tail is pressed backwards with the forefingers and the thumbs are placed on either side of the vent. The thumbs are separated slightly, with a gentle pressure. This opens the vent. As the cloaca is exposed, the penis, if it is present, will protrude. The penis shows 2 stages of development. In immature males the penis is a small, unsheathed organ; in adults it is large and enclosed with a conspicuous sheath (Fig. 11.14C).

The penis of the immature male duck is merely a short, fleshy appendage (Fig. 11.14C) attached to the forewall of the cloaca just within the cloacal lip. It shows a conspicuous left-hand twist, giving it the appearance of a miniature pigtail. It is never more than 12 mm in length. The penis of the immature bird retains its small, unsheathed form, with little or no change in size or appearance until the bird is 5 to 10 months old. Then, when the post-juvenal molt has been completed, the adult penis, 50 to 90 mm or more in length, develops. These 2 growth stages of the penis cannot be confused easily, except during the very short period of transition. The 2 stages show no important variations in different species of ducks.

In the female there is no penis. If the bird is adult, the opening of the oviduct may be seen on the left wall of the cloaca. In immature birds of both sexes the opening of the bursa of Fabricius is present; in mature birds it is absent.

As an age criterion in early-maturing waterfowl, the penis is reliable only during the summer, autumn, and early winter. The period of reliability ceases for all individuals of a species when the earliest developing young drakes assume the adult penis. With respect to this time limit, the species studied at Delta, Manitoba, fall into 2 groups: Group 1—adult penis never assumed by young males before December 31 (gadwall, American wigeon, green-winged teal, blue-winged teal, shoveler, redhead, canvasback, and lesser scaup). Group 2—adult penis sometimes assumed by young males before December (mallard and pintail). The species not studied in suffi-

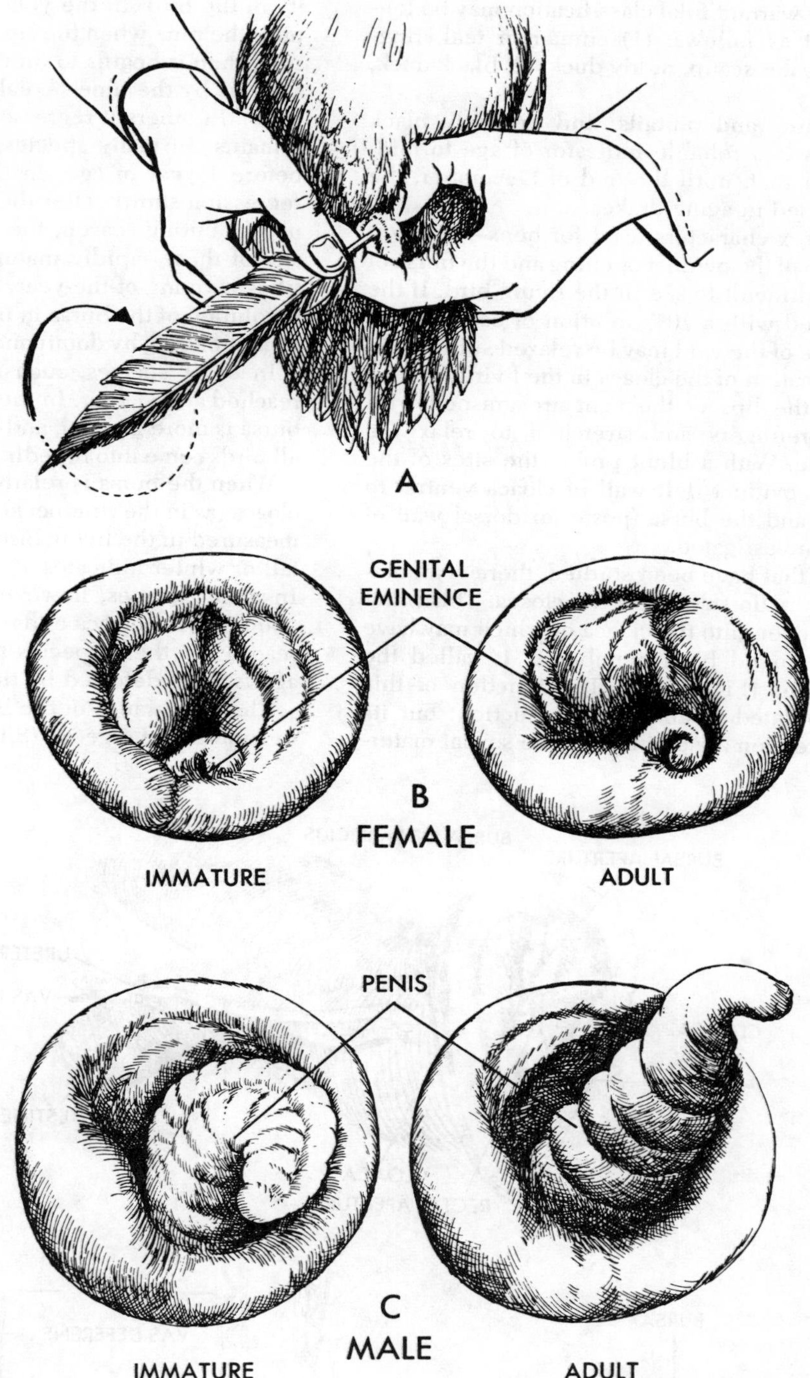

Fig. 11.14. Cloacal characteristics used to determine sex and age in waterfowl. *A* Method of holding and for measuring the bursa of Fabricius. The probe is held in the right hand and rotated into the bursa. *B* Location of oviduct and bursa of Fabricius in female waterfowl. *Left:* Immature. *Right:* Adult. *C* Penis stages in Canada Geese. *Left:* Immature unsheathed penis with conspicuous left hand twist. *Right*: Sheathed penis of sexually mature adult. Bursa is present in both immature male and female; after Addy and MacNamara, 1948 (from Godin 1960).

cient numbers to warrant final classification may be tentatively grouped as follows: (1) cinnamon teal, ring-necked duck, greater scaup, ruddy duck; (2) black duck, and wood duck.

In wild mallards and pintails, and probably black ducks, the penis is a reliable indicator of age to mid-November. After that, until the end of December, the bursa must be used in aging drakes.

The age and sex characters used for hens—the presence or absence of the oviduct opening and the bursa of Fabricius—are difficult to see in the living bird. If the cloaca is swabbed with a 10% solution of cocaine, the sphincter muscle of the vent may be relaxed sufficiently to permit examination of the cloaca in the living female. In dead birds, the lips of the vent are grasped with thumbs and forefingers and stretched to relax the sphincter muscle. With a blunt probe, the sites of the openings of the oviduct (left wall of cloaca ventral to large intestine) and the bursa (posterior dorsal wall of cloaca) may be investigated.

In most birds that have been studied, there is an outpocketing from the dorsal wall of the cloaca. This blind sac, which may open into the cloaca or which may have the opening occluded by a membrane, is called the bursa of Fabricius (Fig. 11.15). The function of this organ may be related to antibody production, but its growth and regression are an index to the sexual maturity of the bird. In the young bird it increases in length until the time when the sex cells are just beginning division, then it begins to diminish. In some species it disappears by the time sexual maturity is reached (Gower 1939). In others it regresses to a certain point, where it remains. In many species, sexual maturity is attained before 1 year of age. In these birds the bursa begins regression shortly after the first of the year. During the usual hunting season, the presence of a large bursa in any of these rapidly maturing species definitely identifies a young-of-the-year. The situation with regard to involution of the bursa in individuals that are prevented from breeding by dominance relations is not yet known.

In other species, such as geese, sexual maturity is reached after 1 year. In these birds the regression of the bursa is more gradual, and also more irregular, since not all birds come into breeding condition at the same time.

When the bursa is relatively large and opens into the cloaca (as in the ring-necked pheasant) its depth may be measured in the living bird by probing. A deep bursa in fall or winter indicates a young bird (Kirkpatrick 1944). In many species, however, the bursa either does not open into the cloaca or has a lumen too slender to probe readily. In these species the bird must be dissected if age is to be detected by this means.

The appearance of the bursa wall is indicative of age in band-tailed pigeons (Silovsky et al. 1968) and Ameri-

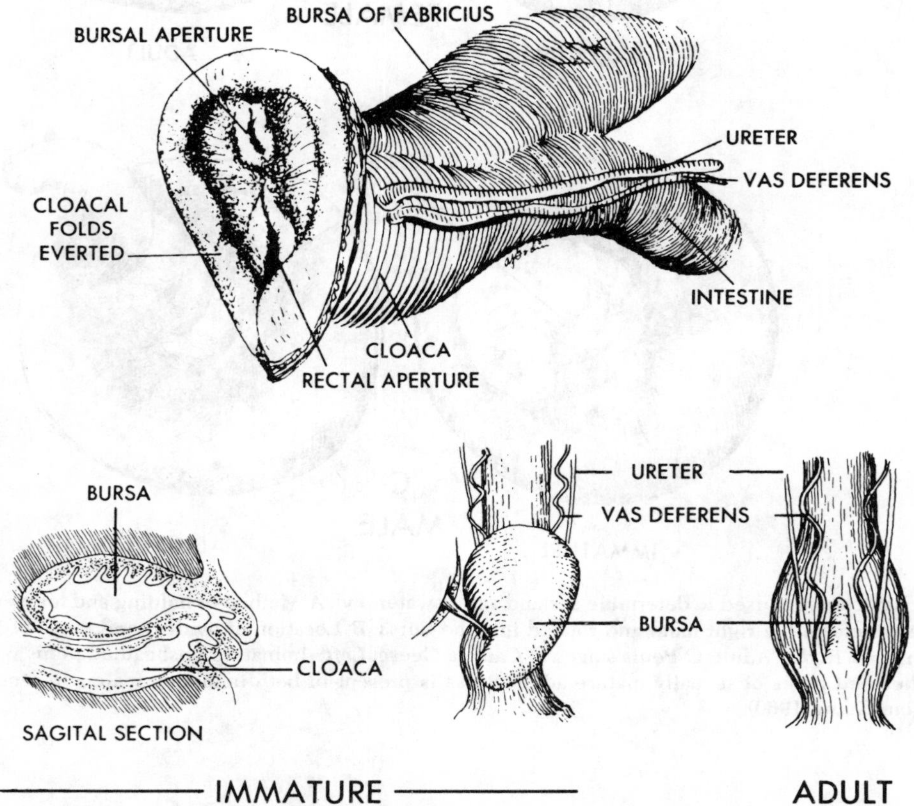

Fig. 11.15. Bursa of Fabricius. *Top:* Excised cloaca and related parts of nonbreeding game birds. (A) Bursal aperture; (B) Bursa of Fabricius; (C) Ureter; (D) Vas deferens; (E) Intestine; (F) Cloaca; (G) Rectal aperture; (H) Cloacal folds everted (from Godin, 1960). *Bottom:* Location and appearance of the bursa and related structures in the California quail (redrawn by Godin from Christman, in Lewin 1960).

can coots (Frederickson 1968). Young birds have fatty or glandular appearing walls as opposed to thin transparent walls in adults.

In mammals, the development of primary and secondary sex organs also can be an index to age-class but not as commonly as in many birds. Development of the baculum already has been described. Penis diameter (Baumgartner and Bellrose 1943) and testes length (Schofield 1955) separate juvenile and adult muskrats. Presence or absence of a vaginal membrane and placental scars are useful for many species. Degree of scrotum development and amount of scrotal hair is a technique useful in squirrels, as is condition of mammary glands (Fig. 11.16B, C). Internal surgical examination for viable sperm, placental implantation sites, and ovarian corpora albicantia also distinguish age-class in mammals.

The behavior of species, particularly in the breeding season, may be an index to age-class. Subadults may not take part in the courtship activity or may form separate groups distinct from the breeding adults and young-of-the-year. Vocalization may separate breeders from younger animals, but the presence of nonbreeding adults may cause confusion. Changes in feeding habits and in appearance of secondary sexual characters may be indices of breeders in some species.

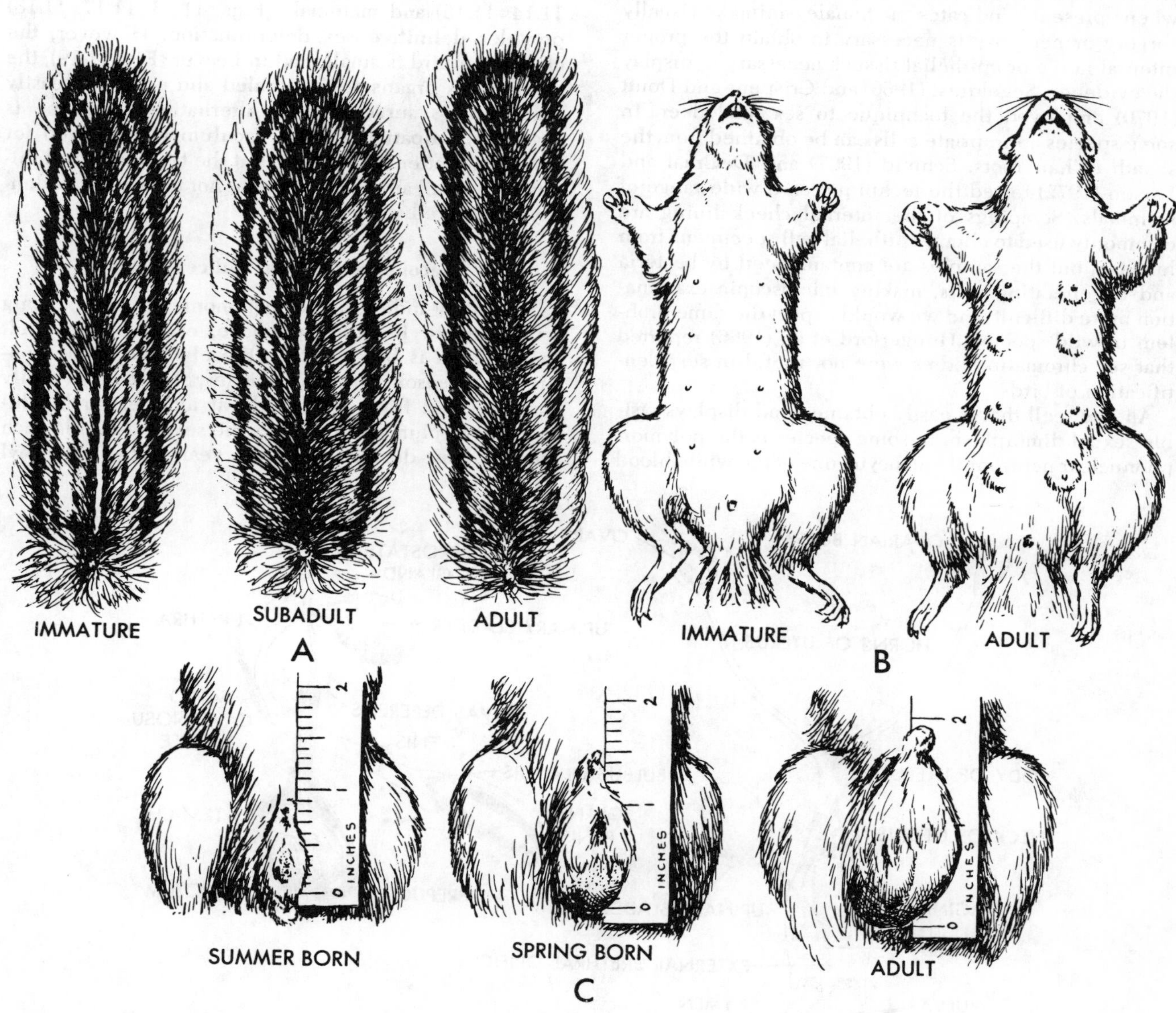

Fig. 11.16. Sex and age criteria for squirrels. *A* Age may be determined by examination of the ventral surface of the tail. *Left:* Juvenile, the shorter secondary hairs are absent on the lower side of the tail bone. *Center:* Subadults, short appressed hairs are present on lower third of the tail bone. *Right:* The appressed hairs obscure the outline of the tail bone in the adult (after Sharp 1958a). *B* Mastology of the female squirrel. *Left:* Juvenile, with nipples minute and barely discernable. *Right:* Lactating adult, nipples black pigmented with most of hair worn off. *C* Scrotal measurements of male squirrels. *Left:* Summer born, the testes are abdominal and the skin is just beginning to pigment. *Center*: Spring born, the testes are large and the scrotum is pigmented but it is heavily furred. *Right*: Adult has shed most of the fur from the scrotum (after Allen 1943; from Godin 1960).

SEX DETERMINATION

Sub-cellular

Wildlife biologists employ techniques on the subcellular level and use primary and secondary physical characters to determine sex of mammals: Subcellular techniques are useful for species such as beaver which conceal their sex, for determining sex of unborn young, or when only a portion of a carcass is available, as is often the case in law enforcement.

Sexual dimorphism occurs in stained preparations of cells in many mammals (Moore 1966). It usually appears as a planoconvex dark-staining mass against the inner surface of the nuclear membrane. Its presence is associated with the second X chromosome in females and, when present, indicates a female animal. Usually surgery or necropsy is necessary to obtain the proper internal nerve or epithelial tissues necessary to display the evidence. Segelquist (1966) and Crispens and Doutt (1970) employed the technique to sex fetal deer. In some species appropriate cells can be obtained from the sheath of hair roots. Schmid (1967) and DeGraaf and Larson (1972) tested the technique on a wide range of mammals. Scrapings of the internal cheek lining are commonly used to obtain epithelial cell specimens from humans, but the samples are contaminated by bacteria and degenerating cells, making microscopic examination more difficult, and we would expect the same problem in wild species. Hungerford et al. (1966) reported that sex chromatin bodies were not useful in sex identification of birds.

Another cell that is easily obtained and displays visible sexual dimorphism in some species is the polymorphonuclear neutrophil leucocyte, one of the white blood cells. Larson and Knapp (1971) have employed this approach to sex beaver, and a well-illustrated review article on sex differences in cells has been published by Mittwoch (1963).

Until recently, subcellular indices of sex have focused on characters associated with the X chromatin. Hoekstra and Carr (1977) have identified white-tailed deer sex through fluorescent Y chromatin techniques, using blood and lymphocytes. Because samples can be taken from dry blood on either permeable or impermeable surfaces, or from meat pieces or frozen samples, it has obvious use in law enforcement cases.

Primary Physical Indices of Sex

Examination of the primary sex organs of birds (Figs. 11.14, 11.15) and mammals (Figs. 11.16, 11.17, 11.18) provides definitive sex determination. However, the cloaca of a bird is small, and in beaver (Fig. 11.19), the primary sex organs are concealed and errors are easily made unless surgery or an alternative technique is available. Palpation for the baculum is employed for beaver and otter (Fig. 11.20), but the technique is dubious with small animals and ought not to be used if identity is required with certainty.

Secondary Physical Indices of Sex

Secondary indices of sex commonly are used among wild species. Breeding plumage, especially in adult males, often is brighter than the plumage of the nonbreeding season. In some species, the male is easily distinguished from the female at any season by differences in plumage. In others the sexes resemble each other at least during part of the year. Thus, waterfowl

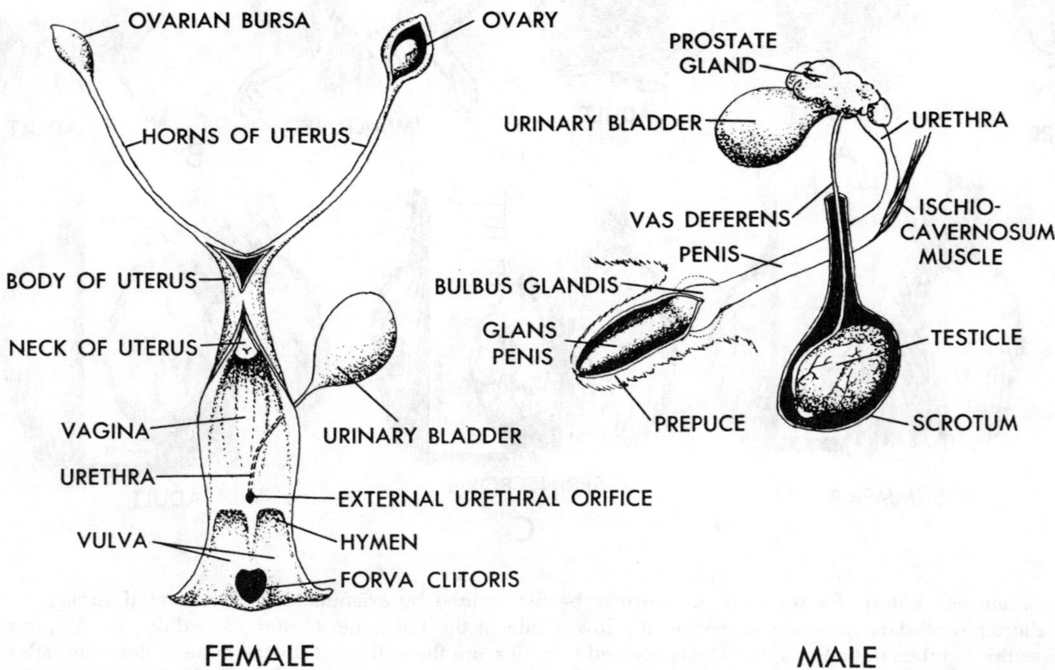

Fig. 11.17. General view of genitalia of female and male animals (Canidae). *Left:* Excised internal female genital organs, dorsal view. *Right:* Lateral view of male genital organs (from Godin 1960).

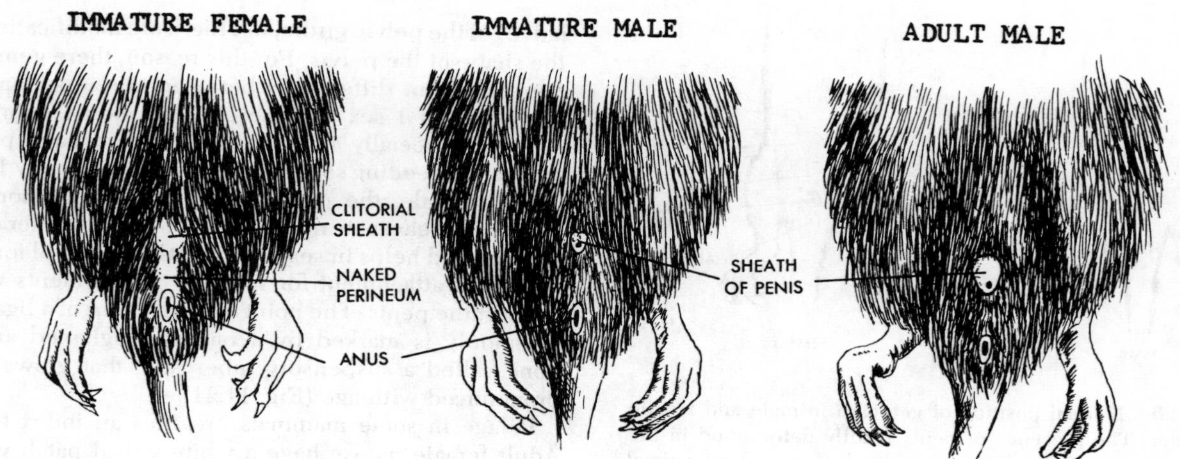

Fig. 11.18. **Sex criteria as shown in genitalia in muskrats. Genitalia: Left—immature female with naked perineum; Center—immature male, note size difference of penis sheath; Right—adult male (after Dozier 1942, from Godin 1960).**

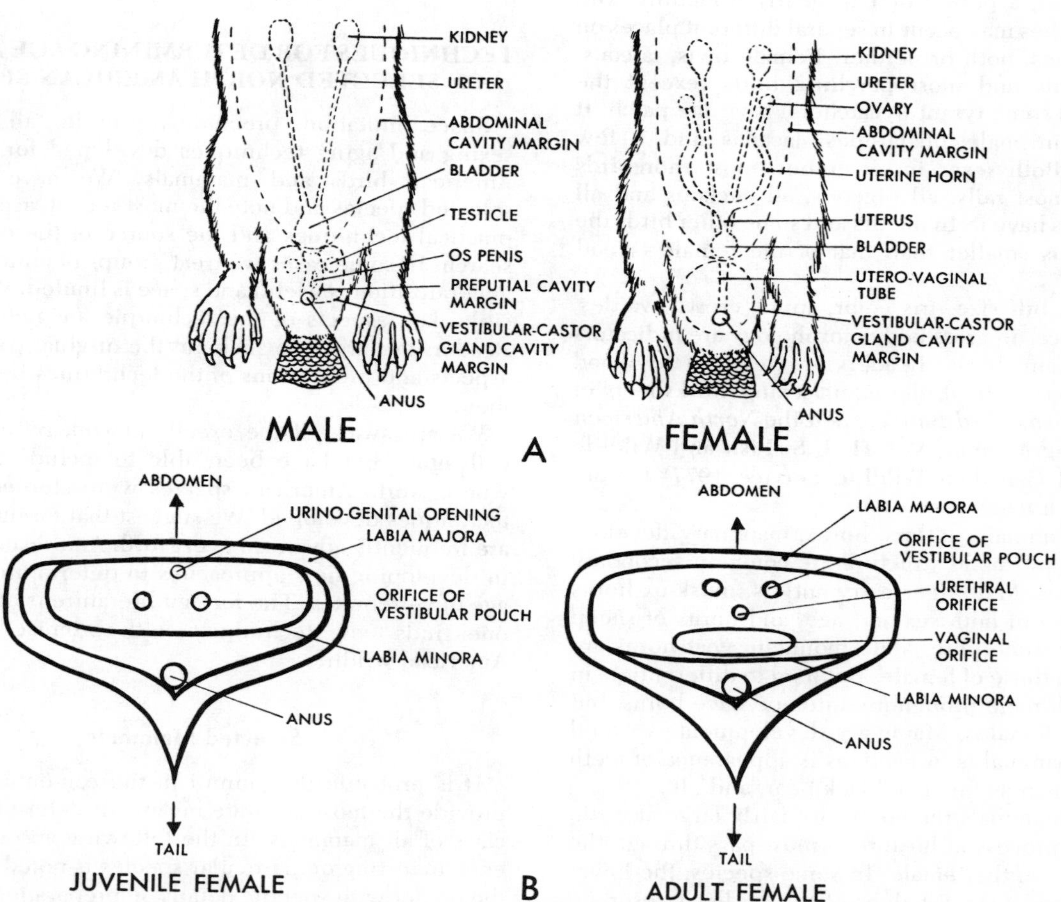

Fig. 11.19. **Some age and sex characteristics of beaver. *A* Schematic representation of penis and testes in the vestibularcastor cavity of male *Left* and normal position of the uterus of the female *Right*. Dissection is required to identify these organs. *B* Diagrammatic representation of the anal-urogenital opening when stretched laterally as by the forefingers. This procedure can be performed on live or dead beaver (sketches by G. J. Knudson *in* Thompson 1958).**

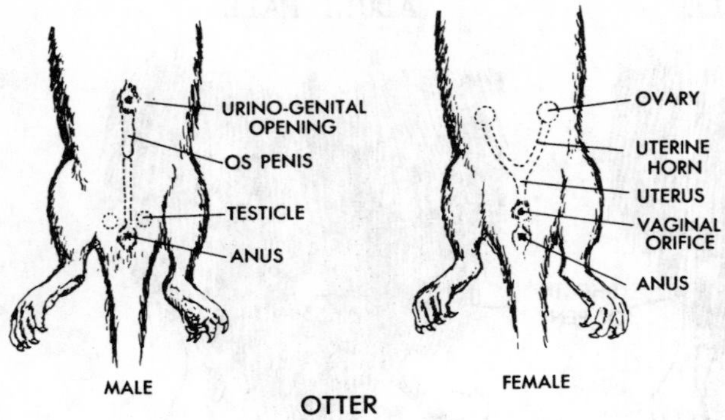

Fig. 11.20. Normal position of genitalia in male and female river otter. The presence of penis readily determined in the male river otter by palpation in the live and dead animal (sketch adapted from Thompson 1958).

may be difficult to sex in the eclipse plumage which follows the breeding season when all the wing feathers are molted simultaneously, and the bird assumes a drab, concealing plumage. In some species, such as geese, the sexes appear alike even during the breeding season.

Most species of birds develop an incubation or brood patch on the breast during egg laying up to the post-breeding molt, a period of 1 to nearly 6 months. The patch or patches may occur in several different places on males, females, both or neither. Female owls, falcons, hummingbirds and most perching birds (except the cowbird and some tyrant flycatchers) have the patch. It is present in male phalaropes, jacanas and a few shorebirds. Both sexes in all grebes, most shorebirds and allies, most rails, all pigeons, all cuckoos and all woodpeckers have it. In the tits and some other birds the male patch is smaller than that of the female (Wood 1969).

Bill color, bill size, iris color, spurs, crests, wattles, and differences in gross body morphology are indicators of sex in many birds. Readers are referred to Wood (1969), Roberts (1955), the aging/sexing worksheets of *North American Bird Bander*, and the *North American Bird Banding Manual*, Vol. II (U.S. Fish and Wildlife Service and Canadian Wildlife Service 1977) for detailed data on many species.

Among mammals, antlers, horns, mammary development, teeth and bone structure are common secondary indices of sex. Male deer carry antlers, musk-ox horns are indicative of both sex and age, and horns of sheep are sexually dimorphic. Male mountain goat horns are heavier than those of females but hard to differentiate in the field. All male pronghorn antelope have horns, but so do some females. Mammary development is useful when the mammal is in hand, as is appearance of teeth in species such as fur seal, black bear, and elk.

In many mammals the young are fairly large at birth. During the process of birth they must pass through the pelvic girdle of the female. In some species, the lower line of fusion of the 2 halves of the girdle is resorbed before giving birth, so that the walls of the girdle may spread. In others, there is a loosening of the ligaments holding the 2 sides of the girdle together. Some species do not have a loosening of the bond between the 2 halves of the pelvic girdle, but there are modifications in the shape of the pelvis. For this reason, there generally are significant differences between the appearance of the pelvis of 1 sex and the other in most mammalian species, especially in individuals which have passed through 1 breeding season (Taber 1956b, Denney 1958).

In the male, the pelvis has a special function that sometimes leaves its mark on the posterior border of the ischium and helps in sex identification—that of forming a point of attachment for some of the ligaments which support the penis. The point of attachment of a ligament commonly is marked by a raised, roughened area of bone called a suspensory tuberosity, that grows more pronounced with age (Fig. 11.21).

Pelage in some mammals provides an index to sex. Adult female moose have a white vulval patch visible during aerial census, female caribou calves have long hairs around the vulva, head pelage is sexually dimorphic in adult bison, and male pronghorn antelope have a complete black facial mask in contrast to the female which has only a black nose.

Behavior is an index to sex during the breeding season in some species. Defense of a territory, vocalization, and creating sounds with the wings are behaviors which some bird and mammal species employ and usually denote a breeding male.

TECHNIQUES FOR DETERMINING AGE AND SEX OF SELECTED NORTH AMERICAN SPECIES

Space limitations preclude presenting all details of sexing and aging techniques developed for all North American birds and mammals. We have included selected species and note the most recent, accurate, and practical techniques and the source of the original research. In some cases we treat groups of animals where generalization is useful and space is limited. Where possible, key aspects of the technique are noted briefly. Readers are urged to seek out the original paper for all aspects and precautions of the techniques before using them.

We are aware of the excellent work by our foreign colleagues but have been able to include them only where North American species were studied or basic techniques developed. We suggest that foreign workers are frequently advanced over North American biologists in developing new approaches to determining sex and age of vertebrates. The foreign literature is often where one finds new techniques with promise for North American wildlife.

Selected Mammals

It is probable that annuli in the cementum of teeth provide the most accurate means for determining year-class of all mammals. In the following accounts, reference to testing on particular species is noted to provide the reader with specific details on preparation and reading of histological sections. Where age-class techniques have been developed or a year-class technique that does not involve thin sections of tooth or bone, the key details are outlined.

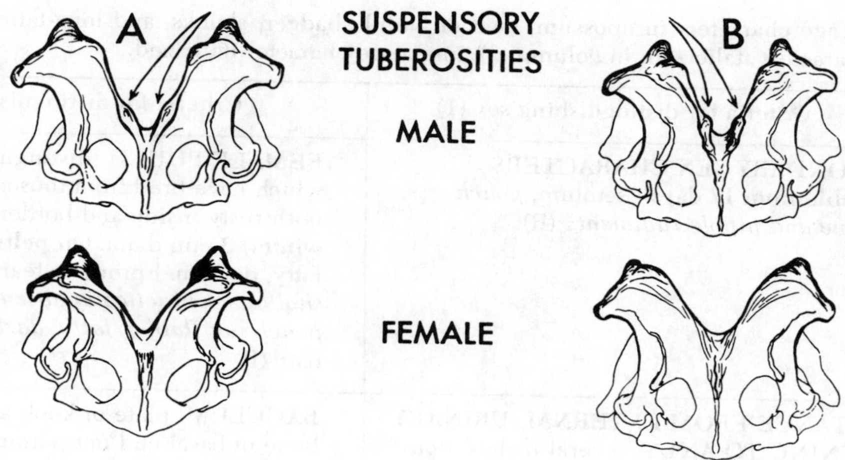

Fig. 11.21. Pelvic girdle of the white-tailed *A* and black-tailed *B* deer, viewed from the rear, showing the suspensory tuberosities for the attachment of the penis ligaments in the male and their absence in the female (after Taber 1956b).

BLACK BEAR

Cementum annuli in transverse sections of canine teeth are evidence of year-class. Sauer et al. (1966) and Allen and Collins (1971) have developed an appropriate cryostat procedure. Willey (1974) reported the canine or first premolar as equally good sources of annuli. Black bear canines are sexually dimorphic and maximum root width and maximum root thickness of lower canines, in combination, are the best criteria of sex. A gauge for sexing Adirondack black bear appears in Figure 11.22.

GRIZZLY BEAR

Cementum annuli in fourth premolar sections are indices of year-class (Craighead et al. 1970).

POLAR BEAR

The length of mandibular and maxillary molar rows are longer in males than in females (Larsen 1971b). Age may be determined by skull characteristics and weight of bacula (Manning 1964).

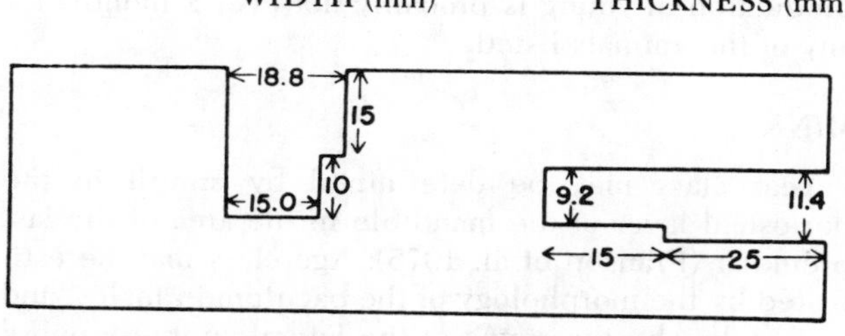

Fig. 11.22. The gauge devised for sexing black bears by the size of the lower canine tooth. It indicates sex as follows.
Female: tooth fits into smaller part of slot for either width or thickness (but not necessarily both).
Male: tooth does not fit into larger part of slot for either width or thickness (but not necessarily both)
If tooth fits into the larger part of both slots, but into the smaller part of neither, it must be measured and a summation of the width and thickness made as described in Sauer (1966).

BOBCAT

Crowe (1972) has shown that histological sections of canines reveal cementum annuli indicative of year-class.

OPOSSUM

See Table 11.4. Young animals may be aged (McGrady 1938) by the dental formula:

$$3 \text{ months} = \frac{5120}{4120}\ ;\ 4 \text{ months} = \frac{5131}{4132}\ ;$$

$$5\text{–}8\tfrac{1}{2} \text{ months} = \frac{5132}{4133}\ ;$$

$$7\text{–}11 \text{ months} = \frac{5133}{4134}\ ;$$

$$10 \text{ months} = \frac{5134}{4134}$$

RACCOON

Llewellyn (1953) developed indices to prenatal age based on crown-rump measurements. During the winter, juveniles may be identified by means of X rays of the distal ends of the radius and ulna, and the epiphyses are distinct and not fused with the shafts (Petrides 1959). However, thin epiphyseal lines (Fig. 11.4) often persist through the following year (Sanderson 1961a). In carcasses of males taken during the winter, the penis of a juvenile cannot be extended over one-half its length, while that of an adult can be extended more than one-half its length (Sanderson 1961a). See Table 11.4. Young raccoons are weaned about 16–20 weeks of age. During this period their age may be determined by tooth eruption, following the data in Table 11.5. Mature animals can be aged by incisor cementum annulation (Grau et al. 1970).

Dried weight of the eye lens is a reliable indicator of age up to 1 year of age only (Sanderson 1961b). However, Montgomery (1963) reported that both freezing

Table 11.4. Sex and age characters in opossum, raccoon, mink, badger, skunks, and long-tailed weasel. Note: In column (1), female characters italicized; in column (2), immature character italicized.

Species	Criteria for distinguishing sex (1)	Criteria for distinguishing age (2)
Opossum	SECONDARY SEX CHARACTERS (reliable from 17 days): scrotum; *pouch outline and nipple rudiments* (R)	FEMALE POUCH (distinguishes those which have bred from those which have not): rusty inside and border, teats (dried winter) 3 mm diam. On pelts, pouch flabby, fatty, dark, and prone to tear; *pouch white, shallow or practically absent; on pelts, pouch not flabby, fatty, dark or prone to tear* (P)
Raccoon	DISTANCE FROM EXTERNAL URINARY OPENING TO ANUS: several inches; *not over one inch* (St). URINARY PAPILLA: penis bone felt by palpation; *no penis bone* (S). CASED SKIN (if not too fat): roughened area near middle of belly (site of preputial orifice), small teats may show through skin; *no rough area, teats large* (S)	BACULUM: plate or knob at distal end (S), bone of basal end not porous (D); *distal end cartilaginous, basal end porous.* UTERINE HORNS (distinguishes those which have had litters from those which have not): opaque, 4–7 mm diam., w/placental scars; *translucent, 1-3 mm diam., w/o placental scars* (S)
Mink	CASED SKINS: penis scar present; *penis scar absent* (P-50a)	TEATS (of female): dark, raised, over 1 mm diam.; unpigmented, *scarcely raised, under 1 mm diam.* (P-50a)
Badger	Same as mink	TEATS (of female): 4–6 mm diam., 4–10 mm long even in dried skins; *1.5 mm diam. and 1 mm long in dried skins* (P-50a). Also see text.
Striped and Spotted Skunk	Same as mink	TEATS (of female): at least 2 mm diam. and 2.5 mm long, usually dark; *under 1 mm, usually flesh-covered* (P-50a). Also see text.
Long-tailed Weasel	Same as mink	TEATS (of female July-October): enlarged; *not visible* (W)

Authorities: (D) = Dellinger 1954; (P) = Petrides 1949; (P-50a) = Petrides 1950; (R) = Reynolds 1945; (S) = Sanderson 1950; (St) = Stuewer 1943; (W) = Wright 1948.

and decomposition tend to reduce lens weight and lead to an underestimate of age.

Delayed Implantation in Mustelidae

Because most members of the weasel family show a delay between the time that the ovum is fertilized and the time that it is implanted, there often is confusion concerning the length of the gestation period and the age at first breeding. In management, the principal question concerning age-classes is: during the harvest period, should a distinction be made between 3 classes (juveniles, subadults which have not yet produced young, and adults) or merely 2 (juveniles and adults)? Data on this question are presented in Table 11.6 for the principal members of the weasel family. In connection with this table it should be noted that the period between the implantation of the fertilized ovum, and the production of young is probably not over 2 months for any of the animals listed.

MINK

Year class may be determined by annuli in the periosteal layer of the mandible in the area of the last premolar (Franson et al. 1975). Age class may be estimated by the morphology of the baculum in males, and in females, by the status of the lateral supra-sesamoid tubercle (Fig. 11.23) and the fugal-squamosal suture. See Tables 11.7 and 11.8 (Lechleitner 1954, Greer 1957). Birney and Fleharty (1968) reported best results from using the status of the tubercle and the texture of the femur in the region of the epiphyseal closure (porous in juveniles, smooth in adults). However, Dellinger (unpublished) found 13.5–18.3% overlap using the tubercle as an age indicator in Missouri, indicating that

Table 11.5. Mean ages of raccoons at eruption of deciduous and permanent teeth (Montgomery 1964).

Tooth	Upper		Lower	
	Mean Age (days)	Sex	Mean Age (days)	Sex
Deciduous				
First incisor	34.0	2.8*	28.5	2.2*
Second incisor	25.4	2.2*	37.3	2.1*
Third incisor	26.2	1.2	33.0	2.4*
Canine	29.3	0.9	29.3	0.8
First premolar	64.5	1.9	60.7	1.8
Second premolar	46.2	1.0	43.4	1.6
Third premolar	49.2	1.2	48.4	1.2
Fourth premolar	48.7	1.0	48.7	1.0
Permanent				
First incisor	65.6	1.4	65.9	1.0
Second incisor	73.3	1.3	72.6	1.2
Third incisor	96.6	1.7	85.5	1.9
Canine	111.7	3.9	105.6	3.6
First molar	81.0	1.2	78.1	1.5

*The following percentages of these teeth either did not erupt or erupted and were shed before examination of the animals; upper first incisor and lower second incisor, 66.7; lower first incisor, 16.7; upper second incisor, 5.5; lower third incisor, 33.3.

there may be distinct variations between different populations.

Birney and Fleharty (1968) found nasal sutures in juveniles and an absence of bony deposits on the ischia of juvenile males. Adults had heavily worn teeth, and eye lens weights separated adults from juveniles but not without overlap. See also Tables 11.4 and 11.6.

Sex of cased skins may be determined by presence or absence of the penis scar (Table 11.4).

PINE MARTEN

See Tables 11.6 and 11.8. Clear-cut criteria of age have not been worked out. Nasal sutures are probably unfused in juveniles and fused in adults. The sagittal crest is more pronounced in males than females and also more pronounced in old than in young. In the female the presence of a sagittal crest indicates probable adulthood; however, some adult females apparently have no crest. In males a sagittal crest under 20.0 mm indicates that the individual is immature. In addition, it seems probable that males with sagittal crests over 30.0 mm and females with crests of over 20.0 mm may be termed "very old" (Marshall 1951). Dagg et al. (1975) found that fusion of the distal femoral epiphysis was not a reliable indicator of age in winter-trapped animals because fusion is a function of size and possibly of sex.

Newby and Hawley (1954), working with live pine marten, distinguished sex on the basis of the presence or absence of the baculum (determined by palpation), through observation of the vulva, or on the basis of the larger over-all size and broader head of the male. These same authors estimated age on the basis of: weight (juvenile females reached adult weight at 3 months, juvenile males at about 4 months); the softer appearance of the juvenile pelage (until late September); development of the sagittal crest; development of the head of the male baculum (enlarged in adults—see Fig. 11.6); and mammae of females (large and conspicuous in adults, inconspicuous in juveniles).

RIVER OTTER

Adults may be sexed by the relative positions of the anus and urogenital opening (see Fig. 11.20). Stephenson (1977) showed that annual layers in the cementum of canine teeth are 99% accurate for year class determination. Juvenile otters could be distinguished from adults by the size of the body, skull and baculum, and morphology of the skull (Stephenson 1977).

WOLVERINE

While known-age specimens are not readily available for this species, Rausch and Pearson (1972) reported that cementum annuli in canines was the most reliable estimate of age beyond 1 year. Reproductive organs, long bones, and cranial sutures separate young-of-the-year from adults only if the young are less than 10–11 months.

FISHER

Known age specimens are difficult to obtain, but Kelly (1977) showed that annuli occur in the cementum of the first premolar. He compared cementum annuli with age estimates based on reproductive status and on morphological criteria (Coulter 1966, Wright and Coulter 1967). He concluded that specimens with no annuli were less than 15 months old, and that where present, each annulus represents a 12-month interval. Wright and Coulter (1967) described skull and baculum charac-

Table 11.6. Some aspects of reproduction in members of the Mustelidae which determine whether there are classes in the harvest in addition to juvenile and adult.

Species	Breeding season	Season of birth	Gestation period*	Delayed implantation?	Age of ♀ at first breeding	Age of ♀ at first parturition	What classes in addition to immature and adult in winter population?	Authority
Mink	Winter	Early May	39–75 days	Yes	10 months	12 months	None	Hanssen 1947, Enders 1952
Pine Marten	July-Aug.	April	220–265 days	Yes	27 months	36 months	Yearling and two-year old	Asdell 1964
Long-tailed Weasel	July	Spring	205–337 days	Yes	3 or 4 months	12 months	None	Wright 1948
Fisher	March	April	338–358 days	Yes	12 months	24 months	Yearling (females only)	Hall 1942, Eadie and Hamilton 1958
Badger	July-Aug. ?	Spring	Probably about 9 months	Yes	15 months?	24 months?	Yearling	Hamlett 1932
Wolverine	July-Aug.?	Spring	Probably about 9 months	Yes	15 months?	24 months?	Yearling	Wright and Rausch 1955
Striped Skunk	Feb.-March	Spring	62 days	No	10 months	12 months	None	Wight 1931
River Otter	Dec.-March	Nov.-Jan.	288–380 days	Yes	36 months?	48 months	Yearling, two and three-year-old	Friley 1949, Liers 1951

*The period between copulation and parturition.

teristics for juvenile and adult fishers, but Boise (1975) found significant variation in skull measurements. Dagg et al. (1975) found that epiphyseal closure was not an accurate indicator of age. Table 11.6 reviews reproductive aspects of fishers.

Body size is markedly sexually dimorphic with males twice as heavy as females. Sex is determined by examination of external genital evidence on live animals or pelts. Parsons et al. (1978) have shown that maximum root width of lower canines is indicative of sex. Widths in excess of 5.64 mm are males.

AMERICAN BADGER

Histological sections of the upper canine show cementum annuli. The first dark annulus is laid down in the second summer or autumn, based on April 1 parturition (Crowe and Strickland 1975).

STRIPED AND SPOTTED SKUNK

Lens weights separate juveniles, subadults, and adult spotted skunks best, while closure of cranial sutures is

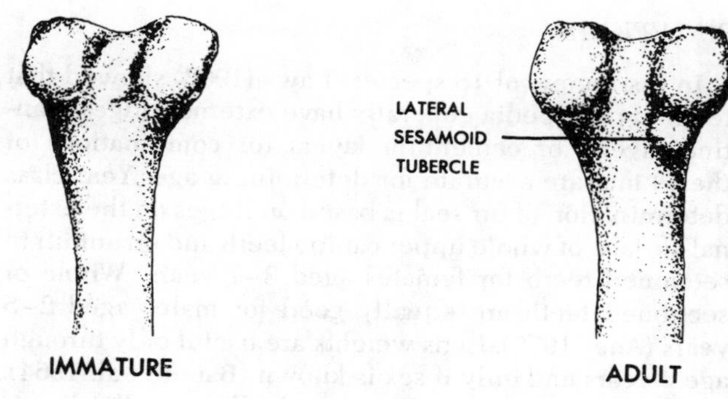

Fig. 11.23. Femurs of mink showing lateral supra-sesamoid tubercle of adult and its absence in the immature (from Lechleitner 1954, by Godin 1960).

second best for age-class determination (Mead 1967). Casey and Webster (1975) used cementum annuli for year class and sex chromatin in neurons for sex determination.

RED AND GRAY FOX

Monson et al. (1973) demonstrated that molars and premolars are superior to canines for cementum annuli in red fox. Allen (1974) reported that red fox canines erupt throughout life. The distance between the enamel line and the alveolar sockets is less than or equal to 2.0 mm for most juveniles. Allen developed a technique for hand-sectioning teeth. Pelts of both red and gray fox are readily sexed by the presence or absence of a "scar" marking the site of the penis.

Table 11.7. Use of femur tubercle (present on at least 1 side) and jugal-squamosal suture (absent on at least 1 side) as aging criteria in combination for mink (after Greer 1957).

Age classes	Total number	Number	Percent
	Femur tubercle absent and jugal-squamosal suture present		
Juveniles	495	468	95
	Femur tubercle present and jugal-squamosal suture absent		
Adults	388	375	97

Table 11.8. Criteria of age based on the baculum of some mustelids (the term "head" means the basal, or proximal, enlargement).

Species	Characteristics of baculum in young*	Characteristics of baculum in old*	Authority
Mink	No ridge. Head not always morphologically distinct. Wt. 172 (1 S.D.) 34.2 mg	Distinct ridge on baculum at head, which is distinct. Wt. 398 (1 S.D.) 97.0 mg	Lechleitner 1954
Long-tailed Weasel	Heads scarcely larger than shafts. Wt. 14–29 mg	Heads greatly expanded. Wt. 53–101 mg	Wright 1947
Striped Skunk	Head not enlarged. Shaft irregularly curved.	Head enlarged. Shaft more straight.	Petrides 1950
Badger	Short light-weight, with only shallow grooves, w/o protuberances and with head only slightly enlarged and never ridged.	Long, heavy, with prominent grooves and protuberances and with head much enlarged and often sharply ridged.	Petrides 1950
Pine Marten	Wt. under 100 mg	Wt. over 100 mg	Marshall 1951
Wolverine	Wt. 653–1458 mg (avg 1134 mg)	Wt. 1780–2940 mg (avg 2338 mg)	Wright and Rausch 1955

*Young means young of the year in the winter; old means older.

Gray fox age criteria based on baculum criteria are shown in Table 11.9, and general age characters for red and gray fox in Table 11.10.

Table 11.9. Measurements (early winter) of gray fox bacula in central Ohio (after Petrides 1950).

Age class (according to baculum shape)	Number	Length (mm)	Weight (mg)
Subadult	5	51 ± 1.7	280 ± 62
Adult	5	57 ± 2.6	528 ± 100

Table 11.10. Age characters for red and gray fox. Characters for young are italicized.

Anatomical structure	Characters
BACULUM:	(♂♂) Larger, heavier, with enlarged and roughened basal area; *smaller, lighter, w/o large, rough basal area* (P)
TEATS:	(♀♀) Over 2 mm diam, dark, obvious to touch in dry pelts; *under 1 mm diam, light colored, scarcely raised* (separates those which have bred from others) (P)
EPIPHYSES OF RADIUS AND ULNA (by X-ray):	No cartilage plate at distal end of radius and ulna; *cartilage plate at distal end of radius and ulna (cartilage plate at distal epiphyseal gap)* separates young up to 8–9 months from adults) (S & H)

(S & H) = Sullivan and Haugen 1956; (P) = Petrides 1950.

COYOTE

The permanent canines erupt at 4–5 months and the root canal of the same tooth closes at 8–9 months. The first dark annulus in the cementum forms at month 20 and 1 forms each year thereafter (Linhart and Knowlton 1967). Allen and Kohn (1976) suggested that there may be considerable variation between geographic regions in timing of deposition of cementum annuli. Roberts (1978) recommended the lower canine as the tooth of choice for examining cementum layers because the number of annuli varied between different kinds of teeth. Nellis et al. (1978) described a technique for estimating age up to 50 months by progressive closure of the canine socket. Crown-rump measurements are the best estimate of fetal age (Kenelly et al. 1977).

WOLF

Wolves do not breed until 3 years for males and 2 years for females but are "fully grown" at 18 months (Young and Goldman 1944). No specific characters have been recorded.

PINNIPEDIA

In his review of 18 species, Laws (1962) showed that teeth of pinnipedia generally have external ridges, dentine layers, or cementum layers (or combinations of these) that are accurate for determining age. Year-class determination of fur seal is based on ridges on the external surface of whole upper canine teeth and on annuli in sectioned teeth for females aged 3–7 years. Whole or sectioned teeth are equally good for males aged 2–5 years (Anas 1970). Lens weights are useful only through age 2 years and only if sex is known (Bauer et al. 1964). Fur seals and their teeth are markedly sexually dimorphic in gross size. Northern sea lion pups up to 15 months can be aged by general size (to the nearest 6 weeks), and the pattern of tooth eruption is also a guide to this age group (Spalding 1966).

Pinnipeds generally display annuli in the dentine deposits within the pulp cavity of canines and cementum deposits on the apex of the root. Both of these may be examined in longitudinal sections of the teeth (Kenyon and Fiscus 1963). In some genera (*Callorhinus, Eumetopias, Zalophus, Odobenus,* and *Mirounga,* at least) there are annuli visible as ridges on the outer surface of the canines (Scheffer 1950, Laws 1953, Mansfield 1958, Kenyon and Fiscus 1963).

COTTONTAIL RABBIT AND HARES

Young-of-the-year may be separated from older animals on the basis of length of hind foot and dry weight of the eye lens. The epiphyseal closure of the humerus allows separation of 2 groups of animals under 10 months of age (Bothma et al. 1972 and see Table 11.11). Conception dates of prenatal animals may be estimated by use of a photographic key developed by Rongstad (1969). Freezing eye lenses dramatically reduces lens weights (Pelton 1970), and weights vary so much among adults that this technique can only separate young-of-the-year from adults (Rongstad 1966). Sullins et al. (1976) showed that periosteal layers are absent in mandibles of young-of-the-year eastern and Nuttall's cottontails and present in those that were 1 year or older. They suggest that the annuli are useful for separating year classes of cottontails older than 1 year, but found that this technique has no particular advantage over lens weight for separating adults from young-of-the-year.

Sex is determined in the live animal as follows: when the cottontail is relaxed, the penis of the male and the clitoris of the female (which somewhat resembles the penis) are withdrawn into the body. For examination, these organs can be erected by applying downward pressure with a thumb and forefinger placed in front of and behind the genital region, respectively.

The penis is a cylindrical organ whose basal sheaths unfold on erection in the manner of a small telescope. A tiny terminal opening is apparent on close inspection.

The clitoris of the female is nearly as large as the penis of a young male and might be mistaken for it. However, it differs in being flattened posteriorly and in having no terminal opening. The vaginal opening is located between the base of the clitoris and the anus but is

Table 11.11. Sex and age criteria for rabbits, hares, and muskrat. Note: In column (1) female characters are italicized; in column (2) immature characters are italicized.

Species	Criteria for distinguishing sex (1)	Criteria for distinguishing age (2)
Cottontail Rabbit	See text	HUMERUS: Epiphyseal line or groove absent; *epiphyseal line or groove present* (up to 9 months) (H)
Hares	Like Cottontail Rabbit (L)	Like Cottontail Rabbit (L)
Muskrat	PELT: nipples absent; *nipples present* (Sch) URETHRAL PAPILLA (fresh or live animals): penis present; *penis absent* (B & B)	PELT PRIMENESS PATTERN: Irregular, spotted or mottled; *regular longitudinal arrangement* (subadult); *lyre-shaped unprime area on dorsal side* (juveniles) (A & P) (see Fig. 11.9) PENIS: Over 5.15 mm diam., dark, w/blunt rounded tip; *under 5.15 mm diam, lighter red, w/knob-shaped tip* (Sch) (B & B) TESTIS LENGTH (fall & early winter): over 11.65 mm; *under 11.65 mm* (Sch) VAGINAL ORIFICE: membrane thin or missing; *closed by thick membrane* (Sch) PLACENTAL SCARS (where there are no barren adults): present; *absent* (Sch)

References: (A & P) = Applegate and Predmore 1947; (B & B) = Baumgartner and Bellrose 1943; (H) = Hale 1949; (L) = Lechleitner 1957; (Sch) = Schofield 1955.

not always visible. In young females it is covered by the vaginal membrane.

Small rabbits are hardest to sex. In a young male the distal portion of the penis may "open up" along the midventral line to somewhat resemble the clitoris. This flattening of the terminal region of the penis does not extend, however, to the base of the organ, as it does in the clitoris. Fox and Crary (1972) developed and illustrated a technique useful on newborn rabbits as young as 27 days based on examination of the urogenital papilla.

Sex and age determination for hares is similar to that for cottontails (Lechleitner 1957).

BLACK-TAILED JACKRABBIT

Connolly et al. (1969a) reported that eye lens weight is superior to ephiphyseal closure, up to 140 days. Tiemeier and Plenert (1964) gave a curve that shows lens weight increased to at least 680 days, but beyond about 200 days their sample size was not sufficient to assess the amount of variability to be expected among individuals of the same age. These authors divided their jackrabbits into 3 age classes on the basis of condition of the proximal epiphyseal groove of the humerus: I—0–5 mo., definite groove; II—5–14 mo., definite line; III—over 14 mo., no line. Ear and hind foot length reached full size within age class I, but age classes II and III could probably be distinguished by lens weight.

MUSKRAT

Sex may be determined by the presence or absence of the penis (Table 11.11) if the urinary papilla is grasped between forefinger and thumb and stripped posteriorly. The penis, if present, will be either felt or exposed. In very young rats, not yet fully furred, the presence or absence of visible nipples will indicate sex.

The molt pattern on the inside of the skin is a good indicator of age (see Fig. 11.9) until the molt is completed, in February or March. Thereafter the most reliable way to distinguish juveniles (almost 1 year old) from adults is by the appearance of the first upper molar. Sather (1954) described the juvenile first upper molar as having fluting which runs deep into the alveolar socket, so that the end is not visible even in the cleaned skull. The adult, in contrast, has fluting which extends only part way along the tooth, so that the end of the fluting is visible in the cleaned skull. In addition, the anterior face of the adult tooth is discernibly humped, while that of the juvenile is straight. Sather suggested that in the freshly killed animal it may be necessary to cut the gum away to see these characters clearly.

Olsen (1959) further refined this technique by distinguishing (in muskrats trapped in March and April) between 3 age classes, as follows (all description applies to the upper right molar): (1) highly developed roots and end of fluting extruded well below the bone line—adults; (2) moderate root development and end of the fluting just barely or not quite emerged from the bone line—subadults of about 10 months of age; and (3) little or no root development and fluting ending deep in the alveolar socket—juveniles averaging about 7 months of age. Doude Van Troostwijk (1976) developed a formula for estimating age, in months, of muskrats 1 month of age or older, based on the crown length and total length of the first molar:

$$\text{age (months)} = \frac{\frac{100 - \text{crown length M}'}{\text{total length M}'} \times 100 \pm 1.98}{3.97} + 1$$

He reported that the formula becomes less accurate as animals approach the age of 2 years. Vincent and Quéré (1972) constructed a curve to estimate age, up to 36 months, based on eye lens weights.

The zygomatic breadth was used to separate freshly-skinned muskrats, with subadults measuring less than 4.16 mm and adults more than this (Alexander 1951). However, this measurement decreases as the skull dries, declining by 0.5 mm over the first 5 days. This shrinkage totalled 0.7 mm by the end of the first year. Summer humidity (70 to 80%) caused an increase of 0.3 mm in this measurement (Alexander 1960).

The ossification of the baculum has been shown to be a reliable age criterion for Missouri muskrats (see Elder and Shanks 1962 and Fig. 11.24).

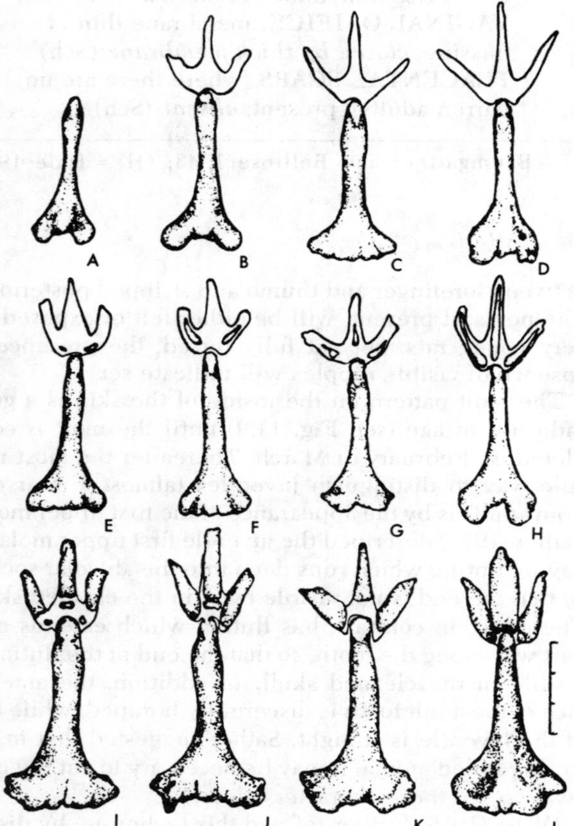

Fig. 11.24. Age changes in the bacula of muskrat. A–D: about 4–8 months old; E–H; about 8–15 months old; I–L: adult—over 15 months old. Scale in mm (from Elder and Shanks 1962).

BEAVER

Cementum annuli from ground and polished teeth indicate year class (Van Nostrand and Stephenson 1964, Larson and Van Nostrand 1968). Nuclei of the polymorphonuclear neutrophil leucocyte are sexually dimorphic when viewed at 1000X (Larson and Knapp 1971). Live adult beaver may be sexed, but only with experience, by palpation, for the testes and penis, with its baculum. The presence or absence of testes may be determined as follows: Place the beaver in a normal standing position, with head covered. Place 1 hand so that it lies lateral to the pubic symphysis with the finger tips anterior to the pubis and resting on the soft abdomen. Press lightly and draw the hand posteriorly. If the animal is a male, the testis can be felt as it slips anteriorly under the finger tips. If no testis is felt, a check may be made by palpation for the os penis, or baculum. This is done by placing the thumb and forefinger immediately posterior to the pubic symphysis and passing them back toward the vent between the castor glands. Care must be taken not to misinterpret concretions in the castors. Another difficulty lies in the variability of the position of the penis. It may be at one side and in close proximity to the castors in old males; in young males it is always in a median position (Osborn 1955). Kennedy (1952) recommended palpation by an insertion of the index finger into the cloaca and urogenital orifice. The finger is passed anteriorly into the vestibule or cavity that exists between the castor glands. About 2.5 cm from the external opening the finger, moved from side to side in the male, will contact the penis. This method was first described by Bradt (1938). Figure 11.19 illustrates the appearance and location of beaver genitalia.

SQUIRRELS (GRAY, FOX AND RED)

Squirrels are born hairless and with the eyes closed; their subsequent postnatal development to 6 weeks is as shown in Table 11.12. Squirrels are sexed by examination of the external genitalia.

Several aging techniques have been developed which enable the aging of squirrels as immatures or adults. Body weights have been used, as presented in Table 11.13, under the reservation that weights are dependent on many external conditions independent of age. Gray squirrels can be aged by cementum annuli (Fogl and Mosby 1978).

The degree of development of the external genitalia (Table 11.13) has also been used, but this also has its limitations since fully adult males may be mistaken for immature males during the sexually quiescent period. Under favorable conditions immature females may breed and appear to be over 1 year old.

A normal November sample will contain spring-born juveniles (8 to 9 months of age), summer-born juveniles (3 to 4 months), and adults (over 1 year). The 3 classes can be separated by the characters of the tail pelage, as viewed from below: young juvenile—2 sometimes 3, dark lines running through the reddish-brown primary hairs of the tail, lower or proximal one-third of tail naked beneath; older juvenile (subadult)—dark lines as in juvenile, lower one-third of tail covered with short appressed hairs; adult—tail bone obscured by appressed secondary hairs that radiate out over and partially cover the long primary hairs of the tail. As shown in Figure 11.16, the lines or bars so prominent in young of the year have become weakened in color intensity and are diffuse in the tails of adults (Sharp 1958a). Pelage characteristics which reveal age are particularly attractive in

Table 11.12. Development of young fox and gray squirrels.

Age	Developmental characters of Fox Squirrel*	Developmental characters of Gray Squirrel**
New born	14.2g	
1 week	28.3g, first hair appears on back of head and shoulders.	
2 weeks		Emerging hair darkens dorsal surface.
3 weeks	56.6g, covered with dark hair beginning to turn brown on tail and around eyes and mouth. Lower incisors appear and ears open.	Hair about 1 mm long. Ears open. Lower incisors erupted.
4 weeks		Silver hair on tail about 2 mm long. Upper incisors erupting.
5 weeks	70.8 to 85g. Eyes open. Hair appearing under tail, the last part to become furred.	At least 1 eye open.
6 weeks		Underside of tail covered with hair.

*After Allen (1943).
**After Uhlig (1955):

that live animals can be aged and then released to give known age individuals in the population.

Another readily applied field aging technique for the gray squirrel that is based upon pelage characteristics is the method developed by Barrier and Barkalow (1967). In winter pelage the late fall harvest can be separated into: summer juvenile—pelage in rump region when separated and laid flat by the thumbs will reveal no yellow prebasal band in the black underfur, and the majority of banded guard hairs will be black tipped; spring-juvenile—using same technique the yellow prebasal band in the black underfur will be absent or indistinct, and all banded guard hairs will be white tipped; adult—there is a distinct, yellow prebasal band in the black underfur, and all banded guard hairs will be white tipped.

One skeletal method to separate juvenile from adult squirrels is the degree of closure of the distal epiphyses of the radius and ulna, which change with maturation of these long bones. X-ray reveals that the epiphyses described remain open through the 18th week of life and that an epiphyseal line may still be detected until the 12th month. Thereafter, the epiphyseal line is absent (Petrides 1951, Carson 1961).

The weight of the eye lens increases with age and has been used to distinguish age classes in fox squirrels shot in October and November in Michigan. The age classes and their lens weights found are: summer born—to about 28 mg; spring born—from 29 to 39 mg; older—with some evidence of different year-classes but with considerable overlap among them (Beale 1962). The lens weight technique can be utilized without known age weights or curves by plotting lens weight by frequency and noting natural breaks in the frequency distribution, provided a substantial sample is processed. This method would allow separation of summer young, spring young and adults.

Gray squirrels may be separated into young-of-the-year and adults on the basis of eye lens weight (Fisher and Perry 1970). McCloskey (1977) tested various aging techniques on the same fox squirrel specimens and concluded that X-ray of the epiphyseal line in the forefoot was the most accurate indicator of age class. Among the field techniques, coloration and appearance of nipples of females, tail pelage (both sexes), and scrotal pigmentation of males were best. Nellis (1969) found too much overlap in cranial measurements to separate sexes of red squirrels. Lemnell (1974) found cementum annuli in premolar and molar roots of red squirrels the most accurate aging method, but suggested that it would be faster to first sort out the juveniles on the basis of ephiphyseal closure and/or eye lens techniques.

While there are several aging techniques that are applicable to squirrels, it is realized that many are subject to external factors not related to age, such as range condition, health, and also the experience and ability of the investigator. With this in mind, it is always desirable to employ as many of the techniques as possible and arrive at a conclusion based on all the information available.

WOODCHUCK

Woodchucks in spring may be divided into young, yearlings, and adults, using the following criteria (Davis 1964):

Table 11.13. Characteristics for distinguishing between adult and juvenile fox and gray squirrels in October and November (from Uhlig 1956).

Adult	Juvenile
MALE	
Ventral and posterior end of scrotum darkened and generally free of hair.	Posterior end of scrotum with smooth skin, brown to black, and possibly free of hair. Summer juveniles with scrotum covered with hair, small testes, may be difficult to detect. Spring males may sometimes be mistaken for adults.
FEMALE	
Mammary glands large and noticeable, not hidden by hair; teats are black-tipped in fox squirrels. On gray squirrels the black spots may be absent, or about the size of a pin point.	Teats inconspicuous, more or less hidden by the hair. Spring females occasionally have young before the hunting season and are classified as adults.
MALES AND FEMALES	
Tails rectangular, blocked-shaped, sides parallel or nearly so. Unless in an emaciated condition, the weight of adults is over 396.2 gm.	Tails pointed, triangular, sides not parallel. Spring juveniles will weigh over 396.2 gm. Summer juveniles will be under 396.2 gm. A rough index to age of summer juveniles is: 8 weeks—141.5 gm; 10 weeks—198.1 gm; 14 weeks—311.3 gm; 16 weeks—367.9 gm and 18 weeks—396.2 gm.

Young: weigh 300–450 g about May 15 and gain about 19 g/day from June through September; do not begin molt until early July, pelage remains short and fine later in season than that of older animals—up to September; incisors narrow, long, pointed, unstained; head small; muzzle narrow and pointed; lens weight mean 12.32 mg (S.D. 2.8).

Yearling (young of previous year): in March and April size, head shape and incisors like young; from February through April testes white (although some yearlings have pigmented testes in March and April); lens weight mean 21.78 mg (S.D. 1.7).

Adult: incisors broader, with worn points and darkly stained; testes light to dark brown; lens weight mean 28.53 mg (S.D. 4.5).

SMALL MAMMALS

Eye lens weights have been used extensively to attempt to age small mammals, but Dapson and Irland (1972) pointed out that because of the small size of the organ the relative magnitude of error is high. They have developed a technique based on insoluble protein (Tyrosine) content of the lens which is accurate up to at least 750 days. Birney et al. (1975) reported that for cotton rats lens weights are acceptable up to 130 days, but the insoluble protein technique is necessary for older animals. Gourley and Jannett (1975) reported that if elaborately careful methods were used, lens weights were good in pine and montane voles up to 112 weeks. Tooth eruption is a good guide, up to 1 year, in Arctic ground squirrels (Mitchell and Carsen 1967). Adhesion lines in the periosteal layer of lower jaws have been used in pika (Millar and Zwickel 1972) and cementum annuli in Uinta ground squirrels (Montgomery et al. 1971) and California ground squirrels (Adams and Watkins 1967). It would appear that as a generalization cementum annuli and insoluble protein content of the eye lens will be the most accurate techniques for most small mammals.

Beg and Hoffman (1977) used the pattern of maxillary tooth eruption and amount of wear on molariform teeth to determine age classes of the red-tailed chipmunk. Three age classes were established for wild juveniles between 39 and 79 days of age and 5 age classes for adults between 10 and 64+ months of age.

To determine sex in small rodent (voles, lemmings, deer mice) skeletons found in raptor pellets, etc., use is made of the proportions of the pelvic girdle (the 3 bones—ilium, ischium, and pubis together constitute the innominate; the 2 innominates constitute the pelvic girdle). The pubic arm of the pelvis tends to be narrower and longer in proportion to the ischial arm in the male (Dunmire 1955).

A vespertilionid bat *(Myotis myotis)* has been studied by Sluiter (1961) who found that young born in June can be distinguished from adults until October by smaller size, darker fur, and relatively longer ears. Sexual maturity is reached during the second year of life. Females that have not yet given birth can be recognized by examination of the reproductive tract during the first and second winters of life. Juvenile males can be recognized by the reproductive tract during the first winter only. Tooth abrasion continues through life, but overlap between age-classes precludes use of the results of tooth wear as a reliable criterion of age.

WHITE-TAILED DEER

Year class is most accurately determined from cementum annuli using histological sections of the first incisor, keeping in mind that split annuli can occur in both sexes (Lockard 1972). The pattern of tooth replacement (Table 11.3, Fig. 11.8, and Severinghaus 1949) can be used to place animals in the fawn or yearling categories, but tooth wear characteristics are too varied for accurate determination among older animals (Gilbert and Stolt 1970). Ludwig and Dapson (1977) have shown that gravimetric and colormetric determination of eye-lens protein can place animals in year classes.

Deer, both mule and white-tailed, may be easily sexed in the flesh, but it is occasionally necessary to determine sex from the skeleton. This is possible, in animals over 2 years of age, by the presence of tuberosities where the ligaments which support the penis attach in the male and their absence in the female (Taber 1956b) (Fig. 11.21).

It is sometimes desirable to age the unborn deer, or fetus, for the purpose of determining the date of conception. Often this is done on the basis of crown-rump length; but since both mule deer and white-tailed deer vary in size from race to race, it is better to determine fetal age by developmental characters. The stages of fetal development are shown in Table 11.1, based on the work of Armstrong (1950) and Hudson and Browman (1959).

MULE AND BLACK-TAILED DEER

For animals up to 33 months, Rees et al. (1966) have described the eruption pattern of mandibular teeth (see also Fig. 11.8, Table 11.2). Connolly et al. (1969b) and Erickson et al. (1970) have found that after 24–28 months, tooth wear, eye lens and molar tooth ratio techniques are grossly inadequate. However, when reference sets of sex specific mandibles are available, the accuracy of the tooth wear technique is improved to an acceptable level (Thomas and Bandy 1975). Thomas and Bandy (1973) reported that cementum annuli from incisor sections is accurate for all ages. McCullough (1965) has reported that the hooves of adult black-tailed deer are sexually dimorphic to the extent that tracks of adult males and larger yearling, which have a larger arc-width, can be recognized with certainty. Sex from the skeleton is determined as in white-tailed deer, above (Fig. 11.21).

ELK

Greer and Yeager (1967) have shown that upper canines removed from the jaw are indicative of sex and place animals in age classes of calves, yearlings and 2 years and older. Keiss (1969) reported that annuli in first incisors were accurate indicators of year-class and that only 50% can be aged to year correctly by tooth wear.

The fetal, or unborn, elk may be placed in its proper stage of gestation by measurements, as shown in Table 11.14. Table 11.15 gives the sequence of tooth eruption.

MOOSE

Cementum annuli of incisors are valid year-class indicators (Gasaway et al. 1978, Haagenrud 1978), and adult antlerless moose and most calves may be sexed from the air by display of a white vulval patch (Roussel 1975).

Table 11.14. Fetal development of the Rocky Mountain elk of Montana (from Morrison et al. 1959). Birth occurs at about 247 days.

Age in days from conception	Development characters and measurements
25	Body not yet C-shaped. C-R* 6.2
30	Body C-shaped; mandible well formed; 4th branchial cleft apparent. C-R 8.2; HL** 0.7
37	Body C-shaped; snout becoming formed; olfactory pits well developed; external ear beginning to differentiate; branchial clefts becoming obliterated. C-R 14.4; HL 3.0
43	Body less C-shaped; head, neck, and body regions well differentiated; mouth open; vibrissae follicles visible around eye. C-R 24.0; HL 5.0
59	Body fish-hook-shaped; hooves and dew claws formed; vibrissae follicles on muzzle and lower jaw; eyelids complete and closed. C-R 65.0; HL 19.5
90	Lachrymal sinuses have a prominent fold of skin around them. C-R 167.5; HL 75.0
123	Body no longer fish-hook-shaped; hooves pinkish with black pigmentation forming on anterodorsal edges; muzzle brown-tipped; vibrissae protrude 1-2 mm from follicles around eyes, muzzle, and lower jaw. C-R 305.0; HL 178.5
182	Entire body well haired except axillae and inner ear surfaces; nose black and reticulated with deep wrinkles. C-R 540.0; HL 378
247	(Full term) C-R 925.0; HL 406

*C-R = the distance in millimeters from the anterior-most to the posterior-most points of the body (early stages) or anterior-most point of the crown to the tuberosity of the ischium (later stages).

**HL = the distance in millimeters between the tubercle of the tibio-fibula and the point of the hoof.

Table 11.15. Tooth eruption in the Rocky Mountain elk (from Quimby and Gaab 1952). Milk or deciduous tooth—D; permanent tooth—P; parentheses indicate that the tooth is in process of erupting at that particular time.

	Incisors			Canine	Premolars			Molars		
Age	1	2	3	1	2	3	4	1	2	3
1/2 year	D	D	D	D	D	D	D	P		
1-1/2 years	P	D P	D	D	D	D	D	P	P	
2-1/2 years	P	P	P	P	D (P) P	D (P) P	D (P) P	P	P	P
3-1/2 years	P	P	P	P	P	P	P	P	P	P

CARIBOU

The eruption pattern of molars and permanent premolars can be used to age Newfoundland caribou up to age 27½ months (Bergerud 1970a) and in barren ground caribou up to 2 years (Miller 1974b). Miller (1974a) has shown the cementum annuli technique valid for barren ground caribou and has developed an accurate eruption pattern chart for the species (Table 11.16, Miller 1974b). The second or third incisors may be removed from living animals for aging (Bergerud and Russell 1966).

MUSK-OX

Sex and age in the musk-ox are best determined by the appearance of the horns, since most animals must be classified while alive. Calves are readily identified by their size. Yearlings are small and have small, straight, horn projections: in males the length of the horn sheath is probably about 100 mm and in females about 66 mm.

Immature animals include bulls of 2½ to 5½ years and cows of 2½ to 3½ years. Sex is difficult to determine in 2½-year-old animals, although the horns of bulls are whiter and project more nearly straight from the head than those of females. During the fourth year the horns of the females have developed to the point where their basal depression reaches the maximum, almost touching the jaw, and the apical portions turn upward and out. They are then considered adults. Bulls are considered adults from their sixth year, which is marked by the growth of their horns completely over the forehead (Tener 1954).

BISON

Frison and Reher (1970) showed that age can be based on tooth eruption patterns up to 4½ years. Novakowski (1965) showed cementum annuli is valid for year-class determination. Shackleton et al. (1975) showed that degree of fusion of cranial sutures can be used to put males in age classes and that cranial measurements distinguish sex as well. Table 11.17 gives the sequence of tooth eruption and replacement. Duffield (1973) developed a table for calculating age, up to about 11 years, based on closure of the epiphyses. He also identified sexual differences in a number of postcranial skeletal measurements.

WILD SHEEP

Cementum annuli are valid criteria of year-class in Rocky Mountain bighorn, Nelson's bighorn, Peninsular bighorn, Dall and Stone sheep (Turner 1977). Horn segment counts are also valid on bighorn (Geist 1966). Sheep, like other North American bovidae, are slower than the members of the deer family in achieving adult dentition, 4 years being required for completion ooth replacement and eruption (Table 11.18 and 11.19).

The most intensively studied wild sheep form has been the bighorn sheep, but sex criteria probably apply equally well to the Dall sheep of the North. At a distance it is possible to distinguish but not sex lambs. Yearlings, especially rams, unless closely examined for the scrotum, cannot be clearly distinguished from adult ewes. Two-year-old and older rams are easily distinguished by their large horns. The younger-adult rams (less than 3/4 curl) may be separated from the older ones (3/4 curl or over) (Jones et al. 1954).

MOUNTAIN GOAT

Sex of all ages may be determined by urination posture. Males stand or stretch while females squat during urination. The scrotum of the yearling and older males is visible during the summer. Male horns are thicker at the base than those of females and, as seen frontally, there is less space between male bases than in females. Female yearlings and older show a black vulval patch under the tail.

Kids (animals born during the current summer) have horns barely visible to less than 1/2 ear length by fall. Yearlings have horns in early summer less than ear length and to about ear length in fall. Two-year-olds and adults have horns longer than ears. Adults have faces larger and more angular than do 2-year-olds but this distinction is difficult by late summer (Nichols 1978).

Aging is possible both by the intermittent growth of the horn, causing the formation of annual rings (see Fig. 11.2) and by the eruption and replacement of the teeth (Table 11.20).

PRONGHORN ANTELOPE

Year class is determined by cementum annuli in the first permanent incisor (McCutchen 1969). Techniques based on wear are not valid and histological sectioning

Table 11.16. Percentage frequency of occurrence of stages of eruption of teeth of Kaminuriak caribou according to age during first 29 months of life (from Miller 1974b).

Age, mon.	i1	i2	i3	c1	p2	p3	p4	m1	m2	m3
	Mandibular incisiform and molariform tooth rows									
0	D*	D	D	D	D E†	D E	D E	A‡	A	A
1	D	D	D	D	D	D	D	A	A	A
3	D	D	D	D	D	D	D	P§	E A	A
5	D	D	D	D	D	D	D	P	E A	A
10	D 46, E 21, P 33	D	D	D	D	D	D	P	A 62, E 38, P 0	A
12	D 14, E 3, P 83	D 41, E 21, P 38	D 52, E 22, P 26	D 59, E 22, P 19	D	D	D	P	A 7, E 77, P 16	A
13	P	D 58, E 0, P 42	D 67, E 0, P 33	D 83, E 0, P 17	D	D	D	P	A 40, E 33, P 27	A
15	P	P	P	D 0, E 8, P 92	D	D	D	P	P	A 92, E 8, P 0
17	P	P	P	P	D	D	D	P	P	A 65, E 35, P 0
22	P	P	P	P	D 74, E 21, P 5	D 86, E 12, P 2	D 95, E 3, P 2	P	P P	A 10, E 89, P 1
24	P	P	P	P	D 34, E 20, P 46	D 28, E 23, P 49	D 50, E 15, P 35	P	P	A 0, E 47, P 53
25	P	P	P	P	D 17, E 11, P 72	D 17, E 6, P 77	D 39, E 3, P 58	P	P	A 0, E 39, P 61
27	P	P	P	P	D 13, E 7, P 80	D 10, E 3, P 87	D 19, E 0, P 81	P	P	A 0, E 6, P 94
29	P	P	P	P	P	P	P	P	P	P

*D—milk tooth.

†E—erupting tooth. An erupting tooth has a stained portion but has not migrated to its position of permanent orientation.

‡A—absent tooth (permanent tooth not yet erupted).

§P—permanent tooth.

‖Numerical values—frequency of occurrence, in percentages, of each type of tooth. When no values are given, occurrence is 100 per cent. Incisors and premolars equal D E P, molars equal A E P.

Table 11.17. Tooth eruption and replacement in the lower jaw of the bison (after Hogben, ms.). Milk or deciduous tooth—D; permanent tooth—P; parentheses indicate that the tooth is in process of erupting at that particular time.

	Incisors			Canine	Premolars			Molars		
Age	1	2	3	1	2	3	4	1	2	3
1 year	D	D	D	D	D	D	D	P	(P)	
2 years	P	D P	D	D	D P	D	D	P	P	(P)
3 years	P	P	D	D	(P) P	(P) P	D (P)	P	P	(P)
4 years	P	P	P	D	P	P	P	P	P	P
5 years	P	P	P	(P)	P	P	P	P	P	P

Table 11.18. Tooth eruption and replacement in the lower jaw of the bighorn sheep (based on Cowan 1940, Deming 1952, and upon specimens at Montana State University). Milk or deciduous tooth—D; permanent teeth—P; parentheses indicate that the tooth is in process of replacement at that particular time.

	Incisors			Canine	Premolars			Molars		
Age	1	2	3	1	2	3	4	1	2	3
Birth	D	D	D	D	D	D	(D)			
1 month	D	D	D	D	D	D	D			
6 months	D	D	D	D	D	D	D	(P)		
12 months	(P)	D	D	D	D	D	D	P	(P)	
16 months	P	D	D	D	D	D	D	P	P	
24 months	P	D	D	D	D	D	D	P	P	
30 months	P	D	D	D	(P)	(P)	D	P	P	(P)
36 months	P	(P)	D	D	(P)	(P)	(P)	P	P	(P)
42 months	P	P	D	D	P	P	P	P	P	P
48 months	P	P	P	P	P	P	P	P	P	P

of teeth to expose annuli is superior to cut and grinding procedures (Kerwin and Mitchell 1971).

The males have horns in this species and the females may or may not. In general, animals with horns longer than the ears are adult males. The adult male is marked with a black mask covering the face up to the horns; the female has a black nose, but only a faint shadow of dark hair extends upward on her face (Einarsen 1948).

Table 11.21 gives the sequence of tooth eruption and replacement.

COLLARED PECCARY

Kirkpatrick and Sowls (1962) have described a technique based on tooth-replacement patterns which place animals up to 21½ months in 6 age classes.

Work on peccaries is still in its infancy but the information given in Table 11.22 will be useful until more precise data are available.

Selected Birds

This section first treats game bird species whose populations have been managed in North America and concludes with nongame species. Basic references to age and sex characters in birds are the *Manual for the Identification for the Birds of Minnesota and Neighboring States* (Roberts 1955), *A Bird Bander's Guide to Determination of Age and Sex of Selected Species* (Wood 1969), and *North American Bird Banding Manual*, Vol. II (U.S. Fish and Wildlife Service and Canadian Wildlife Service 1977).

SWANS

Sexes are alike in trumpeter and whistling swans and can be distinguished only by internal examination (Bellrose 1976). In mute swans the fleshy knob on the forehead is less prominent in the adult female than in the adult male. In aggressive display, the adult male raises the wings to form a hood over its back. Adult males are larger and heavier than females (+10 kg). Immature mute swans can only be sexed by internal examination (Johnsgard 1975b).

Age classes are determined by plumage, color of feet and bills and the pattern of the forehead feather line (Johnsgard 1975b, Bellrose 1976).

Table 11.19. Tooth eruption and replacement in the lower jaw of the Dall sheep (from Hemming, 1969). Milk or deciduous tooth—D; permanent tooth—P; brackets indicate that the tooth is in process of replacement at that particular time.

Age	Incisors 1	2	3	Canine 1	Premolars 2	3	4	Molars 1	2	3
5 days	D	D	D	D	(D)	D	D			
1-1/2 months	D	D	D	D	D	D	D	(P)		
4 months	D	D	D	D	D	D	D	P		
5 months										
8 months										
10 months	D	D	D	D	D	D	D	P	(P)	
11-1/2 months										
13 months	(P)	D	D	D	D	D	D	P	P	
16 months	P	D	D	D	D	D	D	P	P	
17 months										
18 months										
19 months										
20 months										
21 months										
22 months	P	D	D	D	D	D	D	P	P	(P)
23 months										
25 months	P	(P)	D	D	D	(P)	(P)	P	P	P
28 months	P	P	D	D	(P)	(P)	(P)	P	P	(P)
30 months	P	P	D	D	(P)	P	P	P	P	(P)
32 months	P	P	D	D	P	P	P	P	P	(P)
33 months	P	P	(P)	D	P	P	P	P	P	(P)
35 months	P	P	P	D	P	P	P	P	P	(P)
40 months	P	P	P	D	P	P	P	P	P	(P)
45 months	P	P	P	(P)	P	P	P	P	P	P
47 months	P	P	P	P	P	P	P	P	P	P

Table 11.20. Tooth eruption and replacement in the lower jaw of the mountain goat (after Brandborg 1955). Milk or deciduous tooth—D; permanent tooth—P; parentheses indicate that the tooth is in process of replacement at that particular time.

Age	Incisors 1	2	3	Canine 1	Premolars 2	3	4	Molars 1	2	3
1 week	(D)	(D)	(D)		(D)	(D)	(D)			
6 months	D	D	D	D	D	D	D	(P)		
10 months	D	D	D	D	D	D	D	(P)	(P)	
15–16 months	(P)	D	D	D	D	D	D	P	(P)	(P)
23 months	P	D	D	D	D	D	D	P	P	(P)
						(P)	(P)			
26–29 months	P	(P)	D	D	(P)	(P)	(P)	P	P	(P)
38–40 months	P	P	(P)	D	P	P	P	P	P	P
48 months	P	P	P	(P)	P	P	P	P	P	P

GEESE

Geese mature more slowly than most other birds, so the juveniles usually are readily distinguished by cloacal characters and by their plumage (U.S. Fish and Wildlife Service and Canadian Wildlife Service 1977). An illustrated table (similar to Table 11.28) for aging Canada goose goslings, has been prepared by Yocom and Harris (1965).

Hanson (1967) described the cloacal characteristics of Canada geese as related to age, sex and sexual maturity, but Higgins (1969) reported that bursal depths are unreliable for aging lesser snow geese and small Canada geese. Adult small Canada geese have a sharp demarca-

Table 11.21. Tooth eruption and replacement in the lower jaw of the pronghorn antelope (after Dow 1952, Dow and Wright 1962). Milk or deciduous tooth—D; permanent tooth—P; parentheses indicate that the tooth is in process of eruption at that particular time.

	Incisors			Canine	Premolars			Molars		
Age	1	2	3	1	2	3	4	1	2	3
Birth	D						D			
6 weeks	D	D	D	D	D	D	D	P		
15–17 months	P	D	D	D	D	D	D	P	P	P
27–29 months	P	P	D	D	P	P	P	P	P	P
39–41 months	P	P	P?	(P) P	P*	P*	P*	P	P	P

*Total of 24 infundibula.

Table 11.22. Tooth eruption in the lower jaw of the collared peccary (after Kirkpatrick and Sowls 1962). Milk or deciduous tooth—D; permanent tooth—P; parentheses indicate that the tooth is in the process of eruption at that particular time.

	Incisors			Canine	Premolars			Molars		
Age	1	2	3	1	1	2	3	1	2	3
2–6 months	D	D	D	D	D	D	D	D	D	D
7–10 months	D	D	D	D	D	D	D	P	D	D
11–12 months	D	D	D	P	D	D	D	P	D	D
13–18 months	D	D	D	P	D	D	D	P	P	D
19–21-1/2 months	D	D	D	P	D	D	D	P	P	(P)
Over 21-1/2 months	D	P	P	P	P	P	P	P	P	P

tion in neck plumage while juveniles have black necks merging to gray breast plumage (Higgins and Schoonover 1969). Cooper and Batt (1972) constructed a photographic key to age giant Canada goose embryos, day 0 to day 27. For black brant, Harris and Shepherd (1965) reported that the presence of 1 or a few white-tipped secondary coverts on wings of flightless birds in summer is indicative of yearlings. Older birds have black secondary coverts and goslings have a complete set of white-tipped coverts.

The U.S. Fish and Wildlife Service and Canadian Wildlife Service (1977) have developed keys to age and sex snow (including blue), Ross', white-fronted and Canada geese plus brant. Since these are too extensive for reproduction here we suggest consulting the original reference for these species.

DUCKS

The characters of the tail feathers and tertial coverts are generally useful for age determination (Table 11.23) and those of the cloaca for sex (Table 11.24). Standard terminology and banding symbols used in Tables 11.23 and 11.24 appear in Table 11.25.

The U.S. Fish and Wildlife Service and Canadian Wildlife Service (1977) have developed detailed keys to age and sex the mallard, black duck, American wigeon, American green-winged teal, blue-winged teal, cinnamon teal, northern shoveler, pintail, wood duck, redhead, canvasback, greater and lesser scaup, common goldeneye, Barrow's goldeneye and bufflehead. For each there are footnotes comparing and contrasting them with similar species. Since these are too extensive to reproduce here we suggest that for these species, the joint U.S./Canadian publication should be used. As an illustration Table 11.26 presents the key for mallards. Age characteristics for additional species are in Table 11.27. Table 11.28 gives the typical sequence of plumage development in a wild duckling, and Table 11.29 gives the age-span and midpoint for each plumage subclass for several ducks.

Hopper and Funk (1970) have shown that use of the tertials and primary and secondary coverts is valid until March 1 for separating adults from the young of the year. Photographic indices of mallard and wood duck embryos have been developed by Caldwell and Snart (1974) and Burke et al. (1978). Female redheads can be placed in adult and juvenile age classes on the basis of covert markings and width, weight and length of the 5th primary and weight, length and diameter of the 9th primary (Dane and Johnson 1975).

In common mergansers, red bills, red feet or both indicate adult birds. Yellow bills, yellow feet or both indicate sexually immature birds. Male wings are ≥ 264 mm and female wings have a black distal bar on greater secondary wing coverts (Anderson and Timken 1971).

Table 11.23. General key to age determination of ducks by external examination (from U.S. Fish and Wildlife Service and Canadian Wildlife Service 1977).

1A	Tail feathers notched* or with down attached to tip of shaft (A BELOW)	L/HY
1B	Tail feathers not notched; no down present on tail feathers (A BELOW)	*See 2*
	**Note:* Some AHY birds that have not molted worn tail feathers may be confused with L/HY birds with notched tail feathers.	
2A(1)	Greater and middle tertial coverts comparatively narrow and pointed (B BELOW) often frayed and worn, with colours faded *or* some coverts narrow and pointed while others are wider, more rounded, and more richly coloured, i.e., with two types of feathers	L/HY/SY
2B	Greater and middle tertial coverts comparatively wide (B BELOW) rounded and richly coloured *except* rather frayed, worn, and dull coloured in late summer before molt and again in late winter	AHY/ASY

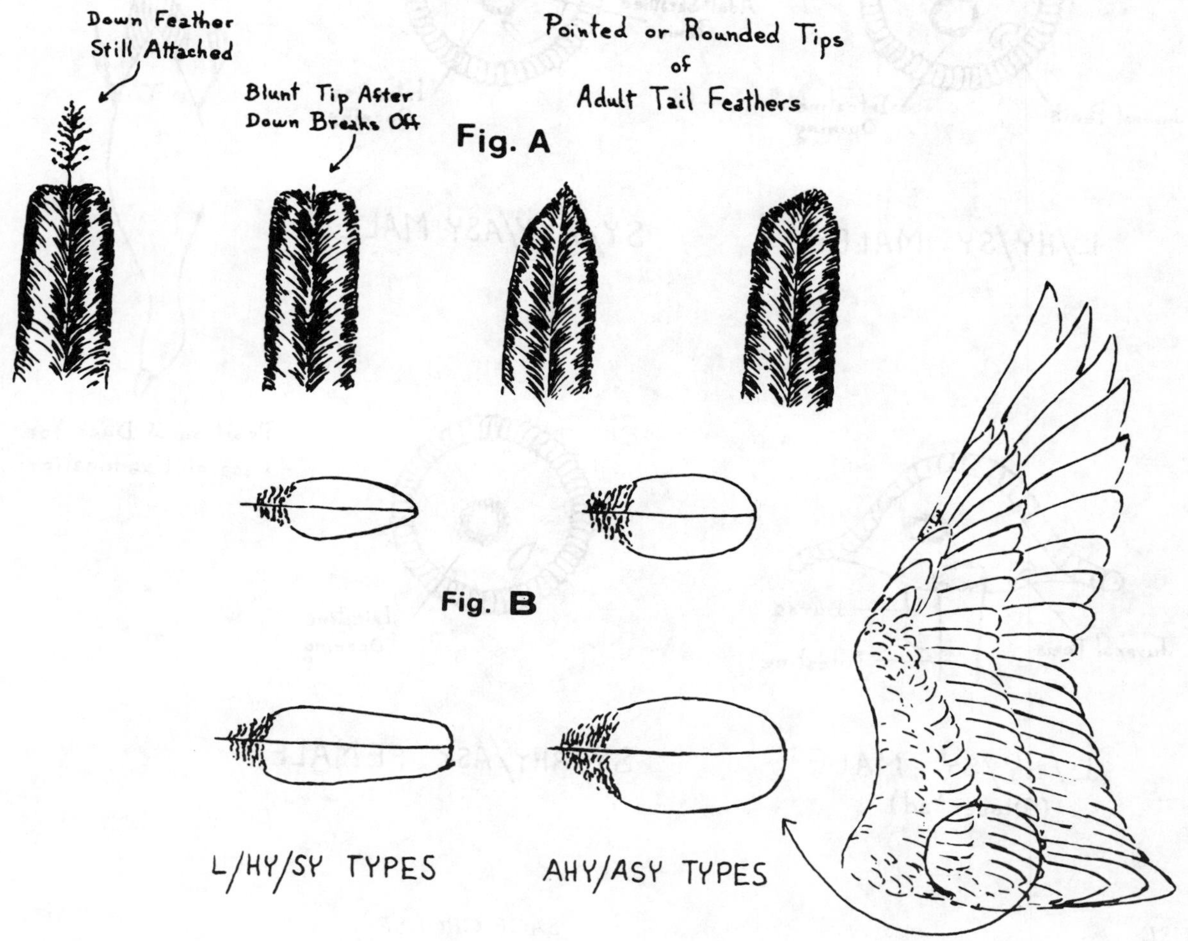

Erskine (1971) constructed growth curves for young mergansers for age 0–85 days and described the sequence of plumage acquisition of flightless birds. In this species males are markedly larger than females.

Trauger (1974) produced a color photographic chart of progressive change in eye color with age for female lesser scaup. Peterson and Ellarson (1978) suggest that gray scapulars indicate nonbreeding subadult oldsquaws.

GALLINACEOUS BIRDS

In gallinaceous birds, the appearance of the cloaca has not been used as extensively to determine sex as it has in waterfowl because plumage and other characters are better sex criteria (Table 11.30). However, the depth of bursa of Fabricius is a reliable age character and often can be determined by probing in the living bird.

Table 11.24. General key to sex and age determination of ducks by cloacal examination (from U.S. Fish and Wildlife Service and Canadian Wildlife Service 1977).

1A	Penis present but may be quite small, especially in young diving ducks (See below)	Male *(see 2)*
1B	Penis absent; oviduct opening present but often difficult to detect, especially in young birds (See below)	Female *(see 2)*
2A (1)	Bursa present; penis unsheathed, small *or* oviduct opening small, often invisible (See below)	L/HY/SY
2B	Bursa absent; penis sheathed, large, *or* oviduct opening large, conspicuous (See below)	AHY/ASY

GROUSE

As a group, the grouse are alike in that both sexes resemble each other superficially (although the male is heavier), and the young in their first fall tend to resemble the adult female.

The young do not molt the 2 outer primaries in their first year. In fact, if the hunting season is held before the fall molt, there will be immature birds in the bag which have adopted adult plumage except for the juvenile outer primaries which have not yet been replaced. If this replacement pattern is understood, it is possible to distinguish the juvenile age-class. Criteria of sex and age in grouse are summarized in Table 11.31.

SAGE GROUSE

Eng (1955), in a study of wings collected in October in Montana, found that sex could be determined in old and young alike by the relative length of the primaries, different primaries being diagnostic for different molt stages (Table 11.32). Measurements were made from the point of insertion to the top of the feather.

Most wings collected before September 20 can be segregated into adult, yearling, and juvenile age classes. Adults have molted all 10 wing primaries at least once and are in the third year of life. Adult primaries are uniform in color and have rounded tips. Yearlings retain juvenile primaries 9 and/or 10, and these are faded and

Table 11.25. Aging codes used for ducks by the U.S. Fish and Wildlife Service and Canadian Wildlife Service (1976).

Numeric Code	Alpha Code	Alpha Designation	Definition
0	U	Unknown	A bird which cannot be placed in any of the year classes below. Except in cases where data were not recorded or have been lost during the nesting season, ONLY BIRDS BANDED AFTER THE BREEDING SEASON AND BEFORE JANUARY 1 CAN BE CORRECTLY CODED "U".
4	L	Local	A young bird incapable of sustained flight.
2	HY	Hatching Year	A bird capable of sustained flight and known to have hatched during the calendar year in which it was banded. *Example:* Banded 1967—Hatched 1967.
1	AHY	After Hatching Year	A bird known to have hatched before the calendar year of banding; *year of hatch otherwise unknown. Example:* Banded 1967—Hatched before January 1, 1967. (Birds which would have been coded "U" on December 31 "graduate" to class "AHY" on January 1.)
5	SY	Second Year	A bird *known* to have hatched in the calendar year preceding the year of banding and in its second *calendar year* of life. *Example:* Banded 1967—Hatched 1966.
6	ASY	After Second Year	A bird known to have hatched earlier than the calendar year preceding the year of banding; *year of hatch otherwise unknown. Example:* Banded 1967—Hatched 1965 or earlier.
7	TY	Third Year	A bird known to have hatched in the calendar year preceding the year before the year of banding, now in its third calendar year of life. *Example:* Banded 1967—Hatched 1965.
8	ATY	After Third Year	A bird known to have hatched prior to the calendar year preceding the year before the year of banding, now in at least its fourth calendar year of life. *Example:* Banded 1967—Hatched 1964 or earlier.

worn in contrast to primaries 1 through 8. A bird retaining juvenile primary 10 and molting primary 9 is a yearling. Juveniles have primaries 9 and 10, and usually 8, all new in appearance, pointed, narrow, and with no frayed tips (Eng 1955, Beck et al. 1975).

SHARP-TAILED GROUSE AND PRAIRIE CHICKEN

See Table 11.31. The sex criterion based on color pattern in the central tail feathers is illustrated in Fig. 11.25.

Sharp-tailed grouse with eye lens less than 30 mg in weight are juvenile, but plumage characteristics are the basic key to age (Dahlgren et al. 1964). Crown feathers are indicative of sex and are more accurate than tail feather criteria according to Henderson et al. (1967). Males have dark crown feathers with a buff-colored edging while female crown feathers have alternating buff-colored and dark cross-bars. Wishart (1977) described a sexing technique based on differences in the patterns that occur on the greater upper tail coverts. He also reported an accurate aging procedure based on first primary calamus diameters and further suggested that lengths of central tail feathers appear significantly different in adults and juveniles. Caldwell (1980) found the ratio of the shaft diameter of primaries 8 and 9 to be an accurate means of aging sharp-tailed grouse.

RUFFED GROUSE

See Table 11.31. Sexing of adult Wisconsin grouse is accomplished by measuring the central tail feathers (Fig. 11.26); males of all ages have (plucked) feathers longer than 15 cm, while females have feathers under 15 cm (Hale et al. 1954).

Dorney (1966) reported that 2/3 of adult birds in Wisconsin and 1/2 of the juveniles can be sexed by measuring a central tail feather at the point 50 mm from the tip of the tail (Table 11.33). In Quebec, 1 white dot on the terminal end of the rump feathers indicates a female and 2 or more dots, a male (Roussel and Ouellet 1975). Ohio ruffed grouse can be aged best on the basis of calamus diameter, length of the mid-retrix, length of the primary and mid-rectrix calamus diameter. Sex is based on the length of the central rectrix (Davis 1969) (Table 11.34).

Gullion (pers. comm.) pointed out that tail feather lengths as reported in Table 11.32 vary regionally, and Wisconsin criteria do not hold in Minnesota. Many young males have tails under 150 mm, so age has to be known for tails in the 142 mm to 149 mm range. If it is

Table 11.26. Mallard key to sex and age (U.S. Fish and Wildlife Service and Canadian Wildlife Service 1977).

MALLARD (MALL) Sp. no. 132.0
Anas platyrhynchos Band Size 7A

KEY TO AGE AND SEX: *Caution—do not* sex locals or molting young by bill colour. Sex these individuals only by cloacal examination.

1A	Bill slate colour	L/HY *(see 2)*
1B	Bill yellow, orange, or green	*See 3*
	2A(1) Penis present	Male
	2B Penis absent	Female
3A(1)	Bursa present; tertials slightly suffused with chestnut-brown *or* broadly edged with buff; penis (if present) unsheathed, small, *or* tail feathers notched or with down attached to tip of shaft	HY/SY *(see 4)*
3B	Bursa absent; tertials strongly suffused with chestnut-brown *or* narrowly edged with buff; penis (if present) sheathed, large, *and* tail feathers not notched, no down present on tail feathers	U/AHY *(see 4)*
4A(3)	No white bar in front of speculum; bill yellow to green, unblotched; penis present	Male
4B	White bar in front of speculum; bill orange to green, blotched; penis absent	Female

SIMILAR SPECIES: The *Mexican Duck* has darker body colour, a darker bill, and more heavily streaked underparts. *Black* has light under-wing coverts; *Mallard* dark under-wing coverts. *Mallards* hybridize with many species of ducks, mostly *Black* (east) and *Pintail* (west).

MOLTS: Post-juvenal complete, May–Dec.; pre-nuptial partial (scapulars, contour feathers), Aug.–Dec.; post-nuptial complete, Jun.–Aug.

INCUBATION: 26 days. FLYING YOUNG: approx. 52–60 days. BANDING: approx. 3 weeks.

NOTES FOR FURTHER STUDY: Other methods appear necessary for separating HY from SY birds. Need reliable methods of ageing SY and ASY into start of nesting season.

adult, the bird is very likely a hen, if a young bird, probably a male. For age separation he found the following criteria useful, based on 673 grouse from the Cloquet Forest Research Center:

Females: Central rectrix shorter than 142 mm, length of central rectrix not over 5 mm longer than the 9th primary, mid-toe shorter than 36 mm, length of tail barb 50 mm from distal end of central rectrix less than 36 mm, eyebrow without pigmentation, terminal band obscured or blotched.

Males: Central rectrix longer than 147 mm, length of central rectrix more than 10 mm longer than the 9th primary, mid-toe longer than 41 mm, length of tail barb 50 mm from distal end of central rectrix over 40 mm, eyebrow brightly colored red or orange, neck ruff feathers conspicuous, terminal tail band clear or fuzzy.

In regions where the gray phase occurs most of the hens have central tail feathers markedly redder than the lateral. It is extremely uncommon for the central rectrices of a male to differ from the color of the laterals. But this is not good in regions where only the red phase occurs, for there is no color difference in the tail of red hens. Hens usually have less than 8 transverse tail bars (not counting the subterminal band) while males usually have 9 or more. A combination of characters is best for accurate sex determination.

Aging during the fall may be accomplished by use of bursal depth, taking 5 mm as the dividing point between juveniles and adults. Aging of ruffed grouse also may be done by wing characters. The outer 2 juvenile primaries are pointed, while those of the adult are usually rounded. In case of doubt, the base of the quill in primary #8 should be examined for scaly remnants of its feather sheath. In the juvenile, primaries #9 and #10 usually do not show these remnants; in the adult they do (Hale et al. 1954). K. E. Hungerford (pers. comm.) used the following criteria for sexing and aging Idaho grouse; length of center unplucked feather (i.e. from tip to skin line). $L>15.2$ cm = adult male; $L\geq 14.0$ cm = adult female; $L<14.0$ cm = juvenile.

Many cocks are mirror-trapped in the spring. At that time young (almost 1 year old) males (in Wisconsin) may be distinguished from older males by the following criteria (Dorney and Holzer 1957):

a. Width of shaft of 9th primary at point where larger proximal barbs begin: Young—2.97 mm or less; old—2.97 mm or more.
b. Length of central tail feather (after 2 months of drying): Young—159 mm or less; old—170 mm or more.
c. Width of shaft of central tail feather (dried: Young—2.21 mm or less; old—2.34 mm or more.

Table 11.27. Winter plumage characters for distinguishing age in diving ducks and tree ducks (after Kortright 1953). Note: immature characters are italicized; ♂♂ are treated first.

Species	Characters
Oldsquaw[2,4]	♂ ♂: SPECULUM: chestnut brown; *dusky*. Two MIDDLE TAIL FEATHERS: greatly elongated and pointed; *not long*.
Harlequin Duck[2,3]	♂♂: BILL: bluish gray; *brown*. RUMP: steely blue black; *brown*. ♀♀: BILL: dusky; *brown*.
Steller's Eider[2,3]	♂♂: SPECULUM: blue black; *dull blue*. OUTER SECONDARIES: tipped with white; *dusky*. ♀♀: SPECULUM: dull blue; *dusky*.
American Eider[2,5]	♂♂: CROWN: iridescent glossy black; (first autumn) *brown*, (second autumn) *black mottled with grayish brown*. BREAST: black; (first autumn) *dull brown*, (second autumn) *dull brownish black*.
King Eider[6]	♂♂: CROWN: pearl gray; (first autumn) *dark brown*, (second autumn) *dull gray*. LESSER AND MIDDLE COVERTS: pure white; (first autumn) *dusky, with paler edges*, (second autumn) *white, margined and shaded with dusky*. ♀♀: BILL: pale greenish or yellowish; (first autumn) *grayish olive*.
Spectacled Eider[6]	♂♂: HEAD: circle of dense silvery white feathers framed in black around eye; (first autumn) *spectacle only faintly indicated*. ♀♀: BREAST AND BELLY: dusky brown; (first autumn) *brown, spotted with dusky*.
White-winged Scoter[4,6]	♂♂: HEAD: black, with small crescent-shaped white spot behind and below eye; (first autumn) *brownish black, with white patch in ear region*. FEET: orange vermillion on inner sides, purplish pink on outer; (first autumn) *light brownish red*. ♀♀: FEET: light brownish red, webs blackish; (first autumn) *outer side of tarsus blackish, inner side of tarsus and toes dull purplish brown*.
Surf Scoter[3,4,6]	♂♂: HEAD: black except for white patch on forehead and long triangular white patch on nape, pointing backwards; (first autumn) *dusky brown, with only light patches on sides of head*, (second autumn) *black with nape patch but no forehead patch*. ♀♀: BREAST: mottled grayish and dusky; (first autumn) *pale gray or whitish*. HEAD: dusky brown with vague whitish patch on back of head; (first and second autumn) *no whitish patch*.
American Scoter[2,3,4]	♂♂: BREAST: black; *whitish, marked with grayish brown*. ♀♀: BREAST: brown; *whitish marked with grayish brown*.
Ruddy Duck[1,3,4]	♂♂: CHEST: rich reddish chestnut; *dusky, broadly tipped with buff*. CHEEKS: white; *no clear white area*. ♀♀: BREAST: bright silvery white, some feathers of forebreast often with gilt tips; *mottled with dusky*. CHEST: marked with broken bars of dark brown and buffy brown; *dusky, broadly tipped with buff*.
Black-bellied Tree Duck[1]	UNDERPARTS: brown chest, black breast; *grayish buff*.
Fulvous Tree Duck[1]	UPPER TAIL COVERTS: creamy; *tipped with brown*.

[1]Species in which males assume adult plumage the first spring after hatching.
[2]Species in which males assume adult plumage the second autumn after hatching.
[3]During their first winter the juvenile males resemble adult females.
[4]No eclipse molt occurs in these species.
[5]Males do not attain full adult plumage until the fourth autumn (i.e. when 4.5 years old). In females the adult plumage is assumed in third autumn.
[6]Males and females do not attain full adult plumage until the third autumn.

Table 11.28. Development of a wild duckling as viewed under ideal conditions (from Gollop and Marshall 1954). See Table 11.29 for use in aging.

Plumage Class	Sub-class	Description
I	a	"*Bright Ball of Fluff.*" Down bright. Patterns distinct (except diving ducks). Body rounded. Neck and tail not prominent.
Downy young; no feathers visible	b	"*Fading Ball of Fluff.*" Down color fading, patterns less distinct. Body still rounded. Neck and tail not yet prominent.
	c	"*Gawky-Downy.*" Down color and patterns faded. Neck and tail become prominent. Body becomes long and oval.
II	a	"*First Feathers.*" First feathers show on side under ideal conditions, stays in this class until side view shows one-half of side and flank feathered.
Partly feathered as viewed from the side	b	"*Mostly Feathered.*" Side view shows one-half of side and flank feathered. Primaries break from sheaths. Stays in this class until side view shows down in one or two areas only (nape, back or upper rump).
	c	"*Last Down.*" Side view shows down in one or two areas only (nape, back or upper rump). Sheaths visible on erupted primaries through this class. Stays in this class until profile shows no down.
III Fully-feathered as viewed from side	a	"*Feathered-Flightless.*" No down visible. Primaries fully out of sheaths but not fully developed. Stays in this class until capable of flight.

d. Bursa: Only used if bursa is closed, in which case the bird is considered old.
e. Contour of 9th and 10th primary, as above.
f. Sheathing at base of primaries, as above.

These authors found that if all these criteria are used, most questionable birds can be aged reliably.

Gullion (pers. comm.) has developed the following criteria of age, based on 673 grouse from the Cloquet Forest:

Young females: 9th and 10th primaries present, fully grown but probably showing foxed tips; 8th primary absent, growing, or with more evident sheathing at its base than the 9th; central rectrix shorter than 132 mm, 9th primary shorter than 132 mm, diameter of 9th primary calamus under 2.67 mm, diameter of rectrix calamus under 1.93 mm, rectrix barb at 50 mm less than 32 mm.

Adult females: 9th and/or 10th primaries absent, growing or more heavily sheathed at base than the 8th; central rectrix longer than 145 mm, 9th primary longer than 141 mm; diameter of 9th primary calamus exceeds 2.79 mm; diameter of rectrix calamus exceeds 2.06 mm.

Young males: Condition of primaries same as in young females, central rectrix shorter than 151 mm, 9th primary shorter than 134 mm, diameter of 9th primary calamus under 2.79 mm, diameter of calamus of central rectrix under 2.08 mm, rectrix barb at 50 mm shorter than 39 mm.

Adult males: Condition of primaries same as in adult females, central rectrix longer than 169 mm, 9th primary longer than 146 mm, diameter of 9th primary calamus exceeds 2.95 mm, diameter of rectrix calamus exceeds 2.33 mm, rectrix barb at 50 mm exceeds 44 mm.

As in sex determination, a combination of characters is most likely to produce accurate age determination. More detail on the Minnesota ruffed grouse age and sex research appeared in Gullion (1972).

Rodgers (1979) found the calamus diameter ratio of primaries 8 and 9 to be accurate for aging ruffed grouse in the spring.

Table 11.29. Approximate age-span and midpoint (in days) for each plumage subclass for 11 ducks, with supplementary data (after Gollop and Marshall 1954).

Species	Plumage Subclass (see Table 11.28)							Flying	Primaries break from sheaths	Areas of last down visible
	Ia	Ib	Ic	IIa	IIb	IIc	IIIa			
Mallard	1-4-6	7-10-12	13-16-18	19-22-25	26-31-35	36-41-45	46-51-55	52-60	35 days	Rump
Black Duck	1-3-5	6-9-12	13-16-18	19-22-25	26-30-33	34-39-43	44-52-60	58-63		
Gadwall	1-4-6	7-11-14	15-17-18	19-23-27	28-33-38	39-42-44	45-48-50	48-52	31	Nape & back
Baldpate	1-4-7	8-10-12	13-16-18	19-23-26	27-31-35	36-39-41	42-46-50	47+	30	Nape & rump
Pintail	1-3-5	6-9-12	13-16-18	19-21-23	24-29-33	34-39-43	44-48-51	46-57	31	Back
Blue-winged Teal	1-3-5	6-8-9	10-12-13	14-18-21	22-26-30	31-34-36	37-39-40	35-44	30	Nape & rump
Shoveller	1-4-6	7-10-13	14-16-17	18-23-27	28-32-35	36-40-44	45-48-50	47-54	33	Nape & back
Redhead	1-4-6	7-13-18	19-22-24	25-29-32	33-39-45	46-50-54	55-58-60	60-63	43	Rump & back
Ring-necked Duck	1-3-5	6-8-10	11-14-16	17-21-24	25-28-30	31-35-38	39-44-49	49-53		
Canvasback*	1-5-9	10-14-18	19-22-25	26-29-32	33-37-42	43-48-53	54-59-65	56-68	40	Rump & back
Lesser Scaup	1-3-6	7-10-13	14-17-20	21-25-28	29-31-33	34-38-42	43-47-50	47+		

*Dzubin (1959) gives a waterline (swim) ratio of length of young: adult hen: 1 day old—1:3; Subclass IIa—2:3; subclass IIIa—3:3.

SPRUCE GROUSE

Franklin spruce grouse can be aged and sexed on the basis of tail plumage (Zwickel and Martinsen 1967) (Table 11.35). In Alaskan birds the black breast feathers are tipped with white, the black breast feathers of females are barred with brown and the tail characteristics are generally similar to the Franklin spruce grouse. In juvenile birds primary 10 is pointed and primary 9 is mottled, edged with brown. In adults primary 10 is rounded and primary 9 is edged with brown (Ellison 1968). Up to 75 days of age, hatch date and age of Alaska juveniles can be estimated from measurements of juvenal primary 7 and 9 and post-juvenal primary 7 (McCourt and Keppie 1975).

PTARMIGAN

Criteria of sex and age in willow ptarmigan have been studied by Bergerud et al. (1963). Age in chicks up to 20 days can be determined by wing length (carpel joint to top of longest primary). The stage of primary replacement (see Table 11.31) can be used to 112 days, by which time the quill of primary #8 is fully hardened. In October, juvenile birds can be distinguished from adults by the gloss and pigment of the distal primaries: in juveniles the gloss on primary #8 is more pronounced than on 9 and 10, whereas there is little or no difference in gloss among the 3 outer primaries in adults; in juveniles the area of black pigment on primary #8 including flecking, is equal to or greater than the area of

Table 11.30. Development of primary feathers of the wing with age (in days) in immature gallinaceous birds and the mourning dove.

Species	*Primary number* (A = begins growth; B = fully grown) 1 A	1 B	2 A	2 B	3 A	3 B	4 A	4 B	5 A	5 B	6 A	6 B	7 A	7 B	8 A	8 B	9 A	9 B	10 A	10 B	Authority
Willow Ptarmigan	18		25		30		35		40		46		53		65	91**	Juvenal not replaced				Westerskov 1956
Ruffed Grouse	14	45	20	49	27	63	35	68	42	77	49	83	61	98	74	119	Juvenal not replaced				Bump et al. 1947
Blue Grouse	21-28		28-35		28-42		35-49		42-56		49-63		63-70		77-91		Juvenal not replaced				Smith and Buss 1963
Hungarian Partridge	24		32		40		46		52		59		73		87	105	Juvenal not replaced				McCabe and Hawkins 1946
Ring-necked Pheasant	28		35		42		48		56		63		70		82		91		98	112	Buss 1946
Bobwhite	26-30	54-58	33-37	56-60	40-44	60-64	44-50	70-76	52-58	81-89	58-62	99-107	69-77	120-128	97-105	146-154	Juvenal not replaced				Petrides and Nestler 1943
Red-Legged Partridge	29		34		41		49		58		70		86		105	130	Juvenal not replaced				Petrides 1951
Coturnix Quail	22-		23-		27-		34-		34-		40-		49-				Juvenal not replaced				Wetherbee 1961
California Quail	29	55	32	62	38	70	46	80	52	90	62	108	72	121	100	141	Juvenal not replaced				Raitt 1961
Mourning* Dove	25 ±4		30 ±4		37 ±5		45 ±6		54 ±8		66 ±10		80 ±14		96 ±16		117 ±18			142 ±20	Swank 1955

*Figures in column A represent age at which the juvenal feather is dropped. The second figure represents one standard deviation.
**Bergerud et al. (1963) point out that this feather can be identified by its soft quill to 112 days.

black pigment on primary #9. Since the willow ptarmigan sheds its 2 outer primaries at 14–15 months of age, it is possible to recognize a yearling class; primaries of the preceding year can be easily recognized by their faded and worn condition.

Rock ptarmigan in Alaska (and Scotland) can be aged on the basis of primary coloration. Adults 15 months and older have the same amount of pigment, or less, on primary 9 than primary 8. Juveniles have more pigment on primary 9 than on primary 8 (Weeden and Watson 1967).

Criteria for ascertaining age and sex of white-tailed ptarmigan have been investigated by Braun and Rogers (1971). Adults lack pigmentation in the distal 3 primaries (8–10) and the tenth primary covert. Yearlings (up to 14 months) and juveniles have pigment extending into the vane in one or more of these feathers. Giesen and Braun (1979) reported that the age of juveniles can be ascertained from wing length (up to 30 days) or molt stage and growth of post-juvenal primaries (17 to 90 days). Sexes can be accurately distinguished for live birds in nuptial plumage only (late April to mid-September). The nuptial plumage of females is characterized by heavily barred black and yellow dorsal feathers and brown and buffy feathers on the breast, abdomen, and under-tail coverts. Males have darker dorsal and upper breast feathers and retain white plumage on the abdomen and lower breast (Braun and Rogers 1971). Techniques for distinguishing sex of live birds in winter plumage based on eye-stripe coloration and primary lengths are only 95% accurate (Braun, unpublished data). No techniques currently exist for accurately distinguishing sex of live chicks less than 15 weeks of age.

Table 11.31. Sex and age characters in the grouse. In column (1) the female characters are italicized; in column (2) the immature characters are italicized.

Species	Criteria for distinguishing sex (1)	Criteria for distinguishing age (2)
Sage Grouse	AVERAGE WT.: 2.72k; *1.84k.* THROAT: black band upper throat, scaly white foreneck feathers; *grayish white upper throat, no scaly feathers.* AVERAGE TAIL LENGTH: 29.2cm; *19cm.* FLIGHT: even; *body dips from side to side* (P). In juveniles the male has a middle toe one full toe-nail length longer than the female (P).	UPPER BREAST: solid feather pattern; *triangular patch of feathers showing dark spots and light vertical streaks* (through early fall). TOE COLOR: dark green; *light yellowish-green* (P).
Sharp-tailed Grouse	CENTRAL TAIL FEATHERS: longitudinal pattern of light and dark markings; *transverse pattern* (S).	OUTER PRIMARIES: unworn, same color as other primaries; *rough and worn, lighter than other primaries* (A).
Prairie Chicken	HEAD AND NECK: longer pinnae, much larger air sacs, orange flesh colors on neck and "eyebrows"; *shorter pinnae, inconspicuous air sacs, no orange flesh colors* (E). TAIL: less barred; *more barred* (E).	OUTER PRIMARIES: same as Sharp-tailed Grouse. For lesser prairie chicken spotting on 9 and 10 not extend to tips. *Spotting on 9 and 10 extend to tips (Co).*
Ruffed Grouse autumn (see text for spring characters)	CENTRAL PLUCKED TAIL FEATHER LENGTH: 15.0 cm. or more; *14.9 cm. or less* (Ha). COLOR BARE SPOT OVER UPPER EYELID, 8–14 WK. CHICKS: subdued orange to bright red-orange; *little or no color* (Pa).	PRIMARIES: 8, 9, and 10 rounded with sheathing at base, *8 rounded, 9 and 10 pointed, with sheathing on 8 only* (Ha).
Blue Grouse	CERVICAL AIR SACS: (from 8 weeks of age) surrounded by white feathers, tipped w/bluish black; *surrounded by grayish brown feathers* (C). HEAD, NAPE, INTERSCAPULARS: no barred feathers; *some barred feathers* (R&F).	Immatures look like ad. ♀ except CONTOUR FEATHERS: shaft streaks dark; *shaft streaks dull white* (G). TAIL: gray bar at end; *no gray bar* (G). BELLY: gray patch; *no gray patch* (G). BREAST: Dark brown; *pale buffy or white* (G). Also see text.
White-tailed Ptarmigan	HEAD: red "eyebrows" prominent; *"eyebrows" not prominent.* COLORED FEATHERS: reddish brown, not heavily barred; *gray-brown or tan, heavily barred* (H).	OUTER PRIMARIES: usually pure white, often with black shafts, 8th primary never shorter than 9th; *usually mottled with brown or black, 8th primary often shorter than 9th* (H).[1]

References: A = Ammann (1944); C = Caswell (1954); E = Edminster (1954); G = Grinnell et al. (1918); H = Hewitt (*pers. comm.*); Ha = Hale et al. (1954); Pa = Palmer (1959); P = Patterson (1952); R&F = Ridgway and Friedmann (1946); S = Snyder (1935); Co = Copelin (1963).

[1]Weeden (1961) found for rock ptarmigan that outer primary shape and pigmentation were not reliable age criteria.

BLUE GROUSE

Zwickel and Lance (1966) developed a method for estimating age of juvenile blue grouse based on the molt and development of primary feathers. While this is a simple and rapid technique, there may be a bias due to the fact that it was based on pen-reared birds. Redfield and Zwickel (1976) reported that wild chicks did not grow as fast and that a more accurate estimate of age is to use the original technique and add 9% of this age to the estimated age. Subadults are distinguished from adults on the basis of pointed outer primaries 9 and 10 and shorter, narrower rectrices (Boag 1965). Bunnell et al. (1977) developed a key for determining age and sex of hunter-harvested dusky blue grouse from wing evidence alone.

RING-NECKED PHEASANT

There is no difficulty in distinguishing sex of adults, except in an occasional intersex. In rare instances, male plumage is found in females whose ovaries are inactive. A shot occasionally lodges in the ovary of a hen, causing an intersex to be produced. These individuals are readily recognized by their partial male plumage and the absence of spurs.

Latham (1942) illustrated the sex differences in the distribution and pattern of down in newly-hatched

Table 11.32. Age of sage grouse as shown by differences in length of primaries #8 and #9 and bursal depth of birds collected in October (after Eng 1955).

	Difference in length (mm) between primary #9 and #8		Bursal depth (mm)	
	Adult	Immature	Adult	Immature
Sample size	13	20	13	19
Maximum	24	−27*	7	25
Minimum	11	−4	0	13
Average	17.3	−12.3	1.6	18.9

*Negative figures indicate #9 is shorter than #8 by mm shown.

Table 11.33. Frequency distribution of barb sizes for adult and juvenile ruffed grouse measured from the central tail feathers of birds whose sex was determined on the basis of the secondary sexual characteristic of tail length (from Dorney 1966).

	Sample Size	Barb Length in mm		
		32–37	38–43	44–52
Adults				
Male	241	2 (1%)	81(33%)	158(66%)
Female	174	114(66%)	53(30%)	7 (4%)
Juveniles				
		30–34	35–40	41–51
Male	554	7 (1%)	282(51%)	265(48%)
Female	549	268(49%)	275(50%)	6 (1%)

chicks. Additionally, in chicks 24–36 hours after hatching, males can be distinguished by the presence of an infantile wattle under and above the eye (Woehler and Gates 1970) (Fig. 11.27). To remove subjective judgments regarding the sex of day-old chicks, Wentworth et al. (1967) developed a sex-linked mutation which produces a wild-type, colored male and a pale blonde female to increase efficiency in game farm operations.

Primaries of females typically show light-colored bars that meet the rachis at right angles along its entire length. Males typically have no pattern on the ends of their primaries, or males have a more diffuse color pattern than primaries of females (Linder et al. 1971).

Immature birds in the fall closely resemble adults. Unlike many other gallinaceous birds they often replace the 2 outer primaries (#9 and #10) during the post-juvenal molt and so display primaries of adult shape during the fall (Wright and Hiatt 1943). However, the first primary shaft diameter of the adult male is 3.30 mm and has a length of 170 mm. The adult female has a diameter of 3.02 mm and a length of 157 mm (Wishart 1969). Etter et al. (1970) developed a method of age determination for Illinois birds based on rate of growth of the 10th primary (Table 11.36).

The use of the bursa of Fabricius is the most reliable technique for aging ring-necked pheasants during the hunting season. Since some adult birds retain a shallow bursa, the question is how to distinguish between young and adult birds. Stokes (1954), working on Pelee Island, Ontario, considered 8 mm and 6 mm as the maximum bursal depths for adult cocks and hens respectively during the hunting season, when the young birds were about 20 weeks old. In California, where the birds are about 27 weeks old during the hunting season, the trough in the bimodal curve of bursal depths of cocks falls at 6 to 8 mm (Harper et al. 1951), suggesting a slightly shallower maximum bursal depth for adults. In South Dakota, Nelson (1948) found that the bursa in adult cocks reached a maximum depth of 10 mm. It appears that acceptance of 8 mm as the maximum depth in adult cocks would involve little error in the populations which have been studied.

Labisky et al. (1969) found that eye lens is an unreliable criterion of age in pheasants due to high variation in weights.

WILD TURKEY

This species, the largest North American upland game bird, requires more time to reach adult size than do most other birds. Therefore, weight differences may be used to distinguish between young and older turkeys. McDowell (1956:18), working with the eastern wild turkey in Virginia, found that first-fall hens weighed less than 3.62 kg, first-fall gobblers normally weighed less than 6.35 kg, older hens usually weighed from 5.44 kg, and older gobblers weighed more than 6.35 kg.

First-year turkeys may be distinguished most easily from older birds by 1) the irregular contour (Fig. 11.28) of the row of greater secondary wing coverts in young turkeys (Leopold 1943, Williams 1961), 2) the unequal contour of the spread tail feathers (caused by the late replacement of the central 4 to 6 rectrices), 3) the pointed outer (10) primary (see Fig. 11.29) and 4) the presence of the bursa of Fabricius in first-fall turkeys (Mosby and Handley 1943:93–96). Kelly (1975) examined 3 age-correlated variables, spur length, beard

Table 11.34. Analysis of feather measurement data as aging criteria for Ohio ruffed grouse; southeast and east-central region samples combined (from Davis 1969).

	Male		Female	
	Adult	Immature	Adult	Immature
Calamus diameter primary 9 (inches)				
Division points	⩾0.118	⩽0.112	⩾0.115	⩽0.110
Percent between division points[a]	19.1	23.8	18.2	13.6
Probability of misclassification[b]	0.03	0.04	0.06	0.04
Length of mid-rectrix (mm)				
Division points	⩾184	⩽171	⩾156	⩽136
Percent between division points	37.7	40.3	87.8	87.3
Probability of misclassification	0.06	0.03	0.03	0.01
Length of primary 9 (mm)				
Division points	⩾155	⩽146	⩾151	⩽142
Percent between division points	35.0	56.7	54.6	44.8
Probability of misclassification	0.07	0.06	0.10	0.05
Calamus diameter mid-rectrix (inches)				
Division points	⩾0.096	⩽0.084	⩾0.089	⩽0.072
Percent between division points	54.3	63.3	87.2	89.5
Probability of misclassification	0.05	0.04	0.03	0.01

[a]The normal curve area between division points.
[b]The normal curve area, exclusive of the overlap or unknown group, that is below or above the division point of the other age class.

Table 11.35. Criteria for classifying age and sex of Franklin spruce grouse from tails (from Zwickel and Martinsen 1967).

Adult Male.—Rectrices a rich, shiny black with little or no grey flecking. Upper greater coverts black, heavily barred or flecked with grey; with relatively large white tips that contrast sharply against rectrices.	*Adult Female.*—Rectrices black to very dark brown; central rectrices usually barred with buffy or cinnamon brown; other rectrices often barred or flecked with buffy or cinnamon brown. Upper great coverts black, heavily barred with buffy or cinnamon brown; with relatively large white tips that contrast sharply against rectrices.
Juvenile Male.—Rectrices dull black to very dark brown, less shiny and rich than in adult males; often lightly flecked with grey. Upper great coverts black, heavily barred or flecked with grey; with relatively small white tips that contrast less sharply against rectrices than in adults. Rectrices tend to be longer than in juvenile females.	*Juvenile Female.*—Rectrices dull black to very dark brown, often heavily barred or flecked with buffy or cinnamon brown. Upper greater coverts black, heavily barred with buffy or cinnamon brown; with relatively small white tips that contrast less sharply against rectrices than in adults. Rectrices tend to be shorter than in juvenile males.

length and body weight, and found that only spur length was correlated closely with age and particularly with older age classes. Stoll and Clay (1975) have produced a photographic guide to the age of wild turkey embryos.

It is difficult to sex the wild turkey with accuracy by external characters until enough of the post-juvenal molt is completed to show the adult breast feathers. Usually by the 16th week of age, young hens may be distinguished from gobblers by the shape and tip-coloring of the breast feathers. The breast feathers of the hen are rounded and buff-tipped whereas these feathers in the gobbler are squamate and black-tipped (Fig. 11.30). Experienced observers can sex turkeys by the larger head and longer neck, longer tarsi, and greater height of the gobbler. The presence or absence of a beard is not completely diagnostic of either sex or age. The beard on the breast of the gobbler may reach 3.8 cm to 5 cm in length in the first fall, seldom protruding far beyond the breast feathers. The second fall the beard seldom exceeds 12.7 cm in length, is spread loosely, and has a burned appearance on the end. Older birds have beards usually 20.3 cm long, or more, and uniform in diameter and

Table 11.36. Ranges in length (mm) of the 10th (outermost) primary feather of juvenile pheasants for each week of age, modified from Trautman (1950:49–50) on the basis of data from recaptured wild Illinois birds (from Etter et al. 1970).

	Sex	
Age in Weeks	Cocks	Hens
15	0–9	0–16
16	10–49	17–48
17	50–82	49–77
18	83–107	78–101
19	108–129	102–122
20	130–144	123–134
21 or older	145–174	135–156

color. However, because of wear beards are not a reliable criterion of age (Latham 1956). The beard is absent from immature hens (first fall) and seldom exceeds about 7.6 cm in length when present in older hens (Edminster 1954).

The sex of adult turkeys can be determined by the relative size and shape of their droppings, according to Bailey (1956). Droppings of the adult male are straighter, longer, and greater in diameter than those of the hen. The typical male dropping has a curlicue on the larger end. In the fall, immature (young of the year) males may be separated from older males by a difference in dropping diameter; young males have droppings seldom exceeding 10 mm in diameter, while older males may have droppings as large as 15 mm in diameter. Female droppings differ from those of the male by their smaller diameter (5 to 8 mm) and their looped, spiral, or bulbous shape (see Fig. 11.31).

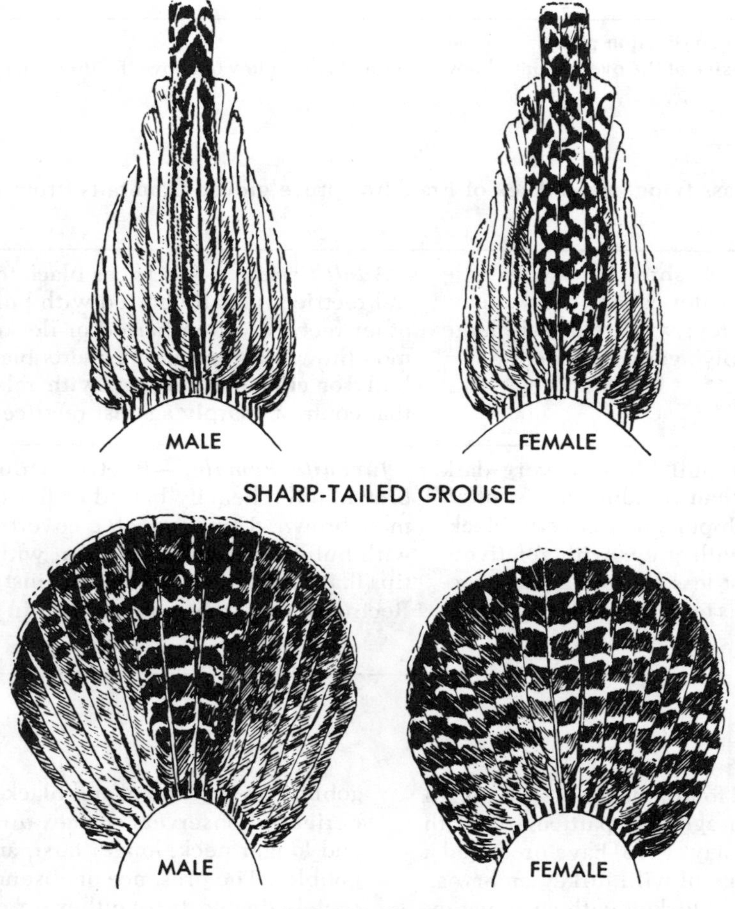

Fig. 11.25. Tail patterns as criteria of sex in prairie grouse. *Top:* Predominantly longitudinal striping in males and cross-barring in females of sharp-tailed grouse. *Bottom*: Absence of barring in outer tail feathers of male and barring of all tail feathers in female prairie chicken (after Thompson 1958).

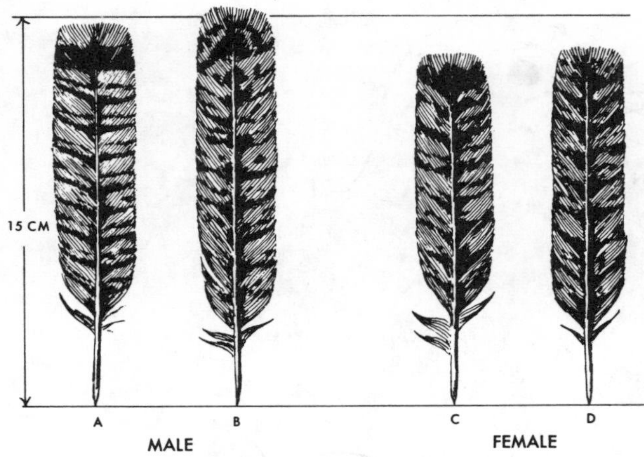

Fig. 11.26. **Central tail feathers of ruffed grouse may be used in aging. Note greater length of male feathers (from Hale et al. 1954).**

BOBWHITE AND OTHER QUAIL

Occasionally difficulty is encountered in determining whether a bobwhite is juvenile or adult from the characters of the 2 outer primaries and the tip coloring of the greater upper coverts. For such cases, it has been found that the shape of greater primary covert #7 is useful. This feather is plucked out and compared to specimens from known young and known adults. In the immature bird this covert has a uniform brownish tint, is usually tipped with buff, and the barbs and vanes separate easily, giving a ragged, mussy appearance. This covert in the adult bird holds together better, giving a sleek appearance, is darker, and without tip markings (see Fig. 11.32 and 11.33). In addition, most adult 7th greater primary coverts have more whitish-downy tipping on the basal 15 to 20 barbs (Haugen 1957). Rosene (1969) published color plates illustrating juvenile with molt in progress; subadult with molt completed; adult with molt in progress and adult with molt completed. He also showed that age of juveniles and hatching dates can be determined by the length of the primary feathers, up to 150 days.

Sex determination of bobwhite is based on the presence of fine black, sharply pointed vermiculations on the middle wing coverts of males and wide, dull gray markings on the same feathers of the female (Thomas 1969). See Table 11.37 for sex and age criteria for several quail species.

In addition to the criteria listed in Table 11.37, the adult breeding coturnix quail male has a swollen cloacal protuberance which is red in color. The cloaca exudes a teaspoonful of froth if squeezed. This froth often is found on the droppings of males (Coil and Wetherbee 1959).

Sex of day-old coturnix may be determined by the morphology of the male genital protuberance (Kazutaka et al. 1966).

HUNGARIAN PARTRIDGE

The sex of an adult partridge can be determined by the scapular and median wing coverts (Fig. 11.34). The male has dark "shoulder" feathers, each with a single median buff stripe; in the female these feathers are lighter and each has a wide median buff stripe and 2 to 4 buff crossbars (McCabe and Hawkins 1946).

Weigand (1977) reported that sex may be determined by facial plumage. Males possessed rust-colored feathers on their orbital, malar and auricular regions; the forehead, crown and occiput were uniformly slate gray. No differentially-colored superciliary line was noted for males. Females exhibited buff-colored orbital and malar regions; these areas terminate at about the posterior edge of the eye. The auricular region characteristically showed mottled gray and white feathers extending posteriorly from the eye to the neck. The forehead and crown of females was also mottled gray and white, with a frequently distinct white superciliary line separating the dorsal from the orbital region.

Male facial plumage appeared at about 10 weeks and was a reliable sex criterion by week 13. Female plumage development was delayed to weeks 13 and 15 respectively.

The immature birds in fall look like adults and may be distinguished from them by the pointedness of the 2 outer primaries (McCabe and Hawkins 1946) and by their yellow feet. Adult feet are blue-gray (Edminster 1954).

CHUKAR PARTRIDGE

Sex of day-old birds is based on the shape of the genital protuberance (Fig. 11.35) in the partially everted cloaca (Siopes and Wilson 1973). Sex and age of fall-shot birds (Table 11.38) is based on coloring, molt stage, and length of primaries (Weaver and Haskell 1968).

WOODCOCK

See Table 11.39. Figure 11.36 illustrates an age character and Fig. 11.37 a sex character in the wing of the woodcock. Martin (1964) gave a key for determining the age (immature, subadult and adult) of woodcock from January through March by wing characters. Artmann and Schroeder (1976) have shown that wings from females were significantly larger than those from males. Wings measuring 133 mm or less were from males, and those 134 mm or more were from females.

MOURNING DOVE

See Table 11.39. The presence of white-tipped primary coverts is indicative of a juvenile bird but these are molted in sequence distally 1 or 2 feathers in advance of the primary molt (1–10). Thus when primaries 8 and 9 are being replaced with adult feathers, the diagnostic primary coverts are usually gone. At this time, immatures usually can be detected by the presence of a buff-colored fringe on the tips of primaries 9 and 10 (Wight et al. 1967). Sadler et al. (1970) reported that all doves with

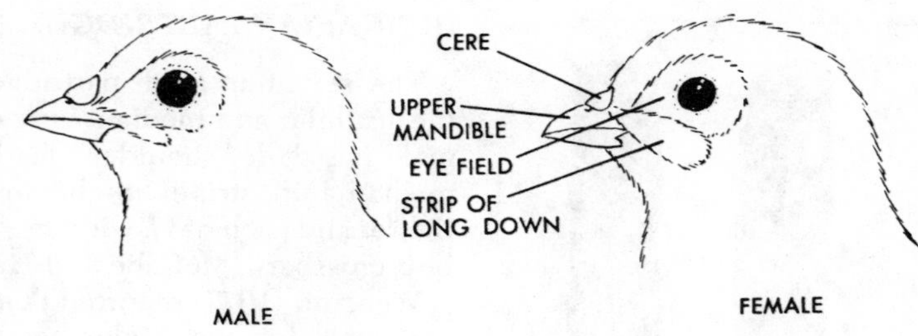

Heads of day-old pheasant chicks showing regions of maximum wattle development. Male chick on left, female at center, and male chick at right from which natal down has been removed. Sketches are slightly schematic and the characteristic may be somewhat less conspicuous than shown here until the natal down is parted as in C.

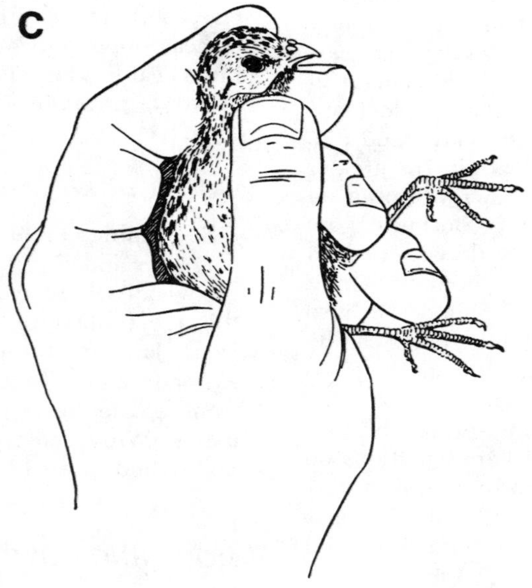

Convenient method of restraining day-old pheasant chicks during examination of cheek region for wattle tissue.

Figure 11.27. Sex characters of newly hatched ring-neck pheasants (from A. Latham 1942; B and C: Woehler and Gates 1970).

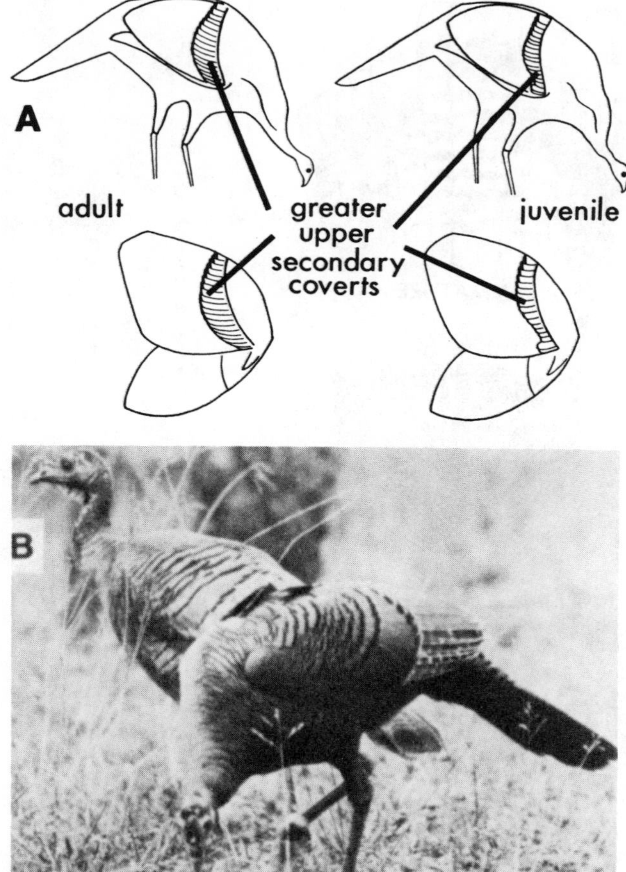

Fig. 11.28. A. Greater upper secondary covert configuration in juvenile and adult turkeys (from Williams 1961) B. Turkey in the foreground is an adult and the one in the background is a juvenile (Lovett E. Williams, Jr., Florida Game and Fresh Water Fish Commission).

Fig. 11.29. Primaries No. 10 of adult and immature Eastern wild turkey. Note that the tip of the adult primaries are broadly rounded and barred, with white almost to the extreme tip; the tip of immature primaries are pointed and plain gray in color and lack definite barring (original report by Petrides 1942; sketch by Grace Smyth).

completed primary molts in September in Missouri can be regarded as immature birds since adults complete their molts later. Haas and Amend (1979) documented that South and North Carolina doves completed their primary molt a month earlier than Missouri doves. Since mourning doves molt all 10 primaries (and primary coverts) in the post-juvenal and postnuptial molts, there are no known external criteria for separating adults from inmatures when molts has been completed after October 1 in Missouri and possibly earlier in more southern latitudes. Holcomb and Jaeger (1978) found highly individual variation in nestling growth but developed a formula, based on several measurements, that estimated age from hatching to fledging:

$-1.13 + (0.15)$ (tarsus length) $+ (0.19)$ (tomium length) $+ (0.12)$ (second primary length, if present) $+ (-0.09)$ (spinal tract feather length, if present) $-1 =$ age in days.

BAND-TAILED PIGEON

Table 11.40 presents a key to age and sex of band-tailed pigeons (Braun 1976). White and Braun (1978) aged immature birds from fledging to 34 days on the basis of primary and secondary feather replacement. During trapping in May and June and in September, sex identification poses little problem (Silovsky et al. 1968, Braun 1976). The plumage of males is brighter with a more rosy hue to the breast and head; females are duller and have brown or gray breasts and necks. Passmore and Jarvis (1979) recommended using a combination of plumage characters and cloacal inspection to reliably sex band-tailed pigeons.

RAILS

The sexes of king rail are similar in plumage. During September and October, the young progress toward adult plumage. By November, they are practically in adult plumage, although they do not attain their full brilliancy of color until the next molt (Bent 1926). Males are usually larger than females and immatures may be distinguished from adults on the basis of color of the soft parts (Meanley 1969).

The adults of both sexes of clapper rails are identical in appearance. The juvenal plumage is similar to that of

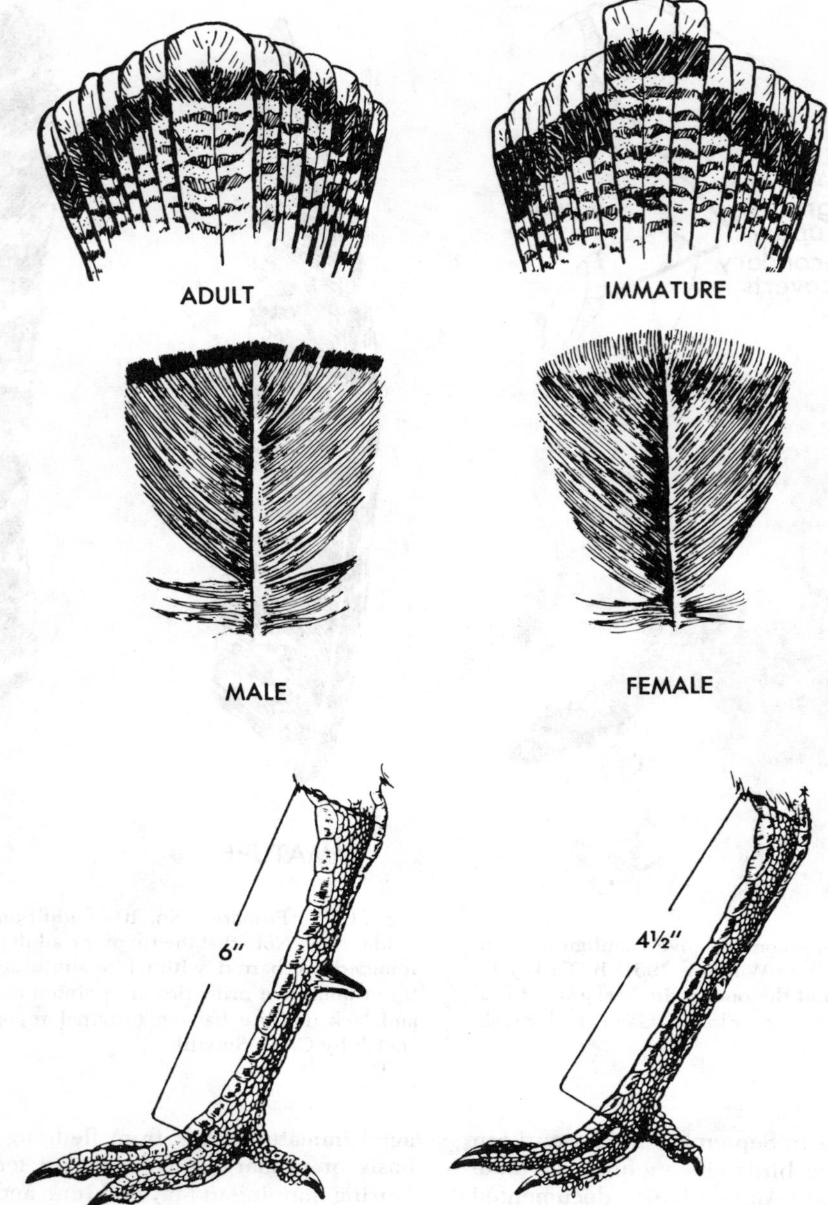

Fig. 11.30. Sex and age characters in the eastern wild turkey. *Top:* The adult shows an even contour of the spread tail *Left* whereas the immature *Right* has an irregular contour. *Middle:* Breast feather of male *Left* is flattened and black-tipped, whereas that of female *Right* is rounded and buff-tipped. *Bottom:* Foot of male is about 15.2 cm and bears a spur while that of the female is only 11.4 cm (from Godin 1960).

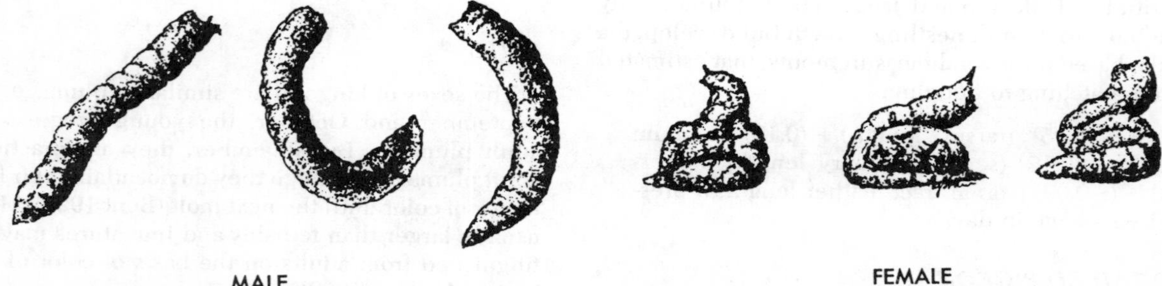

Fig. 11.31. Dropping configurations as indicators of sex for the eastern wild turkey. *Left:* Typical gobbler configurations. *Right:* Typical configurations of the hen; after Bailey 1956 (from Godin 1960).

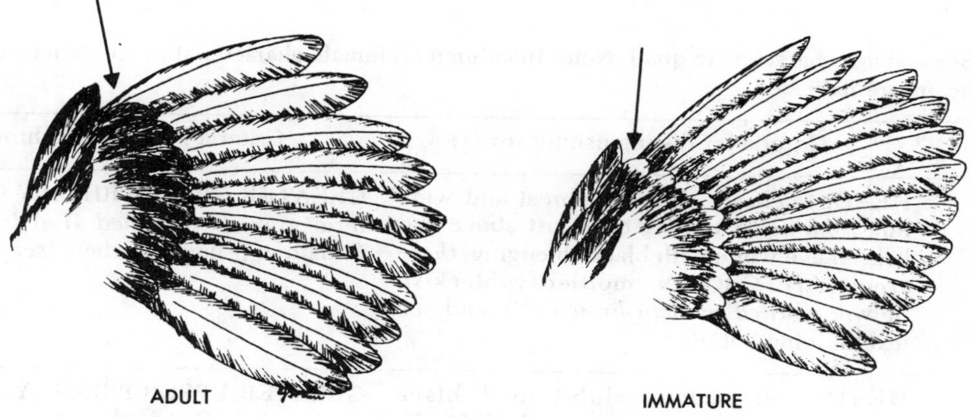

Fig. 11.32. Age criteria, based on wing characters, of all quail in Table 11.37, except coturnix quail. *Left:* Primary coverts in adult are of uniform color. *Right:* Primary coverts in immature individuals have tips of light color (from Godin 1960).

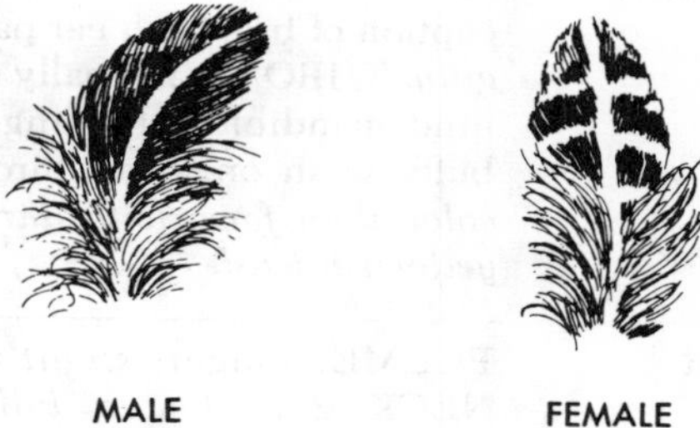

Fig. 11.34. Scapular feathers from Hungarian partridge. Note center stripe in feather from male and barring on feather from female (sketch by Jens von Sivers *in* Thompson 1958, after McCabe and Hawkins 1946).

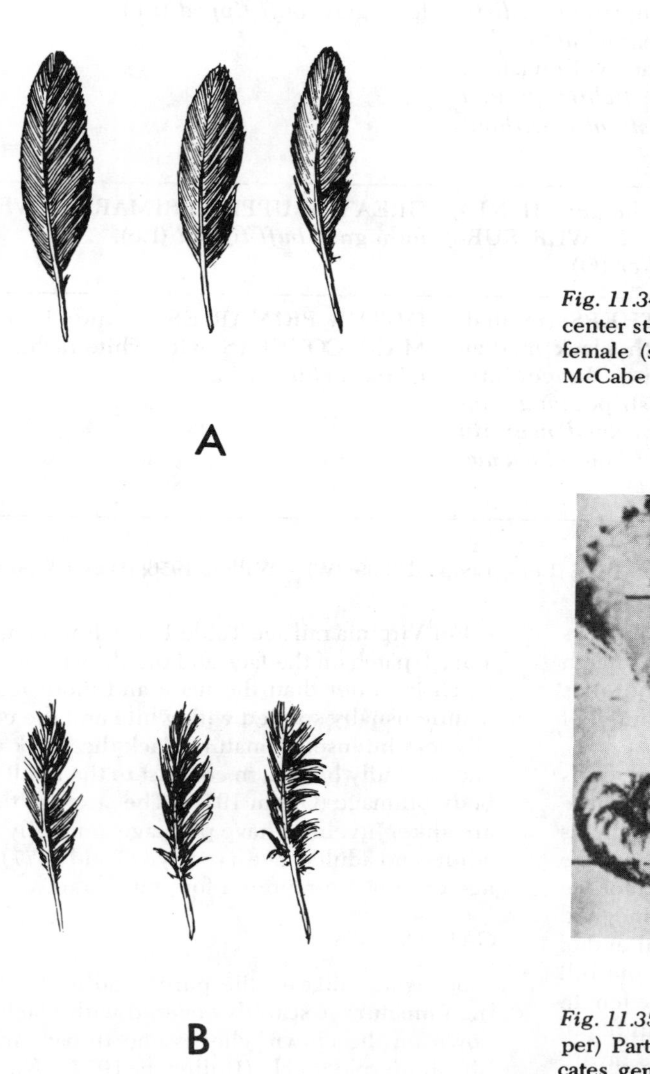

Fig. 11.33. Seventh greater primary coverts of bobwhite, showing sleek appearance in adult (A) and ragged (B) appearance in juvenile (after Haugen 1957). See Fig. 11.10 for location of this feather on the wing (from Godin 1960).

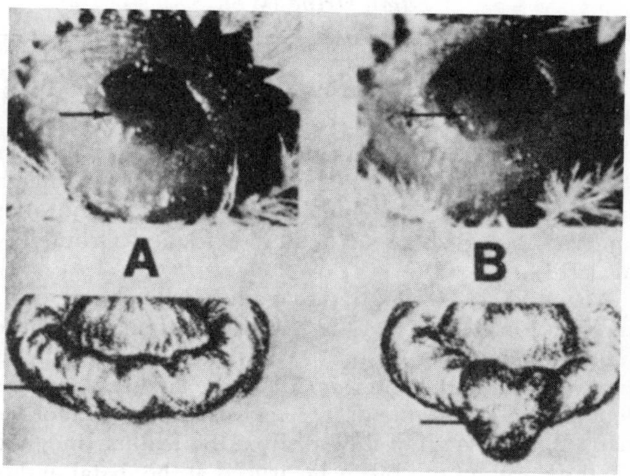

Fig. 11.35. Cloacal sexing of day-old chukar partridge. (A, upper) Partially everted cloaca of a typical female. Arrow indicates genital fold on the ventral rim of the vent. (A, lower) Schematic drawing of a typical everted female type cloca. (B, upper) Partially everted cloaca of a typical male. Arrow indicates genital protuberance on the ventral rim of the vent. (B, lower) Schematic drawing of a typical male cloaca (from Siopes and Wilson 1973).

Table 11.37. Sex and age characters in quail. Note: In column (1) female characteristics are italicized; in column (2) immature characters are italicized.

Species	Criteria for distinguishing sex (1)	Criteria for distinguishing age (2)
Bobwhite	HEAD: forehead, chin and throat and wide line from beak running back just above and behind eye white with blackish edging; *these areas buff.* CROWN: mottled w/blackish brown; *mottled w/rusty brown* (E), and see text for wing criteria.	GREATER UPPER PRIMARY COVERTS: uniform gray; *buff-tipped* (Le) (see Fig. 11.33). Length of primary feathers (see Rosene 1969).
California Quail	HEAD: conspicuous club-tipped black topknot; *topknot inconspicuous.* PLUMAGE: fairly bold and colorful; *dull.*	GREATER UPPER PRIMARY COVERTS: uniform gray; *buff-tipped* (Le).
Gambel's Quail	Similar to California Quail.	GREATER UPPER PRIMARY COVERTS: uniform gray; *buff-tipped* (Le).
Scaled Quail	SIDE OF FACE: uniform pearl gray, with exception of brownish ear patch; *streaked dirty gray.* THROAT: normally clear white just behind mandible, blending into yellowish or buffy wash on lower throat; *lighter ground color than face, with dark streaks, without yellowish wash* (W).	GREATER UPPER PRIMARY COVERTS: uniform gray; *buff-tipped* (Le).
Mountain Quail	PLUME: longer; *slightly shorter.* HINDNECK: gray clearer; *duller.* LOWER SURFACE: brighter; *slightly duller* (G).	GREATER UPPER PRIMARY COVERTS: uniform gray; *buff-tipped* (Le).
Coturnix Quail	CHIN AND THROAT FEATHERS: (nuptial) reddish-brown, rounded with black median stripe; (nonbreeding) long, lanceolate, whitish, with black median stripe; *long, lanceolate, light cinnamon, margined near tip with rufous or black spots, without black median stripe* (We).	OUTER PRIMARIES: rounded; *sharp.* PRIMARY COVERTS: with white rachises; *without white rachises* (We).

Authority: (E) = Edminster 1954; (G) = Grinnell et al. 1918; (Le) = Leopold 1939; (W) = Wallmo 1956; (We) = Wetherbee 1961.

the adult but the streaking on the back is duller and less strikingly contrasted, the lower surface is very much lighter, more buffy in tone, and the barring on the sides and flanks scarcely or not at all in evidence (Grinnell et al. 1918).

Mangold (1974) reported that adult male clapper rails in New Jersey appear to be larger than females. Three measurements were used: (1) the longest toe length, as measured from the anterior side of the tarsus, where the foot is bent perpendicularly backward, to the end of the nail; (2) the length of the bill from the feather line; and (3) the depth of the bill is measured at the distal end of the groove which runs from the nostril. When the bill measured 6.35 cm (2 1/2 inches) or longer, the toe length was 6.35 cm (2 1/2 inches) or longer and the bill depth was 0.64 cm (18/64 inch) or larger, the bird was invariably a male. Birds that measured less in all 3 measurements were females. In a sample of 17 males and 48 females, 29% of the males and 14% of the females did not meet the criteria specified in each of the 3 measurements.

For Virginia rail see Table 11.39. For Sora, males have a black patch on the face and the throat. The female face patch is duller than the male and more restricted, the mantle usually spotted with white and the colors generally less intense. Immatures lack the black throat patch and are buffy brown, in contrast to the adult gray-brown body plumage (Odom 1977). The sexes of the black rail are alike. Juveniles have plumage generally lighter than adults and adults have a red eye (Todd 1977). No sex and age criteria are reported for yellow rail.

GALLINULES

Sexes are alike in the purple gallinule. The head of the immature is scantily covered with black and silvery down on the crown, cheeks and throat. Adults have a bluish purple neck (Holliman 1977). No age or sex criteria are reported for the common gallinule.

COMMON SNIPE

Sexes are alike, but the female is heavier and has a

Table 11.38. A key for determining age and sex of chukar partridge from wings, from mid-September through December (from Weaver and Haskell 1968).

1a. Mottled secondaries absent	2
1b. Mottled secondaries present	*juvenile* 5
2a. Neither primary 9 nor 10 in stage of molt	3
2b. Either 9 or 10 or both in stage of molt	*adult* 8
3a. Upper primary covert 9 is less than 29 mm long	4
3b. Upper primary covert 9 is 29 mm long or more	*adult* 8
4a. Outer two primaries pointed at tips, only slightly faded, showing little wear	*juvenile* 5
4b. Outer two primaries faded, showing wear	*adult* 8
5a. Primary 3 is fully grown, is at least 4 mm longer than primary 2	6
5b. Primary 3 is in stage of molt, not fully grown	7
6a. Primary 3 is less than 135 mm long	*juvenile female*
6b. Primary 3 is 135 mm long or more	*juvenile male*
7a. Primary 1 is 119 mm long or less	*juvenile female*
7b. Primary 1 is longer than 119 mm	*juvenile male*
8a. Primary 3 is 136 mm long or less	*adult female*
8b. Primary 3 is longer than 136 mm	*adult male*

Table 11.39. Sex and age characters in shorebirds, pigeons, doves, and Virginia rail. Note: In column (1) female characters italicized; in column (2) immature characters italicized.

Species	Criteria for distinguishing sex (1)	Criteria for distinguishing age (2)
Woodcock	BILL: usually under 67 mm; *usually over 69 mm* (E). WEIGHT: under 175 grams; *over 200 grams* (G). OUTERMOST PRIMARY WIDTH (2 cm. from tip): average 2.5 mm; *average 3.9 mm* (G).	OVIDUCT WIDTH: not under 3 mm; *not over 1 mm* (G). BURSA: absent; *present* (G). MIDDLE SECONDARIES: dark-tipped; *light tipped* (M).
Wilson Snipe	Adults identical (Gr).	STRIPE FROM SIDE OF BILL TO EYE: dark brown; *black* (Gr). CHEEK AND CHIN: buffy and whitish, flecked w/dusky-diagonal dark stripe on lower cheek beneath ear; *mixed white, black, and cinnamon* (Gr).
Mourning Dove	BREAST: faint pink; *brown* (Gr). CROWN: bluish-gray; *brown* (Gr).	PRIMARY COVERTS: uniform; *white-tipped* (P&M). BURSA: absent; *present* (W). See text.
White-winged Dove	CROWN & BACK OF NECK: purplish; *grayish brown* (E). SIDE OF NECK. iridescent green-gold; *grayish-brown* (E). Cloacal examination needed for accuracy (B).	GREATER PRIMARY COVERTS: tips plain; *tips light colored* (E). FEET AND LEGS: red; *brownish to reddish brown*. EYE: bright red; *brown to yellowish brown* (B).
Virginia Rail	Adults identical (GB&S).	TOP OF HEAD, HIND NECK: blackish, narrowly streaked w/olive brown; *dull black w/traces of buffy feather edgings* (Gr). LOWER SURFACE: cinnamon brown, fading to lighter on belly; *mixed black and white, latter predominating down middle of breast and on belly* (Gr). LOWER TAIL COVERTS: mixed blackish, white and cinnamon; *dull cinnamon* (Gr).

Authorities: (E) = Edminster 1954; (G) = Greeley 1953; (Gr) = Grinnell et al. 1918; (M) = Martin 1964; (P & M) = Pearson and Moore 1940; (W) = Wight 1956; (B) = Brown 1977.

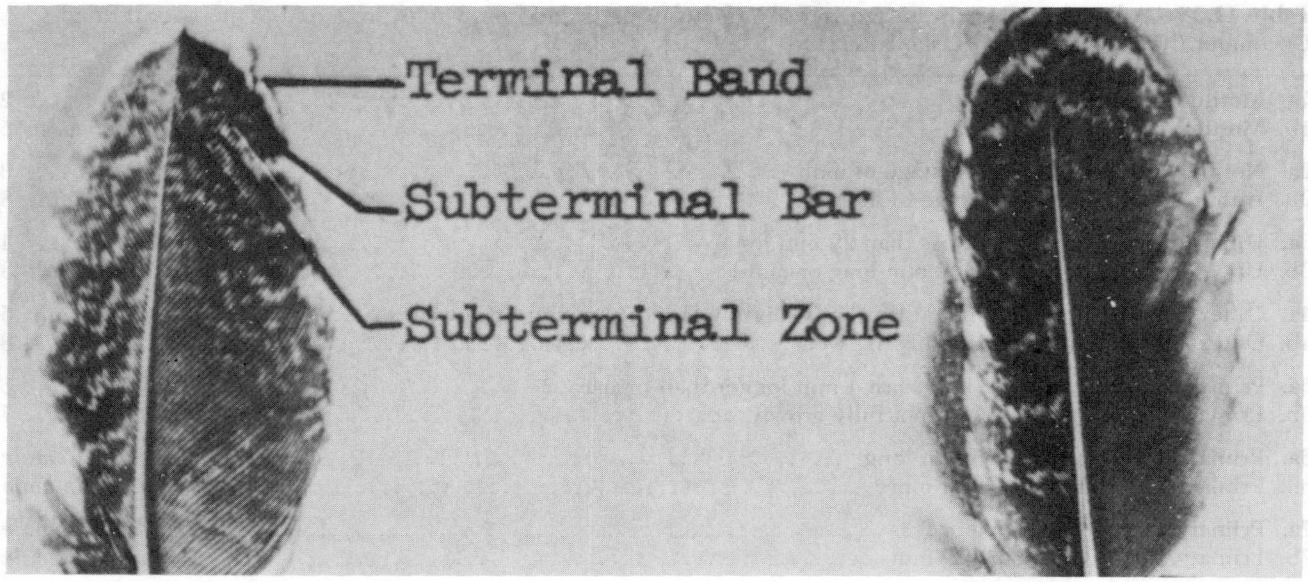

Fig. 11.36. The presence of a light-colored terminal band (*left*) on the secondary flight feathers indicates a woodcock less than 2 years old. Absence of the band (*right*) indicates older birds. (Photo by Richard L. Hall.)

Fig. 11.37. Sex of a woodcock can be determined by examining the 3 outer primary flight feathers. Feathers of female birds are noticeably wider than on male birds. (Photo by Richard L. Hall.)

Table 11.40. Key to age and sex of band-tailed pigeons (from Braun 1976).

1a.	Some or all wing coverts tipped with white, reddish, or pale brown; all or some juvenile secondaries present. (Juvenile secondaries are shorter, narrower, and more pointed than the broad square secondaries of adults.)	.... HY/SY* 2
1b.	Coverts without white, reddish, or pale brown tipping; no juvenile secondaries present; head and breast pink to brown; neck crescent usually pronounced	.... AHY 3
2a.	Some or all coverts tipped with white, reddish, or pale brown; all juvenile secondaries present; primary molt not greater than P6. Sex of immature pigeons molting past P2 can normally be ascertained	.... HY 3
2b.	Some but not all coverts tipped with white, reddish, or pale brown; at least secondary 1 or 2 is adult, primary molt P6 or greater	.... SY 3
3a.	Breast, neck, and top of head bright pinkish to purplish	.... Male
3b.	Breast, neck and top of head dull brownish to gray-brown or pinkish brown	.... Female

*HY, immatures; SY, subadults; AHY, adults.

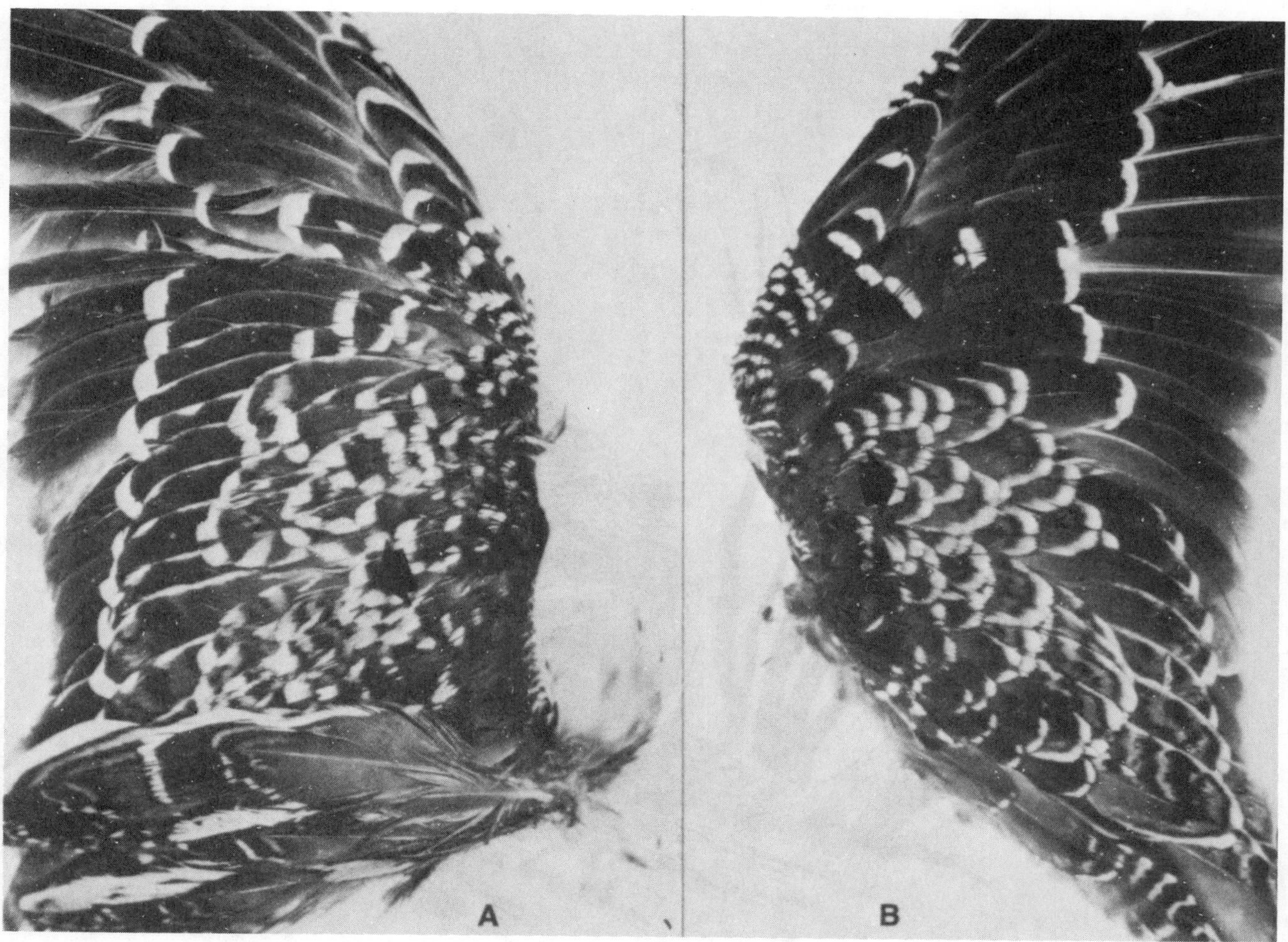

Fig. 11.38. (A) Adult snipe wing. Note the presence of a wide dark terminal shaft line on the lesser and median secondary coverts. (B) Immature snipe wing. Note the presence of faint black tip on some of the lesser and median secondary coverts (Dwyer and Dobell 1979).

longer bill. Dwyer and Dobell (1979) verified the accuracy of Tuck's (1972) technique for using coloration of median and lesser-wing coverts (Fig. 11.38).

SANDHILL CRANE

Sexes are alike. The juvenile has rusty brown plumage on the crown until the post-juvenal molt. The adult has dark red papillose skin on the crown (Lewis 1977).

COOT

Crawford (1978) reported that tarsus color during the breeding season is indicative of age. Juveniles are blue-green; yearlings, green; 2-year olds, yellow-green; 3-year olds, yellow; and all older birds have yellow-orange to red-orange tarsi.

Immature birds have fatty-appearing bursa walls while adult bursa walls are thin and transparent, but internal examination is required (Fredrickson 1968). The most reliable method of sexing coots in the field is by the lower pitch and nasal quality of female notes (Gullion 1952). Frederickson (1968) reported that nesting pairs can be accurately sexed by the large body size of most males and the conformation of the larger culmen-shield.

OTHER BIRDS

Age and sex characteristics have been described for many nongame and other shorebird species. The various characters employed and the species are too numerous for treatment here. Serious ornithologists will refer to the *North American Bird Banding Manual,* Vol. II (U.S. Fish and Wildlife Service and Canadian Wildlife Service 1977) for very complete descriptions for over 60 species, most of which are not covered in this chapter. In addition the publications of the several bird banding associations in North America often carry reports of new or tentative age and sex techniques, e.g., ***Bird-Banding, Inland Bird Banding News, North American Bird Bander*** (combines the former *Eastern Bird Banding Association News* and *Western Bird Bander*), and the *Ontario Bird Banding Association News* and *Contributions.* Major North American periodicals which also publish papers on bird age and sex techniques are *The Auk, The Condor, The Journal of Wildlife Management* and *The Wilson Bulletin.*

Chapter Twelve

Computer Applications in Wildlife Management

J. SCOTT ZIESENIS
Biologist, Texas Instruments Inc.
P. O. Box 237
Buchanan, N.Y.

LOWELL ADAMS
302 Central Blvd.
Pacific Grove, California

Electronic computers and their use touch the daily lives of nearly everyone in America. Bills, advertisements, applications, and many other communications come to us on the now-familiar cropped-corner card. Computers now have become an essential tool for wildlife biologists, and the next generation of biologists and wildlife managers will undoubtedly rely on computer technology as much as the knowledge of natural history.

Computers are useful to ecologists because they can handle large amounts of complex relationships rapidly. Life is a large number of complex relationships, whether examined at the level of the cell, the organism, the population, or the community. Before computers became available, the complexities of life could only be studied as simple, isolated pieces, despite the realization that the pieces should not be studied alone. Because of computers, biology is now in a period of rapidly-growing ability to deal with complex living processes. The wildlife manager and researcher need to know how to obtain the use of a computer, and more importantly, how to use it.

The purpose of this chapter is to describe the kinds of computers available and what they do that is of interest to wildlifers; to introduce basic methods of using computers and to illustrate some of their important uses in wildlife. Reading this chapter will not make anyone an accomplished user of computers, but will only provide an introduction; expertise comes only with formal instruction and actual practice.

KINDS OF COMPUTERS

There are 2 main kinds of computers—analog and digital. Other kinds are combinations of these (hybrid computers), and special purpose computers. Analog computers work by a set of electronic components (resistors, capacitors, transistors, amplifiers, etc.) which act upon a voltage. The voltage is the analog of the biological quantity involved, e.g., the number of animals in a population. The actions by the electronic components are analogs of biological effects, e.g., births and deaths. Births are represented by voltage increases (amplifiers), deaths by voltage decreases (resistors). The solution is displayed as a curve of the changing voltage, over time as the independent variable, drawn by a strip-chart, an x-y recorder, or by an oscilloscope. The voltage curve is converted to a population curve simply by labeling the coordinates "population" instead of "voltage" with proper scales to represent animal numbers instead of voltage. This conversion is much like a slide-rule in which the distance along a rule can be added to, subtracted from, divided, or multiplied by a number. Distance along the rule is the analog of the quantity being manipulated, and corresponds to voltage in an electrical conductor. A wildlifer does not have to be an electronics engineer to operate an analog computer, any more than he needs to be one to use a radio or television set. He does have to know mathematics, however, because the machine can only perform mathematical operations.

The digital computer works with digits (numbers), not voltages. To operate the machine, numbers are put in together with instructions, and numbers are produced printed in tables, punched cards or paper tape, or stored on magnetic tape. How the digital computer manages to push numbers around to achieve the mathematical computation is a problem best left to the computer engineer with his circuits, gates, pulses, registers, etc. The user needs to know only how to "talk to" the machine. This will be discussed later.

The digital computer has become increasingly available over the last 10 years in small desk-top varieties and programmable calculators. These models are especially useful in calculating statistics on small data sets, and their use requires a minimum of knowledge of computer science. In general, they have limited data storage capabilities which limit their usefulness to the wildlife biologist.

In some ways, analog computers can be used more flexibly than digital ones. For example, certain parameters of a model can be changed while the computer is in operation, to see what effect the change has on the model. To illustrate, in a study to measure the effects of different birth rates on the size of a population of animals; it is possible to use any birth rate of interest to set up the model on the analog computer and determine the resulting population size. Then by simply turning the dial of a variable resistor, the birth rate can be varied, and the population levels resulting from a large array of comparative birth rates found immediately. Similarly, death rates and other parameters can be varied at will, either independently or in conjunction with each other. This facility for "playing with the model" by twirling dials and watching effects on the recorder chart has considerable heuristic value for better comprehension of the parameters' effects. The digital computer can also be used to test various hypothetical parameters, but this is done either by manually re-running the program with the test parameters as new input, or by programming a set of inputs to be used automatically in sequential cyclic runs of the program. This process takes more time and lacks the illuminating effect on the wildlifer obtained by the manipulation of the dials of the analog computer and the direct cause-effect observation.

A disadvantage of the analog computer is that it accepts only mathematical models based on linear differential equations. In engineering, where such models are frequently used, the analog computer is especially valuable. Relationships are nonlinear in many biological models, however, and often must be handled by numerical means, rather than by the formal calculus used in analog computers.

The hybrid computer is a digital computer, an analog computer, and the interface equipment designed to transfer information and controls between the two. The use of such a tool requires intimate and sophisticated knowledge of computer technology, and any detailed description of hybrid computers is out of order here. The main point is that analog and digital computers both have certain strong points and weaknesses, and the hybrid assembly provides for use of the best features of both.

Special-purpose computers are used mainly in the automation of manufacturing and military processes, such as running machines, aiming guns, landing aircraft on carriers—wherever logical decisions and consequent adjustments are required in the course of an operation. These special machines are also beyond the scope of this review, since wildlife biologists will rarely use them.

HOW TO WORK WITH COMPUTERS

Computers have essentially 3 capabilities of interest to the wildlife biologist. They can: (1) compute mathematical functions, (2) perform logical decisions, and (3) iterate the same series of calculations many times. A variety of functions, some especially interesting to wildlife biologists, can be derived from these capabilities.

A hypothetical study will serve to demonstrate these capabilities of computers. A study is conducted in which birds are identified in 3 different habitats, each day during spring and summer months. For each sighting, the date, observer, area, species, number of individual birds, and time of day are coded on a data sheet. The information is entered through punched cards or key to disk entry.

The computer reads each data card as an individual observation. Thus, a variable identified as NUMBER on the data sheet would refer to the number of individuals of a particular species seen during that particular sighting. Obviously, it is no great chore for the computer, using its ability to compute mathematical functions, to add up the number of individuals seen. However, totals for individual species are of more interest. These cards could be sorted by hand, putting cards with species code 01 into 1 pile, 02 in another and so on. The computer, however, with its ability to make logical decisions, can do this sorting. Thus the data can be sorted by species, by week, by area, or by any other variable present on the data card. Moreover, calculations can be performed and printed out on the sorted data if this is desired.

The iterative ability of the computer now becomes important. If the data are sorted by species, by day, and by week, the investigator may be interested in the mean number of individuals of a species seen each day, averaged over a week. The computer can be told to add all of a certain species seen each day. The daily totals summed over 7 days and divided by 7 is the mean number of individuals of that species seen weekly. To obtain a variance associated with this mean, iterative calculations must be performed on each daily total to give the sums of squares. The computer will iterate this task as many times as required. Anyone who has calculated sums of squares on a hand calculator will recognize the benefits of such iterative capabilities.

The programming associated with this example may seem complex. However, systems that contain these programs are available on most large computers. Thus, the wildlife biologist need only know how to access a SORT program, not how to write one. Accessing these programs will be discussed in more detail later.

When is a computer needed? Of course, no clear-cut answer is possible because the need depends upon the nature of the job, plus the availability (location, cost, and time) of a computer. However, some guidelines are available.

The decision to use a computer hinges on the amount and repetitiousness of computing to be done. You may have a large computing job to do once, or a relatively simple computation to be repeated often with new dates. If small jobs are to be done only once (or only a few times), use of a computer should be questioned. The key to this decision is the amount of time required to perform the mathematics on a hand calculator, versus the time required to program it, plus the cost of computer time.

Some sample applications of the above principles are described in the following account. First, suppose that data are collected annually on the furbearer harvest in a state, as a basis for management decisions. These data include the species of furbearers, number of trappers, sales prices, etc. by management districts. In any 1 year it costs less to summarize the data by hand than by computer, but the same analysis procedure is used every year. After 3 years of data accumulation, the programming expenditures prorated over time reach the break-even point, where it is equally expensive to do the job by hand or by computer. From the third year on, the computer is the cheaper way and should be chosen in the beginning. Computers might be used in analyses of creel censuses, game-range forage surveys, hunter questionnaire analyses, and similarly repetitious tasks. Once set up for such computer work, organizations may find it profitable to use the facilities for such distantly-related tasks as making pay-rolls, bookkeeping, equipment inventory, and procurement.

Another situation demanding computer use may be a complex analysis of a multifactorial experiment involving, for example, the effects of weather, fertilizers, degree of use, and seasons on forage production on winter deer range. This is a 1-time study, but involves a large set of computations. Other factors permitting, the wildlifer may elect to program the job for a computer rather than use the desk calculator to save time, computational errors, or both.

Desk top and programmable calculators create still another decision to be made. Complex analyses can be computed on many of these machines, but the data are generally not stored. If the investigator decides on another analysis, or finds his data must be transformed to meet the assumptions of his test, he will need to enter the data again. Once the data are on cards or stored in a large computer, there is no need for re-entry. Thus, if you want to analyze data several different ways, or need to make decisions regarding the analysis after an initial examination, then it is best to enter the information and store it for future retrieval.

In essence, then, the job is a candidate for the computer if it will be accomplished repeatedly in the same way or if it is highly complex. Choice of computing method is an administrative decision based largely on relative costs, the time available for the computations, and accuracy of computer versus hand computation.

USE OF COMPUTERS

Assuming a decision has been reached about which computer facility to use, how do you go about it? Computers are instructed to do work through computer programming. The program, or set of instructions, activates or "tells" the computer what data are available and how they are to be analyzed. Learning to program a computer is like learning to weave cloth, to find a book in the library, or to perform other similar tasks requiring the knowledge of a process and its sequential order. Learning to program is an intriguing experience and with present simplifications is not a great task if one has a competent instructor.

The task of programming at first looks formidable. The wildlifer cannot visualize how the computer works, and therefore cannot understand how it is possible to learn to operate it. The same fears apply to learning to drive an automobile or operate any complex machine. The use of a computer involves a set of knowledge and skills quite distinct from the knowledge and skills required to know how a computer works and how to keep it operative. Just as mechanics keep automobiles in running condition, electronic technicians keep computers in working order. Wildlifers are usually concerned with using the computer, not with its working.

Should the researcher know how to program, or should he hire a programmer? If the project can afford a programmer, the researcher need not do his own programming. Nevertheless, the researcher should know how to program for 2 reasons. First, a knowledge of programming technique aids in communicating with a programmer; and, secondly, programming can be a way of thinking scientifically, once it is learned. Just as statistical techniques can teach one to "think statistically," so programming teaches one to "think computer-wise." In some areas of thought (e.g., simulation, neural anatomy), "computer thinking" is a valuable mental tool.

Many texts purport to teach computer programming. To date, all texts we have studied have proved confusing. It is strongly recommended that beginners take a course that requires first-hand use of computers via computer programming. Learning by doing is the only method resulting in successful programming skills. Fortunately, computer manufacturers, computer centers, and most universities now conduct regular courses in programming.

Computer programming is step 2 in a sequence of procedures involved in computer use. Step 1 is the formulation of the problem and step 3 is the operation of the computer. Fig. 12.1 illustrates this entire system. The first step is skipped, assuming that the problem is already organized in mathematical formulation. Programming is the process of stating the solution to the mathematical formulation in a form the computer will accept. Usually the programmer first constructs a flow-chart. The flow-chart is a device for organizing the sequence of computational operations in a pattern acceptable to the computer. A simple example best illustrates the use of the flow-chart.

Suppose the problem is to compute the locations of points on a graph for the mathematical formulation

$$Y = BX^2$$

The flow-chart might look like Figure 12.2.

This simple program has only 1 branch and 1 loop. The branch, or 2 paths that go to "Yes" and "No," is the major logical capability of the computer. The loop is the

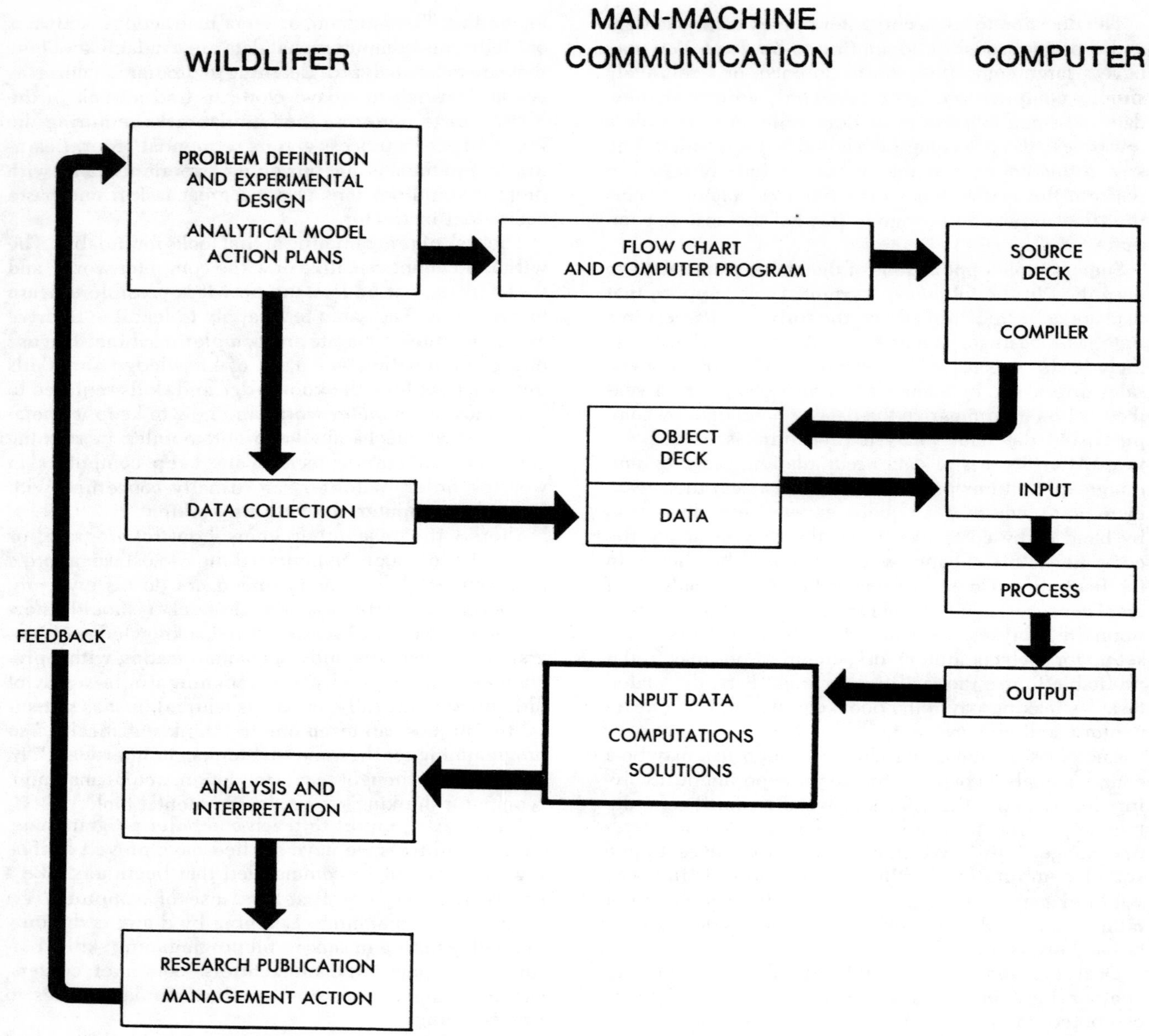

WILDLIFER
MAN-MACHINE COMMUNICATION
COMPUTER
PROBLEM DEFINITION AND EXPERIMENTAL DESIGN
ANALYTICAL MODEL ACTION PLANS
FLOW CHART AND COMPUTER PROGRAM
SOURCE DECK
COMPILER
OBJECT DECK
DATA
INPUT
DATA COLLECTION
PROCESS
FEEDBACK
OUTPUT
INPUT DATA
COMPUTATIONS
SOLUTIONS
ANALYSIS AND INTERPRETATION
RESEARCH PUBLICATION
MANAGEMENT ACTION

Figure 12.1. Generalized flow-chart diagram of the computer-wildlife management research system.

circle of procedures that goes from READ to WRITE, to the branch, to READ, to . . . etc. until the particular set of instructions is complete. When the program becomes more complicated with many branchings and loops (including loops within loops), the need for the flow-chart becomes more apparent.

START
READ B
READ X
Y = bx²
WRITE X & Y
IS THERE ANOTHER X IN INPUT?
NO
YES
STOP

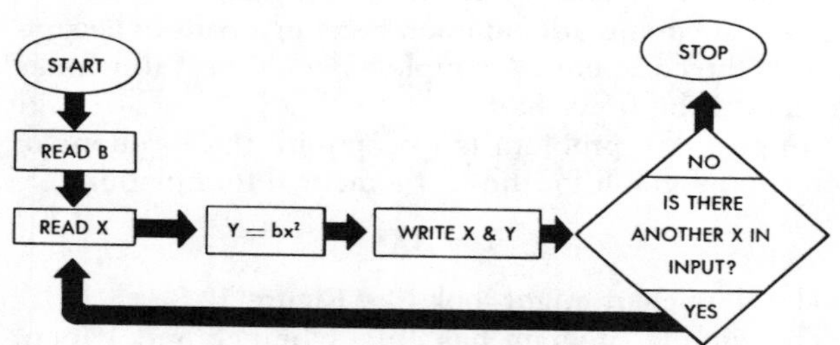

Figure 12.2. A flow chart for a simple Fortran program.

Next, the flow-chart is converted into computer program language. Each block (circle, rectangle, oval, etc.) of the chart is considered in sequence and translated into programming language. In the early years of computers, the programmer wrote his instructions in "machine language." That is, he worked with the computer's memory in mind, placing specific "bits" and "words" in selected locations in memory whose "addresses" were recorded. When an arithmetical procedure was to occur, the computer called forth the "words" by their "addresses." This method of programming places great responsibility on the programmer to keep track of the information in the various localities in memory.

Computer technologists soon overcame much of this burden by programming the computer itself to keep track of the location of information in memory, and to find correct "words" as needed. With this development, it became possible to let the machine translate instructions from a simplified language to machine language. Programming is now done as a 2-step process. First, the programmer writes a "source program" which is fed into the machine along with a "compiler program." The compiler program causes the machine to translate from the programmer language to an "object program," to produce a translation of the "source program" into machine-language. The "object program" is then fed back into the computer, along with the data to be processed. Although this has introduced the additional step of translation by a "compiler program" it has reduced programming time and made programming methods easier to learn.

Many different programming languages, together with their compiler programs, have been developed. Some are for general purpose computation (FORTRAN, ALGOL, PL-1, etc.), and others are for special purposes (LISP, SIMSCRIPT, etc.). A language is selected with the aid of a computer operator, based upon the operations to be performed, abilities of the programmer available, compiler programs, and other considerations. The following program (in FORTRAN) for the simple computation, $Y = bX^2$, illustrates the use of programming language.

```
  PROGRAM EXAMPLE             (1)
  READ 1, B                   (2)
1 FORMAT (F10.2)              (3)
2 READ 3, X, IEND             (4)
3 FORMAT (F10.2, I5)          (5)
  Y = B*X**2                  (6)
  PRINT 4, X, Y               (7)
4 FORMAT (F10.2, 10X, F12.4)  (8)
  IF (IEND) 2, 2, 5           (9)
5 CONTINUE                    (10)
  END                         (11)
  END                         (12)
  0.5                         (13)
  0.2                         (14)
  0.5                         (15)
  1.0                         (16)
  2.0                         (17)
  2.5                         (18)
  3.0 1                       (19)
```

The index numbers in parentheses at the right are to explain the purpose and effect of each statement. (These index numbers are not part of the program actually used).

1. Name of the program for identification and billing. This aspect of programming tends to be specific to the computer system with which you are working.

2. Causes the machine to read the constant B on a data card and put it in memory according to format instruction No. 1—next card, card (3).

3. Format instructions describing the positions of the digits and decimal point on the input card. The F is a code that causes the machine to accept B in the "floating point" form commonly used in many scientific applications. The number is expressed, in the computer, as some number multiplied by a power of 10, e.g., 150 in floating point is 1.5×10^2. In computers this is an efficient form to use. The 10.2, in the format statement (3), indicates that B (13) is allowed enough space to be a 10-digit number in which the decimal point is 2 places to the left of the last digit.

4. Index number (2) used to find this instruction when the machine comes back to it in (9). This instruction causes the machine to READ the next data card according to format 3. This is the first X-value. It also causes a read of the space on the card designated IEND whose location is also designated in (5). This is the indicator of the end of the run as will be explained under (9).

5. Format for reading and storing X and IEND. It also causes a READ of the next 15 columns to see whether anything (IEND) is punched there—see (9) below. The value of X should be punched in card columns 1–10 with the last digit in column 10. The value of IEND should be punched in columns 11–15.

6. Instruction for the actual computation (all other instructions before and after this one are "housekeeping" instructions for moving the data into and out of the computer). Instructions: "Find the value previously stored data—(4) and (5)—at the address for X, square it (**2), find the stored value of B, multiply B times X-squared. Store the result in memory at the address for Y."

7. Instruction to print X and Y according to format 4.

8. Instruction to print X in the first column on the print-out page. This column is spaced for 10 digits, 8 to the left of the decimal place and 2 to the right. Next, skip 10 spaces (10X), then print Y in a column within a space with 12 places, 8 to the left and 4 to the right of the decimal point. Thus the X's and Y's are printed in 2 straight columns as follows:

```
 .20        .0200
 .50        .1250
1.00        .5000
2.00       2.0000
2.50       3.1250
3.00       4.5000
```

9. Instruction to return to instruction 2 if the space for IEND on the last data card was unpunched, i.e., was less than, or equal to, zero. If a number greater than zero is punched in the IEND space, go to instruction 5. In punching the X data cards, the IEND space was left unpunched (=zero or less than zero) until the last X card. This card was punched with a "1" in the IEND space, thus signalling the end of the run.

10. Instruction merely to send the process on to the next instruction. In some FORTRAN languages the machine cannot go from an IF instruction to an END instruction, and a continue instruction is used.

The punched program cards constitute a "source deck." This deck is placed in the computer hopper which processes one card at a time. First, the machine translates the source-deck instructions into machine instructions using a "compiler," which is a set of instructions permanently maintained on magnetic tape, discs, or punched cards. (Programs and compilers for different program languages are called "software" in contrast to the "hardware" of computers, key-punches, etc.). The translated machine-language program, the object deck, may be punched on cards or stored in magnetic-tape memory. In the larger, modern computers, the operator need not be concerned with the compiler and object decks; the computer automatically handles all processes from input to output. The computer and its printout device return the data-object deck and a printed copy of the results arranged in whatever form the program prescribed.

In presenting the general procedures, many supplementary details are omitted. For example, the computer often encounters instructions that it cannot execute because they are improperly written, or for other reasons. The computer may then write a message to the operator explaining the error, and either proceed with the rest of the compilation or stop. It is then up to the programmer to correct programming mistakes and resubmit the program. This is called "de-bugging" the program, and many times is a tedious and exasperating task. Methods of de-bugging and many other details not covered here must be learned from instructors and references. Various manuals exist for programming techniques using the many programming languages. Novice programmers should use these in conjunction with a competent instructor and a computer available for practice runs.

Just as FORTRAN removed the programmer from the inconveniences of machine language, various "packages" allow the computer user greater freedom from the nuts and bolts of programming. With these packages (BMD, SAS, SPSS), the user does little actual programming. Instead, he uses "canned" programs already included in the package. These systems were developed mainly for statistical analysis, but their use goes further. Regression, ANOVA, and chi square are just a few of the statistical tests available. Other routines, such as SORT and RANK, are available on these systems that allow the investigation greater flexibility in the analysis of data.

The advantages of using these packages are many. The wildlifer need not concern himself with writing programs, but need only know how to use them. The programs are written by professionals, and thus are more efficient and flexible than anything an occasional user might write. However, a background in FORTRAN or some other language is still helpful.

Data processing by analog computer is strikingly different from that by digital computer. Instead of the human-language approach, the problem is stated in mathematical form. Then, using plug-in connecting wires, the various components of the computer are wired together in proper configuration to solve the problem. In planning the program a diagram slightly resembling a flow-chart is used with conventional symbols representing components (summing amplifier, potentiometer, etc.). Lines connecting the components represent the connecting wires.

COMPUTER USE IN WILDLIFE MANAGEMENT

The actual use of computers in wildlife biology depends largely upon the stage of the study. An investigation might consist of collecting data, analyzing them to determine relationships, and predicting future occurrences, given a specific set of conditions. The computer is useful in each of these stages. Data management is the process by which data are first stored and organized within the computer. After statistical analysis has described the relationships present in the data, these and other relationships can be combined into a program that models the system, predicting future trends.

Data management is the storage and organization of a large amount of data. Examples of this type of computer use are common in the literature. Programs such as RUN WILD provide inventories, species-habitat associations, and management information for each class of vertebrates (Patton 1978). A variation of this program is being developed for the eastern United States (Cushwa et al. 1978). Ornithological field notes are stored on computers at the University of Wisconsin—Stevens Point (Wisdom 1976). Habitat data are computer stored in conjunction with wildlife sightings in Maryland in a system that has already provided several uses in wildlife management (Antenucci et al. 1979). All of these systems maintain a large set of data in an organized manner, that is easily accessible. Once data are stored in this form, analysis is relatively simple.

Data base management can be a critical phase of computer use since the organization of a stored data set may restrict its use. Recent technological advances have increased storage capabilities while decreasing costs. Computer storage is not limited to data, but line drawings, photographs (Martin 1977), maps (Amidon 1978), and literature (see chapter 2) among others, may be stored. Considering the rate of technological advances, these storage capabilities will undoubtedly be increased. These advances in data storage technology are timely since The National Environmental Policy Act has created a practical demand for inventory type data bases for the preparation of environmental impact statements and input into models (Martel and Lackey 1977).

Data analysis is now commonly conducted on computers. Many calculators and programmable calculators have statistical routines written for them or have the analysis hand wired in the instrument. Desk top computers have these benefits also. For larger data sets, the statistical packages described in the previous section are available. The present dependency of statistical analyses on computer science is evident from the use of techniques such as multiple regression, that have computational procedures so complex that they are essentially not practical to do by hand. In the previous decade, few papers were published in which this technique was used, but now it is a relatively common analysis in the literature. Hocking (1976) evaluated several different multiple regression routines designed to derive sets of independent variables that best explain the variation in the dependent variable.

Analysis may be conducted on raw or transformed data. Data may be transformed for statistical reasons, i.e., normalizing the variance, or for biological reasons.

For instance, vegetation clippings were collected during a study of a grazing community, and later analyzed for nitrogen and acid detergent fiber. A program was written that converted these data to digestible dry matter and apparent digestible protein, which were then converted to parameters of productivity (Church and Rees 1976).

The ability of a computer to analyze data is staggering. We have all marvelled at the space program with its computer enhanced photographs. Certain aspects of wildlife biology are now using highly sophisticated computer routines to analyze data. The most notable of these is in the analysis of movements through biotelemetry where 3-dimensional motion pictures (x, y, and time) have been generated by computers (White 1979). The use of such sophisticated tools is bound to increase in wildlife biology.

The third major use of computers in wildlife biology, modeling and simulation, is in an embryonic stage and has considerable potential. Models serve to organize available knowledge into a series of equations that will predict future changes in the system, given a particular set of circumstances. Any level of organization, ecosystem community or population, can be modeled. The model accomplishes 3 purposes. The first is the obvious prediction of changes in the system under the specified set of conditions. This purpose is particularly important in predicting the impact of man's activities upon wildlife populations. A third of the papers presented at a recent conference on the effects of mortality from power plants on fish populations concerned modeling (Van Winkle 1977).

The second function of modeling is that of sensitivity analysis. In this procedure various functions in the model are varied and the effects on some independent variable such as goodness of fit to observed data are noted. The objective is to determine which dependent variable has the greatest effect on the independent variable. The status of these variables with the greatest effect on the model can then receive special attention. Van Winkle et al. (1976) used this type of analysis to evaluate the sensitivity of a model predicting the effects of increased mortality on a population.

In addition to predicting the future, the model also serves to organize the available information on the system in such a way that deficiencies in our understanding of the system become apparent. For instance, the major question posed at the conference mentioned above was that of the relationship of density to survival. Although much data on mortality rates were available, the notable absence of knowledge regarding density-dependent response to this mortality precluded the accurate prediction of population changes.

Simulations may also be used to evaluate analytical techniques, and to this end, a random number generator is particularly useful. An example of this form of computer use can be found in a publication by Slade (1977); in it, methods of detecting density-dependence in a time series of population census are summarized. A simple population model was developed in which a density-dependent function could be varied. Various statistical techniques for estimating the parameter of the density-dependent function were compared with results obtained from the analysis of a series of random numbers (no density-dependence). This could have been conducted with a programmable calculator and a random numbers table. In the field of modeling and simulation, the investigator is often limited only by his own resourcefulness.

Larry Toschik

Chapter Thirteen

Mathematical Modeling in Wildlife Management

ALAN R. TIPTON

Department of Fisheries and Wildlife Sciences
Virginia Polytechnic Institute and State University
Blacksburg, Virginia

The role of mathematical models has become well established in the general field of ecology. Recent reviews of ecological models can be found in Dale (1970), Reddingius (1971), Royama (1971), Maynard Smith (1974), and Conley and Nichols (1978). In recent years there has been increasing utilization of models in the natural resource field (Davis 1967; Watt 1968; Giles and Scott 1969; Hayne 1969; Lobdell et al. 1972; Gross et al. 1973; Bunnell 1974; Walters et al. 1974, 1975; Dolbeer at al. 1976; Guynn et al. 1976; Nichols et al. 1976; Tipton 1977; Cowardin and Johnson 1979). The migration of mathematical models and modelers into the field of wildlife ecology and management has been met with attitudes ranging from open distrust to awe. Some research and management groups blindly expect models to solve all their problems; others have recognized the potentials and limitations of modeling and have cautiously integrated modeling into their programs; others have categorically refused to consider models and have continued to conduct their research-management programs without evaluating the utility of models.

The purpose of this chapter is to introduce the reader to the basic concepts and philosophy of modeling, discuss the uses and misuses of models, and outline the processes for model development, construction and implementation. It would be impossible to present a complete overview on all aspects of modeling in one chapter. There have been numerous books written on various aspects of modeling (Patten 1971, 1972, 1975, 1976; Jeffers 1972; Maki and Thompson 1973; Thornley 1976; Gold 1977; Hall and Day 1977; Solomon and Walters 1977; deWit and Goudriaan 1978) and many other papers and chapters (Swartzmann and Van Dyne 1972, Streifer 1974, Wiegert 1975). This chapter will attempt to highlight the major topics and provide references for more detailed explanations. The major emphasis will be on mathematical models particularly mathematical population models. However, because there is a great deal that is common to all models, I will draw on information from many fields and in later sections relate these more specifically to wildlife research and management.

DEFINITION OF A MODEL

In its broadest context a model is a representation of something. Models can be physical representations such as a map or a scale model, a graph or a diagram, a mental concept or picture, or a detailed mathematical formulation. Forrester (1961) discussed how we use models in our everyday routines. Our thought processes depend on models. We consciously (and unconsciously) select only certain information from a multitude of data that we are constantly exposed to every second of our waking lives.

This selection process is necessary because of the tremendous amount of data that is constantly bombarding our senses. Only a small amount of this data is necessary for our survival; we select and use it and ignore the rest. A yellow or red traffic light may be ignored by a passenger, but hopefully not by the driver of a car. In our day-to-day existence we actually are dealing with a simplified model of the real world. We develop this model based on past experience; therefore each person will have a unique model of the world. This explains why people from other countries or cultures appear to react strangely in certain situations. The model that governs their actions is based on different customs and traditions. For another example, a deer standing at the side of the road will represent something entirely different to the person who has previously been involved in an accident with one, than it does to the average citizen. It may come as a surprise that we have all been building mental models since birth. It is not surprising that most of us were unaware of this modeling effect because it is automatic or ingrained in our natural thought processes. However, the mental image of our surroundings is, in fact, a model.

Before exploring the realm of mathematical models let us first consider some other types of models that might be more familiar to us. Physical models such as model ships or airplanes have been used by engineers for years in design and development. More recently, physical models have been used in wildlife to measure patterns of air flow and heat loss in deer and quail (Moen 1973:95). Road and soil maps, charts, graphs, and box and arrow diagrams are models that provide specific information in a readily understandable form. Another type of model is a controlled experiment in a laboratory or enclosure where live organisms are reared in an artificial environment that simulates natural situations. For example, the effects of temperature on food intake of small mammals initially could be studied in environmental chambers before attempting to conduct a similar study in natural situations. All the above models are simplifications or abstractions designed to represent more complex systems.

PURPOSE OF MODELING

What are the purposes or objectives for developing a model? What good are models and why is their use increasing? One reason that models are becoming so widely used is that, by their very nature, they are simpler than the real world system; therefore, they offer the researcher or manager a better chance to understand or control the real system. Most natural systems are so complex that it is impossible to consider all the components, their interaction, and the potential impact of even the simplest change. By constructing a model of a natural system we can then study and manipulate a much simpler system. It would be impossible to construct a model exactly like the real system. Even if possible it would serve little purpose to do so. Why study a model if it is as complicated as the real system? Clearly a major benefit of a model is its being simpler than the system that was modeled. Because it is a simplication, there must be some selection of the components to be included in the model. In modeling, especially mathematical modeling, we are forced to be precise. We must discard all but the essential features of the system in order to formulate the model. In this way modeling forces us to synthesize and organize existing knowledge. We must identify assumptions, hard facts, and areas where nothing but educated guesses will provide input into the model. Modeling also forces us to explain and quantify the interactions of the various components in the system. Solomon (1979) points out that in expressing a model mathematically we provide a language with which we can manipulate (subject to the law of mathematics and logic) the elements of the model free from our biases and interpretations. The model's performance will not be influenced by its use for predicting the number of deer to be taken in next year's harvest or how many fish should be stocked in a certain stream. Mathematical models also provide a common language with which scientists from many disciplines may communicate. Solomon (1979) states "Lurking behind every biological model is an economic model—a change of nouns affects the conversation."

The above are benefits accrued from the development of the model. More importantly for natural resource managers may be the benefits obtained from the predictive power of the model. The model can be used to predict future events in the system. The manager can then play "what if" games to evaluate alternate management strategies. This will save not only time, money, and manpower, but improper management decisions will effect only a "paper" system, not cause irreversible damage to the environment.

These different benefits of modeling have prompted several authors, notably Caswell (1976) and Solomon (1979), to classify models as either motivated by the desire to understand the real world (theoretical) or to provide a basis for prediction and control (predictive). These 2 objectives are certainly not mutually exclusive. However, the process of developing the model may be different depending on what the final product is supposed to do.

Modeling efforts whose objectives are to provide insight and further our understanding of the real world usually are governed by rules pertaining to scientific methodologies and hypothesis testing. The model, in this context, becomes inseparable from the hypothesis prediction—experimentation cycle (Conley and Nichols 1978). As part of the modeling process, hypotheses must be generated about the structure and function of the system. The model then becomes a formalization of these hypotheses and can be evaluated via methodology proposed by Popper (1959, 1963). For thorough discussions on the philosophy of modeling and modeling as an inductive-deductive process see Skellam (1972), Caswell (1976), Conley and Nichols (1978), and Innis (1979).

MODEL CLASSIFICATION

There are almost as many types of models as there are modelers, but many of these can be divided or classified into broad groups. We have already mentioned 2 distinct types of models, namely physical and abstract. A physical model is one that is physically similar to the system or object being modeled. An abstract model bears no physical resemblance to the real world system and uses symbols to represent the system; for example, verbal or mental models, box and arrow diagrams, or mathematical equations. Our main concern is with mathematical models, a special subset of abstract models.

A mathematical model consists of an equation or set of equations that represent the assumption or hypotheses about how the real system works. These equations can hopefully be solved, producing predictions about the modeled system. If the model was correctly developed and accurately describes the system, then the predictions should reflect the actual system. However, the mathematical equations do not provide any biological information. The model's output must be interpreted relative to the real world system. The model simply represents a translation from a real world situation into a quantitative language that can be more easily manipulated to provide results which must again be translated back to the real system for interpretation. We will discuss this translation process in greater detail later.

There are a number of ways of classifying mathematical models. The 2 main divisions are based on the intent or objectives for developing the model and the structure or type of mathematical formulation used. These divisions are not necessarily clear-cut nor are they universally agreed upon. Hopefully, however, presentation of some of the more common classifications may provide some insight into the various aspects of model development and construction.

We have already discussed the division based on goals or objectives for modeling. The following distinctions are closely related but are somewhat different.

Simple vs. Complex

Pielou (1969) describes 2 schools of thought on the subject of model building. One school insists that models be simple and the assumptions be kept to a minimum. The other school, mostly having developed since the advent of the high speed computer, strives for more realistic models by including as much information as possible into the model. The problem inherent in the simple model is that it may not be realistic enough to predict adequately the system's behavior. However, the more complex models, although adequately describing the system, may be so complicated that they provide little insight into how the various elements in the system interact.

Mechanistic vs. Empirical

The term mechanistic was used by Thornley (1976:4). Other synonyms for this type model are theoretical (Maynard Smith 1974, Caswell 1976), functional, biological, or heuristic (Solomon 1979). Mechanistic relates to the intent to thoroughly understand the behavior of the system and to construct the model based on this understanding (or on existing theory). It is necessary to make assumptions about how the system works, then quantify these assumptions in the model. Conversely, empirical models are usually developed using simple equations fitted to experimental data. If the equations adequately describe the natural system then mechanistic or functional relationships might then be investigated.

Analytical vs. Simulation or Numerical

Although this distinction, like the 2 discussed above, is not universally held, some researchers use the term model only for those systems that have analytical solutions, i.e., the equations can be solved by mathematical manipulations. Those models based on equations that have no solutions are referred to as simulations or simulation models. These 2 classes are quite closely related to the simple vs. complex categories since many of the simple models also have analytical solutions while the more complex models may not.

Models are also categorized on the structure or mathematical formulation.

Static vs. Dynamic

This dichotomy deals with the model's major independent variable. Dynamic models are those where time is the major independent variable. Static models are those where the independent variable is something other than time. Although most ecological models deal with change over time, there are those models that deal primarily with spatial patterns, distributions, dispersal or migration.

Discrete vs. Continuous

This dichotomy relates to the mathematical representation of the variables in the model. The elements of a continuous model vary continually over time (if a dynamic model), and each element is usually expressed mathematically as differential equations, and calculus is required to solve or manipulate the equations. Discrete models deal with finite time periods which can be expressed by difference equations and algebriac systems. A discrete model of a plant community could deal with the number of individual stems while a continuous model would use percent cover (Solomon 1979). The choice of either type model depends on the available data and the intent or objectives of the modeling effort.

An interesting discussion on whether calculus (and differential equations) is an appropriate mathematical tool for biology is presented in Williams (1977). She suggests that perhaps calculus is not adequate for expressing important biological ideas and perhaps a new mathematics may be needed.

Stochastic vs. Deterministic

A deterministic model is one in which the output of the model is uniquely determined by the input. Stochastic models attempt to include the variability of the biological world through the use of probability functions and distributions. There is quite a philosophical controversy about the use of deterministic vs. stochastic models. On one hand we are aware of the great deal of random variation in the real world, implying that a realistic model should be stochastic. On the other hand, some researchers believe that given sufficient data and understanding there is no need to use stochastic models. In any event, deterministic models can frequently be justified because they are simple and provide insight into the workings of the system. They may sometimes be viewed as a first cut or approximation to stochastic models. Stochastic models can provide information on the effects of random variation of variables and using means for variables actually having statistical distributions.

The above classifications are by no means all the ways to classify models, but these are the ways most commonly used. For further reading on these matters see Forrester (1961), Innis (1979), and Solomon (1979).

DEVELOPMENT AND CONSTRUCTION OF MODELS

Innis (1979) adopts a novel approach toward the construction and development of models by presenting it as a part of the scientific method that is, in turn, a subset of problem solving. He discusses the relationship between the 12 steps in problem solving identified by Bunge (1967:199):

1. State the problem clearly
2. Identify the constituents: What are the parts of the problem?
3. Unearth the presuppositions
4. Locate the problem
5. Select a method
6. Simplify
7. Analyze the problem
8. Plan: Identify all the steps that will be taken in the problem solution process.
9. Look for similar solved problems
10. Transform the problem. If a similar problem has been solved elsewhere, transform the current one to that area.
11. Export the problem. Work on the transformed problem in the arena to which it has been moved.
12. Control the solution. The problem arose and has been solved for some purpose. Control the solution to achieve that purpose.

Innis compares these with the 8 steps by which science is advanced, also taken from Bunge (1967:8):

1. Ask well formulated and likely fruitful questions
2. Devise hypotheses, both grounded and testable, to answer the questions
3. Derive the logical consequences of the assumptions
4. Design the techniques to test the assumptions
5. Test the techniques for relevance and reliability
6. Execute the tests and interpret their results
7. Evaluate the truth claims of the assumptions and the fidelity of the techniques
8. State the new problems raised. In scientific studies the product of one set of experiments often raises more questions than it resolves. This brings us back to step 1.

By comparing the steps of each method one sees the similarities in these 2 efforts and how they relate. Innis then lists and discusses 7 ways for constructing a model:

1. Determine and state the objectives. Model objectives provide the problem statement.
2. Formulate and state the hypothesis. To achieve the modeling objectives we must have hypotheses about the system structure and functions as regards the objectives.
3. Formulation of mechanisms. Each hypothesis must ultimately be converted to a mathematical form for coding into a computer program.
4. Code the model. Convert the collection of mathematical expressions into computer cards.
5. Model experiments. These experiments relate to location of syntax and logical errors in the model.
6. Mechanism analysis and refinement. Part of mechanism analysis is the detection of errors in the formulation of the mechanisms. Another part is to vary poorly known parameters in an attempt to force certain model output.
7. Laboratory or field experiments. Placing the modeling activity before the experiment can be paraphrased as "synthesize what you do and do not know before launching into a collection of data through laboratory and field studies."

The above is but one author's approach to modeling. The comparison between model development, problem solving, and the scientific method should be informative since most of us may be more familiar with the latter 2 endeavors than with model development. Other methods for developing models have been proposed by Holling (1966), Levins (1966), Morris (1967), Hayne (1969), Goodall (1972), Gold (1977), Hall and Day (1977), Conley and Nichols (1978), and Solomon (1979).

For our purposes we shall use a methodology presented by McLeod (1974) and modified and discussed by Harold Rauscher (pers. comm.). McLeod's basic steps for formulating a dynamic systems model are:

1. Verbal description of the system
2. Precise definition of the problem
   a. Reference mode
   b. Definition of boundaries
   c. Time frame or horizon
3. Construction of casual loop
4. Formulation of a flow diagram
5. Writing the equations
6. Instrumentation of the model
7. Analysis of the model
   a. Comparison with the reference mode
   b. Sensitivity testing
   c. Policy testing
8. Evaluation, communication, implementation of recommendations.

Before using the above outline to develop a model, it should first be emphasized that modeling is an iterative, trial, and error process. Regardless of the choice of steps or procedures the model is usually developed in steps of increasing complexity until the results fit the objectives of the modeling effort. This iterative process can be idealized as in Fig. 13.1. The figure emphasizes the cyclic nature of the modeling process; however, the starting point should be with the development of the model and not with the collection of real world data. As Innis (1979) pointed out, experimentation and data collection should follow the modeling effort, not precede it. The model should provide insight into what data is required. All too often, the model is constructed after the data has been collected. The modeling exercise then becomes one of constructing a model with the available data and hoping it will suffice. Obviously a certain amount of advance information is required to develop a model. However, the model should be used to design and guide the research or management program, not salvage it.

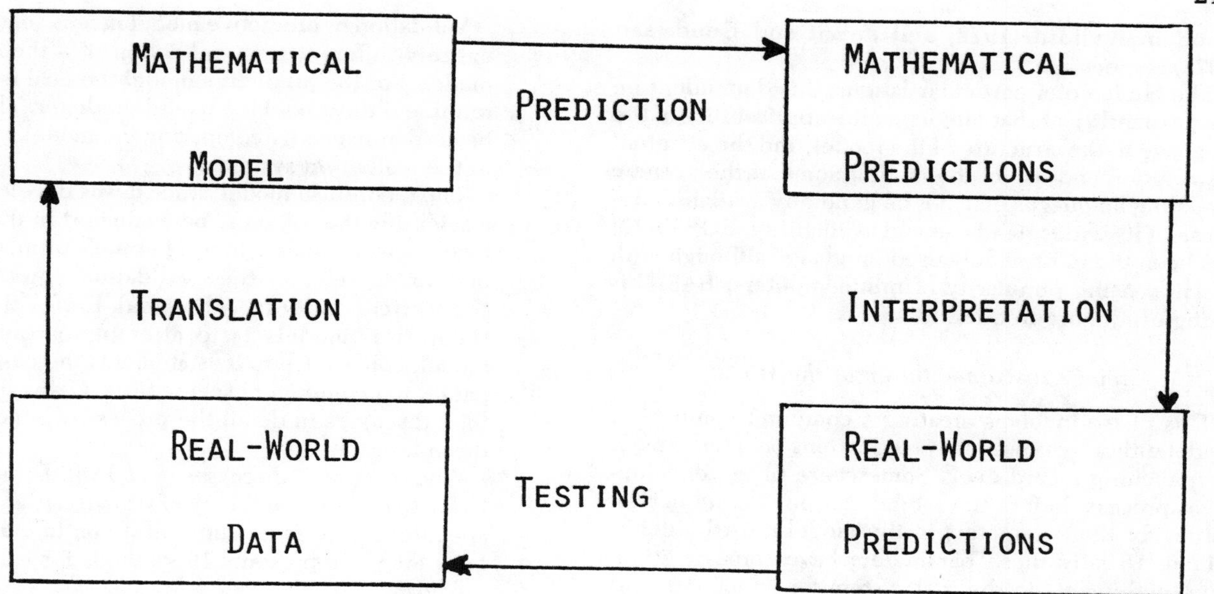

Fig. 13.1. Cyclic nature of model construction (after Roberts 1976).

In our attempt to develop a model we will start with the real world system and the procedure that Roberts (1976) calls translation. Using McLeod's outline we shall discuss the steps in developing a model and then illustrate these procedures for a model of the wild boar population in Great Smoky Mountains National Park.

Step 1. Verbal Description of the System

This represents the verbal summary of the information about the system. This step should involve the collection and synthesis of all past research, summarizing personal experience, etc. In essence this step is the construction of a mental model of the real-world system.

Step 2. Precise Definition of the Problem

This step requires a clear statement of the problem that the model will address. This is a very important step which should include not only problem definition but also a statement of the objectives of the modeling effort. The delineation of the problem requires selecting those factors that are affecting the system, the objectives of the modeling effort, the ultimate role of the model and some standards for its evaluation. This step is similar to Innis' steps 1 and 2.

a. Reference mode
The reference mode is a sketch of the dynamics of the problem as they are already occurring or envisioned to occur in the future.
b. Definition of boundaries
The boundaries that separate the elements of the system must be defined and distinguished from those factors that do not influence the system.
c. Time frame
The time frame is the length of time over which the system behavior develops. Recognition of the time frame directs the choice of dynamic processes to be included in the model, which in turn dictates how the process should be represented mathematically.

Step 3. Construction of a Causal Loop Diagram

This is a preliminary sketch of the causal relationships between the major components. The construction of the causal loop represents the translation of the verbal or mental model into a graphic or diagrammatic model.

Step 4. Formulation of the Flow Diagram

This is a more accurate picture of the system's structure and can take 2 forms. In systems analysis, flow diagrams are used to illustrate flows of information and materials between the components of the model. The flow diagram is also used to design the actual computer program and consists of an outline of the various loops and logical steps in the program. Both uses of the flow diagram are important and should be used in the modeling effort. More recently there have been several good books written on program construction and design (Yourdon 1975, Higgins 1979) that should be consulted before actually writing the computer program.

Step 5. Writing the Equations

This stage constitutes the final step in quantifying assumptions and selecting parameters and mathematical equations representing the dynamics of the system. Innis (1979) thoroughly discusses methodologies for expressing functional relationships and developing mathematical expressions. He points out that quite different hypotheses may have similar formulations in mathematical terms. It is at this stage that decisions must be made on whether the model will be analytical or numerical in structure, will represent time as continuous or discrete, and will have deterministic or stochastic elements. In addition, the computer programming language must be selected. There are several languages that have been developed specifically for modeling ecological systems; they are discussed in Radford (1970). Detailed descriptions of 2 languages, DYNAMO and CSMP, may be found in Radford (1972) and deWit and Goudriaan (1978) respectively.

The choice of a particular language is dependent on the availability of that language, the applicability of the language to the structure of the model, and the eventual distribution and use of the model. Some of the specific modeling languages may not be generally available. Because of its widespread use and availability, FORTRAN has been the most widely used language, although with the increasing popularity of minicomputers, BASIC is being used more frequently.

Step 6. Instrumentation of the Model

This phase involves creating a computer compatible model either by typing in the equations on a teletype or keypunching a card deck. Somewhere in the development process, before the model can be run, numerical values for the parameters in the model must be determined. Usually these parameters have some relationship to elements in the real system for which data has been previously collected. But sometimes it is necessary to modify or manipulate the data to make it compatible with the model, (i.e., yearly birth rate reduced to seasonal, etc.). In other cases there is not available data and estimates must be obtained from the literature or by educated guesses. Goodall (1972) and Innis (1979) discuss several ways to estimate parameter values.

The next step is verification of the model. This includes checking for any typing or logical errors and making sure the program runs as intended. This phase also includes checking the output of the model for gross predictions that indicate either internal problems with the program or with the formulation of the equations. This activity should not be confused with validating the model. Innis (1979) clearly discusses the steps of verification and validation. He separates verification into 2 parts. Verification I refers to checking and debugging the computer program. Verification II is directed toward determining if the program and code truthfully represent the mathematical formulation.

Step 7. Analysis of the Model

This involves using the model to simulate the system and usually involves 3 stages.

a. *Comparison of model's output to the real system.* This is the validation process. In its simplest form this process can be accomplished by comparing the model's output with data collected on the real system. The normal procedure, at least in theory, dictates that the data used for validation is not the same data used to develop the model. However, the validation process is seldom this straight forward. Innis (1979) again breaks the process into 2 steps. Validation I attempts to determine if the mathematical formulation adequately represents the hypotheses. Validation II attempts to determine if the hypotheses were appropriate for achieving the objectives of the modeling effort.

Caswell (1976) points out that the method for validating models should be dependent on the type (theoretical or predictive) and motivation for developing the model.

Validation of predictive model means something entirely different from validation of a theoretical model. For the predictive model the goal is to determine if the model is a useful predictor. This can be accomplished by comparing the model's output to the real world system.

The theoretical model, since it was developed as a scientific theory, must be evaluated in that context. Caswell chooses to use Popper's term, corroboration, to refer to the "validation" process for theoretical models. The goal for evaluating theoretical models is to attempt to refute the model; confidence in its statements increases as it passes more and more severe tests. Caswell (1976) then discusses in detail the process of conducting these tests.

Giles (in prep.) discusses model validation in relation to the general theory of knowledge and more specifically, as an example of a continuous feedback loop. He presents 10 methods for validating models.

1. Sensory—hands on experience in running a model, manipulating variables, etc.
2. Private—assertive validity. This represents the modeler's overall view of the model, its performance and his willingness to accept the risk of using it.
3. Induction—also called empirical validity. Inductive validity is the method generally referred to as validation and involves comparing the model's output with real world. Giles contends that this method, although generally accepted, is perhaps no better than many of the other 9 methods. Because of the problems and errors inherent in inductive validation, he presently places as much faith in mature computer models as in "hard" research results.
4. Contextual—also called face validity. This is achieved by asking people who know the system to evaluate the model.
5. Authority—similar to the above, an expert evaluates the model to see if it represents the system with which he is knowledgeable.
6. Coherence—"Theoretical validity" has been used to describe the extent the model conforms to theoretical and logical principles. This method is similar to Caswell's corroboration.
7. Pragmatism—does the model work? The theorist wants a coherent model, the pragmatist one that works.
8. Correspondence—internal validity, testing a model throughout its extremes to see if outputs correspond to reality.
9. Probability—by generating hundreds of results using different inputs or time frames the outputs can be observed, treated statistically, and compared with acceptable limits of reasonableness.
10. Heuristic convergence—rather than rely on a single "perfect" validation methodology, validity at a point in time is expressed, probabilistically as a function of the above methods and sequential

plans for continued work on validation are specified along with criteria for success.

The above methodology and underlying philosophy represents a somewhat radical divergence from the generally accepted methods for validation. However, with increasing use of models in the mangement-decision making process, for which the systems may be poorly understood and hard data lacking for validation, some of the above methods may be the only means for evaluating these models.

b. *Testing the sensitivity of the model to changes in parameter values.* Assuming at this stage that the model has been debugged and is providing "realistic" results, sensitivity analysis is an attempt to determine for which variables the model is most sensitive. This can be accomplished by varying individual or groups of parameters and observing changes in the model's output. The purpose of this exercise is to determine the relative effects of errors in the estimates of each of the parameters. Additional, more accurate data may be needed for parameters that have large effects on the output. Conversely, data need not be particularly accurate if the model is not sensitive to certain parameters. For large complex models sensitivity analysis becomes exceedingly difficult if not impossible. For discussion of sensitivity analysis see Wiegert (1975) and Innis (1979). Chapter 15 of this manual contains an example of a sensitivity analysis of a simple model.

c. *Assessing the effects of alternate policy of the system's behavior.* This stage involves changing specific parameters to simulate changes in management policy. This represents playing the "what if" game to evaluate changes in model output brought about by changing parameters or relationships, i.e., "What would happen if we implement an either sex deer season for 1 week instead of 1 day?"

Step 8. Evaluation, Communication, and Implementation

The model should now be evaluated on its ability to produce the same behavior as the system. The standard for evaluation should be stated among the objectives for developing the model. If the purpose of the model was to provide additional understanding of the system and determine areas for future research, the evaluation process probably has been carried on throughout the entire development phase. However, if the ultimate goal was predictive power or to suggest management strategies, then the output of the model must be evaluated by some predetermined standards: "How good a fit is good enough?"

The importance of communication cannot be overemphasized. This entails not only communication among those developing the model, if it is a team effort, but also externally with potential users of the model. The model should be well documented so that it can be used by other research groups as well as managers or decision makers. Documentation should consist of a verbal description of all variables, sources for parameter estimates if input data was obtained from literature, a detailed flow diagram with verbal description of subroutines and self-contained portions of the program, and a detailed user's guide or handbook describing how to run the model.

Communication is also important to provide users some understanding of the basic assumptions and potential weaknesses that are inherent in the model. Often modelers tend to oversell the utility of the model to secure funding for the project. At the present time few managers or decision makers, if they were not involved in the development of the model, understand modeling and are forced to accept results of the model at face value. It is the *modeler's responsibility* to point out where the model should or should not be applied and how much faith should be placed in its output. This will be discussed in more detail in the concluding section of this chapter.

Implementation refers to making optimum use of the results of a simulation study to influence the real-world system. The understanding and insight gained in developing the model is often justification for the effort; however, in most cases the model was developed with a more pragmatic goal in mind. Only by integrating the model into the research-management program can the model affect the real-world system.

ILLUSTRATIVE EXAMPLE

To illustrate the development of a mathematical population model, let us consider the population of European wild boar in the Great Smoky Mountains National Park (GSMNP). Much interest, both ecologically and politically, has been generated on this species and will serve as a good example. The model was developed as my Ph.D. dissertation (Tipton 1975), modified as a class exercise for graduate level population dynamics class (Tipton 1977), and used in conjunction with the analysis of population data for the National Park Service (Singer et al. 1978). This process took place over a 6-year period and in 3 phases but will be presented below as if it was a single modeling effort.

Step 1. Verbal Description of the System

The population of European wild boar, an exotic species introduced in North Carolina in 1912 (see Bratton 1975 for details), is presently inhabiting 2/3 of the GSMNP and is expanding its range into the remaining 1/3 of the Park. The boar appears to have no natural predators; and, since hunting is not allowed in the Park, their numbers and range in recent years have greatly increased. It is strongly believed that this species is harmful to the flora and fauna of the Park and that some effort should be made to control population levels or eliminate the species from the Park. There has been sufficient research done on European wild boar in Europe and in the Smokies, in addition to research on feral domestic hogs, to provide data for an initial modeling effort.

Step 2. Precise Definition of Problem

In an effort to reduce the detrimental effects of the wild boar population in GSMNP: (1) A better understanding of the dynamics of the population is needed, and (2) the effects of various control procedures must be evaluated.

a. Reference Mode
   Population density appears to be stable in occupied range of Park, and unoccupied portion will probably be invaded within next several years.
b. Boundary of System
   Because there are no known predators on wild boar in GSMNP and the effects of competition with other species is unknown, the model will contain only the boar population with the capabilities for including the effects of hunting or control. It was reported earlier that the mast crop may influence the survival and reproductive success of the wild boar. Data was obtained from Tennessee Game and Fish Commission (1972) and Frank Singer (pers. comm.) relating to mast influence on litter size and percent breeding. Not enough was known about the effects of other environmental variables such as temperature or precipitation to warrant inclusion of the mode.
c. Time Frame
   The time frame for evaluating management strategies had to be of sufficient length (5 to 10 years) to actually determine the long term effects of control programs. Because females have been known to reach sexual maturity at 6 months of age, it was decided to use a discrete time frame with 6-month time intervals to simulate 2 seasons, only one of which is greatly affected by mast. With a 6-month time step, little detail is lost and multiyear simulations are possible.

Step 3. Construction of Causal Loop

Figure 13.2 is the graphic representation of the causal loop. The population-level parameters of density, age structure, and sex ratio are affected by the (1) reproduction and natural mortality, both of which are affected by the quality and quantity of the mast crop, and (2) the effect of man-caused mortality via the control program.

Step 4. Formulation of Flow Diagram

Because the model is biologically quite simple, Fig. 13.2, representing the causal loop, may also serve as the flow diagram. In most modeling efforts the flow diagram should be more detailed. Because the model selected for this research effort is quite lengthy, no flow diagram of the computer program will be presented here.

Step 5. Writing the Equations

Because of the lack of a detailed data base for the wild boar population it was decided to use a model previously constructed, based on a modified Leslie matrix. Briefly, the model is based on a system of difference equations developed by Leslie (1945). The elements of the equations were variables representing the probability of animals surviving from 1 time period until the next (P_x) and the number of offspring produced by females of a certain age during each time period (F_x). The model had the capability to group animals into different age classes and to separate both males and females. The

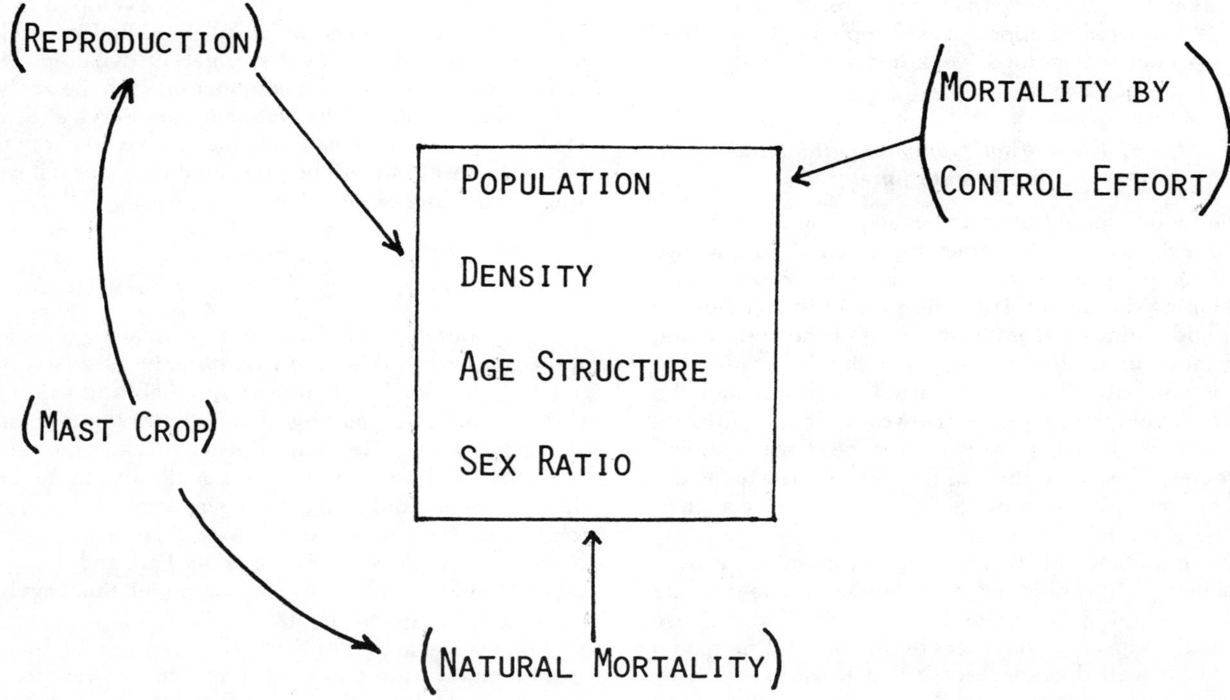

Fig. 13.2. Conceptual model of population parameters and interactions.

model also was capable of simulating changes in the number of females in breeding condition as a result of good or bad mast crops. The model was basically deterministic using mean values for reproduction, percent breeding, and probability of survival although it has the capabilities to use stochastic functions for survival and reproduction. Information from the literature and the data collected in GSMNP was detailed enough to justify separating the population into different age classes. No differences in mortality related to sex could be distinguished so only the female portion of the population was included in the model and numbers doubled to produce total population density. The program was written in FORTRAN IV.

Step 6. Instrumentation of the Model

The model was originally written and run on the Control Data Computer at Michigan State University. The program was verified and debugged at this facility. However, when the model was run on the IBM computer at VPI & SU it was found that several of the FORTRAN statements were not compatible between the 2 systems and had to be modified. This problem can be especially frustrating and time consuming if the program or data happens to be on magnetic tape rather than computer cards since translating magnetic tapes can still pose major problems between different research facilities.

Step 7. Analysis of the Model

The model was used to simulate population dynamics over 10 and 15 year periods with various control strategies employed (Tipton 1977).

Population density data for GSMNP was not being collected so comparison of the model's output with the real world system was not possible. However, the age structure and population trends were considered to be fairly realistic by Park personnel (Frank Singer, pers. comm.). Sensitivity analysis was conducted on the model by decreasing survival rates of different age classes. Results, as expected, indicated that reductions in younger age classes had greater effects on population density than reductions in older age classes.

Step 8. Evaluation, Communication, and Implementation

The evaluation of the model was hampered by a lack of detailed quantitative data on the population. However, the main objective of the modeling effort was to provide insight into the reaction of the wild boar population to possible control strategies. In this sense the modeling effort was successful. Results from the model showed that due to the reproductive potential of the wild boar population and the extreme difficulty of reducing the population, the complete elimination or even a moderate reduction of the population for the whole Park was a biological impossibility using existing control procedures.

Since modeling is an iterative process, the role of field experimentation and additional research aimed at improving parameter estimation and modifying model estimates cannot be overemphasized. The model should provide insight into additional information needed. The iterative process also may involve increasing the biological realism of the model. It might be informative to see how this model could be modified to achieve this goal. Goodall (1972:180) discusses 3 ways to increase complexity in a model.

1. The (state) variables can be subdivided. In simple models there is usually a great deal of clumping. An attempt was made in this direction in modifying the original Leslie matrix model by adding an additional parameter that represented the percent of the females in each class that were in breeding condition. In this way the single reproductive variable, F_x, was now expressed as 2 separate variables, litter size, m_x, and a percent breeding variable and both could vary under changing environmental conditions.
2. Take into account a larger number of variables. In this case if the effects of weather conditions on reproduction or survival could be determined this variable could be included in the model in addition to the effect of mast crops.
3. Include more detailed mechanisms. It has been previously emphasized that the model that was developed was quite simple. There was no feedback loop between the population processes such as reproduction or survival and population density nor was there any functional relationship between mast crop and reproduction. Given adequate bioenergetic information, i.e., physiological effects of protein and energy on survival and reproduction and protein-energy availability in the vegetation, functional relationships could be developed that would increase the biological realism of the model in addition to supplying a density dependent mechanism (Tipton 1975:33).

The above additions or modifications could be made to the existing model. In addition, the separation of animals by sex could be accomplished if data indicated that survival was sex specific. However, the most glaring shortcoming of this model and many other dynamic population models in use today is the omission of a spatial component. The population is treated as homogeneous without reference to individual or group movement patterns or clumping.

In recent studies in GSMNP, the wild boar population has exhibited seasonal movement patterns. These patterns are in response to weather conditions and food availability. Knowledge of these movement patterns and how they are affected by environmental variables and man could be very important in developing a management program that would emphasize reduction or control in certain areas and at certain times of the year. The presently developed model could not, in its present form, be modified to address changes in both time and space, and in some circumstances it may be easier and more efficient to start completely over and develop a new model rather than modify a model that was developed with specialized objectives and structure. Conley and Nichols (1978) review and discuss models that deal with both the temporal and spatial aspect of population ecology.

CONCLUSIONS AND RECOMMENDATIONS

The above sections briefly outline the steps in developing a model and discuss some of the aspects of modeling-research interaction. This chapter has been directed mainly toward model development as conducted by the research scientist. Several years ago there was concern over the lack of modelers who knew any biology and of the lack of biologists who knew any modeling. Through modeling workshops and retraining programs this problem is no longer critical. These 2 groups are now communicating frequently and working on joint modeling efforts. In addition, through modifying and restructuring college curricula a new breed of quantitative ecologist has emerged, equipped to handle both biological and quantitative problems with equal skill. Today more and more management agencies are turning to models as aides in decision making. These models range in scope from purely ecologically oriented models for setting harvest seasons to multidisciplinary models for determining optimum use of the total natural resource base.

The problems inherent in this new use of modeling are probably no greater than the problems inherent in modeling ecological systems. However, one major problem facing managers (and modelers of management systems) is how to measure management (and models') output. What units does one use to measure benefits to society from our natural resources, and how can one construct a model that can quantify these benefits? It is again worth restating in this context that the primary role in modeling may be forcing modelers and managers to formalize their objectives so that the modeling process can be integrated into the management process. This will entail a much closer interaction between these 2 groups, more workshops, and possibly revision and modification of college curricula (Tipton and Lackey 1978).

Giles (1979) discusses the question of whether to model decisions or ecological systems and concludes that although there are major differences in managers and researchers there is a need to model both decisions and ecosystems. The implications are that decisions need to be analyzed if ecosystems are to be designed or shaped. "Once the omnipresent role of human decisions is seen, in even the most basic or fundamental efforts, it would not seem too great a compromise to include decision making in the larger managerial sense in the work to be done and the design of models."

A good example of the use of modeling in management can be found in the many states that have adopted ONEPOP (Gross et al. 1973 and further discussed by Pojar 1977) as a management tool. This simulation model was used during a series of workshops conducted for the potential users (wildlife biologists, area supervisors, etc). This method of using workshops to introduce the manager-decision makers to the potential uses of the model is not as good as having the manager involved in the development of the model, but it is certainly better than no introduction and avoids the time-consuming process of model development.

In conclusion, no paper on modeling would be complete without some words of caution on the use of models. Models appear to be here to stay and will doubtlessly play an increasingly important role in all aspects of management and research of our natural resources. It should be remembered, however, *that a model is only a tool.* It will not solve all the problems involved in understanding and managing, nor will it supercede the need for well-trained biologists and managers. The utility of models can only be as good as the foresight and planning ability of the managers and the basic biological understanding of the biologists.

Chapter Fourteen

Estimating the Numbers of Wildlife Populations

DAVID E. DAVIS

777 S. Picacho Lane
Santa Barbara, California

RAY L. WINSTEAD

Associate Professor
Indiana University of Pennsylvania
Indiana, Pennsylvania

INTRODUCTION

The material presented in this chapter is designed for a wildlifer starting an investigation that requires a knowledge of how many animals are present either now or in the future. It is intended for a person located somewhere in the field who lacks an extensive library and sophisticated computers, although such aids are available with a little effort and planning. The person should examine the methods presented here, try the ones that seem most appropriate, consult with whatever specialists are available, and decide after a few months of trial, whether or not (a) any type of census is necessary for his investigation, (b) these simple methods satisfy his needs, or (c) specialists in census methods should be consulted. Additional help in these decisions may be obtained in the voluminous literature on methods, some oriented for a species and others for the topic. Thus, this chapter is a *manual* for use in estimating wildlife populations rather than a review of research.

The methods of estimating numbers of animals have now achieved a level of sophistication worthy of a mature science. Conceptually the methods have gone from simple counts to complex relations, involving numerous assumptions. Technically the calculations have progressed from pencil and paper to computer. The recent literature is vast and much of it highly mathematical. For example, the excellent article (Eberhardt 1978a) on transect methods can not be abstracted here but must be examined in the journal. This chapter will attempt to achieve 2 objectives: (1) present the conceptual basis for census methods, and (2) describe a few methods in sufficient detail so that with a little effort the field worker can follow them. It would be desirable to include specific instructions for carrying out a census, much as is done in the standard laboratory manuals for bacteriology or engineering subjects. Unfortunately, it has been necessary to refer the reader to original literature for these details.

Several problems occur while attempting to describe census methods. One is that only 2 basic methods exist and hence presentation would either be in 2 big groups or in many small divisions that would inevitably result in some duplication. We decided to compromise and divide the discussion into more than 2 divisions, but have lumped several methods under some headings, recognizing that some methods are very similar. Another problem is where to discuss the evaluation and comparison of methods. It seemed that less confusion results if the comparisons are placed in 1 group at the end of the chapter rather than with each particular method. A third difficulty is the problem of species accounts. It would be very desirable to have a section devoted to each species. Unfortunately space would not allow this detailed treatment.

This revision leans heavily on the organization of the second edition of the *Wildlife Investigational Techniques* (Mosby 1963a). More recent modifications of concepts are noticed and many recent examples are included. Earlier references are retained if the data are needed to provide examples, but the literature is now so voluminous that inclusion of all references would produce an unmanageable list. Therefore many references to older works will be omitted but can be found in the second edition of *Wildlife Investigational Techniques.* Fortunately, many of the recent publications describe attempts to adjust for assumptions made in older methods. Also some recent monographs review various methods for a species or a group of species (e.g., Eberhardt et al. 1979). The recent elaboration of computer programs permits calculations at a level not imagined even a decade ago. However, it is only possible in this chapter to refer to readily available computer programs (Sokal and Rohlf 1969) and to indicate their role in wildlife investigations.

This chapter has been written for the person planning or leading a study that requires knowledge of abundance. It is assumed that the person is familiar with the ecology of the species, with the behavior patterns that affect census methods, and with the elements of sampling. This person must be able to look up references in the original literature and also to follow statistical explanations.

GENERAL CONSIDERATIONS

The purpose of this chapter is to classify and illustrate various methods of estimating numbers in wildlife populations and to explain the advantages and disadvantages of the methods. Also, where data are available, the accuracy of each method will be indicated.

All methods of estimating wild animal populations have 2 basic assumptions which *must* be considered:

1. Mortality and recruitment during the period when data are collected are negligible or, if not, are corrected in the estimates. For example, collection of data about the rabbit, which has a high turnover rate, should be restricted to the shortest possible time or at a season when recruitment and mortality are not appreciable. Movement out of a population is treated as part of mortality; movement into it as part of recruitment.
2. All members of the population have an equal (or known) probability of being counted. For example, in the trapping, marking, and releasing technique of population estimation, the animal must not develop trap-aversion or trap-addiction, must mix randomly in the population after being marked, and must not group by sex, age, or other characteristics. In other words, any sample must be representative of the population.

The wildlife biologist preparing the population estimate must determine if these 2 assumptions are met to an acceptable degree; if they are not, the estimate will be fallacious, irrespective of the accuracy, precision or fineness of the "census" technique employed.

Before describing the methods in detail it is important to clarify several terms. A clear distinction should be made between *accuracy, precision,* and *fineness.* Consider a population of pheasants that is *known* to contain 84 birds. A method might give a result of 82 birds due to bias in instruments, errors of arithmetic, etc. The answer is correct only to an *accuracy* of 2 birds. In contrast, *precision* refers to the repeatability of the measurements. Estimates on 3 different days might be 40, 60, and 152 giving an accurate average of 84; or the estimates might be 82, 87, and 83, also giving an accurate average of 84. The latter is much more *precise.* A third term, *fineness,* is sometimes used to indicate the level of measurement. A fine measurement would be recorded in terms of individual birds; whereas a less fine measurement would be in terms of tens or hundreds.

The word "census" is defined as a count, which includes details as to sex, age, etc. of a given species for a given area. As such, it means an actual count; for example, the number of rabbits in a cage. Since such counts of wild animals are rarely possible, or even desirable because of the cost required, estimates usually are obtained by some sampling procedure. These estimates, being samples, have variability, but permit inferences about the population. Each estimate should be expressed in the statistical form, i.e., "We do not know how many deer are in this forest but the chances are that 95 out of 100 estimates will be between 280 and 340." Such an estimate is usually expressed as the mean (310) plus or minus 2 standard errors of the mean. An estimate is not a census, and biologists should be careful to make that distinction clear.

Another distinction of importance occurs between the terms *bias* and *sampling error.* Bias deprives an estimate of representativeness by systematically distorting it. For example, an estimate based on a sex ratio would be biased in favor of the males if the males are more conspicuous than females. In contrast, sampling error may distort the result on many occasions but not always in the same direction, and so may tend to balance out the average.

The question of determining whether 2 populations differ in number is related intricately to the question of precision. In the example of the pheasant mentioned above, the average in both cases was 84; in the first case, however, the precision was low and in the second it was high. When the precision was low, the standard error was high (29 pheasants) and hence the result is "the chances are 95 out of 100 that between 26 and 142 pheasants are in the area." In the second case, when precision was high, the standard error was low (about 1.3) and so the conclusion is "the chances are 95 out of

100 that between 81 and 87 pheasants are in the area." The advantage of high precision in this case is the narrowing of the probable limits of the estimate. One should remember, however, that the answer may be inaccurate because of some error in the method or failure to meet the basic assumptions. It also could be biased.

When the limits of the estimate are narrow, the detection of small differences is possible. To illustrate this advantage, suppose that in the following year other estimates of pheasant numbers were made, one with low and the other with high precision. Suppose the first estimate indicated between 60 and 182 birds and the second indicated between 118 and 124 (the average is 121 in both cases). The estimates with low precision overlap for both years (26 to 142 and 60 to 182), and hence we cannot conclude that the population increased. The estimates with high precision (82–87 and 118–124) do not overlap and hence we can suspect that the pheasant population has increased. To reach a definite conclusion the actual tests for significance must be done because the "overlap" test is merely a crude way of making a preliminary guess about the significance of differences. The importance of precision has, however, a converse aspect. If the population has changed greatly, then an estimate of low precision is all that is needed to detect the difference. Under these circumstances one need not spend the time and money necessary to obtain an estimate of high precision.

The cost of estimating an animal population requires a few comments here. Estimates with high accuracy and precision cost money due to extra time and manpower needed to obtain large samples and to double-check field records, calculations, and instruments, and may not be justified by the needs of the study. Before an estimate of a population is made, considerable thought should be given to the precision required and the associated cost of attaining that precision. These remarks apply to the results of esoteric experiments as well as to problems requiring administrative decision. More discussion of the need for precision is included under comparison of estimates at the end of this chapter.

Another pair of terms need definition. An *absolute* count or estimate includes the total population and, within the limits of the assumptions, gives a number of animals present within a specified area. From such counts or estimates one can draw conclusions about the size of a population. A *relative* method simply indicates increases or decreases but does not give the numbers. Relative counts may, for example, be presented as + or −, or percentage increasing. Nonparametric statistics usually are appropriate for relative methods (Siegel 1956, Linton and Gallo 1975). Such techniques may satisfy the needs of the manager and may be much cheaper than absolute methods.

It is also important to distinguish clearly between a *count* and an *estimate*. If we find by counting that room A has 20 students and room B has 19, then the answer to the question "Which room has more students?" is obviously A. No sampling or statistical procedures are involved. But if we ask whether the rooms on 1 floor (represented by A) have more students than on another floor (represented by B), then A and B are only samples and the appropriate statistical procedures must be applied to distinguish between the estimates.

The word *estimate* has at least 2 meanings: (1) a vernacular term for a guess at a number as contrasted to a count; (2) a statistical term referring to an average and its range of values, as determined by a definite set of rules (statistics). Only the second meaning is used here.

Estimating the size of an animal population requires 2 basic steps. The *first* is to get the data and the *second* is to calculate the result. The data may be obtained by visual counts of animals (with or without trapping) or enumeration of their signs (here defined as any evidence of their presence that does not require seeing the animal, e.g., tracks, droppings, nest, song). These data are then used to calculate the estimate and its sampling error except when the data are a true count. If a count does not measure the population directly, a variety of estimating calculations may be used, usually employing *ratios* to indicate the number seen per unit (time, trap, etc.). All of the methods described here are techniques for sampling the population and calculating an appropriate ratio.

In studies of populations great effort has been expended on techniques for collecting data and in calculating from them population size. But little study has been made of the basic assumption of all methods; namely, that the unknown ratio is the same as the known ratio. An illustration may make this point clear. By some procedure it may be determined that a pheasant cock crows 10 times per hour. This is a known ratio. Now a count in nature may be 30 crows per hour, and the population estimate is thus 3 pheasants. Should the conditions for obtaining the latter "unknown" ratio be different from those for the former "known" ratio, the transposition to the final estimate will, of course, be in error. It is assumed that this difference is small and has only a trivial effect on the conclusion. The big job of the wildlife biologist is to test this assumption, rather than to be concerned with little changes in the techniques of getting or calculating data.

The term *index* generally refers to the census or estimate of some object related to the number of animals. The reason for using an index is that the object is easier to count than the animal itself. Examples of indices are calling counts of mourning doves, tracks of deer, and houses of muskrats. The use of an index adds an assumption: the ratio of the index to the population is the same in the several populations being compared.

Clarification of the terms ratio and index is necessary. *Every* census or estimate occurs within some unit such as hectare, hour, state, etc. Thus the result is a ratio, although sometimes the denominator is omitted. Thus we have rabbits seen per km, tracks made per square meter, gulls landing per hour and so forth. These are ratios, not indices. An index is a count of an object somehow related to the animal such as feces, tracks, songs, etc. The related object must be studied to determine its ratio to the wildlife population. Thus a study might show that 7 deer are present for 100 cows, or that 0.3 rabbits occur on a square km. Then by counting the related object (the index) a calculation can be made from the ratio to determine the population. To clearly illustrate this confusing concept, consider a study of beaver populations (Table 14.1). A count of houses per pond from an airplane yielded 1.8 houses per pond. Thus the count was 1.8. (Note that the unit is houses per pond.) If one were interested in houses (not beavers) one would stop at this stage since one has a census of houses. But when one wants to determine how many beavers are present, one uses houses as an index. Trapping revealed 3.6 beavers per house. This is the population. (Note that the unit is beavers per house.) One can use the count of houses as an index of beavers. To get those figures one has to use the figure for beavers per house (note units):

$$\frac{1.8 \text{ houses}}{\text{pond}} \times \frac{3.6 \text{ beavers}}{\text{house}} = \frac{6.3 \text{ beavers}}{\text{pond}}$$

These calculations are replete with assumptions that will be discussed later.

A difficult feature of census procedures is to know what proportion of the population is detectable. The estimates mentioned in an earlier example result from techniques that rely upon seeing or hearing the pheasants. No measure of the animals present, but not seen or heard, is taken by these techniques. For example, the number of gobblers seen, pheasants killed, or doves nesting is tabulated, but the number of individuals present but not observed is unknown. Therefore, estimates based on these techniques include only a part of the population. The portion tabulated may be less or much more than the portion not tabulated, but it is never all of the population. In field studies the assumption must be made that the same proportion of the total population is tabulated each time the same technique is used under similar field conditions with the same species.

Remember that the *true census* is a count of all individuals present on a given area. It is not a sample but an actual count of all animals present; hence, there can be no standard deviation. It can be inaccurate because of errors; however if signs, such as beaver houses, are counted, it is a census of beaver houses and an index to the beaver population. A *sampling estimate* is derived from partial counts made on sample plots which are not expected to yield uniform counts, thus are said to have variance. While the count on each plot is a census for that plot, usually the plot is only 1 of many plots from which the estimate for a larger area is derived.

Table 14.1. Number of houses and beaver in several colonies, Colorado (Hay, 1958).

Colony Number	Active Houses	Trapped Beavers
1	2	10
2	1	7
3	2	8
4	1	3
5	1	11
6	3	7
7	1	4
8	1	7
9	1	6
10	1	2
11	3	3
12	3	5
13	3	9

The several techniques of getting data for estimating wild-animal populations may be classified broadly as follows:

- I. Count animals
  - A. Count of all animals present in a given area
    1. No statistical assumptions required
    2. Is true census—not an estimate
       Example: Deer on a small island
  - B. Sample Counts
    1. Assumes samples are random
    2. Usefulness depends upon precision
    3. Is an estimate—not a census
       Example: Average number of quail per farm
- II. Count signs (tracks, calls, etc.)
  - A. Count of all signs in a given area
    1. Assumes that each animal leaves sign and that each individual's sign is observed
    2. No statistical assumptions required
    3. Is a true census—not an estimate
       Example: Territorial songs of certain birds
  - B. Sample count
    1. Assumes that sample is random
    2. Usefulness depends upon precision
    3. Is an estimate—not census
       Example: Count of pellets from deer

Note that counts of signs are simply that. Such counts can be translated into animals (i.e., used as an index) only by calculating from a known ratio of signs per animal as illustrated for beaver houses.

A final general point: the method employed in making the estimate must be chosen specifically for the particular species, time, place, area, and purpose. If possible, several methods of estimation should be used and compared.

An evaluation of the several census and estimation techniques is presented in the latter part of this chapter. The literature is so voluminous that the papers cited will include only those that present an original approach or review several methods. Whenever possible, references from journals readily available to the wildlife manager are used. Recent and nonmathematical papers are preferred. The following methods are presented according to the technique used in getting data (since this comes first in any problem) followed by a discussion of the details of calculations for each procedure.

A major use of census methods is the provision of data for calculation of survival rates. Censuses of a population at 2 or more dates (e.g., spring and summer) provide the data for calculations of survival. Many of the methods to be discussed in this chapter, such as the change in ratio, are frequently used for estimation of survival. These methods are repeated in Chapter 15 but from the viewpoint of calculation of survival rates. Hence slightly different terminology is used.

CENSUS

An obvious method of determining a population is to count or to capture all of the individuals. Unfortunately this method is practical only under special circumstances. The development of innumerable methods for estimating populations is evidence of the fact that trapping or killing all individuals is rarely possible although some attempts have been reported. Nevertheless, the simplest way to determine the size and composition of a population is by a direct count of the number seen. Populations may be described in time (robins per hour), distance (doves per highway km), or area units (quail per ha). These counts are suitable for diurnal or otherwise obvious species and may be divided into several types.

Many territorial species may be readily observed, located within their territory, and thus counted for a specific area. The result is commonly expressed as animals per ha. This method is regularly used for birds and is very satisfactory because the territorial habit makes it unnecessary to mark the individual to prevent duplication. The "mapping method" or "spot-map method" involves recording on a map those individual birds seen or heard on territories in the research area. After a number of censuses a pattern of concentrated records usually appears that indicates the territory defended by each male. Some researchers regard this as an absolute count. However, a controlled study with known territories and population size revealed major problems inherent in this census procedure which could result in large errors (Best 1975). Five different ornithologists, familiar with the method of interpreting "spot-map" census data, made different estimates (all underestimates). In addition to this bias, there are problems of possible observational bias, such as the visual and auditory skill of observers and screening effect of the habitat and environmental noise.

Direct counting of animals that congregate in flocks or groups is one of the more simple census methods. For example, the coveys of bobwhite and the number of individuals present in each covey present on a given area at a given time can be determined by means of a trained dog. The data in Table 14.2 are direct counts. We do not know how many were "not seen." Note that calculation

Table 14.2. Counts of number of bobwhite quail and of coveys for the periods 1935–38 and 1946–49 on the approximately 888-ha Virginia Polytechnic Institute Farms, Virginia. Populations determined by direct count, aided by trained dogs (Mosby and Overton 1950).

	October 1st population		April 1st population	
Year	Number of birds	Number of coveys	Number of birds	Number of coveys
1935–36	195	13	88	8
1936–37	146	10	99	10
1937–38	293	21	176	20
1946–47	204	14	63	8
1947–48	232	17	41	8
1948–49	247	20	118	13
6-year average	220	16	98	11

of the number per covey would permit use of the number of coveys as an index. One need count only the coveys and, making assumptions based on the number per covey, calculate the number of quail.

In those species that regularly call or sing, such as quail, woodcock, grouse, and turkey, the location of vocal animals can be determined by the intersection procedure if 2 or more observers simultaneously plot the direction of the sound. Obviously only the vocal members of the population are counted. Likewise, since vocalizations often stimulate a response by nearby individuals, tape-recorded calls may be used to locate birds and may double the number observed per man-hour (Braun et al. 1973). Management potential in predicting fall population levels and hunting success is illustrated by Brown et al. (1978) with their call-count surveys of scaled quail during spring and summer.

The counting of waterfowl, big game and other wildlife from airplanes is commonly practiced, particularly in open country. A count also can be made from an aerial photograph. Figure 14.1 shows such a photograph of 24,263 greater snow geese. The technique used in determining the number of geese in this flock was to mark out each dot with a pin hole while tallying with an automatic counter. More recent studies indicate problems with aerial counts, since speed of the airplane, height above ground, transect width, and the skill of different observers had significant effects on population estimates (Caughley et al. 1976.). Other factors such as variation of pilots (Hoskinson 1976), snow conditions, terrain, and time of day appear also to bias results (LeResche and Rausch 1974). Although aerial surveys seem to be the only practical way to estimate population densities of some animals (e.g., moose), the method is under serious attack, the validity of estimates are being questioned, and underestimates seem to be inherent in the method (Stott and Olson 1972, LeResche and Rausch 1974). However, the aerial survey method can be used to gather accurate results. For instance, individual moose are not randomly dispersed, but moose aggregations usually are, causing census procedures based on aggregations of moose to obtain better results (Table 14.3). Conditions for good results are extremely rigorous, since the count must be made within a few hours after fresh snowfall with experienced observers. Leatherwood et al. (1978) estimated densities of dolphins and found that strips were more reliable sample plots than quadrats. The percentage difference between aerial and ground counts of 8 species of sea ducks ranged from 20 to 81 (Table 14.4). Ground counts were assumed to be 100% of the population because of the ease of counting and the ducks' habit of staying reasonably close to shore. However the extent of duplication or omission was not entirely known.

One point that can be made here is that no statistical procedure will make data collected under different conditions comparable. In all census techniques employing direct counts, the major problem is to conduct counts under sufficiently similar conditions so that comparisons of counts are valid. For example, the Christmas Bird Count lists the number of birds seen in many places in the United States under relatively similar conditions each year. These data may be used to detect

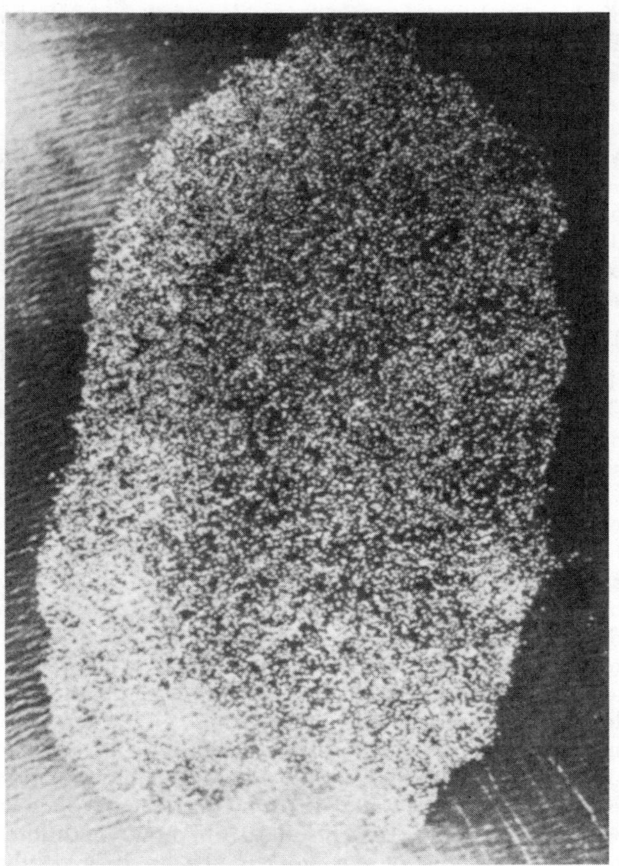

Fig. 14.1. Flock of greater snow geese off Atlantic Coast near Back Bay, Virginia. A total of 24,263 geese was counted from this aerial photograph (photo courtesy Ernest Atkinson).

gross, but not detailed, changes over a period of years for some species.

In migratory mammals, such as the altitudinally migratory Interstate Deer Herd, fairly accurate census data have been obtained by counting the tracks of the animals as they cross roads in the spring on their leisurely way to high country (Table 14.5). Great differences occur when these counts are made on different dates during migration. This technique requires that the roads be dragged between counts to eliminate hoof marks. Such counts may be considered relatively complete but they probably always are conservative due to the difficulty of counting each and every individual track at well-used crossings. Mule deer have been counted as they congregate in meadows. The counting of the deer in meadows is about as accurate, and is one-twelfth as costly, as counting tracks on a road.

In Europe, the total extermination of deer herds on shooting preserves to eliminate old stock before introducing "fresh" deer is sometimes practiced. In such programs a rather complete census of the herd is obtained. It is obvious that the total extermination of wild animals is both costly and time consuming. Furthermore, this method of obtaining a census would have rather restricted use, mainly in detailed research programs.

A method called "minimum number present" calculates the number trapped plus the number known from subsequent trapping to have been present. This figure indicates nothing about the number not captured, and assumes no immigration or emigration. It is not an estimate but is a census.

ESTIMATES

For practical reasons a complete count usually is impossible; hence, samples of some sort must be drawn from the population. Some techniques measure the population directly while others measure an attribute (index) which is related to the population. Of course, a direct count may be used to sample the animal population on a portion of a larger area.

Transects or Quadrats

A very general method is to count the number along a transect or within a quadrat. The number counted is a true census but only of a representative portion of the particular area. Counts of several areas or several counts of the same area provide the numbers needed for calculation of an estimate. Many detailed versions exist (see Anderson et al. 1976 for method).

The strip census method entails walking a predetermined line, counting the animals observed, and record-

Table 14.3. Comparison of moose densities, aggregation size, and dispersal of aggregation (R = 1 random), 1960–66 (from Bergerud and Manuel 1969).

Date of census	Moose per sq. km	Aggregations: Total	Aggregations: Per sq. km	Moose per Aggreg. ± S.E.	R Values	C[a] Values
Jan. 11, 1960	31.0	82	13.2	2.3 ± 0.20	1.08	1.04
Dec. 27, 1961	7.5	25	4.1	1.9 ± 0.21	1.11	0.70
Jan. 13, 1962	17.2	47	7.5	2.0 ± 0.22	0.99	0.14
Mar. 12, 1962	7.8	26	4.1	1.9 ± 0.34	1.07	0.49
Jan. 13, 1964	11.6	35	5.8	2.1 ± 0.22	1.07	0.62
Jan. 25, 1965	9.6	33	5.4	1.8 ± 0.20	1.16	1.44
Feb. 22, 1965	15.6	47	7.5	2.0 ± 0.22	1.10	0.95
Jan. 3, 1966	26.7	80	12.9	2.1 ± 0.14	1.29	4.12
Feb. 20, 1966	20.2	63	10.1	1.9 ± 0.12	1.36	4.38

[a]C is the standard variate of the normal curve; C values of 1.96 and 2.98 indicate departure from random distribution at the 5% level and 1% level of significance.

Table 14.4. Results of 15 simultaneous aerial and ground censuses of 8 species of sea ducks on a 35 km section of the New Hampshire and Massachusetts coastline (from Stott and Olson 1972).

Flight Number	Date	Total Ground Count	Total Air Count	Percent Counted from Air	Aircraft	Sky	Ocean Surface
1	1- 6-68	736	452	61.4	Cessna 150	Clear	Flat calm
2	4- 7-68	976	329	33.7	Cessna 172	Clear	Flat calm
3[a]	11-14-68	419	144	34.3	Beaver	Clear	Rough[b]
4[a]	12-18-68	809	299	36.9	Beaver	Clear	Rough
5	1-28-69	948	718	75.7	Cessna 150	Clear	Light ripples
6	3-16-69	841	451	53.6	Cessna 150	Partly cloudy	Light ripples
7	5- 2-69	1,719	681	39.6	Cessna 150	Clear	Flat calm
8	10-31-69	723	178	24.6	Beaver	Clear	Moderate[c]
9	11-26-69	1,280	817	63.8	Cessna 150	Overcast	Light ripples
10	1- 5-70	1,196	632	52.8	Beaver	Clear	Moderate
11	3-16-70	1,208	242	20.0	Beaver	Partly cloudy	Moderate
12[a]	4- 9-70	735	595	80.9	Cessna 150	Overcast	Moderate
13	4-14-70	747	256	34.3	Cessna 172	Clear	Light ripples
14	12-29-70	1,228	854	69.5	Cessna 150	Overcast	Light ripples
15	1- 6-71	1,247	730	58.5	Beaver	Partly cloudy	Rough

[a]Ground count conducted the day before the aerial survey.
[b]Whitecaps with surf onshore.
[c]Swells with surf onshore.

ing the distances at which they are seen or flushed. The average of the flushing distance is determined and used to calculate the effective width of the strip covered by the observer. The population for the entire area then is considered to be the number of animals flushed, divided by the area of the strip and multiplied by the total area:

$$P = \frac{AZ}{2YX}$$

where P = population
A = total area of study
Z = number flushed
Y = average flushing distance
X = length of strip

The formula can be changed to correct for the angle of flushing. Each count is a sample. All counts should be averaged to give a mean and standard deviation. The mean of Z then is used in the formula as well as the mean of Y. Three assumptions (Hayne 1949a) are made: (1) that animals in a population vary with respect to flushing angle and distances, (2) that the various types of animals are randomly distributed around the path of the observer, (3) that the average flushing-distance observed is representative of the average flushing-distance of the entire population. The first 2 assumptions are regularly true if adequate care is taken in randomization of the area. The third assumption, however, appears to be false. Also in respect to flushing-distance, each class must be computed separately to give the proper average.

The averaging of flushing-distances, or distances to carcasses, from a paced line gives an erroneously small strip-width and a correspondingly large population estimate. In hiking along a strip of a certain vegetative cover-type an observer can see, or cause animals to be flushed, along a strip of a certain average width. This average width should be predetermined by trial and error. As an example, a person searching for deer carcasses finds he can spot all carcasses in a strip 10 m on both sides of a line. In a transect 300 m long he feels confident in having seen every carcass in 6000 m². However, if the average sighting distance is used, only about 3000 m² is considered to be sampled by the transect; thus, the formula P = AZ/2YX gives a population figure approximately twice that actually present. Some carcasses would be seen farther than 10 m, but the farther the distance, the less the chance. Accordingly, population estimates would still be too high.

DEFICIENCIES

The main problem is that this system does not allow for area actually sampled *beyond* the animals observed.

Table 14.5. Track count of Interstate Deer Herd on northward migration in 1947 and 1948 (Interstate Deer Herd Committee 1950).

Date of track count	Number of deer migrating north 1947	1948
April 10	2,152	
15	588	36
20	403	53
25	172	162
30		21
May 5		369
10		392
15		878
25		653
Totals	3,315	2,564

Table 14.6. Testing of Hayne's and King's census methods using 200 burlap sacks and a theoretical sight distance (Robinette et al. 1956).

Survey number	Population Estimated by: Hayne's method	King's method
1	292	156
2	252	150
3	210	152
4	231	147
Mean	246	154
Departure from 200 in percent	+23	−23
Confidence limits	191–302	145–157

This deficiency may be serious for obtaining total population estimates. Index figures for year-to-year comparisons could be obtained either way, as long as the same system is used each time. A modification of this method was to count deer seen from an airplane while flying over strips and to convert the values to deer per square km.

This method must be used with caution. The strip method of estimating winter losses of deer was unsatisfactory as evidenced by the estimates being greatly different from actual counts (Table 14.6). Strip census methods were tested with known populations under field conditions (Table 14.7) to determine the census estimates as percentages of the actual population for 10 different census methods. Charles E. Gates, Texas A & M University, has developed and has available a computer program called LINETRAN that performs 14 different estimators of wildlife populations using line and strip census data.

A method (Anderson and Pospahala 1970) compensates for the number of individuals not counted on sample transects with a fixed width. Observers are reasonably expected to miss individuals as the width of the transect increases and likewise are expected to record a higher proportion of the total number of individuals actually present on narrower transects. The procedure involves first measuring the distance at a 90° angle from the animal to the center line of the transect. The resulting measurements are then grouped into flushing distance class intervals (which will vary according to the biological situation) and a histogram constructed as illustrated (Figure 14.2A). Based on this frequency distribution of recorded data, a mathematically describable curve is found that closely represents the data. The dependent variable (Y) is the number of individuals recorded in an interval, and the independent variable (X) is the distance from the center line of the transect to the midpoint of the class interval. Consult a standard statistics text for curve-fitting procedures, especially the least squares method. For the data in Figure 14.2A a fitted

Table 14.7. Census estimates as percentages of true population for 10 strip census methods (Robinette et al. 1974). The methods of Kelker and of Anderson are preferred.

Census Number	King	Hayne	Gates II	Gates III	Webb	Leopold	Gates I	Frye	Kelker	Anderson
1	82.4	164.8	164.7	115.5	109.6	119.7	119.4	73.3	99.0	99.2
2	94.0	119.0	185.2	106.8	138.5	163.5	161.3	85.7	116.7	96.9
3	93.9	156.6	187.4	111.9	125.2	138.4	138.2	79.3	95.7	99.2
4	105.0	150.1	209.8	120.4						
5	86.0	108.1	171.4	95.5	131.2	142.9	142.8	83.0	90.5	91.3
6	98.4	145.2	195.9	115.7						
7	69.1	134.6	137.9	95.8						
8	93.1	158.2	185.9	115.2						
9	107.5	153.2	214.7	125.9						
10	93.5	139.2	187.1	107.4	137.9	143.0	142.9	86.4	94.4	94.2
11	107.8	161.7	215.2	127.3	167.9	189.7	189.4	115.9	142.7	129.9
12	94.8	135.0	188.6	111.8	147.4	167.8	167.6	102.9	116.9	110.4
13	88.2	145.6	173.7	107.6	149.1	176.9	175.2	104.8	126.9	149.0
14	70.1	111.5	139.7	87.8	119.3	135.2	134.7	78.4	96.3	125.7
15	96.8	132.6	192.9	111.7						
16	97.4	138.9	193.8	113.2						
17	79.9	145.7	158.8	93.6						
18	61.2	82.1	119.5	70.0						
19	106.6	147.5	211.2	123.7	134.6	145.8	144.5	71.3	107.0	97.1
20	99.3	157.2	197.6	126.9	126.2	117.9	117.4	82.4	88.2	87.5
Mean	93.56	142.17	186.26	112.23	135.17	149.16	148.49	87.58	106.75	107.31
C.V. (%) of estimates	12.0	11.7	12.0	9.9	11.8	15.3	15.2	16.1	16.1	18.1
t value	2.439	10.785	16.377	4.675	7.336	7.152	7.116	2.922	1.302	1.250
p	≅0.03	<0.01	<0.01	<0.01	<0.01	<0.01	<0.01	<0.02	≅0.02	≅0.24
Weighted mean	95.2	141.2	189.8	112.2	134.3	145.7	145.4	86.4	99.8	100.7

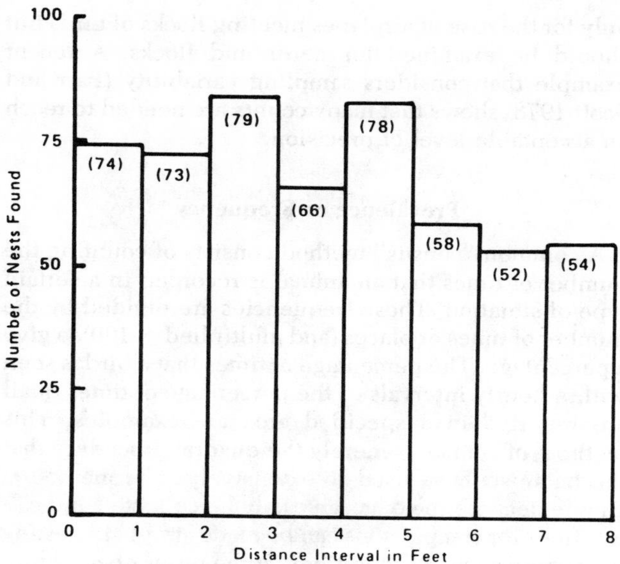

Fig. 14.2A. **Histogram of waterfowl nests located on belt transects, Monte Vista National Wildlife Refuge, Colorado, 1967 and 1968 (Redrawn from Anderson and Pospahala 1970).**

curve is $Y = 77.05 - 0.4039X^2$. The area under this curve represents the proportion of animals actually counted (Figure 14.2B) and may be found from crude techniques or more precisely by using standard procedures found in any calculus text. Then the observed total count for the transect should be multiplied by the reciprocal of the calculated proportion of animals found (e.g., $1/0.881 = 1.135$ in Figure 14.2B). The population estimate for the entire area under study may then be made from the adjusted transect count. This method was actually designed for immotile objects (e.g., nests or dead deer). A large number of objects or individuals is needed for repeatable results.

OTHER PROCEDURES

An additional example of a complete count on sample areas is the estimate of production of mourning doves (Jumber et al. 1957). A sampling scheme was prepared to estimate the number of dove nests in a town. This result was translated into production by determining the young produced in representative nests. From the original counts it was estimated that the total production was 495 doves with a standard error of 60 doves.

Features of several methods can be combined to develop an estimate for birds. The absolute number of birds can be counted in small areas and then compared with the number seen on a transect through the area. A measure of conspicuousness of each species was the ratio of those seen on the roadside count to the absolute number along the road. For example, if 3 robins were seen where territorial counts indicated that 10 robins lived, then the index of conspicuousness is 0.3. Conspicuousness is merely a factor used to relate the birds seen to the absolute number in the area. Thus, if one saw 6 robins, the population is $0.3N = 6$ or $N = 20$. Emlen (1977) reviewed several methods and also derived conversion factors or "coefficients of detectability" for each species before calculating density values.

Eberhardt (1978a), in addition to classifying and appraising different transect methods, suggested improvements.

The study of bird populations in urban areas presents problems that are not encountered in natural habitats. These include differences among areas in visibility and noise, problems of access, uneven or nonrandom distribution of birds, and an abundance of nonterritorial species. To minimize the effects of these problems, the U.S. Fish and Wildlife Service developed a procedure for obtaining indices of bird use of sample plots in urban areas. Transects, divided into segments 100 m long, are established along roads. Each segment is covered in exactly 4 minutes while walking down the road or sidewalk, and observations are confined to birds that are seen or heard within 50 m of the transect line. Birds seen flying from or alighting in the 100- × 100-m plot are counted; however, those flying over are not. Plot size was determined by noting that under a wide variety of habitat conditions relatively few observations were made at greater distances.

A frequently used variant of the transect or quadrat procedure is the roadside census (e.g., Walker and Cant 1977). In this method, the observer travels rural roads for the specific purpose of counting the numbers of individuals which are then related to the number of kilometers traveled. Thus, in the case of rabbits, if 10 rabbits were seen on a 20-km census-route, the census would be 0.5 rabbits per km. Roadside censuses are used widely in the midwestern states to estimate numbers of rabbits

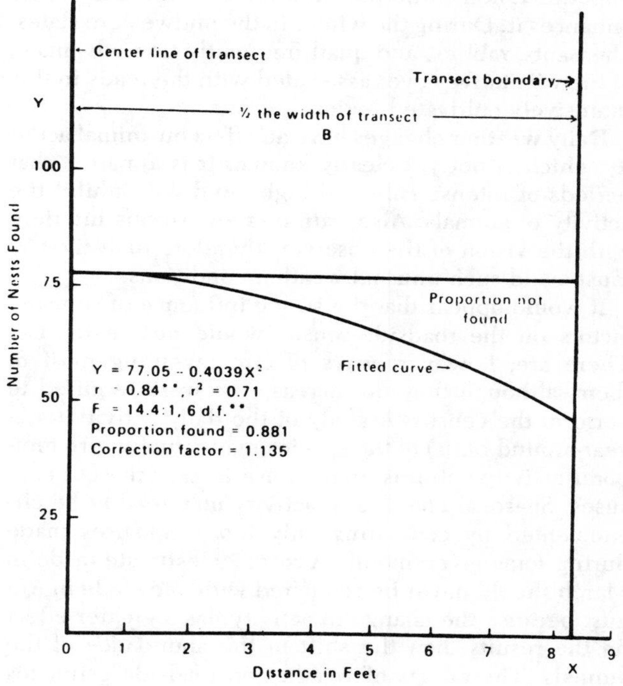

Fig. 14.2B. Quadratic equation used to represent the relationship between distance from the center line of the transect and number of nests found on the Monte Vista National Wildlife Refuge, Colorado, 1967 and 1968. Estimates of the proportion not found in the outer 3 inches of the transect were derived using the quadratic equation; the data representing this small interval were not used in forming the equation. **99% level significance. (Redrawn from Anderson and Pospahala 1970.)

and pheasants. Some states secure the cooperation of rural mail carriers to obtain estimates of the abundance of their principal game species (Greeley et al. 1962). A variation of the roadside census was used (McCaffery 1973) with regression techniques to show that numbers of white-tailed deer killed on roads provide a useful index to deer population changes. Road-kill trends correlated well with trends in registered buck harvests.

The *advantages* of the roadside method are obvious. One can traverse large areas quickly and easily in the comfort of an automobile. Further, this method is about the only one that is useful for large regions such as a state. The *disadvantages* of the roadside census are so many and important that investigators who ignore them are obtaining useless information. Factors other than abundance that determine the numbers of animals seen during a census are: (1) activity of the animals as affected by hour of day, food supply, and weather, and (2) condition of the roadside cover. Activity may vary quantitatively (a) temporally, (b) seasonally, and (c) selectively. For instance, rabbits regulate their activity according to standard time, having evening and early morning peaks of activity which are unrelated to sunrise or sunset. Pheasants, on the other hand, regulate their arousal by the time of sunrise and have an early morning peak in their activity. Likewise, seasonal changes in the amount of activity occur in rabbits and presumably other species which have important effects on the roadside-census results. In addition, seasonal changes in cover use exist. The tall vegetation of late summer seriously impedes vision while the snow cover of the late winter enhances it. During the winter in the midwestern states, pheasants, rabbits, and quail frequently take advantage of the vegetative cover associated with the roads in this intensively cultivated region.

Daily weather changes have an effect on animal activity which is not yet clearly known. It is apparent that periods of intense cold and high wind will inhibit the activity of animals. Also, rain or snow storms interfere with the vision of the observer; therefore investigators must avoid such unusual weather conditions.

It would appear that the strong influence of so many factors on the roadside-census would negate its use. There are, however, ways of circumventing most of them, although they do increase the work required to perform the census. A study of the daily activity (on a year-around basis) of the species may actually turn temporal activity patterns to good use in carrying out censuses. Seasonal changes in activity may readily be circumvented by comparing only those censuses made during some given month. A roadside estimate made in March should never be compared with one made in August because the change in activity has a greater effect on the results than the shift in the abundance of the animals. The effects of weather on roadside estimates may be minimized by avoiding unusual weather conditions and repeating the total census many times each month.

A reverse version of the transect census is for the observer to remain in 1 place and count the individuals that pass by. This system has been used for migratory mule deer, birds and also for species that congregate in roosts. The mathematical treatment has been examined only for the case of airplanes meeting flocks of birds but should be examined for herds and flocks. A recent example that considers sampling variability (Parr and Scott 1978) shows that many counts are needed to reach an acceptable level of precision.

Prevalence or Frequency

A common "census" method consists of counting the number of times that an animal is recorded in a certain type of situation. These frequencies are divided by the number of times or places (and multiplied × 100) to give a percentage. The percentage of times that a bird is seen within hourly intervals or the percentage of times quail are reported in a specified area are examples. This method, of course, is merely the quadrat procedure that the botanists have used so extensively. The method is simple because the data can easily be collected and calculations for comparisons can be made simply by testing the significance of proportions. Some terms need definition. Frequency is the number of times the animal occurs; prevalence (or proportion) is the frequency divided by the number of quadrats; percentage is the prevalence multiplied by 100. This method is often called "frequency index" but it is not an index in the sense used in this chapter. An example of a quadrat of large size is the study of eagles (Grier 1977). From an airplane eagles were counted in 100 km² quadrats.

Serious disadvantages exist because the frequency depends upon the size of the unit. Consider an example in estimating the number of muskrat houses in a marsh. The marsh is divided into 100 units of size X. A count of the number of units that have muskrat houses is, let us say, 20, or a frequency of 20%. If the unit size is doubled to 2X then the frequency that have houses will be higher, say 35%. As the unit size is increased, the frequency is increased, until 100% is attained. It is obvious that the frequency changes with changes of the quadrat size. Also, it is obvious that no comparison of frequency can be made between 2 populations that are present in 100% of the quadrats even though 1 marsh may contain more houses per unit than the other. One problem is that 1 size of plot may be more efficient at 1 density and another size at another density. To overcome this problem quadrats of several sizes should be used. A practical way to do this efficiently is to subdivide a large quadrat and record the data separately for each portion. Then the data can be analyzed at any time in the future by quarters, halves, or wholes. Unfortunately, comparison of populations in quadrats of the same size also may give deceptive results, and the appropriate size may change from year to year. A further difficulty is that most populations are not distributed randomly. However, in spite of its disadvantages, the comparison of prevalence or frequency has value in areas that are fairly similar if the size of the quadrat is chosen so that the prevalences for the important species are about 0.8.

Data on prevalence also may be used to estimate the mean number per quadrat. If the number per unit (of time, space, etc.) has a Poisson distribution, then $e^{-\bar{x}} = q$ where q is the proportion of units that lack individuals, $\bar{x}$ is the mean individuals per unit and e is the base of natural logarithms. From this $\ln q = -\bar{x}$. It is often very difficult to count the number of individuals in a unit, (such as fleas-per-rat, moles-per-hectare) but easy to determine the proportion of units that lack individuals, which is q. Obviously $\bar{x}$ can then be calculated. The method saves work but may underestimate the population (Wadley 1954). An example of an estimate of a fox population is available (Table 14.8). The proportion of stations catching no foxes is 0.807 whose natural logarithm is −0.214. The estimate of 0.214 is close to the observed mean captures-per-station of 0.237. The expected number of stations (Table 14.8) comes from the equation $P_r = \frac{\bar{X}^r e^{-\bar{x}}}{r!}$ where P_r is the probability that a station will capture r individuals. The high chi square value means that the distribution of foxes per station is not random or independent and did not approximate a Poisson distribution well, but was clumped. However note that the procedure gives a reasonable estimate of the mean number per quadrat, even though only the proportion of quadrats lacking individuals was used.

INDICES

A variation of the complete count for a given area is to determine the number of animals from a relation to some obvious environmental feature. The resulting count has merit as it stands or can be converted to an index to be used in areas where it is difficult to count the primary species. For example, a ratio between deer population and cattle may be obtained in sample areas, and then applied with suitable caution to a large area where the number of cattle is known. Counts of deer trails have been used as an index to population size and habitat use in Wisconsin (McCaffery 1976), and tracks of rodents also indicate population levels (Sarrazin and Bider 1973). A thorough exploration of an index is described for beaver (Table 14.1) by comparison of counts of an index (houses) with the number of beaver captured. An aerial count of food caches was a reliable index to colonies because there is only 1 per colony. However the ratio was 7.8 beaver per cache in aspen areas and 5.1 beaver per cache in willow areas. This example illustrates the fact that the relation of an index to a population may vary from place to place. An additional method for translating the index (beaver houses) into an estimate of the number of beaver is from an estimate of the number of beaver per house calculated from the age composition of trapped individual (Novak 1977). He calculated that the average family contained 7.59 beaver or 7.59 beaver per house.

Table 14.8. Distribution of 3,058 trap station subsamples of gray fox census lines showing number of foxes captured in a 7-day period (Wood et al. 1958).

Foxes captured in 7 days	Stations	Expected stations	(Observed-Expected)² / Expected
0	2468	2413.3	1.239
1	475	571.4	16.263
2	98	67.6	13.671
3	15	5.3	
4	2	0.3	23.207
Total	3058	3057.9	54.380

Mean = 0.23675, Chi-square = 54.380

Signs

A variety of methods have been based upon ratios calculated from animal "signs." Basically these methods are the same as techniques based on observing the animals directly and receive the same statistical treatment. One can measure the signs directly or use signs as an index to the number of animals. A few of the signs that may be used are: dens, burrows, nests, houses, tracks, feces, dead individuals, song, calls, and shed antlers. Most of the results are in relative terms. For example, pheasant crowing may be more frequent in March of one year than in March of another year. The number of pheasants is not known, but merely the difference in crowing frequency. The results, however, may be transformed from relative terms into an absolute figure by the following procedure: Suppose that 100 pheasant crows per hour are recorded from a particular area and that 3 pheasant cocks then are removed. Assume that a later investigation reveals that the calls have decreased to 70 crows per hour. Clearly, the 3 pheasants made 30 calls or the cock population is (100) × (3)/30, or 10 cocks. Now the call frequency has been used as an index.

An illustration of a suitable procedure for relating an index to a count is available for ruffed grouse. The first step was to determine a "drumming index" which was a routine count of drummings heard under specified conditions. This index then was compared with the actual population as determined by observation of drumming logs and by banding (Table 14.9). The relation was similar in several years within 1 area (mean of 2.45) but differed greatly from another area (mean of 0.92), showing that this relation must be determined for each area. There was a good correlation between the drumming index and another index, birds flushed per 100 hours.

An example that illustrates the index technique—and its problems—is the counting of dove calls in relation to the number of doves. In several areas the number of pairs was counted and also the number of calls. From

Table 14.9. Comparison of the actual number of cock ruffed grouse with the drumming counts in 1 area (Dorney et al. 1958).

Year	Drumming count (A)	Number of male grouse (B)	Ratio of A:B	Deviation of ratio from average (Per cent)
1954	58	25	2.32	− 5
1955	71	25	2.84	+16
1956	66	30	2.20	−10
Average	65	26.6	2.45	0

these data (Table 14.10) the number of pairs per call was calculated by dividing the number of breeding pairs found in 60 ha by the average number of calls per visit to a station (which encompassed 60 ha). Considerable variability occurred among stations but the averages for 2 years were similar (1.81 and 1.72). Although no correlation coefficients nor estimates of variability were determined, the population for various other areas was calculated by multiplying the "index" (calls per station in these areas) by pairs per calling bird from Table 14.10.

Using the principles from these examples, elaborate procedures are now available for woodcock, doves, and a few other species. The "rules of the game" are so complex that the guidelines must be consulted for each species. Regression coefficients are useful to adjust counts to the day of year, time of day, wind velocity, temperature, and relative humidity, all of which influence the number of calls heard (Robel et al. 1969).

Kozicky et al. (1954) used a formula to determine how many woodcock call-index routes need to be run to detect a change from year to year or from place to place. Let us assume that the standard deviation is 0.4 and that we want to detect a change of 15%. The number of routes which should be run is determined as follows:

$$N = \frac{2(1.96)^2 \quad (0.4)^2}{(\log 1.15)^2} = 332$$

The value 1.96 represents the t value at the 5% level of confidence. Change to some other percentage (say 25%) would require log 1.25 in the denominator. To be safe the investigator should use more than 332 call routes,

Table 14.10. Relationship between breeding density and number of calls in May–June (average number of doves per calling station) on a call-count route (Lowe 1956). To obtain pairs per calling dove divide breeding pairs by calls per station.

Year	Breeding pairs per 60 ha	Number of counts	Calls per station	Pairs per calling dove
1951	4	17	2.60	1.54
1952	3	8	1.28	2.19
	2	8	1.47	1.36
	3	8	2.00	1.50
	2	8	0.50	4.00
	0	8	0.50	0.00
Mean–1952	2.0		1.15	1.81
1954	4	6	1.67	2.39
	2.5	6	1.33	1.88
	3	8	2.67	1.12
	4	8	2.00	2.00
	5.5	8	2.33	2.36
	1.5	8	1.00	1.50
	2.5	8	0.33	0.76
Mean–1954	3.3		1.62	1.72
Average of all data	2.85		2.28	1.74

perhaps 350 in this case. However, this formula applies to log transformed data and persons desiring to use this method must consult the original article for details of assumptions. Hayne (1978) strongly urges repetition or replication of individual observations and entire studies to confirm the results and strengthen the general conclusion. Eberhardt (1978b) examines the problems and offers solutions for determining appropriate sample size for population studies and also gives a classification of population census methods.

A novel index to determine the numbers in a roosting congregation of blackbirds and starlings is to compare the fecal material produced overnight by captive birds to amounts of fecal material from samples collected on papers set under the roost (Table 14.11). In some cases, such as deer and snowshoe hares, pellet count data were so variable that they were useless, although more recent reports are more encouraging. Bowden et al. (1969) fitted different mathematical distributions to pellet frequency data to determine appropriate forms for standard errors and confidence limits. Robinette et al. (1958) described in detail the procedures for pellet sampling during winter. They cautioned against counting too long after the herd has left the area or when pellets were wet. They recommended that, as a trial, circular plots that contain 10 m² be used. These plots should be spaced at 70 or 210 m intervals along parallel randomized transects about 400 m apart. They noted that the detection of a change in pellet numbers may be satisfactory for management purposes. Results of extensive sampling in areas containing a known number of deer showed that, although the number of pellet groups per deer per day varied due to sampling error, diet, age and other factors, the mean from a number of areas was about 15 pellets per deer per day. Variations due to diet and age perhaps can be minimized by limiting the work to a particular season coupled with a knowledge of herd composition. Counts of pellets present many additional problems (Neff 1968) such as clumped distribution, defecation rate, observer bias, deterioration of pellets, effect of rain, and humidity which must be examined by studies on permanent plots. Some of these problems are minimized in a method that essentially treats the number of pellets as a consequence of a "birth" rate (defecation) and a "death" rate (disappearance) (Batcheler 1975). The pellets are sampled by a procedure using distance from other pellets.

A count of a related object need not necessarily be converted to an index; it may be examined for its own merits. For example, scent stations were placed for bears and the proportion of stations visited was determined. The proportions changed from 0.238 in May, to 0.185 in June, to 0.088 in August, and to 0.028 in October. We can conclude that the frequency of visits declined. The authors implied that the proportion was related to abundance but presented no supporting data. They suggested several possible ways to convert the proportion into an index (Lindzey et al. 1977).

In considering indices, it is essential to evaluate the variation among the several investigators participating in the study using a comparison, by analysis of variance, of the results reported by experienced and inexperienced observers. Analysis of pheasant call counts

Table 14.11. Numbers of birds in main part of roost, based on amount of fecal material deposited (Stewart 1973).

Species	Sexes	Fecal material per bird (g)	Percentage of population	Total fecal material (g)	No. birds
Starling	Both	1.3	17.5	398,719	306,707
Red-winged Blackbird	Male	1.2	0.1	2,103	1,753
Common Grackle	Male	1.9	42.4	1,411,904	743,108
Common Grackle	Female	1.6	40.0	1,121,672	701,045
TOTALS			100.0	2,934,398	1,752,613

showed that the data collected by experienced observers agreed closely with one another and also on each day whereas those from the inexperienced persons did not. Although the statistical procedures are laborious, they are essential for problems of this type.

In summary, these methods are simple in principle but have many pitfalls when comparing 2 estimates. The conditions under which the counts were made must be comparable. For example, the number of calls per pheasant declines during the breeding season, dew alters the activity of birds, and population density affects frequency of decline. There also is opportunity for differences between observers. Great care must be taken to account for the magnitude of such variables. Use of detonations to stimulate crowing apparently removes some of the variability.

ESTIMATES FROM CAPTURES

Since it is rarely possible to capture all individuals (but see Tryon and Snyder 1973 and Brown and McGuire 1975), a plethora of methods have been developed to estimate the population from the rate of capture. The data may be obtained by a variety of capture methods. Traps may be set in a grid or in lines; nets or other devices may be used. It is necessary to emphasize that there are several ways of estimating the population from capture data but when the basic data are the same, the estimate can not be verified by using as checks the several methods listed below.

Sum of Daily Captures

A simple plot (Fig. 14.3A) of the number of animals caught per day can be smoothed and extrapolated to zero to estimate the total for the area. For example, had trapping stopped on October 6, the sum of the ordinates for each day on a smoothed curve up to October 20 would give a good estimate.

Cumulative Sum

The number caught may be cumulatively added (Fig. 14.3B) to give an estimate where the line levels off, in this case at 280. The cumulative process smooths the curve.

Probability of Capture

If the number caught each day is plotted against the number previously caught, then a straight line results (Fig. 14.3C). The slope of the line represents the probability of capture and the intersection with the horizontal axis estimates the population. Thus, the slope of the line in figure 14.3C is 0.35 and the population estimate is 13.3. For reasons that will be discussed below, it will be satisfactory for the wildlife manager merely to estimate the population from the intersection point on the graph. This method is best for general use.

Catch-Effort

The decline in catch in relation to some unit (hour, trap, etc.) has been widely used especially for populations of fish. The method relies on a decline in the rate

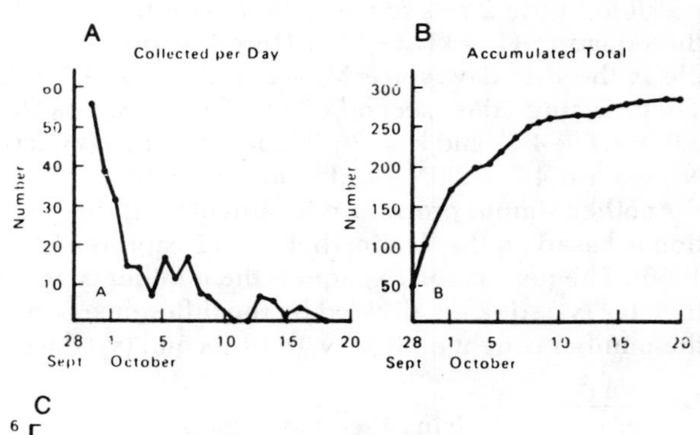

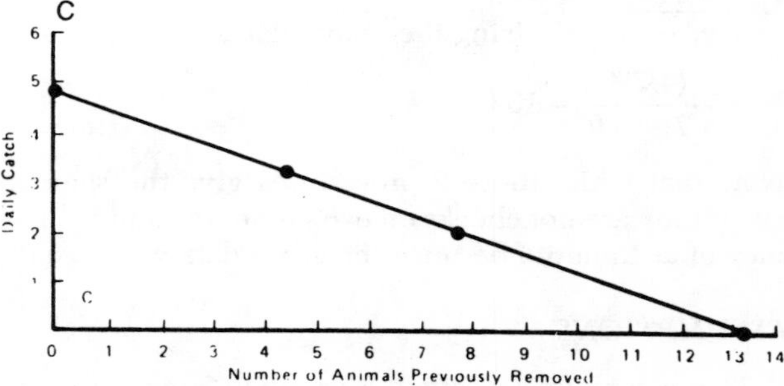

Fig. 14.3. Estimating a population from capture data. (A) Plotting the number caught each day, then summing each day's capture. (B) Plotting the cumulative total until curve levels off, taking population estimate at asymptotic level (280 in this example). (C) Plotting the daily catch (per trap) against the total number previously captured.

(DeLury 1951). In brief, the method states that the catch (C_t) per-unit-effort at time (t) is proportional to the population (N_t) at time (t), if traps do not compete with one another. Therefore: $C_t = k_tN_t$ where k_t is a constant. C_t can, of course, be obtained from the data, but k_t and N_t must be determined. For simplicity we assume that k_t (the probability of capture) is a constant throughout the trapping period and call it k, and also assume that the population is closed. At any time t, $N_t = N_o - M_t$ where M_t is the total catch up to the time t and N_o is the original population. In simplest terms this equation merely says that the number remaining equals the number at the start, less the number already removed. Substituting $N_o - M_t$ for N_t and k for k_t in the equation above gives: $C_t = k(N_o - M_t)$, which is an equation of a straight line. Since k and N_o are constants, a plot of values of C_t against M_t will give a straight line of slope −k exactly as in Fig. 14.3C. For additional refinements and the calculation of confidence limits, one should refer to mathematical texts (Seber 1973, Ricker 1975).

The data in Fig. 14.3C illustrate the method. The results are averages from a large number of trap lines and hence the number of animals are fractions rather than whole numbers.

Day	Caught (C_t)	Cumulative (M_t)
1	4.7	0
2	3.0	4.7
3	2.1	7.7

The slope of the line can be obtained by dividing the projected distance along the vertical axis by the projected distance along the horizontal axis between any 2 points on the line. The simplest example is at the points where the line intersects the axes or 4.7/13.3 = 0.35. It is possible to use 2 sets of values to obtain the slope from the equation $C_t = kN_o - kM_t$. Here the simplest example is the first day, since $M_t = 0$ and hence $4.7 = kN_o$. Then, using the second day, $3.0 = kN_o - kM_t$ or $3.0 = 4.7 - 4.7k$ and k = .36. Then to get the population, N_o, we use $4.7 = .36N_o$, and hence $N_o = 13.1$.

Another simple procedure for calculating the population is based on the decline between 2 captures (Zippin 1956). The population (N) equals the number caught the first day (y_1) squared, divided by the difference between the number caught on first (y_1) and second (y_2) days or:

$$N = \frac{y_1^2}{y_1 - y_2}$$

Using the above data,

$$N = \frac{(4.7)^2}{4.7 - 3.0} = 13.0$$

Note that while these 2 procedures give the same answer, they are not checks on each other (except for accuracy of arithmetic) because the same data were used.

ASSUMPTIONS

The catch-effort method described above involves several basic assumptions about the behavior of the individuals and the nature of captures.

First, that the *population is closed;* i.e., that immigration and emigration, births and deaths are negligible. In nature this assumption may be true for short periods in ponds or on islands. However, DeLury (1951) and Fredin (1954) have developed procedures for estimating the extent of these 4 forces in a population. These procedures are lengthy and should be examined in the original publications.

Second, that the *probability of capture* remains constant during the period of collection of data. The probability may vary for many reasons such as trap shyness, change in weather, food supply, etc. For example, even when using the same number of traps more animals will be caught when their range is large than when their range is small. Thus, the "catchability" is not constant but varies with the size of home range and other factors—place, season and population level. It is permissible to use estimates of populations that have different probabilities of capture if the probabilities are constant for each population. Trouble arises when the probability of capture varies during trapping as may occur if animals learn to avoid traps. While it is possible to develop equations when capture probability is variable, the calculations become very complex.

Third, that the *catch is proportional to the population.* In many cases this relation is not true. A trap density that will provide a catch proportional to the population may exist but that density may not lie within practical limits.

Note that capture success must be sufficiently great to cause a marked decline in the population, otherwise no noticeable change in slope will occur. An intimate knowledge of the biology of each species may be needed to confirm that the assumptions hold. Unfortunately, the problems cited above are rather universal, and hence, there is doubt that the assumptions will frequently be fulfilled.

For a study comparing live-trapping and snap-trapping estimates see Table 14.12 which shows a tendency for snap-trapping to give a higher estimate but no real, significant difference between the 2. Nelson and Clark (1973) presented a method to correct for sprung traps in catch per effort calculations of trapping results.

Change in Ratio

Another form of the catch-effort method is based on a change in 1 of several possible ratios due to removal of some individuals. The fundamental similarity of these methods is that removal changes the ratio of catch-to-traps, or males-to-females or adults-to-young or marked-to-unmarked. Indeed a great variety of ratios could be used. For example, the number of deer tracks per area (T_1) found in the snow in a specified area may be counted, a known number of deer (n) removed and then the tracks (T_2) counted again. The change in number of tracks per area ($T_1 - T_2$) is due to n deer and hence:

$$\frac{T_1 - T_2}{n} = \frac{T_1}{N_1} = \frac{T_2}{N_2}$$

where N_1 is the population before removal and N_2 after removal. The equation can be solved for N_1 or N_2. T can refer to any measurable aspect that is altered by the removal. It must be realized that this formula is general and can be applied to any change in ratio. The method is extremely simple but makes the assumption that the ratio of objects counted (in this case tracks) to animals is

Table 14.12. Estimated population densities of voles for the several areas and dates (Yang et al. 1970).

			Estimate obtained by:			
			Live-trapping		Snap-trapping	
Species	Date	Minimum known alive	Number	95% C.I.	Number	95% C.I.
M. ochrogaster	July 1967	87	91	81–101	108	88–128
"	November 1967	41	44	36–51	47	40–55
"	August 1967	18	22	12–33	45	6–84
"	October 1967	25	27	21–34	42	25–58
"	August 1967	26	28	19–37	31	24–38
"	December 1967	12	13	11–15	16	8–24
M. pennsylvanicus	March 1967	27	28	22–34	27	27–27
"	December 1967	30	32	30–35	39	24–54
"	October 1967	8	9	2–16	14	6–22

the same at the 2 times. To be sure that this assumption holds, one must know the habits of the species thoroughly.

This method also has been used to estimate wildlife populations from changes in sex or age ratios. In these cases T refers to bucks-per-doe before and after the hunting season and n refers to the numbers of bucks killed during the hunting seasons. Dasmann (1952:227) gives a good example of the use of this technique in estimating a deer population, although the procedure is a little complicated because the calculations are based on a denominator of 139 does (which represents the "specified area" above). The prehunting value (T_1) was 74 bucks to 139 does and the posthunting value (T_2) was 50 bucks to 139 does. Hence, the kill ($T_1 - T_2$) was 24 bucks per 139 does. From a check of hunters it was known that 246 bucks (n) were killed. Hence the preseason population of bucks was:

$$\frac{\frac{74}{139} - \frac{50}{139}}{246} = \frac{\frac{74}{139}}{N_1} \quad \text{or } N_1 = 758$$

The arithmetic is a little easier if the numbers are first changed to percent male (or female) for T_1 and T_2. Similarly, $N_2 = 512$.

Another example is worked out with the ratios rather than the actual numbers. Stokes (1954), working with pheasants, obtained the following:

Observed ratio of females per male:	Preseason 1.5 Postseason 7.0
Kill:	Cocks 5000 (including cripples) Hens 500 (including illegal)
Using c for cocks alive before hunting season	$\frac{1.5c - 500}{c - 5000} = \frac{7.0}{1} \quad \therefore \quad c = 6280$

The sex-ratio method is widely used but has the serious deficiency that no estimate of variance is available; thus, the significance of difference between estimates cannot be evaluated. However, Paulik and Robson (1969) gave statistical procedures for calculating variance when numbers (not ratios) are used. Furthermore, serious deficiencies may occur in the assumption that the sexes or ages are equally countable before and after harvesting and that the harvest is known.

The change in ratio method often is useful for calculation of survival rates. Additional examples are given in Chapter 15 using different formulae, but the basic concepts and assumptions are the same.

ESTIMATES FROM RECAPTURES

A large number of studies of populations use methods based upon the recapture of marked individuals. Bands are used for birds and bats; ear tags for mammals; jaw tags for fish and reptiles; clipped toes for mammals and clipped fins for fish; radio-active compounds for small mammals. The method presently considered the best is Jolly's (1965), since it is most realistic and useful (Poole 1974: 307–313, Wilbur and Landwehr 1974, but see Roff 1973a). Because of its length, the method is presented later but the reader is strongly urged to consult the original paper (Jolly 1965) for details. Actually, the animal may not need to be recaptured. It may be captured and marked and then later visually "recaptured." Rice and Harder (1977) estimated white-tailed deer by systematically surveying a research area by helicopter and "recapturing" deer which had been previously marked with a collar. Multiple samples were taken to improve substantially the precision of the estimate.

Procedure

One of the first mark-recapture methods has many names such as "tagging ratio," "Petersen-Jackson Method," and "Lincoln Index" and is considered the most useful by Seber (1973). The method itself depends upon a very simple ratio. The population (N) is related to the number marked and released (M) in the same way as the total caught (n) at a subsequent time is related to the number recaptured (m), or:

$$\frac{N}{M} = \frac{n}{m}, \quad \text{whence } N = \frac{Mn}{m}$$

The population (N), therefore, may be calculated from the equation by substituting the number (M) originally marked and released, the total (n) marked and unmarked that were captured at a subsequent time, and the number (m) of this total that were marked. The confidence limits at 95% level may be calculated (Bailey 1951) from:

$$\text{S.E.} = \sqrt{\frac{M^2n\ (n - m)}{m^3}}$$

To determine the limits within which the population lies (95% confidence), add and subtract 2 standard errors from the estimate. To compare 2 populations, N_1 and N_2, determine the standard errors ($\text{S.E.}_{\cdot 1}$ and $\text{S.E.}_{\cdot 2}$) and calculate the ratio:

$$\frac{N_1 - N_2}{\sqrt{\text{S.E.}_{\cdot 1}{}^2 + \text{S.E.}_{\cdot 2}{}^2}}$$

If this ratio is more than 2, one can claim that the populations are "different" (95% confidence level). Consult a standard statistical text for the "t" test. Methods for calculating the standard errors for more than 2 nights of trapping have been developed by Zippin (1958), and simple formulae for 3 nights of recaptures are given by Bailey (1952). Adams (1951) presented charts for these limits and Chapman (1948) gave a detailed discussion of several types of confidence limits.

Ideally the marking and releasing should all be done at 1 time (a day) and the recaptures also at 1 time (another day). However, in many cases, so few animals are caught in 1 day that the ideal is not attainable. In these cases it is permissible to group the captures for a period (a week perhaps) and assume that all were made on the same day.

An example may be given from the work (Adams 1959) on snowshoe hares on an island, where immigration and emigration were impossible and at a season (winter) when births did not occur. Mortality was assumed to be the same in the marked and unmarked individuals. In January, 27 hares were marked and released. In March, 23 were captured of which 17 had been marked in January. Therefore:

$$N = \frac{27\ (23)}{17} = 36.5;\ \text{S.E.} = \sqrt{\frac{27^2\ (23)\ (6)}{17^3}} = 4.5$$

Upper limits = 36.5 + 9.0 = 45.5

Lower limits = 36.5 − 9.0 = 27.5

The conclusion should be stated that the chances are 95 out of 100 that the population lies between 27 and 46 hares if all assumptions are really fulfilled. It is true that this population is finite and thus a "correction factor" which reduced the S.E. could be used. This factor is rarely applicable because it may not be used for comparisons of differences between populations.

An alternative procedure is to accumulate the captures and recaptures over a period of time. Techniques proposed include those by Schnabel (1938), Schumacher and Eschmeyer (1943), Chapman (1951), and Jolly (1965). The Schnabel Method is illustrated in Table 14.13, using data from a population known to have

Table 14.13. Estimation of cottontail rabbit population by Schnabel (Krumholz) formula from data in Edwards and Eberhardt (1967).

Date	(A) No. of animals captured	No. of animals marked (all released)	No. of (B) animals marked in area	Product (A) (B)	(C) Sum of (A) (B)	No. of animals recaptured	(D) Sum of recaptured	Estimated population (C)/(D)
Oct.								
24	9	9	0	0	0	0	0	
25	8	6	9	72	72	2	2	36
26	9	3	15	135	207	6	8	26
27	14	11	18	252	459	3	11	42
28	8	4	29	232	691	4	15	46
29	5	1	33	165	856	4	19	45
30	16	8	34	544	1400	8	27	52
31	7	3	42	294	1694	4	31	55
Nov.								
1	9	6	45	405	2099	3	34	62
2	3	1	51	153	2252	2	36	63
3	8	1	52	416	2668	7	43	62
4	14	9	53	742	3410	5	48	71
5	2	1	62	124	3534	1	49	72
6	5	5	63	315	3849	0	49	79
7	11	6	68	748	4597	5	54	85
8	0	0	74	0	4597	0	54	85
9	5	0	74	370	4967	5	59	84
10	9	2	74	666	5633	7	66	85
Totals	142	76						

Table 14.14. Estimation of a fox population using recapture data and adjusting for mortality during the trapping period (Lord 1957).

Time period	Number caught A	Marked caught C	Marked Foxes at Large unadjusted B	Marked Foxes at Large adjusted D	AB	AD
Aug. 17–24	35	0	0	0	0	0
Sept. 20–25	6	3	35	33	210	198
Nov. 22–30	19	6	41	35	780	665
Dec. 1–18	11	4	60	54	660	595
Total		13			1650	1458

$$P = \frac{(AB)}{C} = \frac{1650}{13} = 127$$

or

$$P = \frac{(AD)}{C} = \frac{1458}{13} = 112 \text{ foxes in 1954 adjusted for mortality during trapping}$$

135 animals. Several live-trapping techniques were compared and the Schnabel estimates were much too low. Another basic deficiency of this method is that the procedure for calculating standard errors is complex (Ricker 1975). The procedure "smoothes" the data by accumulation and thus the estimates of population are deceptively uniform. Bouffard and Hein (1978) tested different methods to estimate abundance of a particular species (e.g., squirrels) and found that none of the methods were satisfactory for management even though the Schnabel method gave the least variable estimates.

Another illustration may be given using data of marked foxes (Table 14.14). The data were adjusted for mortality during trapping by calculating the deaths of marked foxes based on the annual probability of dying. A further adjustment for trap avoidance reduced the estimate to 101 foxes.

The Schumacher-Eschmeyer calculations may be carried out as indicated in Table 14.15 using rabbit trapping data from 165 traps operated during the month of November.

Table 14.15. Calculation of cottontail rabbit population by Schumacher-Eschmeyer procedure.

Date	k	M	M^2	n−m	m	n	M^2n	Mm	$\frac{m^2}{n}$
Nov.	(1)*	(2)	(3)	(4)	(5)	(6)	(7)	(8)	(9)
1				6	0	6			
2	1	6	36	11	0	11	396		
3	2	17	289	2	0	2	578		
4	3	19	361	2	0	2	722		
5	4	21	441	2	0	2	882		
6	5	23	529	3	1	4	2116	23	0.250000
7	6	26	676	6	1	7	4732	26	.142857
8	7	32	1024	14	0	14	14336		
9	8	46	2116	7	3	10	21160	138	.900000
10	9	53	2809	3	0	3	8427		
11	10	56	3136	0	1	1	3136	56	1.000000
12	11	56	3136	14	2	16	50176	112	.250000
13	12	70	4900	3	4	7	34300	280	2.285714
14	13	73	5329	7	2	9	47961	146	.444444
15	14	80	6400	8	3	11	70400	240	.818181
16	15	88	7744	4	5	9	69696	440	2.777777
17	16	92	8464	0	4	4	33856	368	4.000000
18	17	92	8464	1	3	4	33856	276	2.250000
19	18	93	8649	2	1	3	25947	93	.333333
29	19	95	9025	3	2	5	45125	190	.800000
30	20	98	9604	2	2	4	38416	196	1.000000
31	21	100	10000						

*Column number as substituted in following calculations.

Table 14.15. Continued

$$(1)\ N = \frac{\sum M^2(n)}{\sum Mm} = \frac{(\sum(7))}{(\sum(8))}$$

$$(2)\ s^2 = \frac{1}{k-1}\left[\left(\sum\frac{m^2}{n}\right) - \frac{(\sum Mm)^2}{\sum M^2(n)}\right] = \frac{1}{k-1}\left[\sum(9) - \frac{(\sum(8))^2}{\sum(7)}\right]$$

$$(3)\ S.E. = N\sqrt{\frac{s^2}{\frac{(\sum Mm)^2}{\sum M^2(n)}}} = N\sqrt{\frac{s^2}{\frac{(\sum(8))^2}{\sum(7)}}}$$

When:

N = total population summation
M = number of marked animals in area
m = number of recaptured animals in each sample
n = number of animals in each sample
s^2 = variance
S.E. = standard error of estimate
k = number of samples ($k-1$ equals degrees of freedom)

Note: first marking is not included in calculation of k.

Stochastic models such as Jolly's (1965) acknowledge the many random factors and variances involved in sampling a biological system and should be used more often. The model assumes that each sample is a random sample from the population and that captured animals distribute themselves after release so that marked and unmarked individuals in the population have the same probability of being caught in the next sample. Animals must be marked so that individuals can be identified and each of their captures in a particular sample must be tabulated. Estimates of population size may be made from the following equation:

$$N_i = \frac{M_i}{\alpha_i} = \frac{M_i n_i}{m_i} \quad (i = 2, 3, \ldots, v-1)$$

where

N_i = estimate of the total number of animals in the population when the ith sample is captured (N_1 is put equal to N_2 for subsequent computations)

v = number of samples

$M_i = \frac{s_i z_i}{R_i} + m_i \quad (i = 2, 3, \ldots, v-1)$ = estimate of total number of marked animals in the population at time of sample i ($M_1 = 0$)

$\alpha_i = \frac{m_i}{n_i} \quad (i = 2, 3, \ldots, v-1)$ = proportion of recaptured animals in sample i)

and

s_i = number of animals released from the ith sample after marking

m_i = number of marked animals in the ith sample

n_i = number of animals captured in the ith sample

n_{ij} = number of animals in the ith sample last captured in the jth sample ($1 \leq j \leq i-1$)

$a_{ij} = \sum_{k=1}^{j} n_{ik}$ = number of animals in the ith sample last captured in the jth sample or before

$z_i = \sum_{k=1}^{v} a_{k(i-1)}$ = the number of animals marked before time i which are not caught in the ith sample but are caught subsequently

$R_i = \sum_{k=i+1}^{v} n_{ki}$ = the number of animals released from the ith sample that are caught subsequently

Estimates of "survival" and number of new animals entering the population may be made from the following equations:

$$\phi_i = \frac{M_{i+1}}{M_i - m_i + s_i} \quad (i = 1, w, \ldots, v-2)$$

$$B_i = N_{i+1} - \phi_i(N_i - n_i + s_i) \quad (i = 2, 3, \ldots, v-2)$$

where

ϕ_i = estimate of the probability that an animal (or proportion of animals) alive at the moment of release of the ith sample will survive and remain in the research area until the $(i+1)^{th}$ sample is taken. This also includes resultant changes caused by emigration and immigration.

B_i = estimate of the number of new animals joining the population in the interval between the ith and $(i+1)^{th}$ samples and alive at time $i+1$ (by definition $B_0 = N_1$ and $B_1 = N_2 - \phi_1(N_1 - n_1 + s_1)$)

Variances of the estimates should also be computed using the following formulae:

$$V(N_i) = N_i(N_i - n_i) \left\{ \frac{M_i - m_i + s_i}{M_i} \left(\frac{1}{R_i} - \frac{1}{s_i} \right) + \frac{1 - \alpha_i}{m_i} \right\} + N_i - \sum_{j=O}^{i-1} \frac{N_i^2(j)}{B_j}$$

$$V(\phi_i) = \phi_i^2 \left\{ \frac{(M_{i+1} - m_{i+1})(M_{i+1} - m_{i+1} + s_{i+1})}{M_{i+1}^2} \frac{1}{R_{i+1}} - \frac{1}{s_{i+1}} + \right.$$

$$\left. \frac{M_i - m_i}{M_i - m_i + s_i} \left(\frac{1}{R_i} - \frac{1}{s_i} \right) + \frac{1 - \phi_i}{M_{i+1}} \right\}$$

$$V(B_i) = \frac{B_i^2 (M_{i+1} - m_{i+1})(M_{i+1} - m_{i+1} + s_{i+1})}{M_{i+1}^2} \left(\frac{1}{R_{i+1}} - \frac{1}{s_{i+1}} \right) +$$

$$\frac{M_i - m_i}{M_i - m_i + s_i} \left\{ \frac{\phi_i s_i (1 - \alpha_i)}{\alpha_i} \right\}^2 \left(\frac{1}{R_i} - \frac{1}{\alpha_i} \right) +$$

$$\frac{(N_i - n_i)(N_{i+1} - B_i)(1 - \alpha_i)(1 - \alpha_i)}{M_i - m_i + s_i} + N_{i+1}(N_{i+1} - n_{i+1}) \frac{1 - \alpha_{i+1}}{m_{i+1}} +$$

$$\phi_i^2 N_i (N_i - n_i) \frac{1 - \alpha_i}{m_i}$$

where

$N_i(j)$ = expected number of animals in the population at time i which first joined the population between times j and j+1, i.e., animals which are members of B_j $(1 \leq j \leq i-1)$.

Programming these equations on a computer is very helpful. Terms in the summation $\sum_{j=O}^{i-1} \frac{N_i^2(j)}{B_j}$ needed in the computation of $V(N_i)$ are found from the equations $N_{j+1}(j) = B_j$

and $N_{k+1}(j) = \frac{N_{k+1} - B_k}{N_k} \bullet N_k(j),\ k > j.$

Note especially that values of $N_{k+1}(j)$ depend upon previous values $N_k(j)$. Refer to Jolly (1965) for the theory and development of the previous equations. Details of the method are illustrated in Tables 14.16A, B, C which come directly from an example in Jolly (1965). The number of animals captured in the ith sample (n_i) and number of animals released from the ith sample after marking (s_i) are given in Table 14.16A. Note that they are not necessarily the same. Table 14.16A also gives the tabulated values (n_{ij}) of the number of animals observed in the ith sample (read down the first column) last captured in the jth sample (read across the top). For example, the number of animals in the 7th sample last captured in the 5th sample is 34. The sum of the columns gives the number of animals released from the ith sample that are caught subsequently. For example, the number of animals released from the 7th sample that are caught again is 108. Table 14.16B illustrates the next step of finding the values a_{ij}. Entries in Table 14.16B come from adding across the columns of Table 14.16A. For example, the second entry in column 5 of Table 14.16B comes from adding the entries in row 7 of Table 14.16A, i.e., 56 = 1 + 6 + 5 + 10 + 34. Likewise, the seventh entry in column 4 of Table 14.16B comes from the entries in row 11 of Table 14.16A, i.e., 7 = 1 + 2 + 3 + 1. The values for Z_i are found from Table 14.16B by adding the entries of a column except the first. Note that the values from column i actually sum up to Z_{i+1}, e.g., Z_7 = 110. The top entry of column i in Table 14.16B is m_{i+1}, e.g., m_7 = 112. Table 14.16C shows the final results, giving the estimates and their standard errors for each sampling period. This method does not give good results with small numbers. The large standard errors are regrettable but inherent in sampling biological systems and must be acknowledged.

Methods of this type obviously benefit from the use of a computer both for calculation of populations and for

Table 14.16A. Number of animals captured and released in each sample (Jolly 1965).

i	n_i	s_i	*1*	*2*	*3*	*4*	*5*	*6*	*7*	*8*	*9*	*10*	*11*	*12*
1	54	54												
2	146	143	10											
3	169	164	3	34										
4	209	202	5	18	33									
5	220	214	2	8	13	30								
6	209	207	2	4	8	20	43							
7	250	243	1	6	5	10	34	56						
8	176	175	0	4	0	3	14	19	46					
9	172	169	0	2	4	2	11	12	28	51				
10	127	126	0	0	1	2	3	5	17	22	34			
11	123	120	1	2	3	1	0	4	8	12	16	30		
12	120	120	0	1	3	1	1	2	7	4	11	16	26	
13	142		0	1	0	2	3	3	2	10	9	12	18	35 *13*
R_i =				80	70	71	109	101	108	99	70	58	44	35

testing the appropriateness of the data to the model (Manly 1971, Brownie et al. 1978).

A graphic form is useful for estimating the population from trap-retrap data (Hayne 1949b). In Fig. 14.4 the proportion marked is plotted against the number previously marked. The population can be read on the graph at the point where the slope line would intersect the top horizontal line, which represents all marked individuals. The population can also be determined from the slope by dividing the distance of any point on the plotted line from the vertical axis (x) into the distance from the horizontal axis (y). Then substitute this slope ($b = y/x$) in the equation of a straight line: $R = a + bN$ where $R = 1$ (i.e., all marked), $a = 0$ (since the line must go through the origin), and N is the population. In Fig. 14.4, the slope is (calculated above letter A) 0.42/48 = .00875. Hence $1 = .00875N$ and $N = 114$. An even simpler procedure is as follows. When $R = 1$ (i.e., 100% marked) then $1 = bN$ or since $b = y/x$ then $1 = Ny/x$ or $x/y = N$. Hence, N can be obtained directly merely by determining the value of any point on the line in terms of the number of animals marked previously (which is x) and the proportion marked in the catch (which is y). This is, of course, merely the reciprocal of the slope. In this case 48/0.42 = 114.

The equation ($x/y = N$) can be written $y = (x/N)^z$ where z is some power. When $z = 1$, then, of course, a straight line results. When z is more than 1, the proportion marked is not increasing as rapidly as it should be from the number caught and marked, and one can conclude that a significant increase of unmarked animals has occurred due to births or immigration. When z is less than 1, the proportion marked is increasing more rapidly than it should be from the number caught. Therefore, one can conclude that there is a larger likelihood of capture of marked than of unmarked animals. The value of z can be found from the plotted data by using simultaneous equations for 2 points. Let us use the curved line in Fig. 14.4 and consider the points A and B. At A, $y = 0.42$, and $x = 48$ while at B, $y = 0.17$ and $x = 22$. Then, taking logarithms

$\log y = z \log x - a \log N$ and
$\log 0.48 = z \log 48 - z \log N$; also
$\log 0.17 = z \log 22 - z \log N$. Therefore:
$0.38 = 1.68\,z - z \log N$

Table 14.16B. Procedure for calculations of a_{ij} from values developed in previous table (Jolly 1965).

	1	*2*	*3*	*4*	*5*	*6*	*7*	*8*	*9*	*10*	*11*	*12*
	10											
	3	37										
	5	23	56									
	2	10	23	53								
	2	6	14	34	77							
	1	7	12	22	56	112						
	0	4	4	7	21	40	86					
	0	2	6	8	19	31	59	110				
	0	0	1	3	6	11	28	50	84			
	1	3	6	7	7	11	19	31	47	77		
	0	1	4	5	6	8	15	19	30	46	72	
	0	1	1	3	6	9	11	21	30	42	60	95 *13*
Z_{i+1} =	14	57	71	89	121	110	132	121	107	88	60	

Table 14.16C. Estimates and standard errors resulting from calculations in previous tables (Jolly 1965).

i	$\hat{a}_i$	$\hat{M}_i$	$\hat{N}_i$	$\hat{\phi}_i$	$\hat{B}_i$	$\{V(\hat{N}_i)\}^{\frac{1}{2}}$	$\{V(\hat{\phi}_i)\}^{\frac{1}{2}}$	$\{V(\hat{B}_i)\}^{\frac{1}{2}}$
1	—	0	—	0.649	—	—	0.114	—
2	0.0685	35.02	511.2	1.015	263.2	151.2	.110	179.2
3	.2189	170.54	779.1	0.867	291.8	129.3	.107	137.7
4	.2679	258.00	963.0	.564	406.4	140.9	.064	120.2
5	.2409	227.73	945.3	.836	96.9	125.5	.075	111.4
6	.3684	324.99	882.2	.790	107.0	96.1	.070	74.8
7	0.4480	359.50	802.5	0.651	135.7	74.8	0.056	55.6
8	.4886	319.33	653.6	.985	13.8	61.7	.093	52.5
9	.6395	402.13	628.8	.686	49.0	61.9	.080	34.2
10	.6614	316.45	478.5	.884	84.1	51.8	.120	40.2
11	.6260	317.00	506.4	.771	74.5	65.8	.128	41.1
12	.6000	277.71	462.8	—	—	70.2	—	—
13	.6690	—	—	—	—	—	—	—

$0.77 = 1.34\ z - z \log N$. Subtracting gives:
$0.39 = -.34z$ and $z = -1.15$. Then
$0.77 = 1.34\ (1.15) + 1.15 \log N$ and rearranging
$1.15 \log N = 2.31$
$\log N = 2.01$ and $N = 102$

An ingenious method may be useful to estimate a small population (Davis 1963). Obviously, if all individuals have been marked, subsequent samples cannot contain unmarked individuals. A table can be prepared, from probability considerations, showing the number of successive collections (in which all animals are marked) necessary to permit the conclusion that, at a level of 90% confidence, the population is less than the specified total. This method has not been tried on wild populations, and obviously is suitable only for very small populations.

The recapture method can be used for estimation of various objects in addition to the animals themselves. In a study of the number of nests built by robins in orchards (Johnson et al. 1976) the number of nests found in spring was the number marked (M), the total nests after the trees lost their leaves was n, of which m had been observed in spring. The usual calculation of the recapture method gives the number of nests in spring.

To convert this estimate of nests into an index of robin populations one should know how many robins per nest were present.

Assumptions

The recapture method, however, requires several assumptions: (1) no loss (or gain) of marks; (2) no recruitment (births or immigration); (3) no difference in mortality of the marked and unmarked individuals; (4) catchability is the same in marked and unmarked individuals. Although the method is simple mathematically, the habits of the species rarely fulfill the assumptions. Assumption (1) is usually true at least for short periods of time but may fail for birds because of band loss. As-

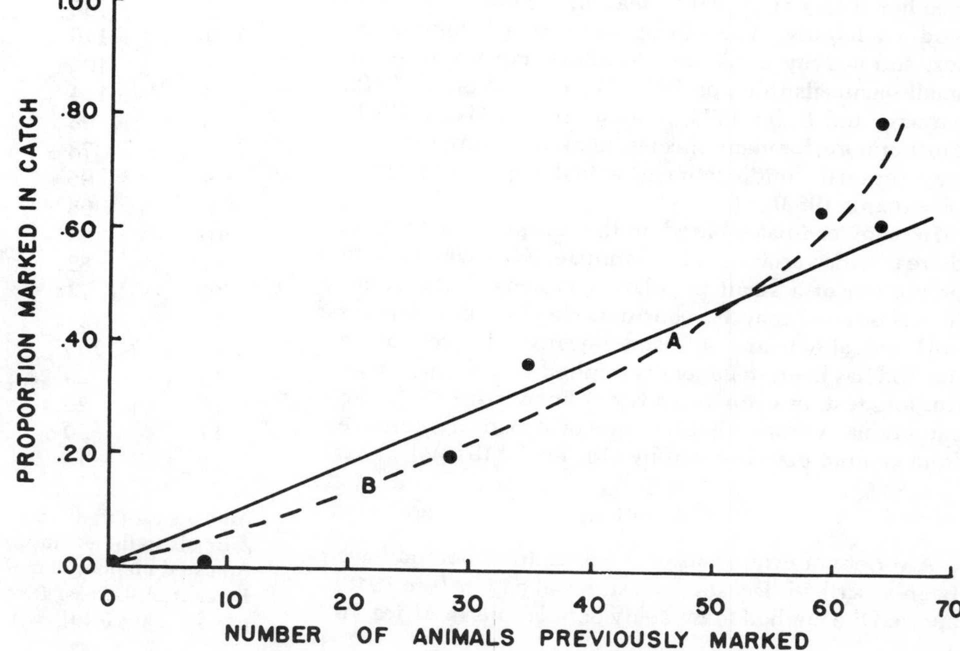

Fig. 14.4. Graphic method of estimating a population by plotting the proportion in the catch that are marked against the number already marked. The straight line is taken from Hayne (1949b) and represents a condition when there is no bias in retrapping. The curved line shows the slope when individuals are retrapped more frequently than expected by chance.

sumption (2) may be true in the nonbreeding season or for short periods of time. It may be circumvented by determining which individuals are the newcomers and rejecting them from the total captures, n. Assumption (3) is probably often true, but should be proven for each case of estimation. An important bias occurs during hunting. Assumption (4) is perhaps true enough for general purposes but rarely is completely true because of home range behavior in mammals and territorial behavior in birds. Also many weather factors affect trappability such as cloudiness, temperature, precipitation and wind (Perry et al. 1977). Furthermore, some individuals become trap-happy or trap-wise. This difficulty has not been tested for most species. In many cases, recapture by a procedure different from the capture procedure will minimize the difficulty. For example, woodchucks may be trapped for marking and shot for recapture. However the mark must not be conspicuous or a biased recapture may result. Nevertheless, if sight of the mark itself is the means of "recapture" then it must be conspicuous.

Problems with mark-recapture methods cause serious inaccuracies, and therefore some recent references dealing with these problems should be examined in detail, because while useful for general estimates, these methods may have limited value in many situations (Roff 1973a,b; Sarrazin and Bider 1973). Assumptions behind the methods are often violated and estimates must be considered imprecise because of large variances. Also differences in the probability of capture related to age cause estimation errors (Hall 1974, Joule and Cameron 1974). For example, probability of capture (p) may be related to weight (age). Population estimates may be based on these probabilities. In particular (Table 14.17) the ratio 1/p may be used as the correction factor to compensate for age bias. This example is one of many that illustrate the need to verify the assumptions.

Wilbur and Landwehr (1974) suggested ways to test for equicatchability from recaptures of marked individuals and emphasized its importance to the mark-recapture methods. Indeed, a number of factors such as weather (Perry et al. 1977), season, population density, food availability, type of trap used, social dominance, sex, and activity are known to affect trap responses of small mammals (Sheppe 1972, Wiener and Smith 1972, Sarrazin and Bider 1973, Summerlin and Wolfe 1973). Furthermore, for many species, mark-recapture methods may seriously underestimate actual population levels (Eberhardt 1969).

In many estimates based on the recapture technique, there is wide variance of the estimate. Even when a high proportion of a small population is marked the confidence interval may be considerable. The deficiencies outlined above are stressed because the recapture method has been so generally applied without adequate caution, test, or even an apparent knowledge of the assumptions. A thorough discussion of statistical inference from capture date is given by Otis et al. (1978).

Elaborations

A variety of extensions of the recapture method have been described. Jackson, in a series of papers (see 1948) applied the method to tsetse fly populations in Africa. In 1939 he incorporated the calculation of birth and death rates into the method. This inclusion is possible because repeated recaptures over a period of time showed a decline in the ratio of marked-to-unmarked individuals due to mortality and to births. In 1944, Jackson discussed some environmental factors and in 1948 he refined some of the calculations. Many recent elaborations and descriptions are available in Seber (1973).

A few comments on the elaborate mathematical developments of this method are pertinent. Numerous papers make assumptions about particular animals and develop appropriate mathematical equations. However, the development of the mathematics has proceeded far more rapidly than has the testing of the assumptions. Only recently have serious attempts been made to make these tests. In some cases the assumptions hold for 1 species but not for another living in the same field. Unfortunately, each investigation must involve a testing of the assumptions for that species, time, and place. The fact that the assumptions held for species "A" at place "X" does not mean that they will hold for place "Y" nor even for another season at place "X". The task of testing these assumptions is tremendous but must be done in any investigational program. Because of these deficiencies, the mathematical elaborations are not described here in detail.

Another aspect that requires comment is the fact that many of these mathematical methods are closely related versions employing the same principle. Thus, methods which appear to be very different are really based on the

Table 14.17. Adjusting a population estimation by weight-capture probabilities (from Hall 1974).

Animal number	Weight (g)	Probability of capture (p)	Observation adjustment factor (1/p)
1	88	0.83	1.20
2	85	0.83	1.21
3	116	0.87	1.15
4	104	0.86	1.17
5	114	0.87	1.15
6	98	0.85	1.18
7	78	0.81	1.23
8	95	0.84	1.19
9	68	0.79	1.26
10	84	0.82	1.22
11	82	0.82	1.22
12	74	0.81	1.24
13	97	0.84	1.19
14	108	0.86	1.16
15	20	0.57	1.76
16	25	0.62	1.60
17	20	0.57	1.76
18	19	0.56	1.80

Animals captured: 18
Animals in the enclosure: 28
Adjusted number of animals captured: 22.4
Percent of success: $18 \div 28 = 64$ or $22.4 \div 28 = 80$
$p = 79.764 + 0.101\ (wt) - 496.312\ (1/wt),\ r^2 = 0.86.$

same basic relations. For example, the removal method is the same in its simplest form and in such complex forms as the catch-per-unit-effort, change in sex or age ratios, gas model, artificial predation and many others. This same situation occurs for the techniques based on the recapture method. Thus, unfortunately, we do not have a large number of estimation methods available in these mathematical papers, but only numerous modifications of 2 methods.

SURVIVAL

Another method of estimation of population size must be included for completeness, although it rarely is useful. When the survival rate (p) is known one can determine the population size at both a previous or subsequent date if one has an estimate for only one of these times. Thus, if the population at time 2 is N_2, then the population at time 1 is given by $N_1p = N_2$ or $N_1 = N_2/p$. Similarly, the population at time 3 is $N_2p = N_3$. The reason this method is rarely used is that when one has an estimate for a particular time, it is usually easier to get another estimate than to get a value for p. But the method should not be overlooked in searching for suitable census procedures.

COMPARISON OF METHODS

Thus far, this review has been concerned with a description of the various methods. It now remains to evaluate these methods as they relate to wildlife species. Unfortunately, little true evaluation has been done. Rarely has a thorough investigation been made to compare a population estimate with a known population. However, some comparisons between methods have been made on the same but unknown population. A few comparisons were noted earlier in the text as illustrations of methods and more will be mentioned here.

Total Counts

Some counts have been performed by different observers to give some notion of the variation between observers. An estimate of song bird populations calculated from the number seen per-unit-area was compared to an independent count. When this estimate was compared with the known number of birds in the area, the average error in 6 different months was only 15%. Drives by a group of trained persons were made on a known number of deer in a large enclosure. The drive recorded about 65% of the deer when the men were 280 m apart but almost 100% when the drivers were 40 m apart.

A notable comparison concerns estimating the winter-kill of deer. (It obviously lacked many of the variables associated with counts of live animals). Four versions of the strip census were used; primary differences involved details of calculating the average distance between observer and dead deer. The results of these 4 versions differed in 1 test by 3, 74, 19, and 12% from the true number of dead deer. Even though some estimates were close, the confidence limits had a wide spread. In several comparisons the various strip-census methods differed from a simple recapture ratio. A further examination of estimates were made by various methods on a known population of 200 burlap bags, placed so as to resemble dead deer. When the lines were 32 km long, the error of recapture ratio was only 1%, but when the lines were 8 km it was 10%. The errors associated with strip censuses varied from 4 to 65%. Even when the estimate differed by only 1% from 200, the confidence limits were wide (Robinette et al. 1954). The important conclusion from their investigation is that several methods should be used to estimate a known population at a particular time and place as a basis for appraising estimates of populations of unknown size.

Two types of census of pheasants along the same routes were compared: (1) cocks-seen per mile and (2) cock-calls per 2-minute intervals. Elaborate statistical analysis showed that strong wind reduced the count of cock-calls and dew reduced the count of cocks-seen. Neither of these methods is absolute, but joint use has advantages.

Estimates from Indices

A precise check on the relation of signs to a known population was made (Rasmussen and Doman 1943) when a fire killed all the mule deer in an enclosure of 300 ha and thereby permitted a comparison of a known number of deer with previous counts of fecal pellets. In this unique situation it was possible to establish the value of 12.7 pellet-groups per deer per day for this place and season. However, this ratio has been applied innumerable times to populations in other places and in other seasons without allowing for the fact that the pellet count must be calibrated in each area. A comparison of the number of deer from an airplane and the number of pellet-groups showed variation from 370 to 1280 pellets per deer, thereby giving an estimate with so much scatter as to be practically useless (Bennett et al. 1940). An appraisal of the results of the pellet-count procedure and the results of 3 other methods showed that the pellet-count procedure gave very different results that were presumably erroneous. The "pellet-groups" per deer per day varied from 10 to 17 in various months (Dasmann and Taber 1955).

Estimates From Captures

A number of authors have compared results obtained by various types of traps, especially for small mammals. Considerable differences occur in the numbers trapped using different types of traps; also different sizes of the same type of trap may catch different numbers. A comparison of live traps and snap traps shows that the 2 types can give comparable results when only 3 days were used. It is obvious, therefore, that the effectiveness of the removal equipment must be established before using the removal technique to estimate animal numbers. It may be advisable to use the same kind of trap for 2 populations if they are to be compared.

Estimates by Recapture Method

In spite of its wide use, the recapture method has rarely been checked against a known animal population. An estimation of the deer in a yard was possible from accidentally-marked individuals. Three variations of the recapture method gave 714, 803, and 902 deer, whereas the number actually observed in the yard was 473 (which was less than the true number) (Kabat et al. 1953). In some cases estimates of pheasant populations based on the recapture method agree fairly well with estimates based on the change in sex ratio during the hunting season (Harper et al. 1951).

A comparison of 2 methods is available in a study of blackbirds (Albers 1976). Territorial males, which are conspicuous along roadsides, can be readily counted so that one has a figure for x territorial males per km. In addition, one can make several visits to an area and treat a male seen in a particular place as "marked" to be, or not be, "recaptured" on subsequent visits. In this recapture formula, N is the population (unknown) on the first visit, M is the number of territorial males seen on the first visit, and n is the number of males on subsequent visits of which m were "marked" previously. N may be calculated from 2 visits or calculated by the Schnabel or Jolly method using many visits. A comparison for 1973 (Fig. 14.5) shows that the direct count of males gave higher numbers than did the recapture estimate. (The original publication gives various calculations in detail.) The problem now is to decide which is the more *accurate*. Numerous opportunities for bias and for duplication of counts exist. Other persons using these methods have had similar problems, but it seems likely that the direct count is more accurate than the recapture method.

A serious effort to compare methods (Bouffard and Hein 1978) for gray squirrels in a 31.5 ha forest indicated that the Schnabel gave the best (most precise) estimate and the Jolly the worst. The time-area counts were most efficient and thus cost the least.

Many opportunities exist for using several methods simultaneously. Indeed, populations studies should be organized at the outset so that real checks can be made upon the census estimates. The same data used in the recapture method may be used for the catch-effort method if a marked (recaptured) individual is considered in the records to be dead. Two methods of calculation can be used on the same data, but both may be affected equally by biases.

Precision

From the few examples given in detail, it is evident that comparison of methods requires high precision that can only be attained by a high number of captures. In case after case, the confidence limits of the estimate have been at least 25–50% of the total. The only way to reduce these limits is to increase the probability of capture or observation. The only way to accomplish this is to spend more time in capturing or observing. When the removal technique is used, it is necessary to catch 90% of the animals in order to have the limits of an estimate of 50 animals be within 40 and 60 individuals, and a 95% catch is necessary for the limits to be within 45 and 55 animals (Zippin 1958). Table 14.18 shows the proportion of the population that must be captured during removal to achieve a certain coefficient of variation (ratio of standard error to the mean). Note that the necessary proportions get higher when fewer animals are present. Since such a high proportion must be captured to obtain a precise estimate, biologists should ask why use an estimate at all. Wildlife managers will have to spend much greater time and money on estimates than has been done in the past if they wish to detect changes of much less than 25–50% of the population.

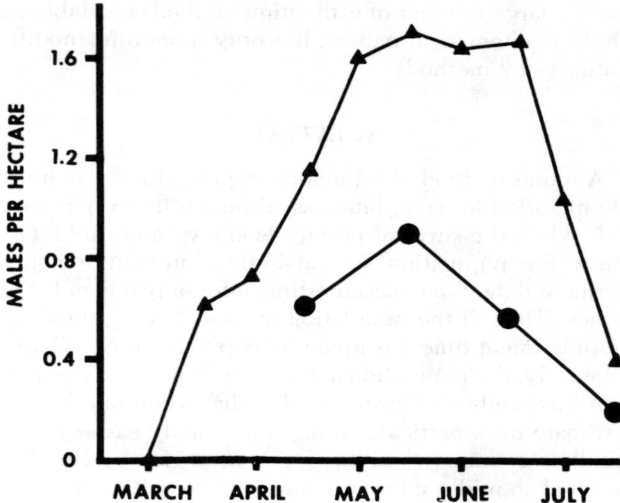

Fig. 14.5. Comparison of counts (triangles) and estimates (circles) of red-winged blackbirds along roadsides in preferred habitat during the breeding season of 1973 (Adapted from Albers 1976).

CONCLUSION

The failure of wildlife investigators to check population estimates against a known population is a deplorable situation. Further progress in the study of populations requires concentration on improvement of estimators but, more particularly, a detailed study of biases and the appropriateness of assumptions. Furthermore, most present-day techniques of estimation have such low precision that only large changes of the population—or large influence of a factor—can be detected. For example, if the population estimate has a precision of only 15% then we cannot detect the effect of, say predation, unless its effect is more than 15%. If there is a change in this population of, say 14%, we

Table 14.18. Proportion of total population required to be trapped for specified coefficient of variation of N (Zippin 1958).

N	Coefficient of Variation 30%	20%	10%	5%
Proportion (to nearest .05) of population to be captured (in 100 or fewer trappings)				
200	.55	.60	.75	.90
300	.50	.60	.75	.85
500	.45	.55	.70	.80
1000	.40	.45	.60	.75
10000	.20	.25	.35	.50
100000	.10	.15	.20	.30

cannot say whether it is due to sampling variability or to predation. Fortunately, however, at this stage in the development of management of wildlife populations, low precision population estimates may be adequate. The administrator is not impressed by some management procedure that will increase the quail population by only 5%. To be worth the effort, the management technique must have a large effect; fortunately even a method of low precision can detect a large effect.

Another discouraging aspect is that we have so few basic methods. Actually there are only 3 basic population estimation methods—direct count, change in a ratio, and survival—and the first is difficult and the last is rarely useful. When one remembers that even the catch-effort method of DeLury and the recapture method of Peterson, Jackson, and others merely reflect changes in ratio, one realizes that there is little hope of adequate comparison of methods.

A fundamental problem in population dynamics is to determine the density of a population where density means the number of animals per unit area. Density is an important parameter because it directly relates the population to habitat conditions. Preferably density should be expressed in reference to the factor that is limiting the population at that time and place (e.g., "birds-per-budworm," "deer-per-kg of forage," etc.). Since this procedure is difficult, density is usually expressed as animals-per-unit area. This definition assumes that the limiting factor is proportional to the size of the area. This expression requires a further determination of the abundance of forage per unit area, for example, to be meaningful in judging how near the population is to carrying capacity.

Another complication of the density problem results from the fact that we are interested in an "instantaneous" density. A little reflection will make it clear that if we study an area over a period of time (which is necessary to secure adequate data), we will include all immigration regardless of whether it is due to births or to movements. Consider, for example, a case of a farm (100 ha) in which there are 100 quail. Suppose that during the month 10 quail die and are immediately replaced by 10 immigrants. The population at any time is 100 (the instantaneous population), but 110 different quail are involved. Obviously the density is 1.00 quail per ha; not 1.10 quail per ha. Swift and Steinhorst (1976) present a technique for defining the area associated with a population estimate based on captures on a grid. This method gives an estimate of density by taking into account both the animals which are normally found entirely within the grid area and those which are active both on and off the grid. Assessment trap lines intersect grid lines to give an estimate of the area actually being sampled by the traps on the grid. O'Farrell et al. (1977) concluded that livetrapping gave better estimates of density than did removal trapping when using assessment lines. O'Farrell and Austin (1978) recommended that the census lines include assessment lines rather than a simple grid to estimate density because this modification gave similar results with less effort.

It is important to note that new variations of the basic methods for estimating population numbers are constantly being developed. Techniques useful to the wildlife biologist also may come from other fields, such as the nearest-neighbor method used by botanists for estimating plant populations (Blackith 1958). This procedure could be tried for the enumeration of animal forms such as dead deer or woodchuck burrows. Refinements of techniques may be reported in relatively unexpected places, such as an ingenious procedure for determining the probability of capture (Sluiter et al. 1956). In closing, it is important to note that the possibilities for developing new techniques of estimating population numbers have by no means been exhausted.

Chapter Fifteen

Vital Statistics of Animal Populations

ROBERT L. DOWNING

Wildlife Research Biologist
U.S. Fish and Wildlife Service
Denver Wildlife Research Center
Clemson, South Carolina

INTRODUCTION

Vital statistics, such as sex and age ratios, natality and rearing success, and survival and mortality rates, should be known to judge intelligently the welfare of animal populations. Census techniques (presented in another chapter) are important for measuring population size, but do not identify which recruitment and/or mortality factors are responsible for observed changes. Thus, techniques for estimating vital statistics are indispensable "tools-of-the-trade" of every practicing wildlife biologist.

The purpose of this chapter is to present, in terms understandable by novice and experienced biologists, the basic techniques for estimating vital statistics and to point out some of the many biases to consider when making biological measurements. Each technique is presented by example, usually without symbols and formulas. In addition to the basic, time-honored techniques, this chapter presents a new technique for population reconstruction, unused variations of the change-in-ratio technique, and suggests changes in nomenclature for life tables. Formal training in population dynamics, statistics, sampling, or differential calculus is not required to understand this chapter.

SAMPLING CONSIDERATIONS

Population analysts should ask themselves "How much information do I need?" Only 1 indicator of population welfare, such as a census or a measure of recruitment or mortality, may be needed every 3 to 5 years to detect gross changes in a long-lived, slow-changing population of low economic, scientific, or recreational value. However, highly reliable data on population size or density, plus several key vital statistics, must be obtained frequently for a short-lived, rapidly fluctuating population of high value (either positive or negative). Highly reliable and detailed data are always needed in research situations.

Unfortunately, the needed information cannot always be obtained with the available resources. Money and manpower are usually limited; therefore, the investigator must choose between the various data-gathering schemes, selecting those which are affordable but meet the objectives of the study. Budgets often can be stretched by gathering data during "off" seasons, by gathering several kinds of data at the same time, or by designing the study so that maximum use can be made of unskilled or seasonal labor. For example, more good age data can be obtained per dollar by hiring students to collect wings, teeth, etc. for later analysis than by hiring experienced biologists to determine the age on the spot. Free data on poaching, road kills, and other scattered losses can be obtained by enlisting the help of enforcement personnel, clerks-of-court, insurance adjustors, foresters, extension agents, etc. Such efforts often assure good will and acceptance of the study if the biologist keeps the cooperators informed and makes them feel they are part of the team.

A recurring question is "How long should data gathering continue for a population?" Continuous, prolonged accumulation of data without meaningful analysis, interpretation, and reporting may lose the support of cooperators. Reporting of progress should begin as soon as possible, and an annual updating should be made as long as there are significant fluctuations in any vital statistic. However, if the population and its habitat appear to be reasonably stable, the sampling scheme could be changed from continuous to periodic with little loss of information. After a baseline has been established for each statistic, future measures will be easier to interpret.

Vital statistics are calculated from samples of the living population at some point in time or from samples of those which die during some interval. Every sample, whether living or dead, must be "representative" to depict accurately the vital statistics of a population. Unfortunately, biases often deprive samples of their representativeness.

Many techniques for sampling a living population have bias due to differences in size, activity, and distribution of each sex and age group in the population. Differences in observability (Downing et al. 1977) or problems in determining sex and age from a distance may make it necessary to capture or kill a sample of the living population. Hunters frequently provide large samples rather economically, but there are inherent biases due not only to differing behavioral characteristics of each sex and age class in the population but also to the behavior and selectivity of the hunter (Coe et al. 1980). Most of these biases have been poorly described.

Representative samples of those dying may be even more difficult to obtain than samples of the living population because several causes of death are involved, and each cause removes each sex and age at a different rate. Each cause of death also is sampled at a different rate because some causes of death are easier to observe than others. Hunter kills usually are sampled at the highest rate (approaching 100% if a well-enforced, mandatory check is employed), followed by accidental highway deaths, crippling, poaching, starvation, disease, and predation. This order should not be confused with their relative importance as mortality factors. For example, predation or starvation may be the most important cause of death in lightly hunted populations, but may be sampled at a low rate because humans are not involved in the death.

The problem of obtaining representative samples can be complex; first, the analyst must be sure that the subsample for each cause of death is representative of those that died from that cause. Then, each subsample must be "weighted" so that it makes up the same portion of the total sample as that cause of death contributed to the total deaths. The problem deserves a great deal of thought, and the solution may require an elaborate sampling scheme. Schemes designed to disclose the total number dying, not just a representative sample, require extra effort but are needed to fill the gap in our knowledge of mortality factors. One of the many possible techniques for enumerating deaths is described in this chapter under "Population Reconstruction."

Bias is not always bad. When the same estimator is used repeatedly to detect a temporal change (a trend) in a vital statistic, bias may have little effect providing both estimates are equally biased. Such a measure often is called an index. Biases vary between areas, seasons, etc.; consequently, an index should be used with caution.

There also is variability between samples to consider. Standard statistical texts describe how variability between samples can be measured and controlled. The early help of a biometrician also is needed to define study objectives and hypotheses in the proper terms and to design an efficient sampling scheme. Periodic statistical consultation is helpful during data collection to make sure sample sizes and numbers are adequate, but not excessive, in view of the precision required (also see Eberhardt 1978b). A biometrician should then guide the analysis to be sure the appropriate techniques are being used. This is especially important because many wildlife data do not conform to normal frequency curves and are more appropriately analyzed by nonparametric and other methods which do not assume normality. Finally, a biometrician should help interpret the results, because there are many pitfalls for the inexperienced or unwary biologist.

SEX RATIOS

Sex ratio should be measured periodically to determine if it is within the range needed for normal reproductive performance. A knowledge of sex ratios is essential to understand and interpret other vital statistics, many of which are expressed separately for each sex. Sex ratios also are raw data for calculating other vital statistics, especially change-in-ratio estimators. Techniques for determining sex of a variety of species are contained in a separate chapter in this manual.

Every sample of sex ratio should be critically examined to determine if it is biased. Selection of males by hunters results in biased sampling of many species. Deer hunters often hunt near buck rubs or scrapes, follow the largest tracks in snow, or let groups of deer pass hoping that other groups will contain a buck. Some data (Roseberry and Klimstra 1974) suggest that male fawns are killed at a higher rate than doe fawns, possibly because males are more active and/or less inclined to remain with family groups (Coe et al. 1980). Duck hunters often select male mallards from the flock because of their bright coloration and lower "point" value. Sometimes one sex is easier to trap than the other (Bellrose et al. 1961). Sex ratios of some migratory species are biased geographically because males migrate at a different time than females.

Even if an accurate sex ratio cannot be obtained directly due to biased sampling, an adult sex ratio sometimes can be estimated if the sex ratio of the young is known (or if equal numbers of male and female young can be assumed) and if the relative difference between sampling rates of young and adults is the same for both sexes. For example, suppose that a population contains 600 young males, 500 young females (a young sex ratio of 54.6% males and 45.4% females), 400 adult males, and 1400 adult females. Also, suppose that a sample from this population contains 10% of the adult females (140), 15% of the young females (75), 20% of the adult males (80), and 30% of the young males (180). The only common denominator of these highly biased sampling rates is that the young of both sexes were sampled at a 50% higher rate than the adults of that sex. Adult sex ratios can be estimated as follows:

$$\frac{0.454 \times 140 \times 180}{0.546 \times 75 \times 80} = \frac{11{,}440}{3276} = 3.5 \text{ adult females per}$$

$$\text{adult male or} \quad \frac{3.5}{1.0 + 3.5} = 77.8\% \text{ females}$$

The above method may not be appropriate for species in which the young males travel with and behave similar to females. Deer, for example, are inappropriate because the male fawns remain with their mothers throughout the first year and are harvested at similar rates under antlerless regulations. Thus, there is a greater difference between harvest rates of young and adult males than between young and adult females. However, it may not be necessary to include fawns in the calculation. Yearling bucks behave more nearly like adult bucks, and since yearling and adult does also behave similarly, yearlings can be used as the "young" portion of the sample. This variation of the method (Severinghaus and Maguire 1955) will then estimate the sex ratio of deer 2 years old and older. The reader is cautioned that it may be difficult to verify if relative sampling rates are truly equal for both sexes.

Several biologists have apparently misinterpreted the paper by Hayne and Gwynn (1977) as suggesting that the sex ratio of the *harvest* is a statistic indicative of deer herd welfare. Hayne and Gwynn merely gave theoretical support to the practice of limiting harvest sex ratios (usually to 30–40% female) to prevent overharvest. I have prepared a paper (in press) that refutes the "welfare indicator" idea. I also point out that exceptional herds, those with low rates of nonhunting mortality, can be unknowingly *underharvested* by limiting the percentage of does in the harvest unless several other herd and habitat statistics are closely monitored. I contend that if limited data are available, it is better to monitor and adjust the *number* of each sex harvested, rather than the sex ratio.

David E. Davis (pers. comm.) has pointed out that the conventional expression of sex ratio, the number of males per 100 females, is awkward and generally requires extra calculations when such sex ratios are used in other computations. He suggests that all ratios be expressed in percent because this gives males and females a common base. As an example, only 1 formula is needed to perform a variety of change-in-ratio calculations if the ratios are expressed in percent, while 2 and sometimes 3 formulas are needed if sex ratio is expressed as males per 100 females. All ratios used in this chapter are expressed in percent.

AGE RATIOS

Age ratios (or other expressions such as the number of animals in each age class) are an important source of information. Young/adult ratios are a measure of the natality and rearing success of a population. A knowledge of the relative size of each age class of females is needed to interpret age-specific reproductive rates. For example, older mothers usually are more successful than young ones, but as a group may not contribute as much to the productivity of the population if they are less numerous. The number of animals in each age class is the raw data for most calculations of mortality and survival, as illustrated later in this chapter.

Age ratios are obtained in various ways. Some species can be differentiated into 2 or more age classes in the field while others must be captured or killed to determine age. The sampling scheme should be carefully chosen to assure that all age classes are equally represented. Hunters usually are not a bias-free sampling medium because of their tendency to select the larger, more colorful animals. Many field counts and hunting and trapping samples are further biased by the behavioral characteristics of certain age groups which are manifested in certain orders of travel, grouping tendencies, and the use of different habitats. A separate chapter describes methods for determining age of a variety of species.

A popular misconception among biologists is that one can use age distributions to indicate if a population is increasing or declining. An "old" age distribution is sometimes interpreted as a characteristic of a declining population while a "young" distribution is thought to characterize an increasing population. However, age-ratio interpretation is more complicated; the "old" distribution also might be indicative of populations experiencing poor rearing success while the "young" distribution could be the result of good rearing success. Caughley (1974a:562) stated "Age ratios are a resultant of all these factors and cannot be broken down to reveal the component effects." Further, he said: "To sum up: age ratios cannot be interpreted without a knowledge of rate of increase, and if we have an estimate of this rate we do not need age ratios."

While it is difficult to interpret age ratios observed at any one time, it may be possible to make useful inferences from changes in these ratios. For instance, if the percentage of younger animals in the population is declining, management should be designed both to increase natality and to reduce juvenile mortality until better information reveals which one is causing the decline. Grier (1979) presents an interesting discussion of the problems inherent in interpreting changes in age ratios.

NATALITY AND REARING SUCCESS

Measures of natality and rearing success are good indicators of population health and suggest how much annual mortality a population can endure without suffering a decline. Natality and rearing success are also measures of the maximum rate at which a population can rebound following decimation. Some biologists, assuming that reproduction is sensitive to habitat conditions, monitor natality and rearing success as an index to range conditions rather than attempt to quantify and interpret complex, seasonally changing, or inaccessible habitats.

Estimates of the number of young per adult female are often difficult to obtain because the young are born in a protected, inaccessible, or cryptic location. Investigators should be sure that the habitat which is most convenient to sample is representative of that used by the entire population. For example, mourning dove nests can be found easily in almost any grove of trees in the Great Plains and several studies of their nesting success have been made in such locations. However, 71% of the doves in northwestern Oklahoma nested on the ground (Downing 1959), and these are not sampled in most such studies. High winds, which destroy many tree nests, have little effect on ground nests. Heavy rains, on the other hand, may flood ground nests without harming tree nests. Bias is also present in most nesting studies because successful nests are more likely to be found than unsuccessful ones (Miller and Johnson 1978).

Young animals often stay in the den or nest until they are capable of escaping predators and do not become a part of the active and visible population for some time. When the young do become active, they do so gradually, perhaps never becoming as visible as adults because of differing behavior and smaller size. For example, field counts of fawns per white-tailed doe (Downing et al. 1977) are low in summer and fall because of the secretive nature of the fawns. Field counts in winter, when fawns and does are seen at about the same rate, are not practical because of difficulty in distinguishing between fawns and yearlings. Similar biases are not uncommon with other species and thus present difficult problems in estimating natality and survival.

Fall populations of a few species may not be "ageable" in the field, but if they are "sexable," an estimate of recruitment rate may still be possible. The change-in-ratio formulas presented in detail later in this chapter under "Mortality and Survival" may be used in reverse to calculate recruitment. Suppose, for example, that a population contains 70% females prior to the nesting season (Symbol R), that the young are 50% female (Symbol K), and that the fall population of young and adults combined contains 60% females (Symbol P). The portion of the fall population made up of young is

$$\frac{P-R}{R-K} = \frac{60-70}{70-50} = \frac{10}{20} = 0.500.$$

The number of recruits per adult female is

$$\frac{0.500}{0.500 \times 0.700} = \frac{0.500}{0.350} = 1.428.$$

Sex ratios are not the only kinds of ratios useful in this kind of estimate. Antlered : antlerless ratios would work just as well, for example.

Catch-effort techniques, discussed briefly under "Mortality and Survival" are also potentially useful for estimating recruitment.

Relatively large numbers of nests and young can be found if the species uses a specialized and/or scarce habitat type. Such species are often colonial or nest at a relatively high density. If a total count of nests and young is not possible, these may be estimated using normal plot-sampling census techniques. The author has roughly estimated the number of young least terns in a colony by banding a large number 1 day, then capturing another sample the next day and recording how many were previously banded. The same principle (Lincoln Index) was employed for estimating the number of fawns born at Radford Arsenal. Fawns were tagged over a period of a month and the tagged-untagged ratio was observed repeatedly 2 to 3 months later to estimate the number born. Use of individual tags also made it possible to determine how many of the tagged fawns survived. Census techniques such as the above are discussed in detail in another chapter.

Indirect measures of rearing success may be available for some species. For example, measurements of teat size and the presence of milk in the udder may be reliable for some mammalian species. A brood patch indicates that a bird has recently incubated eggs. Signs of abundant activity at the entrance of a fox or coyote den may indicate that large pups are (or were) present. Songbirds usually can be considered to have fledged if the edges of the nest and the ground underneath are covered with droppings or the nest has a worn, flattened appearance. The pattern of eggshell fracture and the appearance of the inner membrane may indicate whether eggs were hatched or were broken by predators. Fecundity, fertility, and natality can also be determined by examining reproductive tracts, a special field of investigation discussed in Chapter 8.

MORTALITY AND SURVIVAL

Natality and mortality, the beginning and end of life for each animal, obviously are equally important in their effect on populations. Natality often can be determined by direct observation but the difficulty in observing deaths has encouraged the development of methods for mathematically determining their magnitude.

Four general classes of mortality analysis have been developed in the last 30 years or so: 1) catch-effort techniques; 2) mark-recapture techniques; 3) change-in-ratio techniques; and 4) life tables (I prefer to call them survival and mortality tables). Each of these techniques has been used widely to solve special problems and a number of seemingly different variations have been developed. To avoid confusion and hopefully to standardize these methods, the formulas and examples presented here are the simplest and most generally applicable now available. No attempt is made to review the voluminous literature on the subject other than to point out how a few specialized analyses, such as the recoveries of bird bands, are related. Censuses and density measurements, which provide essential raw data for survival tables, are covered in another chapter. Methods for finding dead animals and for diagnosing the cause of death are beyond the scope of this chapter.

Catch-effort Techniques

If an estimate of the number of animals in a population is available at 2 different times, survival rate for the interval can be calculated by dividing the number present at the end of the interval by the number present at the beginning. Unfortunately, population size is often difficult to estimate accurately. However, an index to population size, such as the number captured or shot per unit of effort, can be substituted if seasonal differences in weather, behavior, and/or habitat do not change the probability of capturing, shooting, or observing animals. Variations of the catch-effort technique are also used to estimate population size, as discussed in another chapter.

Mark-recapture Techniques (including modern bird-band analysis)

Numerous mark-recapture methods for estimating survival have been developed to satisfy specific species, habitats, and capture combinations. These methods are generally improvements over the previously mentioned catch-effort techniques because the survival estimates are derived by sampling 2 or more groups at the same time(s), thereby eliminating effects of time-related changes in weather, habitat, and behavior. The simplest such technique is the "triple-catch" method (Ricker 1958:128) that requires capture and marking at the beginning and end of the interval for which survival rate is desired. A third capture or shooting effort (elapsed time not important if an adequate sample can be obtained) is used to sample both marked groups to compare their abundance; the difference in the portions recovered is attributed to mortality (and possibly emigration) in the interval between the first and second markings. For example, suppose that 500 and 200 adult rabbits were captured and marked in the spring and fall, respectively. A third sample taken by hunters in early winter, when both groups were considered equally vulnerable to shooting, contained 20 of those marked in the spring and 40 of those marked in the fall. Any of those shot that had been captured during both spring and fall must enter the calculations in both groups. Survival rate of adult rabbits from spring to fall is calculated as

$$\frac{20 \times 200}{40 \times 500} = \frac{4{,}000}{20{,}000} = 0.20.$$

Seber (1973:219–223) outlined variance computations for the triple-catch and related methods.

Several modern bird band analysis models employ this principle; the major difference is that "third captures" are performed repeatedly each hunting season. An example, based on data (Table 15.1) from Brownie et al. (1978:14), illustrates the basic method. Survival rate from fall 1964 to fall 1965 can be estimated as follows:

Table 15.1. Wood duck banding and recovery data from Brownie et al. (1978:14).

Year Banded (Fall?)	No. Banded	Year of Recovery 1964	1965	1966	1967	1968
1964	1603	127	44	37	40	17
1965	1595		62	76	44	28
1966	1157			82	61	24

$$\frac{(44 + 37 + 40 + 17) \times 1595}{(62 + 76 + 44 + 28) \times 1603} = \frac{138 \times 1595}{210 \times 1603} = 0.654.$$

Similarly, survival rate from fall 1965 to fall 1966 is estimated as

$$\frac{(76 + 44 + 28) \times 1157}{(82 + 61 + 24) \times 1595} = \frac{148 \times 1157}{167 \times 1595} = 0.643.$$

The reason these estimates differ slightly from those in Brownie et al. (1978:16) is that their model includes a correction for small-sample bias. Brownie et al. presented 13 additional models to use when the portion recovered is dependent on age of the bird, year of banding, etc. Two computer programs are available from them to select and test models, to analyze the data, and to perform standard statistical tests.

Change-in-ratio Estimators

Change-in-ratio estimators originally were developed to calculate the portion of a population taken by hunters, lost over winter, or otherwise removed. Sex ratios are the most commonly used ratios but the technique will work equally well with age ratios, marked-unmarked ratios, species ratios, etc. The technique requires that a population containing 2 kinds of animals be divided into 2 groups, usually by removing one group. One kind of animal must be removed at a higher rate than the other so that the ratios of these animals in all 3 groups, in the population before removal, in the portion removed, and in those remaining, are considerably different. If the ratios are not greatly different, small biases in any of the ratios will cause large biases in the final estimate. Of course, estimates of each ratio must be representative of that particular group, but one need not sample each group at comparable rates. The portion of each kind of animal removed is calculated entirely on the basis of the percentage composition of each group.

The basic, general formula, $\frac{P-R}{R-K}$, estimates the portion removed from the population (both kinds combined) where P is the percentage of one kind of animal in the population prior to removal, K is the percentage of that kind among those killed or otherwise removed, and R is the percentage of that kind among those remaining after the removals. If it is necessary to estimate the percentage of *each* kind removed, the product of $\frac{P-R}{R-K}$ must be multiplied by $\frac{K}{P}$ using percentages specific to that kind of animal. A comprehensive review of change-in-ratio techniques is contained in Hanson (1963). Statistical treatment of change-in-ratio estimates is discussed by Paulik and Robson (1969).

The following example illustrates the technique. The preseason sex ratio of pheasants was 40% cocks and 60% hens, the kill contained 75% cocks and 25% hens, and the postseason ratio was 20% cocks and 80% hens. The portion of the total population removed by hunting was

$$\frac{P-R}{R-K} = \frac{40-20}{20-75} = \frac{20}{55} = 0.364.$$

Sex-specific removal rates were

$0.364 \times \frac{K}{P} = 0.364 \times \frac{75}{40} = 0.364 \times 1.875 = 0.682$ for cocks and $0.364 \times \frac{25}{60} = 0.364 \times 0.417 = 0.152$ for hens.

The technique is also useful as a population estimator if the *number* removed is known. If the total kill of cocks and hens is known to be 150 and 50, respectively, the number of cocks and hens in the population before the hunt was $\frac{150}{0.682} = 220$ and $\frac{50}{0.152} = 329$, respectively.

One difficulty with the above technique is that 2 field counting periods are necessary to obtain the P and R sex ratios and relative observability of the 2 sexes must not change between counts. Since these counts must be separated in time by at least the length of the hunting season, changes in weather, density of cover, and behavior must be considered. Changes in behavior may be especially important since hunting may cause 1 sex to become more wary than the other. Deer and other ungulates present a special problem because the breeding season may coincide with and affect 1 of the counts. White-tailed bucks are less observable than does early in the breeding season and more observable late in the breeding season (Downing et al. 1977). The months when observability was most nearly equal were August and November. Unless hunting is conducted in September, October, or early November, an observability correction factor must be developed for each locality. Wallmo (1964) suggested September and February as the most comparable months to count mule deer in Texas.

It would be advisable at this point to illustrate the effect a difference in observability or similar bias can have on change-in-ratio estimates. Suppose 100 bucks and 25 does (80% bucks) were removed from a deer herd containing 200 bucks and 300 does (40% bucks), leaving a postseason herd of 100 bucks and 275 does (26.7% bucks). If bucks and does were equally observable before the hunts, but bucks were 10% more observable than does after the hunt, then the postseason herd will be erroneously classified as having 28.6% bucks. Change-in-ratio calculations will indicate that only 44.4% of the bucks were removed, an error (relative to the 50% removed) of approximately 11%, which may be acceptable for some purposes.

However, the effect of a bias is greater if the difference between the sex ratios is less. For example, if only 50 bucks and 25 does (66.7% bucks) had been removed, 150 bucks and 275 does (35.3% bucks) would remain. If bucks were 10% more observable after the hunts, the herd would be erroneously classified as containing 37.5%. Change-in-ratio calculations will indicate that only 14.3% of the bucks were removed, an error (relative to the 25% removed) of more than 40%. Estimates of each of these ratios must be quite accurate when there is little difference in the rate of removal of each sex. Conversely, accurate estimates of sex ratios may not be needed if all 3 sex ratios are greatly different. Robinette et al. (1977:95) were experiencing this phenomenon when they noted that a bias of 3.5% in the fawn crop estimate caused a 42% bias in their population estimate.

The change-in-ratio technique is versatile enough to be used with a number of different ratios and for a number of different purposes, examples of which are contained elsewhere in this chapter under "Population Reconstruction" and under "Natality and Rearing Success." One additional example is presented here to stimulate thought and to encourage additional uses. Suppose that 1,000 mallards and 500 gadwalls (an M/G percentage of 66.7 : 33.3) were banded at the same time on a large study area where hunters were encouraged through publicity and personal contact to return (report) bands from ducks they shot. After all banded ducks were presumed dead, the band returns were tabulated, disclosing that 48 mallards and 12 gadwalls (an M/G percentage of 80 : 20) were reported dying on the area while 45 mallards and 30 gadwalls (an M/G percentage of 60:40) were reported dying off the area, including out-of-state. It is doubtful that the proportion of ducks dying on the area was really $\frac{48}{48+45} = 0.516$ for mallards, $\frac{12}{12+30} = 0.286$ for gadwalls, or $\frac{12+48}{48+45+12+30} = 0.444$ for both species because the publicity and personal contact may have caused differences in return rates on and off the area.

Change-in-ratio formulas should be tried as an alternative method. The portion of both kinds of ducks dying on the area can be estimated as

$$\frac{P-R}{R-K} = \frac{66.7-60}{60-80} = \frac{6.7}{20} = 0.335$$

The portion of mallards dying on the area is estimated as

$$0.335 \times \frac{K}{P} = 0.335 \times \frac{80}{66.7} = 0.335 \times 1.20 = 0.402.$$

The portion of gadwalls dying on the area is estimated as

$$0.335 \times \frac{20}{33.3} = 0.335 \times 0.601 = 0.201.$$

The possibility of hunters selectively killing 1 kind of duck at a higher rate because of later migration, greater size, lower point value, etc. does not introduce bias as long as the band return rates (the percent reported of the total killed) are the same for both species. Those dying on the area can be returned at a different rate than those dying off the area as long as the return rate in each location is the same for both species. In other words, the M/G ratio must *represent* the ratio of mallards to gadwalls which died in each location. Since hunting causes only a portion of the total deaths, the returns, which come mostly from hunting, probably do not represent all deaths. Nevertheless, the change-in-ratio treatment of the returns probably comes closer to describing the distribution of deaths than the direct proportion method illustrated in the previous paragraph.

The imaginative analyst will think of many more uses for this change-in-ratio formula. The only requirements are that the population contain 2 kinds of animals and that this population is subsequently divided into 2 (and only 2) groups. If the population is divided into more than 2 groups, these must be recombined into only 2. Preferably, all 3 ratios, P, K, and R, should be greatly different to minimize the effect of sampling errors.

Survival of two classes of animals *relative* to each other can be calculated using the method in Hanson (1963:29) even if the sex ratio of those dying is unknown. For example, using the pheasant data employed previously in this section, cocks survived at only $\frac{60 \times 20}{40 \times 80} = \frac{1200}{3200} = 0.375$ or 37.5% as high a rate as hens. A bias in the observability of males and females has no effect if it is the same during both observation periods. For example, if cock pheasants were at all times 10% more observable than hens, the ratios would have been recorded as 42.3% cocks and 57.7% hens before the hunts and 21.6% cocks and 78.5% hens after the hunts. Relative survival rate of cocks to hens is the same:

$$\frac{57.7 \times 21.6}{42.3 \times 78.4} = \frac{1246.3}{3316.3} = 0.376.$$

Life Tables, Survival Tables, and Mortality Tables

Human demographers and actuaries developed life tables as a means of presenting mortality and survival statistics. Mortality rates are the raw data for life tables (Dublin et al. 1949:11); these rates are calculated as the number of known deaths during a period of time divided by the number known to have been alive (initially) in each age class in the population. Complete records of deaths at each age are kept continuously and a complete census is taken every decade or so to supply this information about many human populations. With such data, few assumptions are necessary and relatively few sampling problems are encountered.

However, biologists usually have only one-half of the life-and-death picture, either censuses or death records, but rarely both. The other half must be inferred from the age structure of the available data. The basic life table format of 3 columns (q_x, the mortality rate at each age; l_x, the number initially alive at each age; and d_x, the number dying during each age interval) has been adopted by biologists as a convenient format for showing how mortality rate by age was inferred and calculated from censuses or death records. The difference between a table showing how mortality rates were calculated (the biologist's life table) and a table *presenting* mortality rates and survival statistics (a true life table) may seem subtle and inconsequential to some, but apparently has resulted in widespread confusion over data requirements, methods of calculation, nomenclature, and interpretation among wildlife biologists. Hopefully, this brief discussion will place wildlife *survival* and *mortality* tables, as I prefer to call them, in their proper perspective and restore the original use and meaning to life tables. An example of a true life table will be presented later using wildlife data.

Four distinctly different types of age structure data have been used by biologists to calculate age-specific survival and mortality rates. These are discussed briefly below:

SINGLE CENSUS DATA

A single census or representative sample of population age structure cannot be used to calculate age-specific survival and mortality rates unless the population is known to be "stationary" in size and age structure. This is because the differences in size between *different* cohorts, all censused at the same time, are assumed to be due to mortality, when these differences could just as realistically be due to unequal size of the cohorts at birth and/or to unequal death histories of each cohort since birth. Since truly stationary wildlife populations are rare and because the necessary mathematical calculations tend to magnify biases, this technique cannot be recommended for use with most populations.

If further discouragement is needed, bear in mind that mortality level *per se* does not directly affect age structure and thus cannot be determined by analyzing a single sample of age structure. Recruitment rate is the primary determinant of age structure; mortality rate modifies this structure only if there are considerable differences in the mortality rates of the various age classes. Studies by Keyfitz and Flieger (1971: 33–35) have shown that fertility has a much greater effect on the age structure of many human populations than does mortality. In comparing populations in the United States and Venezuela, they said: "Evidently, the proportion at any age in the two countries, including the proportion of old people, differs in the long run mainly because they differ in birth rates." Smith (1974:299) presents a simple explanation of the methods used in arriving at this conclusion. Caughley (1974a) made a detailed study of the relationships between natality, mortality, and age structure, and concluded that other information, such as rate of increase, is needed to interpret age structure.

A composite of several years of census data largely avoids the problem of unequal cohorts by averaging out the differences, so to speak. However, 2 or more annual censuses are more appropriate for analysis as "multiple census data" which are not affected by changing recruitment rates, mortality rates, or population size.

SINGLE SAMPLE OF DEATHS

Many of the previously stated shortcomings of single census data also apply to single samples of those dying. The common assumption is that the population is stationary, which could happen only if all cohorts were the same size at birth and experienced the same rates of death ever since. Truly stationary wildlife populations are rare, thus the technique should not be used with most populations. As previously discussed, there is also the basic question of whether mortality level or recruitment rate determines the age structure of such "kill curves" (Gill 1953, Caughley 1974a).

A composite of several years of representative mortality data averages out many of these problems unless a strong upward or downward population trend is evident. However, if 2 or more years of representative mortality data are available, these can be used with the population reconstruction technique presented later. The primary advantage of the population reconstruction technique is that it is affected very little by fluctuating natality, mortality, and population levels and yields several vital statistics simultaneously. If the death records span the lifetimes of one or more cohorts, these data can be analyzed as "death history" data in an appropriate mortality table which is discussed later.

MULTIPLE CENSUS DATA

These data are obtained by 2 or more censuses; the decline in size of a cohort between censuses is assumed to be due to mortality. If the data are not complete censuses, sampling intensity must be equal for each age each year. Hunters are often not acceptable for sampling population age structure because hunters harvest the younger age classes at different rates than adults (for various reasons). Even if the overall harvest rate was the same from year to year, the sampling rate for each younger cohort would change because they change vulnerability as they become older.

Complete censuses have their disadvantages, too, because most species must be captured to determine their age during each census. Wildlife biologists have enough difficulty obtaining good censuses without this added requirement. Because biases in estimates of cohort size are magnified by the mathematical calculations, caution is recommended in the use of multiple census data. The principle is sound, but sufficiently accurate data are difficult to obtain.

Gray squirrel recapture data presented by Mosby (1969:62) (Table 15.2) appear to be sufficiently accurate and are used here to illustrate 4 variations of survival tables (Tables 15.3–15.6). The 4 tables are not necessarily inconsistent; the reason for their disagreement is that each represents a different span of time and different individuals. Because of the difficulty in devising brief, yet descriptive names for each of these variations, I suggest that each be called simply a "survival table," making sure that an adequate description of the source of data is contained in each heading. To further avoid confusion, it is suggested that the raw data always appear in the left 2 columns.

Table 15.2. Squirrel census data from Mosby (1969:62, Fig. 1).

Age (Years)	Number Captured or Known to be Alive								
	1952	1953	1954	1955	1956	1957	1958	1959	1960
0–1	29	27	42	30	44	38	30	19	18
1–2		22	27	20	22	35	26	22	10
2–3			19	12	10	9	20	13	7
3–4				8	8	3	4	3	
4–5					1	2	1		1
5–6							1		

Bird band analysts sometimes assume that the rate of band recoveries (a composite of harvest rate and the band reporting rate) is constant and therefore that the number recovered is a constant proportion of the number alive in the cohort at the beginning of each year. Analysis of such data is similar to the composite survival table (Table 15.6). When it is recognized that recovery rate varies between juveniles and adults, such an analysis should be restricted to adults, because the technique is quite sensitive to biased "censuses" of this sort. For the same reason, this method is not recommended if there are year-to-year variations in recovery rate.

DEATH HISTORY DATA

If all the animals born (or tagged) at one time are eventually recovered at death, the number alive in the cohort each year can be reconstructed by adding the deaths, 1 year at a time, starting backward from the old end of the age spectrum. Hesselton et al. (1965) simultaneously reconstructed the minimum size of deer cohorts at Seneca Army Depot in this way. In fisheries practice, this is known as the "virtual population" technique (Fry 1949). From this minimum population, mortality rate can be calculated as the ratio of deaths at each age to those known alive at that time (the number which died at that age and older). If the deaths are accurately enumerated (or representative samples are obtained with similar effort each year), there are no problems with this technique; the population need not be stationary or numerically stable, have equally vulnerable age classes, or have equal harvest rates each year.

Unless the species is short lived, however, the investigator must wait a long time for the last cohort member to die before beginning the analysis. Few of us are willing to wait 10 years or so to begin analyzing an ungulate cohort, for example, and by then we may not be interested in what happened a decade ago. If a constant rate of change in mortality rate with increasing age can be assumed, a graphical analysis of the annual decline in number dying (Overton 1971:450) may be used to predict how many more will die and when the last death will occur, thus shortening the time-lag. The population reconstruction technique presented later is a practical alternative because it requires only 2 years of data to reconstruct the population, which in turn provides the data needed to calculate mortality rates and recruitment rates.

Numerous examples of "death history" data are available in the literature, but it is important for comparison purposes that all the examples of survival tables and mortality tables given here be derived from the same population. Mosby (1969) did not find many dead squirrels, but for the purposes of this presentation it is as-

Table 15.3. Survival table based on censuses in Table 15.2 during 1957 and 1958. Calculations in parentheses.

Age (Years)	Population Size: Begin (1957) (Raw data)	Population Size: End (1958) (Raw data)	Survival Rate	Mortality Rate
0–1	38	26	0.684 (26/38)	0.316 (1−0.684)
1–2	35	20	0.571 (20/35)	0.429 (1−0.571)
2–3	9	4	0.444 (4/9)	0.556 (1−0.444)
3–4	3	1	0.333 (1/3)	0.667 (1−0.333)
4–5	2	1	0.500 (1/2)	0.500 (1−0.500)

Table 15.4. Survival table based on composite of censuses in Table 15.2 during 1956, 1957, and 1958. Calculations in parentheses.

Age (Years)	Population Size: Begin (1956–1957) (Raw Data)	Population Size: End (1957–1958) (Raw Data)	Survival Rate	Mortality Rate
0–1	82 (44+38)	61 (35+26)	0.744 (61/82)	0.256 (1−0.744)
1–2	57 (22+35)	29 (9+20)	0.509 (29/57)	0.491 (1−0.509)
2–3	19 (10+9)	7 (3+4)	0.368 (7/19)	0.632 (1−0.368)
3–4	11 (8+3)	3 (2+1)	0.273 (3/11)	0.727 (1−0.273)
4–5	3 (1+2)	1 (0+1)	0.333 (1/3)	0.667 (1−0.333)

Table 15.5. Survival table based on annual censuses in Table 15.2 of cohort born in 1954. Calculations in parentheses.

Age (Years)	Population Size (The Raw Data): Begin	Population Size (The Raw Data): End	Survival Rate	Mortality Rate
0–1	42 (1954)	20 (1955)	0.476 (20/42)	0.524 (1−0.476)
1–2	20 (1955)	10 (1956)	0.500 (10/20)	0.500 (1−0.500)
2–3	10 (1956)	3 (1957)	0.300 (3/10)	0.700 (1−0.300)
3–4	3 (1957)	1 (1958)	0.333 (1/3)	0.667 (1−0.333)
4–5	1 (1958)	0 (1959)	0 (0/1)	1.000 (1−0)

Table 15.6. Survival table based on a composite of annual censuses in Table 15.2 of cohorts born in 1954 and 1955. Calculations in parentheses.

Age (Years)	Population Size (The Raw Data): Begin	Population Size (The Raw Data): End	Survival Rate	Mortality Rate
0–1	72 (42+30)	42 (20+22)	0.583 (42/72)	0.417 (1−0.583)
1–2	42 (20−22)	19 (10+9)	0.452 (19/42)	0.548 (1−0.452)
2–3	19 (10+9)	7 (3+4)	0.368 (7/19)	0.632 (1−0.368)
3–4	7 (3+4)	1 (1+0)	0.143 (1/7)	0.857 (1−0.143)
4–5	1 (1+0)	0	0 (0/1)	1.000 (1−0)

sumed that he found all that died. These "death history" data are presented in Table 15.7 and analyzed in 2 variations of "mortality tables." Note that the raw data again are presented in the left column and that the heading fully describes their source. Each of these tables is accurate, the only difference being that Table 15.8 applies to only 1 cohort while Table 15.9 is a composite of 2 cohorts.

In interpreting these tables, it is interesting to note that juvenile squirrels had a relatively low mortality rate at this location. Usually, the prime-age animals 1 to 3 years old have the lowest mortality rate, but this was not the case. Before accepting the low juvenile mortality rates of 1954 and 1955 (Table 15.9) as normal, the analyst should try to determine if the years covered by the table were exceptional in any way, and if so, extend the analysis to other years. Mortality records seem complete for each cohort born from 1952 through 1955 because no additional animals in those cohorts died in 1959, the last year of record. A composite mortality table covering all 4 cohorts yields a similar pattern, thus low juvenile mortality seems normal for this population.

If bird band recoveries were a representative sample of the ages at death, these could be analyzed as death history data. However, because fewer than 10% of all deaths of banded birds are usually reported, it is unlikely that these recoveries represent the proportion which dies at each age. Burnham and Anderson (1979) present a detailed analysis showing the inappropriateness of this method for most bird band analyses. Mortality tables based on death history data probably are useful only with nonmigratory species for which a high percentage of the deaths are recorded, and then only if the unrecorded deaths occurred at the same rates for each age as the recorded deaths.

Table 15.7. Death records (assumed by the author for purposes of this presentation) of squirrels from Mosby's (1969:62) Crumpacker Woods data.

Age (Years)	Year Death Recorded 1952	1953	1954	1955	1956	1957	1958	1959
0–1	7	0	22	8	9	12	8	9
1–2		3	15	10	13	15	13	15
2–3			11	4	7	5	17	13
3–4				7	6	2	4	2
4–5					1	1	1	
5–6							1	

A LIFE TABLE USING WILDLIFE DATA

This life table (Table 15.10) presents in a logical manner the essential survival and mortality characteristics (Tables 15.6 and 15.9) of the squirrel cohorts born in 1954 and 1955. The life table says that for each 1,000 squirrels which are born, 791.5 are alive at midyear (on the average) and 583 at the end of the year, for an annual mortality of 417 squirrels or 41.7%. Each of the 1,000 squirrels which are born have a life expectancy of 1.46 years. Among the 583 which reached 1 year of age, 423.5 should reach midyear and 264 should live to the end of the second year. Additional life expectancy of the 583 1-year-olds is 1.14 years.

I recommend that survival and mortality rates be calculated separately from life tables in the future, so that all life tables can take the form of Table 15.10. Mortality rates (q_x) should always be the raw data for life tables. Including the various kinds of census and death records from which these mortality rates were calculated invites confusion and should be discontinued.

Table 15.8. Mortality table based on annual death records in Table 15.7 of cohort born in 1954. Calculations in parentheses.

Age (Years)	Deaths (The Raw Data)	Initial Cohort Size (By Backward Accumulation)	Mortality Rate
0–1	22 (1954)	42 (1+2+7+10+22)	0.524 (22/42)
1–2	10 (1955)	20 (1+2+7+10)	0.500 (10/20)
2–3	7 (1956)	10 (1+2+7)	0.700 (7/10)
3–4	2 (1957)	3 (1+2)	0.667 (2/3)
4–5	1 (1958)	1	1.000 (1/1)

Table 15.9. Mortality table based on composite of annual death records in Table 15.7 of cohorts born in 1954 and 1955. Calculations in parentheses.

Age (Years)	Deaths (The Raw Data)	Initial Cohort Size (By Backward Accumulation)	Mortality Rate
0–1	30 (22+8)	72 (1+6+12+23+30)	0.417 (30/72)
1–2	23 (10+13)	42 (1+6+12+23)	0.548 (23/42)
2–3	12 (7+5)	19 (1+6+12)	0.632 (12/19)
3–4	6 (2+4)	7 (1+6)	0.857 (6/7)
4–5	1 (1+0)	1	1.000 (1/1)

Table 15.10. A life table based on the mortality rates obtained in Survival Table 15.6 and Mortality Table 15.9. Calculations shown in parentheses.

Age (Years)	q_x (Raw Data)	l_{x1000}	d_{x1000}	L_x	e_x
0–1	0.417	1000	417(1000×0.417)	791.5 $\left(\frac{1000+583}{2}\right)$	1.46 $\left(\frac{7.0+55.5+180.5+423.5+791.5}{1000}\right)$
1–2	0.548	583(1000–417)	319(583×0.548)	423.5 $\left(\frac{583+264}{2}\right)$	1.14 $\left(\frac{7.0+55.5+180.5+423.5}{583}\right)$
2–3	0.632	264(583–319)	167(264×0.632)	180.5 $\left(\frac{264+97}{2}\right)$	0.92 $\left(\frac{7.0+55.5+180.5}{264}\right)$
3–4	0.857	97(264–167)	83(97×0.857)	55.5 $\left(\frac{97+14}{2}\right)$	0.64 $\left(\frac{7.0+55.5}{97.0}\right)$
4–5	1.000	14(97–83)	14(14×1.000)	7.0 $\left(\frac{14+0}{2}\right)$	0.50 $\left(\frac{7.0}{14}\right)$

q_x = age specific mortality rate
l_{x1000} = number attaining this age from a beginning cohort of 1000
d_{x1000} = number dying each age from a beginning cohort of 1000
L_x = mean number alive between age classes
e_x = mean expectation of life (average additional lifespan of those reaching this age)

POPULATION RECONSTRUCTION

The population reconstruction technique presented here for the first time estimates both recruitment and mortality and relates these dynamic functions to population size and/or population trends. The required data are enumerations of the animals which die in each sex and age class for at least 2 consecutive years. These data could be only a fraction of those that die, but this fraction must be the same each year for each sex and age class. In practice this is difficult for populations that suffer more than 1 source of mortality because all sources have to be sampled at the same rate each year. Fractional data will reconstruct "minimum" populations which accurately depict mortality rates, recruitment rates, and sex and age ratios. However, the reconstructed population will be smaller than the actual population in the same proportion that the fractional sample of deaths was to the total number dying.

In many situations, it is almost as easy to estimate the total number dying as it is to obtain a constant fraction. The extra difficulty in estimating the total number dying usually is offset by the extra usefulness of the full-sized reconstruction.

The following example illustrates how the change-in-ratio technique can be used for estimating the total number dying in each sex and age class, and how these data can then be used to reconstruct the population. This example is based on 13 years of mule deer data collected at Oak Creek, Utah, by Robinette et al. (1977). As part of the intensive study conducted on that herd, the workers routinely checked most of the deer removed by hunters. Removed deer not routinely examined were estimated by spot-checks of hunters who used parts of the area not served by the check station. A total of 3,537 bucks and 2,368 does was estimated (Robinette, pers. comm.) to have been removed by hunters during the study (Table 15.11).

Robinette (1966) reported that 28% and 14% of the tag returns for bucks and does, respectively, were from outside the 137 km² study area. These deer may also belong in the hunter-killed category because they were mostly returned by hunters and/or encouraged to move off the area by the disturbance of hunting. A further reason for including dispersals in this category is that it is desirable to lump all buck-biased causes of mortality into 1 group and all doe-biased causes into the other, thus assuring that each group's sex ratio will be greatly different. The greater the difference between sex ratios, the less sensitive the change-in-ratio technique is to sampling errors. The total of harvest and dispersal can be calculated as

$$\frac{3537}{1-0.28} = \frac{3537}{0.72} = 4912 \text{ males and}$$

$$\frac{2368}{1-0.14} = \frac{2368}{0.86} = 2753 \text{ females.}$$

If dispersals are assumed equal for each year, this amounts to

$$\frac{4912-3537}{13} = \frac{1375}{13} = 105.8 \text{ bucks and}$$

$$\frac{2753-2368}{13} = \frac{385}{13} = 29.6 \text{ does per year.}$$

These are further distributed in proportion to the ages at which the tags of dispersed deer were returned (Robinette 1966:342) so that 4 buck fawns, 57 yearling bucks, 27, 2-year-old bucks, and 18 older bucks (a total of 106) are added to the hunter kills each year. Similarly, 2 doe fawns, 9 yearling does, 6, 2-year-old does, and 13 older does (a total of 30) are added. The overall sex ratio of harvested and dispersed deer is

$$\frac{4912}{4912+2753} = \frac{4912}{7665} =$$

64% bucks and 1–0.64 = 36% does.

Table 15.11. Sex and age of mule deer estimated to have been removed by hunters, Oak Creek, Utah (Robinette, pers. comm.).

	Males (ages)				Females (ages)			
Year	0–1	1–2	2–3	3+	0–1	1–2	2–3	3+
1947	28	171	58	37	23	41	45	105
1948	18	172	83	54	17	46	30	69
1949	14	85	69	44	8	27	33	75
1950	17	102	68	44	20	19	31	73
1951	40	140	50	31	26	57	35	84
1952	31	125	87	56	25	49	42	72
1953	33	120	77	51	24	59	42	92
1954	32	104	63	32	25	20	15	54
1955	31	135	83	55	21	21	24	47
1956	41	119	87	51	39	60	45	75
1957	23	82	63	45	29	47	34	83
1958	46	124	72	64	33	53	49	134
1959	37	117	76	50	45	42	29	75
Annual dispersals (see text)	4	57	27	18	2	9	6	13

Next Robinette et al. (1977) attempted to determine how many deer died of starvation, crippling, abandonment, predation, etc. by using systematic strip counts (Robinette et al. 1974). A total of 907 "range losses," all deer mortalities other than those removed by hunters, was found (Table 15.12). However, because the effort expended and the success in finding young fawns were not comparable to that for older deer, fawn data must either be weighted in some way or removed. Young fawns will be removed hereafter from consideration, so that the vital statistics from this reconstruction can be compared to those in Robinette et al. (1977) which apply to the fall population. Many workers are most interested in the status of their herds just prior to the hunting season, so beginning the year on 1 October presents no serious problem. All deaths (except young fawns) which occurred from 1 October 1957 through 30 September 1958, for example, are entered and analyzed as 1957 data.

One class of loss, poaching, was not specifically studied and did not show up frequently on strip counts because most of the poached deer were removed. To illustrate how within-sample and between-sample weighting can be used to equate the causes of loss,

Table 15.12. Sex and age of known range losses at Oak Creek, Utah (Robinette et al. 1977:119, Table 62).

	Age															
	0–4.3 mos			4.3 mos–1 yr			1–2		2–3		3+		"Adults"		
Cause of Loss	M	F	?	M	F	?	M	F	M	F	M	F	M	F	?
Malnutrition	0	0	0	45	61	27	2	2	0	3	1	39	1	5	4
Predation	4	1	43	20	33	37	6	8	1	3	1	14	1	6	0
Accidents	1	1	1	3	5	1	2	3	1	4	1	12	0	1	2
Poaching[a]	0	0	0	1(10)	0	2(20)	1(10)	1(10)	1(10)	0	1(10)	6(30)	0	0	0
Hunt related	0	0	0	30	34	13	43	27	12	27	13	117	1	19	6
Other + ?	6	3	50	6	10	17	4	2	3	0	2	35	0	4	4
Total	11	5	94	114	143	115	67	52	27	37	28	247	3	35	16
Redistribution[b]	Not analyzed			165	207		70	59	29	42	30	282			
Percent by sex	Not analyzed			56.1	35.1		23.8	10.0	9.9	7.1	10.2	47.8			
Total estimated losses[c]	Not analyzed			676	856		287	244	119	174	123	1167			

[a]Weighted poaching losses shown in parentheses.
[b]Includes unaged and unsexed deer redistributed in proportion to known sex and age.
[c]Based on change-in-ratio technique, see text.

known poaching losses were weighted (arbitrarily) to partially compensate for the obviously poor sample in this category (Table 15.12). Weighting was not uniform because more poached 3+-year-old does were found on strip censuses than any other sex or age class; these does often were in poor condition and may have been abandoned after being poached. This group was multiplied by a factor of only 5, instead of the 10 used to weight the other age classes, because 3+ does were more likely to be found than other sex and age classes. The 884 "representative" range losses at 4.3 months of age or older in Table 15.12 contained 33% bucks and 67% does. Recruits into the population were considered to be 54% males and 46% females, the captured fawn sex ratio.

The change-in-ratio formula presented previously can be used to estimate the portion of the total annual mortality due to hunting and dispersal. In this case the recruits (symbol P) are divided into 2 groups according to the cause of their eventual death, K symbolizing hunting and dispersal and R symbolizing the remaining causes of death. Sex ratios within these groups are assumed to have been stable over the 13 years of study. Using this formula, the portion of deaths attributable to hunting and dispersal is:

$$\frac{P-R}{R-K} = \frac{54-33}{33-64} = \frac{21}{31} = 0.6774.$$

The portion of male deaths attributable to hunting and dispersal is $0.6774 \times \frac{K}{P} = 0.6774 \times \frac{64}{54} = 0.6774 \times 1.1851 = 0.803$. The portion of female deaths due to hunting and dispersal is $0.6774 \times \frac{36}{46} = 0.6774 \times 0.7826 = 0.530$. Total deaths of males is calculated as $\frac{4912}{0.803} = 6117$ and of females as $\frac{2753}{0.530} = 5194$. A total of $6117 - 4912 = 1205$ males and $5194 - 2753 = 2441$ females are calculated as lost to causes other than hunting and dispersal.

A detailed study of Table 15.12 will reveal how the 1205 males and 2441 females were allocated by age. Because range losses were not sampled with the same effort each year, these losses also were distributed among the years in proportion to the number found per mile during the annual searches (Table 15.13). Table 15.14 presents total mortality estimates (combination of Tables 15.11, 15.13, and the annual dispersal estimate) in 4 age classes, the maximum that most biologists can recognize on the basis of tooth replacement and wear. This should satisfy another basic requirement of the population reconstruction technique—that the last 2 age classes have equal mortality rates—a requirement which often dictates that the last 2 classes be adult.

Population reconstruction can now begin, using the female data in Table 15.14 as the example. It is strongly recommended that persons interested in this technique actually reconstruct a population, because a word description of the principles involved usually is not sufficient to bring about an understanding.

Backward reconstruction, the principle employed in this technique, theoretically works perfectly if the mortality rate of adults in the last year is known. Because this is rarely true, an extra year of *average* mortality data can be used as a starting point. This average number of deaths at each age is added as a projection of what will happen in the future if average conditions prevail. However, this average may need to be adjusted by projecting it upward slightly if the population is known to be increasing, and downward if the population is declining. The starting point is not critical because errors here are soon absorbed and become less and less significant as the reconstruction proceeds backward through the years.

It seems appropriate to base the starting point in this example on an unadjusted average of all 13 years of data. The downward trend in mortality exhibited in 1959 can be ignored because it probably reflects a lower mortality rate, not a significantly lower population.

First, the average number of deaths of 2-year-old and 3+-year-old does (54.4 and 182.6, respectively) must be used to calculate their average survival rate, as follows: $\frac{182.6}{54.4+182.6} = 0.770$. Average mortality rate is $1 - 0.770 = 0.230$. Next, the average mortality rate and the average number of deaths can be used to calculate how many 2-year-old and 3+ does entered the average year, here called 1960, as follows:

$$\frac{54.4}{0.230} = 237 \text{ and } \frac{182.6}{0.230} = 794.$$

Those which begin 1 year are those which survived from the previous year; thus the number of 3+'s at the beginning of each year is the total of 2-year-olds and 3+'s which survived the previous year. If 794, 2-year-old and 3+'s survived the 1959 data year and entered 1960 as 3+'s, the total number of 2-year-olds and 3+'s entering 1959 must have been 794 + 42 + 140 = 976, the number present before the 42, 2-year-olds and 140, 3+'s died that year. Survival rate in 1959 was thus $\frac{794}{976} = 0.814$. The number of 2-year-old and 3+ does entering 1959 can be calculated separately as

$$\frac{42}{1-0.814} = \frac{42}{0.186} = 226 \text{ and } \frac{140}{1-0.814} = \frac{140}{0.186} = 753,$$

respectively.

These calculations can now be repeated for the previous year of data. If 753, 3+ does entered 1959 (survived from the 2-year-old and 3+ classes in 1958), the total number of 1-year-olds and 3+'s entering 1958 must have been 753 + 69 + 246 = 1068, the number present before the 69, 2-year-old and 246, 3+ does died that year. Survival rate during 1958 was $\frac{753}{1068} = 0.705$ and the number of 2-year-olds and 3+'s entering 1958 was

$$\frac{69}{1-0.705} = \frac{69}{0.295} = 234 \text{ and } \frac{246}{1-0.705} = \frac{246}{0.295} = 834$$

respectively. Obviously, these calculations can be repeated year after year to reconstruct the last 2 age

Table 15.13. Distribution of estimated 1205 male and 2441 female range losses by year, based on density of carcasses found, Oak Creek, Utah (Robinette et al. 1977).

			Estimated Range Losses[2]							
			Males (ages)				Females (ages)			
Year	Carcasses[1] Per Mile	Percent of Total	0.4–1	1–2	2–3	3+	0.4–1	1–2	2–3	3+
1947	0.154	7.7	52	22	9	9	66	19	13	90
1948	0.395	19.7	133	56	24	25	169	48	34	230
1949	0.194	9.7	65	28	12	12	83	23	17	113
1950	0.148	7.4	50	21	9	9	64	18	13	87
1951	0.104	5.2	35	15	6	7	45	13	9	61
1952	0.121	6.1	42	18	7	7	52	15	11	72
1953	0.114	5.7	38	17	7	7	49	13	10	66
1954	0.124	6.2	42	18	7	8	53	15	11	72
1955	0.143	7.2	49	20	9	9	61	18	13	84
1956	0.132	6.6	45	19	8	8	56	16	12	77
1957	0.110	5.5	37	16	6	7	47	13	10	64
1958	0.170	8.5	58	24	10	10	73	21	14	99
1959	0.091	4.5	30	13	5	5	38	12	7	52
Total		100.0	676	287	119	123	856	244	174	1167

[1]Transect data provided by Robinette (pers. comm.).
[2]Based on change-in-ratio formula, see text and Table 15.12.

classes for each year of data. (Continue $834 + 50 + 160 = 1044, \frac{834}{1044} = 0.799$, etc.)

The younger classes are reconstructed by simple addition. For instance, the number of yearlings entering 1958 is the 226, 2-year-olds of 1959 plus the 84 yearlings dying during 1958, which equals 310. Similarly, the number of fawns in October 1957 is 388, the 310 yearlings of 1958 plus the 78 fawns which died during fall and winter of 1957. Table 15.15 presents complete population reconstructions based on mortality data of Table 15.14. Fawns born in the last year have been sampled only once, thus, there is little basis for estimating the size of that group. A simple estimate based on the usual number of fawns and the relative size of the single sample is all that is justified.

Vital statistics now can be calculated from the population reconstruction. Mortality rates were calculated by sex and age for the last 2 classes during the process of reconstruction and can be easily calculated for the remaining classes. For instance, the mortality rate for fawn does in 1957 was $\frac{78}{388} = 0.201$ and for yearling does in 1958 was $\frac{84}{310} = 0.271$ (Tables 15.14 and 15.15).

Recruitment rates are obtained by dividing the reconstructed number of fawns by the number of does. For

Table 15.14. Estimated total annual mortality of mule deer at Oak Creek, Utah (combination of Tables 15.11, 15.13, and dispersals).

	Males (ages)				Females (ages)			
Year	0.4–1	1–2	2–3	3+	0.4–1	1–2	2–3	3+
1947	84	250	94	64	91	69	64	208
1948	155	285	134	97	188	103	70	312
1949	83	170	108	74	93	59	56	201
1950	71	180	104	71	86	46	50	173
1951	79	212	83	56	73	79	50	158
1952	77	200	121	81	79	73	59	157
1953	75	194	111	76	75	81	58	171
1954	78	179	97	58	80	44	35	139
1955	84	212	119	82	84	48	41	144
1956	90	195	122	77	97	85	63	165
1957	64	155	96	70	78	69	50	160
1958	108	211	109	92	112	84	69	246
1959	71	187	108	73	85	62	42	140
Means			108.2	74.7			54.4	182.6

Table 15.15. Reconstruction of the Oak Creek, Utah, mule deer herd based on the estimates of total mortality in Table 15.14.

Year	Male (ages)				Females (ages)			
	0.4–1	1–2	2–3	3+	0.4–1	1–2	2–3	3+
1947	545	454	182	124	399	274	278	904
1948	493	461	204	148	445	308	205	912
1949	423	338	176	121	349	257	205	736
1950	476	340	168	115	416	256	198	686
1951	454	405	160	108	385	330	210	664
1952	453	375	193	129	311	312	251	668
1953	449	376	175	120	324	232	239	704
1954	494	374	182	108	411	249	179	713
1955	461	416	195	135	418	331	205	720
1956	421	377	204	129	400	334	283	740
1957	458	331	182	133	388	303	249	796
1958	478	394	176	149	411	310	234	834
1959	450±	370	183	124	380±	299	226	753
1960			183	126			237	794

instance, recruitment rate in 1957, expressed as female fawns per 2+-year-old doe, is calculated as $\frac{388}{249 + 796} = 0.371$. Male and female fawns can be combined for a calculation of total fawns per 2+-year-old doe, or for any other age of doe, for that matter. Table 15.14 provides all the information that is needed, so the manner of expression is the choice of the analyst. Sex ratio calculations for fawns and adults are obvious.

The accuracy of any technique is only as good as the data and assumptions on which it is based and every opportunity should be taken to check the results using independent estimates. Table 15.16 contains some vital statistics calculated from this reconstruction, compared to Robinette's independent estimates. Posthunt population size is quite similar for both methods. Overall recruitment rates are similar, but there are unexplained disagreements in 1956 and 1959. The slight disagreement between adult sex ratios may be due to the secretive nature of bucks or to their distribution, because some may not have migrated to their winter range when Robinette's counts were made in October. Some of the disagreement in mortality rates may be due to tag losses of older deer having elevated Robinette's estimates.

It is difficult to predict what effect different inputs would have on the reconstruction, but, with very little extra effort, several levels of poaching, of dispersal, and several fawn sex ratios could have been used in preparing data for additional population reconstructions. The manager could then choose the reconstruction which best fits his knowledge of the population. This technique has been computerized, thus multiple reconstructions using different data should present no problem. Consult the next section of this chapter entitled "Do the Vital Statistics Agree?" for more discussion on this subject.

Differing inputs may indicate higher or lower population levels, but the same trends should be detected with considerably different inputs, within reason. To illustrate this principle, you may wish to reconstruct a *minimum* population for Oak Creek using only the harvest data in Table 15.11. You will find that population levels are much lower, ranging from about 1,200 to 1,500 and that recruitment rate is higher, ranging from about 0.7 to 1.2 fawns per doe. However, the trends are similar, suggesting that harvest-based minimum reconstructions may be useful for monitoring many populations.

The reader is cautioned that a minimum population reconstruction spanning a period in which the harvest rate was increased will, at least temporarily, erroneously indicate an increasing population size simply because a higher percentage of the total deaths is included in the analysis. In other words, a constant fraction of the total deaths is needed to perform a minimum reconstruction and this requirement may be violated by any change in hunting regulations and perhaps by weather or other conditions that affect hunting success. For these reasons, I intuitively feel that attempts to estimate the magnitude of all deaths and thereby reconstruct the whole population are worth the effort, even if these attempts are rough.

For most big game herds, measurement of deaths due to causes other than hunting will indeed be rough because the reports come from a variety of unrelated sources. Enforcement personnel report most of the highway and poaching deaths but these personnel usually do not know what portion of the total highway and poaching deaths these samples represent. Hunters report most of the crippled and abandoned deer in the sample, but the proper weight to give these samples depends on hunter density and length of season; the higher the hunter density and the longer the season, the greater the chance of these losses being reported (Downing 1971). Unless systematic surveys are made, few animals dying from starvation, predation, and other causes will be found or considered in managing the population. Obviously, better results can be expected from minimum reconstructions if hunting is the dominant cause of death, because harvests are relatively easy to measure and the remaining deaths may not be numerous enough to greatly increase the size of the re-

Table 15.16. Comparison of vital statistics calculated from population reconstruction (Table 15.15) with independent estimates from Robinette et al. (1977) and Robinette (pers. comm.).

	Population size			Recruitment Fawns/doe 1 year and older		Percent does among deer 1 year and older	
	Reconstruction		Robinette[a]				
Year	Prehunt	Posthunt	Posthunt	Reconstruction	Robinette[b]	Reconstruction	Robinette[b]
1947	3160	2175	2706	0.648	0.620	66	76
1948	3176	2265	2269	0.658	0.706	64	73
1949	2605	1893	2013	0.644	0.566	65	81
1950	2655	1929	1878	0.782	0.756	65	75
1951	2716	1953	2019	0.697	0.678	64	73
1952	2692	1897	2007	0.621	0.624	64	78
1953	2619	1815	2108	0.658	0.573	64	71
1954	2710	2110	2186	0.793	0.681	63	70
1955	2881	2176	2516	0.700	0.610	63	73
1956	2888	2048	2274	0.605	0.748	66	79
1957	2840	2151	1691	0.628	0.663	68	74
1958	2986	2070		0.645	0.694	66	73
1959	2785	2019		0.649	0.856	65	74
Overall	2824	2039	2151	0.671	0.670	65	75

Overall mortality rate, excluding fawns:

	Reconstruction	Robinette[c]
Bucks	0.554	0.603
Does	0.240	0.348

[a]Based on pellet group counts.
[b]Based on prehunt classification counts.
[c]Based on tag return analysis.

constructed population or influence management recommendations derived from it. However, the relative importance of the harvest cannot be known until the other causes of death have been measured at least once. Reconstruction of the whole population is recommended.

Lang and Wood (1976) presented another system for reconstructing deer populations based primarily on kill data and reproductive information. Their system is an excellent example of how vital statistics can be employed to manage populations. The admitted inaccuracy inherent in their method of calculating average annual reduction rate (AARR) probably could be reduced by substituting the following formula:

$$AARR = 1 - \frac{\text{No. } 2\frac{1}{2} \text{ bucks} + \text{No. } 3+ \text{ bucks}}{\text{No. } 1\frac{1}{2} \text{ bucks} + \text{No. } 2\frac{1}{2} \text{ bucks} + \text{No. } 3+ \text{ bucks}}$$

Because this improved formula always yields a higher AARR, total size of the reconstructed population is always lower. Unfortunately, a system to produce higher, not lower, population estimates is needed, as evidenced by the fact that the predicted harvests of bucks in Pennsylvania averaged 12.3% lower than those that actually occurred. One or more data biases are suspected to be causing most of this minor inaccuracy.

DO THE VITAL STATISTICS AGREE?

Suppose that you have carefully analyzed all the available population data and have obtained what are apparently good estimates of natality and mortality, the primary elements. If these are both within the range reported in the literature as characteristic of that species, you may be willing to accept them at face value. However, it may be worthwhile to study further the interaction of these vital statistics to see if they agree with each other. This requires the construction of a simple model (Table 15.17).

The summary at the bottom of Table 15.17 indicates that females could not replace themselves at the natality and mortality rates modeled. The 100 females lived only long enough and/or reproduced only fast enough to produce 70 female young in their lifetimes, a condition that should cause a sharp annual decline of more than 20%. Before discounting either estimate because they do not agree, however, consider the fact that sizable disagreements between natality and mortality often occur for short periods. Populations are indeed dynamic, constantly changing in size and structure due to short-term imbalances. A perfect balance between natality and mortality is a temporary condition; thus, the presence or absence of a balance may not be a good criterion for deciding whether either estimate is good or bad.

A long-term discrepancy between natality and mortality, however, is quite another matter. If the natality and mortality rates modeled here actually occurred for several years, we should have noticed that the population was declining rather rapidly. If censuses did not indicate a population decline, something was definitely wrong with 1 or more of our estimates and an effort should be made to identify and correct the bias.

Table 15.17. A model depicting the interaction of natality and mortality in a single cohort of 100 females (species not defined).

Age (Years)	Year 1	2	3	4	5	6
0 (no young)	100(0)					
(Mortality* 70%)	(−70)					
1 (1 ♀ young)		30(+30)				
(Mortality 60%)		(−18)				
2 (2 ♀ young)			12(+24)			
(Mortality 60%)			(−7)			
3 (2 ♀ young)				5(+10)		
(Mortality 60%)				(−3)		
4 (2 ♀ young)					2(+4)	
(Mortality 60%)					(−1)	
5 (2 ♀ young)						1(+2)
(Mortality 70%)						(−1)
Summary: total ♀ young 70						
young–adult ratio 2.00:1 (100:50)						

*Could include immigration and emigration.

Prior to reexamining the estimates, it may be useful to perform a sensitivity analysis of the model. Sensitivity analyses are easy to perform and involve nothing more than repeated modeling; 1 parameter is changed by a standard amount in each simulation. Table 15.18 contains a sensitivity analysis of the model in Table 15.17 and shows that a bias in the mortality rate of the younger age classes has the most effect on the ability of the 100 females to replace themselves. This does not necessarily mean that the mortality rate of the younger age classes is biased; it merely means that a bias in these sensitive parameters will have the greatest effect on the model's performance. Furthermore, it may be fruitless to search for biases in parameters that have little or no effect. The confidence one has in an estimate, both biological and statistical, is equally important in identifying biases.

Assuming that mortality rate has been identified as the vital statistic most likely to be in error, we are still faced with the problem of quantifying the bias. When searching for biases, the analyst should go all the way back to the raw data, critically examine the observations and assumptions, and if any item is found to be suspect, correct it and repeat the calculations. The basic calculations must be repeated because a bias in 1 age class sometimes affects several other age classes due to the mathematics involved. Furthermore, the analyst should carefully examine the basic data in order to understand and agree thoroughly with the biological and statistical implications of any change.

Suppose, for example, that the mortality rate used in Table 15.17 was obtained by analyzing multiple census data and that due to a bias in both censuses there were actually 50% more 1-year-old females at the beginning of each year. The recalculated mortality rate of juvenile females is thereby decreased from 70 to 55% and the mortality rate of 1 year olds is increased from 60 to 73.3%. These new, partially offsetting rates are modeled in Table 15.19.

An examination of Table 15.19 reveals that the number of female young which 100 females are capable of producing at these new mortality rates has increased to 85, but this is still somewhat short of the 100 needed for a stable population. A further reexamination now should be made of the data, searching primarily for biases which could reduce mortality estimates for all age classes. If, for example, the entire first census was found to be too high (or the second too low) by 10%, this would cause the recalculated mortality rate to be approximately 10% lower for each age class. If this lower rate of loss is modeled, approximately 110 female young are producible in the lifetimes of 100 females, the equivalent of a modest annual *increase* in population size. At first glance this, too, seems unrealistic since we had previously stated that population size was stable. However, if the assumption of stable population size was based on these same biased censuses, then that assump-

Table 15.18. Sensitivity analysis of model in Table 15.17.

Single Parameter Changed	No. Female Young Produced
No change	70.0
Reproductive rate 10% higher age 1	73.0
Reproductive rate 10% higher age 2	72.4
Reproductive rate 10% higher age 3	71.0
Reproductive rate 10% higher age 4	70.4
Reproductive rate 10% higher age 5	70.2
Mortality rate 10% lower age 0	85.0
Mortality rate 10% lower age 1	82.0
Mortality rate 10% lower age 2	74.0
Mortality rate 10% lower age 3 (and older)	70.0

Table 15.19. A model depicting the interaction of natality and mortality in a single cohort of 100 females. Natality same as in Table 15.17, but mortality is adjusted as described in text.

Age (Years)	Year 1	2	3	4	5	6
0 (no young)	100(0)					
(Mortality* 55%)	(−55)					
1 (1 ♀ young)		45(+45)				
(Mortality 73.3%)		(−33)				
2 (2 ♀ young)			12(+24)			
(Mortality 60%)			(−7)			
3 (2 ♀ young)				5(+10)		
(Mortality 60%)				(−3)		
4 (2 ♀ young)					2(+4)	
(Mortality 60%)					(−1)	
5 (2 ♀ young)						1(+2)
(Mortality 70%)						(−1)
Summary: total ♀ young 85						
young–adult ratio 1.54:1 (100:65)						

*Could include immigration and emigration.

tion, also, was wrong and the population was slowly increasing, which agrees fairly well with the trend suggested by the model.

Exercises such as the one just discussed can quickly become mind-boggling, but this does not mean they are useless. To the contrary, such an exercise is highly beneficial because it forces the analyst to critically reexamine the basic data and assumptions.

The analyst also may use simple models like the one just discussed to obtain a rough estimate of natality or mortality when only 1 of these statistics is known. If natality is known, for instance, the analyst constructs several models, each using a different "guess" of the mortality rate until 1 is found which balances with natality. This rough estimate of mortality may be accurate if natality was accurately estimated and if population size does not change.

If a population is known to be increasing, and if its reproductive and mortality rates can be accurately modeled, it is a simple matter to model higher mortality rates on a trial-and-error basis to see how much more exploitation the population can endure. The effect of strategies to harvest some age classes at a higher rate than others can be predicted. "What if" games can be played to disclose what would happen if reproduction suddenly declined, for example. A separate chapter on modeling discusses this technique in greater detail.

A complex, necessarily computerized model has recently been used by Jack Gross (pers. comm.) to "align" the vital statistics of big game herds throughout the United States. Separate computer runs are made, changing 1 questionable statistic at a time, until everything one knows about a population seems to agree. One problem with such modeling efforts is that some of the required information often is not available. When this happens, the biologist is encouraged to "guess" the missing statistic and proceed with the modeling effort. It is conceivable that some models are as sensitive to biased sex ratio estimates, for example, as the change-in-ratio technique presented previously. If so, filling the data gaps with seemingly logical guesses (assumptions), such as a 50–50 fawn sex ratio or equal vulnerability of each sex and age class to poaching, may cause the modeled population to respond peculiarly. It would be helpful if model builders would thoroughly study the sensitivity of their models to various input parameters; such an analysis would be an aid for identifying research priorities and plans could be made to measure with greatest accuracy those types of data to which the model is most sensitive.

USING LIMITED DATA TO MONITOR AND ADJUST HARVESTS

Few agencies have sufficient resources and manpower to obtain detailed scientific information for all their hunt units, and their biologists sometimes are forced to regulate those units "by the seat of their pants," so to speak, on the basis of rather limited, often spontaneous information. The following brief discussions outline many of the possibilities (some of which are obviously inappropriate for most species) and point out some consequences of making erroneous assumptions and actions.

1. *Monitor* the number of animals harvested each year. *Assume* that fluctuations in harvest are caused entirely by fluctuations in population size. *Regulate* by liberalizing or restricting hunting pressure as long as an increase or decrease continues, respectively, and stabilize hunting pressure when the harvest stabilizes. One *problem* is that you may increase hunting pressure too rapidly and unknowingly stabilize the population at too low a level because there is nothing inherent in this system to indicate when carrying capacity has been

reached. Another problem is that a steadily increasing trend in the harvest could be caused by other factors, such as an increasing number of hunters, increasing opportunities, or an increasing reporting rate. Short-term increases also are possible due to such factors as weather and feeding behavior. If short-term factors are suspected of being the primary ones contributing to an increase, it may be best to observe 2 or 3 years of increases to be sure the population trend is real before liberalizing regulations. In *conclusion,* the number of animals harvested is useful for detecting population trends, but additional information usually must be collected to indicate when carrying capacity has been reached.

2. *Monitor* the physical condition of adults. *Assume* that significant declines occur immediately if carrying capacity is exceeded. *Regulate* by increasing harvest when a decline in condition is first noted. One *problem* is that adult size usually is not a sensitive indicator of their present environment because their bones and musculature were formed before the population became too high. Once the habitat has declined enough to cause a deterioration of the animals' physical condition, it may be extremely slow to recover. It may be difficult to know how much to increase hunting pressure, since there will be no immediate improvement in physical condition by which to judge. It is usually not possible to compare one population with another due to basic genetic, habitat, and geographical differences; and for these same reasons the "normal" level must be defined for each population. In *conclusion,* this approach usually is not recommended, but the following one has possibilities.

3. *Monitor* the physical condition of young animals. *Assume* and *regulate* as above. Young usually are much more sensitive to environmental and behavioral stress than adults. Nevertheless, habitat recovery is slow if damage occurs, and the physical condition of young animals may not, after the initial change, provide information to fine-tune hunting pressure. Populations cannot be compared, for the reasons given previously. In *conclusion,* the physical condition of young animals is a better population indicator than that of adults but should be used with caution.

4. *Monitor* the number and quality of harvested trophy animals. *Assume* range conditions are reflected in the percentage of trophies. If trophy animals decline, *regulate* by increasing hunting pressure to guard against overuse of the habitat. This assumption and action overlooks the fact that advanced age also is necessary to reach trophy size, in many cases, and that few animals reach advanced age under high hunting pressure. However, reducing harvests when trophies decline may cause habitat deterioration so that no animal is well fed enough to reach trophy size. Selective removal is necessary; but careful control, requiring much more than simple data, will be needed to produce a large number of male young, keep them healthy through population control, and let them live to trophy age.

5. *Monitor* several high-preference "indicator" plants in the habitat. *Assume* that these will show overuse only when carrying capacity is reached. *Regulate* by increasing harvest pressure as soon as overuse is noted. It is a good theory, but one *problem* is that few plants have been adequately studied to determine how much use is too high. Furthermore, highly-preferred species are sometimes consumed to the point of overuse at almost any population density. Some foods, such as seeds and mushrooms are completely consumed, and thus nothing remains to indicate the degree of use. In *conclusion,* this often used but sometimes difficult concept requires an intimate knowledge of the animals' food habits and the quality of the environment.

6. *Monitor* several low-preference "indicator" plants. *Assume* these will not be used until carrying capacity is reached. When use is detected, *regulate* by increasing hunting pressure until use stops. Most plants vary considerably in their palatability from season to season and many otherwise unpalatable ones will be eaten considerably just as they begin spring growth, especially if they are the first to emerge. In severe winters or during high water, animal movement may be so restricted that they may use low-preference foods considerably, even though animal density is not too high for "normal" conditions. Obvious signs of general overuse, such as "browse lines," may be noticed far too late, after the population has become too high and the habitat has been damaged. In *conclusion,* the concept is sometimes useful, but only if the proper cautions are exercised.

7. *Monitor* crop damage and damage complaints. *Assume* that animals prefer native foods and will not consume crops in large quantities unless there are too many animals for the native habitat to support. Choose a "normal" level of crop damage and *regulate* by increasing hunting pressure each time this level is exceeded. One *problem* is that some crops, such as corn and beans, are *more* palatable than most native foods and will be eaten extensively at almost any population level. Furthermore, research to establish a "normal" or "target" level of crop damage would be difficult and that level might be politically indefensible. Farmers may force you to keep the crop damage low, even if this means the animal population must be kept much lower than the native habitat will support. In *conclusion,* it is a factor to consider and may be helpful, in combination with other information, in setting hunting regulations.

8. *Monitor* reproductive and recruitment rates. *Assume* these parameters decline significantly when habitat carrying capacity or territory saturation is reached. *Regulate* by increasing hunting pressure if a decline is detected and continue to increase it until reproduction returns to normal. The complex relationship between habitat, territoriality and other behavior, and reproduction is presently poorly known for many species. Even when reproduction is sensitive to habitat quality, the change may begin before carrying capacity is reached or, even worse, not occur until long afterward, depending on the species. A return to normal, if it occurs, may be quite slow, due to the slow rate of recovery of the habitat. In *conclusion,* reproduction holds much promise as a basis for regulating harvests. However, the information costs may be excessive.

9. *Monitor* "natural" or nonhunting mortality rates. *Assume* that natural mortality increases significantly when carrying capacity is reached. *Regulate* by increasing hunting pressure each time natural mortality exceeds some low "normal" level. The *problem* is, these data are expensive to obtain and therefore cannot be

considered simple. Catastrophic die-offs can be detected without elaborate studies, but these usually occur only after the habitat has been damaged severely. The population may be greatly reduced by a catastrophic die-off and may need to have the hunting pressure reduced for a few years, not increased. The system is appealing because of its direct relationship to the fundamental reason for hunting—to replace "natural" mortality. If inexpensive measures of nonhunting mortality are available, the system is promising.

10. *Monitor* road kills. *Assume* the number of kills is in proportion to population size. As road kills increase, *regulate* by increasing hunting pressure until road kills stabilize. One *problem* is that road kills are also related to vehicle traffic volume, vehicle speed, weather, season, location of feeding areas, and other factors. Many states have insufficient reported road kills to provide the needed sample size for small management units. Many of these occur too late in the year (usually fall) to be useful in setting current-year regulations. Furthermore, road kills do not indicate when carrying capacity has been reached. In *conclusion,* even though road kills are seldom useful as a sole source of information, they may help support other data to confirm a population trend.

11. *Monitor* harvested age ratios. *Assume* that a "young" age distribution is indicative of an increasing population. *Regulate* by continuing to liberalize hunting regulations until age structure returns to "normal." As mentioned previously in this chapter, age structure is primarily a reflection of recruitment rate, (see possibility No. 8), and the idea of it reflecting an increase or decrease in population size is outdated. A low density population is the kind most likely to have a young age distribution, and this population would be made even smaller by increasing hunting pressure. In *conclusion,* the system as stated is *not recommended.*

12. *Monitor* harvested sex ratios. *Assume* that all populations have essentially the same rate of "natural" losses. *Regulate* by limiting the percentage of females in the harvest, generally within the range of other populations with which you have more experience. This practice is usually *not recommended* because it is not realistic to assume that all populations have the same rate of natural losses. An exceptional population with few natural losses will eventually produce approximately a 50–50 sex ratio in the harvest, and it would be a grave mistake to limit the harvest sex ratio of such a population. If the rate of natural loss and the percentage of harvestable surplus animals are known, an appropriate harvest sex ratio can be prescribed, but this approach is usually not practical because of the difficulty in measuring both of these statistics. The harvest sex ratio itself contains no information about population welfare to help fine-tune the system.

13. *Monitor* the number of hunters and where they hunt. *Assume* that hunters go only where there is plenty of game. As hunters increase, *regulate* by liberalizing seasons to attract even more hunters to the area. Hunters often go to areas that have been most publicized and may not have any personal experience with the area. Hunters may interpret the liberalized regulations as an indication that the agency has scientific proof that there is more game in the area, when the agency is actually getting all its clues from the hunters. The number and distribution of hunters is also related to tradition, the abundance of competing hunting areas and seasons, the price of gas and meat, and even to local economic conditions, such as a coincidental strike at a large manufacturing facility nearby. In *conclusion,* this system has many pitfalls and should be used with caution.

14. *Monitor* hunter success rates using an end-of-season questionnaire or a similar method. *Assume* that hunter success rate is primarily related to the game species' population size. *Regulate* by increasing or decreasing hunting pressure each time the hunter success rate increases or decreases, respectively. Like possibility No. 1, there is no indication when carrying capacity has been reached. Other problems are that hunter success rates also are affected by the number and density of hunters (see the system above). Additional, short-term influences on success rates are weather conditions, access, day of week the season opens, habitat factors such as food abundance and distribution, and even biases in questionnaire response caused by the attitude of the people toward the agency. In *conclusion,* the system is potentially useful if the possible pitfalls are kept in mind and avoided.

15. *Monitor* animal sign, such as tracks, scats, and calls. *Assume* that fluctuations in sign are caused entirely by fluctuations in population size. *Regulate* by liberalizing or restricting regulations as long as an increase or decrease continues, respectively, and stabilize hunting pressure when the amount of sign stabilizes. There is nothing inherent in the abundance of sign to indicate when carrying capacity has been reached. Hunting pressure may be increased too rapidly and thus stabilize the population at too low a level. Like possibility No. 1, it may be necessary to monitor additional statistics, such as habitat or animal condition. Data acquisition costs may be high. In *conclusion,* the system is frequently useful, but its shortcomings should be kept constantly in mind.

16. *Monitor* internal or external parasite burdens. *Assume* that any increase in parasite burden above some "normal" level is indicative of excessive population density. *Regulate* by continuing to increase harvest presure until parasite burdens return to normal. Parasite studies have been made for many species (Eve and Kellogg 1977), but in most cases it was not known if the animal population was below or above carrying capacity, thus the "normal" level is poorly known. Furthermore, if host density has been high in the recent past, parasite incidence may remain relatively high even though host populations are reduced. Parasite studies are expensive but may be justified because this information helps the public understand the need for population regulation. In *conclusion,* the system has considerable potential provided the supporting relationships are well known.

17. *Monitor* predators, one step up the food chain from the "subject" species. *Assume* that predator population levels are related to the population size of the subject species. If predators increase, liberalize harvest regulations until the predator returns to normal population levels. A confounding *problem* is, most predators are adaptable to several food sources and may be reflect-

ing an increase in other foods, not the subject species. Furthermore, if you reduce the subject species' population, the predator may shift to another species and maintain near-normal levels. There are far too many variables for this technique to work effectively, in most cases.

18. *Monitor* public opinion, especially hunter complaints. *Assume* that a certain ratio of negative to positive comments is normal and increase or decrease hunting pressure (as appropriate) when this ratio is exceeded. The *problem* is that one person who feels strongly about something can sometimes influence the opinions of others and generate a flood of criticism. "Infectious" opinions, no matter how widely accepted and frequently voiced, may not be as useful to the agency as a few that have arisen independently and thoughtfully from careful, objective observers. Unfortunately, it may be impossible to encourage the latter without also stimulating the former. Furthermore, if you ask for the public's opinion, you may be obligated to accept the majority view. Most agencies have administrative policies concerning public involvement and the role of these opinions in decisionmaking. Nevertheless, the biologist should be aware of the inherent biases.

19. *Monitor* nothing. *Assume* that the relationship between hunters and game populations is largely self-regulating. Do not *regulate* each species separately, but use a common, traditional season for all species, especially small game. The law of diminishing returns works fairly well on small game, and hunters tend to lose interest or shift to other species when their success declines. Fortunately, many small-game species have high reproductive rates and hunters are too inefficient to reduce populations below those needed for replacement. However, the desire to harvest a big game animal, especially a trophy, may be so high that hunters will persist even when their chances are slim. Big game have relatively low reproductive rates and often cannot be safely reduced more than 30% by hunting. In *conclusion*, while the law of diminishing returns operates with all species, this "system" may work *well* only with small game.

Summary

Systems for using limited data are usually poor substitutes for comprehensive, well-designed, statistically controlled studies. Nevertheless, time and budget limitations are a reality and the choice for some hunt units often is "regulate based on limited data or do not regulate at all." This section recognizes that fact of life and points out some of the biases and pitfalls to be aware of and avoid, if possible.

There is one final point to consider. Each kind of information discussed in this last section is indeed limited. However, the number of *kinds* of information is not so limited, and there may be opportunities to simultaneously compare several indicators of population trends or habitat quality and get a clearer picture. The biologist can proceed with greater confidence if several independent bits of information agree that the population is increasing, for example. I urge that investigators use as many kinds of information as possible, especially when these are of limited quality.

Chapter Sixteen

Measurement of Ecological Diversity

JAY D. HAIR

Coordinator of Fisheries and Wildlife Sciences
Departments of Zoology and Forestry
North Carolina State University
Raleigh, North Carolina

INTRODUCTION

Establishment and maintenance of ecologically diverse wildlife communities are important objectives of contemporary wildlife management. Interest in ecological diversity has developed, particularly in recent years (Schoener 1974), because of the realization that technological "progress" has resulted in a world of rapidly diminishing natural resources (Pimlott 1969). Human alteration of wildlife habitats inevitably brings changes in species composition and population densities. Measures of ecological diversity are important tools for evaluating or predicting potential impacts of alternative land-use practices on the structure and function of wildlife communities.

The purpose of this chapter is to introduce the basic concepts of ecological diversity and the most frequently used diversity indices along with their respective manual calculation. Emphasis will be placed on species diversity at the community level of organization.

ASSUMPTIONS AND DATA REQUIREMENTS

The community concept is one of the most important principles in ecologic theory because it emphasizes that diverse organisms live together in an orderly manner. The species composition of communities has been used as an approach to community analysis for at least 50 years and has been analyzed by species frequency, species per unit of area, the spatial distribution of individuals, and the numerical abundance of species (Hairston 1959). One of the most important aspects of community structure is that of species diversity. When measured by appropriate indices this permits the summarization of large amounts of data about the number of species and their relative abundances as a mathematical value (Wilhm 1968). The reason for measuring a community's diversity is usually to judge its relationships to other community properties (e.g., productivity, habitat structure, environmental conditions) or compare it with other communities.

Several different indices of species diversity have been suggested. They differ in the assumptions made about the relative abundance of species, in their sensitivity to different types of change in community structure, and in their degree of independence of sample size (Peet 1974, Pielou 1975). The measurement of diversity is not as simple as might be expected. Before diversity can be measured there must be a precise definition of the collection of organisms that comprise the community concerned (Pielou 1975). Communities vary tremendously: one might define as a community the shorebirds inhabiting a coastal island; the small mammals in a southern Appalachian deciduous forest; the passerine birds using a clear-cut area; the plants in an alpine meadow; the invertebrates from a mountain trout stream; the fish from a creel sample; or the abomasal parasites from a population of deer. Consequently, a number of assumptions regarding the data to be analyzed are required. In summary these include the following major points:

1. The spatial boundaries of the area containing the community, the way in which sampling was conducted,

and the time limits during which observations were made must be specified.

2. Measurement of diversity requires a clear taxonomic classification of the subject matter. Reference in the literature is usually made to species diversity, but nothing precludes treatment of any taxon rank, structural components of the habitat or even trophic diversity. Pielou (1967) has discussed some of the problems associated with simultaneous treatment of different levels of hierarchic classification.

3. All individuals assigned to a specific class are assumed equal. Different forms (e.g., sexes, larval stages) of the same species may have very different functional roles in the structure of a particular community (Preston 1969).

4. All species are assumed to be equally different. Lloyd (1964) and Johnson and Raven (1970) questioned the assumption of species equivalency and suggested a factor for weighting individuals by reproductive value in calculating species diversity.

5. Most diversity indices require an estimate of importance. Abundance is not always the best indicator of a species' importance. If necessary before comparisons are made the data should be weighted by use of appropriate conversion factors (e.g., biomass, dry weight) (Wilhm 1968). The actual weighting factor used will depend on the area of research, but the choice can greatly influence the results obtained (Dickman 1968).

6. Many organisms are not distributed randomly throughout a given area or sample. This necessitates careful randomization in sampling (Pielou 1967, Fager 1972) and correct use of statistical procedures.

7. Three levels of diversity have been distinguished: (1) Alpha diversity, the within-habitat or intracommunity diversity, (2) Beta diversity, or between-habitat diversity, defined as the change in species composition along environmental gradients, and (3) Gamma diversity, the diversity of the entire landscape which can be considered a composite of alpha and beta diversity. These forms are not always easily distinguished. Many alpha diversity measurements are influenced by habitat variations, which could also be interpreted as beta diversity. Whittaker (1972), Allan (1975), and Pielou (1975) provide further consideration of this aspect of ecological diversity.

DIVERSITY INDICES

Species Counts

The simplest measure of species diversity is to count the *number of species* (S) occurring per unit area, sample etc. There are 2 principal drawbacks to using species counts as a measure of diversity. First, it is an unweighted measure since it fails to account for the relative abundances of the species present. For example, it is desirable that a community with 97 individuals of 1 species and 1 individual of each of 3 other species have a lower diversity index than a community of 4 species, each with 25 individuals (though both have 4 species and 100 individuals). Second, species counts depend on sample size. Although none of the diversity indices proposed to date show complete independence of sample size, its influence on species counts is more unpredictable than it is on the other measures of diversity (Hurlbert 1971, Whittaker 1972).

Several alternative indices for measuring diversity have been suggested (see reviews by Fager 1972, Peet 1974, Pielou 1975). They are generally intercorrelated (DeBenedictis 1973), differ markedly in ease of calculation, and measure somewhat different features (Hurlbert 1971). The diversity indices described below are the ones used most extensively by ecologists. They are called dual-concept measures of diversity since they are sensitive to changes in both the number of species ("species richness" component) and to changes in the distribution of individuals among the species present ("evenness" or "equitability" component).

Simpson's Index

The first dual-concept index of diversity used in ecology was proposed by Simpson (1949). This index measures the probability that 2 individuals selected at random from a population of N individuals will belong to the same species. If a particular species i ($i = 1, 2, \ldots, S$) is represented in a community by p_i (proportion of individuals), the probability of picking 2 individuals at random that belong to the same species is the joint probability $[(p_i)(p_i)$, or $p_i^2]$. If each of these probabilities for all the i species in the community are summed, then Simpson's diversity index for an infinite sample is:

$$SI = \sum_{i=1}^{S} p_i^2 \quad , \qquad (1)$$

or when the sample is being treated as a complete or finite sample,

$$SI' = \sum_{i=1}^{S} \frac{n_i\,(n_i - 1)}{N\,(N-1)} \quad , \qquad (2)$$

where N is the total number of individuals in the population and n_i is the number of individuals of the ith species.

As formulated above, Simpson's index varies inversely with heterogeneity (i.e., index values decrease [or increase] as a diversity increases [or decreases]). For clarity, it is desirable that higher (or lower) index probability values correspond to higher (or lower) diversity values. To account for this, it has been proposed that Simpson's index be subtracted from its maximum possible value of 1 (Pielou 1977).

Therefore, when a sample is being regarded as a random sample from an infinitely large population, Simpson's index of diversity is:

$$D = 1 - \sum_{i=1}^{S} p_i^2 \quad , \text{or} \qquad (3)$$

as Pielou (1977) has suggested, it is statistically more correct to use a formulation adjusted for finite sample size:

$$D' = 1 - \sum_{i=1}^{S} \frac{n_i\,(n_i - 1)}{N(N-1)} \qquad (4)$$

The following hypothetical data will be used to illustrate the manual calculation of the species diversity indices considered in this chapter:

Species	Individuals (n_i)	Proportions (p_i)	P_i^2
1	50	0.50	0.250
2	30	0.30	0.090
3	15	0.15	0.023
4	5	0.05	0.003

Total (N) = 100

Example 1—Simpson's Index (D) for an infinite sample (equa. 3):

$$D = 1 - \sum_{i=1}^{S} p_i^2$$

$$= 1 - [(0.50)^2 + (0.30)^2 + (0.15)^2 + (0.05)^2]$$

$$= 1 - [0.250 + 0.090 + 0.023 + 0.003]$$

$$= 1 - 0.366$$

$$= 0.634$$

Example 2—Simpson's Index (D') for a finite sample (equa. 4):

$$D' = 1 - \sum_{i=1}^{S} \frac{n_i\ (n_i - 1)}{N\ (N-1)}$$

$$= 1 - [\frac{50\ (49)}{9900} + \frac{30\ (29)}{9900} + \frac{15\ (14)}{9900} + \frac{5\ (4)}{9900}]$$

$$= 1 - [0.247 + 0.088 + 0.021 + 0.002]$$

$$= 1 - 0.358$$

$$= 0.642$$

The Simpson measure of diversity is sensitive to the abundances of the 1 or 2 most common species of a community (Poole 1974), and can be regarded as a measure of "dominance concentration" (Whittaker 1965). Simpson's index is, therefore, most appropriately used when the relative degree of dominance of a few species in the community is of primary interest, rather than the overall evenness of the abundance of all species.

Hill (1973) interpreted Simpson's index as a weighted mean of the proportional abundances and concluded that the reciprocal of Simpson's index (i.e., $\frac{1}{D}$ or $\frac{1}{D'}$) was more appropriate as a measure of diversity than 1–Simpson's index (see Hill 1973 for details). Regardless of the formulation used, the important point for comparative purposes is that diversity measures be expressed on a uniform scale.

Information Theory Measures of Diversity

The most frequently used species diversity indices are those based on information theory. This approach was first used by Margalef (1958) and as Pielou (1969) pointed out, its use is appropriate since it can be "... equated with the amount of uncertainty that exists regarding the species of an individual selected at random from a population. The more species there are and the more nearly even their distribution, the greater the diversity." The most frequently used information measures of diversity are Brillouin's (1962) H and Shannon and Weaver's (1949) H'.

BRILLOUIN'S FORMULA (H)

If all of the individuals of a collection or community can be identified and counted, the absolute diversity of the community can be measured by the Brillouin formula:

$$H = \frac{1}{N} \log_b \left(\frac{N!}{n_1!\ n_2! \ldots n_S!}\right) \tag{5}$$

where N is the total number of individuals, and n_1, $n_2 \ldots, n_S$ are the number of individuals of each species and, N! = (N factorial) = N (N–1) (N–2) . . . (1), e.g., 5! = 5 (4) (3) (2) (1) = 120. The choice of logarithmic base ($\log_b$) is arbitrary. If logarithms to the base 2 are used, the unit of H is called a "binary digit" or "bit." If natural logarithms (1n) are used (base e), the unit is termed a "natural bel" or "nat." When common logarithms (log), base 10, are used the unit of H is called a "decit" (Pielou 1977).

Because H measures absolute diversity (i.e., the diversity of an entire community), it has no standard error. Any 2 different values of H are, therefore, significantly different (Poole 1974). To avoid the problem of evaluating factorials when H is calculated manually (since it is only their logarithms that are needed) it is convenient to use the equivalent equation:

$$H = \frac{C}{N} (\log_{10} N! - \sum \log_{10} n_i!) \quad , \tag{6}$$

where "N" and "n" are as defined above and C is a constant for conversion of logarithms from the base 10 to the base chosen for the measure. For base 2, C = 3.321928; for base e, C = 2.302585; for base 10, C = 1. For convenience, the appropriate values for use in equation (6) for all integers from n = 1 to 100 are given in Table 16.1 (modified from Lloyd et al. 1968). For values of $\log_{10}$ n! greater than 100, Sterling's approximation for factorials can be used:

$$\log_{10} n! \simeq (n + 0.5) \log_{10} n - 0.434294482n + 0.39909 \tag{7}$$

Example 3—Brillouin's H:

The hypothetical data given previously will be used to illustrate the calculation of Brillouin's H using formula (6). The measure will be based on natural logarithms (base e), so, to convert from logarithms base 10 to logarithms base e:

$$\frac{C}{N} = \frac{2.302585}{100} = 0.023026$$

Table 16.1. Functions for use in manual calculations of ecological diversity and equitability. Logarithms are to base 10.

N	LOG(N)	LOG_N!	N_LOG_N	N	LOG(N)	LOG_N!	N_LOG_N
1	0.0000	0.0000	0.0000	51	1.7076	66.1906	87.0861
2	0.3010	0.3010	0.6021	52	1.7160	67.9066	89.2322
3	0.4771	0.7782	1.4314	53	1.7243	69.6309	91.3866
4	0.6021	1.3802	2.4082	54	1.7324	71.3633	93.5493
5	0.6990	2.0792	3.4949	55	1.7404	73.1037	95.7199
6	0.7782	2.8573	4.6689	56	1.7482	74.8519	97.8985
7	0.8451	3.7024	5.9157	57	1.7559	76.6077	100.0849
8	0.9031	4.6055	7.2247	58	1.7634	78.3712	102.2788
9	0.9542	5.5598	8.5882	59	1.7709	80.1420	104.4803
10	1.0000	6.5598	10.0000	60	1.7782	81.9202	106.6891
11	1.0414	7.6012	11.4553	61	1.7853	83.7055	108.9051
12	1.0792	8.6803	12.9502	62	1.7924	85.4979	111.1283
13	1.1139	9.7943	14.4813	63	1.7993	87.2972	113.3585
14	1.1461	10.9404	16.0458	64	1.8062	89.1034	115.5955
15	1.1761	12.1165	17.6414	65	1.8129	90.9163	117.8394
16	1.2041	13.3206	19.2659	66	1.8195	92.7359	120.0899
17	1.2304	14.5511	20.9176	67	1.8261	94.5619	122.3470
18	1.2553	15.8063	22.5949	68	1.8325	96.3945	124.6106
19	1.2788	17.0851	24.2963	69	1.8388	98.2333	126.8806
20	1.3010	18.3861	26.0206	70	1.8451	100.0784	129.1569
21	1.3222	19.7083	27.7666	71	1.8513	101.9297	131.4393
22	1.3424	21.0508	29.5333	72	1.8573	103.7870	133.7279
23	1.3617	22.4125	31.3197	73	1.8633	105.6503	136.0226
24	1.3802	23.7927	33.1251	74	1.8692	107.5196	138.3231
25	1.3979	25.1906	34.9485	75	1.8751	109.3946	140.6296
26	1.4150	26.6056	36.7893	76	1.8808	111.2754	142.9418
27	1.4314	28.0370	38.6468	77	1.8865	113.1619	145.2598
28	1.4472	29.4841	40.5204	78	1.8921	115.0540	147.5834
29	1.4624	30.9465	42.4095	79	1.8976	116.9516	149.9125
30	1.4771	32.4237	44.3136	80	1.9031	118.8547	152.2472
31	1.4914	33.9150	46.2322	81	1.9085	120.7632	154.5873
32	1.5051	35.4202	48.1648	82	1.9138	122.6770	156.9327
33	1.5185	36.9387	50.1110	83	1.9191	124.5961	159.2835
34	1.5315	38.4702	52.0703	84	1.9243	126.5204	161.6395
35	1.5441	40.0142	54.0424	85	1.9294	128.4498	164.0006
36	1.5563	41.5705	56.0269	86	1.9345	130.3843	166.3669
37	1.5682	43.1387	58.0235	87	1.9395	132.3238	168.7382
38	1.5798	44.7185	60.0318	88	1.9445	134.2683	171.1145
39	1.5911	46.3096	62.0515	89	1.9494	136.2177	173.4957
40	1.6021	47.9116	64.0824	90	1.9542	138.1719	175.8818
41	1.6128	49.5244	66.1241	91	1.9590	140.1310	178.2728
42	1.6232	51.1477	68.1765	92	1.9638	142.0948	180.6685
43	1.6335	52.7811	70.2391	93	1.9685	144.0632	183.0689
44	1.6435	54.4246	72.3119	94	1.9731	146.0364	185.4740
45	1.6532	56.0778	74.3946	95	1.9777	148.0141	187.8837
46	1.6628	57.7406	76.4869	96	1.9823	149.9964	190.2980
47	1.6721	59.4127	78.5886	97	1.9868	151.9831	192.7169
48	1.6812	61.0939	80.6996	98	1.9912	153.9744	195.1402
49	1.6902	62.7841	82.8196	99	1.9956	155.9700	197.5679
50	1.6990	64.4831	84.9485	100	2.0000	157.9700	200.0000

Species	Individuals (n_i)	*$\log_{10} n_i!$
1	50	64.4831
2	30	32.4237
3	15	12.1165
4	5	2.0792
Total (N)	100	Σ = 111.1025

*$\log_{10} 100! = 157.9700$

$H = 0.023026\,(157.9700 - 111.1025)$

H = 1.079 natural bels per individual

*see Table 16.1 for values

The total information content for the collection is, B = HN or, B = 1.079(100) = 107.9171 natural bels.

SHANNON-WEAVER FUNCTION (H')

In most instances it is not possible to identify and count every individual in a community. For such cases it is necessary to take a random sample of individuals from the populations of all species present. Under these circumstances, the Shannon-Weaver (1949) information theory function (also referred to as Shannon-Wiener function) is the correct measure of diversity. It is one of the simplest and most extensively used diversity indices and measures the average degree of uncertainty of predicting the species of a given individual picked at random from a community. The formula for the Shannon-Weaver function is:

$$H' = -\sum_{i=1}^{S} p_i \log_b p_i \quad , \qquad (8)$$

where S is the number of species, and p_i is the proportion of the total number of individuals consisting of the *i*th species. The proportions (p_i) are intended to be the true proportions from the population being sampled. In practice, these are usually estimated from the sample as $p_i \simeq n_i/N$. Since the p_i's are estimated, it is feasible to compute Shannon's H' directly in terms of the observed n_i's to avoid the inconvenience (and attendant rounding errors) of calculating sample proportions (Lloyd et al. 1968).

The logarithmic base is arbitrary, but when H' is calculated manually (without a computer program) it is convenient to use the equivalent equation:

$$H' \simeq \frac{C}{N}\left(N \log_{10} N - \sum n_i \log_{10} n_i\right) \quad , \qquad (9)$$

where C is the constant for conversion of logarithms from base 10 to the chosen base (see p. 272), and N and n_i are as defined previously. This permits the use of the precalculated values for the components of the index ($\log_{10}$) provided in Table 16.1.

Example 4—Shannon-Weaver Function (H'):

Using formula (9) and with H' based on natural logarithms (base e),

$$\frac{C}{N} = \frac{2.302585}{100} = 0.023026$$

Species	Individuals (n_i)	$n_i \log_{10} n_i$
1	50	84.9485
2	30	44.3136
3	15	17.6414
4	5	3.4949
Total (N)	100	Σ = 150.3984

$N \log_{10} N = 100 \log_{10} 100 = 200.0000$

$H' \simeq 0.023026(200 - 150.3984)$

$H' \simeq$ 1.1421 natural bels per individual

One of the merits of the Shannon function is independence of sample size because it estimates diversity from a random sample which presumably contains all of the species of the community (Poole 1974). Practically, this type of random sample may be impossible to obtain in diverse communities, because increasing sample size almost always results in finding individuals of the more uncommon species. However, this bias will be minimized if statistically valid sampling procedures are followed (Pielou 1966).

EQUITABILITY INDICES

Incorporated within the dual-component concept of diversity is the feature concerning the evenness with which individuals are divided among the species present. This component, termed "equitability," is logically independent of the second component, "species richness" (Peet 1974). The maximum possible diversity for a given number of species occurs if all species are present in equal numbers. For the Brillouin formula this is referred to as "H maximum" and correspondingly, for the Shannon function, "H' maximum."

Several approaches to the measurement of equitability have been proposed (see reviews in Hurlbert 1971, Hill 1973, Peet 1974, Pielou 1975). Of these the most frequently utilized are Pielou's "J" and "J'" (Pielou 1966, 1967). Their formulations are:

$$J = \frac{H}{H \text{ maximum}} \quad , \qquad (10)$$

where H is as defined previously for Brillouin's measure of absolute diversity, (equa. 5), and where the maximum possible diversity is calculated as:

$$H \text{ maximum} = \frac{1}{N} \log \frac{N!}{[N/S]!^{\,S-r}\,([N/S]+1)!^{\,r}} \quad , \qquad (11)$$

where [N/S] is the integer part of N/S, S is the number of species, and r = N−s [N/S].

Example 5—Equitability Measurement (J):

Using the same hypothetical data used previously, equitability (J) would be calculated from equation (10) as follows:

$$J = \frac{H}{H \text{ maximum}}$$

H = 1.079 (see example 3)

$$N/s = \frac{100}{4} = 25$$

$$\begin{aligned} r &= 100 - 4\,(100/4) \\ &= 100 - 4\,(25) \\ &= 100 - 100 \\ &= 0 \end{aligned}$$

$$\begin{aligned} H \text{ maximum} &= \frac{1}{100} \log_{10} \frac{100!}{(25!)^4\,(26!)^0} \\ &= \frac{1}{100} \log_{10} 100! - (4 \log_{10} 25! + 0 \log_{10} 26!) \\ &= \frac{1}{100}\, 157.9700 - (4 \times 25.1906 + 0) \\ &= \frac{1}{100}\, 157.9700 - 100.7624 \\ &= \frac{57.2076}{100} \\ &= 0.5721 \text{ decits per individual} \end{aligned}$$

For purposes of comparing maximum diversity with logarithms to the base e (used in calculating H) this value is multiplied by the appropriate conversion factor and, H maximum = (0.5721) (2.302585) = 1.3173 natural bels per individual. H maximum was calculated initially with logarithms to the base 10 in order that the precalculated values given in Table 16.1 could be used for manual calculations.

Now, substituting into equation (10), the calculated equitability for the sample data is:

$$J = \frac{1.079}{1.3173} = 0.8191$$

The appropriate measure of equitability for use with the Shannon-Weaver measure of diversity is:

$$J' = \frac{H'}{H' \text{ maximum}} \quad , \qquad (12)$$

where H′ is the diversity value as defined previously for the Shannon Weaver function, and H′ maximum is equal to the logarithm of the number of species (Log S), using the same base of logarithms used in the calculations of H′.

For the sample data used previously, where H′ = 1.149 and using values for $\log_{10}$ in column 1, Table 16.1, where H maximum is defined as the logarithm of the number of species, then

$$\begin{aligned} H' \text{ maximum} &= \log_{10} 4 \\ &= 0.6021 \end{aligned}$$

Using the correct conversion factor for logarithms to the base e used in calculation of H′,

$$\begin{aligned} H' \text{ maximum} &= (0.6021)\,(2.302585) \\ &= 1.3863 \text{ natural bels per individual} \end{aligned}$$

Substituting into formula (12) the equitability value for the data is,

$$J' = \frac{1.142}{1.3863} = 0.8238$$

While both of the above equitability indices are used widely, their limitations are frequently ignored. The most important limitation is their dependence on species number. For an accurate calculation of either measure, it is necessary to know the total number of species in the community (sample). For most ecological applications this is virtually impossible to determine. Most investigators (particularly those using the Shannon-Weaver function) have substituted the number of species in the sample as the value for the total number of species present in the community. As a result, (S) is almost always underestimated and consequently, equitability (J′) is overestimated. See Peet (1974) for further discussion on this topic.

CONCLUDING REMARKS

Several factors are important in the determination of the ecological diversity of a wildlife community. Individual species of animals respond to and select habitats primarily on the basis of differences in habitat structure (Anderson and Shugart 1974). As structural complexity or heterogeneity of a habitat increases, the number of microhabitats potentially available also increases. This, in general, corresponds to an increase in the number of species in a given area (Rosenzweig and Winakur 1969, Brown 1973, Cody 1974, Wiens 1974, Willson 1974, Roth 1976, Abramsky 1978, Gauthreaux 1978, Shugart et al. 1978). When interpreting diversity indices it is important to remember that 2 or more sets of data could possess (assuming corresponding relative abundances) totally different species yet have identical diversity index values. Alternatively, 2 habitats could be suitable for identical species of animals, but have different diversity indices due to asynchronous population changes that shift the equitability component without modifying the species number (M'Closkey 1972).

The values obtained from the calculation of diversity indices do not in themselves provide answers for solving specific wildlife management problems. They do, however, serve as useful focal points for evaluating spatial, temporal, and trophic variables associated with field observations. To be most useful to the natural resource manager, these variables should be quantifiable and associated with wildlife management practices.

Prior applications of measures of species diversity are numerous and involve most plant and animal taxons. Of particular interest to wildlife research and management are those dealing with the inter-relationships between faunal diversity and components of the habitat. For example, it has been well documented that vegetative characteristics (MacArthur and MacArthur 1961, Karr 1968, Kricher 1973, Noble and Hamilton 1975, *inter alia*), structural features (Karr 1968, Dwyer 1972, Tomoff 1974, Balda 1975, Ferguson et al. 1975, Reese and Hair (1976), and size (Forman et al. 1976, Galli et al. 1976, MacClintock et al. 1977, Whitcomb 1977, Whitcomb et al. 1977) are important factors in determining avian species diversity of terrestrial habitats. These relationships have a number of important management implications, and their details warrant careful review.

Overall, habitat management is the key to wildlife diversity. It is, however, important to point out that, although maximizing the diversity of a particular group of animals (e.g., passerine birds) may be an important wildlife management objective, the ecological impact will be quite different than maximizing diversity at a particular trophic level. Also, managing solely for species diversity may not be an appropriate strategy since some management practices may exclude valuable but uncommon species from a given habitat (Balda 1975).

The application of measures of ecological diversity are not limited to the types of comparisons mentioned in the preceding paragraphs. Diversity measures can be used whenever the subject matter can be classified and objectively measured. For example, diversity indices would be useful tools for food habit analyses, comparative ethology studies, environmental monitoring, land-use planning etc. Like all scientific investigations the application of diversity measures should follow sound research principles where meaningful hypotheses are identified and tested statistically.

Chapter Seventeen

Reconnaissance Mapping and Map Use

HENRY S. MOSBY

Professor, Wildlife Management
Department Fishery and Wildlife Sciences
Virginia Polytechnic Institute and State University
Blacksburg, Virginia

Maps are the most convenient and universally understood means yet devised to show graphically the spatial relations between the various features and structures on the earth's surface. These relations are expressed so that it is possible to determine from a map the distance and bearing (angle) from any point on the map to any other point. In wildlife management, as in other activities dealing with areas of land, a map is indispensable for recording and communicating the information relating to a specific area (War Department 1939, 1944).

Recording all data about a specific area on 1 map would result in such a jumble of symbols that the map would be unintelligible. For this reason, a map is normally prepared to show a specific set of data. Thus there are many types of maps showing, for example, cover types, vegetative distributions, land use patterns, soil types and characteristics, distribution and abundance of animals, topography, future plans, and even fieldnote locations.

In most instances, wildlifers prepare reconnaissance-type maps that do not have to be of a high order of accuracy. If great accuracy, such as distances accurate to 1 meter or less are required, standard surveying instruments and techniques must be employed. The preparation of maps of such accuracy will require considerable training and experience in surveying and therefore the services of a professional surveyor should be used. Thus, this chapter is concerned only with the preparation of reconnaissance maps or the utilization of available maps.

The wildlifer, when working in new and unfamiliar country, should first assemble maps of the area. Adequate and satisfactory maps can usually be secured. Highway maps are usually available from the state highway department or the district highway engineer's office; soil maps for those areas which have been mapped usually are available from the state agricultural extension service, located at the state college, or from the local office of the Soil Conservation Service; topographic maps are available for many sections from the Map Information Officer of the U.S. Geological Survey or the Superintendent of Documents, Washington, D.C., and often are in stock at local stationery stores; local offices of the Soil Conservation District can supply information on the availability of aerial photographs; local and state planning commissions usually have various types of maps which they will make available to interested individuals; and, finally, the Army Map Service, Washington, D.C., acts as a map coordinating agency for the federal government. They have available for sale a vast number of maps for most regions of the United States.

It may be necessary to prepare special maps or to redraft, enlarge, or reduce existing maps for particular uses. These techniques will be discussed briefly.

RECONNAISSANCE-MAPPING INSTRUMENTS

Perhaps the mapping tools most often used by the wildlife worker who prepares his own maps in the field are the hand-held (box) or staff-held (forester's) compass (Fig. 17.1A), Abney level (Fig. 17.1B), and tape (either 100-ft or Gunter's chain-66 ft). Details of the construction of the compass and Abney level are supplied in the manufacturers' manuals. Kjellstrom (1975) presented an excellent discussion of the compass and its use; de-Moisy (1949) described both the compass and Abney level and their use. Table 17.1 shows the accuracy in distance which may be expected with these instruments.

MAP DISTANCES

All map distances are horizontal, not ground, measurements. The ground measurement, the hypotenuse of a triangle, (see Fig. 17.2) is greater than map distance. Slope measurements may be reduced to horizontal measurements for mapping by holding the tape horizontal (Fig. 17.2A), by "breaking" the tape (Fig. 17.2B), by formula, or by the use of a "trailer tape." Since the first 2 methods are illustrated, slope correction by formula and by the use of a trailer tape will be discussed.

Several formulae for reducing slope distances to horizontal distances may be used when a tape and Abney level are employed (Fig. 17.2C). An Abney level may have a topographic or a percent scale, each of which has advantages in certain situations. When employing the topographic scale on the Abney, a chain tape should be used with built-in graduations on the back showing the difference between slope and horizontal distance at various Abney level readings. The use of the topographic Abney and surveyor's chain tape is described and shown in Forbes and Meyer (1955:17:30–31). The degree Abney measures to the nearest degree the angle between the slope and the horizontal. Normal geometric calculations and trigonometric tables are then used. The percent Abney scale measures the number of feet rise per 100 ft of horizontal distance. The percent reading expressed as a decimal is also the tangent of the slope angle.

Table 17.1. Distance accuracy expected using reconnaissance-mapping techniques (Virginia Polytechnic Institute, Dept. of Forestry and Wildlife).

Measurement Technique	Allowable Error in Feet
Pacing	1 in 80
Hand-held compass (box)	1 in 80
Staff-held compass (forester's)	1 in 300
Abney level—elevation	1 in 500
Taping	1 in 5000

The distance FE in Fig. 17.2C is obtained from the approximate formula.

$C = \frac{P^2}{200}$ where C = correction

P = percent slope

where the slope is 20%, $C = \frac{(20)^2}{200} = 2.0$

Therefore 100 ft on the 20% slope is equivalent to 98 ft; 102 ft equivalent to 100 ft. This equation is approximate and suitable generally below slopes of 23%.

The precise method is:

The cosine of the angle A whose tangent is 0.2 (20%) or 11°•20″ is 0.98.

Table 17.2 provides similar corrections for the percent and topographic Abney arcs.

Most tapes are 2 (or more) Gunter's chains in length (132 ft) and are equipped with a "trailer" to facilitate the reduction of slope to horizontal distances. At the 1-chain length (66 ft), these slope conversion units are found on the backside of the second chain; at the 2-chain length,

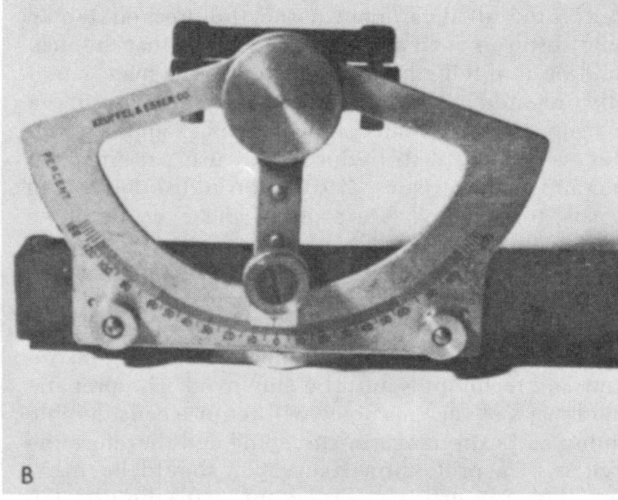

Fig. 17.1. The most frequently used reconnaissance-mapping tools are the staff-held, or forester's compass *A*, and the Abney level *B*.

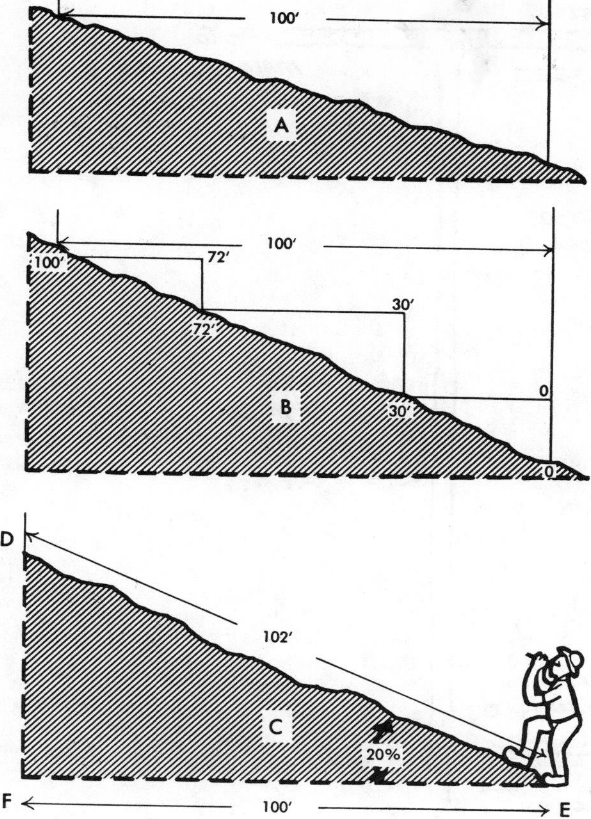

Fig. 17.2. Measurements along a slope may be corrected to horizontal distances by holding the tape horizontally *A*, by "breaking tape" into smaller horizontal measurements *B*, by a special "trailer" tape (see text), or by tape and Abney level *C*.

Table 17.2. Corrections for Abney level measurements.

Abney Reading	Percent Arc Correction in Feet per 100 Feet	Topographic Arc Correction in Links per Chain
5	0.2	0.3
10	0.5	1.0
15	1.1	2.5
20	2.0	4.5
25	3.1	6.9
30	4.4	9.9
35	6.0	13.2
40	7.7	16.9
45	9.7	21.1
50	11.8	25.3
55	14.1	30.3
60	16.6	35.2
65	19.3	40.4
70	22.1	45.7
75	25.0	51.4
80	28.1	57.0
85	31.2	62.9
90	34.5	69.0
95	37.9	75.0
100	41.4	81.8

they are attached to the tape as a trailer, extending beyond the 2-chain mark. These units, which represent the difference between slope and horizontal distance at various Abney topographic arc readings, are used as follows:

> The head chainman with the zero end of the tape goes up the slope a distance of 2 chains. The rear chainman reads +20 on the Abney. The rear chainman finds the 20 reading on the trailer, and has the head chainman move out this distance. The rear chainman again reads the Abney. If the reading is still +20 (if elevation change is great, the reading could be greater than +20), the head chainman locates that point on the ground as being 2 chains of horizontal distance.

MAKING RECONNAISSANCE MAPS

All maps should include scale, date, surveyor's names, descriptive title, North (magnetic or true), and, if applicable, the contour interval.

Sketch Maps

A sketch map is nothing more than a sketch of an area to give the approximate location of various land and structural features. Such maps may involve no measurements of distances and no accurate determinations of bearings. All features are placed on the map in their approximate relationship by eye and by estimation. A map made in this manner should be clearly labeled as a sketch map. Such sketches, despite their limitations, are far superior to resorting to a written description of the location of various features. An example of a sketch map is shown in Fig. 17.3.

Compass-Traverse Maps

Traverse-survey maps may be prepared by the wildlifer with reasonable accuracy by: (1) staff compass and taped distances, (2) hand-held (box) compass and paced distances, or (3) variations on these combinations. In the preparation of a compass traverse map, the use of the forester's compass and Jacob staff is a more accurate method of determining the bearings than by means of a box compass held in the hand. The box compass and paced distance method of preparing a map is much more rapid, of course, than forester's compass and taping, but less accurate. However, an experienced worker can prepare a surprisingly reliable and usable map by compass and pacing.

The bearings and distances can be recorded in field notes, and these notes can be plotted later in the office. This method of preparing a compass-traverse map is not recommended if it can be avoided. Rather, the map should be prepared in the field as the survey progresses. When the latter method is utilized, as errors become apparent they can be corrected immediately. Plotting a map in the office from field notes does not offer this opportunity.

Plotting the map in the field on coordinate paper is highly desirable for the vertical lines may be used as the north-south bearing. Thus coordinate paper, a rule, pen-

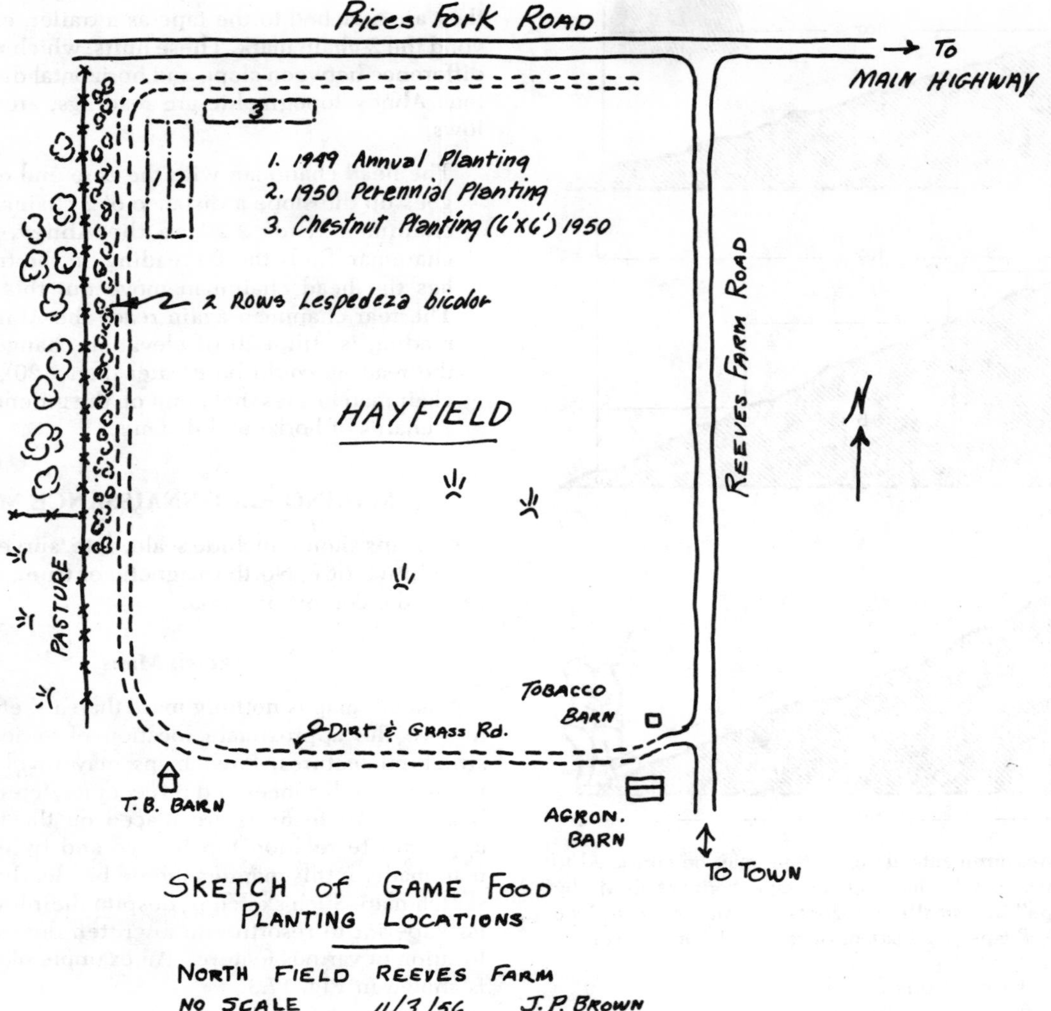

Fig. 17.3. Sketch maps are superior to word descriptions in locating points of reference.

cil, protractor, and clipboard or datum holder are required when preparing the map in the field. A rubber band placed across the bottom of the paper on the clipboard or datum holder prevents the paper from flopping in the wind. The Redy-mapper (deMoisy 1949) employs this concept and is an efficient field device for reconnaissance maps.

The scale of the map should be adjusted so that it can be plotted on a single sheet of coordinate paper. After the scale is determined, care must be exercised to locate the known starting point on the coordinate paper so that the plotted map will be contained on a single sheet of paper. With a known starting point established, set up the compass over this point, determine the bearing to some other prominent object (turning point), such as a tree, stake, or building. Plot this bearing on the coordinate paper, and then tape or pace the distance to that point. Turning points may be established at any convenient interval desired. Other points to be located within the traversed areas may be determined by intersection from 2 known points or by running a traverse line to them. Normally, determination by intersection of the bearings from 2 or more known points is the quickest and easiest method of locating such objects as trees, buildings, and similar features. Other data such as cover type, fence rows, types of crops in the fields, and related data should be recorded on the map as the survey progresses.

An example of a field map prepared by the compass traverse and compass intersection method is shown in Fig. 17.4.

Topographic Maps

Topographic maps graphically show the differences in elevation of a specific area. Normally, these differences in elevation are shown by means of contour lines, which are lines which pass through points of equal elevation. The vertical interval between the contours may vary widely, depending upon the accuracy desired. Usually these contour intervals are 5, 10, 20, 50 and 100 feet in most reconnaissance maps.

Many sections of the United States have been topographically mapped by the U.S. Geological Survey and, near navigable water, by the U.S. Coast and Geodetic Survey. Many of the earlier Geological Survey topographic maps were prepared by means of aneroid barometers. For this reason, a high degree of accuracy is

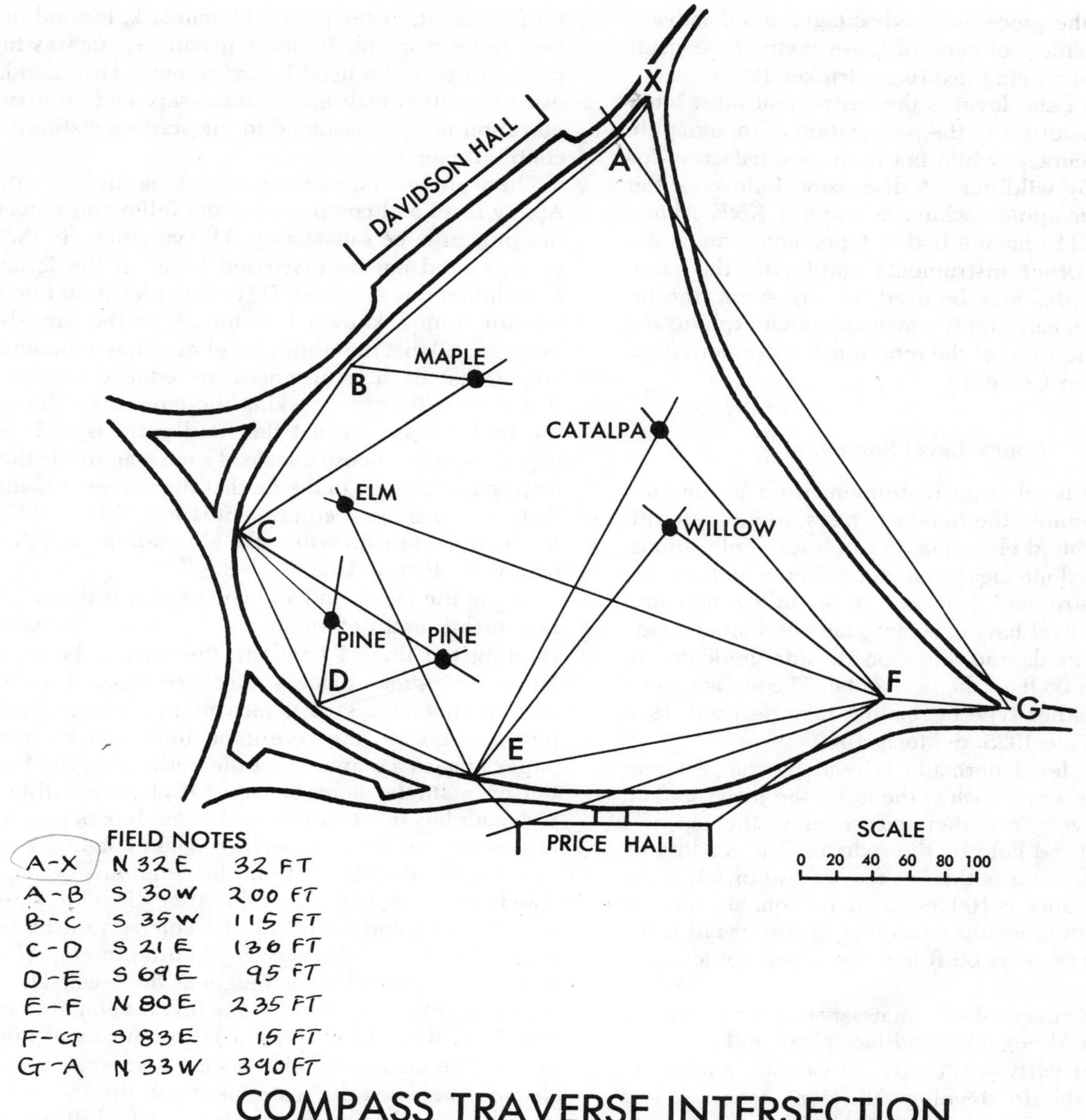

Fig. 17.4. Field map prepared on coordinate paper by the compass traverse and intersection method. For report use, this field map would have to be redrafted, usually by tracing.

not claimed for these earlier maps. Both the Geological Survey and the Coast and Geodetic Survey maps should prove of great value to the wildlife manager, especially when he is concerned with large areas. The Geological Survey maps usually are prepared as quadrangles, and an index map is available for most states showing those sections of the state which have been mapped and the quadrangle name of each mapped section. Common sizes are 7 1/2″ and 15″ latitude and longitude. When ordering topographic maps, the name of the quadrangle desired should be stipulated. If the quadrangle name is not known, give the specific locality desired by naming the county or parish, a post office in that specific locality, and the state.

The wildlife manager who is concerned with manipulating the habitat on a relatively small area may find it desirable to prepare his own topographic map. For example, he may wish to lay out a farm pond, drain or flood a marsh, or determine the difference in elevation on various parts of a watershed. The accuracy desired will vary widely, and it will be the responsibility of the wildlife manager to determine the contour interval and accuracy necessary to meet the requirements of his specific problem.

Contour maps may be prepared by various methods, such as by the stadia method with a plane table and alidade, from aerial photographs, by the use of aneroid barometers, by level surveys, and by hand levels. For a discussion of the procedures, advantages and disadvantages, and accuracy of each of these methods, consult any standard surveying text (e.g., Brinker 1969).

Perhaps the hand level is the instrument most often used by the wildlifer in the preparation of topographic maps. The accuracy, while not high, is satisfactory for normal uses by wildlifers. A discussion follows of the topographic mapping technique using a K&E Abney level (Fig. 17.1B) having both a topographic arc and a percent arc. Other instruments employing the same general principles may be used. In any event, the instrument maker can supply a manual which explains the uses and applications of the individual instrument (e.g., Keuffel & Esser Co., n.d.).

Abney Level Surveys

The Abney level is an instrument used to measure slope, to determine the height of trees, to measure differences in ground elevation, to run lines of elevations, and to reduce slope measurements to horizontal equivalents. The instrument discussed in the following pages is the Abney level having an arc graduated on one side in percent of grade and the opposite side graduated in rise or fall per 66 ft on the horizontal. The arc is reversible so that either type of reading may be used. (See Calkins and Yule 1935, deMoisy 1949.)

The Abney level normally is read by the observer from the top of a rod (such as the top of the Jacob staff or, for tall observers, a higher rod), reading the top of a similar-height rod held by the rodman. The reading by the instrument man is then in feet of rise or fall if the horizontal distance is 100 ft and the percent arc is being used; the reading would be in feet of rise or fall if the horizontal distance is 66 ft and the topographic arc is being used.

Topographic maps of reconnaissance accuracy can be made with an Abney level and Jacob staff and compass. A 2-man field party, with only a moderate amount of experience, should develop sufficient accuracy and speed to map in the field from 8 to 12 ha of rolling to hilly terrain per field day. With additional experience, it is possible to double this acreage in favorable country. Of course, the acreage mapped per day would vary widely, depending upon such factors as the amount and type of cover, extremes in elevation, and the accuracy (contour interval) employed.

In the following discussion, a reasonable familiarity with the construction and operation of the Abney level and the Jacob staff and compass (Fig. 17.1) is assumed. Those who do not possess such information should consult the manuals supplied by the manufacturers of such instruments (cf. deMoisy 1949).

The equipment needed by a 2-man field party engaged in topographic mapping should include: Abney level with either a percent arc or a topographic arc, Jacob staff and compass, chain tape, pins, stakes, protractor, rule, clipboard, cross-section paper, flashlight (for signaling) and field notebook. An axe may be needed in heavy cover.

If the topographic map is to be tied in with other existing topographic maps it will be necessary to run an elevation line from a benchmark of known elevation to a turning point, or temporary benchmark, located on the area to be mapped. In some instances, such as topographic maps to be used in laying out a farm pond, the exact elevation may not be necessary and an assumed elevation may be assigned to the starting station of the control traverse.

There are several methods of making surveys with the Abney level and compass, but the following procedure has proven to be satisfactory. The variations in the procedure need not be discussed here. In the following description it is assumed: (1) that an elevation line must be run from a known benchmark to the area being mapped; (2) that the Abney level used has a topographic arc; (3) that all slope distances are reduced to horizontal distances, either by breaking the tape or by the use of the trailer tape; (4) that the field party is sufficiently experienced to choose a scale of such magnitude that the map can be plotted in the field as the survey is made; (5) that the above listed equipment is available; and (6) that the instrument man will make all readings and the rodman will plot the data.

Set up the Jacob staff and compass over the reference benchmark and determine the bearing to be taken in running the line of levels to the area to be mapped. Have the rodman place a reference stake at a convenient, but not necessarily a measured, distance along this bearing. Locate the reference benchmark on graph paper in such a manner that the entire area can be plotted on a single piece of paper if at all possible. The rodman plots this bearing on the graph paper by means of a protractor. The rodman then goes to Station 1, which is a measured distance from the reference benchmark. The instrument man places the Abney level on the compass housing and by tilting the compass on its swivel head, aligns the reference crosshair on the top of a rod, which is exactly the same height as the level. The arc is adjusted until the bubble in the level is centered on the crosshair; then the arc is locked by means of the turn screw. The instrument man reads the arc scale and if the distance between the instrument and the rod is 1 horizontal chain, the arc reading is the actual difference in elevation between the 2 points. If the distance between the 2 points is a multiple or fraction of a chain, the arc reading must be multiplied by this whole or fractional number for the elevation change. The instrument man should call the difference in elevation to the rodman who plots the distance and elevation at the appropriate point along his bearing line. In addition to the data plotted by the rodman, it is advisable for the instrument man to record field notes, such as the station number, arc reading, distance between stations, difference in elevation between the 2 stations, and the bearing reading between the turning points. Such data permit the instrument man to check the plotted data of the rodman and facilitate the location of errors should the traverse fail to close or the elevations fail to check out due to mathematical mistakes.

After recording and plotting the information at the first location, the instrument man moves and places his Jacob staff and compass at Station 2. The rodman moves a measured distance along the bearing line and is aligned by the instrument man. At Station 2, and until Turning Point No. 2 (TP-2) is reached, it is unnecessary for the instrument man to take another bearing reading from the compass. Thus, the Jacob staff and compass are used only as a support for the Abney level between the several TPs. This process is repeated until a traverse line, with elevations, is run around the area to be mapped, and the traverse is closed on either the original reference benchmark or on a turning point. Both the traverse and level lines should close within the accuracy which would be acceptable for the purposes of the map. The traverse should close within at least one-half chain for every 80 chains of line, and the level should close within at least 1 contour interval. If this degree of accuracy is accepted, the error of closure, both in the traverse and level lines, can be distributed equally among each of the turning points.

After the traverse line, with elevations, has been established, level lines can be run between the several turning points. The number of level lines necessary would vary with the differences in elevation and must be determined by the survey party. In any event, a sufficient number of elevations must be determined to permit the survey crew to put in the contour line with reasonable accuracy. If possible, these contour lines should be placed on the map before the survey crew leaves the area. By doing this, it often is possible to check the contours by a visual inspection of the area. Figure 17.5 shows an example of a field map plotted in the above manner.

The Abney level can be set at 0 on the arc and used as a lock level to stake out contour lines. If this is to be done, the exact location of the contour must be determined; and with this known point, the instrument is set up over this point. From this known point he can direct the rodman to points of the same elevation, and the rodman can indicate these points by stakes. Staked contour lines are often used in locating the water level of a proposed pond or in the establishment of farm contour strips.

A rapid and simple method for determining degree and aspect of slope using a slope-meter was described by Koeppl (1979).

Mapping by Intersection

Fairly accurate maps of small areas may be made by intersection even when crude instruments are used. This type of mapping is especially suited for areas of 0.4 or 0.8 ha, the entire area being visible from some vantage point. Mapping a pond by intersection using readily available instruments will be briefly described as an example. Reference should be made to Fig. 17.6.

The equipment needed for this type of mapping is: a plane table (or improvised plane table), an alidade or triangular scale, straight pins, tape to measure the base line, coordinate paper, pencil, and several stakes. A compass to indicate North on the map is desirable, but not absolutely essential.

Choose a position near the pond which will afford as unobstructed a view of the pond as possible. Lay out a carefully measured base line (A–B in Fig. 17.6) of a measured distance and choose a scale which will permit the entire map to be plotted on a single piece of paper. Set up the plane table over point "A," choose a straight line on the coordinate paper, and lay off the measured base line on the coordinate paper. Insert straight pins at points "A" and "B," place triangular scale on the table with one edge touching the pins and align the table by turning it until the scale edge is in line with the stake at point "B." After so aligning, set table securely so it will not jar out of alignment. Choose convenient points around the periphery of the pond and sight along the top of the triangular scale or alidade to each of these points. Draw a light pencil line along the edge of the alidade or ruler, making this line extend well beyond the point being located. These points should be located in a clockwise direction, numbering each line as it is located. After all points have been marked from point "A," take up the plane table and move it to point "B." Align, as described above, by sighting back on the stake at point "A." After alignment, draw lines from point "B" to each of the previously selected points along the pond shore. Thus, by intersection, convenient points around the pond are located. The shore line of the pond is then sketched in by eye while in the field.

Maps from Aerial Photographs

Aerial photographs are now available for most of the United States and for large sections of Canada; the wildlifer can make good use of these photographs. The interpretation of aerial photographs will yield a vast amount of data to the experienced photo-interpreter (Dalke 1937, Leedy 1948, Spurr 1948). The various techniques and equipment utilized by photo-interpreters will not be discussed here as this is a large and complex field. Rather, this discussion will be concerned only with the use of aerial photographs as a convenient way of preparing reconnaissance base maps.

Reconnaissance maps can be prepared from aerial photographs by: (1) the use of the individual photograph itself for small areas (810 ha or less); (2) blueprints made from photographic negatives (Moessner 1963); (3) making a mosaic from several aerial photographs for larger areas; (4) making a direct tracing of individual prints or of a mosaic; (5) a tracing made by equipment designed for this purpose, such as the aerial sketch-master or radial-planimetric plotter, and (6) tracing the desired data in India ink directly on the aerial photograph, then bleaching the photo, leaving the inked record.

Aerial photographs are often available to the wildlife investigator through loan from local public agencies. Prints also may be purchased. The identification number on each print, as well as the source from which it may be purchased, usually is available from the local office of the Soil Conservation Service, County Agricultural Agent, U.S. Forest Service, or Production and Marketing Agency.

If the wildlife investigator acquires his own copies of aerial photographs, the individually-owned prints make excellent field maps. Making an accurate mosaic of a series of aerial photographs is rather involved (Kelsh 1940, Am. Soc. Photogrammetry 1966) but the wildlife worker can put together a serviceable mosaic if high accuracy is not required (Fig. 17.7). The mosaic itself may be traced to give an inked map.

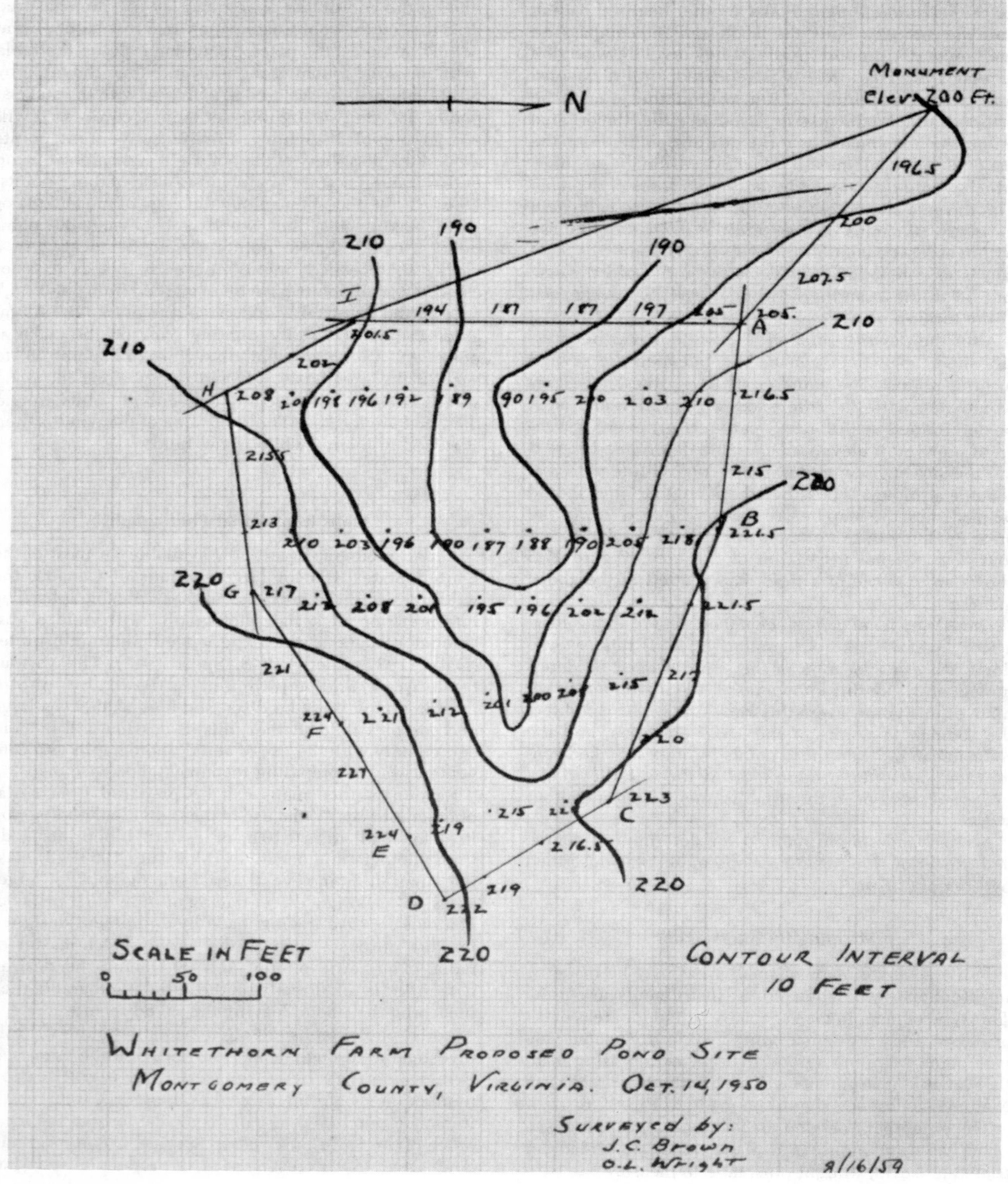

Fig. 17.5. Field copy of topographic map prepared by the compass traverse and Abney level method. The map was plotted on coordinate paper and then the contour lines were sketched on the field map.

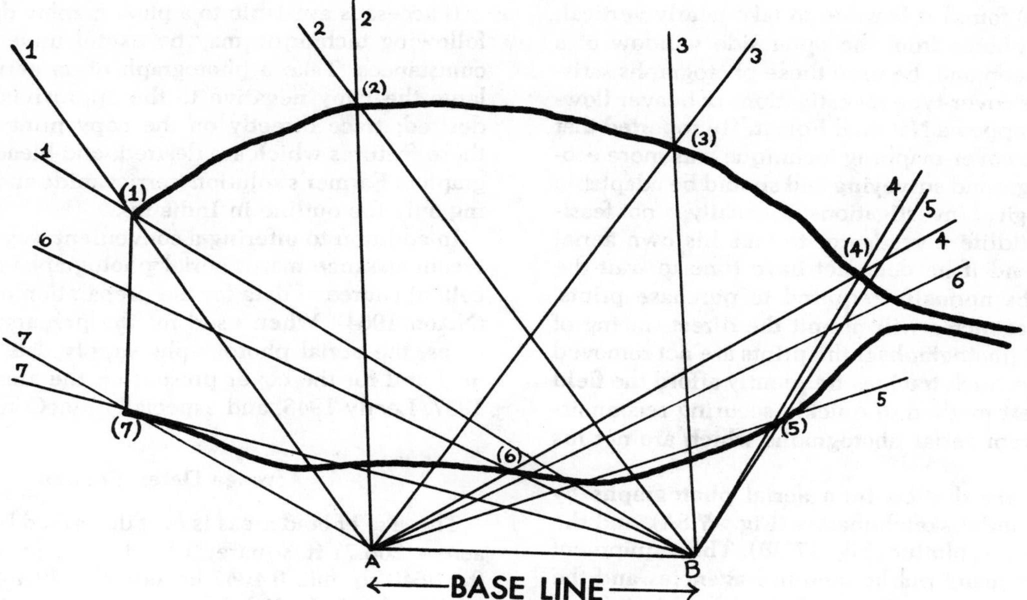

Fig. 17.6. **Farm pond mapped by the intersection method. The base line (points *A* and *B*) is a measured distance. The plane table is placed over point *A*, aligned on point *B*, then the numbered points are located by sighting along an alidade or triangular scale. The plane table is moved to point *B*, aligned on point *A*, and each of the numbered points fixed by a second intersection line.**

Fig. 17.7. Composite aerial photos, or mosaics, are of limited accuracy but serve as excellent maps for many areas.

Kirby (1976) found it feasible to take nearly vertical, 35-mm color photos from the open side window of a high wing monoplane; he used these photographs satisfactorily in his cover-type investigations of beaver flowages in the Chippewa National Forest. He reported that this waterfowl cover-mapping technique was more economical than ground surveying and should be adaptable to other ecological investigations. It usually is not feasible for the wildlife investigator to take his own aerial photographs and if he does not have time to wait the several months normally required to purchase prints, many public agencies will permit the direct tracing of specific aerial photographs if the prints are not removed from the office. Such tracings frequently afford the field worker the best method of quickly securing reconnaissance maps from aerial photographs which are not his property.

Base maps are drafted from aerial photographs by means of the aerial sketch-master (Fig. 17.8A), and the radial-planimetric plotter (Fig. 17.8B). This equipment is available in many public land-use agencies and the wildlife investigator may prepare the map he requires by borrowing the use of this equipment and the necessary photographs.

The scales used in aerial photographs will vary with the size of the print (degree of enlargement). Since there is a change in scale from the center to the edge of aerial prints (and with rough topography), it is advisable not to accept the listed scale for the prints of aerial photographs. The scale should be checked on the ground. This is done by selecting 2 conspicuous landmarks on the aerial photograph, measuring the distance in cm on the photo, then measuring the horizontal distance on the ground between these 2 points. The scale is expressed as follows:

$$\text{Scale} = \frac{\text{Distance in cm on aerial photograph}}{\text{Distance in cm, measured on ground}}$$

Whenever possible, maps should be prepared and traced from the center of aerial photographs, due to distortion near the photo edges.

If access is available to a photographic darkroom, the following technique may be useful under special circumstances. Take a photograph of an aerial print; enlarge the copy negative to the approximate size print desired; trace directly on the copy print in India ink those features which are desired; and bleach the photograph in Farmer's solution (ferricyanide and hypo), leaving only the outline in India ink.

In addition to offering a convenient way of preparing reconnaissance maps, aerial photographs afford an excellent source of data for the preparation of cover maps (Nixon 1964). When used for the preparation of cover maps, the aerial photographs supply data for the base map and for the cover present on the area (See Dalke 1937, Leedy 1948, and especially MacConnell 1957).

Acreage Determination

The size of land areas is best described by acreages (1 acre = 208.71 ft. square; 3.16 chains square; 43,560 sq. ft., 1/640 sq. mi., 0.4047 hectares, or 40.468 ares). Conversion from English to metric is facilitated by Table 17.3. Even approximate acreage figures are better than such terms as "a large boundary of land" or similar expressions. Rough acreage figures can be determined by dividing the map into convenient rectangles and measuring the 2 sides of each rectangle. From these measurements it is a simple matter to determine from the map scale roughly the square feet or square miles in the area. Of course, if the data so calculated are in square feet, the number of acres can be determined by dividing by 43,560.

A compensating polar planimeter is an instrument designed to measure area from maps (Fig. 17.9). Planimeters measure the number of square inches or the number of square centimeters. In each case, it is necessary to determine, from the map scale, the area of a square inch or square centimeter. A square drawn to 1 unit of the map scale and planimetered will provide a useful factor for converting the planimeter readings to areas. When this information is available, the reading from the

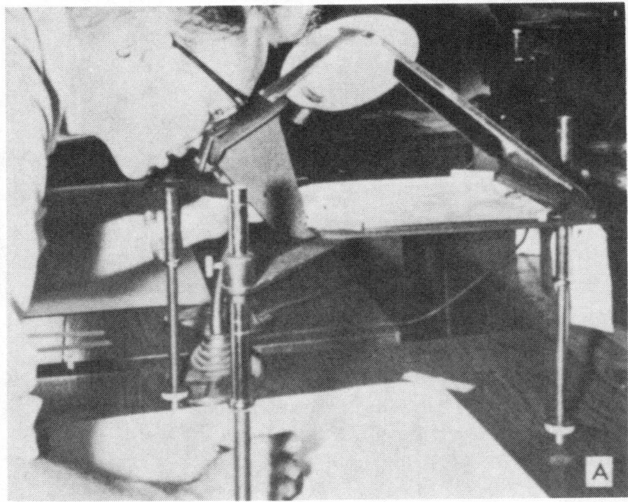

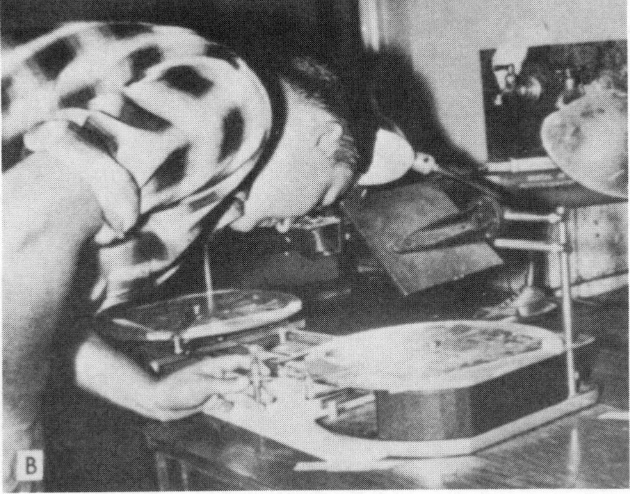

Fig. 17.8. Maps may be drawn from aerial photographs by means of *A* the aerial sketch-master (camera lucida principle) or *B* by means of the radial-planimetric plotter (stereoscopic principle).

Table 17.3. Conversion factors useful in making 2-way translations of English-metric length-area units.

To convert	Into	Multiply by
Acre	Feet square	208.71
	Square chains (Gunter)	10.0
	Square feet	43,560
	Square meters	4,042.42
	Square yards	4,840
	Hectare	0.4047
Chain	Feet	66.0
	Inches	792.0
	Meters	20.12
	Yards	22.0
Feet	Centimeters	30.48
	Kilometers	3.048×10^{-4}
	Meters	0.3048
	Millimeters	304.8
Hectares	Acres	2.471
	Square feet	107,637
	Feet square	328.08
Meters	Centimeters	100.0
	Feet	3.281
	Inches	39.37
	Miles (statute)	6.214×10^{-4}
	Yards	1.094
Miles (statute)	Feet	5,280
	Kilometers	1.609
	Meters	1,609
Millimeters	Inches	0.03937
Square feet	Square meter	0.09290
	Square yard	0.1111
Square kilometer	Acre	247.1
	Square meters	10^6
	Square yard	1.196
Square mile	Acres	640.0
	Square feet	27.88×10^6
	Square kilometer	2.590
	Square meters	2.590×10^6
Square Yard	Acres	2.066×10^{-4}
	Square feet	9.0
	Square meter	0.8361
Yard	Centimeters	91.44
	Kilometers	9.144×10^{-4}
	Meters	0.9144
	Miles (statute)	5.682×10^{-4}
	Millimeters	914.4

planimeter dial can be translated into area measurements.

On small areas, acreage can be determined by plotting the map on coordinate paper and, with the number of square feet per block of coordinate paper known, it is a simple matter to count the blocks or fractions and thus determine acreage.

The transparent grid developed by Bryant (1943) is a simple and reasonably accurate method of determining acreage (Fig. 17.10). This grid is marked in blocks and dots, which are fractions of a square inch. The grid is placed over the map, the number of blocks and dots counted within the area being measured, and the area determined from the scale of the map (acres, or square miles per square inch).

Acreage may be determined mathematically from the bearing and distances of a traverse survey. This method is more complicated and achieves a level of accuracy rarely needed by wildlifers. For a description of the method used in calculating the acreage mathematically, see a standard surveying text (e.g., Brinker 1969).

Millar (1973) developed a procedure for estimating area and circumference of wetlands of 4 ha or less by dividing the area into single or multiple ellipses and employing the ellipse formulae for calculating area and circumference. He reported that 95% of the calculated values were within 13% of actual values.

MAP PREPARATION AND REPRODUCTION

Whatever the primary purpose of a map, it should convey the pertinent data with clarity and in an easily understood manner. The map, therefore, must be neatly drawn using conventional symbols and usually be acceptable for duplication. Mappers must have knowledge of drafting and an understanding of the several techniques employed in map duplication. If the field worker is familiar with the technique of duplication which he proposes to use, this knowledge will greatly decrease the time spent at the drafting table.

Drafting

The drafting of a neat map is a time-consuming matter that requires experience to acquire proficiency. Some persons are more gifted than others in drafting, but the neatness and efficiency of the neophyte and the expert alike are increased by the use of conventional tools. Most wildlifers are familiar with the normal drafting instruments such as the ruling pen, compass, speedball pens, protractors, crow quill pens, T-squares, and triangles. Mechanical lettering and numbering sets, glass-top tracing tables, mechanically-printed types of hatching and lettering (such as Zip-A-Tone), and related equipment of the draftsman are very helpful. Such equipment, if available to the casual mapper, may be used to excellent advantage.

Usually, the working copy of a map is redrawn on tracing paper or tracing cloth before it is reproduced or filed. Such tracings may be made on a tracing board or a glass-top tracing table. If a mechanical lettering set is available, this instrument will greatly speed up the lettering of maps. Black waterproof ink is used in preparing tracings, especially if the tracings are to be reproduced photographically, photostatically, by B & W or blueprint processes, or by any of the engraving processes.

Enlarging and Reducing

Most maps prepared by the wildlifer will be used in reports or in manuscripts submitted for publication. The

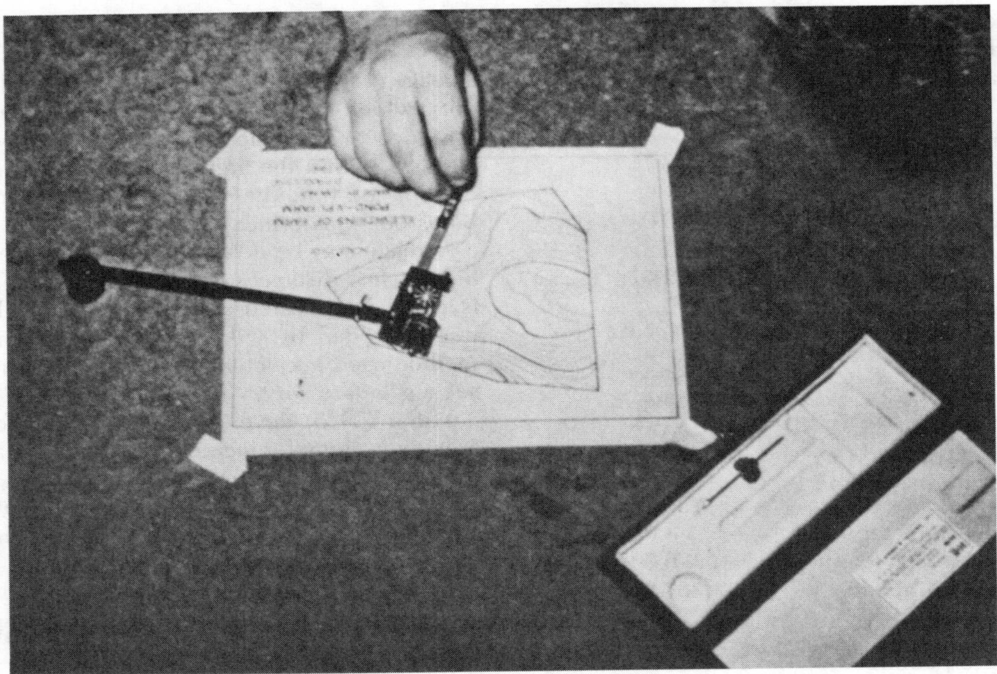

Fig. 17.9. Compensating polar planimeters are used to measure the square inches (or centimeters) within a given area. This measurement is then translated into acreage figures according to the scale of the map.

maps should be prepared and submitted in such a form that either the superior officer or the publisher can use them without time-consuming adjustment or redrafting of these maps. For example, if the map is to be used in a report on standard-size paper (8 1/2 × 11 inch), the map should be submitted in this size, or multiples of this size, so that it may be folded and fitted into the report. Likewise, if the map is to be used in mimeograph form, it should be submitted on a mimeograph stencil, thus saving trouble, as well as avoiding the possibility of errors if copied by inexperienced clerks. If the map is to be reproduced by photography or engraving, it should be drafted in a size that will permit a 50% reduction.

Adjusting the scale of the work map to a suitable scale for the finished map often presents a problem. For example, if the map is for use in an administrative report, the finished map should be of such size as to fit on a letter-size page (6 × 9 inches). On the other hand, this scale is not always acceptable in the field map and it may be necessary either to enlarge or reduce the field map. Enlargement or reduction may be accomplished by the use of a pantograph, or by photography. The pantograph is a mechanical device for either copying a map or diagram in the same scale, enlarging the scale, or reducing the scale (Fig. 17.11). This instrument is available in an inexpensive form or as a very elaborate and costly piece of apparatus. The pantograph may be adjusted by means of perforated, adjustable rules in such a manner as to copy, enlarge, or reduce according to the scale desired. The following method of determining the most suitable scale may be used: Assume that the work map is to be reduced from a larger size to a tracing which will fit on 8 1/2- × 11-inch tracing paper; estimate the percentage reduction which will be necessary and set the adjustable arms at this estimated reduction scale as printed on each pantograph rule face. Then, select a specific section of the larger map and measure the distance in inches and tenths. Put the pantograph in place and, on a piece of scratch paper, trace the above-measured distance. Measure the line as reduced by the pantograph and use this figure as the numerator and the distance traced on the larger map as the denominator of a fraction. With this reduction fraction determined, measure the outside measurements of the larger map and multiply these measurements by the reduction fraction. If the resulting figures are less than 8 1/2 by 11 inches, this scale is satisfactory; if it is not, adjust the scale on the pantograph, either up or down, and repeat this procedure.

Drawings made with an inexpensive pantograph are not finished products and will have to be "dressed-up" before they can be inked. Most of the lines made by the pantograph will be wavy and of unequal density. Thus, it is well to locate accurately the important points on the reduced map by means of dots so that they can be checked when making the final inked tracing.

Maps may also be reduced, copied, or enlarged photographically. The map must be photographed, using special film and developer (e.g., Eastman Contrast Process Ortho film and D-11 developer), and the resulting negative contact printed or projected to secure either a reduction or enlargement. It is important that a map which is to be photographed for reduction should be inked with heavy lines and the lettering should be of such a scale that it will be legible (at least 1/16 inch) in the reduced copy of the map. This latter point cannot be overemphasized as it often causes trouble. A reducing lens is useful for checking such scaling.

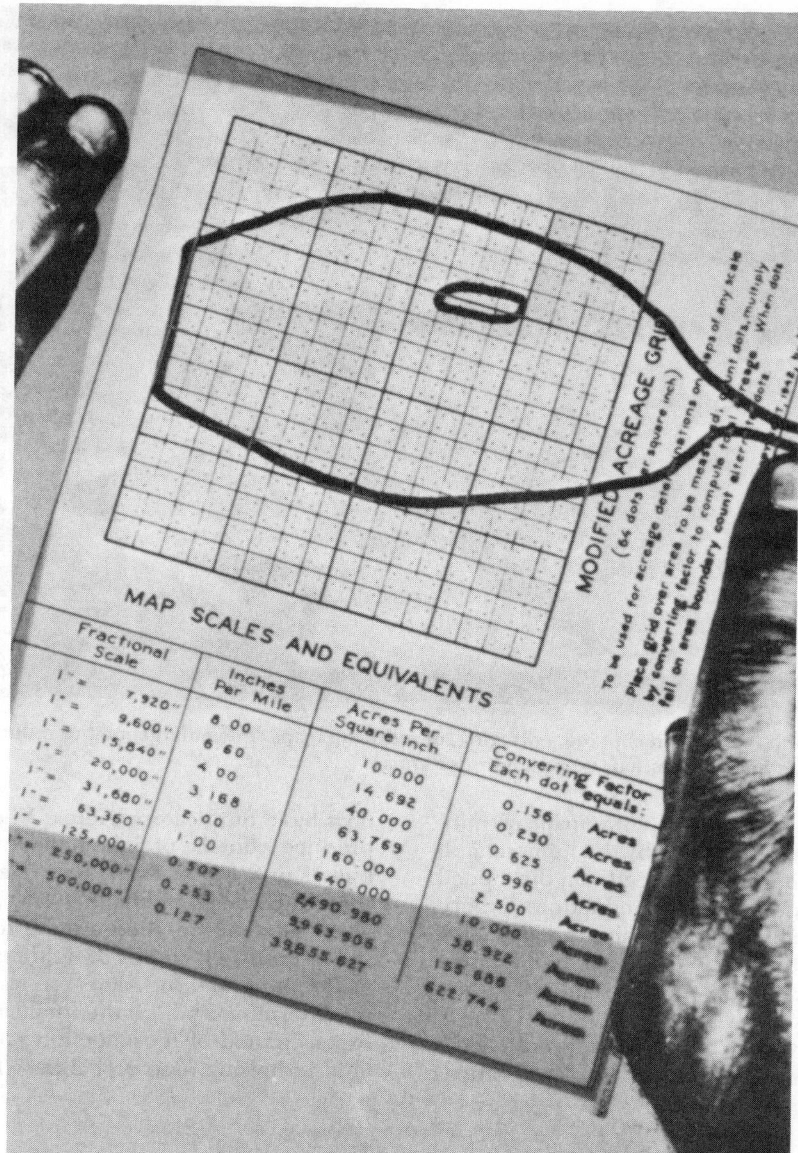

Fig. 17.10. The Bryant transparent grid is a quick and reasonably accurate method of determining acreage. See text for explanation of how this grid is used.

Reproducing Maps

Maps may be reproduced in a number of ways, including blueprinting, blue-line or black-line printing, mimeographing, lithoprinting, photostating, dittoing, line-cut printing, or photographic printing. In all instances, except when maps are to be reproduced by mimeographing or dittoing, the map should be on tracing paper or tracing cloth in dense waterproof ink. It is possible to make a blueprint and blue or black-line print from a penciled tracing on opaque paper, but such prints are not entirely satisfactory. Most engravers prefer that the maps from which they prepare line-cuts be made on white bond paper although they will accept inked copy on tracing paper or cloth. Likewise, they will accept clear and sharp photographic copies of maps, but their preference is for copies made in black ink on white bond paper.

Lithoprinted or multilithed maps can be copied by a photographic process from inked tracings, or the map

Fig. 17.11. A pantograph is useful in copying, enlarging, or reducing maps. The enlargement or reduction is determined by selecting the appropriate holes in the four perforated ruler arms.

may be drawn directly on a special lithoprint or multilith stencil. Maps to be reproduced by the mimeograph or ditto process should be copied directly on the stencil used in the respective process of reproduction. Experience is necessary in making a reasonably good tracing on a mimeograph or ditto stencil and the amount of fine details which may be included on these stencils is limited.

Maps for use in reports may be contact reproduced by several commercial "blueprint" processes. Many offices now have duplicators (Xerox, Verifax, etc.) that will reproduce contact of inked maps in sizes 8 1/2 by 11 inches or 8 1/2 by 14 inches. The photostat process can reproduce maps either the same, enlarged, or reduced size. Whatever method of map reproduction is used to secure multiple copies of field maps, a thorough understanding of how the maps are to be reproduced should be determined before the final tracings are made. If the exact method of reproduction is determined, considerable redrafting time probably will be saved.

Chapter Eighteen

A Guide to Remote Sensing Information for Wildlife Biologists

WILLIAM H. ANDERSON
EROS Data Center
U.S. Geological Survey
Sioux Falls, South Dakota

W. ALAN WENTZ
Department of Wildlife and Fisheries Sciences
South Dakota State University
Brookings, South Dakota

B. DEAN TREADWELL
Applied Remote Sensing Program
Office of Arid Lands Studies
University of Arizona
Tucson, Arizona

Today's wildlife manager is confronted with increasing pressure to address problems that extend beyond the scope of traditional wildlife management and often appear overwhelming in complexity, size, and cost. Tasks such as determining the wildlife values in an area proposed for large-scale energy development or preparation of a comprehensive environmental impact assessment require access to timely and accurate information over large areas. In such cases, traditional field methods are often impractical due to manpower and funding limitations. New techniques such as computer modeling and remote sensing—the subject of this chapter—are being developed to help meet the challenges facing the wildlife biologist now and in the future.

Remote sensing describes the practice of gathering data about objects or conditions on the ground using cameras or other sensing and recording devices carried aboard aircraft or spacecraft. Remote sensing is, in essence, collecting data about an object from a distance. The definition of remote sensing has been expanded in practice to include a wide range of activities and technologies involving aerial photography, satellite images, supportive field data, radio telemetry, thermal sensors, and radar as well as various interpretive and analytical procedures. The scope of remote sensing is multidisciplinary and can include physics, mathematics, electrical engineering, computer science, natural sciences, and other disciplines. The *Manual of Remote Sensing* (Reeves 1975) devotes more than 2000 pages to the subject and is the most comprehensive source book available on the topic.

The contents of this chapter have been selected to serve as a useful guide for wildlife biologists. The chapter is not a comprehensive analysis of remote sensing techniques, but it is a selected review of the literature designed to call attention to various applications and how other wildlife biologists are using remote sensing. The chapter also serves as a brief introduction to some of the basics of remote sensing technology and, most importantly, can be used as a guide to obtaining additional information, images, and assistance.

SOME BASICS OF REMOTE SENSING

Technological advancements during the last 30 or more years have broadened the scope and increased the sophistication in many areas of remote data gathering and associated data manipulation. In some instances, a highly specialized knowledge is necessary to work effectively with the latest developments. However, as with computers, it is not necessary to understand every aspect of remote sensing technology to use it effectively. A working-level understanding of the basic principles, approaches, and limitations is sufficient to begin applying remote sensing methods in many situations.

Most conventional remote sensing systems of interest to wildlife managers operate within the visible light and near infrared portions of the electromagnetic spectrum. Every object interacts with incoming solar energy in a characteristic way: absorbing, reflecting, transmitting, and emitting radiant energy at different rates and in different portions of the electromagnetic spectrum. This interaction produces a *spectral signature* (a pattern of reflected and emitted energy that varies according to wavelength) that can often be used to characterize the object.

The aerial photograph is the most common type of remote sensing image; it results from chemical reactions between reflected energy and the sensitive emulsions of the photographic film. Nonphotographic systems, such as multispectral scanners, use electronic detectors in place of film. The detectors respond to the amount of reflected or emitted energy and produce an electrical signal in proportion to the signal strength. A light meter is a common example of this principle. The signal produced by the scanner is usually digitized for transmittal, storage, and manipulation. The resultant electronic data can be displayed as an image similar to a television picture or, as in the case of earth resource satellite data, converted to a hard copy, photo-type image.

When most people first view an aerial photograph, they tend to interpret it in terms of the objects they are familiar with and recognize. This approach is basically a function of the photograph's *spatial resolution*.

Spatial resolution, however, is only one of the image characteristics used in the interpretation process. Indeed, by analyzing all inherent characteristics of an image such as tone, color, size, shape, texture, association, and so forth, it often is possible to infer the presence of objects even though they cannot actually be seen on the photograph.

Equally important for many applications is *spectral resolution*. This characteristic of the remotely sensed image is usually manifested by the sensor's ability to detect and measure variations in tone and color (wavelength). Other image characteristics also play a role in the interpretation process. Relative size and shape of an object provide important clues to the feature's identity. Image *texture* is another characteristic On small-scale photography, grasslands will appear smooth while shrub-lands will appear mottled. Finally, *patterns* and other associated objects can provide additional clues to aid the interpreter in making a valid identification of features and conditions.

The initial step in image interpretation involves delineating areas on the photograph that exhibit a similar appearance. The next step is identifying or classifying the units delineated on the image. This activity involves the incorporation of corollary information such as ground data, existing maps, and reports, as well as the interpreter's personal knowledge and understanding of the physical and biological aspects of the area.

Finally, the collection of *ground truth*, or *ground data*, is vital to any project based on remote sensing. These activities serve to verify preliminary delineations and inferred identifications, and to identify units that could not be identified through photo interpretation alone. One of the major benefits of surveys supported by remote sensing, compared with those based only on traditional groundwork, is the capability to extrapolate information from sample sites to unsampled, remote areas. Careful selection of representative ground truth sites greatly enhances this capability. The aerial perspective enables the interpreter to provide accurate boundaries and identify map units, but the quality of the final product (resource map) is often directly proportional to the intensity of ground data collection activities.

Perhaps an example will help illustrate the operation of this interpretation process. At the common mapping scale of 1:24,000, individual grass plants cannot be resolved. On color-infrared film exposed during the growing season, however, the herbaceous understory will appear smooth textured and bright red (texture and spectral resolution image characteristics). Knowledge of the plant communities in the study area might suggest whether this herbaceous material is annual or perennial, grasses or forbs, or some combination; perhaps some of the common species could even be inferred from corollary data. The preliminary vegetation map based on this image then could be verified in the field through ground truth collection in 1 or 2 of the areas delineated on the photos. If the boundaries and identifications are correct, then other areas appearing similar on photos can be inferred to be the same through extrapolation.

This discussion of remote sensing and image interpretation principles is certainly not a complete discourse on the subject. Rather, it is intended only to introduce the fundamentals of applied remote sensing, diminish notions that remote sensing is a highly esoteric discipline, and hopefully interest potential users to pursue further background knowledge and to ultimately evaluate the technology as it applies to their specialty.

Fortunately many excellent texts on remote sensing (including airphoto interpretation) are currently available (Spurr 1960, Way 1973, Estes and Senger 1974, Harper 1976, Kroeck 1976, Avery 1977). Several general references emphasize remote sensing specifically with respect to ecology (Johnson 1969, Howard 1970, Lintz and Simonett 1976, Barrett and Curtis 1977). Strandberg (1967) and Paine (1975) offer general instruction in the basics of airphoto interpretation in the form of a workbook. As interest in remote sensing grows and knowledge of the subject increases, the number of texts will also increase. The material available in any well-designed, comprehensive volume should be more than sufficient to provide a working level understanding of remote sensing methods and materials.

Remote Sensing Systems for Wildlife Management

Remote sensing may involve gathering data across a large portion of the electromagnetic (EM) spectrum, from ultraviolet to radio frequencies. This necessitates the use of a variety of sensor systems, each capable of detecting and recording EM radiation within certain portions of the spectrum. Aerial cameras, for example, are limited to the visible and near infrared region. Optical-mechanical scanning systems, using sensitive detectors rather than photographic film, have greatly expanded capabilities for gathering data in the ultraviolet, visible, near infrared, and thermal (heat) infrared portions of the EM spectrum. Much has been written about the operation of various sensor systems and a detailed discussion of their characteristics is beyond the scope of this chapter. It may be instructive, however, to consider briefly the types of data produced by the 2 most widely used remote sensing systems in wildlife management—aerial cameras and multispectral scanners.

AERIAL PHOTOGRAPHY

Aerial photography has been, and will continue to be, the workhorse of operational remote sensing. Millions of frames of aerial photographs have been acquired and are currently available. In spite of advances in the state-of-the-art of sophisticated computer-assisted data gathering and analysis, it is unlikely that aerial photography will ever become obsolete. For example, some of the latest strategies of computerized data analysis include the incorporation of data derived from the interpretation of aerial photographs. The role of aerial photography and human interpretation probably will become more important in future years.

Conventional aerial photographs can be acquired in scales ranging from approximately 1:120,000 to 1:1,000 and larger. The smaller photographic scales generally are used for interpretation of large areas. Due to ground resolution limitations at very small scales, interpretation usually is limited to relatively broad information categories of land cover or terrain.

Photographs with scales in the range of 1:40,000 to 1:10,000 can be used to meet many of the typical information requirements of the wildlife biologist. Very large scale photographs (1:1,000 and larger) are used in situations that require extreme detail, such as the intensive analysis of small areas. At the larger scales, individual plants often may be identified and mapped.

As a general rule, it is most cost-efficient to use the smallest scale that satisfies the information requirements. If a map differentiating between forest, range, and agriculture is all that is needed, then a small scale photograph is likely to be suitable, thus eliminating the cost associated with assembling and interpreting numerous larger scale photographs of the same area. Conversely, if a species-level vegetation map is required, then large scale photographs become a necessity.

Many comprehensive resource management operations could benefit by using various scales of photography in the same project. Such a stratified design provides all the benefits of the variety of remote sensing capabilities without sacrificing either the small scale synoptic coverage or the level of detail associated with large-scale coverage.

A multiscale or multistage design typically begins with small-scale coverage of the entire area of interest using 1:125,000 high altitude photography (or even 1:250,000 satellite imagery). At these scales, broad physiographic and vegetative cover types can be identified along with general geographic relationships. From this base map, representative areas can be selected for medium-scale coverage. On medium-scale photographs, additional resource categories can be separated according to management information needs. Finally, large-scale coverage can be acquired for selected sample sites. Ground data collection activities typically are associated with these local sites. Data from all sources can be combined using multistage statistical procedures.

THE LANDSAT SERIES OF EARTH OBSERVATION SATELLITES

The first Earth observation satellite, originally called ERTS-A (Earth Resources Technology Satellite) was launched on 23 July 1972. Renamed ERTS-1 when orbit was achieved, it was joined in space on 22 January 1975 by the second Earth observation satellite, ERTS-2. At that time ERTS-1 was renamed Landsat 1, and ERTS-2 became Landsat 2. Landsat 1 ceased operation on 10 January 1978 after 5 years of almost continuous operation. Landsat 3 was launched in March 1978. A comprehensive discussion of the technical characteristics of the Landsat series of Earth monitoring devices is given by Short et al. (1976) and Taranik (1978).

A typical frame of Landsat imagery is shown in Fig. 18.1. An individual Landsat scene records an area of approximately 185-by-178 km (32,930 km^2). More than 3,000 frames of 1:20,000-scale aerial photography would be required to record the same area. Landsat satellites pass over the same area every 9 days and offer the opportunity to acquire continual coverage of most of the world. Rabchevsky (1977) has summarized in tabular form examples of repetitive surveys based upon Landsat data. Ashley and Rea (1975) provide an excellent example of using repetitive surveys in their study of the phenology of crop and forest vegetation and the use of these data to define growth and yield characteristics. The synoptic view and frequency of Landsat coverage can be highly significant to wildlife applications involving regional analysis and monitoring (Fig. 18.2).

The majority of imagery available from Landsat 1, 2, and 3 was derived from Landsat's multispectral scanner (MSS). This type of sensor simultaneously measures the intensity of reflected light from 4 different portions of the electromagnetic spectrum—2 in the visible and 2 in the near infrared. The resolution element (minimum area from which reflectance data are recorded) of the

MSS is a 79 × 79 meter square, or approximately 0.44 ha. Data are electronically telemetered to Earth and can be stored in digital form on a computer compatible tape.

These data can be processed into a color image. This color image can be made by optically combining 3 MSS bands in registration and sequentially exposing them through appropriate filters to produce an image commonly called a "color composite" or "false-color composite" (FCC). Fig. 18.1 is an example of this process. A wide capability for enhancing various features exists by varying the color and intensity of the light passed through the images of the different spectral bands.

In addition to the MSS, Landsat carries a Return Beam Vidicon (RBV) camera. This camera transmits a single panchromatic image rather than separate bands like the MSS. In addition, RBV images from Landsat 3 have twice the nominal resolution (40 meters) of the MSS.

Another capability of the Landsat satellites is the Data Collection System (DCS) that has been used, among other things, to monitor the movements of wild animals (Buechner et al. 1971, Craighead 1976). This system acts as a relay mechanism. It collects signals from Earth based instruments (radio transmitters, thermometers, rain gauges, etc.) and retransmits the data to receiving stations when Landsat is within reception distance.

In addition to optical data processing and visual image interpretation, Landsat data are stored and analyzed in digital format on computer compatible tapes. Work and Gilmer (1976) have documented a computer classification approach to mapping prairie wetlands to provide information vital to studies dealing with waterfowl nesting habitat. Craighead (1976) used digital techniques to inventory and map vegetation cover related to grizzly bear habitat requirements. The literature contains many examples of vegetation cover mapping using Landsat digital data and computer classification techniques.

Reeves (1975: Vol. 2) is a useful reference on digital data and computer classification techniques. Other pertinent references appear in symposia proceedings and research reports. Many of these sources, however, are of relatively limited distribution. For instance, a recent bibliography (Rohde 1977) on Landsat digital processing applications listed only 3 of 83 citations published as journal articles; the remaining 80 citations were from limited distribution sources that require considerable effort to obtain. Because of the rapid rate of development and increased usage, technical symposia are likely to continue to be the prime source of information about advances in digital analysis. As the technology develops, the value and applicability of digital analysis to wildlife management will undoubtedly be enhanced.

In summary, the Landsat system was designed to provide synoptic information for regional resource evaluation. Landsat data provides adequate detail for producing general resource maps at scales in the order of 1:250,000 by either visual image interpretation or, for some applications, by computer classification techniques. Other documented applications of Landsat data to wildlife management include: (1) selecting potential areas for more detailed investigations; (2) determining optimal dates for larger scale overflights; (3) updating general land use maps and monitoring habitat encroachment by agricultural or mining activities; and (4) locating areas of early ephemeral forage production.

WILDLIFE APPLICATIONS

The use of remote sensing data in wildlife management is not new. Leedy (1948, 1953) discussed the fundamentals of aerial photo interpretation for wildlife management long before the phrase *remote sensing* was coined. Today, wildlife biologists use remotely sensed data primarily for animal census, habitat inventory and assessment, and environmental impact assessment. Remote sensing also has significant potential for related areas, such as recreation use surveys and various planning activities.

Animal Census

VISUAL SURVEYS FROM AIRCRAFT

Direct visual observation from light aircraft is a well-established and often used technique for estimating wildlife population numbers. Aerial surveys by experienced observers often are the only practical method to census many animals. These surveys typically involve cataloging the number, age, and sex of animals seen while flying systematic, low altitude transects.

Norton-Griffiths (1975) and Caughley (1977b) have detailed the operational aspects of designing and conducting an aerial survey. Caughley (1974b, 1977a), Caughley and Goddard (1972), and Caughley et al. (1976) have discussed the problems of aerial surveys and provided guidelines for correcting visibility bias and maximizing the precision of population estimates. Visual survey techniques have been applied to a wide variety of species, including caribou (Bergerud 1963, Siniff and Skoog 1964), rhinoceros (Goddard 1967), salmon (Kalez 1947, Eicher 1953), bald eagles (King et al. 1972, Grier 1977), golden eagles (Hickman 1972), white-tailed deer (Rice and Harder 1977) and moose (LeResche and Rausch 1974).

AERIAL SURVEYS WITH PHOTOGRAPHIC RECORDS

A logical extension of visual censusing from aircraft is the addition of cameras to provide a permanent record of the ground scene or animal groups for analysis at a later date (Norton-Griffiths 1974). Aerial photography for census work has been used on many species, including waterfowl (Chattin 1952), sandhill cranes (Leonard and Fish 1974), flamingos (Grzimek and Grzimek 1960), elephants (Croze 1972), seals (Lavigne and Oritsland 1974), and salmon (Kalez 1947). Muskrats, pocket gophers, moose, walrus, wildebeest, whales, and polar bears also have (both directly and indirectly) been the subjects of aerial censusing using remote sensing.

A variety of camera systems can be used to obtain aerial photographs. The most sophisticated are the 9-inch film format aerial mapping cameras used by most commercial firms and government agencies. Smaller format cameras, however, (70 mm and 35 mm) are becoming popular for aerial photography because they are easy to use and inexpensive to operate (Anderson and Wallner 1978). Although the smaller format cameras can be used to obtain hand-held, oblique photos, vertical photographs usually produce better results for animal surveys (Heyland 1973).

Woodcock (1976) described a 70 mm format camera system and belly-port mount adapted for light aircraft such as the Cessna 182. Woodcock also provided information on calibrating the camera, planning the overflight, and producing a photo index. Meyer and Grumstrup (1978) have developed an extremely versatile 35 mm aerial photography system and have prepared a guidebook that describes film and filter combinations, camera and mounting, flight preparation, enroute operations, film processing, image interpretation, field checking, and example applications.

Black-and-white films are the most cost-effective, but color films may offer advantages in censusing certain animals. Most aerial films require some type of filter to reduce the effects of atmospheric haze. Haze causes a bluish tone in color films and reduces the contrast in black-and-white films. Appropriate film-filter combinations are referenced in Eastman Kodak Co. (1971).

Large animals, such as elk and cattle, may be identified on photos with scales ranging from 1:8,000 to 1:5,000. Larger scales (1:3,000 or larger) are required for smaller animals, such as deer or sheep (Poulton 1975). Heyland (1973) provided a comprehensive introduction to the subject of animal censusing using aerial photography, and he discussed films, filters, processing, mission planning, and interpretation.

Cost-efficient use of aerial photography in censusing wildlife usually precludes acquisition of very large-scale photos in which the animals appear as they would when viewed through binoculars. Accordingly, characteristics other than resolution, such as gross morphological features, behavior, habitat preferences, associated species, and changes in appearance from season to season, often are used to identify animals. For example, wing size, shape, and position may be used to identify many species of birds in flight. Flocking patterns are diagnostic for some species of waterfowl. The shadows of antlers often are more apparent than the actual antlers and can be used to differentiate sex for some of the large ungulates. Knowledge of habitat preferences and seasonal movements of large animals can reduce photography costs because cameras can be turned off over unsuitable areas (Heyland 1973). Stereo overlap photography during a census overflight provides an additional capability for separating animals from inanimate objects by detecting movement between adjacent frames.

THERMAL INFRARED AERIAL SENSING

Thermal infrared sensing offers another method for censusing animals. These systems detect emitted radiation, or heat, rather than the reflected light that is imaged on conventional photographic films.

Several factors limit the practical application of thermal sensing systems. Infrared radiation from animals hidden beneath tree cover does not penetrate the foliage, and such animals cannot be detected. Therefore, animals must be in the open or in very light cover to be recorded. Animals can be detected only if there is a sufficient radiant temperature difference between themselves and their background (Reeves 1975). Other terrain objects, such as rocks, may retain solar heat and produce radiant temperatures greater than animals for several hours after sunset (Parker 1972). These objects can therefore be mistaken for animals.

Although thermal scanning has not been proven as a cost-effective operational technique for censusing wildlife at this time, it does offer possible applications in the future. Further information is available in Croon et al. (1968), Graves et al. (1972), and Poulton (1975).

Habitat Inventory and Assessment

Perhaps the most common application of remote sensing in wildlife management is habitat inventory and assessment. Foresters have used aerial photography for many years to aid in timberland inventory and management (Thorley 1975). Soil surveys have been based on aerial photo interpretation for 40 years (Soil Conservation Service 1966). Poulton (1975) provided an extensive discussion on range resources and remote sensing that included methods and applications for wildlife management.

TERRESTRIAL HABITATS

Remote sensing can provide information on a variety of terrestrial habitat parameters, including:

1. The type of habitat as defined by physiography, substrate, and plant cover.
2. Particular features of a habitat that may be especially significant for certain animals (waterholes, snag trees, cover types, etc.).
3. The areal extent of habitat types.
4. Spatial distribution and degree of interspersion. The concept of edges as an important attribute of wildlife habitat was first stated by Leopold (1933:132) when he suggested that population densities for species with low travel radius are proportional to the sum of the habitat type peripheries. Patton (1975) indicated that edge measurements could be used as diversity indices. The perspective provided by aerial photography is ideal for measuring edge lengths and for analyzing the spatial arrangements between important habitat components.
5. Certain aspects of forage quality. Healthy, vigorously growing plants exhibit a strong response in the near infrared wavelengths and appear bright red on color-infrared film. In contrast, dormant plants are a duller red to brown, and diseased plants often show radical changes in color. Herbaceous understories often can be identified by a characteristic reddish blush. Preliminary studies by Bentley et al. (1976) included a potential for predicting ephemeral range production through analyses of Landsat digital data.
6. Trends or changes over time. Since the remotely sensed image is a permanent record of the ground scene at the time of the overpass, it provides a unique and

cost-effective method for monitoring changes in an area over time. Old aerial or ground-level photography can be compared with recent coverage to determine the effects of such activities as overuse by animals, fires, woodcutting, agricultural encroachment, certain forms of pollution, flooding, and off-road vehicle use. Hastings and Turner (1965) provided excellent examples of some of these comparisons. Aerial photography also can be planned to monitor recovery of an area following a change in management strategy.

Habitat maps derived from remotely sensed information can serve a variety of purposes, including:

1. Relating results of animal surveys to particular spatial arrangements and sizes of habitat types to facilitate extrapolation of population densities.
2. Selecting potential areas for introducing native or exotic species.
3. Selecting sites for improvement practices such as controlled burning, water development, etc.
4. Identifying critical areas for preservation.
5. Developing maps depicting types and sizes of habitats that might be used for quantitative compensation requests for mitigation alternatives.

Merchant and Waddell (1974), Craighead (1976), Meyer (1976), and Grumstrup and Meyer (1977) described the use of remote sensing for terrestrial habitat analysis.

WETLANDS AND AQUATIC HABITATS

Numerous researchers have used remote sensing in wetlands habitat analysis. Multispectral photography (i.e., film and filter combinations selected to limit exposure to specific segments of the electromagnetic spectrum) has shown great promise for identifying and mapping wetland types and plant species (Nelson et al. 1970, Anderson and Wobber 1973, Cowardin and Myers 1974, Boland 1976, Work and Gilmer 1976). Meyer et al. (1974) indicated that some forms of remote sensing are both economically feasible and efficient in estimating a wide range of wetlands habitat variables useful in waterfowl management. Reeves et al. (1976) used both Landsat and meteorological satellite data to monitor arctic habitat conditions to predict snow goose production for use in setting annual harvest regulations. Brown (1978) found remote sensing to be a versatile tool for meeting a variety of specific and diverse wetland mapping requirements.

Some applications of remote sensing to fisheries management are described in Poulton (1975). A brief but comprehensive evaluation of remote sensing capabilities for describing features of rivers is provided in a study conducted by the Civil Engineering Department (1972) of Colorado State University. Austin and Adams (1978) found remote sensing to be effective in establishing baseline data for marine macroalgae resource management. Caron et al. (1976), in a comparison of natural color, color-infrared, and water-penetrating aerial films for underwater feature detection, determined that natural color film provided the greatest amount of subsurface information, but color-infrared film was best to obtain information on submersed, emersed, and terrestrial vegetation.

Environmental Impact Assessment

Many researchers have indicated that one of the most promising uses of remote sensing technology is in environmental impact monitoring and assessment (Austin and Adams 1978, Brown 1978, Doyle 1978, Henderson and Ondrejka 1978). Numerous resource agencies are in the process of developing remote sensing techniques to replace or supplement more expensive ground survey methods for monitoring environmental change. A variety of resource data can be obtained by present-day aircraft and satellite sensing devices. These data describe soil erosion, sedimentation of reservoirs, industrial development, land use patterns, plankton content of water bodies, sources of air and water pollution, crop and forest activities, snow distribution, mining activity, and human recreation activities.

AN EXAMPLE OF ENVIRONMENTAL IMPACT ASSESSMENT

Carneggie and Holm (1977) have provided a demonstration of the applicability of remote sensing techniques to environmental impact assessment. The following paragraphs summarize their approach for determining the impacts of phosphate strip mining on wildlife resources of the upper Blackfoot River watershed in southeastern Idaho. The watershed is approximately 1000 km^2 in size and contains excellent wildlife and fish habitat.

Three phosphate strip mines currently operate in the watershed. A fourth mine closed in 1969 after operating for 17 years. Eight phosphate mining companies have developed plans for 17 new strip mines, 15 of which are to be within the watershed. Development plans include establishing several processing plants, new roads, railways, conveyer lines, and other means of transporting the phosphate bearing ore to loading facilities and processing plants.

Before the development could proceed, an environmental impact assessment had to be completed to determine the effects of the development on the area. It was decided that remote sensing techniques would yield useful information on the problem.

A Landsat color composite of the area, acquired 6 September 1975, provided an overview of the study area and a base for delineating the watershed boundary, land use, landform characteristics, and a vegetation cover map of 8 primary cover types. Interpreting and verifying the general vegetation map of the watershed required less than 1 man-day. The resulting vegetation map was more detailed and accurate than the vegetation map prepared for the 1976 Draft Environmental Impact Statement for southeastern Idaho, especially in those areas where vegetation maps had not been prepared previously (Carneggie and Holm 1977).

The Landsat image was used to display: (1) the areal extent and distribution of mines; (2) the location and distribution of support services to sustain the mining; and (3) the relationship of proposed developments to existing land use, vegetation types, and wildlife habitat.

T1 S D E011-1.0 C004-043

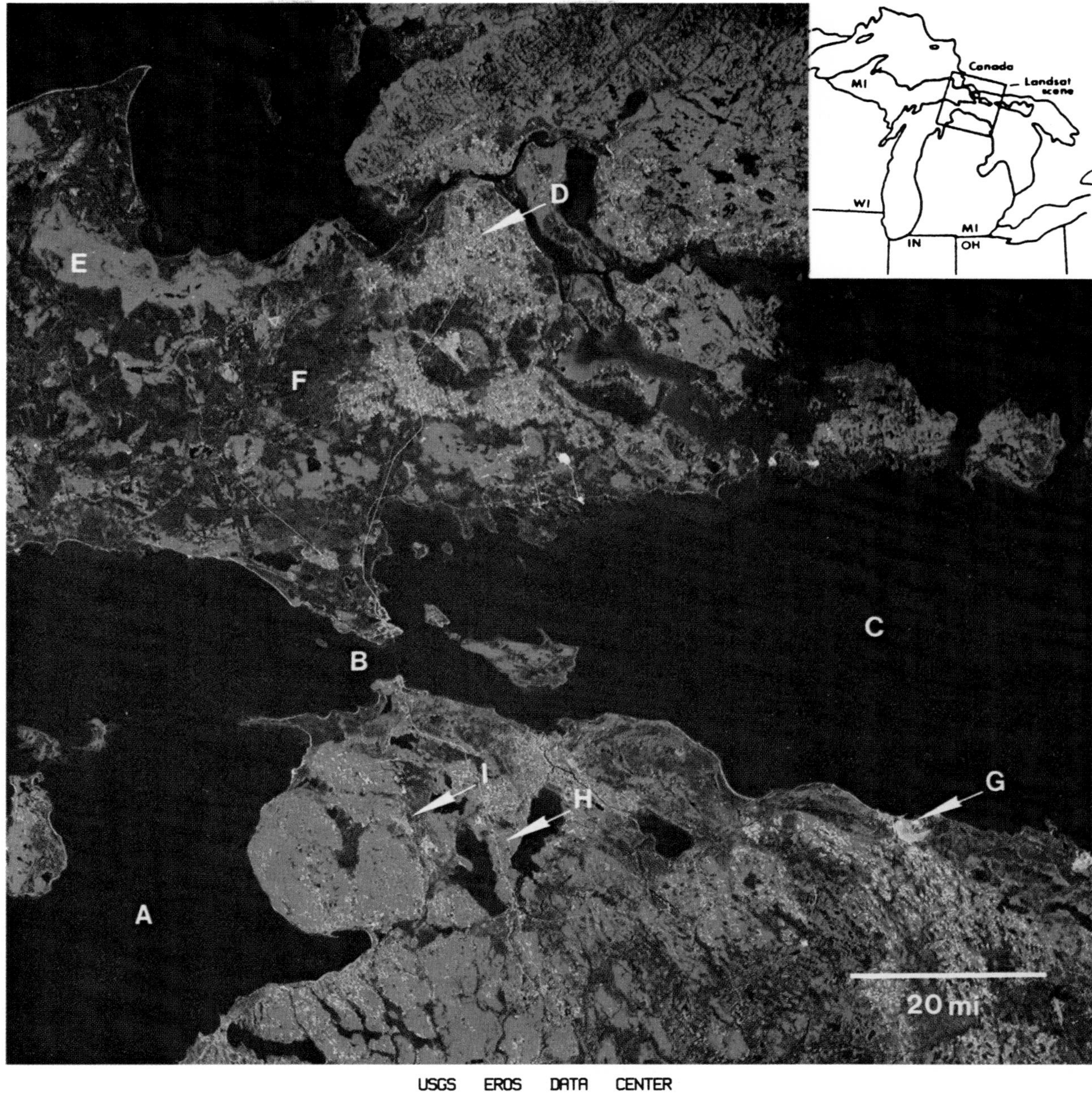

02JUN76 C N45-57/W084-21 N N45-56/W084-16 MSS 5 7 SUN EL56 AZ125 192-6929-N-1-N-P-2L NASA ERTS E-2497-15400-5 01

023-028

Figure 18.1. Digitally processed Landsat image of an area of northern Michigan, acquired 2 June 1976 (identification number E-2497-15400). The color image is made by optically combining 3 multispectral scanner (MSS) bands in registration and sequentially exposing through appropriate color printing filters to produce a colored image commonly referred to as a "color composite" or frequently "false-color composite (FCC)." In this early summer image, there is a great deal of contrast between hardwoods (mainly aspen) and conifers (mainly northern pines and spruces). Later in the growing season the distinction becomes less obvious. As in all Landsat color composites, water appears nearly black unless it is silt laden. Agricultural areas are identifiable by their pattern (a heterogeneous mixture of various field sizes and cover types). Major highways, airports, and other manmade features are often visible. Other noteworthy features include Lake Michigan (A), Straits of Mackinac (B), Lake Huron (C), Agricultural activity (D), Hardwood forest (E), Conifer forest (F), Quarry (G), Highway (H), Airport (I).

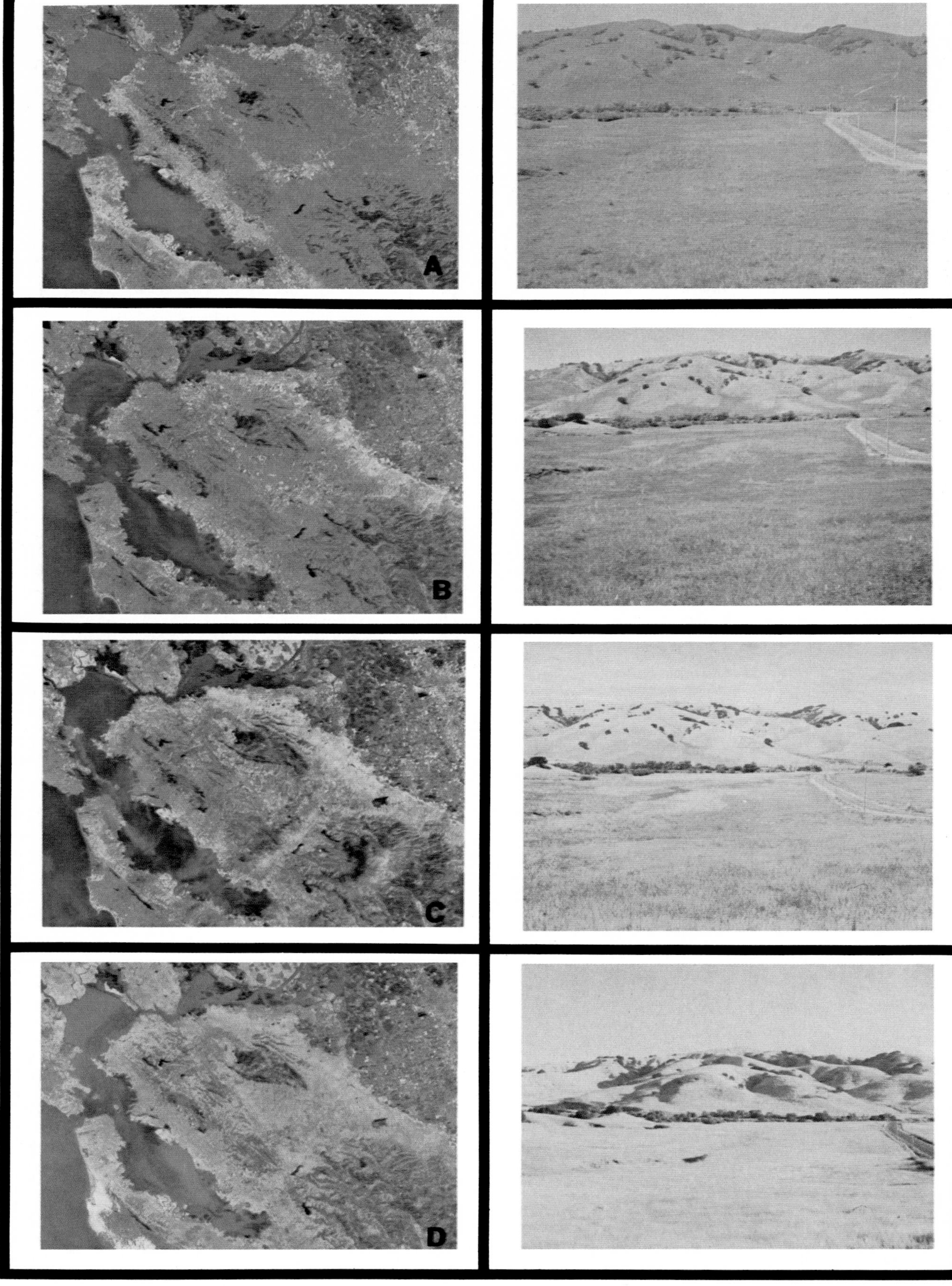
A
B
C
D

Color-infrared aerial photographs of southeastern Idaho were taken on 26 August 1975 by a NASA high-altitude research aircraft. Eight 9- by 9-inch photographs were required to allow stereo analysis of the entire watershed area from which vegetation cover delineations were produced (Fig. 18.3). Seven man-days were required to delineate and verify the vegetation types on the 1000 km^2 area. Drainage patterns and land-forms were delineated by stereoscopic examination. Through careful analysis of drainage patterns and density in the vicinity of an existing or proposed mine, information regarding permeability of surface soil materials and erosion potential was derived. It also was determined whether critical fish spawning areas or other aquatic resources were likely to be jeopardized by sedimentation resulting from proposed or existing strip mines.

Certain kinds of sensitive cover types including marshlands, wet meadows, areas adjacent to streams and water bodies, and beaver ponds were identified and mapped from aerial photographs. Supplemental habitat information, such as critical winter ranges and calving grounds for big game, were superimposed on the photographs to complete the assessment of wildlife values that were potentially threatened by mining or other proposed disturbances.

The vegetation, terrain, and wildlife habitat delineations on an aerial photograph did not constitute a true planimetric representation of the data because of distortions introduced due to topographic relief. To make relatively accurate acreage estimates and display features in true planimetric positions, the interpretative overlays were transferred to a planimetrically accurate map base for measurement (Fig. 18.4). The final products included map overlays that depicted land ownership, vegetation, drainage patterns, and sensitive wildlife habitats.

According to Carneggie and Holm (1977), additional analyses could have been performed to: (1) detect and assess alterations and unavoidable impacts to the environment; (2) identify development stipulations for the mine plan and monitor compliance with the plan; and (3) monitor the cumulative impacts of mining on a regular basis. Image analyses of the color-infrared photographs could be used to locate potential or actual soil erosion and other point and nonpoint sources of pollution, thus aiding in assessing potential impacts on aquatic environments from increased sedimentation. Additional uses of the images include locating transportation and utility corridors and determining suitable locations for overburden waste materials and settling ponds. Another important application could be determining specific sites where more intensive field investigations are warranted. Although remote sensing will not directly solve all of the problems associated with preparing an environmental impact assessment, it has been demonstrated to be a powerful tool in the complex evaluation tasks associated with this critical issue.

Figure 18.2. A series of Landsat images and ground photographs from the same area illustrating the use of sequential imagery for vegetation change detection and environmental monitoring. Manual interpretation procedures can be used to monitor changing conditions during the annual growth and development cycle of vegetation, as illustrated by this 4-date sequence of the San Francisco Bay area, California.

A Portion of a Landsat image acquired 4 April 1973 showing the annual forage crop near the peak of foliage development. Healthy green vegetation appears red. The accompanying ground photograph, taken in the Pinole Valley area east of Berkeley, CA, documents the vigorous state of annual grass development on both the upland and meadow areas.

B Same area as recorded on 10 May 1973. The ground photograph reveals that the grass is beginning to dry in the upper, less moist, areas. The Landsat image provides a synoptic view of the situation.

C This image, acquired 18 days later on 28 May 1973, reveals the extent of drying. Most grassland forage crops on the upland sites are completely dry. The lowland areas are beginning to dry also, as shown in the ground photograph.

D By 15 June 1973 the grassland is nearly completely dry. Only forested areas, riparian vegetation and some agricultural crops still are green and therefore appear red on the Landsat color composite.

Other Applications

In addition to censusing animal populations, inventory of habitats, and environmental impact assessment, remote sensing can be helpful in certain other areas of wildlife management. Hazzard (as cited in Poulton 1975:1474) used aerial photographs to determine the number of boats, and sometimes the number of boat occupants, in an area. Under proper conditions, it is likely that the number of hunters afield also could be estimated using large-scale aerial photography. The aerial perspective provides an accurate and permanent record of entries into restricted areas and has been used as evidence during litigations (Leedy 1948). Aerial photographs also could be useful in planning activities such as locating scenic sites or environmentally sensitive areas and designing access trails. Jensen and Meyer (1976) summarized other uses of remote sensing by the Minnesota Department of Natural Resources including engineering, environmental protection, and recreation applications.

SOURCES OF INFORMATION AND ASSISTANCE

The successful design and operation of a project involving remote sensing depends upon access to suitable remote sensing expertise. To meet this need, a growing interest has developed for university level programs, shortcourses, and user-oriented workshops about remote sensing.

Numerous universities now offer specific courses related to various aspects of remote sensing—photogrammetry, aerial photo interpretation, and photographic sensors, for example. Bidwell (1975) listed those universities actively publishing research material in remote sensing technology and applications of benefit to researchers and others who wish to obtain the most recent information. Nealey (1977) has prepared a list of university courses, programs, projects, and textbooks in common use.

Figure 18.3. An example of the image interpretation process applied to vegetation cover mapping. Vegetation types were mapped from color-infrared aerial photographs. The key to mapping symbols is given below:

FOREST TYPES		*SHRUB COMMUNITIES*		*HERBACEOUS*	
Fa Aspen dominated	Cx Clearcut	Si Lowland sage	Sd Treated sage/herbaceous	M Wet meadow	P Seeded pasture
Fc Conifer dominated	W Woodland	Su Upland sage	T Tall shrub		A Croplands
Fm Mixed	R Riparian				

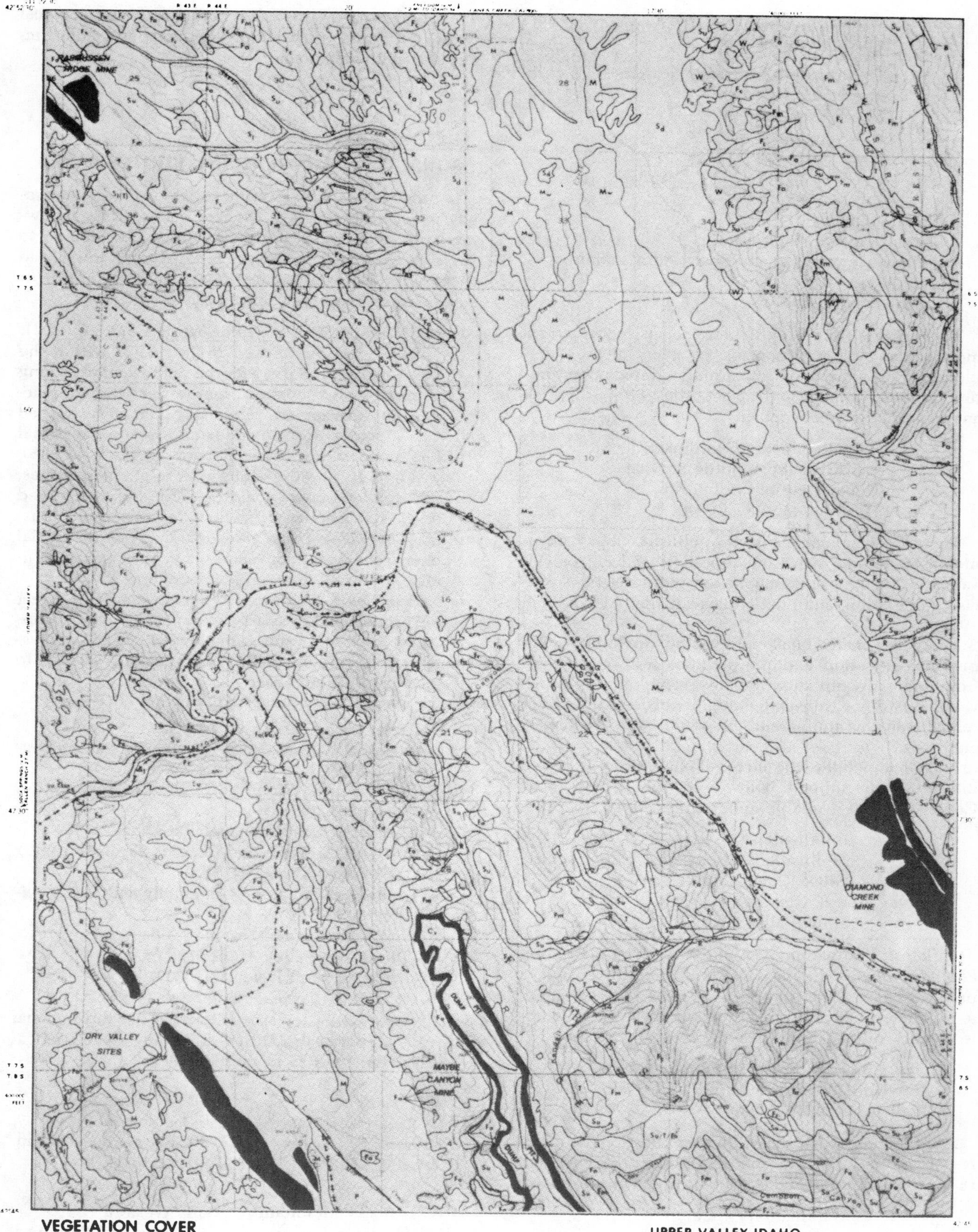

Figure 18.4. The vegetation cover map for the Blackfoot River watershed derived through an interpretation of color-infrared aerial photographs. The vegetation cover delineations from the photographs have been manually transferred to a 7.5 minute series topographic map sheet as the final step in preparing the vegetation cover map. This final step minimizes mapping errors due to distortions inherent in the aerial photographs. The legend system is the same as in Figure 18.3.

General information about available shortcourses and workshops can be obtained from:

Training and Assistance Section
Applications Branch
EROS Data Center
U.S. Geological Survey
Sioux Falls, SD 57198

and

Training Officer
Goddard Space Flight Center
National Aeronautics and Space Administration
Code 902.1
Greenbelt, MD 20771

The U.S. Fish and Wildlife Service has sponsored remote sensing training courses for many of their employees. For information concerning training opportunities and other remote sensing activities within the Fish and Wildlife Service, contact:

Remote Sensing Coordinator
U.S. Fish and Wildlife Service
Department of the Interior
Washington, D.C. 20240

The U.S. Geological Survey publishes many documents, including maps and reports, that have proven valuable in support of remote sensing projects. A concise guide to this information is available (Clarke et al. 1978).

There are many image processing (including computer classification) and interpretation services, ranging from university-affiliated remote sensing groups to private industries. A substantial number of companies offer remote sensing equipment and services on a commercial basis.

A list that includes all sources of image processing and interpretation support known to the EROS Data Center/USGS is available upon request from:

Information Officer
Applications Branch
EROS Data Center
U.S. Geological Survey
Sioux Falls, SD 57198

The latest information can often be obtained from *Photogrammetric Engineering and Remote Sensing*, a publication of The American Society of Photogrammetry, the principal organization of remote sensing professionals. Address inquiries to:

The American Society of Photogrammetry
105 North Virginia Avenue
Falls Church, VA 22046

A bibliography listing wildlife applications is maintained at the Earth Resources Observation Systems (EROS) Data Center and is available upon request from:

Information Officer
Applications Branch
EROS Data Center
U.S. Geological Survey
Sioux Falls, SD 57198

This bibliography includes citations from technical notes, bulletins, symposia proceedings, and from limited distribution sources.

SOURCES OF IMAGERY AND PHOTOGRAPHS

In order to facilitate locating suitable aerial photography and satellite imagery, we have compiled the following guide to the most common sources. In addition to those sources listed below, it is usually worthwhile to check with the appropriate state planning bureau (or equivalent) for catalogs of available photographs.

1. <u>National Cartographic Information Center (NCIC)</u>.

NCIC was established in July 1974 within the U.S. Geological Survey for the purpose of providing a single-point contact source for cartographic-related information, including remotely sensed data. A computerized indexing system, the Aerial Photography Summary Record System (APSRS), will initially show all holdings of Federal agencies, with the long-range goal of including data acquired on the state and local levels as well as private industry. Coverage will be categorized as planned aerial photo coverage, photo acquisition programs in progress, and existing aerial photo coverage.

Inquiries through the APSRS system will direct the requestor to the particular agency that holds imagery in the requestor's area of interest. The requestor must then contact the holding agency directly to place an imagery order.

Among the cooperating Federal agencies are:

—U.S. Geological Survey (USGS)
—National Oceanic and Atmospheric Administration (NOAA)
—Agricultural Stabilization and Conservation Service (ASCS)
—Bureau of Land Management (BLM)
—National Archives and Records Service (NARS)
—U.S. Forest Service (USFS)
—Library of Congress, Geography and Map Division
—Soil Conservation Service (SCS)
—Tennessee Valley Authority (TVA)
—Department of Defense (DOD)
—U.S. Army Corps of Engineers (USACE)

To provide easier access to NCIC at the regional level, support capabilities are being developed at each of the 4 USGS mapping centers:

NCIC Eastern
U.S. Geological Survey
536 National Center
Reston, VA 22092

NCIC Midcontinent
U.S. Geological Survey
1400 Independence Road
Rolla, MO 65401

NCIC Rocky Mountain
U.S. Geological Survey
Stop 510, Box 25046
Denver Federal Center
Denver, CO 80225

NCIC Western
U.S. Geological Survey
345 Middlefield Road
Menlo Park, CA 94025

2. EROS Data Center (EDC).

The EROS Data Center was established in 1971 as part of the Earth Resources Observation Systems (EROS) program of the Department of Interior (DOI) and is managed by the U.S. Geological Survey. It provides primary access to Landsat data, aerial photography acquired by the DOI and NASA, and from Skylab, Apollo, and Gemini spacecraft programs.

Landsats 1, 2, and 3 have acquired approximately 275,000 individual scenes in 4 separate spectral bands. Nearly complete coverage of the world land areas, except the polar areas, is available.

More than 40,000 frames of Skylab, Apollo, and Gemini coverage have been archived at EDC. Only selected coverage was taken on these missions.

High-altitude (60,000–65,000 feet) aerial photography has been acquired by NASA for much of the United States at the request of investigators participating in the NASA Earth Resources Program. The most common scales are 1:60,000 and 1:120,000. Generally, black and white, color, and color infrared are available in a 9-inch film format.

Conventional aerial photography flown by the USGS accounts for approximately 2,000,000 frames. The most common scale is 1:24,000 typically on 9-inch black-and-white panchromatic film.

A final category includes aerial photography acquired by various Federal agencies at various scales and film types. The following have put approximately 1,000,000 frames into the EDC archives:

—U.S. Army Map Service (AMS)
—U.S. Air Force
—U.S. Navy
—U.S. Bureau of Land Management
—U.S. Bureau of Reclamation
—Wallops Flight Center (NASA) [Chesapeake Bay Ecological Program]
—Marshall Flight Center (NASA)
—U.S. Army Corps of Engineers
—South Dakota State University
—Mississippi Test Facility (NASA)
—University of Michigan

The EROS Data Center does not necessarily hold all the aerial photography acquired by these individual groups. It will be necessary to contact the originating agency for possible additional coverage. Contact:

EROS Data Center
User Services Branch
Sioux Falls, SD 57198

3. U.S. Bureau of Land Management (BLM).

The BLM has acquired photography in recent years at various scales and film types. For more information contact:

Office of Special Mapping
Bureau of Land Management
Denver Federal Center
Building 50
Denver, CO 80225

4. Agricultural Stabilization and Conservation Service (ASCS).

The ASCS has acquired coverage over about 80% of the United States excluding Alaska. Most photography is black-and-white panchromatic at scales of 1:20,000 and 1:40,000. Coverage is usually flown on a county-by-county basis on a 7-year cycle, dating back to the 1930's. Indexes of coverage for specific areas are available for inspection through local ASCS offices. For more information contact:

Aerial Photographic Laboratory
ASCS-USDA
2222 West 2300 South
P.O. Box 30010
Salt Lake City, UT 84125

5. Soil Conservation Service (SCS).

The SCS has acquired conventional black-and-white photographs for many areas of the United States. Coverage was generally acquired at a scale of 1:20,000 on 9-inch black-and-white panchromatic film. Most recently, coverage has been acquired at scales ranging from 1:31,680 to 1:85,000. The SCS is currently undertaking orthophoto mapping projects with cooperation from the USGS. Surveys are not flown on any type of repetitive basis. For more information contact:

Soil Conservation Service, USDA
Cartographic Division
Federal Center Building
Hyattsville, MD 20782

6. National Archives and Records Service.

This center is the archive for historical (pre-1940) resource photography acquired by such agencies as the ASCS, SCS, and USGS. A catalog entitled "Aerial Photographs in the National Archives" is available upon request. For more information contact:

National Archives and Records Service
Cartographic Branch
General Services Administration
Washington, D.C. 20408

7. U.S. Forest Service (USFS).

The USFS has acquired aerial photographs of most of the National Forest lands. Photography is primarily at scales of 1:20,000 to 1:24,000 on standard black-and-white 9-inch panchromatic film, and dates back to 1934. Standard coverage through the 1960's was at a scale of 1:15,840. More recently, color and color-infrared photography at smaller scales ranging up to 1:80,000 has been acquired. Coverage is updated as is deemed necessary by the USFS. Inquiries should be directed to the appropriate regional headquarters or:

Division of Engineering
U.S. Forest Service, USDA
Washington, D.C. 20250

8. National Park Service (NPS).

The NPS has acquired aerial photographs of the national parks at various scales and film types. For more information contact:

National Park Service
Department of the Interior
Denver Service Center
655 Parfet Street
P.O. Box 25287
Denver, CO 80225

9. U.S. Environmental Protection Agency (EPA).
In 1974 the EPA established a Remote Sensing Branch at the National Environmental Research Center in Las Vegas, Nevada. The data acquired are of various types and formats. For more information contact:

Environmental Protection Agency
Remote Sensing Branch
P.O. Box 15027
Las Vegas, NV 89114

EPA Interpretation Center
P.O. Box 1587
Vint Hall Farms
Warrenton, VA 22186

10. Environmental Satellite Imagery (Meteorological or "Weather" Satellites).
Low resolution imagery of the Earth is being acquired by a variety of environmental satellites such as the SMS-GOES, TIRDS, Nimbus, ATS, and ESSA using visible and thermal infrared sensors. For more information contact:

Satellite Data Services Branch D543
Environmental Data Service
National Oceanic and Atmospheric Administration
World Weather Building—Room 606
Washington, D.C. 20233

11. National Oceanic Survey—Coastal Mapping Division.
The Coastal Mapping Division (formerly the Coast and Geodetic Survey) has acquired coverage over the nation's coastal areas. Coverage at scales ranging from 1:10,000 to 1:40,000 has been acquired in recent years. This agency also has the responsibility for acquiring aerial photography over the nation's major airports, dating back to World War II under the "Airport Obstruction Chart Survey Program." Coverage is typically black-and-white panchromatic with scales varying from 1:24,000 to 1:60,000. For more information contact:

Coastal Mapping Division
NOAA
Rockville, MD 20852

12. Department of Defense (DOD).
Estimates of the number of aerial photographs acquired by the DOD range between 100 to 200 million frames. The primary agency responsible for archiving this collection is the Defense Intelligence Agency (DIA). Photography was generally acquired by conventional means at scales of 1:15,000 to 1:40,000 on 9-inch black-and-white panchromatic film. Coverage dates back to the 1930's. Some of the early coverage, such as the Army Map Service small-scale coverage of the 1950's and the Navy/Army acquired coverage of Alaska has been transferred to the EDC archives. NCIC is currently handling the task of producing plots and indexes of DOD unclassified coverage.

The Defense Mapping Agency (DMA) was established in 1972, with primary responsibilities for mapping and charting within the DOD. Most current activities are done in conjunction with the USGS. For more information contact:

Defense Intelligence Agency
Attn: DS4A
Arlington Hall Station
Washington, D.C. 20301

Defense Mapping Agency
Topographic Command
6500 Brooks Lane, NW
Washington, D.C. 20315

13. U.S. Army Corps of Engineers (USACE).
The USACE has extensive involvement in civil projects such as dams, shoreline and flood protection, and waterway navigation. Coverage dating back to the 1930's has been acquired generally with standard 9-inch black-and-white panchromatic film with scales varying considerably with the particular project requirements. More recently, coverage has been acquired using color and color-infrared film. Although officially part of the DOD, most of the more recent coverage remains in the particular project office collecting the data. Most recently, the Coastal Engineering Research Center at Ft. Belvoir, VA, has taken on the responsibility of indexing much of the imagery collected by the Corps. For more information contact:

U.S. Army Engineer Waterways Experiment Station
Mobility and Environmental Systems Laboratory
P.O. Box 631
Vicksburg, MS 39180

14. Defense Meteorological Satellite Program (DMSP).
Data acquired by the United States Air Force Global Weather Satellite Program are archived at the Space Science and Engineering Center at the University of Wisconsin. These data originate out of USAF Global Weather Center, Offut AFB, Omaha, NE. For more information contact:

DMSP Satellite Data Library
Space Science and Engineering Center
University of Wisconsin
1225 West Dayton Street
Madison, WI 53706

15. Wallops Flight Center (NASA).
Wallops Flight Center has an active remote sensing program centered around its Chesapeake Bay Ecological Program. Generally, the Center has acquired low- to middle-altitude multispectral photography. For more information contact:

Chesapeake Bay Ecological Program Office
NASA-Wallops Flight Center
Wallops Island, VA 23337

16. Tennessee Valley Authority (TVA).
The TVA has acquired conventional aerial photographs of the Tennessee River watershed area, which includes the state of Tennessee and adjoining portions of Alabama, Georgia, Kentucky, Mississippi, North Carolina, and Virginia. Coverage, dating back to 1933, was taken at various scales, although typically at 1:24,000. Recently, some special purpose color and color-infrared coverage has been acquired. For more information contact:

Map Information and Records Unit
Maps and Surveys Branch
Tennessee Valley Authority
101 Haney Building
Chattanooga, TN 37401

17. Aerial Survey Companies.
Aerial survey companies are often an excellent source of existing aerial photography. They often hold originals of their photography flown for map-making purposes. If existing coverage is not suitable, it may be necessary to contract for new photography to be flown. A good source for names and addresses of aerial survey firms is:

American Society of Photogrammetry
105 North Virginia Avenue
Falls Church, VA 22046

18. Acquiring Your Own Reconnaissance Photographs.
It is often desirable to take your own aerial photographs from a light aircraft using readily available cameras. An annotated bibliography on the subject is available from the National Technical Information Service (Anderson and Wallner 1978).

CONCLUDING REMARKS

At the pace at which remote sensing technology is advancing, especially in the area of sensors and computer processing, improvements in image quality, digital analysis results, turn-around time, and cost-effectiveness are inevitable. For example, Landsat imagery has been improved significantly by digital enhancement as illustrated by Rohde et al. (1978). High resolution film cameras are scheduled to be carried into space by the NASA Space Shuttle, introducing a new dimension to aerial photography. An excellent account of the next generation of remote sensing satellites can be found in Colvocoresses (1977) and Doyle (1978).

It should not be surprising that basic research in remote sensing has progressed more rapidly than have operational applications. The discussions and references in this chapter show that many aspects of remote sensing are currently being evaluated and utilized for wildlife applications.

We believe that remote sensing technology offers a powerful tool to those who learn what it can do and how to use it. Hopefully, this chapter will serve as a useful introduction and guide to further information sources.

The authors wish to acknowledge the valuable contributions to this chapter made by Dr. David M. Carneggie, Mr. Larry R. Pettinger, and Mr. John R. Kaliszewski, all of the EROS Data Center, Sioux Falls, South Dakota.

Chapter Nineteen

Habitat Analysis and Evaluation

LESLIE W. GYSEL

Professor, Fisheries and Wildlife Department
Michigan State University
East Lansing, Michigan

L. JACK LYON

Wildlife Research Biologist
Intermountain Forest and Range
Experiment Station
U.S. Forest Service
Missoula, Montana

INTRODUCTORY STATEMENTS

Trefethen (1964) summarized the importance of wildlife habitat in his book, *Wildlife Management and Conservation*, in a chapter titled, "Habitat—The Vital Element." He stated that habitat is the sum total of the environmental factors—food, cover, and water—that a given species of animal needs to survive and reproduce in a given area. Each wild animal has specific habitat requirements, and the possible distribution and numbers of any species of wild animal are limited in any given area by the quality and quantity of available habitat.

A consideration of the relationships of components of habitats to the growth and survival of wildlife species has been the subject of many research projects and management proposals. The methods that have evolved for the analysis of habitats were developed by plant, range, forest, and wildlife ecologists.

Obviously, it is necessary for the wildlife ecologist to possess some knowledge of the situation being evaluated. The following discussion presupposes that the wildlife investigator has knowledge of the ecology of the animal species involved; without such a knowledge, it is impossible to determine the importance (value) of various habitat factors.

It is also impossible to apply any technique intelligently for measuring habitat unless the objectives of such measurements are clearly stated. Evans (1959), in commenting on the statistical aspects of the various papers presented at a symposium on vegetative analysis, said: "It seems abundantly clear that we understand the need for unambiguous objectives. It would seem that we are quite conscious of the dangers of gadgeteering and peering into small places. But we seem to have spent an appalling amount of time discussing what might be done on a variety of plots, without much consideration of whether or not we belong on the plot to begin with." As

Gates (1949) pointed out, habitat evaluation may unintentionally become so involved with instrumentation and procedure that these become the major concerns, rather than the ecological question under investigation. The field investigator, therefore, must constantly keep in mind the desired objective(s) and guard against the danger of overemphasizing instrumentation and gadgeteering in his efforts to assess wildlife habitat. Hamilton (1978) in a discussion on precision in natural resources inventories suggested the following steps: (1) develop a statement of objectives, (2) identify the population or unit to be sampled and data to be collected, (3) specify the precision of data collection, and (4) select an efficient sampling design.

Methods presented in this chapter can be classified in a general way into reconnaissance-type techniques, which can be used for preliminary investigations, and more intensive sampling techniques which are ordinarily used to obtain specific data from measurements or estimations. Such a division is arbitrary but is of practical value in keeping the techniques used *in line with the objectives of the investigation.* Detailed vegetative analysis techniques, due to practical considerations, are not suitable to large area habitat evaluation and reconnaissance-type techniques will usually not produce detailed data suitable for statistical testing. The various methods can be used in different ways to provide data for: (1) general wildlife management decisions and manipulations, (2) research projects and intensive management procedures, (3) land use surveys and planning and natural resource inventories, and (4) environmental assessments and impact statements.

The analyses and evaluation procedures discussed in this chapter are based primarily on ground sampling and estimation methods. Remote sensing procedures, which are also commonly used to provide the data required for the description and evaluation of wildlife habitats, are described in Chapter 18.

SITE DESCRIPTION AND COMMUNITY DEFINITION

To orient the field biologist as well as the reader of a report, general site classifications and descriptions of various site factors affecting both flora and fauna are often necessary. These descriptions generally precede presentation of habitat analysis and evaluation. The amount of detail necessary is related to the importance of each factor to growth and survival of vegetation and to use of the habitat analysis. Ordinarily the entire site description section is brief.

Associated with a consideration of the site factors is the delimitation of the communities which will be the basis for analyzing and utilizing the data.

Classification Systems

ECOSYSTEMS

Classification systems that can be used throughout the country are important for orientation and to establish general ecological relationships. Different schemes have been used. Dice (1943), in delineating the biotic provinces of North America, described a province as a considerable geographical area over which the environmental complex produced by climate, topography, and soil is sufficiently uniform to permit the development of characteristic type of ecologic associations. His reference book has a map with 29 provinces and a short description of soil, topography, climate, and dominant vegetation. Shelford (1913) recognized the biome as the largest community which he characterized by the climax vegetation, seral stages, and animal constituents. Maps of the biomes and regions as well as descriptions of climate, soil, vegetation, and associated animal species are given in a reference book. Bailey (1976) recognized ecoregions, continuous geographical areas, each characterized by 1 or more ecological associations. His hierarchical classification scheme includes domains and divisions related to climates with 2 broad topographic ecoregions divided into provinces and sections related to vegetation units, delineated on a map. The provinces are briefly described in a separate publication (Bailey 1978).

In the handbook, *Vegetation and Environmental Features of Forest and Range Ecosystems,* Garrison et al. (1977) described 34 ecosystems that cover all of the land area of the 48 contiguous states. Each description contains brief sections on physiography, climate, vegetation, fauna, soils, and land use. For some ecosystems approximations of herbage and browse production are also given. Classification of the vegetation was based on Küchler's (1964) scheme of mapping vegetation and his revised map, Potential Natural Vegetation. The ecosystems map with the handbook is a combination of Küchler's map and the USDA Forest Service Map. Both maps are in *The National Atlas of the United States* (U.S. Geological Survey 1970), an excellent source of information about land forms, geology, soils, climate, and water resources.

Modified Ecoclass, a Forest Service method for classifying ecosystems described by Buttery (1978), links terrestrial and aquatic ecosystems to provide a unifying framework for the various functional interests within which research and management can be planned. This is a relatively complex hierarchical 4-system method including vegetation, landform, soil, and aquatic systems.

HABITAT AND LAND TYPES

In order to classify forest ecosystems within a state to provide a basis for land management, habitat types based on potential climax tree and undergrowth species were recognized by Pfister et al. (1977) for Montana and by Hoffman and Alexander (1976) for Wyoming. An example of a habitat-type designation is one that has been reorganized in Montana—*Pseudotsuga menziesii/Calamagrostis rubescens.* Maps developed from an intensive study of habitat types can be considered permanent since they reflect the potential of the land units. Although this system does not include a description of young seral communities, the site classifications and descriptions provide a basis for the study of these early successional stages which may be important for wildlife.

Land types as used by Thomas et al. (1979a) in the Blue Mountains of Washington and Oregon are a combination of land features and vegetation components used to predict vegetative and animal responses to vegetation management. Type descriptions include soil characteristics, topographic features, and juxtaposition of the tract under consideration in relation to the location of roads, fences, water or streams, position on the slope, adjacent vegetation, and tract shape and size.

The biophysical land classification system used in Canada is based on the recognition of landscape characteristics as an ecological framework for the evaluation of natural resources (Gimbarzevsky 1978). Four classification levels are used to express the intensity of delineated map units—Land Region, Land District, Land System and Land Type which is the fundamental land classification unit. Categories of the system are determined from the topography, geological data, and vegetative structure and composition.

WETLANDS

Since wetlands have a unique and valuable role in supporting diverse food chains, providing fish and wildlife resources, and maintaining natural hydrologic systems, biologists have studied these habitats for many years and have developed different types of classification systems. Most of these systems are regional in scope and are related to special ecological conditions. For the glaciated prairie region, Stewart and Kantrud (1971) based classes on permanency and alkalinity with each class distinguished by 1 of 6 phases of vegetational zones. In a classification of the freshwater wetlands of the glaciated Northeast by Golet and Larson (1974), the principal criteria delineating classes are surface water depth during the growing season, degree of water level fluctuation, and dominant life-forms of vegetation.

To construct a new national classification system for wetlands, an interim classification of wetlands and aquatic habits has been developed by Cowardin et al. (U.S. Fish and Wildlife Service 1976a). Objectives are: (1) to group ecologically similar habitats, (2) to furnish habitat units for inventory and mapping, and (3) to provide uniformity in concepts and terminology. An example of the classification structure for 1 of the 5 ecological systems is given in Figure 19.1.

In situations where the relative size of a stream or drainage basin is important, stream classification based on order number as described by Horton (1945) and Strahler (1957) is often used. A major advantage of this system is that a stream can be classified by reference to a large-scale topographic map.

Site Factors and Indices

GEOLOGY AND TOPOGRAPHY

Various types of rock formations or glacial deposits may affect the composition and structure of vegetation. Descriptions of the underlying rock formations as well

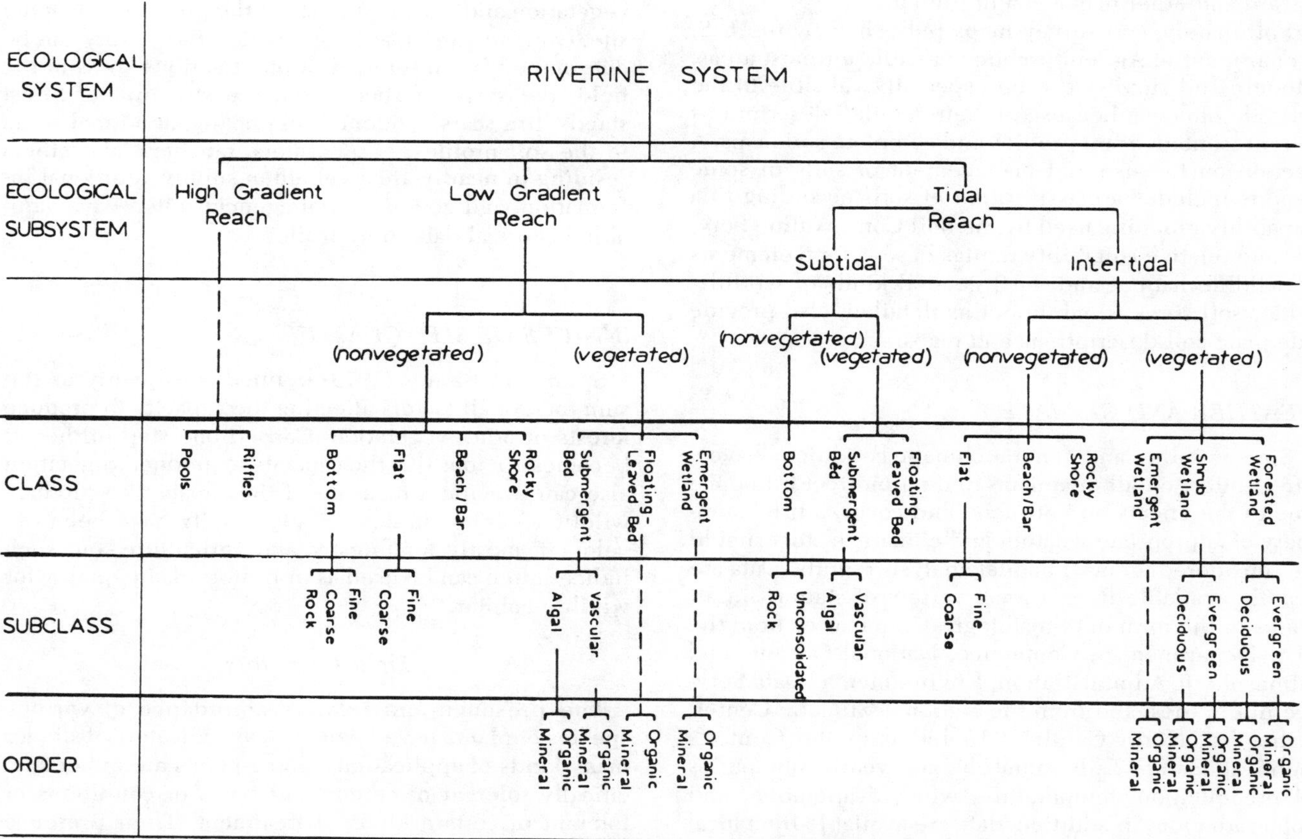

Fig. 19.1. Diagram of the wetland classification hierarchy for the riverine ecological system (U.S. Fish and Wildlife Service 1976a).

as the surface geology may be obtained from numerous reports, bulletins, circulars, and professional papers of the U.S. Geological Survey, from memoirs and special papers of the Geological Society of America, and from the *Structural Geology of North America* by Eardley (1951). Regional and state publications are also possible data sources.

The surface features which result from various geological formations are often extremely important in their effect on other ecological factors affecting organisms. Therefore descriptions should be made at least in general terms—flat, rolling, hilly, mountainous—and often with more definite data including percent of slope, length of slope, and aspect. The presence of marshes, ponds, streams and lakes should be indicated with appropriate classifications and data.

SOILS

A knowledge of soil characteristics can be useful in understanding many ecological relationships. Plant species composition, density, and growth are related to the characteristics of soils. In some sections of the country, minor variations in soil structure or texture can have a marked effect on the growth of both wildlife food and cover. A biologist with a knowledge of soils can predict fairly accurately the species composition and density of successional stages on a site as well as the growth and survival of planted species. For wildland management, soils information is often useful in identifying erosion hazard and other management limitations.

Fortunately, soil survey maps published by the U.S. Department of Agriculture are available for most areas. Modern soil surveys can be especially valuable to the wildlife biologist because of their detailed descriptions of representative soil profiles and complete soil maps. A section on the use and management of soils in some reports includes a classification of soils according to a capability grouping used by the Soil Conservation Service and relative suitability ratings of soils for 8 elements of wildlife habitat and for 3 general kinds of wildlife. Older soil surveys, while not as detailed, also provide adequate soil descriptions and maps.

WEATHER AND CLIMATE

Since weather and general climatic conditions have a direct effect on all organisms and an indirect influence due to the effects on both food and cover, a brief summary of appropriate weather and climatic factors should be considered for most habitat analysis reports. Data are readily available from a great variety of stations in all states in the form of climatological summaries from the U.S. Department of Commerce, National Oceanic and Atmospheric Administration, Environmental Data Service in libraries, and from the National Climatic Center, Asheville, North Carolina. Included in the Center's publications are daily, monthly, and yearly summaries of precipitation, temperature, wind, evaporation, and solar radiation. In addition, data are available from local weather bureaus. Ruffner and Blair (1974) also included summaries of weather and climatic data in their Weather Almanac.

CULTURAL FEATURES

In many areas, the location of cities, towns, separate buildings, power lines, airports, highways, and fences must be considered when evaluating wildlife habitat. This is especially important if management procedures are to be considered or if the analysis is to be used as a part of an environmental impact statement. The best source of information for the location of these features will ordinarily be aerial photographs available from various governmental agencies such as the Soil Conservation Service, the U.S. Forest Service, the Bureau of Land Management, and EROS (Earth Resources Observation Systems), Sioux Falls, South Dakota.

Additional data may be required for impact statements since social and economic as well as environmental impacts must be considered according to the requirements of the National Environmental Policy Act. Demographic data as well as agricultural and industrial summaries are often available on a county or multicounty basis from county Cooperative Extension Offices, and from modern soil surveys and data from the U.S. Bureau of the Census.

HISTORY

In order to understand the ecology of an area, a biologist should know its history. The cutting of forest stands, fire, cultivation, grazing, flooding, and abandonment ordinarily have a marked effect on the original vegetation and may greatly affect the productivity of the site. On many areas, at least a part of the history can be determined by an interpretation of various signs in the field, the stage of succession, the structure of forest stands, fire scars, evidences of grazing, abnormal strata in the soil profiles, etc. Farmers, ranchers, and others residing in nearby areas can often supply additional information, and governmental agencies often have valuable historical data in their files.

INDICES OF SITE QUALITY

Spurr and Barnes (1973) defined site quality as the sum total of all factors affecting the capacity to produce forests or other vegetation. Carried one step further, it becomes obvious that the capacity to produce vegetation also can provide a measure of the capacity to produce wildlife. Various indices of site quality have been developed, mostly for forestry and agriculture, but such indices often can be used as indicators of site quality for wildlife habitat.

Plant Indicators

The presence and relative abundance of various species of plants have been used as indicators of site for many kinds of applications. Some plants are either specifically tolerant of certain soil types or conditions or tolerant of certain kinds of treatment. Their presence often can supply valuable information about the site. Farmers have used plants as indicators of sites for the growth of crops and range managers use plants to judge the condition of the range and as an aid for determining the grazing capacity. In a similar way, wildlife biologists, utilizing their experience and results of research, judge the value of habitats for wildlife species by the presence or absence of plant species.

Foresters in the United States, Canada, and Europe have also utilized plants as indicators of site productivity, and have developed fairly definite correlation schemes using understory shrubs, herbs, ferns, or lichens as indicators (Linteau 1955, Crandall 1958, Rowe 1967). In addition to undergrowth plant distribution, Mueller-Dombois and Ellenberg (1974) also considered physiographic position and surface soil characteristics for identifying habitat types and productivity.

It is true that plant indicators and what they tell of habitat conditions are difficult, if not impossible, to reduce to instrumental measurement. They do permit the observant field worker to deduce a great deal about conditions in the field provided he has a good grasp of the ecology of the area in which he is working. Care must be exercised in translating too freely ecological experience obtained in one region to another region or area.

Site Index

Foresters have used *site index* as a measure of site productivity for many years. This is based on the generalization that the height of trees of a given species and of a given age is more closely related to the capacity of a given site to produce wood of that species than any other one measure (Spurr and Barnes 1973). The height of the dominant portion of a forest stand at a specified standard age is commonly termed *site index*. This can be determined in the field by measuring the height of a sample of the larger trees of a single species in the stand, determining the mean age from increment borings and by referring to site index curves or tables for the species in various government bulletins, in a compilation by Hampf (1964), and in the *Forestry Handbook* (Forbes and Meyer 1955). A site index of 30 as compared with a site index of 60, for example, indicates that the height growth of the larger trees on the latter site is double that of the first site at the same age. With some experience, a biologist can relate the presence and growth of a variety of plant species providing food and cover for wildlife to site index values.

Community Definition and Designation

When making a habitat analysis, the plant community is often the ecological basis for taking observations and establishing some order for data analysis. Plant community classification, however, involves a variety of ecological concepts ranging from the holistic approaches of Clements (1916, 1928), Tansley (1920) and Braun-Blanquet (1928, 1965) through the individualistic viewpoint of Gleason (1926, 1939). These approaches and later developments (Curtis and McIntosh 1951, Daubenmire 1952, Curtis 1955, Daubenmire and Daubenmire 1968, Pfister et al. 1977, and many others) are descriptive and useful in the area for which they are developed. Perhaps the simplest practical definition of a biotic community is: *an aggregation of plants and animals having a unity of taxonomic composition and relative uniformity in size and density*. In terrestrial ecosystems the most practical method of defining a community in terms of the plant components will probably be through the recognition of plant groupings in accordance with the above definition. This means taking into consideration the species composition, the size or age of the plants, the density, growth forms, and distribution patterns. Communities commonly recognized are the various successional stages in an area such as grass-forb, shrub-sapling forest, pole forest, and mature forest. For example, an old field and an oak-hickory forest can be easily recognized as separate communities. Within the forest, other communities can be recognized on the basis of differences in the size classes of the dominant species, such as oak-hickory mature, oak-hickory pole, and oak-hickory sapling. Although the community designation may seem simple in scope, the ecological differences are often great and complex, and the determination of boundaries may be difficult.

DESIGNATION OF COMMUNITY COMPONENTS AND MAPPING

The initial investigation of an area is divided into 2 steps by Cain and Castro (1959)—the reconnaissance and the primary survey. Both are extensive and general and are used to provide maps of plant communities and other associated data. A reconnaissance, the first step in characterizing the landscape and its vegetation, can be made by ground study or from the air with the aid of aerial photos and various kinds of maps that may be available. A knowledge of the flora and fauna of an area is important.

The second step, the primary survey, consists of recognizing, mapping, and describing the plant communities utilizing topographic maps, other types of ground surveys and aerial photos. After the community boundaries are mapped, the development of an appropriate symbolism should fit the immediate needs of the user and should be as uncomplicated, or as detailed, as seems necessary to meet those needs.

For some maps different colors or crosshatching to represent different vegetation types are used. In general, strong colors symbolize forests and pale colors lesser vegetation while the amount of crosshatching is related to vegetation density (Gaussen et al. 1964, Küchler 1967). The addition of letters, numbers, and symbols further increases the detail available on the map itself. In addition to general phytosociological and physical site information about mapped communities, structural definition or biotic components may be especially important ecological factors. Graham (1945) developed a method for describing strata of communities with a formula. Components of the formulas can be various characteristics of the dominant plant and animal species which are determined by observations and signs in each community. The following symbols and formula are an example of a modification of Graham's method used in Michigan:

Plant species—use the first letter of the common name, e.g., Red maple—Rm when important as component of habitat; otherwise, designate plant groups, e.g., forb (f), grass (g).

Amount of Cover	Range in Percent
I—open tree and shrub cover; sparse forb and herb cover	0–40
II—partially closed crown or stem cover	40–80
III—fully closed crown or stem cover	80–100

Plant sizes—for trees 4.5 m in height and over, indicate the size by dbh in centimeters. Indicate "dbh" with diameter measurements in the formula. For trees, shrubs, and herbs under 4.5 m, indicate size by height in centimeters with no dbh designation.

Strata division within a community—designate by horizontal lines. Select strata according to height and by potential value for food or cover for designated animal species.

Animal species—designate by the first letter of common names.

A single habitat community formula is as follows:

Rm–Ro^{III} 25–38 dbh Fs

Rm–Bc^{II} 15–240 Wd

g–f^{I} 2.5–15

This means—

Red maple–Red oak, fully closed, 25–38 cm dbh—Fox squirrel (Overstory)

Red maple–Black cherry, partially closed, 15–240 cm in height. White-tailed deer (Understory)

grass–forbs, sparse cover, 2.5–15 cm, in height (Ground cover)

All symbols and abbreviations should be described in a legend. Different combinations of numbers and symbols might be developed to fit the specific needs of any investigator.

The composition and structure of a habitat can also be indicated by a profile diagram (bisect), a method used for many years. The diagram can be relatively simple showing the crown form and heights of the vegetation along a transect or it can be more complicated with many symbols as described in a system for recording vegetation by Dansereau et al. (1966). In this system 6 main categories of symbols are used for the structural description of vegetation types: habitat form, leaf shape and size, leaf texture, seasonality, stratification, and coverage.

For additional detail, a relevé analysis based primarily on estimations from a single plot as described by Mueller-Dombois and Ellenberg (1974) could be used. These authors indicate that the relevé record always has 3 basic items of information: (1) geographic and physiographic, (2) species composition, and (3) description of soils.

For describing and comparing avian habitats specifically, Emlen (1956) recognized 16 measureable features: 8 for vegetation (by strata)—height of the top and bottom of a canopy, screening efficiency of the upper and sub-canopy, foliage type, twig type, coverage and dispersion of plants. For the substrate 3 features are recognized: ground slope, ground water, and soil type. Special features such as bodies of water, barren areas, and buildings were also recognized. Direct linear measurements or percentage values were used whenever possible; for other cases appropriate symbols were used. The data can be organized and tabulated in formulae and habitat diagrams or it can be statistically analyzed.

Range ecologists have developed special combinations of methods for describing and making ecological evaluations of rangelands. Francis (1978) summarized the basic inventory interpretative units used by federal agencies which include the Range Allotment used by the Forest Service, Range Sites, Woodland Suitability Groups, and Native Pasture Groups used by the Soil Conservation Service and the Site Writeup Area used by the Bureau of Land Management. Parameters for inventory and analysis include physical environmental data, cover type mapping, range suitability for animals, production and utilization for livestock, and big game grazing capacity.

Special methods must be used to map and describe floating or submersed vegetation. According to the *Standard Methods for the Examination of Water and Wastewater* (American Public Health Association 1980), preliminary surveys should include making a plant collection, determination of water depths and distribution of vegetation according to depth and breadth. Mapping of pure stands of floating or submersed vegetation in small areas can be made with a viewing box, snorkel, or SCUBA (self-contained underwater breathing apparatus) using an established baseline for reference. Vegetation maps of mixed stands and/or large areas are made by using transect lines perpendicular to the shore to the maximum depth of plant growth. Snorkel or SCUBA is used to determine the plant species intercepting the line at 0.5 m intervals.

As resource information and knowledge about environmental interrelationships increase in complexity, a point is reached when computer techniques may be the most effective and efficient method of handling data. Beeman (1978) described a computer-assisted data handling technique, IMGRID, that provides for a highly efficient manipulation of geographical data for the production of maps with site specific resource interpretations. Of value in planning processes in which wildlife is a consideration will be the capability of programs to identify habitat data such as soil type, percent of slope, location of plant communities, location of mast and browse, and the proximity of selected habitat parameters on computer-generated maps. With this system data can be stored, updated, and manipulated.

A PRIMARY SURVEY PROCEDURE

When large or even small areas are to be analyzed with time and manpower restrictions, efficient methods must be used to obtain required habitat data. Primary survey procedures based on estimations (with experience) can often be used. From aerial photos, land use patterns and community boundaries can generally be designated. By making observations and estimations in selected communities, details for a community formula such as composition, amount, and height of cover (previously described) can be determined. This can be accomplished with a knowledge of plant taxonomy, general ecological principles, and a few simple measurements. Similar communities can be recognized on the photos and the formulas applied to the entire area.

Observations and estimations can be made throughout a community, or an area can be selected as "characteristic" within the community (a single plot) to obtain the data. At the same time, the observer can look for animal signs such as tracks, scats, and browsed plants. Additional valuable information about the history of the area and animals seen, hunted, or trapped can generally be obtained from local residents or from regional, state, and federal agencies. For some areas a storage and retrieval system for wildlife habitat like one for the Southwest, RUNWILD, developed by Patton (1978) may be especially valuable and efficient. A management file of this system provides information on species distribution, protection status, key habitat factors, and food and cover requirements.

MEASUREMENTS OF VEGETATIVE COMPONENTS OF COMMUNITIES

Sampling Procedures

The acquisition of data describing a wildlife habitat can be time consuming and costly. It is important that the biologist consider the kind of data actually needed and select or design a sampling system that will meet those needs without producing vast amounts of unnecessary data.

Most of the commonly used vegetation sampling methods can be arrayed along a rough scale of increasing precision and decreasing efficiency. Presence and constancy data, for example, are easily obtained but are not very precise. Frequency, density, and cover measurement are increasingly precise but less efficient; and very precise weight or biomass sampling may require major sacrifices in efficiency. Some sampling systems replace actual measurements with estimation procedures that increase efficiency substantially without necessarily reducing accuracy or precision.

Ordinarily, a complete count or measure of various components of wildlife habitats cannot be made because of the large size of the units or because the objectives of the survey do not warrant expenditures for great accuracy. Some form of sampling is usually used; however, choices have to be made in regard to the type and characteristics and size of the sample unit. Data can be obtained by using plots, plotless techniques, or a combination of the two methods.

PLOTS

Shape

The most commonly used shapes have been square, circular, and rectangular. There seems to be general agreement among ecologists that a rectangular plot is more efficient than other shapes. Bormann (1953) noted that the variance per unit area decreased as the sample plots were increased in length only if the long axis of the plots cut across any banding in the vegetation pattern.

Ordinarily plot borders are measured with a tape; however, less precise methods can be used when absolute values are not imperative. Penfound and Rice (1957) indicated that relative frequency, density, basal area, and importance values obtained by the arms-length rectangle method closely approximated the values obtained by a complete census in a 5.5-ha forest stand and required a small amount of time and effort. After the length of a pace and the width of the spread of the arms are determined, the biologist then paces off with arms outstretched a distance equal to the size of the plots desired along predetermined compass lines. It should be noted that the length of a pace can vary with the percent of slope and various kinds of obstructions.

Size

The size of plots for density measurements is ordinarily related to the size and spacing of individual plants due to the problems in obtaining accurate counts. In forested areas, plots of decreasing size for measurements of large trees to seedlings and herbs can be used. Plot sizes suggested by Oosting (1956) are 10 m × 10 m for the tree layer, 4 m × 4 m for all woody undergrowth to 3 m in height, and 1 m × 1 m for the herb layer.

Various investigators have indicated the relative efficiency of small plots for a variety of habitats. This principle led to the point intercept method developed in New Zealand by Levy and Madden (1933) and further described in a subsequent section.

In regard to the determination of plot size, Cain and Castro (1959) described the *minimal area* as the smallest area that provides sufficient space or combination of habitat conditions for a particular segment of a community type to develop its essential combination of species or its characteristic composition and structure. To determine the size of the minimal area based on species composition, Cain and Castro showed how a species-area curve can be used by plotting sample units of different sizes on the x-axis and species number on the y-axis and by determining a point on the curve where a specified increase in area of the sample yields only a small specified increase in the total number of species. This minimal area can be used as a single plot sample. For multiple plots in a habitat, a similar type of curve can be used for sample units in sets of different sizes increasing from smaller to larger on the x-axis and number of species sampled on the y-axis.

Number

The species-area curve can also be used to determine the number of plots required for an adequate sample of the species composition of a habitat by plotting the number of species sampled on the y-axis according to an increasing number of plots of a given size on the x-axis and then determining a point in the break of the curve beyond which added sampling effort produces diminishing returns.

The adequacy of sample size for measuring density can be determined by plotting the running means of 2 or more plot samples. By determining a point on the curve indicating an insignificant variation in means, the investigator can find the number of plots required (Kershaw 1964).

A statistical evaluation of the number of sample plots required is also possible. For a rather simple method, it is necessary first to decide upon the accuracy desired before sampling intensity can be determined. It is also necessary to know the confidence level limit (e.g., 0.05, 0.10, 0.25, etc.), margin of error (d), and the normal deviate (t) corresponding to an acceptable confidence limit.

The size of the sample (n) cannot be determined without some previous knowledge of the standard deviation (s) of the population. Preferably, s is estimated from previous preliminary sampling of the same or of a similar population; however, the value of s may be chosen by estimate.

If the total population being sampled (N) is very large (n/N being less than 0.05), a formula (Snedecor 1956) for estimating the approximate size of the sample (n) is:

$$n = \frac{s^2 t^2}{d^2}$$

in which n = number of plots required

s = standard deviation

t = normal deviate at confidence limit level and given degrees of freedom (from t table)

d = margin of error (arithmetic mean times designated accuracy)

For example, suppose we desire to determine the available browse by clipping studies and want to know the number of 0.004-ha plots which should be taken. It would be necessary to know (or assume):

1. that cover type is homogeneous so far as the particular investigation is concerned
2. the size (acreage) of the cover type
3. the acceptable accuracy
4. the acceptable confidence limit
5. the acceptable degree of freedom, which is n minus one.

Let us assume that the cover type being sampled is 40 ha and that a 10% accuracy at a 0.05 confidence limit level is satisfactory. In order to estimate the variation, suppose we randomly sample 10 plots which are 0.004 ha in size and these samples supply the following data:

$\bar{x}$ = 19.2 kg = arithmetic mean of the kg of browse per 0.4 ha

s = 2.5 = standard deviation

n = number of plots required.

t = 2.26 = (9 degrees of freedom [n − 1] at 0.05 confidence level).

d = designated accuracy (10% times $\bar{x}$).

Then, solving for n under the above conditions:

$$n = \frac{s^2 t^2}{d^2}$$

$$n = \frac{(2.5)^2 \ (2.26)^2}{[(19.2) \ (0.10)]^2}$$

$$n = \frac{31.92}{3.69} = 8.65$$

Under the above assumptions, it may be concluded that 10 plots "probably" (i.e., 95%+) will give a "reasonable" (i.e., within 10%+) estimate of the available browse in this cover type.

A different method for determining sample size which can greatly reduce the coefficient of variation and consequently the sample size has been described by Wiant and Michael (1978). It facilitates the selection of samples with a probability proportional to predicted size and is referred to as 3 P sampling.

Distribution

There are 2 choices for distributing plots—a systematic method in which the plots are spaced at regular intervals along lines spaced at regular intervals and a random placement of the plots. Some investigators prefer the former method because the plots can be easily located in the field and relocated for additional measurements if necessary. If an unbiased estimate of the population variance is necessary, the sampling should be done from a random distribution of the plots.

Bourdeau (1953) found that stratification of the random sample always yielded a gain in precision over the unrestricted form, especially in sampling sporadic distributions. Variations of the stratified sampling procedures and details of other statistical sampling methods are given in a publication of the National Academy of Sciences (1962).

The final decision in regard to a systematic or random distribution of plots will generally depend upon the objectives of the study. Oosting (1956) indicated that the interests of ecologists and statisticians may not always be the same in regard to the way plots may be distributed by the 2 methods. With random placement, samples can be in close proximity and some areas left unsampled. These unsampled areas may be of great concern to the ecologist. He concluded that systematic sampling may be quite satisfactory for most ecological sampling and, in fact, is likely to be better than random sampling for certain ecological purposes.

Tally of Sample Data and Analysis

Before making measurements of estimations in sample plots and tallying the data, an investigator should have tally sheets or cards with a listing of parameters and approximate space for the data. For large habitats with many sample plots, a more efficient method may be to use field data coding forms for computer analysis. Ohmann and Ream (1971), for example, described the data forms and program output for an ecological research program in the interior zone of the 202,430-ha Boundary Waters Canoe area of the Superior National Forest in which data were taken in plots and by a plotless method.

Van Dyne (1960) explained a method for the rapid collection, processing, and analysis of line intercept data utilizing a tape recorder to record data in the field, a method of coding the intercept data on special forms, and the transferal of data to keypunch cards.

PLOTLESS METHODS

Sampling is also done without definite plot boundaries. These methods can be considered in 3 different categories. When using the line or point intercept methods, sample determinations are made at a point or along a line. Distance methods involve measuring distances between selected points and trees or between 2 trees. In the application of the variable radius method, a tally of plants is made from sample points according to the diameter of plant stem or crown width and the distance of the observer to the plant. Measurements also are made with an angle-gauge. Additional details about these methods are given in the following section.

Measurements and Estimates

DENSITY

Density refers to the number of individuals per unit area and is a commonly used habitat parameter because it can provide an indication of the structure of a habitat and the amount of wildlife food and cover. It also has the advantage that data collected by different sampling methods can be compared. The direct measure is a complete count of all plants or stems in an area or in sample plots, which can be tedious but otherwise is not difficult. Before counting, particularly with shrubs, it is necessary to define whether stems or individual plants are to be counted. To provide a measure of the structure of a habitat, density counts are ordinarily tallied by height or diameter classes.

Since the counting of individual plants can be very time consuming, the ultimate value of these data must be considered in comparison with other possible measurements. In addition, for efficiency, quadrat size should be related to the number and size of the individuals being counted.

When an exact count is not necessary, satisfactory estimates can be recorded in abundance classes. Cain and Castro (1959) provided a summary of the various kinds of abundance designations that have been used. Abundance classes proposed by Tansley and Chipp (1926) are as follows:

Abundance Class

1: Rare
2: Occasional
3: Frequent
4: Abundant
5: Very Abundant

Since these abundance classes are subjective, they can be used mainly to convey a general impression of density. In order to make the abundance class designations more definite, other investigators have related each class to a range of plant units or to an average spacing.

In another approach to density sampling, plotless techniques or distance measures can be used. The point-centered quarter method (Cottam and Curtis 1956) has gained wide acceptance because it does not require a correction factor and because it provides more information per sampling point than other distance methods (nearest neighbor, closest individual, and random pairs). For the point-centered quarter method, 4 quadrants are established at each sampling point; within each the distance from the point to the center of the nearest plant, ordinarily in a specified size class, is measured. The average of the 4 measurements at all points is equal to the square root of the mean area per plant. Estimates of density can then be obtained by dividing the mean area into the unit of expression, i.e., if the mean area = 2 m^2/plant, then 100 m^2/2 = 50 plants/100 m^2. This method is applicable only to random distributions, and in common with other distance techniques, it tends to produce underestimates of density in populations with contagious distributions and overestimates in regular distributions. Most authors caution against using distance methods in sampling either shrub or herbaceous life forms because of nonrandom distributions. Modifications of distance techniques intended to overcome this possible bias have been suggested by Catana (1963) and Batcheler (1971).

Despite the apparent simplicity and objectivity of density sampling, there are a number of inherent problems and disadvantages associated with the density parameter. Cottam et al. (1953) remarked on the characteristic extreme variability of density samples, and Lyon (1968a) suggested that "... the standard deviation of any density sample will be nearly as large as the mean." As a result, density sampling may require a virtually prohibitive sample to attain barely acceptable precision for a statistical test which may fail to detect density differences that are probably obvious on visual inspection.

COVER

Cover, or percent cover, generally refers to the proportion of an area covered by the vertical projection of plant crowns or basal area to the ground surface. Cover is usually considered to be of greater ecological significance than density (Daubenmire 1968), and it supplies considerably more precise information about the actual structure of vegetation. Cover has the additional advantage that "... nearly all plant life forms, from trees to mosses, can be evaluated by the same parameter..." (Mueller-Dombois and Ellenberg 1974).

The implications of the value of vegetative cover for wildlife are well documented. Among the most important are the protection it provides from various components of weather and from other competing forms of wildlife; however, the precise manner in which a species utilizes cover is often not known.

There are a variety of methods for measuring or estimating cover. The choice will depend upon the required precision of the measurements and efficiency of the method. Estimations may often be adequate. For example, Daubenmire and Daubenmire (1968) estimated cover of shrubs and herbs in 2 × 5-dm plots using 6 canopy coverage classes (0–5, 5–25, 25–50, 50–75, 75–95, and 95–100%), and Braun-Blanquet (1965) used a cover-abundance scale with 7 classes (solitary, few, under 5, 5–25, 25–50, 50–75, and 75–100%) on sample areas of 200 m^2 and larger.

When density information is also being collected, crown cover of shrubs can be determined by obtaining 2 diameter measurements with a tape or an appropriately marked staff. The area of the crown can be calculated

$$A = d_1 \times d_2 \times 0.7854$$

and density × mean crown area (A) = cover.

Basal Area

This measurement can be used as an index of cover in forest stands and on rangelands although it is used in different ways in each of these habitats. Foresters determine the basal area of a tree by measuring its diameter at 1.4 m above the ground and by calculating the cross section area. Basal area is usually specified for all the trees of a unit area, either an acre or hectare. Instead of measuring and tallying each tree by diameter, foresters commonly use Bitterlich's variable radius method by counting trees from a sampling point with an angle gauge. Hovind and Rieck (1970) described the use of various types of angle gauges and explained applications of the method. Cooper (1957, 1963) described an application of the Bitterlich method in open shrub stands utilizing a simple angle gauge calibrated in percent of cover. Details of the Bitterlich method are also given in forest mensuration text books.

Although the basal area concept has been mainly used by foresters as a measure of stocking, as a guide for marking, and as an aid in timber estimation, it can be used by the wildlife biologist to indicate in a general way both stem density and cover especially if the range of diameters of the dominant species is specified.

In grassland research, the basal area of grass clumps 2 to 3 cm above the ground is considered a better parameter than foliage cover because of the large variations caused by grazing, trampling, and weather (National Academy of Sciences 1962).

Line Intercept

Another relatively common method of measuring cover is the line intercept as described by Canfield (1941). Measurements are made of the crown intercepts on a tape stretched tightly along the ground or between stakes above ground for low-growing herbs and shrubs; however, special methods must be used to project high tree crown perimeters to a point on a tape on the ground. Different instruments for this purpose have been described by Buell and Cantlon (1950) and Dealy (1960). The "stick method" described by Andresen and McCormick (1962) appears to be as practical and as accurate as methods that use more complex instruments. In this method, the surveyor first straddles the tape line, approximately beneath the perimeter on one side of the crown which is to be measured, and then points toward either end of the tape line. By raising the stick through a vertical arc until the perimeter of the crown is intercepted, he establishes point X at which the plane of the tape line passes through the crown perimeter (Fig. 19.2). The surveyor then makes a quarter turn in either direction so that he faces the tape, with his shoulders parallel to it, and with his feet about a meter from the tape. Next the surveyor points the stick straight ahead, at a right angle to the tape line and inclined upward toward the tree crown, then adjusts his position to the left or right until he is immediately opposite point X. By bringing the stick down in a vertical arc until he touches or points to the tape line, the surveyor establishes a second plane, perpendicular to the plane of the tape line, which is tangent to the tree crown at point X and which intersects the tape line at a place directly beneath point X. A reading is made on the tape line and recorded as the beginning or end of the tree crown.

In layered vegetation where the crowns overlap, crown intercepts should be measured for each layer separately. The calculation of percent of cover is made by totaling the length of the separate crown intercepts and by calculating the percentage of the total length of line covered by each species or by all plants regardless of species.

Point Intercept

Measurements of cover can also be made by counting point intercepts along a tape, or on a transparent dot-grid overlaid on an aerial photograph. For herbaceous or dwarf-shrub vegetation, the point frame has been used frequently (Levy and Madden 1933). This consists of a wooden or metal frame with guide holes for pointed pins. When the pins are lowered, hits are counted by tallying only the first interception with crown or shoot cover. Evans and Love (1957) described a variation of this method in which a single pin is guided by a notch in the boot of the investigator. In order to eliminate some of the errors with methods involving mechanical contact for determining percentage of cover by the use of point intercepts, a short focus telescope was developed by Reynolds and Edwards (1977) which made ground cover assessments with a high degree of accuracy. It has an objective focusing lens coupled to an orthoscopic focusing eyepiece complete with a crosswire reticule at focal length. Measurements with this device could be used as standard for the correction of assessments carried out with established techniques.

For application of the point intercept method to the determination of the percentage of cover of tree crowns, instruments were designed by Robinson (1947) and Lemmon (1956, 1957) for projecting a view of a crown on a dot-grid.

Another variation of the point intercept has been widely used in range analysis. The sample unit is a very small circular plot or loop, ordinarily 1.9 cm in diameter formed by a metal ring attached to a shank about 40 cm long. If any portion of a root crown, a stem for forbs, and a crown canopy for shrubs is within the loop, a hit is recorded for that species.

The Chart Quadrat

In situations which require a detailed record of coverage by species, a map of plant crowns within a quadrat can be made. For a high degree of accuracy a square meter quadrat with subsquares described by Mueller-Dombois and Ellenberg (1974) or a pantograph can be

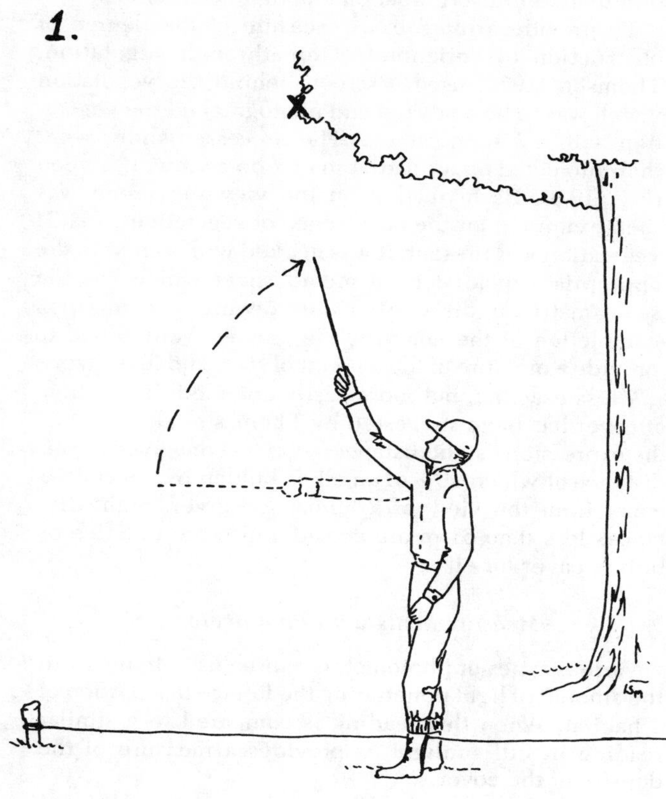

Fig. 19.2. **In this illustration of the stick method (Andresen and McCormick 1962), the observer first straddles the tape line (1) and determines the point where the outer boundary of the crown is above the tape line, designated as point X. Standing at a right angle to the tape (2), he adjusts his position until he is directly opposite point X; by bringing the stick straight down (3), the point at which the crown is intercepted by the line is determined.**

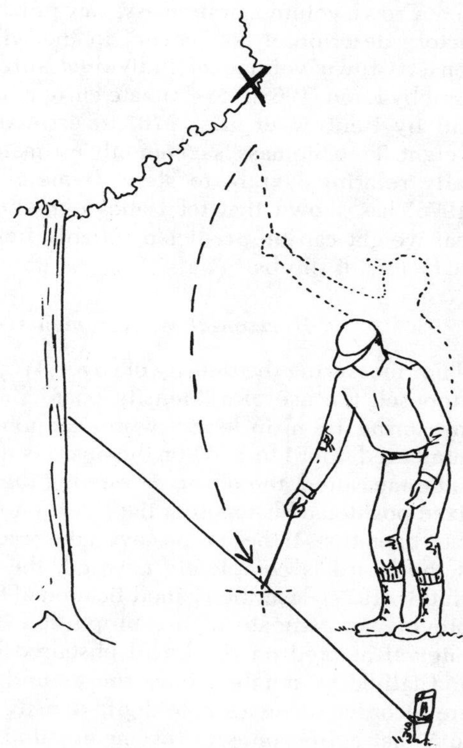

used. Photographs of the quadrat can also be taken. Since this method is time consuming, it would probably be used for special research projects and for documenting changes in coverage. Mack and Pyke (1979) described a field-portable sonic digitizer with a remote activated stylus which minimizes some of the limitations of the mechanical technique for mapping. This instrument combines mapping and digitizing into one rapid procedure. Linear coordinates of any point within a quadrat defined by 2 perpendicular linear microphones can be measured by causing a penlike stylus to emit a hypersonic impulse at that point. The time required for the impulse to travel from the point to each microphone is measured by 2 scalers. The coordinates then appear on the display of the digitizer.

For a less precise analysis of cover, ocular estimations can be made by establishing a grid within a quadrat frame as a reference and reporting the results in ranges of percentages. This can be a useful method for many applications in habitat analysis for large areas.

Stratification and Biomass

An even higher level of precision in vegetation sampling is available when height is used in conjunction with cover to evaluate biomass. Ordinarily, such estimates are derived by stratifying the community into layers and recording cover within each layer or stratum. A few investigators have obtained absolute biomass by removing and weighing all vegetation from sample sites. However, this level of sampling is obviously very expensive and for most habitat evaluations will produce far more information than is actually needed.

Biomass sampling in wildlife management is usually confined to describing cover or weight of edible vegetation. Crown volume, or biomass, may prove to be a satisfactory description for "cover" in the wildlife habitat sense. Crown volume of individual shrubs has been used by Lyon (1968b) to estimate current annual growth and by Bentley et al. (1970) to estimate shrub dry weight. Tree biomass is commonly estimated by empirically relating weight to stem diameter, and Brown (1976) has shown that total above-ground weight and leaf weight can be predicted reliably from basal stem diameters of shrubs.

Horizontal Measurements

For measuring the density of cover, Wight (1938) first proposed the use of a "density board," approximately measuring 1.8 m in length with each foot marked and numbered from 1 to 6. When the board is set in the cover to be measured, the observer viewing the board from a fixed position adds together the figures not obscured by the vegetation. If there is no cover, the reading is 21, and if the board is completely covered, the reading is 0. Nudds (1977) described a modification of this method to provide an estimate of the proportion of each 0.5-m interval marked on the board obscured by vegetation and tallied by heights above the ground surface. Data are recorded using a single digit "density score" from 1 to 5 that corresponds to the mean value of a range of quintiles (e.g., 1 corresponds to a range of 0 to 20%, 2 to a range of 21 to 40%, etc.). The standard observing distance was determined by recording densities at different distances and choosing the one with the greatest variation to assure discrimination among microhabitats.

To provide a more exact measure of the degree of obstruction to horizontal vision through vegetation, Thomson (1975) used a screen behind the vegetation which was to be analyzed and photographed the vegetation with a 35-mm camera. The processed slides were then projected on a quadrat matrix on a viewing screen (Fig. 19.3). Each quadrat on the viewing screen was then examined for the occurrence of vegetative parts. If vegetation was present, it was marked with a cross in the appropriate quadrat on a record sheet which has the same matrix as the one on the viewing screen. Upon completion of the analysis, the crosses were added to provide a measure of the amount of stem and leaf cover.

A less exacting, but more easily obtained description of cover has been suggested by Thomas et al. (1976) in the expression "sight distance." This is conceived as the distance at which 90% of an elk is hidden by vegetative cover from the view of a human observer. Sight distances less than 61 m are considered representative of hiding cover for elk.

Measurements with Photometers

Various types of photometers can be used to measure the amount of light penetrating the foliage in a portion of a habitat. When this reading is compared to a similar reading in full sunlight, it provides a measure of the density of the cover.

A method used at the Virginia Cooperative Wildlife Research Unit (Giles 1969a) is simple and consists of making simultaneous photoelectric readings of the light conditions beneath various types of cover and in full light. The photometers are supported on a frame 20.3 cm above a 20.3 cm square board which has been painted with aluminum paint. The light reading is taken with the photoelectric cell facing downward, measuring reflected light. However, Sather (1950), using a phototronic cell with a diffusing disc, obtained the most reliable results with the cell pointed directly upward. As a result of a comparison of light meters, Fick (1972) stated that different light meters are likely to give different results, and therefore the results should not ordinarily be compared.

Photographic Evaluations

Frequently, it is desirable to depict the cover conditions in as graphic a manner as possible. One method of showing the changes which take place in cover composition from 1 season of the year to another, under different land uses or abuses, and as a result of normal ecological succession, is by means of photographs. Such photographs often tell the story in a way that is superior to all other methods. If photographs are used for this purpose, care should be taken to frame the sequence pictures adequately. The placing of white stakes at intervals throughout the area being photographed is an excellent method for giving some recognizable points of reference within the photographs. A small chalkboard with area, name, and date shown within the picture is desirable for identification.

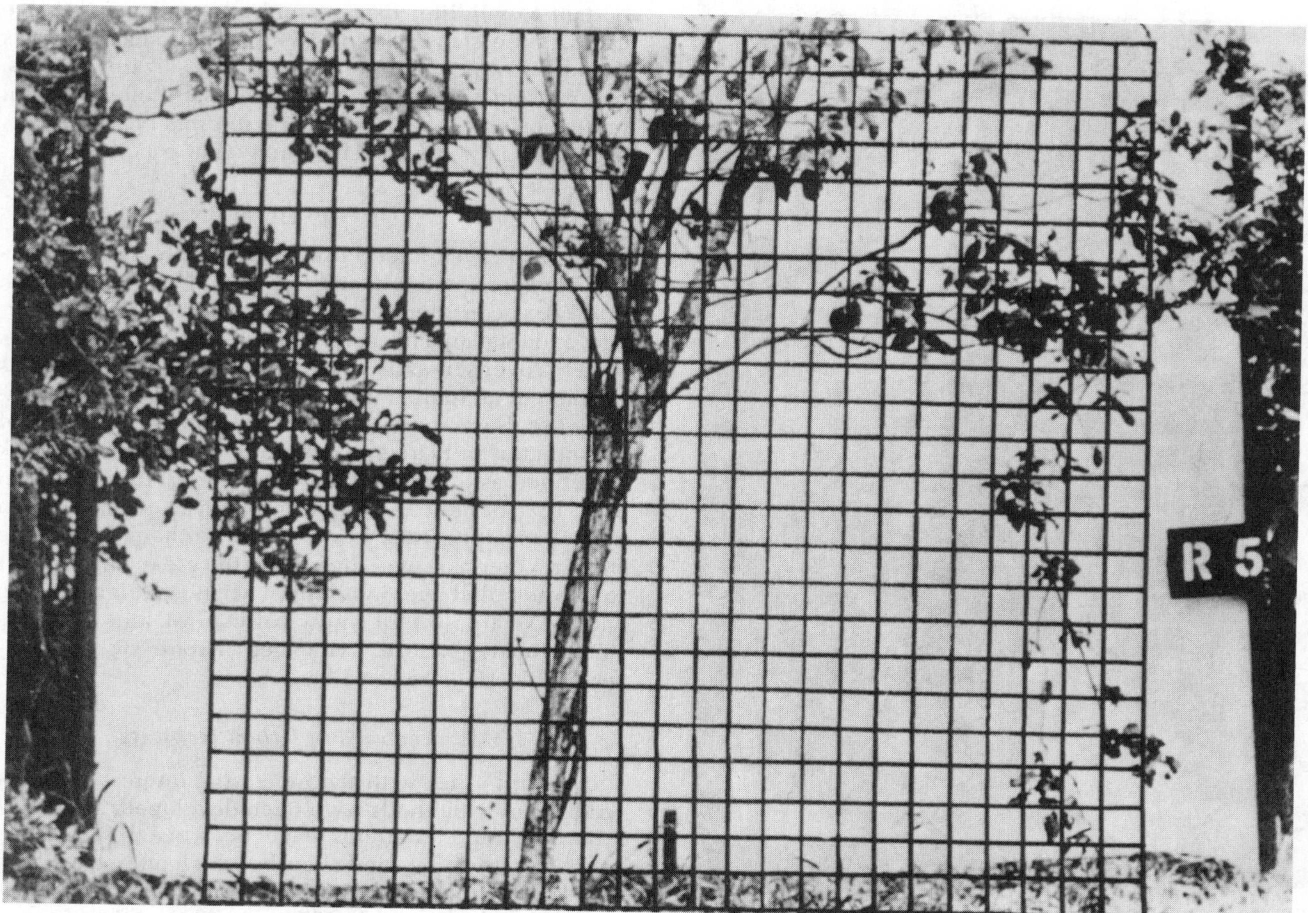

Fig. 19.3. A photograph of vegetation projected on a quadrat matrix on a viewing screen used as an aid in the determination of the degree of obstruction to horizontal vision (Thomson 1975).

Cavities in Live Trees and Snags

In most wooded areas the recognition of cavities in live trees and snags as wildlife cover will be essential for a complete habitat analysis. Although tree cavities are an important type of cover for a variety of bird and mammal species, methods for determining their presence and size are generally described in brief only in separate studies of animal species. Gysel (1961) in a study of tree cavities and ground burrows utilized by a variety of species made a complete tally in 6 forest stands, first from the ground with binoculars and later from various heights in the trees which proved to be necessary to determine the actual number of cavities available. Measurements of the horizontal cross section and the vertical extent of the cavities were necessary to determine their potential value for wildlife (Fig. 19.4). Many cavities, which appeared to be usable from the ground, could not be used because of small interior dimensions or poor drainage. The number of cavities per unit area can be determined by a sampling procedure along transect lines, in plots, or in conjunction with a plotlesss method as described by Prince (1968) for nest cavities of wood ducks and goldeneyes.

Snags as defined by Thomas et al. (1979b) are any completely or partially dead trees still standing, at least 10.1-cm d.b.h. and at least 1.8 m tall. They indicated the value of snags for 39 bird species and 24 mammal species in the Blue Mountains of Washington and Oregon and listed the following types of cavity development or use: (1) excavation in sound wood, (2) excavation in soft or decayed wood, (3) occupation of cavity made by another species, (4) occupation of "natural" cavities created by decay, etc., and (5) occupation of space under loose bark. For uses of cavities the following were listed: (1) as part of a courtship ritual, (2) for nesting and/or raising young, (3) roosts, and (4) overwinter cover including hibernation.

Use of the cavities can be determined by direct visual observations and by the presence of scats, hair, feathers, fleas, odors, nesting materials, food particles, and the amount of wear on the sides of the cavity. In addition, photographs of animals entering or leaving through some cavity entrances can be obtained with a small camera with an automatic shutter release (Gysel and Davis 1956).

Logs

Logs can be utilized as hiding and thermal cover and can provide moist microclimatic conditions for wildlife. In recognition of the structural changes of logs with age,

Fig. 19.4. **A biologist examining a tree cavity. Climbing gear is a rope and saddle. To determine the value and use of this type of cover, it is often necessary to make detailed observations at various heights in trees.**

Maser et al. (1979a) described 5 classes: (1) essentially sound with support points intact and utilized by animals such as snowshoe hares and porcupines; (2) weakened and sagging slightly on support space points with duff and soil building up on the sides and used by snakes and small rodents; (3) bark loosened with interspaces between bark and wood used as hiding and thermal cover and for the moist microclimate by small animals; support points are gone and the log sags; (4) log completely on the ground and may be partially buried with the inside usually soft enough for small mammals to burrow into; (5) logs soft and powdery, partially buried and with long-established burrow systems both within and under them and used primarily by mammals. Where hollow logs occur, the size and location of a hollow area within a log affects the various types of utilization such as escape cover or for rearing of young.

Cliffs and Caves

Cliffs and caves provide ideal cover for some wildlife species and are sometimes an important component of the habitat in some areas. Maser et al. (1979b) indicated that cliffs offer relatively high security, distinctive internal environment, predictable airflow patterns, diversity in plant communities and abrupt, relatively stable edges. The authors recognized 4 types of cliffs important to wildlife: fissures and edges; deep cliff-face caves; loose slab-rock and fissures; and shallow caves used by a variety of raptors, swifts, bats, lizards, snakes, rodents, and cats. Underground caves also offer physical protection and in addition stable internal environments especially important for the survival of bats.

Thermal Cover

Thermal cover, a term used to designate a major function of vegetative cover and recognized by Thomas et al. (1979a), is considered in 3 dimensions—height, coverage, and total area of cover in units of forest stands. This type of cover serves as an aid for ameliorating the effects of ambient air temperature, radiant heat loss, and insulation for deer and elk. For the Blue Mountains of Washington and Oregon, optimum thermal cover for elk is defined as a stand of coniferous trees 12 to 24 ha in area, 12 m or more in height, and with an average crown cover exceeding 70%. Verme (1965), although not using the term thermal cover, described the ideal winter cover for white-tailed deer in northern Michigan for providing the least amount of snow and wind and a stable microclimate—dense, even-aged mature swamp conifers in blocks of 16 to 64 ha.

Measurements in Urban Habitats

In recent times with the increasing interest in urban wildlife, new methods have been developed, and adaptations of older methods have been used to analyze habitats in the cities and suburbs which often have food and cover that is much different from that in wild environments. Thomas et al. (1977) described methods used to study the habitat associations of 10 songbird species in a suburban area in Massachusetts. For deciduous and coniferous tree volumes, crowns were classified as 1 of 5 profile shapes and 1 of 3 plan view shapes using crown height and radii measurements. Shrub volumes were determined by treating each plant or cluster as a rectangular prism. Each house was treated as a rectangle with height to determine volume. Also considered were building densities, traffic flow, number of gardens, fields, woodlots, feeders, nest boxes, dogs, cats, and people. Geis (1974) in his study of the effects of urban development on bird populations also considered details of the structure of buildings, such as type of eaves and lattice work. During a study within the city of Cincinnati, Ohio, Schinner and Cauley (1974) found that raccoons utilized a variety of cultivated foods and garbage and for cover—tree dens, sewers, and culverts. In the city of Detroit, Cauley (1974) observed fox squirrels using seed in bird feeders and foods in gardens and for cover—a chimney, exhaust ductwork for a furnace, and an attic.

DISTRIBUTION OF PLANTS

Plant distribution throughout a community can be very important for wildlife species in regard to the availability of food and cover. It can be measured quantitatively by determining the percentage of plots in which a species occurs expressed as ***frequency***. Mueller-Dombois and Ellenberg (1974) recommended selection of a frequency quadrat large enough to include about 3 to 8 species per observation, and Daubenmire (1968) has proposed that quadrat size should be reduced when more than 1 or 2 species show a frequency of 100%. Cain and Castro (1959) discussed the effects of plot size, number, shape, and distribution on frequency values. Although all factors should be considered, plot size and number appear to be the most important.

While easy to obtain, frequency information from quadrats suffers major disadvantages. Results from different areas can only be compared when the quadrat size and shape are similar, and data are difficult to interpret because frequency confounds the 2 parameters of density and dispersion. Frequency can be made an absolute measure of cover by reducing the quadrat to a point, but it will then only detect the more abundant species.

The most common use of frequency in habitat analyses involves the distribution of food, cover, or some specific wildlife habitat requirement. The distribution of snags in woodpecker habitat, for example, might be expressed quantitatively by determining the percentage of plots in which suitable snags occur. Depending on the species of woodpecker, these plots could be several hectares in size. A much smaller plot size might adequately describe the distribution of a single plant species or of habitat niches suitable for cottontail rabbits.

Braun-Blanquet's (1965) Sociability or Dispersion Rating is an example of a qualitative method for showing how individuals of a species are grouped or how they are distributed in a habitat. The rating is as follows:

1. growing solitary
2. forming clumps or dense groups
3. forming small patches or cushions
4. growing in small colonies or forming larger carpets
5. growing in large, almost pure population stands

Despite widespread acceptance of a theoretical relationship between wildlife populations and plant community diversity (Odum 1971), diversity has only recently been recognized as a measurable parameter of wildlife habitat. Part of the reason, as Thomas et al. (1979a) has pointed out, is that standard ecological diversity indices (see Pielou 1975) ". . . require measurements of species numbers and frequency that are far too detailed and expensive to acquire . . . ." In addition, wildlife management texts (Leopold 1933, Trippensee 1948, Grange 1949, Moen 1973) usually develop the concepts of edge, juxtaposition and, sometimes, niche theory without considering diversity indices. Diversity, if mentioned at all, refers to structural pattern on a horizontal plane.

A designation of diversity has been proposed by biologists who identify the presence of "edge" or the border between 2 vegetative types with a possible increase in animal species and number as compared with interiors of the adjacent, more homogenous communities. Wertz (1965) determined values of soil management areas for wildlife on a comparative basis in part by measuring the linear extent of natural edges that coincided with soil boundaries. Patton (1975), also relating "edge" to diversity, proposed a diversity index (DI) by relating the linear extent of a measured edge (TP) of a habitat to the perimeter of a circle derived from the area (A) of the habitat according to the formula:

$$DI = \frac{TP}{2\sqrt{A \cdot \pi}}$$

Since a circle has the least perimeter for a given area, any irregularity or increase in the edge of an area will be indicated by a figure proportionately greater than 1.0. To make the DI of greater use, the number of types and the acreage can be added to the index. For example, a DI of 1.69 (4) 400 would indicate a 1.69 index for 4 types for a 400 ha area.

Thomas et al. (1977) have proposed a modification of Patton's DI which would recognize the difference between inherent edges, those that are site related, and induced edges, which occur when 2 successional states or conditions meet within a community. This is a significant concept because induced edges can be produced when and where desired by management action. Thus, a DI of 1.69 (4) 400 might be converted to a DI of 1.97 (8) 400 by creating 4 openings, 1 in each of the 4 type communities, with a combined additional edge of 2 km.

Using a line transect method to obtain a quantitative evaluation of edges from aerial photographs, Schuerholz (1974) found that overlays with radial line transects gave a high correlation between edge length and edge points. He considered line transect sampling more suitable than other sampling methods for the quantitative description of edge occurrence on aerial photos as well as in the field.

AMOUNT OF AVAILABLE FOOD

The most commonly used measure of the value of a habitat for the production of food is weight because weight can often be related to established requirements of animal species; however, care must be taken to measure only parts of plants that are actually utilized. Oven-dry weights are ordinarily used to provide a common base for comparative purposes.

Herbage

Clipping and weighing of grasses and forbs from plots is a simple and direct method; however, it is a time-consuming process. In addition, the structure of the vegetation on the plot is completely changed. An adaptation of this method for deer forage is described by Harlow (1977).

Weight estimates such as the method described by Pechanec and Pickford (1937) to increase efficiency can be used. They specified a training period for the observer to relate his estimates by species to weights determined by clipping and also a check on estimates each day during an inventory.

Robel et al. (1970) reported on the relationship of visual obstruction measurements to weight of grassland vegetation. They used a round probe with alternating decimeter units painted light brown and white, and they suggested a viewing distance of 4 meters at a height of 1 meter. The lowest half-decimeter mark visible was recorded. Because this visual obstruction measurement was so strongly correlated with the weight of vegetation, it is possible to use this visual index as a measure of total forage production.

The potential of electronic capacitance instruments for estimating standing herbage has been known for many years and recently new instruments have been described. Neal and Neal (1973) indicated that the new types of electronic circuits and techniques have been proven to be useful under a wide variety of range conditions.

Browse

The clip and weigh method can be used for browse with the same constraint as for herbage. Weight estimates can also be used, but they may be especially difficult in habitats with a variety of species and growth forms.

The twig-count method described by Shafer (1963) can be as accurate as the clip and weigh method and about as fast as the weight estimation method. It is also nondestructive and the results can be analyzed statistically. First the investigator must determine the average portion of the twig that a species actually consumes; and from a sample of twigs clipped to the size of the average portion consumed, a weight per twig per species is determined. Counts of twigs suitable for browsing by species are then made in plots throughout a habitat and the totals are multiplied by the weight per twig to determine weight per plot which can be converted to total weight per unit area.

Another approach to measuring browse weight is suggested by a number of papers reporting relationships between twig diameter, twig length, and weight (Basile and Hutchings 1966, Telfer 1969, Lyon 1970, King 1975). For most browse species it is possible to establish an accurate correlation which will allow prediction of twig weight from nondestructive measurement of either diameter or length.

Fruits and Seeds

Fruits of low-growing herbs, shrubs, and trees can ordinarily be collected easily with a complete count or by collections made within specified areas of a crown surface. For tall trees, counts can be made within open quadrats beneath the crown or in seed traps as described by Gysel (1956) for acorn crops (Fig. 19.5). Consideration must be given to the size and construction of the seed trap, the number and location of traps per tree, and the number of sample trees. Before weighing, fruit should be analyzed for damage, since a major part of the production during some years may have little value as food.

Fig. 19.5. **A funnel-type seed trap made of treated canvas with a 3.2-mm (⅛ inch) iron pipe frame. This was a durable and efficient trap that was used for many years (Gysel 1956). Other types of traps have been made from a variety of materials including paperboard and plastic.**

Buds

Buds are used as food by a variety of wildlife species. Svoboda and Gullion (1974) reported that the buds of quaking aspen and to a lesser extent bigtooth aspen are essential in the winter diet of ruffed grouse in Minnesota, and they described a method for monitoring this food source. From a count (with binoculars) of the number of staminate flower buds on 10 to 20 randomly selected twigs in tree crowns and from a determination of the percentage of living branches bearing staminate buds, a Relative Productivity Index (RPI) is derived by multiplying the 2 values. An average flower bud count of 5 with 80% of the twigs having flower buds would result in an RPI of 400. The authors suggested making the counts annually as soon as possible after leaf fall and using the RPI as a comparative index.

In a study of the spring food habits and feeding behavior of fox squirrels and red squirrels, Reichard (1976) used binoculars and a spotting scope to observe the use of buds and flowers. In the field he was able to determine the numbers and species of buds eaten per unit of time as well as the feeding behavior and interaction between squirrels during feeding. And by measuring the energy values of the parts of buds used as food, he estimated the quantity of buds needed to meet the energy requirements of the squirrels.

FOOD UTILIZATION

Palatability and Preference

Stoddart et al. (1975) stated that raw utilization data have little utility in range management, and they indicated the importance of knowing what level of use plants can withstand and of knowing how animals select among plant species. This leads to a consideration of *palatability* which refers to the attractiveness of plants to animals as forage and *preference* which refers to the selection of plants by animals and may vary by season or year.

Petrides (1975), in a review of food preference ratings, defined a *preferred food species* as one which is proportionally more frequent in the diet of an animal than it is available in the environment, and *food preference* as the extent to which a food is consumed in relation to its availability. His preference rating is derived from the relationship of the availability of a forage species to its occurrence in the diet:

$$p = \frac{d}{a}$$

p = preference rating

d = percentage of each species removed as related to all species removed and consumed

a = percentage of each species available as related to all available species

Species with preference ratings above 1.00 are those sought out as preferred foods, and ratings below 1.00 represent forage species that are neglected or avoided as foods. For example, for a plant species making up only 10% of the available forage (a) but providing 30% of the diet of an animal species (d) would have a preference rating of 3.00. Another plant species comprising 25% of the available forage (a) and making up 7% of the diet (d) would have a preference rating of 0.28.

Herbage

A simple and direct measure of the amount utilized by animals can be obtained by clipping and weighing in plots immediately before and after grazing or on adjacent grazed and ungrazed areas (Beruldsen and Morgan 1934). In order to include the effect of grazing on herbage production during a growing season, vegetation can be clipped from temporarily caged and ungrazed plots at designated periods. Cassady (1941) suggested clipping and weighing a predetermined number of plant units of key forage species before and after short periods of grazing. Ocular estimates of utilization can be made on a plot basis or with individual plants when actual measurements are not considered necessary.

Browse

Direct measures such as clipping and weighing used for the utilization of herbage would generally not be feasible for sampling the utilization of browse over large areas. Instead, methods involving changes in twig length according to measurements before and after browsing have been used (Varner et al. 1954). This method consists of tagging branches on selected browse plants along a transect to measure the percentage of utilization. It is most effective with browse species where the seasonal growth tends to be linear.

The recommended procedure to follow in establishing browse-utilization transects is as follows:

1. Locate the transect to obtain a representative sample of the key area.
2. Establish the transect along a compass course or a line described by bearing and distance to recognizable landmarks or map points.
3. Tag only branches that are available to the game animal under study. In addition to tagging 2 twigs to be measured on each plant, tag or flag each plant in an identical place for ease in relocating.
4. Classify each tagged plant according to its form and age-class.

With shrubs like sagebrush and snowberry on which seasonal growth is not easily measured, the following procedure is used:

1. The shrub is examined to reveal the extent of cropping.
2. The shrub is mentally reconstructed as it would have appeared had it not been cropped.
3. An estimate is made of the percentage twig length utilized (National Academy of Sciences 1962).

Browse utilization may also be estimated by predicting the prebrowsing twig length from diameter measurements (Basile and Hutchings 1966, Telfer 1969, Lyon 1970) or by simply counting the numbers of browsed and unbrowsed twigs (Stickney 1966). Jensen and Scotter (1977) found that by estimating the percentages of browsed twigs or by calculating percentages from twig counts the results gave higher utilization values than by measuring twig lengths. They also indicated that the twig length measurements provided equal sensitivity over a wide range, that the data were more consistent among observers, and that the time required for measurements was about 4 times that required for estimating.

Extensive methods, such as the one described by Dahlberg and Guettinger (1956), consist of a random walking-cruise of as large a portion of the total area of a deer yard as the cruiser feels is desirable. He notes the distribution, composition, density, and availability of the various deer browse plants as well as the evidence of current and previous browsing pressure and the degree of yarding. When he has completed the survey, he makes a report about the present range conditions classified into 3 categories based on the following appraisals:

Poor—range probably not capable of supporting its present number of deer.

Medium—range currently capable of supporting the deer population, but range condition changing.

Good—no immediate browse shortage and no shortage foreseeable for several years.

Next, the present browse utilization is classified in relation to the carrying capacity of the range.

Dasmann (1948) reviewed the literature on methods of browse analysis and evaluated some extensive methods relating to the general distribution, composition, and availability to deer of food plants on winter range and the degree of current utilization by deer. He suggested that a reconnaissance method based on range indicators be used where rapid, extensive utilization checks are wanted.

A disadvantage of extensive methods, in which the surveyor makes estimates only, is that they will be no better than the experience, memory, and judgment of the man making the survey. However, qualified observers will produce faster results from a management standpoint when using these surveys than when using intensive methods.

Exclosures, or fenced plots, are used by biologists to indicate the amount and kind of food utilized by a comparison with an unfenced area. Single plants can be en-

Fig. 19.6. **An exclosure in a deer yard in Michigan. As a result of browsing by deer, plant species composition and density are often greatly different within the exclosure and in the unfenced area outside the exclosure.**

closed, or fenced areas up to 30.5 m square or larger may be required. The height of the fence and size of the mesh of the fencing must be considered in regard to the size and characteristics of the animals to be fenced out. This method, which often provides spectacular results, can be used for demonstrations, as well as for research (Fig. 19.6). Details of the construction of exclosures are described by Krefting (1951) and Cooley (1961).

For a more direct analysis of the consumption of vegetation, especially by the larger ungulates, it is possible to observe tame animals at close range. In a summary of this method, Wallmo and Neff (1970) indicated the following advantages: (1) identification of all foods taken; (2) determination of species and plant parts eaten; (3) determination of the relationship of selections and rejections to availability; (4) opportunity for sampling in conformance with a predesigned plan; (5) collection of large amount of data compared to other methods. Disadvantages are the lack of a satisfactory method for quantifying the intake, variability between animals, and lack of a method for establishing an acceptable degree of similarity between tame and wild animals. Costs for acquiring, rearing, and training the animals must also be considered.

PREDICTION OF FRUIT PRODUCTION

The prediction of fruit production of species of value to wildlife can often be an aid in management and research. This can be done rather easily for species having flowers and fruits that can be observed for varying lengths of time depending on the period of maturation of the fruit. Whether or not flowers are produced is the first indication of the potential for fruit production. However, observations for a prediction must be made during the period following flowering due to various factors affecting germination and the formation and maturation of the fruit. For many species of angiosperms and gymnosperms, this period may be for a few weeks or up to 6 months, but the seeds of pine and the red oak group require 2 years for maturation and a potential prediction period can be considered for that length of time. Gysel (1958) described the results of a study of the prediction of acorn crops by making counts of flowers and immature acorns at different periods with binoculars and by checking the size of the crop of mature acorns with seed traps. He concluded that early prediction can indicate the potential size of the crop; however, the actual size can be determined only by later observations and check counts. Sharp (1958b) used a method for ranking acorn production for a state survey based on numbers of acorns of the terminal 60 cm of thrifty branches in the upper one-third of selected crowns a month or 2 before complete maturation.

EVALUATION OF HABITATS

Measurements, estimations, and descriptions are only a part of the wildlife habitat evaluation job—the determination of the value of a habitat for wildlife and related uses. The weakest link in evaluation is usually the amount of data available to describe the habitat requirements of a species of interest. Even if the amount of available forage and cover are known, there are few wildlife species for which optimal conditions, or even minimum limits, have been described accurately. Thus, the final step in evaluation may be a subjective judgment by the manager or researcher.

Managers or researchers can obtain habitat data by the variety of methods previously described and can utilize many different evaluation procedures, often with the aid of various statistical analyses. A definite interest has been developing for more systematic procedures for collecting and evaluating field data utilizing various rating schemes. These methods can be considered in 2 categories—capability ratings which are based on values of the environment for wildlife and impact evaluations or the effect of environmental modifications on habitats and wildlife.

Capability Ratings

A method described by the U.S. Fish and Wildlife Service (1976b) for the evaluation of land use impacts on wildlife habitats is based on a ranking that utilized a combination of biological judgment and rating criteria. Although the Fish and Wildlife Service's Habitat Evaluation Procedures were designed initially to determine impacts of water resource projects, they also have application to other actions involving land use changes. The FWS method is an adaptation of the techniques described by Hamor (1970) and Daniel and Lamaire (1974). This approach makes the assumption that the value of a unit area of land for wildlife can be estimated and displayed as a habitat quality index from 1 to 10. Moreover it is assumed that the value of a given segment of land for wildlife is proportional to the product of the habitat quality index and the amount of habitat involved. Implicit in the procedures is the assumption that the habitat quality index is proportional to carrying capacity of the habitat. This approach provides a quantitative estimate of the impacts to wildlife of land use changes that alter either the quality or quantity of wildlife habitat. The procedures may, therefore, have application in refuge planning and in assessing other types of wildlife management activities. A general summary of the evaluation procedures is as follows:

Step 1:

The biologist obtains maps, aerial photographs, and other pertinent graphic materials to assist in the preparation of a vegetative cover type map of the study area.

Step 2:

A number of sample sites are chosen within each cover type. At each sample site, the capability of the habitat to meet the requirements of a given wildlife species or group is rated using a scale of 1 to 10. Any number of wildlife species or groups can be considered. The number of sample sites is statistically tested to determine the adequacy of the sample size for attaining chosen accuracy and confidence constraints. If necessary, additional sample sites are selected and evaluated. The average of the sample site values for each cover type represents the "habitat type value" (Fig. 19.7).

Step 3:

The above value of each cover type, when multiplied by the number of acres of that type in the project area, yields the total number of "habitat units" for that type.

Step 4:

Analyze project impacts. This involves decisions concerning probable future habitat conditions that would occur throughout the life of the project. Project impacts are measured from a baseline condition called the "Future Without Project" projection. Essentially this projection considers probable future habitat conditions that would occur should the project not be implemented. The difference between the "with" and "without" project projections (usually to 50 or 100 years) provides a measure of the net project impacts ("habitat units" lost or gained).

Step 5:

Display beneficial and adverse effects. The above losses or gains are then displayed to show differences between project alternatives.

Step 6:

The amount and type of compensation, needed to offset losses, is calculated for each habitat type.

A method for adjusting the habitat type value for interspersion juxtaposition of types is also described. Evaluations are made by a team of biologists and the criteria for making the evaluations are recorded.

As an alternative to the "team scoring" approach to habitat evaluation, the FWS method can be applied by individually scoring discrete habitat characteristics as described by Flood et al. (1977). They developed a method for rating habitat types for groups of animal species based on a multiple scoring method for a variety of habitat characteristics. The habitat value index for each group of species is obtained by calculating a weighted average of individual characteristic values (Fig. 19.8). Included in their handbook are concise but quite complete units describing the food, cover, water, and reproductive requirements for animal groups such as forest game. Special requirements related to season or competition with other animal species are also provided to enable the investigator to score habitat characteristics.

Whitaker et al. (1976) proposed a similar method that uses graphical techniques (line charts) to inventory characteristics of the habitat and to convert measurements of habitat characteristics to an index of habitat quality (habitat type value). The FWS is currently developing a set of "Key Criteria Handbooks" for each Ecoregion (Bailey 1976) that will provide rating criteria for selected wildlife species, utilizing the approach of Whitaker et al. (1976) and Flood et al. (1977). An example of the presentation of these criteria in graphic form for wood ducks based on a variety of literature sources and a formula for the integration of these criteria is given in Figure 19.9.

A method for regional landscape evaluation for wildlife developed by Hawes and Hudson (1976) required the identification of land systems—patterns of landforms with associated vegetation and soil types. Field identification was made from surficial material, vegetation zones, major habitat types, soil development, drainage, and topography. Specifically considered for wildlife were food, cover, and interspersion of major habitat elements. Suitability ratings were then based on the relative ability of each land system to provide habitat requirements of representative species, including the capacity to respond to management techniques and the degree of effort to provide optimum habitat.

In synthesizing the best landscape data and existing procedures into a landscape planning mode, Fabos and Caswell (1977) described the use of special assessment procedures for wildlife habitats based on the natural suitability of the soil for each wildlife type and the degrees to which the overlying land use detracts from that suitability. Habitats are first classified according to SCS capability classes for openland, woodland, and wetland and are assigned a rating according to 1 of 4 soil suitabil-

U.S. FISH AND WILDLIFE SERVICE
DIVISION OF ECOLOGICAL SERVICES

FISH AND WILDLIFE HABITAT FIELD EVALUATION SHEET

Page ________ of ________ pages

PROJECT NAME

DATE

HABITAT CODE	HABITAT TYPE	ALTERNATIVE PLAN

SAMPLE SITE IDENTIFICATION NUMBER	EVALUATION ELEMENTS										LINE TOTAL
TOTAL EVALUATION ELEMENT VALUES											

Grand Total of All Evaluation Elements / Number of Sample Sites = ________ =

HABITAT TYPE UNIT VALUE	MANAGEMENT POTENTIAL UNIT VALUE *(Wildlife habitat only)*

INSTRUCTIONS

In order to evaluate the impact of the plan on the fish and wildlife habitat, it is necessary to know the value of the habitat itself. Here, each habitat type is assigned a value according to its worth for fish or wildlife. These resources are to be evaluated separately, and impacts and compensation needs are also computed separately. To determine this habitat type unit value, the evaluation team will complete a Form No. 3-1101 for each habitat type as follows:

1. Select ten representative species that are dependent to some degree on the habitat type being evaluated and which best express its diversity. These will be used in rating the sample sites. List them across the top of the chart at the left. The reasons for selecting these particular species should be noted and appended to this form. The objective is to consider the full range of animal life in assessing habitat quality. Normally ten species are selected, however the number of species used to evaluate a particular habitat type may vary. If another number is chosen, the rationale for this must be noted on the back of this form. These species, or evaluation elements, may not vary within a habitat type.

2. Select a number of sample sites agreeable to all members of the evaluation team. This number may vary with different habitat types.

3. Rate the capability of the habitat to meet the requirements of each of the evaluation elements on a scale of 1 through 10 at each sample site, the higher rating being given to the more desirable sites. All evaluation elements must be rated at each sample site.

4. The key criteria involved in making the above judgement should be recorded on the back of this form or on a separate sheet and attached.

5. Sum the values in each Evaluation Element column vertically, and write this number at the bottom of the column.

6. Sum each Sample Site line horizontally and sum the Total Evaluation Element Column. Write the totals in the spaces provided. Note that if more than ten evaluation elements are used, a second Form No. 3-1101 must be used and the line totals from one sheet carried forward to the second.

7. Divide the Grand Total of All Evaluation Elements by the Number of Sample Sites. If ten evaluation elements were used, this number is the Habitat Type Unit Value for the habitat type being evaluated, and this number should be written in the box provided at the bottom of the Form No. 3-1101. If more or fewer than ten evaluation elements are used, then the number obtained by this division operation must be prorated, for example: if only five evaluation elements are used, then the quotient must be multiplied by 10/5. If twelve evaluation elements were used, then the quotient must be multiplied by 10/12. This product is the Habitat Type Unit Value in these cases and is the number that should be written down in the box at the bottom of the form.

SIGNATURE OF LEAD PLANNING AGENCY REPRESENTATIVE	LEAD PLANNING AGENCY
SIGNATURE OF STATE REPRESENTATIVE	STATE AGENCY
SIGNATURE OF FWS REPRESENTATIVE	ES FIELD OFFICE

(Additional instructions for wildlife habitat types)

8. Using professional judgement, the evaluation team now estimates the increase in wildlife habitat type unit value possible by proper management of the resources present. This is the Management Potential Unit Value. Write this number at the bottom of the form in the box provided. The sum of this number and the Habitat Type Unit Value must not exceed 100. If they do, the Management Potential Unit Value must be reduced accordingly.

9. For wildlife habitat, an interspersion value may be determined. If this is done, the evaluation continues on Form No. 3-1102.

Fig. 19.7. Habitat field evaluation sheet with instructions for determining Habitat Type Value (U.S. Fish and Wildlife Service 1976b).

ity groups (Mott and Fuller 1967) that are based on the relative value of the soil for the establishment, development, or maintenance of habitats. Habitats are then rated according to 4 land use detractor groups based on the similarity of land use types in terms of: (1) the degree to which they modify the natural productivity of the soil for wildlife, and (2) the likelihood of their reverting or the effort required to revert them to productive habitat. Final steps involve the determination of normalized Resource Value Ratings from the interaction of ratings given for the soil suitability and land use detractor groups.

McCall (1979) devised a home-range scale as a tool for wildlife habitat assessment. The clear plastic scale, which shows approximations of the average home-range areas for selected species, is designed to be used as an overlay on standard 12.63 cm: 1 km (8 in: 1 mile) aerial photos. The habitat assessment is to be made onsite first by determining the species or group of wildlife species to be considered and by identifying key habitat edges for these species. The edge line on the scale is then placed over the edge of key habitat on the photo. By using the scale a determination can be made of the area of each major habitat of similar quality and the gross area within the home range area of the species designated. An estimate is then made of the quality of each vegetative type according to quality rating criteria developed by an interdisciplinary team. A habitat unit value can be determined by multiplying the gross habitat acreage of each type by the assigned quality rating.

The concept of *carrying capacity*, a type of capability rating, is commonly used in wildlife and range management literature. The ideas involved in the concept were used by Hadwen and Palmer (1922) in relation to the number of animals that could graze on an area without injury to the range. However, Paul Errington is considered to have developed the concept (Andrewartha and Birch 1954). In his work on bobwhite quail, Errington (1934) found that overwintering numbers of quail were remarkably constant for the same areas year after year, although they varied from one area to another.

As the concept evolved, many definitions were proposed in the literature; however, Edwards and Fowle (1955) in a review paper stated that most of these definitions were vague and that some were almost meaningless. They proposed a definition in more definite terms—the maximum number of animals of a given species and quality that can, in a given ecosystem, survive through the least favorable conditions occurring within a stated time interval. These authors stressed the importance of recognizing that carrying capacity is not a stable property of a unit of environment, but the result of the ebb and flow of the interaction of organisms and their environment.

In summarizing the important ways in which the term *carrying capacity* is used, Dasmann (1964) presented 3 definitions: (1) the number of animals of a given species that a habitat *does* support, determined by observation over a period of years; (2) the upper limit of population growth above which no further increase can be sustained; and (3) the number of animals that a habitat can maintain in a healthy, vigorous condition. He considered that it is too late to do anything about the loose and conflicting meanings assigned to the term *carrying capacity* and that it is best to use it in a general rather than in a specific sense.

For actually calculating the *carrying capacity* of a range under common use (domestic and wild animals), the assumption is made that the key species makes up approximately the same part of the animals' diet throughout the grazing season (Stoddart et al. 1975). Their method involves: (1) identification of the key species which both animals use; (2) finding the maximum level of use that the key species can tolerate; (3) determining the proportion of the diet that the key species makes up for each animal; (4) determining the grazing capacity for each animal alone; and (5) determining the attained utilization of other species when the key species is fully utilized by either animal.

In assessing a biological basis for the calculation of *carrying capacity*, Moen (1973) stated that there is an obvious need for the knowledge of the requirements of an animal for maintenance and productive purposes—a costly and time-consuming process involving feeding trials and measurement of animal response. He also pointed out that it is necessary to know the quality of resources available to supply the requirements of the animal in terms of units that are biologically meaningful such as the kilocalorie for energy and weight units for protein, with the relationship between the animal and range analyzed through the use of net values.

The concept of *carrying capacity* is complex and simple definitions do not seem to be applicable. Since there appears to be no general agreement about an exact definition of *carrying capacity*, its use may be restricted and the implications confusing. However, the concept is generally considered important for some phases of wildlife management and therefore will be used in some form. Biologists, therefore, should consider the various complexities when using the concept and denote the factors and conditions considered.

Impact Evaluation

In line with current requirements for impact assessments for a great variety of projects affecting habitats, special methods of analysis are being proposed utilizing ranking or rating schemes. Impact analysis is also a part of the FWS evaluations previously described.

A variety of methods have evolved for the general assessment of the environment which generally includes habitats and wildlife. In a summary of these methods Munn (1975) selected 3 general approaches representing a range of options. The Leopold Matrix (Leopold et al. 1971) is a well-known example of a checklist type of analysis which includes 100 project actions along a horizontal axis and 88 environmental characteristics and conditions along the vertical axis. With the Overlay Method (Nehman et al. 1973), a series of transparencies is used to identify and predict as well as to assign relative significance and communicate impacts in a geographical frame. In the Battelle Environmental Evaluation System (Dee et al. 1973), 4 main categories were considered: Ecology, Physical/Chemical, Aesthetics, and Human Interest/Social. For each of these compo-

Evaluation Element: FOREST GAME — Habitat Type: UPLAND HARDWOOD

CHARACTERISTICS	POSSIBLE SCORE	ACTUAL SCORE*
I. Tree size class and canopy closure		I.________

CODE

CANOPY CLOSURE	SIZE CLASS OF 50% OR MORE OF STAND
1=70-100%	S = sawtimber (9" and above dbh)
2=40- 69%	P = poles/small trees (2-8.9"dbh)
3=10- 39%	R = reproduction (less than 2"dbh)
	NO SIZE CLASS MAKES UP 50% OF STAND
	M = mixed

CHARACTERISTICS	POSSIBLE SCORE	ACTUAL SCORE*
A) 2-S	10	
B) 3-S	9	
C) 1-S	8	
D) 3-M	7	
E) 2-M	6	
F) 1-M	5	
G) 1-R; or 2-R; or 3-R	4	
H) 3-P	3	
I) 2-P	2	
J) 1-P	1	
II. Preferred food plant diversity (consider only species in significant amounts)		II.________
A) many species	8-10	
B) some species	4- 7	
C) few species	1- 3	
III. Browse availability (vegetation up to 7')		III.________
A) abundant	8-10	
B) moderately abundant	4- 7	
C) sparse	1- 3	
IV. Vegetative cover (shrubs and herbs)		IV.________
A) covers more than 50% of forest floor	8-10	
B) covers 20-49% of forest floor	4- 7	
C) covers less than 20% of forest floor	1- 3	
V. Openings (less than 10% canopy closure)		V.________
A) many	5	
B) some	3- 4	
C) few	1- 2	
VI. External edge		VI.________
A) meandering/dense vegetation	5	
B) slightly meandering/moderately dense or discontinuous vegetation	3- 4	
C) straight/sparse vegetation	1- 2	
VII. Diversity of non-preferred plants (consider only species in significant amounts)		VII.________
A) many species	5	
B) some species	3- 4	
C) few species	1- 2	

*IF CHARACTERISTIC NOT APPLICABLE, ENTER NA AND DO NOT COUNT IT AS A CHARACTERISTIC USED

(1) Total scores I-IV	(1)____
(2) Number of CHARACTERISTICS used in (1)	(2)____
(3) (1) ÷ (2)	(3)____
(4) Total scores V-VII	(4)____
(5) Number of CHARACTERISTICS used in (4)	(5)____
(6) (4) ÷ (5)	(6)____
(7) (3) + (6)	(7)____
(8) (7) x 2÷3	(8)____ HABITAT UNIT VALUE

Fig. 19.8. A habitat evaluation form used in Missouri with ranges of ratings for habitat characteristics and the procedure for determining a habitat value (Flood et al. 1977).

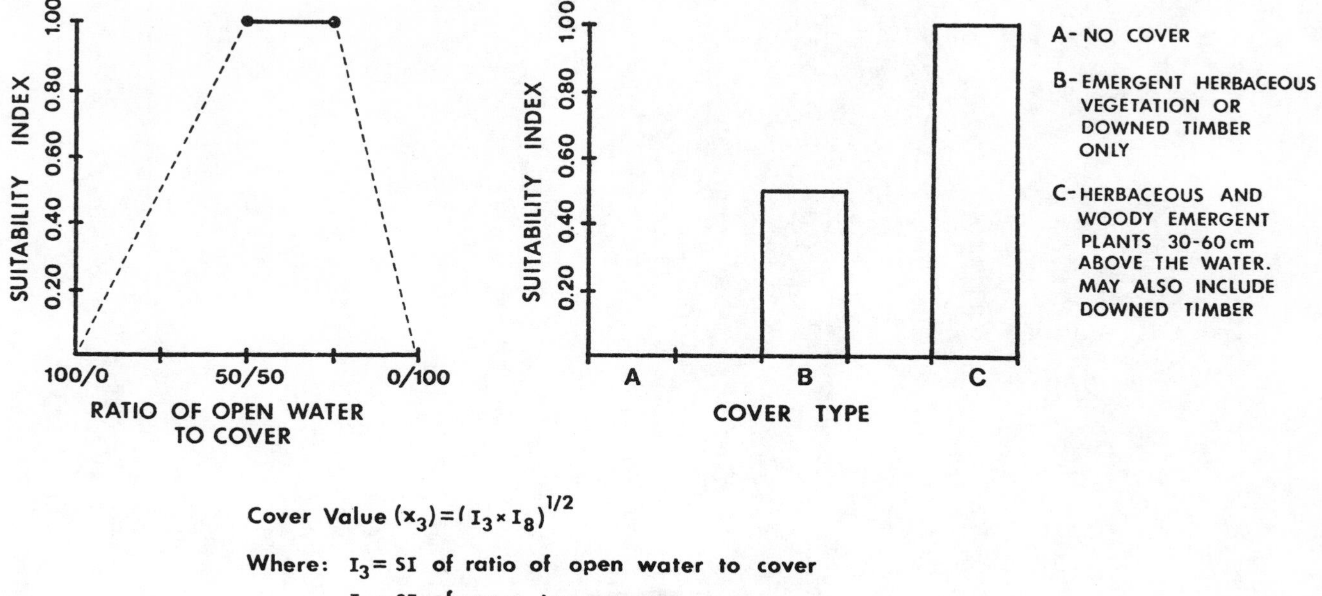

Cover Value $(x_3) = (I_3 \times I_8)^{1/2}$

Where: I_3 = SI of ratio of open water to cover

I_8 = SI of cover type

Fig. 19.9. Suitability indices for 2 types of habitat measurements for wood ducks in cypress-gum swamps and an integration formula. (U.S. Fish and Wildlife Service 1978).

nents, an index of environmental quality is developed on the basis of rankings by groups of individuals. A numerical measure of each impact indicator is obtained by determining the difference between the without-action and with-action states.

Daniel and Lamaire (1974) developed a habitat evaluation system to analyze the effects of water resource developments on wildlife habitats, based on the concepts that all land has some value to wildlife with or without project development and that the effects of a water resource project on wildlife habitat can be expressed numerically in units of habitat value. A rating scheme for characteristics like the one previously described for Missouri was used to determine a habitat value for habitat units lost and project credits due to development. Net units lost with the project were then used to determine the area of mitigation needed.

To identify areas where the risk for adverse impacts to wildlife communities is relatively greatest, Thompson (1977) has developed an "impact risk" technique. Briefly, this method involves the following steps: (1) species of greatest concern are identified and ranked numerically based upon several measures of relative importance and the relative magnitude of impacts using a matrix; (2) a habitat map is prepared, and the habitat categories are rated according to potential suitability for each species; (3) the distributions and seasonal use areas of each species are mapped; (4) the distribution maps and the habitat map are digitized by means of a raster scanner and combined; and (5) each resultant category is weighted according to the numerical ranking of its resident species as well as its suitability as habitat for those species. The composite map which results from this process depicts 5 "impact risk" categories, ranging from 1 (smallest relative impact risk) to 5 (greatest relative impact risk). The highest-ranking of these may be considered "critical" wildlife habitat.

As with other evaluation methods based in part on subjective ratings, this method for identifying critical wildlife habitat can be no better than the quality of the data which goes into the model. According to the author, much of the information necessary to rate wildlife values adequately is lacking. However, the method has been proven to be useful in utility siting studies and can probably have its greatest value for assessments which are relatively site-specific.

Russell (1979) proposes the use of a Wildlife Management Information System, WILDMIS, for estimating the cost for replacement, through wildlife management actions, of wildlife lost as a consequence of proposed projects or land use changes. Three computer programs are used: EIDA, a mapping system; PATREC, a habitat evaluation system; and MANALT, a wildlife management evaluation system. Immediate products of WILDMIS include cost and benefit estimates of wildlife management actions, species population density estimates, and quantitative descriptions of relevant environmental features.

Chapter Twenty

Habitat Improvement Techniques

JIM YOAKUM

Wildlife Management Branch
U.S. Bureau of Land Management
Reno, Nevada

WILLIAM P. DASMANN (Retired)

Wildlife Management Branch
U.S. Forest Service
San Francisco, California

H. REED SANDERSON

Range and Wildlife Habitat Laboratory
U.S. Forest Service
La Grande, Oregon

CHARLES M. NIXON

Section of Wildlife Research
Illinois Natural History Survey
Urbana, Illinois

HEWLETTE S. CRAWFORD

Northeastern Forest Experiment Station
U.S. Forest Service
Orono, Maine

INTRODUCTION

Wildlife management is the science and art of the interrelationships between wild animals, habitats, and man (Giles 1969b:1). Therefore, the maintenance or manipulation of habitats is a major component of the wildlife biologists' responsibilities. This responsibility cannot be slighted because wildlife habitats in North America are undergoing tremendous changes. These changes are primarily accomplished by man for man's needs: grazing rangelands for red meat; logging forests for building materials; or constructing towns, cities, and highways for concentrated human activities. Man's manipulation of the environment for his needs is the most prevalent factor affecting wildlife habitat and, consequently, wildlife populations. Often it is not the *act* of using natural resources, but the *way* man uses these resources that determines the total impact on wildlife.

There are many examples of how the manipulated environment can be beneficial or detrimental to wildlife. For example, logging dense old-growth forests may be disastrous to the spotted owl's nesting and feeding requirements, but could greatly increase preferred forage for elk. Wildlife biologists must recognize the factors that affect wildlife habitat, specifically those not designed or implemented for wildlife, and understand the habitat and animal interrelationships. The wildlife biologist has the responsibility to show how such practices can be modified to increase habitat diversity for the benefit of wildlife and man. These interrelationships are well documented by Thomas et al. (1976) for habitats in the Northwest and Holbrook (1974) for habitats in the South.

Wildlife habitat management is basically concerned with 2 major objectives: (1) to maintain quality habitat as it exists in a natural ecosystem; and (2) to provide quality habitat where it has deteriorated, or where a specific habitat component is lacking such as water, food, or shelter. The following basic principles should be included in planning and implementing habitat manipulation practices:

1. Projects must be justified according to biological needs based on intensive investigation.
2. Proposed practices must be evaluated for their effect on other natural resources and land uses.
3. Projects must be economically practical and should specify if the objective is to maintain, improve, or completely alter the existing habitat character.
4. Improvements must simulate natural conditions. Generally native flora and fauna should be perpetuated.
5. Manipulation projects must be designed to follow natural topographical features as opposed to geometrical squares or strips.
6. Projects must be evaluated at intervals to determine if the objectives have been accomplished.

Aldo Leopold's (1933) list of "axe, plow, cow, and fire" as major habitat management tools has expanded with new understandings and technological advances. All of the land-use tools available to the farmer, forester, and construction engineer have been used to manipulate wildlife habitat. However, all the habitat manipulation techniques cannot be described in 1 chapter; consequently, a guide for selection of projects and ways to "accomplish management goals" is presented. Each method must be judged critically for each site and for the goal to be accomplished.

Many of the methods discussed are from the following major periodicals: (a) *Western Browse Research* published annually by various western state wildlife agencies from 1955 to 1963; (b) *Game Range Restoration Studies* published annually by the Utah State Department of Fish and Game from 1956 to date; and (c) *Range Improvement Notes* published by the USDA Intermountain Forest and Range Experiment Station, Logan, Utah. By far the most important compendium on habitat manipulation is the *Wildlife Habitat Improvement Handbook* (U.S. Forest Service 1969). This handbook is the best available compilation of State, Federal, and private findings regarding food, cover, and water practices for the benefit of wildlife in North America. Consequently, we have incorporated much of the information in this chapter.

The *Wildlife Habitat Management Handbook* (U.S. Forest Service 1971), which has a "field reference" for popular game species (Byrd and Holbrook 1974), is also an excellent forest management guide for modifying silviculture practices to maintain or improve wildlife habitat. Although this handbook was developed for the southeastern United States, much of the information is applicable over a much wider area. Wildlife habitat managers in western North America would also do well to consult Vallentine's (1971) book *Range Development and Improvement*, because there is considerable information that can be used to develop habitat.

Other important sources of information are monographs and symposia on specific wildlife species, including those concerned with nongame species (U.S. Forest Service 1970, D. R. Smith 1975, U.S. Dept. Agric. 1976, U.S. Fish and Wildlife Service 1977b, DeGraff 1978).

This chapter concentrates on methods and techniques of habitat manipulation specifically designed to increase food, water, or cover for wildlife. The primary objectives are to provide the basic principles for the variety of techniques available. By being aware of these various procedures, the wildlife or resource manager has the basic tools to provide food, water, or shelter for wildlife.

FOOD AND COVER PRODUCTION

Here, the goal is to improve habitat by providing food and/or cover for a particular species, or group of species. In general, there are 3 major methods: Propagate "new" plants, release existing plants by destroying "undesirable" competing species, and protect existing habitat from such factors as nonprescribed livestock grazing, fire, or draining.

"Propagation" is the direct planting of desirable seeds or transplants; but it may also include the manipulation of residual cover to produce mixtures of species important to wildlife, such as even-aged forest management. "Release" encompasses such practices as mechanical crushing, controlled burning, and creating openings by mechanical or chemical means to favor increased production of desirable understory species. "Protection" includes preserving those species producing food or cover important for wildlife.

Propagation

Although the art and science of plant propagation is very old, information on propagating wild plants is limited to relatively few species. However, there is considerable information on ornamental plant propagation that can be readily applied. The same scientific rules apply; the challenge is to apply these rules and the art of plant propagation to establish "new" plant species successfully for improved wildlife habitat.

Land reclamation efforts in the 1930's to revegetate wind- and water-eroded land and find suitable plants for windbreaks, waterways, and wildlife cover provide an information source which may require a diligent literature search for information on some plant species. More recent efforts to revegetate drastically disturbed areas as a result of surface mining provide valuable information on both plant propagation and site preparation.

The interested habitat manager would do well to consult further with the following major publications pertaining to the propagation of plants by Koller and Negbi (1961), Plummer et al. (1968), Gill and Healy (1974), U.S. Forest Service (1974), Hartmann and Kester (1975), Czapowskyj (1976), and U.S. Soil Conservation Service (1976).

Sources for nursery stock and seed are listed in such publications as *Source of Planting Stock and Seed of Conservation Plants Used in the Northeast* (Northeast Regional Technical Center 1971), *The Oregon Interagency Guide for Conservation and Forage Plantings* (Oregon Interagency n.d.), and *Provisional Tree and Shrub Seed Zones for the Great Plains* (Cunningham 1975).

The U.S. Soil Conservation Service maintains offices in most counties and is a good source of information for plant species best suited for a particular area. Such publications as *Grasses and Legumes for Soil Conservation in the Pacific Northwest and Great Basin States* (Hafenrichter et al. 1968), *Shrub Plantings for Soil Conservation and Wildlife Cover in the Northeast* (Edminster and May 1951), or *Plants Useful in Upland Wildlife Management* (McAtee 1941) also provide such information. The general rule is to use native trees, shrubs, and vines because they are adapted to the site and offer a better opportunity of surviving. Exotic species generally have poorer initial survival, frequently require more cultural treatment, often grow slowly, and may produce less seed.

The planting of food and cover species for wildlife is often expensive and results are not always predictable. Planting is no easy cure-all. From the standpoint of cost, there is no good substitute for natural regeneration of native species. Where possible, management should aim at maintenance or improvement of existing native species. Where it becomes necessary to introduce or restore species, this may be done by direct seeding or use of transplants (Plummer et al. 1955, Brown and Martinsen 1959, Holmgren and Basile 1959, Hubbard 1964, Plummer et al. 1966).

The most important considerations leading to a successful plantation are: site selection, site preparation, planting depth, and soil moisture. The best results may be expected on sites which are known to have supported the species concerned in the past. A knowledge of plant requirements is essential, including answers to the following questions: Should the soil be coarse or fine textured; should it be well-drained or poorly drained, acid or alkaline? At what depth should seed be planted?

An important cause of plantation failure is the competition for soil moisture given the transplants or seedlings by established vegetation. Whether planting is done on selected spots or over a broad acreage, care must be taken to eliminate or reduce competition by existing herbaceous and woody vegetation. With spot plantings, reduction of competition can be secured through either hand or mechanical scalping. For broad plantations, the best results follow the preparation of the site by regular farming methods. The objective is to plant in a clean, firm seedbed. This may involve plowing or disking as well as the drilling of seed.

TRANSPLANTING

Some native and exotic woody species suitable for habitat improvement can be obtained from commercial nurseries. Some will have to be found growing wild or propagated. Regardless of source, transplants must be kept moist until planted. Planting procedures should follow accepted nursery practices.

Elaborate facilities, although convenient, are not needed to propagate transplants. If a greenhouse is not available, cold frames or a plastic-covered greenhouse can be readily constructed. Milk cartons and coffee cans make convenient containers. However, one should become thoroughly familiar with propagation facilities and techniques before deciding on the course of action.

When a seed source is limited or not available, cuttings, layering, and suckers are appropriate methods for propagating transplants. Grafting also may be a useful means to establish a particularly desirable plant trait for a seed orchard or nursery.

The following discussion provides some general information on plant propagation techniques that could improve existing wildlife cover and/or food. Detailed instructions for these techniques are available from most state agricultural experiment stations and horticultural textbooks such as Hartmann and Kester (1975).

Cuttings are a portion of a leaf, stem, or root that has been removed from the parent plant and placed in a suitable rooting medium to form roots and shoots. Although some species are difficult to propagate by cuttings, other species root readily and only simple facilities are needed to achieve success. Tree species, which generally do not root from cuttings, may be stimulated to form root primordia by girdling the shoot 4 to 8 weeks before cutting (Hare 1977). For those species that root readily, cuttings are an inexpensive, rapid, and simple method of propagating many new plants in a limited space.

The following general factors must be considered when selecting cutting material:

1. Rooting ability varies greatly, even among individual plants. Botanical relationships give a general indication, and the rooting ability of some wild plants may be predetermined by reviewing the literature on related cultural species.

2. Stems with low-nitrogen and high-carbohydrate content are firm and stiff, and break with a snap, which can be confused with firmness due to tissue maturity. Succulent, rapidly growing plants should be avoided. Starch content, an indicator of nitrogen-carbohydrate ratio, can be determined by the iodine test: Immerse the ends of freshly cut stems in 0.2% iodine solution (potassium iodide) for 1 minute. The darkest stained cuttings have the highest starch content and are best suited for propagating. It may be desirable to fertilize selected wild stock plants to improve the rooting success of cuttings.

3. Usually cuttings taken from young plants root more readily than cuttings taken from older plants. In some cases, juvenile growth can be induced in mature plants (Hartmann and Kester 1975).

There are also some specific factors that should be considered, such as lateral versus terminal shoots: lateral shoots may produce horizontal spreading plants; terminal shoots may produce erect plants. Other factors are flowering versus vegetative shoots, cuttings from different parts of the shoot, or cuttings that retain part of the old wood, as well as the best time of the year to take cuttings from specific plant species. Because plant species respond differently to these specific factors, no generalized statements can be made to guide rooting success. Specific data on individual species must be obtained from the literature or through experience.

Layering stimulates root development on a stem while it is still attached to the parent plant. Basically, layering consists of covering a portion of a plant stem with a suitable rooting medium until it develops sufficient root mass. The disadvantages of layering are that it requires considerable hand labor, and the layered plants need individual attention. The advantages to the layering technique are that it can be used by an individual with little plant propagation experience and that larger plants can sometimes be produced in a shorter time than starting with cuttings.

Suckers are shoots produced from adventitious root buds and should not be confused with watersprouts that are produced from latent buds on the trunk or main branches of established plants. Suckers are usually removed in the dormant season by digging down and cutting the shoots from the parent plant. In cases where no roots are formed, suckers can be treated the same as cuttings.

Grafting is a specialized propagation technique of joining parts of plants together so they unite and continue to grow as 1 plant. Although grafting has only limited application for habitat improvement, it may be the best method to obtain transplants of species that do not readily reproduce by other means. Grafting may also be used to establish a more convenient parent stock with desirable fruiting or growth characteristics for later vegetative or seed production. Grafting can also be used to obtain desirable fruiting qualities on root stocks that are more tolerant of unfavorable soil conditions.

Regardless of the grafting method used, the following requirements must be met:

1. Scion (upper portion of the graft that develops stems or branches) and stock (lower portion of the graft that develops the root system) must be compatible. Generally only closely related plants are capable of uniting.

2. Cambial region of the 2 plant parts must be in intimate contact.

3. Stock and scion must be in the proper physiological stage. Depending on the grafting method, stock may be either active or dormant, but the scion must be dormant.

4. All cut surfaces must be covered with grafting wax to prevent drying.

5. Grafted plants must be given proper care. Shoots from below the graft must be removed to stimulate the scion growth. Also, shoots from the scion may need extra support to prevent breakage.

Smith (1973) recommended that clones of crab apples that produce large annual seed crops be located and protected as a source of scion wood for grafting on young, vigorous trees 7.6–10.2-cm dbh.

DIRECT SEEDING

The establishment and improvement of interspersed forage and cover species is a wildlife habitat improvement measure of broad application (Sampson et al. 1951, Plummer et al. 1955, Edmundson and Cornelius 1961). Frequently there are opportunities for forage or cover improvement by coordinating wildlife needs with other resource activities. It is important that such opportunities be recognized and used when available.

Some land management activities which offer opportunities to establish forage or cover at low costs are forestry (such as thinning, harvest, and postharvest treatments), utility transmission corridors, soil stabilization projects (such as after fires, road and ski-slope construction, and surface mining), range improvements (such as reseeding and brush control), and any other project that modifies the vegetative cover. It is often possible to choose species best suited for wildlife habitat requirements.

Coordination of this kind is an economical way to improve wildlife food and cover.

Sharecropping agreements with local farmers offer an opportunity to maintain unharvested grains for wildlife food and cover on lands in public ownership. In Illinois, sharecrop farmers use a crop rotation of corn or corn and soybeans, which may or may not be followed by small grain (wheat or oats); then 1–2 years of legumes and volunteer forbs. Farmers are not allowed to use herbicides or insecticides or to fall plow under these sharecropping agreements. Sharecropping is also a more economical and efficient method of maintaining unharvested croplands than developing food patches for wildlife. In most cases, it has been amply demonstrated that small plots (less than 2 ha) of unharvested grain are not effective in increasing the production of game species. Further, development costs for a grain planting program have risen to such high levels that their use cannot be justified on the basis of the amount of game harvested (Ellis et al. 1969).

Food patches are certainly no substitute for management programs based on a thorough knowledge of wildlife ecology and the culture of native vègetation.

Wildlife management is, after all, applied ecology. To be cost effective it must be based on manipulation of natural successions. Cropping and fallowing lands, prescribed burning, and timber sales are all techniques designed to manipulate natural succession. While food plots have been used for many years in the East (Shomon et al. 1966), their effects on wildlife have not been well documented. Food plots should be only used in areas where sharecropping or burning is not feasible.

Seed Collection and Treatment

If seeds of native plants are not available commercially, it will be necessary to collect them, which requires specific information on time of seed ripeness and the proper method of handling, storing, and treating seed before planting. Such information is available in the following publications: *Collecting and Handling of Seeds of Wild Plants* (Mirov and Kraebel 1939) and *Seeds of Woody Plants in the United States* (U.S. Forest Service 1974). Specific information is occasionally available from regional botanical gardens such as Santa Barbara Botanical Gardens which specializes in native California plants (Emery 1964).

Many plant characteristics are genetic, such as growth form, seed production, and palatability. Therefore seed collections should be confined to plants that display characteristics desirable for propagation.

Seedbed Preparation

The first step ordinarily will be to get rid of woody vegetation by crushing and burning or other disposal. For some species, it is necessary to have a seedbed of exposed mineral soil for the seed to germinate and grow. Others do best on duff or litter. The type of equipment needed for seedbed preparation will vary with species to be planted, site and cover conditions. If domestic livestock are in the area, they will need to be fenced from the reseeded area until it is well established.

Fertilization

It is advisable to secure a soil test as a basis for deciding about the need for fertilizer. The County Agent can assist in getting the soil test, interpreting the results, and recommending the time of application.

Williams (1972) attempted to show how commercial fertilizers may be used to increase wildlife production by improving forage production and the nutritional quality of forage available to wild animals. The response to fertilizers varies greatly among plant species; however, nitrogen fertilizers have been used successfully to increase shrub and forb dry-matter production. Nitrogen fertilizers also have increased crude protein in plants. Sulphur and phosphorus applications have produced the best results for increasing legumes and other plants possessing nitrogen-fixing nodules on their roots. One of Williams' major summary points is that plants growing on soils of low fertility or soils having an improper nutrient balance have responded more to fertilizer applications than plants growing on fertile soils or soils having proper nutrient balance.

Barrett (1979), working on pronghorn winter range in Alberta, concluded that nitrogen and phosphorus fertilization on sagebrush-grassland steppes: (1) increased total forage production and hence protein production, and (2) that antelope use showed a definite preference for treated areas.

Equipment

There are several kinds of equipment commonly used for direct seeding. This equipment is described in the *Range Seeding Equipment Handbook* (U.S. Forest Service 1965) and information on new developments is generally available from the U.S. Forest Service Missoula Equipment Development Center (Fort Missoula, Missoula, Montana 59801). The commonly used equipment is briefly discussed below.

- Deep-furrow Drill

The deep-furrow drill provides a furrow 5.1–7.6 cm deep, spaced at 35.6-cm intervals. Wider spacing is achieved by removing drops. The 71-cm spacing is regarded the most practical for planting browse. Spacers in the seedbox can be quickly provided to permit seeding of different species in alternate rows. The drill is mounted on rubber tires and can be pulled by a light tractor or jeep. It was not designed for seeding rough rangelands. On more level lands, the drill does an excellent job of seeding as well as leaving a good seedbed for emergence. The machine can be hauled on a 1364-kg truck. Maneuvering ability of the drill limits its use. It is not a practical tool for seeding small openings.

- Hansen Browse Seeder

The Hansen browse seeder can be equipped with either 40.6- or 81-cm scalping wings. Whether equipped with 1 or 2 scalpers, the seeder can be pulled by a jeep or small tractor (either with wheels or tracks). The equipment is small enough to operate in small spaces as well as larger areas. Arrangements can be made to pull 2 drills at a time for large-scale seeding operations (Fig. 20.1). Successful plantings have been effectively made with a variety of shrubs, broadleaf herbs, and grasses (Plummer et al. 1968).

- Cutout Disk

The horse-drawn cutout disk used a decade ago has been satisfactorily used in rocky and partially brushy areas. This small disk pits the ground with many small impressions or gouges. The seed is broadcast either ahead of the disk or behind it. The gouges or impressions aid in retaining moisture in the soil. The disk is light in weight, compact, and rugged. It can be pulled by a single horse or by a team.

- Seed Dribbler

Observations have indicated that soils disturbed by crawler tractors are excellent seedbeds for browse, forb, and grass species. Some of the best stands are often obtained in these tracks. Because of the availability and

Fig. 20.1. **Two Hansen browse seed drills hooked on a tandematic bar behind a tractor. The purpose of this arrangement was to drill over 1020 ha burned by wildfire on critical deer ranges.** (U.S. Bureau of Land Management photo by Jim Yoakum.)

high cost of native browse, forb, and grass seed, it is important that a cost-efficient method be used in seedings. Consequently, the seed dribbler was constructed. This attachment dribbles seed onto the track-pad just as it breaks over the front idler. The seed drops off the pad and is imbedded in a compacted seedbed.

Seed dribblers are mounted on the deck of a D-8 or similar size tractor. The seed-drop mechanism has a direct drive from a rubber-tired wheel riding on the tracks of the tractor. The seeders may be mounted as a pair, one on each side of the tractor, and are adaptable to various types of seed. The hopper holds enough seed for approximately 1.5 hours of operation. With some modifications, it could be used to broadcast in front of plows or pipe harrows.

• Rotaseeder

The rotaseeder, a 1.78-m rototiller equipped with special slot cutting blades and a seed drill, has been used to seed ditch banks in the Midwest (Fig. 20.2). The blades cut narrow grooves in existing sods and when used with a chemical defoliant, can be used to seed areas subject to erosion.

Fig. 20.2. **The rotaseeder features a 1.78-m series of blades that cut grooves and allow seed placement in established sods.** (Illinois Department of Conservation photo by Larry M. David.)

• Broadcast Seeding

Seed can be broadcast by aerial, ground, or hand equipment. Aerial broadcasting is particularly useful on extensive areas following wildfires, on terrain too irregular, rocky, or steep for drills, or on areas covered with slash from tree or brush removal programs (including logging). Cyclone seeders can also be attached to about any type of ground equipment: pickup trucks, jeeps, all-terrain-vehicles, or crawler tractors. Hand broadcasting is also an effective method of dispersing seed on small areas or selected sites. Excellent results have been obtained by seeding up to 32.4-ha areas with a 5-man crew using hand operated cyclone seeders. Two days were required to seed such areas with 10.7–13.4 kg of seed per ha. Many species of seed require covering after broadcasting by mechanical procedures such as harrowing, cabling, or chaining. However other species do not require covering and need only be seeded into the ashes after prescribed burning (Crawford and Bjugstad 1967).

- Seed Spots

Shrub seeds, such as bitterbrush, can be planted either by hand, by a modified corn planter, or by a "Schussler"[1] planter in areas 0.6–0.9 m in diameter that have been cleared and 1.27–2.5 cm of topsoil has been scraped away. Bitterbrush seed spots are particularly applicable following fire on terrain where large equipment cannot be used (Sanderson and Hubbard 1961).

- Seed Mixtures

On most lands, the use of "mixtures" of 2 or more adapted species is advisable. Crawford and Bjugstad (1967) successfully used grass and legume mixtures on mesic sites. In Utah, Plummer et al. (1968) recommended seed "mixtures" to include a minimum of 6 species each of grasses, forbs, and shrubs. Such mixtures are consistent with natural vegetative communities which most often have an endemic mixture of a variety of grasses, forbs, and shrubs. Soil and moisture conditions often change so markedly within short distances that there may be great variation in the success and productivity of a single species within a seeded area. If a species does poorly because of an unfavorable site condition, or is killed by rodents, insects, disease, or frost, one or more of the others may take its place. Another advantage of "mixtures" is that some species develop stands quickly and supply forage while slower developing species become established. "Mixtures" also produce vegetation with a more varied and often higher food value. The adaptation and relative values of 56 most promising species for seeding western rangelands with precipitation above 20.4 cm are shown in Table 20.1.

If adapted legumes are available, their use with grasses usually increases total production and improves the nutritive value of the forage for many species of wildlife. They also help increase soil nitrogen through the action of associated nodule bacteria which converts free nitrogen from the air into available soil nitrogen.

The introduction of dryland Nomad variety alfalfa was one of the most successful techniques accomplished on antelope ranges in southeastern Oregon (Kindschy 1974). In excess of 22,700 ha involving 36 separate seedings have been planted to date. The alfalfa was generally aerially seeded onto plowed sagebrush ranges following drilling to adapted grasses and shrubs. Recent analysis of the seedings disclosed that the majority have maintained alfalfa composition at a level of 10% of the vegetation present over a 6-year or longer period. The seedings have increased the forb composition from 2% in untreated areas to 7% in seeded areas. During August 1976 antelope census, more antelope does with fawns were observed in grass and forb seedings than on adjacent, shrub-dominated rangelands (Yoakum 1978).

Browse species can be mixed with grass and forb seeds and drilled or broadcasted concurrently. Over 30,375 ha of rangelands in Utah alone have been planted by such methods. On one 1,620 ha project in central Utah, there was a 7-fold increase in forage production 3 years after treatment. Forage increased from about 89 kg per ha to an average of nearly 623.5 kg per ha. Deer use averaged 1.6 deer-days per ha on the adjacent untreated lands and 34 deer-days of use per ha on the seeded areas 3 years after treatment—about a 20-fold increase. It was noted that deer were attracted to the seeded areas from adjacent untreated ranges. While the degree of deer use apparently had not damaged the forage plants at the time of inspection, such heavy use might prove deleterious if continued over many years. Average deer use of seeded range over the state of Utah is much less than reported here, but it appears possible to increase the carrying capacity on many thousand hectares of critical deer winter range by seeding and planting (Plummer et al. 1966).

Forage on seeded areas is generally available earlier in the growing season and is more palatable than on untreated ranges. An adequate supply of green forage on seeded areas during the critical early spring period, when fetuses are developing rapidly in pregnant does, is of special value. The improved forage reduces winter and early spring mortality and increases fawn survival. Seeded ranges have been especially helpful in keeping deer out of cultivated fields. Experience and knowledge gained from seeding projects to date indicate that the wildlife range manager obtains greatly increased livestock grazing capacities and watershed values—both of which greatly add to multiple-use values.

On reclaimed surface mining or strip mining areas, Riley (1963) successfully established 57 species of trees, grasses, legumes, and shrubs that enhance wildlife habitat. He tested these species on different soil types having critical site factors such as extreme acidity, high total salts, and compacted surface soil. Successful seedings grew on soils having a range of pH values from 3.4 to 7.2; most of the sites exhibited acid to extremely acid soil reaction. Many species of shrubs, grasses, and legumes displayed a tolerance to very acid soils, high concentrations of trace elements, sulfates, and soluble salts.

For reclaimed areas on which forest plantations presently grow, the technique of seeding strips of grass and legume through the plantations has proven highly beneficial to wildlife. Older deciduous forests often consist of hardwoods with a high percentage of black locust, often in a decadent condition. For such areas, a bulldozer can create seeding strips. Recommended minimum widths are no less than 15.2 m and a maximum of 30.5 m. On strips less than 15.2 m wide, black locust usually invades and closes the area within 5 years, often making treatment of such areas uneconomical. Seeded strips

[1]Bitterbrush seed planter designed by Mr. Howard Schussler and sold by Crookham Seed Company, Caldwell, Idaho.

Table 20.1. Adaptation and recommended use[1] of species for seeding in various precipitation and vegetation zones on lowland and mountain areas in the Intermountain region (Plummer et al. 1955).

GRASSES

Species	Lowlands				Mountain lands		
	Below 20.3 cm precipitation	20.3–30.5 cm precipitation	Above 12 inches precipitation	Salty soils	Mountain brush[2]	Aspen[3]	Subalpine
Sand dropseed	C	C	.....	.....	.....	.....	.....
Bottlebrush squirreltail	C	C	.....	.....	.....	.....	.....
Indian ricegrass	C	C	C	.....	C	.....	.....
Russian wildrye	C	B	B	B	C	.....	.....
Crested wheatgrass (Standard)	B	A	A	.....	B	.....	.....
Crested wheatgrass (Fairway)	B	A	A	.....	A	C	.....
Bulbous bluegrass	.....	X	X	.....	X	.....	.....
Bluebunch wheatgrass	.....	B	B	.....	B	C	.....
Beardless wheatgrass	.....	B	B	.....	B	C	.....
Pubescent wheatgrass	.....	C[4]	A	.....	A	B	.....
Intermediate wheatgrass	.....	C[4]	A	.....	A	B	.....
Western wheatgrass	.....	C[4]	B	.....	C	C	.....
Beardless wildrye	.....	C[4]	B	C	C	C	.....
Big bluegrass	.....	C[4]	C	.....	C	.....	.....
Mountain rye	.....	.....	X	.....	X	.....	.....
Great Basin wildrye	.....	.....	B	.....	B	C	.....
Tall wheatgrass	.....	.....	B	A	B	C	.....
Tall fescue	.....	.....	.....	B[4]	.....	C	.....
Bulbous barley	.....	.....	.....	.....	B	C	.....
Blue wildrye	.....	.....	.....	.....	B	C	.....
Bearded wheatgrass	.....	.....	.....	.....	B	B	.....
Smooth brome (southern strain)	.....	.....	C[4]	.....	A	A	B
Smooth brome (northern strain)	.....	.....	.....	.....	C	A	A
Slender wheatgrass	.....	.....	.....	.....	B	B	C.
Mountain brome	.....	.....	.....	.....	B	B	C
Meadow brome	.....	.....	.....	.....	B	B	B
Kentucky bluegrass	.....	.....	.....	.....	X	X	X
Tall Oatgrass	.....	.....	.....	.....	A	A	A
Orchardgrass	.....	.....	.....	.....	B	A	C
Reed canarygrass	.....	.....	.....	.....	B[4]	B	B[4]
Timothy	.....	.....	.....	.....	B[4]	A	B
Meadow foxtail	.....	.....	.....	.....	B[4]	A	B
Sheep fescue (Sulcata)	.....	.....	.....	.....	.....	C	C
Red fescue (sod-forming)	.....	.....	.....	.....	.....	C	C
Subalpine brome	.....	.....	.....	.....	.....	.....	B
Winter rye	.....	X	X	.....	X	.....	.....

Table 20.1. Continued.

Species	Lowlands				Mountain lands		
	Below 20.3 cm precipitation	20.3–30.5 cm precipitation	Above 12 inches precipitation	Salty soils	Mountain brush[2]	Aspen[3]	Subalpine
LEGUMES							
Alfalfa	....	C[4]	B	....	B	C	....
Sicklepod milkvetch	....	C[4]	B	....	B	C	....
Chickpea milkvetch	....	C[4]	B	....	B	B	C
Yellow sweetclover	....	....	X[4]	B[4]	X	C	....
Strawberry clover	....	....	....	X[4]	....	....	....
Birdsfoot trefoil	....	....	....	....	C	C	....
Mountain lupine	....	....	....	....	....	C	B
Alsike clover	....	....	....	....	....	C[4]	C[4]
OTHER BROADLEAF HERBS							
Summercypress	....	....	....	X	....	....	....
Fivehook bassia	....	....	....	X	....	....	....
Palmer penstemon	....	X	X	....	X	....	....
Wasatch penstemon	....	....	....	....	X	X	....
Showy goldeneye	....	....	....	....	X	X	X
Common cowparsnip	....	....	....	....	C	C	C
Sweetanise	....	....	....	....	C[4]	C	C
SHRUBS							
Winterfat	C	C	C	....	C	....	....
Fourwing saltbush	C[4]	C	C	....	C	....	....
Antelope bitterbrush	....	C	C	....	C	C	....
Oldman wormwood	....	....	X	....	X	X	....
Blueberry elder	....	....	X	....	C	C	....

[1]A—Proved to be productive and widely adapted for seeding throughout the zone or type.

B—Valuable over much of the zone or type, but value or adaptation either more restricted or not as well determined as species designated A.

C—Value or adaptation more restricted than those species designated B, but useful in some situations.

X—Recommended for special uses or conditions, usually as pure stands.

[2]Applicable also for seeding openings in the ponderosa pine zone.

[3]Applicable also for seeding openings in Douglas-fir and spruce timber.

[4]Adapted only to better than average sites in the zone or type.

through hardwood plantations, without black locust, have remained open for 6 years with practically no invasion by tree species. Large, nonforested areas supporting grasses and legumes can be improved for wildlife by planting strips not over 6.1 m wide with shrub species. Such woody plants, along with selected tree species, may be used around the perimeter of croplands, on slopes of strip-mine lands, or in abandoned fields.

The use of native grasses should also be considered in those areas where they will grow and where controlled burning or haying (in late summer) can be used to rejuvenate old sods annually or at 3- to 5-year intervals (burning). Use of such species as little bluestem on dry sites, Indian and switchgrass on sites with intermediate moisture, and big bluestem on moist sites offers a means of creating forage and nest cover at a reduced cost of maintenance. These grasses should be sown in early summer on ground disked just before seeding to remove weed competition. Seeding rates of 2.7 to 3.6 kg/ha have proven successful. For the first few years, mowing may be necessary to control competition until the grasses achieve dominance on the site.

TEN BASIC PRINCIPLES FOR SUCCESSFUL PLANTINGS[2]

There are 10 fundamental principles for making ranges more productive by planting of browse, forbs, and grass. They are based on over 25 years of research and field-tested procedures developed at the Intermountain Forest and Range Experiment Station (Plummer et al. 1968). Recommendations usually cover broad areas and need to be modified to fit local conditions, availability of seeds, and facilities for doing the work. Such modifications will usually be satisfactory if they conform to the following principles:

1. *Reduce competition.*—Seedlings and suppressed plants must have moisture to develop. Established plants that use all or most of the available moisture must be greatly reduced before seedlings or transplants can develop into satisfactory wildlife cover or food.

2. *Determine when and where planting will improve the range.*—Where good forage plants are present, reduction of competition may be all that is necessary for the desired restoration. On western ranges, usually 1 shrub, on the average, to each 9.3 sq. m and 1 herb to each 0.93 sq. m is an approximate minimum. Sometimes, there is need to round out an existing forage resource by introduction of a scarce element. For example, there may be ample browse on a big game winter range, but a lack of grasses and broadleaf herbs. Departure of deer and elk from their native ranges to cultivated fields in late winter and early springtime in search of succulent plants is a particular problem in some states. A good balance of browse and herbaceous plants on the winter range may help to reduce such depredation. The establishment of early spring-growing herbaceous species, such as crested wheatgrass, Russian wildrye, intermediate wheatgrass, a range-type alfalfa, small burnet, and balsamroot can provide desirable succulent herbs on intermountain big game winter ranges.

3. *Annual precipitation should be adequate.*—Ordinarily, artificial seeding should not be undertaken on sites where precipitation is less than 25.4 cm. The amount of precipitation along with occurrence of indicator species are the important guides in selection of species to be used. Where precipitation is near the lower limits, species which may be successfully seeded are limited in the West to such plants as crested wheatgrass, Russian wildrye, and range alfalfa. As precipitation increases, the number of species that may be successfully established also increase.

4. *Terrain and soil should be suitable to support the desired forage species and to permit restoration treatments.*—Shallow, infertile soils naturally produce little forage and may not justify restoration. On such sites, using native species will usually result in better success at less cost than attempts to use exotic species. While some improvement is usually possible on unfavorable sites, similar effort on favorable tracts will usually be more effective and more productive. With improvement of forage on good sites, game animals may shift use to the better forage, and as a result, more severe sites will improve naturally. There will be instances, of course, where poor sites may require restoration treatment solely to fill a critical need such as control of soil erosion.

5. *Plant adapted species and strains.*—Returns on the investment for restoration and seeding depend on a lasting improvement. It is essential that the planted species be able to maintain themselves and, preferably, to spread by natural means. Sometimes it may be wise to include rapidly developing short-lived species to meet a planned objective, such as a nurse crop or a quick forage supply. Such species as mountain rye, small burnet, short-lived perennials, and yellow sweetclover, a biennial, are useful for this purpose. A low seeding rate of annual winter rye may achieve the same goal. Planting rates of transient species in the mix should not be so great as to offer serious competition to more desirable and persistent species. Usually 2.7–4.4 kg per ha is adequate for the short-lived perennials and sweetclover, and 13.4 kg of winter rye per ha is adequate. Slower developing but more persistent plants such as antelope bitterbrush, fourwing saltbush, balsamroot, crested wheatgrass, and bluebunch wheatgrass, will gradually replace the short-lived plants. Where there is no need for the rapid developing species, then only long-lived perennials should be used.

It is particularly important that adapted sources or strains be used. Ordinarily seed from plants growing on greatly different soils, or in different climatic zones, are much less preferable than seed from sites similar to that planned for treatment. For example, it has been observed that antelope bitterbrush seed collected from acid granitic soils may develop chlorotic plants on basic soils originating from limestone. Fourwing saltbush collected in the blackbrush type in southwestern Utah has failed to survive well in the higher elevation mountain brush type. Similarly, Indian ricegrass from salt desert shrub types has failed to survive on mountain brush and higher elevation juniper-pinyon range. It appears that sources from colder areas with greater precipitation can survive better in warmer and drier areas than the reverse. There may be exceptions, but these are rare.

6. *Plant mixtures, especially on variable sites.*—A major reason for using mixtures is to put different species in the site conditions where they are best suited. Site characteristics can change often and dramatically within a limited area. Another advantage of mixtures is that they provide a variety of forage. The total production of a well-chosen mixture is considerably greater than of single species stands. Where possible, seeds of

---

[2]Editor's Note: Although this section deals primarily with semiarid range, it has been included because the principles have wide utility, because more millions of hectares of land for which these principles apply are manipulated for wildlife than any other land type, and because of the need for making this information available to wildlifers and land managers in the U.S. and abroad where semiarid land management is critical.

slower growing shrubs and herbs should make up the initial seeding and fast growing, aggressive species introduced later. Thus, grasses drilled in alternate rows with shrubs permits better establishment of the slower establishing shrubs than when both seeds are planted in the same rows. Also, broadleaf herbs generally establish better if they can be similarly separated from the grass. Some species are better suited to specific sites, such as north versus south slopes or shady versus open areas. Therefore, it may be best to confine them to such sites. Of course, the practicability of separating species for localized conditions depends on the size of the area. Often it is not practical to segregate sites, so mixtures are used.

7. *Use sufficient seed to insure a stand.*—One reason to avoid heavy seeding is the unnecessary cost entailed. Stands are usually not materially improved by excessive seeding. Usually, 7.1–17.8 kg per ha of total mixture is adequate, depending on the sites involved and the method being used. Ordinarily, when drilling, 7.1–8.9 kg per ha are advised; in broadcasting 13.4–17.8 kg are recommended. With proper planting, 2.7–7.1 kg of shrub seed per ha is usually sufficient. Proper planting depths and spacing of seed by drilling is often far more effective than heavy broadcast seeding. However, there are many sites where, because of terrain and obstacles, broadcasting must be used in spite of its being more wasteful.

8. *Proper planting and coverage of seed is essential.*—Provision for some seed coverage must be made. Seeds placed under 0.64–1.9 cm of soil are usually satisfactorily covered. A few species with large seeds may emerge from depths deeper than 2.54 cm, but most are suppressed by excessive planting depths. Seeds which are very small should be sown no more than 0.64 cm deep. Establishment of seedlings from uncovered seed, as from broadcasting, requires unusual moisture conditions for successful establishment.

9. *Seed in late fall and early winter but transplant in early spring.*—Seeding in October, November, December, and even January is essential for those that need to lie over winter to break dormancy. With a few species, notably alfalfa, fourwing saltbush, and winterfat, spring planting is superior to fall. This results from their tendency to germinate during a warm period in winter or early spring only to succumb later as a result of freezing temperatures. The major advantages of late fall or winter seeding are: (1) inherent dormancy is overcome; (2) some stimulation is provided by the cold temperatures and seedlings are induced to more rapid growth; (3) a longer period of adequate moisture is available so that seedlings are larger and better able to withstand the drought and heat of summer; (4) many seed-collecting rodents tend to be inactive after late fall so seed loss from this factor is reduced.

There are exceptions to this rule. Native grasses, such as big and little bluestem, Indian and switch grasses, are warm weather grasses and should be sown in early summer.

Where rodent predation on seeds is a problem, as it is on fall-sown black walnut seed in eastern forests, spring sowing of seed may increase the chances of seedling establishment (Engle and Clark 1959). This problem of depredation is well documented in reports for birds (Goebel and Berry 1976) and small mammals (Everett et al. 1978). Sowing seed in the spring reduces the time that rodents have to find the seed before it germinates.

10. *Eliminate or reduce livestock and wildlife use.*—Young plants and seedlings do not develop well when cropped off or severely trampled by large or small animals. Livestock use of planted areas should be eliminated until the seeded stand is established. Control of game animals can be achieved by increasing the harvest during the hunting season. Mice, chipmunks, rabbits, kangaroo rats, and ground squirrels can also devastate plantings if control measures are not employed. Personnel in the Division of Animal Damage Control of the U.S. Fish and Wildlife Service, as well as county agricultural agents, can give up-to-date information on animal control methods (see Chapter 22).

Regeneration

The acceptance of clear-cutting as a means of regenerating most of the forests of the United States, both soft and hardwood types, has created the opportunity for increasing forage yields at little direct costs to wildlife. The key to coordination of timber and wildlife lies in the long-term scheduling of timber harvests using *small* units of land (Roach 1974). Clear-cuts should be large enough so deer and other wildlife will not eat much of the tree reproduction, yet small enough so wildlife adapted to the old-growth forest, such as squirrels and wild turkeys, will not be seriously damaged by the practice. Narrow clear-cuts (<152.4 m wide) totaling about 8.1 ha in size seem to be a suitable compromise.

It should be remembered that nonyarding deer do not eat large quantities of woody browse but subsist mainly on mast, fungi, forbs, and grasses (Cushwa et al. 1970, Nixon et al. 1970). There are presently little data available on methods for increasing many of the forbs native to the eastern hardwoods. Crawford (1976) summarized the response of understory vegetation to overstory cutting in eastern hardwood stands.

For browse cutting, clear-cuts 1 and 1/2 times as wide as the uncut trees have been recommended. Rinaldi (1970) found that strip clear-cutting spruce-fir stands in patches 40.2 m wide yielded more forage for deer and hares than did strips cut 20.1 m or 60.4 m wide.

In the northeastern states, regular periodic winter-harvested strip clear-cuttings are encouraged in and adjacent to winter deer yards. Within the yards, strips of conifers 40.2 m wide are left along streams and lake shores for winter shelter for deer (Schemnitz 1974). In eastern Canada, Boer (1978) recommended cuts in strips or patches no wider than 60 m in deer wintering areas.

Many of the procedures used to release desirable browse plants from the competition of less desirable species are the same as those used for complete removal of existing vegetation. The results of such treatments depend upon the intensity of application. For example, chemical sprays may be used only to dessicate the crowns of woody species, or to kill the plants completely, depending on strength of the mix and the number of applications (Pechanec et al. 1954, Plummer et al. 1955).

There are 4 general methods of eliminating competition—mechanical and manual treatment, chemical sprays, and prescribed burning. Often these methods are used in combination to meet specific needs. Mechanical methods and hand methods are more expensive than either chemicals or burning, but have much wider application.

MECHANICAL AND MANUAL METHODS

The *Range Seeding Equipment Handbook* (U.S. Forest Service 1965) contains descriptions of equipment that may be used to treat areas for release from competition, together with the advantages and limitations of each method. Only a few of the more common procedures will be described briefly. Other important references on these practices include Plummer et al. (1955), Sampson and Jesperson (1963), Box and Powell (1965), Pechanec et al. (1965), Roby and Green (1976), and Green (1977).

Chaining

Chaining consists of dragging a heavy chain through vegetation to break off or uproot plants. The general procedure is for 2 tractors, 1 attached to each end of the chain, to travel on parallel courses 18.3–30.5 m apart. Additional disturbance can be gained with 1 tractor ahead of the other so the chain rides in a "J" configuration (Roby and Green 1976). The spacing is dependent upon density of vegetation, weight, and length of the anchor chain, size of tractor, bite of tracks, and slope. Ordinarily, tractors with a minimum of 110 horsepower on the draw bar are used. The chain size is dependent upon the degree of kill desired. For dense stands of target species with little desirable understory, a heavy anchor chain weighing about 45.4 kg per link achieves the best results. Dense young stands of trees or brush require a heavier chain than older stands because of the need to have the chain ride close to the ground. Links of 12.2–18.1 kg are used on areas where it is desired to leave a fairly dense residual stand of browse plants.

A better kill can be ensured by chaining when the soil moisture is at a minimum or when the first several cm of the soil are frozen. Chaining efficiently removes young, flexible trees. Chaining also can create a good seedbed for aerial broadcast seeding. In areas planned for twice-over chaining along with aerial seeding, the second pass should be timed so it will cover the seed. Properly planned chaining projects will leave fingers or islands of unchained trees to simulate natural openings in the landscape (Cain 1971).

Vegetative type manipulation projects such as chaining can change the aesthetic and biological values of an area. Consequently the manager should be well instructed in the principles and procedures for pretreatment, treatment, and posttreatment as described by Cain (1971). The habitat manager should likewise be concerned with and plan aesthetical values and designs into vegetative conversion projects.

Chaining projects in Nevada increased forage quality, quantity, and diversity for deer (Tueller and Monroe 1976). Deer utilization was 139% higher in treated area and a 7-fold increase in deer-days use per hectare was attributed to increase forage availability.

A "ball and chain" technique was developed to crush brush on steep sideslopes. The equipment consists of 45.7 m of chain and a 1.5-m-diameter steel buoy filled with water. Chain weight varies from 13.6 to 108.9 kg per m depending on the length of chain used and steepness of slope. Long chains should be of low weight per meter so the ball will drop down the slope far enough to work effectively (Roby and Green 1976).

Scalping

Scalping consists of scraping off the plants and part of the top layer of soil from planting sites. It is a simple and highly effective method of removing vegetation as well as most of the seed in the soil beneath it (Brown and Martinsen 1959, Holmgren and Basile 1959, Box and Powell 1965) . The scalping of broad areas often leads to soil losses from erosion.

There are a number of methods for scalping. The simplest is with a hand hoe. The fastest and least expensive is with mechanical equipment. However, mechanical scalping is limited to terrain that can be negotiated by a tractor or jeep. A practical method for scalping and planting gentle slopes fairly free of rocks involves the use of a Hansen seeder equipped with a wide moldboard plow. Hand scalping is effective on steep slopes and rocky areas. Scalps 0.19 sq. m and at least 5.1 cm deep or deeper than the effective depth of the annual roots are cleared with a hoe. Heavier, narrower hoes are required for rocky, compact soils with perennial vegetation. In scalping, the material scraped off is piled on the lower side of the plot to form a catch basin. Care should be taken to avoid dirt spilling over the top of the blade back into the plot, since this may contaminate the seedbed with annual weed seeds. Sloughing of the soil into the scalp from its upper edge is common on slopes steeper than 50%. This sloughing can be minimized by gradually increasing the scalp in depth as the hoe is pulled downhill rather than by vertically chopping.

Conventional Tillage

Where soil and vegetative conditions permit, plowing is a desirable method to eliminate competitive vegetation (Pechanec et al. 1954, Plummer et al. 1955). Disk-type plows, such as a heavy offset disk or wheatland plow, are good for controlling nonsprouting species on soils with relatively few rocks. The brushland plow is best for rough, moderately rocky areas.

Plowing to a depth of 7.6 to 10.2 cm is recommended for most nonsprouting plants such as sagebrush. Depths of 10.2–15.2 cm are required to control plants which spread by underground root stocks or from the crown. A heavy-duty root plow is required to eliminate root-sprouting species.

The Holt plow is effective in reducing competition on slopes up to 40% where watershed measures are also needed. It will create a continuous furrow in either direction. This double disk furrower is attached to a crawler-type tractor by means of a specially built 3-point hitch. The depth and angle is controlled by a hydraulic ram. The tractor must have more than 100 horsepower on the drawbar to handle the Holt plow effectively.

Chipping

Wood chipping machines are replacing some of the traditional cutting and hauling equipment for timber harvesting. Whole tree chippers used for clear-cutting will leave a postcutting site almost devoid of tree limbs. Because this technique is new, it deserves close observation to determine its appropriate value.

CHEMICAL APPLICATION

Herbicides offer possibilities for improving wildlife habitat (Crawford 1960, Krenz 1962, Sampson and Jesperson 1963, Halls and Crawford 1965, Kearl 1965, Oregon State University 1967). Selective spraying may be used to reduce stands of undesirable browse plants. Basal sprouting of browse species that have grown too high or dense for deer and elk can be stimulated by killing the aerial crowns with chemicals (Wilbert 1963, Mueggler 1966). The variable sensitivity of different species to the formulation, concentration, and time of application of herbicides should enable discriminating manipulation of the habitat, once these sensitivities are known. Unfortunately, not a great deal is currently known about this subject. Most big game ranges, for instance, support a mixture of shrub species that differ in sensitivity to chemicals. This often makes the effects of sprays unpredictable. It is known, for instance, that mixed stands of big sagebrush and bitterbrush may be sprayed with 2,4-D butyl or isopropyl ester at the standard sagebrush control rate without serious loss of bitterbrush, provided spraying is done while bitterbrush is still in bloom. On a California project, a 0.9-kg acid equivalent 2,4-D spray with diesel oil as a carrier, at a volume of 4.6 l per ha, resulted in 95% removal of sagebrush and 18% kill of the most severely hedged and decadent bitterbrush plants. The remaining bitterbrush plants, however, rapidly developed good form and vigor. Leader growth of treated plants was 1.1 times greater than that on controls 2 seasons after treatment even though crested wheatgrass was planted in the treated area. However, until more is known about selective sensitivities, caution is needed in application of chemical sprays on mixed browse stands. Opportunities to observe effects of forest or range management spraying on plants of various species should not be overlooked. The advantages of hand- or power-operated ground sprayers for control of individual undesirable species should be considered.

Pelletized picloram (4-amino-3,5,6-trichloropicolinic acid), a 10% acid formulation in an extruded clay pellet with low dermal toxicity, was effective in maintaining forest openings in northern Wisconsin (McCaffery et al. 1974a). Picloram pellets (30–50) applied by hand at the base of stems or suckers during the growing season, achieved adequate control of aspen, willows, fir, and alders at a cost of $23.47 to $46.93 per ha depending on labor costs and distance travelled to the work site. Because picloram also kills broadleafed forbs, broadcast applications are not recommended.

CONTROLLED BURNING

Controlled burning is one of the more economical procedures for removing a stand of vegetation for a prescribed purpose (Pechanec et al. 1954, Biswell and Gilman 1961, Hiehle 1961, Sampson and Jesperson 1963:27, Cushwa 1968) and is a valid habitat improvement technique (Beardahl and Sylvester 1974, Page 1975, Lovaas 1976). It can be used as a first step in seedbed preparation to reduce competing plant species, to create openings in dense stands of brush, or to create essential habitat for wildlife species that have adapted to fire climax vegetation such as the Kirtland's warbler (Radtke and Byelich 1963).

Investigators have reported direct, immediate stimulation of plant growth due to fire which results in greater forage yield. Soils are warmer on burned areas and spring growth starts earlier. On burned areas, soil fertility is usually increased. Plant vigor is promoted by removal of old shoots and foliage, and in many situations, burning of the mulch favors plant growth. Longer term increases in growth have been achieved by timing the fire to favor the species with highest yields, by removing undesirable, competing plants and by preparing seedbeds for successful reproduction. In addition to measurable increase in forage yield, greater forage availability was reported where unpalatable plants became palatable after burning, where physical barriers to utilization were burned, or where large plants were reduced in size by burning. Most prescribed fires lead to an increase in protein content and palatability of resprouting plants.

Fire has been a natural action changing vegetation through all biomes of North America for centuries. Fire is therefore a natural force in plant succession and has always been a factor in wildlife habitat manipulation. Uncontrolled, man-caused fires, which often have been devastating, are one of the biggest problems to wildlife. Such fires often have been started during the wrong seasons of the year and sometimes repetitively set, which in turn have created plant successional stages not always beneficial to endemic wildlife. Consequently, fire as a tool for habitat manipulation has been received with hostility at times during the twentieth century.

The Tall Timbers Research Station was organized in 1958 near Tallahassee, Florida, to explore the role of fire in land management. One of the station's primary interests is basic research regarding the influence of fire on the environment and the application of fire in land management. It further recognized the right of the public to be adequately and honestly informed as to the usefulness of fire in land management as well as to its destructiveness (Komarek 1962).

The Tall Timbers Station has held annual conferences on fire ecology since 1962. Most of these meetings have been held in Florida; however, some have been conducted in California, Montana, Canada, etc. Each conference has been summarized in a proceedings volume containing papers presented. An example would be Number 14, 1974, which was published in cooperation with the Inter-mountain Fire Research Council and totaled 675 pages in 3 parts: Fire Management Section; Fire Ecology Section; and Fire Use Section. Included are some of the most current papers on the values, procedures, and techniques of planning and implementing prescribed burning. Each annual proceeding contains papers on the role of fire practices in relation to wildlife habitat management. The proceedings are concerned with fire ecology throughout the world as exemplified in the 1971 edition devoted to "Fire in Africa."

The following is a suggested outline for planning, execution, and evaluation for prescription burning (A. Becker, pers. comm.):

1. *Analyze Project*
   a. Ascertain present successional patterns for the area in question. Utilize historical references, photographs, fire history (long term), environmental influences and present vegetation patterns.
   b. Project where you wish to be. What vegetation composition do you wish to manage for (short term and long term)?
   c. Assess site potential. Soil, moisture, residual plants and/or seeds, etc.
   d. Evaluate projected fire effects on resources (vegetation, watershed, etc.). Utilize literature.
   e. Determine: Can fire meet management objectives?
2. *Prepare Prescription*
   a. Gather field data such as:
      Fuel loading (by size class)
      Depth and structure of fuels
      Fuel continuity
      Type of fuels (volatility)
      Slope
      Aspect
      Litter Depth
      Existing firebreaks
      Access
      Adjacent fuels
      Weather patterns
   b. Determine the projected fire intensity needed to meet objectives.
   c. Utilizing the above, fuel models[3] (if applicable) and/or expertise, formulate prescription and document. Acknowledge risk areas and mitigating measures. Prescription should include:
      Temperature
      Relative humidity
      Ignition points
      Wind speed and direction
      Fuel moisture
      Soil moisture
3. *Execute Burn*
   a. Follow prescription and burn plan. If changes are needed, document.
   b. Document fire behavior (flame length, rate of spread, etc.).
4. *Evaluate*
   a. Immediate followup: Map intensity of burn. Record amount of biomass left (by species such as sagebrush skeletons, etc.), amount of litter left, scorch height, etc.
   b. Document vegetation recovery, percent kill by species, sprouting, production changes.
   c. Insure proper management after burn. Document wildlife use, location, etc.

The wildlife habitat manager planning a controlled burn should review the reports by the Tall Timbers Research Station (Komarek 1962). We urge the manager to contact local authorities as to liability and seek expertise during the initial planning stages for a controlled burn.

Rejuvenation

Many species of shrubs and trees can regenerate by sprouting from adventitious buds on the stem or from the root crown. The seed of chaparral species and other species are heat resistant and germinate in abundance after fire. When such species have grown too tall, dense, or decadent to produce available browse, it is possible to rejuvenate the stand by burning (Biswell et al. 1952, Hiehle 1961). With many species, it has been found that the sprouts and young plants are considerably higher in protein and other food values for several years after burning than in older growth stages. However, some species of shrubs and trees are killed by fire and may not reestablish on an area naturally for decades after a hot burn. These plants will, however, often respond by high production of adventitious growth to a rejuvenation treatment: crushing, cutting, or mowing. Chemical spraying that burns back the tops but does not kill the shrubs, has a similar effect on many kinds of woody plants. The root systems remain largely undamaged; the plants respond to the reduction of aerial growth by rapid and expansive root and leaf development. However, there is evidence that deer are reluctant to browse heavily on plants where a multitude of dead stems are intermingled with new growth. Dead stems may be a disadvantage if moderate to heavy browsing is needed to hold the growth at heights available for browsing. Crushing of brush either before or after burning results in better utilization of rejuvenated forage.

REJUVENATING BITTERBRUSH

Bitterbrush is an important browse species on mule deer winter ranges in several western regions. Many procedures have been used to rejuvenate tall, decadent stands of bitterbrush (Driscoll 1963, Ferguson and Basile 1966, Ferguson 1972). Results from railing or by crushing with a bulldozer, with blade 30.5 to 61 cm above the ground, indicate a great increase in growth the first year after treatment. This increase has been followed by a decline in growth the second and third year and by an actual loss of forage production. The evidence at hand indicates that dozing and railing cause severe mortality and diminishment of the total area of crown.

Rolling bitterbrush with a heavy log covered with rubber tires and pulled by a rubber-tired tractor shows promise for plant rejuvenation. Although there was little response the first year after rolling on a project in California, bitterbrush leader growth averaged 54% greater than that on the control area the second year, and

[3]Most fuel models are averaged over a large area, and do provide good information. However, additional data gathered for each site will assist in more closely predicting fire effects for similar sites and altering prescriptions.

most of the treated plants showed excellent vigor. Only 2% of the rolled plants failed to resprout.

Roto-cutting bitterbrush in early spring with blade set 45.7 cm above the ground level resulted in a 47% increase in leader growth the same year on 1 project. Long-term results have not yet been evaluated. Pruning of stems from an average height of over 1.5 m to heights under 1.2 m coupled with removal of all shrub competition resulted, after 2 growing seasons, in an increase in leader growth 2.1 times greater than on an adjacent control area. Again, long-term evaluation has yet to be made (Schneegas and Zufelt 1965).

CRUSHED BROWSE-WAYS

Many chaparral-type brushfields are practically impenetrable to deer and offer little habitat to other wildlife. Such brush ranges can be improved for wildlife by creating interspersion of brush sprouts and herbaceous vegetation through development of small openings connected by lanes (Biswell et al. 1952, Hiehle 1961). The primary objectives of such work are the development of both food and access.

Release

On many sites, seed growth and production can be improved for some species by removing the surrounding competition. For example, Halls and Alcaniz (1968) found that seed yields for some understory plants were up to 32 times greater in openings compared to yields beneath a moderately stocked pine stand.

Small group selection cuts or row thinnings can be designed to admit more light, moisture, and nutrients to potential seed- or browse-producing understory species. In stands too young for commercial timber sales, individual stems of important seed and browse species can be released from surrounding competition using fire (such species as sassafras and flowering dogwood resprout vigorously after burning), herbicides, or cutting.

Release cutting of trees in older forest stands is best accomplished in conjunction with some type of commercial timber harvest. In the oak types, trees needing release should be selected in the fall during a good seeding year to insure that released trees will bear seed crops. Due to genetic factors, some oaks never bear much seed. In oak types, about 6.4 to 6.9 m^2 of basal area of seed producers should be reserved per ha (Shaw 1971).

In clear-cuts made in hardwood types, 0.5–0.9 m^2 per ha of basal area for seed-producing understory species, 5.1–12.7-cm dbh, should be reserved from cutting to insure that some seed is available for wildlife during the early years of regrowth after clear-cutting.

In addition, certain species important to wildlife, such as the hickories and American beech, are slow growers and are frequently overtopped by the vigorous growth of intolerant tree species that generally follow clear-cutting. If these slow-growing species are to reach seed-bearing size in these clear-cut stands, they must be released from competition. Nixon et al. (1975) recommended that 20–25 suppressed hickory poles greater than 15.2-cm dbh be left per ha after clear-cutting. Some of these stems may die after complete release but the remainder would have a good chance of reaching seed-bearing size. Similar recommendations have been made for beech and sugar maple in northern hardwood stands (B. A. Roach, pers. comm.).

Another method of increasing fruit production is to select trees, such as apple (wild or in abandoned orchards), wild cherry, hackberry, oak, or hickory, and apply one of the orchardist's methods for producing more fruit. This method involves measuring the diameter of the tree in cm at 1.37 m above ground. The diameter is divided by 2.78, and m are then substituted for cm. The resulting figure is the length of each side of a square from which all trees are to be removed except the fruit tree to be favored. Not only will this give the tree an opportunity to produce more fruit, but the interspaces are open for increased production of grasses, forbs, and shrubs (Shomon et al. 1966).

With many fruit-producing chaparral species in the West, such as manzanita, California redberry, and toyon, decadent stands can be renewed by mechanical crushing, chemical spraying, and especially by controlled burning.

BROWSE

Browse is defined as leaves, shoots, and twigs of shrubs and trees used as food. In some situations, such as a range recently burned by wildfire, there may be a need to plant desirable browse to introduce or restore a supply of forage. Elsewhere, increased food production may be a goal.

Twig growth has been found to be up to 7 times greater for browse plants growing in the open compared with those beneath trees (Halls and Alcaniz 1968). Creation of openings for browse production, like release cuttings, are best made in conjunction with a timber harvest. Browse manipulation practices can be grouped into the following categories:

1. Release through thinning to remove competition with less desirable species.
2. Rejuvenation through breaking, crushing, herbicide spraying, pruning, or burning rapidly regenerating species.
3. Planting to introduce seed stock.

MECHANICAL METHODS

Cabling

Cabling is suited to areas where it is planned to save residual stands of desirable shrubs and herbaceous cover and where the target species are not young and resilient (Plummer et al. 1955). Cabling is conducted essentially the same as the procedure described in chaining except a 45.7- to 61-m-long 3.8-cm cable is used in place of a chain.

Hula Dozer

This mechanical device is a 100 to 125 drawbar-horsepower crawler-type tractor with a "hula dozer" blade. The blade consists of hinged pusher bars and hydraulic tilting attachments. The pusher bar is used to tip trees, while the corner of the blade is used to lift them from the ground. Hula dozing is economically advantageous in areas where target trees are clustered, and clusters are widely spaced, or where trees do not exceed 240 per ha. This method is used primarily where stands of browse plants are present, and it is desired to leave them undamaged.

Mechanical Thinning

Equipment used to precommercially thin coniferous forest species such as the Tomahawk and Hydroax may be used to release browse or seed-producing species. Other equipment that rolls, chops, or flails the vegetation also might prove useful depending on the objective of a particular project and the availability of equipment.

Special Considerations

Vegetative manipulation projects, such as chaining, burning, and spraying, are designed to alter the habitat structure—both plant species and shape. Therefore, depending on the individual involved, vegetative manipulation projects can be unsightly areas to observe. Consequently, project planners must be concerned with aesthetic values and plan projects to simulate natural openings in the landscape. Project planners should also be well instructed in the principles and procedures for pretreatment, treatment, and posttreatment as described by Cain (1971).

The size and pattern of food and cover treatments should be geared to the requirements of the target wildlife species involved and aesthetical values for ecological conditions. With nonmigratory deer, for instance, many small, treated spots or strips scattered over a large area will benefit more deer than a large, single project. There are several reasons for this. In the first place, the home ranges of bucks or doe-yearling-fawn family groups can be quite small. Only the deer whose home ranges impinge on or are immediately adjacent to the treated area will move into and use the new forage. In addition, deer often are reluctant to travel more than 61–91 m from cover and may use only the circumference of a large opening. Of prime importance, also, is the need to gear the amount of forage produced to the number of animals that will use it. If use is too light, the new sprouts and young plants may grow rapidly out of reach or become as dense as the original untreated stand. If, however, the treated areas are small enough so that moderately heavy browsing of forage holds plants in desirable forms, value will be prolonged over much longer periods. If deer respond to better forage conditions by increase in numbers, the frequency and size of treated areas can be increased. Treatments can be rotated so that no one area will be manipulated more often than once in 10–20 years. In any case, no more than 30% of the area should be treated to create better forage areas and the other 70% left in cover, with size of cover patches at least 16.2 ha or more (Taber and Dasmann 1958).

The prescribed treatments for key portions of migratory deer winter range will necessarily differ from those described above. Because heavy snows and other conditions force deer to concentrate during mid-winter, deer densities and hence food demands tend to be high in these areas. For this reason, it is essential that treatments be large enough to prevent decimation of new forage. Even here, the most productive patterns will be in extensive broad strips or openings interspersed with patches or strips of cover rather than in single large projects. Retention of cover should not be neglected in such projects and should be given special emphasis where winters are severe. In northern Maine, for instance, dense conifer winter cover for deer should be intermixed with open feeding areas not exceeding 91 m. in width.

This brief description of requirements for deer will show the need for analysis of the requirements of the wildlife species to be favored and the importance of tailoring the program to fit these requirements.

Finally, it should be pointed out that managing habitat for a single species of wildlife has essentially ended, at least on public lands in the United States. Today, the wildlife manager must strive to produce a mosiac pattern of different habitats providing niches for an array of wildlife species. A variety of techniques will be needed to do the job. We reiterate again that wildlife habitat management, to be successful, must be based on the manipulation of natural plant successions. Techniques that duplicate natural forces (such as fires that create openings) offer the cheapest and most effective means of providing wildlife with habitats they have adapted to through time. There will be situations where more artificial techniques such as planting will be required; but whenever practical, native species should have priority in any planting program.

COVER PRACTICES

Cover fulfills varied habitat requirements for wildlife. A hedgerow may provide escape cover for quail from predators, or the same shrubs may provide nesting cover for song birds. Cover can be provided by a variety of items; rock piles, ground burrows, brush piles, or trees (including cavities). The absence of cover, its sparceness, or its poor distribution can be the factor limiting the use of an area by wildlife. The habitat manager can improve wildlife numbers or area of use by improving cover quality or quantity. When manipulating food or water, wildlifers should be careful to assure enough cover of various kinds is left to meet wildlife needs.

Cover includes escape, nesting areas, and refuge from inclement or adverse weather. It most often consists of a form of vegetation—herbaceous, shrubs, or trees—that provides protection from hunters or predators, mechanical or thermal protection from winter storms or summer sun, or a combination of these factors which provide a secure nest site.

Hedgerows

In some areas, cover plantings are not necessary due to rapid natural revegetation. However, other regions may require the planting of cover such as hedgerows. Hedgerows provide desirable escape, refuge, and nesting cover, as well as travel lanes for many species of wildlife. Low, woody vegetation can be planted along fence rows, in gullies, and along streams or around ponds, springs, food patches, and breeding grounds. Such plantings generally are established by transplanting seedlings or wildlings. Planting can be done by hand or with a mechanical planter depending upon the size of the project. Three to 4 rows of different size plants should be planted in a stairstep pattern so varied degrees of cover exist. For instance, rows of Russian olive, squawbush, and Siberian pea spaced appropriately will provide travel lanes, cover, and food for many wildlife species. Spacing of plants varies with species. The smaller plants are planted every 45.7 to 61 cm in rows 0.9 to 1.2 m apart. Larger plants are planted every 2.4 to 3.7 m in rows about 2.4 to 3.0 m apart. For most wildlife species, hedgerows 4.6 to 6.1 m wide are adequate. Row lengths vary, depending on the needs and available space. One strip to each 49.4 to 61.8 ha in open country appears adequate.

Hedgerows can also be established by plowing a strip where a hedgerow is desired, then lining or staggering fence posts about every 6.1 m down the strip. Wire or twine is strung between the posts for a bird perch. Droppings of birds that perch are laden with viable seed and will "plant" the prepared seedbed. These "plow-perch" plantings grow almost as fast as those produced from root stock.

Brush Piles

When cover is limited in wildlife habitat, brush piles may be provided. If possible, brush piles should be a by-product of other land treatments, rather than a specific practice. Timber harvest, timber stand improvement, pasture or cropland clearing, release cutting for trees or shrubs all provide woody limbs suitable for brush piles. Brush piles when correctly constructed and located provide nesting and protection cover as would a good stand of natural vegetation. Their values include (Warrick 1976):

1. Concealment cover from predators—an overhead canopy and surrounding brush hide nests from the view of predators.
2. Protection from predators—the tight network of strong twigs and small openings eliminate entry of many predators.
3. Protection from the elements—nests are sheltered from the cooling rains, wind, and excessive sunlight.
4. Harbor for various seeds to sprout in—the network of twigs and grass provide a medium for seed germination and young plant growth.

Spacing of brush piles will depend on the mobility of the species that are to use them. Brush piles for quail, for example, should be within 61 m of other escape cover and (for western quail) no more than 0.4 km from water. The carrying capacity of large clearings for many upland game birds can be increased by providing brush pile cover.

Top pruning of trees on scaled quail range not only provides slash that can be piled for cover but promotes a bushy tree growth that makes preferred loafing cover. Such piles should be about 1.5–1.8 m in diameter and about 0.9 m high. It is best to elevate the pile about 15.2 cm above the ground by using rocks or heavier limbs for support. Where large clearings (40.5 ha or more) are made on quail range, brush should be piled at an optimum rate of about 1 pile per hectare.

Long brush piles placed in the upper portion of broad arroyos or low profile ravines may be used to increase cottontail rabbit populations. For rabbits, the pile may be 7.6–15.2 m long, 1.5 m wide, and 1.2 m high (Shomon et al. 1966). Brush piles should be at least 3.7–4.6 m in diameter and 1.5 m high to provide rabbit cover for several years.

Both white-crowned and Harris' sparrows often are found in association with brush piles. In Kansas, Harris' sparrows often are found in winter wherever there are brush piles (R. Graber, pers. comm.).

Turkey nests have been found in slash piles, thickets, fallen tree tops or at the base of bushes and trees. There are indications that carefully located brush piles may provide nesting cover, and there may be advantages to simulate turkey nesting cover preferences by piling brush or slash at the bases of trees or around logs. Such brush piles should be within 0.8 km of water.

Use of slash remaining after a timber harvest offers a means of creating turkey nesting habitat adjacent to openings created by the logging operation. Openings are sought as feeding sites by hens with poults.

Brush or trees piled loosely in field corners or along fence rows may extend pheasant habitat. Grass, forbs, and vines will grow up through the brush and add density and permanence to the pile.

Javelina range may be extended by brush piles. A wooden platform about 0.9 m high supported by rocks or creosoted posts, with brush piled on top and on 2 sides, may be used for this species. The structure may be placed against a bank or overhanging cliff. Such javelina brush piles should be at least 1.8 × 1.8 m and located in an area protected from wind and near food.

Natural and Artificial Roosts

Some species of wildlife, such as quail and turkeys, require adequate perching or roosting sites. Where roosts are lacking, such cover can be provided through natural vegetation plantings or by artificial roosting structures.

Since 1958, the Rio Grande turkey has extended its range into the scrub mesquite prairie of west Texas, in part because of the installation of electric transmission poles that are used as roost sites (Kothmann and Litton 1975). Use by these turkeys suggests the installation of similar towers in other areas that lack roost sites but offer food supplies and adequate rainfall.

The California quail is an example of a species that needs at least a good roosting site per 12 ha for desirable habitat. The lack of adequate sites may be corrected by planting thick foliaged trees such as live oaks, olives, citrus, and juniper. Where it is not practical or feasible to plant trees, artificial quail roosts, e.g., brush piled on a wire-covered frame held off the ground by 4 posts, can be made with little cost and used as temporary roosts while waiting for permanent natural vegetation to grow (McMillan 1959). These roosts are constructed of pipe or wood and should be approximately 2.4 × 5 m in diameter and installed 1.8 m above the ground when completed (MacGregor 1950, Fig. 20.3).

Another method to improve protective roosting sites for quail is to cut the limbs of large trees above the primary forks and pile these same limbs in the forks. This also causes the tree to bush out, which creates good dove nesting cover as well as quail roosting cover (Bauer 1963).

Eagles near Klamath Falls, Oregon, benefited from the construction of a huge artificial tree. The traditional roost was near a favored fishing lake. However, the few trees used for perching were blown down by a heavy wind. Recognizing their plight, an artificial tree was installed which has 3, 18.3-m poles placed in a tepee formation with 3, 6.1- to 9.1-m cross perch poles. Fast-growing poplars and elms were planted around the base of the artificial tree to provide eventually a more natural and permanent roosting site. Within less than a month, bald eagles used this new structure and have been using it each year since (Oregon State Game Commission 1972).

The extensive open grassland prairies of the West provide good food sources for raptors but frequently lack roost and nest sites. Olendorff and Stoddart (1974) noted that raptors readily used trees and buildings made by man, and, consequently, recommended planting trees to improve raptor habitat. They observed that trees planted near water are most frequently used. Until the natural trees are large enough for nest sites, it may be necessary to place an artificial nest structure (see "Specialized Nest Structures: Platforms" for further specifications).

Nesting Cover

Mixtures of brome grass and alfalfa, each applied at the rate of 8.9–10.7 kg/ha, have been found to produce suitable nesting cover for ring-necked pheasants and other grassland nesting avifauna along roadsides in otherwise intensively cultivated landscapes (Joselyn and Tate 1972). Such seedings, once established, have provided pheasants with 15 years of quality nest cover at an amortized cost of less than $24.70/ha (R. E. Warner, pers. comm.). Seedings are mowed once each growing season after August 1.

On Wisconsin upland sites, canary grass, Blackwell switchgrass, and brome grass produced the best nesting cover for grassland nesting species. On muck or peat soils, canary grass and timothy gave the best results (Frank and Woehler 1969). Plantings on upland soils were most successful when seeded in April or May with a nurse crop of oats; the oats were then harvested in late July or early August. They used 3.6–5.3 kg/ha of fine seeded grasses such as canary grass, and 5.3–7.1 kg/ha of the large seeded varieties such as brome grass. Oats were seeded at 42.8 l per ha. August seedings were most successful on muck soils because heavy weed competition occurred following spring planting. Forage sorghums and sorghum-sudan grass hybrids, established annually, provided good winter cover on Wisconsin upland sites. Such cover was useful on diverted acres or as interim winter cover until woody plantings furnished protective cover. For pure sorghum stands best results were obtained using 7.1–13.4 kg/ha. In seeding corn and sorghum-sudan mixtures, 0.1 l of Hi-Dan 35 seed were added to 17.6 l of seed corn. Corn planter boxes were kept about 1/2 full and 55–80 g of Hi-Dan were added to the plant boxes at regular intervals. As few as 4 rows received use by pheasants, but 0.4–1.2 ha were usually seeded (Frank and Woehler 1969). Cost of establishing nest cover ranged from $37 to $91/ha, including seed, fertilizer, site preparation, and planting. Winter cover costs averaged $59 to $89/ha, if such planting were renewed annually.

For prairie grouse, a successful seeding per ha of 1.8–2.7 kg of redtop, 0.45 kg of timothy and 0.45 kg of red clover, Korean lespedeza, and alsike clover, plus 0.45 kg of alfalfa when the pH of the soil is suitable, has provided attractive nest cover in Illinois (Sanderson et al. 1973).

Redtop seedings have been most attractive to nesting prairie chickens the second nest season after seeding and the second nest season after controlled burning of redtop sods 4 or more years old (Westemeier 1973). Nest cover for prairie chickens should be managed in 2.0–8.1-ha blocks, because most prairie chicken nests have been located near breaks in cover types.

If native grasses (bluestems, switchgrass, Indian grass, sideoats grama) are used for nest cover, they must be mowed, burned, or grazed frequently to break up the dense cover that will develop. The warm season grasses mature late and can be mowed for hay in late July or August after eggs are hatched and young are flying. These grasses should be rotation burned in early spring at 3- to 5-year intervals. This burning rotation benefited prairie chickens, sharp-tailed grouse, pheasants, upland plovers, and Hungarian partridge in North Dakota (Kirsch and Kruse 1973).

Additional suggestions for maintaining or improving nesting cover by Shomon et al. (1966) are as follows:

1. Maintain permanent, undisturbed cover along fences, ditch-banks, roadsides, railroad rights-of-way, and in waste areas (such as cattail sloughs) and odd corners, where possible.
2. Encourage farmers and ranchers to enter into 1 or more of the several government programs which provide financial aid for planting vegetation which is suitable for wildlife cover.
3. Work with state and local highway departments to discourage burning of cover along roadsides during the winter and spring; encourage the delay of mowing until after July 1; and encourage the planting of grasses and legumes for use by nesting pheasants.
4. Refrain from dryland fallowing operations between the period of April 15 and June 20 to enable ground-nesting birds to hatch in important stubble field nesting areas.
5. Use flushing devices on mowers to save nesting females during the first cutting of alfalfa.
6. Fence nesting cover to prevent grazing by livestock.
7. Plant shrubby thickets along gulleys and draws for use as cover.

Snags

Over 85 species of North American birds use cavities in dead or deteriorating trees (Scott et al. 1977). Thomas

Fig. 20.3. Installation of an artificial quail roost in southern California (photos by I. McMillan).

et al. (1976) observed that 24 mammal and 38 bird species used tree cavities for a mountain range in Oregon and Washington. Such trees are often called "snags." The removal of snags can reduce wildlife populations. For example, in Arizona the removal of snags reduced cavity-nesting bird populations by 50%. Much of this decline was in populations of violet-green swallows, pygmy nuthatches, and northern three-toed woodpeckers. Swallows alone dropped 90%, whereas a low woodpecker population was eliminated (Scott et al. 1977).

Foresters and recreation managers are now more aware of the economic and esthetic values of cavity-nesting birds. The majority of snag-dependent wildlife species are insectivorous and fill a major role in the control of forest insect pests (Thomas et al. 1976). Recognizing these wildlife values, the U.S. Forest Service (1977) issued a new policy to "provide habitat needed to maintain viable, self-sustaining populations of cavity-nesting and snag-dependent wildlife species." An example of placing this policy into effect was the Arizona-New Mexico Forest Service Regional Office recommendation that 7 good quality snags per ha be retained within 152 m of forest openings and water, with 5 per ha over the remaining forest. Some agencies are now placing signs on snags and other valuable wildlife used trees identifying them as "Wildlife Trees" not to be harvested or cut down for firewood.

SPECIALIZED NEST STRUCTURES

Many species of wildlife that use tree cavities have declined due to the loss of primeval forests. Examples are the ivory-billed and red-cockaded woodpeckers which are presently on the endangered species list due mainly to the loss of habitat (Scott et al. 1977). There are many mammals that also rely heavily on tree cavities for part of their life cycle. For example, the best nest den sites for the eastern gray or fox squirrel are tree cavities with specific dimensions. For fox squirrels, cavity dimensions averaged 16 × 17.5 cm in diameter and 38.1–40.6 cm deep, measured from the top of the den entrance, with an entrance opening 6.1 cm × 9.4 cm in diameter (Baumgartner 1938). Blackgum, beech, maples, gums, basswood, and elms decay readily and form dens within a few years; oaks decay slowly and form dens in their later years. Sanderson (1975) recommended a mixture of trees that decay and form cavities at different rates.

Man should husband existing den or nest trees and should look to artificial structures only as a secondary technique after full evaluation of the need. It is more realistic and justifiable, in view of the many human and ecological values at stake, to make ample den or nest trees continuously available as a natural and vital component of the living forest.

At times, however, man-made structures must be used or a species will not survive. As an example, nest trees for double-crested cormorants have become scarce along the upper Mississippi River in Illinois and Wisconsin. In Illinois, an artificial nest tree was provided. A single 14.6-m utility pole was anchored adjacent to 2 existing natural nest trees about 1.6 km from shore and in water about 5.5 m deep. Twelve nesting platforms were attached to the pole using 6 cross arms spaced 0.9 m apart (Fig. 20.4). The nest platforms consisted of boxes 5.1 cm × 40.6 cm × 1.8 cm deep with 3, 7.6 × 40.6-cm slats on the bottom. The boxes were lined with 2.5-cm-mesh chicken wire (Kleen 1975). Another type of platform with 2 cormorant nests was built on the Agassiz National Wildlife Refuge in Minnesota (Fig. 20.12).

The U.S. Forest Service system of managing nesting trees for rare and endangered native wildlife such as the bald eagle, ivory-billed woodpecker, red-cockaded woodpecker, and osprey provides an example of how the important, but seldom understood, technique of nest tree protection is currently being practiced:

1. Maintain an inventory of all nest sites and identify in detail the location of each.
2. Check nests periodically and record a cumulative history of nest use.
3. Within 100 m of any nest tree, development activities will be limited to management measures beneficial to maintaining the nesting site.
4. A special buffer zone, 201 m in radius, will be established and marked on the ground around each nest site.
5. Timber cutting, timber stand improvement, prescribed burning, road construction, recreation construction, and other disturbing activities will not be allowed within the buffer zone during the period from November 1 to June 15.
6. All practices such as insecticide spraying, aquatic plant control, and the use of fish toxicants, will be critically evaluated regarding their effects on nesting sites within the forest and areas outside of the forest, but within 0.8 km of the forest's boundary.
7. Three to 5 old growth trees will be reserved as roosting and potential nest trees within the buffer zone surrounding the nest. For red-cockaded woodpeckers, an aggregate of cavity containing live pines, 25.4–63.5-cm dbh, 70–100 years old, are needed for each colony.
8. The location of all nests and their buffer zones will be shown in the forest's "Multiple Use Atlas." These special management considerations will stay in effect until it has been conclusively determined that the nesting site has been abandoned.

Artificial nest structures can substitute for a deficiency of natural sites in otherwise suitable habitat. Where primeval forests are primarily gone in the eastern United States, purple martins now depend almost entirely on man-made nesting structures (Allen and Nice 1952). Bird houses have been readily accepted by many natural cavity nesters, and increases in breeding density have resulted from providing such structures (Grenquist 1966, Strange et al. 1971, Hamerstrom et al. 1973). Nest boxes are useful for wood ducks and squirrels, as well as various nongame species, such as bluebirds, screech owls, kestrels, and barn owls. Nest baskets and platforms are readily used by waterfowl.

Bird houses have been built by man all over the world for eons. Sometimes this was merely the placing of a large gourd with a small hole in a nearby tree. At other times it would be the elaborate construction of a 18-compartment complex for the gregarious purple martin. The practice continues today as attested by the variety of different bird house designs and styles (Fig. 20.5). Detailed plans for these structures are often available from the National Audubon Society, local bird clubs, Cooperative Extension Service (McDowell 1972), and other sources (Shomon et al. 1966).

The very popular and helpful pamphlet *Homes for Birds* published by the U.S. Fish and Wildlife Service (Kalmbach et al. 1969) provides many excellent examples for constructing bird houses. The authors stress that the bird house should be designed and constructed according to the needs of the target species. These specifi-

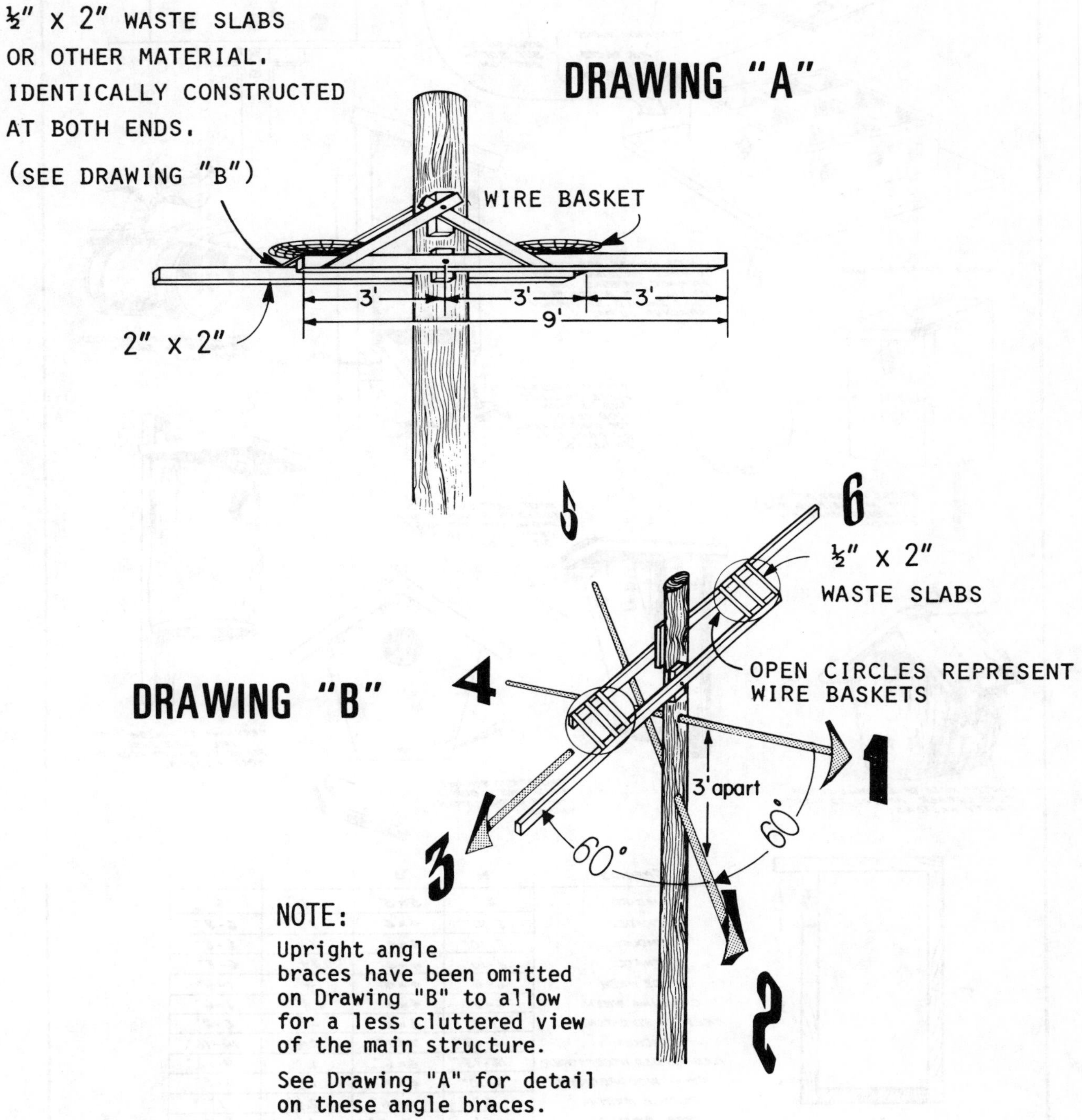

Fig. 20.4. Nest tree for double-crested cormorants. The crossarms and nest baskets are attached to a 14.6 m telephone pole as shown in Drawing "A." Crossarms spiral up the pole 60 degrees apart as shown in Drawing "B." The numbers in Drawing "B" refer to crossarms. (Illinois Natural History Survey drawing by Lloyd Lemere.)

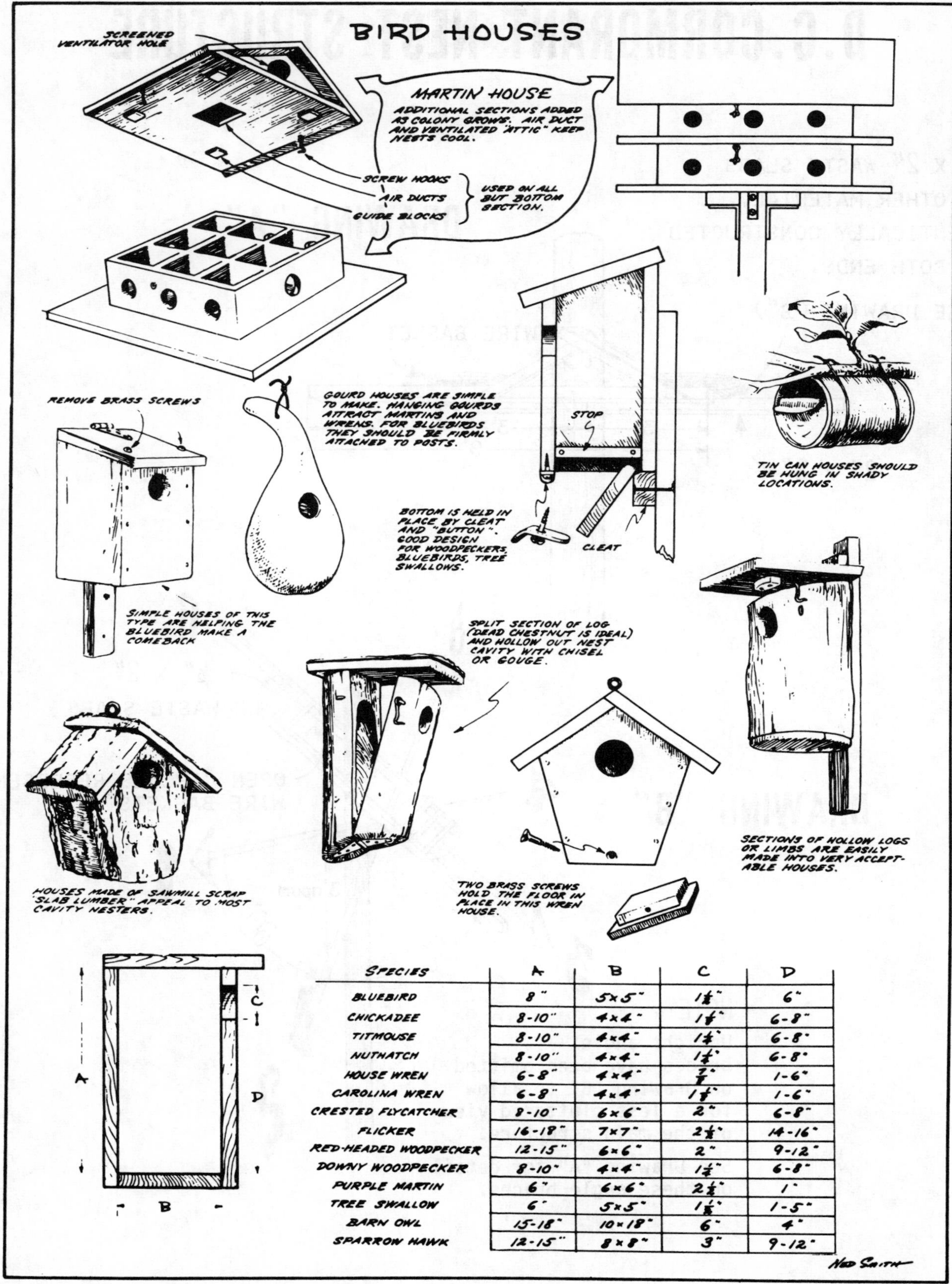

SPECIES	A	B	C	D
BLUEBIRD	8"	5×5"	1 1/2"	6"
CHICKADEE	8-10"	4×4"	1 1/8"	6-8"
TITMOUSE	8-10"	4×4"	1 1/4"	6-8"
NUTHATCH	8-10"	4×4"	1 1/4"	6-8"
HOUSE WREN	6-8"	4×4"	7/8"	1-6"
CAROLINA WREN	6-8"	4×4"	1 1/8"	1-6"
CRESTED FLYCATCHER	8-10"	6×6"	2"	6-8"
FLICKER	16-18"	7×7"	2 1/2"	14-16"
RED-HEADED WOODPECKER	12-15"	6×6"	2"	9-12"
DOWNY WOODPECKER	8-10"	4×4"	1 1/4"	6-8"
PURPLE MARTIN	6"	6×6"	2 1/2"	1"
TREE SWALLOW	6"	5×5"	1 1/2"	1-5"
BARN OWL	15-18"	10×18"	6"	4"
SPARROW HAWK	12-15"	8×8"	3"	9-12"

Fig. 20.5. There are many styles or varieties of bird houses. The 1 main criteria for design is to build the nest facility to the size and needs of the target species (Shomon et al. 1966).

cations vary greatly and can make the difference in the success or failure of a newly constructed bird house producing nestlings. Table 20.2 provides the various specifications for 26 different birds.

In the U.S.S.R. and some eastern European countries, increasing emphasis is being placed on the role of forest birds in preventing irruptions of harmful forest insects. While the role of birds is generally considered prophylactic and contributive as a component in integrated pest control (Khramtsov and Timchenko 1976), certain species are believed to depress insect numbers during high insect populations (Blagosklonov 1977). Research efforts in attracting birds for insect utilization have significantly increased (Kuteev 1977). Blagosklonov (1977) discussed the results of an evaluation of artificial nesting structures, differing in construction material, dimensions, construction form and color. Evaluation criteria were based on the habitat requirements of 5 bird species important as insect predators.

Where intensive forest management has eliminated dead and dying trees, the placing of artificial bird nest boxes can be a beneficial wildlife management technique (Bruns 1960, Franz 1961, Williamson 1970, Beebe 1974). The installation of bird nest boxes can increase bird abundance which in turn can be an important factor on the control of insects injurious to forests.

Nest Boxes and Tires

Nest boxes must be properly designed, located, erected, and maintained for beneficial results. They must also be durable, predator proof, weather tight, lightweight and economical to build. The boxes also must meet the biological needs of the target species.

WOOD DUCK

No one type of nest box or placement meets all the requirements imposed by the diversity of habitat and predators. Consequently, each nest box program needs to be designed for local conditions. However, certain generalizations are warranted (Bellrose 1976):

Table 20.2. Dimensions of nesting boxes for various species of birds that regularly use them, and the height at which they should be placed above the ground (Kalmbach et al. 1969).

Species	Floor of Cavity	Depth of Cavity	Entrance above Floor	Diameter of Entrance	Height above Ground[1]
	Inches	Inches	Inches	Inches	Feet
Bluebird	5×5	8	6	1½	5–10
Robin	6×8	8	(2)	(2)	6–15
Chickadee	4×4	8–10	6–8	1⅛	6–15
Titmouse	4×4	8–10	6–8	1¼	6–15
Nuthatch	4×4	8–10	6–8	1¼	12–20
House wren	4×4	6–8	1–6	1-1¼	6–10
Bewick's wren	4×4	6–8	1–6	1-1¼	6–10
Carolina wren	4×4	6–8	1–6	1½	6–10
Violet-green swallow	5×5	6	1–5	1½	10–15
Tree swallow	5×5	6	1–5	1½	10–15
Barn swallow	6×6	6	(2)	(2)	8–12
Purple martin	6×6	6	1	2½	15–20
Prothonotary warbler	6×6	6	4	1½	2–4
Starling	6×6	16–18	14–16	2	10–25
Phoebe	6×6	6	(2)	(2)	8–12
Crested flycatcher	6×6	8–10	6–8	2	8–20
Flicker	7×7	16–18	14–16	2½	6–20
Golden-fronted woodpecker	6×6	12–15	9–12	2	12–20
Red-headed woodpecker	6×6	12–15	9–12	2	12–20
Downy woodpecker	4×4	9–12	6–8	1¼	6–20
Hairy woodpecker	6×6	12–15	9–12	1½	12–20
Screech owl	8×8	12–15	9–12	3	10–30
Saw-whet owl	6×6	10–12	8–10	2½	12–20
Barn owl	10×18	15–18	4	6	12–18
Sparrow hawk	8×8	12–15	9–12	3	10–30
Wood duck	10×18	10–24	12–16	4	10–20

[1]Many experiments show that boxes at moderate heights mostly within reach of a man on the ground are readily accepted by many birds.

[2]One or more sides open.

1. Initially, wooden boxes are more acceptable to wood ducks than metal boxes. But metal boxes have a higher nest success rate and in a few years may have a higher occupancy rate than wooden boxes. However, wood ducks need to be conditioned to using metal boxes by prior use of wooden boxes. For wooden boxes, rough-cut lumber is best. Smooth lumber can be used if a "ladder" of 0.64-cm mesh hardware cloth is attached inside so the day-old ducklings can climb out. Vertical metal boxes should be provided with either a hardware cloth "ladder" inside or with a car undercoat material sprayed or troweled inside to permit ducklings to exit.

2. Nest boxes should be made as predator-proof as possible or mounted in such a way to prevent predators from entering. Both wooden and metal boxes should have elliptical, raccoon-proof entrances, or be protected with inverted metal cones, or be attached to a steel pipe.

3. All nest boxes must be provided with 7.6–10.2 cm of sawdust, wood chips, or shavings to form a nest base and cover the first few eggs.

4. Groups of 4 to 8 nest boxes per ha ultimately have the highest use because of successful nesters and the associated young birds' homing behavior. However, grouped boxes have higher predator exposure and must have adequate protection.

5. Wood ducks use nest boxes on poles in water at a higher rate than those in woods. In woods, the nearer the water the better; up to 0.4 km is good, 0.8 km satisfactory, and 1.6 km a possibility for nesting. The more open and parklike the woods, the better for wood ducks and, unfortunately, for starlings. Dense woodland deters starlings more than wood ducks. Houses in trees should be placed 3.7 to 6.1 m above the ground where the canopy is open and does not overhang the entrance.

A design for both wooden and metal nest boxes for wood ducks is shown in Figs. 20.6 and 20.7.

Where starlings are a problem, a horizontal nest box can be substituted for the vertical box (McGilvrey and Uhler 1971). This nest box is constructed of galvanized duct pipe 30.5 cm in diameter and 61 cm long with 2.5-cm-thick wooden ends. The back is solid and the front has a 10.2 × 27.9-cm semicircular opening. Cylinders are mounted on steel fence posts over water and equipped with 61–91 cm lengths of aluminum downspout sleeves (7.6-cm diameter) to act as predator guards. A shallow partition may be placed in the center of the cylinder to prevent eggs or ducklings from moving forward and becoming chilled.

Cylinder structures should be used in combination with the metal or wooden vertical boxes to allow wood ducks gradually to accept the horizontal cylinders. It should be possible to switch the nesting population of an area from vertical boxes to cylinders over a 5–6 year period. Kestrels, tree swallows, grackles, purple martins, and great crested flycatchers have also nested in these cylinders (Heusmann et al. 1977).

The British Columbia Fish and Game Branch erected 30 wood nest boxes for buffleheads. Most were used by starlings and tree swallows from the start. However, 6 were used by buffleheads on 3 consecutive years. Reports indicate that buffleheads also used nest boxes in Alberta and California (Erskine 1971). Norman and Riggert (1977) reported 36% of nest boxes examined were used by ducks in Australia.

SQUIRRELS

The nest box designed by Barkalow and Soots (1965) has been slightly modified to provide a more durable and maintenance-free structure. See Fig. 20.8 for design specifications. The use of rot resistant or treated wood enhances durability of nest boxes; however, creosote treated wood should be avoided. The wooden nest boxes should be fastened to the tree with nonferrous nails.

The dimensions of this box also meet the specifications of nest boxes for kestrels and screech owls. Other species of wildlife known to use squirrel nest boxes for shelter or nurseries include flickers, nuthatches, red-bellied woodpeckers, starlings, flying squirrels, and tree frogs.

Tire nests have also been utilized for nesting by eastern gray squirrels (Burger 1969). The construction details are shown in Fig. 20.9. Tire nests should be hung over a branch at least 4.6 m from the ground with the open throat towards the tree trunk.

Nesting structures for squirrels should be erected at densities of 5–7.4 per ha in areas producing 45.4 kg or more mast per ha (Sanderson 1975). They are most effective in hardwood stands between 30 and 60 years when mast crops are abundant, but tree cavities suitable for sheltering squirrels are scarce. Nesting structures should not be placed in trees already containing tree cavities; squirrels will not readily accept artificial nesting structures if natural cavities are available in the same tree.

BLUEBIRDS, SWALLOWS

During the past 40 years, eastern bluebird populations appear to have plummeted as much as 90% (Zeleny 1977). The western bluebird and the mountain bluebird of the Rocky Mountain region have suffered less, but gradually they are experiencing similar declines. The loss is due in part to decreased old, decadent cavity trees needed for nesting and competition with starlings and house sparrows for limited nest sites.

Today's bluebirds are taking more readily to artificial nest boxes due to the scarcity of natural nest sites. During the past 5 years, nearly 1,000 bluebirds were raised in 85 nest boxes along a "bluebird trail" 11.3 km from Washington, D.C. (Zelený 1977). Canada boasts a 3,218-km "bluebird trail" through the prairie regions of Manitoba and Saskatchewan. Some 8,000 nest boxes were installed which produced more than 8,000 young bluebirds and 15,000 young tree swallows in 1976.

Bluebirds prefer open areas with scattered trees. Nest boxes may be constructed of almost any type of wood. They should be placed 0.9–1.5 m off the ground. Fence posts make good sites. Boxes should be spaced at least 100 m apart to eliminate fighting among highly territorial males. Figure 20.10 provides detailed plans for constructing a top-opening bluebird nest box.

Tree swallows also readily use nest boxes of the same specifications. Ponds and marshy areas are ideal locations to place nesting boxes. Backyards are another good place as swallows readily adapt to human activity and are welcomed for their habit of consuming numerous mosquitos. Nest boxes should be spaced 22.9–30.5 m apart on poles about 1.2 to 2.7 m above the ground. Fig-

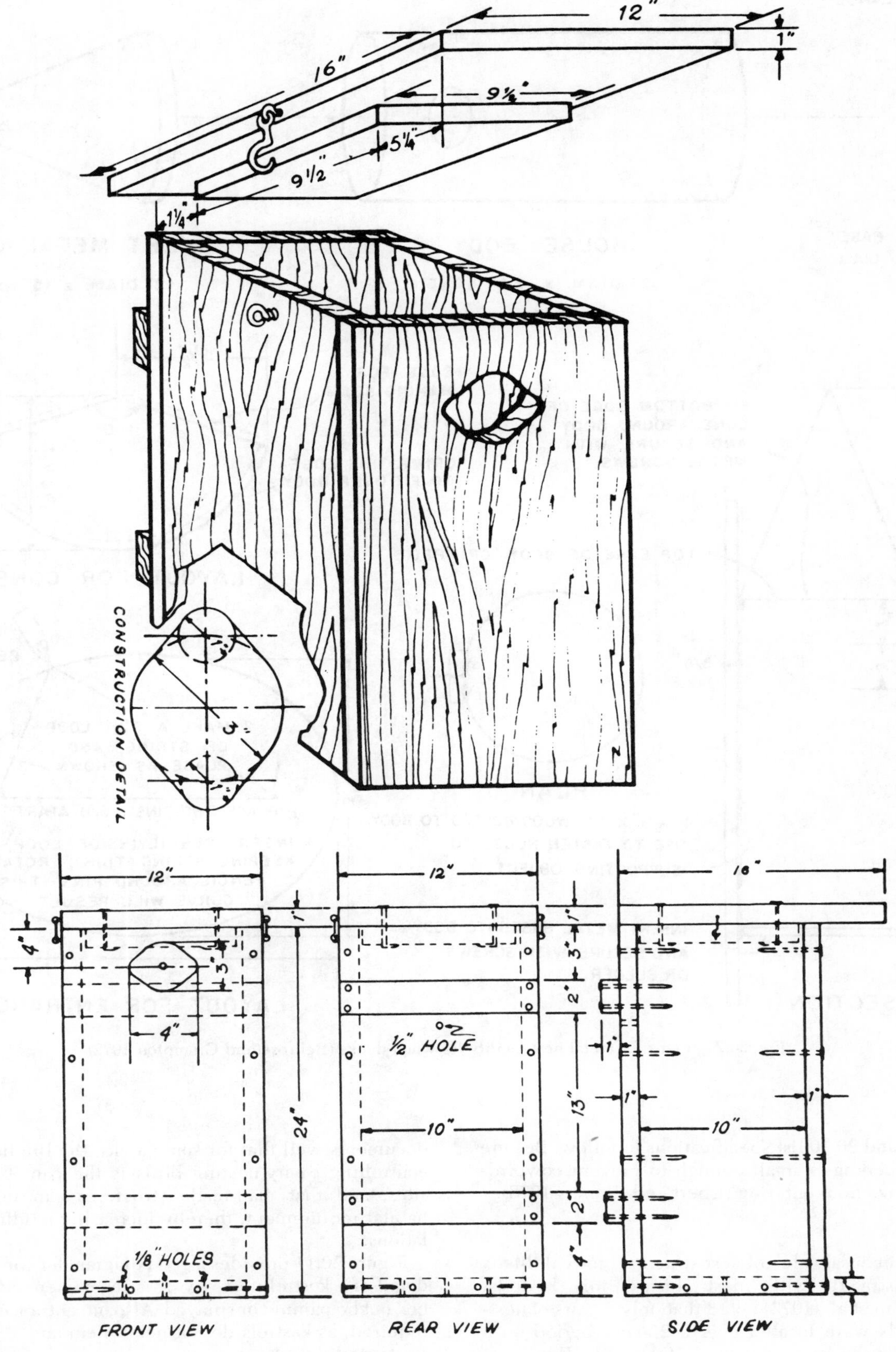

Fig. 20.6. Plans for a wooden nest box for wood ducks (Bellrose and Crompton 1972).

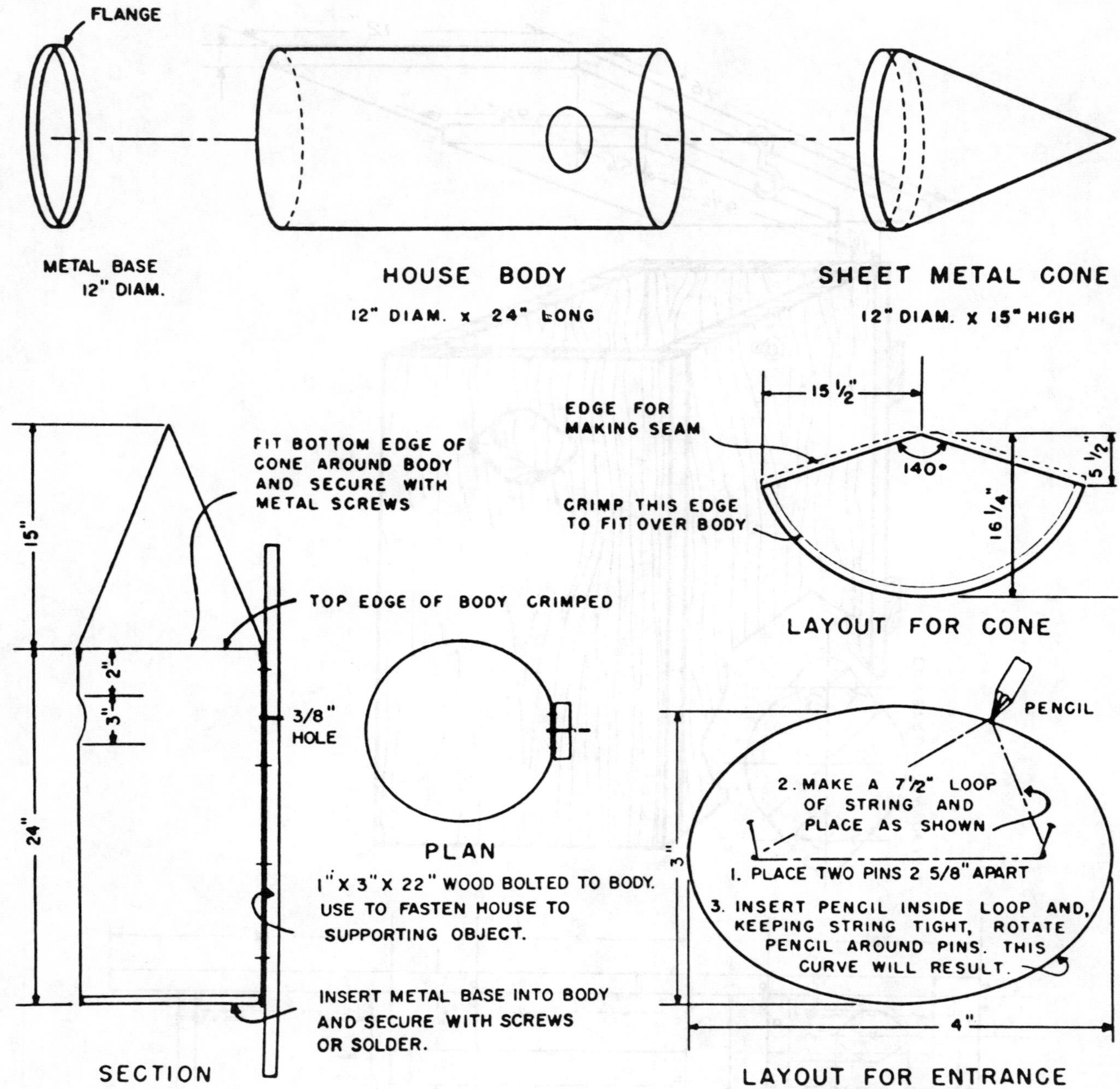

Fig. 20.7. Plans for metal nest facility for wood ducks (Bellrose and Crompton 1972).

ures 20.5 and 20.10 list specifications to follow. Be sure the box opening is small enough to prevent cowbirds and starlings from entering (Ebert and Francis 1978).

KESTRELS

The commensal value of nest structures for wildlife is well illustrated with nest boxes for kestrels. Hamerstrom et al. (1973) noted that only 3 pairs of nesting kestrels were located over a 20-year period on a 20,243-ha study area in central Wisconsin. Fifty nest boxes were put up from 1968 through 1972. These boxes successfully produced 8 to 12 broods per year, totaling 204 birds, or 1,600% increase in kestrels compared to natural production in the same study area. This study documents well that for some areas, the limiting factor controlling cavity-nesting birds is the paucity of nest sites, and that man-made structures can fulfill this habitat requirement, thereby increasing wildlife populations.

Figure 20.11 provides a good diagram for construction detail of a kestrel nest box. It is recommended that the box not be painted or sprayed. Also, no entrance perch is required, as kestrels do not need them and a perch attracts starlings.

Kestrel nest boxes can be placed in towns and urban communities, but they are most successful in rural areas. Place the nest box on a lone tree or post in or on the edge of a field. Kestrels generally nest 6.1–7.6 m from the

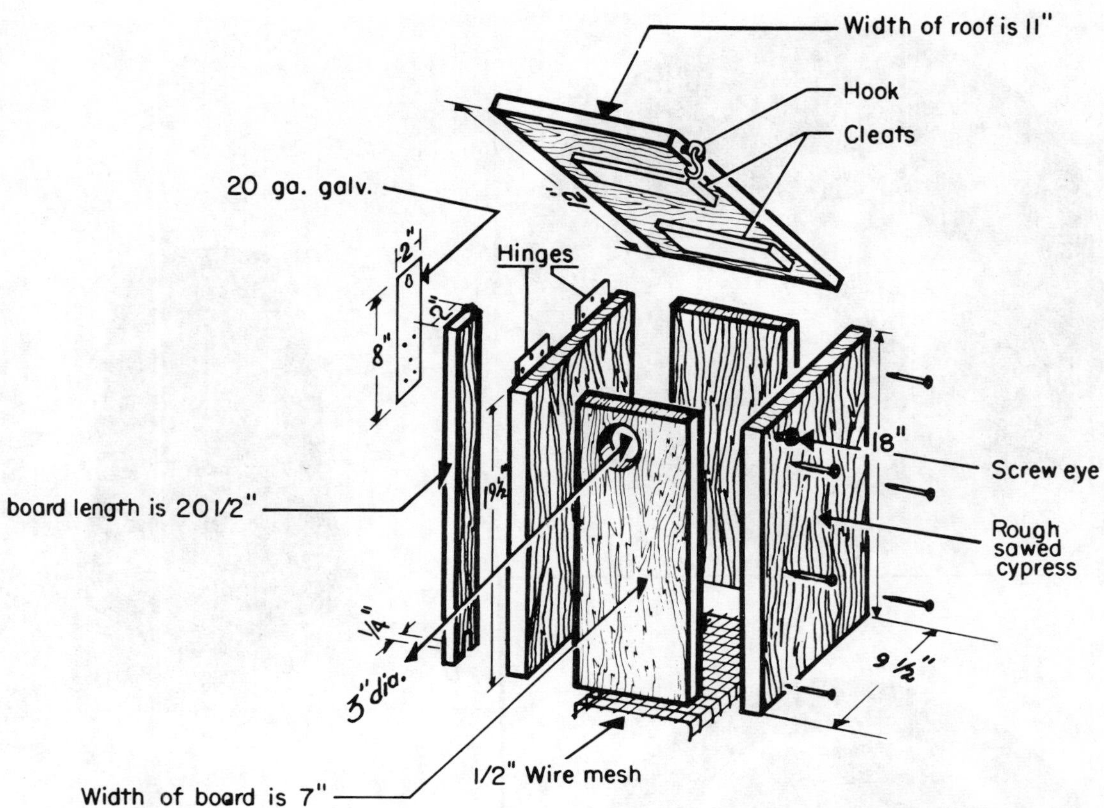

Fig. 20.8. Plan for wood nest box for tree squirrels (modified from Barkalow and Soots 1965).

ground and the nest usually faces south or east. They apparently prefer a clear flyway, so the space in front should be free of shrubs, limbs, or obstructions. Another favored site is old barns or buildings. Place 7.6 cm of coarse sawdust or wood chips in the bottom. This should be cleaned out and new material replaced annually following the nesting season.

Kestrel nest boxes have proven so successful and easy to install during the past decade, they are now located across the country in both Canada and the United States. This is another wildlife habitat improvement technique popular as a conservation project for youth and education groups.

MICE

Natural control of harmful insects is receiving increased emphasis to help offset massive chemical spray projects. H. R. Smith (1975) recommended the use of nest boxes to increase populations of deermice to prey upon larvae and pupae of the gypsy moth in young, even-aged hardwood stands. These nest boxes followed the design of Nicholson (1941) and were 12.7-cm cubes of 9.5-mm (3/8-inch) exterior plywood with a hinged lid and a 2.5-cm hole for an opening. Cotton bedding was supplied and replaced as it became fouled.

Platforms

WATERFOWL

Structures, such as illustrated in Figs. 20.12 and 20.13, have been constructed for the benefit of geese in the West (Saake 1968, Grieb 1970). Their value is especially great in areas where predation by feral dogs is a problem. Many construction variations may be employed; such as, 4 bales of hay instead of the tire, 1 stout pole instead of 4, and a large metal washtub instead of the wooden platform. The single pole specification is better than 4 steel posts in regions where ice movement is a problem.

Canada geese also will nest on floating nest structures constructed of a 20.3- × 55.9-cm canoe-like platform which supports a 48.3- × 66-cm nest box, an anchor, and an equalizer (Will and Crawford 1970). To give extra buoyancy to the platform, a sheet of Dyfoam 5.1 cm thick is encased with lumber. Splash shields are a necessity during high winds to keep the nest and eggs dry: 1 shield to the side of the nest box and an additional V-shaped shield to the bow of the platform. A dark-colored preservative should be applied to the nest box and box splash shield, not only to preserve the wood, but to camouflage the newly cut lumber. Prairie hay or coarse wood shavings should be packed tightly into the

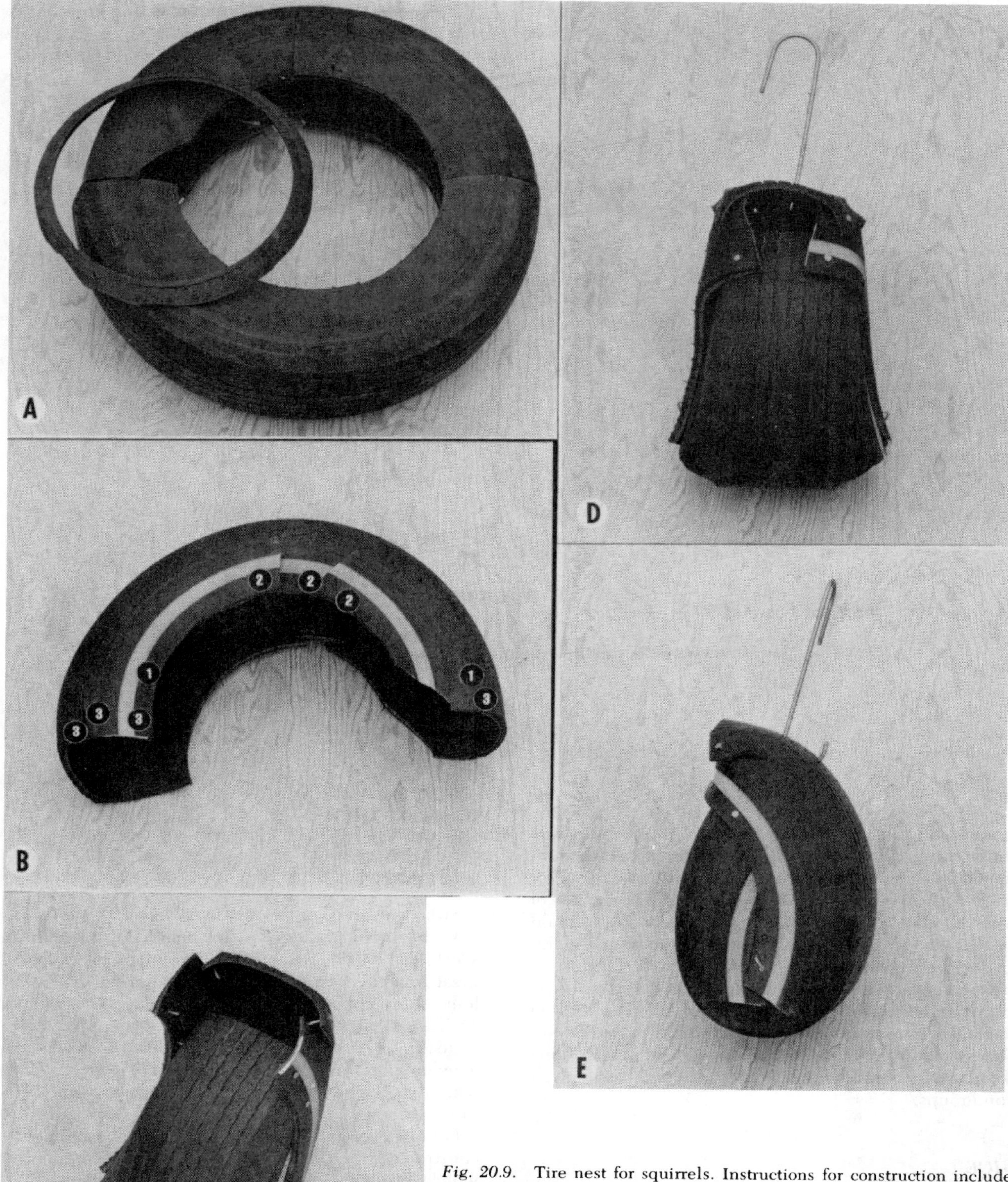

Fig. 20.9. Tire nest for squirrels. Instructions for construction include: (A) Remove steel bead from inner rim; (B) Cut tire in half, and cut ears off both sides at one end. Cut 7.6 cm slits in the middle on each side; (C) Fold tire and attach at # 1 hole inserting roofing nail from inside on both sides. Insert roofing nails in hole # 2 on each side; (D) Squeeze the top 2 edges of the tire together and attach nails in # 3 holes with roofing nails. Cut 7.6 cm slits on outside edges of tire. Make sure upper side overlaps to keep out rain; (E) Use steel rod or heavy wire and insert 6.4 cm from end of tire. Hang tire nest with throat towards tree trunk at least 4.6 m from ground (Maryland Game and Fish Commission 1966). (Photos by Larry Farlow, Illinois Natural History Survey).

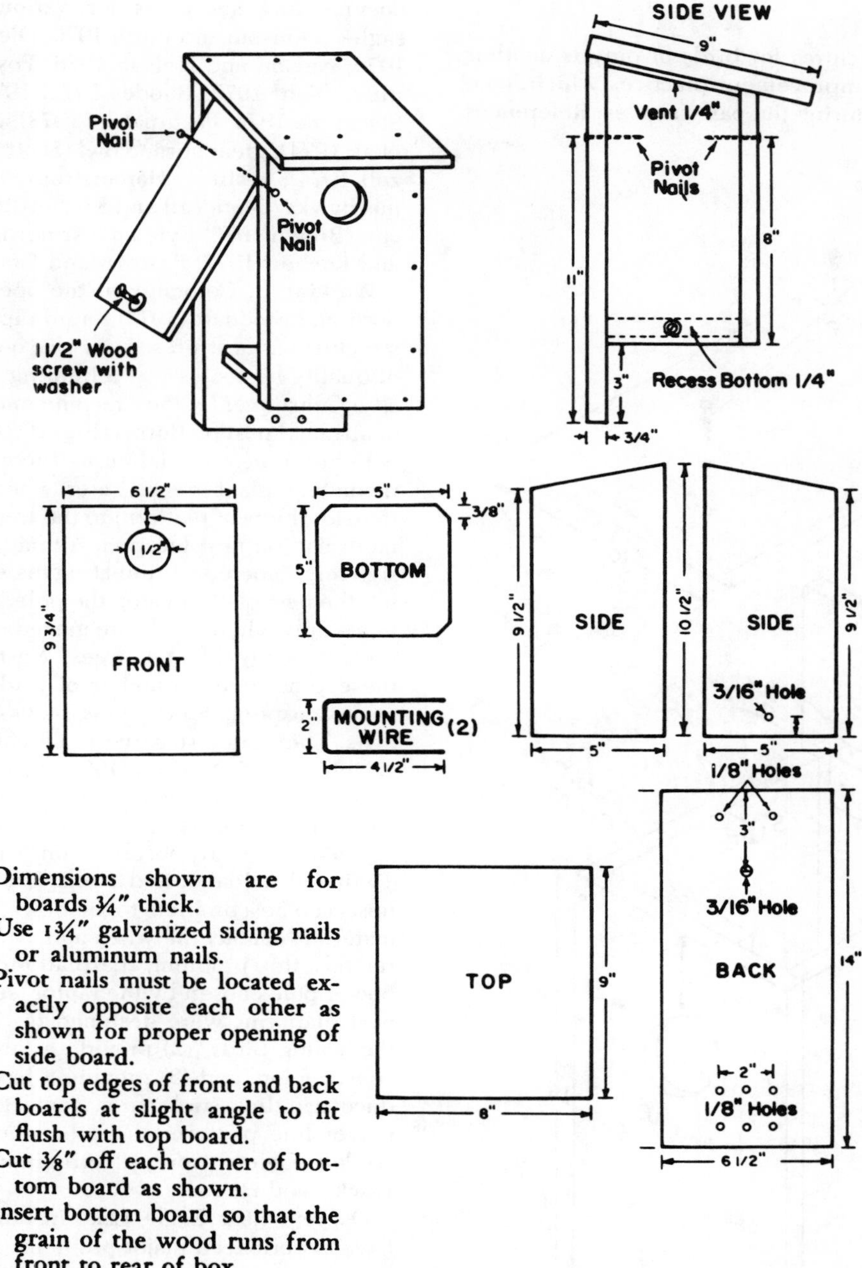

Fig. 20.10. Plans for a side-opening bluebird nest box (Zeleny 1976).

nest box to provide nesting material. The structures are easily stored by removing the nest box and splash shield.

In early experiments with floating structures, high winds dragged the anchor if it was attached directly to the floating structure. To prevent this, an equalizer was placed between the anchor and the structure, where it rode broadside against the wind. Structures anchored in this manner were not moved by winds exceeding 128 kph.

Forty-five kg of large rocks placed in a basket made from a 76.2- × 91.4-cm section of V-mesh wire laced together with galvanized wire has proved to be a satisfactory anchor. A new anchor was recently developed using heavy plastic bags obtained from the Ralston Purina Company, St. Louis, Missouri. Two bags, one inside the other, are large and durable enough to hold 49.9 kg of fine sand. Just before the anchor is dropped into the water, a number of small holes are punched into the bag to allow trapped air to escape.

For best acceptability, floating structures should be made available to Canada geese as soon as water areas are completely free from ice.

RAPTORS

Artificial nest structures for birds of prey is another example of habitat improvement practices which have greatly accelerated during the past decades. References documenting successes for various raptors include: eagles (Dunstan and Borth 1970, Olendorff and Stoddart 1974, Nelson and Nelson 1976, Postupalsky 1978); ospreys (Kahl 1972, Rhodes 1972, 1977, Postupalsky and Stackpole 1974, Postupalsky 1978); great gray owl (Nero et al. 1974); great horned owl (Scott 1970, Doty and Fritzell 1974); kestrels (Hamerstrom et al. 1973); ferruginous hawks (Olendorff and Kochert 1977); and prairie falcon (Brown 1976, Fyfe and Armbruster 1977, Olendorff and Kochert 1977, Postovit and Crawford 1978).

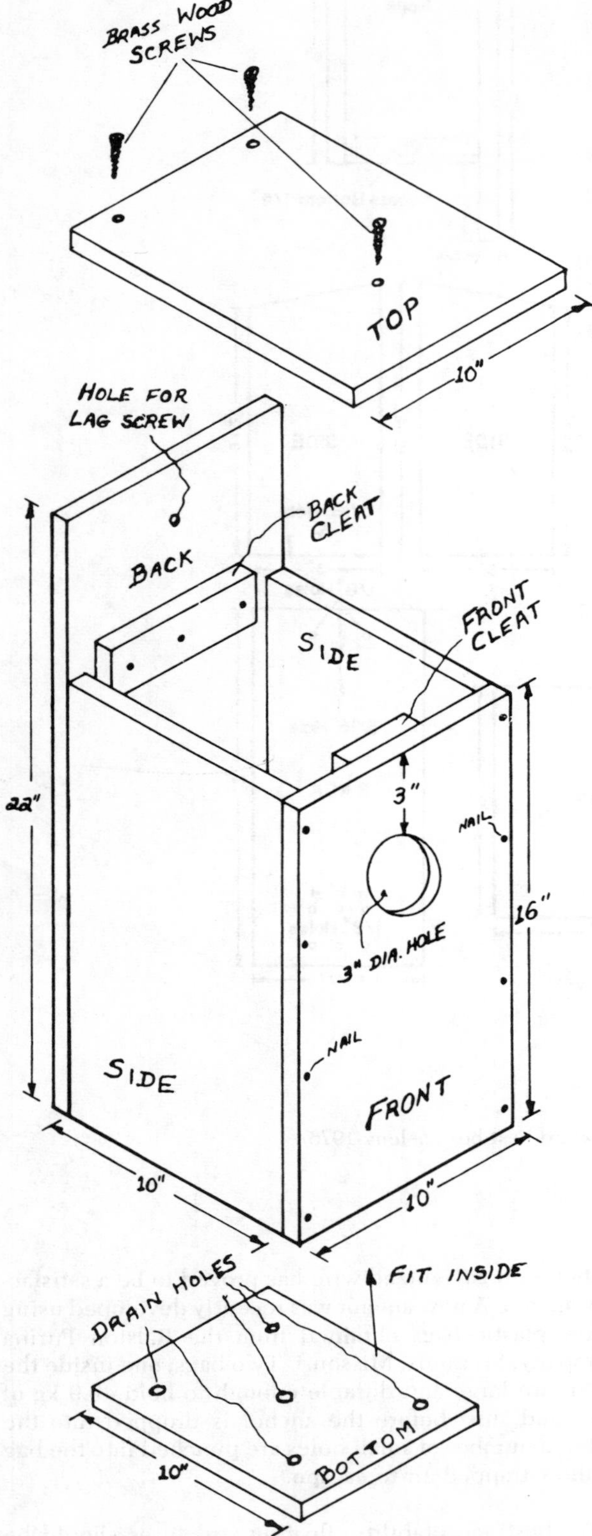

Fig. 20.11. Plans for a kestrel nest box.

Working in Colorado on the open grasslands, Olendorff and Stoddart (1974) found raptors using windmill structures as nest sites. They also noted that the absence of quality nest sites was a limiting factor to raptor density. Consequently they recommended the construction of artificial nest platforms (Fig. 20.14). A major objective is to build the artificial nest structure first and then immediately plant trees. Later when the trees mature, transfer the nest platform to the trees which results in a more natural nest location. Alterations of this basic design might include eliminating the shading device, placing the nest platform atop the pole, and constructing the fence only where cattle are grazed or when necessary to protect newly planted trees. Nest structures such as these can serve a number of birds of prey including eagles, osprey, ferruginous hawks, and great horned owls. They can also serve as perching or roosting sites.

Nelson and Nelson (1976) proposed a habitat improvement technique developed to accommodate eagle and other raptor nests on power lines. During 1973, 32 raptor nests were observed on a power line between Twin Falls, Idaho, and Hells Canyon, Oregon. These nests can be a problem to the power company when nest materials contact the wires and cause power outage. To remedy this problem, the platform was placed on the power pole chosen by the raptor (see Fig. 20.15). These nest platforms were designed to (1) provide shade for the young birds, (2) provide a large platform for nest construction, and (3) provide a base for the nest to reduce dangling sticks from contacting the wire. These power line platforms have been used successfully by golden eagles, ospreys, ferruginous hawks, red-tailed hawks, and ravens.

Ospreys near Eagle Lake in northeastern California have experienced major problems including the loss or deterioration of nest sites. State and federal agency personnel joined efforts and developed 2 techniques to improve nest sites, especially for these raptors (Kahl 1972). One practice required the topping of 15 large trees along the lake shores (Fig. 20.16). These trees ranged from 22.8 to 38.1 m in height and from 1.2- to 1.8-m dbh. To provide a good foundation for potential nests and reduce windstorm losses, 30.5-cm spikes were driven into the outer edges of the topped trees and a 61-cm-diameter platform was nailed on the topped tree. Osprey acceptance was especially good, and within a month a pair built their nest.

The second technique was to erect poles 7.6 m high and from 0.9-m to 1.5-m dbh near deteriorated snags used for nest sites. A 61-cm diameter nest box was nailed on top of each pole to anchor and protect it from windstorm damage. These structures were also readily accepted by the ospreys (Fig. 20.16).

Fig. 20.12. Various artificial nest structures used by wildlife: "A" placing wood chips in a wood duck box; "B" floating raft nest structure for Canada geese; "C" newly hatched Canada geese in a plastic tub; and "D" 2 double-crested cormorant nests on a platform. (Photos "A" and "B" courtesy of Minnesota Department of Natural Resources. Photos "C" and "D" courtesy U.S. Fish and Wildlife Service, Agassiz National Wildlife Refuge.)

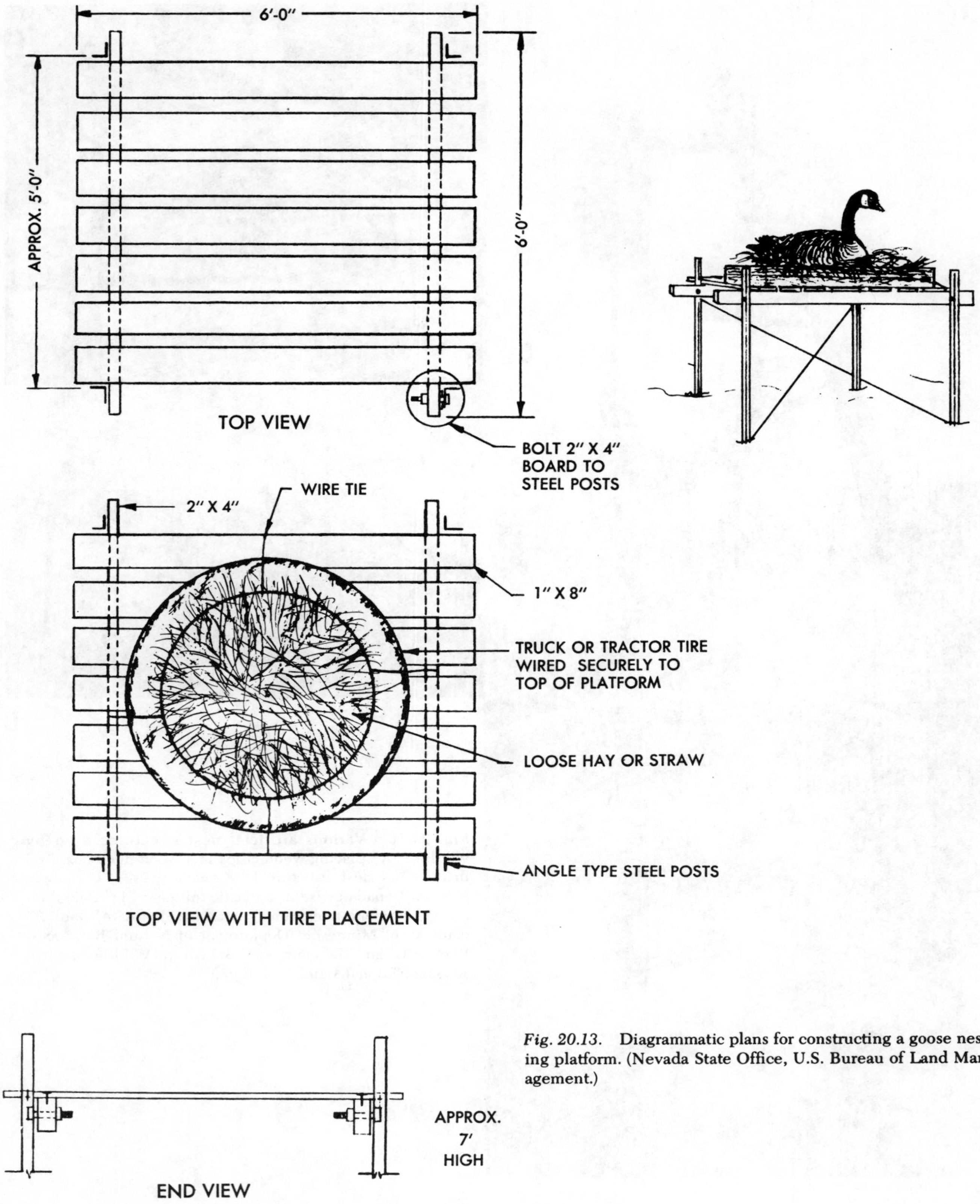

6'-0"
APPROX. 5'-0"
6'-0"
TOP VIEW
BOLT 2" X 4" BOARD TO STEEL POSTS
WIRE TIE
2" X 4"
1" X 8"
TRUCK OR TRACTOR TIRE WIRED SECURELY TO TOP OF PLATFORM
LOOSE HAY OR STRAW
ANGLE TYPE STEEL POSTS
TOP VIEW WITH TIRE PLACEMENT
APPROX. 7' HIGH
END VIEW

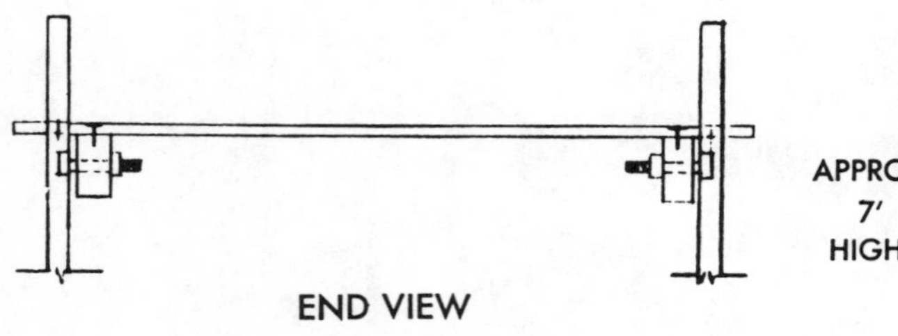

Fig. 20.13. Diagrammatic plans for constructing a goose nesting platform. (Nevada State Office, U.S. Bureau of Land Management.)

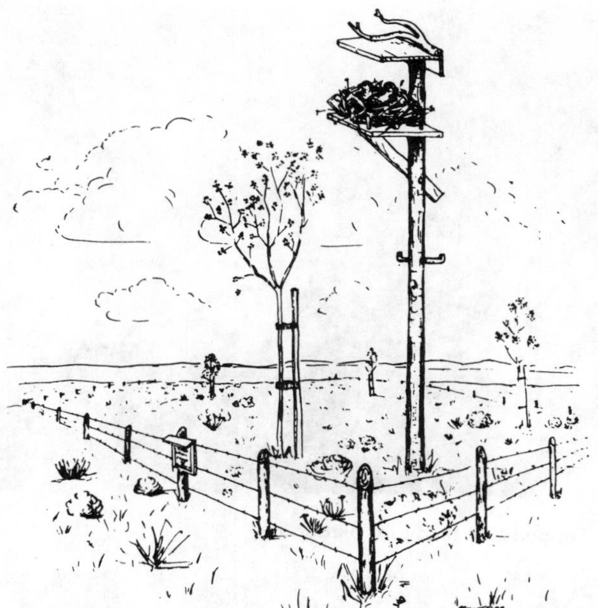

Fig. 20.14. Plans for an artificial nest structure for raptors (modified from Olendorff and Stoddart 1974).

Baskets and Cones

WATERFOWL

The following specifications have been used in the construction of durable and economic nest baskets for use of waterfowl. Materials needed include:

4 black metal rods, 53.3 cm × 0.6 cm (¼ inch)
1 black metal rod, 2.1 m × 0.6 cm
1 sheet of 0.6-cm (¼-inch) hardware cloth, 91.4 cm × 91.4 cm
1 I.D. (inside diameter) galvanized pipe, 45.7 cm × 3.2 cm (1 ¼ inch)
1 machine bolt and nut, 9.5 mm (⅜ inch) × 2.54 cm
12 medium pig rings
1 I.D. galvanized pipe, 3.1 m × 2.54 cm

Recommended procedures for construction of nest baskets are:

a. Cut cone from hardware cloth according to pattern "A" in Fig. 20.17, bend to shape, and fasten with 4 pig rings.

b. Bend 2.1-m rod to form a hoop and weld.

c. Bend the 4 braces (53.3 cm) according to pattern "B" in Fig. 20.17.

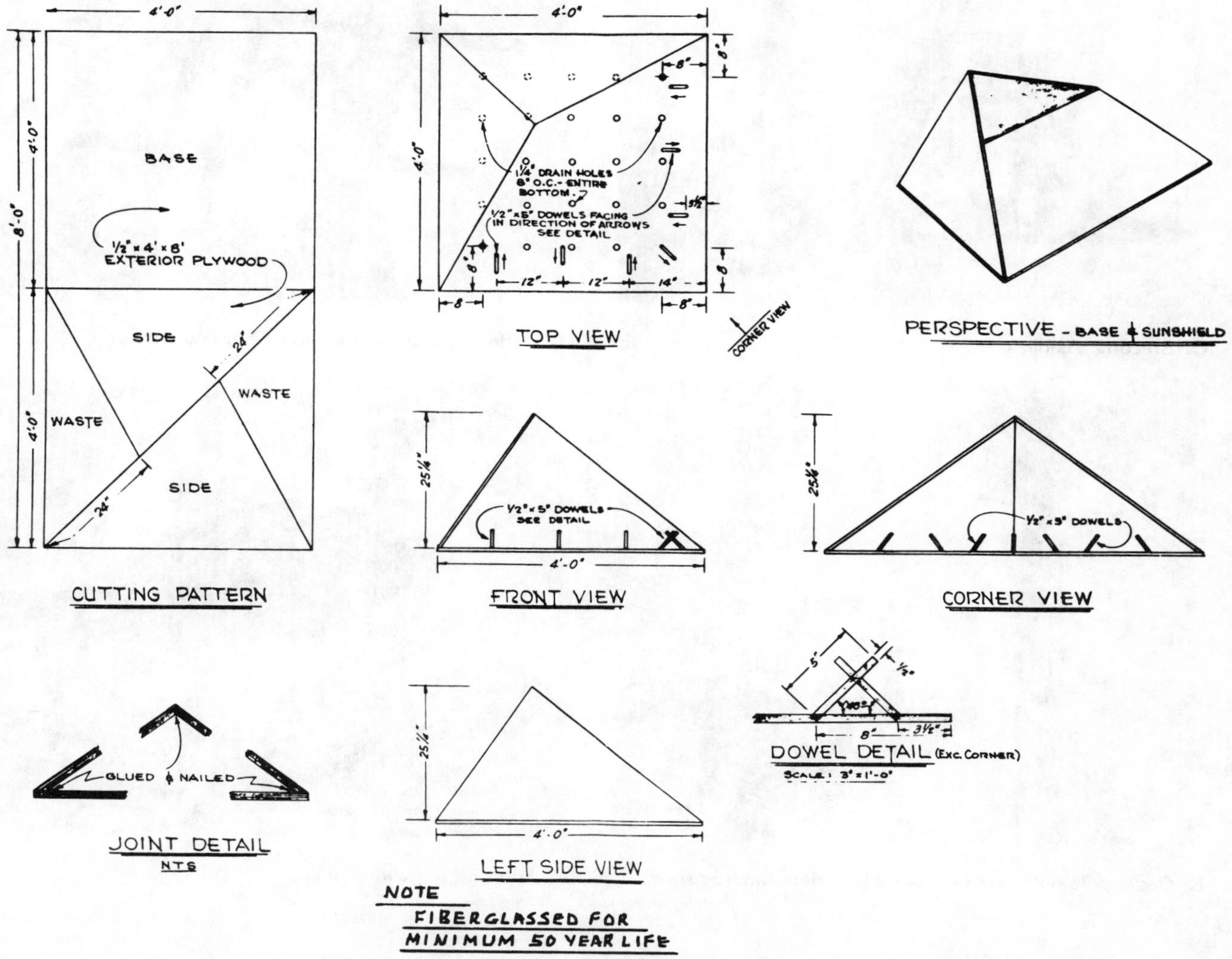

4'-0"
8'-0"
BASE
1/2" x 4' x 8' EXTERIOR PLYWOOD
SIDE
WASTE
24"
CUTTING PATTERN
TOP VIEW
1 1/4" DRAIN HOLES 8" O.C.- ENTIRE BOTTOM
1/2" x 5" DOWELS FACING IN DIRECTION OF ARROWS SEE DETAIL
CORNER VIEW
PERSPECTIVE - BASE & SUNSHIELD
25 1/4"
1/2" x 5" DOWELS SEE DETAIL
FRONT VIEW
1/2" x 5" DOWELS
CORNER VIEW
GLUED & NAILED
JOINT DETAIL
NTS
LEFT SIDE VIEW
DOWEL DETAIL (EXC. CORNER)
SCALE: 3" = 1'-0"
NOTE
FIBERGLASSED FOR
MINIMUM 50 YEAR LIFE

Fig. 20.15. Plans for a raptor nest platform for placement on power lines (Nelson and Nelson 1976).

A. Topping a pine tree.

B. Topped tree ready for platform.

C. Erecting a cedar pole.

D. Platform placed on topped tree or cedar pole.

E. Cedar pole without nest placed by a deteriorating snag.

F. Adult osprey with chick.

Fig. 20.16. Constructing artificial platforms for osprey (after Kahl 1972).

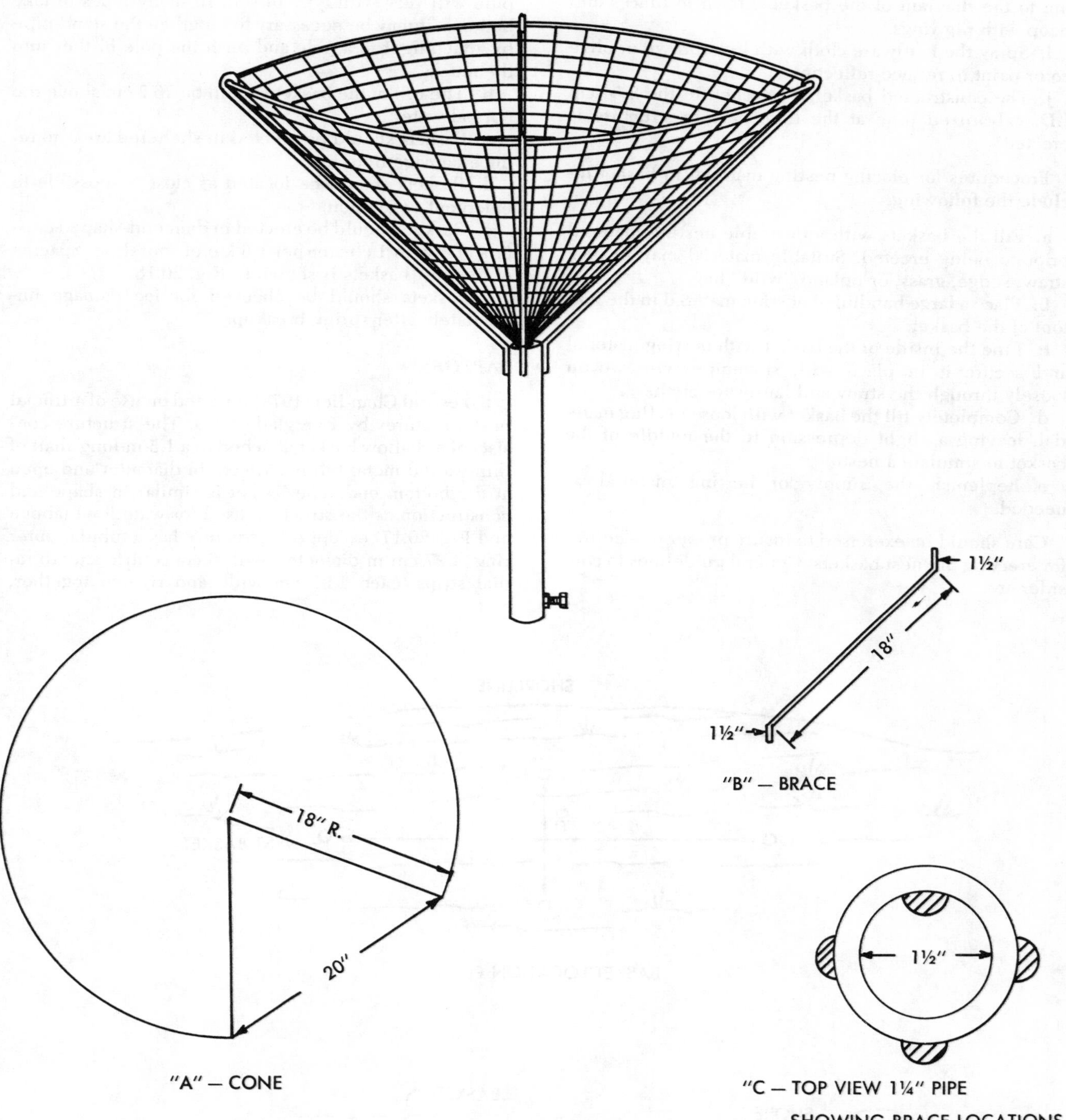

Fig. 20.17. Patterns for construction of waterfowl nest baskets.

1) Bend short hook in 1 end to fasten over hoop.
2) Bend other end of rod and place flat against pipe for welding.

d. Drill 1 hole, 11 mm (7/16 inch), in 3.2-cm (1 ¼-inch) I.D. pipe, 5.1 cm from end. This will be referred to as the bottom of the pipe.

e. Weld nut to pipe over hole and insert 9.5-mm (⅜-inch) machine bolt as set screw.

f. Weld braces to top end of 3.2-cm I.D. pipe according to pattern "C" in Fig. 20.17 (1 brace is welded inside to serve as a stopper in case the set screw loosens, allowing the basket to slip on the pipe stand).

g. Hook braces to hoop and weld in place.

h. Place hardware cloth cone inside of hoop according to the diagram of the basket. Attach to braces and hoop with pig rings.

i. Spray the hardware cloth with light brown or olive color paint to reduce reflection.

j. The constructed basket is attached to the 2.54-cm I.D. galvanized pipe at the time nesting structure is erected.

Procedures for placing nesting material in basket include the following:

a. Fill the baskets with a desirable nesting material prior to being erected. Suitable material may be flax straw, sedge, grass, or upland "wild" hay.

b. Place a large handful of nesting material in the bottom of the basket.

c. Line the inside of the basket with nesting material and secure it in place with stovepipe wire woven loosely through the straw and hardware cloth.

d. Completely fill the basket with loose nesting material, leaving a slight depression in the middle of the basket to simulate a nest.

e. Replenish the supply of nesting material as needed.

Care should be exercised to insure proper procedures for erecting the nest baskets. General guidelines to consider are:

a. Baskets should be erected in a minimum of 30.5 cm of water on a 2.54-cm I.D. galvanized pipe. Length of pipe will vary with type of soil. In many types of lake bottoms, it may be necessary to lengthen the stand-pipe by attaching it to a pole and push the pole further into the muck.

b. The rim of the basket should be 76.2 cm above the normal water level.

c. Baskets should be erected in sheltered areas to reduce damage from ice.

d. Baskets should be located as close as possible to emergent vegetation.

e. Baskets should be erected in diamond-shaped clusters of 4 with 1 cluster per 1.6 km of shoreline. Spacing of the nest baskets is shown in Fig. 20.18.

f. Baskets should be checked for ice damage immediately after spring breakup.

RAPTORS

Sykes and Chandler (1974) reported on use of artificial nest structures by Everglade kites. The structure consists of a shallow basket attached to a 1.5-m-long shaft of thin-walled metal tubing, 7.8 cm in diameter and open at the bottom end. The basket is similar in shape and construction as the structure used for waterfowl (above and Fig. 20.17) except this structure has a tubular outer ring, 1.27 cm in diameter, with 6 concentric and 15 radial strips, each 1.27 cm wide and riveted together,

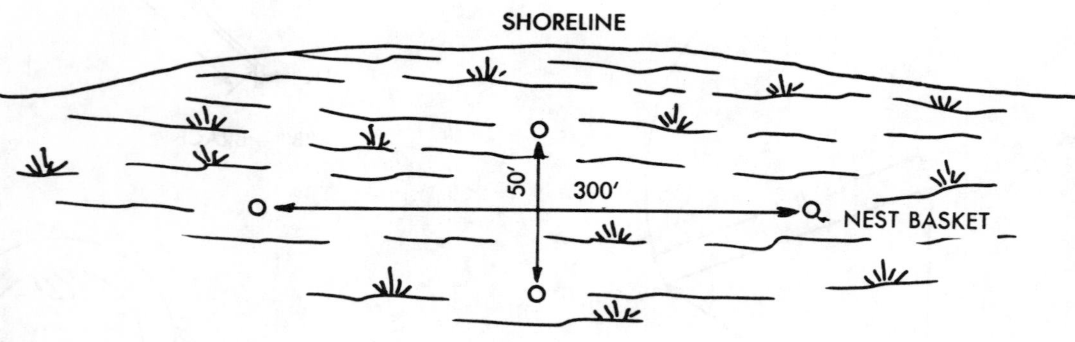

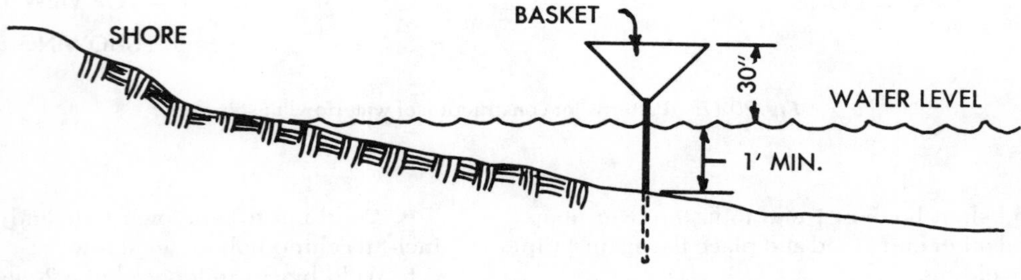

Fig. 20.18. Diagram of cluster placement of waterfowl nest baskets.

forming the nest. The basket measures 55.9-cm inside diameter and 7.6 cm in depth. It is supported on the bottom by 3 braces, which are woven into the basket and are attached by rivets to the main support tubing. Stainless steel, aluminum, or galvanized sheet metal all produce a reusable structure. Care should be taken to place the structure close to and at the same height above water as the existing nests. Young fledged in the artificial structures after eggs were transferred from natural nests to the artificial structures (Sykes and Chandler 1974). Perhaps egg transfer will not be necessary once a population adapts to artificial structures.

DOVES

Mourning doves generally build a loose, flimsy platform of twigs for a nest. Many are destroyed by heavy winds and rains. Artificial wire cone nest structures improve nestling survival (Cowan 1959). These wire cones are made of 6.4-mm (¼-inch) or 9.5-mm (⅜-inch) mesh hardware cloth. They are easy to construct and install (Fig. 20.19).

The best location usually is along limbs where branches are forked and where there is moderate shade. Most doves seem to prefer a height of 1.8 to 4.4 m above

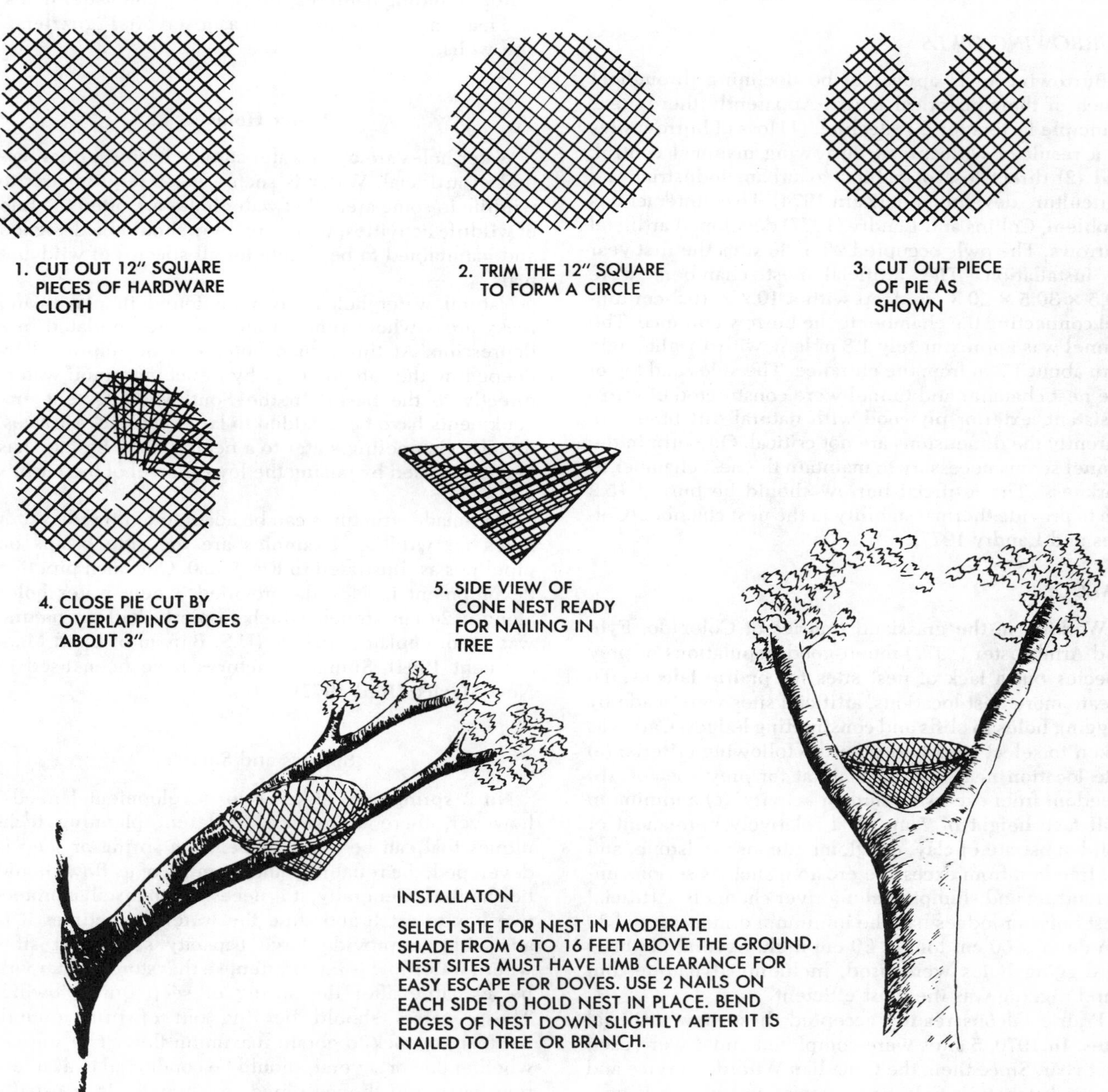

Fig. 20.19. Construction and installation of wire nest cones for mourning doves (Cowan 1959).

the ground for their nests. Sites must command good visibility and have enough clearance of brushy limb growth so the birds can escape danger easily. After the nest cone is properly secured, bend the outer rough edges down slightly to form a smooth place for the birds to alight. Best results in the Central Valley of California were obtained by installing the wire cones in late February, March, and April before most doves selected their nesting territories.

Periodic checks should be made to see that the wire cones remain securely fastened and that they are not obstructed by new branches. Clean out old nest material from the cones each year.

Burrows and Ledges

BURROWING OWLS

Burrowing owls appear to be declining throughout much of their historical range. Apparently there are 2 principle factors for this decline: (1) loss of burrow sites as a result of widespread burrowing mammal control, and (2) direct loss of habitat to urban, industrial and agriculture development (Zarn 1974). To counteract this problem, Collins and Landry (1977) developed artificial burrows. The owls occupied 20 of 30 sites the first year of installation. The artificial nest chambers were 30.5 × 30.5 × 20.3 cm deep with a 10.2 × 10.2-cm tunnel connecting the chamber to the burrow entrance. The tunnel was approximately 1.8 m long with 1 right-angle turn about 1.2 m from the entrance. The sides and top of the nest chamber and tunnel were constructed of warp-resistant, exterior plywood with natural dirt base. Apparently the dimensions are not critical. One turn in the tunnel seems necessary to maintain the nest chamber in darkness. The artificial burrow should be buried 15.2 cm to provide thermal stability in the nest chamber (Collins and Landry 1977).

FALCONS

Working in the grassland prairies of Colorado, Fyfe and Armbruster (1977) found good populations of prey species but a lack of nest sites for prairie falcons. To create more nest locations, artificial sites were made by digging holes in cliffs and constructing ledges. Care was taken to select sites based on the following criteria: (a) site location near suitable habitat for prey species, (b) freedom from excessive human activity, (c) a minimum cliff face height of 7 m, (d) a relatively permanent or solid substrate of clay, conglomerate, or sandstone, and (e) freedom from excessive erosion, such as serious undercutting and slumping along river channels. Artificial nest holes or ledges had the minimum dimensions of 30 cm deep × 60 cm long × 30 cm high. Several methods of digging holes were used, including dynamite, but hand digging was the most efficient.

Prairie falcons readily accepted these new artificial sites. In 1970, 5 sites were completed and 4 were used that year. Since then, the Canadian Wildlife Service and the Saskatchewan Falconry Association have made over 200 similar artificial sites and one-fourth have been occupied.

WATER DEVELOPMENTS

The amount, availability, and presence of water throughout the year can be improved for purposes of increasing wildlife numbers or expanding the use of habitat. Water can be "removed" to reduce animal numbers and feeding in areas where they are undesired. Frequently water is developed for various other uses than specifically for wildlife. For one 11-year rangeland rehabilitation program in a 96- by 282-km area of southeastern Oregon, 1,600 water developments were completed primarily for the needs of domestic livestock (Heady and Bartolome 1977). When these uses are properly planned, water also can provide benefits to wildlife. Consequently, the habitat manager should be familiar with the various techniques for development of water including natural springs, seeps, and water holes; and man-made structures such as reservoirs, "guzzlers," and wells.

Water Holes

Water holes are open water storage basins, either natural or artificial. Water is such a basic requirement to wildlife in some areas that water holes are often the hub of wildlife activities; therefore, they should be designed and maintained to be usable for all species of wild animals.

Natural water holes are often found in playas and rocky areas where runoff waters are accumulated in a depression. At times such holes can be improved by deepening the catchment or by trenching runoff waters directly to the basin. In the Southwest, cement embankments have been added to large, flat rock surfaces, thereby channeling water to a nearby hole. Storage has been increased by raising the lowest level of the basin's edge.

Man-made structures can be adapted to provide water holes for wildlife. Examples are the side basins on pipelines as illustrated in Fig. 20.20. One such pipeline development in Nevada provided 3 new water holes along a 24-km stretch which formerly had no natural waters for chukar partridge (U.S. Bureau of Land Management 1964). Similar structures have been used in New Mexico (Bird 1977).

Springs and Seeps

No 2 springs are alike as to developmental needs; however, there are several different planning techniques that can be applied. Before a spring or seep is developed, the reliability and quantity of its flow should be checked. Generally, it is necessary to install a protective box to catch and store the water. Sometimes it is advisable to provide large capacity storage at sites where waterflow is intermittent so that stored water will be available after the spring or seep quits flowing. These waters should be dug out of firm ground, hardpan, or rock to obtain maximum flow. The source, whether one or several, should be conducted to a collection basin and thence piped to a trough. It is usually necessary and desirable to fence the water source and collection basin from human or livestock use.

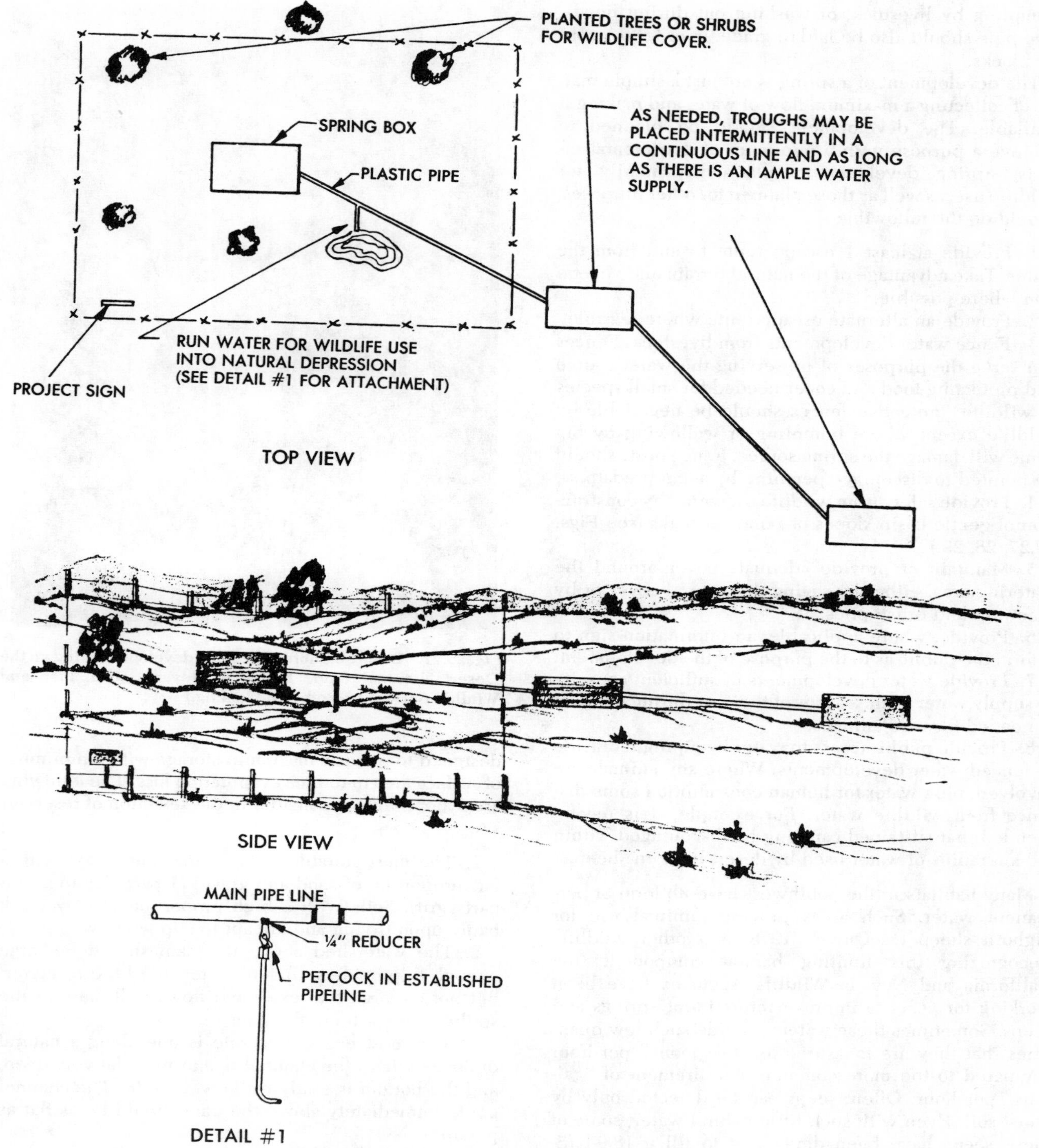

Fig. 20.20. Water developments for many uses can be modified for the benefit of wildlife. This drawing of a spring improvement for livestock in Nevada included a side basin installation for chukars. (Nevada State Office, U.S. Bureau of Land Management.)

In the central and western U.S., many springs are found in canyon bottoms and when developed often become a maintenance problem due to storm flood damage. Flood damage can be reduced for canyon bottom projects by burying a short length of perforated asphalt soil pipe in packed gravel at the water source from which the water is piped to a basin out of the canyon bottom. This technique allows storm water to flow over the buried source of spring water without damage to the development work (Weaver et al. 1959).

For wildlife water developments, plastic pipe is usually preferred to galvanized iron pipe since it is lighter and easier to transport and lay. The pipe should be buried deep enough to escape damage by freezing, trampling by livestock, or washing out during floods. The pipe should also be laid to grade, in order to avoid air blocks.

The development of a spring is not just a simple matter of collecting a maximum flow of water and making it available. The development should be planned to achieve a purpose with a minimum of detrimental effects. Spring developments planned primarily for wildlife use, as well as those planned for other purposes, should do the following:

1. Provide at least 1 escape route to and from the water. Take advantage of the natural terrain and vegetation where possible.
2. Provide an alternate escape route where feasible.
3. Fence water developments from livestock. Fences can serve the purposes of preserving the water source and protecting food and cover needed for small species of wildlife. Protective fences should be negotiable by wildlife except where trampling or wallowing by big game will damage the spring source. Fence posts should be pointed to discourage perching by avian predators.
4. Provide safety from wildlife drowning by construction of gentle basin slopes or ramps in tanks (see Figs. 20.27, 28, 29.)
5. Maintain or provide adequate cover around the watering area, either by saving the natural cover or by plantings and brush piles.
6. Provide, where applicable, an information sign to inform the public as to the purpose of the development.
7. Provide water developments of sufficient capacity to supply water at all seasons of the year during which it is needed for wild animals.
8. Provide public access to water by piping it outside of fenced water developments. Where shy animals are involved, pipe water for human consumption some distance from wildlife water. For example, it is recommended that sustained camping be discouraged within 0.8-km radius of water used by desert bighorn sheep.

Many habitats in the Southwest have no form of permanent water. Such areas provide minimal use for bighorn sheep (McQuivey 1978) and other wildlife. Recognizing this limiting habitat component, the California and Nevada Wildlife Agencies have been working for years to improve intermittent springs and seeps. Sometimes these waters provide such low quantities that they are measured as "teaspoons" per hour compared to the more common measurement of "gallons" per hour. Often, seeps can be detected only by moist soil. Even with such little natural water, some of these seeps have been developed to fill a 18.9-l (5-gallon) or 37.8-l (10-gallon) container. Bighorns have been seen to wait their turn for such available drinking water (C. Hansen pers. comm.). Figure 20.21 illustrates desert bighorn sheep using a spring development.

Fig. 20.21. **Desert bighorn sheep at a developed spring on the Desert National Game Range in Nevada. (U.S. Fish and Wildlife Service photo by O. Deming.)**

Reservoirs and Small Ponds

The term "reservoir" as used here refers to water impounded behind a dam. It may be formed by building a dam directly across a drainage or by enclosing a depression to one side of a drainage and constructing a diversion ditch into the resulting basin. Reservoirs should be designed to provide maximum storage with a minimum of surface area to reduce evaporation loss. The following are major points to consider in the selection of reservoir sites:

1. The most suitable soils for dams are clays with a fair proportion of sand and gravel (1 part clay to 2 or 3 parts grit). Soils with a high proportion of clay crack badly upon drying and are apt to slip when wet.
2. The watershed above the dam should be large enough to provide sufficient water to fill the reservoir, but not so large that excessive flows will damage the spillway or wash out the dam.
3. The most economical site is one along a natural drainage where the channel is narrow, relatively deep, and the bottom is easily made watertight. The channel grade immediately above the dam should be as flat as possible.
4. Wildlife should have easy access to the water.
5. The dam should be located, if possible, to take advantage of natural spillway sites. Otherwise, an adequate spillway must be incorporated into the development.

The dam site should be surveyed and staked prior to construction. If there is any question as to the suitability of material for dam construction, an examination should be made by a soil scientist. Trees and shrubs should be cleared from the dam site and flooded basin. The foundation area of the dam should be plowed or scarified in the direction of the main axis of the dam so there will be a good bond between the foundation and the fill material. On sites where stability and permeability of the foundation material is questionable, a narrow core trench should be dug lengthwise to the dam, then refilled and packed with damp clay soil. Where suitable material is available above the dam, it should be obtained there so the borrow pit will become part of the reservoir and add depth to the impoundment. General specifications for the construction of dams should include these items:

1. The base thickness of the dam must be equal to or greater than 4½ times the height plus the crest thickness. The slopes of the dam should be 2½:1 on the upstream face and 2:1 on the downstream face.

2. Minimum width of the top of all dams should be 3.1 m.

3. The fill of the dam should be carried at least 10% higher than the required height to allow for settling.

4. Freeboard (depth from the top of the dam to the high-water mark when the spillway is carrying the estimated peak runoff) should not be less than 61 cm. The spillway should be designed to handle double the largest known volume of runoff and should be constructed at a level which will prevent the water from ever rising higher than within 61 cm of the top of the dam. A natural spillway is preferred. It should have a broad, relatively flat cross section, take the water out well above the fill, and re-enter the main channel some distance downstream from the fill. When a spillway is built, it should be wide, flat-bottomed, and protected from washing by riprapping (facing with rocks). The entrance should be wide and smooth and the grade of the spillway channel mild so the water will flow through without cutting (Hamilton and Jepson 1940).

New reservoirs usually do not hold water satisfactorily for several months. It may be necessary to spread bentonite over the bottom and sides of the basin and face of the dam to "seal" the impoundment so it will hold water. Samples of soil from the reservoir, the dam material, and the bentonite can be laboratory tested to determine how much bentonite should be applied. Another method of sealing reservoirs to prevent excessive loss of water is to line the basin with polyethylene (U.S. Bureau of Land Management 1966). After the basin has been made, it is covered with plastic sheets, then 15.2 to 20.3 cm of dirt rolled evenly over the plastic. Where there is the possibility of damage to the plastic by animals, 30.5 cm of soil must be placed over the liner.

While working in the Southwest, biologists for the U.S. Fish and Wildlife Service found that water-cut canyons offer suitable sites for small concrete dams and reservoirs to provide water for desert bighorn sheep (Halloran and Deming 1956). These small reservoirs were most effective where canyons narrowed down with steep, vertical sides of bedrock. Such arroyos make good construction sites, particularly on east or north facing drainages which provide protection from the sun and reduce evaporation. Dams should be firmly keyed into the bedrock on both sides and bottom. A pipe outlet should be incorporated into the dam. Water loss will be prevented if rock formations are checked from cracks and fissures. Rock sealing is, at times, an important phase of sound construction. Commercial sealers can be quickly applied to the dam after completion. Usually, such canyon dams should be under 12.2 m long and not over 3 or 3.7 m high. During the first several years after construction, the small ponds formed behind the dams will provide water for wildlife. After the reservoir becomes filled with gravel and sand washed in by rain floods, the water soaking into the gravel and sand is stored and protected from excessive evaporation. The stored water is piped through the dam to natural rock basins below or to cement troughs constructed away from the main water course (U.S. Bureau of Land Management 1964).

Small ponds can often be constructed quickly and efficiently for wildlife needs. Their small size and strategic distribution provide not only an animal's water requirements but add new diversity to habitats. One example is an area that was devoid of natural surface waters. Then an unsuccessful agricultural experiment left an uncapped artesian well. Wildlife managers channeled water from the well to a small excavated pond which now services over 155 different species of wild mammals, birds, fishes, and amphibians. It can be said that in this case, man created a new environmental niche which in turn provided a richer habitat for endemic wildlife.

Water Catchments

During the past 2 decades, there have been several types of self-filling watering devices designed for the use of wildlife. Probably the greatest numbers have been constructed for primary use by quail. However, many of these structures have been built specifically to benefit other wild animals, including antelope, bighorn sheep, deer, sage grouse, and turkeys. The California Department of Fish and Game (Glading 1947, Leopold 1977) constructed over 2,000 catchments for quail between 1943 and 1974. Since so many of these devices were installed for upland game birds (Galliformes) they have been referred to as "Gallinaceous Guzzlers" or recently, just "Guzzlers."

GUZZLERS

The guzzler is a permanent, self-filling water catchment similar to a cistern. The whole structure is so simple there is very little that can get out of order, and so a minimum of maintenance is required. Essentially, the guzzler installation consists of a watertight tank set in the ground which is filled by a rain-collecting apron. This apron collects rainwater and drains it into a tank where it is stored for use by wildlife. Where the device is intended for watering birds or small animals, they may enter the covered tank through an open end and walk down a sloping ramp to the water level. If the birds and other animals drink directly from the storage tank, all floating valves or other mechanical devices that are subject to failure are eliminated (see Fig. 20.22).

The most important step in the installation of a guzzler is locating an adequate site for its placement. A guzzler should not be placed in a wash or gully where it may collect silt or sand, or be damaged by flood waters.

Fig. 20.22. Water catchments for small wildlife species have been constructed in the western states. They have been an important factor in increasing suitable habitat (U.S. Bureau of Land Management photo by Ed Smith).

The size of the water-collecting apron should be proportioned so that the cistern will need no water source other than rainfall to fill it. Since the cost of digging the hole for the cistern is one of the largest expenditures, a site should be chosen where digging is comparatively easy. The tank should be placed with its open end away from the prevailing wind and, if possible, facing in a northerly direction in order that a minimum of sunlight will enter the tank. Such placement will cut down the growth of algae, temperature of water, and evaporation.

The cisterns used for guzzlers usually are made of either concrete or plastic. Occasionally steel tanks are used. The plastic guzzler is a prefabricated tank constructed of fiber glass impregnated with a plastic resin. If the construction site is a long distance from a source of washed aggregate, or if labor costs are high, the plastic guzzlers offer savings in transportation and labor costs.

With concrete guzzlers, only washed gravel aggregates should be used for construction; otherwise the concrete may start to disintegrate after 5 or 10 years. Tanks made of steel are used for guzzlers in some areas and are reported as giving satisfactory service.

Collecting aprons have been made of many materials. Concrete sealed with bitumul, galvanized metal sheet roofing, glass mat and bitumul, rubber or plastic sheets, asphalt, and plywood have all been used successfully. From the standpoint of maintenance costs, however, durable materials such as concrete or metal have proven most satisfactory.

The size of the water collecting apron or surface needed to fill a guzzler will depend on the size of guzzler and the minimum annual rainfall that can be expected at the construction site. Actually, the size of the needed interception area will prove surprisingly small because nearly 100% of the rainfall is collected. Calculation of the potential yield of the rainfall collection surface can be determined by the following formula:

Surface area in square meters of apron $\times$ 9.9 = liters per cm of rainfall. It is important that calculations be made on the basis of the minimum of precipitation expected, rather than the average or maximum, to prevent guzzler failing during drought years. Table 20.3 gives the size of aprons in square feet needed to fill 2271 l, 2649.5 l, 3046.5 l tanks at different minimum rainfall rates.

General instructions for installation of a concrete guzzler are summarized as follows:

1. Select the site and clear the apron. Lay out the excavation site for the guzzler. To square the outline, measure diagonally from each rear corner to opposite front corner and adjust stakes until these distances are equal. Excavate the rear portion to required depth and slope ramp at front to ground level. Line excavation with laminated Kraft paper.

2. Assemble reusable plywood forms for inner walls and hang in position with 10.2-cm clearance between forms and walls and floor. Level the forms and pour

Table 20.3. Size of apron needed for 600, 700, and 900 gal "guzzlers."

Minimum Annual Rainfall (inches)	Square Feet of Collecting Surface Required			Apron Dimension in Feet					
				Square			Circular		
	600g.	700g.	900g.	600g.	700g.	900g.	600g.	700g.	900g.
1	965	1,127	1,453	31	34	38	36	38	43
2	482	563	726	22	24	27	25	27	31
3	322	376	485	18	19	22	20	22	25
4	242	282	365	16	17	19	18	19	22
5	192	225	290	14	15	17	16	17	19
6	162	189	243	13	14	15	15	16	18
7	138	161	208	12	13	14	13	14	16
8	121	141	182	11	12	14	12	13	15
9	107	125	161	11	12	13	12	13	14
10	97	113	146	10	11	12	11	12	14
11	87	102	132	9	10	11	10	11	13
12	80	94	121	9	10	11	10	11	12

concrete between forms and walls of excavation. Tamp and vibrate walls. Pour enough concrete to complete floor and ramp. Trowel smooth, allowing 1.3-cm clearance between edge of form and ramp.

3. Remove wall from carriers, assemble reusable roof forms, place in position and cover with 3 thicknesses of Kraft paper. Place dishpan in position for manhole. Cover roof with 7.6 cm of concrete, place 7.6 cm of concrete inside the dishpan. Insert a loop of heavy wire or 0.6-cm reinforcing rod at center of manhole cover to serve as a handle. Provide a 15.2-cm curb at front end of guzzler roof. Pour a 7.6-cm skirt 0.9 m wide in front of guzzler ramp and provide a 15.2-cm trash wall.

4. Outline apron. Excavate a settling basin 45.7 cm in diameter and 20.3 cm deep in front of skirt. Cover entire apron and basin with Kraft paper and pour concrete 7.6 cm thick. Trowel smooth and provide a 15.2-cm trash wall around circumference of apron. Provide a hole of 7.6-cm diameter through trash wall for screened inlet to guzzler. Make holes for 1.3-cm-diameter iron coyote guard at 10.2-cm intervals across front of guzzler. Cover all fresh concrete with paper to ensure proper curing.

5. Allow to set for 24 hr, remove paper and forms, wash inside of guzzler with cement and water. Apply asphalt emulsion to apron. Install coyote guards. Cover roof with 25.4 cm of dirt to stabilize temperature within cistern. If domestic livestock graze the area, fence the entire guzzler against stock so there will be no chance of damage to apron, tank, or lid. When guzzler is constructed after the rainy season, it is best to fill it with water to aid in curing concrete and to develop bird or animal acceptance.

Although incorporating the same general principles as the concrete guzzler described above, the quail guzzler illustrated in Fig. 20.22 is dissimilar in many respects. This illustrates the flexibility and diversity of design that has been characteristic of guzzler development in various regions. The iron roof should have a gentle slope of around 5% for best performance and should be relatively smooth to prevent water from standing on surface. Runoff is caught at the bottom of the aprons and carried in pipes to the storage container.

In some localities the storage tank has been closed at all ends, or a storage bag is used, and the water piped by gravity flow to a small trough (Lauritizen and Thayer 1966). Here the flow is regulated by a float valve. Where such a valve is in use, a regular schedule of maintenance is needed to keep the valve functioning during the season when water is needed. Possibly the greatest value of this design facility is that it directly allows wildlife to use the water in the storage tank. This eliminates additional construction and maintenance costs experienced with additional items such as troughs and float valves.

Although most guzzlers have been constructed for game bird use, their values to big game were well analyzed by Roberts (1977). He researched the literature thoroughly to identify the needs and values for antelope, bighorn sheep, deer, and elk. Roberts' final comment was that water catchment devices for big game are a practical means of increasing wildlife habitat and distribution in arid areas.

Figure 20.23 portrays a guzzler adapted for bighorn sheep. Similar structures have been designed for and used by deer. The catchment provides for a precipitation collecting apron and underground storage tanks. From the storage tanks the water proceeds to a trough with a control valve. The project is designed to use water more efficiently through excess surface exposure causing high evaporation. However, it can require a higher maintenance frequency schedule and has a more limited use value for other species of wildlife.

The installation of precipitation catchment facilities on ranges lacking adequate water has been successful for pronghorns (June 1965, Sundstrom 1968). Figure 20.24 provides specifications for the catchment used. At first, a fence was constructed to control livestock use; however, this was later dismantled when its need was no longer justified. This construction type of catchment was installed in a variety of habitats and was used by deer, elk, sage grouse, doves, rabbits, ground squirrels,

Fig. 20.23. A water catchment constructed in the Southwest on a critical summer range inhabited by desert bighorn sheep. (U.S. Bureau of Land Management photo by Jim Yoakum.)

and many other species of wildlife. Possibly its greatest value is that it provides ready access of water to a tremendous variety of wildlife. Not only was the water used for drinking, but it was used frequently for bathing by songbirds, thereby qualifying as a genuine multiple-use improvement!

DUGOUTS

As cattlemen moved into the West, they constructed large earthen catchment basins to collect water for livestock. These excavations were commonly called "dugouts" by early pioneers and "charcos" by early settlers along the Mexican border. Lately, government agencies have been constructing many of these charco pits on public lands. Deer and antelope frequently make use of such improvements and rely heavily upon their use during critical dry summer months. Bighorn sheep are not frequent users of these projects but do benefit occasionally during seasonal movements to and from their ranges in rocky, mountainous terrain.

Dugouts may be located in almost any type of topography. They are, however, most satisfactory and commonly used in areas of comparatively flat but well-drained terrain. Flat slopes facilitate maximum storage with minimum excavation. A natural pothole or intermittent lake bed is often a good location for a dugout. Dugouts should not be located in wet or muddy areas because of the difficulty for large animals to get to the water.

Fig. 20.25 shows a small rectangular dugout with specifications. For larger dugouts the length, width, or depth may be increased, but the side slopes should be about the same. All sides should be sloped sufficiently to prevent sloughing (usually 2:1 or flatter) and 1 or more relatively flat side slopes (4:1 or flatter) should be provided for livestock or big game entrances (U.S. Bureau of Land Management 1964).

Modified Water Developments and Safety Devices

The habitat manager may construct water developments, such as tanks, troughs, or wells strictly for the

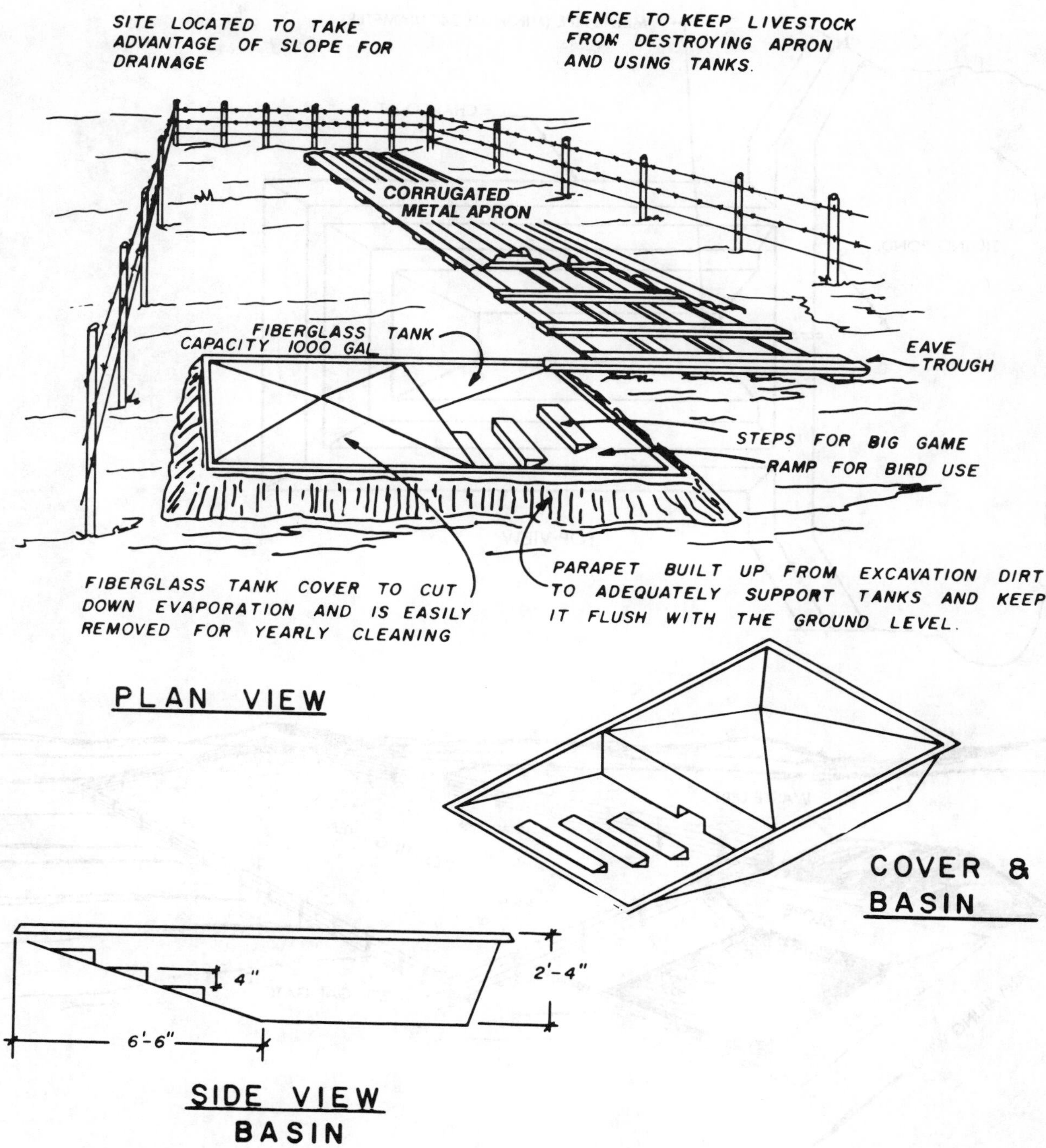

Fig. 20.24. A water catchment designed for antelope use on the Red Desert of Wyoming (adapted from June 1965).

benefit of wildlife. More commonly, water developments will be constructed for other purposes, i.e., for livestock, campground water storage, and fire suppression. Often a slight modification or addition to such developments can be made that will make water available to wildlife. Managers desiring additional information on specifications, plans and construction details for water improvements will find the following sources of value: *Range Improvement Standards Handbook* (U.S. Forest Service 1960), *Engineering Handbook and Construction Manual* (U.S. Bureau of Land Management 1967), and Vallentine's (1971) book: *Range Development and Improvement.*

Where water is scarce in dry environs, wildlife often readily seek and use man-made water improvements. Some of these are designed without proper considerations for wildlife use and, consequently, can become a problem by entrapment and drowning. This is especially true for young animals. The hazard of drowning can be reduced by floats, ramps, or ladders that allow avenues of escape. The best design will incorporate such escape facilities as a part of the improvement.

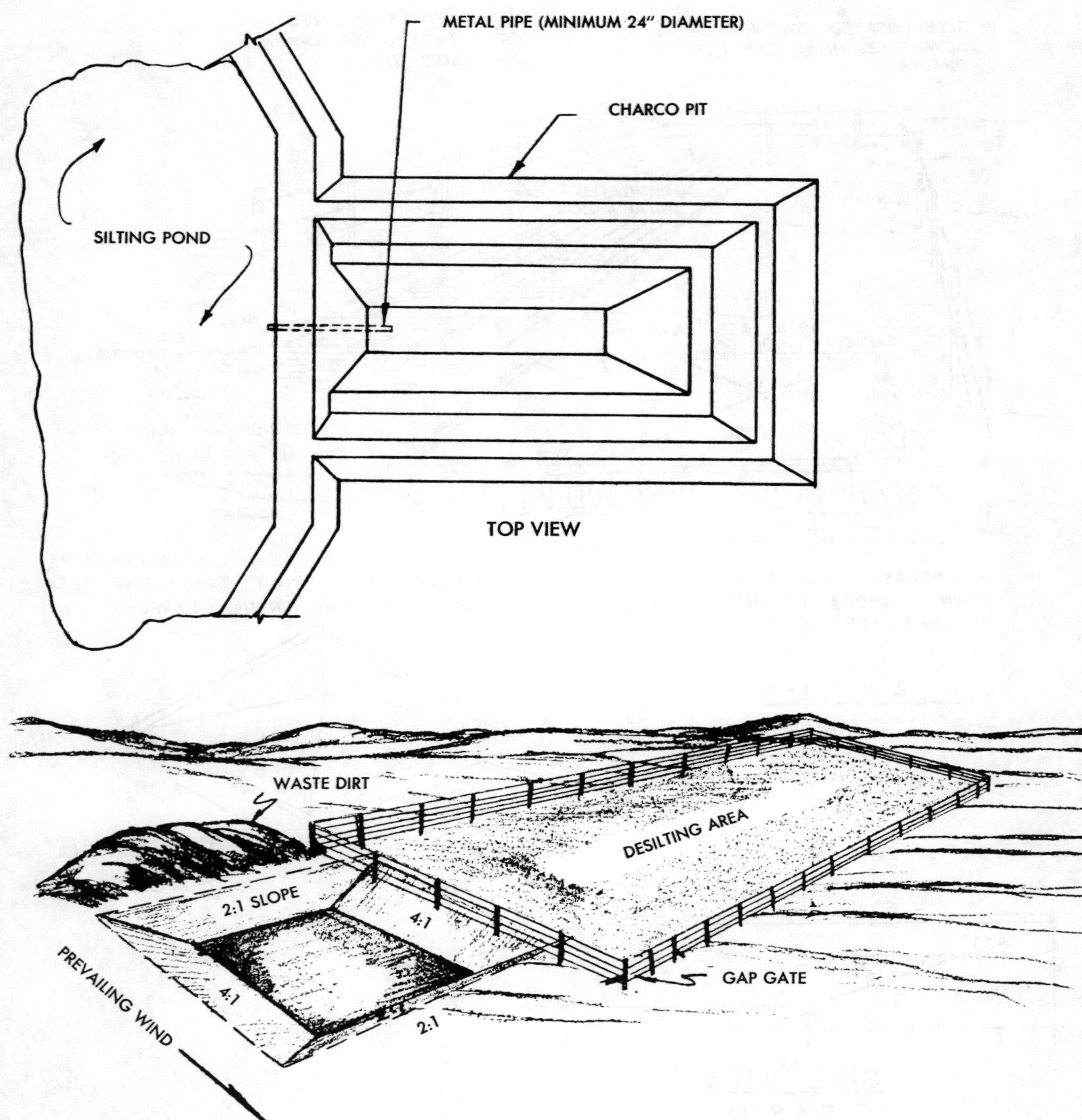

Fig. 20.25. Schematic sketch of a "dugout" or charco pit used in the west for providing water on the ranges for livestock and wildlife. Nevada State Office, U.S. Bureau of Land Management.)

Where this has not been done, it becomes necessary to improvise. Any float, ramp, or ladder placed in a water development should be relatively maintenance free and designed so that it neither interferes with nor can be damaged by livestock. Wilson and Hannans (1977) surveyed the subject of water development for livestock and listed the following guidelines:

1. Rarely are livestock water developments located in areas where terrain and cover conditions promote maximum utilization by wildlife; therefore, separate watering facilities for wildlife should be provided in association with the livestock development.

2. Fencing the wildlife water facility in a manner allowing wildlife use, but excluding livestock, is nearly always necessary to preserve water quality and insure growth of protective cover.

3. Water should be available in all water developments at all times, except in those areas where freezing during the winter could result in damage to the project.

4. Wherever ground-level wildlife drinking facilities are not provided in association with other water developments, the height of livestock troughs or other containers must not exceed 50.8 cm (Fig. 20.26).

5. Consider installing safety barricades in all livestock watering developments to prevent accidental entry and possible drowning (Fig. 20.27).

6. Consider installation of concrete blocks and/or rocks to form escape ramps on all livestock water developments where water depth exceeds 50.8 cm (Fig. 20.27).

7. When the lip of water troughs prohibits small wildlife from the water, construct wildlife ladders which allow the animals access. These ladders can be constructed of expanded metal or rebar and hardware cloth and should be protected by posts or protective fencing (Fig. 20.28).

8. An alternate method of providing small animal access to the water from outside the trough is to construct concrete ramps or rock ramps topped with cement (Fig. 20.28).

9. Large troughs posing survival problems inside the facility need escape ladders. These escape ladders must be constructed to intercept the line of travel around the edge of the tank. They should be attached to the structure by a hinge or bracket. Wildlife escape ladders should have a minimum slope of 30 degrees, but the incline should not exceed 45 degrees. A minimum of 1 ladder should be installed per 9.14 linear m of trough perimeter (Fig. 20.29).

In many livestock rangelands, large open water storage tanks are used which are out of reach for many species of wildlife (except birds and bats). For these developments, a floating wildlife platform should be installed. Figures. 20.30 and 20.31 provide examples of floating ramps.

WETLAND IMPROVEMENTS

Development of Water Areas

Techniques for improving wetlands will vary and are dependent to a large degree on the prior structural development of the area, water quality, water level management, soil, climate, topography, and plant succession. Sometimes wetlands can be manipulated by use of biological and physical forces to develop an improved environment for wildlife.

A biological need should be established before any plans for wetland improvements are made. The chief use or uses of the area should be the prime consideration in judging its potential development, although these uses are also largely determined by the location of the area and physical characteristics. Some areas may best be developed primarily for waterfowl, others for muskrat or other fur production. There will be other areas where these 2 features can be combined. The habitat manager can often use various practices to create interspersion of open water with marshland, interlace ditches and high spoil lands, plant vegetation for food and cover, and thereby create wetlands favorable to ducks and geese, beaver, muskrats, mink and warm-water fishes. For the habitat manager seriously concerned with techniques of preserving, managing, or manipulating wetlands, we recommend the *Techniques Handbook of Waterfowl Habitat Development and Management* published by the Atlantic Waterfowl Council (1972). A sizable portion of this book is devoted to making preliminary evaluations prior to development in order to establish need. There are also sections on improvement techniques, many of which are incorporated in this Chapter.

Fig. 20.26. A water trough financed for livestock use; however, a wildlife habitat manager added the following specifications for wildlife requirements: (1) that the trough be placed low to the ground for easy wildlife access; (2) that water be available for wildlife during critical dry seasons even though livestock are not in area, and (3) that an escape ramp (right distance end covered in part by vegetation) be installed for small wildlife. (U.S. Bureau of Land Management photo by Jim Yoakum.)

A. When trough height is 20 in or less wildlife have better access to water

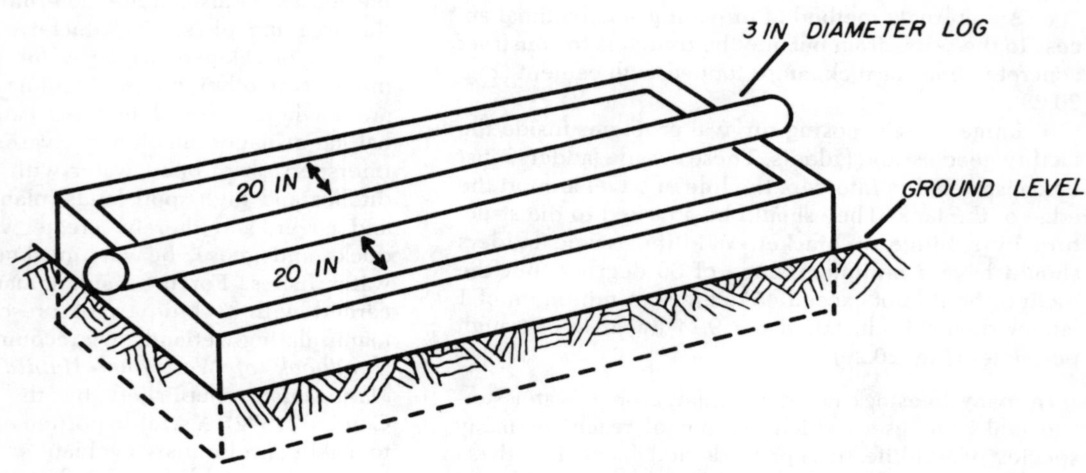

B. Possible barricade development depending on livestock trough configuration

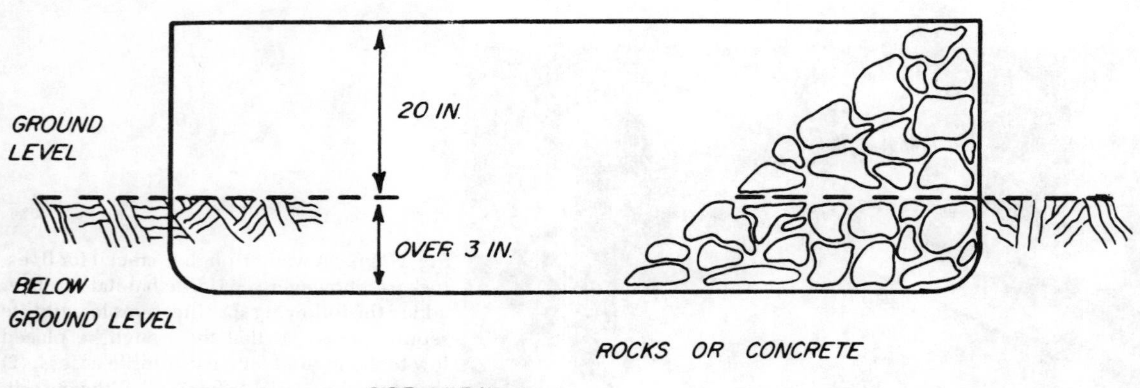

C. Placing of rocks, concrete blocks or other ramp facilities provide on escape route for wildlife where the water depth exceeds 20 inches

Fig. 20.27. Design modifications beneficial to wildlife for water troughs constructed for domestic livestock (adapted from Wilson and Hannans 1977).

A. Concrete ramps or rock ramps capped by concrete into livestock trough

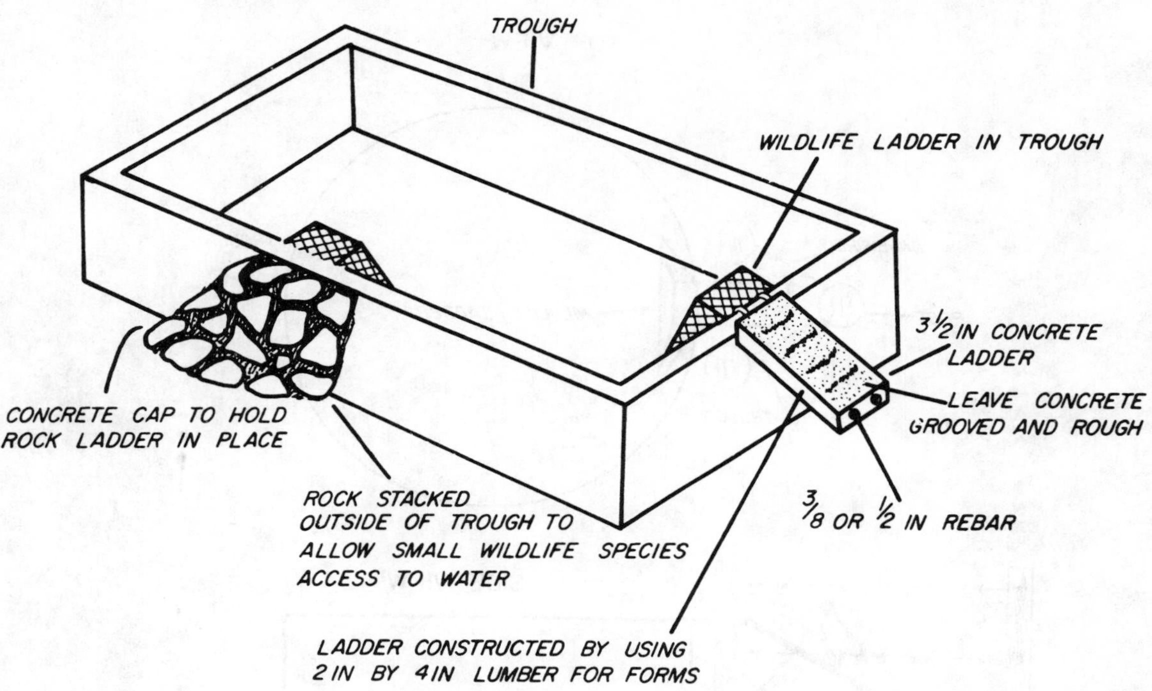

B. Details for a triangular shaped wildlife ladder

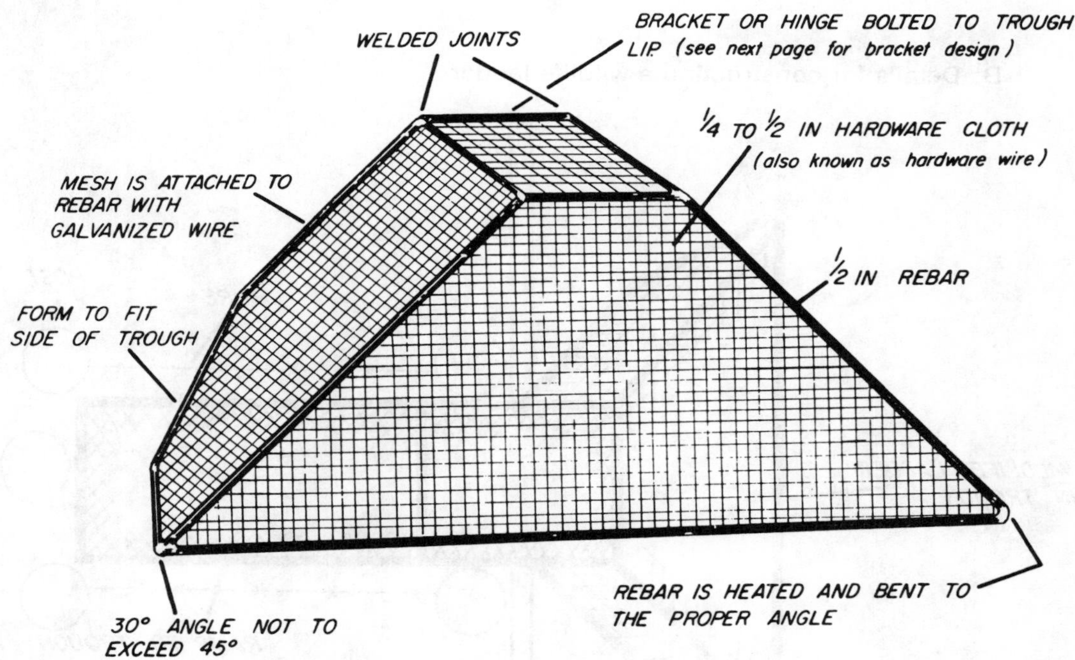

Fig. 20.28. Construction details for adapting a livestock water trough for wildlife use (Wilson and Hannans 1977).

SHALLOW MARSHES

Marshes provide nest sites, cover, and food for waterfowl and for muskrats and other furbearing mammals, such as mink and otter. Herons, cranes, rails, plovers, and sandpipers are the chief bird families that require marshes. Many forms of reptiles, amphibians, and fish complete the vertebrate fauna. A marsh should have open water areas if it is large, or an adjacent pond, if small, for maximum wildlife value.

Artificial impoundment is a common practice used to improve existing marshes or to create new ones. The objective is not merely to flood an area, but to control

A. Fencing and post arrangement to protect wildlife ramp leading into a livestock watering facility.

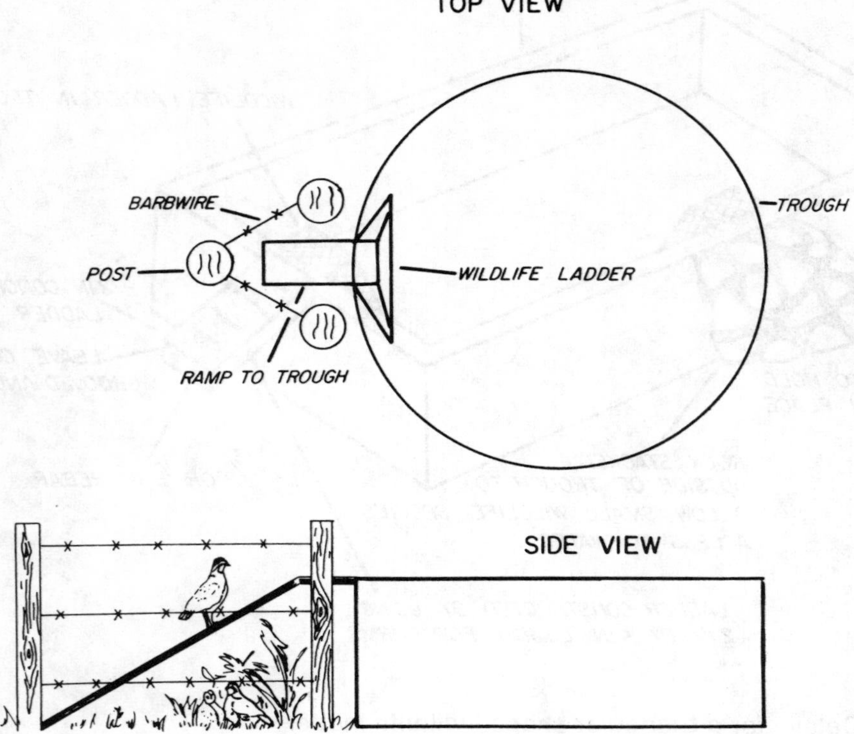

B. Details for constructing a wildlife ladder.

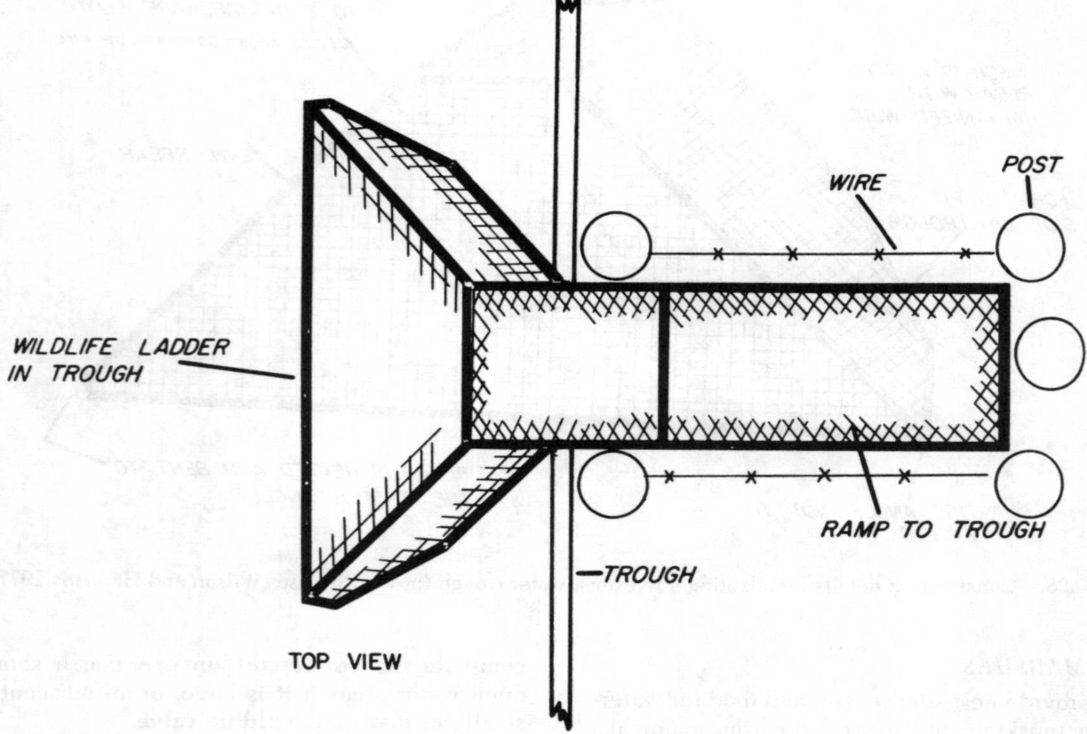

Fig. 20.29. Plans for modifying a livestock water trough by providing both an outside and inside wildlife ladder (Wilson and Hannans 1977).

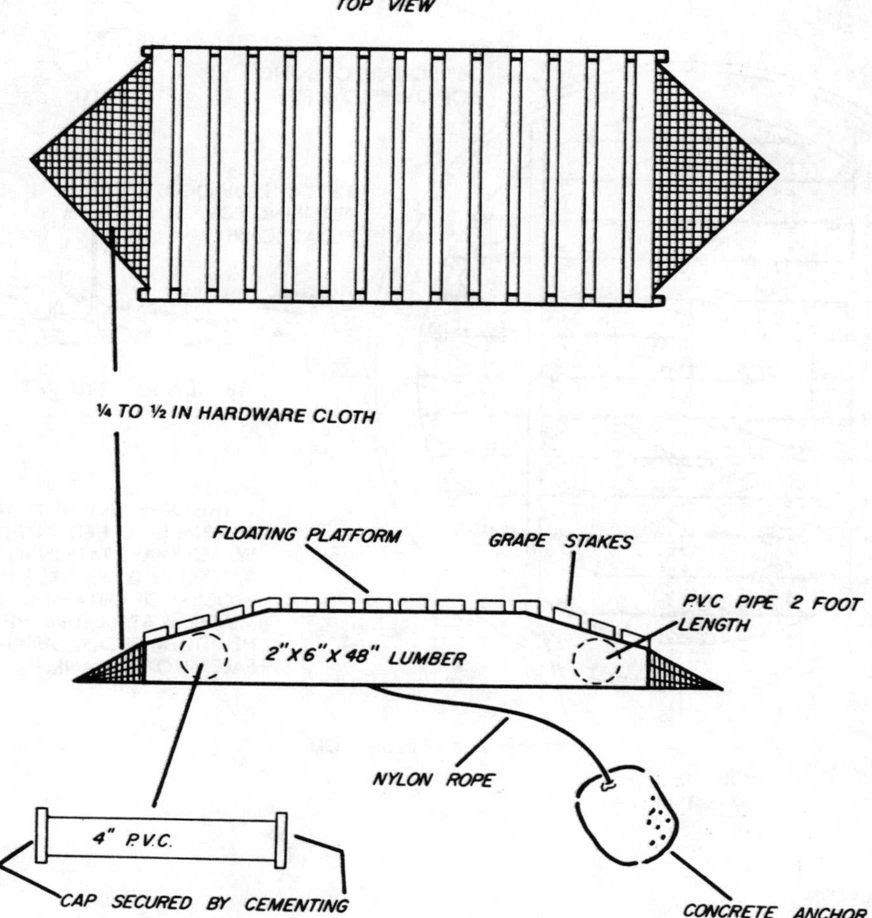

Fig. 20.30. Floating wildlife platform recommended for large open water storage tanks (Wilson and Hannans 1977).

water levels after impoundment as a method of managing food and cover conditions. Stoplog controls should be designed so that water level can be manipulated, including complete drawdown when needed. In most instances the average water depth should be 45.7 to 61 cm depending on site condition and amount of edge.

Ditching marshes increases the variety of habitat for furbearers as well as waterfowl. Deeper water in ditches helps animals find food and cover during dry periods. The spoil banks, on the other hand, offer dry resting sites, feeding areas, and shelter during flood periods. Ditches also facilitate access for hunters, trappers and maintenance crews.

Dredging has been found superior to blasting as a method of ditch construction. Blasted ditches tend to be shallower and loosened muck along the edges of the ditch is highly susceptible to wave and wind erosion. The lack of high spoilbanks desired for waterfowl nest sites and muskrat dens further reduces the value of blasting.

In constructing improvements in shallow marshes, the use of scoops, draglines, bulldozers, or combinations of the 3, are recommended so that the material removed may be piled along the edges. The high areas should be planted to a grass-brush cover.

POTHOLES, SUMPS, PONDS

Potholes may be defined as small, shallow, open water retention areas or basins with surface areas usually under 1.6 ha in size. These areas, when developed in conjunction with large, permanent water areas, can be a particularly valuable tool in waterfowl management. The purpose of making potholes is to create or increase water area lost to geological change and plant succession. An ideal wetland for waterfowl has one-third open water and two-thirds marsh.

Draglines and bulldozers have been used in construction of potholes, but they are of most use when ditching, damming, and diking are required. The use of a blasting agent is the most expeditious and economical method to employ in creating new small potholes. Recent experience has shown ammonium nitrate to be a very effective agent. It is less expensive and safer than dynamite. Best results are obtained with commercially prepackaged ammonium nitrate fuel oil charges (U.S. Forest Service 1969). In pastured areas potholes should be fenced. Fences should be located at least 7.6 m and preferably 12.2 m or more back from the waterline (Mathiak 1965).

Beavers, when skillfully managed, can create much desirable habitat. Their ponds in intermediate stages of

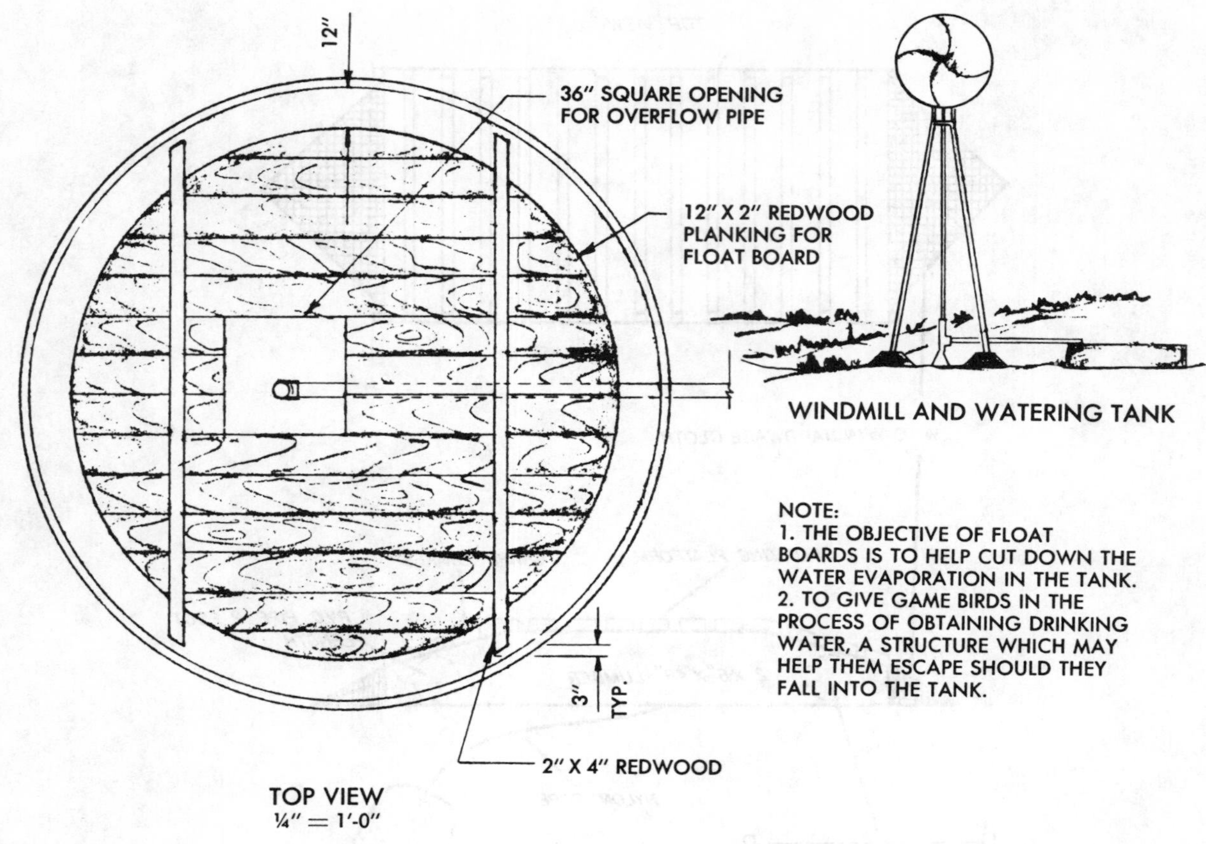

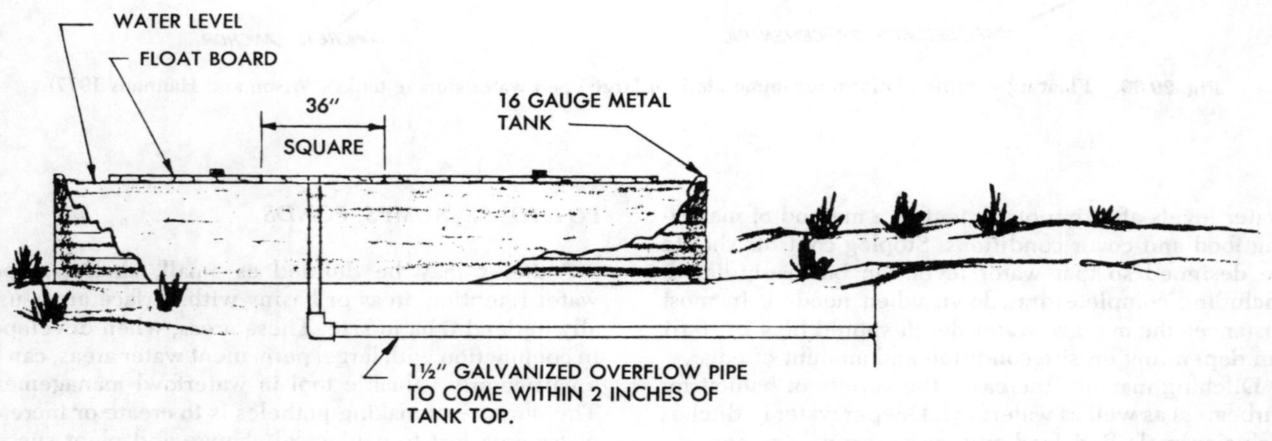

Fig. 20.31. **The simple round float board illustrated in these drawings has saved hundreds of wild birds by providing an area for them to drink at round water troughs. One such trough without the board flat contained 13 sage grouse carcasses, however, after the "wildlife saver" had been installed, no further mortalities were observed (Nevada State Office, U.S. Bureau of Land Management).**

development are major attractions, not only for waterfowl, but also for other wildlife. But the typical beaver impoundment is a changing affair that evolves through several stages. For this reason, the manager should not be as concerned with maintenance of individual ponds as he is with rotation of favorable habitat elements within the entire area of beaver influence.

During the past 25 years, the states of Maine and New Hampshire have developed and refined beaver management techniques as part of their waterfowl management programs. Hundreds of hectares of selected beaver-created impoundments, including problem flowages which otherwise might have to be destroyed, are preserved annually through a program of beaver population control and stabilization of water levels.[4]

The life expectancy of a beaver-created impoundment is determined by the available food supply and the number of beaver utilizing the food. From a food supply standpoint, a beaver flowage in which the beaver population is maintained at low numbers (2–3 beaver) will remain active for a much longer period of time than if the same flowage were occupied by a full colony (10–12) of beaver. Beaver populations in desirable flowages can be managed by annual trapping, live trapping and transfer, and beaver sterilization techniques.

New Hampshire has developed a "beaver pipe" (Laramie 1978) or water level stabilization device which can be used in alleviating flooding conditions caused by beaver building dams in culverts or flooding valuable timber, fields, or roadways. A "beaver pipe" is a 7.3-m-long, 30.5-cm-sq wooden tube with 1 solid end and a bottom of 5.1 × 10.2-cm wire mesh. For ease of handling, a "beaver pipe" is constructed in 2 sections which are joined together at the installation site. When pushed through or set on top of a beaver dam (wire side down with the solid end extending out into the pond) and secured by steel posts, water flows freely through the bottom of the pipe out over the dam. The pipe can be set at almost any level and the beavers' efforts to stop the flow are usually futile. Experience has shown a minimum of 0.6 m of water must exist between the bottom of the upstream end of the pipe and floor of the pond for the pipe to work efficiently.

In the case of a plugged culvert, the dam is removed and a heavy wire mesh fence (15.2 × 15.2-cm #6 concrete reinforcing wire) is installed around the mouth of the culvert and secured with steel posts. When the beaver build a dam on the fence, a "beaver pipe" can then be placed through the fence to keep the water at a desired level (Fig. 20.32).

For beaver flowages where no culvert is involved (a situation where the water level must be maintained or lowered) installation of a "beaver pipe or pipes" alone will do the job. A single "beaver pipe" can handle the normal runoff from a 8.7-sq-km drainage area and installations have been made utilizing up to 3 pipes (Fig. 20.33). Beaver flowages with drainage areas exceeding 26–28.8 sq km are not feasible to manage using "beaver pipes."

The State of Maine in turn has developed a water level control pipe (Boettger and Smart 1968) constructed from aluminum culvert stock which they use to achieve and maintain optimum water levels in beaver flowages and prevent damage through excessive flooding.

GREENTREE RESERVOIRS

Greentree reservoirs are bottomland hardwood areas shallowly flooded for short periods during the dormant growth period for the purpose of attracting waterfowl.

Fig. 20.32. **Wire mesh fence to protect culvert from flooding with a "beaver pipe" (H. Nevers, N. Hampshire Fish and Game Department).**

Fig. 20.33. **Water level can be maintained or lowered in a beaver flowage by installing a "beaver pipe" (H. Nevers, N. Hampshire Fish and Game Department).**

---

[4]Material provided by Harold Nevers, New Hampshire Fish and Game Department, Concord.

Short-term flooding makes possible attractive feeding conditions on mast from various oaks (pin, willow, Nuttall, and cherrybark) supplemented by understory food plants, such as wild millet and smartweed. Flooding may be scheduled so as not to adversely affect tree growth or plant succession.

Acorns are the staple wildlife food item for which such areas are managed. Ducks (mallards and wood ducks) are the principal target species; but greentree reservoirs are also good for turkey, squirrel, deer, quail, raccoon, other furbearers, and many species of nongame mammals, birds, reptiles, amphibians, and fish.

Water depth of 30.5 to 45.7 cm is considered most suitable for "puddle duck" feeding. It is not necessary that the ground be completely flooded; narrow ridges may remain dry and still be utilized by waterfowl.

The selection of a site for a greentree reservoir should be based on 3 main considerations:

1. The area should be flat and contain impervious clay soils and be close to a low gradient stream to prevent excessive diking cost.
2. There must be mast-bearing oak timber that can be flooded and is adapted to flooding. The opportunity for this appears to be largely limited to broad, geologically old-age valleys such as those of the south central and southeastern United States.
3. There must be an ample and dependable water supply which can be removed from the area before tree growth starts in the spring.

In the operation of a greentree reservoir, it is desirable to begin flooding sufficiently early in the fall to attract early flights of waterfowl. Drainage of flooded areas should be accomplished during late March to mid-April to prevent loss or damage to timber stands.

An open marsh constitutes an ideal supplement to a greentree reservoir. Such marshes add to the variety of habitat conditions and probably increase nesting and brood rearing values. Marshes may be improved by the methods suggested in the "Shallow Marshes" section of this chapter. Technical engineering guidance and planning are needed for all proposed greentree reservoirs. A detailed plan of the area to be flooded should be made prior to construction including proposed water levels, soil samples, and location and design of levees and diversion channels or dams. Engineering features that should be included in the plan include:

Levees

a. Levees should be wide enough for small vehicles, a minimum of 1.2 m wide at top.

b. Levees should have a 3 to 1 slope downstream, 4 to 1 slope upstream.

c. Levees should be seeded or sodded to permanent vegetative cover including wildlife food plants.

Borrow Areas

Areas where soil is taken should be outside the greentree reservoir, preferably on high ground where the spillway will be located. Taking soil from within the greentree reservoir creates a deep water hazard for hunters.

Spillways and Drainage

a. The borrow area, if properly located, may be incorporated into the spillway. The spillway should flow onto undisturbed earth.

b. When a system of levees is needed to make flooding possible or to divide large areas into management units, the spillway may be incorporated into the structures.

c. Spillways built into levees must be stabilized by using soil, cement, concrete, or paving material.

d. Flooding of the feeding range may be accomplished by several methods, all of which require use of low contour levees with control structures.

Retention of Rainfall or Flood Waters

This method is best adapted to flat bottoms with low gradient. It requires minimum investment and is economical to operate. This method depends on rainfall for flooding at the proper season. Since soils on these sites generally are heavy clay and difficult to drain, sites should be chosen which will allow draining the impoundment early in the spring to guard against loss of tree growth.

Diversion of Inflowing Streams

This method may be used where small streams enter terraces and well-drained bottomlands. It consists of a gate-type structure in the stream to permit diversion of the stream-flow into the diked area at the proper time. Initial cost is largely governed by the size of the diversion structure and extent of facilitating levees. Flooding by this method, however, is not dependent on rainfall.

Pumping

Pumping is used where groundwater is readily available and where other water sources are unreliable. Flooding, of course, is completely controlled, but requires a relatively fixed annual cost for pumping. Pumping costs usually range from \$2.03 to \$4.05 per 1000 m^3.

Habitat Manipulation Practices

WATER LEVEL CONTROL

Production of submerged aquatic vegetation will generally require stable water levels. Actual depths will depend upon topography, clarity of the water, plants used, and species of wildlife involved. Operating depths will usually vary from 0.5 to 3.7 m with the optimum being about 1.2 or 1.5 m. Water levels of 0.3 or 0.6 m during the production season for submerged aquatics proved most beneficial to waterfowl on the Montezuma National Wildlife Refuge. Depths greater than this were of little value to dabbling ducks. Water levels should be managed so as not to allow freezing to occur in the bottom soils. It should be pointed out, too, that where sufficient water level control is possible to permit growth of wet-soil plants, food production usually exceeds that of submerged aquatics. In all improvement projects, means should be incorporated in the control structures to allow maximum flexibility in manipulating water levels.

For management of emergent vegetation, the drawdown practice of water level controls is used in areas where waters are acid, turbid and light penetration is inhibited, and also where soils are of low quality. Perennial and annual food plants may be managed by drawdown dependent upon whether the objective is to encourage permanent muskrat populations, or to provide needed habitat requirements for waterfowl. Drawdown should be as late as possible yet still early enough to allow seed production for such fast growing aquatics as wild millet, rice cutgrass, and annual smartweeds which may become established on moist mud flats. The drawdown date will vary according to latitude. In the Middle Atlantic states, June 20 is the approximate drawdown date. Reflooding is usually done by September 1 in order to serve early migrating waterfowl.

If the impoundment is in an estuarine area, tide gates should be in operation during the period of drawdown to prevent ingress of saline waters. For most marshland plants drawdown is to meadow level in order to furnish subirrigation waters. For millet, the water level should be raised above meadow level after the growing millet has attained a height of 15.2 cm or more. As the millet grows, water levels can be raised accordingly, but in no case should the water be allowed to flood over the top of the growing plants. Preventing overflooding has the advantage of inhibiting the growth of undesirable and perennial plants.

Reservoir drawdown is an effective method of manipulating cover around waterfowl impoundments. Species composition of cover can be controlled by time and length of drawdowns. If the soil remains wet, cattail and bulrush are favored. If it is allowed to dry, sedges and such species as woolgrass are likely to invade. Late spring and early summer drawdowns favor submerged plants; mid and late summer drawdowns favor weedy growth. In some regions, willow and red-osier dogwood may invade rapidly where the drawdown is sustained for 2 years or more. Drawdowns also improve the growth of submerged aquatic plants once the area is reflooded because of both physical and chemical improvement of soils.

In Ohio, drawdowns during May in a managed marsh were the most successful in producing plant successions beneficial to waterfowl (Meeks 1969). Semiaquatic species such as rice cutgrass and nodding smartweed were abundant after May drawdowns. In addition, drawdowns in May did not impair duck nesting and did not limit muskrats to single litters as occurred following drawdowns in March, April, or June.

Although water drawdowns are a valuable tool in marsh management, they must be used with care, and should be predicated on knowledge of physical and biological characteristics of the marsh. Bottom topography, soils characteristics, existing plant communities, current waterfowl use and productivity, and seasonal water supplies all are important factors that will affect the decision to use drawdown as a habitat manipulation technique.

PLANTINGS FOR FOOD AND COVER

Efforts to propagate plants for waterfowl food should be undertaken only after thorough survey of existing conditions. The important native species first must be identified and inventoried. Consideration needs to be given to the distribution and environmental requirements of all the important duck food plants that are, or should be, present on the area. Planting, the last step in the program, is done only when it is known that important species are missing and that conditions for their introduction are right. A very important first step in providing food plants for waterfowl is covered in this Chapter under "Shallow Marshes." This is to create the kind of shallow, marshy-edged type of impoundment that encourages the favored flora. A constant, stabilized water level is very important for growth and reproduction of most aquatic life, whether it be plant or animal. This is especially true during late spring and summer.

Artificial introductions are of most value to small areas where the site can be managed and controlled intensively. Planting of large marshes, river bottoms, or extensive impoundments is frequently very costly. When starting a planting program, small plantings should be made, thereby determining the adaptability of test species for the site.

To realize best results from the planting program, the work must be conducted at the proper period of the year, usually during spring or early summer months. Second, the planting site must be of a nature that promotes growth. If the site is already supporting a cover, there is little reason to expect planting success, as the plants growing on the site will be much more adapted than introduced species (Singleton 1965).

The job of the habitat manager is similar to that of the farmer as he implements the principles and practices of crop production. In order to insure successful growth, the crop producer first removes all competing growth from the land and tills the soil in an effort to create conditions favorable to the growth and production of the target crop. Recommended sources of good information pertaining to plantings, especially for waterfowl, include the following: for the Gulf states (Singleton 1965); for the eastern states (Atlantic Waterfowl Council 1972); for the Pacific Northwest (Scheffer and Hotchkiss 1945); for the Great Lakes areas (Pirnie 1935); for the Pacific Southwest (Miller and Arend 1960, George 1963); and in general for North America (Addy and MacNamara 1948).

For immediate reference, the following are some of the more important food plants for waterfowl and suggested techniques for planting them:

Pondweed

Pondweeds can best be introduced into new waters by transplanting of the rootstock early in the spring season. Whole plants should be pulled or dug, the roots balled with mud, and immediately transplanted. Soft, muddy bottoms make the most satisfactory growth sites.

Smartweed

Smartweed is best propagated by transplanting rootstocks. Successful establishment has also been accomplished by 30.5-cm long stem cuttings. About one-half of each cutting should be stuck into mud bottoms in shallow water. Rootstocks or cuttings should be transplanted during late winter or early spring.

Duck Potato

This species may be established by transplanting the entire plants in the spring or early summer. The transplants should be set in water equally as deep as that from which they were collected. Soft, muddy bottoms make the best growth sites.

Spike Sedges

Rootstalk or entire plants can be propagated. All transplanting should be completed in the spring or early summer months.

Duckweeds

Transplant the entire plant. This is done simply by collecting the floating plants in a bucket or basket and then scattering the material in the site to be planted. Duckweed makes its best growth in sites having emergent vegetation which will protect the duckweed from excessive wind or wave action.

Coontail

New plants grow from fragments of coontail stems. The stem fragments may be planted at any time during the growing season and can be transported whenever it may be gathered, either from the masses of live plants in the fall or by rakes and drags used on the bottom in winter or spring. They may be planted in packages or merely pushed by hand into the soft soil.

Grasses

There are hundreds of grasses, both natural and domesticated grains, used by waterfowl in North America. Two native species commonly planted are wildrice and wild millet. Wildrice is broadcasted and requires no covering, for each good seed sinks at once and becomes embedded in the bottom soils. Best planting sites are those that have shallow, fresh, nonstagnant water, mud bottoms, and are open to the sunlight. A great deal of wildrice seed has been wasted in water too deep for the young plants to reach the surface or on sludge bottom into which the seed worked down too deep by means of its tiny slanting barbs.

Wild millet, or watergrass, will not sprout if the water depth exceeds 15.2 cm. Usually no seedbed preparation is necessary if the wetlands are newly formed on agricultural land or on annual grassland. The seed can be broadcast and the pond flooded. The same treatment can be given bare pond bottoms. However, a seedbed must be prepared if the bottom is covered with cattails, tules, and saltgrass, or rushes and spikerushes, since millet cannot compete with these plants. In such cases the soil must be plowed or disced 2 or 3 times and then harrowed to break the sod. The seed may be planted by a field broadcaster, airplane application, or by use of grain drills. When using drills, plant the seed no more than 0.6 cm deep since deeper plantings often fail to germinate. The usual planting rate is 22.4 to 33.6 kg of seed per ha. May and June plantings produce the best yield. Millet germinates rapidly when soaked and must not be left dry afterwards or the germ will die (Miller and Arend 1960).

Alkali Bulrush

For many of the southwestern salt wetlands, alkali bulrush may be established. Generally seedbed preparation is not needed unless competition is severe with other plants such as cattails, tules, and saltgrasses. Spring seedings are recommended at a rate of 33.6 kg per ha. Seed may be aerially broadcast (seed should be presoaked for 5 days) for large areas or a standard 20 × 6 grain drill used for operations smaller than 10 ha. If drilled, be sure not to cover the seed more than 1.27 cm otherwise germination will be retarded or lost. Very small areas (of less than 0.4 ha) can be hand transplanted by digging up the entire plant, including rhizomes and tubers.

Proper water management is exceedingly important to establish this species. First, as much of the field as possible should be preflooded to a depth of 2.5 to 7.6 cm. After seeding, the water should be held at this 2.5- to 7.6-cm level for 2 to 3 weeks, then the water should be drawn down to a mud flat stage for 2 or 3 days. This allows the seedlings to emerge and firm their rudimentary root systems. The wetland should then be reflooded to the original depth (2.5 to 7.6 cm) and maintained at this depth until the plants have full mature seed heads. After this plant has become established, it may be flooded to almost any depth without adverse effects (George 1963).

RESTING SITES

Often it is necessary to create loafing islands or nesting sites on wetland development projects for waterfowl. Brood-rearing territories can be increased on improved marshlands exceeding 0.8 ha by partitioning the tract. Partitions are made by ridging or building chains of islands across the project. Ridges and islands can be constructed with a bulldozer or dragline during dry periods or by depositing rocks and boulders on the ice in winter. Snow fences strung across potholes is another practice to serve as temporary partitions (Atlantic Waterfowl Council 1972).

Floating "islands" can be anchored in shallow low water ponds. Metal barrels are sometimes attached underneath to adjust the height of flotation. The "islands" can be constructed from green logs with rough mitred corners made by a chain saw and held together with lag screws. Each "island" should be landscaped with grass or willows to provide shade and protection from predators (Shomon et al. 1966). Loafing and resting places may also be made by anchoring a couple of logs or 1.2 × 1.2-m rafts in open water, or by stacking rocks, old straw or hay bales in shallow water.

NEST STRUCTURES

For suggested techniques on nest boxes, nest platforms and cones, see "Nesting Cover" and "Specialized Nest Structures" in this Chapter.

MAN-MADE ISLANDS

During the past hundred years, over 2,000 man-made islands have been constructed throughout U.S. Coastal, Great lakes, and riverine waterways. These islands have created new habitats for many species of wildlife, especially colonial birds. Landin (1978) provided an evaluation of these structures and listed some 50 references documenting the use of man-made islands by wildlife.

Most man-made islands are constructed with dredged materials. They vary greatly in size and characteristics and range in age from newly formed to 50 years. Commencing in 1976, the Dredged Material Research Program's Habitat Development Project located at the U.S. Army Engineers Waterways Experimental Station, Vicksburg, Mississippi, initiated studies of these structures. Most results published to date relate plant succession to bird utilization of islands. One report (Soots and Landin 1978), provides helpful information pertaining to the development of avian habitat through dredged material islands.

Small man-made islands were attractive, relatively safe nesting sites for mallards and Canada geese in prairie wetlands (Johnson et al. 1978).

Constructing Water Control Devices

There are various development structures used to control water to improve wetlands for wildlife. A general list of techniques is presented here with references on construction methods and specifications. The importance of working with expert engineers in developing construction requirements cannot be overemphasized.

DIKES AND EMBANKMENTS

All discussions relating to earthen water impounding embankments are limited to fills 3 m high or less. If higher embankments are required, detailed soil studies must be undertaken in order to design and construct a safe structure for the most reasonable cost.

For a well-documented review of principles and methods of making dikes or impoundments, see the excellent *Techniques Handbook of Waterfowl Habitat Development and Management* compiled by the Atlantic Waterfowl Council (1972). The material presented here was obtained from that book. The handbook describes the following types of embankments:

Simple Embankments

Simple embankments are those consisting of reasonably uniform material throughout. They are generally located in marsh or swamp areas where on-the-site soils must be used. They generally involve the least expenditures for construction and in many instances are the only feasible type to use (Fig. 20.34).

Core Type Embankments

Core type embankments are those whose central portion or core is constructed of selected soil, usually the least pervious material. The outer surface is comprised of on-the-site, more pervious soils. This type of embankment seldom is used on low-head fills unless the supply of less pervious materials is readily available or unless the soils of different permeability are separated naturally by distinct layers, readily available to the earth-moving equipment being used. However, on-the-site soils can be so poor that stability of the embankment will be questioned by competent engineers. In such cases it may be economically sound to haul the core material from some distant borrow pit (Fig. 20.35).

Diaphragm Type Embankments

Diaphragm embankments are those which incorporate a relatively thin section of concrete, steel, or wood to form a barrier to percolating water. The "full diaphragm" type has the barrier extended from the level of the impounded water down to a seal in an impervious foundation. A "partial diaphragm" or cutoff wall type is one which does not meet the conditions of the full type (Fig. 20.36).

Although the need for complete, detailed investigations of the properties of soils and subsurface conditions is less on the low-head fills, on-site inspections must be

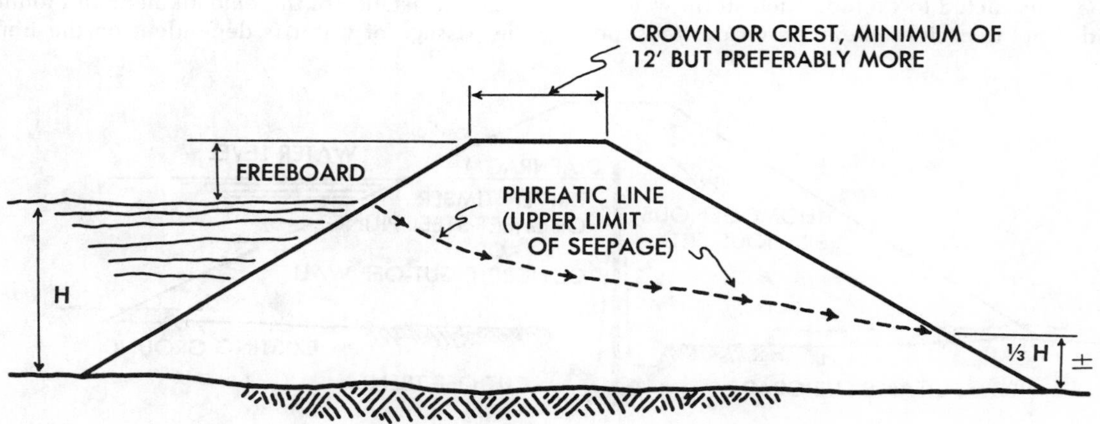

Fig. 20.34. Plans for construction of a homogenous fill typical dike (Atlantic Waterfowl Council 1972).

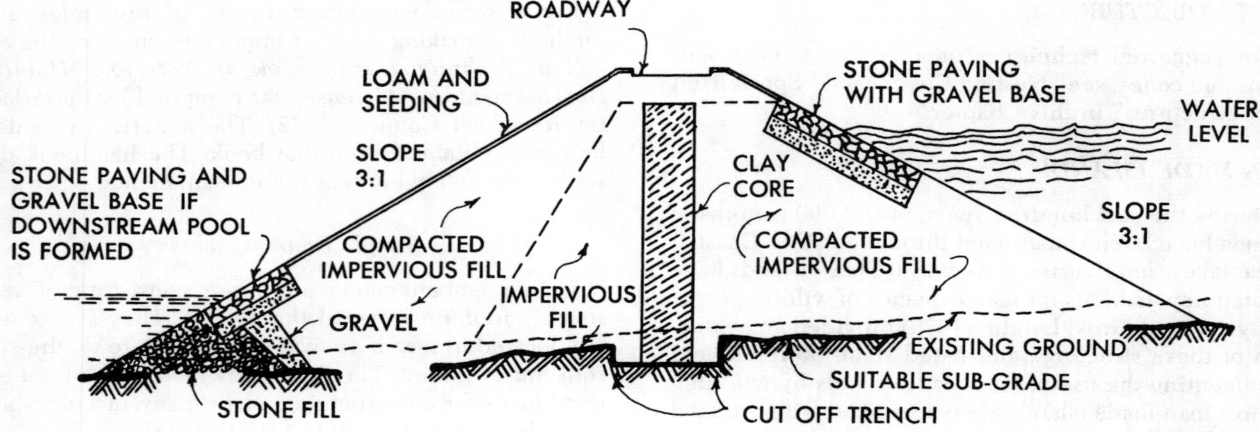

Fig. 20.35. Plans for construction of a typical clay core dam (Atlantic Waterfowl Council 1972).

made and "rule-of-thumb" criteria based on experience, must be used in designing the embankment and selecting the type of earth moving equipment for the job.

All earthen embankments should meet the following recommended criteria:

The dam shall be designed so that destruction through erosion is prevented. In order to meet this condition: (1) the spillway should have sufficient capacity to safely pass the expected peak flow for the drainage area, and (2) freeboard should prevent overtopping by wave action at maximum high water. The final top elevation of the embankment, after settlement, in areas of runoff water should be designed by adding to the maximum high-water elevation (resulting from flood flows) an amount at least equal to the wave height plus wave run up the slope. These amounts are determined by standard construction formulas. In areas of deep frost, an additional amount must be added to allow for damage from frost action. The elevation so determined considers overtopping by water originating upstream from the embankment.

For construction of sites in tidewater areas, overtopping by storm waters from outside the impoundment should be given consideration. The type of management within the impounded area, type of material available, and the cost of construction will have to be weighed to determine whether or not embankments in these locations will be constructed to exclude such storm waters. If it is decided not to exclude them, provisions must be made in spillway and control structure sizes to admit the storm water into the impoundment in such quantities that the water surface elevation within the impoundment rises at approximately the same rate as the water outside. Then, when overtopping occurs, dike erosion will be reduced to the minimum.

For some wildlife management purposes, extremely low fills may be desirable to temporarily impound shallow water. Under these conditions, a comparison of construction plus annual maintenance costs must be made between dikes which would allow for overtopping and those which would prevent overtopping.

The foundation should be able to support the load imposed by the embankment and live loads placed on it. Foundation soils will usually be stable enough to support the load of the embankment and live loads for low-head fills. In some areas, however, the soils may be highly plastic so special precautions must be taken to insure stability. If such soils are not too deep they can be removed and replaced with more stable material. In other areas, however, it may not be feasible to remove and replace them and some method of treating them in order to realize stability will have to be devised. Rows of sheet piling or round piling can be used, but the cost per meter of dike is high. If extensive areas of such unsuitable foundation soils are encountered, it may be wise to abandon the site.

The resistance of the embankment and foundation to the passage of water is dependent on the impervious-

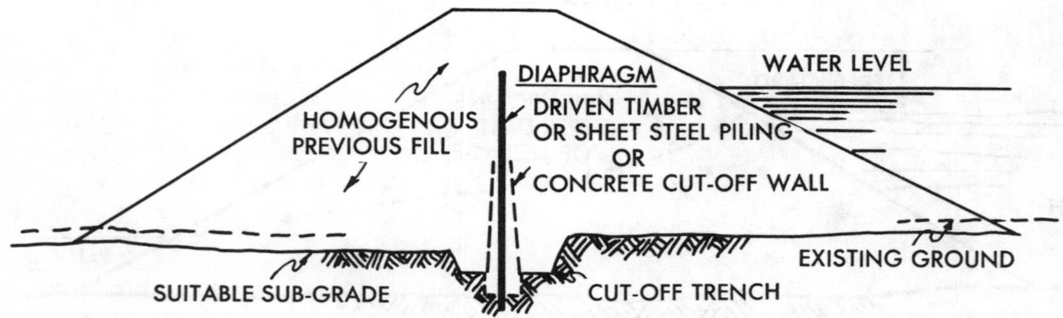

Fig. 20.36. Plans for construction of a typical diaphragm embankment (Atlantic Waterfowl Council 1972).

ness and compaction of the material used. Loss of water is not dangerous if the supply retained in the impoundment is sufficient for operational needs and the seepage of water does not cause flotation of soils. Care must be taken to establish the minimum slopes and top width of dike which will provide this embankment safety and bury the seep line. A 3.5 or 4 to 1 slope is considered the minimum for maintenance because tractor mowing equipment usually cannot safely operate on steeper slopes. Any embankment used for travel or maintenance mowing should have a minimum 2.4 m crown width with 3.1 m preferable.

The sites for habitat impoundment projects cannot always be limited to those having suitable foundation and fill materials. It is frequently necessary to compensate for poor onsite material by safe design and construction of the embankment. However, under such conditions, the initial construction cost and future annual maintenance costs will increase proportionately with the decrease in soil stability. In all cases, the typical section (slopes, crown width and freeboard) should be such as to keep the impoundment seep water line within the fill. Wet spots on the downstream slope of any embankment could indicate the seepage line is not covered and remedial action should be taken. The type of embankment will be governed by the depth of water to be impounded, the materials available, and costs of both initial construction and later maintenance. All of these factors are interrelated but any one of them can outweigh the others on the specific project.

SPILLWAYS

Spillways are provided in major wetland developments to release surplus or floodwater which cannot be contained in the impoundment basin. Inadequate design of the spillway structure may result in failure of the retaining dam and possible downstream damage. The spillway design should be considered in relation to the management potential of the marsh and to drawdown or stable pool operation. A spillway design of maximum flexibility of water levels will, in most cases, be the best suited to the management of a wetland impoundment. Flexibility should be carefully judged against its benefits as related to structural costs. Standard types of spillways include the following:

Free Overfall or Straight Drop

This type is used most frequently in the Northeast in low-head design, common to most large shallow area impoundments. It is necessary to provide artificial protection below the spill crest, as scouring and structural damage is likely to occur. A concrete or plank apron combined with cutoff walls is, therefore, an integral part of the free overfall design. The free overfall spillway of reinforced concrete or wood planking is usually designed for fixed water level impoundments. In low-head waterfowl impoundments, the design is usually modified to provide for drawdown or limited increase in storage capacity.

The reinforced concrete spillway is usually the most satisfactory design. The initial cost of concrete design is higher than log cribbing or Wakefield piling, but maintenance of the structure is minimized since concrete longevity is much greater than other materials. The location of the impoundment site and availability of material may warrant use of material other than concrete. The spillway should be designed for access so structural maintenance can be performed.

Ogee

The ogee spillway, usually designed of reinforced concrete, has a weir that is ogee or (S) shaped in profile. The flow is over the crest and along the profile of the structure with minimum interference and therefore attains near maximum discharge efficiency. In many low-head designs for waterfowl, storage of water is important and discharge efficiency is not a factor limiting design. The ease of construction and cost-related considerations may limit construction of ogee spillway design. In cases where ogee designs are contemplated for waterfowl impoundments, consideration should be given to incorporating drawdown features. This may involve drop boards, gates, or valves, so that water levels may be dropped below normal operational levels. Drawdown features should be considered even where management planning is based on stable pools. The installation cost of a drawdown feature may well pay for itself by improving the future maintenance of the prime structure.

Natural

This spillway is one that provides for impoundment runoff over natural undisturbed ground. A spillway of this type is unusual in a large fresh water impoundment design. The possibility of locating a natural spillway with runoff capacity, soil type, and vegetative cover that will meet design criteria is unlikely. If a design can take advantage of such a spillway, substantial savings in development cost may result. It should be noted that maintenance of this type spillway may in some instances be rather high. The obvious disadvantage is that unless this type is supplemented with gates or other mechanical devices, it is not possible to provide for drawdown or drainage.

Pipe or Culvert

A culvert spillway is a simple type spillway with the inlet opening placed either vertically or inclined upstream, with a uniform profile grade. The approach to the conduit may have flared or tapered sidewalls with a level or sloping floor. Conduits are usually metal, with a bituminous coating, and may have paved inverts. Concrete or fiberglass conduits have been used some. In low-head design, this type spillway is adaptable for either part or full capacity operation. Construction is simple and economical.

There are disadvantages, however, in the use of culvert-type spillways in managed wetland impoundments. The capacity does not increase greatly with increased head, and there are limitations imposed in drawdown unless a gate valve is incorporated.

Log Crib

The log crib spillway used in wetland impoundment is limited to locations where the use of permanent materials would be too costly. Logs should be selected that have uniform taper and are highly resistant to deterioration. Logs treated with preservatives such as coal tar, creosote, or pentachlorophenol solution are desirable where longevity is important. The abutments and spillway are usually faced with 7.6 cm treated planking. The maintenance of this type spillway is often very high in relation to cost of a more permanent type installation.

Because standard design plans are not often used in these structures, it is important that a plan be designed to meet local needs. The plan should be based on competent engineering standards. In general log spillways are constructed of toe piling driven on the upstream face of a bed log with the spillway having a maximum incline of 30°. All bark should be peeled from logs not completely underwater. It may be desirable to include a stoplog section if drawdown is a consideration in the impoundment.

Drop Inlet

A drop inlet is one in which the water enters over a horizontal positioned lip, drops through a vertical box or shaft, and is discharged through a pipe or conduit. In waterfowl impoundments, a concrete drop inlet in conjunction with reinforced metal pipe may be suited to small drainage areas. The most usual design is a monolithically reinforced concrete box, with stoplog slots on the upstream side. Provisions may be made for trash screens to prevent pipe constriction. Emergency spillways are incorporated in the design.

Stop Planks

Stop planks provide a means of adding flexibility to an ungated spillway. These are planks spanning horizontally between grooved recesses in supporting piers. Stop planks may be removed during floods to pass excess waters or when partial or complete drawdown of the pond is desirable. This type control is the most economical and provides adequate area to pass debris. The passage space should be a minimum of 1.2 m wide on larger dam structures. A lifting type device may be desirable if the stop planks are to be removed frequently since manual removal may entail considerable time and work. If water loss is to be minimized, stop planks should be planed on all 4 sides and free from warp. Leaks between planks can be easily sealed by placing soft coal ashes in small quantities (handful) immediately upstream and over the leak. Dry cinders are best as they float more quickly into the leak. Planks should be naturally resistant or specially treated, and a minimum width of 5.1 cm.

Gates

Gates are used in spillways where higher frequency and greater control of drawdown may be desirable. Lift gates span horizontally between guide grooves in supporting piers. Gates are usually cast iron or steel and raised or lowered by an overhead hoist device. Radial gates are usually constructed of steel (prefabricated). Water thrust operates the radial type of gate which may be set at a predetermined level so as to operate automatically. Cost of the installation of radial gates may be appreciably higher than lift gates, stoplogs, or drop inlet installations. If continual drawdown in the impoundment is contemplated, gate installation should be considered.

LEVEL DITCHING

Level ditching means constructing upgraded ditches on lands having a high water table. These ditches are installed to improve water distribution, provide open water for waterfowl, furnish nesting sites, and aid in increasing or maintaining aquatic food and cover plants for waterfowl and furbearers (Mathiak and Linde 1956). This practice is applicable on wetlands where soils are suitable for ditch construction and require a minimum of maintenance for a long period of time. Suitable soils include peats, muck, clays, and silt. Sands, sandy loam, and clay high in salt content generally are not suitable. Generally, ditching is applied to marshes exceeding 0.8 ha.

It is helpful to consult with soil scientists, hydrologists and agricultural engineers for planning level ditching. On large wet areas, an aerial photo or topographic map is useful in locating natural drainage patterns and in laying out ditch systems. A sufficient number of levels should be run to determine the general slope of the wet area. Where slopes exceed 0.5% the ditches must be laid out on the contour level. The ditching pattern is designed to avoid interception of natural channels except where desirable for circulating systems. Usually blocks are left between level ditches and the natural channels, but these are designed to allow flood or high tide flows into the ditches or else water circulation is regulated by means of control devices. As a rule, level ditches are installed at approximate right angles to natural channels.

Level ditches are generally constructed with a dragline or with ditching dynamite. Occasionally a backhoe or a bogharrow may be used. In the use of ditching dynamite, the supervision of a licensed and experienced explosive expert is recommended. When a dragline is employed for ditching, spoil material is stacked 3 m from the ditch edge in piles alternated from side to side at 15.2 m intervals. This spoil serves an important function in providing nesting areas. The breaks between piles are said to reduce nest predation. In small marshes ditching usually is done in straight lines or, where there is a slope, on the contour. Whether straight or curved, these ditches must not have a fall. On flat marshes exceeding 4 ha, the ditch is constructed in zigzag pattern, with each reach about 30.5 m long. Such a design reduces influences of wave action during high winds. Multiple ditches are laid out with parallel reaches 61 to 121.9 m apart.

Minimum dimensions recommended for level ditches are 1.2 m depth and 3.7 m top width. Such ditches provide, at intervals given above, about 275.5 square m of open water per ha.

PLUGS

Plugs are usually recommended for marshes where diking is not a feasible management tool due to either improper physical conditions of the area (size, location, water, or terrain) or economic reasons.

Plugs can prevent the fluctuation of water levels in existing water areas or increase the water area in the marsh. Various types of plugs as defined by the Atlantic Waterfowl Council (1972) include the following:

Nonspilling earth plugs are usually used to repair marsh damage caused by mosquito or other marsh drainage projects. The same principles are used as in building a dike across a tidal creek. The plug must be keyed in to both sides of the ditch and a good bond must be made between the fill material and the bottom of the ditch.

Nonspilling wooden plugs serve the same purpose as the earth plug type. Wakefield piling of creosoted lumber is used. Care must be taken to use piling long enough to prevent undercutting and the wing walls must be of sufficient length to prevent water from cutting around the end of the plug.

Spilling gut plugs are designed to reduce water fluctuations due to tidal action and thereby to make more food available to waterfowl for longer periods. The most common material used in this type of construction is creosoted lumber.

STRUCTURAL IMPROVEMENTS AND FACILITIES

Modern society creates a variety of structural improvements and facilities that affect wildlife populations. Most of these are built for other than wildlife management objectives, e.g., fences to control domestic livestock, bypasses for vehicular access on highways, etc. Since these structures are being built continually and design specifications can adversely or beneficially affect wildlife populations, techniques are provided stating how they can best be implemented with considerations for wildlife. Then too, there are certain practices needed in wildlife management, such as fences to control wildlife access.

Fences

Most fences are constructed today to control domestic livestock. However, fences are also constructed to restrict vehicular access on highways and other reasons. Fences have had their most serious impact on big game; consequently, techniques are listed on how best to construct fences to (1) allow wildlife movement through fences built to control livestock, and (2) design specifications that will control wildlife access.

LIVESTOCK FENCES AND PRONGHORNS

Fences constructed to control domestic livestock often have been documented as a problem to the free movement of antelope on western rangelands. Caton (1877) first noted this problem a century ago. More recently, wildlifers report (Martinka 1967, Sundstrom 1970, Oakley 1973) that fences can be major obstacles where antelope mobility is restricted to procure food and water, or escape deep snows.

During the 1960's, there was an accelerated increase in livestock fences constructed on western private and public rangelands. The effects of these fences was the subject for an in-depth research project conducted in Wyoming during 1963 and 1964. Results from this research provided scientifically designed and tested data regarding the interrelationships between pronghorns and livestock fences. However, the true importance of fencing to antelope mortality was not well accepted into the 1970's; consequently, a regional workshop pertaining to the problem was conducted during March 1974, in Cheyenne, Wyoming. Some 150 people representing state, federal, and private workers met to establish guidelines for the construction of fences in relation to the pronghorn's welfare (U.S. Bureau of Land Management 1974).

There are 2 major interagency conferences that periodically meet to exchange information and provide recommendations on pronghorn management. Relative to fences, each of these conferences documented their findings and recommendations in the following publications: Interstate Antelope Conference (1962) and Antelope States Workshop (1974).

It can, therefore, be stated that the controversy between livestock fences and antelope has been a long one with many studies and recommendations. Recognizing these interrelationship problems, the following are basic principles that should be considered during the planning of all fences in pronghorn habitat:

1. Any fence has the potential of becoming a problem to antelope welfare if the fence restricts access to food and water or causes physical injury through entanglement. These potential biological problems should be recognized during the initial planning justification for all fences in pronghorn habitat.

2. How the fence is specifically designed will determine the true effects the fence will have on the antelope population. A fence can be designed to allow no antelope movement; it can be designed to allow limited antelope movement; or it can be designed to allow easy movement for most antelope.

3. The design of the fence should allow for movement of all antelope age groups in order to maintain healthy populations. This is particularly important for fawns.

4. Fences that are constructed on migration routes or seasonal movement areas can be especially deleterious. Antelope traditionally need to have freedom of access from areas with deep snows. Likewise they need unrestricted access for seasonal movements to obtain water and preferred forage. They also need unrestricted routes to seek traditional fawning grounds.

5. Keep fenced areas as large as possible to allow antelope to obtain basic habitat requirements. Pronghorns maintain best populations on ranges where there is an abundance of forage and water with no undue movement restrictions.

6. Existing or planned fences constructed through traditional antelope migration routes or important seasonal movement areas should contain an alternative to use "lay-down panels" during time of antelope use. The choice of such an alternative decision means that these

panels must be properly maintained; otherwise, they may be ineffective and could be even disastrous to a population if not functioning during a crisis (e.g., extreme early season deep snowfall).

7. Although a number of devices known as "antelope passes" have been recently developed, they are a mitigating alternative and have limited value in providing movements for all aged pronghorns. This mitigating alternative needs to be recognized in the initial planning and justification of the fence project.

Net or Woven Wire Fences

Antelope workers are adamant in their professional opinion that net or woven wire fences are a serious restriction to movement of pronghorns. Such fences can be the primary cause of death for individual animals when deprived of access to waters or forage, or restricting herds when inclement weather conditions result directly in mortality. Therefore, it is strongly recommended that no woven wire fences be constructed in antelope habitat. This is especially true for the so called "wolf-proof" fences on domestic sheep ranges in New Mexico and Texas. These fences are constructed of woven wire (of which 15.2 to 45.7 cm is buried underground) and topped with 2 to 4 stands of barbed wire. Fence heights average 1.4 to 1.8 m. The objective is not to allow coyote access under, through, or over such fences. They also are 100% effective in preventing pronghorn access.

Barbed Wire Fences

1. The bottom wire should be at least 40.6 cm from the ground.

2. Because antelope generally go under barbed wire fences and the barbs can cause injury, it is recommended that this wire be smooth.

3. No stays should be placed between fence posts to provide a more flexible fence for antelope attempting to go between wires.

4. Spillett et al. (1967) documented that 81 cm high fences contained most livestock on rangelands. It is therefore recommended that this fence height be constructed on antelope rangelands. Antelope can and do jump fences in some areas, and the lower the top wire the better. This would also hold true for other wildlife such as deer, elk, and moose.

5. Based on findings of the "Regional Fencing Workshop" (U.S. Bureau of Land Management 1974), the following specifications for barbed wire fences on livestock ranges (see Fig. 20.37.) are provided:

Type 1: Ranges occupied by cattle only
3 strands of wire spaced at intervals of:
—bottom wire 40.6 cm from ground (smooth wire only)
—next wire (barbed) up 27.9 cm
—top wire (barbed) up 27.9 cm more for a total wire height of 96.4 cm from ground

Type II:
Ranges occupied by domestic sheep only
4 strands of wire spaced at intervals of:
—bottom wire 25.4 cm from ground (smooth wire only)
—2nd wire (barbed) up 17.8 cm
—3rd wire (barbed) up 17.8 cm
—4th wire (barbed) up 20.3 cm for a total of 81 cm from ground

Type III: Ranges occupied by domestic sheep and cattle
4 strands of wire spaced at intervals of:
—bottom wire 25.4 cm up from ground (smooth wire only)
—2nd wire (barbed) up 22.9 cm
—3rd wire (barbed) up 22.9 cm
—4th wire (barbed) up 25.4 cm for a total of 96.6 cm from ground

Antelope workers would be quick to evaluate these fence specifications and to note that types II and III could provide limitations to easy movement of certain antelope age groups.

Antelope Passes

Standard cattleguards will allow the movement of adult antelope. Fawns, however, have difficulty in crossing them. They must be placed where antelope can readily locate them. Advantages have been realized by placing cattleguards in fence corners. The fences then act to "drift" the antelope to the pass opening. In long sections of fences, it is helpful to build a jog in the fence line for placement of the cattleguard. Care needs to be taken in locating the placement site to minimize the cattleguards filling with debris and silt.

Structures described as "antelope passes" were developed and tested in the Wyoming sheep-antelope-fence study (Spillett et al. 1967). Unfortunately few of these structures have been tested under range conditions. More recently, Mapston and ZoBell (1972) field tested one such structure in Wyoming. Their conclusion was that antelope passes are used but they have limited value in relation to properly planned and fully implemented range fences such as Type I in Fig. 20.37. Figure 20.38 depicts a 4–5 month fawn pronghorn negotiating one of these facilities. Figure 20.39 provides detailed plans for constructing antelope passes. After studying the effects of passes on antelope movements under field conditions, Mapston and ZoBell (1972) provided guidelines as to when they are advantageous and where they have limited values. Antelope passes can facilitate antelope movement through fences, but only when properly located and installed. For maximum effectiveness, passes should be placed in fence corners or offsets (see Fig. 20.40) and supporting fence post braces kept to a minimum. Although antelope have an innate jumping ability, it takes considerable time in certain areas for pronghorns to learn to use passes. The authors emphasized that passes have limitations and should not be viewed as a substitute for fences that permit ready passage of pronghorns. The manager responsible for making the decision as to whether a livestock fence should or should not be constructed should also consider the fence's effect.

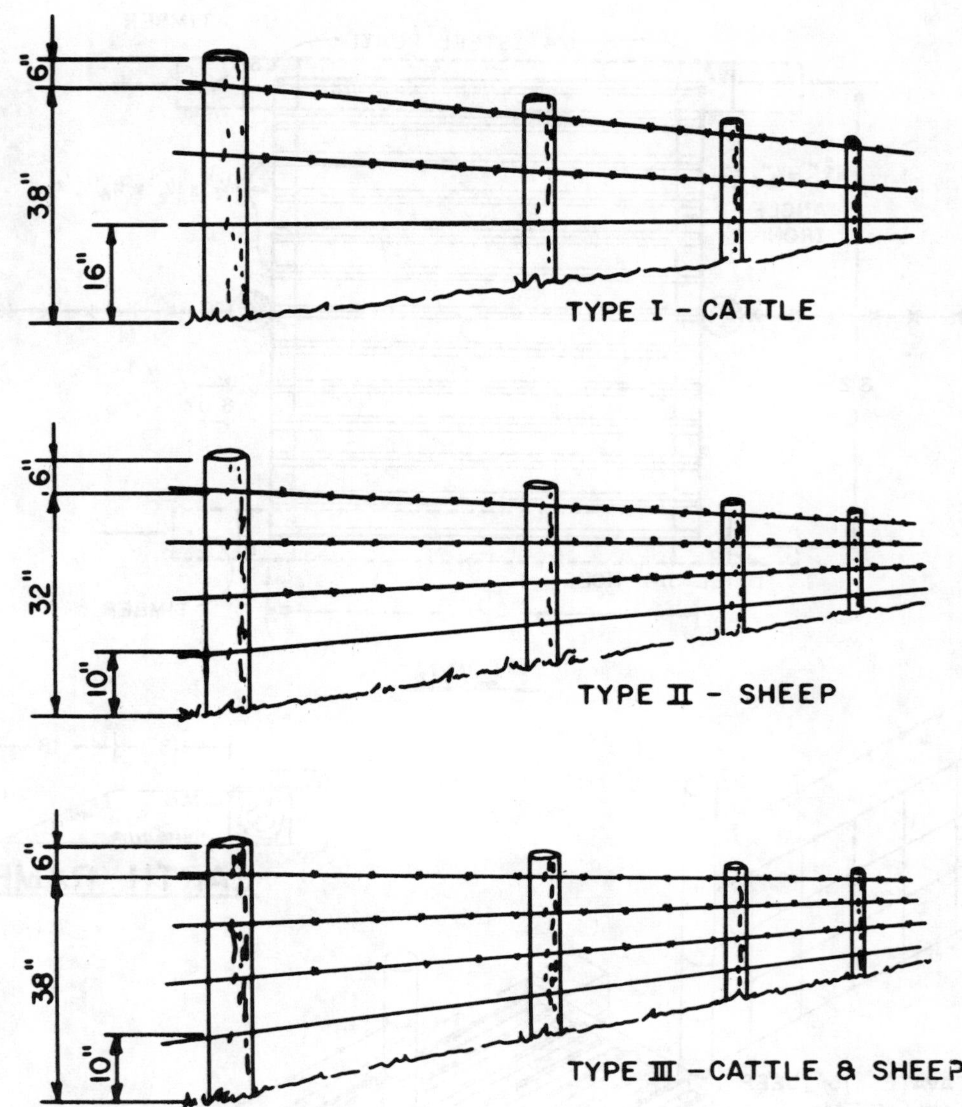

Fig. 20.37. Details of specifications for livestock fences constructed on antelope ranges as recommended by the Regional Fencing Workshop (U.S. Bureau of Land Management 1974).

Fig. 20.38. A 4-5 month fawn pronghorn leaps through a break in a livestock fence known as an "antelope pass" (U.S. Bureau of Land Management photo by Ray Mapston).

LIVESTOCK FENCES AND DEER

The interrelationships of domestic livestock fences and native deer have not raised the political furor that it has for the American pronghorn. However, throughout North America where livestock fences have been built, they have undoubtedly caused a far greater mortality problem to deer than they have to antelope. Deer are more subject to being victimized on an individual basis whereas antelope at times are entrapped in large winter concentrations. Then too, deer are frequently caught in fences in isolated areas not readily witnessed, whereas antelope mortalities in wide open country are easy to observe.

Deer characteristically jump over fences and this often leads to their demise. While the adult deer is jumping, its hind feet can become entangled between the top 2 wires of range fences. Such a case generally results in eventual death. A case investigated in north-

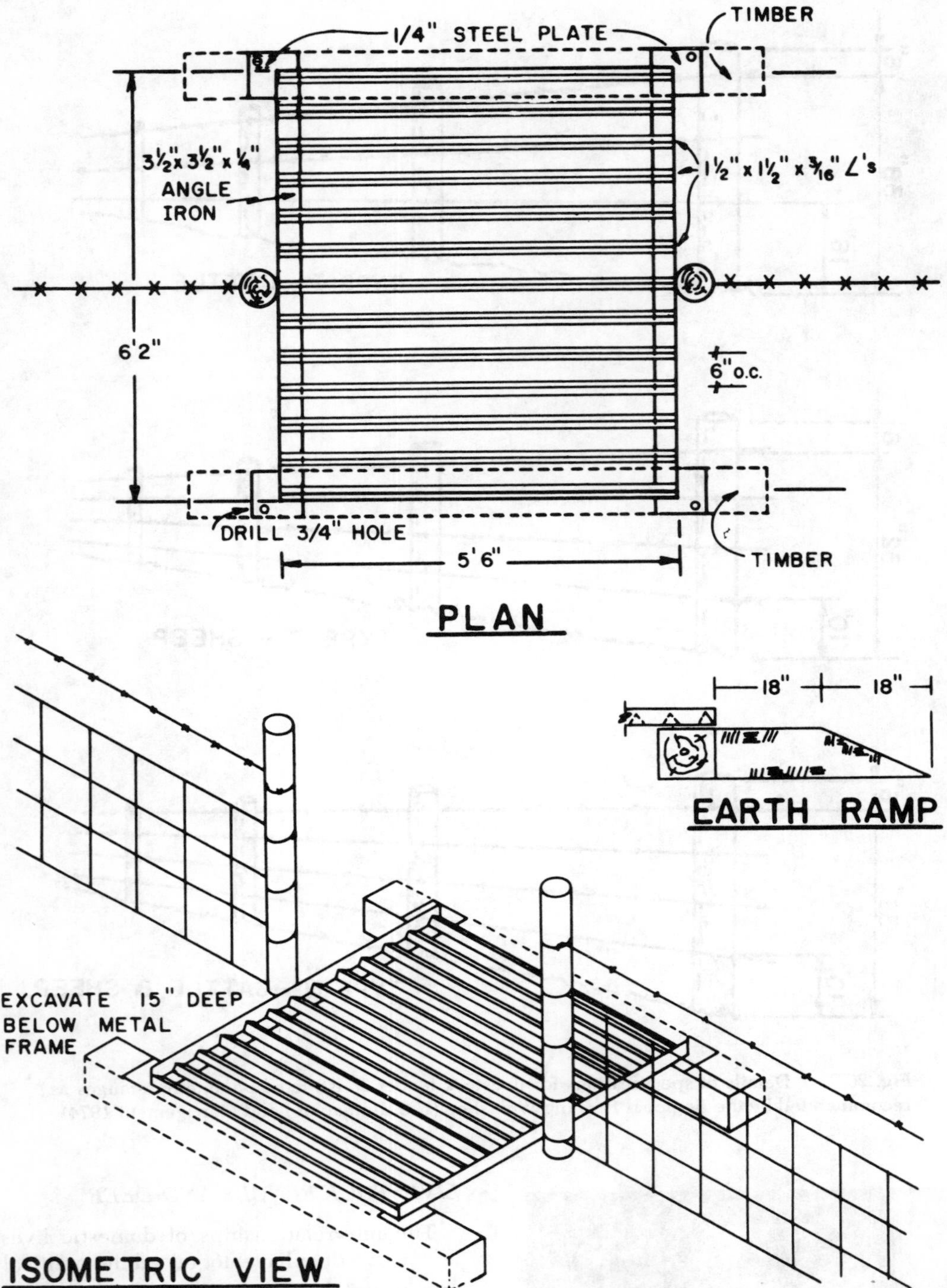

Fig. 20.39. Antelope pass specifications and recommended method of installation (Mapston and ZoBell 1972).

west Colorado disclosed a major deer death loss due to a combination 81-cm net wire and 2-stranded barbed wire fence. The 1.6-km-long fence was placed across a traditional migration route. For years the winter snows were not deep and no problems were recorded. Then during 1974, heavy snows fell. The deer migrated through the area as they normally did. However, the short yearling class of deer did not have the ability to negotiate the fence with a result of 12 perishing in the fence and some 50 others succumbing through entrapment.

Guidelines for Barbed Wire Fences

Nevada has experienced many cases where deer have become entangled in barbed wire fences. Recognizing this problem, state and federal wildlife managers designed a barbed wire fence best adapted for deer ranges. It stresses 2 major points: (1) keep the bottom wire up to allow movement of fawns, and (2) keep the top wire down to allow ease for jumping over. Figure 20.41 provides a schematic drawing for this specially designed

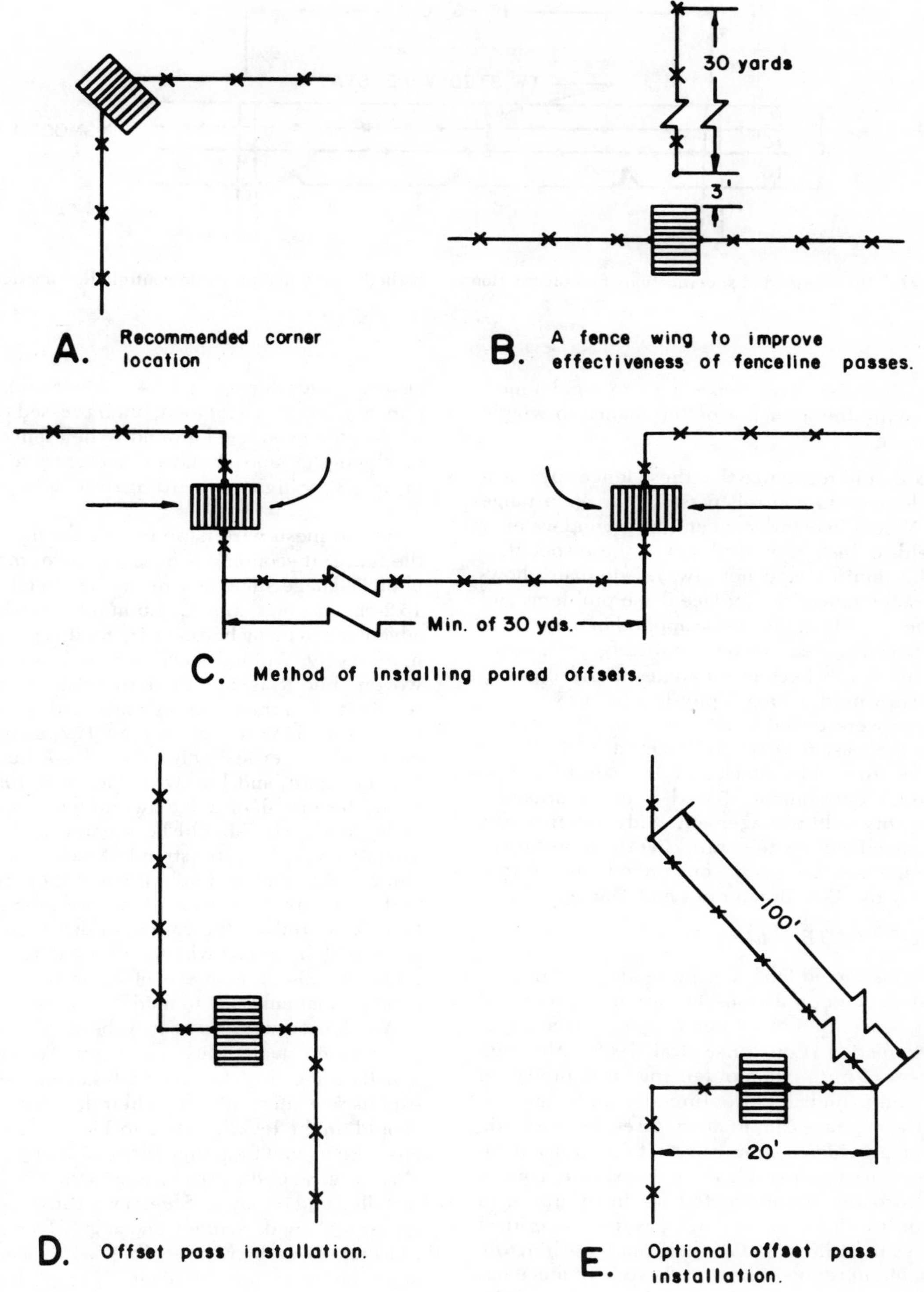

Fig. 20.40. Recommended methods for installing antelope passes (Mapston and ZoBell 1972).

deer fence. Note these specifications designed for deer requirements:

1. Bottom wire up 40.6 cm from ground—thus allowing for movement of fawns.
2. Only 3 strands of wire required. Fences were constructed on large open rangelands where livestock were not restricted. Under these circumstances, 3 wires are all that were needed to control cattle.
3. Top wire is smooth and 91.4 cm from ground, thus allowing deer greater ease in jumping over the fence.
4. Stays are placed between fence posts. Since deer frequently become entangled when the top 2 wires twist

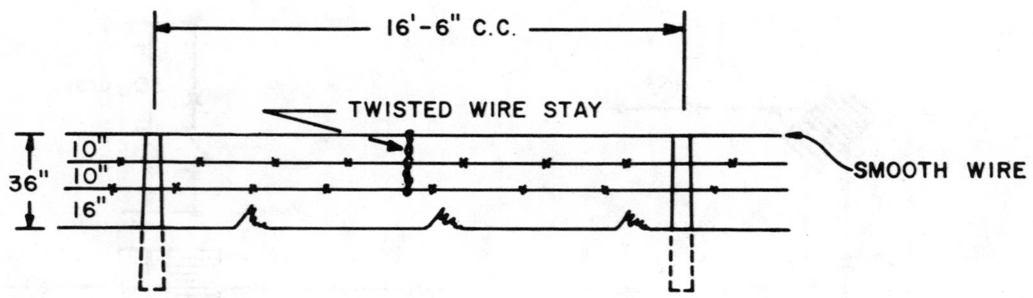

Fig. 20.41. **Recommended specifications for construction of a barbed wire fence for cattle control allowing deer access.**

around the legs, the stays make a more rigid fence, thereby allowing the animal a better chance to wiggle out of the fence.

Managers should recognize that these fence specifications are adequate to control livestock for open range conditions. Where livestock concentrate around water or adjacent fields of lush, preferred forage, these specifications will be minimal and not always adequate; however, most range fences do not face these problems and therefore the specifications can be applied in more cases than not. Because deer characteristically jump over fences and frequently become entangled in the top wire, a smooth wire would decrease physical injuries.

Two fences were tested with these specifications in Nevada for the past 6 years. In each case, the fence adequately controlled livestock and decreased the incidence of deer entrapment. Based upon information gained from this field management study, other fences with these specifications to control livestock on important deer ranges have been constructed on western rangelands by the U.S. Bureau of Land Management.

FENCES FOR CONTROLLING DEER

Properly constructed fences can provide good protection against deer depredations to various agricultural crops, high concentration winter ranges, and areas of timber reproduction (Longhurst et al. 1962). Although the initial cost of installation of fencing for depredation controls is often high and continued maintenance is necessary, the expense can, in many cases, be justified.

Fences can provide economic protection against damage that deer can cause to high-value crops. Deer control fences are also being constructed for the purpose of rotating deer use of forage in range pastures on critical winter ranges in California, Colorado, and Washington. Under most circumstances the upright style of fence has proven most satisfactory, but under some conditions the slanting fence is cheaper to construct and is advantageous because of its lower height. Specifications for both fence types are presented here as adapted from Longhurst et al. (1962). The use of electrical fences has been a third technique used to a limited degree in deer habitat control.

Upright

While a height of 1.8 m is usually adequate for upright fences on level ground, a 2.4-m fence may be necessary against larger deer (Fig. 20.42). Deer normally will not jump a 1.8-m fence for food, but if pressed they can jump a 2.4-m fence on level ground. When fences are located on sloping ground, it may be necessary to build them 3 m or 3.3 m high to guard against deer jumping from above.

Woven mesh wire is preferable for the full height of the fence; if economy is necessary, 2 or more strands of 9- or 10-guage smooth wire can be stretched at 10.2- to 15.2-cm spacings above a 1.5-m mesh wire. There is no advantage in using barbed wire for this purpose, and it is more costly. Welded mesh wire is less expensive than woven, but it is too rigid to conform readily to irregularities in the ground surface and is most useful on even ground. Wire lighter than 12½ gauge is not recommended. Vertical stays should not be over 15.2 to 20.3 cm apart, and line wires not over 10.2 to 15.2 cm apart. Because deer will crawl under a fence when possible, mesh wire should be secured and kept close to ground level. An extra strand of barbed wire stretched along the ground will help prevent them from crawling under. In any depressions between posts, wire should be staked firmly to the ground or depressions should be filled with materials which will not deteriorate or wash away. A 0.9–1.2-m piece of angle-iron post makes a good permanent stake to hold wire close to the ground.

Wooden or steel posts may be used, the choice depending on availability and costs. Wooden posts are usually somewhat cheaper, with sawed ones being more expensive than split posts. Their dimensions at the ends should not be less than 10.2 to 12.7 cm across. If fences are to be moved from time to time, steel posts are preferable because of the greater ease with which they can be installed and removed. Steel posts can be purchased in 3 types: T-shaped, channel, and angle. The T-type is more rigid and is perhaps preferable, with channel next and angle last in order of strength; prices also decrease in that order. Posts should generally be set about 3 to 3.7 m apart, but extra posts may be necessary to hold the wire to the contour of uneven ground. When building with steel posts it is often advisable to intersperse them with wooden posts in order to strengthen the fence—1 wooden post for every 3 to 5 steel posts is the approximate ratio. Proper bracing along fence lines is important to give sufficient strength. Wooden corner posts should be at least 15.2 cm across the ends and are preferable to steel posts unless the latter are in concrete and are well braced.

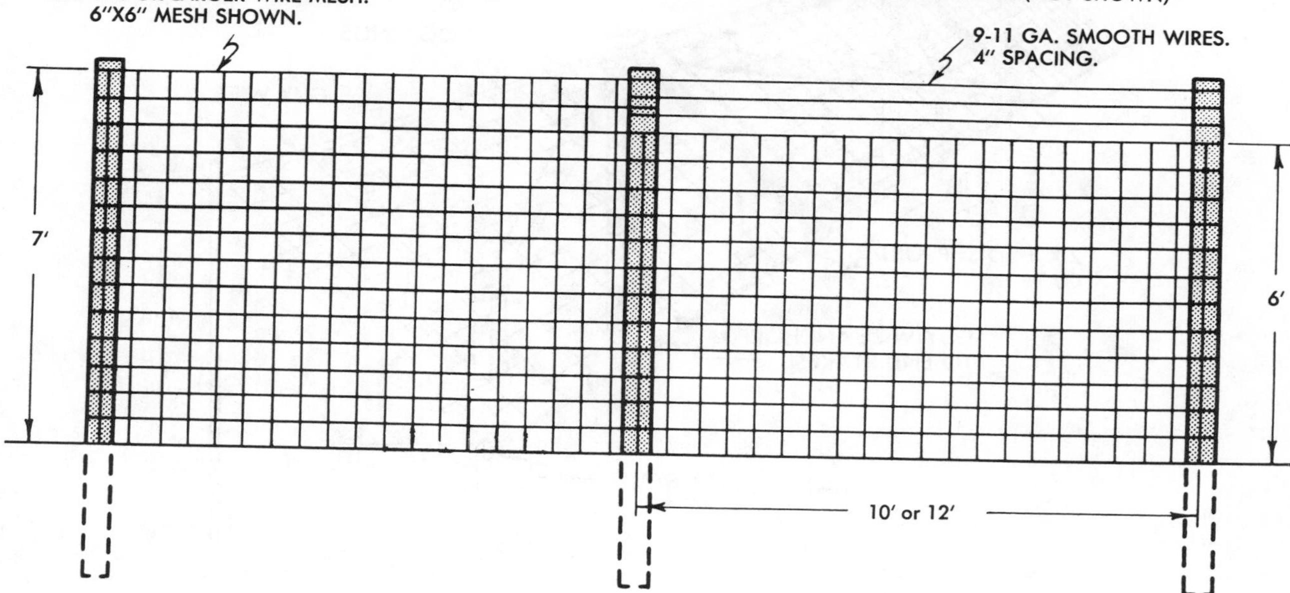

Fig. 20.42. Drawing showing 2 methods of using wire, either mesh above or combinations of mesh and smooth, to construct an upright fence for controlling deer damage (Longhurst et al. 1962).

With upright fences the gate height should be approximately equal to fence height. Weight should be kept to a minimum. A light wooden frame over which mesh wire is stretched is often satisfactory. If factory-made aluminum gates are used, metal extensions may be bolted or welded on and mesh wire stretched over them. It is always advisable to sink a metal or treated wooden base frame in the ground below the gate to give a uniform surface and to prevent deer from working under the gate.

In Colorado, a 3-m-high upright fence was constructed to control deer movements on a rotational basis for a key winter range. The fence was effective in controlling both deer and elk movements. The fence was also effective in increasing plant diversity and abundance through controlled use of big game foraging (J. Clark, pers. comm.).

Overhanging or Slanting

This type of fencing is less expensive to construct than upright fencing because fewer and shorter posts are needed and lighter gauge wire can be used. Slanting fences are particularly suitable for temporary fencing, as the few posts can easily be removed and the wire more readily rolled. This type of fencing is also suitable for locations where an upright fence would be unsightly or otherwise unsuitable.

Slanting fences are believed to be effective because they act primarily as a psychological barrier to deer. Deer usually first try to crawl under such a fence and then, finding this impossible and with the wire extended above them, they are discouraged from jumping. For this reason slanting fences are effective in 1 direction only. Overhanging woven wire mesh fences are not recommended in heavy snowfall areas since the fence is subject to being crushed by the settling snow pack. Under such circumstances the fence can be modified by using smooth wires stretched horizontally at 10.2-cm spacings.

The basic design for the slanting fence consists of approximately 1.8 m of mesh wire supported by a guy wire stretched between widely spaced posts (Fig. 20.43). The high side of the fence is the side away from the area to be protected.

For temporary installations, light chicken wire or stucco mesh may be used. For permanent installation, wire no lighter than 12½ gauge is advisable. If woven wire is used, vertical stays should not be over 15.2 to 20.3 cm apart and horizontal line wires should not be over 10.2 to 15.2 cm apart with 1.8-m steel posts recommended and spaced up to 9 to 12 m apart.

A hinged gate is needed if there will be considerable traffic. Adequate side wings should be provided (Fig. 20.44). If little traffic is expected, a panel consisting of a light wooden frame with wire mesh stretched over it is often satisfactory. For easy access where no gate is needed, a stile is simple to construct.

The California Department of Fish and Game (Blaisdell and Hubbard 1956) used this type fence to control deer use of game range vegetation study plots. They found slanting fences (also termed outrigger type deer fence) controlled deer entry whereas regular barbed wire was inadequate. The authors suggest that this fence technique could have values for protecting haystacks, orchards, gardens, and other places where extensive

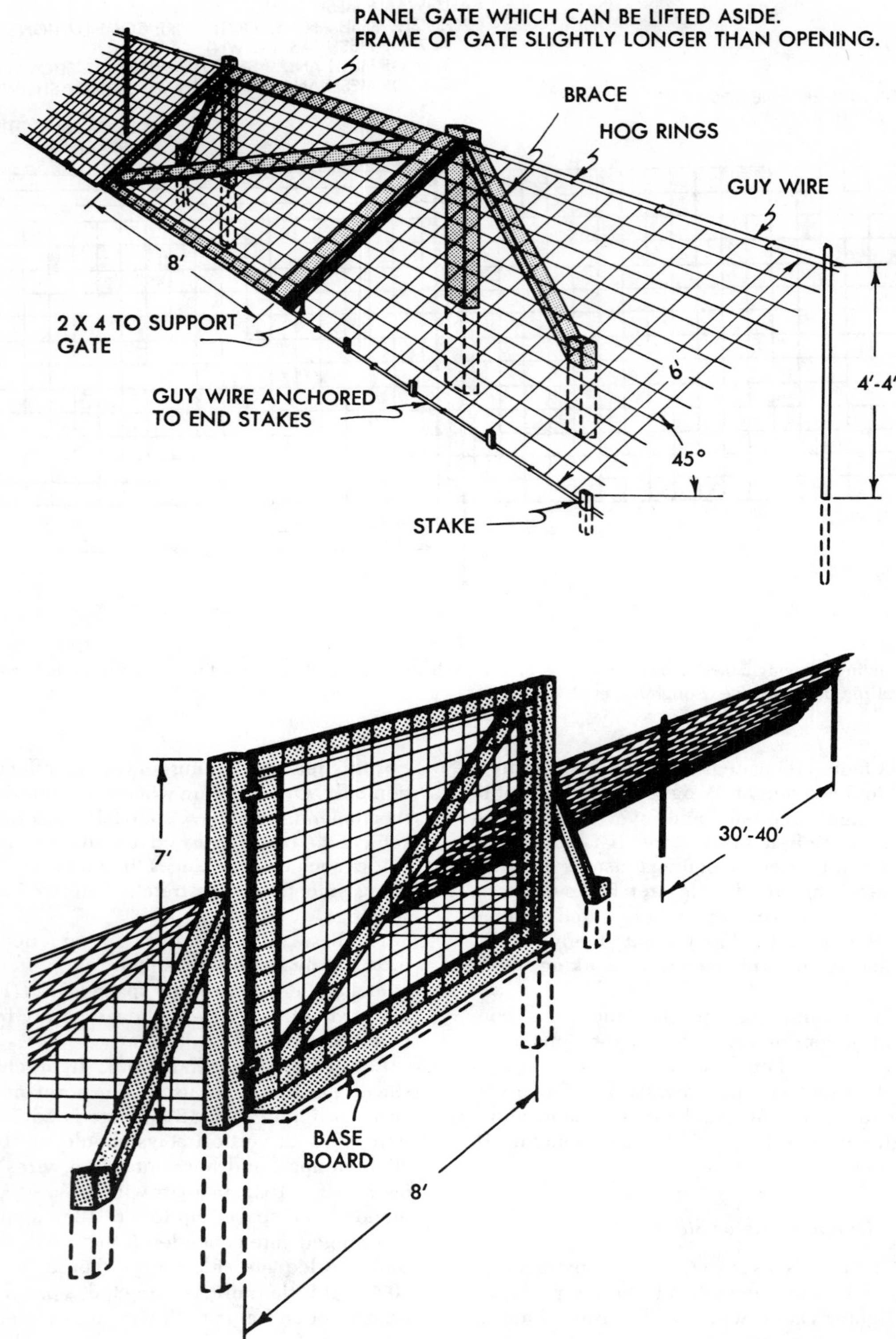

Fig. 20.43. Typical slanting deer fencing with examples of placing the gates either slanting or vertical (Longhurst et al. 1962).

fencing is not needed. Fig. 20.45 depicts an outrigger fence on site to control deer access on key winter ranges near Bishop, California.

Working in South Dakota, Messner et al. (1973) modified the slanting fence described by Longhurst et al. (1962) with several major improvements (Fig. 20.46). These changes included less mesh wire and shorter posts, both contributing to a less expensive structure. The authors also credit their design as blending well into forest and meadow environments and capable of

Fig. 20.44. Hinged gate for an upright deer control fence (U.S. Bureau of Land Management photo by Jim Yoakum).

Fig. 20.45. "Outrigger" fence used to control deer movement on rangelands in California (U.S. Bureau of Land Management photo by Jim Yoakum).

withstanding greater snow loads than other designed slanting deer fences. During 5 years of testing, white-tailed deer and livestock were successfully excluded by this slanting fence.

Electric

Experience has shown that electric fences can be used for deer control. The standard electric fence design used for livestock, however has proven unsatisfactory at times for big game control in parts of the West and Southwest. This is generally during the dry season when lack of moisture in the ground prevents good grounding of current. Researchers in California found that the use of 2 rows of posts and ground wires with leads deeply imbedded in the ground worked best (Longhurst et al. 1962). Fig. 20.47 depicts how the double electric wire fences were used in California.

Managers in Virginia had better experiences with electric fences controlling deer damage to agricultural crops. Here too, the conventional 1-wire fence used to control livestock was not effective for deer. However, with new designs specific for deer management, the electric fence proved effective in reducing deer foraging (Myers 1977). Myer's recommendations for electric fence are:

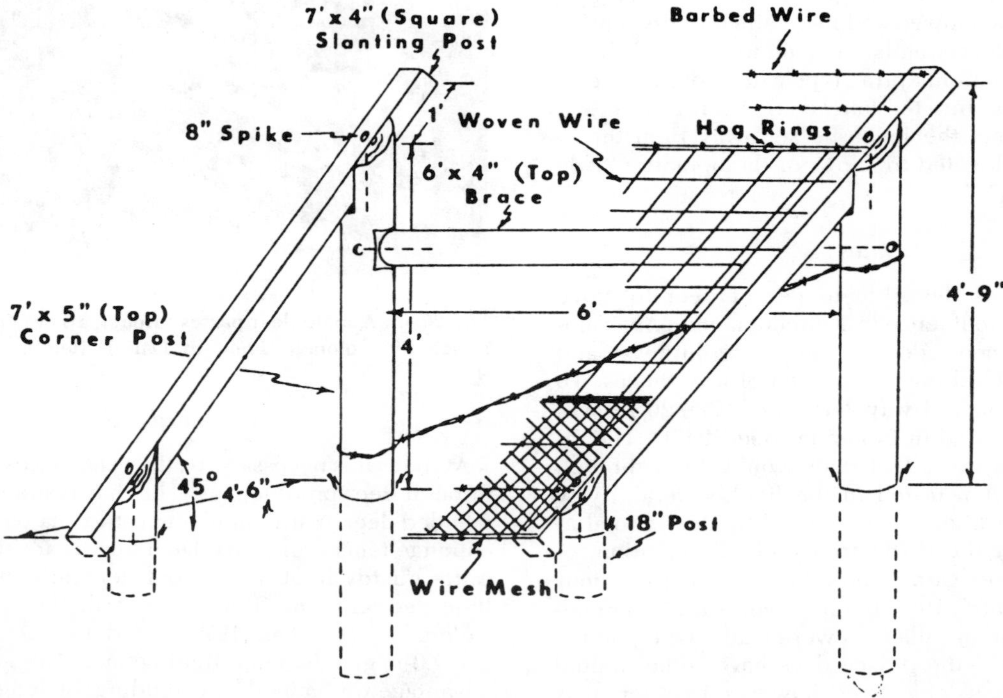

Fig. 20.46. Modification of slanting fence developed in South Dakota (Messner et al. 1973).

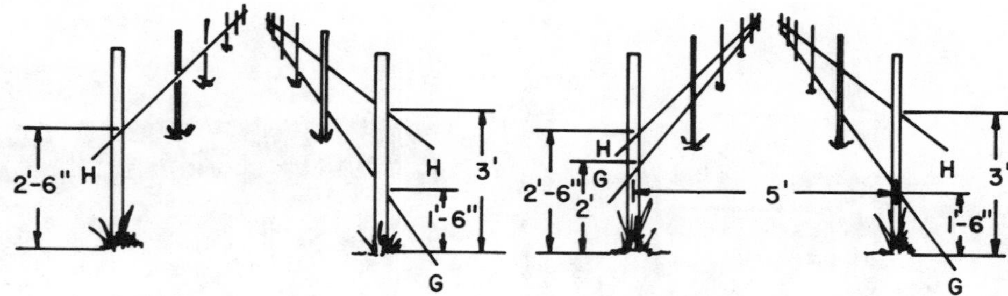

Fig. 20.47. Plans for double electric fence to control deer (Longhurst et al. 1962).

In construction, three strands of 12 or 14-gauge, smooth type, galvanized wire is recommended. Posts spaced approximately 9 m apart can be of either metal or wood with 1.5 m extending above ground level. Corner posts need to be braced properly and all posts must be placed deep enough in the soil to hold wires securely. Measuring from the ground, the bottom wire is attached 45.7 cm up on the post. The second wire is spaced 45.7 cm up from the bottom wire, and the third wire another 45.7 cm higher. This results in a fence that is 137.2 cm high from ground level to the top wire. Either plastic or porcelain insulators can be used. The porcelain insulator is recommended, as the wire can be wrapped around the insulator when needed and does not cut through to cause shorting out when pressure is applied. All three wires are charged with a controller (or box) that operates from 110 volts which must be properly grounded. An electric fence tester is also recommended for checking the fence to assure that it is operating properly. The ground underneath the fence has to be mowed and maintained to prevent electrical short circuits or grounds caused by growing vegetation. Spring type gate hooks can be used for access into the fenced area. It is also recommended that the fence be set away from the area to be cultivated to allow for the operation of equipment.

Gates

Sometimes it is desirable to permit deer to move through a deer-proof fence in 1 direction only. An example would be when a deer has entered a highway and needs to get back through the right-of-way fences. To meet this situation a "1-way deer gate" (Fig. 20.48) was developed and tested in Colorado (Reed 1971). The rationale for this gate is that deer would jump through heavy brush. When tested in the field, several 1-way gates on a major highway were used by deer a total of 146 times during the 1976 spring and fall migration.

The 1-way deer gate is now being used in various parts of the country. Its value has been varied depending on where the installations were made. One point is apparent to date—the device does have some limited value in meeting its objectives; however, in other areas it has received very little use and should be so realized when planning.

Fig. 20.48. A mule deer passes through a 1-way deer gate constructed in Colorado (Photo by Dale F. Reed).

Guards

At times it is necessary to allow easy access of vehicles through deer-proof fences. This has resulted in recommended deer guards similar to cattle guards constructed on range fences for years. Deer guards are similar to the cattle guards in structure, but generally are longer to limit deer crossing (Longhurst et al. 1962). Working in Colorado, Reed et al. (1975) tested deer use of 3.7-, 5.5-, and 7.3-m guards. Their findings substantiated that little advantage was gained by extending the length of guards for deer; when these animals were motivated, they walked, trotted, or bounded across the guards. Consequently, the use of modified deer-cattle guards to control deer movements appears to have limited value, based upon structures designed to date.

Interstate Highways

Movement of big game over country roads and low standard highways has not been a serious problem. Normally, barbed wire fences previously described are used on most rights-of-way. Leedy et al. (1975) published 2 lengthy volumes containing extensive literature reviews on highway-wildlife relationships and suggested research and management approaches to protect and enhance environmental quality for wildlife habitats. These reports are especially timely because currently there over 10 million hectares in highway rights-of-way. The authors cited various reports on practices including fencing, underpasses, traffic warning signs for animals, and other measures.

FENCES

With the creation of the federal interstate highway system, a serious problem has developed. Highway construction is cutting across important big game migratory and access routes. It's important to maintain these big game travel routes, yet the human hazard caused by animals seeking to cross high-speed highways also must be given consideration. When fences are constructed to reduce hazard to life and property on super-highways, alternate methods of allowing game to cross need to be devised. Otherwise, highway fences can have a serious detrimental effect on big game. In some instances, migratory habits may be impeded sufficiently to eliminate a complete big game herd. Mitigation of wildlife losses due to fence barriers must be done through state wildlife agencies. The following approaches to the problem should be considered:

Traversable game fences are described in this section in "Guidelines for Barbed Wire Fences." These fences will hold livestock but will allow game relatively free crossing. They should be used only in areas of light automobile traffic and in stretches where there are no center or island fences. They should be wide enough to allow game to make crossings without entrapment.

There are many areas where game normally winter or summer adjacent to interstate highways. While highways present no barriers to wildlife, the 2.4-m high woven wire fences used in some areas not only block game from crossing the right-of-way, but commonly entrap animals that manage to get inside. Also, in narrow canyons, interstate highways sometimes abandon the separate opposite lanes of traffic and place roadways adjacent to one another, separated by a chain-link fence to reduce collisions and headlight glare. The fence may or may not have a space at the bottom and may exceed the maximum height game animals can jump. This type of fence not only creates an unnatural barrier to wildlife, but a hazard to the driving public as well, because it holds animals in the traffic zone. For such cases as this, the manager may consider the "1-way deer gate" referred to under "Gates." Where chain link fences are used, a 10.2 cm space should be left on the bottom to allow small animals to cross. The maximum height should not exceed 1.0 m where consistent with highway needs.

Regelin et al. (1977) experimented with snowfences to relocate snowdrifts to influence forage availability. Snowfences reduced snow depths in shrub stands so that deer could use them and created drifts deep enough to protect overused and newly seeded areas from grazing by deer.

OVERPASSES

Underpasses and overpasses will need either natural terrain or else wing fences to guide and funnel migrating animals to them. Research in Colorado showed that underpass openings 4.3 m square with dirt floors were accepted by mule deer (Reed et al. 1975). Small skylights or artificial lights were not necessary for deer to use the underpass. Overpass use by game shows a marked reduction as the structures increase in length or decrease in width. Fenced wings to guide big game to these structures have been used with some success, but more study is needed to discover ways of improving their effectiveness.

Power Lines and Raptors

The problem of hundreds of raptors being electrocuted by electric distribution lines became a national conservation issue in the 1970's (Olendorff and Kochert 1977). The problem is greatest in the western United States. Nelson and Nelson (1976) documented that for 1974, over 300 eagles were electrocuted in the U.S. The count showed 98% were young birds just learning to fly. The young birds lacked skill necessary to land smoothly on power lines and were electrocuted.

Efforts to decrease this mortality problem were accelerated in the last decade. State and federal wildlife agencies pooled their biological knowledge with power company's engineering technical skills. The result was the development of several guidelines on how best to construct power lines to minimize electrocution of raptors. These are well documented and available through the U.S. Rural Electrification Administration (1972) and the Raptor Research Foundation (n.d.). Since there are many different power line designs and corrective measures need to be specific to the problem line, the manager should consult with these sources or other specialists.

Two examples of habitat improvements recently developed to enhance power lines for raptors are nesting platforms and wood perches. Nesting platforms are discussed in detail under "Specialized Nest Structures." Figure 20.15 is an example. Wooden perches are structures added 0.9 m above power lines. These have been well used as preferred landing sites by eagles and other raptors (Nelson and Nelson 1976). Figure 20.49 depicts how these perches are mounted. It is estimated that 95% of raptor electrocutions can be prevented by correcting 2% of power line poles. The authors also stated that power line poles properly constructed are a means of improving raptor habitat, for they are often constructed in vast open areas of the West, lacking cliffs or trees. Consequently, the raptors use power line poles for hunting, feeding, and nesting sites.

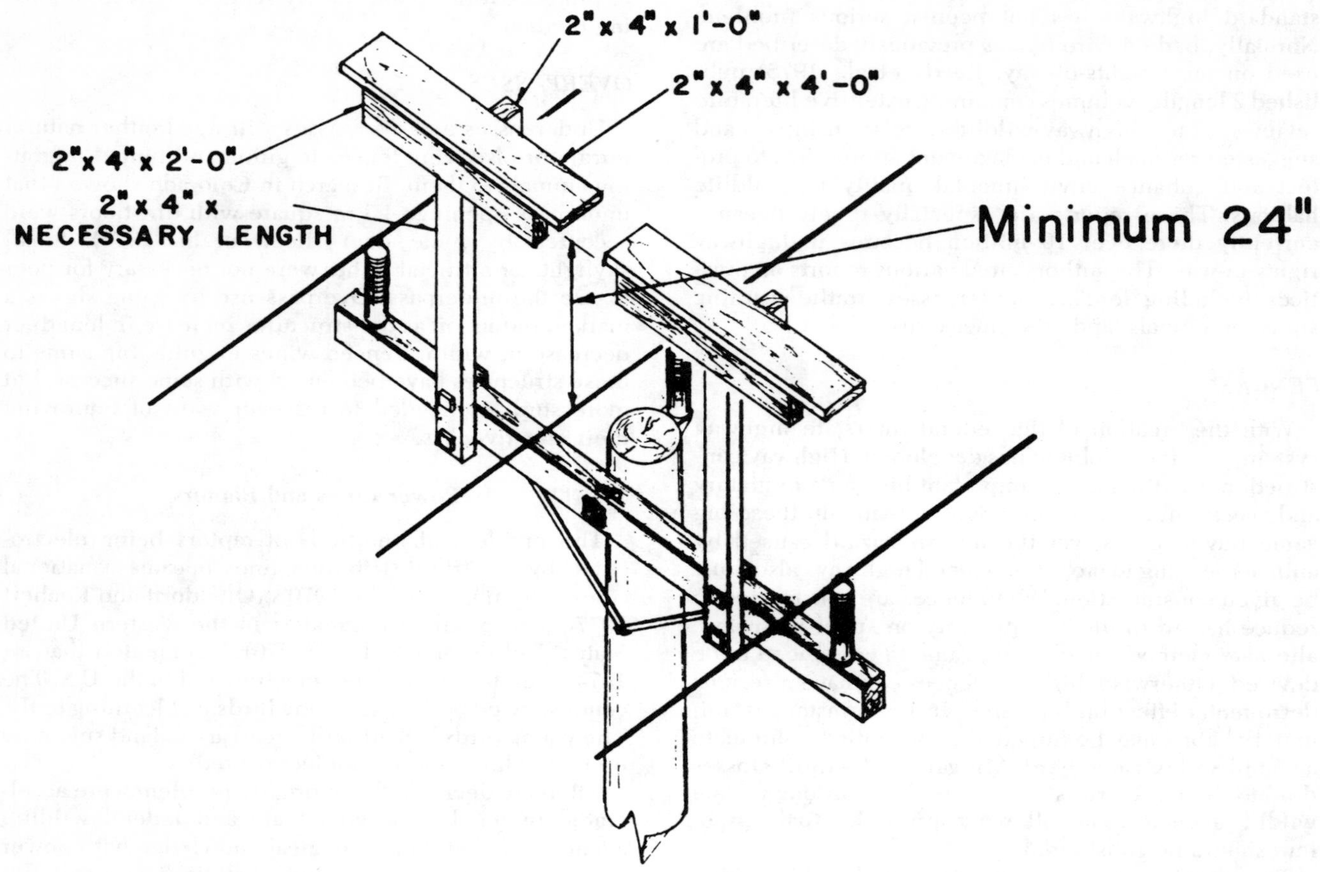

Fig. 20.49. Plans for perches on power lines to help reduce cases of raptor electrocutions (Nelson and Nelson 1976).

Study Exclosures (Big Game)

Exclosures are constructed for a number of purposes, but are mainly used to exclude or control livestock or big game use within the fenced area. These exclosures provide a basis for comparison of grazing or browsing with that on adjacent open range. Exclosures also serve as a method to determine proportionate use on ranges grazed by both big game and livestock.

Permanent exclosures should not be less than 0.4 ha in size—1 to 2 ha are frequently more desirable. Extra strong construction is needed on all parts of the fence to withstand heavy pressure by animals against these small, fenced areas of better forage. Gates should not be constructed in exclosure fences. Stiles, steps, or ladders will provide access to the plot.

Three-way exclosures are often used to compare big game and livestock use of vegetation in an area (Fig. 20.50 and 51). These exclosures are constructed with 2 fenced plots and 1 unfenced or open adjacent control plot. They are generally not less than 0.4 ha each. One fenced exclosure (a) is game and livestock-proof; the second livestock-proof (b) but readily accessible to game. The third plot, (c) or control, is established on open range nearby. This unfenced control plot (c) should be an equal-sized area marked on the ground. The following specifications apply to the fenced plots.

A 2.1-m high fence usually is adequate to exclude both elk and deer. However, if the exclosure is so located, or of such a size that it forms a barrier to concentrated game movements, the fence should be at least 2.4 m high. If areas subject to drifting snows cannot be entirely avoided, it is necessary to construct a higher fence through the drift zone. Fences should not be located on steep ground unless necessary. This will minimize the influence of water drainage from outside the plot.

A square exclosure with wire fence 2.1 m high with 64 m on all sides, will enclose about 0.4 ha and will require the following materials:

20 corner wooden posts	15.2-cm diameter at small end and 3 m long, peeled and penetrated
48 steel line posts	"T" stud, 3 m long

16 line wooden posts,	15.2-cm diameter at small end and 3.0 m long, peeled and penetrated
8 braces, horizontal	12.7-cm diameter at small end and 2.4 m long
8 braces, diagonal	12.7-cm diameter at small end and 3.1 m long
2 spools, barbed wire	80-rod (401.6 m) spool
No. 9 smooth wire, galvanized	91.4 m
9.1 kg staples	3.8 cm
1.8 kg nails	40 d.
hog wire	1.1 m, galvanized, 256 m
Rabbit-proof wire	5.1 × 10.2 cm, galvanized, 256 m
200 hog rings	Heavy duty, galvanized

The livestock-proof plot (b) will be enclosed with 1.0-m fencing; 4-m spacing between posts (64 m to a side). On livestock range, 4 barbed wires shall be spaced 12.7, 28, 45.7 and 66.1 cm from the ground with a smooth wire on top, 25.4 cm above the top strand of barbed wire.

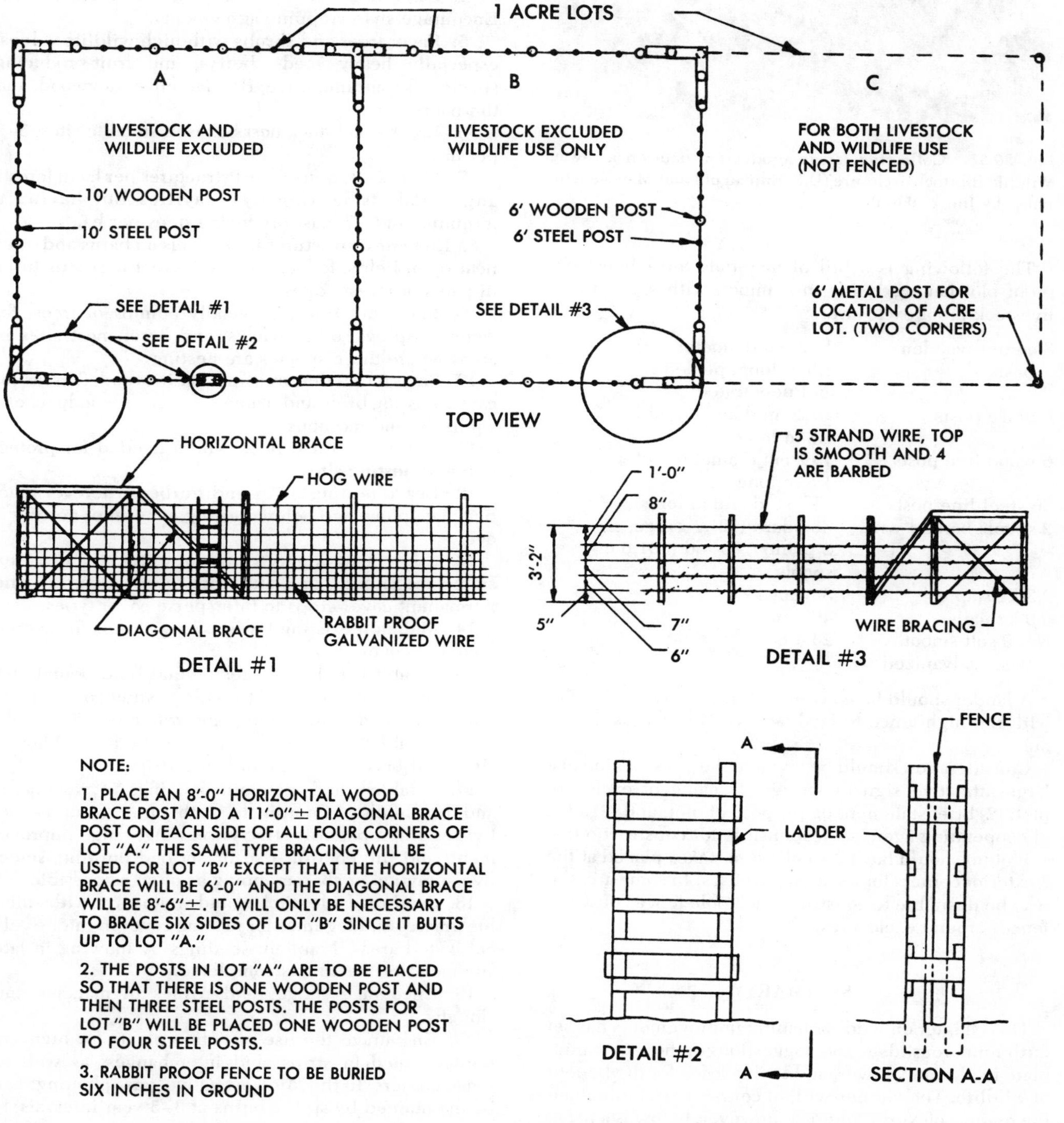

NOTE:

1. PLACE AN 8'-0" HORIZONTAL WOOD BRACE POST AND A 11'-0"± DIAGONAL BRACE POST ON EACH SIDE OF ALL FOUR CORNERS OF LOT "A." THE SAME TYPE BRACING WILL BE USED FOR LOT "B" EXCEPT THAT THE HORIZONTAL BRACE WILL BE 6'-0" AND THE DIAGONAL BRACE WILL BE 8'-6"±. IT WILL ONLY BE NECESSARY TO BRACE SIX SIDES OF LOT "B" SINCE IT BUTTS UP TO LOT "A."

2. THE POSTS IN LOT "A" ARE TO BE PLACED SO THAT THERE IS ONE WOODEN POST AND THEN THREE STEEL POSTS. THE POSTS FOR LOT "B" WILL BE PLACED ONE WOODEN POST TO FOUR STEEL POSTS.

3. RABBIT PROOF FENCE TO BE BURIED SIX INCHES IN GROUND

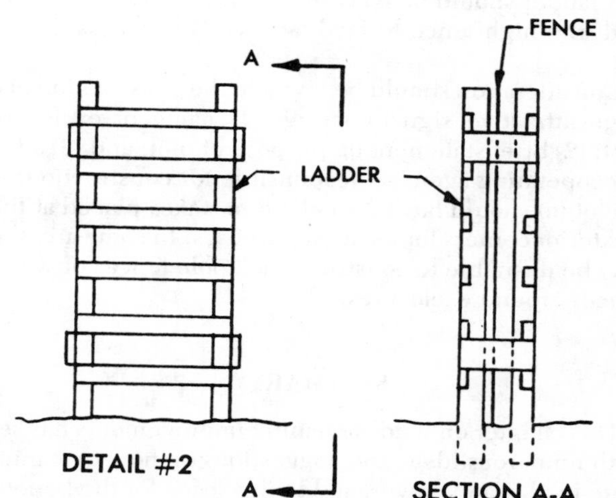

Fig. 20.50. Plans and specifications for the installation of a 3-way wildlife-livestock exclosure.

Fig. 20.51. Collecting forage production data on a 3-way Wildlife lifestock exclosure (U.S. Bureau of Land Management photo by Jim Yoakum).

The following is a bill of materials for a livestock-proof plot having 1 side in common with a game and livestock-proof exclosure:

8 corner wooden posts	15.2-cm diameter and 1.8 m long, peeled and penetrated
6 brace posts	15.2-cm diameter and 1.8 m long
6 wood line posts	15.2-cm diameter and 1.8 m long
36 steel line posts	"T" stud, 1.8 m long
2 spools barbed wire	Standard (12-½ gauge, 2 points), 80-rod (401.6 m) spools
2.3 kg staples	3.8 cm
0.9 kg nails	40 penny
No. 9 soft smooth wire, galvanized	24.4 m

A ladder should be constructed in 1 corner of the plot with the high fence to facilitate workers access in and out.

Consideration should be given to the construction of a large attractive sign denoting: (1) name of exclosure plot; (2) brief statement on purpose of plot; and (3) a list of cooperating agencies responsible for construction.

Plot (c) should have 2 steel 1.8-m stakes placed at the 2 exterior corners for location purposes. In some areas, it may be desirable to construct buck pole fences or worm fences around exclosures.

SUMMARY

This chapter on wildlife habitat improvements has set forth numerous ideas and suggestions on how to manipulate food, water, cover, and living space for the benefit of wildlife. Techniques will, of course, vary throughout the regions of North America; however, below is a list of the main principles and methods:

1. Develop "edge" because many wildlife species are a product of the places where 2 habitats meet. Examples are the borders of woods, fields, ponds, orchards, meadows, rivers, potholes, marshes, brushlands, clearings, and swamps.
2. Maintain mast trees. For oaks, 112 kg of mast per ha is needed to sustain reasonable wildlife densities or 5.7–6.9 m² of basal area per ha for trees old enough to produce seed (25.4 + cm dbh). For hickory and beech 0.7–1.4 m² per ha has been recommended.
3. Encourage fruit trees; also woody cover in hedgerows and fence rows.
4. Discourage fall plowing of harvested grain crops. Encourage sharecropping agreements.
5. Favor trees and shrubs with high wildlife values, especially heavy seed-, berry-, and fruit-producing species like autumn olive, Russian olive, dogwood, and thornapple.
6. Erect wood duck nest boxes in suitable sites, 5–9 per ha.
7. Erect 2–3 squirrel nest structures per ha in forests and woodlots lacking tree cavities but having a minimum of 5–7 mast-producing trees per ha.
8. Erect nest structures for kestrels on barns and trees near open fields, for screech owls erect nest structures in parks or forest edges.
9. Favor tall trees, especially clumps of trees, for eagles, ospreys, other hawks, and heron nest sites in areas where these species are nesting.
10. Save 5 to 9 den trees per ha in wooded areas for cavity nesting birds and mammals such as woodpeckers, squirrels, and raccoons.
11. Construct brush piles where needed for protection and nesting sites.
12. Leave nesting cover undisturbed wherever practical, i.e., plow land before nesting; mow after nesting is over.
13. Allow natural succession to revegetate areas not suited for farming or plant them to trees, shrubs, and permanent cover crops to intersperse cover types.
14. Maintain existing low-growing shrubs for natural food and cover.
15. Establish living hedges around field boundaries to reduce soil erosion and provide nesting cover, travel lanes, and food. Use native plants when possible.
16. Establish windbreaks along roads, around homesites, and between fields and crop strips.
17. Establish and maintain openings in woodlands and brushfields. Coordinate with other resource activities when possible: tree harvesting, range improvement, and fire control. Use prescribed burning, selective spraying, or sharecropping as often as possible.
18. Seed roadside ditches and waterways with suitable grasses and legumes for nesting cover in intensively cultivated areas. Maintain seedings by mowing in late summer after nesting is completed.
19. Encourage sedges and rushes in marshes and sloughs.
20. Encourage the use of native plants for highway borders, median strips, and interchanges, as well as fence corners. In the Midwest native grass plantings can be maintained by spring burns at 3–5 year intervals.

21. Keep certain fields open on old farmland by mowing hayfields or keeping certain areas in cultivation.

22. Vary cover as much as possible. The more varied the cover, the more wildlife.

23. Mix small plantings (0.4 ha) of evergreens with hardwoods for cover; do not plant in extensive solid blocks and reserve the bottoms for hardwoods.

24. Control excessive weed growth in canals, streams, lakes, and ponds.

25. Provide floating logs or rafts as loafing sites for waterfowl.

26. Establish water holes at springs or in seepage areas.

27. Provide potholes and other small open-water areas for nesting or resting waterfowl.

28. Develop ponds and lakes for waterfowl, water birds, and aquatic mammals.

29. Protect forests, marshes, swales, and fields from uncontrolled fires. However, consider a "let burn" program. Fire is a natural force in many ecosystems and can provide benefits for man and wildlife.

30. Avoid burning when vegetative habitat is critical for nesting cover or food for young wildlife. In some areas cool, late season burns can be used to rejuvenate herbaceous species needed for wildlife food and cover. Depending on successional trends and wildlife needs, burns should be used on a 3–5 year rotation.

31. Perpetuate sand and small, natural gravel along roads and trails to supply birds with grit.

32. In February–March, place mourning dove nest cones 1.8–4.9 m above ground in suitable trees.

33. Fence woodlots and planted areas against uncontrolled grazing to protect food and cover.

34. Stabilize streambanks with shrub and conifer plantings. Fence livestock and wildlife away from eroded streambanks where their use restricts recovery of vegetation.

35. Reserve undisturbed buffer strips of riparian vegetation alone streams to provide shade, insect food for fish, and dens for mammals.

36. Control water levels in marshes to favor habitat for waterfowl and other water birds.

Chapter Twenty-One

Sustained Yield Management

IRVIN R. SAVIDGE

Biologist
Texas Instruments
P.O. Box 237
Buchanan, New York

J. SCOTT ZIESENIS

Biologist
Texas Instruments
P.O. Box 237
Buchanan, New York

INTRODUCTION

The primary goal of wildlife management is to optimize the utilization of wildlife resources by man. This utilization can be either consumptive or nonconsumptive. The magnitude of this utilization may be regarded as the yield of the wildlife resource to man. Yield is normally applied only to the consumptive utilization (harvest) of the resource. The consumptive utilization of the resource includes both quantitative and qualitative aspects. The management of wildlife populations must take these 2 aspects into account. The management of small game species such as cottontail rabbits and gray squirrels to provide maximal numbers harvested on a sustained basis will also maximize the recreational aspects of the harvest. For other species in which trophy value provides an additional qualitative aspect to the resource utilization, management for maximum sustainable yield in terms of numbers or biomass usually will not provide the maximum sustained yield as measured by trophy animals harvested. Management schemes must therefore balance the relative quantitative and qualitative aspects of wildlife harvest to ensure optimal harvest of the resource. Optimal sustainable yield as a concept in fisheries management has been the subject of a recent symposium (Roedel 1975). Definition of the optimal harvest of these populations is a sociological as well as a biological decision. The biological problems of wildlife management can be resolved only after defining the specific management goals.

Management of wildlife populations is largely a matter of habitat management and application of a harvest strategy to maximize the qualitative and quantitative aspects of the yield of the population. Management of habitat involves manipulation of food and cover. Removal of predators to increase the yield of a wildlife population is in reality only a reallocation of the yield from predator to man although some net increase or decrease in yield may result from the change in the timing of the harvest.

Management of yield of a wildlife population consists of the application of an appropriate harvest strategy. Two aspects of the harvest strategy are immediately apparent: magnitude and timing. Magnitude may refer to numbers or may be age class and sex specific. Timing may refer to annual timing of harvest or to age of animals to be harvested. The effects of annual timing of harvest of wood pigeons in England is described by Murton et al. (1974). The potential of increasing big game yield through periodic harvest has been modeled by Walters and Bandy (1972).

Data on wildlife populations generally available to the manager usually are limited to harvests, density estimates, and hunter effort. Unfortunately, this information is of limited duration or absent for many management problems. Management of populations for which more extensive data are available can be based on mathematical models and simulation of the population response and yield under alternative management procedures. (See Chapter 13). With more limited data, however, insights into management alternatives can be obtained through the use of simplified yield relationships. The simplified approach to developing harvest strategies in this chapter will be based on population growth equations, parent-progeny relationships, and empirical procedures. No attempt will be made to deal with the development of complex management strategies that are best formulated through the use of simulation techniques.

BASIC CONCEPTS

In managing wildlife populations for maximum sustained yield, the basic concepts of population ecology must be applied. The mechanisms involved in density dependent population regulation also provide the ability of the population to compensate for additional mortality imposed by man's harvest of the resource. This harvest may be imposed as either a density dependent or density independent mortality.

The carrying capacity of the habitat is defined as the number of animals the habitat can support and encompasses both density independent and density dependent environmental facets. As viewed by the wildlife manager the carrying capacity of a habitat need not be constant and in most cases will change on a short-term or long-term basis. Changes in carrying capacity may occur through environmental changes resulting from succession, fluctuations in weather, or destruction of habitat through overpopulation. The destruction of habitat through overpopulation is an example of a population modifying the carrying capacity of its habitat.

Rates of increase, birth rates, and death rates may be defined in several ways using either finite or exponential notation. These rates may be broadly categorized as physiological under optimal environmental conditions, intrinsic under existing environmental conditions excluding density dependent feedback and realized rate under existing environmental conditions including density dependent feedback. These rates in exponential notation are summarized below:

Rate	Physiological	Intrinsic	Realized
birth	b_{max}	b_o	b
death	d_{min}	d_o	d
increase	r_{max}	r_o	r

The factors interacting to determine these rates are extremely complex. Fortunately the relationships between population growth and density can be simplistically modeled even when the functional relationships of the various density dependent mechanisms are poorly understood. For all species b_{max} must exceed d_{min} to avoid extinction. For a population to be maintained without supplemental stocking b_o must also exceed d_o ($r_o > o$). In a population which is neither increasing nor decreasing over a period of time, b=d, and r=o. Note that r_{max} is equivalent to Andrewartha and Birch's (1954) r_m, and r_o above is equivalent to Caughley and Birch's (1971) r_m.

SIMPLIFIED POPULATION GROWTH AND STOCK RECRUITMENT RELATIONSHIP

Sustained yield is the numbers or biomass of animals that can be removed from a population over a long period of time while assuring persistence of the resource. A population can stabilize at different levels of sustained yield, but 1 level of sustained yield will provide the maximum sustained harvest. This level is the maximum sustained yield. The maximum sustained yield may not be the optimal sustained yield when the exploitation is intended to maximize some qualitative characteristics of the harvest such as trophy value.

A convenient and familiar starting point for developing the yield concept is the exponential and logistic equations. In the exponential equation the rate of increase is the intrinsic rate of increase and population change is proportional to the population size, (N).

$$\frac{dN}{dt} = r_o N \quad (1)$$

The rate of increase per individual is constant, and the realized rate of increase is equal to the intrinsic rate of increase.

$$\frac{dN}{Ndt} = r_o \quad (2)$$

Populations do not increase indefinitely in nature as would be the case with the exponential relationship obtained by integrating equation (1) with respect to time.

$$N_t = N_o \exp r_o t \quad (3)$$

where N_0 is the initial population size and t is time. Changes in the realized birth and death rates eventually result in the realized rate of increase becoming zero or varying around a mean of zero when the population reaches the carrying capacity of the habitat.

The logistic equation incorporates the assumption that the realized rate of increase decreases in proportion to the ratio of population size (N) to the carrying capacity of the habitat (K).

$$r = r_o N(K-N)/K \quad (4)$$

Density dependent feedback is thus incorporated so that the realized rate of increase of the population decreases as the population increases

$$\frac{dN}{dt} = r_o N\ (1-N/K) \quad (5)$$

In the logistic model, the realized rate of increase is always less than the intrinsic rate of increase and becomes negative when the population size exceeds the carrying capacity of the habitat.

$$\frac{dN}{Ndt} = r_o\ (1-N/K) = r \quad (6)$$

The logistic equation incorporates a density dependent feedback response of the population and produces a symmetrical S-shaped population growth curve (Fig. 21.1). The shape of the curve can be modified by changing the formulation of the density dependent feedback. It is an algebraic expression that represents an empirical relationship rather than a functional relationship. The data required for building a functional mathematical relationship to describe the effects of density on reproduction and mortality are not available for most wildlife populations. For those species having density dependent regulatory mechanisms acting with an intensity approximately proportional to population density, the

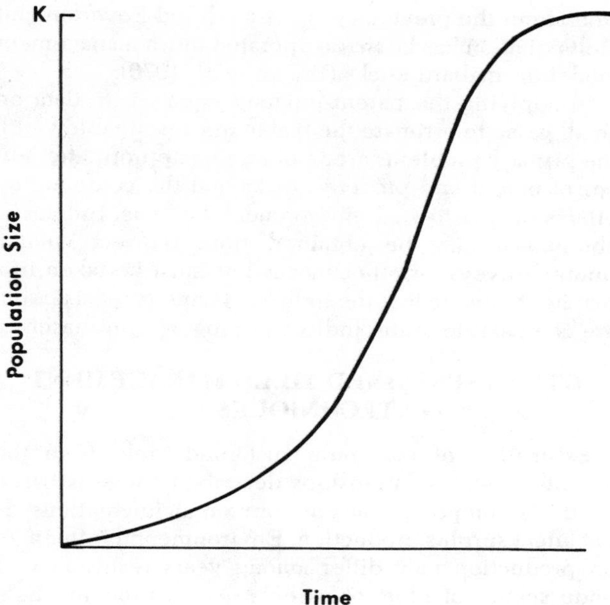

Figure 21.1. Logistic growth curve.

logistic equation provides a tool for making management decisions. It has been used by Mentis (1977) for evaluating stocking rates of African ungulates.

Equation (6) can be solved for the population at time t relative to the population size at time t-1.

$$N_t = N_{t-1} \exp r_o (1-N_t/K) \tag{7}$$

Although the realized rate of increase per individual decreases with population size in the logistic equation (Fig. 21.2), the increase in numbers per unit of time is greatest when the population size is approximately one half of the carrying capacity (Fig. 21.3). The shape of these curves is a result of the assumed mathematical form of density dependent feedback. Other formulations can shift the population size at which maximum recruitment occurs to higher or lower levels.

From the relationship of population growth to population size one can estimate the sustainable yield at any population size less than the carrying capacity. The sustainable yield is the difference between the progeny produced and the number of progeny required to maintain the parental stock size (Fig. 21.3). The increase in stock size (or surplus production) can be harvested to maintain the parent stock size. Since this increase will be constant for a constant parental stock size, the harvesting of the increase to maintain the parent stock size will result in a sustained yield. The relationships between parent and progeny might be evaluated empiri-

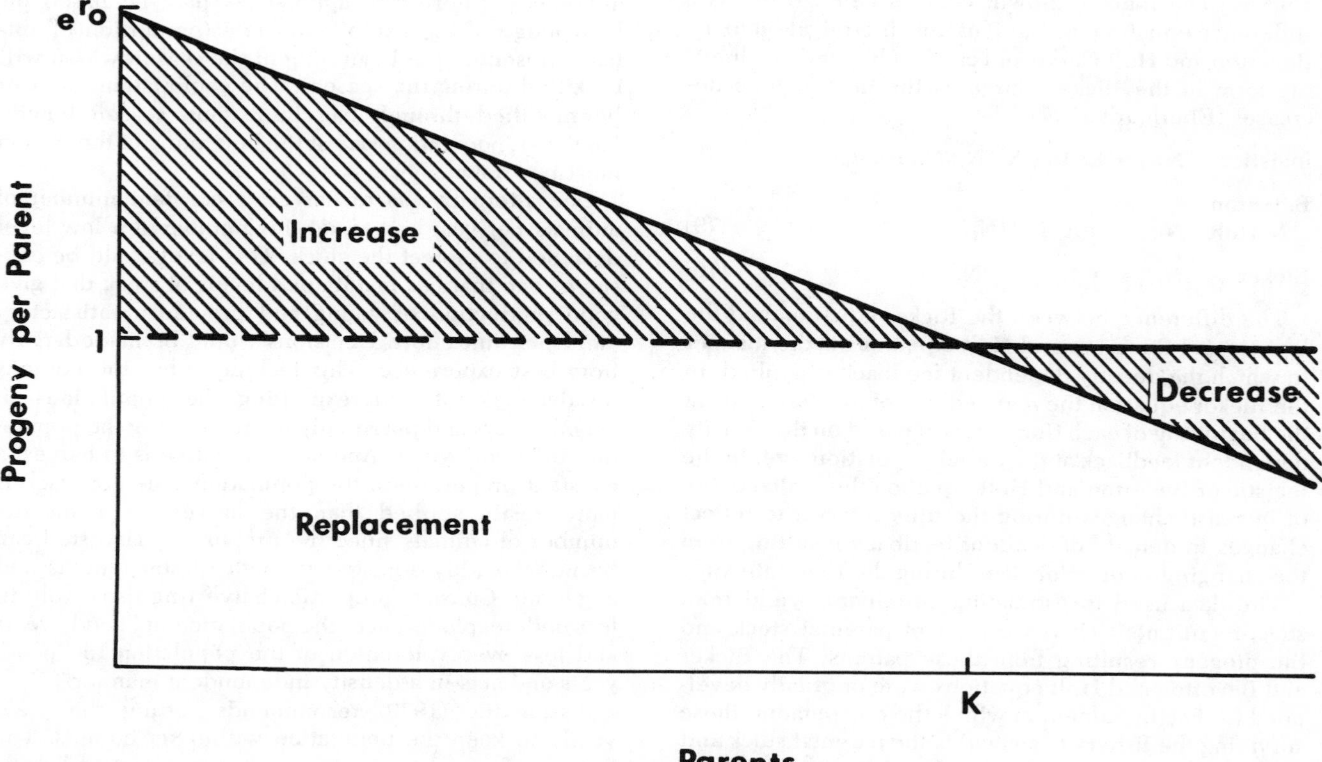

Figure 21.2. Progency per parent at differing parental densities. At the carrying capacity (K) the number of progeny equals the number required to replace the parents.

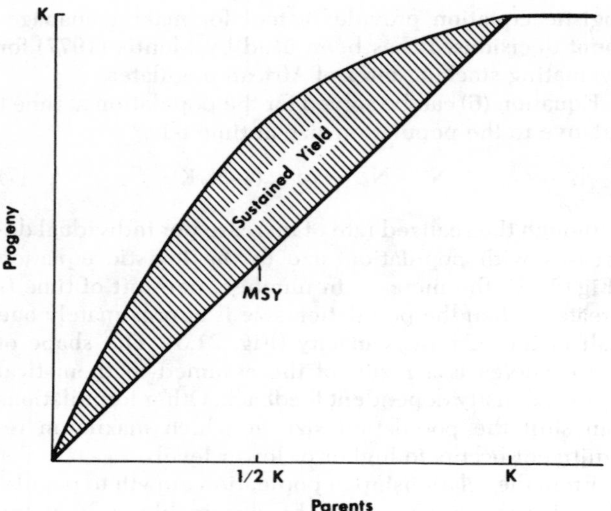

Figure 21.3. **Parent progeny relationship from logistic growth curve. Shaded area represents production of progeny in excess of numbers required for replacement of parents. The samples production can be harvested as a sustained yield.**

cally from field data, or theoretically from population growth and stock-recruitment equations.

The 2 major parent-progeny curves in current usage are the Beverton and Holt (1957) and Ricker (1975) Curves. The logistic growth curve when written as a difference equation for 1 unit of time is equivalent to the Beverton and Holt Curve and can be obtained as a limiting form of the Ricker Curve as the unit of time decreases (Eberhardt 1977).

logistics $N_{t+1} = K/(1+((K-N_t)/N_t)\exp{-r_o})$ (8)

Beverton & Holt $N_{t+1} = 1/(A + \beta/N_t)$ (9)

Ricker $N_{t+1} = \propto N_t \exp{-\beta N_t}$ (10)

The difference between the Ricker equation and the logistic and Beverton and Holt equations is the manner in which the density dependent feedback is applied. In the Ricker equation the realized rate of increase is set at the beginning of each time interval based on the density dependent feedback at the initial population size. In the logistic or Beverton and Holt equation the realized rate of increase changes during the time interval to reflect changes in density dependent feedback resulting from the changing population size during the time interval.

The data used in estimating sustainable yield from stock-recruitment curves consist of parental stock and the progeny resulting from those parents. The Ricker and Beverton and Holt equations were originally developed for Pacific salmon in which the escapement (those surviving the fishery to spawn) is the parental stock and the spawning run (prior to the fishery) 1 generation later is the progeny. This situation is roughly comparable to estimating posthunting season stock size for a given year and later estimating prehunting season stock size the following year for small game species; annual mortality is so high that stock in any year is largely the progeny of stock from the previous year. A modified Beverton and Holt equation has been incorporated into a management model for mallard ducks (Brown et al. 1976).

In applying the parent-progeny equation to data on small game to estimate the maximum sustainable yield, the primary problems are in obtaining appropriate indices of parent and progeny stocks and the confounding effects of year-to-year environmental effects. Indices of abundance may be obtained from transect counts, hunter surveys, or other means but must be taken in a manner to insure that the indices of parents (postseason) are comparable to the indices of progeny (preseason).

OTHER SUSTAINED YIELD MANAGEMENT TECHNIQUES

Estimation of maximum sustained yield from the parent-progeny relationships described above is based on the assumption that environmental fluctuations do not affect surplus production. Environmental influences on production may differ among years resulting in a wide scatter of plots of parents versus progeny. Estimates of maximum sustained yield under average conditions can be obtained by fitting parent-progeny equations to these data. Through use of additional information on preseason population size, the long-term harvests may be further increased by adapting the harvest to the fluctuating densities without jeopardizing the population. Sissenwine (1979) has demonstrated that MSY can be seriously underestimated if surplus production varies randomly through time due to environmental influences. Alternative approaches may be based on knowledge of the exploitation rate (proportion of animals present at the beginning of the season which will be killed during the season). The exploitation rate can be modified through bag limits and season length. However, population size at the beginning of the season must be known.

One alternative is to harvest a constant number of animals per year and to set this number at a low level designed to protect the stock. This level could be chosen as one that has maintained levels of stock that give good production of young and provide a satisfactory yield per unit effort. Decisions would be made largely from past experience. This technique has the obvious disadvantage of underexploiting the populations in "good" years and potentially overexploiting the population in "poor" years. Another alternative is to harvest a constant proportion of the population. The approach is more easily applied than the harvest of a specific number of animals since the proportion harvested can be more readily adjusted through season lengths and bag limits. Constant proportion harvesting also results in less underexploitation of the population in "good" years and less overexploitation of the population in "poor" years and acts in a density independent manner.

Sissenwine (1979) recommends setting the yield yearly to keep the population within set bounds. The bounds of population size can be set to protect habitat and farmland from overutilization. A similar strategy of harvesting populations in a density dependent manner, based on rate of increase of the population after harvest, is suggested by Caughley (1977b) for harvesting fluctuating populations.

An interesting blend of these approaches has been suggested by Ricker (1975). He suggests that the exploitation rate be increased each generation. Exploitation of the first generation displaces the population from the equilibrium point and effectively increases production. Thus increased exploitations will give an increase in harvest the next generation until the exploitation equals the maximum sustained yield. After this point, harvest will decline with increases in exploitation rate. The relationship between exploitation of the parental generation and harvest of the progeny generation can be plotted and the maximum sustained yield can be derived from the point on the curve where increasing exploitation causes reduced yield in the next generation. These relationships may be obscured, however, if the population is subjected to high variation from environmental influences.

SUMMARY

The concept of sustainable yield is a natural outgrowth of the relationship of population density to the rate of growth of the population. At densities below the carrying-capacity, production must be greater than that required to maintain the population at that level; the excess production can be harvested. Most management practices to increase yield either increase the excess production by raising the carrying capacity (habitat management) or through reallocation of the harvestable excess (predator control).

For a specified environment, a population density exists that will produce the maximum sustainable yield. This stock level and the associated sustained yield can be approximated through the use of simple stock-progeny models. As a first approach, the logistic equation indicates that the maximum sustained yield will result when the harvest is adjusted to maintain the parental stock size at approximately one half the carrying capacity of the habitat. As data become available for more detailed analyses, or the management objective incorporate qualitative as well as quantitative goals, more complex simulations should be considered in formulating the management scheme.

Chapter Twenty-Two

Wildlife Damage and Control Techniques

DONALD W. HAWTHORNE[1]

State Supervisor
Division of Animal Damage Control
U.S. Fish and Wildlife Service
San Antonio, Texas

INTRODUCTION

The purpose of this chapter is to discuss various forms of wildlife damage and control techniques. Obviously, all species have beneficial and positive aspects; however, most species at one time or another may require some form of management. Animal damage control is one of the many tools of resource management, and like all the others it is a means to accomplish an objective and never an end (Berryman 1971). Some examples are a forester conducting a pocket gopher control project to re-establish a forest area; a manager doing bird control to protect agricultural production to meet the increasing need for food and fiber; or a biologist controlling a competing or depredating species to give an endangered species an edge. Of course, there are many similar examples which also might be used as illustrations. Nevertheless, one thing is certain—as the human population increases, so will the man-wildlife related conflicts. Therefore, the individual or agency faced with resolving these conflicts must be able to identify the species causing the problem, and have knowledge of the methods or techniques available that can limit or reduce the conflicts to a tolerable level.

Wildlife-caused damage is primarily associated with feeding activity, and to a lesser extent, related to denning, nesting or roosting behavior, or the animals involved may just be in the "wrong place" at the "right time." Every conflict does not necessarily call for corrective action, but it is the sustained damage, "the total picture," that demands the manager's attention. Animal damage control is complex. There is no "cookbook" guide or barometer to tell when control is needed. Each damage situation must be weighed individually on its own merits and in relation to other ecological considerations.

Berryman (1972) suggested several areas to be considered when planning control: (1) control decisions should not be made independently; (2) management objectives and plans should be developed cooperatively with others having management responsibilities and talents from many disciplines; and (3) input of accurate

[1]The author wishes to express his appreciation to personnel in the U.S. Fish and Wildlife Service, and State Extension Wildlife Specialists who provided material for and critical review of this chapter.

data is essential. The criteria for determining need is not based solely on economics or impact on other wildlife but may include aesthetic, social, ecological, political, and administrative considerations. Animal damage control measures should be applied at a time, point, and place when the animal is most vulnerable and with least effect on nontarget species. Control methods available to the manager include habitat modification, biological control, mechanical barriers and repellents, trapping and transplanting, controlled killing, and economic reimbursement. To achieve maximum effectiveness, they should be applied in combination. Two approaches can be used to accomplish control: (1) extension methods (giving individuals the knowledge to solve their own problems) and (2) professionals. Animal damage control should be carried out by professionals when it may affect sensitive species, requires hazardous control methods, or is conducted on public lands. Once the control project has begun, it should be applied only to the extent necessary to accomplish planned objectives. Costs should be related to the overall worth of the ultimate management objectives and should be equated to social and aesthetic values (Berryman 1972).

Each of the major sections of this chapter has 3 parts—1 on the assessment of the damage; 1 on identification of damage by individual species; and the final one on the control techniques, which is an elaboration of those listed under each of the species.

RODENTS AND SMALL MAMMALS

Damage Assessment

While assessment of damage and the determination of the responsible species may be rather simple for one with experience, the untrained observer may have a difficult time. In examining the damage, one must look for "clues." Obviously, the best clue is actually observing the species doing the damage, but the investigator may not have this opportunity. Therefore, "signs" such as tracks, tooth marks, droppings, dens, burrows, and trails must be sought. Together with these "signs," familiarity with the habits of wildlife will aid in the determination of the species.

Different species will damage different parts of a plant, for example; root damage—gophers and mice; root collar barking—mice and gophers; trunk barking—voles, mice, squirrels, porcupines, wood rats, rabbits, and mountain beavers; stem and branch cutting—beaver, rabbits, mice, mountain beavers, pocket gophers, wood rats, squirrels, and porcupines; needle clipping—mice, squirrels, mountain beavers, porcupines, and rabbits; debudding—red squirrels and chipmunks. These are only indications of the animals that might be suspected doing the damage.

Identifying the species is difficult at times, since similar types of damages can be caused by more than one animal. For example, rabbits and porcupines may clip young seedlings in identical fashion. When small animals are involved, snap trap lines are useful in determining species and population levels present.

Species Damage Identification

ARMADILLO

The armadillo's diet generally consists of earthworms, insects, insect larvae, and tender roots and shoots. On rare occasions, they will find a ground nesting bird's nest and eat the eggs. They cause urban damage by rooting in lawns, golf courses, vegetable gardens, and flower beds. A few people have complained that the armadillo's shell rubbing against their house or other structure has kept them awake at night. When looking the area over for signs, one usually will find a small path leading to a den. Also, armadillos may be observed, particularly during the twilight hours. They are persistent diggers and have a distinctive three-toed track which shows sharp claw marks.

Control techniques: Conibear traps, shooting, and live traps with wing fencing, exclusion fencing (25 cm high poultry wire) and insecticides (removal of food source).

BEAVER

The presence of beaver damage is readily evident by noting the cone-shaped stumps of trees, freshly peeled sticks scattered around the area and floating in the water, and broad, chisel-like tooth marks left on the stumps. Beavers favor deciduous trees such as sweetgum, cottonwood, willows, alder, and aspen. If large pools or lakes are being utilized by a beaver colony a dam may not be present, but generally, a bank den or lodge will be in the vicinity.

The major damage caused by beaver is not just the timber they cut, but more importantly the timber, pastures, croplands and roads flooded by their dam building activities. They also feed on corn, soybeans, or almost any convenient and palatable plants.

Control techniques: Habitat modification, live trapping, conibear traps, shooting (using a spotlight with red lens), and leg hold traps (No. 3–4).

CHIPMUNKS

Occasionally, chipmunks may damage grain fields or garden seeds and plants, and have been known to dig up flower bulbs. They have been observed destroying eggs and nestling birds, but this is not a common occurrence (Eadie 1954). Chipmunks often cause major problems in reforestation areas. The extent to which the forest suffers from this species is not easily determined. They not only eat and cache great quantities of seed, but they also may feed heavily on emergent seedlings and terminal buds of older plants. Chipmunk damage is not readily apparent to the casual observer, but a careful search near sheltered areas—rotten logs, large rocks or stumps—should reveal accumulation of opened seed hulls. Their presence can best be determined by direct observation or the use of either live or snap traps.

Control techniques: Snap traps, live traps, and toxic grain bait, (zinc phosphide and strychnine).

COTTON RAT

Cotton rats normally are vegetarian; however, they do have carnivorous tendencies. They are active both day and night, and feed on seeds, grasses, sugar cane, fruits, vegetables, berries, nuts, and insects. They also have been observed preying on eggs and young of ground nesting birds, particularly quail. After a crop begins to grow, the rats move into fields and develop runways and burrow systems. They remain as long as shelter and food are available.

Evidence of cotton rat presence is grass cuttings 7.5 to 10 cm long placed in piles at various points along the runway systems. Also, droppings may be present along the runway, usually of a pale greenish-yellow color and approximately 9.5 mm in length and 4.8 mm in width (Caroline 1953). Droppings, grass clippings, and runways are all similar to, but larger than those made by the meadow mouse.

Control techniques: Habitat modification, treated grain (zinc phosphide and strychnine), and snap traps.

DEER MICE

Deer mice are very prolific, but not noticeably cyclic. Their populations may fluctuate markedly from year to year, with a population varying from a few to as many as 10 per hectare, depending on the habitat.

There are a number of small mammals that feed upon tree seeds; however, none affect reforestation as much as deer mice. These mice are nocturnal and active all year. They consume and cache great quantities of tree seed. Even low populations can consume most of the seeds of a normal seed fall. Laboratory studies have revealed that a deer mouse in captivity will eat approximately 200 Douglas-fir seeds per day. In agricultural areas, they can be very destructive to grain and other crops by digging up planted seeds or feeding on ripening crops. They have been known to invade suburban and summer homes or cabins, where they have caused havoc by eating stored food and shredding bedding and furniture upholstery (Eadie 1954). Generally, more than 3 animals per 100 trap nights indicate a need for control (Packham 1970).

Control techniques: Habitat modification, snap traps, live traps, and toxic grain baits (strychnine grain, zinc phosphide, or anticoagulants).

GROUND SQUIRRELS

Ground squirrels can be quite destructive to forest regeneration projects. They not only seek out tree seeds, but also feed on emergent seedlings. A ground squirrel may consume as many as 340 ponderosa pine seeds daily (Siggins 1933). A careful search of the affected area will reveal opened seed hulls and caches. Several ground squirrel species may inflict serious damage to pastures, rangelands, grain fields, vegetable gardens, and fruit trees. At times, ground squirrels may prey on ground-nesting birds. One study in California found that 30 of 96 valley quail nests were destroyed by *Spermophilus beecheyi* (Glading 1938). Ground squirrels in a duck nesting area destroyed 19% of 126 nests, in addition to killing young ducks as they strayed from broods (Sowls 1948). In Modoc County, California, using exclusion cylinders, preliminary investigations in damage assessment indicated that 49 squirrels per hectare removed an average of 4,000 kg of spring growth alfalfa and downy brome per hectare in 44 days (Sauer 1976). The same study revealed that the average daily food consumption is greater earlier in the year (May) than later (July). The damage caused by ground squirrels is similar to that of chipmunks. However, since both are active during the day, observation is one of the methods of making positive identification; live or snap trapping is another.

Control techniques: Habitat modification, shooting, fumigants, snap trapping, and toxic bait (strychnine, 1080, zinc phosphide, or anticoagulant treated grain).

KANGAROO RATS

High populations of kangaroo rats can be destructive to various crops, especially grains. Most damage occurs at the margins of fields adjacent to uncultivated areas. These animals may feed exclusively on available grasses and grass seeds, thus competing directly with livestock for forage. This may not be of great economic importance during normal years except for local situations; however, during extreme drought, it has an important impact on the carrying capacity for livestock in grazing areas.

The presence of kangaroo rats is evident by small burrows with surface runways leading to feeding areas or adjacent burrows. Snap trap surveys may also be used to make identification.

Control techniques: Habitat modification, snap traps, and toxic grain bait (strychnine, zinc phosphide and 1080).

MARMOTS

Marmots (woodchucks, rock chucks, ground hogs) like ground squirrels, can cause damage to many crops. Damage to legumes and truck gardens is often severe, with most damage caused by the animals consuming the plants. Earthen mounds near their burrows and the burrows themselves may damage haying and other farm equipment. Their burrows also may cause a loss of irrigation water when dug along water conveying ditches. Marmots may sharply reduce forage production by their feeding. Additional evidence includes droppings, burrows, and trails leading to and from the damaged area to dens or loafing areas. During spring, occupied woodchuck burrows are easily recognizable by the presence at the burrow entrance of dirt pellets ranging from marble size to fist size (Anderson 1969).

Control techniques: Fumigants, shooting, conibear traps, leg hold traps (No. 1 1/2–2) and strychnine-treated bait.

MEADOW MICE

Meadow mice, voles, prairie voles, and pine mice may cause damage to forests, orchards, ornamentals, and crops. Normally, mouse damage does not extend into bare openings, but occurs under cover of snow or matted vegetation. These mice normally gnaw the bark from small trees near the root collar and up the trunk as far as the snow extends. They may fell small trees or shoots up to approximately 6.2 mm in diameter, leaving stumps like miniature beaver work. Distinctive tooth marks sometimes are lacking. Occasionally, roots are stripped of their outer layers of bark by meadow mice, but this damage is usually the work of pine mice which live in subterranean tunnels. This root damage, primarily to orchard trees, may be undetected until spring or later.

The presence of mice may be discovered by pulling away the grass and other debris from the base of the tree and exposing their runways, or the burrows can be detected by probing the area close to the tree suspected to be harboring mice. Their gnawing is less uniform than that of other rodents. Tooth marks will be at all angles, even on small branches. These marks will vary from light scratches to channels 3 mm wide, 1.6 mm or deeper and about 9.5 mm long.

Control techniques: Screening, habitat modification, and toxic grain bait (zinc phosphide or strychnine) applied by hand baiting, fertilizer spreader, or by mechanical trail builder.

MOLES

Moles feed on insects and insect larvae; however, over three-fourths of their normal diet is earthworms. Approximately 20% of their food is plant material, which may include tulips, bulbous iris, carrots, parsnips, potatoes, peas, beans, vetch, oats, corn and wheat. Often, such items form a substantial part of an individual's diet (Silver and Moore 1941).

Mole mounds and burrow systems may reduce pasture production, make harvesting difficult by breaking or plugging machinery, contaminate hay and silage, and contribute to soil erosion. In some localities, moles have damaged lawns and golf greens extensively through their burrowing activities, leaving the surfaces marred by mounds of earth and ridges of raised turf.

Their presence is usually detected by the mounds of earth they throw up from the extensive tunnels dug in search of food. These surface mounds can be distinguished from those made by pocket gophers by the more rounded contour and by the absence of a burrow entrance in the center of the mound surface (Eadie 1954).

Control techniques: Harpoon and scissor traps, habitat modification, treated bait (strychnine and arsenic), and insecticides (removal of food source).

MOUNTAIN BEAVER

Mountain beavers cause serious economic loss by burrowing through and feeding on garden vegetables, berry plants, and young trees. They may use drainage ditches for burrow sites, and block them with refuse and soil. Springs also are often polluted by the mountain beaver's activities (Eadie 1954). Their burrows may undermine roadways and result in collapse of the road.

Mountain beaver can adversely influence forest reproduction. They may clip seedlings and gnaw saplings as well as stems and bark of larger trees. Seedlings normally are clipped clean at 45 degree angles. On small seedlings this may be difficult to distinguish from rabbit damage; however, rabbits seldom clip stems larger than 6 mm in diameter or 50 cm above ground level, whereas mountain beavers often cut stems larger than 12.7 mm in diameter or up to 3 m or more above ground (Lawrence et al. 1961). Mountain beavers will leave cut branch stubs protruding from the main stem. These branches may be cut at a 45 degree angle. The bark of the main stem will show horizontal tooth marks and vertical claw marks (Packham 1970). Runways and burrows will be present in or near the damaged area.

Control techniques: Live traps, conibear traps, leg hold traps (No. 1½–2), and habitat modification.

MUSKRAT

The most serious damage done by muskrats results from its burrows. The burrow entrance is below water level and penetrates the embankment at an upward angle to allow for a room above the water level. Damage occurs when the water level rises and forces the animal to dig deeper and higher to construct a new dry chamber, thereby increasing chances of washouts and embankment cave-ins. At times, muskrats have caused severe damage to grain, such as rice and garden crops growing near water. They commonly construct houses of grass and cattails in marshes and ponds. These are typically cone-shaped and project 0.5 to 1 m above the water surface. They are used primarily as resting, loafing and feeding areas.

Muskrat presence is indicated by its houses, underwater dens visible at low water, slides, cave-ins along banks caused by the undermining of their burrows, visual sightings of individual animals, tracks along trails and at the water's edge, and droppings.

Control techniques: Conibear traps, leg hold traps (No. 0–2) toxic baits (anticoagulants and zinc phosphide), live traps and habitat modification.

NUTRIA

Nutria are herbivorous and feed on a wide variety of aquatic plants, roots, seeds, and other succulent plants. They may cause severe damage when rice, corn, sweet potatoes, sugar cane, and other agricultural crops are grown close to waterways. Nutria are competitors of waterfowl and muskrats for natural plant food in marshes. Their burrows are made in banks, dams, and dikes, and may cause cave-ins.

Their presence is evidenced by tracks, droppings, and trails to and from the damage area. They also may be observed in the damage area (Anderson 1969).

Control techniques: Conibear traps, leg hold traps, (No. 1–2) and toxic baits (zinc phosphide and anticoagulants).

POCKET GOPHERS

Pocket gophers, found only in the western hemisphere, cause problems in cultivated lands, lawns, ranges, forests, and orchards. Orchards offer suitable habitat for pocket gophers in areas where weeds become established among the trees. The trees are damaged or killed by the gophers feeding on the roots (Anderson 1969).

Pocket gopher burrows have caused dams and roads to wash out and loss of water from canals. Gopher mounds in hay fields can cause equipment breakage and increased wearing rate of haying machinery. Gophers may damage hay and feed crops such as alfalfa by feeding on the leaves, stems, and roots. Many plants are killed by the animal cutting the roots and stems. Pocket gophers also have caused serious damage to buried cable and plastic water lines.

Pocket gophers can cause damage to pine and fir plantations. Their root cutting can prevent reproduction in forest clearings (Moore 1943). A recent study showed that pocket gophers damaged 2% of ponderosa pine within 24 hours of planting and approximately 14% within 1 month (Capp 1976). Similarly, Black et al. (1969) reported that pocket gophers destroyed about one-third of all conifer seedlings within 6 months after planting. Gopher infested roadways, power line rights-of-way, and meadows adjacent to plantations will insure a much greater rate of infestation of the plantation site. Root damaged trees are frequently unnoticed until the crowns turn yellow and then brown in summer. Large trees seem healthy until tilted at odd angles by the wind. Once discovered, they can be easily pulled up to reveal root cutting and barking. Pocket gophers forage above ground and tunnel in snow to gnaw off tree branches. Coniferous trees have been found barked to a height of 3.5 m by pocket gophers working under the snow (Capp 1976). Gophers also fill some of the snow passages with soil, thus forming long tubular "casts" which remain after the snow melts. When these casts are deposited on young trees 2 to 4 years old, deformity of severe proportions may occur.

Flat, fan-shaped mounds of soil are evidence of the presence of pocket gophers. These mounds contrast with the volcano-shaped mounds pushed up by moles. Above ground barking injuries caused by pocket gophers show small tooth marks. This differs from the distinct broader grooves left by porcupines, and the finely gnawed surface inflicted by meadow voles. Gophers may at times pull saplings and other small plants into the burrow.

Control techniques: Macabee, Victor, or California pocket gopher traps, fumigants, toxic grain bait (strychnine or 1080) placed into burrow by probe or burrow builder, and habitat modification (flooding).

PORCUPINE

The porcupine is most active at night, usually spending the day asleep in a cave or perched in a tree. During the summer, porcupines may be found in open meadows, fields, and along the banks of streams and lakes. They eat succulent plants of many species and are especially fond of garden and truck crops. In the fall, they may seek fruit in orchards. In winter, the porcupine retreats to forested areas and feeds largely on bark of certain evergreens, such as white, ponderosa, pinon pine, and hemlock. Basal girdling may occur on seedlings, the thinner barked Douglas-fir, and young, pole-sized trees. Damage can be particularly severe during winter months when porcupines are concentrated around den areas. In addition to damaging crops and forests, porcupines cause considerable damage to man-made structures, such as camps and summer homes that are unoccupied during the winter.

Porcupines are extremely fond of salt and are attracted to anything which may contain salt or salt residue. They have been known to gnaw on saddles, harnesses, belts, and salt placed for livestock.

Porcupine damage may be identified by broad incisor marks on the exposed sapwood. Also, oblong droppings about 2.5 cm in length may be found under freshly damaged trees. Roost trees are recognized by the large deposits of droppings beneath them. Top girdling in pine produces a characteristically bushy crown.

Control techniques: Shooting, strychnine salt block, leg hold traps (No. 1–3) and proofing and screening.

PRAIRIE DOGS

Prairie dog damage to rangelands, pastures, and growing crops often may be severe. Also, damage to irrigation systems is common, and badgers digging for these rodents cause even greater damage.

Prairie dogs clip the vegetation in their towns to a point where livestock often are unable to find forage. During seasons of extended drought native grasses are killed, leaving the soil barren, which supports only unpalatable weeds (Buell 1953). This is, of course, compounded by the size of the town, which may grow to be quite large. One of the larger towns recorded covered 140,000 square km and contained an estimated 400 million individuals (Eadie 1954).

Crops planted near prairie dog colonies may receive serious damage from feeding and trampling. Livestock, primarily horses, have been known to sustain broken legs from stepping into burrows while running across "dog towns."

Prairie dog colonies are characterized by the cone-shaped mounds around their burrows, and the presence of the animals watching invaders from their mounds.

Control techniques: Fumigants, shooting, toxic grain bait (zinc phosphide, strychnine, or 1080), and leg hold traps (No. 0–2).

RABBITS AND HARES

Rabbits and hares may damage or completely destroy a wide variety of tree plantings, gardens, ornamentals, agricultural crops, and rehabilitated rangeland. They can also strip bark from established fruit trees and conifers (Pearce 1947).

Both rabbits and hares produce similar clipping injuries to tree seedlings. Clipped trees have a clean oblique knifelike cut on the stem. They usually clip stems off 6 mm in diameter or less at a height not more than 50 cm above the ground (Lawrence et al. 1961). Repeated clipping will deform seedlings.

Quite often, rabbits or hares may be observed doing damage. Other evidence of their presence are tracks and trails leading to and from the damage area, as well as droppings at the base of the damaged area.

Control techniques: Habitat modification, fencing and proofing, repellents, live traps, body snares, shooting, and toxic baits (anticoagulants and strychnine).

TREE SQUIRRELS

Tree squirrels are found in most forested areas and have many local names; however, they can be placed into 5 groups—gray, fox, tassel-eared, flying, and red (or chickaree) squirrels. Squirrels may be quite destructive by eating plants and fruit, digging up newly planted bulbs, stripping bark and leaves from trees and shrubs, invading attics, and entering homes by way of the chimney. Utility companies report that squirrels cause them considerable work and expense when they gnaw through cables, causing power failures. In late summer, they often invade orchards and destroy large amounts of fruits and nuts. They may be troublesome at bird-feeding stations.

Red squirrel damage is indicated by green, unopened cones scattered on the ground under mature conifers. Accumulation of cone scales and "cores" mark their favorite feeding stations. Both red and gray squirrels will chew and strip bark from mature conifers, leaving ragged edges and allowing many pieces to fall to the ground. They also will cut the tips of twigs and branches, leaving ragged ends and rasping tooth marks, typical of rodent cuts (Packham 1970).

Control techniques: Fencing and proofing, repellents, live traps, shooting, conibear traps, and leg hold traps (No. 0–2).

WOOD RATS

Wood rats, also called pack rat, brush rat, or trade rat, may be attracted to food supplies left in buildings and will remove small objects such as spoons, forks, knives, and other items, sometimes leaving sticks or other items "in trade." The conspicuous stick houses on the ground are indications of their presence. They may construct their home in old buildings, abandoned vehicles, or in the upper branches of trees (Elliott 1953). Sure signs of occupancy are freshly cut twigs or leaves laid on or stuck into the upper walls of the house.

Wood rats are semiarboreal and agile climbers, able to jump like tree squirrels from branch to branch. They consume a variety of fruits, seeds, and green foliage of both herbaceous and woody plants (Lawrence et al. 1961). They strip patches of bark from conifers and fruit trees. The bark is apparently not eaten (Hooven 1959), but is finely shredded to line nest chambers. They also may clip small branches for food and building material. Their damage may be confused with tree squirrels and porcupines; however, wood rats leave a relatively smooth surface with a few scattered tooth marks, and tend to litter the ground beneath the tree less than tree squirrels.

Control techniques: Shooting, snap traps, live traps, toxic bait (strychnine, anticoagulants, and zinc phosphide), and proofing.

COMMENSAL RODENTS

There are 3 species of commensal rodents (those that live primarily around human habitation): Norway rats, roof rats, and house mice. These rodents consume millions of bushels of grain each year. They destroy it in the field, on the farm, in the elevator, mill, processing plant, store, home, and in transit. In addition, these rodents waste many more millions of bushels by contamination. Food may be severely contaminated, since each rodent drops 25 to 150 pellets every 24 hours, voids 10 to 20 cc of urine each day, and constantly sheds fine hairs.

Rats are omnivorous. They eat nearly every kind of grain, fish, fruit, meat, milk products, and vegetables. These rodents can destroy hundreds of chicks in 1 night. They attack broilers and even adult hens, ducks, geese, and wild birds. They have been known to seriously injure new born pigs, lambs, and calves. Health departments annually report hundreds of human babies being bitten by rats. Many viral and bacterial diseases are transmitted to man by rodent feces and urine which contaminate food and water.

Rats gnaw to keep their incisor teeth sharp and worn down, as these teeth grow about 13 cm a year. This gnawing causes considerable property damage. Fires are sometimes started by these rodents when they damage the insulation of electric wiring. They may also use flammable materials like oily rags and matches for building nests, which may cause fires from spontaneous combustion. Extensive damage is sometimes done when Norway rats burrow under buildings. Foundations and lower floors of buildings have been weakened and some have collapsed when rats burrowed under them. Concrete slabs crack when burrows undermine them. Burrows into dikes and outdoor embankments cause erosion and floods.

Signs of commensal rodents are gnawing, droppings, tracks, and darkened or smeared areas along walls where they travel. Bait acceptance may be tested by placing food where these rodents can find it and observing the results. Bullard and Shumake (1977) found that Philippine ricefield rats accustomed to eating rice grain showed greatly increased preference for granulated rice when it was enriched by the volatiles from ground unpolished rice.

Control techniques: Habitat modification, proofing and screening, snap traps, toxic baits (multiple and single dose), tracking powder and fumigants.

Control Techniques

HABITAT MODIFICATION

All animals are dependent on food and shelter; therefore, elimination of one or both of these requirements will force them to move from the immediate area. This method of control, where practical, is the most desirable and usually has the most permanent effect in stopping damage problems. Therefore, habitat modification should be seriously considered in all situations.

Many rodents and small mammals may be discouraged from using damage areas by removal of brush piles, weeds, old lumber piles, and other debris. Reducing the vegetative cover near cultivated areas and cleaning fence rows by brush cutting or burning are deterrents to rodents and small mammals as well as other species. Elimination of mixed shrub-grass types of environments seems to reduce the number of kangaroo rats. The number of mountain beaver in cultivated areas may be lessened by removing surface shelters such as stumps, logs, and brush piles (Eadie 1954).

Grass or weed infested orchards are frequently invaded by mice, while continuously cultivated, clean orchards usually will be free from mice. The elimination of weedy or brushy margins or fence rows near the orchard will prevent rapid reinfestation of mice. Davis (1976) reported that pine mouse damage in an apple orchard was reduced by the following program: mowing 5 times a year; clearing vegetation from under the trees; removing prunings; restricting distribution of fertilizer; and after harvest, inspecting and cleaning especially vulnerable parts of the orchard. In northern areas having prolonged snow, cover is provided for mice, and damage may occur at that time.

In poultry operations, keep manure piles away from chicken houses and place brooder houses in open, clear areas to reduce rat problems. It is good practice to keep portable houses well off the ground and open and free beneath.

Water level modification can be used in conjunction with beaver dams. Water level can be controlled by installing a perforated pipe through the beaver dam. Perforated stove pipe, standard steel pipe, or even rectangular wooden box pipe will work. The upper opening of the stove pipe and steel pipe must contain an elbow which is turned downward, and the wooden pipe should have slots in the bottom to prevent the beaver from plugging them (Laramie 1963).

Armadillos and moles feed largely on grubs, soil insects, and earthworms. The elimination or reduction of these food sources by use of insecticides will afford protection to turf where mole damage is a constant threat.

Steep banks with good protective covering are choice locations for muskrat burrows. Conversely, a slope, if not steeper than 3 to 1 on the water side of the dam or dike, will lessen damage. Damage will also be reduced if water is maintained at a constant level, and if the water level is not less than 0.9 m below the dam or dike (Merrill 1953). Also, if the water is drained for a period of time each year, it will force the rodents to find other cover. Short cropped grass will discourage muskrat or nutria usage.

In the control of commensal rodents, it is essential that garbage and refuse be placed in airtight covered metal containers and the premises be kept clean. To reduce cover, materials stored outside should be off the ground and not stacked against or near walls.

PROOFING AND SCREENING

Proofing and screening includes several types of barriers which prevent access into structures or areas and prevents a specific animal from damaging a specific object. This approach solves many problems, but usually is costly. Correctly done, it does afford prolonged protection. Rats and mice may be kept out of buildings by making sure the doors are kept tightly closed. Cover all air vents and openings with sheet metal or hardware cloth. Close unnecessary openings with concrete or sheet metal, particularly around pipes, and place covers over all floor drains.

In small orchards, rabbit and rodent damage can be eliminated by wrapping trees with hardware cloth or burlap. Be sure to bury it about 5 cm around the tree base to keep mice from crawling under the barrier.

Tree squirrels and chipmunks can be kept out of buildings by closing openings with 1.2-cm mesh wire or sheet metal. Observe travel routes to locate entrances. Look for eave openings, unscreened attic vents, knot holes, loose flashing around chimneys and vent pipes, and openings around cables. Screen chimney openings. A 0.6 m wide metal band around tree trunks and 2 m off the ground will keep squirrels out of individual, isolated trees. The band should be adjustable to allow for tree growth. Trim back branches within 2 m of the ground or buildings. Conical or round metal guards will prevent squirrels from getting into bird feeders.

Sand or gravel topping may protect earthen structures from muskrat damage. This material should be placed on the inner face of the dam to a depth of 0.3 m or more below the water surface and extend 0.6 or 1 m above it.

Fence type barriers can be used to protect small areas against a variety of nonclimbing rodents and small mammals. The fence should be made of 1.2- to 2.5-cm mesh net wire and be 0.7 to 1 m high. To prevent burrowing under, it must be buried 15 cm deep with an "L" shape on the outside of the fence.

Pocket gophers cause extensive damage to underground power and telephone lines. Thus far, no effective repellents have been found. The telephone and power companies may use steel sheathed wire on their underground lines in potential damage areas.

Campbell and Evans (1975) reported excellent success in preventing Douglas-fir seedling damage by mountain beavers and rabbits by using VEXAR(R) seedling protectors. These protectors are netted plastic tubes, 90 cm tall and 5 cm in diameter, and are placed over the seedlings at planting. They allow the branches to grow through the netting and provide protection for the terminal bud for about 3 to 5 years as it grows up through the tube. The VEXAR(R) seedling protector photodegrades during that time, leaving no environmental contaminants.

FUMIGANTS

Fumigants are effective against most burrowing rodents. Calcium cyanide, one chemical used in fumigation, releases deadly hydrocyanic gas upon contact with moisture. A tablespoon of the compound should be inserted into the burrow and the entrance carefully sealed with soil, sod, or rocks. Make sure the cyanide crystals are not covered with dirt. This substance is quite dangerous and should be handled with caution. Some of the other registered fumigants are carbon disulfide, chloropicrin, methyl bromide, ethylene dibromide, ethyl dichloride, and sulphur dioxide.

A foot pump duster may be used to dispense calcium cyanide dust into burrow systems. Caution should be taken when it is used around buildings to prevent the gas from entering and creating a hazard to humans. One advantage of this material is that it kills ectoparasites within the burrow system and therefore prevents spread of diseases.

Gas cartridges may be used for a variety of burrowing rodents. The cartridge contains chemicals that cause death by suffocation when burned in a burrow. The entrance must be covered tightly with sod to prevent the gas from escaping. A number of gas cartridges or smoke cartridges are manufactured by several commercial firms, and may be available from farm supply outlets.

TOXICANTS

Multidose Toxicants

These toxicants are also known as anticoagulants because of their mode of action. As the name suggests, these compounds inhibit blood coagulation, thus causing the animal to bleed to death internally or from external wounds. These chemicals generally must be ingested for 3 to 14 days consecutively to be effective. The animals apparently do not associate the hemorrhage with the food supply; therefore, bait shyness is avoided. The toxicants in this group include, among others, Warfarin, Pival, Fumarin, Diphacinone, Prolin, PMP, and Chlorophacinone.

These anticoagulants may be obtained in prepared baits or purchased as concentrates for mixing with fresh bait. The baits should be placed where the rodents feed, water, or travel. Since anticoagulants require continuous exposure, bait stations are particularly useful in protecting the bait from weather and nontarget species. Ready-to-use stations (bait boxes) may be purchased from pesticide supply houses or constructed from wood or metal (Fig. 22.1). The openings at the ends of the stations where the rats and mice enter should be no larger than 7.5 cm in diameter. The box may be built with a bottom and a lid that can be locked.

Some anticoagulants are also registered for use as tracking powders, and dusted into house mice or Norway rat holes and along runways where these animals travel between shelter and feeding places. The animals pass through the toxic dust picking it up on their feet and fur, and receive a lethal amount of the chemical while grooming themselves.

Many anticoagulants are available in a paraffin impregnated cereal bait for use in sewers or other excessively damp locations where unprotected bait would rapidly deteriorate.

Single-Dose Toxicants

Single-dose toxicants are those that require only 1 feeding to be lethal. Zinc phosphide is one of the most commonly used single-dose poisons. Its pungent odor and dark color generally are offensive to humans and other animals; however, rodents seem to like it. This gives a measure of safety to this technique. Zinc phosphide baits are prepared using sweet potatoes, carrots, or apples for nutria and muskrat; apples, cracked corn, or oats for vole and pocket gopher control; oats for prairie dog control; and ground fish or meat for commensal rodent control.

Prepared cereal rodent baits may be purchased from a variety of commercial sources. To prepare fresh bait such as apples, sweet potatoes or carrots, coat the bait with a small amount of vegetable oil and tumble in a plastic or paper bag to insure even distribution.

For muskrat and nutria control, bait can be placed on 110- by 125-cm size rafts anchored in the proximity of the damage area or area of use. The rafts (Fig. 22.2) should be constructed of marine plywood, and floated on styrofoam. Prebaiting is necessary on each raft to assure success in nutria control. The amount of bait needed will depend on the amount of prebait consumed (Evans 1970).

Control methods for meadow mice vary with the situation. The bait may be scattered along surface runways or placed in underground runways. In orchards, the bait may be placed under small boards or asphalt shingles inside the drip line of fruit trees. This will cater to the mice habit of burrowing under such objects for cover and nesting, and will protect the bait from the weather.

Zinc phosphide is used to control certain black-tailed and white-tailed prairie dogs. This toxicant is placed on steamrolled oats, but requires prebaiting before use. After 1 to 3 days of prebait acceptance, a heaping teaspoon of bait is scattered around each burrow (Tietjen 1976).

Strychnine-treated grain may be used to control a variety of field rodents. The prepared bait is available from a number of commercial sources. When using this bait, it must be thinly scattered near, not in, the target species' burrow or den, and along travel ways, or in damage areas. Strychnine-treated milo and wheat are effective on mice, but not rats of the genus *Rattus*.

Although compound 1080 (sodium monofluoroacetate) use is prohibited in federal programs and on federal lands, some states and counties are using this toxicant in their rodent control programs. When used the bait should be thinly scattered near burrows and along feeding trails or damage areas. Bait may be distributed from a vehicle or horseback. In areas where the problem is widespread, an aircraft may be used (Schilling 1976). Bonded pest control operators may use compound 1080 for commensal rodents by mixing with water and making it available for the rodents to drink.

Red squill is a relatively selective toxicant for Norway rats since it causes most animals to vomit, and it is physically impossible for rats to do so. This toxicant has the greatest acceptance when mixed with meat or fish as bait materials since they will mask the bitter taste. The imported product varies widely in toxicity and must be fortified before it is consistently effective.

Antu is an effective Norway rat toxicant; however, it should not be used more than once or twice a year since bait shyness develops if used more frequently. Antu can be dusted on fresh baits such as apples and sweet potatoes, or it may be used as a tracking powder in the rat burrows and along travel ways.

TALON®, a single-dose anticoagulant, is used in baits for the control of commensal rodents.

BURROW BUILDER

The burrow builder (Fig. 22.3) is a tractor-drawn mechanical tool which dispenses a toxic bait for controlling pocket gophers. The burrow builder constructs an underground artificial burrow and places 1080 or

Fig. 22.1. For baits that are exposed for long periods, protection from weather and non-target animals is important. Therefore, bait stations are recommended such as those commercially available (a) or homemade from plywood (b), cardboard box (c), and modified ammunition box (d).

strychnine-treated grain baits in the simulated gopher burrow. The artificial burrows are constructed 6 to 9 m apart, usually at a depth of 20 to 30 cm. The proper depth to set the machine can be determined by locating the gopher burrows by probing with a pointed instrument and measuring the depth of the burrow. The machine can then be set accordingly. Thirty-two to 40 hectares of gopher-infested land can be treated in a day with this tool. During their underground travels, the gophers intersect the artificial burrows, consume the toxic bait, and die underground.

The trail builder is a variation of the burrow builder. The burrow is shallower and its diameter less than that constructed by the burrow builder. Trail builders construct artificial burrows to control vole damage in orchards or tree plantings. Zinc phosphide-treated grain is the bait most commonly used in this machine (Anderson 1969).

TRAPS

Live Traps

Live traps, also known as box traps, are used to capture animals alive and unharmed. They are an excellent tool to use in residential areas or in situations where animals doing the damage may be transplanted to another location. These traps come in various shapes and sizes. They can be homemade of wire or wood, or can be bought commercially. Some traps have doors at both ends which allow the animals to see through, therefore reducing reluctance to enter. These traps are placed near the animal's travel lane or at the entrance to its den, and are often most successful when baited. Some suggested baits are pumpkin or sunflower seeds, peanuts, peanut butter, rolled oats, or similar foods. When the animal enters the trap it trips a trigger device which allows the door to close.

The Bailey and Hancock live traps, used to capture beaver, are made of flexible mesh wire. When set, the Bailey trap resembles an open suitcase; the Hancock trap resembles a half open suitcase. When the triggering device is tripped the trap closes with the animal uninjured between the 2 halves. These traps are best suited for use at the beaver's entrance and exit routes or in water travel lanes. Both traps can be baited with an ear of corn or a fresh piece of aspen, cottonwood, willow, or other edible woody plant (Anderson 1969).

Leg Hold Traps

Leg hold traps, also called steel traps, are manufactured in several different sizes. Squirrels, rats, woodchucks, ground squirrels, and chipmunks may be trapped using a number 0 to 2 size trap. Traps may be set in travel lanes or near burrow openings without bait.

Fig. 22.2 Floating bait stations made of wood with styrofoam floats are an effective method for controlling nutria, using zinc phosphide-treated carrots. The stations should be anchored so they will rise and fall with the water level.

These are called blind sets. These traps may be tied or wired to tree limbs used by squirrels to get to a house attic, or on pipes or beams traveled by rats inside buildings. When setting in the soil, the trap pan should be covered with a canvas cloth or leaves.

Traps placed underwater for beaver and muskrat usually are set at burrow entrances or exit points from the water. Stakes or anchor material should be placed in the water in such a way that the trapped animals will seek the deep water and drown, thus preventing them from twisting out. A number 4 is the best size trap for beaver, and a smaller trap (No. 0–2) is recommended for muskrat.

Prairie dogs, ground squirrels, and mountain beavers may be caught by burying the traps near the burrows using a pan cover and covering the traps with soil. Scattered grain is then placed on the traps. Prebaiting may improve trapping success.

Body Gripping Traps

Conibear traps are the best known of the body gripping traps and are chiefly used in water sets for muskrat, nutria, and beaver. They are manufactured in 3 sizes, and have the humane feature of killing quickly. This may also be a disadvantage because any nontarget animal caught is killed as well. These traps have a pair of rectangular wires that close like scissors when released, killing the animal with a quick body blow. Conibear traps are light weight and easy to use. They may be placed at the entrances of burrows, lodges, in dams, runs, and slides. Care should be taken when using the large conibear traps because of the hazard to pets and children.

There are somewhat similar body-gripping traps for moles and pocket gophers. The mole choker trap is one. To use it, press the runway down, and with a garden shovel make a slit on each side of the depression for the loops of the trap to fit into so the loops encircle the runway and the trigger is firmly on the depressed area. The trap is activated when the mole traveling the runway raises the depression, trips the trap, and is caught by the loops. The scissor-type mole trap works on the same principle, but instead of loops, the trap has 2 scissorlike devices that catch the mole when the trap is sprung.

The harpoon trap is also used in a similar fashion, but instead of the mole being caught, it is speared by a spring-loaded harpoon. Make sure this trap is set deeply enough to penetrate the runway. The prongs should be raised and released several times so that soil or rocks will not prevent full trap action.

The Macabee trap is effective in ridding pocket gophers from small acreages, but trapping is also time consuming. The trap is set in an enlarged burrow located by probing around a fresh mound. The mound normally has an indentation on 1 side which is a clue as to the location of the burrow. Probing should begin about 30 to 45 cm out from the mound (Fig. 22.4). Dig down to the burrow and enlarge the opening of each burrow to allow room for the trap to operate. Place a trap (Fig. 22.5) in each burrow opening, and secure the trap by tying a string or light wire through the spring and stake it on the surface. This will prevent the gopher from dragging the trap into the burrow. The gopher is caught when it pushes soil to plug the burrow opening.

Snap Traps

There are several advantages to using snap traps to control rats and mice; there is less danger to children or

Fig. 22.3. The burrow builder constructs an underground burrow and places a toxic treated bait in the burrow.

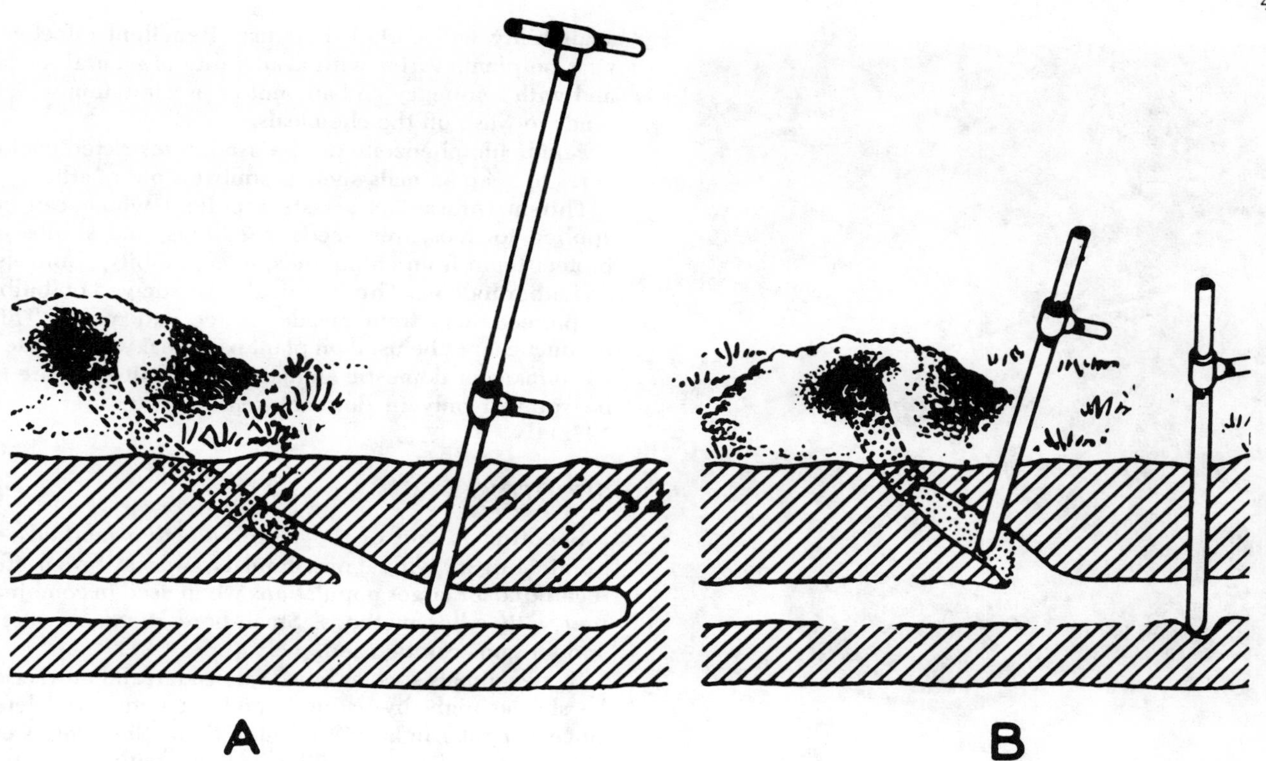

Fig. 22.4. (A) Right way to probe. The probe was inserted about 30 to 45 cm from the indented side of the mound and was allowed to just penetrate the main runway. (B) Wrong way to probe. The probe was inserted too close to the mound and penetrated a plugged lateral burrow. The second probe is too deep which allows the bait to be deposited below the floor of the tunnel.

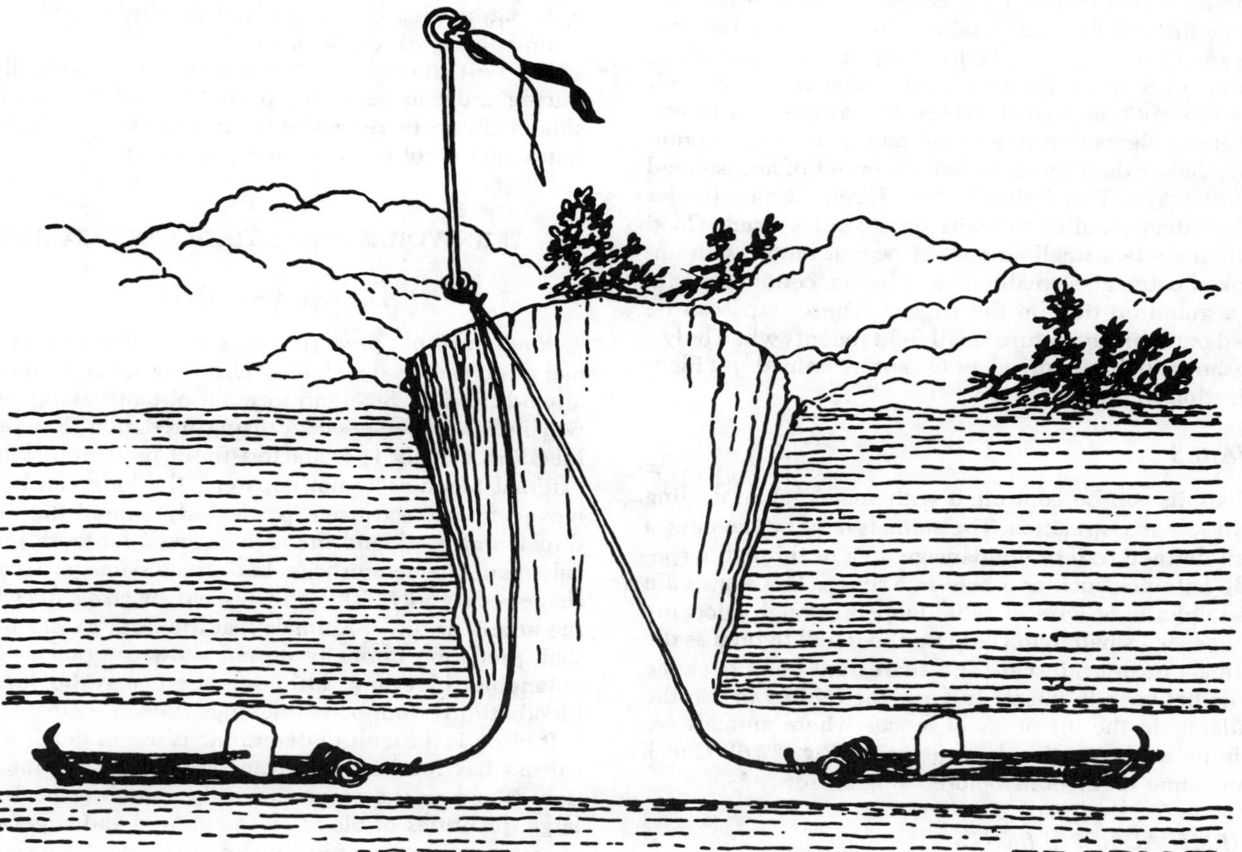

Fig. 22.5. After excavating the main runway, traps are set—1 in each direction. Stakes help located the sets and anchor the traps so they will not be lost.

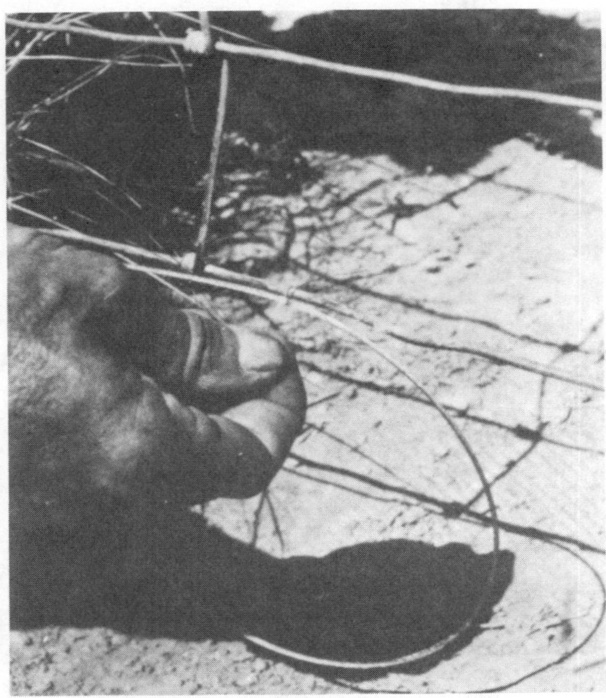

Fig. 22.6 The body snare is set in a trail between 2 objects or under a wire fence. A light wire supports the snare in a proper position.

pets than with lethal chemicals; there is no odor of dead rodents which cannot be recovered; and there are no contaminants. An easy modification that will increase the snap trap's efficiency is to enlarge the bait pan with a heavy piece of cardboard or stiff screen wire and use it as a runway trap. Use obstacles such as boxes or boards to force rodents to run over the trap. Place traps in runways rather than trying to bait them out of accustomed travel ways. Traps should be placed perpendicular rather than parallel to walls or obstacles used. Good baits include a small amount of peanut butter with uncooked oatmeal, a small piece of bacon, cotton, a raisin, or a gumdrop tied on the trigger. These traps can be used outdoors to capture small field rodents when only a few animals are involved, or to capture animals for identification purposes.

SNARES

Rabbits can be controlled with snares when dealing with a small population. The animals must be traveling a well-defined trail to the damage area or through a specific entrance such as a hole in a fence. The snares are made of a light wire or cable looped through a locking device, or a small nylon cord tied so it will tighten as the animals push against it. The snares are hung over the trails between 2 objects to force the rabbits to use the trails, or in the openings of fences where animals are gaining access to the damage areas (Fig. 22.6). Check state game regulations before using snares.

CHEMICAL REPELLENTS

There are a number of repellents registered with the Environmental Protection Agency; however, limited availability will curtail their use. Repellent effectiveness on plants varies with availability of natural foods, and with frequency and amount of precipitation which tends to wash off the chemicals.

Paradichlorobenzene can be used in restricted enclosures to keep animals such as squirrels out of attics.

Thiram (Arasan) is a taste repellent which can be applied to trees, tree seeds, seedlings, and shrubs to protect them from chipmunks, mice, rabbits, squirrels, and other rodents. Thiram can also be sprayed on bulbs to protect them from meadow mice and moles. This product cannot be used on plant parts that will be eaten by humans or domestic animals. Also, fruit trees are to be sprayed only in dormant season (Fitzwater et al. 1972).

SHOOTING

Shooting is one of the more selective methods of eliminating individual pest animals, and may be a useful technique for larger populations when used in combination with other methods. Small-bore shotguns, rifles, and air guns can be used.

Some animals such as beaver, muskrat, and nutria can be shot at night by using a spotlight with a red lens, since a regular light will frighten them. Shooting is especially useful in controlling animals with low reproductive rates, such as porcupines. Dogs may be used to track the animal in snow during late fall, winter, and early spring. During breeding season in early fall, road hunting at night using a spotlight is productive. Early morning hunting in low, moist areas during spring and summer also will produce good results.

The best time to shoot specific animals normally is during their most active period. Local game codes should always be reviewed before any shooting is done; hunting at night is not legal in some states.

CARNIVORES AND OTHER PREDATORS

Damage Assessment

Whether or not predation caused the death of an animal often can be decided by checking for signs on and around the kill. Size and location of tooth marks often will indicate the species causing predation. Extensive bleeding usually is characteristic of predation. Where external bleeding is not apparent, the hide can be removed from the carcass, particularly around the neck, throat, and head, and the area checked for tooth holes, subcutaneous hemorrhage, and tissue damage. Hemorrhage occurs only if skin and tissue damage occurs while the animal is alive. Animals that die from causes other than predation normally do not show external or subcutaneous bleeding, although there may be loss of bloody fluids from body openings (Bowns 1976).

It often is difficult to determine cause of death if the carcass has reached an advanced stage of decomposition. Blood on the ground near the mouth or neck and large quantities of blood on the ground and vegetation near the carcass are indicative of predation. Care should be taken to distinguish blood from other body fluids that drain from a decomposing carcass.

Animals that are pulled down from the side or rear will often have blood on the sides, hind legs, and tail areas. Calves may have their tails chewed off and the nose may have tooth marks or be completely chewed by the predator when eating the tongue (Bowns 1976).

Tracks and droppings alone are not proof of depredation or of the species responsible, but are useful evidence when combined with other characteristics of depredation.

Species Damage Identification

BADGERS

The diet of badgers primarily consists of rodents such as mice, prairie dogs, pocket gophers, and ground squirrels. They also will prey on rabbits, the young being most vulnerable. They destroy nests of ground-nesting birds and occasionally kill small lambs and poultry, parts of which they may bury in holes resembling their dens.

Badgers usually consume all of a prairie dog except the head and fur along the back. This characteristic probably holds true for most larger rodents they eat; however, signs of digging near prey remains are the best evidence of badgers (Anderson 1969).

Control techniques: Leg hold traps (No. 2–4) and shooting.

BEAR

Black bear damage to trees has been a concern to foresters for many years. It can be recognized by the large vertical incisor and claw marks on the sapwood and ragged strips of bark hanging from the tree. Pole size trees to small sawtimber are preferred. Most bark damage occurs during May, June, and July (Packham 1970). After the bark is pulled away, bears will scrape off the cambium layer of the tree with their incisor teeth, leaving vertical tooth marks (Murie 1954).

Both black and grizzly bears prey on livestock. Black bears usually kill by biting the neck or by slapping the victim. Torn, mauled, and mutilated carcasses are characteristic of bear attacks. Often, the bear will eat the udders of females, possibly to obtain milk. The victim usually is opened ventrally and the heart and liver are consumed. The intestines often are spread out around the kill site, and the animal may be partially skinned during feeding on the carcass. Smaller livestock such as sheep and goats may be consumed almost entirely by a bear, leaving only the rumen, skin, and large bones. Fecal deposits generally are found within the kill area and a bed often is found nearby. They use their feet while feeding so they do not slide the prey around as do coyotes. If the kill is made in the open, it may be moved to a more secluded spot.

The grizzly has a feeding and killing pattern similar to the black bear. Murie (1948) found that most cattle are killed by a bite through the back of the neck. A large prey often has claw marks on the flanks or hams where the bear grabbed it. The prey's back is sometimes broken just in front of the hips where the bear simply crushed it down. However, personal observation by Gretz, U.S. Fish and Wildlife Service (1977) indicated that some yearling calves were killed by a bite through the forehead as the animals were seized while facing the grizzly. The bear apparently grabbed the calves by the head and neck and bit them through the forehead.

The presence of bears has been known to stampede range sheep causing them to pile up with death resulting from suffocation, or to frighten them over cliffs. A marauding bear may also play havoc with beehives, food storage areas, summer cabins, autos, and camping facilities.

The bear track resembles that of a human, but has distinctive claw marks. Quite often the little inside toes leave no marks in dust or shallow mud so the print appears to be four-toed (Murie 1954).

Control techniques: Dogs, livetrapping, foot snares, fencing, and shooting.

BOBCAT AND LYNX

These related species prey on sheep, goats, deer, antelope, porcupine, poultry, rabbits, rodents, and birds. The bobcat has been known to kill domestic cats.

Bobcats most often kill adult deer by leaping on their back or shoulders, usually when the victim is lying down, and biting them on the trachea. The jugular vein may be punctured, but the victims usually die of suffocation and shock. Bowns (1976) reported that a lamb killed by a bobcat had hemorrhages produced by claws on both sides of the carcass, indicating the bobcat was holding the lamb with its claws while biting the neck. Stiles (1967) identified deer killed by bobcats by the sheared clumps of hair along the back and neck, and deep open wounds caused by biting the throat and lower jaw. Saunders (1963) described a caribou which had been attacked by a lynx as bleeding from the neck and shoulder. Very small fawns, lambs, and small prey often are killed by a bite through the top of the neck or head (Young 1958).

In most cases, the hindquarters of deer or sheep seem to be preferred by bobcats, although the shoulder and neck region or the flank sometimes are eaten first. Often, the rumen is untouched. In many cases the carcass is partly covered with litter or snow, particularly the parts that have been fed upon. Stiles (1967) observed that a bobcat partially buried the stomach, intestines, and hind feet of one rabbit kill while only the hind feet and intestines were buried on another.

Poultry usually are killed by biting the head and neck (Young 1958); the heads usually are eaten. Also, both species reportedly prey on bird eggs.

Bobcat and lynx droppings are similar; their feeding habits are identical (Murie 1954). In areas inhabited by both species, the tracks will help determine the responsible animal. The lynx has larger feet with much more hair, the toes tend to spread more and help distinguish lynx tracks from the smaller, more compact bobcat tracks.

Feline predators usually attempt to cover their kills with litter. Bobcats reach out 30 to 35 cm in scratching litter, while cougars reach as far as 90 cm (Young 1958). The distance and diameter of the canine teeth marks will also help distinguish a cougar kill from that of a bobcat.

Control techniques: Dogs, snares, calling and shooting, leg hold traps (No. 3–4) and aircraft (under some specific circumstances).

COUGAR

This large animal, also called mountain lion or puma, preys on deer, elk and domestic stock particularly colts, lambs, kids, grown horses, and cattle. They also utilize rodents and other small mammals when available.

Cougars, having relatively short, powerful jaws, kill with bites inflicted from above, often severing the vertebral column and breaking the neck. They also may kill by biting through the skull (Bowns 1976).

Laughlin (pers. comm.) observed that cougars often killed more animals than they could utilize, citing over 50 sheep that were killed in 1 attack. In 1 instance, according to Young (1933), a lone cougar attacked a herd of ewes and killed 192 in 1 night.

Cougars usually first feed upon the front quarters and neck region of their prey. The stomach generally is untouched. The large leg bones may be crushed and ribs broken. Many times, after a lion has made a kill, the victim may be dragged or carried into bushy areas to be covered with litter (Laughlin, USFWS, pers. comm.). Whether the cougar will return depends on whether it is disturbed, on weather conditions, and on its ability to find prey elsewhere (Young 1933).

Adult cougar tracks are approximately 10 cm in length and 11 cm in width. There are 4 well-defined impressions of the toes at the front, roughly in a semicircle. The cat family has retractable claws; therefore, no claw prints will be evident. The untrained observer sometimes confuses large dog tracks with those of the cougar; however, dog tracks normally show distinctive claw marks, are less round than cougar tracks, and the rear pad marks are distinctly different.

Control techniques: Dogs, snares, and leg hold traps (No. 4½–114).

COYOTES, WOLVES, AND DOGS

These 3 canids prey on a wide variety of animals ranging from big game and livestock to rodents, wild birds, and poultry. Complaints of pets being killed, particularly by coyotes, also have increased with urbanization (Swick 1974). Avocado producers who rely on drip irrigation systems report that coyotes chew holes in plastic pipe and disrupt irrigation (Cummings 1973). Watermelons are damaged by coyotes biting a hole through the melons and eating the center out. This differs from raccoon damage to melons; raccoons make small holes in the melons and scoop the pulp out with their front paws. Coyotes also will damage other fruit crops.

Wolves prey on the larger ungulates such as caribou, moose, and elk. Big game animals and livestock attacked by wolves usually are brought down by cutting or damaging the muscles and ligaments in the back legs, commonly called hamstringing, or by seizing the victim in the flanks. Slash marks made by the canine teeth may be found on the rear legs and flanks. The downed animals usually are disembowelled.

Domestic dogs can be a serious problem to livestock, especially to sheep pastured near cities and suburbs. Dogs often attack the hindquarters of ewes in the same manner as coyotes, but normally little flesh is consumed. They are likely to wound the animal in the neck and front shoulders; the ears often are badly torn. Attacking dogs often severely mutilate the victim (Bowns 1976).

Coyotes can cause extensive livestock losses. They normally kill with a bite in the throat, but may pull the animal down by attacking the sides, hindquarters, and udder. The rumen and intestines may be removed and dragged away from the carcass. On very small lambs, the upper canine teeth may penetrate the top of the neck or the skull. Calf predation by coyotes is most common when calves are young. Calves attacked, but not killed, exhibit wounds in the flank, hindquarter, or front shoulders; often their tails are chewed off near the tip. Bowns (1976) reported that mature deer were killed in a manner similar to that used on adult sheep. Large animals may be grabbed by the throat, but often are pulled down from behind. Fawns often are bitten through the neck or head. Deer carcasses often are completely dismembered and eaten.

Control techniques: Fencing, den hunting, calling and shooting, aircraft, snares, M-44s and leg hold traps (No. 3–4½).

FOX

All fox species feed primarily on rabbits, hares, ground squirrels, mice and other rodents, poultry, birds and insects. They also will consume fruits such as grapes, figs, dates, and wild berries. In addition, the gray fox eats fish and the swift and kit fox may eat reptiles, 2 forms of prey that the red fox often does not eat. Foxes may kill turkeys, chickens, and lambs (Garlough 1945). Foxes sometimes will kill wantonly. One farmer in New York State found 80 pullets freshly killed in a single morning (Eadie 1954). Normally, foxes will take 1 fowl, leaving behind only a few drops of blood and feathers and carry the prey away from the kill location, often to a den. Eggs usually are opened enough to be licked out. The shells are left beside the nest and rarely are removed to the den, even though fox dens are noted for containing the remains of their prey, particularly the wings of birds (Anderson 1969).

Einarsen (1956) noted that the breast and legs of birds killed by foxes are eaten first and the other appendages are scattered about. The toes of the victims usually are drawn up in a curled position because of tendons pulled when the fox strips meat from the leg bone. Smaller bones are likely to be sheared off. The remains often are partially buried in a hole scratched in the soil.

Foxes dig their dens in a variety of places; in wooded areas or open plains. They have been known to use hollow logs as dens. Dens may be identified by tracks which resemble a small, narrow doglike track or by fox hairs clinging to the entrance. The gray fox is the only fox that readily climbs trees. They have been known to den in a hollow tree. Murie (1954) reports a distinctive scent which some people can detect as they near a den.

Control techniques: Dogs, leg hold traps, (no. 2–3) denning, shooting, fencing, aircraft, M-44s, snares.

OPOSSUM

Opossums are omnivorous; eating fish, crustaceans, insects, mushrooms, berries and other fruits, vegetables, eggs, and carrion. They are well known for predation on birds and eggs. They also will raid poultry houses. The opossum usually kills 1 chicken at a time, often mauling the victim (Burkholder 1955). Eggs will be mashed and messy. Eggshells often are chewed into small pieces and left in the nest. Opossum usually begin feeding on poultry at the anal opening. Young poultry or game birds are consumed entirely with only a few wet feathers remaining (Anderson 1969). Occasionally, they cause damage to cornfields when the corn is in the milk and dough stage.

Control techniques: Live traps, leg hold traps (No. 1–1½), shooting, dogs, and exclusion fencing.

RACCOON

Availability seems to govern the raccoon's diet. Most often the animal eats whatever is encountered such as mice, small birds, snakes, frogs, insects, crawfish, grass, berries, acorns, corn, melons—the list is almost endless. During lean periods or when living in urban areas, they will raid garbage cans and dumps; these may be a major source of food in urban areas. Field crops or gardens grown near wooded areas may suffer severe damage from raccoons. Corn in the milk and dough stage frequently is eaten and much is wasted. Raccoons may be severe predators on various kinds of turtles, taking both adults and eggs. They sometimes may affect wood duck numbers by raiding nesting cavities (Eadie 1954). They also will take the eggs of alligators. Rarely, they have been known to kill small lambs, usually by chewing the nose.

Occasionally, raccoons enter poultry houses and take many birds in one night. The breast and crop may be torn and chewed, and the entrails sometimes are eaten. There may be bits of flesh near water (Anderson 1969). Eggs may be removed from poultry or game bird nests and eaten away from the nest. However, Rearden (1951) found that the eggshells were somewhere within 9 m (most were within 1.75 m) of the nest.

The raccoon track is distinctive, resembling a small human handprint. It has 5 toes on both the front and hind feet. Murie (1954) stated that raccoon tracks usually are paired with the left hind foot placed beside the right forefoot. The pattern of the raccoon tracks is similar to that of the opossum, and in soft sand where toes do not show, identification may be difficult.

Control techniques: Dogs, live traps, leg hold traps (No. 2–3), exclusion fencing, and shooting.

SKUNKS

Skunks consume a large number of insects, and their fondness for these may result in depredations on beehives. They usually dig small cone-shaped holes in lawns, golf courses, and meadows in search of beetle larvae and grubs. A less serious but common complaint of objectionable odor occurs when 1 or more skunks take up residence under buildings used by humans.

Skunks, although often accused of killing poultry and small game species, kill few adult birds, but are serious nest robbers (Einarsen 1956). Eggs usually are opened at one end, the edges are crushed as the skunk punches its nose into the hole to lick out the contents (Einarsen 1956, Davis 1959). The eggs may appear to have been hatched, except for the edges. When in a more advanced stage of incubation, the eggs are likely to be chewed into small pieces (Anderson 1969). The eggs may be removed from the nest, but rarely more than 1 meter away.

Most rabbits, chickens, and pheasant carcasses found around skunk dens are carrion that have been dragged to the den site (Crabb 1948). When skunks do kill poultry, they generally will kill only 1 or 2 birds and maul them considerably. Crabb (1941) observed that spotted skunks are effective in controlling rats and mice in grain and corn storage buildings. They kill these rodents by biting and chewing the head and foreparts; the carcasses are not eaten.

Inhabited dens may be recognized by fresh droppings containing undigested insect parts near the mound or hole. Hair and rub marks also may be present. There usually is the characteristic skunk odor, although it may not be strong.

Control techniques: Live traps, leg hold traps, (No. 1–1½) and shooting.

WEASELS AND MINK

Weasels and mink have similar feeding behaviors. They kill their prey by biting through the skull, upper neck, or jugular vein (Hamilton 1933, Cahalane 1961). When they raid poultry houses at night, they may kill many more birds than can be utilized and often eat only the head of the victim. Burkholder (1955) noted the head and breast may be eaten by either of these animals. Predations by rats usually differ in that portions of the body may be eaten and the carcasses are dragged into holes or concealed locations (Anon. 1953).

Errington (1943) noted that mink, while eating large muskrats, make an opening at the back or side of the neck. As it eats away flesh, ribs, and pieces of the adjacent hide, it skins the animal by pulling the head and hindquarters out through the same hole. McCracken and Van Cleve (1947) noted the same feeding behavior in weasels eating small rodents.

Teer (1964) observed that blue-winged teal eggs destroyed by weasels were broken at the ends, with openings 15 to 20 mm in diameter. Small punctures, often in pairs, were found in the sides or ends of all broken eggs, and embryos were missing. Close inspection of the shell remains frequently will disclose finely chewed edges and tiny tooth marks (Rearden 1951).

A weasel may den in the ground (in a mole or pocket gopher burrow), under a barn, in a pile of stored hay, or under rocks. Mink may dig dens approximately 10 cm in diameter into banks. Mink also use muskrat burrows, holes in logs and stumps, and other ready made shelters.

Control techniques: Leg hold traps (No. 0–1) and conibear traps.

DOMESTIC CATS

Domestic cats rarely prey on anything larger than ducks, pheasants, rabbits, or quail. Einarsen (1956) noted the messy feeding behavior of these animals. Portions of their prey often are strewn over several square meters in open areas. The meaty portions of large birds are consumed entirely, leaving loose skin with feathers attached. Small birds generally are consumed with only the wings and scattered feathers remaining. Cats usually leave tooth marks on every exposed bone of their prey (Anderson 1969). Nesting game birds particularly are vulnerable to cat predation. In areas managed for game birds or waterfowl production, vagrant cat control is almost a necessity. Unlike their native cousins, domestic cats are observed readily in the daytime, although feral cats often are extremely wary.

Control techniques: Live traps, shooting, and leg hold traps (No. 1–1½).

Control Techniques

AIRCRAFT

Fixed-wing aircraft were used in the northern plains states prior to 1925 to remove predators for protection of livestock (Wade 1976). There have been a number of such aircraft used to control wolves, coyotes, bobcats, and foxes, but the Piper Super Cub, with a 150-horsepower engine, has proved to be the best suited for the job. The pilot and gunner sit in tandem in this 2-seat aircraft. This gives both occupants the advantage of being able to see out both sides of the aircraft. Hunting is more effective on snow because the target animals can be seen and tracked more easily. When the hunted animal is found, the pilot makes an approach over it at approximately 15 m of altitude and preferably into the wind. The ground speed of the aircraft is around 60 to 85 km per hour at this point, but the airspeed should never be near the stalling speed of the aircraft. The gunner will shoot either out the window on the left side if right handed, or the door of the right side if left handed. This reduces the likelihood of the gunner shooting the propeller. A 12-guage semiautomatic shotgun is the most common weapon used with number 4 buck-shot, BB, or number 2 shot.

There have been several modifications made to the Super Cub which have increased safety and effectiveness. These modifications include: a larger propeller and drooped wing tips to provide added power, stability and maneuverability, particularly at higher altitudes. Larger balloon tires have been added to provide clearance for the longer propeller and to better utilize primitive runways, dirt roads, and pastures for landing.

Rotary-wing aircraft (helicopter) have been used in recent years for animal damage control. The helicopter, with its ability to hover, can be used more effectively than fixed-wing aircraft in rougher and brushier terrain. The down draft from the rotor occasionally will flush animals from their hiding places. However,the helicopter has a much higher cost of operation than the fixed-wing craft. In models with the plexiglass bubble enclosed cockpit, the visibility and consequent tracking ability are very good. The gunner may shoot out of either door, depending on the model. He may use a 12-gauge pump or semiautomatic shotgun.

The fixed-wing craft and helicopter sometimes are operated together. The helicopter is used for dispatching the animal while the fixed-wing flies above the helicopter and maintains surveillance. This combination works well in areas that have been hunted heavily with the helicopter where "chopper-wise" animals try to evade the hunters, but can be spotted with the fixed-wing. There must be radio contact between the 2 aircraft.

To be most effective in either the fixed-wing aircraft or helicopter, the pilot and gunner must work as a team, each knowing what the other is doing. Aerial hunting is no place for the novice or amateur. The pilot *must* be trained by another pilot with many hours logged in this operation. The U.S. Fish and Wildlife Service requires that each gunner and pilot be trained thoroughly before being certified for this type of operation.

Aerial hunting can be more efficient if 1 or more ground crews work in conjunction with the aircraft. The ground crew induces the coyotes to howl by using a horn, siren, voice, or recorded howl. When the animals respond, the aircraft is directed into the area by 2-way radio communication. Early morning and late afternoon are the most productive times for aerial hunting.

Federal law requires each state where hunting is allowed to issue aerial hunting permits. Also, most states require low level flying waivers for hunting from aircraft.

CALLING AND SHOOTING

Calling and shooting is a very selective control tool used primarily for coyotes, bobcats, and foxes. It has become a popular sport, and for some people it is not calling and shooting, but calling and photographing.

There are several commercial calls available as well as recorded calls. Open reed duck calls work well, but require more practice. Some hunters make their own calls. The call is blown to imitate the sound of a distressed rabbit. This sound either rouses the predator's curiosity or indicates a free meal; the predator responds to the call and comes within shooting range. Of course, there are predators that become wise to the call. Conversely, the call may be an effective method to remove a trap-wise animal.

There are 3 factors that must be kept in mind when calling:

(1) Make sure the wind is blowing from the area being called. This will prevent the predator from detecting the caller's scent before the animal comes into shooting range. (2) Have a full view of the area being called so that the predator will not be able to approach unseen. (3) To avoid being seen, the caller should never be silhouetted. He should be hidden in or behind some type of vegetation. Camouflage clothing will aid in concealment. Some hunters use grease paint or head covers to conceal their face.

The most effective time of day to call is early morning and late afternoon. The hunter can gain an added advantage by locating the coyotes before beginning the call. This is done by inducing the coyote to howl as previously described under aerial hunting.

Calling at night using a spotlight is also effective; however, local game laws and regulations should be checked before beginning such a project.

DENNING

In the spring, depredation on livestock and poultry by coyotes and foxes may be an indication of a nearby den which has increased the food requirement for support of the pups as well as the adults. In most cases, removal of the entire litter will end the losses of livestock; however, this is dependent on the availability of other food sources and preferences.

Dens are located by tracking or observing the adults. Den hunting is based on the principle that the adults tend to follow irregular routes while searching for prey, but once the food is secured, the animal returns to the den in the most direct route possible. The experienced observer can distinguish between these tracks. Close to the den site there will be many tracks which form a trail leading to the den itself.

The den is evident by hairs around the entrance, fresh tracks, and if the pups are large enough to come out of the den, vegetation around the den will be matted and worn from their activity. Fox dens usually will have remains of prey brought in for food. This is not common at coyote dens.

Den hunting is hard work and takes time, particularly on hard ground, in heavy cover, and during high winds. A good dog is a great help in locating dens. Some dogs are trained to return to the hunter when the adult predator tries to chase them out of the den area. This usually will get the target animal within rifle range. A call blown to imitate a frightened or injured pup sometimes will bring adult coyotes within rifle range. Care should be taken while digging out dens because of the possibility of cave-ins and ectoparasites.

DOGS

There are 2 types of dogs that may be utilized in predator control work. The dogs that hunt by sight, such as greyhounds, are hauled in a box or cage until the predator is seen, then released to catch and kill the animal. This type of dog is only effective in relatively open terrain (Wade 1973). The other type of dog is the trail hound. These dogs are able to follow an animal by its scent, whether it is on the ground, snow, or vegetation. Trail hounds hunt on bare ground; however with the aid of snow or heavy dew, trailing is made easier. Hot, dry weather makes trailing difficult; therefore, early morning with dew is much more effective. These trail hounds consist of several breeds such as bluetick, black and tan, Walker, and redbone. They usually are run in packs of 2 to 5.

Trained trail hounds also are used to catch and "tree" raccoons, opossums, and bobcats. In the western states, these dogs are effective in capturing depredating bears and cougars. Many times these dogs are able to track the offending animal from a kill, thus making this control method highly selective.

Local game codes should be checked before this type of control is exercised.

SNARES

Snares are made of varying lengths and sizes of wire or cable looped through a locking device which allows the snare to tighten. There are 2 types of snares—body snares and foot snares. The body snare (Fig. 22.6) is used primarily on coyotes; however, it may be used for a number of other animals. This snare is set where the animals crawl under a fence, a trail under brush, a den entrance, or some other narrow passageway. The device is looped in such a manner that the animal must put its head through the snare as it passes through the restricted area. When the snare is felt around the neck, the animal normally will thrust forward and tighten the noose.

The foot snare (Fig. 22.7) is spring activated. When the animal steps on the trigger the spring is released,

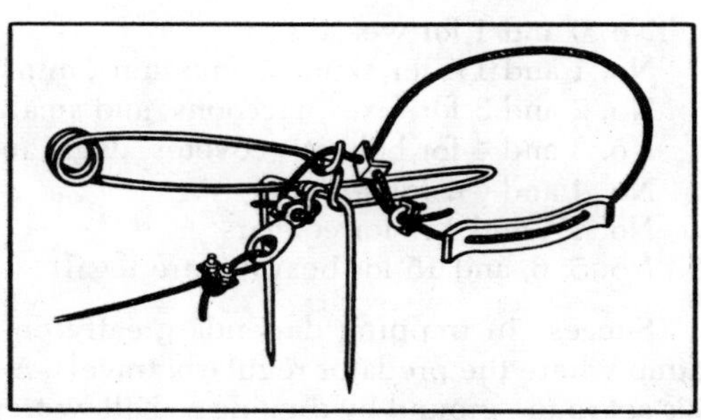

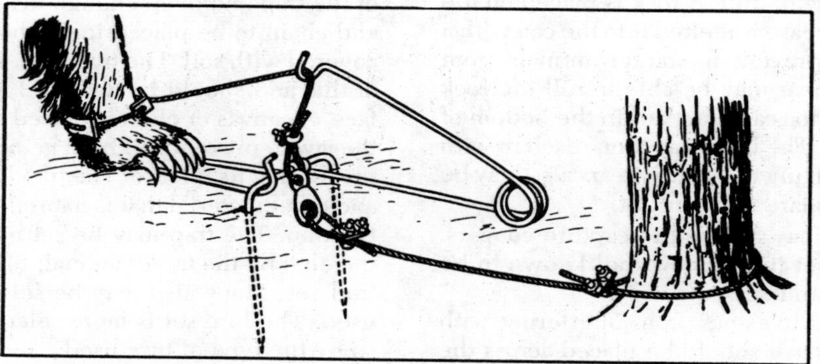

Fig. 22.7. The Aldrich spring-activated animal snare is effective in trail sets or when placed at a bear pen or cubby set.

Fig. 22.8. The bear pen or cubby set may be used with the bear trap, or preferably, the spring activated foot snare. Clearance must be allowed so the spring can work properly.

lifting the noose and tightening it around the foot. This device has been used effectively to capture cougar, grizzly, and black bear. The foot snare can be used in a bear pen or cubby set (Fig. 22.8). This pen is just large enough to accommodate the bait, which usually is the carcass remains of the animal killed earlier by the predator. The pen can be built of brush or poles and has an open end where the snare is set. The pen and guide sticks will force the bear to step into the snare while trying to reach the bait. Bacus (1968) described a pipe snare set which consists of a 2-pound coffee can (or a similar length of 13 cm pipe) with a 2.5-cm slot cut down the side to accommodate the trigger. The can is buried and the loop laid loosely on the ground around the outside of it and covered with duff. A rock is placed on top of the can, and bacon grease is melted into the can with a torch. The rock will prevent nontarget animals from tripping the snare. A bear may be able to roll the rock off, but will be unable to reach the bait in the bottom of the can with its mouth. The bear may then reach in with its front foot, thus springing the snare. Bears also may be caught using the foot snare in a trail set.

The foot snare also may be used to capture cougars. The snare should be set in a narrow trail known to be traveled by the target animal.

To prevent deer and livestock from interfering with the snare, a pole or branch should be placed across the trail, directly over the set and about 0.9 m above the ground.

The selectivity of the foot snare may be improved by placing sticks under the trigger which break only under the weight of the heavier animals. Foot snares have advantages over large bear traps in that they are lighter, easier to carry, and are less dangerous to humans and nontarget animals.

TRAPS

Live Traps

Live traps, as discussed in the rodent section, are available in various sizes and may be used to capture small predators as well as the larger ones, such as bear. Coyotes and foxes are difficult to live trap because of their caution and reluctance to enter the confined area of the trap.

Problem bears can be caught in live traps made from steel culverts equipped with a trap door and trigger device. They normally are mounted on trailers for easy transport of the traps and to permit bears to be easily moved to other locations for release.

Commercial dog or cat foods are effective baits to entice opossum, skunks, and cats into live traps. In trapping skunks, the traps should be covered with a canvas or heavy cloth, and a flap provided for the door. When a skunk is captured the trapper should walk up to the trap on the covered side and drop the flap over the door. Once this is done the skunk can be transported to the release site. To release, the trapper should stand beside the trap and ease the flap and door open; the animal will head out and usually not look back.

Leg Hold Traps

As stated earlier, leg hold traps or steel traps are manufactured in a variety of sizes. The following trap sizes are recommended for the animals listed:

No. 0 and 1 for weasels
No. 1 and 1½ for skunks, opossums, minks, and cats
No. 2 and 3 for foxes, raccoons, and small dogs
No. 3 and 4 for bobcats, coyotes, dogs, and badgers
No. 4 and 4½ for wolves
No. 4½ and 114 for cougars
No. 5, 6, and 15 for bear (where legal)

Success in trapping depends greatly on placing the trap where the predator regularly travels. A trap usually is set in the ground by digging a shallow trench the size of the trap and deep enough to allow the stake (or drag) and chain to be placed in the bottom of the trench and covered with soil. The trap (Fig. 22.9) is set firmly on top of this and should be about 12 mm below the soil surface. A canvas or cloth is placed over the pan and under the jaw to prevent soil from getting beneath the pan and preventing its release. The trap is then covered with soil and other material that is natural to the area surrounding the trap. The trap may be set unbaited in a trail being traveled by the target animal; this is called a "blind" or trail set. Traps also may be set off the trail and a lure used. The lure set is more selective, and is made more so by the type of lure used.

Fig. 22.9. The leg hold trap in a lure set.

The dirt-hole set is effective for raccoon, fox, and mink. The trap is set in the same manner as the baited set, but instead of placing the scent on the vegetation or ground, a small hole, about 15-cm deep, is dug on a slant behind the trap and the lure is placed in the hole.

Traps may be placed in water for mink and raccoon. The trap pan may be covered with aluminum foil and placed in shallow water for raccoon. The shiny foil attracts the animal.

The bear trap is extremely large, powerful and dangerous to humans, livestock, and pets. The trap should be used in a pen as described under snares, and prominent warning signs posted nearby. Trap clamps, which are used to depress the springs, should be located within easy reach of the trap. Since the bear foot snare is as effective and much safer to use, bear traps are not recommended and no longer legal in some states.

The location of the trap set has an influence on its selectivity. When placed by a carcass, it may catch nontarget animals such as vultures, eagles, badgers, and other carrion-feeding birds and mammals. Nine meters away from the carcass normally is a safe distance to set traps. Weather also can affect the operation of traps. Frozen or wet ground may prevent the trap from springing.

Leg hold traps must be checked often to prevent the needless suffering of captured animals. Check state game laws before trapping; many states have laws affecting the type of trap that is legal, trap visitation, legal baits, and types of sets.

FENCING AND BARRIERS

There are a number of ways to protect livestock, poultry, and crops from predation by using properly placed fencing and barriers. Ordinary fencing will not keep most predators from gardens or poultry ranges—if they cannot go under it, or through it, they will climb over it. However, it is possible to keep out many of them by adding a single wire strand electrified by a commercial fence charger, 20 cm out from the fence and 20 cm above the ground. Storer et al. (1938) reported success in keeping bears out of storehouses and other areas by the use of a specifically designed electric fence.

An anticoyote electric fence has been tested with good results and may evolve as an effective method of preventing coyote depredation of livestock. This fence is 1.5 m high and has 12 alternating ground and charged wires spaced from 10.0 cm at the bottom to 15.2 cm at the top (Gates et al. 1978).

Burrowing beneath a fence can be prevented by burying a 0.6-m wire mesh extending 15 cm below the surface and 45 cm outward at that depth.

For skunk control around a poultry range, surround the range with a 0.9-m wire netting fence set 0.6 m above ground and 0.3 m below the surface. Bend outwardly at right angles, 15 cm of the part below the surface, and bury 15 cm deep. When the skunk digs down along the vertical wire fence, it will stop when it strikes the horizontal wire.

Close or screen all holes in foundations of buildings to prevent skunks from living in or under them. If they have already established a home, close all entrances except one. With a gardening tool, loosen the soil so a track can be detected, or remove the vegetation and sprinkle flour in and in front of the hole. Check for tracks after dark, and if they indicate the animal has left the location, seal the opening securely.

M-44

The M-44 (Fig. 22.10) was developed as an alternative for the coyote getter. The M-44 is registered for the control of coyotes, foxes, and feral dogs. This is a mechanical device which ejects sodium cyanide into the animal's mouth. The unit consists of a case holder wrapped with cloth, fur, wool, or steel wool; a plastic capsule or case that holds the cyanide; and a 7-cm ejector unit. The M-44 case is loaded with 12 grains of sodium cyanide and an additive to reduce caking. Ejection is provided by a spring loaded plunger. These components, when assembled, are encased in a tube driven into the ground. The cocked ejector with the case in the holder is screwed on top, placed into the tube, and baited. The bait usually is made from fetid meat, musks, and beaver castors. When an animal is attracted to the bait and tries to pick up the baited case holder with its teeth, the cyanide is ejected into its mouth. The fright caused by the coyote getter has been reduced with the development of the M-44, resulting in recovery of the animals closer to the devices.

Dogs, skunks, raccoons, bears, and opossums sometimes are attracted to the bait used on M-44s; however, selectivity is enhanced by proper site and bait (scent) selections.

Before use, state regulations should be checked for registration, and the 26 restrictions outlined in the Environmental Protection Agency M-44 Sodium Cyanide Use Restriction Bulletin must be carefully followed.

UNGULATES

Damage Identification and Assessment

Forbs, which occur naturally in some reforestation projects, sometimes are preferred over young trees by deer, elk, and moose. Therefore, a close examination of

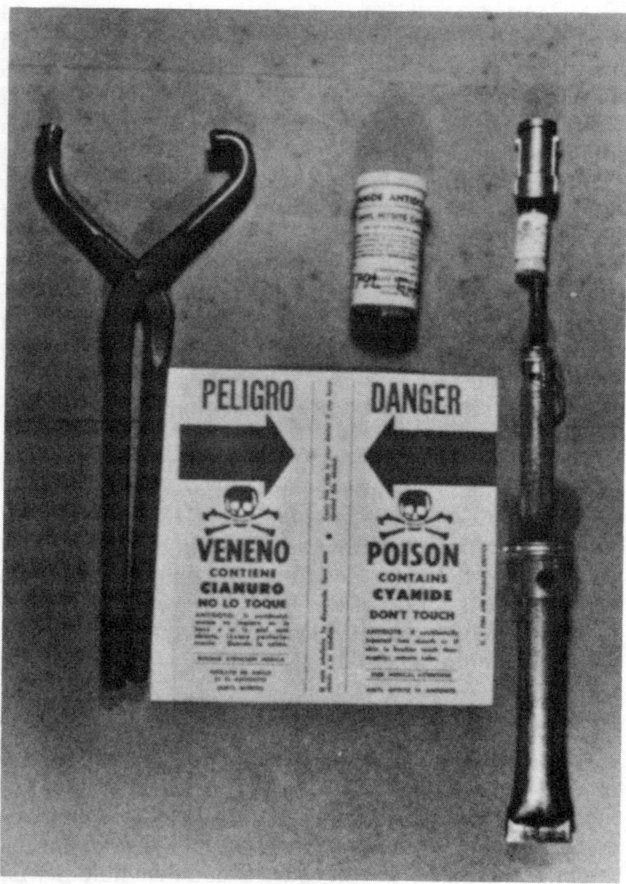

Fig. 22.10. The M-44 device consists of the case holder, case containing the sodium cyanide, ejector, and tube which is driven into the ground and the other components are placed in it. Also pictured are the special cocking pliers, the antidote kit that must be carried on the person setting the M-44s, and the unit warning sign that EPA requires to be within 1.8 m of the M-44 unit.

the branches must be made to determine if damage is indeed occurring. Dried shoots that have been killed break easily after a time, leaving an end resembling that of deer damage. However, frost damage to a tree will be uniform, and the dead tips will not fall off at the same time. Observations in late evening, early morning, or at night using a spotlight, are of course, one sure way of determining the species causing damage. Tracks, droppings, and location of the orchard or forest trees also will provide evidence to make a determination of species.

Once the guilty species is determined, the next step is to decide if the amount of damage justifies the expense and effort of control.

DEER, ELK, AND MOOSE

Overpopulations of deer and elk can have adverse effects on forest regeneration and maintenance of habitat for other wildlife. They may also compete with livestock on rangelands, and cause damage to crops and orchards. Damage to fences by elk often results in secondary damage by permitting livestock access to other areas. Winter wheat or hay fields sometimes are badly damaged by trampling and bedding of large herds of elk. In some areas, elk persistently raid haystacks and cattle feedlots (Eadie 1954).

When buck deer are rubbing the velvet from their antlers, they may scar saplings, break some of the limbs, and bruise the bark. Any of the antlered animals will leave this evidence of the approaching rutting season (Murie 1954). According to Pearce (1947), the rub will be confined to the trunk area between 0.04 m and 1 m above the ground. Small trees may be killed, according to Eadie (1954). This damage can be important economically when it occurs in orchards, and the value of the individual trees is high.

In Douglas-fir regions, populations of black-tailed deer increase dramatically in response to improved forage supplies after forests are logged or burned. In these clear-cut areas, incidental browsing on young trees lowers forest productivity by reducing growth rates and occasionally contributes to complete plantation failures (Crouch 1976).

In winter, moose will trim the limbs of fir trees, aspens, and other favorite foods, as high as they can reach. A much used willow range will be characterized by numerous dead, broken tops, which slant across or downward in various directions. Moose and elk will gnaw the bark of aspen trees.

Twigs or plants nipped by hoofed animals do not show the neat, sharp cut edge left by most rodents, but instead show a rough, shredded edge, and usually a square or ragged break. The stems browsed by these 3 ungulates show no appreciable difference in appearance. Pearce (1947) observed that deer in the Northeast seldom browse higher than 1.8 m from a standing position, but are able to reach 2.5 m or more by rearing up on their hind legs. He also reported that elk and moose browse to a height of about 3 m. Deer rarely browse on branches over 2.5 cm in diameter.

All 3 species of animals will ride down small trees to feed on by straddling the tree with their front legs and pushing it over with their chests. Seedlings may be uprooted by browsing animals.

Control Techniques

HABITAT MODIFICATION

Recently, research has revealed several forbs which appear in newly slash-burned or mechanically scarified plantations. Deer and elk prefer these to Douglas-fir seedlings. Studies have shown that these forbs can be seeded in reforestation areas and reduce damage to the trees, but not increase the attractiveness of the areas to the deer and elk (Campbell 1974).

FENCING AND BARRIERS

These methods of reducing damage by ungulates can be rather expensive; however, they may be considered for individual or small groups of trees. Also, high value crops may justify fencing. One of the most expensive fences is the conventional 2.5 m high fence. It is constructed of net wire and topped with barbed wire; if maintained, it will effectively exclude deer (Loomis 1975).

The New Hampshire Fish and Game Department has developed an electric fence which has been used with some success. The fence is constructed of a 1.3 m high post, with 2 cross-arms fastened to the post and attached to 1 end to form a triangle. An insulator and wire are affixed to each point of the triangle. There is 1 electric wire on 1 side of the post about 0.7 m from the ground, 2 wires on the opposite side with the bottom wire 3 cm from the ground, and the top wire about 1 m from the ground. All 3 wires are electrified. The vegetation must be mowed or killed with herbicides to prevent it from touching and grounding the bottom wire.

Individual trees can be encircled with hardware cloth or poultry wire to prevent browsing or antler rubbing.

The VEXAR(R) seedling protectors, as described under the rodent section, are very effective in reducing damage to young conifer trees of reforestation (Campbell and Evans 1975). They are relatively inexpensive compared to fencing.

REPELLENTS

There are commercial repellents available on the market that have been proven effective during dormant seasons; however, during the growing season, the new growth must be treated regularly or damage will occur. The success of the repellent also will depend on the availability of other foods. In situations where the animals do not have an alternate food source, repellents will give little protection.

Thiram (Arasan) is registered for use on plants for protection against deer damage. This product is available in an aerosol spray, a 20% solution to be diluted with water, and in a 42% concentrate to make a mixture of water and sticker (Fitzwater et al. 1972). To use, spray the plant thoroughly before damage begins. One application can protect up to 6 months during the dormant winter season but should be repeated when new growth begins.

A new repellent, cooperatively developed by the U.S. Fish and Wildlife Service and the Weyerhaeuser Company, has recently been registered by McGlaughlin, Gormley, and King Company, Minneapolis, Minnesota. This product is made of reformulated, fermented eggs and is called BGR (Big Game Repellent) (Rochelle et al. 1974). At present, it is only distributed in the Portland, Oregon, area for use in the Pacific Northwest.

Although not registered with the Environmental Protection Agency, Loomis (1975) reported that fresh blood and bone meal in a one-to-one mixture, or tankage, is a popular and readily available repellent. It can either be broadcast around the perimeter of a field, mixed with water and sprayed on trees, or attached to individual orchard trees in small "Bull Durham" type cloth bags. An insecticide should be mixed with the tankage or bone and blood mixture to prevent insect damage.

SCARING

A wide variety of noise makers, flashing lights, and visual repellents have been used to frighten deer out of gardens, tree plantings, and orchards. Most such devices enjoy fair success when first used, but prove to be ineffective as long-term repellents. Animals become accustomed to the noise or light and eventually ignore them. Propane or acetylene exploders, shell crackers, flashing lights, lanterns, and "scare crow" type devices all fit into this same category.

A sonic device emitting an unpleasant sound to deer has been used successfully over a small area. Fireworks triggered at sporadic intervals at night have had limited success (Harder 1968).

SHOOTING

In large areas where significant damage occurs and the state wildlife agency has determined that there are excess numbers of deer, special hunts may be organized to reduce the overpopulation. In local damage situations, the wildlife agency may shoot a number of animals using spotlights, and donate the carcasses to a state institution. Loomis (1975) reported that some states will give the first animal killed to the person suffering the loss with the hope that it will make the owner more tolerant of the other deer.

TRAPPING

As an alternative to shooting, the wildlife agency may wish to livetrap the depredating animals in problem areas and move them to areas having low populations. This method is costly, time consuming, and may prove to be ineffective because the damage may be occurring faster than the animals can be trapped and moved.

BIRDS

Damage Assessment

Bird damage to agricultural crops is a multimillion dollar problem in the United States, according to reports by Guarino (1975). Studies of damage to ripening field corn showed that birds caused a loss of approximately 6.5 million bushels each year in 1970 and 1971 (Stone et al. 1972, Stone and Mott 1973). Bird damage to fruit crops also is extensive. Nationwide damage to grapes was approximately 4.4 million dollars in 1972; more than 3.7 million dollars in damage occurred in California (Crase et al. 1976). Damage in local areas can be severe to other crops such as peanuts, lettuce and other truck crops, sweet cherries, pecans, and other fruits and grains (Guarino 1975).

Bird damage to corn can be measured by using the number or percentage of kernels damaged. The length of the damaged area on the ear, or the percentage of the ear affected, is translated into either an absolute loss (bushels per hectare), or a percentage of the crop destroyed (Linehan 1967).

Methods of alleviating bird problems depend on the number and species involved, whether the birds are local or migratory, type of damage incurred, the extent and magnitude of the problem, the time of year damage occurs, weather patterns, and public opinion (Guarino 1975). Control efforts also will depend on the determination of whether a particular problem is temporary in nature, or whether it will persist and recur.

With the exception of some of the nocturnal birds, most bird damage is done during daylight hours. The best way to identify the species doing the damage is by observation.

The 3 important factors in dealing with bird problems are: timing, persistence, and diversification. Control measures must begin at the first indication of damage, and vulnerable crops should be watched closely. As long as there is a potential problem, control measures should be continued. A variety of control techniques usually is more effective than any single approach in controlling damage.

Most birds have federal and/or state protection. Refer to the discussion of bird permits later in this section, and contact the local state wildlife officer.

Species Damage Identification

CROWS, RAVENS, AND MAGPIES

Crows, ravens, and magpies are well-known predators of other birds' nests. Crows usually remove the egg from the nest before breaking a hole in it. The raven and magpie break a hole in the egg up to 2.5 cm in diameter. The raven leaves a clean edge along the break, never crushed, whereas the magpie often leaves dented, broken edges. Ravens also eat young birds (Anon. 1936).

In certain areas, crows, ravens, and magpies will kill new-born lambs by pecking their eyes. At times, they also may injure cattle, horses, and sheep by pecking on fresh brands or sores which may cause infection of the area, loss of weight, severe wounds, or in extreme cases, even death (Anderson 1969).

Crows cause serious losses to pecan growers throughout the growing areas. They also damage peanuts, corn, and other crops, as well as winter roosts causing hazards around airports.

Control techniques: Mechanical frightening devices, shooting, trapping, and chemical frightening agents.

PIGEONS

Excessive numbers of pigeons can cause property deterioration, and also can constitute a health hazard. Pigeons are associated with the transmission of ornithosis, encephalitis, Newcastle disease, aspergillosis, thrush, histoplasmosis, cryptococcosis, toxoplasmosis, pseudotuberculosis, avian tuberculosis, salmonellosis, and coccidiosis (Anon. 1969). Geis (1976) cited an example of a nursery school being held in violation of health codes by the local health department because of pigeon droppings in the play yard.

Grain spillage around elevators, railroad sidings, and other such sites are attractive feeding sites for pigeons. Pigeons can also become quite a problem around stockyards. Defacing of buildings by pigeon droppings is a serious problem in locations where they roost or loaf. There are many incidents where food stored in large warehouses has been condemned because of pigeon droppings. The New Orleans Port Commission, in 1974, complained that pigeons in their 27 sq km of warehouses were costing port leasers thousands of dollars yearly because of condemnation by the Food and Drug Administration (Abraham, pers. comm.).

Control techniques: Mechanical frightening devices, toxic bait (strychnine), toxic perches, shooting, traps, proofing and screening, and chemical frightening agents.

GULLS

Gulls have adapted to existing in close proximity to man and have taken advantage of municipal dumps, fishing ports, and sewage outfalls. This has resulted in an increase of gulls which concentrate around metropolitan centers and cause problems. The major culprit is the herring gull in the East, and the California gull in the West. A wide range of complaints levied against gulls include hazards to public safety at airports, damage to blueberries and golf courses, depredation to fish at hatcheries, losses of duck eggs and ducklings, contamination of public water supplies, and defacing of property.

Control techniques: Habitat manipulation, proofing and screening, mechanical and chemical frightening agents, and shooting.

SPARROWS

In many parts of the country, reports are received of depredation by house sparrows on relatively small acreages of grain, with damage particularly severe when the grain plantings ripen earlier or later than in larger commercial fields.

For many years, the 65-ha Branch Experiment Station at Mesa, Arizona, sustained severe sparrow damage to ripening barley and wheat from March to mid-June. The problem was acute because only 6 ha or less of wheat and barley were grown each spring for experimental purposes. Damage was chiefly in terms of lost research effort (Royall 1969).

House sparrows cause problems when they roost in garages, aircraft hangars, and warehouses. They also may cause damage to ripening fruits in local situations. These birds build their nests in open eaves of houses, and in rain spouts, causing them to plug. In some poultry operations, sparrows will consume feed and deface property. They have caused the introduction of the northern fowl mite *(Ornithonyssus sylviarum).*

Control techniques: Trapping, toxic bait (strychnine), chemical frightening agents, shooting, repellents, habitat manipulation, proofing and screening, and toxic perches.

STARLINGS AND BLACKBIRDS

Serious economic losses to large agricultural crops by starlings and blackbirds are reported in many parts of the United States. Stockdale (1967) reported a study of red-winged blackbirds that showed 90% of their diet during late summer and early fall was composed of soft seeds, primarily milk and dough stage corn. In 1967, the estimated loss to crop depredating birds in Ohio was $15 million.

Blackbirds are a major concern of the rice growers in this country. Heaviest damage usually occurs in the first fields to ripen and the last fields to be harvested, and in fields adjacent to bayous, river bottoms, and wooded areas (Meanley 1971).

Large flocks of starlings and blackbirds can cause serious losses to poultry and livestock feedlot operations where they not only consume, but contaminate large quantities of feed.

Starlings have a high food requirement, which causes them to be economically important pests. The starling goes through a complete digestive cycle in about 30 minutes, which is due to its high metabolism and relatively inefficient digestive tract (Clore 1976). Bird species as numerous and adaptable as starlings, with this high food requirement, create a large variety of damage problems. In addition, starlings have an impact on the native bird species by competing for nest sites, cover, and food.

Perhaps more dramatic than economic losses are the losses of human lives as occurred in 1960, when 62 people were killed in an Electra turboprop aircraft at Logan Airport in Boston. The crash was attributed directly to starlings entering 3 of the 4 engines continually for several seconds during the critical power requirement period just after the plane had taken off. A similar incident occurred to a Lear jet in 1973 at an Atlanta airport.

Control techniques: Habitat manipulation, proofing and screening, mechanical and chemical frightening agents (Avitrol[R]), repellents, toxicants (Starlicide), trapping, shooting, and toxic perches.

HAWKS AND OWLS

Hawks and owls obtain food by preying on a wide variety of birds and mammals, including rodents, skunks, and pigeons. They also are opportunists, and occasionally may kill poultry. They maintain large hunting areas and usually are not numerous in any 1 area. Removal of 1 or 2 individuals usually will alleviate a problem. Great horned and snowy owls are highly effective predators on other birds. They usually capture their prey by an attack in the middle of the back, between the wings. Sometimes marks on an owl kill are difficult to distinguish from those of a canine, except for the spacing of the puncture wounds (Pfeifer, pers. comm.). The carcass of a bird with its head bitten off close to the body usually indicates owl predation.

All hawks and owls are federally protected. The U.S. Fish and Wildlife Service may issue special permits for control if raptors present a serious predation problem.

Control techniques: Pole trapping, frightening devices, proofing and screening, and habitat modification.

HERONS, BITTERNS, AND CORMORANTS

Herons, bitterns, and cormorants normally do not cause many problems; however, some fish hatcheries have experienced heavy losses. Scars on the backs of fish in raceways are a good indication that herons or bitterns are working the hatcheries. A check at night using a spotlight may confirm the predator. Salmon smolts released in rivers in the Northeast have suffered heavy depredation by cormorants.

Control techniques: Frightening devices, proofing and screening.

WOODPECKERS AND SAPSUCKERS

Woodpeckers and sapsuckers at times may cause damage to houses with natural wood siding, particularly cedar. The birds peck holes in the siding in search of insects, or to establish territories prior to the nesting season. They also cause damage to utility poles. Occasionally, woodpeckers may annoy homeowners by knocking on metal rain gutters to mark their territories. The sapsuckers attack trees to feed on the sap and bark tissues. Their attacks can kill the trees or seriously degrade the wood. One common kind of damage attributed to sapsucker attack is known as bird peck, and another is the discoloration associated with sapsucker wounds (Rushmore 1969).

Control techniques: Frightening devices, repellents, live traps, snap traps, and shooting (permit needed).

DUCKS, GEESE, AND SANDHILL CRANES

These migratory birds are capable of causing serious crop damage as they travel up and down their migration routes. Depredation primarily is on grain crops, but damage has occurred to melons, lettuce, corn, and soybeans as well. In 1974, a mail survey revealed that about 1% of the total grain crop was lost to waterfowl, amounting to approximately $25 million (Schwilling 1975). A large number of geese walking over a field will cause soil compaction. Problems in Texas and Louisiana are caused by snow geese grazing in rye grass pastures. Damage usually begins in spring with sprout pulling and trampling of plants. Heavier damage is caused when grain fields begin to ripen, and waterfowl not only eat grain, but knock seeds from the stalks onto the ground. Any delay in harvest or control at this time will result in more severe damage.

Research has revealed that waterfowl grazing on the dormant winter wheat during February and March does not reduce the yield. In fact, moderate grazing tends to increase the yield.

Control techniques: Mechanical frightening devices, lure crops, and feed stations.

GOLDEN EAGLES

There are numerous reports each year of golden eagles killing range lambs. Most of the reported complaints are concentrated in western Texas, eastern New Mexico, and the Rock Creek and Sweetwater Basin areas near Dillon, Montana. Miner (1975) reported 44 verified eagle-killed lambs, 76% of all recorded deaths, during a short study in Montana.

Close examination is needed to identify an eagle kill. The victim will have subcutaneous hemorrhages and deep puncture wounds on the back and head. The wounds caused by the toes will be about 2.5 cm apart and in a straight line or small "V", and hallux wounds will be about 10 to 15 cm from the middle toe. With all mammalian predators, 4 punctures or bruises from the canine teeth are almost always evident. Talon punctures are generally deeper than tooth punctures, and there is seldom any crushing between the talons. If a puncture cannot be seen from the outside, it is best to skin the carcass to determine the pattern of talon or tooth marks. Often, a young lamb is killed with a single puncture from the hallux in the top or front of the skull and the 3 opposing talons puncturing the base of the skull or top of the neck (O'Gara 1978).

Control techniques: Mechanical frightening devices, trapping and shooting. A permit is required from the U.S. Fish and Wildlife Service before any control is conducted.

LINNET

The linnet or house finch, now common in the West and spreading eastward, may cause damage to more than 20 different crops; however, the depredation usually is localized. The presence of linnets in an agricultural area should not be taken as evidence that they are doing damage; however, sighting combined with debudding, seed removal, or fruit pecks are good indications (Palmer 1970).

Control techniques: Mechanical frightening devices, traps, and toxic bait (strychnine-treated seed).

Control Techniques

HABITAT MANIPULATION

Habitat manipulation is the change of some practice or factor that will reduce the amount of damage to a specific area. Guarino (1975) provided several examples: planting less valuable and more attractive lure crops, such as millet, adjacent to the more valuable crops to divert the birds; changes in cultural practices, for example, harvesting earlier or changing crops; burning roosting areas, thereby reducing vegetation, thinning branches and trees, making the site less desirable for roosting; changing to more bird-resistant crops or crops that are not as susceptible to bird damage.

Mott (1975) suggested that fields near woodlots or marshy areas vulnerable to bird damage be planted early to get an earlier harvest, before the birds arrive. Some crops may be harvested early and artificially dried.

Winter blackbird roosts may be moved from urban and suburban locations by altering the habitat. Most roosts in these locations are in live oaks, magnolias, evergreen shrubs, ornamental bamboo, and pine trees. Where possible, the long-range approach is to alter the roost areas so that they are less attractive to the birds. This is done by thinning and pruning the trees or other plants within the roosting site. This procedure can be accomplished without destroying the esthetic value of the environs. For example, young live oaks have a very thick growth inside the crown, and as the tree ages, this intergrowth diminishes making the tree unattractive to the birds. Young trees can be pruned to provide the same affect. This procedure will not only eliminate the roosting habitat, but also will improve the appearance and health of the tree (Abraham, pers. comm.). The most drastic measures in altering roost sites is to remove completely all vegetation that is being utilized by the birds.

Bird problems at airports can be eliminated in a majority of the cases by habitat modification. The removal of dumps, landfills, or sewage disposals near airports will eliminate food sources which may attract large numbers of gulls, starlings, and other birds to the vicinity. All berry- or seed-producing shrubs and weeds that may attract wildlife should be removed. Tall vegetation that may be potential roosting sites for such birds as starlings, crows, or blackbirds should be cut (Aldrich et al. 1961). Drain or fill marshy areas in the proximity of airports. To discourage birds from loafing on the runways, the grass should be mowed no closer than 15 cm. However, grasses allowed to grow taller will attract mice and, subsequently, hawks and owls. This may add to the bird/aircraft problem. Removal of dead snags from an area may help reduce hawk and owl damage.

Sugden (1976) found that lure crops which were left out and lying in the fields had varying degrees of success in reducing waterfowl damage in the Prairie Provinces of Canada. Also the use of feeding stations combined with a scaring program has proven effective (Hammond 1961).

PROOFING AND SCREENING

Small mesh nettings, usually made of nylon, plastic, or cotton string are effective in protecting individual fruit trees, ornamental shrubs, and to some extent, high value, low-growing berry plants such as blueberries and strawberries. To protect fruit trees, it is necessary to cover the entire tree. In cases of low-growing plants, supporting stakes or a frame may be required to keep the birds from feeding through the mesh. If proper care is taken of the netting, it will last for several years.

Ledges or other structures on buildings can be covered with slanting boards, sheet metal, or mortar placed at a 45 degree angle or greater to discourage birds from using them as roosting or nesting sites. Electrically charged wires have been permanently installed on roost sites on some buildings. Steeple's, towers, poultry houses, barn lofts, and similar places can be birdproofed with 1.9 cm or smaller mesh wire.

McAtee and Piper (1936) described a wire grid that is constructed about 0.7 m above the pond or raceway to deter fish-eating birds from preying in the hatcheries. The space between the wires depends on the wingspan of the species involved. They also suggested a poultry wire fence around the perimeter to prevent birds from walking into the pond. Modern nylon netting installed in the same manner over the fish rearing areas will accomplish the same results.

To prevent sapsucker damage, Ostry and Nicholls (1976) suggested wrapping the affected tree with hardware cloth or burlap around the area tapped.

FRIGHTENING

Mechanical Devices

One of the better known of these devices is the exploder, which is available in propane, acetylene, or carbide models (Fig. 22.11). The exploder produces a loud explosion at timed intervals, and has been used in a variety of bird problems. To be effective, this device must be moved often, preferably every 2 or 3 days, and regular maintenance is needed for proper function. To project the sound over a greater area, the exploder may be mounted on a platform or tower. Changing the time

Fig. 22.11. There are 3 types of exploders commercially available—carbide, acetylene, and propane. Exploders should be placed on platforms above the crop to be protected and their location changed every 2 or 3 days. One exploder will protect 2–14 ha depending on local conditions and bird pressure.

interval between explosions prevents birds from becoming accustomed to the exploder.

Shellcrackers are widely used to move birds out of problem areas. These shells are fired from a 12-gauge shotgun, and shoot a projectile which explodes approximately 65 to 70 m away. Care should be taken if dry vegetation poses a fire hazard (Mitchell and Linehan 1967).

Rockets are available for the purpose of scaring birds. The rockets do not require a shotgun; however for better accuracy, they should be launched from a launching rod. The rocket has a much greater range than shellcrackers, and the hissing sound, as it travels through the air, adds to its frightening power.

Recorded alarm and distress calls of birds broadcast over a speaker system sometimes work well, especially in combination with other frightening devices. These biosonic devices are available commercially, and produce an amplified noise to frighten birds.

At one time class 3 fireworks, such as "silver salutes" and "cherry bombs" were widely used; however, they have been banned for use by the general public. They are still available to governmental agencies for bird control. The fuses of firecrackers are inserted through a saltpeter-soaked cotton rope. The rope is hung from a tree or a wooden frame, and the bottom end lit. As the rope burns, it ignites the firecrackers.

Small pistols are available that shoot a modified shellcracker, a whistle bomb, or flare. The pistol uses a .22-caliber blank to start the projectile which has a range of approximately 65 to 70 m before it explodes.

Blackbird roosts containing up to several million birds can be moved by using a combination of recorded distress calls, shellcrackers, and pistol rockets. Several amplified distress call units are stationed throughout the roost. A person armed with a shotgun and shellcracker or a bomb pistol is stationed at the perimeter of the roost where the flight lines are coming into it. The operation begins as the first birds arrive, and ends at dark. The birds usually will move to another roosting site after 3 to 5 days.

Care should be taken that the birds do not relocate in another area which would be objectionable to the public. If they do begin using an undesirable location, they should be moved before the new site becomes an established roost. It is possible to move a roost, depending on circumstances, with only electronic distress calls or pyrotechnics, but coverage must be adequate and generally takes a combination of these techniques to do an efficient job. Once the roost is moved, the site should be inspected periodically. If the birds attempt to reestablish the roost, a few shellcrackers and bird bombs usually will discourage them. In many instances, even though the roost is relocated and stays relocated for the winter, the birds may return the next winter. This behavior emphasizes the importance of habitat alteration (Abraham, pers. comm.).

Firing a .22-caliber rifle over a field is effective in frightening birds, but extreme caution must be taken when using this method. Mitchell and Linehan (1967) reported that 1 rifleman using a .22-caliber rifle and positioned on a silo, rooftop, or tall platform, can protect a solid block of corn, as large as 40 ha, by firing earthward into the midst of the depredating birds.

The scarecrow is one of the oldest control devices, and if used properly, can be fairly effective—the larger number used, the better. At least 1 scarecrow is needed for every 4 to 6 ha. The scarecrow may be made from a variety of materials; old clothing, grain sacks stuffed with straw, or a black plastic flag hung from a tall pole. The important thing is that it moves or swings in the wind. Like the exploders, it is important that the scarecrows be moved every 2 to 3 days.

Balloons have been used successfully to keep waterfowl from damage areas. These balloons are 50 to 75 cm in diameter, filled with helium or hydrogen, and tethered to a stake with a 15 to 20 m, 22 kg monofilament line. The balloons are placed about 175 m apart. Good all-weather balloons that are not sensitive to ultraviolet light must be used; they require frequent checking and refilling. White and yellow balloons have been effective in keeping geese out of fields at night; red balloons are best for day operations.

Different types of lights have been used with varying degrees of success. These include searchlight beams, blinking lights such as those used in highway construction, rotating lights, and strobes.

Ribbons, pie pans, and aluminum foil strips tied to string so they can be moved by the wind, have some scaring effect. For woodpecker damage on homes, take an aluminum foil strip about 5 cm wide and 0.9 m long, tie to a string, and hang on the side where the damage is occurring.

Any of the scaring devices placed in the field should be removed as soon as the harvest is completed.

Chemical Agents

Avitrol(R) is a registered frightening agent. The chemical, when ingested, causes the affected bird to emit distress cries while flying in erratic circles. This behavior frightens the rest of the flock away from the damage area. The product is relatively safe, affects only 1% of the target species, and has no secondary hazards. It is registered for control on feral pigeons, gulls, sparrows, starlings, and blackbirds around structures, nesting and roosting sites; for starlings in feedlots; gulls at airports; crows in pecans; starlings and blackbirds in corn; and for protection of peanuts from blackbirds. It is available in concentrate to use on fresh baits, treated pellets, or on treated grain.

For the protection of standing corn from blackbirds, a 1 to 99 mixture of cracked corn bait is spread evenly on about one-third of the field. The bait can be applied by ground or aerial methods, and the first application is made when the birds are first seen in the field. Additional applications may depend on the bird concentration and rainfall (Pfeifer, pers. comm.); however, 3 to 5-day intervals are recommended. The treatment of other field crops is conducted in similar manner. The use of AVITROL(R) is limited to state certified applicators.

REPELLENTS

There are 3 groups of bird repellents—odor, tactile, and taste.

Naphthalene flakes are currently registered for sparrows, pigeons, and starlings in indoor roosts. Use about 2.2 kg of crystals for every 56.6 cubic m. After the birds leave, seal off all openings used as entrances.

A number of tactile repellents have been registered, but few have demonstrated much success. Most of these repellents are for use on window sills, gutter edges, or other ledges, and require the surface to be painted or taped to prevent the material from absorbing into porous surfaces. Warm temperatures may cause them to run, and dust may cause them to lose their sticky properties. Pentachlorophenol may be troweled into holes made by woodpeckers to discourage them from enlarging the holes. It also may be applied to areas subject to woodpecker attacks (Fitzwater et al. 1972), and Ostry and Nicholls (1976) recommended the sticky repellents to prevent sapsucker damage on a small number of trees. The material should be put around the area tapped.

Some of the taste repellents, such as THIRAM(R), are sprayed on trees to discourage birds from landing on them; however, this product cannot be used on fruit trees. Other taste repellents are used to prevent seeding, digging, or sprout pulling.

MESUROL(R) (methiocarb), is used to curtail blackbird damage to seeds and sprouts of field or sweet corn and popcorn. This product must be applied to seed at the time of planting. It is also registered for use in some areas to protect ripening cherries.

STRESSING AGENTS

In 1974, the U.S. Fish and Wildlife Service registered PA-14 (commercially known as Tergitol 15-9-9) for use as an avian stressing agent. This wetting agent is used to reduce large populations of blackbirds and starlings in roosts. PA-14 lowers the surface tension of the bird feathers, allowing the inner feathers to become wet and the bird to lose body temperature until a lethal level is reached. It is applied to roosting birds immediately before or during cold, wet weather, at temperatures near 4–9°C., and preferably with at least 1.3 cm of rain predicted immediately after the treatment. The registration allows use by, or under the supervision of, government personnel trained in bird control (Lefebvre and Seubert 1970).

TRAPS

There are a number of sizes and styles of bird traps, some homemade and others available from commercial sources. Most traps are used to reduce sparrow, starling, pigeon, and blackbird populations. One of the most common is the pigeon trap, used to remove birds from urban areas, or to control bird damage in orchards and vineyards.

The trap most often used for starlings and blackbirds is an adaptation of the "Australian Crow Trap" (Fig. 22.12). Although it can be of any size, the most common is 2 × 2 × 2.5 m. The trap frame is made of pipe or lumber, and covered with small mesh poultry wire. The birds enter through small openings in the top, and the trap design prevents them from escaping. The trap is baited with food and live decoy birds. The decoy birds are important to the success of the trap, so ample food and water must be provided to keep them active. Generally, the trap should be placed near the damage area, but Bogatich (1967) found that cherries could be protected before ripening by locating the traps near loafing areas or along flyways. He also reported good success was gained by mounting the trap on a trailer, thus enabling it to be pulled and set up quickly in areas where damage was developing. The plans for constructing this trap are available from most U.S. Fish and Wildlife Service offices.

Miner (1975) reported success in livetrapping golden eagles using the "Lockhart Method." This involves using 4, weak spring, No. 3 or 4 steel traps with padded jaws. These traps are set by the head, back, rear, and belly of a dead jackrabbit or lamb, staked down for bait. The traps are set using pan covers, and covered with soil. A decoy eagle equipped with leather jesses is tethered far enough out to prevent it from reaching the

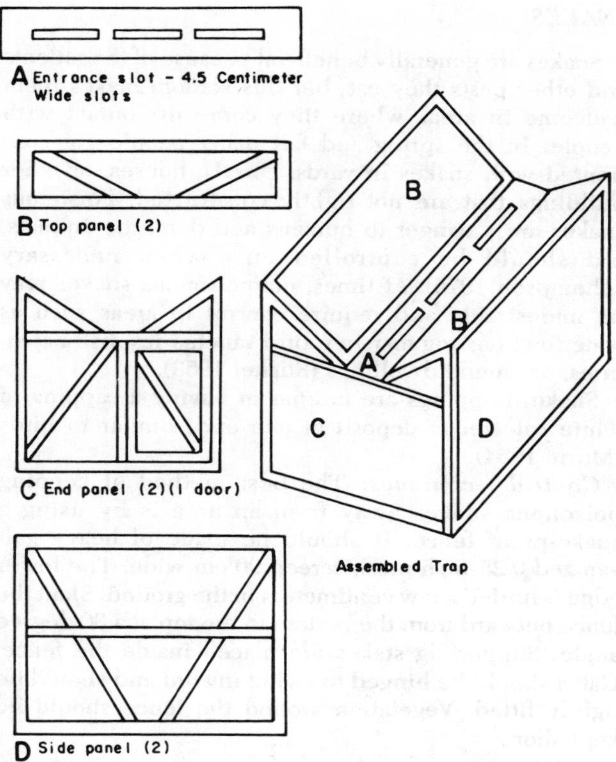

Fig. 22.12. "Australian Crow Trap" used for capture of starlings and blackbirds.

bait or the traps. The trap site should be checked at approximately 1-hour intervals using a spotting scope. A 15-m drag rope is attached to the trap chain to facilitate capturing the trapped eagles.

Before any eagle trapping operations are initiated, a permit *must* be acquired from the U.S. Fish and Wildlife Service.

Pole trapping is an effective method for capturing problem hawks and owls because of their preference to perch on tall isolated poles. A No. 1½ steel trap with foam rubber or slit surgical tubing padded jaws is recommended. Verbail Loop traps also will work, but they are more difficult to set. The trap is placed on a pole in the area where the damage is occurring. Drive 2 heavy staples near the top of the pole, and secure the trap on the pole by running a thin wire from the staples over the trap base, and lightly tie it to the opposite side. Attach the trap chain to a heavy gauge wire running from the top of the pole to the ground to allow the trap and bird to slide to the ground.

SHOOTING

This method may be effective if only a few birds are involved. When dealing with large numbers of birds, shooting has little effect other than the repelling value. Where permissible, persistent shooting with a .22-caliber rifle, .410 gauge shotgun, or air rifle can eliminate a small flock from a given area.

Gramlich (1972) reported success in removal of pest birds in some situations using .22-caliber CB caps. The CB caps have a killing range of about 30 m—15 to 22 m is optimum. They will not penetrate 2.5-cm board or corrugated steel at close range. CB caps may be used inside buildings without fear of ricochet.

A kill permit is required from the U.S. Fish and Wildlife Service to shoot all migratory birds, except blackbirds, crows, and magpies, when they are doing or about to do damage. See "Permit Requirements" later in this section.

TOXICANTS

STARLICIDE(R) is the trade name for a toxicant used in controlling starlings in livestock feedlots and poultry yards. Decino et al. (1966) reported that it is highly toxic to starlings, and less toxic to most other birds. Hawks are particularly resistant, so there is little danger to them or to mammalian carnivores that might eat STARLICIDE(R) poisoned starlings. This toxicant is only available on poultry pellets; therefore, prebaiting with untreated pellets improves the success. The prebait and treated bait should be broadcast outside the feed bunker. After receiving a lethal dose, the starling will die up to 48 hours later, usually in the roost. The material is most effective when snow covers the birds' normal food supply, forcing the birds to concentrate on the feedlots. This product is now also registered in the Northeast for gull control.

Strychnine-treated whole corn can be used to effectively control pigeons. The size of the whole kernel bait adds some selectivity; however, the corn used should be recleaned before treatment to remove corn particles, weed seeds, and other grains which could be easily ingested by smaller birds. Also, strychnine-treated corn chops may be used for sparrow control. Prebait for several days in areas close to buildings to minimize hazards to nontargets. Do not put out toxic bait until prebait has been eaten or swept up. The amount of bait needed is determined by the daily consumption of the prebait.

Endrin and Fenthion treated wick-type perches are available for pigeon, sparrow, and starling control in buildings.

Permit Requirements

Federal regulations require that a depredation permit be obtained from the U.S. Fish and Wildlife Service before any person may take, possess, or transport migratory birds for depredation control purposes. No permit is required merely to scare or herd depredating migratory birds other than endangered or threatened species, or bald or golden eagles.

A federal permit is not required to control yellow-headed, red-winged, tri-colored, Rusty, and Brewer's blackbirds, cowbirds, all grackles, crows, and magpies, when found committing or about to commit depredations upon ornamental or shade trees, agricultural crops, livestock, or wildlife, or when concentrated in such numbers and manner as to constitute a health hazard or other nuisance.

All birds taken under the above provisions without a permit cannot be sold or removed from the area where killed. Also, the above regulations do not circumvent any state laws or regulations. (Part 20, Chapter 1, Title 50, Code Federal Regulations, paragraphs 21.11–21.43.)

OTHER SPECIES

Damage Identification and Assessment

BATS

Bats feed almost exclusively on night-flying insects; therefore, their eating habits are not objectionable. When they select a building for roosting, they often become a nuisance. Bats have a characteristic pungent and offensive odor that develops from their droppings and urine. Another source of complaint is the scratchy, scrambling noise they make while entering and leaving their roosting places. Annoyance results from their fondness for such roosting places as between roofs and ceilings, in walls, in chimneys, and behind shutters or rafters (Bruce and Knowlton 1953). Kincaid (1975) reported that at 1 air base, in 8 months' time, there were 50 cases of bats striking airplanes, with damage approaching $200.000.

A number of bats such as the gray bat, Indiana bat, and the Hawaiian hoary bat are protected as endangered species. Control of bats classified as endangered can only be undertaken if they demonstrate a threat to human safety (Kincaid 1975).

Control techniques: Smaller species of bats can crawl through an opening as narrow as 9.5 mm; therefore, when bat-proofing a building, a very careful inspection is necessary to close all possible entrances. Larger openings can be covered with sheet metal or 0.25-inch mesh hardware cloth, if ventilation is desired. Narrow cracks can be filled with oakum, tow, or similar packing materials and sealed with caulking compound. All bats should be out of the building before bat-proofing is completed. During warmer months,when bats are active, all occupants normally leave the roost within 15 to 20 minutes. If a number of entrances have been used, wait 2 or 3 days before closing the last one, allowing all bats to learn to leave through the last opening.

Repellents sometimes are useful when the areas to be protected have large outside openings, and proofing is impractical. The only chemical currently registered is naphthalene flakes. The odor of naphthalene is apparently extremely offensive to bats and they begin to leave immediately, even in broad daylight. Flakes are usually spread under the area where bats are roosting (Kincaid 1975). The area will have to be retreated often, for the odor of naphthalene dissipates rapidly.

Greenhall and Paradiso (1968) described a number of methods for capturing bats which include hand nets, Constantine traps, modified tunnel nets, as well as other devices. Bat traps are sold commercially, but little is known of their effectiveness. Do not handle bats with bare hands.

In rabies situations, bats can be controlled by using 50% wettable DDT powder in their roosting area. The bats ingest the toxicant while grooming their feet and body. Each request for use must be authorized by the Environmental Protection Agency and the Center for Disease Control, except under emergency circumstances which permit state agencies to proceed with control activities with notification of federal agencies to follow immediately.

SNAKES

Snakes are generally beneficial because of the rodents and other pests they eat, but this seldom makes them welcome in areas where they come in contact with people. In the spring and fall many people are confronted with snakes in yards, corrals, houses, or other buildings that are not tightly constructed. Poisonous snakes are a danger to humans and domestic animals, but should be controlled only when necessary (Thompson 1975). At times, nonpoisonous snakes may be undesirable and require control in areas such as waterfowl nesting marshes, bird sanctuaries, fish hatcheries, or around dwellings (Stickel 1953).

Snake droppings are unique in having a capping of white calcareous deposit at one end, similar to birds (Murie 1954).

Control techniques: The best method of keeping poisonous snakes away from an area is by using a snake-proof fence. It should be made of heavy galvanized 0.25-inch mesh screen 90 cm wide. The lower edge is buried a few centimeters in the ground. Slant the fence outward from the bottom to the top at a 30 degree angle. Supporting stakes are placed inside the fence. Gates should be hinged to swing inward and should be tightly fitted. Vegetation around the fence should be kept short.

Another type of snake-proof fence is a strip of concrete, approximately 10 to 15 cm wide and 5 cm deep, placed around the area to be protected. An electric wire is strung along the top, 12 mm above the concrete.

Eliminate food and cover by closely mowing lawns and fields, removing board piles, trash and debris. Along water margins remove driftwood, rocks, old boats, and other debris. Snakes are seldom seen in clean, open areas where they are exposed to direct sunlight and enemies. Many snakes feed on rodents so it is advisable to rodent-proof buildings.

If a snake has entered a house and hidden, one way to lure it out is to put wet cloths on the floor near the area where you think the snake is, and cover them with dry cloths or burlap bags. Snakes like moisture and shelter and normally will crawl between the cloths. They can then be disposed of. If this method does not work, fumigation by a pest control operation may be the only alternative.

To keep snakes from entering buildings, all openings must be blocked. Snakes can pass through extremely small openings, usually near or below ground level. Cellar doors, windows, and screens must fit tightly. Search walls and floors for crevices. Plug spaces around pipes that go through outside walls. Galvanized screens can be fastened over drains or ventilators.

Snakes hibernate singly or in large groups. Sometimes hundreds of rattlesnakes are found in a single den, and den trapping can be quite successful. In using this technique, all openings to the den except the one leading to the trap are blocked with stones, wood, or by sealing them with concrete. Packed earth or sod usually is not resistant enough. Large openings may be closed with screen tacked to a wooden frame that is set deeply in the ground.

A snake trap is made of 1 by 12 lumber, and is 0.3 m wide by 0.9 m long. It has a hinged door on the end opposite the den for removal of snakes, and will accommodate approximately 60 snakes. A chute acts as a one-way entrance into the trap. The end of the chute projects into the trap, cut at an angle so that the bottom projects out further than the top. The entrance hole is covered with a round piece of plexiglass, mica, or celluloid, hinged at the top but free to swing at the bottom to form a one-way gate. Snakes, upon leaving the den, enter the chutes and pass through the hole into the cage by lifting the transparent gate which closes automatically after the snakes have passed through, preventing their return to the den. The hole is near the top of the chute, 10 to 13 cm above the floor level, so that the snakes in the trap cannot easily pile up in front of the entrance and prevent others from entering (Thompson 1975). These traps usually are set in early spring, although with some modifications, they may be used in the fall.

Often, the most practical way of controlling snakes is by clubbing or shooting. Poisonous snakes are scarce enough in many areas that this method will provide adequate control.

In considering the type of control to use on snake infested areas, it is important to estimate the cost of the method selected and decide if the expense and effort is justified.

SNAPPING TURTLES

When snapping turtles become overabundant in an area, they may prey heavily on waterfowl, muskrat, and some species of fish. They usually inhabit slow-moving streams, ponds, and lakes with mud bottoms. In the bottom ooze, turtles wait for prey to come within striking distance. These animals are not always still hunters, as cautious stalks of swimming ducks indicate. Observers have reported that these turtles attack waterfowl on shore. The victims invariably are dragged beneath the surface of the water, since the heads of the snappers must be submerged in order to eat (Anon. 1939).

Control techniques: Methods of controlling snappers vary with the seasons. Late spring and summer capture is most effective with submerged or floating traps, hooks, and lines. Most traps follow 2 general designs. One variety is constructed to catch in a submerged net any turtles which might drop into it from a basking log or plank. The other, designed for subsurface trapping, utilizes various adaptations of the funnel principle. The hook and line method is to put a fresh piece of meat, about the size of an egg, on a stout hook (pickerel size). A wire leader, usually not more than 0.9 m in length, is attached and the line anchored in fairly shallow water with the bait resting on the bottom. Check state game codes before using this method.

Egg gathering is another effective turtle control measure. In early summer, the female moves to a damp spot, often in loamy or sandy soil near the water, and scratches a hole into which she lays about 20 round, white eggs with a thin, hard shell. Turtle tracks will often help locate nests.

Turtle-proof fences are occasionally used to prevent ingress of the species to areas of waterfowl concentration. Sometimes, wire screens placed as baffles across waterways or swampy areas, with traps placed at both ends, will help control migratory snappers.

Probably the most effective method of snapper control is winter gaffing. When the water temperature is low enough to induce hibernation, the turtles congregate in muddy recesses not reached by the ice. Muskrat burrows, springy places, or brush piles in the mud are characteristic areas. A sturdy pole with a stout and well-sharpened, firmly attached gaff hook is used to prod likely hibernation recesses until a turtle is encountered. The turtle offers little resistance to removal because of its lethargic state.

Chapter Twenty-Three

Human Surveys in Wildlife Management[1]

FERN. L. FILION

Coordinator, Social Studies Division, Migratory Birds Branch,
Canadian Wildlife Service
Environment Canada
Ottawa, Canada

INTRODUCTION

In an ecological sense, people, land and wildlife are closely interlinked. Changes in any 1 component induce changes in the other 2. At some point in time, wildlife management invariably results in the management of people. This implies that wildlife managers must have some understanding of wildlife—people interactions. Government wildlife agencies attempt to regulate and enhance wildlife resources for human benefits. This implies that management agencies have some understanding of the values, needs, perceptions, and actions of people. One way to gain a better understanding of people and their relationships with wildlife is to conduct social surveys.

The varied applications of social surveys in wildlife management have been reviewed by Hendee and Potter (1971) and their importance illustrated by Hendee and Schoenfeld (1973). In brief, they may be used to study a wide range of wildlife-based and wildlife-related human activities, values, and characteristics (Filion 1980). Hunter surveys, for example, have been used to measure the size and distribution of harvests and are helpful in setting hunting regulations. Survey of humans can help gauge the attitudes, preferences, satisfactions and motivations of wildlife users and can be used in decisionmaking or in resolving specific management problems. Through social studies Kellert (1976) developed a typology of 9 attitudes held by the American public towards animals. He reported substantial differences among age groups, rural and urban dwellers and participants in various types of wildlife-related activities. Such findings may have an impact on conservation education and government activities and serve to buffer potential conflicts between hunters and antihunters. Surveys of humans can also play an important role in wildlife valuation by assessing user costs and benefits and examining the trade-offs people are willing to make for use of the

[1]Much of what is written in these pages is a product of my stimulating association with H. J. Boyd, F. G. Cooch, A. R. Sen., and G. E. J. Smith of the Canadian Wildlife Service. Special thanks are due to the following persons for their encouraging reviews and suggestions on an earlier draft: J. Beaman (Parks Canada), J. M. Barbowski (Ontario Ministry of Natural Resources), A. Geis (U.S. Fish and Wildlife Service), J. C. Hendee (U.S.D.A. Forest Service), T. J. Peterle (Ohio State University), L. A. Ryel (Michigan Department of Natural Resources, V. L. Wright (Louisiana State University).

resource (Davis 1964, Horvath 1974, Langford and Cocheba 1978, Bart et al. 1979). Such information could play a crucial role in measuring the effects of wildlife management actions and in attempting to optimize the benefits accruing to the public.

Although social surveys can play a vital role in wildlife management, there is an ever present danger that they may be misused by researchers unfamiliar with the techniques, underlying assumptions, and potential biases. This chapter offers advice on how to conduct mail and interview surveys by focusing on their main pitfalls. It is a cautionary note on the liberal use of social surveys in wildlife management which is intended to help decisionmakers and researchers use them more effectively.

STUDY METHODS AND DIFFICULTIES

Techniques

Humans can be studied using a broad range of techniques. Social studies can be conducted on secondary or primary data which are collected to solve a specific problem. Secondary data may consist of statistical records (government—private statistics, etc.), personal documents (diaries, letters, etc.) and media (newspapers, television, etc.). Primary data may be collected using observational methods, projective and other indirect methods or survey questionnaires. Each method has advantages and disadvantages which have been reviewed by several researchers (Selltiz et al. 1959, Parten 1966, Sudman 1967, Clark 1977). In their broadest sense social studies might also include "public involvement techniques" (Vindasius 1974) which utilize workshops, public hearings, day-to-day public contacts and special task forces to elicit public input in decisionmaking. Aney (1974) has reviewed the various survey methods commonly used by western states in estimating fish and wildlife harvests.

The questionnaire sample survey is the most widely used method in social studies. This technique relies heavily on personal answers to specific questions obtained from a representative group of a larger target population. It provides investigators with firsthand data that could only be obtained, if at all, by more time-consuming, costly, or even less accurate methods such as those described in the preceding paragraph. Questions may be administered by an interviewer or self-administered as in the case of mail surveys. Choosing the form of administration may be a difficult task and requires consideration of many factors. They include: available resources, time constraints, accessibility and characteristics of the target population, size and dispersion of the sample, complexity of the topic, the threatening nature of the subject matter, etc. Further details are provided in Table 23.1 which contrasts the interview and mail questionnaire methods. Although the table does not distinguish between face-to-face and telephone interviews, the choice entails advantages and limitations regarding sampling and other matters which are clearly beyond the scope of this chapter. Sometimes, distinguishing characteristics of mail and interview techniques may enable the researcher to integrate both methods in a complementary manner. For either the mail or interview survey to be used successfully, the potential respondent must (a) have some understanding of the terms of reference under which he is being asked to provide information, (b) have ready access, from memory or otherwise, to the data requested and (c) be motivated to report the information. The design of the questionnaire or interview form obviously plays a central role in these matters. An annotated bibliography prepared by Potter et al. (1972) contains many useful references on the design, construction and use of questionnaires. An excellent, comprehensive and concise discussion of the interview method and the central role of the interviewer has been prepared by Cannell and Kahn (1968). Invaluable advise on the conduct of mail and telephone surveys can be found in Dillman (1978).

Potential Sources of Errors

Depending on the complexity of the topic and the nature of the methods employed, sample surveys are potentially subject to important sources of error (Deming 1944, Filion 1979). These are summarized in Table 23.2 where they have been categorized as sampling and nonsampling errors. While it is not my intent to dwell on sampling and residual errors, they are mentioned for the sake of completeness.

The principles and techniques of sampling are well documented by Cochran (1977) and Kish (1965). Much of the theory is understood by statisticians but can be difficult to apply in specific situations. A more novel and practical approach to sampling may be found in Sudman (1976). Samples must be selected in a manner which makes them representative of the target population and must be large enough to yield results at an acceptable level of statistical precision. Only then may researchers draw inferences from survey results to the general population. The advantages of selecting a manageable sample rather than attempting to conduct a census of the target population are documented in Hawn and Ryel (1969). One sampling error which has received little attention concerns the identity of the respondent to mail questionnaires. By asking for age on the questionnaire and checking replies against official records, Wright (1978) found that 7% of the respondents to a game harvest questionnaire were not the individuals initially sampled. This is an indication of bias introduced when questionnaires are either delivered to the wrong address or handed to the wrong person at the correct address. The potential problems listed under "other errors" are worthy of attention in every social survey. Errors in coding, editing, and computer packages, as well as incorrect use of statistical methods and underlying assumptions, may distort results substantially.

Response and nonresponse biases and ways of dealing with them are the focus of this chapter. They are more difficult to measure than errors related to sampling and comparatively little is known about them. In many cases where a special effort has been made to study them, they have emerged as being considerably larger than sampling errors.

Table 23.1. Selected strengths and weaknesses of interview and questionnaire methods.

Study Concern	Method	
	Interview	Mail Questionnaire
Population types	–suitable for most types of human populations	–best suited for literate individuals and persons or groups that can be addressed by name
Sampling	–difficulty and cost of contacting greatly increases with size and dispersion of sample –potentially high control over who responds and possible consultation or any substitution –surveys conducted during the day may over-represent people outside labor force	–large dispersed samples can be used easily to increase accuracy –reaches people who are protected from solicitors and investigators and those temporarily away from home –requires addresses of individuals or households selected –may be difficult to verify that respondent is addressee
Complexity of topic	–suited for various question types including lengthy, complex and open-ended ones –filter questions and question sequence are more effective –suited for various types of data including complex nonfactual information	–most effective for short, simple and structured questions on factual data –open-ended and complex questions must be restricted to avoid overtaxing
Response rate and validity	–generally high response rate with callbacks –generally high item response –may be sensitive to socially desirable or threatening questions –sensitive to interviewer effects (tone of voice, language, sex, appearance, social class, etc.) –potential for probing and observing respondents in specific settings –high potential for variability among interviewers	–variable response rates. Generally highest for homogeneous or specialized populations. Response rate dependent on survey procedures used –some item nonresponse for boring or complex questions –greater potential for nonresponse bias –sensitive to questionnaire design –uniformity in wording, instructions and questions order
Administrative constraints	–stringent personnel needs (skilled interviewers, interviewer training and supervision) –complex organization for selecting, training and supervising interviewers –costs increase rapidly as size and dispersion of sample increase –completion time is variable and depends on sample size and number of field staff available	–requires fewer skilled personnel with some clerical support –insensitive to increasing geographical dispersion. Potentially least expensive method –requires at least 4–8 weeks from first mailing

NONRESPONSE BIAS

Definition and Examples

It is almost impossible to obtain replies from every person in a large sample irregardless of the data collection method used. Nonresponse usually results from the fact that persons refuse to answer questions or because they are not at home when an interviewer calls. It also may result from persons unable to respond due to illiteracy, illness, and other reasons, or from situations where a person cannot be located following a move, or from conditions whereby the interviewer cannot or does not want to reach the person selected. Nonresponse may bias survey results considerably. Assuming that the sample is representative of the population studied, it is likely that respondents, who are self-selected, will not represent the sample. If respondents do differ from nonrespondents, the best sample design, based on incomplete response, may result in population estimates which are inaccurate and misleading. Many sociological surveys have found that nonrespondents differ signifi-

Table 23.2. Potential sources of error in social surveys.

1) ERRORS RELATED TO SAMPLING	a) *Nonrepresentative sample* –results from improperly defined universe or –inaccessible universe or –lack or randomness in selection
	b) *Sampling error* –results from fact that only a portion of the universe is selected and is inherent in all sample surveys –is increased by inadequate sample size or design
2) NONSAMPLING ERRORS	a) *Nonresponse bias* –results from failure to get responses from designated individuals (not at homes, refusals, etc. . . .) –related to rate of nonresponse and extent of difference between respondents and nonrespondents –may be affected by kinds of canvass, response burden, sponsorship, question design, time frame, operational procedures, anonymity, nature of content (threatening or socially undesirable)
	b) *Response bias* –results from the difference between the true answer and the respondent's answer to a question –may be affected by kinds of canvass, interviewer, response burden, sponsorship, question design (clarity, wording, concepts), time frame, operational procedures, anonymity, nature of content (socially desirable or undesirable)
	c) *Other errors* –editing, coding, processing errors –tabulation and analysis errors –interpretation errors –changes in universe resulting from public knowledge of survey results –changes in universe before survey results are available

cantly from respondents in demographic and socioeconomic characteristics. Several researchers observed that nonresponse in various hunting surveys resulted in overestimates for harvests of game birds (Overton 1953, Sen 1971, Filion 1975, Wright 1978), upland game (Martinson and Whitesell 1964) and big game (MacDonald and Dillman 1968). Filion (1975) also found that nonrespondents were characterized by a higher proportion of inactive hunting permit buyers, a higher incidence of rural residents, less previous hunting experience, and young persons. He suggested that nonrespondents are not highly motivated to respond to questionnaires because they are less interested and involved in the topic of the survey and may in fact derive less satisfaction from hunting than respondents. The Advertising Research Foundation recommends an 80% or better response on mail surveys, which brings the rate of nonresponse in line with the rate of substitution in well-conducted personal interview studies (Erdos and Morgan 1970:144).

Solutions to Nonresponse Bias

In theory, the degree of nonresponse bias (B) is directly related to the proportion of nonrespondents (R_2) in the total sample and the extent of the difference between respondents (μ_1) and nonrespondents (μ_2) on the variables investigated (Cochran 1977). That is to say:

$$B = R_2\,(\mu_1 - \mu_2)$$

Minimizing nonresponse bias requires a reduction in the nonresponse proportion as well as information on the characteristics of nonrespondents. Over the years, researchers have developed several ways of dealing with the problem. Several methods have been briefly reviewed by Daniel (1975). Some methods lend themselves well to mail questionnaire surveys while others are most suited to interviewing. There are 2 general approaches to the problem of nonresponse. The researcher may attempt to maximize response or try to correct for bias by weighting. I recommend a combination of both methods. The various techniques are presented in order of personal preference.

MAXIMIZING RESPONSE

The most logical approach to nonresponse bias is to reduce the nonresponse proportion to a minimum. But this may not be an easy task for many researchers. Interview surveys usually have a higher response rate than mail surveys. However, interviewers not selected and trained meticulously usually have a higher refusal rate than those who are. Durbin and Stuart (1951) found the refusal rate for inexperienced amateur interviewers to be about 3 times that of experienced professional interviewers. Useful guidelines on the art of interviewing are provided in Sheatsley (1959), Atkinson (1971), and Institute for Social Research (1976). The most effective solutions to the problem of nonresponse in interview surveys are based on motivational models that treat the interview as a social process between the interviewer and interviewee (Cannell and Kahn 1968). The interview product is thus affected by the attributes of each person, their mutual social positions, the nature of the topic discussed and their mutual perceptions of each other. Interviewee motivation is increased when the interviewer successfully emphasizes the importance of factors such as the prestige of the research agency, interviewee's self-image as a dutiful citizen, loneliness or liking for the interviewer while playing down factors such as dislike of interview content, embarrassment at ignorance, and pressures from competing activities.

Questionnaires administered by mail suffer most frequently from a low rate of returns. This is due largely to the fact that investigators do not make complete use of the response induction techniques available to them. The most effective techniques were reviewed by Kanuk (and Berenson (1975), Linsky (1975), Heberlein and Baumgartner (1978), and Filion (1978a). The following is only a partial summary of the reviews. Mail questionnaires yield the highest returns when researchers develop a comprehensive survey plan which deals specifically with (a) respondent preparation and involvement, (b) design and construction of the questionnaire, and (c) use of follow-ups and other motivational aids. The work process throughout these phases promotes a meaningful relationship between the investigator and the sample members, develops a questionnaire that will appeal to the potential respondents, and carefully selects effective peripheral techniques to motivate recipients to respond.

The covering letter is one of several methods of preparing and involving the respondent. A covering letter always should be sent with the questionnaire. The purposes of the letter are to explain the nature of the survey, to request cooperation, and to convince the recipient that a response is truly needed. The letter should emphasize the utility of the research undertaken, the important role of the respondent, and the ease with which the questionnaire can be completed. It also should draw the reader's attention to such conveniences as a self-addressed, postage-paid return envelope. Letters should be brief, written in simple language, use relatively short sentences, be printed on letterhead paper, and signed by a person with a prestigious title or whose name is well known and respected.

Since the mail questionnaire must be its own salesman, its format, appearance, and overall attractiveness most definitely affect response. As a general rule, mail questionnaires not only should be as short as possible but also designed to appear short, simple to understand, and complete. A 1-page questionnaire containing logical, interdependent questions should generate highly meaningful answers and reduce nonresponse to individual questions to a minimum (Bauer and Meissner 1963). Response tends to be lower when a large amount of work is demanded of the respondent (Scott 1961, Filion 1976a). As a general rule, the questionnaire will be shorter and have a better design if the investigator has formulated clear research objectives and has a reasonable idea of how the data will be analyzed. Questions should be clearly separated and numbered to avoid overcrowding and confusion, and to ensure adequate space for answers. The print may be varied to emphasize important words, phrases and instructions. There should be a simple and standard method of answering the questions. The more objective and factual the information sought, the more highly structured the questionnaire format can be. Highly structured forms that list closed questions and offer fixed alternate answers such as the dichotomous "yes" or "no," multiple choice, or check lists usually can be completed by using a simple check mark. However, when using structured questionnaires, care must always be taken to offer full alternatives (Noelle-Neümann 1970). Closed, fixed alternative questions should be used when the possible replies are clear-cut, limited, and known by the researcher; otherwise they may bias replies. Structured forms tend to increase the efficiency of the questionnaire by speeding its completion and accelerating the analysis since editing, coding, and keypunching are simplified.

The attractiveness of the questionnaire should not be offset by its content. The questionnaire's heading should clearly define the subject under investigation and show the official backing of a sponsor, preferably one who is known and respected by the population sampled. In some cases, government sponsorship brings an advantage in the total response rate (Scott 1961). Brief and clear instructions must be given to help the addressee complete the form correctly. The sequence of the questions may affect the rate and quality of response. Several short, simple and preferably interesting questions should be asked first to encourage the respondent. Questions should flow from general to more specific items and show some logical interdependence. Simple vocabulary, clear and straightforward syntax, and a neutral style of wording are recommended. Format and content must be coordinated to achieve questionnaire attractiveness. The appeal of the questionnaire may be increased by using a central motivating theme, or motto, and a graphic symbol. Attractiveness may be increased by using quality paper of appropriate color, size, and style of print that is easy to read. Some of these aspects of questionnaire design are illustrated in Figs. 23.1 and 23.2.

Follow-ups are one of the most effective techniques used to increase response. Return envelopes, special postage, and monetary incentives also have been used successfully. Research conducted by the Canadian Wildlife Service (Filion 1974) indicated that the use of precontacts, follow-ups and registered mail had a significant effect on response rates in game harvest surveys. Follow-ups sent with another copy of the questionnaire were about twice as effective as follow-ups using a letter reminder only. Follow-ups sent by registered mail induced response rates that were almost twice as high as with first-class postage. The overall design of the questionnaire emerged as an important variable affecting the rate of returns. In an experiment, improvements in the

CONFIDENTIAL

CANADIAN WILDLIFE SERVICE

SURVEY OF
CANADA MIGRATORY GAME
BIRD PERMIT BUYERS

PURPOSE

Permit buyers and hunters are a very important part of Migratory Game Bird management. For this reason we need to know more about you, your needs, your likes and dislikes. Your answers to this questionnaire will help us design programs to maintain and improve your hunting enjoyment.

INSTRUCTIONS

Please answer and return the questionnaire as soon as possible. Most questions can be answered quickly by placing a simple check mark ☑ in the small boxes. The questionnaire has 5 parts: Please complete each part as well as you can. All answers are strictly confidential.

The heading emphasizes the confidential nature of the survey and identifies the sponsor and the topic. It summarizes the purpose of the study and gives brief instructions on questionnaire completion. It captures attention with the waterfowl symbol and provides a short motivational theme.

Fig. 23.1. Sample heading from a mail hunter questionnaire.

design of the Canada Migratory Game Bird Harvest Survey questionnaire increased the rate of returns by about 30%.

When used in combination, these techniques may achieve impressive total response rates. For example, Filion (1974) obtained an overall response rate of 84% in a Canadian Wildlife Service Migratory Game Bird Harvest Survey with the following methods: preseason contact of the sample, redesigned survey questionnaire, provision of a return envelope, 2 follow-ups of nonrespondents including another copy of the questionnaire, and use of registered mail in the final wave. In another survey conducted among Canada Migratory Game Bird Permit purchasers, a response rate of 92% was obtained from a 20-page bilingual questionnaire dealing with hunting activities and related sociological parameters (Filion 1978b). The survey used a carefully designed questionnaire, covering letters, prepaid return envelopes, and 3 follow-ups of nonrespondents. Follow-ups including another copy of the questionnaire and a return envelope were sent at 3-week intervals. Registered mail was used in the final mailing. A postcard reminder was sent 4 days after the initial mailing of the questionnaire; the response rate prior to the first follow-up was 52%.

High response rates do not necessarily imply added costs but definitely provide important benefits. For example, it does not cost more to administer a well-designed questionnaire than a poorly designed one. Postcard follow-ups are effective and inexpensive. Substantial increases in response may lead to savings due to reduced sample size without sacrificing precision. Follow-ups not only increase response but enable researchers to examine the presence, direction, and extent of nonresponse bias.

WEIGHTING TO CORRECT FOR NONRESPONSE BIAS

Correcting for nonresponse bias is a very difficult task since the information needed is, by definition, not available. There are 2 basic approaches to the problem. The first seeks to correct for bias using replies to follow-ups as a proxy for the characteristics of nonrespondents, while the other does not.

Weighting Using Follow-ups

Follow-ups enable the researcher to adjust survey data for nonresponse bias in either of 2 ways: extrapolation across successive mailing waves or simple weighting of responses to follow-ups. The method of extrapolating change observed in an estimated parameter value over successive cumulative response waves seems to be increasing in popularity. This technique is based on the assumption that replies to an initial questionnaire and to successive follow-ups of nonrespondents represent distinct categories forming a continuum of respondent types ranging from highly motivated to unmotivated individuals. Successive waves, it is assumed, probe deeper into the core of nonrespondents and the continuum is indicative of both the direction and extent of nonresponse bias. This method or a variant has been used or suggested by Hendricks (1949), Scott (1961), Sen (1971), Filion (1976b), and Armstrong and Overton (1977). Sen (1971) and Filion (1975) have obtained similar results by applying this technique to estimate the

A REDESIGNED QUESTIONS

3 SHOW ONE PROVINCE WHERE YOU DID **MOST** OF YOUR HUNTING FOR MIGRATORY GAME BIRDS THIS SEASON.

NFLD.	☐ 1	P.E.I.	☐ 2	N.S.	☐ 3
N.B.	☐ 4	QUE.	☐ 5	ONT.	☐ 6
MAN.	☐ 7	SASK.	☐ 8	ALTA.	☐ 9
B.C.	☐ 10	N.W.T.	☐ 11	YUKON	☐ 12

4 PRINT THE NAME OF THE TOWN (WITH A POST OFFICE) **NEAREST** THE PLACE WHERE YOU DID **MOST** OF YOUR HUNTING THIS SEASON. ☐

5 HOW FAR IS THE HUNTING PLACE FROM THAT TOWN ☐ MILES

6 SHOW THE DIRECTION OF THE HUNTING PLACE **FROM** THAT TOWN

NORTH	☐ 1	EAST	☐ 2	SOUTH	☐ 3	WEST	☐ 4
NORTH EAST	☐ 5	NORTH WEST	☐ 6	SOUTH EAST	☐ 7	SOUTH WEST	☐ 8

B PREVIOUS QUESTION DESIGN

5. Please circle the province or territory where you did most of your hunting for migratory birds this season.

Prière d'encercler le nom de la province ou du territoire où vous avez surtout chassé, cette saison, les oiseaux migrateurs.

Nfld. – *T.-N.*	01	Que. – *P.Q.*	05	Alta. – *Alb.*	09
P.E.I. – *Î.-P.-É.*	02	Ont.	06	B.C. – *C.-B.*	10
N.S. – *N.-É.*	03	Man.	07	N.W.T. – *T.N.-O.*	11
N.B. – *N.-B.*	04	Sask.	08	Yukon	12

6. Print Name of City, Town or Village (with Post Office) near place where most of your hunting was done, in rectangular box.

Inscrire en lettres moulées dans le rectangle le nom de la localité (Bureau de poste) la plus proche de l'endroit où vous avez chassé le plus.

Indicate with "X" in appropriate circle showing direction from town to place where most of your hunting was done.

Indiquer par un "X" dans le cercle approprié dans quelle direction se trouve par rapport à la localité, l'endroit où vous avez chassé le plus.

Give the distance in miles (Approx.) from town nearest to place where most of your hunting was done.

Donner approximativement, en milles, la distance entre la localité et l'endroit où vous avez chassé le plus.

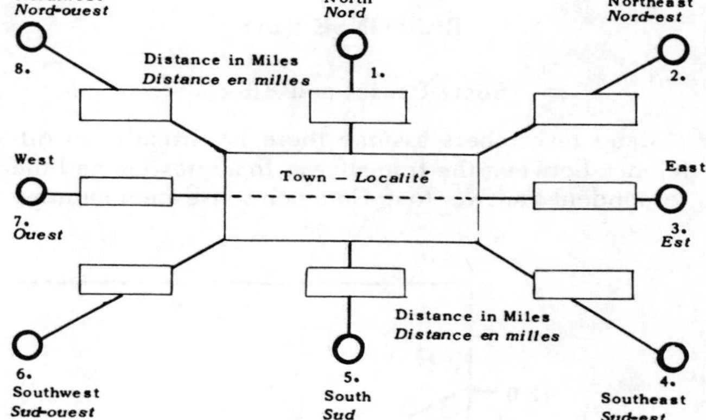

The redesigned version (A) makes use of a standard answering procedure and places the French questions on the back side to create the illusion of a shorter questionnaire. Question 6 in the previous design (B) has been subdivided into 3 questions to simplify understanding and completion.

Fig. 23.2. Redesigned questions on place of hunting.

direction and extent of nonresponse bias in game harvest surveys using different regression models. Their conclusions are compatible with the direction of bias observed by others on harvest surveys (Overton 1953, Martinson and Whitesell 1964, MacDonald and Dillman 1968, Wright 1978). The linear regression method is illustrated in Fig. 23.3. It has the advantages of being inexpensive, requires no data from other sources, and utilizes the variables with which the study is concerned. One danger in extrapolation is that "hard core" nonrespondents may differ from late respondents and upset observed trends. Results of this technique usually will be the most valid when based on data from at least 3 mailing waves and a total response rate exceeding 60%.

Another approach to the treatment of nonresponse is to assume that nonrespondents have the same characteristics as those who respond to follow-up questionnaires. This method differs from the extrapolation technique since it is not concerned with the trend over successive waves. Consequently, estimates of a population parameter (μ) are obtained by combining a value ($\bar{y}_1$) based on respondents (n) to the first wave in a sample (N) with the value ($\bar{y}_2$) based on respondents to the follow-up and weighting the latter value to represent all nonrespondents (N-n). That is to say:

$$\mu = \frac{n\bar{y}_1 + (N-n)\bar{y}_2}{N}$$

The Hansen and Hurwitz (1946) method is based on this approach. It utilizes a mail questionnaire to collect data in the first wave and interviewers to follow up a subsample of nonrespondents in the second wave. El-Badry (1956) has extended the technique to maximize the response rate in the mail questionnaire phase before resorting to personal interviews. Bartholomew's (1961) two-call technique makes use of interviewers in both the initial questioning and follow-up stages.

By simply weighting responses to a follow-up, nonresponse remains a potential problem if the nonresponse proportion is quite large and no attempt is made to examine possible trends in characteristics over successive waves. Furthermore, the variance will be increased if the number of respondents to the follow-up is a relatively small portion of the nonrespondents. The use of 2 different data collection techniques (i.e., mail questionnaires and personal interviews) may introduce an additional bias in the results.

Weighting Without Follow-ups

The following techniques do not require the use of any data on nonrespondents. They include the "disproportionate returns" method (U.S. Bureau of Census 1967, Fuller 1974), the Kish-Hess (1959) replacement technique, the Politz and Simmons (1949) probability technique for "not at homes" and the "time trends" (Scott 1961) method. In view of the assumptions on which they are based, these techniques may not be very effective in reducing nonresponse bias especially when the response rate is small.

RESPONSE BIAS

Some Causes and Effects

Many researchers assume there is virtually no difference between the true answer to a question and the respondent's answer to it. Common sense and mounting evidence suggest that this assumption is at best questionable. For example, most postseason game hunting surveys seem to yield exaggerated harvest estimates. Questioning people is a social process and the resulting information is necessarily affected by the respondent's perceptions of interviewers or survey sponsors and the nature of questions asked. Many factors may place excessive demands on the respondent's understanding of survey questions, his privacy and memory, and contribute to invalid responses. They include the method of canvassing, the words, concepts and time frames, the threatening nature of questions, and the amount of work involved in responding. The interview technique may be very sensitive to this type of bias. A review of some of the biases, risks, and costs of the interviewer method is found in Cannell and Kahn (1968). One of the difficulties in the telephone or personal interview is that the respondent is usually not given much time to recollect accurately before answering a question. Another problem relates to the respondent's unwillingness to report information. Most respondents have a need to maintain self-esteem and to present an image of consistency and worthiness. For example, research by MacDonald and Dillman (1968) suggested that "prestige bias" in harvest surveys results in unsuccessful hunters reporting being successful while other hunters who kill antlerless deer report killing an adult buck. Most respondents need to be perceived by the interviewer as a person who does not violate important social norms. The use of direct versus indirect questions to study the nature and extent

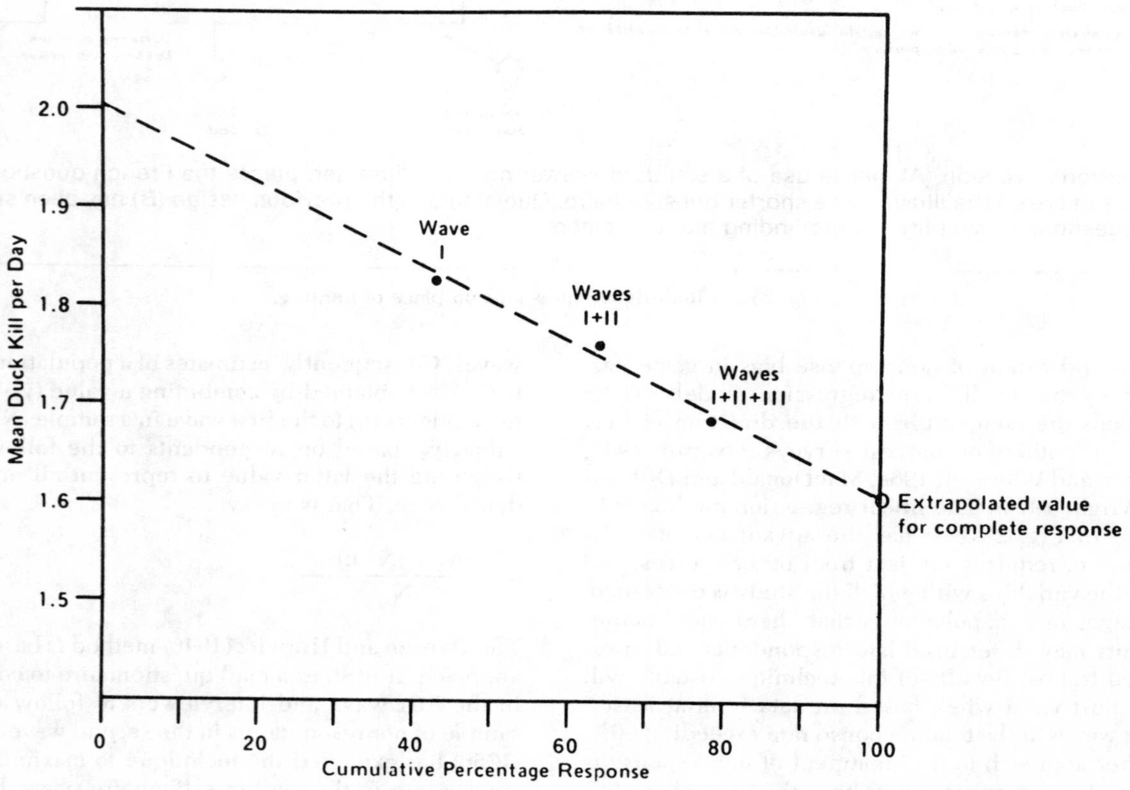

Fig. 23.3. **Illustration of linear regression method for exploring and correcting for nonresponse bias using data from 3 cumulative mailing waves.**

of game law violations would likely yield very different results. For example, asking a hunter whether he had violated certain laws would probably reveal a lower incidence of violations than if the hunter was asked if he knew violators or if he was of the opinion that laws were being violated by hunters. Also, whether or not the anonymity of the respondent was protected would very likely affect responses to such questions. Some response bias may be explained in terms of interviewer-interviewee characteristics and their interaction. Several studies have shown a direct relationship between the interviewers' attitudes and the information they reported obtaining from respondents. Socio-economic, cultural, and demographic characteristics are a source of many attitudes and behavior and affect the interviewer-interviewee relationship by providing cues to each participant about the other.

Research undertaken by Sudman and Bradburn (1974) indicated that task, time, and memory factors as well as respondent and interviewer characteristics may affect responses to social surveys. The effect of time lapse, salience, and social desirability on survey responses was examined by Cannell et al. (1977). They drew the following conclusions: (a) as the time between the event and questioning increased, there was increased underreporting of information about that event, (b) events which were important to the respondent were reported more completely and accurately than those of less importance, and (c) reporting of an event was likely to be distorted in a socially desirable direction. The following review and discussion deals primarily with the problems of recall, question wording, and response burden.

Recall Bias

THE NATURE OF THE RECALL PROBLEM

Researchers always must be concerned about the respondent's ability to recall accurately if an event happened, and its frequency, time and place. Some research in experimental psychology indicates an inverse relationship between an individual's ability to retain information and the time elapsed since the occurrence of the event (Hilgard and Atkinson 1967). This relationship generally resembles an exponential function in which the ability to recall decreases most rapidly during the initial units of time elapsed. The nature of forgetting also may be influenced by the individual's motivation or interest in the event, the individual's emotions and perceptions during the event, and the frequency with which he talks about it or utilizes the information.

Neter and Waksberg (1964) examined the accuracy in recall of expenditure data in household interviews over a period of time which varied from 1 to 3 months. Increasing the recall period resulted in decreasing the ability of individuals to recall the number of expenditures. The problem was most serious for small expenditures and resulted in a net underestimate of the frequency of expenditures. They also found a tendency for individuals to report events at a time which differed from the time when the event actually occurred (telescoping effect). The telescoping effect was forward in time and highest for large expenditures. Forward telescoping can bias responses in 2 ways: (1) for a specific time interval respondents may tend to report events closer to the time of questioning than in reality (internal forward telescoping); and (2) respondents may tend to report events which actually happened outside the specific time period (external forward telescoping). There is evidence that game hunting surveys, for example, are subject to internal forward telescoping that results in reported harvests being more evenly distributed throughout the season than actually occur.

THE CASE OF GAME HARVEST SURVEYS

Example of Recall Bias

In the last 2 decades there have been several attempts to assess the nature and extent of recall bias in hunter surveys. The classic method has been to interview sportsmen leaving a specific hunting area using bag check stations to register their harvest and to question them at a later time to determine how accurately they could recall the event.

One of the best-known studies on response errors in postseason hunting surveys was conducted by Atwood (1956). He reported that survey responses of waterfowl hunters differed from bag checks by as much as 168%. Kills reported in postseason surveys were generally higher, had a longer seasonal distribution, and showed more hunters in upper kill intervals than kills observed at bag-check stations. Postseason survey kills were frequently reported as multiples of the daily bag limit and tended to be rounded to the nearest 0 or 5. He attributed these response errors to pride, prestige, and memory failure of waterfowl hunters.

The work of Atwood (1956) has been replicated by Hayne (1964) and Wright (1978). Wright's findings were similar to Atwood's. He found harvests reported in postseason survey data to be more than twice that observed in check stations. His findings were similar to Atwood's with respect to kill intervals and multiples of daily bag limits. Survey data on the number of waterfowl hunting trips were higher than the field data by as much as 30%. Very special care was taken by Hayne (1964) to exclude from the study the effect of any misunderstanding the respondent might have over the precise geographic area of reference. His observations differed somewhat from the above. He found that bias arose from reports from about 25% of the respondents. This resulted in waterfowl harvest estimates which ranged from 11–57% higher than the field records. He also found evidence of some slight internal forward telescoping in the postseason survey responses. Results from other studies similar to Atwood's generally support the direction of the above findings. Sen (1971) found waterfowl survey kills to range from 16–80% higher than bag-check data. Martinson and Whitesell (1964) found survey data on upland game harvests to be as much as 98% higher and trip data to be 19% higher than field records showed. Data collected by MacDonald and Dillman (1968) on big game hunting show deer harvest survey estimates to be about 9% higher than field data.

A Word of Caution

The reader should be cautioned against accepting the above special survey results at face value. The results are almost certainly affected by the methods employed in testing for recall bias. The time elapsed between the bag-check phase and the survey phase varied from study to study, and none of the studies attempted to examine the effect of variable time intervals on ability to recall. None of these studies indicates the exact question wording used in both the bag check phase and the questionnaire survey phase. A major part of the observed bias may be explained by the way in which questions were worded. Atwood (1956) attributed a substantial amount of bias to pride and prestige. However, wording in his questionnaire covering letter suggests that not killing any waterfowl may be interpreted as socially undesirable and may have contributed to the extent of the bias he observed: "If you were one of the *unlucky ones* who hunted but killed no birds, please fill out the forms anyway . . . " (Atwood 1956:2). Also, the way in which his questions were worded may have resulted in at least some hunters reporting kills originating outside the specific areas under study. The wording used by Wright (1978:252) may also have inflated response bias. The wording of the question on recreational hunting days is of a personal nature: "How many days did *you* hunt waterfowl?" However, the questions on waterfowl harvests are not as personal and may have been interpreted as intended to measure party kills: "Total ducks killed and retrieved."

There are additional difficulties readers must be cautioned against before generalizing beyond the response bias studies reviewed. They include the nature of the sample questioned, the particular hunting area, the time specific nature of the questions asked, and the use of at least 2 different data collection methods in each study.

The information from the above studies refer, first and foremost, to a sample of hunters using a restricted class of public hunting areas. Hayne (1964:22) questioned whether information obtained from such studies can be applied beyond the particular areas studied: " . . . the areas chosen cannot realistically be considered a random sample, either of all public hunting areas, or much less, of all areas where there is waterfowl hunting. Nor can the patrons in these study areas be viewed as a good sample of all waterfowl hunters." The fact that the hunter is asked about his hunting trips and harvests on only a part of his potential hunting season and on only a part of his potential hunting area may have confused respondents. It seems reasonable to expect hunter replies to such site and time specific questions to be biased upwards to some degree by a telescoping effect or a transfer of information from the total hunting area into a potentially smaller one. The substantial difference in the magnitude of the bias reported between Atwood (1956) and Hayne (1964) is likely explained by Hayne's special follow-ups of respondents and his rejection of some returns to eliminate the effect of misunderstanding on the part of the hunter regarding the exact area of reference.

One final difficulty in evaluating the validity of survey data concerns the different methods employed within each study. The bag-check data were collected by relatively inexperienced interviewers while the postseason data were usually collected by mail questionnaires. It usually has been assumed that the bag-check data were accurate. There is no way of knowing what biases may have been introduced by untrained interviewers or the manner in which questions were asked. In some cases hunters may have deliberately reported lower kills to the interviewers because they had personally exceeded daily bag limits. In other cases hunters may have arbitrarily divided the total bag evenly among themselves. Wright (1978:259) goes as far as saying "the value obtained at the check station cannot be considered the true value for that particular hunter." In some cases the mail questionnaire data may in fact be closer to the true value than the bag-check data.

I know of only 1 survey in which most of the above-mentioned difficulties in response validity studies were partly or completely controlled. Sen (1973) used a single survey method (the mail questionnaire) to study recall bias among a representative sample of about 1600 Canada Migratory Game Bird Hunting Permit buyers. One half of the sample received a single postseason questionnaire on hunting activity during the 4-month hunting season while the other half received 2 questionnaires—a midseason questionnaire dealing with activity during September and October only and a postseason schedule dealing with November and December only. This design is immune to potential interview bias and confusion due to the site and time specific nature of previous studies on the subject. The question wording was identical in all questionnaires and emphasized the personal nature of the question: "Show the number of game birds *you* killed and retrieved by month this season." The design also minimized the effect of external telescoping by covering the entire hunting season while enabling the researcher to study the effect of internal telescoping. The results indicate that lengthening the recall period from 2, 2-month periods to a single 4-month period did result in higher estimates of waterfowl harvests and hunting days. However, unlike previous studies the increase in harvest was only 13% and was not statistically significant ($P<0.05$). Days hunted increased significantly by 46%. A slight internal forward telescoping effect was also detected.

Bias Due to Questionnaire Design

GENERAL EXAMPLES

Responses to questions may be affected by the design of the questionnaire, the manner in which questions are worded, and the amount of effort involved in responding. Examples of the potential effect of some of these factors were mentioned above. Results from a few studies dealing specifically with social survey methodology further support this claim. Belson and Duncan (1962) reported that close-ended "checklist" type questions yielded a much higher estimation of participation in an event than open-response questions. Guest (1962) found that attitude studies using 4 choice answers to indicate agreement or disagreement produced results which were significantly different from those using 2 choice answers. Belson (1966) observed that reversing the presentation order of verbal rating scales resulted in a significant effect on the degree of favorableness reported.

EFFECT OF WORDING AND BURDEN

Special studies dealing with the effect of questionnaire design on wildlife-related issues are very sparse. Langford and Cocheba (1978) acknowledged the importance of proper question wording in surveys dealing with the problem of wildlife valuation. Meyer (1975) conducted a special study to determine the relationship among 4 ways of wording questions dealing with recreation and preservation values associated with salmon in British Columbia. He found the question, "What would I have to pay you?" yielded an economic value 18 times higher than another which asked, "What would you pay?" Less traditional questions worded either as a "community decision" or as judicial "award of damages" resulted in intermediate estimates.

Filion (1976a) conducted a special study to assess the effect of changes in migratory game bird harvest mail questionnaires on survey estimates among a stratified sample of 4,200 hunting permit buyers in eastern and western Canada. He designed several different questionnaires in which the definitions of hunting days and migratory game bird harvests were systematically varied, and the amount of effort required to respond to the schedule was systematically increased. Estimates of migratory game bird hunting days were derived using 3 different definitions as shown in part A of Table 23.3. Estimates of migratory game bird harvests were derived using 2 different definitions as shown in part B. The amount of effort required to complete the questionnaire was defined as response burden. Three levels of response burden were identified as shown in part C.

The analysis was based on a response rate of 86% which did not vary significantly among the questionnaires tested. The estimates of total migratory game bird hunting days based on definition 1 exceeded those based on definitions 2 or 3 by as much as 17%. Estimates of migratory game birds harvested based on definition 4 exceeded those based on definition 5 by as much as 34%. Questionnaires with a low level of response burden yielded estimates of hunting days and harvests

Table 23.3. Differences studied in special questionnaire survey.

A. *Differences in the definition of recreational hunting days*

1)–Number of different days on which you hunted ducks
–Number of different days on which you hunted geese
–Number of different days on which you hunted other migratory game birds

2)–Number of different days on which you hunted ducks and geese
–Number of different days on which you hunted other migratory game birds

3)–Number of different days on which you hunted migratory game birds

B. *Differences in the definition of migratory game birds bagged*

4) Number of migratory game birds you bagged:

sea ducks	other ducks	Canada geese	other geese	other M.G.B.

5) Number of migratory game birds you bagged:

ducks	geese	other M.G.B.

C. *Differences in response burden*

	Burden level	*Description*
6)	low	1-page questionnaire having optional duck calendar and asking for the 1 place where most hunting occurred.
7)	medium	1–2-page questionnaire with optional duck and goose calendars and requesting up to 3 hunting places.
8)	high	1-page matrix-type questionnaire requesting up to 14 hunting places with mandatory migratory game bird calendar for 8 species.

which were as much as 128% and 49% higher, respectively, than schedules with a high response burden. Questionnaires with the highest response burden also yielded a lower estimate of active hunters (47% versus 58%), produced the highest proportion of unusable returns (8% versus 1%), and showed the potentially lowest response rate (46% versus 55% after only 2 mailing waves). These findings indicate that the choice of word definitions in questionnaires may result in serious over- or under-reporting about the subject of inquiry. For example, combining narrow hunting day categories that may not be mutually exclusive into a broader category results in a lower and probably more realistic estimate of total days of recreation. On the other hand, combining narrow bird species categories (e.g., sea ducks and other ducks) into broader species categories (e.g., ducks) results in harvest estimates which are significantly higher. Wording emerges as an important cognitive factor in question formulation and deserves further attention from researchers. The depressing effect on reported hunting involvement caused by an increase in response burden suggests that respondents who would normally report information that is readily accessible with some accuracy, may not work hard enough to retrieve information from memory and to structure their responses in time and space as tasks become more demanding. These findings should serve to caution wildlife managers contemplating changes in the design of questionnaires used in recurring annual surveys. Such changes may affect year-to-year comparisons and jeopardize long-term management efforts.

Dealing with Response Bias

SOLUTIONS TO RECALL BIAS

Two mathematical techniques have been proposed to adjust for recall bias in post-season game harvest surveys. The method proposed by Atwood (1956) consists of plotting the harvest data on semi-logarithmic paper and hand fitting a smooth curve from which corrected means are derived for days hunted and birds bagged. All data which are a multiple of the daily bag limit or a multiple of 5 are excluded and the curve must approximate a specific shape. Wright's (1978) method assumes that the true seasonal bag distribution is continuously decreasing in approximately a geometric form. It consists of fitting the mid-points of intervals within which hunters are likely to round off when guessing on the harvest estimate with a geometric curve based on a specific formula. Although Wright's method is more rigorous than Atwood's, both techniques have limitations and should be used with caution. Atwood's method may result in the regrettable loss of more than half of the data (Wright 1978:260) and may be subject to considerable variability depending on the person fitting the curve. Wright's method should yield consistent results in view of its explicit assumption, but he reports that the overall reduction in mean and variance of the fitted curve explains only 30% of the observed response bias. If one assumes that the methods employed by Wright overestimated the true recall bias, it is possible that his correction technique is more effective than he indicates. MacDonald and Dillman (1968) proposed a linear correction technique for response bias in big-game hunting surveys. Although they do not describe the method in detail, it appears to be suited best for situations when the response bias is linear and relatively low, and the rate of successful hunters approaches 50%. Consequently, it may not be very useful in waterfowl harvest surveys.

It may be premature to utilize any of the above correction techniques on postseason game harvest survey data for several reasons. The extent of the bias reported in various studies appears to depend on (a) the possible misunderstanding the respondents have of the questions asked, (b) the methodology used to measure errors, and (c) the type of hunting surveyed.

More stringent research is required on the topic. An important contribution to this field would be a replication of the approach developed by Sen (1973) with appropriate controls over varying time intervals and game species. Experimentation with shorter recall intervals, panels, or even the diary method might yield some effective solutions. The recall problem might be alleviated by providing a sequence of questions that helps the respondent reconstruct the past and by wording questions that require recognition rather than recall of the event. For example, questions concerning hunting as a comprehensive recreational experience rather than questions segmenting the experience and thereby restricting reports to certain species and specific hunting areas might yield lower estimates of activity. Further insights regarding the characteristics of specific groups of hunters are needed and should consider age, sex, region, income, and ethnic response differences in detail.

SOLUTIONS TO WORDING ERRORS, RESPONSE BURDEN, AND INTERVIEW BIAS

I know of no mathematical formulae to correct for errors created by inappropriate wording, unreasonable burden placed on respondents, or interviewer bias. As a general rule, questions should be formulated in a language that conforms to the vocabulary and syntax of the target population. They must be phrased clearly, using simple and objective words in a consistent manner. They should be sequenced to arouse interest and facilitate recall. Questions should be short, yet contain enough detail to help the respondents structure accurate responses without imposing an unreasonable amount of burden. Additional guidelines may be found in Payne (1951), Selltiz et al. (1959), Oppenheim (1966), Parten (1966), Cannell and Kahn (1968), Dillman (1978), and Filion (1978a). Pretesting of questionnaires, special experimental studies, knowledge of the current literature on the merits and pitfalls of social survey techniques, a basic understanding of human nature, and good common sense are absolutely essential in minimizing these problems. For the results of the pretest to be meaningful, pretesting should be conducted among persons who are as similar as possible to the target population. The research reviewed on these matters indicates that errors due to wording and burden may at times be far greater than we would normally expect. Interviewer bias can be reduced by selecting interviewers who will minimize undesirable interactions with respondents, by training them in techniques that maximize respondent motivation, and devising procedures that minimize the amount of interviewer improvisation. It is vital for anyone contemplating surveys of humans in wildlife management to seek professional advice from experts in social survey research.

DISCUSSION AND CONCLUSIONS

Social studies play an important role in helping wildlife managers gain a better understanding of people when managing the resource. The complexities, assumptions, and potential sources of errors are such that great care must be exercised when conducting questionnaire sample surveys. A good understanding of these difficulties and expert advice are necessary to obtain precise and valid results. The cautionary notes and procedural guidelines presented in this chapter are intended to enlighten current and future managers contemplating the use of this promising tool. I have devoted more attention to the mail questionnaire than to the interview method because I believe it is potentially the most useful, and inexpensive technique, and one which is often misunderstood and misused. Since interview surveys are more complex and subject to additional biases which may be very difficult to control, it is advisable to leave this technique to experts in the field.

The current abundance of social studies in wildlife management is not typified always by an adequate concern for the quality of data. Social survey research is founded on 2 major premises. It assumes that responses to questions are (a) valid and (b) that human responses are quantifiable and amenable to statistical analysis. Questionnaire surveys also are subject to various potentially serious errors summarized in Table 23.2. Investigators must seek study designs, survey methodologies, and statistical procedures that are compatible with the premises and least sensitive to potential errors.

This chapter has focused on response and nonresponse biases because there is relatively little known about their nature, extent, and ways of dealing with them. Although some wildlife studies have suggested that response bias may be more serious than nonresponse bias, I do not believe the methods employed in the studies enabled the investigators to draw firm conclusions. Furthermore, the extent of the bias due to nonresponse is probably related to the subject matter and complexity of the questionnaire. Based on the studies reviewed, nonrespondents are characterized by a lower level of interest and involvement in the subject investigated. This could be used as a point of departure for building a sociological theory of nonrespondents.

Current research indicates that response bias is affected by temporal, salience and social desirability factors, wording of questions, and amount of burden involved in responding. Although sociological findings generally indicate that an increase in time between the event and questioning results in underreporting, the reverse trend has been observed in game harvest surveys. This may be accounted for partly by the importance of recreational hunting in the respondent's life and the prestige associated with harvesting game. In view of the complexity of the recall process and the influence of telescoping and transfer effects, some hunters (particularly those involved in several types of hunting and those involved in party hunting) report total hunting activity rather than species related activity and party kills rather than personal harvests. Although question wording may bias responses upwards or downwards, an increase in response burden likely will depress reported involvement.

Several partial solutions have been proposed to the problems in surveys of humans. The most effective ones, in my opinion, are those that are people-oriented and of human scale. Whenever possible, nonresponse bias should be minimized by motivating people to respond in the first place. Only then should weighting procedures be considered. Response bias may be reduced by using shorter recall intervals and by questioning respondents in a comprehensive manner (in the context of the total event and its component parts) rather than on fragments of the event at distant points in time. Increased knowledge of the target population, appropriate question wording, and minimum response burden are necessary. Pretesting of survey instruments and more experimental research are invaluable in this area.

It should be encouraging for wildlife managers to note that decisions which have been based on game harvest survey estimates that are biased upwards have generally favored the preservation of species. This, however, may not be the case for other variables in wildlife related social studies. Decisions based upon inaccurate or invalid information seldom result in sound management practices. Further research on the topic should examine the "total" survey error which is comprised of elements shown in Table 23.2. Hopefully, we will find that errors in well-executed surveys are small, tend to cancel each other, and result in data which are sufficiently accurate for our needs. Another encouraging point is that ongoing surveys that are known to be consistently biased may still provide excellent indicators of trends in the variables under study. For example, obtaining accurate trend data in game harvests over the years may be as important for long-term management of game populations as accurate estimates of annual harvests.

An alternative to the problems that I have discussed is to avoid using questionnaire sample surveys where there are effective alternates. There are almost certainly situations where this technique is neither the best nor only method available to provide needed information. The alternative methods enumerated previously under "techniques" should at least be considered before undertaking surveys. There may be times when sampling and related errors may be avoided by conducting a census of the target population; such might be the case in a small localized study. In some situations participant or nonparticipant observational methods may be used although extrapolation to a larger target population may not be as objective as properly designed sample surveys. The participant observational technique, for example, may be very effective when questions are of an open-ended exploratory nature and there is a general lack of information available on the topic investigated. Selection of the most desirable research strategy should be guided by factors such as the type of questions being asked, the research design being adopted, the characteristics of the target population, and the advantages and limitations of the various data gathering techniques available.

Chapter Twenty-Four

Wildlife Program Planning

KENNETH H. ANDERSON

Director, Planning and Coordination Division
Maine Department of Inland Fisheries and Wildlife
Augusta, Maine

FREDERICK B. HURLEY, JR.

Wildlife Resource Planner
Maine Department of Inland Fisheries and Wildlife
Augusta, Maine

INTRODUCTION

In recent years, there has been a conscious effort to increase the scope and emphasis of fish and wildlife program planning in response to the ever increasing loss of habitat, fluctuating populations, and restricted budgets. The California Department of Fish and Game was one of the first fish and wildlife agencies to develop and promote a comprehensive fish, wildlife, and marine planning process, and many agencies have patterned their planning activities after the California approach. Today, program planning is actively contributing to the development and maintenance of comprehensive fish and wildlife conservation efforts ranging from single species to complete fish and wildlife management programs.

However, "planning" is not new to the fish and wildlife management profession. It is little more than the thought and decisionmaking process utilized to define the "who, what, when, where, why and hows" for any activity we are about to undertake (Fig. 24.1). Most fish and wildlife managers accept the necessity for "planning" at the project level, but seem reluctant to apply the same thought process to the development of state-wide, national, or continental wildlife management plans. The considerations remain the same; but the "who, what, when, where, why, and hows" are simply broadened in scope to apply to more than one species, the entire jurisdiction of the agency, and all administrative subdivisions of an agency supporting the management of wildlife resources.

Answers to the "who, what, when, where, why, and hows" must be based on an assessment of present and future species abundance and distribution, resource use (the act of taking or observing wildlife), use opportunity (the opportunity to take or observe wildlife), supply (the number of animals which are available for harvest or observation), and demand (the public's desire to harvest or observe wildlife at a given success rate). This assessment provides the basis for selecting management goals and objectives which lead to the design and selection of specific jobs based upon cost-need and effectiveness considerations. The final phase of the process includes jobs scheduling, implementation, and evaluation.

As stated previously, planning is not new. What is new is the concept that agency program planning must be comprehensive in nature if the greatest benefits from planning are to be achieved. To accomplish this, planning must begin at the broad agency level with the development of specific management goals and objectives and proceed to the design and implementation of specific activities to support the selected goals and objectives. This requires that planning be done along functional rather than administrative lines (Fig. 24.2). Fisheries and wildlife agencies have only 2 basic functions: to provide for the management and use of the fishery and wildlife resources. In the past, most fish and wildlife agencies developed their agency program by melding programs independently developed by each of their administrative subdivisions. These programs were often designed to solve problems, real or imaginary, as identified by the individual administrative units of the

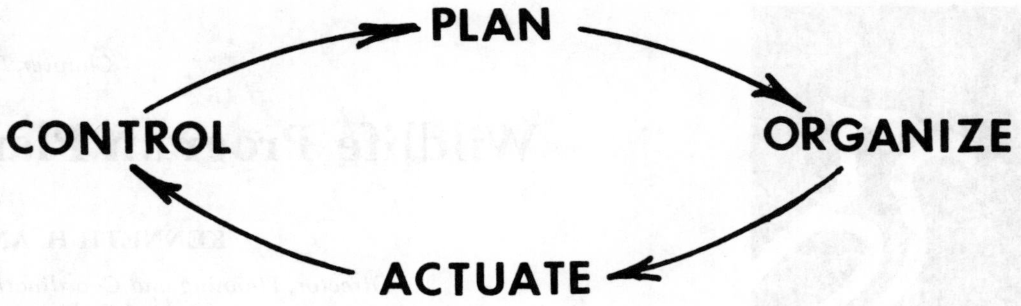

Fig. 24.1. Planning is the initial step in the management process.

agency. This fragmented approach to program development leads to uncoordinated management efforts, ineffective use of available funds and manpower, competition for position in the pecking order, and funding based upon individual desires and not the real problem needs of the agency.

Functional Lines	Administrative Lines
Wildlife Conservation	Wildlife Management
Fish Conservation	Wildlife Research
	Information & Education
	Law Enforcement
	Hatchery
	Engineering
	Land Acquisition
	Administration
	Legal Services

Fig. 24.2. Fish and wildlife program planning is structured along functional lines rather than administrative lines.

The best agency program will contain the mix of specific jobs which provide the most effective use of available materials and manpower in solving the problems interfering with selected management goals and objectives. To accomplish this a departmental program must be developed with fisheries and wildlife management goals and objectives as the focal point. The activities of each administrative division of the agency are then designed to focus on problems affecting selected agency goals and objectives in the most cost-effective manner possible. Before this can be accomplished, species assessments must be developed, problems identified, and alternative jobs discussed, reviewed and discussed again—not just within the biological divisions, but within and among *all* of the divisions in the agency with the hope that this will result in a better understanding of the contribution each division must make to the total effort (Fig. 24.3).

This concept is new and admittedly an idealistic approach. Nevertheless, it must be done if the resources are to be managed in the most cost-effective manner—a necessity that has been created by the times. This will not be accomplished overnight, since many of the old ways are not easily discarded. This philosophy, the philosophy of the development of an agency rather than a divisional program, is the basis for the discussion which follows.

In summary, agency program planning endeavors are bringing together, into a single program development effort, the many forces which have traditionally influenced fish and wildlife related programs. Success of such a task requires a strong commitment to an orderly assessment, discussion, and decisionmaking process. The end product is the implementation of programs designed to focus on the most pressing problems at hand, thus providing for the greatest benefit for each dollar of expenditure.

We wish to point out that there are many aspects of wildlife resource planning ranging from management plans for a unit of forest or wetland to the interdisciplinary approach to ecosystems management which have not been discussed in this chapter. In addition, no detailed discussions of the numerous analytical tools such as computer software packages for modeling, cost-benefit analysis, and mapping of remote sensing information are presented. Discussion of these techniques or methodologies was purposely omitted in this chapter in order to direct emphasis to the process of agency program development: an area which has been frequently overlooked in the past.

PREPLANNING

If there is one prerequisite for planning, it is total commitment: a commitment which must be expressed forcefully in thought, work, and action by the chief administrator. Less will only result in a paper plan—a shelved plan—nice to look at for a while and great to gather dust when the newness is gone. Without a total commitment from the top administrator, the effort will result in a hot-and-cold approach and do nothing more than confuse and frustrate the participants and fuel the fires of skeptics and status quo advocates.

Once a commitment to planning is made, the process begins with the formulation of a "plan for planning." This describes exactly what the planning process will include and how it will be done. Exactly how a plan will be developed depends on what the plan is for, what needs to be assessed, who will ultimately be affected by the implementation of the plan, and the interests that will have to be integrated into the planning process if it is to be successful (Fig. 24.4). The latter consideration is

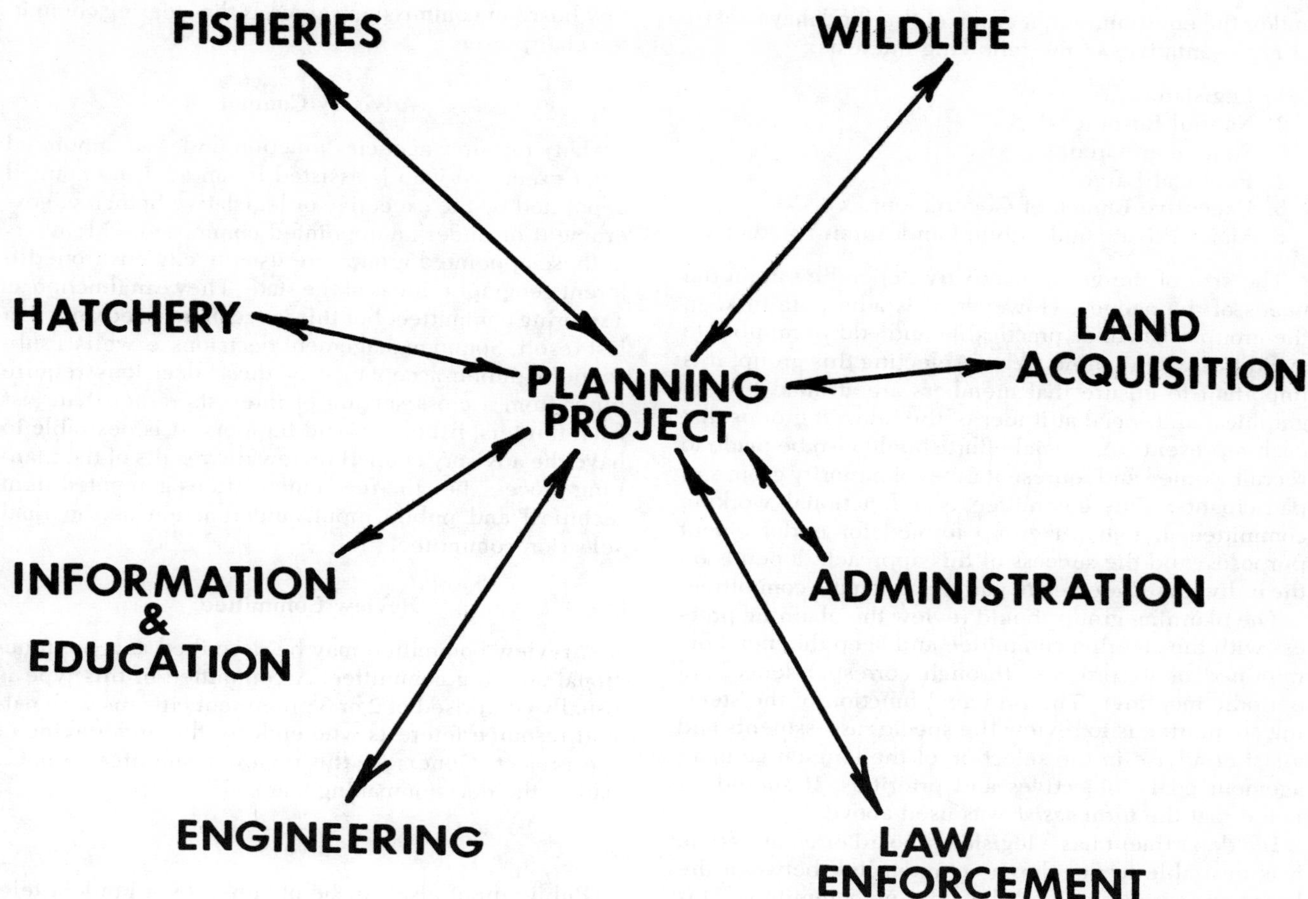

Fig. 24.3. **Comprehensive planning must consider all aspects of fish and wildlife management.**

frequently overlooked, and is probably the principal reason many plans never become operational.

Before a planning process can be designed, however, several questions must be answered. First, the scope of the planning effort must be clearly defined. A review of a public agency's enabling legislation is the initial reference which should be considered. The latter establishes the overall responsibilities of an agency and the extent of the responsibilities determines the overall scope of planning efforts. Secondly, the duration of the planning period must be defined. Many states have adopted a comprehensive planning approach with 15-year projections, 5-year programs, and 3-year updates. Thirdly, the question of who will do the planning must be resolved. Traditionally, this was an easy question to answer, since most planning has been done at the project level. Comprehensive agency program development (program planning), however, requires an expansion of the thought process to include the summarization, assessment, and evaluation of many interrelated factors, and the integration of technical, institutional, social, political, and economic considerations into a sound decisionmaking process. Comprehensive planning can be most efficiently and effectively handled by an interdisciplinary planning group which works hand in hand with individual project personnel, agency administrators, and the public. A planning group of this nature can be composed of either existing members of an agency, consultants, or a combination of both. In most cases, fish and wildlife departments are utilizing their own personnel to staff planning groups and utilizing consultants with special expertise as the need arises. The use of agency personnel has the advantage of utilizing people who are intimately familiar with the conditions within which the planning process must operate. It is extremely important that members of the planning team represent all the administrative subdivisions of an agency affected by its efforts.

It should be understood that comprehensive plans are not being written for the department, division, or individual expert, but for the benefit of the species and the user—the public, e.g., the hunter, trapper, fisherman, environmentalist, or bird watcher. In order to do this effectively, it is extremely important to involve the user in the planning process. There is no best way of accomplishing this, and each agency must decide what will work best for it. The suggestions which follow merely scratch the surface, but they will assist in demonstrating the concept.

Steering Committee

A steering or advisory committee is composed of private citizens representing a cross section of interests. In most instances this is a nonpaid volunteer group who have an active interest in the resource, conservation, and/or the environment. A group of this kind may consist of representatives of the following interests:

1. Legislators
2. Natural Resources
3. Sportsmen Groups
4. Public at Large
5. Executive Branch of Government
6. Major Private and Public Land Administrators

The size of the group may vary depending upon the needs of the agency. However, it is advisable to keep the group as small as practicable and odd in number to avoid ties when voting. When selecting this group, it is important to ensure that members are attuned to geographical and social attitudes of the interest groups that each represents. A special effort should also be made to recruit women and representatives of minority groups as participants. This committee is a functional working committee, not just a group formed for endorsement purposes, and the success of this approach depends on the individuals selected to participate on the committee.

The planning group should review the planning process with the steering committee and keep the members informed of its progress through correspondence and periodic meetings. The principal function of the steering committee is to review the species assessments and assist or advise in the selection of the long-range management goals, objectives and priorities. It should be noted that the term *assist* was used above.

If a department has a legislated board or commission, it is desirable to develop a common link between the board or commission and the steering committee. This can easily be accomplished if a member of the mandatory board or commission serves as the steering committee chairperson.

Advisory Council

Many resource agencies function under an appointed chief executive who is assisted by an advisory council appointed by the executive or legislative branch of government or under an appointed commission. Members of these appointed groups are usually citizens from different geographic areas of the state. They can function as a steering committee, but this is recommended only as a last resort. Sound management decisions as well as subsequent public acceptance of these decisions require input from a cross section of interests rather than just from hunters, fishermen and trappers. It is desirable to have the advisory council review the results of the planning process, i.e., the recommendations generated from technical and public input, and function as the final selection committee.

Review Committee

A review committee may be described as a nonfunctional steering committee. A committee of this type is usually comprised of 2 or 3 prominent citizens with natural resource interests who endorse the undertaking of the project. Generally, the review committee is not a part of the decisionmaking team.

Surveys

Public input also can be obtained by a random telephone or mail survey. In our opinion, surveys of this

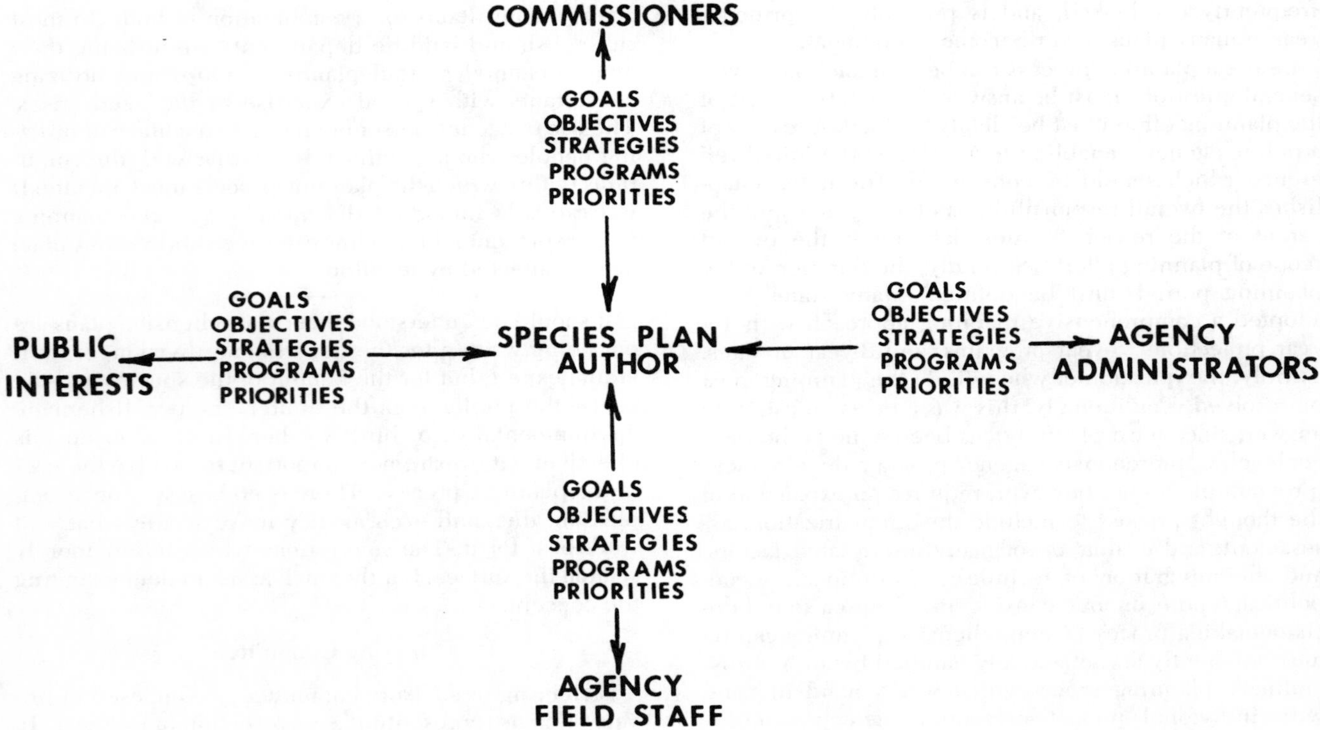

Fig. 24.4. Comprehensive planning must involve everyone affected by a plan.

type should only be used to provide information concerning the very broadest of questions; for example, should the state initiate a wild turkey stocking program?, should there be an open season on moose?, Sunday hunting?, and so on.

Surveys must be carefully prepared to avoid misunderstood or confusing statements and to ensure compatibility with analysis methodology. In addition, the sampling scheme must be carefully designated to minimize reporting bias. This may require the use of special sampling techniques to ensure that respondents are providing a representative sample.

Public Hearings

Formal public hearings strategically held throughout the area of concern provide another method of obtaining input from the public. As in the case with mail and telephone surveys, vocal individuals with strong feelings concerning particular matters may overshadow the opinions and feelings of the less vocal cross section of the public. Public hearings combined with a steering committee may be a useful combination if approached correctly.

Whatever the approach, public input is vital to the long-term success of any planning effort. The selection of long-term goals, objectives, and the development of a program without user involvement is open to criticism, and the program proposal often will end up on the shelf collecting dust. To be successful, the alternatives must be publicized well in advance of public meetings and the meetings moderated in a manner which will direct the attention to the alternatives under consideration.

As soon as the commitment has been made and before the planning methods are selected, thought has to be given to just how a project of this magnitude is going to be kept on track and headed in the right direction. This task is usually assigned to the first member chosen for the planning team, and his or her only function is to coordinate the activity—to smooth the ruffled feathers, to keep all the divisions involved and informed, to see that time schedules are met, and, perhaps the most important of all, to keep the interest and commitment sustained with the administration. Planning assignments are often made to personnel throughout an agency in addition to the responsibilities required by ongoing jobs. Under these conditions, even the most dedicated professionals begin to question the necessity for such an undertaking. Tempers frequently flare and time and time again the commitment is tested, and the coordinator has to continually reassure personnel and resell the worth of the endeavor. A successful coordinator will learn to read people—to have a feel for the time and place to force the issue, and to push the project forward.

Because an effective planning process requires group action, a multitude of problems arise as planning is integrated in the administrative arm of an agency. The major problem is that of communication. It comes as a shock when the person assigned planning responsibilities realizes that not only is he misunderstood within the planning group, but also that the planning group is misunderstood by the divisions within the department, by the public, and by other groups within state government.

The reasons for a communication gap are many, but perhaps the most pronounced is the fact that effective communication systems have not been established between the various administrative divisions of an agency. In addition, personnel assigned to the planning group begin to acquire a broader perspective. Consequently, people who have worked for years in their respective divisions suddenly find themselves in the position of frequently having to explain and defend their newly developed point of view to their former peers as well as to those of other disciplines. To illustrate, imagine yourself trying to convince your former waterfowl project associates that black bear, quail, or perhaps even largemouth bass should be given a higher priority than waterfowl, or trying to explain to a resource economist or an urban planner why you cannot describe deer habitat in precise, *measurable* terms, or why you do not know how many cottontail rabbits you have in your district or state. Additionally, the planner is likely to become so involved with his new activities that the opportunity to converse with former division colleagues diminishes. He also may have a tendency to forget the problems of field personnel and the possessiveness that researchers have for incomplete or unpublished data. Perhaps most important of all, he forgets that the "lingo" he has acquired is not completely understood by all.

Within the group there is also a tendency for each member to develop the attitude that his discipline is paramount, e.g., wildlife, fisheries, law enforcement, etc., and that he alone is responsible for the project's success or failure. As a result, he may (in his zeal) inadvertently make decisions without the knowledge and consent of the project administrator or group members. The same problem applies to his relationship with the administrator of the home division. As planning duties become more demanding, there is a tendency to rationalize: "I am too busy today and the division chief will be out tomorrow so I'll discuss the situation with him some time next week." When the meeting finally takes place, so much has happened that the division chief may never be fully brought up to date.

The last and perhaps the most important area of concern is criticism from other professionals (university personnel, consultants, etc.) as well as the general public that the planners have not solicited input from without and have failed to state the people's wishes. Any plan not tested to determine if it meets the needs of the department or its constituency will have little chance of success no matter how well conceived.

Human nature prevents us from attaining that utopian goal of complete understanding. However, we should realize that misunderstandings result because someone did not hear (or listen) to what was being said or did not understand what was being said. Communication is a 2-way street (1) listening and understanding, and (2) informing. The following suggestions are offered as ways of minimizing the communication gap:

General

1. State the case briefly in *simple* terms.
2. Avoid the use of jargon peculiar to your field or specialty.

3. Encourage questions and constructive criticism.
4. Avoid the position of defending an action if at all possible.
5. Learn to be a good listener!

Within and Between Other Divisions or Agencies

1. Keep the administrator and/or project leader informed of what you plan to do, whom you plan to see, and the subject to be discussed.
2. Prepare minutes of all meetings and circulate them promptly throughout this group.
3. Frequently inform the agency administrators of the planning process, progress, and problems.
4. Keep in personal contact with members of other divisions. Submit your material to them for review and comment.
5. Always follow the established chain of command when arranging meetings with personnel from other divisions.
6. Always contact the person responsible for the required data well in advance of any deadline. *Never* ask someone else to secure data for you without prior arrangement with the researcher or manager.
7. Establish an information flow through you as the divisional representative, e.g., changes in data collection forms, project or program changes, etc.

THE PLANNING PROCESS

A "plan for planning" must be developed which describes exactly what the planning process will include and how it will be done. Basically, the "plan for planning" should provide for an assessment of the current and projected distribution, abundance, and appropriative and nonappropriative use of wildlife resources, as well as the coordination and decisionmaking process which will be used to formulate management goals, objectives, and programs (Fig. 24.5).

During preparation of the basic species assessments, a frequent reaction will be "I don't have the information to estimate species abundance, species use, sustained harvest levels, . . . or evaluate carrying capacity, land use trends, ..." Wildlife planners, as well as those assigned to write specific wildlife assessments, continually must remind themselves that the objective of the planning effort is not to produce detailed, statistically defendable resource evaluations, but to assemble available information into a species assessment which will provide the basis for selecting management goals, objectives, and developing specific job recommendations. Planning should not be stymied by what one feels is a lack of information, since planning is the vehicle by which critical data gaps are identified and a program developed to provide the needed information. It is a continuing process which requires periodic updates and improvements as new information becomes available.

It is important that the species assessment be as clear and consise as possible, and that it focus on the principal planning considerations—current and projected supply and demand relationships. Although certain life history considerations are an important component of supply and demand evaluations, the inclusion of detailed life

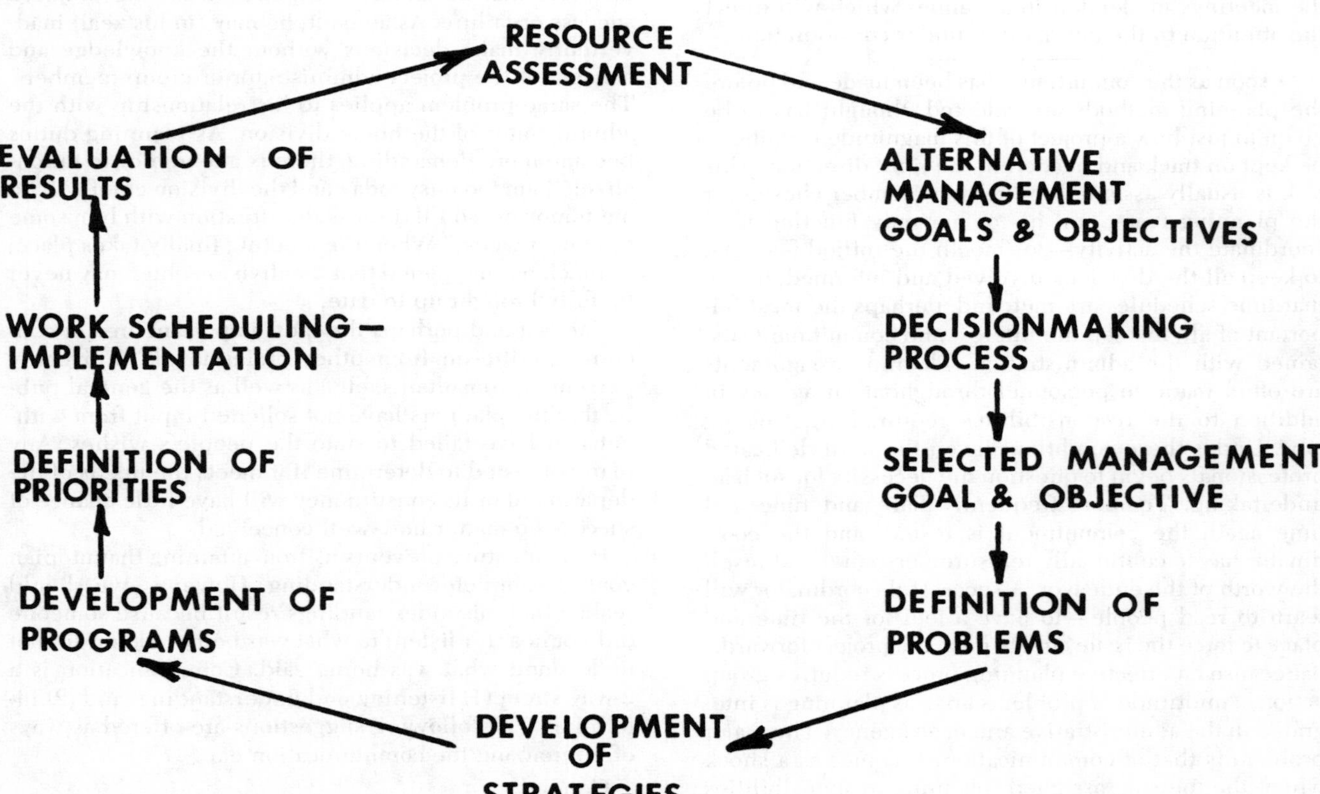

Fig. 24.5. Comprehensive planning provides for a logical thought and decisionmaking process.

history information in the assessment should be discouraged. In most cases, this information provides little direct support to the planning process and may tend to distract from the real planning considerations at hand.

Exactly how projections are made will depend on the type, form, and amount of information available. Projection techniques include: simple extrapolation of historical data; statistical evaluation of the past and projected relationship between various independent and dependent variables over a period of time or at the same point in time but over many geographical areas (Davis and Seneca 1972); and analysis of the subjective or intuitive opinions of a representative group of technical people (Ayres 1969:148–153).

Individual species assessments, as well as alternative management goals and objectives, are then developed and reviewed by the various planning committees at the technical, administrative, and public level. The consensus of each group is then determined. Species assessments, alternative management goals and objectives, and the consensus obtained from the various planning committees are then presented to the director(s) or commission(s) and specific goals and objectives are then selected.

Goals should provide a broad statement of purpose which focuses on the end product and not the means of providing the product, lend themselves to quantifiable measures of output or benefit, and be defined with sufficient precision to permit the identification of competing or inconsistent goals. Goals are necessarily subjective because they state what we hope to achieve and not how or when we hope to achieve it. An example would be: to increase the hunting opportunity and success for white-tailed deer. Objectives define the specific level of achievement desired by a specific point in time. An example would be: increase the deer population to between 200,000 and 300,000 animals by 1990 and provide for an annual harvest of 30,000 to 50,000 animals with a resident hunter success ratio of 25%.

The selection of specific goals and objectives provides the basis for defining problems or obstacles which can be expected to prevent the agency from achieving specific management goals and objectives. Planning efforts are then focused on the development of solutions to specific problems. An operational strategy is formulated which defines the course of action which will be followed to solve the problems at hand. The strategy is then translated into specific jobs containing an objective, procedure, work schedule, and manpower and funding requirements.

Planning will likely result in the identification of far more goals, objectives and needs than can be accomplished by an agency. A logical thought process is required to aid in establishing management strategies, priorities, and selecting specific jobs for implementation. The procedure to follow depends upon the structure of the organization and whether or not it is engaged in intensive or extensive management of wildlife resources. Departments with limited personnel and funding generally practice extensive management—management by regulation—and, of necessity, confine their activities to the surveys and inventories which provide the basis for regulation. These activities do not lend themselves to the standard cost-benefit analysis because of the difficulty of assigning measurable benefits or outputs.

It might be more meaningful to think of the basic survey and inventory projects necessary to establish reasonable seasons and harvest limits as an expansion of the business term, "overhead," i.e., those things which must continually be done to meet the legislative mandates of the organization. We have redefined "overhead" to include not only the physical plant and salaries but also those basic projects which must be conducted in order to function. In this situation, a logical thought process is required to aid in establishing priorities and selecting specific jobs for implementation. Subjective evaluation techniques are frequently the only way to evaluate many wildlife jobs. The decision matrix is an extremely useful tool in this regard. One approach uses subjective evaluations of staff professionals expressed as a rank or a score to evaluate alternatives on a cost-benefit-need basis. For example, participants are asked to indicate the priority they place on specific job proposals using a scale of 1 to 10 with 1 being the highest. Another variation of the decision matrix provides for the comparison of any number of alternatives based upon the evaluation of all alternatives on a one-to-one basis (Morrisey 1977: 80–84). These approaches can also be used to canvass groups such as steering committees and advisory councils for opinions relating to species management priorities and the percentage of the budget which should be devoted to each species or group of species. Analysis of these data will aid in establishing management priorities.

Those agencies which practice intensive management, e.g., development of wildlife habitat and public use facilities, and nonnative game introductions, may find input-output techniques such as MAST—Management Allocation Selection Techniques (Lobdell 1972)—useful when choosing priorities based on input (cost) and output (man-days of use-benefits) considerations.

Once job priorities have been established, selected jobs must be merged into an agency program. Existing programs within the administrative divisions of the agency must first be reviewed to determine: budget and staffing levels; the type of jobs which are currently pursued; and the time required to accomplish day-to-day administrative or public relation type functions which must be done regardless of program direction. Based upon the above, selected jobs are then placed into the work schedules of the appropriate administrative divisions of the agency. This requires establishing a job implementation sequence and specific work schedules designed to implement the selected jobs in accordance with budget and staff limitations.

Finally, program monitoring, control, and change procedures must be implemented to ensure that the agency's program is progressing on schedule towards the stated management goals and objectives.

One of the most sensitive tasks in the agency planning process is the integration of specific jobs into the ongoing programs of the various administrative divisions of the agency, such as Law Enforcement, Information and Education, and Realty. Each has traditionally developed programs independently and may offer some reluctance to alter existing programs. Completion of this step requires an extensive amount of coordination and communications with all administrative levels of the agency. These efforts must continually be aimed at creating an understanding and acceptance of the agency's program planning effort.

THE MODEL PLANNING PROCESS

Presented in the following pages is a step-by-step example of the wildlife portion of a comprehensive fisheries and wildlife program planning process patterned after the California approach (Stokes et al. 1968) and the Maine approach (Goggins et al. 1971, Maine Department of Inland Fisheries and Wildlife 1975). The same principles presented in the following pages apply to the fisheries aspect as well.

Step 1—Inventory of Current Land and Water Cover

Objective—To collect land and water cover data for the purpose of determining habitat conditions for wildlife.

Justification—Wildlife resources are a product of the land and water, and the types of land and water cover, to a great degree, determine the kinds and amounts of wildlife present in an area.

Procedure—Estimates of the current type and amount of land and water cover within wildlife management units will be generated to support wildlife habitat evaluations. An inventory of land and water cover information available from state, federal, and private agencies will be made and appropriate information compiled and entered into available data processing systems. Examples of the type of land and water cover summaries utilized in the Maine Department of Inland Fisheries and Wildlife's comprehensive planning process are shown in Tables 24.1 and 24.2.

Step 2—Inventory of Current Wildlife Habitat

Objective—To define the current quantity, quality, and distribution of habitat for wildlife resources.

Justification—A thorough assessment of the quality, quantity, and distribution of existing habitat for wildlife resources is essential to maintaining current and projected species abundance assessments.

Procedures—The assessment of current wildlife habitat conditions will be based on land and water cover summaries developed by the land and water inventory. Of particular importance are summaries of the type and amount of forest, agricultural, and wetland habitats on a management unit basis. Habitat quantity and quality for each species will be determined by comparing available land cover information to known harvest figures, censuses, direct observations, and habitat and population information existing in the wildlife literature.

Harvest and census data will be obtained from appropriate studies that have been conducted within the region of concern. Direct observation information will be obtained from field biologists and district wardens (Fig. 24.6) and will include factual information for nonseasonal wildlife mortalities, crop damage complaints, and/or wildlife nuisance complaints. In addition, opinions resulting from direct observations and contacts with the general public will be evaluated. Following careful analysis of all available information, the land cover required for each species will be defined, and the amount and quality of habitat will be estimated on a wildlife management unit basis as accurately as possible.

Step 3—Current Wildlife Abundance

Objective—To estimate current population levels, population trends, and the capacity of the habitat to support selected wildlife species.

Justification—A thorough assessment of wildlife abundance is essential to maintaining current and projected wildlife supply and demand assessments in support of the development of management goals, objectives, and specific jobs directed towards the optimum abundance and use of the resource.

Procedures—Estimates of the abundance of wildlife species will be made for specific habitat types within wildlife management units using the best information available. Numerical estimates will be made whenever possible, utilizing the results of census work and population reconstruction from harvest data. Where insufficient information is available to allow for direct population estimates, density, distribution, and habitat information will be obtained from the literature and the subjective observations of district game wardens (Fig. 24.6), fire tower observers, biologists, and selected members of the public. Estimates obtained from these sources will be reported as a relative abundance, e.g., as not present, scarce, common, or abundant. When such data can be sufficiently refined, estimates will be reported in appropriate ranges of animals per ha or square km. An expected population range for each species will be made on a wildlife management unit basis using the habitat estimates generated in Step 2 and population densities which appear likely to occur within the habitat types occurring in each wildlife management unit.

Time series analysis and standard statistical evaluation techniques will be used to further evaluate the current status of a species. Information which will be evaluated in this manner includes harvest and use data from big game registrations, fur tagging, hunter and trapper questionnaires, license sales, and other harvest and use surveys. In addition, population modeling will be utilized when appropriate models and information are available.

Step 4—Current Wildlife Use

Objective—To estimate the current appropriative and nonappropriative use of wildlife.

Justification—A thorough assessment of the current uses being made of wildlife resources is essential to maintaining current and projected wildlife supply and demand assessments in support of the development of management goals, objectives, and management programs directed towards the optimum abundance and use of these resources.

Procedure—Demand is a term used to express the amount of desire by the public to harvest or otherwise utilize specific wildlife resources. The level of use of a wildlife species is a measure of the demand that has been exhibited and, in our opinion, is the most useful measure of demand available to wildlife planners. Demand can be more precisely measured utilizing market

Table 24.1. Maine Land Cover Estimates By Wildlife Management Units.

WMU*	Total Area[1]	Tidal Flats[2]	Urban Rural-Urban[3]	Railroad Beds (Acres)[4]	Rural Road Beds (Surf.) (Mi.)	(Acres)[5]	Rural Road Beds (Unsurf.) (Mi.)	(Acres)[6]	Year A. Dwl. (#)	(Acres)[7]
1	1,553,423	0	15,193	2,782	(1,294)	4,887	(890)	2,849	(7,358)	7,358
2	5,970,378	0	0	588	(123)	518	(1,277)	3,182	(454)	451
3	2,544,753	0	1,178	598	(1,138)	4,100	(1,643)	6,564	(6,417)	6,417
4	3,636,155	0	36,193	3,188	(2,784)	19,012	(2,408)	7,807	(17,873)	17,873
5	1,884,023	309	4,506	828	(797)	2,896	(1,042)	2,909	(5,514)	5,514
6	1,670,291	34,105	6,317	1,036	(1,492)	5,410	(1,232)	3,547	(14,704)	14,704
7	1,365,573	12,652	26,088	930	(2,379)	8,996	(1,695)	5,312	(18,135)	18,135
8	1,781,715	12,448	138,513	1,543	(3,252)	12,811	(2,044)	6,398	(30,536)	30,536
Total	20,406,311	59,514	227,988	11,493	(13,259)	58,630	(12,231)	38,495	(100,911)	100,988

WMU*	Seas. Dwl. (#)	(Acres)[7]	Farms (#)	(Acres)[7]	Other (#)	(Acres)[8]	Water and Wetland[8]	Forest Land[9]	Agricultural Land[9]
1	(2,032)	1,016	(2,860)	8,580	(1,420)	1,420	58,460	1,044,632	406,246
2	(904)	452	(30)	90	(348)	348	462,668	5,447,060	55,021
3	(5,960)	2,980	(752)	2,256	(2,009)	2,009	227,521	2,291,130	–
4	(7,441)	3,721	(3,498)	10,494	(3,457)	3,457	248,439	3,088,813	197,158
5	(2,964)	1,482	(543)	1,629	(1,182)	1,182	213,467	1,616,315	32,986
6	(6,418)	3,209	(386)	1,158	(3,014)	3,014	118,228	1,390,764	88,772
7	(9,354)	4,677	(2,991)	8,973	(3,592)	3,592	95,642	1,003,490	177,066
8	(19,074)	9,537	(7,094)	21,282	(5,149)	5,149	149,878	1,225,594	167,126
Total	(54,147)	27,074	(18,154)	54,462	(20,171)	20,171	1,574,303	17,107,798	1,124,375

* Wildlife Management Unit

1. Total area from the Maine State Planning Office by minor civil divisions. Tidal water and island which are not connected to the mainland by an intertidal flat, except for the principal island municipalities, are not included.
2. Area of tidal flats from the Maine Department of Inland Fisheries and Wildlife's wetland inventory.
3. Area of urban and rural-urban land as defined by the State of Maine Department of Transportation and measured from "A General Highway Atlas of Maine."
4. Area of railroad bed taken from "A General Highway Atlas of Maine" utilizing a right-of-way of 8 acres per mile.
5. Area of surfaced road beds in rural areas taken from the State of Maine, Dept. of Transportation's Highway System Mileage Inventory utilizing road bed widths of 30 for town ways, 20 for private roads, 30 for the various types of state/or federal roads, and 130 for the 4-lane interstate or toll road in units 8 and 7 and 65 for the 2-lane interstate in units 1, 5, 2, and 4.
6. Area of unsurfaced road beds in rural areas taken from the State of Maine, Dept. of Transportation's Highway System Mileage Inventory utilizing road bed widths of 30 for town ways, 20 for private roads, 30 for the various types of state/or federal aid roads.
7. Year-Around-Dwellings, seasonal dwellings, farms (dwellings and structures) and other establishments along rural roads from the State of Maine, Department of Transportation Highway System Inventory and area directly affected utilizing one acre for year-around-dwellings, ½ acre for seasonal dwellings, 3 acres for farms, and 1 acre for other establishments.
8. Area of wetland to include open water from the Dept. of Inland Fisheries and Wildlife Wetland Inventory. Wooded swamp has been excluded, since this type is included under forestland.
9. The total of nonforested and nonagricultural land was subtracted from the total area within each management unit and the remainder was divided into forested and agricultural land according to the ratio of forested sample plots to agricultural sample plots (within management units) in the U.S. Forest Service's Land Use Data from their study of the timber resources of Maine. The number of sample plots occurring within forested and agricultural land within each unit was as follows: 1–126, 2–453, 3–200, 4–258, 5–137, 6–139, 7–88, 8–117.

Table 24.2. Maine wetland acreages (and number of areas) by Wildlife Management Unit.*

Wildlife Management Unit	Tidal Flats	Seasonally Flooded Basins or Flats (# Areas)	Fresh Meadow (#Areas)	Shallow Fr. Marsh (# Areas)	Deep Fr. Marsh (# Areas)	Open Fr. Water (#Areas)	Shrub Swamp (# Areas)
1	—	192 (6)	871 (46)	101 (4)	360 (1)	34,838 (147)	13,137 (492)
2	—	2,705 (30)	9,874 (243)	2,462 (37)	1,891 (5)	322,309 (905)	58,353 (2,094)
3	—	3,462 (37)	8,851 (263)	97 (9)	1,867 (11)	174,379 (476)	31,764 (822)
4	—	7,639 (41)	9,495 (239)	6,451 (98)	10,656 (153)	150,285 (543)	42,304 (928)
5	309	801 (18)	10,829 (218)	2,953 (44)	1,719 (23)	123,754 (275)	28,418 (763)
6	34,105	245 (5)	5,757 (90)	3,775 (52)	1,819 (32)	81,651 (256)	11,493 (205)
7	12,652	— (—)	5,539 (77)	4,738 (63)	3,581 (51)	63,493 (209)	12,658 (174)
8	12,448	1 (1)	6,467 (97)	2,379 (74)	4,008 (128)	96,869 (312)	12,386 (301)
Total	59,514	15,045	57,683	22,956 (381)	25,901 (404)	1,047,578 (3,123)	210,513 (5,779)

Wildlife Management Unit	Bog (# Areas)	Shallow Fr. Marsh-C (# Areas)	Deep Fr. Marsh-C (# Areas)	Salt Meadow (# Areas)	Reg Flood Salt Marsh (# Areas)	Total**	Rank
1	8,961 (124)	–	–	–	–	58,460	8
2	65,074 (1,119)	–	–	–	–	462,668	1
3	7,101 (109)	–	–	–	–	227,521	3
4	21,609 (238)	–	–	–	–	248,439	2
5	44,993 (417)	–	–	–	–	213,467	4
6	9,257 (138)	56 (1)	–	2,677 (49)	1,498 (18)	118,228	6
7	3,408 (33)	–	586 (2)	1,639 (8)	–	95,642	7
8	5,921 (79)	9,478 (10)	1,274 (14)	10,954 (60)	141 (3)	149,878	5
Total	166,324	9,534 (11)	1,860 (16)	15,270	1,639	1,574,303	

The figures are subject to change when the data edit is completed. Any additional changes should be relatively minor and the above figures should be utilized for species planning purposes.

* Department of Inland Fisheries and Wildlife, Wetlands Inventory.

** Does not include Tidal Flats or Wooded Swamp.

analysis techniques, but most agencies do not have the resources to conduct such studies, to say nothing of utilizing the results to implement programs to satisfy latent demand.

The estimated number of people hunting and trapping wildlife species, and/or man-days of hunting or trapping effort, as well as the total harvest and harvest per person, will be summarized for the past 15 years, or to the extent of the available information. Included in the latter are harvest and effort data from hunter and trapper questionnaires and surveys, big game registrations, fur tagging, and license and permit sales. These data will be supplemented by information obtained from questionnaires distributed to field personnel and to selected nonagency employees. Where possible, the data will be analyzed on a 5-year basis to minimize any distortion due to weather or socioeconomic conditions.

Nonappropriative use levels will be difficult to determine. The type and amount of nonappropriative use will be initially estimated from information supplied by organized bird and nature study groups and by agency personnel. Other information such as the wholesale sale of bird seed should also be identified and used in nonappropriative use determinations. Estimates should

Warden Service Survey–1973

Wildlife Abundance and Distribution

Name ______________________ Division ______________________ Date ______________

Note: Indicate on the attached sheets, under the species heading and opposite the townships or part of townships within your division, the approximate (overall) abundance of the species over the last two years (1971 & 1972). Utilize the following definitions and abbreviations.

Absent or not known to be present (abs)

Scarce (sc)2—Insufficient numbers to provide any hunting; any kill strictly incidental to hunting for other species.

Low (lo)–Populations which could provide limited hunting; usually for local hunters knowing where the species is likely to be found.

Common (co)–Fair hunting success could be experienced. For example, in a township:

(1) 1 to 2 out of every 10 deer hunters *could* be successful.
(2) 1 out of every 10 hunters strictly after bear *could* be successful.
(3) Upland game and waterfowl hunters *could* partially fill daily bag limit on most trips afield.
(4) Furbearer hunters *could* be successful on one-half of their trips afield.

Abundant (a)–Good hunting success could be experienced. For example, in a township:

(1) More than 2 out of every 10 deer hunters *could* be successful.
(2) More than 2 out of every 10 hunters strictly after bear *could* be successful.
(3) Upland game and waterfowl hunters *could* frequently fill daily bag limit on most trips afield.
(4) Furbearer hunters *could* normally be successful on each trip afield.

Over *each* species heading indicate the degree of accuracy which you feel the majority of your answers have according to the categories listed below.

Accurate (a)–Answers which you feel are based upon a sufficient knowledge of local conditions to ensure their correctness.

Probably Accurate (PA)–Answers which you are not absolutely certain about; although they are based on an extensive knowledge of local conditions and most likely correct.

Good Guess (GG)–Answers which you feel are fairly accurate; although they are based on a limited knowledge of local conditions.

Wild Guess (WG)–Answers which you are not certain about.

Fig. 24.6. Instruction to the 1973 Maine warden service wildlife abundance survey.

be reported as user days of effort. Where specific information is lacking, species should be grouped and their use evaluated in a subjective manner.

Step 5—Current Human Opportunities to Use Wildlife

Objective—To determine the availability of current supplies of wildlife for public use.

Justification—In addition to a knowledge of the current and projected habitat conditions and species abundance, the availability of these resources for public use must be determined to evaluate wildlife supply and demand relationships properly.

Procedure—A variety of restrictions on the use of available wildlife affect the opportunity for the public to utilize these resources. Of primary importance are legal restrictions, statutes regulating use, "posted lands," and physical restriction.

Sample areas will be selected, and complete surveys will be periodically made of the lands within these areas in order to estimate the amount of legal and physical restrictions occurring within wildlife management units. In addition, regulations controlling the legal supply will be identified. These estimates will be utilized in conjunction with current and projected habitat conditions and species abundance information collected in Steps 2, 3, and 5 in order to estimate the current availability of wildlife for public use.

Step 6—Land and Water Cover Projections

Objective—To estimate land and water cover trends.

Justification—Estimates of the type, amount, and quality of habitat which will be available for wildlife at some future date must be based on land and water cover projections. The analysis of these data will provide a basis for estimating future wildlife distribution and abundance and for identifying potential imbalances between projected supply and projected demand.

Procedures—Land and water cover projections will be developed using all available sources of information, as well as the consensus obtained from agency personnel and others with expertise in specific land use categories. Projections for specific types of land and water cover will be obtained when available from state, federal, and private agencies which have collected and evaluated pertinent data. These agencies may include state forestry, agriculture, wildlife, water resources, environmental protection, and transportation departments; the U.S. Department of Agriculture, Forest Service, and

Soil Conservation Service, the Department of Interior, Bureau of Land Management, U.S. Fish and Wildlife Service, and the U.S. Geological Survey. Where projections are not available, the planning staff should encourage and support the development of programs in appropriate agencies to supply data needs.

Special emphasis and consideration will be given to the factors which will influence future land and water use patterns and subsequently affect wildlife habitat.

Forest Lands

The following activities will greatly affect habitat for the major wildlife species:

(1) fire suppression; (2) timber harvests; (3) reforestation methods and programs; (4) recreational development; (5) water resources, including flood control projects, hydroelectric developments, and developments for public water supplies; (6) demands for wood products; (7) subdivision of extensive land holdings; and (8) the legal aspects which will include zoning of wildlands, taxation, and public use, that will result from state or federal legislation.

Agricultural Lands

The following factors, which will affect agricultural lands, will also have a pronounced effect on wildlife habitats:

(1) future demands for agricultural products; (2) land ownership patterns, size of holdings, and proposed use; (3) encroachment by housing developments, urbanization, mining, flood control, hydroelectric facilities, public water supplies; (4) recreational development, including the lands used for golf courses, camping areas, shooting preserves, and lands acquired by the state or federal government for parks, etc.; (5) farm subsidies; and (6) cost and availability of fossil fuels and fertilizers.

Industrialization and Transportation

Industrial expansion and demands for increased transportation facilities (roads and airports) also will exert a measurable influence on future wildlife habitats.

Department field personnel will participate in the analysis and projection of these data for their areas of responsibility.

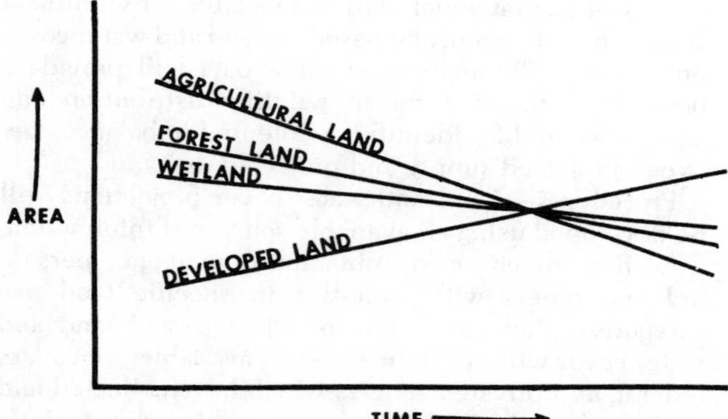

Fig. 24.7. **The availability of suitable habitat will be the principal factor influencing future supplies of wildlife.**

Step 7—Projection of Future Wildlife Habitat Quality and Quantity

Objectives—To project the type, quantity, and quality of habitat which will be available for wildlife at some future date.

Justification—The future status of wildlife resources is dependent on the type, amount, and quality of habitat available to them. A hypothetical example of land cover trends is given in Figure 24.7. As a result of natural succession and man-made alterations to the land, the type, amount, distribution, and quality of habitat is ever changing. These changes must be identified and their impact on wildlife assessed if management objectives and programs are to be responsive to the conditions at hand.

Procedure—The impact of changes in land and water use identified in the previous work item will be assessed in relation to the future type, amount, and quality of habitat available for individual wildlife species. Habitat for individual species of wildlife is often quite variable from one geographical area to another. As a result, the definitions of habitat which are acceptable from the biological point of view do not adequately support quantitative evaluation. As quantitative land and water cover projections become available, it will be necessary to determine future habitat conditions from an analysis of current and projected land use and vegetative cover type estimates. Habitat projections will be based upon the habitat types used by the species and the direct comparisons of the current estimate of land and water cover types to the land and water cover-type projections.

Step 8—Project Future Use-Opportunity for Wildlife

Objectives—To project the future opportunity to utilize wildlife on a state-wide and wildlife management unit basis.

Justification—It is important that planning efforts provide for the evaluation of land use, land ownership, legislation, and other factors which affect use-opportunity to determine the amount of wildlife that will be available for use in the future. The future use-opportunities will then be compared with projections of future use in order to ascertain whether the supply of a species is sufficient to meet the demands. This analysis will be the basis for the development of refined objectives, policies, and programs.

Procedure—The future opportunity for the public to utilize available wildlife resources will be estimated, utilizing subjective or intuitive projection techniques such as the Delphi Method (Ayres 1969). Time series analysis will also be conducted if sufficient supporting data are available. The analysis includes past changes in habitat area, species population levels, acreage of posted land, miles of road construction, and other factors influencing the opportunity for resource use.

Step 9—Projecting Future Use of Wildlife Resources

Objective—To develop both short-term (5-year) and long-term (15-year) wildlife use predictions.

Justification—Estimates of future levels of wildlife use are needed to evaluate future supply and demand relationships.

Procedure—Projection will be based on an analysis of harvest and use records, as well as the many factors influencing the use of wildlife resources. The latter includes economic conditions, human population levels, amount of leisure time, habitat availability, resource abundance, equipment requirements, success rates, and aesthetic conditions. All variables concerned in the analysis will be subjected to regression analysis, and significant linear relationships will be extrapolated into the future, using time series and cross-sectional analysis techniques. Finally, all predictions will be reassessed in regards to the likelihood that they will actually occur or not occur in view of apparent changes in use levels, as well as the factors affecting use.

Predictions are a major component of the planning process, and the process is never complete. All projections must be periodically reviewed and updated if they are to support planning efforts adequately.

Step 10—Analysis of Current and Projected Supply and Demand Relations

Objective—To evaluate the current and projected relationship between the available annual surplus of wildlife resources and the use which is being made of them.

Justification—Analysis of current and projected supply and demand relationships is needed to identify future supply and demand imbalances. This will provide the basis for establishing management goals and objectives and for the development of management programs designed to meet the most pressing problems at hand.

Procedure—The current and projected available supply of individual or groups of wildlife species will be compared to current and projected levels of use to identify potential supply and demand imbalances (Fig. 24.8).

Step 11—Species Management Plans

Objective—To develop and maintain detailed species management plans.

Justification—Evaluations of the current and projected status of the wildlife resources are of little value until they are synthesized into an evaluation and decisionmaking process which results in:

1. The establishment of species management goals, objectives, and priorities.
2. A management program which provides for the most cost-effective solutions to problems at hand.

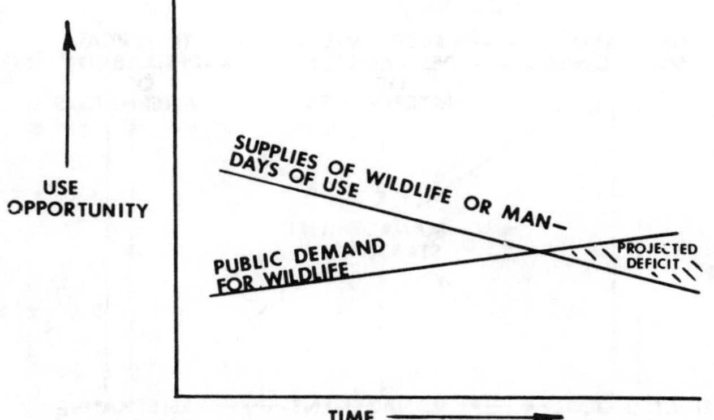

Fig. 24.8. Projected supply and demand imbalances must be identified to guide the development of management goals, objectives, priorities, and programs.

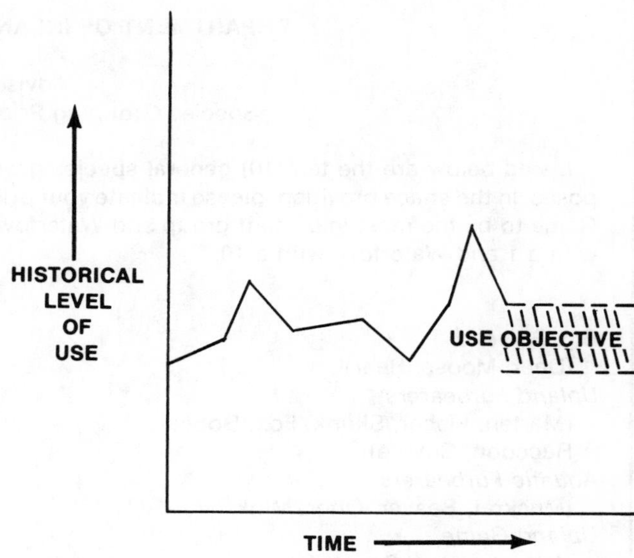

Fig. 24.9. Planning requires the development of precise goals and objectives defining what we wish to do by a specific point in time.

Procedure—Information collected under previous work items will be used as the basis for assessing the current and projected quantity and quality of habitat, species abundance, supply and demand. A diverse array of alternative species management goals and objectives and associated cost will be presented and each generally evaluated in regard to the capacity of the habitat to provide desired use levels, desirability, feasibility, and possible consequences.

Individual species assessments and alternative management goals and objectives will be reviewed by agency planning committees at both the technical and administrative levels, as well as by a steering committee (representing a cross section of the public). Members of each review committee will be asked to select what they feel is the most desirable species management goal and objective. Species assessments, alternative management goals and objectives, and a summary of the reaction of the individual planning committees to alternative management goals and objectives will be presented to the Director or Commissioner and his Advisory Council or Commission for consideration. A management goal and objective for each species or species group will then be selected by the Commissioner and his Advisory Council (Fig. 24.9).

Concurrent with the above, members of the individual planning committees will be asked to rate the management priority they feel should be placed on the major groups of species. The latter will be accomplished utilizing a subjective evaluation ranking scheme (Fig. 24.10). In addition, the estimated economic value, projected supply and demand, and management potential for each species group will be summarized to aid in the development of management priorities.

Once specific species management goals and objectives are selected, management problems (conditions standing in the way or preventing the agency from

DEPARTMENT OF INLAND FISHERIES AND WILDLIFE

Advisory Council
Species Grouping Priorities—Program Allotments

Listed below are the ten (10) general species groupings which will be used for program development purposes. In the space provided, please indicate your priority rating on a scale of 1 to 10, i.e., if you consider Upland Game to be the most important group and Waterfowl to be the least important you would mark Upland Game with a 1 and Waterfowl with a 10.

	Priority Rating	*Percentage of Budget*
Big Game (Deer, Moose, Bear)	____	____
Upland Furbearers (Marten, Fisher, Skunk, Fox, Bobcat, Raccoon, Coyote)	____	____
Aquatic Furbearers (Muskrat, Beaver, Otter, Mink)	____	____
Upland Game (Grouse, Hare, Squirrel)	____	____
Waterfowl (All waterfowl plus Geese)	____	____
Migratory Birds (Woodcock, Snipe, etc.)	____	____
Non-Native Game Birds (Pheasant)	____	____
Non-Game Wildlife (Song Birds, Protected Wildlife Species)	____	____
Rare and Endangered (Those species on federal list–as well as those unique to Maine–Lynx, Eagle, etc.)	____	____
Herptiles (Amphibians & Reptiles)	____	____

In the second column on the right (% of Budget) please indicate in percent, that portion of the total program budget which you feel each group should receive. If you felt that all groups should receive equal consideration, you would indicate by allowing each group 10%.

Remember—the allotments should add up to 100%.

Fig. 24.10. A subjective evaluation system used to guide the development management priorities.

reaching management goals and objectives) must be identified. This is one of the most important phases of the planning process, since the agency's program will be designed to solve the most pressing problems at hand. Problems affecting management objectives include: conditions affecting resource abundance, conditions affecting resource use, conditions caused by the resource, and conditions caused by the public which affect management alternatives. All problems should be identified as precisely as possible and documented in clear, concise problem statements. Identified problems must be carefully screened to ensure that each is a true problem; i.e., a condition which must be eliminated or solved if a management goal and objective is to be reached.

Management goals, objectives, and problems are then translated into a management strategy (Fig. 24.11). This is normally composed of a series of clear and concise statements describing specific courses of action which will be taken to solve the problems at hand. These should cover all needs to include: habitat preservation, inventories, regulations, research, surveys, law enforcement, information and education, hunter safety, engineering, and hatcheries. Obviously, alternatives

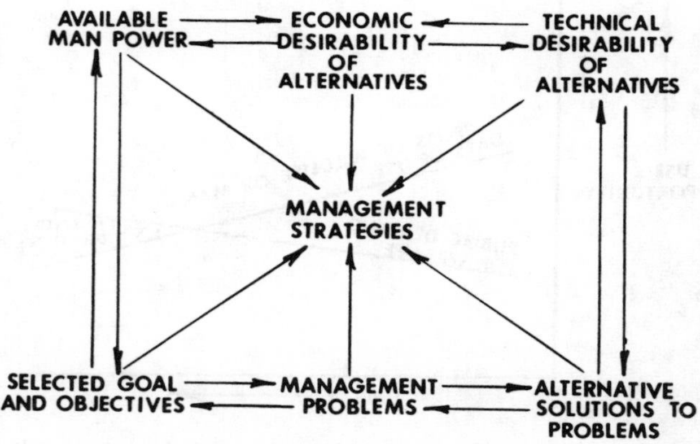

Fig. 24.11. Management strategies provide the framework for management programs.

STATE: Maine

PROJECT NO: W-67-R-7
PROGRAM EVALUATION BASED UPON COST-BENEFIT-NEED CONSIDERATIONS

List of Active Jobs

Study No.	Study Title	Job No.	Title	Total Cost	Species* Group Rank	Job** Rank
I	Deer	54	Deer Study Administration	$ 5,229.	______	______
		58	Deer Cover Density Requirements	601.		______
		59	Minimum Deer Shelter Unit Size	601.		______
		161	Analysis of Deer Legal Harvest	6,928.		______
		162	Analysis of Deer Biological Data	18,582.		______
		164	Deer Registration Errors	1,821.		______
		165	Deer Wintering Conditions	12,043.		______
		166	Deer Mortality Other Than Legal	714.		______
		167	Deer Density Level Studies	4,944.		______
		170	Deer Winter Mortality	1,336.		______
		172	Update Deer Species Plan	441.		______
		173	Deer Regulations	1,440.		______
		175	Deer Population Analysis	3,268.		______
		221	Deer Wintering Area Aerial Inventory	10,284.		______
			STUDY TOTAL	$ 68,232.		
II	Bear	55	Bear Study Administration	$ 2,264.	______	______
		176	Bear Registration and Kill Compositon	1,918.		______
		177	Sampling of Bear Legal Harvest	12,049.		______
		178	Bear Exploitation Rate Study	11,473.		______
		179	Bear Population Reconstruct	774.		______
		180	Bear Regulation Adjustments	482.		______
		186	Update Bear Species Plans	466.		______
			STUDY TOTAL	$ 29,426.		
III	Moose	56	Moose Study Administration	1,669.	______	______
		185	Update Moose Plan	100.		______
		190	Moose Census	2,643.		______
		195	Winter Range Measurements	1,145.		______
		196	Moose Census Errors	3,206.		______
			STUDY TOTAL	$ 8,763.		
	PROJECT W-67-R TOTAL			$106,421.		

*Rank emphasis which you feel should be placed on individual species groups based upon cost-benefit and need considerations, utilize ranks from 1 through 11.

**Within individual specie(s) groups, i.e., Upland Furbearers, Deer, etc., rank the importance of individual jobs.

Fig. 24.12. Program evaluation form used to evaluate proposed species management programs.

and associated costs and benefits must be defined and evaluated before a specific strategy is selected. Use of the decision matrix discussed in a previous step can be of great assistance in evaluating alternatives.

Upon finalization of specific species management strategies, jobs must be developed that focus on discrete components of the strategy. Each job should define exactly what, when, how, by whom, and at what cost the task will be done on an annual basis for a 5-year period or the length of the job if less than 5 years.

In the majority of cases the proposed work program will exceed the department or division's financial and manpower capabilities. Priorities must be established and assigned to various species and species groups based upon such factors as species management goals and objectives, supply and demand, management potentials, economic importance, and public interest. These priorities should reflect the consensus of all interests affected by the planning process. Cost/benefit evaluations utilizing subjective evaluations of staff professionals (Fig. 24.12) or variations of the decision matrix are useful tools and may be used to good advantage.

The agency program is then formulated based upon species or species group priorities, job priorities within

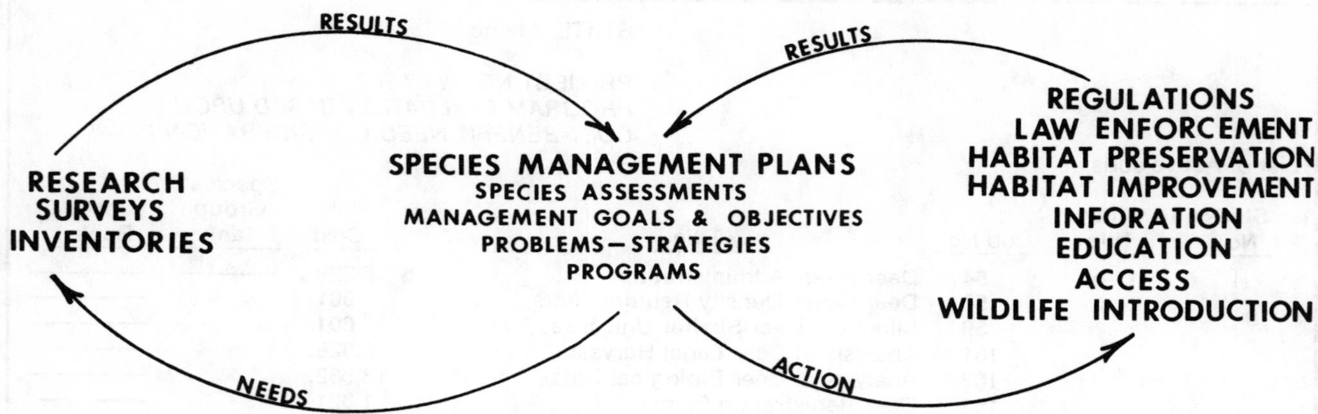

Fig. 24.13. Comprehensive program planning—a self-defining process.

each, and the availability of funds and staff. In order to accomplish this, selected jobs must be integrated into the operational programs of the appropriate administrative subdivision of the agency. This is the most important step in the entire process and requires the evaluation of ongoing work, the phasing out of activities which do not directly support the selected management strategies and priority jobs, and the final selection of the jobs to be included in the agency program based upon established priorities, as well as scheduling and budgetary considerations.

DISCUSSION AND SUMMARY

An attempt has been made to cover the most important points of the wildlife program planning process in a cookbook fashion. We purposely omitted direct reference to strategies and operational plans as separate entities; for we feel planning is the entire process and 1 phase cannot exist without the other. Planning is not a 2-front attack but 1 main spearhead with implementation as the focal point. If one follows "the planning process" section carefully, one will discover that implementation has occurred with the completion of Step 11, entitled "Species Management Plans."

At this point, one may think the job is done and all is well. Nothing could be further from the truth! Implementation of a program is only the beginning—the beginning of the most critical aspect of the entire process—that of making sure that all support divisions are providing the input necessary to meet the selected goals and objectives. This point in time is also critical from the planner's point of view in that it marks the beginning of the 3-year update period. The biota are dynamic, which in turn require that viable plans and programs reflect the changing conditions; and thus the process continues. Nothing remains static: a continual appraisal of goals, objectives, and predictions is essential. It has often been said that if you do not know where you are going, you will not have any problem getting there. Problems are conditions which can be expected to interfere with goals and objectives and which must be changed if management is to meet its selected goals and objectives.

In summary, planning is not a quick solution to crisis problems. It is an orderly thought and decisionmaking process to determine where we have been, where we are, where we want to be in the future, and how best to get there. It is a self-refining process (Fig. 24.13) designed to identify what we really need to know and do versus what we think we would like to know and do if we are to manage a species or group of species adequately now and in the future in a realistic cost-effective manner.

Selected Sources of Information

In addition to the literature cited, the following sources of information are of value to wildlife resource planning efforts:

Source/Reference	Subject
Arnfield, R. V. 1969. Technical forecasting. Aldine Publ. Co., Chicago, Ill. 413 p.	Projections
Ashton, P., R. Wykstra, and K. Nobe. 1974. Optimum supplies of recreation days under conditions of uncertainty: a case study application to wildlife resources. Dept. of Econ. Colorado State Univ., Fort Collins, Colo. 93 p.	Supply and Demand Analysis
Baier, K., and N. Rescher. 1969. Values and the future. The Free Press, N.Y. 527 p.	Projections
Booz, A. 1973. Guidelines for developing a comprehensive plan for the management of fish and wildlife resources. Public Adm. Serv. Inc. U.S. Fish Wildl. Serv. 133 p.	Comprehensive Fish and Wildlife Planning

Reference	Subject
Boyd, H. 1975. Planning for wildlife in Canada. Trans. N. Am. Wildl. Nat. Resour. Conf. 40:97–102.	Planning
Conlin, W. 1976. Demand analysis as an aid to decision making. U.S. Fish Wildl. Serv. Region 5, Fed. Aid Coord. Meet., Alexandria Bay, N.Y. 26 p.	Demand Analysis
Davis, R. K., and J. J. Seneca. 1972. Models for supply and demand analysis in state fish and game planning. Trans. N. Am. Wildl. Nat. Resour. Conf. 37:234–246.	Supply and Demand Analysis
Dorfman, R. 1976. Forty years of cost-benefit analysis. Harvard Inst. Econ. Res. Discuss. Pap. No. 498. 28 p.	Cost-Benefit Analysis
Fish and Wildlife Reference Service, 3840 York St., Denver, Colo.	Published and unpublished research reports resulting from Federal Aid in Fish and Wildlife Restoration
Fuhriman, J. W., and E. S. Crozier. 1974 Planning for wildlife and man. U.S. Fish Wildl. Serv. 56 p.	General Planning
Gill, J. D., J. W. Thomas, W. M. Healy, J. C. Pack, and H. R. Sanderson. 1975. Comparison of seven forest types for game in West Virginia. J. Wildl. Manage. 39(4):762–768.	Habitat Evaluation
Hampton, E. L., and R. T. Lackey. 1975. Management objectives and planning process. Tri-State Fish. Conf., Huntington, W. Va. 17 p.	Management Objective and Planning
Lodico, N. J. 1976. Forecasting demand for hunting and fishing, a bibliography. Inf. Serv. Branch Nat. Resour. Libr. Bibliogr. Ser. No. 33. 19 p.	Demand Analysis
Meshenberg, M. 1976. Environmental planning: a guide to information sources. Gale Research Co., Detroit. 492 p.	Source of Planning Information
Padbury, P., and D. Wilkins. 1972. The future: a bibliography of issues and forecasting techniques. Counc. Plann. Libr. Exchange Bibliogr. No. 279. 102 p.	Projections
Phenicie, C. K., and J. R. Lyons. 1973. Tactical planning in fish and wildlife management and research. U.S. Fish Wildl. Serv. Resour. Publ. 123. 19 p.	Management Objectives and Planning
State Natural Resource, Transportation and Planning Agencies	Land Use Inventories
United States Department of Agriculture, Forest Service	Timber Resource Inventories
United States Department of Agriculture, Soil Conservation Service	Conservation Needs Inventories
United States Department of Commerce, Social and Economic Administration, Bureau of Census	Agricultural Census
United States Department of Interior, Fish and Wildlife Service	National Wetlands Inventory
United States Geological Survey	Land Cover Inventories
U.S. Fish and Wildlife Service, Office of Endangered Species. 1976. Endangered species priority system Admin. Rep. 27 p.	Priority System Based Upon Subjective Evaluations
Williamson, J. F., Jr. 1976. The feasibility of a subjective habitat evaluation technique. M.S. Thesis. Mississippi State Univ. 49 p.	Habitat Evaluation
Willis, R. 1975. A technique for estimating potential wildlife populations through habitat evaluations. Pittman-Robertson Game Manage. Tech. Ser. No. 23., Kentucky Dept. Fish and Wildl. Resour. 12 p.	Habitat Evaluation

Larry Toschik

Chapter Twenty-Five

Preparing and Evaluating Environmental Assessments and Related Documents

JON GHISELIN
Consulting Ecologist
Reading, Pennsylvania

INTRODUCTION

Wildlife in Environmental Impact Documents

Environmental impact "assessment" is a fairly new specialty which requires integrating engineering with several natural and social sciences to predict consequences of proposed developments. Full examination of potential effects is valuable in several ways. It gives decision makers fuller information on which to base their decisions. Not every proposal becomes a project; weighing the advantages expected against the tangible and intangible expenses sometimes results in a decision to abandon the project. If an assessment is comprehensive, it will show the public both what is planned and also unplanned effects. Alternatives to planned actions, including no action, must be considered at the same time. For some projects, the assessment may include recommendations for monitoring the effects of constructing and operating a facility. Sometimes, measures are proposed to mitigate predicted undesirable effects, or to accentuate desirable ones. Wildlife can both affect and be affected by many kinds of developments. Therefore, professional wildlife specialists are often called on to predict the effects of proposed actions. Many wildlifers judge the adequacy of such reports prepared by others.

In depth environmental impact reports, under law and by their nature, require interdisciplinary effort. This chapter will explain how analyses and predictions involving wildlife can best be integrated with the contributions of other specialists in producing finished reports.

The Need for Predicting Environmental Change

Public and governmental concern for environmental quality has increased worldwide almost in parallel with growing human populations. This interest has stimulated legislation at all levels. That legislation has created a need for specialized information and predictions about wildlife and wildlife habitats.

The basic U.S. federal law involved is the National Environmental Policy Act of 1969 (NEPA). NEPA requires that the environmental effects of every "significant" federal action be considered before it is undertaken. Further, it establishes mechanisms to insure that this consideration will be effective and comprehensive.

The fundamental tool of NEPA is the environmental impact statement (EIS). Federal agencies prepare and publish EIS's to predict the effects of many kinds of actions. The data base may be gathered from a variety of sources. Often, these sources include environmental reports (ER's) prepared by applicants for licenses or permits. It is important to recognize the distinction between the 2 types of documents, even though an EIS is "in part a summarization and analysis of information presented in . . . [the] ER" (Dinger 1976:52). Drafts of EIS's are first made available to other agencies and the public for comment. The comments are considered, often together with testimony in public hearings, in preparing final EIS's. Agencies respond to comments by correcting or amplifying parts of draft EIS's; sometimes developments are changed or abandoned. Wildlife biologists participate at all stages in arriving at a final EIS.

Legislation patterned after NEPA exists at many state and local levels. Judicial decisions have helped define the types of studies and predictions required by NEPA, especially since the Calvert Cliffs decision of 1971 (Pastore 1972). Separate agencies meet their responsibilities under NEPA in different ways. Consequently, the wildlife specialist must be aware of each agency's requirements if he is to work effectively. These differences are considered subsequently, and the more prominent among them are pointed out. This chapter does not suggest needed changes in laws or regulations except perhaps by implication. Space limits discussion to describing the requirements of the regulations, principles used in meeting them, and major pitfalls and obstacles confronting the worker. This chapter is a guide to designing and interpreting investigations in a specialized area. It is not a handbook which somehow could replace the background, training, and experience of a wildlife professional. It is not intended to serve as a manual of practice for the wildlifer who prepares the wildlife sections of environmental impact statements, except to consider the extent that the needs of one kind of activity meet the requirements of the other.

Baseline Studies

Before predicting change, it is first necessary to know what already exists. Perhaps because engineers dominated environmental assessment in the earliest days of the EIS, the engineering term *baseline study* has been borrowed for investigations meant to describe conditions existing presently at the site of a project. This is perhaps unfortunate. Engineers deal ordinarily with nonliving materials which rarely change except in predictable ways. Biologists often are less certain about the complex living systems with which they deal. An often overlooked fact is that whether or not a highway is built or a valley flooded, there will be biological change at the site of the proposed project. Consequently, the biologist must make 2 basic predictions in the so-called baseline study. He must predict what change will take place if a project is or is not undertaken.

NEPA calls for describing "the environment without the proposed action." Practitioners often fail to recognize everything this means. Both those who write reports and those who evaluate them frequently regard an instantaneous "baseline" study as adequate to satisfy NEPA's requirement. Clearly it is not. The next section describes how the wildlifer should perform his portion of a baseline study.

Conditions Without Introducing Change

No biotic community is changeless. The nearest approach to permanence in a natural community is the state of dynamic equilibrium called the ecological climax. A climax community is self-sustaining, and the plants and animals that comprise it are replaced by others of the same species. The climax is probably never achieved; climax may be viewed as an ideal condition toward which seral or successional stages trend. The approach is asymptotic, and the climax is never quite attained in the real world. For example, fallen trees in a forest are replaced through localized successions.

Early successional stages replace one another quickly. Later seral communities last longer. Recognizing the current stage of succession in an area is perhaps the first step in predicting what will occur there.

If the site of a proposed action is undisturbed, natural succession can be anticipated with some confidence. The ecological literature will show the communities to be expected in a given region. The best description of the biotic communities of the entire North American continent is by Shelford (1963). Later or more regional works (e.g., Küchler 1964, Bailey 1976) provide detail, but discuss only plants, or only climax conditions. Soil surveys are published for counties or similar areas by the U.S. Department of Agriculture, Soil Conservation Service. Recent ones often describe native vegetation and discuss its value as wildlife habitat.

Local experience is invaluable. Talking with game managers, academics of various kinds, and county agricultural extension agents is frequently the best way to begin a baseline study. Librarians and newspaper editors often know of other knowledgeable people. Any of these may know of hidden sources of information such as theses and old aerial photographs.

Biotic communities are rarely unaffected by man. People compete with other organisms for resources. Changing the use of land changes its suitability as habitat for particular plants or animals. For example, creating a reservoir obviously denies the river bottoms to the terrestrial animals that once lived there, and may reduce cropland. Conversely, the reservoir may provide habitat for fish and waterfowl and function as a recreational area as well. Since critical habitat for some rare species is designated under law, preserving that habitat may be regarded as a resource allocation: a decision no different from setting aside a city park for human use.

Baseline studies must consider a variety of so-called preexisting stresses. These include timber harvesting, air pollutants, and hunting. Many of them are changeable by political whim. Others are even more difficult to predict. For example, it would have been difficult several years ago to predict the present popularity of off-road vehicles.

A baseline study, therefore, should state what exists presently and, when appropriate, should identify foreseeable trends in biotic communities and uses of natural resources. It is a basic, predictive part of the more inclusive environmental report. Though a baseline study may incidentally provide information which is valuable for other purposes, its goal is primarily to facilitate decisionmaking by predicting the environmental effects of a proposed action.

Conditions if Changes Are Introduced

The effects of introducing change must be predicted in the context of existing conditions. The design of a bridge, a pipeline, or a power plant is usually changeable. The wildlife biologist, by predicting the environmental effects of such a facility, may suggest to the engineer how modifications in the plan could result in fewer environmental conflicts. The earlier in the design process the interaction of engineer and ecologist begins, the less the chance of blunders by either.

The environmental effects of many projects also include changes away from their sites. The right-of-way of a transmission line may divide and significantly alter the habitat of a wide-ranging animal. Siltation from a construction site can damage aquatic communities some distance downstream. Therefore, the predicted impacts must consider much more than the biota whose habitat will be altered at the site itself.

Site Selection

The goal of all prediction, including alternatives, under NEPA is to improve decisionmaking. Such decisionmaking frequently requires understanding and careful examining of several choices and rejecting all but one. Very often, more than one site is available for a particular project. Several different plans might seem equally workable for managing a natural resource. The choices are frequently varied and include many more possibilities than whether or not to build a facility or whether or not to harvest a population. The locations of bridges and highways, for example, are flexible. They can serve the same functions at several different locations. Some developments can be put at many places. The wildlife biologist may predict the effects of similar proposed projects at numerous alternate sites. Sometimes this will require long study.

Conducting siting studies is a separate art. When many potential sites must be considered, the interaction of several specialists in a multidisciplinary team becomes especially important. The wildlife biologist, or other ecologist, should work with a meteorologist, an engineer, a planner, and others. Efficiency may justify use of aircraft. Such efforts usually seek first to reject proposed sites because of their definite unsuitability from the viewpoint of one or another specialist. When there is an overriding need to choose quickly, siting studies often can employ profitably the most experienced, even though the most expensive, participants.

Some sites can be recognized as unsuitable on biological grounds. Potential habitats for endangered species should be avoided if possible, partly because of the likelihood that they would require costly study to evaluate their actual suitability. Usually, one should recommend rejecting estuaries and wetlands. Unusual habitats, such as relict plant communities, should be protected. Other participants will recommend rejecting sites for other reasons, such as proximity to historic places or high development costs. If several sites can be found which are both acceptable to representatives of all disciplines and financially feasible for a proposed project, it may be needless to consider others. But if no site is suitable to all team members, restudy will be warranted. Such a restudy often will be greater in depth than the original effort.

The later stages of site-selection investigations usually concentrate on choosing the best among several acceptable sites. This kind of activity involves reconciling the diverse opinions of several experts. It is vital in such situations that artificial values, such as monetary payoff, not be allowed to intrude needlessly into decisionmaking. An obvious hazard is attempting to measure different values which by their natures cannot be compared on the same scale. This problem, characteristic of most cost-benefit analyses, has been widely discussed (reviewed in Ghiselin 1978b), but solutions satisfactory to everyone have not appeared. Perhaps the best advice is to resist and reject strict, formalized procedures, such as assigning numerical values to the opinions of several members of a team (cf. Sackman 1975) to overcome professional judgments by the mob rule of a committee.

WILDLIFE STUDIES

Levels of Community Organization

Some plants and animals can be managed effectively at the level of specific populations. Others can practicably be controlled only at higher levels of integration. For example, deer and other big game are customarily dealt with as species, with each having its special hunting season. Seasons for panfish and most ducks, in marked contrast, often apply to larger groups of species. The latter situation doubtless exists largely because many sportsmen cannot distinguish one duck from another, and the same bait attracts many fish. Consequently, management actions are applied to particular lakes or counties.

Environmental reports must deal with organisms at both higher and lower levels of organization. For this reason, the wildlife biologist must deal with communities at the highest and lowest levels practicable.

For practical description, one must be able to apply 1 term, or a very few, which will describe inclusively the biota of an area. These broad communities of plants and animals are typically (if perhaps archaically) termed biomes and associations (Shelford 1945, 1963). Though the term *ecosystem* is widely used in the literature, and in regulations, practical workers rarely encounter a community which includes all the interacting components. Classically, and strictly, an ecosystem is a community of plants and animals together with its nonliving habitat, complete in itself with the addition of radiant solar energy. Environmental reports rarely consider entire ecosystems, though they may consider several adjacent (but separate) ones. If a proposal called for changes throughout an isolated oceanic island, a report might consider the entire island as an ecosystem. A watershed is another example, though obviously not a particularly good one. Development projects are often not restricted to watersheds in practice because management actions, such as issuing plans for grazing or timber harvest, are usually prepared for political rather than natural units. The Soil Conservation Service, however, fairly often considers watersheds separately.

Davis (1977) recognized the special use of the term *ecosystem* in the context of environmental analysis and land use, describing 13 "primary ecosystems" in New York state and dividing some into "secondary ecosystems," in a classification linking "the concepts of ecosystem and geomorphology." The association also is somewhat too broad a term for many practical uses. Less inclusive levels of community organization and description (Oosting 1956:254) are formations and lociations. As a somewhat faulty rule, a formation can usually be distinguished in the field, or on a large-scale aerial photograph. Examples include oak-hickory forest (Braun 1950:35) and cold desert (Oosting 1956:320–322). Lociations are subdivisions of associations which may be distinguishable only after careful analysis of the species present. Although all of these levels of organization consider both plants and animals, in practice it is usually necessary to infer the animals from the plants.

Habitats of particular species may be important in environmental reports. Because of laws regarding endangered species, definition of critical characteristics of their habitats may be extremely important. Thus, prairie dogs and their towns should be recognized as indicating the potential presence of black-footed ferrets. Cliffs of suitable form are potential nest sites for peregrine falcons.

Populations of particular species may deserve special attention while others do not. If the goal of a study is to describe the range of conditions in an area, it may be necessary to define the populations of irruptive species such as voles (Microtinae) to give meaning to predator data. Other sections and other chapters in this manual give specific methods for particular forms.

Baseline studies must describe the workings of biotic communities so that changes in them can be predicted. Consequently, the wildlife biologist must investigate communities more broadly than if studying only game or pest species. This need for comprehensive investigation carries with it the danger that one will be caught up in trivia in the attempt to gather information about all organisms and all processes in which they participate. One pitfall for an investigator, especially a novice, is to collect detailed quantitative data merely because he knows how. The most important aspect of conducting any study is delimiting the investigational design properly. A later section discusses how statistical techniques should be used to optimize effort. The remainder of this section is concerned with some practical values of wildlife studies in environmental reports.

Practical Wildlife Impacts

Public concerns for wildlife may both overlap and conflict. The same people are often concerned both with consumptive uses of wildlife resources and with other sometimes conflicting kinds of outdoor recreation. Maintaining wildlife is only 1 part of a fairly well-defined conservation ethic. At the same time preserving or enhancing wildlife resources may interfere with more immediate public or individual goals. For example, oil drilling has been prohibited within the breeding habitat of the California condor. Blokpoel (1976) discussed bird hazards at airports. NEPA explicitly requires considering reconciliation of conflicts between immediate and long-term uses of resources. Because wildlife resources are renewable, wildlife biologists' findings and recommendations can be especially important for mitigating undesirable effects of a project.

GUIDES TO ENVIRONMENTAL ASSESSMENT

Agency Publications

This section discusses the requirements of various federal agencies in the United States for environmental reports and related documents. Examples are chosen from the requirements of a variety of U.S. government agencies, but the requirements either of smaller political subdivisions or of other countries will not be included. Although differing demands of various agencies for other kinds of information are touched upon, the purpose here is to compare and analyze what is presently required of wildlife biologists and other managers of renewable resources in meeting the needs and regulations of individual agencies.

NEPA sets forth requirements for environmental assessment by all federal agencies. That basic law also establishes the Council on Environmental Quality (CEQ) to oversee its application. Individual departments and independent agencies publish their own regulations to meet the requirements of NEPA. The result is a profusion of regulations which seek to meet a single goal in varying ways. It is arguable whether or not there need be so many separate sets of rules, and also whether or not they are equally suitable to meet the goals of NEPA and of the agencies themselves. In any case, for a specific project, the regulations of a single "lead" agency must be met. Since the lead agency may not be designated at the time one begins a study, it is prudent to perform an analysis which will meet the most demanding regulations that may be applied in a particular case.

One reason why regulations vary is that NEPA and other laws have been varyingly interpreted by different courts. Another is the historically differing philosophies of separate agencies. Though a tendency toward compliance with the intent of NEPA can be discerned in most agencies, the law is sometimes resisted by conservative elements in several.

The Council on Environmental Quality oversees the implementation of NEPA by 2 principal means. These are (i) by issuing regulations for implementation of procedural provisions of NEPA, and (ii) by reviewing the contents of selected draft EIS's for conformity with those guidelines before final impact statements are published. Federal lead agencies file draft EIS's with the Environmental Protection Agency. The CEQ retains control by resolving disputes among agencies, though it reviews closely only a small proportion of draft EIS's.

The regulations appear in the Code of Federal Regulations in Title 40, Chapter V, Part 1500. Special instructions are issued occasionally by memorandum, and specific agencies are given individual guidance by the CEQ staff. The regulations give general information on the preparation and review of environmental impact statements. They are meant to improve decisionmaking in the "NEPA process" by standardizing the format and content of EIS's among agencies, and reforming procedures to reduce delay and needless paperwork. However, because individual agencies retain control over the process, wildlifers are still concerned with specific rulings and procedures of individual agencies.

The individual guidelines of specific agencies often differ and, at times, conflict in what they require. This variety results partly from differences among agencies in their goals and methods and partly from the effects of citizens' actions. A range of requirements is reviewed here, but it is not a current summary. It is important for the wildlife biologist to obtain current copies not only of departmental regulations but also of those issued by agencies and independent activities.

Of all federal agencies, the Nuclear Regulatory Commission (NRC) issues the most demanding guidelines. The reason is that interest in nuclear projects resulted very early in public intervention in licensing proceedings and, consequently, in numerous, demanding court decisions. Regulations of the Nuclear Regulatory Commission are amplified in regulatory guides which, though not strictly regulations, are usually honored as if they were. The most important of these for the wildlife biologist is Regulatory Guide 4.2 (USNRC 1976). This is modified by Regulatory Guide 4.11 (USNRC 1977), and others, for particular kinds of proposed actions.

Section 2.2 of Regulatory Guide 4.2 describes what is required in treating the ecology of the site of a proposed plant. The guide calls for an initial inventory to identify the species which are "important" in the affected biotic communities. Ghiselin (1978a) examines the logical underpinnings of the criteria set forth by the NRC in determining whether or not particular species should be treated as "important," and "concludes that the regulation itself makes it impossible wholly to satisfy all of its requirements." The NRC generally requires a quantitative study of the biota of a large area, encompassing all seasons. Special attention is to be given to species designated as "endangered or threatened with endangerment." Other publications amplify the special requirements needed for considering the effects of releases of radioactive materials. The NRC further requires identification of bioenergetic pathways and other relationships among species. Later chapters in Regulatory Guide 4.2 call for predicting the effects of constructing, operating, and decommissioning a facility.

Additional, separate directions have been developed for particular kinds of investigation to be performed in connection with nuclear facilities. Among these is an industry publication (Battelle Laboratories 1975). American National Standards are being developed as well.

The Army Corps of Engineers (COE) is similarly exposed to intense public scrutiny, and its present regulations are almost as demanding as the NRC's. The COE differs from many agencies in that it not only takes actions having significant environmental effects but issues permits to other entities. For example, the COE is responsible for dredging waterways and also for licensing coal-fired power plants which draw cooling water from navigable streams. The same regulations govern COE actions in both cases. Wildlife biologists working either for the COE itself or for applicants for licenses must prepare environmental reports which conform to COE regulations.

The COE regulation governing EIS's (U.S. Army 1974) specifies the format of tables to be used for biological inventories. These tables are to include all "species of mammals, birds, fishes, reptiles, amphibians, mollusks, crustaceans, etc., that normally inhabit the project area or may be influenced by the project." The tables must include for each species its "Habitat and/or Seasonal Status." The tables also must list for each species its regional range as well as its range in the United States and give its "Abundance in Region" in such comparative terms as abundant, common, occasional, and rare. Endangered species and game species are to be given "specific and detailed analyses." A somewhat less detailed treatment is required for plants.

All this information is to be used to predict the effect of a proposed project on its area. The table is to list the "Project Impact" for each species in such terms as none, minimal, and moderate. COE regulations presently do not require identification or description of biotic communities. Because the numbers of individuals are to be given only in comparative terms, it is sometimes difficult to infer from such a species list what actually lives in the area to be affected by a project, or how it lives there. Ghiselin (1980) described more fully the problems associated with using species lists in ecological assessment.

Predicting the effects of changes with tabular information is difficult. The large mass of undigested data obscures what may be significant, while its tabular organization precludes extensive presentation of experts' interpretations. Data listed in phylogenetic order say little about the relationships of populations. Simultaneously, the regulation fails to require the organized information which is essential for understanding biotic communities. A truly predictive study will require more, in order to satisfy NEPA. Furthermore, to attempt to satisfy the COE alone will produce a document which meets the needs of few other agencies. It is hard to suggest how conflicts between regulations and needs should be dealt with by a wildlife biologist, or any other ecologist. It seems likely that each situation will require individual treatment. It is usually worthwhile to discuss procedures with representatives of responsible agencies early in the preparation of an assessment. The regulations for the implementation of NEPA (Council on Environmental Quality 1978) formalize an interagency "scoping" meeting to establish the responsibilities of various participants in preparing an EIS. The principle could be extended to include others, such as state agencies and consultants, whose responsibilities may be affected.

Other agencies' requirements also differ in both approach and detail. Some barely recognize biological considerations. For example, the Central Intelligence Agency (1974) asks that reports consider "alternative measures to compensate for losses to wildlife and alternative design approaches that significantly affect consumption of energy or other resources."

Regulations of the Department of the Interior govern many agencies whose activities may require EIS preparation. Such actions include leasing mineral lands and managing wildlife in national parks.

An example of an agency manual likely to be used by wildlifers is that of the Bureau of Land Management (1976). Like other agencies, the BLM requires that applicants for permits provide information to support their applications. Consulting firms often provide the data for utility companies or other clients. Information from a consultant's report may be incorporated in the draft EIS issued by the agency, but the responsibility for its accuracy and comprehensiveness remains with the BLM.

It is obviously necessary for the private consultant to insure that his report will satisfy the BLM's requirements; this can be done only with the cooperation of the BLM itself, since it will employ the report in preparing the EIS. The same regulation governs preparation of EIS's on actions proposed to be taken wholly by the Bureau itself.

The BLM manual calls for describing in some detail a proposed action and alternatives. Few federal agencies require considering seral change or other natural alterations extending much beyond the "economic project life" of a proposed action. But the BLM comes closer than many. It requires both describing the "existing environment" and predicting "what the future environment, for the area of consideration, would be without project implementation." The manual emphasizes the importance of professional judgment in predicting impacts, and also calls for reducing the bulk of detail.

Agencies of the Department of Agriculture include the Forest Service and the Soil Conservation Service. Both have long manuals governing conformity to NEPA, but neither is sufficiently detailed to allow someone inexperienced in working with the agency to proceed without first seeking detailed guidance.

The differences among agencies' goals and plans are a primary reason for review of draft EIS's by other agencies. Another important function of review is to suggest changes and correct technical deficiencies. This review is needed both for documents prepared within an agency and for reports submitted by applicants for licenses or permits. Because of the widespread requirement for review of the work of others, the wildlife biologist should be aware of the likelihood that his own work will be evaluated elsewhere, and also should be prepared to perform such review himself.

The principal concerns of each agency are implicit in its mission (and usually in its name); but specialists in other disciplines often have important roles as well. Thus the proposals of the Department of Transportation require consideration by experts in fish and wildlife, and conversely proposals for refuge acquisition receive scrutiny by Soil Conservation Service biologists.

With a welter of differing requirements, it is difficult for anyone to master all. While the preparer must meet all agency requirements, a reviewer rarely needs to master the format of another agency. He must, though, insure that his comment covers the review requirements and responsibilities of his own agency. If the information provided in the draft EIS is insufficient to predict the potential effects of a project, a reviewer should point out the deficiencies. Still another reason for review of draft EIS's by other agencies and by the public is to detect unanticipated effects of planned actions. These may include, for example, altering the habitats of endangered species. If the draft EIS ignores an important "secondary" consequence of its proposed action, the reviewer should identify this weakness. To the degree that the information available makes possible predicting what might happen, the reviewer should suggest it—with caution because of his isolation from the situation.

Useful suggestions for reviewing and commenting on draft EIS's are those of the U.S. National Marine Fisheries Service (1975). This document emphasizes the need for scientific and technical soundness. A draft EIS should be a specialized scientific document, and it should be reviewed like one. Each comment should stand up to scrutiny by the reviewer's peers. For this reason, the reader must scrupulously avoid "making judgmental, reproachful, abusive, sarcastic, derisive, discourteous, contemptuous, or disparaging remarks." Each comment employing technical data should be documented (in the format of the Council of Biology Editors [CBE Style Manual Committee 1978]) whenever possible.

Other Publications

Examples given in the foregoing passage show something of the variety and differing emphasis found in regulations of several federal departments and agencies. These examples do not include the special viewpoints of many agencies. Several handbooks seek to resolve the differences among agencies, to provide a unified approach to environmental assessment under NEPA, and to guide the preparation of environmental reports. Publications at the departmental level, and some prepared by the Council on Environmental Quality, have been issued by government sources. This section attempts to guide the reader through further examples.

Nongovernmental handbooks and textbooks generally deal with both federal and local regulations. These treatments have varying usefulness. The better ones try to identify related characteristics of environmental assessment at various levels and to point up mechanisms, purposes, and difficulties which are common to several. It is regrettable that none quite achieves the goal; but careful foraging will yield some nutrition.

Nuclear power plants are subject to stringent controls. The most comprehensive manual on impact assessment (Battelle Laboratories 1975) was produced to meet the specialized needs of the nuclear power industry. Its 2 volumes recommend methods not only for preparing baseline statements, but also for the design of monitoring programs.

NRC regulatory guides presently require that impacts be reported largely in quantitative terms. Doing so necessarily requires using quantitative methods during both baseline and monitoring studies. However, when early, qualitative studies suggest that no significant effects will occur at a plant site, it is not necessary, under current guidelines, to undertake quantitative studies.

Two sections of Battelle's (1975) publications are of particular interest and value for wildlife biologists. Bell and Rickard describe methods for inventorying plants, birds, mammals, cold-blooded vertebrates, and invertebrates. They discuss measures of biological productivity, warn of pitfalls in using biological indicators, and describe several topics of concern to other specialists. Eberhardt and Gilbert lucidly discuss the statistics of designing surveys and interpreting data. Their section on community analysis seems less satisfying, largely because of the practical difficulty of interpreting either productivity or species diversity at the level of the biotic community. The book contains an extensive review of the literature.

It is especially important for wildlife biologists to recognize the hazard of oversimplification, because many ecological problems are apt to be more difficult to describe than others concerned with environmental assessment. Moreover, the sorts of issues which are important to biologists frequently resist translation into monetary terms. Recreational values, habitat for endangered species, and integrity of biotic communities are examples.

When NEPA began to call explicitly for interdisciplinary analyses, it was recognized early that the interactions of different disciplines' concerns, and the number of factors to be evaluated, made it almost essential to have a formalized, structured mechanism to insure that all were considered. In one of the first proposed, Leopold et al. (1971) presented a matrix which is best used "as a checklist or reminder of the full range of actions and impacts." Though the authors pointed out its tentative nature, the very existence of the document has led to ill-considered applications. Among the most pernicious of these has been the devising and using of numerical rating systems for comparing different kinds of potential effects. These schemes can give the appearance of mathematical precision and impartiality to processes which are innately neither precise nor impartial. This is a hazard of cost-benefit analysis and similar techniques which, though recognized by law and by regulatory agencies, is not always understood by practitioners. Ghiselin (1978b) discussed the topic more fully and considered certain mathematical inexorabilities of the situation.

The handbooks and other commercial publications which have thus far appeared include annotated syllabi (Corwin et al. 1975), proceedings of symposia (Karam and Morgan 1976), and other miscellaneous compendia (Dickert and Domeny 1974). Most of these seem to aim at audiences of supervisors, rather than working biologists. Consequently, such publications have only limited value as aids for the design and preparation of environmental reports. They do provide entries to the scientific literature and suggest approaches and hazards peculiar to what is becoming in some ways a separate discipline in applied ecology. Technical information is presented later in this chapter and elsewhere in this manual. More will appear in the increasing number of specialized journals in the field. These include the *Journal of Applied Ecology*, the *Journal of Environmental Management*, and *Environmental Management*.

Several publications discussed earlier in this section seek to describe procedures for environmental assessment. All fall into one or another pedagogical trap. A common danger for technical people, whatever their specialties, is to do things because they are familiar activities. People in general may succumb to mumbo jumbo and accept the trappings of science as somehow superior to their own experience. These tendencies can lead to 2 errors which commonly appear in manuals and many environmental reports.

The first mistake is overemphasizing aquatic studies. Complex instrumentation is needed to gather data on most aquatic communities, while terrestrial studies of comparable predictive value can be done by simpler methods. Consequently, aquatic studies may seem more precise and hence more significant than those done on land. Impressive apparatus and showy procedures can be permitted similarly to dominate information gathering. Insect-sampling machines and elaborate sampling designs are of this kind. Those who keep in mind why investigations are performed will hardly be caught in this confusion. Field biologists often understand that machines do not necessarily improve scientific reliability, but such sophistication may impress engineers and others who are concerned either with utilizing professional resources within their organizations, or with contracting for them from outside.

Shortsightedness is the second difficulty. The potential effects of public works often persist long beyond the so-called useful lives of the projects. Reservoirs silt in. Power stations become obsolete, but their ash dumps remain. Abandoned canals and old railroad grades show how long the marks of a technology may persist.

Few agencies have yet begun to require consideration of impacts beyond the short term. Manuals presently available, understandably, suggest no more. Cultural considerations may be appropriately considered in a time scale beginning in the remote past, and stopping right now; this is how historic sites and land-use planning appear to be addressed in the present. Water supplies are provided, and their usefulness predicted, on the basis of demand projected during the project's anticipated life. But most projects have actual effects beyond their expected usefulness. Biological changes of long duration include altering succession and obliterating habitats. It is, therefore, almost inevitable that in an "interdisciplinary" team, the wildlife biologist is often—if not usually—the primary one to consider long-term effects. He considers interactions of information originating in separate disciplines in more breadth than others do.

Prediction is the purpose of environmental assessment under NEPA; but prediction is rarely mentioned in manuals and guidelines. The substitute they give is description of the *status quo*. The reader is often left to infer his own predictions from variously adequate descriptions. Descriptions are often insufficient because of inappropriate design or unwisely chosen methods. Both design and performance of studies are—or should be—the responsibilities of the various sorts of professionals who prepare sections within environmental reports. Those who write EIS's based on those reports should themselves be prepared to plan and perform the studies.

TASKS FOR WILDLIFE PROFESSIONALS

Describing Communities

It was pointed out earlier that biotic communities can be discriminated at many levels. These range from lociations to biomes in various notations. Odum (1977) has argued that the ecosystem is a useful level for organizing thought and comprehending relationships, and few ecologists would disagree. The synthetic process is essential to formulating a holistic conception of interacting organisms in any biotic community, whatever the level at which it is discriminated. It is rather obvious, therefore, that species-list ecology is not the best practice in preparing environmental reports, but very nearly the worst. Odum appropriately calls for organizing impact assessment in energetic terms at the level of ecosystems, but it is usually impractical to achieve that ideal in our present state of ignorance.

There are 2 principal reasons why. One is the problem of time (or money, or manpower). The other is the less tractable difficulty of scale. It might be possible to mass an interdisciplinary force sufficient to predict the consequences, say, of melting the Antarctic ice cap to irrigate the Sahara. It requires, however, quite a different scale of thought—or at least of execution—to predict the effects of building a sewer main. Wildlifers will chiefly work on the latter class of jobs; and therefore, it is chiefly to the more probable kinds of work that this section is addressed.

It is useful to separate biotic communities only to those subdivisions significant in a particular analysis. Valuable communities, in that sense, are usually those one would discriminate in a detailed cover map or a modern soil map. (Cover mapping is discussed in Chapter 17.)

Aerial photographs are especially useful in discriminating habitat types, provided that the accuracy of interpreting photographs is verified by "ground truth." Moreover, an aerial photograph may serve as a detailed base for a cover map. Orthophotoquads, which relate aerial mosaics to topographic maps, are valuable. Color infrared and false-color aerial photographs are often useful. LANDSAT or other satellite imagery has value in certain types of study, usually of large areas.

Certain habitats or kinds of biotic communities which require special treatment are discussed below. Though for several reasons it may be necessary to delineate such special community types, it is rarely necessary to work at the same level of detail throughout a study. A sense of tidiness in planning a study should not justify otherwise unwarranted effort.

Endangered Species

The potential occurrence of endangered, or threatened, species requires special effort in describing communities. If such species range into a study area, it is usually essential to describe in detail any available habitat. For example, the peregrine falcon has the potential for occurring in many parts of North America, but suitable nesting habitat is of most concern in assessing the effects of proposed developments. "Critical" habitat is designated for certain species by the U.S. Fish and Wildlife Service.

Life history studies are especially important in delineating habitat which is potentially critical for rare species, whether or not they have been declared to be endangered or threatened. Since a species may be both rare and secretive, it may not be encountered in a particular investigation. However, it should be possible to reach a judgment as to whether or not suitable habitat exists in an area during the course of a study. The actual or potential presence of a rarity in or near a project area does not necessarily preclude developments. The potential impact of a proposed action on a particular species should be the determining factor in recommendations regarding it. Also, taking actions which could mitigate potentially adverse effects on, or possibly benefit, a particular species should be considered.

Sensitive Habitats

Another reason for emphasizing particular areas is the commercial or recreational value of certain segments of biotic communities. Animals of this kind include game species, furbearers, commercially valuable fishes, predators, and forest and crop pests. Agricultural crops and timber are important floral components. Considerations of commercial or recreational resources may require consultation with experts in other fields, such as forestry.

Potential disruptions of estuaries should be considered carefully. A classic categorization of wetlands (Shaw and Fredine 1956) has been incorporated in the legal definitions of wetland types given in the Water Bank Act (P.L. 91–559, 1970). Though more modern treatments of wetlands are available (Darnell 1976, Cowardin et al. 1977), descriptions in environmental assessments should be compatible with legal requirements. Wetlands are important not only for their production of fish and game but also for such other values as purifying polluted water (Odum et al. 1977).

Potentials for forest production should not be ignored. Some areas can be revegetated, even though their normal soil profiles have been destroyed. Hutnik and Davis (1973) provide entries to the literature. Other possibilities are locally important; an example is catfish farming. Many potentials are limited by soil characteristics; the local Soil Conservation Service wildlife biologist and soil conservationist are usually helpful.

Predicting Changes

The purpose of the environmental assessment required by NEPA is to consider all the effects of proposed actions beforehand, rather than risk being surprised by significant impacts. Predicting environmental impacts is, consequently, not new to planning. It is merely an orderly way of looking before one leaps. Its purpose does not differ from boring to plan the foundations of buildings, conducting clinical tests of new drugs, or tasting food before one salts it. Its practical effects on a project can range from causing no change in good plans to forcing the total abandonment of disastrous ideas.

The unanticipated consequences of a plan may be more extensive than its intended results. This is conspicuously so of biological effects because of the interrelationships of organisms. Perturbations of living systems affect organisms which at first glance seem unconnected. One special contribution of wildlife biology is identifying situations sensitive to such "indirect" alterations and anticipating further changes that might result from them. One potential class of effects caused by changing natural systems is often overlooked by nonbiologists when they consider biological impacts of a project. This is that a proposed activity may cause population growth that can subsequently reduce other populations of interest. Examples include algal blooms and plagues of insects.

Computer simulation is sometimes useful for predicting the effects of proposed alterations in natural processes. The practical value of this aid depends on providing accurate data initially, and subsequently validating the model (Caswell 1976). The techniques of systems ecology are usually costly, and they have limited use in environmental assessment. They probably find greatest application in dealing with predictable changes, such as the thermal effects of power stations on cooling waters. Chapter 12 of this manual, describing the use of computers in wildlife management, presents material which is also valuable in this context.

The most important contribution a participant can make to an interdisciplinary study can be to indicate areas of potential difficulty. Prediction in such a study, therefore, should emphasize factors critical to the integrity of affected communities or of particular species which are important. For example, because such factors as cover, food, water, or migration routes may be limiting, the prediction of impacts most logically begins by considering the effects of changes in such factors.

Identifying populations which are especially sensitive to the effects of proposed actions usually begins by gaining a basic understanding of the proposed activity. Once again, the interaction of ecologist with engineer should begin as early as possible in the development of a project.

Recommending Mitigative Methods

The logical step following prediction is recommending changes to limit the effects which one foresees for a particular development. Recommendations about ameliorating effects often will come almost simultaneously with recognizing the potentialities for inducing them; but in other cases, trade-offs will be developed late in project planning. For example, the wildlife biologist may recommend developing habitat for a particular game species specifically to compensate for destruction of similar habitat by construction. Decisions to undertake such actions will commonly be made in the contexts of politics or public relations, but their feasibility should be considered early in the process of design development.

DEFINING PROBLEMS IN IMPACT ASSESSMENT

Baseline Studies

Baseline investigations are fundamental to all other inquiries: they provide the information on which to base predictions of changes. Such changes include those that will occur in the absence of human intervention and also those that may result from it.

Baseline studies are conducted like most basic research and both must first consider biotic communities unaltered by man. Baseline studies are given extra impetus by their relationship to potential developments. Nonetheless, baseline studies should draw upon all literature of ecology, and they should contribute by publication and otherwise to the accumulation of ecological knowledge whenever possible.

A baseline study cannot consider equally all aspects of the biology of an area. It must be planned to evaluate principally the elements of a biological situation which are most vulnerable to change, either directly or consequentially. These are usually important alterations in the habitats of organisms. The significance of such changes, of course, varies among species; but some generalization is possible.

Disruption of large areas of contiguous habitat denies it to populations both as places to live and as routes for emigration from affected places. Because of behavioral interactions within populations, it is unlikely for animals to flee from construction sites into adjacent regions; most will die. Exceptions might be found in understocked habitats, but these are likely to occur principally among cyclical or exploited species, and not whole biotas.

Large organisms are more apt than small ones to show the effects of a project. This applies to both plants and animals; and in both cases it is related to the size-volume relationships of physiology, to trophic relationships, and to the usually longer generation time in large organisms than small.

There are principles in wildlife ecology which hardly need presentation here, but which should be emphasized because of their special pertinence to baseline studies. One axiom of management is to identify and manage the weakest link in an organism's life cycle. The interpretation of this generalization for baseline studies is to identify critical stages in order to predict impacts. Welfare factors give wildlife managers a kind of leverage in this regard, as well as being the obvious place to begin in planning ameliorative steps.

Siting and Other Studies of Large Areas

It was suggested earlier that siting investigations are almost a separate, special type of investigation for wildlife biologists. In this section, that theme will be expanded and extended to other kinds of investigations which deal extensively with large areas. These are contrasted with the more intensive investigations which characterize baseline studies. One should not lose sight of the fact that the goal of all impact assessment is predictive, and that its reason is always practical and directed to a specific goal.

What are generally termed siting studies include 2 types of investigation. The first is intended to choose a site for a particular installation. These are typified by interdisciplinary studies to choose the best site within a power company's service area for construction of a power station. There is seldom a question whether or not such a plant should be built; the chief problem is where.

The second class of investigation covering a large area is concerned with deciding whether or not to do something. Such evaluations are often called feasibility studies. They are included in this discussion because some aspect of a proposed action's environmental impact may be limiting. A member of an interdisciplinary study team may show at an early stage that a proposal is not feasible before much effort has been invested. Examples of this kind of proposed action include constructing recreational reservoirs and opening surface mines. Deciding to do such things depends in large measure on whose "bread is buttered" and whose "ox gored."

In this second case, it usually will be more important to initiate discussion among disciplines as soon as possible. Engineering considerations probably will have less weight, socioeconomics more, and the concerns of such natural sciences as biology may be in danger of being lost. Moreover, the wildlifer often will find himself anticipating the work of another sort of specialist. Kitchen middens and old millponds are properly the concerns of archeologists and specialists in historical preservation. Nonetheless, the wildlife biologist should be alert to such things, because they may indicate historic features whose disruption would call forth public opposition, whatever one's own feelings might be.

Whichever sort of investigation is at hand, one should be ready to discuss related issues, especially those which seem at first to be quite unaffected by a proposal. Two reasons are most important. First, the wildlifer should be prepared to speak in council with representatives of other fields, especially since it may be his lot to resolve differences among them because of his breadth of training and outlook. Second, it may be necessary to explain one's opinions and recommendations under oath in a hearing.

Corridor Studies

One class of facility presents special difficulties because of the scope of work involved. This includes all projects which look very thin on a map but may be very long. Examples are pipelines, transmission lines, and highways. They are distinguished most by the variety of ecological situations they affect.

Such investigations as these often involve both site selection and an attenuated prediction and comparison of potential effects. A particular concern often is the influence of a proposed facility on an area which, on a map, it would barely seem to touch. Such problems are caused by the often needless clearing of vegetation along rights-of-way, siltation of streams below highway crossings, and fragmentation of habitats by facilities built across them. Remedies and attenuating measures vary but usually require early and continuing consultation among the various members of the environmental assessment team. Egler and Foote (1975) described abuses of rights-of-way by conventional treatment and recommended methods of management dealing chiefly with vegetation.

INVESTIGATIONAL DESIGN

The investigators' time is the major cost of most studies. Smaller "out-of-pocket" costs, such as travel and computer use, also must be considered. All can be minimized by planning investigations to limit waste effort while insuring that they achieve their purposes. One rarely has the luxury of being able to work at a leisurely pace. Conversely, since almost every hour is charged, and there are deadlines to meet, one must optimize his own efficiency to meet competition. The complexity of these circumstances makes planning more detailed in environmental assessment than in most other classes of work a wildlife biologist might do. Slightly different emphases guide those responsible for writing environmental reports. These include biologists who work for utilities or other applicants for licenses, and those who work in agencies responsible for preparing EIS's. All should make certain the predictive purpose of environmental assessment is met.

The first step in planning should be to set and clarify the goals to be met. Failing to recognize the reason why one is beginning a study will tempt one to overemphasize some aspects of the study and to neglect others because of personal predilections and other less defensible reasons, such as the availability of unassigned investigators.

Baseline studies are intended to provide information needed for predicting the effects of either continuing or changing priorities in land use. Moreover, they are needed to monitor changes in newly undertaken projects and also may support future studies designed to test predictions of impact. However, more extensive studies are rarely justified.

Statistical Control

Professional judgments often are based on limited information and influenced by personal experiences and outlooks; but in every technical area, experts usually reach agreement as information is increased. In science and engineering, the reliability of information is measured and described by statistical confidence limits (Clopper and Pearson 1934).

Other chapters in this manual describe the use of statistical controls in experimental design. Schultz et al. (1976) provide a current bibliography. This section discusses only some special applications useful in preparing environmental reports. It considers optimizing investigational effort and emphasizes reasons for avoiding the use of mathematical methods when they are not appropriate.

It is important that investigators recognize the intended uses of information to be collected, and thereby avoid the collection of unneeded data. Probably the most useful generalizations are that one should use the least costly level of measurement which will meet the needs of a study, and that one should avoid methods that produce data which cannot be interpreted at the level of measurement chosen.

Two categories of statistical inference are widely used. These are parametric and nonparametric statistics. Because the differences between them are not always recognized, it should be helpful to contrast the two. Parametric statistics are based on specific, preconceived distributions; each distribution is derived from unique parameters that describe a population. In parametric statistics, the normal distribution is used most often by biologists. However, some populations do not conform to the normal distribution or any other known or familiar distribution.

A large class of nonparametric or distribution-free statistics has been developed to deal with such cases. These aids to statistical inference have found much application among wildlife ecologists for 3 principal reasons. First, it is difficult to determine whether or not many populations conform to a particular distribution. Second, many biotic populations clearly do not conform to any known distribution. Finally, biological data are often expressed in measurement scales which cannot be treated by the usual parametric methods.

Tests assuming a normal distribution have greater power efficiency than nonparametric counterparts. It is, therefore, advantageous to apply parametric tests wherever they can be used legitimately. The levels of measurement employed often dictate which class of test is appropriate. Following Siegel (1956:21–30) and Conover (1971:65–67), one may discriminate among 4 levels of measurement. These, with the measures of central tendency appropriate for each, are (i) nominal (mode); (ii) ordinal (median); (iii) interval (mean); and (iv) ratio (geometric mean). In analyzing data at these 4 levels, nonparametric statistical tests can be employed for all, but parametric tests can be applied only to measurements made at the interval and ratio levels. This is because only these latter 2 are truly quantitative scales. The difference between ordinal and interval scales is clearly set forth by Hailman (1969). He gives as a rule of thumb that measurements are actually recorded at the interval and ratio scales only if they can be expressed in an internationally recognizable unit, such as time or length or weight.

There are 2 main keys to minimizing the costs of both quantitative and qualitative studies of biotic communities. These are (i) to insure that data gathered can be analyzed at the same level of measurement, and (ii) to prevent giving disproportionate effort to gathering certain classes of data. The first is achieved by experimental design, and the second by care in execution.

For many types of population estimates, such as the familiar Lincoln or Petersen index, the results are at the interval or ratio levels of measurement. The critical parameter here is the standard deviation, σ, which, of course, is obtained in practice from the variance, σ^2. Small calculators are now available which permit one to estimate σ, and thus to insure that population data do not exceed the fiducial limit. Exceeding that limit will gain the investigator nothing, but nonetheless will cost time and effort.

A more important problem can result from a blunder in designing a study. If a population estimate is made, for example, at the interval level of measurement, every constituent measurement must be at the same (or a higher) level. Thus to include a single measurement at the ordinal level will "poison" an entire mass of related statistics. No mean, and no variance, calculated for a population as a whole will have any usefulness in such calculations as estimating the flow of energy in an area. It should follow that if equally good data are not collected or otherwise available for all parts of a population, it is senseless (in the absence of some special need) to gather good data on some parts and bad data on others.

Optimizing Effort

Optimization of investigational effort, and therefore project costs, is actually a part of investigational design. Acceptable values for fiducial limits should be established in the design and maintained in executing it. Again, the important parameter is σ. If one can predict (i.e., guarantee) the value of σ to be achieved, he can make either of 2 plans. These are either (i) to provide a given precision at a fixed price or (ii) to meet an estimated price for a specified precision. Depending on the precision required and the complexity of the study, several refined techniques for optimizing the collection of data are available. Stratified sampling is described in Southwood (1966:21), Watt (1968:189–225) and Cochran (1977). Sequential techniques are considered in Finney (1960:140–141, 145–148); Southwood (1966:43–46); and Poole (1974:321–325). The influence of species diversity on the adequacy of sample size is discussed in Chapter 16 of this manual.

Habitat Analysis

Describing biotic communities is probably more time consuming than any other aspect of environmental assessment. Certainly it is as near being a universal duty as any for wildlifers. Consequently, it will receive considerable attention here.

Workers experienced in virtually any region should be able to describe the principal biotic communities occurring there. This description should certainly be at the level of the plant association, as discussed earlier, and perhaps below. The vertebrates of each area should be similarly predictable. Invertebrates and lower plants may be less well known, but such information also will probably be less important at the time. In almost all instances, the most profitable activity for the investigator is to conduct a detailed reconnaissance of the area of a proposed project and of adjacent places where related investigations will be conducted.

This kind of reconnaissance should in most cases aim at describing and discriminating plant communities. At this time, one may begin a cover map (see Chapter 17). Consulting with project engineers and other specialists whose own decisions may affect the project will be especially appropriate at this stage. When plans for a project have been refined, it will be time to begin an analysis of areas which may be affected by the project, and of nearby areas which may serve for comparisons.

When a general description of an area has been largely achieved, it often will be useful to begin to describe its bioenergetics. This will initially require merely describing the most important species of plants and animals and their roles in their communities. For example, in a mature hardwood forest, one might identify several dominant species of trees, and identify the most important herbivores and their predators.

After the purely descriptive stage has passed and the investigator has developed a basic assessment of the biotic community, it may be appropriate to begin quantitative studies of potentially affected communities. These usually will include analyses of the proportional composition of such cover types as marshes or woodlands by studies of sample plots (see Chapter 19) or by plotless or nonparametric techniques (e.g., for one method, Catana 1963, Ashby 1972). At the same time, quantitative analyses of animal populations should ordinarily begin.

Throughout an investigation, one should remember both the reason for conducting a study and how the results will be presented—graphically, tabularly, or pictorially. Regulations or the usual practice in an organization may require the inclusion of species lists (e.g., U.S. Army 1974). In such cases, the redundant and inefficient use of separate lists describing the biotas of several communities discriminated in an area may be necessary to permit discussion of relationships.

METHODS OF STUDY

General Considerations

Though the goal of preparing environmental reports is predicting consequences of actions, it often will be impossible to test the accuracy of such forecasts. Some predictions may not be testable for many years. Even forecasts that can be judged almost immediately are often moot; actual events may make prognostications about them meaningless. Thus, it is understandable that trying to predict environmental impacts sometimes may seem futile. Schindler (1976) called the whole process a boondoggle. Unquestionably, the costs of EIS's are sometimes excessive. Most people, though, now acknowledge their value for improved decisionmaking. This is why environmental assessment is so well established.

Reasonable objections to requirements for environmental reports are numerous, but they represent only a few classes of complaint. It is argued that costs are too high, and that investigations take too long. Perhaps a more telling argument is that reports and EIS's based on them mean almost nothing when they are at last submitted. This section considers practical ways by which the effort may be made more useful.

One of the most difficult concepts to handle in practice is that of "important" species. This idea occurs in many agencies' guidelines. Its most extreme development is in those of the NRC. The reason for requiring special treatment for some species or populations is to reduce the waste of effort if exhaustive studies of all species were to be performed. As a device for coping with environmental complexity, the idea is attractive; but in practice, as mandated by NRC regulatory guides, the concept is more a trap than a haven. Uncertainties about which species are to be treated as "important" may persist until late in a study, even though they must be identified at its beginning if approved procedures are to be followed. The resulting situation forces the adoption of investigational designs which are extremely conservative, because doubts about many species must be given the costly benefit of overemphasis in gathering data. This and related concepts are treated more extensively in Ghiselin (1978a).

Methods for Studying Plant Populations

Plant populations are emphasized here as the basis for discriminating among biotic communities. There are 2 reasons. First, plants are usually immobile. Second, plants have a trophically inescapable preponderance in biomass as contrasted with animals. Yet despite this ecological position, plants usually have a subsidiary role in the ecology of man and other animals. This is more conspicuous in studies of the autecology of man, as represented in environmental impact assessment, than in other aspects of ecology.

Natural populations of animals and plants change through ecological succession. Methods for studying plant communities should be adapted to dealing with succession, both in predicting changes which may be caused by man and in describing the changes which will take place if an area is not disturbed. Because seral change will vary from point to point in an area, it will be essential to replicate sampling in several representative places. An exception is an important community which occupies so small an area that it can or must be studied in its totality.

Studying plant populations to provide information for an environmental report differs somewhat from studying the plants which occur in the habitat of a game animal, because of differing objectives; but the methods described in Chapter 19 are generally useful. A later section in the present chapter considers endangered species.

Methods for Studying Animal Populations

Many methods described in this manual are appropriate for studying both game animals and other vertebrates. But they are not as useful for populations of invertebrates, even though invertebrates are food for some vertebrates and competitors for others. This section suggests field methods useful in preparing environmental reports. However, wildlifers should be aware that investigations of invertebrates may require significant help from specialists.

Animals should be considered with regard both to the plants and other animals in their habitats and to their own populations. The distinction is needed because of animals' differing mobility. Springtails (Collembola) have minuscule ranges and may reasonably be dealt with (if at all) in the context of a lociation; some migratory birds have ranges so large they give difficulty when one considers the idea of an ecosystem.

Studies of vertebrate populations should emphasize those subject to rapid change because these may be more sensitive than others to environmental alterations. Most of these species will be small and short-lived. Special attention should be given to some species because of such extrinsic reasons as their importance as game or pests. Most populations, however, need be described only well enough for an expert to detect unusual situations, and little more. The goal of such a description is to permit predicting the consequences of taking various actions. For this purpose, indices of population change may be as valuable as absolute numerical data. Indices are discussed further, and cautions about their use are given in Chapter 14.

As a general rule—with numerous obvious exceptions—vertebrates indicate perturbations within their communities better than other organisms. Invertebrates may reveal those disturbances faster, and plants faster still. Thus, no single group of organisms should be studied to the exclusion of others. However, within these groups, some species are known to be less adaptable and therefore are more sensitive to change than others.

Methods for studying mammals and birds are so well known (see Chapters 28 and 29) that they are passed over here. Reptiles and amphibians are sometimes overlooked. Their trophic significance, however, makes them important in many communities. It is rarely necessary under the current standards for studies to treat them quantitatively, but incidental collections and observations should be made when amphibians or reptiles are encountered.

Like aquatic herpetofauna, fishes and their habitats are beyond the scope of this chapter; but the effects they may have on land organisms should be assessed. This is particularly true of food organisms. Examples are prey for ospreys and the mass emergence of aquatic insects which attract swallows to feed over streams.

Invertebrates are difficult to study because of their diversity and the sporadic and unpredictable occurrence of some species; but many are important as pests, predators, pathogens, or prey for plants or other animals. Such soil organisms as nematodes (Nematoda) are still less obvious and, consequently, still more difficult to investigate. Yet the trophic function of such detritivores is clearly important. As methods advance, study of these inconspicuous animals will probably become routine; at the present, one should be aware of the potential need to seek specialized aid in assessing their importance in particular systems. Southwood (1966) presents methods for their study, emphasizing insects.

Endangered Species

Some species of plants and animals are so rare they are near extinction. Since extinction is the destiny of every species, this is hardly a cause for concern in every instance; but many human activities are stressful to populations of other organisms, hastening their disappearance. Recognizing this, the Endangered Species Act of 1973 and several later laws provide for special treatment for species or subspecies designated as either "endangered" or "threatened with endangerment" by the U.S. Fish and Wildlife Service. In the present context, the most important aspect of such designation is that either known or suspected presence of an endangered organism where it might be affected by a proposed action can prevent the project from going forward.

At present, most "threatened" and "endangered" species are vertebrates, but lists of plants and invertebrates are being enlarged. In any case, administrative designation of a population as being endangered may have little relation to its actual status in a particular place. (One might hope that all populations in danger of being extirpated would receive the same sort of solicitude from wildlife biologists.)

The practical importance of endangered and threatened species is that ecologists must concern themselves both with the organisms themselves and with their habitats. Obviously, the rarer an animal, the less likely it is to be observed. Therefore, the wildlifer must be prepared to point out the importance of habitat for rarities, even when he cannot report observations. The law recognizes this and explicitly protects critical habitat for endangered species.

Bioenergetic Studies

The importance of describing energy flux in living systems can easily be overemphasized, as I have noted. Nonetheless, an analysis of the principal trophic pathways in a community permits the reader of an ER to grasp quickly many relationships which could be obscure in a species list. Figure 25.1 is an example of a graphic presentation of such relations, somewhat modified from its source in a report of a reconnaissance of an estuary on the East Coast of the United States. Such diagrams present observations and conclusions at the ordinal level of measurement, at best, but they have proven helpful for reviewers of reports.

Bioenergetic investigations revealing the relationships among all the members of a biotic community are now beyond the state of the so-called art of environmental assessment. However, as Odum (1977) points out, a way already exists to use certain characteristics at the level of the community or ecosystem as indicators of the functioning of the whole.

Because much of the information required for bioenergetic studies is botanical and physiological, collection and analysis of the data will be beyond the usual expertise of the wildlife biologist. Nevertheless, it is well to understand something of the reasoning and the techniques involved.

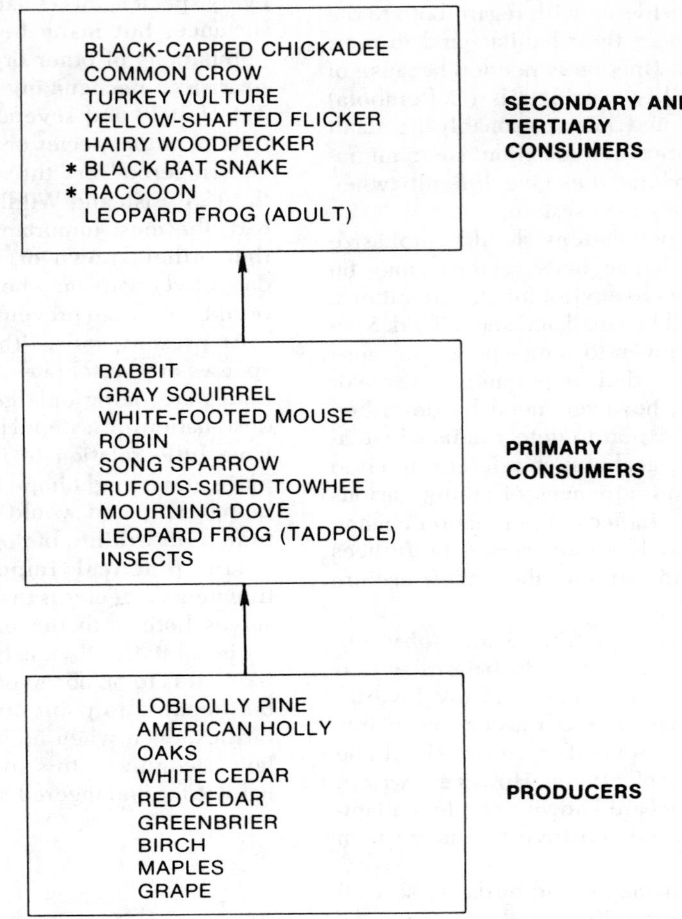

Fig. 25.1. **Diagram setting forth the major trophic relationships within a proposed project area.**

PREDICTING CHANGES

Comparing Biotic and Abiotic Systems

Most activities now requiring EIS's are engineering works—dams or power plants—or related to such extractive activities as surface mining. Almost all of these have the principal intention of changing the nonliving world or removing the materials of which that world is composed. Almost all are meant to be permanent, in the sense of lasting out their designed lives. Biologists' involvement with such projects is almost restricted to the inadvertent or consequential effects which the engineers do not intend. The difference in outlook between ecologists and engineers appears to lie largely in the different time scales associated with effects on living and nonliving materials.

Engineers' predictions for what they design are, like most pragmatic forecasts, restricted to the useful lives of what they plan to make. Thus, the effects of a power plant on its surroundings are assumed to end with decommissioning the plant, and the benefit of a dam should last forever because the dam theoretically has no limit to its durability.

An ecologist, by contrast, may view the same projects in a different light, because he sees a different period during which each project will affect its surroundings. Retiring a power station will not hide its fuel wastes and by-products; a nuclear plant may require the use of tens of hectares somewhere to store its waste, and a coal-fired plant the use of thousands. The principal effects of a dam will be expected only during the time before its reservoir silts up—unless the dam should ultimately fail.

Biotic systems tend to be affected differently in the long and the short terms, while abiotic systems are not, or at least less so. Thus, the effects of building a highway will be prominent while it is being constructed, but it will remain a barrier to animals' movements, for example, long after. The influence of a strip mine on vegetation will persist long after the mine site has been recontoured and planted.

I think this difference in temporal appreciation or extent of consideration may be the chief reason why field biologists, and especially ecologists, sometimes disagree with engineers, politicians, and utility executives about the magnitude of the consequences of proposed actions. The disparity perhaps does not warrant a remedy so much as mutual understanding.

Changes Without a Proposed Project

Predicting the effects of proposed actions, or of alternatives to those actions, often is improved by understanding what will happen in an area if man introduces no change. This prediction should be made as a result of the baseline study; but sometimes it is not. I emphasize the matter here because of repeated experience. This is related, I believe, to the difference in how engineers and ecologists apprehend time, which was discussed in the last section. The remedy I suggest is much the same: Early and repeated discussion among wildlife biologists, design engineers, and client representatives should bring forth a satisfactory performance and understanding from all.

Chapter Twenty-Six

The Legislative Process and Wildlife

DANIEL A. POOLE
President
Wildlife Management Institute
Washington, D.C.

Ownership of wildlife in the United States is held by the government in trust for the people. This grew out of the colonists' reliance on the common law of England, arising from the Magna Charta, which placed ownership of wildlife in the King in sacred trust for the people. In time, the states came to act as King, and when the Constitution was written, the states retained that authority. Their vesting of authority in the new Federal Government to make treaties and to regulate interstate and foreign commerce ultimately led to the creation of agencies to discharge that level of government's responsibilities for fish and wildlife.

Although the organizational arrangement has changed over the years and well may change in the future, the federal responsibility mainly is exercised today through the U.S. Fish and Wildlife Service and the National Marine Fisheries Service. State duties and obligations are exercised through agencies in each of the 50 states that are vested with power to protect the public's interest in fish and wildlife. While there is some overlap and contention, the responsibilities of each level of government are generally well understood and respected by the agencies, if not completely by all their employees and some interest groups.

Under our system of government, the authority of the agencies to mount and conduct programs for fish and wildlife, or for any other purpose desired by society, rests in laws. In essence, laws create, assign, and define authority in conformance with society's needs and wishes.

In his Farewell Address of September 1796, George Washington observed: "The basis of our political system is the right of the people to make and alter their constitutions of government." How that right may be exercised in the Congress of the United States is the subject of this chapter. Congress is the focal point because its actions apply more widely and because its recorded proceedings and reports are more accessible than those of State Legislatures. Although the organization, rules, and operating procedures of Congress and State Legislatures may differ in detail, the opportunities available to individuals and groups to influence the content and outcome of legislative proposals are essentially alike in both.

A WORD OF CAUTION

The right of the people to petition government is guaranteed in the first amendment to the Constitution. But those wishing to influence legislation must understand that the right to petition applies differently to them as individuals and as members of groups such as The Wildlife Society, and its affiliated sections and chapters.

Individuals may contact legislative bodies and urge others to do likewise without limitation, providing they act in their own behalf. But individuals acting in concert as members of certain organizations, including The Wildlife Society and its affiliates, may not seek to influence legislation as freely. Other ground rules come into play.

The reason for this is that some organizations, at their own request, are classified as scientific and educational organizations under Internal Revenue Service law. To those that qualify, this classification holds certain advantages; among them, exemption from federal taxes on income and from sales taxes, access to lower nonprofit organization postal rates, and tax deductibility for federal income tax purposes to individuals and others making contributions in support of the organization's program and activities.

Organizations having and wishing to retain such a classification are restricted by an IRS regulation that no substantial part of their activities can involve carrying on propaganda or otherwise attempting to influence legislation. Despite a general rule of thumb that "no substantial part" means less than 5% of an organization's annual expenditures, IRS has not formalized that interpretation and various court tests have failed to establish a firm guideline. Furthermore, there is some apprehension that, if challenged, the test of "substantial" might be applied to efforts rather than to expenditures. Rather than risk their tax exemption, therefore, most scientific and educational groups initiate few attempts to influence legislation. Exceptions to this are suggestions that may be offered and positions that may be taken in response to specific written invitations from congressional committees and on matters directly relevant to an organization's well-being.

This long-standing situation was modified by the Tax Reform Act of 1976, which offers a new option to qualified scientific and educational organizations electing to engage in efforts to influence legislation. It sets forth a scale of expenditures, based on percent of budget, that must not be exceeded. So long as an organization electing the option stays within the expenditure limitation, and complies with record-keeping and other requirements, it may engage in prescribed lobbying efforts without loss of tax exemption.

The reason for explaining this is to make sure that members of The Wildlife Society and organizations holding the same IRS classification are aware of the significant difference between what they may do on their own as citizens and what they may do in the name of their organization. Guidance should be sought from the headquarters office before any action is taken in the name of the parent organization or an affiliate.

What course a scientific and educational organization may follow under the 1976 Tax Reform Act—retain its present mode of operation or elect the lobbying option—rests on the decision of its governing officers. Until that decision is made and members are advised, persons anticipating legislative activity in any way linked to the name of their organization, such as The Wildlife Society or any affiliate, should consult with the organization's headquarters office. Contact also should be made to ascertain if the parent group may have adopted a policy position on any subject receiving legislative consideration.

HOW CONGRESS IS ORGANIZED

The House of Representatives and the Senate, commonly and inaccurately referred to as the "lower" and "upper" houses of Congress, comprise the Legislative Branch of the Federal Government. They are, in fact, proud and competitive co-equals, each protective of its prerogatives, with the House having the distinction, under the Constitution, of responsibility for initiating actions to raise revenue.

Each uses the committee system as the basis of organization for conducting its work. The responsibilities of the committees are spelled out in the House and Senate rules. With few exceptions, committees are further divided into subcommittees, each again assigned a specific part of its parent committee's province.

Under prevailing rules of the House, the committees normally handling legislation pertaining to fish, wildlife and their habitat are the Committee on Merchant Marine and Fisheries, Committee on Interior and Insular Affairs, Committee on Agriculture, Committee on Public Works and the Committee on Appropriations. Cognizant Senate committees are the Committee on Energy and Natural Resources, Committee on Environment and Public Works, Committee on Agriculture, Nutrition and Forestry, and the Committee on Appropriations. Proposals relating in some way to fish and wildlife may be handled infrequently by other committees, but those named will be involved most of the time.

HOW CONGRESS OPERATES

Legislative Branch scholars hold that Congress has at least 10 functions, one of which, not surprisingly, is to legislate. A second and related power is to sit as a board of directors to the government and to the people. This is the important oversight authority whereby the activities and programs of agencies may be examined in detail by cognizant committees. Oversight hearings ostensibly lead to the drafting of legislation to ease difficulties or to correct situations disclosed by such proceedings. Their purpose is to seek to identify problems susceptible to legislative action. There is some suspicion that the oversight authority, on occasion, is used for political, rather than legislative, purposes.

Any Member of Congress may introduce a bill. Several Members may join in cosponsoring a bill. A number of dissimilar bills may be introduced on the same subject. From time to time, the President may forward draft legislation to Congress along with explanatory material in furtherance of the Administration's program. The President's offerings are introduced routinely in the Senate and House by the Chairmen of the committees having jurisdiction over the subject matter covered. Sometimes a bill will bear the words "by request" to show that the introducer does not necessarily endorse its content or espouse its need. This occurs mostly when The White House and the Congress are controlled by different political parties.

A bill originating in the House is identified by H.R. followed by the number assigned to it. A Senate bill bears an S. and the number given to it. The bill number, date of introduction, the name or names of its sponsor or sponsors, and the committee to which it was referred appear on the proposal, which is printed as an official document. There are 3 other kinds of lesser bills or resolutions, but they are not pertinent to a discussion of major legislation. Copies of bills may be obtained from the House or Senate Document Room or, better yet for those residing away from Washington, from their Representative or Senator.

The initial number assigned to a bill may not remain with it all the way through Congress. The turns and twists of the legislative process frequently require or accommodate the substitution of numbers or entirely new numbers. It has been alleged, and with some reason, that the assignment of a new number is done to throw legislative opponents off stride.

Following introduction, a bill, under the rules, is referred to the committee having jurisdiction over its subject matter. Sometimes, the jurisdiction of 2 committees is involved and an accommodation is reached by the committee chairmen on how it will be handled. Once in committee, the bill normally is referred to a subcommittee, and the lion's share of the work is done at this level.

In due course, the subcommittee may schedule a public hearing on the bill singly, with others involving the same subject area, or with others also within its jurisdiction. Major bills normally are heard alone. The hearings mainly are in Washington, but field hearings may be called if the subject is controversial or sweeping or the political interest of prominent members is involved. Public announcement of a hearing is made routinely through committee news releases and required formal notices, but word seldom is carried in most of the nation's press. The newsletters and other publications of conservation organizations generally announce hearing dates on major issues.

Persons or groups wishing to appear before the committee for the purpose of commenting on a proposal may file a written request to that effort. Others may prefer to write letters expressing their views to the committee, addressed either to the parent committee chairman, or preferably, to the subcommittee chairman. Those filing a letter or written statement should specifically request that their comments be included in the printed hearing record. Otherwise, the letters simply will be held in the committee file and will not be made a part of the public record on the proposal. Because congressional action on a bill sometimes may precede printing of a hearing record, the record's value frequently is historical. If final congressional action takes a year or longer, which is not unusual for complex issues, then the hearing records have much informational value for lobbying actions. On simpler measures, a committee sometimes merely will solicit written comments by a certain date rather than suffer the time and expense of a public hearing.

Following a hearing or the receipt of comments, the subcommittee will block out time to consider the proposal in executive session. There is no prescribed deadline by which this must be done, if, indeed, it is done at all. Various amendments may be considered as the subcommittee proceeds to "mark up" the bill. Not infrequently several meetings may be required before action is completed on major legislation. If the subcommittee wishes to advance the proposal, its handiwork, in time, will be presented to the parent or full committee. A favorable recommendation by the full committee readies the proposal for consideration by the House or Senate. In Washington terminology, the bill, at this stage, has been "reported."

A reported bill normally is accompanied by a printed, numbered, and dated report that explains its need and effect on existing law, a section-by-section analysis, agency comments, and other pertinent and supportive information. These reports, intended primarily for, but not restricted to, the members, are helpful to individuals and groups following the legislation. They may be obtained from one's Representative or Senator, from the issuing House or Senate committee, or from the House or Senate Document Room. The request for a copy should refer both to the subject matter and to the report number, if known.

After committee clearance, major House bills are routed to the Committee on Rules, which sets the terms for floor debate—total time allotted for consideration, whether floor amendments will be allowed, etc. Senate scheduling is determined by the Majority Leader. Proposals may reach the floor by other routes, such as suspension of the rules in the House, but these are of greater interest and concern to individuals and groups regularly engaged in day-to-day efforts to influence legislation. Those who must do their lobbying work from afar can, of course, urge their Congressman to support or oppose "suspensions." However, the turnaround times are short, situations change quickly, and guidance should be sought from Washington-based contacts.

In due time a bill is taken up on the floor. When approved in final form, it is forwarded to the other body where it again is referred to the appropriate committee. When approved by either the House or the Senate, a bill becomes known as an Act and remains an Act until it is presented to the President and signed into law. In the opposite body, the Act again is subjected to a repeat process—public hearings, executive sessions, and mark-up. If reported from the committee it will be accompanied by a numbered committee report.

Legislative proposals may not always receive equal attention on both sides of the Capitol. The body originating action sometimes may hold more extensive hearings. An approval of a bill by one side is no guarantee of its eventual acceptance by the other, in that form, in that year, or at any subsequent time.

A Congress consists of 2 one-year sessions: viz. 95th Congress, First Session, 95th Congress, Second Session, 96th Congress, First Session, etc. A bill that fails to navigate the legislative ladder during the 2-year period expires at the close of the second session. Its revival in a succeeding Congress requires reintroduction, and it begins again at square one even though it may have progressed quite far in a previous Congress. It is not unusual for major legislation to be considered over several years before approval is won.

If a bill clears the House and Senate in different form, it normally is referred to a House-Senate conference committee whose members are chosen from the committees that initially handled it. Their compromises to obtain a single version are subject to subsequent House and Senate approval. Bills have died in conference because agreement could not be reached—so strongly have both sides held their separate views. After clearing the conference committee and the House and Senate in its compromised form, the proposal is forwarded to the

President. With his approval, the Act becomes a law. The President's veto or disapproval is subject to House and Senate override votes.

There are 2 basic reference books on Congress—the *Congressional Directory* sometimes available without charge from your Senator or Representative, but regularly for sale at the Government Printing Office, and the *Congressional Staff Directory* which may be purchased through Post Office Box 62, Mount Vernon, Virginia 22121. These books work well as a pair. The first, in addition to offering pertinent information about Congress and its members, also lists the names, titles, addresses, telephone numbers, and similar useful facts about Executive Branch agencies and officials. The latter's chief value is its in-depth listing of the names and titles of the staffs of members and committees, addresses, telephone numbers, and allied information, including biographical sketches of assenting staff members.

There are a number of books on the rules and procedures of the House and Senate, but these mainly are technical in nature. Understanding such details is not a prerequisite to undertaking intelligent and well-organized actions to influence legislation. Such information is of most value to individuals and groups directly and regularly involved with legislative activity.

GETTING EQUIPPED FOR A CAMPAIGN

Individuals, acting on their own, have few restrictions, beyond civility and good taste, imposed on their efforts to influence legislation. Individuals or groups acting in the name of the organization of which they are members, or an affiliate, should check with the organization's headquarters to make sure that a contemplated action is consistent with legal constraints and policies.

Knowing what is going on is the first necessity for legislative activity. Whether a group's focal point is Washington or a state capitol, being well informed is the primary need. Newspapers seldom cover a legislative subject adequately or accurately, if at all, so better and more detailed sources of information must be secured.

Fortunately, several sources are available. Among the best are the National Wildlife Federation's "Conservation Report," the National Audubon Society's "Audubon Leader," the Sierrá Club's "Bulletin," the Wilderness Society's "Wilderness Report," "Outdoor America" of the Izaak Walton League of America, and the Wildlife Management Institute's "Outdoor News Bulletin." Some of these publications are available only to an organization's members or on a subscription or restricted basis. These and other groups also make special mailings to alert interested individuals and organizations on specific situations.

The dean of legislative news services is the "Conservation Report" of the National Wildlife Federation. Issued weekly when Congress is in session, it covers introductions of environmental and conservation legislation, hearings, and other legislative events. Its regular use enables readers to follow a proposal, step-by-step, through Congress.

A second Federation publication, indispensable to legislative activity, is the "Conservation Directory," on sale through national headquarters. Although it provides some information about congressional committees, chairmen, and so forth, it is most useful as a reference source for the names of federal and state resources agencies, including addresses and principal staff, and for regional, national, and international conservation and environmental organizations. New editions are issued annually.

Persons and groups that follow Congress closely regularly read the "Congressional Record," which is the printed journal of the debates, proceedings, and actions of that body. Subscriptions are available and a member's office sometimes can arrange free distribution. Use of the "Congressional Record" is not recommended as a casual reference, however. In the course of a year, it runs to thousands of pages, and its greatest value is to those who have the time and interest to follow Congress closely.

Another useful publication is the "Weekly Bulletin" of the Environmental Study Conference. Information about the subscription cost and availability may be obtained from 3334 House Office Annex 2, U.S. Congress, Washington, D.C. 20515. This service's editorial slant in favor of preservation and away from scientific management should become obvious to careful readers.

The organization of a lobbying effort is equally important as securing a regular flow of reliable information. If done by an individual only, the arrangement is simple. But if it is to be a group undertaking, then it is necessary to assign responsibility for alerting the group to issues, preparing analyses, briefing group members, drafting letters or testimony, making and following through on contacts, and charting other courses of action.

The most effective lobbying work is done on a deliberate and continuing basis. A few major legislative targets should be singled out, rather than skipping across a broad range of subjects. These major targets, in effect, should be followed from birth to disposition, and one's point of view should be pressed at every opportunity along the legislative path.

Letters, statements, and other communications should be typewritten, dated, and correctly addressed. Copies always should be retained. Telephone and personal conversations should be noted and filed with references to subject discussed, date, participants, and important reactions and information.

PUTTING IT ALL TOGETHER

The greatest need of a member of Congress and his staff is for individuals and groups on which they can rely for accurate information and mature judgment. Professional staff members of committees also share this need. Normally more conversant with the subject matter of a proposal than the personal staff of a Senator or Representative, committee staff professionals welcome contact by knowledgeable persons and groups outside of government.

Recognizing this need—and taking advantage of it—provides individuals and groups with their most important first step toward influencing the outcome of legislation. Establishing personal and group contact with a Senator or Representative, where possible, and certainly with one or more principal members of their staffs, should be given first priority. Members of Congress normally have offices in their districts in addition to their Washington offices. Visit them, introduce yourself to the staff, and discuss your legislative concerns. Determine your Senator's or Representative's schedule to learn when he will be visiting in his district or state. Make an appointment to visit with him or invite him to speak to your chapter or group. If you are concerned about watershed channelization, a public land timbering operation, a wildlife refuge, or any other conservation problem, invite him or a member of his staff to accompany you on a well-planned field trip where you can point to and explain the things that concern you. Note the words "well-planned." Field trips and visits should be designed to yield maximum opportunity for examining problems and imparting information and ideas. Avoid, at all costs, poorly planned, time-consuming field trips.

Members of Congress and their staffs exist to serve you. Make requests of them for reports and other information. Deliberately plan to provide opportunities for exchange of information. Be courteous, reasonable and persistent. Sensitize them to your concerns. Personal contact is the strongest weapon in a lobbyist's arsenal. Praise the legislator when he does right; patiently explain his errors when he does wrong.

Remembering that Congress operates on the committee system is a key to targeting a lobbying effort. Senator X or Representative Y may be sincerely interested in fish and wildlife, but neither can deliver much more than his floor vote or a timely speech if he is not a member of the Senate or House committee handling a bill. Congress' division of responsibility makes it impossible for a member to know what is going on at all times. Noncommittee members occasionally will testify on a bill under consideration, particularly when it relates to the interest of their state or congressional district. That usually is the extent of noncommittee member's participation other than when the bill comes to the floor for a vote.

The next step, then, is to examine the membership roster of the committee and the subcommittee to which a bill has been referred. With luck, the full committee chairman, subcommittee chairman, or one or more members of the committee or subcommittee may be from your state. In this case, it is possible to enlist closer attention to your views. Additionally, key committee and subcommittee staff invariably are selected by senior committee members. If your Senator or Representative is a committee or subcommittee chairman, you can rely on attentive service from the committee staff.

If your Representative or Senator is not a member of the committee, then your next best move is to advise him or your interest, keep him informed, and seek to enlist his support where he can conveniently give it. If your initial effort to establish contact and identity is by letter, it generally will stimulate a platitudinous response, which will read something like " . . . Thank you for taking the time to write and tell me your views on the wildlife refuge bill. I will keep your thoughts in mind when the bill comes to the floor for a vote."

Never accept this as proof of having successfully lobbied your Senator or Representative. If you let matters rest at this point, your time and postage have been wasted. Write or telephone periodically to ask about a bill's legislative status, its content, for copies of pertinent reports, and for an assessment of its chances of enactment. This serves the good purpose of sensitizing the member and his staff to your interest. He will build an office file on the subject, begin to keep a count of contacts, and begin to follow the proposal's progress.

More satisfying service can be received from a Senator or Representative who serves on a committee handling a bill of interest to a constituent group. First, should the individual or group wish to testify on the proposal, he can arrange it. This is helpful when many groups are seeking to testify and time is limited. Many times, he can be encouraged to appear at the hearing to personally introduce your spokesman and to lend support to his views. Secondly, he can arrange for the insertion of the individual's or group's comments and recommendations in the hearing record. Finally, his position and vote can be guided by the individual's or group's analysis of the proposal, by its good or bad effects, and by what may be needed to improve it.

By frequently contacting his office and requesting status reports, an individual or a group can force the Senator or Representative to keep in touch with an issue. He can be the source of committee reports, printed hearing records, and other information. The longer one's Senator or Representative has served and the higher he sits on a committee, as indicated by the order of listing of members' names on a committee roster, the greater influence he wields.

Efforts to influence legislation can be as casual or as highly structured as one wishes. They can range all the way from an occasional letter, telephone call, or personal conversation to a tightly run campaign, including many mailings and frequent contact and coordination with others. Within the constraints of good taste and civility, approaches to influencing legislation are limited only by the imagination of those involved, providing, of course, that the participants have basic understanding of the issues and the rules of the road. Above all, be reasonable, realistic, factual and brief. Longwindedness, emotional idealism, and inability to substantiate what you say and recommend will prevent you from gaining a position of trust.

When writing to a Senator, he may be addressed: The Honorable John Doe, Senate Office Building, Washington, D.C. 20510. The salutation should be Dear Senator Doe, unless, of course, he is known personally and can be greeted in more familiar terms. A Member of the House of Representatives, while technically addressed as Representative, invariably prefers to be called Congressman. Letters to House members may be addressed: The Honorable John Smith, House Office Building, Washington, D.C. 20515. The salutation can be Dear Congressman or Congresswoman Smith, unless, of course, you know the individual personally.

As noted earlier, your letter should be brief and to the point, courteous, and organized to present your views in an orderly and persuasive way. Never be threatening. Always word your letters so as to require an answer. Share copies of your letters and any pertinent responses received with the headquarters office of the organization with which you are associated and with offices of Washington-based organizations that you believe or know are interested in the subject matter.

Larry Toschik
1975

Chapter Twenty-Seven

Gaining Public Acceptance of Wildlife Management

RON E. SHAY

Chief, Information & Education
Oregon Department of Fish and Wildlife
Portland, Oregon

Although some wildlife biologists would like to think otherwise, an important part of most wildlife management is people management. This has been true almost from the time individuals started manipulating the resource as a public trust and became even more evident following the environmental movement of the 1960's.

People management should not be looked upon as something out of George Orwell's *1984*, but instead should be considered a positive force that can play an important role in wildlife management plans. Indeed, lack of good public relations often can virtually scuttle the best laid plans of the biologist. Conversely, public support and understanding can save time, money, and effort in accomplishing management goals.

In the eyes of some individuals, trying to "manipulate" people by influencing their ideas and desires is considered less than honorable and something left to the sellers of soap, cars, corn flakes, and other products. The word propaganda smacks of dictatorships and mind control, and yet these same individuals utilize all of the techniques they consider rather shady when arguing strongly against the use of public information methods.

As the wildlife manager competes more and more with other land uses, with a variety of user interests, and with the so-called information explosion, he must gain public confidence by putting forth sound information in a form understood and acceptable to the public, or run the risk of accomplishing few of his goals.

In considering public relations and wildlife management we are not going to discuss the hunting versus antihunting debate. This is a philosophical issue that has been argued at length in many places and probably will continue to be argued as long as there are 2 individuals with opposite views. Suffice to say, there are individuals who, for various reasons, oppose wildlife management and the tools used, including hunting.

There is a large segment of the public that is interested in wildlife. This may be a passive interest that is manifested only by watching animal shows on television or it may be very active as in the case of hunters. A great many of these people will react if they think wildlife is being mistreated or if they think some agency is planning to do something detrimental to the resource. Some individuals have sincere differences of opinion concerning management policies of agencies, but usually the most commotion is caused by those who don't understand what is being done.

At one time, the public relations attitude of the railroads was to keep the public in the dark as much as possible. However, over a period of time they found that even in the case of serious train wrecks they had fewer troubles if they did their best to keep the public fully informed as to what had happened and what was being done. It sometimes appears that wildlife biologists are still at the darkness stage of development concerning the public. Sometimes this lack of information is created purposely; more often it occurs through lack of planning or consideration of the public.

Consideration of the public should take place during the planning stages of any project. As soon as the management plans have been formulated, the manager should do a bit of reflecting and try to put himself outside the project. He should try to look at the project from the viewpoint of as many publics as he is apt to affect. Citizens are not just 1 great amorphous mass of folks who will all react the same. No 2 individuals see things in exactly the same manner. However, one can identify major, broad groups such as hunters, bird watchers, garden clubs, sportsmen's clubs, civic groups, and landowners. Though the individuals within these groups are just that, individuals, they generally have some things in common or they couldn't be identified as a group or public.

By identifying the publics you are likely to affect by your project, you can better compose your materials to answer their questions and hopefully allay any fears. In some instances a management project may be such that it will be noticed by virtually all the publics. In this case materials must be prepared that are very general in nature yet effectively explain what is being done. A project such as controlled burning on a management area near a city might be this type of operation. Everyone gets concerned with fires in the outdoors. Explanations ahead of time will not only preclude panic but also explain a valuable management tool.

By taking the specific public into consideration in the planning stages of a project, you may well save much time and confusion as the project progresses. At the same time, be sure your colleagues know what you are up to. If the local fishery biologist, the local enforcement officer, hatchery personnel, and even personnel of other related agencies are kept abreast of your plans and operations, they not only will be informed sources for the public to call on, but will not give misinformation.

USE OF THE MASS MEDIA

When an individual thinks about informing the public, the use of the mass media usually comes to mind. There are a great number of books and pamphlets available on preparing material for the media; therefore we will not discuss the topic here.

One of the major things to remember is to keep the newspaper and radio and television stations informed—not only of the project you may be planning, but also of the things that occur regularly that are of interest. If you become established as a source of honest, interesting information about wildlife in your area, your chances of getting media help when you need it are much better. The biologist who has lived in an area for 10 years and hasn't made himself known to the local media isn't really doing a complete job.

Immediately, the cry comes up, "But I haven't enough time to do that!" Time spent letting the media know who you are today may save much more time in the future when you are trying to squelch rumors or get public support for a special project.

Getting to know the media doesn't have to be an elaborate thing. It can be as simple as dropping in at the newspaper and chatting with the sports editor or the person who handles outdoors news and leaving your business card for his reference. If you can invite him out on a field trip, so much the better. Show him how you count deer or what kind of range problems you're having. He'll remember you in the future.

With the current nature of radio, it is doubtful that you will be able to get someone from the station out into the field unless he has a strong personal interest in wildlife. However, if you think you have a story, give the station a call. They may not be able to send someone out, but very often they will let you talk about the story over the telephone and then put your voice on the air as an "actuality."

If you're in a city large enough to have a television station, don't miss getting acquainted with its staff. A 1- or 2-minute story on the local television news will reach a great share of the people in your area. Even though you think it may be time consuming to haul these people around, think of the number of people in the public you are reaching in just 1 television news report. This is the medium from which most people get their news today.

Obviously, the best way to get the word out the way you want it is to do it yourself. If you can write a short weekly column for the paper, or do a few weekly spots on radio and television, you have the inside track. The media people almost consider you one of them if you have such things going, and when something big comes up, it's easy to get them involved.

Above all, be impartial with the media and most especially with 2 different outlets of the same medium. Give everyone the same news at the same time. If an individual gets on a story and is following it because of his own initiative, this doesn't mean you have to call everyone else to let them know, but if you are initiating the information, do it for everyone.

You needn't be a Hemingway to get usable material to the media. Any basic journalism book will tell you how to write a story. However, a fact sheet including the five W's and H is almost as good as a story. Just a simple listing of Who, What, Where, When, Why, and How will do the job. Such a sheet is handy if you call on the paper to tell them the story. Give them the sheet and then go through it with them if you can tie them up that long. Such a sheet is essential if you have media people in the field on operations such as release of exotics or marking of animals. They will take notes but you can be more certain the basic facts of the event are going to be accurate if you give out a fact sheet. The reporter then can add his own descriptions around your fact sheet.

You are going to get burned at times or be very disappointed in the way something was covered. Either the reporter didn't understand, perhaps was biased (there is no such thing as complete objectivity!), or perhaps the editor cut the story and left a wrong impression. Don't let this discourage you from use of the media in the future. Just use it as a lesson to see where the foul-up occurred and correct it next time. If it concerns a regulation, give the errant person a call and explain the problem—they want to be accurate.

Don't assume any knowledge on the part of the reporter you are dealing with. This doesn't mean you should assume he is a dummy but there is considerable turnover in the news media operations, especially in smaller towns. You may be dealing with someone who is unfamiliar with even the local landmarks as well as your operations and your department.

Regardless of which medium or group you may be working with, don't get bogged down in technical jargon. Though you have been trained as a specialist and precision in word use is part of the game, be willing to accept a generality to explain what you want to get across. It may not communicate quite as precisely as you would if you were writing a technical paper, but if you get the idea across to the public, you've accomplished your purpose. This doesn't mean you have to be inaccurate; it means you should communicate with your audience in terms they understand!

Above all, be honest with media personnel. If there is a risk to wildlife involved, explain what it is but also explain the reason why the risk is necessary. This may not satisfy some young reporters who have been raised on the "Bambi" syndrome, but in most cases the reporter will keep things in perspective. Again, you may get burned, but if one medium does it, chances are the others won't or even other reporters won't. Knowing your reporters from past association helps you know how to discuss things with them.

Make yourself available for further questions. Be sure to put your telephone number on any materials you hand out, and if the project is a long-range one or one you've announced well ahead of time, check back to see if any questions have arisen in the minds of the reporters. This doesn't mean you should harass a newsman to try to get him to use your material, nor should you try to make up news. It simply means you provide information and as the project progresses, you should follow up with new information when it seems appropriate.

Each mass medium has its own characteristics. Basically, television is always pressed for time, wants visual material, and just skims the news. Radio is the immediate medium. It is where people turn when they hear about something and want to be sure about what they've heard. It has taken the place of the "extra" newspaper. Newspapers still are the in-depth news source. The broadcast media do not compete with the newspapers. In fact, it has been found that in many cases broadcast news stories stimulate people to read the paper to find more information. Obviously newspapers are not as immediate in most cases as radio and probably are not as dramatic as television. Each has its strengths and weaknesses.

THE INDIVIDUAL APPROACH

Just as the news media can reach large audiences with general impressions, appearances at various clubs can reach very specific audiences with very specialized information. For a controversial situation, nothing can beat the individual approach.

Obviously sportsmen's clubs and other outdoor clubs are likely to have an interest in what you're doing. Hopefully, it would be routine to keep them informed at their regular meetings. However, if something special comes up, get in touch with the president and get a special meeting or a mailing to the group. These people should be staunch supporters who can spread the word for you.

The service clubs such as the Kiwanis, Rotary, and Lions contain many of the civic leaders and businessmen of the community. If you can inform them of your project, and convince them of its merit, you have a strong base of support in the community. These groups are always looking for speakers; and, even though their schedules may be made up well in advance, you may be able to get a brief spot to give them an explanation of what is going on even though it's on short notice.

If you have a university or college in the area or can talk with the high school biology classes, you may get the youth of the area on your side and properly informed.

The most in-depth informational technique has to be the "Show-Me" trip. It is the most time-consuming but has the strongest influence over people. You take them to the location where your project or problem exists and show them the situation. Obviously, the number of individuals that can be handled this way is limited and participation may not be good. However, there is a good chance that those who do attend will end up being strong supporters—if you do your job. Such trips should include reporters whenever possible.

I have tried to suggest a few ways of gaining public acceptance of your wildlife management projects and operations. Your information and education or public relations staff should be able to help you plan such a campaign if you give them enough advance notice. However, if it is a local project you are working on, the bulk of the convincing job is going to be on your shoulders and those of your local colleagues. Having a good ongoing relationship with the press and local clubs will make this chore much easier.

There are numerous leaflets and books that will assist you in the actual mechanics of the job. Gilbert (1971) covered the subject of natural resources public relations in detail. Cutlip and Center (1971) discussed the subject in broad general terms in their book, which is probably the most used text and is possibly the best single PR reference for one's library.

SUMMARY

Plan ahead, include public relations as part of your initial plan. Don't decide to apply it after the fat is in the fire and rumors and misunderstandings are well underway.

Establish media relations early. Work with the media all of the time. Don't run to them when you have a problem and expect them to drop everything to bail you out. Become established as a reliable, honest source of information on a regular basis.

Be honest. If the project has risks or something doesn't go right, don't try to cover it up. Explain risks, explain accidents, give background and reasons.

Learn to communicate. Knowing which medium to use does little good if you can't tell what needs to be told in everyday language. Get rid of jargon. Don't be afraid to generalize. Organize your material and if you're working with broadcast media, be able to summarize things in a couple of minutes.

Make yourself available. This may be inconvenient at times but the best way to prevent the press and public from getting the wrong information is to give them correct information yourself.

Inform your fellow workers. On major projects or problems, be sure your co-workers know what is going on. They still may want to refer calls to you but they will be able to handle some of the inquiries.

And once more—incorporate your public relations plan into your original biological plan. Practice fire prevention, not fire fighting. It is easier, more efficient, and much more satisfying!

Chapter Twenty-Eight

Instrumentation

SANFORD D. SCHEMNITZ

Professor and Head
Department of Fishery and Wildlife Sciences
New Mexico State University
Las Cruces, New Mexico

ROBERT H. GILES, JR.

Professor, Wildlife Management
Department of Fisheries and Wildlife Sciences
Virginia Polytechnic Institute and State University
Blacksburg, Virginia

Within 50 years, wildlife research has moved from subjective field observations to highly complex, precise, objective measures of mammal and bird morphology, physiology and behavior. Though recent trends are toward greater use of instruments for obtaining quantities of valid numerical data, the researcher must continue to seek perfection in making observations of field events and in taking records that can be compiled and analyzed. The tendency toward gadgeteering is strong; the means can easily overshadow the end which is knowledge of wildlife, its relation to its total environment, and ways of influencing this relationship.

Instrumentation is the use of any device for measurment and data collection. Instruments are an extension of people's perceptual abilities. Instrumentation encompasses almost every device from knotting a string for counting birds flushed to an electronic computer for processing data.

The advance of instrumentation in wildlife research has been hampered not only by limited funds for proper equipment, but also by field transportation difficulties, lack of power sources, and adverse environmental factors. The great mobility and secretiveness of wildlife also has retarded the use of instruments. Only recently have wildlifers plunged deeply into the previously remote but interrelated fields of electronics, radioisotopes, light physics, and communications. This chapter is a literature review of some special investigational instrumentation developed for, or applied to, wildlife problems. There are few biological or physical techniques that will not eventually be applied to problems of wildlife management and investigation. The chapter attempts to show only some of these uses, to stimulate modifications of an additional use of instruments to obtain more accurate observations and more reliable data. Davis (1954) provided the precautionary word for the need for knowledge of being able to acquire statistically adequate samples of observations of animal activity before investments are made in instrumentation. Chapters 12, 18, 29, and 30 also deal with instrumentation.

General books on instrumentation useful for those seeking advice on a particular problem or background on advice are given by Lion (1959), Stacy (1960), Aronson (1961), Studer (1963), Kay (1964), Newman (1964), Dewhurst (1966), Lenhoff (1966), Considine (1971), Ewing (1974), Tagg (1974), and Todd (1975).

The series, *Physical Techniques in Biological Research*, edited by W. L. Nastuk, provides fundamental guides and discussions. This series is largely for fundamental biological research. It covers topics of electrophysiological methods pertinent to some current wildlife research efforts. Newman (1964) and Alt (1966) also treat these and related topics.

Most departments of universities and natural resource agencies have catalog libraries of their specialties that are available to investigators. A publication of potential usefulness is *Instrument and Apparatus News* (Instruments Publishing Co., 845 Ridge Street, Pittsburgh, Pennsylvania). *Pollution Equipment News* (Computer Center, 8550 Babcock Blvd., Pittsburgh, Pennsylvania

15237) is a good source of information on available equipment for lab and field studies.

POWER SOURCES

Field sources of electrical power create problems where portability or accessibility is a factor and where instruments must be operated for long periods.

Gasoline-operated generators have the disadvantages of being expensive, noisy, and heavy. With adequate extension wires they can be removed from the site of instrument operation. Hand-operated generators may be suitable for some purposes. Instruments operating on direct current (DC) can be attached directly to a storage battery for short runs (depending, of course, on the drain). Most instruments are designed for AC and so require a DC to AC converter (e.g., Terado Co., Raymond Ave., St. Paul, Minn.) when operated from a storage battery or from an automobile lighter jack. Loveless et al. (1963) reported on the use of an AC to DC converter in a remote situation to operate an 8-day strip chart recorder. Dry and wet cell batteries can be connected to provide the exact energy requirement with minimum size, weight, and cost. Rechargeable D-size "flashlight" batteries can be purchased. Miniature batteries are now available through electronics dealers. Taylor and Jean (1964) reported on recharging batteries used for wildlife photography.

Workers should consult a textbook for basic electrical considerations, definitions, and answers to such practical problems as wire sizes, current requirements, and minor adaptations in instruments. Cornsweet's book (1963) also may be helpful.

AUDIO INSTRUMENTS

Bird songs have attracted much attention in the field of instrumentation. When word descriptions of bird songs failed and even musical notations were unable to handle the complexities of bird notes, other methods were sought for studying and recording sound.

The phonographic recording of bird song was unsatisfactory for detailed study of song but has proven of benefit in learning bird identification, producing sounds repellent to crop pests, hunting and predator calling, and other uses. "Photographing" bird songs on motion picture film was the first technique allowing detailed bird song study (Brand 1935). Microscopic examination of the sound track allowed measurement of the length of a song and of individual notes accurately to 1/500 second. It allowed determination of details of rhythm and frequencies of the fundamentals, but nothing could be measured on harmonics or the other frequencies present. Notes inaudible to the human ear and the pitch of a note could be accurately measured. Microscopic examination and manual recording were very time consuming; amplitude or tone intensity was difficult to measure accurately.

These major disadvantages were overcome by devices that automatically transfer recorded sounds to a stylus marking a cylindrical drum. Borror and Reese (1953), Collias and Joos (1953), Thorpe (1954), Bennet (1961), Saunders (1961), Collias (1963), Davis (1964), Lanyon and Gill (1964), and Dewolfe (1967) utilized a vibralizer or sound spectrograph. These devices allowed measurement of high and low tones, time, rhythm, amplitude or loudness, sound quality, and fundamental frequencies and overtones inaudible to the human ear. Vibrograms are made electrically on 14.3- × 32.4-cm facsimile paper on a rotating drum.

Graber and Cochran (1959) used a 184.2-cm-diameter parabolic reflector with 36.8-cm maximum depth to "collect" and study the calls of nocturnal migrant songbirds (see Hamilton 1962). The use of a horn instead of a parabola was suggested as a less expensive possibility. The maximum distance of sound detection will vary directly as the diameter of the parabola. Doubling the diameter may more than double the detection distance. The range depends on the size of the parabola, the sensitivity of the microphone and amplifier, and the amount of external noise. This fourth factor will be limiting. Graber and Cochran used a 10.2-cm permanent magnet speaker with voice-coil-to-grid matching transformer. A preamplifier instead of a self-contained amplifier found with most tape recorders was used. The power source, 110AC, was a 6-v storage battery and 90-v dry cell battery for the amplifier. In personal correspondence, Graber speculated that if the parabola were turned on edge, the range for detecting game sounds, e.g., pheasant's crowing, would be over 8 km. Bradley (1977) described equipment and procedures for making animal sound recordings. Gans and Bonin (1963) have developed an acoustical activity recorder for burrowing animals.

Sound has been used to attract and repel animals for centuries by man. Game calls for "bugling up" elk or moose, calling waterfowl, or calling predators and other animals have a long history. "Squeaking" animals out of cover or causing them to freeze is easily done with the mouth and hand or blade of grass between the thumbs (Loring 1946). Kinne (1960) suggested calling animals for photography.

Frings and Jumber (1954) reported on use of tape-recorded calls to repel starlings from roosts. Diem (1954) reported the use of deer calls for locating fawns which, if they were present, were always seen within 137.2 m of the doe. Tape-recorded fawn calls were useful in attracting mule deer (Arthur et al. 1978). Doe behavior at the sound of the call clearly indicated whether fawns were present. Bohl (1956) used recorded calls of chukar partridge in the field to attempt census but was only partially successful in stimulating a calling response. Frings et al. (1955) and Frings and Frings (1957) were successful in using tape recordings of gull and crow vocalization to attract and repel flocks. They used a continuous-loop cartridge in a special player ("Bird-E-Vict") with amplifers and speakers. By playing a food-finding or assembly call at high sound intensity they attracted birds; distress or alarm call at low intensity repelled birds.

Nesbit (1959) used a modified goose call operated by a 12-v battery to increase the waterfowl use of Powell Marsh in Wisconsin from 82 to 12,000 geese. The player simulated feeding and flight calls which attracted geese. The flight call was more attractive.

Morse and Balser (1961) reported on the use of a portable battery-operated, high-fidelity record player with amplifier and loud speaker to call foxes for hunting. They reviewed the literature on game calling as a hunting technique for coyotes, wolves, deer, raccoon, bobcat, and fox.

Stirling and Bendell (1966) used recordings of the precopulatory calls of blue grouse hens for censusing birds and suggested use for searching, detecting, censusing, observing, and capturing male and female grouse. Levy et al. (1966) recorded the calls of Mearns' quail during the breeding season. By moving over a route and playing the calls at stops, males and their territories could be located. They also developed tapes for Gambel's, scaled, and masked bobwhite quail. On some occasions birds flew to the recorder. They suggested uses of locating birds in an area (e.g., the rare masked bobwhite) for relative population density estimates and trend counts (see Chapter 14), for observing movement in territory, for relating mated to bachelor males, for determining breeding season behavior, and, thus, to improve call-count census techniques.

Borror (1956, 1959, 1965) distinguished individual songbirds by sonagram (voice-prints). Beightol and Samuel (1973) successfully identified individual woodcock by their peent call using sonograms. "Peents" were recorded on a cassette tape recorder. A parabolic reflector was used to magnify the calls. The recordings were processed through a Kay Electric Company Sona-graph, Model 6061-B. Marshall (1977) suggested a log pitch scale to enhance the interpretation of sonograms.

VISUAL INSTRUMENTS

No one field glass or binocular can serve all needs. By knowing the requirements for and the characteristics and capabilities of the glasses, a wise selection can be made. Reichert and Reichert (1961) presented a comprehensive treatment of the selection of binoculars and scopes. Binoculars differ from field glasses by having internal optical prisms, adjustments for opthalmic differences, reduced length, increased field of view, and improved clarity. Binoculars are usually "named" by 2 numbers, e.g., 7 × 50. The magnification, 7x, specifies that objects will appear one-seventh as distant. However, a higher magnification also magnifies movement so that the resolving power of a 10x glass when handheld is only 6x or 7x. The second number is the diameter in millimeters of the objective lens (the larger lens). The larger this lens, the greater will be the light-gathering capabilities and consequently the brightness of the image. The field of view is governed, not by the objective lens, but by the angular degrees and focal length of the binoculars which is a function of the number and arrangement of internal prisms. Wide fields of view are desirable for keeping moving objects such as warblers in view. Coated lenses are generally more desirable than uncoated lenses, for they reduce internal reflection and thereby increase the brightness and detail of the image.

The light-gathering power of a binocular is numerically the square of the diameter in mm of the exit pupil (the white spot seen in the eye lens when the binocular is held at arm's length and pointed toward a light). The diameter of the exit pupil is obtained by dividing the diameter in mm of the objective lens (D) by the magnification (M).

Thus the light-gathering efficiency equals $\left(\frac{D}{M}\right)^2$.

This figure should be increased by 50% for coated lenses. For example the light efficiency of a pair of 6 × 30 coated binoculars is

$$\left(\frac{30}{6}\right)^2 = 25 + (25)\,(0.50) = 37.5\% \text{ light efficiency.}$$

The significance of the exit pupil size (usually 3–8 mm) is that its diameter need be no larger than the size of the observer's pupil (approximately 2 mm in daylight, maximum of 7 mm in darkness) to obtain the maximum light efficiency, not the diameter of the exit pupil lens. The 7 × 50 glass was adopted by the armed forces as a "night glass" because its large exit pupil works extremely well in poor light.

Center-focus and individual lens focus are largely matters of preference. Focusing is needed for all binoculars at distances of less than 91.4 m. Objects moving rapidly toward or away from the observer require rapid focusing such as provided by a center-focus mechanism that adjusts both lenses by the turn of a single knob. The construction of center-focus glasses is not as moisture or dust proof as individually focusing glasses, and they are usually more expensive.

Telescopes follow the same general characteristics as binoculars. Due to their variety, expense, limitations in mobility, and adaptability for photography, they must be carefully tailored to the research job.

Richter (1955) used a 5-cell flashlight to spot rabbits tagged with Scotch-lite ear discs. A spotting head lamp fitted to a battery unit combined with coated 7 × 50 binoculars further enhanced night-observation capabilities.

Demong and Emlen (1975) and DeWeese et al. (1975) developed a battery-powered optical scope to observe nesting activities of burrowing and tunnel nesting birds. Though many animals seem unaffected by artificial light or photo flashes, some are. Since this light prohibits extensive observations of animals at night under "normal" conditions, infrared lighting has been used. Southern et al. (1946) and Seubert (1948) first described an infrared "snooperscope." Swanson and Sargeant (1972) described the advantages of a night vision scope for study of nocturnal feeding behavior of waterfowl. Carpenter (1976b) equipped a similar night-viewing device with a 300-mm telephoto lens to observe deer at distances of 182.9 m. This scope could also be used to observe illegal activities of hunters.

Ultraviolet light has some possible applications in wildlife research. When invisible ultraviolet light or black light irradiates certain substances they absorb the light and reflect it at longer wave length. The light is visible then as fluorescence. Ultraviolet sources are available in mercury, fluorescent, filament and glow lamps with filters (e.g., General Electric, Cleveland, Ohio, Pamphlet LS-141, Black Light). The use of fluorescent materials and ultraviolet lamps has possibilities for special tagging and banding, for feces coloration and location at night (Brown and Conaway 1961), tracking, verification of predators and scavengers on prey dusted with fluorescent powders, and many other uses. The spot bulb of a Black-ray B-100 unit (Ultra-Violet Products, Inc., Walnut Grove Ave., San Gabriel, California) will effectively cover a 4.6-m wide area at 9.1 m. Insects are greatly attracted by ultraviolet light which may be a field disadvantage. The property of ultraviolet attractiveness is used in insect light traps (e.g., Gardner Manufacturing Co., Horicon, Wisconsin). Such traps might be used in measuring the effectiveness of habitat management programs in producing insects for game food.

Research results can be very effectively presented using fluorescing charts, maps, and diagrams illuminated with ultraviolet light.

The use of an x-ray fluoroscope was first suggested by Whitlock and Miller (1947) as a means of detecting lead shot in live waterfowl to measure hunting pressure. Roscoe et al. (1977) perfected a compact hematofluorometer for detecting lead in a drop of blood which reveals lead shot ingestion in waterfowl. Elder (1950, 1955) described a safe, portable fluoroscopy apparatus for field use. Lewis (1962) and Verme et al. (1962) used x-ray equipment to assess fetal development and deer productivity.

Ability to make observations is not entirely a function of light and magnification but also of position. Aircraft towers (Klett 1965) or moving observation platforms are useful.

Gauthreaux (1969) and Avery et al. (1976) described the use of a portable ceilometer, a beacon light, for studying nocturnal bird migration.

ACTIVITY RECORDING INSTRUMENTS

Besides direct visual and audial observations of animals, many simple and complex devices and techniques have been devised for getting expressions of animal presence and activity. Simple devices for collecting hair samples of animals using specific areas have been suggested by Hartesveldt (1951). Radio-location telemetry is presented in Chapter 29.

Between these extremes, sophisticated techniques have been developed. Extensive use has been made of photography in wildlife studies since 1927 (Gregory 1927). Publications of general interest are by Herzfeld (1962), Ledley (1964), and Blaker (1965). Gysel and Davis (1956), Pearson (1959), Osterberg (1962), Abbott and Coombs (1964), Buckner (1964), Cowardin and Ashe (1965), and Gans (1966) have explained use of 35-mm and motion picture cameras and triggering devices with photoelectric flashes. Green and Anderson (1961) and Amos (1965) have used time-lapse and preset interval photography in entomological studies. These techniques have some application in caged or confined animal studies and habitat studies. Dodge and Snyder (1960), like Pearson, circumvented the variable-producing problems of returning to reset such devices as described by Gysel and Davis. They used an electronic flash gun, a 16-mm movie camera and a photoelectric actuating mechanism operated by a pack of five 67½-v batteries. The unit was portable and independent of an AC source. About 2,000 flashes could be obtained from 1 set of batteries.

Sohn (1968), Patton et al. (1972), Temple (1972), Weller and Derksen (1972), and Diem et al. (1974) described time-lapse photographic systems involving compact, portable, and inexpensive 8-mm cameras for wildlife surveillance. Reed et al. (1973) developed a silicon diode camera and a time-lapse video recorder surveillance system useful at low light intensities.

Dane et al. (1959) used moving pictures to examine and describe the actions of the goldeneye. Watt (1966) described computer analyses of behavioral patterns taken from film. Novacek and Hudec (1961) and Cowardin and Ashe (1965) described equipment they used in studies of bird behavior.

Loveless et al. (1963) reported on a photoelectric cell device which they developed and installed in 20 areas in Colorado. They were able to record deer activity and relate it to measures of environmental variables at the same sites. Their paper is particularly valuable because of a literature review of uses of photoelectric cells with animal studies. Harder (1969) found a high correlation between the number of deer counted per night by the Loveless photoelectric cell system and the total number of tracks counted the following morning.

Bayfield and Hewson (1975) developed a device to monitor automatically the trail use by mountain hares. A nylon bristle along the trail when touched by a hare triggered a switch connected to an event recorder. Kolz and Johnson (1976) perfected an inexpensive event recorder using coulometers to monitor ricefield rat feeding activity. Fox (1978) reported a procedure for determining the capture time of small mammals.

Many ingenious devices have been developed for studying animal activity. Justice (1961) reported on the use of smoked kymograph paper in studying small mammals. Papers are placed in open, empty milk cartons and put out on an area after a brief period of trapping and marking by toe-clipping. The animals can be further studied without recapture as they leave tracks on the carton-protected papers. A similar technique was used earlier (Mayer 1957) for determining activity at mammal holes.

In order to obtain an activity pattern of moles, Arlton (1936) used many box-housed alarm clocks with a weighted lever that stopped the clock when a mole passed through a tunnel. Ozoga and Gysel (1965) used a similar mechanical device for measuring deer activity along a trail. Their modified alarm clock rotated a spool of paper tape into which was punched a hole when a trip wire was activated. A photocell, connected to an event recorder, was rigged by Harlow (1979) to monitor directional movement of badgers into and out of burrows.

Godfrey (1954a, see Chapter 30) used a Geiger counter to trace field voles carrying subcutaneous radioactive gold wires. Godfrey (1953) also used radioactive nest material for finding vole nests. Godfrey (1955), Gifford and Griffin (1960), and Breckenridge and Tester (1961) have also reported on use of radioactive tags for studying animal movement.

Other types of movement studies, (besides those possible through capturing marking, or similar studies) are those of Sowls and Minnamon (1963) who used glass beads for marking feces, Brown and Conaway (1961) who used several fluorescing dyes, and Gast (1963) who used Rhodamine-B dye. Gast (1963) used a rhodamine dye which could be detected to 1 part in 10 billion to stain feces which, once collected, fluoresce under a fluorometer. Frantz (1972) employed a fluorescent pigment in bait and detected the fluorescent green feces with a battery-powered fluorescent lantern equipped with an ultraviolet fluorescent tube.

Heath (1961) developed an ingenious spool which he attached to the tail of Gila monsters. During the animals' travels, the spool of nylon thread unwound behind them, thereby providing a record of their movement. Activities such as burrowing and resting along the routes were determined from sign. The device was originally designed for studies of the physiological ecology of small animals.

Nesting activity has been recorded by a thermocouple and recording potentiometer (Baldwin and Kendeigh 1927, Kendeigh 1963). Body heat activated the thermocouple, and presence and departure were recorded. Klonglan et al. (1956) modified a device of Fant (1953). He used an electrical switch projecting into a pheasant nest to activate a pen marking a rotating chart to record the movements of the nesting hen. An itograph and electromagnetic devices were used by Kendeigh and Baldwin (1930) and Bussmann (1933) to record nest activity of birds. Marples and Gurr (1943) used an electrical mercury-contact device. Gurr (1955) used a pneumatic device. He fit a copper tambour with a sheet rubber membrane snugly into the bottom of a nest. The movements of the bird depressed the membrane. A similar tambour nearby, on which rested a recording pen, was activated by the air pressure created by the nesting bird. The pen recorded on a clock-operated kymograph. Cooper (1978) modified a weight-activated nest platform developed by Breckenridge (1956) to measure Canada goose nest attentiveness. Kendeigh (1952) reviewed the automatic nest recording instruments used in songbird study. Farner and Mewaldt (1953) obtained caged bird activity from birds activating a 2-way microswitch attached to a perch. Recordings were on kymograph paper. Kessler (1962) used Yates' (1942) method of photoelectric cells (with an infrared filter) to record nest attentiveness of ring-necked pheasants.

Salter (1966) presented a device for recording the activity within intact game bird eggs. The laboratory device is a vibration transducer.

Animal activity in the laboratory has been extensively studied by animal behaviorists. Kavanau (1961) used ferromagnetic collars on mice to unbalance an excited inductance bridge, thus triggering recording circuitry. He later described (1963) a device for continuous monitoring of the activity of a single animal using a system of electromechanical transducers and electric eyes. He had available 22 independent channels of information. Edwards' (1962) note on the actograph and Kavanau's reply shed further light on animal activity instrumentation. A series of treadles with electrical contacts has been used by Dice (1961) to study animal activity in cages and in the field by Voisey and Kalbfleisch (1962). Behney (1936) used swinging wire doors whose electrical contacts were recorded on an itograph. He studied the 24-hr activity of mice, *Peromyscus leucopus*, caged indoors. Hendrick (1963) reported on a mechanical counter for bird activity. Lawrence and Sherman (1963) reported on a resistor-capacitor traffic counter unit for recording the burrow use of the mountain beaver. The device was operated by a 30-v battery. Weiland (1964) wrote of trap activation by solenoids.

Fallon (1965) described an "eatometer," a device for recording the feeding behavior of caged animals. It was less refined than the drinkometer (Weissman 1962) in that it simply measured animal contacts with the feeding cup. Morton (1965) employed strain gauges as the principal transducer of continuous feeding activity of caged birds. He was able to detect weight changes in supplied food of 0.05 g in 15 g with 99% accuracy.

Harned et al. (1952) presented a method for studying the movements of individually caged small animals. The animal was suspended in a cage, and its movements (from respiration to jumps) were transmitted by a silk thread to a heart lever equipped with a wooden stylus. Recordings were made on smoked kymograph paper.

Lieberman and McCarty (1976) perfected a recording system which recorded the direction of movement of an animal. Fox (1978) devised an inexpensive and simple battery-powered apparatus to record time of capture of small mammals. The timing unit could be readily attached to a collapsible aluminum live trap and did not interfere with a normal trapping program. Teicher and Green (1977) developed a system to monitor and record the vibrational activity of newborn captive animals. Viaud and Le Cain (1975) described an apparatus for recording the motor activities of caged small mammals that employed a strain gauge attached to the cage floor. The rate and pattern of water consumption was measured with a photocell system by Boyles and Wright (1977). To facilitate behavioral ecology studies, Wiens et al. (1970) devised an inexpensive metronome tuning device which emitted a tone "blip" at intervals varying from 1 to 20 seconds.

WEIGHT MEASUREMENT AND ESTIMATION

One of the most taken but least used observation of wildlife is total body weight. The field notes of hundreds of workers are filled with thousands of weight observations of animals but rarely are these presented in reports or used in research conclusions. There are several reasons for this lack of use. Mammals and birds vary widely in weight by sex, age, migration, seasons, time of day, breeding condition, molt, range conditions, length of time since death, and cause of death. One meal can frequently vary the weight of a mammal over 20%. Daily fluctuations of from 3.5 to 10.8% occur in birds' weights (Nice 1938). With such great variances within relatively small numbers of animals examined at any one time, conclusions based on total body weights must be general and cautiously made.

Nevertheless, weights, particularly live weights, are a major concern of biologists, ecologists, and game managers. They are interesting to sportsmen, used by those studying bioenergetics and production, and used in appraising population vigor through age-weight correlation. Facilities for weighing large animals in the field often are lacking (Smith and Ledger 1965b). Murie

(1928) described weighing the sections of butchered moose and elk to determine total weight. With this approach, loss of body fluids creates an error usually well within the significant figures needed or obtainable. Doutt (1940) described the use of a tripod and gallon container of water (about 3.628 kg) as counterweights on a lever arm to measure big game weight. He employed only a 1.020-kg capacity spring balance.

Craighead et al. (1960) described weighing bear in a culvert trap by putting the trap on a trailer, then rolling trap, bear, and trailer onto portable scales. The weight of the bear was gained by subtraction.

Beam scales have a capacity of 181.4 kg and are more accurate than large capacity spring scales. They weigh only several pounds and can be lifted with the animal to be weighed with a sportsman's nylon rope hoist.

Support for scales in treeless or open areas may be difficult to find. Talbot and Talbot (1962) developed a truck-mounted hand-winch for their work with big game. Greer and Howe (1964) used a 226.8-kg Chatillion spring scale suspended from the 4.6-m boom of a hoisting truck for weighing elk carcasses. Smith and Ledger (1965a) described a 7.62-cm iron-pipe tripod for suspending spring balances for weighing whole large African animals. They suspended 5 spring balances each with a 544.3-kg capacity across a bar suspended from a chain-hoist attached to the apex of the tripod. They preferred a chain hoist to a block and tackle because it gave greater control.

Talbot and Talbot (1962) and Pan et al. (1965) devised supports or sling harnesses useful for suspending dead animals or weighing experimental animals (pigs) alive.

Greer (1965) developed an attachment for a metabolism cage useful for easily weighing a small pugnacious animal, a grison, *Galicitis cuja*. Geese (Beer and Boyd 1962) can be placed in a sack and weighed suspended from a spring balance. Sherwood (1965) presented a photo of an efficient goose weighing station and tripod.

Tension spring scales with direct-reading gauge or geared circular gauge are available from 20 g to 545 kg. Some smaller scales have accuracies to the nearest 14.2 g.

Single, double, and triple balances have increasingly greater weighing capabilities without accessory weights. They vary widely in make, construction, and cost. Their capacities range from a single-beam 10 g to 0.1 g to a triple-beam 610 g to 0.1 g. With additional weights their capacities are 2,600 g. A triple-beam is most satisfactory for weighing live, small mammals but is bulky, needs a carrier for field use, and must be level for accurate readings. Movements of animals add to inaccuracies.

Bookhout and Harger (1964) recommended the use of a modestly priced powder and bullet scale that reads up to 21.06 g. Its units are grains but easily converted (grams = grains × 0.0648).

Analytical balances are well known and, depending on quality, have measurement capabilities of from 200 to 0.05 mg. Semimicro balances have capacities from 100 to 0.005 mg. Prices range from $200 to $1,500 depending on quality and characteristics. More recently developed are electrical analytical balances that cost approximately $1,200 to $2,500. Although 4 to 8 times more expensive than an "adequate," general-purpose analytical balance, they allow accurate weights to be very rapidly obtained to 0.005 mg. Where many small, accurate weights must be obtained, these balances are economical.

Although the weights of body organs do not show the extreme variability of total body weight, their collection, just as the collection of total body weight, must be guided by the principle: seek a measuring instrument that will allow observation within one's ability to express and analyze them in mathematically significant figures.

Weights of large animals are difficult to take no matter what the conditions or techniques. Halloran (1961) presented impressive measurements of over 200 bison made under near-slaughterhouse conditions. Rapid field use estimation equations are needed. Because of the great variability in weights previously discussed, efforts to convert hog-dressed weights to live weights have been largely unsuccessful.

Five terms often used are *live-* or *whole-weight*, with self-evident meaning; *field-dressed* weight, a gross measurement meaning the weight of an animal with viscera removed but with heart and liver (and often lungs) included in the weight; *hog-dressed* weight is weight of animals with all organs removed but with hide, feet, and head intact (i.e., whole weight minus all viscera and blood); *skinned-weight*, which is hog-dressed weight minus the hide only; and *skinned-dressed weight*, self-evident.

Blood and Lovaas (1966) reported that hog-dressed weights of Rocky Mountain elk were 67% of live weight and that Manitoba elk on the average weighed 75% of live weight but ranged from 67 to 81%. Mitchell (1971) found that mean hog-dressed weights of Alberta pronghorns averaged 71% and ranged from 66 to 75% of live weight for mature animals. Jonkel (1964) reported that black bear hog-dressed weight was 85% of live weight and varied from 79 to 88%.

Patrick (1961) developed 2 regression equations relating skinned weight of black bear to total weight, $y = 1.86 + 0.86x$, (where x is total weight) and skinned dressed weight to total weight, $y = 2.10 + 0.699x$. Correlation was strong and no differences were noticeable in the weight relationship between the sexes.

Hamerstrom and Camburn (1950) also found no significant difference between equations from animals of different sex or age. With their equations, they concluded that one could predict live weight within plus or minus 2.3 kg from hog dressed weight of Michigan white-tailed deer two-thirds of the time. However, one might miss the true figure as much as 8.2 kg and possibly even more. The average for a large series, such as a checking station, could be calculated from the equation. Their equation for 1941–42 (males and females) was $x = 2.62 + 1.251y$ (where x = live weight and y = hog-dressed weight), and for 1942–43, $x = 8.55 + 1.265y$. The equation for skinned dressed weight, y^1, was $y^1 = -1.48 + 0.538x$.

Other correlations also have been useful. Smith and Ledger (1965b) found that the weight of a single leg was closely correlated to live weight. Prediction is limited by the amount of body fat, but the method has use for large and small animals that are eviscerated in the field,

Table 28.1. Single leg-weight/live weight regression equations, where $y = \bar{y} + b(x - \bar{x})$ and **y = live weight in kilos and x =** leg weight in kilos (adapted from Smith and Ledger 1965b:507).

Species	Regression Equation	
	Hind leg/live weight	Fore leg/live weight
Uganda kob	$y = 67.2 + 10.9\ (x - 7.8)$	$y = 67.2 + 26.4\ (x - 2.6)$
Thomson's gazelle	$y = 18.7 + 10.4\ (x - 2.1)$	$y = 18.7 + 21.8\ (x - 0.8)$
Waterbuck	$y = 163.8 + 10.7\ (x - 18.2)$	$y = 163.8 + 21.4\ (x - 7.0)$
Wildebeest	$y = 149.8 + 12.9\ (x - 13.5)$	$y = 149.8 + 28.4\ (x - 7.1)$
Wart hog	$y = 60.0 + 13.3\ (x - 5.0)$	$y = 60.0 + 17.4\ (x - 1.8)$
Hippopotamus	$y = 1109.2 + 16.0\ (x - 71.0)$	$y = 1109.2 + 3.1\ (x - 38.8)$
Oryx	$y = 169.1 + 9.4\ (x - 17.1)$	$y = 169.1 + 16.6\ (x - 8.1)$
Lesser kudu	$y = 92.1 + 10.0\ (x - 10.2)$	$y = 92.1 + 24.8\ (x - 4.2)$
Brahma steers	$y = 403.1 + 11.1\ (x - 35.3)$	$y = 403.1 + 27.0\ (x - 14.9)$
Brahma cows and heifers	$y = 312.0 + 9.9\ (x - 26.5)$	$y = 312.0 + 25.7\ (x - 10.7)$
Brahma bulls	$y = 375.0 + 11.1\ (x - 32.6)$	$y = 375.0 + 22.7\ (x - 14.2)$

then brought to a place where they can be weighed. Their regression equations are shown in Table 28.1.

Bandy et al. (1956), McCulloch and Talbot (1965), Talbot and McCulloch (1965), McEwan and Wood (1966), and Mitchell (1971) used heart girth as a reliable predictor of live weight. Heart girth is the circumference of the chest immediately behind the axilla, usually measured with a flexible steel tape. Talbot and McCulloch (1965) found their equations (Table 28.2) independent of stomach content and concluded that heart girth may provide as close an estimate of the true mean live weight as the single spot weighing of animals at the time of collection.

Bandy et al. (1956) found the live weight (W) of Columbian black-tailed deer as related to heart girth (HG) was as follows:

$$W = 0.0037HG^{2.64}$$

McEwan and Wood (1966) found a similar equation for caribou of

$$W = 0.0016HG^{2.51}$$

Smart et al. (1973) and Urbston et al. (1976) devised a tape that converted heart girth measurements of white-tailed deer to weight. This tape alleviates the need for cumbersome weighing equipment. Similar tapes have been developed for black bears by Payne (1976) and LeCount (1977).

Table 28.2. Equations of the relation of live weight (w) to heart girth (HG) from Talbot and McCulloch (1965).

	W = wt. in lbs., heart girth in meters correct to 5 mm.
Uganda kob	W = 468 × HG − 276
Thomson's gazelle	W = 175 × HG − 62
Wildebeest	W = 646 × HG − 519
Oryx	W = 495 × HG − 318
Grant's gazelle	W = 319 × HG − 156
Hyena	W = 274 × HG − 117
Impala	W = 309 × HG − 149
Topi and hartebeest	W = 347 × HG − 132
Zebra	W = 645 × HG − 325

Loftin and Bowman (1978) perfected a device to measure accurately bird egg volume.

MISCELLANEOUS DEVICES

Barney (1972) devised a 31-day battery-operated recording weather station. Fowler (1975) described an instrument with low power requirements for measuring and recording wind speed and direction at bimonthly intervals at remote weather stations. Coleman and Wiegert (1967) designed a simple, inexpensive temperature integrator employing a mercury coulometer, mercury battery, and thermistor.

Swanson (1978a,b) perfected a lightweight core sampler for collecting waterfowl foods and a water column sampler for invertebrates in shallow wetlands. A core sampler for extracting lead and steel shot from wetland soil was devised by Quist and Kirby (1978).

Kristiansson et al. (1977) described a bird altimeter to determine the altitude of a bird's flight using an alpha particle source of ^{210}Po attached to a small aluminum sheet.

Higgins et al. (1969, 1977) devised a cable-chain drag device to facilitate nest searches.

Simple devices to expedite ornithological studies include a tube or jacket for holding birds during examination of molt (Seel 1975), weighing (Evans and Kear 1972, Fuller 1975, Schreiber 1976), and taking blood samples (Bolen et al. 1977) and an easily built portable blind (LeCroy 1975).

A telescoping pole apparatus with a mirror attached allows examination of nests at heights of 6.4 m or more (Parker 1972, Smith and Spencer 1976).

Richens and Madden (1973) described a portable snow study kit to measure snow temperature, hardness, density, and structure. A snow penetration gauge was developed by Hepburn (1978) to simulate and measure deer track sinking depth.

Larry Toschik

Chapter Twenty-Nine

Wildlife Telemetry

WILLIAM W. COCHRAN

Associate Wildlife Specialist
Section of Wildlife Research
Illinois Natural History Survey
Urbana, Illinois

DEFINITION, CLASSIFICATION, AND GENERAL LITERATURE

Wildlife telemetry encompasses a variety of techniques associated with obtaining biologically related measurements at a distance from the subject(s) of measurement. Radio waves are the most common "carrier" of information but sound or light may be used in special applications. Radio-location telemetry (radio tracking) involves techniques for radio transmission and reception. Where other data are required, techniques for transforming information into transmissible form, e.g., transducers, must also be utilized. Techniques for processing received information, e.g., notebooks, recorders, or computers, although involving disciplines outside the realm of telemetry, are usually considered a part of a wildlife telemetry system. Figure 29.1 illustrates a wildlife telemetry system in its most elementary form.

Whether or not to use the telemetric technique was, in earlier years, often a question of the cost effectiveness of the technique compared to some other technique that was capable of yielding similar information. It was natural for some researchers to use this new tool in seeking objectives formulated around capabilities and limitations of older tools. However, telemetry for wildlife investigations, like all new tools in the history of science, must alter and shape the direction of research to which it is applicable. Although telemetry opens new areas of wildlife investigations, users should conform to conventional responsibilities of experimental design and project planning.

For purposes of discussion, it is useful to classify biological telemetry as either wide-band or narrow-band. This division, although only one of many, is not arbitrary; it is founded on what might be considered a quirk of nature—the unique electro-mechanical properties of quartz. Quartz crystals can be fabricated for use in radio transmitters to provide frequency stability hundreds of times better than that attainable with inductors and capacitors alone. This stability permits the use of system bandwidths on the order of 50 Hz. Approximately 50 Hz is the effective bandwidth of the human ear in discerning coherent tones in the presence of noise. In contrast, systems with bandwidths on the order of 50,000 Hz are required to accommodate the instability of transmitters without crystal control of frequency. Noise, which is always the limiting factor in weak signal detection, is proportional to bandwidth. Thus, to realize equal signal-to-noise ratio in a given telemetry system, a transmitter with crystal control has a thousandfold advantage over its noncrystal-controlled counterpart. Another way of stating this: For the same battery and antenna, crystal control provides P times as much power and T times as much life where the product of P and T is 1000.

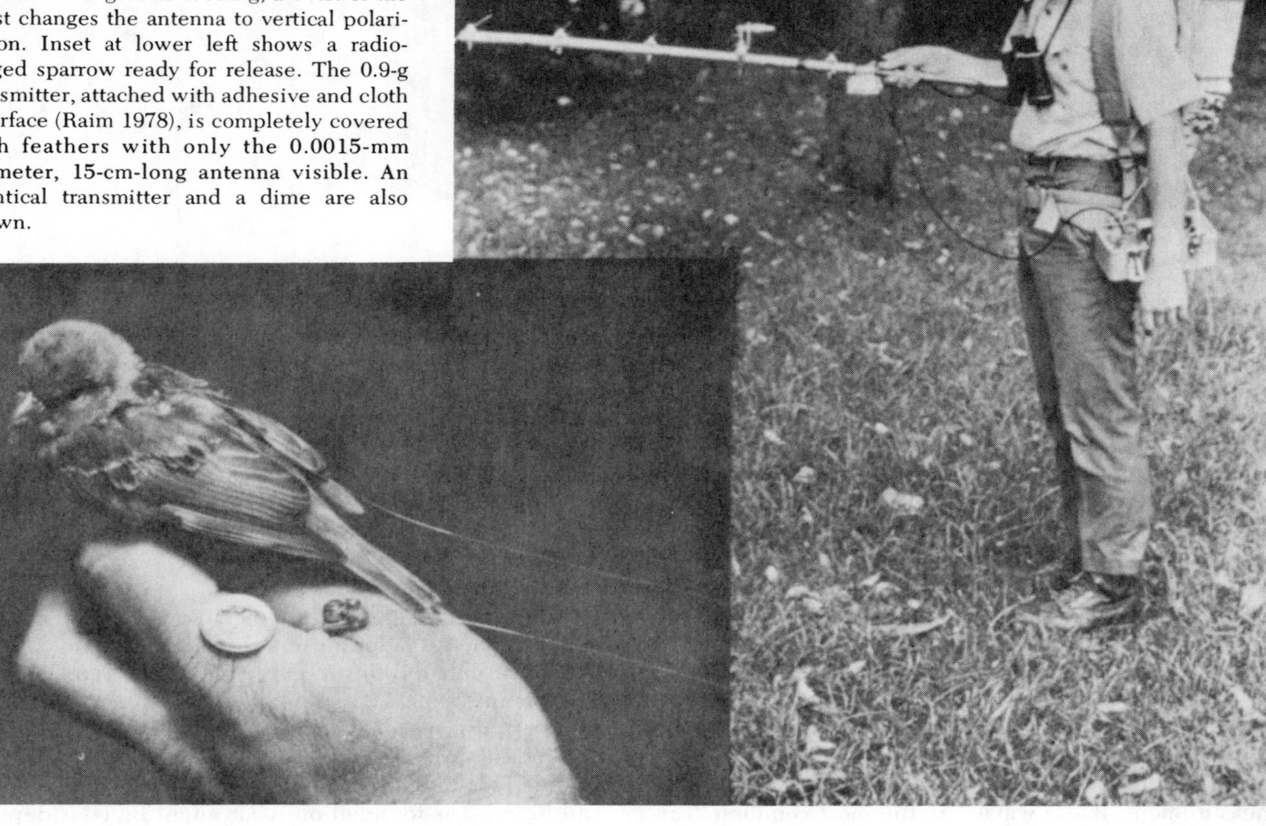

Fig. 29.1. Living with his radio-tagged birds from dawn to dusk, this researcher carries binoculars, tape recorder, notebook, maps, compass, and sandwiches in addition to the hand-held yagi directional antenna and a telemetry receiver. The tape recorder is actuated by a switch on the handle of the antenna and is used with a lapel microphone. On windy days, headphones (in backpack) are used instead of the receiver speaker. Data are a mixture of remotely obtained locations, visual observations, and habitat evaluations. The hand-held antenna is shown held in the horizontal polarization position for best reception from a bird in a tree or on a post. For birds that are ground feeding, a twist of the wrist changes the antenna to vertical polarization. Inset at lower left shows a radio-tagged sparrow ready for release. The 0.9-g transmitter, attached with adhesive and cloth interface (Raim 1978), is completely covered with feathers with only the 0.0015-mm diameter, 15-cm-long antenna visible. An identical transmitter and a dime are also shown.

In practice, narrow-band systems (crystal control) allow for the use of radio tags which have size, longevity, and range characteristics suitable for the study of free-ranging animals, whereas wide-band systems do not.

The use of narrow-band systems is so universal among users of wildlife telemetry that few wildlife researchers are aware of the existence of wide-band techniques, not to mention the performance chasm which separates wide- and narrow-band systems. Physiological and medical researchers, conditioned by at least 3 decades of telemetry dominated by wide-band techniques, are probably equally unaware of the narrow-band techniques. For example, Ysenbrandt et al. (1976), in their physiologically oriented literature survey, listed 1750 titles which included less than 5% of the papers relevant to wildlife telemetry. The literature of several thousand titles on the subject of physiological measurements of animals and humans via telemetry (almost exclusively wide-band) is of immediate value to the wildlife researcher when his objectives are served by systems with limited range. Furthermore, most of the techniques and devices associated with electrodes and sensors and their interfacing with animals are adaptable and applicable to narrow-band systems. This base of information will become an increasingly valuable resource as wildlife investigations include physiological measurements. Coverage of wide-band telemetry and related techniques for physiological measurements will be limited here to brief mention and then only where these border on usefulness in the study of free-ranging animals. For those involved in physiological telemetry, the book by Mackay (1970) is an excellent general reference, and the bibliography by Ysenbrandt et al. (1976) is a good source for work published outside the realm of wildlife literature. A broad spectrum of recent biomedical telemetry techniques may be obtained in Klewe and Kimmich (1978). Will and Patric (1972) produced the most recent bibliography emphasizing wildlife tracking. Underwater telemetry will not be given specific treatment in this chapter although most of the technique information presented here will be applicable if aquatic tracking is done by radio. Stasko and Pincock (1977) reviewed underwater telemetry techniques, with emphasis on ultrasonic methods. Another useful source is the *Underwater Telemetry Newsletter.* For information write Charles C. Coutant, Editor, Environmental Sciences Division, Oak Ridge National Laboratory, P.O. Box X, Oak Ridge, Tennessee 38730.

WIDE-BAND TELEMETRY

Transmitters, without crystal control and of a size and longevity useful for biological studies, have ranges from less than 1 meter to 1 kilometer. Their ranges depend on a variety of factors including frequency of operation, size of transmitting antenna (if any), longevity requirements, and sophistication of receiving equipment. Their 2 principal advantages are that they can be made smaller than their crystal counterparts (a crystal may be larger than all other components combined) and the ease with which they may be frequency modulated with physiological information.

One class of wide-band telemetry devices includes small ingestible transmitters often called endoradiosondes or radio pills. The range of these devices is usually adequate to send signals from within the body and no more. They are useless for the study of free-ranging animals.

Slightly larger transmitters of similar design may be useful for short-range applications. Rawson and Hartline (1964) used 2.6-gram 27 MHz transmitters for tracking mice. Langman (1973) and Anderka and Dyer (1967) described lightweight 88–100 MHz transmitters for telemetering temperature and heart-rate, respectively, from small birds. McKinley et al. (1976) described a "wireless microphone" collar for vocalization studies of domestic cats. Their wide-band, 88–92 MHz system provided ranges from 10 to 65 meters.

Low frequency (0.5 to 1.5 MHz) transmitters can be detected at distances up to about 1 meter on commercial A.M. broadcast receivers. These are usually equipped with a thermistor to make the pulsing (ticking) rate a function of temperature. Lifetimes of several months may be obtained from transmitters of a size suitable for implantation in small animals such as mice. A year or more may be expected from larger units. Several implant transmitters are shown in Fig. 29.2. An observer may find fossorial animals by moving over the ground to search for the ticking sound which, when found, provides location and temperature. Goodman (1971) provided extensive design and construction information for accurate temperature telemetry from these low frequency type transmitters.

Many free-ranging animals have places they regularly visit, such as nests or dens. This habit makes possible other applications for short-range devices. A receiving antenna may be located close to such places and connected by cable to a distant receiver. Recorders are usually connected to the receiver to provide continuous measurement when the animal is present. For examples see Folk (1966) and Shallenberger et al. (1974). In addition to temperature or other physiological information, the time and duration of presence may be obtained. Nest or egg temperatures also have been recorded in this way (Eklund and Charlton 1959, Varney and Ellis 1974, Schwarly et al. 1977).

Location information can be obtained with short-range transmitters from receiving antennas distributed at selected places throughout all or part of an animal's home range (Merriam 1963) or in a grid (Moore and Kluth 1966, Chute et al. 1974). These methods have certain advantages in data uniformity and in automation of data acquisition but are practical only for animals with small home ranges. Each of the above studies was unique in certain particulars, and all should be consulted along with alternatives presented by Banks et al. (1975) and Mineau and Madison (1977).

The range of moderately small noncrystal VHF transmitters with external antennas is generally a few dozen to a few hundred meters, although favorable propagation via radio line-of-sight, as with birds in flight or animals in trees, may extend range to more than a kilometer. Although this range is insufficient to keep in contact reliably with many species over their entire home ranges, the fact that contact can be recovered at known denning, nesting, or roosting sites makes it possible to obtain measurements intermittently over considerable spans of time. Recent examples include Sawby and Gessaman (1974), Morrow and Taylor (1976), and Torre-Bueno (1976).

For larger animals and short periods of observation, large and powerful noncrystal VHF transmitters can provide ranges adequate for tracking. For example, Van Citters and Franklin (1966), and Van Citters et al. (1966) reported ranges of 300 to 3000 meters and longevity of about 200 hours for the system they used to obtain blood pressure measurements from free-ranging giraffes and baboons.

SIMULTANEOUS USE OF NARROW- AND WIDE-BAND SYSTEMS

Cupal et al. (1975, 1976) described a system that has a wide-band link from an implanted transmitter to a collar-mounted receiver and a narrow-band link from the collar to the observer. Variables transmitted to the collar included heart rate and heat flow. The information was relayed via the crystal-controlled, collar-mounted transmitter over distances sufficient for tracking. One of the distinct advantages of noncrystal controlled transmitters is that they may be frequency modulated in a nearly linear manner with simpler circuitry than that required for crystal control. This makes them ideal for transmission of ECG, EEG, and other variables where linearity is important. In the system of Cupal et al., mentioned above, both variables were in digital form (a pulse rate) prior to transmission over the wide-band link, and thus linearity was not important in their application. However, the technology they present is suggestive of the possibilities for measurements from free-ranging animals by complementary use of narrow/wide-band technology.

Fig. 29.2. The smaller units to the right of the nickel are low frequency temperature transmitters made for implantation in small animals. The 5-g unit at the left and the 2-g unit at right have longevities of 1 year and 4 months respectively. Both give less than 1 m range and temperature accuracy better than 0.2 degrees C. Encapsulation is a mixture of paraffin and beeswax. The upper unit is a crystal-controlled temperature transmitter with an accuracy better than 0.2 degrees C. and a range of about 2 km. Its large size limits its use to large animals and mounting inside the body cavity. Predicted longevity is many years with the "D" sized lithium battery pictured. The transmitter is in the hermetically sealed metal housing to the right, and package size can be reduced by using a smaller battery with a corresponding reduction in longevity. The outer coating is a mixture of paraffin and beeswax which provides an adequate long-term seal for the low-impedence battery circuit. A coating of silicone rubber usually is applied to provide good tissue compatibility.

Complementary use does not dictate that the 2 systems be in tandem as above. For example, an externally mounted narrow-band tracking transmitter may be used by an observer to "home in" on a subject until the distance to the subject is small enough that signals can be received from a short-range physiological telemeter, perhaps one which is implanted. This permits data sampling to be a matter of experimental design rather than chance or special situations.

NARROW-BAND SYSTEMS

The remainder of this chapter is primarily directed at the narrow-band systems commonly used in wildlife research. When comment or comparison to wide-band techniques is pertinent, wide-band will be specified. Other comments and generalizations may or may not apply to wide-band systems.

ACTIVITY DETECTION AND MOVEMENT-INDUCED SIGNAL CHANGE

One characteristic of an animal-mounted transmitter is that slight movements of the radioed animal usually cause a change in the amplitude or frequency of the received signal. Therefore, by listening to the signal, it is possible to tell when an animal is moving. Kjos and Cochran (1970) and Gilmer et al. (1971) used recorders to obtain indices of activity based on signal changes. Figure 29.3 shows one kind of recording of circadian activity. Wind-blown vegetation can cause signal changes that may be misinterpreted as activity, although the former has a regularity that is distinct.

Movement-induced signal changes may correlate with specific behaviors. For example, signal changes caused by wing movement and respiration-induced changes in body shape were recorded from a flying duck by Lord et al. (1962). The 2 variables were separable on chart recordings of signal because they were cyclic at significantly different rates.

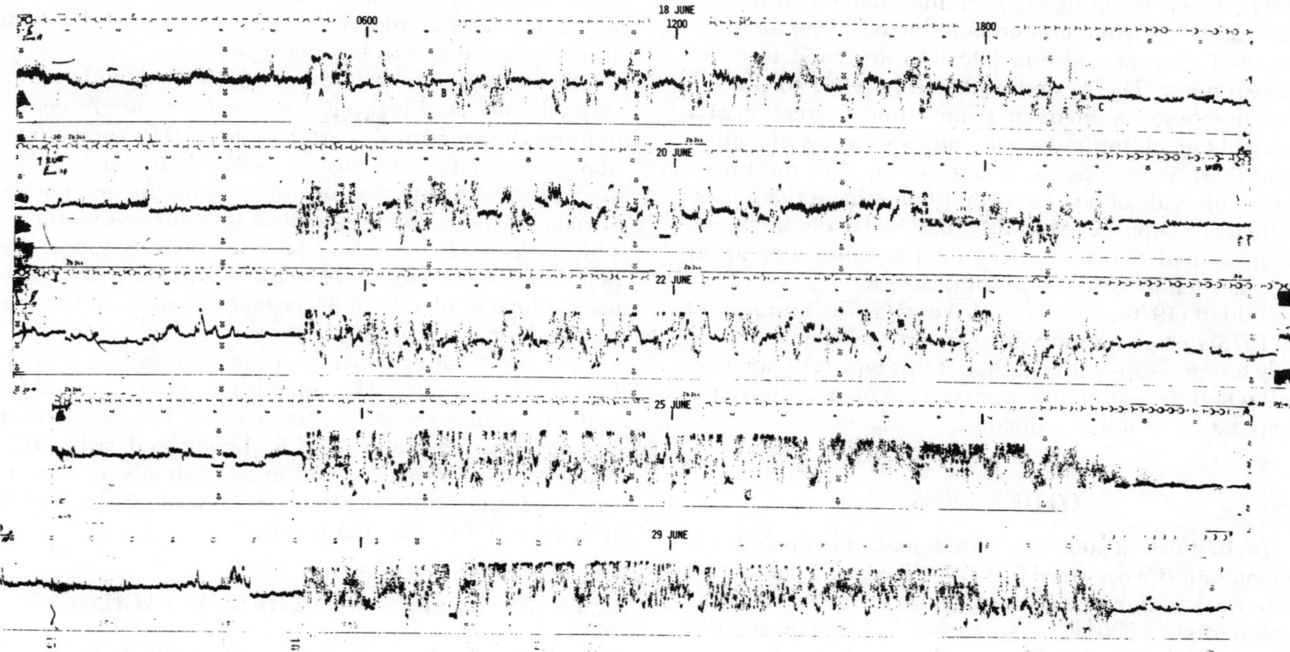

Fig. 29.3. The chart recordings of the logarithm of signal strength (automatic gain control voltage) show the circadian activity pattern of a nesting female brown thrasher. Stronger signal is up with the lower baseline representing an absence of signal. Near mid-range signal strength is that received with the bird in or near its nest in a bush about 1 meter above ground. The recordings were taken from a receiver about 1 km from the bird's home range. Extended periods of inactivity (at mid-range signal level) during daylight on the upper 3 records indicate brooding. The more intense activity of the lower 2 records, and the short, often indistinguishable, nest visits indicate the almost continuous feeding of young. Some of the nocturnal activity indicates singular perch movement, but the more extended periods of nocturnal activity remain unexplained. The fuzziness of the right side of the record of 25 June was caused by accidental disabling of the receiver automatic frequency control combined with transmitter frequency shift due to changing temperature.

Various investigators have reported the detection of feeding, bathing, grooming, preening, carrying of young, and fighting behavior from the "sound" of the signal. Visual correlation usually is needed to establish these relationships and quantification is difficult.

Knowlton et al. (1968) described a motion sensor which used a ball bearing and photograph cartridge to produce motion-related voltage spikes. These spikes triggered the generation of extra transmitter pulses. The system of Kolz et al. (1973), described below, is also capable of generating extra pulses as the result of motion. Activity measured by these methods is immune to the effects of wind mentioned above.

Movement-induced signal changes are often a problem. Simple direction finding involves operator interpretation of signal changes as a function of the rotation of a directional receiving antenna. Movement-induced changes can interfere with this process and make direction finding difficult, especially for inexperienced operators.

Wide-band transmitters are particularly susceptible to frequency shifts caused by animal movement. This can completely mask physiological information. To reduce the masking effect of movement, it is general practice to use an attachment method that provides a minimum of movement of the transmitter, its antenna, and electrodes relative to the subject. Implantation is better than external mounting in this regard. Further improvement can be made by amplification of the biopotentials before they are sent to the transmitter. Some of the movement-induced noise (including electrode noise) can be removed by electronic filtering at both the receiver and transmitter. The use of subcarrier techniques eliminates the problems of movement-induced noise at the expense of complexity (Morrow and Taylor 1976).

MORTALITY MONITORS—MOTION SENSORS

Lack of the signal variations discussed above, for periods of time dependent on animal habits, suggests death. In some cases movement-induced signal changes are difficult to interpret in terms of mortality because a living animal may spend significant periods of time without moving. The critical measurement is the length of time since the subject last moved. It is not practical, for a number of reasons, to use lack of activity as a mortality indicator on a real-time basis without automatic recording. The latter is not possible in most field applications and manual monitoring would be very time consuming. Kolz et al. (1973) and Kolz (1975) described a system which circumvents these problems. In their system an interval timer was used to change the pulse rate of the transmitter whenever the elapsed time equalled the interval. However, the elapsed time accumulator was reset to zero by closures of a motion-sensitive switch, thus preventing elapsed time from equalling the interval except when motion failed to occur for an uninterrupted time period equal to that designed into the interval timer. This system makes it possible to check a large number of animals in a short time. Detection of a changed transmitter pulse rate indicates a lack of motion for at least as long as the design interval of the timer. Timer intervals of one to several hours have been used with large mammals. Mortality may be falsely indicated for an animal that is inactive for the time interval for reasons such as sickness or hibernation.

Stoddart (1970), Osgood and Weigl (1972), and Kolz et al. (1973) described mortality sensors based on a drop in body temperature with death, but this type will not work well when the ambient temperature is near or above the temperature of a live animal.

OTHER USES

The first useful and successful long-term animal tracking via satellite occurred in 1977–78 when 3 polar bears were tracked. One bear was tracked for 1600 km over a time period of 390 days (Kolz et al. 1978). The satellite system used for receiving was designed for other purposes and was not optimal for animal tracking. The required compromise was achieved with sophisticated transmitter design, both expensive and large. In the polar bear study mentioned above, transmitter size was not critical because of the large size of the animal. Also, transmitter cost was insignificant when measured against the dangers, difficulties, and expenses which would have been incurred with conventional tracking from aircraft in polar regions. These considerations apply to animal movement studies involving truly inaccessible geographic areas and animals that can carry transmitter packages without behavioral effects that subvert the study objectives, for example, in the extreme—death. Although the 5 kg packages used on the polar bears could be reduced to perhaps 200 g (Kolz, pers comm.), a 200-g package would limit the usefulness of the system to relatively few of the many wide-ranging species for which satellite surveillance would be ideal. Wildlife researchers interested in obtaining data from spacecraft should consider the possibilities that will be presented by the space shuttle system planned by NASA for the 1980's. The low orbits of these vehicles combined with the reduced costs for dedicated orbitting equipment will provide opportunities for a tracking system capable of being used with transmitters weighing as little as 10 grams, perhaps less.

Charles-Dominique (1977) described a method of monitoring urination. In his system a body harness included a carefully positioned moisture sensor which, when wetted, increased the transmitter pulse rate.

W. Evans (pers. comm.) surgically implanted vaginal transmitters into the reproductive canal of adult female mule deer and elk in New Mexico. The transmitter is expelled at birth. The pulse rate of the transmitter's motion sensor increases rapidly when immobile for a predetermined interval and can be readily located.

Tester and Heezen (1965) used telemetry to observe the movement behavior of deer during a drive census. If a sufficient number of animals are radio-marked, an estimate of the percentage of animals missed can be obtained and tests of effectiveness of drives with different observer spacings can be conducted.

Other census techniques can be tested with radio-marked animals. Flushing distance for different conditions can be measured (see Chapter 14). If a known fraction of animals with visual markers are also radio-marked, an estimate may be obtained for the percentage of visual markers counted with various surveys methods. This percentage can then be used in estimating the population from counts of marked and unmarked animals. Floyd et al. (1979) described this method for censusing deer.

The use of radio transmitters in tranquilizer darts is becoming common. This enables trappers to find an animal that has gone into heavy cover before the drug has had time to immobilize it (Lovett and Hill 1977). Another application in capturing animals is a trap-mounted transmitter that is turned on by a switch tripped when the animal is caught.

TRANSMITTERS AND THEIR ATTACHMENT

Transmitters with predicted longevities of several years are of a size and weight which pose few difficulties in attachment to most animals larger than a wolf. The 260-gram transmitter-collar shown in Fig. 29.4 is typical, consisting of a 15-gram hermetically sealed transmitter, an 85-gram "D"-size lithium battery, and 160 grams of encapsulant and collar material. The large proportion of weight devoted to the encapsulant and collar is consistent with the general practice of providing attachment and protective covering which will last as long as the predicted battery longevity of 3 or more years.

The most common attachment method is a neck collar. Rubber impregnated cotton or nylon webbing (machine belting) and the more pliable nonimpregnated nylon webbing used for seat belts are the most popular materials for collar construction. Plastics are sometimes used, especially for smaller animals and harnesses. Low temperature and aging tend to weaken and stiffen some plastics such as flexible PVC. Plastics with the same name may have a variety of formulations with varying amounts of filler and plasticizer and varying degrees of polymerization, all of which affect physical properties.

A number of factors should be considered in relation to their importance for the particular application when constructing or specifying collar or harness attachments. Among the more obvious are shape, width, contouring, inside smoothness, durability, flexibility, size adjustability, protruding versus enclosed antenna, and ease of attachment. Improvements in 1 factor are seldom accomplished without compromise in others. Factors affecting compatability and reliability usually should be given higher priority than cost or convenience of attachment. Desirable or undesirable features may not be immediately obvious. For example, Garcelon (1977) stated:

> Another concern was to make the transmitter package and collar assembly as compact and inconspicuous as possible, because changes in nor-

Fig. 29.4. The deer transmitter on the left weighs about 260 g and uses a flexible nylon webbing for a collar. All transmitter components are in the hermetically sealed housing between the battery and antenna. The spring is a strain relief for the stainless steel cable antenna. When the transmitter is mounted on the neck, the antenna will be on the right and slant back away from the head. The 9-g squirrel collar to the right is constructed of plastic-covered brass which serves also as the loop antenna. A small bolt and nut at top may be removed and the collar spread while it is being slipped over an animal's head. Longevity of this unit is several months.

mal silhouette of familiar objects tend to upset a mountain lion (Bogue and Ferrari, Alexander Lindway, Jr., Museum, pers. comm.). Bogue and Ferrari also stated that a large transmitter package located under the chin of a mountain lion would be a possible source of injury during attacks on large prey. They pointed out the need of a lion to tuck its chin to avoid being kicked by hooves while trying for a neck bite on a deer. This defensive tucking action would be hindered by a large transmitter package under the chin.

Sharp edges or points should be avoided or placed where there will be minimal stress caused by contact pressure. For example the inside end of a collar lap-joint should be placed as low as possible on the side, where its edge and rivet or bolt ends will not be pressed against skin by the weight of the collar. Pressure may be important, thereby favoring a wide collar to distribute weight over a larger area. However, for animals with short necks a wide collar may impede neck movement. If the neck is tapered markedly, a smaller diameter that stays near the head versus a larger diameter that permits sliding back and forth may present a difficult choice. Trial and error, and a knowledge of anatomical and behavioral function are necessary for development of optimal attachment methods and specific designs. Mech (1974) traced the development of collars and problems encountered in a long-term study of wolves.

Collars that are both reliable and allow for growth (expand) have not been reported convincingly in the literature, although many commercial suppliers make them. Collars that contract and expand present additional design problems (Hamilton 1962, Beale and Smith 1973, Garcelon 1977). The temporary use of 1.5-gram to 3.0-gram transmitter packages of the type used on small birds is an alternative for tagging newborn animals. These could, for example, be affixed to ear-tags. Their 15-day to 60-day longevity may be sufficient for tracking during the period of rapid growth and limited mobility and aid in recapturing an animal for attachment of a more permanent transmitter.

The major problem with transmitters having predicted longevities of several years has been reliability. Early attempts to improve reliability, by making the transmitters physically stronger at the expense of increased weight and bulk, were largely unsuccessful. However, moisture was a greater problem than breakage, and doubling or tripling the amount of encapsulation slowed but did not stop moisture invasion, which is destructive to electronic circuitry. To solve this problem, most commercial suppliers of transmitters seal the critical components hermetically in metal enclosures. The enclosures have leads that exit through hermetic ceramic-to-metal seals. All traces of moisture are removed from the transmitter with dry nitrogen prior to filling the enclosure and final sealing. Moisture leakage into such an enclosure is infinitesimal. The enclosure and batteries are then cast into a block of epoxy or plastic formed to fit the collar. The cast block also serves to anchor the antenna and physically protect interconnections.

Design margins become more restrictive for smaller transmitters. Predicted longevities for the simplest transmitters range from 20 to 70 days per gram of battery. The weight of the smallest of these transmitters is less than 1 gram, including a small amount of encapsulation, see Fig. 29.5, or about 6 grams if a hermetic enclosure is used. They are commonly used with batteries weighing 0.6 to 13 grams and are attached to animals in a wide variety of ways. When the additional weight of a hermetic enclosure cannot be tolerated, multiple coatings of beeswax and acrylic give protection from moisture for several months or more depending on the environment in which they are used. For a complete discussion of the moisture barrier and physical properties of various materials see Chapter 4 in Fryer (1970) and Mackay (1970).

Implantable and ingestible tracking transmitters may be useful in applications where external attachment is impractical, such as for snakes or fish, (Fig. 29.6). Ranges are less than for external mounting because of flesh losses and the necessity for using quite small transmitting antennas.

The number of attachment methods for birds (and variations in each of the methods) given in Table 29.1 is an indication of the uncertainties inherent in affixing a foreign object to an animal so greatly dependent for its survival upon the unimpeded use of its natural endowments. The diversity in physiognomy, size, and behavior among birds limits generalizations on the use and attachment of telemetry devices. Methods of attachment

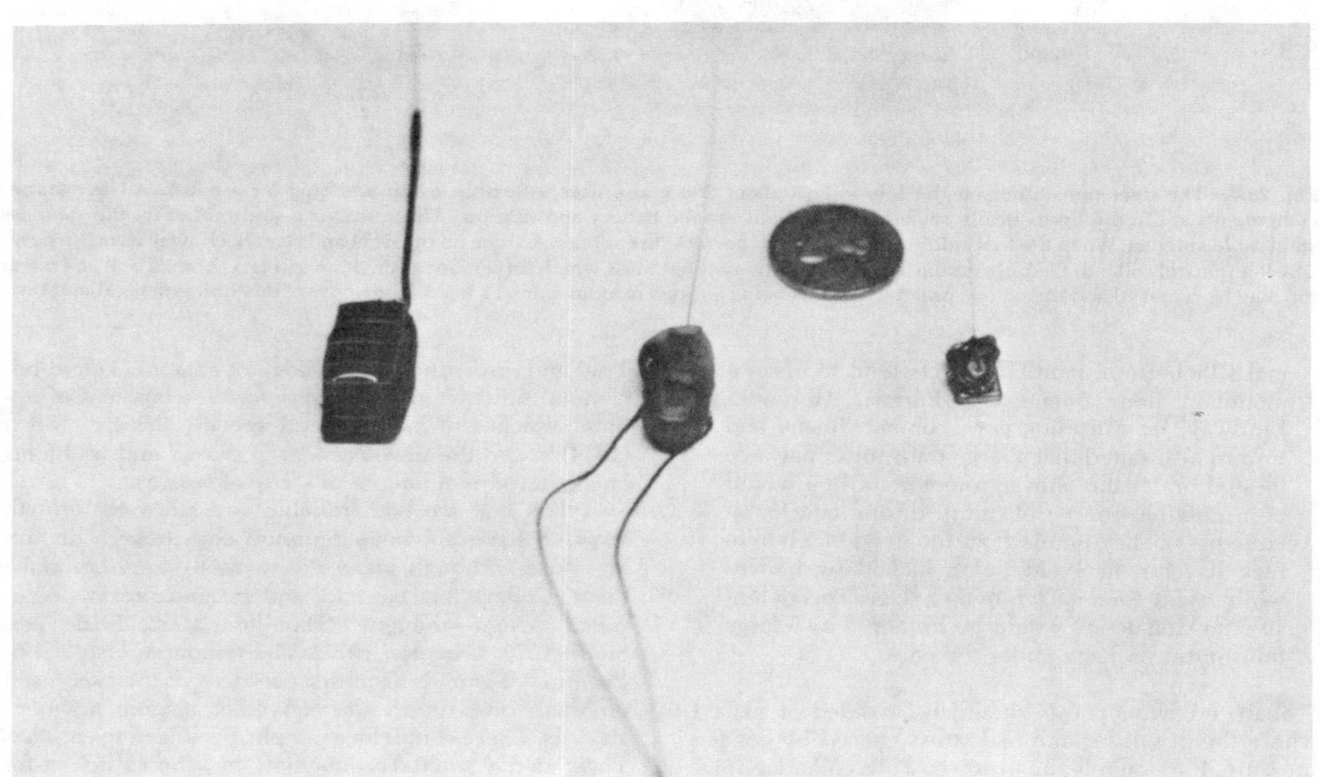

Fig. 29.5. These transmitters are typical of those used for birds. The 4-g unit at left is powered by photocells. Lateral holes in the package (not visible in photo) accommodate plastic tubing or wire for various harnessing schemes. The 1.8-g transmitter at center was designed by W. W. Cochran for attachment to the underside of an outer tail feather. The transmitter is held in place by the thread which is passed through a small hole made in the feather shaft by a hot needle. Rigidity is provided by filleting with 5-minute epoxy. The 30-cm antenna also is tied to the feather shaft at several points. Air-to-air range of this unit is 250 to 400 km depending on the height of the aircraft. The 1.1-g transmitter to the right is electrically identical to the center unit but has a smaller battery and a very thin coating of acrylic plastic to conserve weight. Ground-to-ground range of all 3 units is 2 to 3 km. The whip antennas of the 2 battery-powered units can be replaced with an integral loop antenna making them implantable with a range of about 100 m.

Fig. 29.6. This "padlock" transmitter was designed by W. W. Cochran in 1964 for use in fish and has been used extensively at the Illinois Natural Survey for fish tracking in freshwater. The unit is first coated with beeswax followed by a coating of acrylic plastic and a final coating of beeswax. Frequencies of 30 to 50 MHz. seem to give the best results although some success has been achieved in the 150 and 216 MHz bands in shallow water. Longevity of the 18-g unit is 1 year; units approximately half this size last about 8 months. In water with a conductivity of about 600 mho, range is about 1 km with the transmitter next to the surface and is approximately halved for every meter of depth. Doubling water conductivity reduces range by a factor of about 10 (R. W. Larrimore, pers. comm).

are dependent upon the body form of the animal under investigation. Techniques designed for big game are only generally applicable for use with birds.

The use of a particular kind of harness will not insure the reported performance for that harness because fitting may be the critical factor; such things are likely to remain an art. Many investigators use radio packages that are heavier and bulkier than the best that are commercially available; the reason for this failure to use the best equipment available is obscure. There may be species to which it is impossible to attach telemetry devices without serious side effects, even if package weight is a reasonably small percentage of the subject weight. Many species "seem" to tolerate packages that are 4% of their body weight and "appear" to behave "normally" not "too long" after such a package has been attached. However, there is nothing magic about 4%; distribution of weight and a variety of other factors may be more important. Anyone contemplating the use of telemetry with birds should read all literature available on the subject and then interact actively with the supplier of the transmitters. This interaction should fully explore and exploit the trade-offs in weight, life, range, antenna length, attachment options, and research needs. Similar considerations and difficulties may apply to many nonavian species as well.

EQUIPMENT

Transmitters and other equipment for most wildlife tracking applications are commercially available. The construction of transmitters by persons unfamiliar with transmitter fundamentals can be frustrating and usually is not cost-effective unless large numbers are involved or labor is free. One pitfall for the one-time builder is the variability in components listed in the various circuits available from the literature. This is especially true for crystals and somewhat less so for transistors. In some cases component variability can be accommodated by slight circuit modification. In others, discarding the component is the only solution. For those interested in construction, circuit information is given by Cochran and Lord (1963), Tester et al. (1964), Mackay (1970), Corner and Pearson (1972), Kolz et al. (1972), and Skutt et al. (1973).

POWERING TELEMETRY DEVICES

Four types of batteries are in common use for powering telemetry devices. Lithium and mercury types have nearly identical energy-to-volume ratios, but the energy-to-weight ratio of lithium cells is about twice that of mercury cells. Neither type is rechargeable. Photocells can be used to recharge nickel-cadmium batteries a number of times depending primarily upon how much discharge occurs between charges. This recharging capability is a function of several variables including the size of the battery, the charging capability of the photocells, and the light regime which controls the utilization of this charging capability. Without recharging, the life of nickel-cadmium cells will be about one-third that of mercury cells of the same weight. Silver-

Table 29.1. Avian studies reporting techniques for attachment and/or behavioral effects of telemetry transmitters.

Study	Species	Bird wgt. (g)	Trans-mitter wgt. (g)	Percent of bird body wgt.	Note**
Archibald (1975)	Ruffed grouse	*	21–25	*	h,d
Bartholomew (1967)	Bobwhite quail	165	10	*	h,d,t,b
Boag (1972)	Red grouse	*	25	3.5–4.5	h,b
Boag et al. (1973)	Red grouse	590–650	25	3.8–4.2	h,b
Brander (1968)	Ruffed grouse	*	20	*	h,t
Bray and Corner (1972)	Red-winged blackbird, Starling	93	4.1	4	f,t,b
Bray et al. (1975b)	Starling	95.5	3.2	3.4	f,d,b
Cochran et al. (1967)	Thrush *(Hylocichla)*	30–40	2.3–2.8	8	a,d,t
Cochran (1972)	Waterfowl, shorebird, hawk, pigeon, thrush	*	1.5–110	1–8	h,a,t,b
Cochran (1975)	Peregrine falcon	*	1.4–1.7	.3	h,f,d,t,b
Coon et al. (1976)	American woodcock	186–204	4.5–6.0	3	h,a,d,b
Dunstan (1972)	Raptor (17 species)	*	5–120	7	h,t,b
Dunstan (1973)	Screech, great horned owl, red-tailed hawk	*	3–24	4	f,t,b
Dwyer (1972)	Mallard, pintail, gadwall, blue-winged teal	*	17–26	*	h,t,b
Fitzner and Fitzner (1977)	Swainson's hawk	*	7–8	*	f,t
Gilmer et al. (1974)	Mallard, wood duck	*	23–27	2.0–4.1	h,b
Godfrey (1970)	American woodcock	130	5.5	4.2	h,t
Graber and Wunderle (1966)	Robin	30–100	4.7–6.9	4.7–15.0	h,a,d,t,b
Greenwood and Sargeant (1973)	Mallard, blue-winged teal	*	9–36	1.4–5.3	h,t,b
Hammerslough and Bjorklund (1968)	Heron	*	12–13	1–3	n1,d,t,b
Hanson and Progulske (1973)	Ring-necked pheasant	*	*	*	h,d,b
Herzog (1979)	Spruce grouse	*	13.5	2–5.5	h,t,b
Jackson et al. (1977)	Red-cockaded woodpecker	*	2.7	*	a,t,b
Langman (1973)	Zebra finch	*	1.7	*	a,t
Marshall and Kupa (1963)	Ruffed grouse	*	30	*	h,t,b
Martin and Bider (1978)	Red-winged blackbird	55–70	2.8	5	h,a,t,b
Michener and Walcott (1966)	Rock dove	*	30	*	h,d,b
Nesbitt et al. (1978)	Red-cockaded woodpecker	*	3.6	*	a,d,b
Nicholls and Warner (1968)	Barred owl	*	70	*	h,d,b
Owen and Morgan (1975)	American woodcock	*	5.8	*	h,d,b
Owen et al. (1969)	Blue-winged teal	*	10	*	n2,t
Raim (1978)	Brown-headed cowbird	*	1.8	3.5	a,t,b
Ramakka (1972)	American woodcock	*	4.2	3	h,t,b
Southern (1964)	Bald eagle	*	80	*	h,d,t,b
Southwick (1973)	White-crowned sparrow	25	.9	3.5	n3,d,t,b
Swanson et al. (1976)	Mallard	*	9	*	n4,t,b
Williams et al. (1974)	Herring gull	*	50	*	h,d,b

*These data were not provided in the paper.

**Attachment method: h = harness, a = adhesive, f = tail feather, n1 = leg/neck, n2 = safety pin, n3 = implant, n4 = bill/forehead.

Appreciable comment: d = biological data, t = attachment technique, b = transmitter affects.

oxide cells are available in the smaller sizes and have an energy-to-weight ratio identical to mercury cells but have a higher voltage (1.5) and slightly smaller ma-day (milliampere-day) rating. They find use in small transmitters when power output is at a greater premium than longevity, or where their very flat voltage versus discharge is desired. Table 29.2 contains data on some of the battery types used for powering telemetry devices. Predicted longevity for a typical wildlife transmitter current drain (0.1 ma.) is included for each entry in the table, but the given value may be tripled for the very lowest drain transmitters (circa .03 ma.) and divided by 3 for the higher power multistage transmitters. Most multistage transmitters require 2.5 to 3.0 volts which, for all types except lithium, require 2 cells connected in series. The series connection does not increase the ma-day rating of the pair.

Predicted longevity is always based on a calculation from the current drain of the transmitter and the battery current-time specification. The latter is most conveniently specified in ma-day for wildlife applications. The predicted life in days equals the ma-days rating of the

Table 29.2. Specifications for batteries commonly used in wildlife telemetry applications.

Battery Type	Common Manufacturer's Number	Approximate Weight g	Dimensions (mm) D × L	Ma-day Rating	Predicted Life at Drain of 0.1 ma
Mercury	212	0.33	4 × 5	0.75	7.5 days
Silver-oxide	212	0.37	4 × 5	0.75	7.5 days
Mercury	312	0.57	7.8 × 3.5	1.9	19 days
Silver-oxide	312	0.57	7.8 × 3.5	1.5	15 days
Silver-oxide	13	1.0	7.8 × 5.3	2.9	29 days
Mercury	575	1.45	11.5 × 3.5	4.6	46 days
Silver-oxide	41	1.7	11.6 × 4.2	5.0	50 days
Mercury	675	2.8	11.6 × 5.3	9.2	92 days
Silver-oxide	76	2.8	11.6 × 5.3	7.5	75 days
Mercury	630	4.8	15.6 × 6.0	14.6	146 days
Mercury	640R	8.0	15.9 × 11.2	20.8	208 days
Mercury*	1	12.2	15.9 × 16.4	41.6	1.1 year
Mercury	828	13.4	23.0 × 5.3	41.6	1.1 year
Mercury	601	22.0	16.0 × 26.4	75.0	2.1 year
Lithium	**	9–11	16 × 22	31.3	313 days
Lithium	**	12–14	16 × 33	52.0	1.4 year
Lithium	**	30–40	25 × 41	104.0	2.8 year
Lithium	**	40–50	25 × 50	146.0	4.0 year
Lithium	**	80–90	33 × 60	375.0	10.2 year
Nickel-cadmium	1/3A		16 × 17	7.0	70 days
Nickel-cadmium	1/2AA		15 × 33	11.5	115 days

*Available in medical grade

**Varying type numbers, sizes, weights, and ratings depending on manufacturer, and types of packaging used.

battery divided by the current drain of the transmitter. In practice the predicted longevity is usually overly optimistic. The overestimate increases with greater predicted longevity, especially for values in excess of about 6 months. Fortunately, battery manufacturers are gradually improving reliability. Modern high energy density batteries are complex electrical-mechanical-chemical devices which require time for perfection. Premature failures must be expected at the rate of 10 to 20%; medical grade batteries will reduce these failures to 1 or 2% but are available in only a few sizes. For more details on power sources consult Fryer (1970, Chapter 8), Mackay (1970:62–70), Patton et al. (1973), Williams and Burke (1973), and Harding et al. (1976).

RADIO-LOCATION AND FACTORS AFFECTING ACCURACY AND RANGE

Grid and multiple pick-up location systems have been mentioned above. For most telemetry studies, direction-finding is a fundamental part of the process of locating an animal. The location may be inferred from a single bearing. For example, the position of a fish in a stream may be taken as the area where a bearing intersects the stream. Similarly, a bearing to a nest, watering hole, den, etc. may be equally informative when previous experience with the animal's habits is supportive. I have inferred the location of a peregrine falcon from a single bearing toward an off-shore tanker when the steadiness of the signal indicated that the bird was perched. Conditions where a single bearing will suffice generally are uncommon.

Homing is a method where the observer moves toward the animal until a desired degree of proximity is achieved. Proximity may be determined by visual contact, more often for the purpose of behavioral observation than for location although the latter is concomitant. Homing approaches should be cautious if flushing is not desired or if the animal is dangerous. Proximity may be estimated from signal strength or from rapid changes in direction during a close pass. Hoskinson (1976) described an aerial tracking technique involving one or more close passes followed by tight circling to pinpoint the subject. Homing is often an intermediate tactic employed to bring an observer into a position favorable for triangulation. A comprehensive application of the several location strategies is discussed by Mineau and Madison (1977).

The intersection of bearings from two or more locations may be used to geometrically determine an animal's position relative to these locations. If the locations are known relative to a reference system, such as a map, then the animal's position is also known in that reference system. For a moving animal the bearings must be taken simultaneously. Where each bearing is represented as 2 lines, with the true bearing assumed to fall between, analysis is a matter of elementary trigonometry (Fig. 29.7). The addition of positional errors in the locations from which bearings are taken slightly complicates analysis. Map considerations as

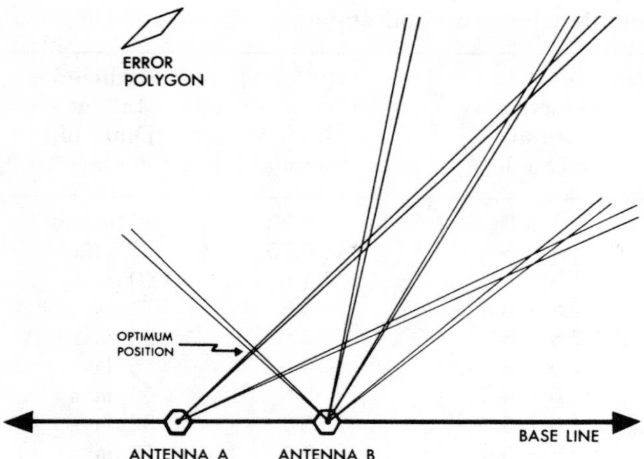

Fig. 29.7. Relative sizes and shapes of error polygons in relation to two tracking antennae. Any true location within an error polygon would be recorded at the center of that polygon (from Heezen and Tester 1967).

well as some of the geometric aspects of triangulation are covered in Chapter 17.

Potential location errors that result from nonsimultaneous bearings taken to a moving animal are calculable using trigonometry and estimates of maximum animal speed. In general, 3 bearings will provide more information when taken from 2 locations than when taken from 3. When animal movement can be assumed to some degree to be uniform in speed and direction it is possible, to a corresponding degree, to determine this movement from multiple nonsimultaneous bearings. Cochran (1972) described such methods used in tracking migrating birds.

The use of 2 or more observers can provide simultaneous bearing measurements but costs twice as much. It is good practice to evaluate all sources of error and their effects on project objectives before taking the additional expenses needed to circumvent them.

Wildlife biologists, with practice, can grasp the essential features of the directional properties of the various types of antennas. However, the actual reception patterns are often distorted in field situations for a variety of reasons. A knowledge of antenna and propagation theory is required to determine the causes and cures, if any, for unexpected results. A review of antenna and propagation theory is beyond the scope of this chapter. Jasik (1961) is an excellent engineering reference on antennas and propagation.

Rotating a receiving antenna in search of a null or minimum signal is somewhat easier than estimating the direction which yields a peak (maximum) signal. Null detection schemes, employed in many types of instrumentation, are useful because of the rapid relative changes in the observed quantity in the vicinity of the null. With a strong signal, the null position of a loop antenna (figure eight pattern) may be ascertained quickly with a resolution of 1 or 2 degrees. Performance deteriorates as the signal strength decreases until the no-signal condition occurs over a wide angle. In the case of low signal strength, a better estimate of bearing can be made from the maximum-signal position of the loop. When homing on a subject, the signal (and bearing accuracy) will improve as homing proceeds. At frequencies above about 100 MHz, loop antennas are small and easy to handle but will provide only about half the range obtainable with a 3-element yagi. At these higher frequencies, for fixed or vehicular use, the signal gain of the yagi can be combined with the accuracy inherent in null detection by using 2 yagis, spaced 1 or 2 wavelengths apart, pointing in the same direction, and connected to the receiver such that the signal from one cancels that from the other. The null condition (cancellation) will exist along the axis of symmetry of the 2 antennas; a slight rotation in either direction from the null will result in a large increase in signal. Resolution is of the order of 1 degree for strong signals. Increased spacing between antennas sharpens the null but also creates off-axis nulls. For spacings greater than about twice the length of the yagis used, the off-axis nulls are difficult to differentiate from the central null. Cochran et al. (1965) described this type of system mounted on large permanent towers and reported an accuracy of plus or minus 0.5 degree. Banks et al. (1975) described a similar system that was semiportable; an excellent illustration of the antenna array was also shown. Null systems are inherently sensitive to errors caused by loss of symmetry due to the presence of nearby objects (such as trees) or due to physical damage (such as bent or corroded antennas). Commercially available versions of double-yagi antennas usually include a phasing switch that allows the operator to select either a null or a peak mode.

Where consistent accuracy of 1 degree or better is needed, extraordinary attention must be given to calibration and to achieving physical and electrical stability and symmetry. Thus, fractional-degree systems are subject to exponentially increasing costs, and to be useful they may require map accuracy better than that commonly available. In addition, hilly terrain or nonhomogeneous vegetation patterns may introduce wavefront distortion (by signal refraction and scattering) which makes the direction of arrival different from the inverse of the true direction to the signal source by an amount greater than system resolution.

Two yagis are usually used for tracking from aircraft, one pointed to the left and the other to the right. The operator alternately switches from one to the other as the aircraft is turned. When equal signals are heard the aircraft is pointed at the animal. The homing accuracy is limited only by the skill of the operator and pilot and the care taken to mount the antennas symmetrically with respect to the aircraft.

The directional properties and gain of receiving antennas used for wildlife tracking are valid only when the antennas are oriented so that their polarization is the same as that of the received energy, which can be (with respect to the Earth) horizontal, vertical, or diagonal depending on the orientation of the transmitter antenna and propagation factors. Polarization can change from moment to moment due to propagation changes caused by animal or observer movement, or it can change as the animal turns, lies down, perches etc. Signal variation due to these changes can be very confusing to an operator trying to take a bearing. An effort should be made to design the transmitter mounting to provide the desired polarization of its antenna. As indicated above, animal posture will affect polarization. Therefore, a mounting which optimizes polarization for the most frequent posture is usually best. Of course, the type of mounting may dictate the polarization. When a choice is possible, the following should be considered. For radio line-of-sight propagation there is no preferred polarization. Vertical polarization gives greater range across water or over conductive soil. Horizontal polarization penetrates dense forest better than vertical polarization (Anderson and De Moor 1971). When variations in polarization are regularly expected, a circularly polarized yagi can be used, or a vertical and horizontal yagi can be mounted on the same mast and selected by a switch as needed. Loop antennas have no directivity for horizontal polarization (the plane of the loop parallel to the Earth) and must be used with vertically polarized transmitters. The following authors describe mountings or calibration techniques for vehicular mounted directional antennas: Hallberg et al. (1974), Bray et al. (1975a), Kolz and Johnson (1975), Hutton et al. (1976), and Whitehouse and Steven (1977). Theory and construction details for variety of antennas, including loops, yagis, and omnidirectional types, are given in Jasik (1961), Mackay (1970), Tilton (1972), and the ARRL Antenna Book (1974).

A common misconception involves the term "line-of-sight." The term refers to vision. Curiously, radio signals may pass readily along a path which blocks or absorbs light, but they may be rapidly attenuated along another path over which light passes freely. Radio line-of-sight refers to a propagation condition where energy falls off inversely as the square of the distance, or approximately so. This condition is not met when the signal grazes the earth's surface. For this type signal path, transmitter power must be increased by a factor of 100 to quadruple range (Kolz pers. comm.). Radio line-of-sight is approximated for signal paths making an angle of about 20 degrees or more with the earth's surface, and range will quadruple when transmitter power is increased by a factor of only 16. For receiving or transmitting antennas operated more than about 2 wavelengths above the surrounding terrain, propagation will change from radio line-of-sight to earth-grazing as the distance increases, and doubling antenna height will result in about a 50% increase in range. Considerable variation from the above can be expected because of differences in soil conductivity, vegetation, and polarization. For example, through dense forest, quadrupling range may require a power increase by a factor of 1000. For distances beyond the general visual horizon (as viewed from the antenna) attenuation is orders of magnitude greater than that for earth-grazing propagation, thus defining an upper limit for practical wildlife telemetry operation. Situations where an increase in power will result in a more proportionate increase in range occur when signals leaving the transmitter undergo high initial attenuation before reaching a more favorable path. For example, a transmitter in dense woods may have only enough power to produce detectable signals above the immediate vicinity of the canopy less than 100 meters away. By quadrupling power, enough signal could be left over, after penetration of the canopy, to reach altitudes of 500 to 1000 meters via comparatively low attenuation radio line-of-sight propagation. Similar considerations exist for transmission from underwater or underground.

The gain of the receiving antenna affects range in the same way as transmitter power. The power gain of antennas is conventionally referenced to a dipole whose gain is considered to be unity. The vertical "whips" employed on vehicles have a gain of about 1. The 3-element yagi has a gain between 8 and 10 and an 11-element yagi a gain between 20 and 25. A carefully tuned resonant loop antenna has a gain between 1/2 and 3/4. Antenna gains are conventionally measured as decibels where gain (in decibels) is equal to 10 times the base-ten logarithm of the power ratio. For example, the factor of 20 mentioned above is plus 13 decibels, usually abbreviated dB. Decibels will hereafter be used in this chapter because the user of telemetry equipment will continually be confronted with them in the process of purchasing equipment and interpreting papers.

Another factor affecting range is noise generated in the receiver or picked up by the receiving antenna. The use of a narrow bandwidth to reduce this noise has been covered in preceding sections. Receiver noise figures usually are quoted in dB, smaller numbers being better. Commercial receivers for wildlife tracking have noise figures of circa 2.5 to 3.5 dB. This 1 dB variation has an insignificant effect on range. In contrast, the portable VHF "police band" receivers sold in department stores will have noise figures ranging from 10 to 20 dB. This is a reason, among several others, that they are not suitable for wildlife tracking. Noise gathered by the receiving antenna is a problem in urban areas. When tracking from aircraft, the combined noise from the thousands of motors, powerlines, etc. in a large city up to 100 km away, can degrade reception by a factor of 10 to 20 dB. Ignition noise from the tracking vehicle or aircraft can degrade performance by 15 dB unless the ignition system is extremely well shielded. Most aircraft have shielded systems but these vary in their effectiveness. This type (impulse) noise is the only type that can be eliminated in the receiver. This requires a noise blanker, an important consideration when purchasing a receiver that will be used in a moving vehicle.

Another factor affecting range is the transmitter pulse-width. Tracking transmitters are usually pulsed (turned on) for a fraction of a second every second or so. If the period between pulses is much longer than 1 second it becomes difficult to take bearings. If the pulse is shorter than about 20 milliseconds, range is reduced. This is because the 50 Hz effective bandwidth of the human hearing process, mentioned earlier, is applicable only to pulses 20 milliseconds or longer. Thus the human ear places an upper limit to battery conservation at a factor of about 50. Pulses as short as 10 milliseconds can be used, but there is no net battery saving because the transmitter power during the on-time must be proportionally increased to compensate for the increase in effective bandwidth. Pulses shorter than 10 milliseconds should never be used because a disproportionate increase in power is required for the same range capability.

Although variations in circuitry and component quality have an effect on the power generating capability of a transmitter, these factors are minor compared to the losses introduced by the necessarily inefficient radiation from animal-mounted antennas. For example, a collar transmitter with an antenna running along the collar will suffer as much as a 20 dB loss in radiated power when placed on the neck of an animal, a power factor of 100! This is a reason not to pay too much attention to the impressive "fence post" tests engineers are so fond of conducting. There are no "magic" designs, fancy names not withstanding, which will alter this fact although poor antenna design can make matters worse. A transmitter with even a small portion of the antenna away from flesh will make a considerable improvement.

Another factor affecting the power radiated from a transmitter is ground loss (Pienkowski 1965). If the animal is within about a half-wavelength from earth (1 meter at 150 MHz), energy loss is noticeable and is greater at lesser heights above earth, another advantage for the fence post and larger animals.

The numerous factors affecting an optimal choice of frequency for a particular application preclude precise treatment. In general, increasing or decreasing frequency by 50% from an existing system will not result in significant changes in performance. However, frequencies available to wildlife research range from 30 MHz to over 450 MHz. One factor which often is interpreted incorrectly as favoring the higher frequencies is receiver antenna gain. The capture area of a receiving antenna is the factor affecting range, all else being equal. The equation for capture area contains an inverse square wavelength factor which exactly cancels antenna gain. For example, a dipole at 50 MHz will gather as much energy as a 3-element yagi at 150 MHz. However, a range advantage does exist for the higher frequencies due to the increased radiation efficiency of the necessarily short, animal-mounted transmitting antennas. For example, a quarter-wave dipole at 450 MHz (length 0.16 meter) will radiate 10 to 20 times as efficiently at 450 MHz as it will at 50 MHz. Slightly offsetting the latter is a decrease in power-generating efficiency in transmitter circuits at the higher frequencies. The directivity of a given physical size receiving antenna is roughly proportional to frequency, but improved directivity is partially offset by the increased problems with reflection and refraction (bending the direction of travel of a signal). The latter can be so severe in dense vegetation that frequencies in the 30-MHz to 50-MHz range are decidedly preferable, although good results can be obtained under the canopy in a rain forest at 150 MHz and 450 MHz (Montgomery et al. 1973). For tracking flying birds, frequencies above 200 MHz are decidedly preferable. For animals which must be tracked while submerged in freshwater, 30 MHz is probably best, but good results are being obtained by some workers at 150 MHz. When vegetation is intermittent, sparce, low, or nonexistent, frequencies in the range 148 MHz to 220 MHz represent a good compromise among those legally available for wildlife tracking. From the standpoints of ease in handling and directivity of receiving antennas, radiating efficiency of animal-compatible transmitting antennas, efficiency in transmitter circuitry, relative freedom from interference by other services, and the number of channels available, the 216-MHz to 220-MHz band is probably the best overall choice for most applications. Some additional information on frequency selection may be found in Mackay (1970:252–258).

Federal Communications Commission authorization is required for all wildlife telemetry operation in the United States. Volume II, Part 5, Subpart C, Article 5.108 of the FCC Rules and Regulations defines 2 frequency bands and the technical standards for wildlife tracking. This publication may be ordered from the Superintendent of Documents, U.S. Government Printing Office, Washington, D.C. 20402.

Wildlife telemetry for nonfederal government researchers is permitted in the frequency bands of 40.66 to 40.70 and 216 to 220 MHz. Other frequencies may be authorized under experimental service assignments. Federal government researchers must apply for authorization through the National Telecommunications and Information Administration (NTIA). For example, the U.S. Fish and Wildlife Service is licensed to operate at 30 and 164 MHz by NTIA. There are no frequencies specifically designated only for wildlife telemetry, hence the spectrum is shared and some rf interference is to be expected. FCC forms 403 and 440 may be obtained to apply for licensing. Commercial telemetry equipment suppliers can provide the technical information required for these forms.

Chapter Thirty

Radioisotopes and Their Use in Wildlife Research

TONY J. PETERLE
Professor, The Ohio State University
Columbus, Ohio

Techniques of wildlife research must become more sophisticated and precise to assure their beneficial application to broadening questions of resource management. The use of radioisotopes can meet some of these research and management needs. Tracer methodology and radiation assay procedures can be very simple or extremely complex.

The growing application of radioisotopes (or nuclides) to a wide spectrum of physical and biological research suggests that unique areas of wildlife research might also benefit through the intelligent application of radiological methods. In some cases, the use of nuclides might be the only method for obtaining some types of physiological information on animal metabolism. A careful appraisal of the benefits should precede any incorporation of these techniques since, in many instances, standard chemical methodology may be simpler, cheaper, and in some instances less hazardous.

Special training is required for principal investigators and is desirable for laboratory personnel prior to the use of isotope or tracer techniques in a research program. Courses are available at many colleges and universities; at the Oak Ridge Institute of Nuclear Studies, Oak Ridge, Tennessee; and at Argonne National Laboratories, the University of Chicago, Chicago, Illinois. Many foreign nations have also developed Nuclear Institutes where training in the biological aspects of tracer methodology and radiology is readily available at low cost.

Many agencies and organizations have Radiation Health and Safety Offices, and formal training and experience are prerequisites to the use of isotopes in research. The health and safety of the research staff, the general public, as well as that of the animals involved are predicated on prescribed procedures and practices regulated by the U.S. Nuclear Regulatory Commission. Laboratory use, release of isotopes in natural systems, and ultimately the disposal of wastes are carefully monitored to insure adherence to safety procedures. Written, detailed procedures are required by Radiation Health and Safety Officers prior to the issuance of a license for use. *The Radiological Health Handbook* (USHEW 1970) is a useful and necessary guide in the preparation of research procedures. Significant general books on the subject include: Atomic Energy of Canada Ltd. (1960), Overman and Clark (1960), Sheppard (1962), USAEC (1962, 1964), Eisenbud (1963), Overman (1963), Shilling (1964), Wolf (1964), Thornburn (1972), Hendee (1973), Wang et al. (1975). A major source of information concerning the use of isotopes in ecological studies has been made available as transactions or proceedings of the 4 National Radioecology Symposia that have been held since 1961. These symposia, sponsored primarily by the U.S. Atomic Energy Commission, now the Department of Energy, contain numerous examples of field use, effects of radiation on species and ecosystems, studies of fallout and power plant effluent as well as laboratory investigations. They have been made available as government publications through the various outlets. These have been edited by Schultz and Klement (1963), Nelson and Evans (1969, 1971) and Cushing (1976), and are probably the best sources of reference for wildlife biologists interested in reviewing the potential for use of isotopes in research.

RADIONUCLIDES AND TYPES OF RADIATION

There are about 105 chemical elements occurring, either naturally or artifically, as approximately 1,200 isotopes. Isotopes are collections of nuclei with the same number of protons (hence belonging to the same chemical element) but with different atomic weights, indicating a different number of total particles in the nucleus. Examples are ^{12}C, ^{13}C, and ^{14}C which are all isotopes of the element carbon with the same atomic number 6, but differing atomic weights indicating 6, 7, and 8 neutrons, respectively. The first 2 are stable, but ^{14}C is an unstable, or radioactive, isotope with a half-life of 5730 years. Radioactive isotopes are called nuclides assuming they are capable of more than transient existence. Half-life is a term denoting the time required for one half the nuclei in a collection of radioactive atoms of a particular isotope to decay to another element that might be radioactive or to a stable state. Thus, to start with 1,000,000 ^{14}C nuclei today, there will only be 500,000 in 5730 years. As isotopes decay to their daughter elements, characteristic types of radiation are emitted as a result of the energy loss. Ultimately they decay to stable daughter elements. Most environments have characteristic levels of background radiation which results from man-made isotopes (bomb fall-out), power plant effluent, and natural radioactive elements such as ^{40}K.

Alpha Radiation

There are about 100 isotopes which emit charged alpha particles while they are decaying to more stable daughter isotopes with 4 less mass units and 2 units lower in atomic number. Polonium-210 having a half-life of about 138 days decays to lead-206, a decrease of 4 mass units and 2 less protons. A = Atomic mass. Z = Atomic number.

$$(A)\ {}^{210}_{84}Po \xrightarrow{138.4\ \text{days}} {}^{206}_{82}Pb + \text{alpha particle emission}\ (Z)$$

The emitted alpha particle is much heavier than the particles from beta emissions, has an electrical charge of +2, an energy of 4 to 10 Mev (million electron volts), a range in air of only up to about 9 cm, and a very limited range (microns) in tissues. Usually alpha emitters have only a single range and energy. High specific ionization over a short distance makes alpha radiation very hazardous. Tissue damage might be 20 times greater than for either beta or gamma radiation. Although alpha particles will not penetrate the skin, they are dangerous when inhaled or ingested. The alpha emitters (uranium, plutonium, and thorium) are becoming more common as nuclear energy programs progress. It is unfortunate that the unique characteristics of alpha particle radiation, of great potential for select research projects, have been of only limited use in biological research to the present. This is due, in part, to the difficulty of measurement and possible tissue damage.

Beta Radiation

Beta particles are lighter and emerge from the nucleus with much higher velocities (some close to the speed of light) than alpha particles. They are physically similar to orbital electrons. Some isotopes decay to more stable isotopes through the emission of a beta particle which increases the atomic number by 1, but the mass number remains the same. One of the frequently used beta emitters, ^{14}C, decays to ^{14}N through the change of 1 neutron to a proton and a beta particle with the subsequent emission of the beta particle.

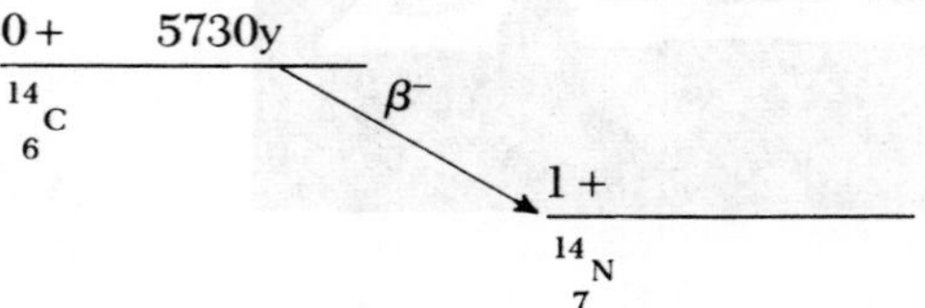

The mass number remains at 14, but the atomic number increases from 6 for carbon to 7 for nitrogen. There are also some beta emitters that release a positron (β^+) which, when captured by an electron, produces through annihilation radiation sufficient gamma energy for measurement. Zinc-65 is an example of a positron emitter.

A wide range of maximum energies (E_{max}) are available to the researcher since each element has a characteristic energy or spectrum of energies. Beta particles can emerge from any given nucleus with a range of energies from nearly zero up to the maximum energy which is characteristic of the isotope under consideration. Some characteristic E_{max} values from common beta emitters potentially useful in wildlife research are: ^{32}P, 1.7 Mev.; ^{14}C, 0.155 Mev.; ^{45}Ca, 0.25 Mev.; ^{35}S, 0.167 Mev.; and ^{36}Cl, 0.714 Mev. Other potentially useful beta emitters include ^{33}P, ^{99}Tc, ^{147}Pm, and ^{90}Sr. All have unique physiological and ecosystem kinetics and must be selected for specific objectives. All have varied half-lives ranging from hours to thousands of years. As beta particles pass through matter they lose energy by the formation of radiation and ion pairs (ionization and excitation). It is this energy loss which is so important, since the ability to use isotopes is directly related to their energy and its measurement. Typically, beta particles can penetrate about 100 times farther than alpha particles with the same energy and are capable of passing through about 1 cm of tissue depending on their energy. As with alpha particles, inhalation and ingestion are considered the greatest safety hazard. Some beta emitters (e.g., ^{32}P) are important in many phases of biological research and are commonly used in clinical medicine studies of humans. This use is now being replaced by ^{99m}Tc. Beta emitters are of limited use for field application and detection. Their low energy makes measurement problems complex. Field beta detectors (see Fig. 30.1) are delicate and the results variable. Applications

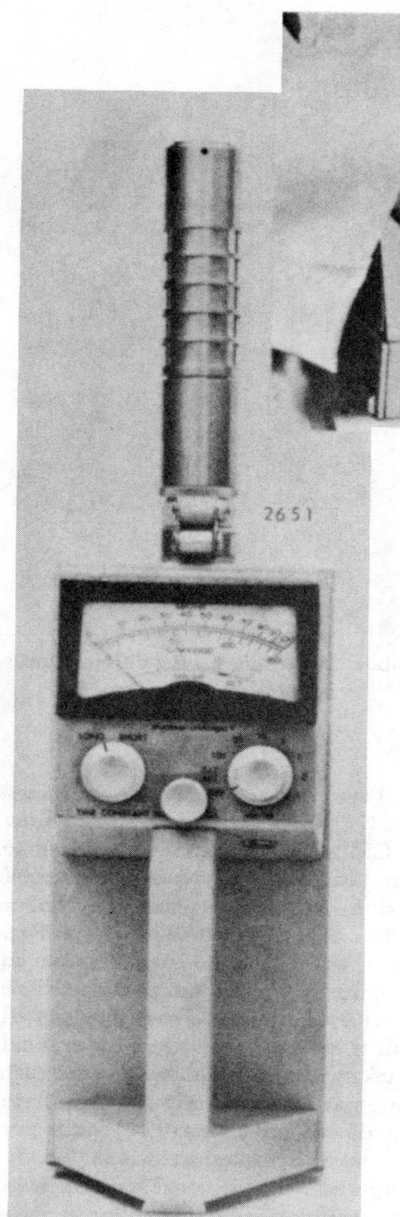

Fig. 30.1. **The portable Geiger-Mueller survey meter is useful for measuring hard beta and gamma radiation. Probes are available for alpha, soft beta, and gamma measurements. Radiation is detected from the dial or from earphones.**

combined with laboratory analyses, however, have great research potential.

Gamma Radiation

Gamma radiations are emitted by the nucleus and are of short wavelength. They are similar to x rays, radio waves, and visible light. They are part of the electromagnetic spectrum and are of high energy ranging from 0.01 to 10.0 Mev. Gamma ray emission is usually accompanied by alpha or also beta radiation. While photons (quantity of radiation) are emitted from the nucleus, the radioactive element decays to a less energetic form of the same nuclide. Alpha or beta energies are emitted from a parent nucleus to form the excited state; then the emission of gamma rays reduces the excess energy, and the nuclide decays to the ground state of the daughter nucleus. Gamma ray energies are dissipated in 3 major ways as they pass through matter. These are: the Photoelectric Effect, in which the gamma ray gives up all of its energy to an orbital electron; the Compton Effect, in which the ray collides with an electron and gives up part of its energy; and Pair Production, in which positron-electron pairs are formed as the gamma ray is annihilated near the nucleus of the absorbing atom. X rays are comparable to gamma rays but originate from electron orbits, not the nucleus. Gamma rays have high penetrating power, produce secondary ionization, and are consequently very dangerous to animal tissue. Some common emitters and their energies are ^{137}Cs, 0.662 Mev.; ^{65}Zn, 1.12 Mev.; ^{60}Co, 1.17 and 1.33 Mev.; and ^{24}Na, 1.37 and 2.7 Mev. Other useful gamma emitters include ^{54}Mn, ^{51}Cr, ^{22}Na, ^{99m}Tc, ^{125}I, ^{131}I, ^{198}Au, ^{182}Ta, and ^{203}Hg. Half-lives of these isotopes listed range from 6 hours to slightly over 30 years. Gamma emitters should be used only under carefully controlled conditions. They have widespread and important use in biological research. The most commonly used isotope in nuclear medicine is ^{99m}Tc.

MEANS OF MEASUREMENT

Because of the unique amounts of energy and mode of decay of isotopes, each requires electronic assay equipment especially designed for highest efficiency. A probe or survey meter designed to measure gamma radiation (Fig. 30.2) would not be very useful for assessing the levels of alpha particles with limited penetrating power. Conversely, gamma rays would pass undetected through some survey equipment with very low counting efficiency. As with the automobile, an assay instrument is outdated when it leaves the manufacturer. Sophisticated scintillation detectors or pulse-height analysers with built-in computers cost thousands of dollars. These may not be needed, for as with the automobile, progress can be made with the Model-T as well as the Cadillac, only it takes a little longer.

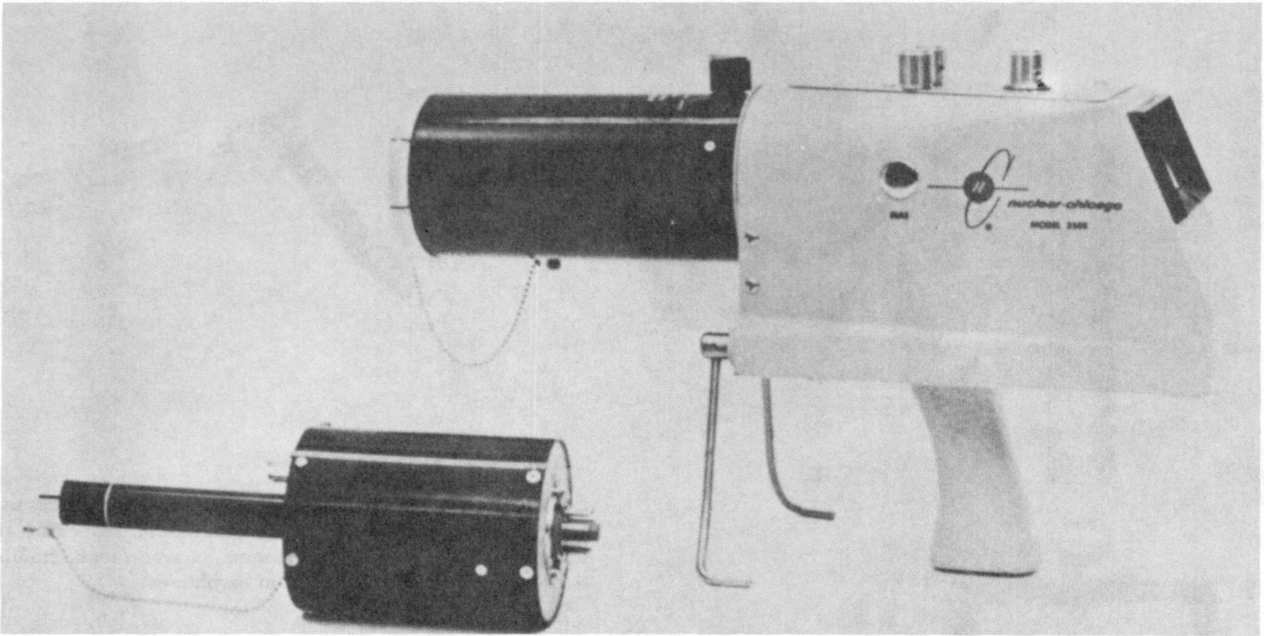

Fig. 30.2. **The "cutie-pie" portable battery-operated survey meter can be fitted with chambers (lower left) having different measurement capabilities.**

Portable Survey Meters

Portable survey meters (Figs. 30.1 and 30.2) and some laboratory survey equipment (Fig. 30.3) are designed to collect the ions produced along the path of radiation particles or rays as they interact with matter. Frequently, these meters are designed for better geometric efficiency as a cylindrical probe. These probes have a central wire as one electrode and the outside case as the other. As ionizing radiation passes through the tube charged ions are formed. These ions are collected and as a quantity of electricity are measured and displayed either on a meter or with some type of digital scaler. Frequently, the efficiency of the collection of ions is enhanced by filling the tube with mixtures of gases, e.g., commercial Q gas, usually a mixture of helium and butane. The windows of the probes for survey meters are variable. Some probes have very thin windows to admit alpha particles or less energetic beta particles, while others designed for gamma ray assay do not have windows. Some meters are made with interchangeable probes, where the suitable probe is attached for measuring specific kinds of radiation. Some gamma survey meters are equipped with scintillation crystals as part of the probe. In biological research, beta emitters are most commonly used, so a probe with a thin window is desired. Usually, detecting equipment must be within 0.6 or 0.9 m of the animal to determine any radioactivity.

Laboratory Systems

Two main types of laboratory assay systems are the gas-flow or Geiger-Mueller counting devices, similar in operation to the portable meters, and the scintillation systems, (Fig. 30.4) where fluors or phosphors (a phosphorescing substance) are used to permit the measurement of the radiation by photoelectric tubes. Gas-flow systems are usually GM tubes housed in shielding to reduce background radiation and to which an external gas supply is attached. Results are recorded on a scaler read directly or attached to a printout device (See Fig. 30.5). Various levels of sophistication are available in these systems. Automatic sample changing devices are available (Fig. 30.6) which can handle over 100 plated samples. The operator is able to preset the time or total count of the assay. Background subtractions and the data can be printed on tape providing sample number, time of count, total counts, counts per minute, or counts per minute minus background. Some systems can be directly coupled to computers for analyses. Thin windows can be purchased for separating the gas from the sample itself. Windowless counters are available where the sample is inserted in the gas chamber, as are gas assay systems where the radioactive gas is directly mixed with the Q gas for assay. Each particular type of system has advantages for specific types of radioactive assay. The selection of a versatile system, suitable and efficient for a wide range of measurements, is difficult and should be given careful consideration.

Scintillation detectors or assay systems detect ionization by measuring the scintillation produced in a phosphor or fluor. These scintillators may be crystalline (such as sodium iodide), liquid, plastic, or gaseous. The substance to be assayed is placed within or near a scintillator placed in intimate contact with a photomultiplier tube. The resultant light measured by the tube is proportional to the energy of the radiation causing the scintillation. Some systems are housed in freezer cabinets to improve the efficiency of the photoelectric tubes, but others are operated at ambient temperatures.

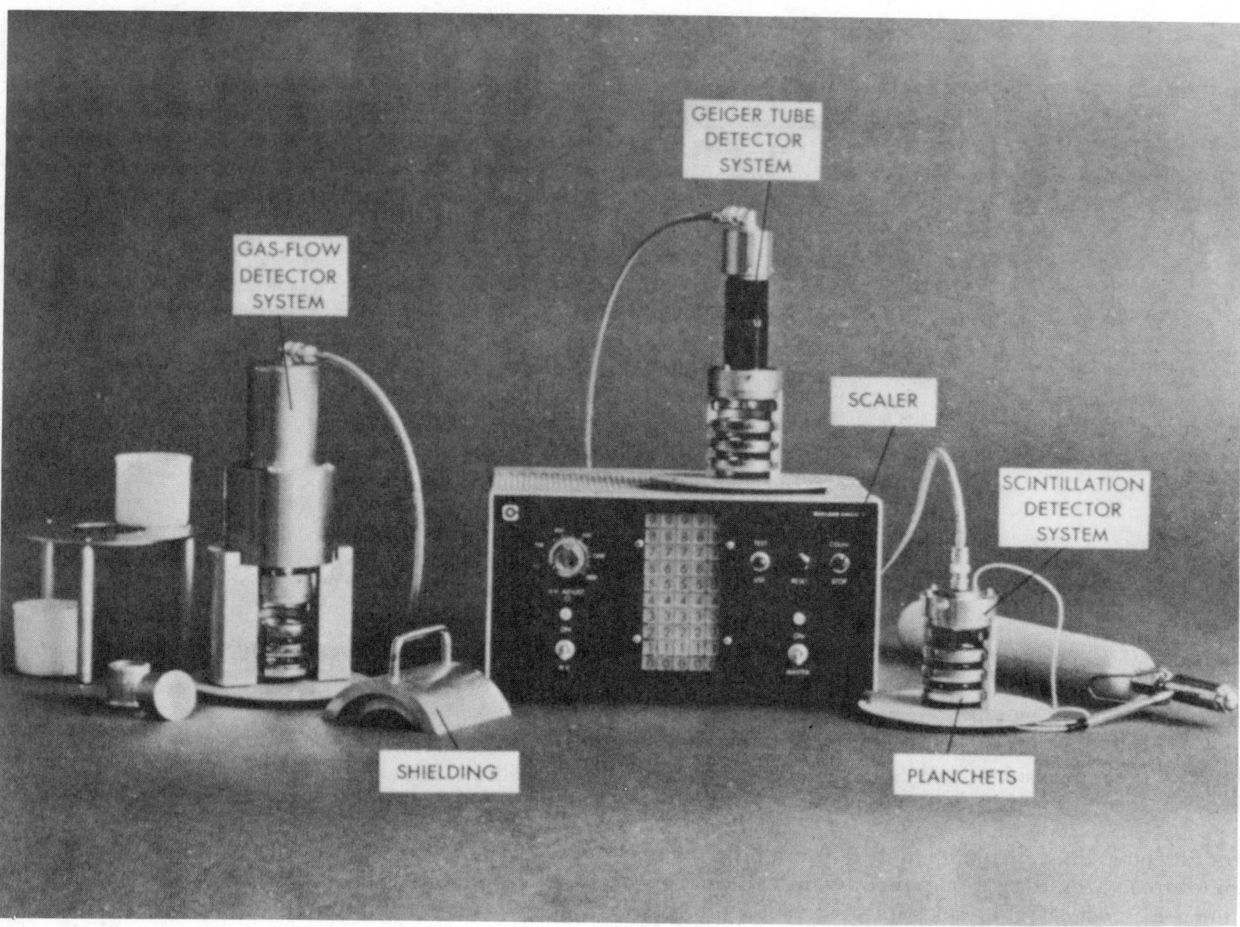

Fig. 30.3. The Nuclear-Chicago, Inc. alpha, beta, and gamma educational laboratory system includes Geiger, gas-flow, and scintillation measurement systems.

Shielding and anticoincidence circuitry reduce the background level from cosmic and other types of radiation. Liquid scintillation systems are most efficient for low energy beta emitters such as carbon and tritium. The sample is mixed directly into a liquid phosphor or fluor and the vial inserted between 2 photomultiplier tubes to improve efficiency. Assay problems occur because many biological materials including water act as quenching agents to the phosphor, but newer counting systems (Fig. 30.4) have an external standard which automatically provides a correction ratio for each sample. The external source of radiation is moved to the vicinity of the sample vial at the termination of the preset counting period, and a standard 1-minute count rate is printed on the tape, allowing corrections for quenching. Liquid phosphors or "scintillation cocktails" can be mixed according to the dictates of the isotope characteristics. Suspendors or emulsifiers can be added to keep particulate matter from settling in the vials, and samples of various consistencies can be assayed. Strips of paper cut from chromatograms can be successfully assayed for radioactive content when immersed in the scintillation liquid. Normal precautions for preparation efficiencies, standards, peak electronic responses and effects of quenching must be taken in determining the most expedient and satisfactory method for sample preparation.

Solid crystals, primarily thallium-activated sodium iodide, are directly coupled to photomultiplier tubes to provide a high efficiency for transferring the photons of light produced by the radioactivity from the crystal to the tube. Housings for the crystals are coated with reflectors to enhance the collection of light. Sodium iodide crystals are primarily used to assay gamma radiation, since each element provides characteristic radiation pulse heights. Pulse-height analysers are available which assign the various voltage pulses to a series of channels or addresses ranging from 100 to several thousand. As the equipment scans the preset energy range, the counts per minute, reflecting the radioactivity of the sample, are reproduced visually on an oscilloscope, graphically on a chart, or numerically in printed tabular form. Other equipment is available to record this information directly on magnetic or punched tape or on machine data cards for subsequent analysis.

Recently, solid state semiconductor detectors providing higher resolution between gamma rays of nearly equal energy have become available. These are called GeLi detectors because of their make-up. Semiconduc-

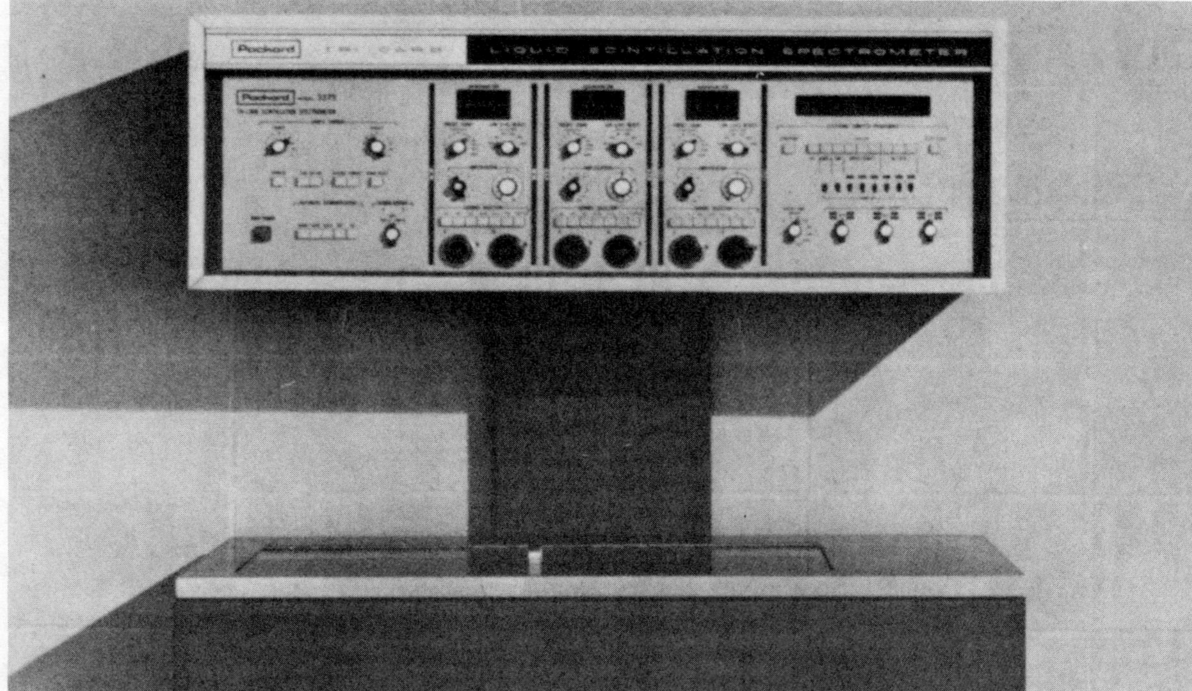

Fig. 30.4. The Packard Tri-Carb liquid scintillation spectrometer automatically or manually handles up to 200 samples in a continuous belt. Counting is by 2 photomultiplier tubes.

tor detectors must be maintained at liquid nitrogen temperatures, providing some inconvenience and additional expense. Higher costs must be balanced against greater resolution and lower efficiencies. Technological developments in this area of radiation detection are being made very rapidly and most equipment is soon outdated, but by no means no longer useful. Resolution for crystal detectors is about 5–10%, while for solid state semiconductors, the range is 0.5 to 3%. Current costs of semiconductors are about 5 to 10 times higher than crystal scintillators.

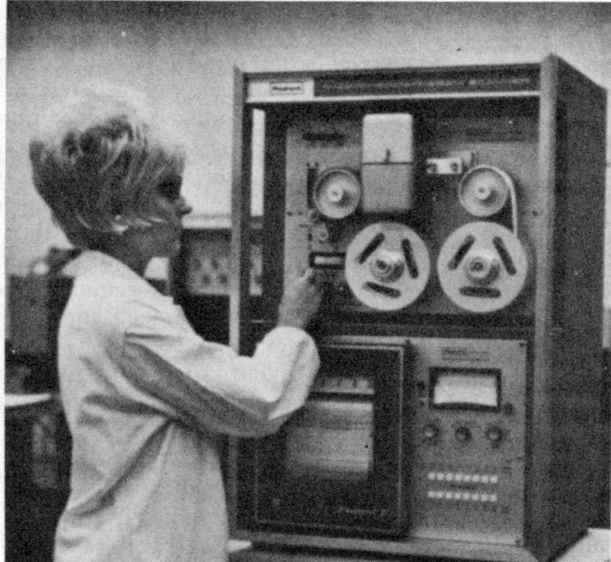

Fig. 30.5. The Packard Instrument Co. radiochromatogram scanner measures and records the beta-emitting nuclides deposited on thin-layer plates or paper strip chromatograms. The scanner employs 2 Geiger detectors for 4-pi scanning of both sides of the paper strip.

COSTS

Equipment

There is such a wide variety of equipment available and prices are so temporal that any estimates of cost would be out of date immediately. But if radiological methods are to become an integral part of an established laboratory, modern automatic equipment is not only desirable but necessary. Minimum basic assay equipment could be purchased for under $2,000. Automated sample changers, printouts and built-in calculators could increase the cost to $8–12,000 for gas-flow systems. Automated liquid scintillation systems (Fig. 30.4) are available for $8–20,000. Multichannel analysers and other computational and printout equipment with new semiconductor detectors would cost $25,000 and higher. The scope of the research, the estimated results, the predicted life of the laboratory, and the available and predicted financial support are all important considerations in the selection of assay equipment. If a single limited application of isotopes is anticipated, the expenditure of large sums of money for highly automated equipment cannot be justified. Obtaining rental equipment or contractual services at universities or national laboratories may be feasible.

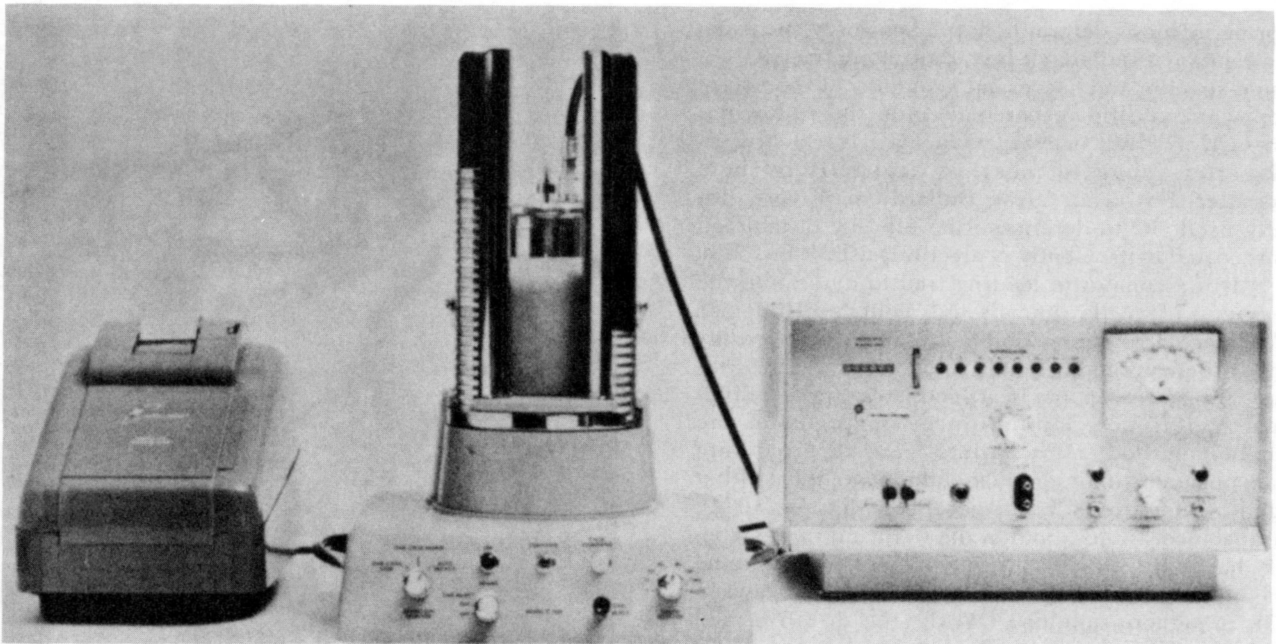

Fig. 30.6. **Automatic sample changer (center) with gas-flow, thin-window, or scintillation detector heads automatically count the activity of 35 solid beta samples for a preset number of counts and have the number of the sample and the time required to reach the counts printed on the timer (left). A binary scaler is at the right.**

Labeled Compounds and Isotopes

There are a number of reputable commercial firms and national laboratories both in the U.S. and abroad which supply a wide variety of isotopes in various forms and can supply a remarkable number of labeled compounds. One commercial firm recently listed over 1,200 labeled compounds (radiochemicals) incorporating the use of 170 isotopes. Many firms will specially synthesize labeled compounds requested by researchers at added cost. Since prices vary widely it is desirable to get several estimates for the purity and specific activity required.

EXAMPLES OF USE

Extensive bibliographies have been prepared on the uses of radioisotopes. Several of importance are: Dahm (1957) on use in pesticide research; Hooper et al. (1961) on use in hydrobiology and fish culture; Jenkins (1957) on use, generally, in entomology; McCormick (1958) select list on use in animal physiology; Gessaman (1973) on energetics of homeotherms; Schultz (1963) on use in ornithology; and general reviews of ecological techniques utilizing isotopes by Schultz (1969) and Schultz and Whicker (1974).

In addition, the select bibliograhies of Klement and Schultz (1962–66) on terrestrial and freshwater radioecology and the annotated bibliography of Klement (1965) on natural environmental radioactivity are notable.

Early expectations for isotope-tracer solutions to many wildlife problems have not materialized (Griffin 1952, Pendleton 1952, 1956, Godfrey 1954b), but other uses have developed and greatly added to the ability of wildlife research scientists to obtain relevant data on the biology of a variety of species.

Tracers

Tracer methodology dates back to the 1920's when lead was used in studies of plant physiology. The many isotopes available from controlled atomic fission since that time have greatly expanded this area of research. (See Schultz and Klement 1962, Schultz 1969.) Using a radioactive label in a compound or in an animal is the same as attaching a band or tag to an individual to distinguish it from the group. It is assumed that the behavior of the labeled or tagged individual is the same as the rest of the group. Most isotopes, except for tritium and carbon-14 (Buchanan et al. 1953) will not affect behavior. The atomic weight of tritium is nearly 3 times higher than for normal hydrogen. In some reactions this might produce an isotope effect. Most isotopes of higher atomic weight are little affected by this small difference. Tracers, such as ^{32}P, ^{45}Ca, ^{35}S, ^{59}Fe, ^{64}Cu, and others, can be used as single elements in nutrition and metabolism studies. Clinical diagnosis for certain diseases and glandular functions are possible through the use of isotopes such as ^{131}I and ^{99m}Tc. A number of isotopes have been used to label or mark individual animals. Grouse, ducks, fish, toads, reptiles, and a number of mammals have been labeled with radioactive gold, phosphorus, cobalt, silver, tantalum, and others. The potential anatomical or physiological effect on the animal must be assessed, and the possibility of human ingestion, particularly of game animals must be weighed against advantages of use before some of these strong gamma emitters are used in the field.

Nest materials, as well as animals, have been marked, movements studied by radioactive excrement, parent-offspring relations determined, predator-prey and food-chain relations studied, all by radioisotope tracers.

Some specific and successful examples of the use of isotopes in wildlife research include the following: 1–15 uCi of ^{106}Ru, or ^{90}Sr, were used to construct a backscatter gauge to measure eggshells by beta backscatter (Fox et al. 1975); Bullard (1970) very efficiently used ^{14}C to determine the efficacy of tableted versus coated baits; Gentry et al. (1971) used ^{59}Fe, ^{65}Zn, and ^{131}I in a composite feeding trial to determine the movements of small mammals and Wolff and Holleman (1978) injected ^{65}Zn into adult female *Mus* and *Microtus* to label their progeny; Pelton and Marcum (1975) injected ^{65}Zn and ^{54}Mn into bears and later sampled droppings to derive a population estimate using the Schnabel method; ^{45}Ca pellets were inserted into female pheasants in order to label the bone tissue of her progeny (McCabe and LePage 1958, McCabe 1974); water balance studies, both in the field and in the laboratory have utilized HTO, tritiated water, to determine in vivo turnover in marsupials (Denny and Dawson 1973), pronghorn antelope (Wesley et al. 1970), and mule deer (Knox et al. 1969). Doubly labeled water (HTO^{18}) and ^{22}Na have been used to measure field energetics, turnover of elements, growth rates, and estimation of milk intake of sucklings (Nagy 1975, Nusetti and Aleksiuk 1975, Green 1978, Green and Dunsmore 1978, Nagy et al. 1978, Green and Newgrain 1979). Other metabolic and forage utilization studies include those of Cowan et al. (1969) utilizing ^{45}Ca and ^{89}Sr in adult buck deer; food passage rates in white-tailed deer utilizing ^{51}Cr as the tracer (Mautz and Petrides 1971); radioiodine kinetics (Fig. 30.7) in mule deer (Gist and Whicker 1971); and the use of fallout ^{137}Cs to determine forage intake (Fig. 30.8) in mule deer (Alldredge et al. 1974). New uses and techniques are being developed very rapidly (e.g., Figs. 30.9, 30.10, 30.11), so recent journals should be consulted during project design.

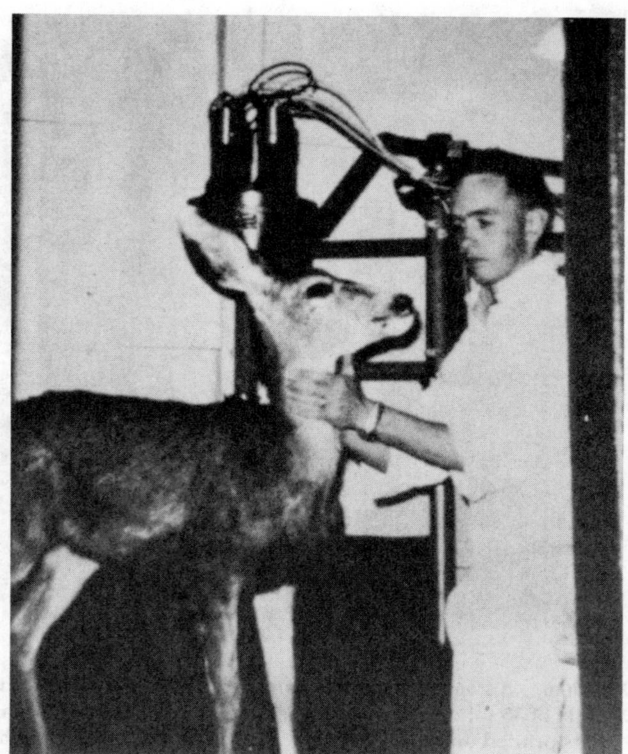

Fig. 30.7. The uptake and elimination of numerous radionuclides including strontium-90, cesium-134, iodine-131, and calcium-45 have been studied in mule deer (*Odocoileus hemionus*). In this figure a mule deer is positioned below a scintillation detector in order to determine its radionuclide body burden. Data from such studies have been used to describe and predict the fate of radionuclides in the environment, to calculate forage intake rates by deer and investigate antler growth (A. W. Alldredge, Dept. of Radiology and Radiation Biology, Colorado State University).

The advantages in marking with a radiolabel are that the animal does not have to be handled to sense the mark, a number of individuals can be scanned quickly, the label is easy to apply, and can be useful for a limited time if desirable.

Recently one of the most important uses of isotope-labeled compounds has been to study the distribution, translocation, and bioaccumulation of pesticides in natural environments as well as within closed laboratory systems. Ease of pesticide sample preparation and residue determinations are major advantages, but a serious drawback is that sophisticated assays of metabolic products are not possible. As an example, ^{36}Cl ring-labeled DDT could not be used to assay for DDE, DDD, or the other metabolites by using only radioassay procedures. Some examples of the use of isotopes in the study of pesticide kinetics include those of Meeks (1968), Dindal (1970), and Forsyth and Peterle (1973), reporting the use of ^{36}Cl labeled DDT in a marsh and meadow ecosystem; and Giles (1970) who studied the distribution of ^{35}S labeled malathion in a forested area.

Neutron Activation Analysis

The determination of minute quantities of various elements is possible by bombarding a sample of the unknown with neutrons or charged particles and subsequently analyzing the induced radiation. Since each element has a characteristic energy spectrum, the composition of the unknown can be determined quantitatively and qualitatively. Using this method, mercury, bromine, sodium, and other elements can be determined at nanogram (10^{-9} gm) levels. Gold can be measured at levels of 10^{-11} grams. Radioassay of trace elements can be an aid in taxonomic work, residue determinations of various pollutants, and in tracer studies. Devine and Peterle (1968) reported on the use of neutron activation analyses to determine mineral content of waterfowl feathers; Kelsall and Calaprice (1972) utilized x-ray irradiation and subsequent x-ray spectrometry with a lithium drifted silicon detector to determine mineral content and possible natal areas of migrant waterfowl. Neutron probes and gamma analysers used in conjunction with scanning electron microscopes are now available for a much faster and more economical determination of elements in tissue samples. Proton activation of stable oxygen-18 in water samples and subsequent assay has also been very effective (Wood et al. 1975).

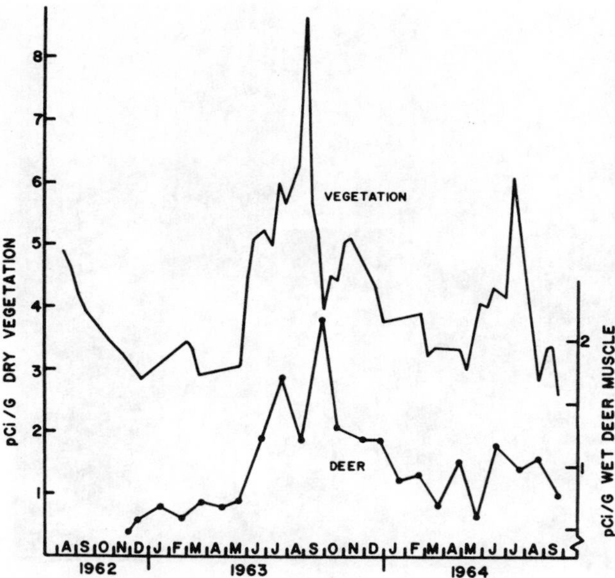

Fig. 30.8. This figure illustrates the similarity in patterns of cesium-137 concentrations measured in mule deer muscle tissue and vegetation that makes up the deer diet. Data from this study were used to calculate daily forage intake rates for free-ranging mule deer in north-central Colorado (A. W. Alldredge, Dept of Radiology and Radiation Biology, Colorado State University).

Isotope Dilution Analysis

Dilution analysis (Radiochemical Centre 1965) is an additional means for determining low levels of specific compounds in mixtures. A known radioactive quantity of the compound to be measured is mixed with the unknown mixture. The compound to be measured is then extracted, and the total radioactivity of the extracted portion is measured and compared in ratio to the original mixture. The total quantity in the unknown mixture can then be computed. This method can produce a considerable savings in time since only a small quantity of the original mixture need be extracted for the compound to be measured. Some pesticide residue work has been developed using these methods.

Miscellaneous

Autoradiography can be an important adjunct to research projects where radioactive compounds are already being used. Macro or micro sections of animal tissue can be placed in contact with x-ray film and exposed for adequate periods of time. Some exposures require a month or longer when residues in tissues are low and the isotope is a weak emitter. As an example, the location of pesticide residues within cells can be determined by feeding labeled compounds to the animal. Techniques for microautoradiography are quite exacting, and considerable experience is necessary to produce and interpret results that are meaningful.

Instruments in which the whole body of specimens as large as a human can be put for counting are now available. The whole-body method of measuring essentially gamma radiation is unique in that it permits periodic assay of a single living individual facilitating the study of bioaccumulation and excretion rates of various elements and compounds. Radioactive dating of fossils and biological materials based on the ratios of various isotopes, and known decay rates has been useful in the study of geologic time. Such dating might also be used in a more modern context for taxonomic studies or predicting environmental trends, particularly in the study of pollen and invertebrates from lake sediment cores. The use of naturally occurring radioisotopes such as ^{40}K and those more recently added to our environmental contamination as fallout products (^{90}Sr, ^{137}Cs, ^{131}I) can be most useful in the study of natural ecosystems. There has been a great body of literature developed in this area of radioecology which has not been generally appreciated by most wildlife workers. Information, techniques, and data from the study of radioisotopes can be useful for solving current problems in pollution research. The parallels are clear.

Health and safety are considerations and practices of paramount importance in the use of isotopes. Ward (1952) wrote of the proper design of laboratories for safety. The *Radiological Health Handbook* (USHEW 1970) is an important general reference. Most installations require a trained radiation safety officer, employed by licensee, to supervise those aspects of research programs where quantities of radioactive materials are used. Licensing requirements are clearly set forth by the

Fig. 30.9. Soil erosion and deposition, in amounts of a few milligrams per square centimeter, have been successfully measured in a shortgrass plains ecosystem using this portable detection system to measure beta particles emitted from a buried strontium-90 source (A. W. Alldredge, Dept. of Radiology and Radiation Biology, Colorado State University).

Fig. 30.10. In conjunction with a bighorn sheep study, investigators estimate alpine plant biomass using the principle of beta particle attenuation in a nondestructive sampling method (A. W. Alldredge, Dept. of Radiology and Radiation Biology, Colorado State University).

Fig. 30.11. The effects of ionizing radiation on a shortgrass plains ecosystem were studied using a cesium-137 source which is located in the structure above. The area devoid of vegetation is a sector that has been chronically irradiated for several years (A. W. Alldredge, Dept. of Radiology and Radiation Biology, Colorado State University).

U.S. Nuclear Regulatory Commission and requests for use of materials above certain minimum levels (^{14}C, 50 uc; ^{32}P, 10 uc; ^{3}H, 250 uc) are reviewed by that agency. (See Atomic Energy of Canada Ltd. 1961). Waste disposal in both air and water is regulated according to published standards. These standards are set and enforced by the USNRC to protect both the people in intimate contact with radioactive materials and the general public. They do not materially hamper use of radioactive materials in ecological or laboratory research.

Chapter Thirty-One

Use of Dogs in Wildlife Biology

FRED C. ZWICKEL
Department of Zoology
University of Alberta
Edmonton, Canada

"When dogs were first domesticated, some eight to ten thousand years ago, they became a part of human society, and they have undergone most of the cultural and environmental changes that have affected their masters." (Scott and Fuller 1965).

In this day of complicated instrumentation, computerization, and fascination with building mathematical models, a discussion of the use of dogs in wildlife research and management may seem rather unsophisticated. Yet all of the technological sophistication in existence will lead to naught if it cannot be applied to the real world. In wildlife biology, field studies are a must, and here is where dogs can contribute.

Dogs are an essential part of some techniques, or simply add to the effectiveness of others. Dogs often decrease costs and human labor, reduce human biases, and increase sample sizes. Many breeds can do things for which man has no ability or do some things better than man. They can also increase the morale of a field crew (and thus its effectiveness), an advantage often overlooked. Conversely, if improperly used, they may have the opposite effect on both morale and biases.

The use of dogs in wildlife biology can be grouped into 6 broad categories: (1) locating wildlife, (2) collecting specimens, (3) capturing wildlife alive (which may or may not include initial location of the animal), (4) studies of behavior of birds or mammals, (5) protection of property from damage by wildlife, and (6) facilitating harvests of certain species. The use of dogs as laboratory animals will not be considered here.

TYPES OF DOGS

The American Kennel Club recognizes about 115 different breeds of dogs, and there are some 800 true-breeding types in the world (Hafez 1962). The proper breed, or breeds, must be chosen for a given purpose. Most working dogs can be classified into the following general types: herding, flushing, pointing, retrieving, and trailing.

Most dogs used in wildlife biology are hunting varieties and many breeds have been selectively developed for different reasons. Davis (1962) and Griffen (1964) each gave a good background to hunting breeds and to their abilities and qualities. Burns and Fraser (1966) and Scott and Fuller (1965) discussed the heritability of some traits of selected breeds. There are many kinds of dogs from which to choose, as well as a potential for developing new breeds, or crossbreeds. Winge (1950) discussed inheritance and crossbreeding in dogs, with emphasis on hunting breeds.

LOCATING WILDLIFE WITH DOGS

Dogs have been used widely for censusing wildlife. In its broadest context, censusing includes counting animals directly or gathering sex and age ratios that are used to estimate density, indexes to density, or productivity.

Wight (1930) estimated that a Gordon Setter increased the efficiency of his census of upland birds by 3 times. Later, Bennett and Hendrickson (1938) reported that a hunting season for bobwhite quail in Iowa was opened principally as the result of censuses made with the aid of bird dogs, and Kozicky et al. (1956) described the adaptation of this technique on a statewide basis. Bergerud and Mercer (1966) compared direct counts of willow ptarmigan by using dogs to estimates of density by other methods. An October count with dogs was the only method that gave an objective measure within specified limits of statistical precision. Good dogs often would scent ptarmigan at 150 m, and up to 275 m.

Jenkins et al. (1963) used setters and pointers to census red grouse. Although the ability of different dogs varied, the chief errors resulted from differences between observers. Also, counts made with the aid of dogs were consistent with those made by other methods, and repeated counts by experienced observers were consistent from day to day. Jenkins and Watson (1962) discussed methods for censusing red grouse with dogs in some detail and claimed an accuracy of plus or minus 10%.

Dogs have been widely used by both management and research biologists for making brood counts of galliform birds. A good dog is especially valuable for locating juveniles in late summer when they are more widely scattered than earlier in the season.

Pointing breeds, especially, have been useful for relocating color-marked blue grouse (Zwickel and Bendell 1967a) and spruce grouse (Stoneberg, Table 31.1) for identification. In some cases marked:unmarked estimates of density were computed from these data (Redfield 1974). Marked:unmarked ratios of roe deer were also obtained with the help of dogs (Anderson 1961).

Caldwell (1963) used hounds for obtaining an index to the relative abundance of raccoons on different habitat types in Florida, and Cunningham (1962) used hounds to recover raccoons after trapping and marking to obtain a Peterson-Lincoln estimate of population size. Goodrum (1940) found dogs an aid in estimating the relative abundance of squirrels, and Babakov (1961) suggested the use of Huskies for censusing squirrels. The Finnish Barking Dog, the Pystikorva (Koskimies 1954), is used for hunting squirrels and it (or similar breeds) may be of value for census purposes. Shtil'mark (1963) counted chipmunks with dogs by recording the number of encounters along specified census routes.

Censuses of big game, especially in mountainous country, may be hindered by areas of "dead ground" which the observer does not have time to cover adequately. Since well-trained sheepdogs will work to hand signals at distances up to 0.6 km (Hafez 1962), such dogs might be used to drive game from these areas so they can be counted. Sheepdogs might also be helpful for keeping game already counted from areas still to be counted. The color of the dog may be important here as Darling (1937) noted that light-colored collies do not move sheep as well as dark ones.

Locating nests often poses special problems. Bennett (1938) used Chesapeake Retrievers, Irish Water Spaniels, and pointers; Sowls (1950), Labrador Retrievers; and Keith (1961), both pointing and flushing breeds of dogs for finding nests of waterfowl. Sowls reported that dogs could find most or all nests on a given area, and Keith's dogs found many nests that were terminated.

Pointing breeds are especially valuable for finding nests of upland game birds (Jenkins et al. 1963, Klebenow 1969, Zwickel 1975). There might be some concern about the effects of the dogs on subsequent success of the nests, but Keppie and Herzog (1978) reported that nests of spruce grouse located by dogs were as successful as those located by radio-telemetry. Pointers also often locate nests of birds other than galliforms, nests of microtines, and a variety of different mammals.

Schemnitz (Table 31.1) used a Weimaraner to locate drumming sites of ruffed grouse that were not actively occupied during midday. This dog also found sporadically used drumming sites that might not have been found otherwise.

Dogs have been used to locate dens of some mammals. Allen (1943) found dogs would trail trapped squirrels, after marking and release, to their dens. Harington (1968) used Huskies to locate dens of polar bears, a technique borrowed from the Eskimos. Smith and Stirling (1975) adopted the Eskimo technique of hunting seals in their dens with dogs for finding birth lairs of ringed and bearded seals. They used a trained Labrador Retriever; training her by giving her a dead seal pup to smell. The use of a dog allowed them to compare densities of birth lairs among areas.

COLLECTING SPECIMENS WITH DOGS

The general use of dogs for collecting museum or laboratory specimens of game birds and game mammals needs no documentation. There are some special cases, however. Gashwiler (Table 31.1) found Beagles very useful for retrieving songbirds that he shot. Dogs have been used to help remove all blue grouse (Bendell and Elliott 1966) and roe deer (Anderson 1953) from experimental plots. They were also used to help remove cottontail rabbits from enclosures (the late Howard Wight) and doubtless would be useful for helping to remove ungulates from large enclosures or exclosures.

Other specialized uses include searching for birds dying from natural causes (Jenkins et al. 1963) or from insecticides (Finley 1965). Dogs also can find crippled bobwhite quail (Robel 1965), ring-necked pheasants (Stokes 1954), band-tailed pigeons (Brown, E. R. Table 31.1), and waterfowl (Marshall, Table 31.1). Marshall used a Springer Spaniel and a Labrador Retriever to pick up ducks stricken with botulism. He found that dogs readily learned that only living ducks were desired and that a good dog can pick up ducks at a rate 3 to 4 times greater than man. Dogs have also served to pick up carcasses of botulism victims so they could be destroyed (Rodgers, Table 31.1).

Small "den" dogs are regularly used for bringing fox pups from their dens in the Midwest and might be of

Table 31.1. Names and addresses of persons who have used dogs in wildlife work as described in the text, but about which nothing has been published. This list is presented so that persons with interests in the techniques involved can contact the handlers for necessary details.

Bailey, E. D.	Dept. of Zoology University of Guelph Guelph, Ontario, Canada N1G 2W1
Bandy, P. J.	Fish and Wildlife Branch Ministry of the Environment Victoria, B. C., Canada V8W 2Z1
Bendell, J. F.	Faculty of Forestry University of Toronto Toronto, Ontario, Canada M5S 1A1
Bowhay, E. J.	Washington State Dept. of Game 600 North Capitol Way Olympia, WA 98501
Brisbin, I. L.	Savannah River Ecology Laboratory Savannah River Project Aiken, SC 29801
Brown, E. R.	Washington State Dept. of Game 600 North Capitol Way Olympia, WA 98501
Brown, R. L.	Arizona Game and Fish Dept. P.O. Box 480 Fredonia, AZ 86022
Conway, M.	New Mexico Department of Game and Fish Santa Fe, NM 87503
Dalke, P. D.	640 N. Eisenhower St. Moscow, ID 83843
Downing, R. L.	U.S. Fish and Wildlife Service Clemson Univ. Clemson, SC 29634
Gashwiler, J. S.	2004 N.E. 7th Street Bend, OR 97701
Hornocker, M. G.	Idaho Cooperative Wildlife Research Unit University of Idaho Moscow, ID 83843
Klimstra, W. D.	Cooperative Wildlife Research Laboratory Southern Illinois University Carbondale, Il 62901
Marchinton, R. L.	School of Forest Resources University of Georgia Athens, GA 30601
Marshall, D. B.	4264 SW. Chesapeake Ave. Portland, OR 97201
Rodgers, R. S.	Williamette Valley National Wildlife Refuge Rt. 2, Box 208 Corvallis, OR 97330
Schemnitz, S. D.	Dept. of Fishery and Wildlife Sciences New Mexico State University Box 4901, Las Cruces, NM 88003
Scott, T. G.	U.S. Fish and Wildlife Service Aylesworth Hall Colo. State Univ. Ft. Collins, CO 80523
Simard, B. R.	Ecole de Medicine Veterinaire University of Montreal St. Hyacinthe, P. Q., Canada J2S 7C6
Stoneberg, R.	Limestone Rte. Nye, MT 59061
Yoakum, J. D.	P.O. Box 9098, Univ. Sta. Reno, NV 89507

value to biologists who need young foxes or other canids for their studies (Scott, Table 31.1). Kalela (1961) collected wandering lemmings with dogs. He felt that dog-caught animals gave less biased sex and age ratios than trap-caught animals. Cunningham (1962) and Johnson (1970) noted that sex ratios of raccoons collected with dog and gun may be less biased than those of animals caught in traps.

Collections of animals with dogs may be the best way of obtaining unbiased data on food habits of some species. For example, Johnson (1970) said that collections of raccoons at night with dogs probably gave his most representative data on food habits of this species. Also, the stomachs of trap-caught animals often contain no food.

Taber and Dasmann (1958) pointed out that a good dog can find wounded deer, and Downing (Table 31.1) used a Weimaraner to trail crippled deer so as to estimate crippling losses. Of 69 wounded deer that were found by Downing, 41 left no visible trail, so could not have been trailed by man. Biologists have sometimes used dogs for finding dead deer in connection with studies of mortality (Marchinton, Table 31.1).

CAPTURING WILDLIFE ALIVE WITH DOGS

The efficiency of waterfowl banding programs may be increased by the judicious use of dogs. Retrieving breeds are helpful for capturing flightless ducks (Addy 1956, Gollop 1956); but, a word of caution, retriever-caught birds may have a higher mortality rate than those caught in traps (Lensink 1964). Bowhay (Table 31.1) used a crossbred sheepdog, and Addy (1956) used Chesapeake and Labrador Retrievers to chase, knock down, and hold flightless Canada Geese. Addy also noted the use of dogs for herding flightless waterfowl into drive-traps.

Several breeds of small dogs have been trained for "tolling" ducks. The dog lures ducks into a "decoy" trap at the command of a handler who is hiding nearby (Anon. 1947, Eygenraam 1959). In practice, the dog is commanded to appear and disappear from among a series of louvre-like blinds arranged along the shore of a narrow waterway. Many ducks become curious and are led by the dog, at the handler's commands, down the waterway into a large, curved and covered funnel that leads into a trap. The handler then appears at the mouth of the funnel and drives them into the trap.

Dogs are used to help capture other birds for banding. Pointers helped to find and "pin down" blue grouse prior to their capture with a "noosing" pole (Zwickel and Bendell 1967b). Stoneberg (Table 31.1) adapted this technique to treeing spruce grouse for capture. The Finnish Barking Dog, used for hunting capercaillie (Koskimies 1954, 1957), may be ideal for treeing species such as spruce grouse for capture with a noosing pole.

A staunch pointer often finds very small, flightless galliform chicks that tend to "freeze" or run and hide. Hundreds of young blue grouse have been wing-tagged after capture with this method (Bendell, Table 31.1 and Zwickel, unpublished). Most of these chicks would have been missed without the help of dogs.

Scott and Fuller (1965) reported that in Britain, prior to the development of the shotgun, Land Spaniels were trained to lie down when on scent, after which a net was drawn over the dog and a covey of partridge. Substituting pointers for spaniels, this technique was used by poachers for capturing red grouse in 19th century Britain (Leslie and Shipley 1912). The technique should be adaptable to wildlife work. Mendall (1938), Blankenship (1957), and Lehman (1966) described the use of dogs for pointing woodcock so they could be netted for banding. Entire broods were sometimes captured in one netting.

A very specialized technique for capturing quail was described by Enderlin (1946). Dogs ran the quail into bags—up a funnel-shaped trough dug in the ground. Klimstra (Table 31.1) found dogs an effective aid when night-lighting bobwhite quail, as did Brown (1975) when night-lighting Mearn's quail. Stoddard (1931) captured bobwhite quail that were flushed by dogs into hand-held clapnets.

Dogs are used more often for capturing mammals for marking than for counting them. A Redbone Hound (Brown, E. R. Table 31.1), a Labrador Retriever (Bandy, Table 31.1), a Vizsla (Downing and McGinnes 1969), and sheep dogs (Bowhay, Table 31.1, Zwickel unpublished) have been used to run down and capture white-tailed or black-tailed deer fawns for tagging. Both twins often were caught, where only one might have been caught without dogs. Also, dogs may catch fawns up to one week older than can normally be captured by man.

Brown, E. R. (Table 31.1) used a Labrador Retriever and a Black and Tan Hound to capture elk calves for tagging, and Murie (1951) noted that dogs were used for capturing elk calves for domestication. Ritcey and Edwards (1956) used Labrador Retrievers to help capture moose calves; and Russian biologists captured calves of caribou with the help of dogs, but the breed of dog is unknown. Yoakum (Table 31.1) found that a Labrador Retriever tripled his efficiency in catching kids of prong-horned antelope.

Many people believe that young cervids have no scent. However, English Pointers often point fawns of black-tailed deer that are bedded down (at times out of sight) and young enough to be captured (Zwickel unpublished) and Brown, E. R. (Table 31.1) noted that his dogs could locate elk calves by smell.

Scott and Fuller (1965) described how pygmies in the Congo used Basenjis to run small antelope into nets, and Bramley (1966) developed a similar technique for capturing roe deer. The deer were run into 1½ m high nets with the aid of trained Beagles. Bramley captured and marked about 80% of the deer population on 1 study area, principally with this technique.

Hornocker et al. (1965), the late Doug Pierson, and Cunningham (1962) used hounds for bringing mountain lions, black bears, and raccoons, respectively, to bay for immobilization with drugs. Animals were individually marked and often relocated for identification by running with dogs. Pierson instrumented some bears with radios and found dogs valuable for recapturing these animals so they could be re-instrumented. He noted, however, that only about 1 in 10 good "cat or "coon" hounds will run black bears successfully. Feral hogs have also been captured for marking with the aid of dogs (Brisbin, Table 31.1).

Simard (Table 31.1) used a pack of 3 Norwegian Elk Hounds to bring moose to bay for immobilization. His hounds also trailed and located drugged moose that were lost from sight before becoming immobile. Merriam (1962), Hill (1966), and Downing (Table 31.1) found dogs valuable for trailing drugged deer that had been lost from sight before the drugs took effect. When using a dog, Downing reduced the recommended dosage of the drug, and consequently the mortality. He made 60 consecutive captures (using nicotine) without a loss. A Vizsla trailed the deer, found the immobilized animal, then returned and led him to the deer. He estimated that 19 of 48 deer that he immobilized would have been lost without the help of his dog.

STUDYING THE BEHAVIOR OF WILDLIFE WITH DOGS

Hamerstrom et al. (1965) described some reactions of displaying prairie chickens to intrusions by domestic dogs. However, the study of behavior of birds, as determined by using dogs, is an almost untouched field. Cursory observations from our studies with blue grouse indicate that much might be learned by keeping close observations and records of both the dogs and reactions of birds to dogs.

Several workers have studied the behavior of wild lagomorphs being pursued by dogs. Carr (1939) noted escape reactions of marsh rabbits running ahead of Beagles, and Lowe (1958) and Toll et al. (1960) studied home ranges of swamp rabbits being chased by Beagles. The latter authors found these determinations of home range similar to those determined from trapping individually marked rabbits. They suggested that running rabbits with dogs is a simple and rapid technique for determining their home ranges.

Moore and Marchinton (1971) used hounds to detect scent left by deer in a study of marking behavior. Their dogs could detect scent markings several days old. Tyson (1959) trailed deer with dogs to determine the extent of their movements during the night. He developed a workable track-count census method partly from this information. Marchinton (1964), Corbett et al. (1971), and Sweeney et al. (1971) used hunting hounds to study the behavior of deer fitted with radios that were being pursued by hounds. Conway (Table 31.1) used trained Labrador Retrievers to detect the scent of black-footed ferrets in attempts to confirm their presence in prairie dog towns. Johnson (1970) found that trailing raccoons with hounds gave him an insight into their feeding habits, activity sites, and refuge behavior. The running of birds and mammals with dogs might be adaptable for studying behavior in many different species.

Scott and Fuller (1965) noted that man's selective breeding has modified the dogs' behavior mainly quantitatively, rather than qualitatively. Thus, some breeds might be used as simulated predators to study the basic hunting patterns of canids and escape reactions of their prey, e.g., Corbett et al. (1971). The growing field of biotelemetry adds still greater possibilities. Since dogs can be instrumented much easier than wild animals, radio-equipped dogs might be used to secure information on the behavior of both predators and prey. This technique could be adapted to study feral dogs, an area of growing concern to wildlife biologists (Scott and Causey 1973, Denney 1974); note, however, that recent studies indicate that the "problem" of feral dogs may be exaggerated (Marchinton et al. 1970, Corbett et al. 1971). More research is needed in this area.

CONTROL OF DEPREDATIONS AND FACILITATING HARVESTS WITH DOGS

Leopold (1933) and Longhurst et al. (1952) pointed out that dogs could be used to herd big game from agricultural areas. The herding of other depredatious wildlife could also prove fruitful.

Hunting raccoons with dogs and gun may be an effective way to control damage caused by this species (Johnson 1970). In fact, hounds are often used to track down depredating bears, cougars, bobcats, foxes, coyotes, and wild hogs by putting the hound on the track at the site of depredation. In this way, specific animals that may be causing problems can be removed.

Many breeds of dogs are used for tracking wounded game while on leash (Bailey, Table 31.1), and numerous papers report that hunters using dogs have greater success than those without dogs. Also, Marchinton (Table 31.1) believes that hunting deer with dogs may simulate natural predation and could offset some of the deleterious genetic effects that may result from the extermination of natural predators. The encouragement of the use of dogs by sportsmen for increasing their hunting success, for reducing crippling losses, and for adding to the enjoyment of their hunt should not be overlooked by biologists as a management technique (Marchinton et al. 1970).

GENERAL ASPECTS ON USE OF DOGS

Most uses of dogs in the wildlife field involve their sense of smell. If dogs are used properly, this is equivalent to adding a new sense to the observer. One may even be able to improve on this ability of dogs as Krushinskii and Floess (cited in Hafez 1962) found that 10–20 mg injections of amphetamine markedly increased the sense of smell and trailing accuracy in hunting dogs. However, amphetamine must be used with caution; and, before use, a veterinarian should be consulted. Whitney (1937) noted that dogs can be taught to discriminate among different odors.

Although pointing breeds are usually considered specialists for working with upland game birds, they will locate many other birds and mammals and could prove useful for finding and capturing species for which they have not been used to date. Other breeds can be useful to biologists for jobs for which they have not been selected, e.g., Labrador Retrievers for capturing young ungulates.

The use of dogs as pack animals has not been exploited to its fullest by wildlife biologists. Hafez (1962) noted that dogs can carry up to one-half their own body weight; sled dogs are an outstanding example.

TRAINING AND HANDLING

The value of a dog to a wildlife biologist is dependent on its inherent ability and training. After finding a suitable breed, *one must bring the dog under control.* A fine dog, ill-trained may be more bother than it is worth.

Training and handling dogs comes easier for some people than for others. However, there are many good books on training and practically anyone with a little patience and understanding can train dogs for most purposes. Some useful general references are *Bird Dogs in Sport and Conservation* (Yeatter 1948), *Sports Illustrated Book of Dog Training* (Sports Illustrated 1959), *Modern Dog Encyclopedia* (Davis 1970), and *The Training and Care of the Versatile Hunting Dog* (Winterhelt and Bailey 1973).

Training is considered by some to be a long and laborious procedure, and in some cases it may be most economical and satisfactory to purchase trained dogs. Others train their dogs during the normal course of field work.

A trained dog today will probably cost at least $500. A puppy, initially acquired for less but trained by the biologist, may cost much more if one's time is included. On the other hand, the type of skill expected from a dog for biological work, e.g., to capture and hold a deer fawn, may require very special training. Wildlife needs are often unrelated to sport hunting abilities, the usual professional training that is available.

The decision to purchase or self-train a dog depends partly on the skills required. A few simple commands, well learned, will bring most dogs under adequate control for many types of field work. Basic training includes a response by the dog to its name and the commands "go," "come," "sit," "heel," "no," and "whoa," and, for some types of work, "fetch." "Go," "no," and "whoa" sound much alike and one may wish to modify these commands. In our work with English Pointers, we use "OK" to replace "go," but find that our dogs discriminate adequately between "no" and "whoa." With intensive training, we have taught several different breeds to respond adequately to all these commands within 3 weeks or less, with some of the dogs being less than 6 months of age, and one more than 5 years of age, at the time. Nevertheless, training procedures for one type of dog may be ineffectual for another (Fox 1965); e.g., Fox noted that mild punishment inhibits Beagles, but punishing a terrier caused resistance as terriers associate pain with fighting. Consistency and patience are important keys to successful training. It cannot be stressed too strongly that for effective use, *the dog must be under control of the handler*.

A wildlife biologist is sometimes dissatisfied with his dog, often because he expects a dog of one breed to do something for which it has little or no ability. Usually, if available, one is better off selecting a purebred dog that has been selected for characteristics needed for a specific purpose. While some crossbred or mongrel individuals may work very well, long-term selection for true-breeding characteristics has a higher probability of giving predictable characteristics. Also, there are differences within breeds, or within litters, and particular individuals may be of no value for field work. Some professional trainers estimate that only about one-half the pups from a given litter will be worth keeping, and trainability cannot be evaluated when the puppy is very small. One must be prepared to put useless dogs aside as they may be more of a liability than an asset.

One often hears the question, "What sex is best for field work?" Each may have some advantages. In terms of inherent abilities, our experiences with pointers indicate that either sex may be equivalent; we have had very good males and very good females. We find, on average, that females are a little more easily trained than males, perhaps because they are more sensitive (Burns 1952). At the same time, females may be a problem during periods of "heat." One solution is to keep only one sex as this causes fewer problems in the field. When dogs are not working, we find that females are less likely to "run" than are males. However, in populated areas one should always kennel valuable dogs.

The proper care, feeding, and handling of dogs while in the field is an important consideration if they are to perform most efficiently. Dogs cannot work long hours on a maintenance diet only. The *Guide to Waterfowl Banding* (Addy 1956) gives a good general coverage of this subject.

Kennels may be a necessary capital investment for maintaining a stock of working dogs for biologists. For example, the Idaho Cooperative Research Unit has maintained dogs for wildlife studies (Dalke, Table 31.1; Hornocker, Table 31.1); the Institute of Terrestrial Ecology in Scotland maintains dogs for work with red grouse; Bendell (Table 31.1) and Zwickel (unpublished) maintain a stock of dogs for work with blue grouse; and The Alabama Cooperative Wildlife Research Unit has a kennel with raccoon hounds, deer hounds, and bird dogs for research purposes.

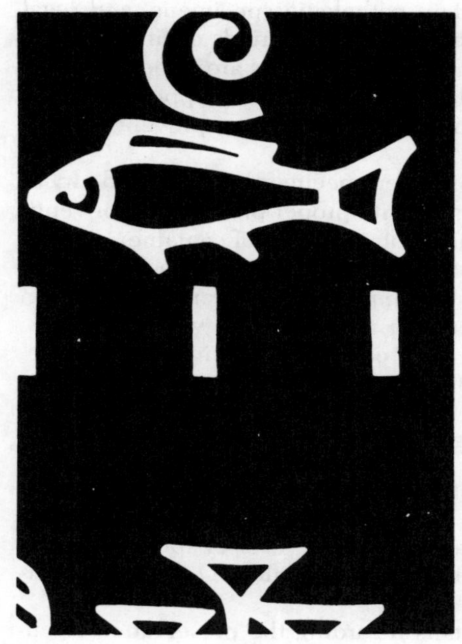

Chapter Thirty-Two

Collection and Field Preservation of Biological Materials*

GARY A. WOBESER

Department of Veterinary Pathology
Western College of Veterinary Medicine
University of Saskatchewan
Saskatoon, Saskatchewan, Canada

TERRY R. SPRAKER

Veterinary Diagnostic Laboratory
School of Veterinary Medicine
Colorado State University
Fort Collins, Colorado

V. L. HARMS

Fraser Herbarium
Department of Plant Ecology
University of Saskatchewan
Saskatoon, Saskatchewan, Canada

GENERAL CONSIDERATIONS

The collection of biological specimens is a part of any field investigation, and proper planning and equipment can greatly enhance the value of any specimens obtained. No attempt will be made here to catalogue the techniques for the preservation of all types of specimens; the discussion will be limited to techniques which may be utilized under normal field conditions.

Many of the specimens collected in the field will of necessity be examined or used by persons other than the collector. Since there is a great deal of personal preference involved in techniques for handling specimens, it is vital that the collector consult with the "user" and agree in advance on the most suitable methods.

Proper and adequate labeling is of paramount importance. Specimens, no matter how carefully collected and preserved, are of little or no scientific value if the supporting documentation is lost or not supplied. The type of data collected will vary with the specimen, but care should be taken to ensure that the information cannot become separated from the specimen. Waterproof linen tags, written on with pencil and tied securely to the specimen with string, are highly satisfactory for identification of many types of material.

Specimens placed in liquid preservation should be labeled in 2 ways. One label is attached to the container and a second label is placed inside the container with the specimen. Such data may be written on paper or cardboard (provided it does not have a starch filler) in soft lead pencil or with carbon (waterproof) ink. Regular ink should not be used because it will wash off in preservatives. It is good practice to write full data on both sides of the label so that at least 1 set of data is preserved.

Whenever possible, specimens should be delivered directly to the laboratory rather than being sent by mail or express. Perishable specimens, in general, should not be sent by mail; if express delivery is used, the receiver should be notified by telephone in advance of shipping

*Revised from the 1969 Chapter by Karstad.

so that specimens are processed immediately upon arrival.

A variety of convenient plastic specimen containers are commercially available. These include vials, bottles with snap-on or screw-on tops, bags with a variety of closures, and tightly closing dishes (Fig. 32.1). Some types of plastic become brittle when cold and thus plastics must be carefully selected to withstand rugged use in cold weather or during frozen storage or shipment. Disposable plastic gloves provide convenient protection against exposure to pathogenic organisms when collecting samples from animal carcasses.

COMMON METHODS OF PRESERVATION

Refrigeration and Freezing

Refrigeration (4°C) is an excellent way to preserve most biological materials if the specimens are to be held for only a short period of time. Cooler chests containing wet or dry (CO_2) ice can be readily taken into the field. If dry ice is used, the outer container must not be completely airtight to prevent a minor explosion due to sublimation of the dry ice. If wet ice is used, the specimen must be placed in a waterproof container.

Freezers (approximately −10° C) are generally available and are excellent for the preservation of many specimens. Storage in freezers of study mount specimens, hides, certain pathologic specimens, and legal evidence, is possible for short periods of time without any special treatment. If specimens are to be frozen for more than a few days, they should be wrapped in freezer paper or placed in airtight containers to prevent dessication.

When chilled or frozen specimens are shipped, dry or wet ice may be used, with proper precautions for ventilation of dry ice and waterproofing of containers for wet ice. Containers of rigid plastic foam which are specifically designed for shipping of refrigerated or frozen biologic specimens are available in a variety of sizes. They are light, waterproof, have good insulating value, and usually are protected by outer boxes of cardboard.

Common Preservatives

Table 32.1 presents a general summary of the more commonly used techniques for preserving biological materials. As noted earlier, the user of specimens may prefer other techniques and should be consulted wherever possible.

For greater details regarding the preservation of entire specimens of vertebrates, reference should be made to Chapin (1946), Anthony (1950), Anderson (1965), and Knudsen (1972). Instructions for the preparation of preservatives are shown in Table 32.2., and details regarding the preparation and limitations of various preservatives and reagents are given in Mahoney (1966), Faulk-

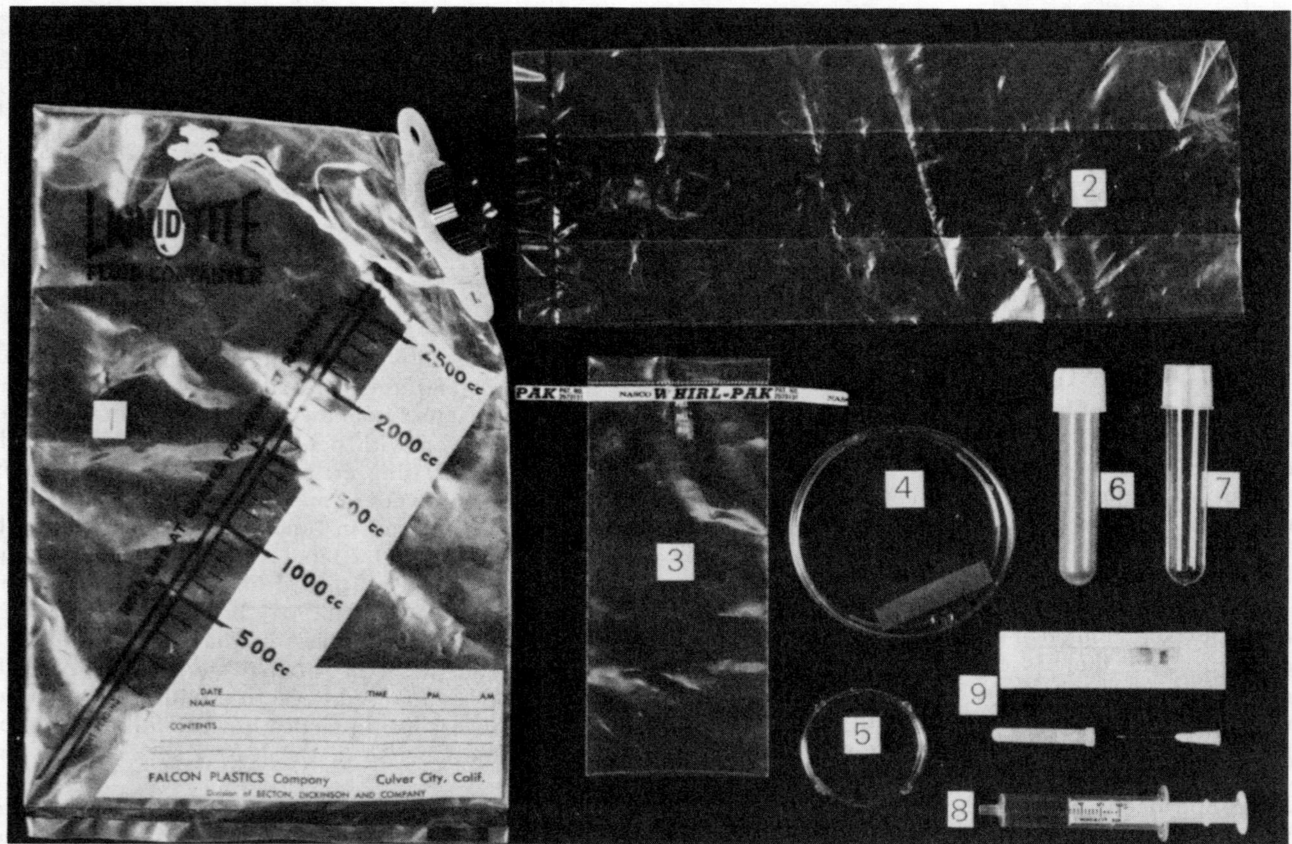

Fig. 32.1. **A variety of plastic containers highly suitable for field use are available. Many, such as items 3, 4, 5, 6, and 7, may be obtained in sterile condition.**

Table 32.1. Techniques for the preservation of biological materials.

Biological Material	Techniques (in order of preference)	Reference
Mammals and Birds		
Whole	Formalin (10%)[a] with injection	Knudsen (1972)
Skin—pelts	(1) Clean thoroughly and air dry; (2) salt thoroughly (NaCl), (3) use alum on pelts which are "slipping"	Anderson (1965)
Skin—study	(1) Arsenic trioxide-borax in equal proportions; (2) arsenical soap. (*Powdered borax is preferable for student use*)	Anderson (1965), Hall & Kelson (1959), Knudsen (1972).
Food material Stomachs	Small stomachs—5% formalin, large stomachs—10% formalin (wrap stomachs in cheesecloth)	U.S. Fish & Wildlife Service (1941)
Feces	Dry quickly, fumigate with carbon disulfide	
Reproductive Tracts	(1) AFA[a] (preferably) or Bouin's; (2) 10% formalin	Forbes (1941)
Reptiles and Amphibians		
Whole	Fix in 8–10% formalin with injection, store in 5–10% formalin, 70% ethyl or 40–50% isopropyl alcohol	Knudsen (1972)
Snake skins	Rolled flat, placed in 10% formalin	Anderson (1965)
Amphibian skins (to preserve color)	Kill with chloroform, skin and place skin in water, float skin onto cardboard, dry quickly	Anderson (1965)
Fish	Fix in 10% formalin, store in 70% ethyl or 40–50% isopropyl alcohol	Anderson (1965), Knudsen (1972)
Insects		
Hard body	Kill, store dry	Knudsen (1972)
Soft body	Kill, store in 70% ethyl alcohol	Mahoney (1966)
Miscellaneous		
Skeleton-field	(1) Clean thoroughly, dry quickly (may treat with arsenical soap for shipment);[b] (2) 70% ethyl alcohol (formalin, unless buffered, dissolves Ca from bones)	Anderson (1965)
Skeletons—in laboratory	Clean by (1) hot water maceration; (2) use of dermestid beetles; (3) cold water maceration. Degrease with carbon tetrachloride	Anderson (1965), Knudsen (1972), Mahoney (1966)
Fumigants—(for specimens in pelt, study or standing mount form)	Carbon disulfide as gas to kill insects, paradichlorobenzene as insect deterrent	Knudsen (1972)
Animal Carcass for Necropsy	(1) Refrigerate or keep cool and transport to laboratory as quickly as possible; (2) freeze; (3) necropsy in field and preserve appropriate specimens[a]	
Blood		
Serology	(1) Collect, separate serum and refrigerate or freeze (2) whole blood or serum dried on paper discs[a]	
Hematology, Clinical Chemistry	Prepare several blood smears, collect blood for serum, collect blood into tubes containing anticoagulant, refrigerate, transport to laboratory as soon as possible[a]	

Table 32.1. *Continued*

Biological Material	Techniques (in order of preference)	Reference
Tissues		
Bacteriology	(1) Sterile container, refrigerate, transport to laboratory as soon as possible; (2) sterile container, freeze; (3) saturate sterile swabs with tissue fluid, transport in special media[a]	
Virology		
Rabies	Submit head as soon as possible to Public Health or Veterinary Diagnostic Laboratory (use care to prevent human exposure)	
Other viruses	(1) Refrigerate (4C), submit to laboratory as soon as possible; (2) freeze on dry ice; (3) freeze	
Histology	Fix small pieces (5 mm in one dimension) in 10% buffered formalin (10X volume of specimen). *DO NOT FREEZE.*	
Toxicology	Refrigerate or freeze blood, liver, kidney, brain, fat and stomach and intestinal contents in separate containers. Also food if suspect is source of toxin.	
Parasites		
Ectoparasites	Remove by hand or with ether, chloroform or absorptive silica powder (Dri Die). (1) ship live in nonairtight container with moist cotton, refrigerate if possible; (2) kill with ether, chloroform of HCN and ship dry between layers of cotton; (3) freeze	
Helminths	(1) Relax in cold water or saline. Fix nematodes in hot 70% ethyl alcohol or 5% formalin. Fix cestodes and trematodes in 10% formalin	Anon. (1971)
Protozoa	(1) Refrigerate tissues, feces, citrated blood; (2) make smears of blood, feces and tissue impressions; (3) fix tissues in 10% buffered formalin	
Plants[a]		
Terrestrial vascular	Press, dry and mount	
Bryophytes & lichens	Collect with substrate, dry	
Fungi	(1) Dry, make spore prints (mushrooms); (2) Preserve in AFA	
Aquatic vascular	Press, dry and mount	
Macrophytic algae	Preserve in AFA or press, dry and mount	
Microphytic algae	(1) Iodine-acetic acid-formalin solution; (2) AFA (Samples of blue-green algae should be dried)	

[a]—See text for description of formulae and techniques.
[b]—Do not use poison on skeletons to be cleaned by dermestid beetles.

ner and King (1970), Frankel et al. (1970), and Knudsen (1972). Knudsen (1972) discussed preservation of plants and animals, and Post (1967) presented a complete field book for the wildlifer for specimen collection and preservation.

Note in Table 32.1 that several concentrations of alcohol and formalin are required. When alcohol is stipulated in this table, reference is made to ethyl alcohol because methyl (or wood alcohol) is not a satisfactory preservative. Normally, alcohol is 95% strength, and

Table 32.2. Composition of commonly used preservatives.

Preservative	Composition		Usage
Alcohol-acetic acid-formaladehyde (AFA)			
	Ethyl alcohol (95%)	50 parts	Preservative and fixative
	Formaldehyde (commercial)		
	(for animal)	10 parts	
	(for plant)	2 parts	
	Acetic acid, glacial	2 parts	
	Water	40 parts	
Arsenic trioxide-Borax	Arsenic trioxide (As_2O_3)	1 part	Preservative, skins
	Sodium tetraborate ($Na_2B_4O_7$)	1 part	
Arsenical soap*	White bar soap	906 g	Preservative skins, skeletons
	Arsenc trioxide (As_2O_3)	906 g	
	Potassium bicarbonate ($KHCO_3$)	170 g	
	Camphor	142 g	
	Ethyl alcohol (95%)	227 ml	
Bouin's fluid	Picric acid (saturated aqueous solution)	750 ml	Fixative, tissue
	Formaldehyde (commercial)	250 ml	
	Acetic acid, glacial	50 ml	
Formalin, neutral buffered	Formaldehyde (commercial)	100 ml	Fixative, tissue
	Distilled water	900 ml	
	Sodium phosphate monobasic ($NaH_2PO_4.H_2O$)	4 g	
	Sodium phosphate anhydrous (Na_2HPO_4)	6.5 g	

*—available from taxidermy supply dealers.

formaldehyde solution is 40% strength in commercial quality. The formula used in diluting either of these chemicals is as follows:

$$\frac{\text{Desired concentration} \times \text{desired volume}}{\text{Concentration of stock solution}}$$

$$= \text{Volume of stock solution to be diluted to desired volume}$$

For example, suppose 200 ml of 60% alcohol is wanted and a stock solution of 95% alcohol is on hand. Then, according to the above formula:

$$\frac{60 \times 200}{95} = 126.3 \text{ ml of 95\% alcohol}$$

to which is added 73.7 ml of water to make 200 ml of 60% alcohol. Likewise, 40% formalin is available from which to prepare 250 ml of 5% formalin. Then:

$$\frac{5 \times 250}{100} = 12.5 \text{ ml of stock formalin}$$

which is mixed with 237.5 ml of water.

COLLECTING SPECIMENS FROM LIVING ANIMALS

Methods for capturing and restraining animals are given elsewhere (Chapter 6), as are some of the reasons for collecting specimens from these animals (Chapter 8). The single most valuable sample for a variety of purposes is blood. Blood should be taken as cleanly as possible, usually by means of venapuncture. Regardless of the site of venapuncture, good restraint is necessary to prevent the animal injuring itself during the procedure. In large animals a number of large veins are available, with the jugular being the most commonly used. It is often difficult to obtain an adequate sample in animals of rabbit size or smaller except by cardiac puncture. This is a somewhat dangerous procedure for the animal and should not be attempted without anaesthesia of the animal.

Blood samples can be collected from veins in either the wing or leg in large birds, and a small sample may be obtained from the jugular vein in small birds. If only a few drops of blood are required, clipping of a toenail is a safe, rapid method for use in most animals.

A very useful system for bleeding animals employs evacuated glass tubes[1] which permit the automatic withdrawal of a measured amount of blood. A double-pointed needle and plastic tube holder are used and multiple samples can be withdrawn once the needle is positioned in a vein. These tubes, containing various anticoagulants, are available in a variety of sizes.

Types of blood samples required for various purposes are shown in Table 32.3.

Table 32.3. Methods for collection and preservation of blood samples.

Test	Sample required
Protein	Serum*
Protein electrophoresis	"
Serum electrolytes	"
Blood urea nitrogen	"
Creatinine	"
Cholesterol	"
Serum enzymes	"
—Alanine amino transferase (GPT)	"
—Aspartate aminotransferase (GOT)	"
—Alkaline phosphatase	"
—Creatine phosphokinase	"
Serology	"
Hematology	2 ml of unclotted blood collected into tube containing EDTA as anticoagulant
Blood glucose	1 ml of unclotted blood collected into tube containing sodium fluoride anticoagulant
Blood parasites	blood smear

*The amount of serum required for any test is dependent upon the method used in the laboratory. In general 10 ml of blood will yield sufficient serum for most purposes.

[1]Vacutainer System, Becton, Dickinson and Company, Rutherford, N.J.

Blood for serum collection should be collected as cleanly as possible in sterile glass or plastic vials and allowed to clot. Normally, a fresh clot will contract during the first few hours after it forms, exuding clear straw-colored serum. This is to be expected if blood is obtained from the veins of a live or dying animal. Under ideal circumstances, serum can be poured off a clot; centrifugation is an aid to remove free cells. Small hand-operated centrifuges can be taken into the field. Small electric centrifuges are suitable for use in areas where electricity is available.

Hemolysis may render a sample unsuitable for some serological tests, and therefore must be avoided. Some of the causes of hemolysis are: freezing, agitation, bacterial contamination, contamination with water or snow, and drawing blood under high vacuum.

If blood is collected before coagulation occurs, it should be allowed to clot at near body temperature and should be kept warm until serum has separated from the clot. This can be done by placing the tube in a shirt pocket, providing undue agitation does not occur. Serum should then be poured off into a second vial and refrigerated or frozen. If serum cannot be removed at once, the tube containing serum and clot should be refrigerated (*not frozen*). Refrigeration of a blood sample immediately after it is collected will do no harm except to reduce the yield of serum. Blood collected from a carcass after death should be refrigerated promptly, since it is certain to contain bacteria.

Blood smears made from fresh blood offer a simple way of preserving evidence of blood-borne parasites and other disorders of the blood. Place a clean slide (Fig. 32.2) on a horizontal surface and put a drop of fresh blood on this slide near one end. A second (spreader) slide, held at an acute angle, is placed on the horizontal slide and drawn into the drop of blood. Allow the blood to spread evenly until it is distributed most of the way across the end of the spreader slide. Before the blood spreads to the ends of the spreader slide, push the spreader quickly across the bottom slide. This places a thin film of blood on the bottom slide.

A number may be placed on the specimen slide with a glass-writing pencil. The blood-smear slide should be dried as quickly as possible, and stored in a dust-proof container for later staining and examination.

Special 17-mm-diameter paper discs have been used to collect and preserve (by air drying) specimens of both

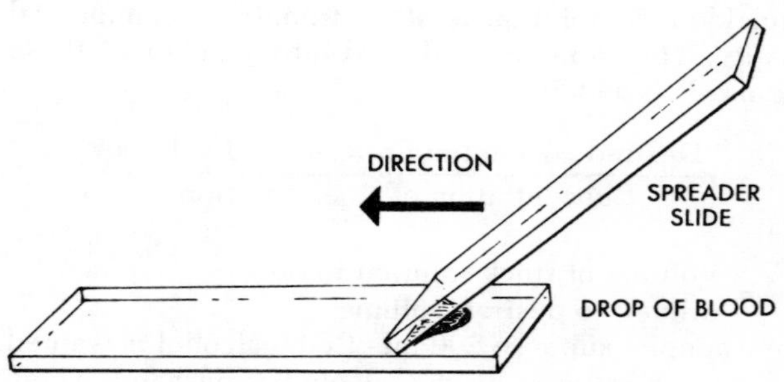

Fig. 32.2. Position of the spreader slide prior to spreading of the smear. The final motion is in the direction of the arrow in a smooth fairly rapid stroke (from Coffin 1945:93).

whole blood and serum (Karstad et al. 1957). These discs may be of value to the field worker as they are simple to transport and store, but are less desirable than frozen sera. Discs to be saturated with whole blood or serum are placed on a smooth nonabsorbent surface, such as a glassine envelope or a plastic or glass petri dish. For quantitative tests each disc must be thoroughly wet (approx. 0.2 ml). Discs are dried by exposure to air, after which they may be stored without refrigeration in glassine envelopes or mailed directly to the laboratory. Each disc-absorbed specimen must be accompanied by a card bearing data on where, when and from what species collected, condition of animal, etc.

Occasionally there may be a need to collect other specimens from living animals. These might include feces for parasitologic examination, fur or feathers for toxicologic studies, and specimens for microbiological examination. Feces can usually be obtained either by observing the animal until it spontaneously defecates or by removing feces from the rectum with a gloved finger. Samples should be preserved by refrigeration.

When collecting hair samples for toxicologic determinations, particularly heavy metals, it is important to select specimens which reflect the time period of importance. Elements are deposited in hair only during the growing phase, so that in situations of recent exposure to a toxin, no residue may be present in the hair, or the concentration may not be uniform along the length of a hair shaft.

Sterile swabs may be used to collect samples from body orifices for bacteriologic or virologic studies. Detailed information on methods for the collection, preservation and examination of clinical material is available in Davidsohn and Henry (1969) and Frankel et al. (1970).

COLLECTION AND PRESERVATION OF SPECIMENS AT NECROPSY

It is usually necessary to preserve specimens at necropsy for further study. These specimens often will be examined by individuals other than the prosector, and the joint effort of several specialists may be required to arrive at a complete diagnosis. The only way to be certain that the correct specimens are collected and that proper preservation methods are used is to consult the person who will examine the specimens.

General rules which can be followed for collecting and preserving specimens are:

(1) It is better to collect and save extra specimens that may later be discarded than to regret not having specimens available. This is particularly true in diagnostic cases for which the cause of death is not evident.

(2) Refrigeration at 4° C or on ice is generally suitable for short-term preservation of specimens.

(3) Specimens always should be placed in individual leak-proof containers and clearly labeled. When submitting specimens to another laboratory, provide a complete history for the case including the gross necropsy findings together with a request for the specific test or procedure which you desire.

(4) Perishable specimens should be delivered directly to the laboratory and should not be mailed. If they must be shipped by express, pack in insulated containers together with wet or dry ice and notify the recipient by telephone so they may be picked up directly upon arrival.

Specimens for Histopathology

The standard fixative for histopathology is 10% neutral buffered formalin. Specimens must be trimmed of excess tissue to allow penetration and proper fixation. In general, portions of tissue should be no thicker than 5 mm in 1 dimension. Neural tissue is an exception; and if tissue is not required for other studies, the entire brain and the spinal cord after opening the dura mater should be fixed in 10–15 volumes of 10% buffered formalin. Tissues may be left in formalin for extended periods of time. Other fixatives such as Bouin's fluid may be used in special cases; however, tissues tend to become extremely hard if left in most other fixatives and must be changed after a few to 24 hours fixation.

Tissues for histopathology should include portions of grossly visible lesions. Whenever possible, the section should be cut so that it not only passes through the lesion but also includes a portion of adjacent normal tissue. In most diagnostic cases, sections of the major organs (liver, spleen, kidney, lung, heart, stomach, intestine and brain), together with any other obviously involved organ, should be fixed. All tissue sections should be cut cleanly with a sharp knife or scalpel, as blunt instruments and scissors tend to crush and distort tissue. *Tissues intended for histopathologic examination should not be frozen.*

Specimens for Microbiology

Results from microbiologic examinations usually are dependent upon isolation of living organisms; therefore, the submitter must be concerned not only with preventing decomposition but also with maintaining the viability of microorganisms within the specimen. Refrigeration at 4° C is the method of choice for preservation of specimens for most bacteriologic, mycologic and virologic examinations. Prompt delivery to the laboratory is more critical with these specimens than with any other type. Small carcasses may be submitted intact to the laboratory. In the case of large animals, tissue should be removed as soon as possible after death, using care to minimize contamination of the specimen, and placed in individual, clean (and if possible sterile) labeled containers. A variety of container types are available from laboratory supply houses; among the most useful for microbiologic specimens are presterilized, disposable plastic petri dishes and bags.

Specimens must be collected where the suspected organism is likely to be found and must be of sufficient quantity to allow a thorough examination. Small organs such as lymph nodes should be submitted intact, and portions of other organs should be at least several centimeters in all dimensions if possible. Lengths of intestine can be submitted after ligation of the ends. If an animal has been dead for some time prior to necropsy, bone marrow is less apt to be contaminated with saprophytic bacteria than are other tissues, and culture for both pathogenic bacteria and viruses may be attempted from this tissue.

Sterile swabs can be used for collection of feces or body fluids for bacteriologic culture. Care must be taken to ensure that drying does not occur prior to delivery to the laboratory. If delivery must be delayed, the swab may be immersed in bacteriologic transport media or special culture units consisting of sterile tube, swab and, culture media[2] may be used. Most bacteria and fungi will withstand freezing and specimens should be frozen if delivery to a laboratory will be delayed.

All specimens for virology should be chilled at 4° C since many viruses are unstable at temperatures above that point. Freezing and thawing is very deleterious for viruses; specimens should be held on ice or at refrigerator temperature rather than being frozen, provided they can reach the laboratory within 48 hours of collection. If specimens must be frozen, they should be kept at −40° C or below. Ordinary freezers are generally above −20° C so that if virus specimens are an important part of a study special provision must be made for freezing, perhaps through the use of dry ice or liquid nitrogen. Standard 28-ml glass screw-capped bottles are suitable for most virus specimens.

Specimens for Parasitology

Ectoparasites collected at the time of necropsy should be submitted live in nonairtight containers, particularly if they are to be examined for infectious agents. For this purpose they may be shipped in glass or plastic vials, with the mouths covered with gauze cloth. These should be placed in an outer container which allows some ventilation and contains moistened cotton or sponge to prevent desiccation of the arthropods enroute. Dead ectoparasites may be shipped dry between layers of cotton or frozen.

Most parasitology texts include a variety of methods for the preservation of helminths. Specimens should be relaxed in cold water or saline for a period prior to fixation. Nematodes can be fixed in hot 70% alcohol or 5% formaldehyde and trematodes and cestodes in 10% formalin. If protozoan parasites are suspected, tissues should be refrigerated for submission and direct wet mounts and tissue impression smears made and examined. Further details are available in Anon. (1971).

Specimens for Toxicology

There is no general laboratory test to detect all toxicants; thus one is unlikely to receive a significant answer if tissues are submitted to a toxicology laboratory with a general request to "check for poisons." Rather, the submitter must make every effort to identify the class of poison suspected, (e.g., chlorinated hydrocarbon, organophosphate, heavy metal, mycotoxin) and provide as much information as possible with regard to potential toxicant sources. Specimens should be placed in clean containers and refrigerated or frozen. Specimens of blood, liver, kidney, brain, fat, and stomach and intestinal contents are sufficient for most toxins. If a food-related toxicant is suspected, samples of the food eaten prior to intoxication also should be included. Buck et al. (1976) provided detailed instructions for sample collection of most toxicants.

[2]Culturette, Scientific Products, Division of American Hospital Supply Corp., Evanston, Illinois.

PRESERVATION OF STUDY SKINS

Field workers often have the opportunity of preserving valuable study skins when specimens become available from highway kills, accidents, trapping operations, sportsmen, and in other ways. Such specimens may be saved and put to good use if the wildlife worker is familiar with the simple technique of preparing study mounts—and is equipped to prepare such specimens.

Full descriptions of the techniques used in skinning and mounting study skins are given in Chapin (1946), Anthony (1950), Hall and Kelson (1959), Anderson (1965), and Knudsen (1972). A label should be attached to the skin as soon as the specimen is completed. Identification is not necessary in field prepared mounts (positive identification may be made later), but sex, age, date, locality, collector, collector's number, measurements, and remarks should be entered on the label. This should be done *when the specimen is prepared* in the field and the tag should be attached to the specimen at that time. The original label tag should *never* be destroyed. Steps in preparing mammal study skins are shown in Fig. 32.3.

The principal steps in the skinning of a bird are given in Fig. 32.4. The major differences between skinning a mammal and a bird are: (1) the skull is left in bird study mounts (after the brain, eyes, and the fleshy portions are removed); (2) wire is normally not needed to strengthen the legs and wings of birds as the flesh is removed from these appendages and cotton is wrapped around the bones; (3) a wire or small stick, usually inserted in the skull and extending to the tail, is used to strengthen bird mounts; and (4) finished bird mounts normally are wrapped in thin "sheets" of cotton or cheesecloth when left to dry. The same type of label is used for birds as is used for mammals.

The preparation of neat, quality mammal and bird study mounts becomes easier with practice. Thus, the wildlife investigator should develop the art of preparing study mounts so that he can preserve specimens in a reasonable manner and length of time. If the ability to work quickly and neatly is not developed through practice, the field worker is prone to discard specimens under the excuse that he does not have sufficient time to preserve them.

PRESERVING BIG GAME TROPHIES

The biologist should be familiar with the general techniques used in preserving game trophies and game meat because sportsmen will assume that he possesses such knowledge.

For purposes of illustration, the preservation of the meat and trophies of the deer will be used in the following discussion. For further details regarding the preservation of game meat, reference is made to Low and Pierce (1950), Rawley et al. (1950), and Field et al. (1972, 1973a,b).

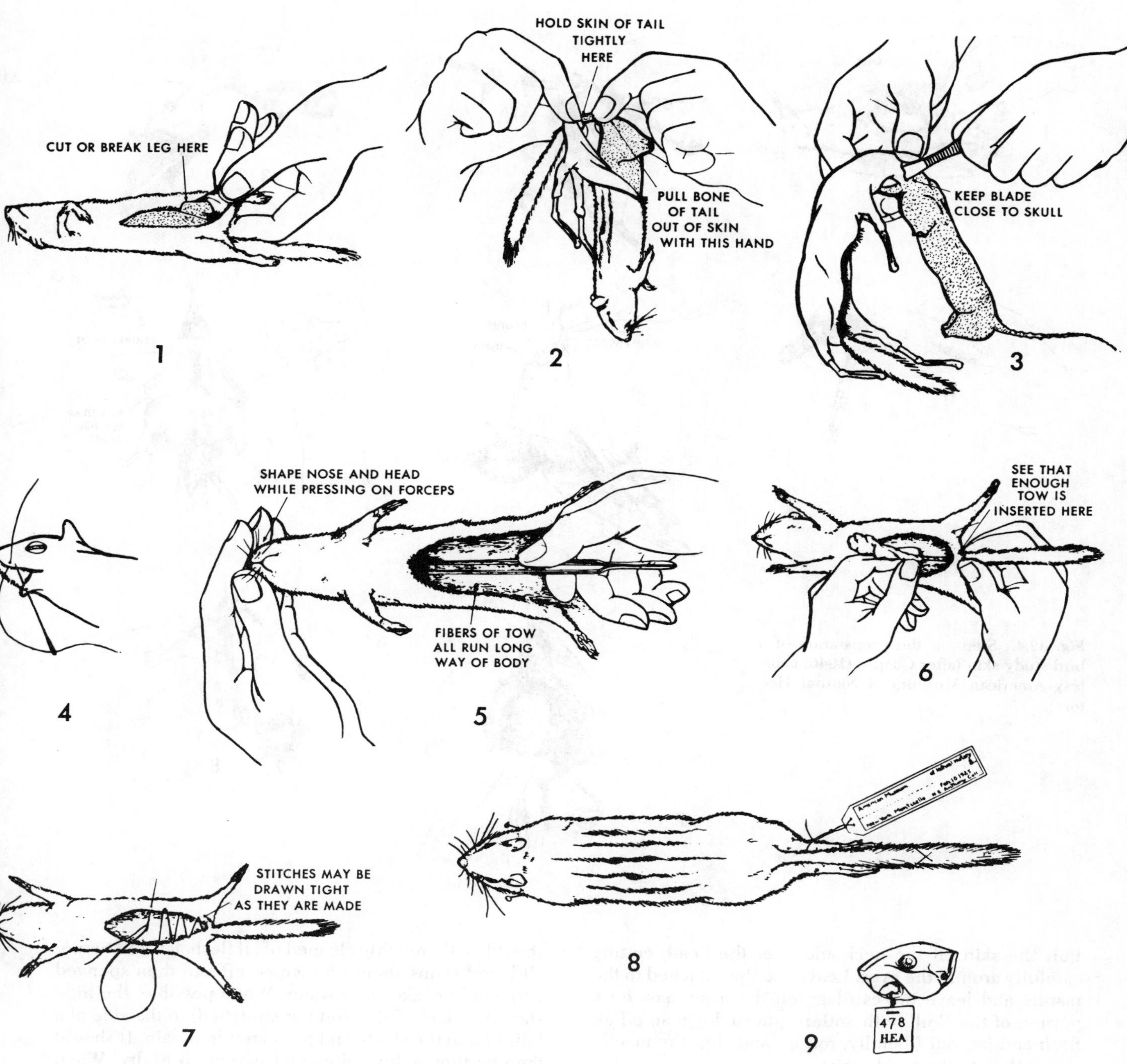

Fig. 32.3. Steps in the preparation of a mammal study skin: (1) The opening belly-cut and 1 leg freed from the skin at the knee; (2) removing the tail vertebrae; (3) cutting around the ears; (4) stitching the lips; (5) the start in filling the skin; (6) filling the tail with a covered wire; (7) sewing the filled skin; (8) top view of finished study skin; and (9) tagged skull (from Anthony (1950), courtesy of American Museum of Natural History).

The preservation of the head, hide, and feet of the deer will be briefly discussed to illustrate the general principles. Fish and birds require special treatment (Hornaday 1929), but the general considerations are essentially the same.

To save a deer "head" for mounting by a professional taxidermist, make a cut through the hide along the top of the neck from the shoulder to about 8 cm from the midpoint between the base of the antlers (Fig. 32.5). Next, make a cut to and around each antler. This will leave a V-shaped flap of skin over the skull. Cut the ears free from the skull, making sure to cut as close to the skull as possible. Then, make an encircling cut around the base of the neck *at the shoulder*. Many hunters cut too far up on the neck, thus giving the taxidermist such a short mantle that he cannot prepare a good head mount.

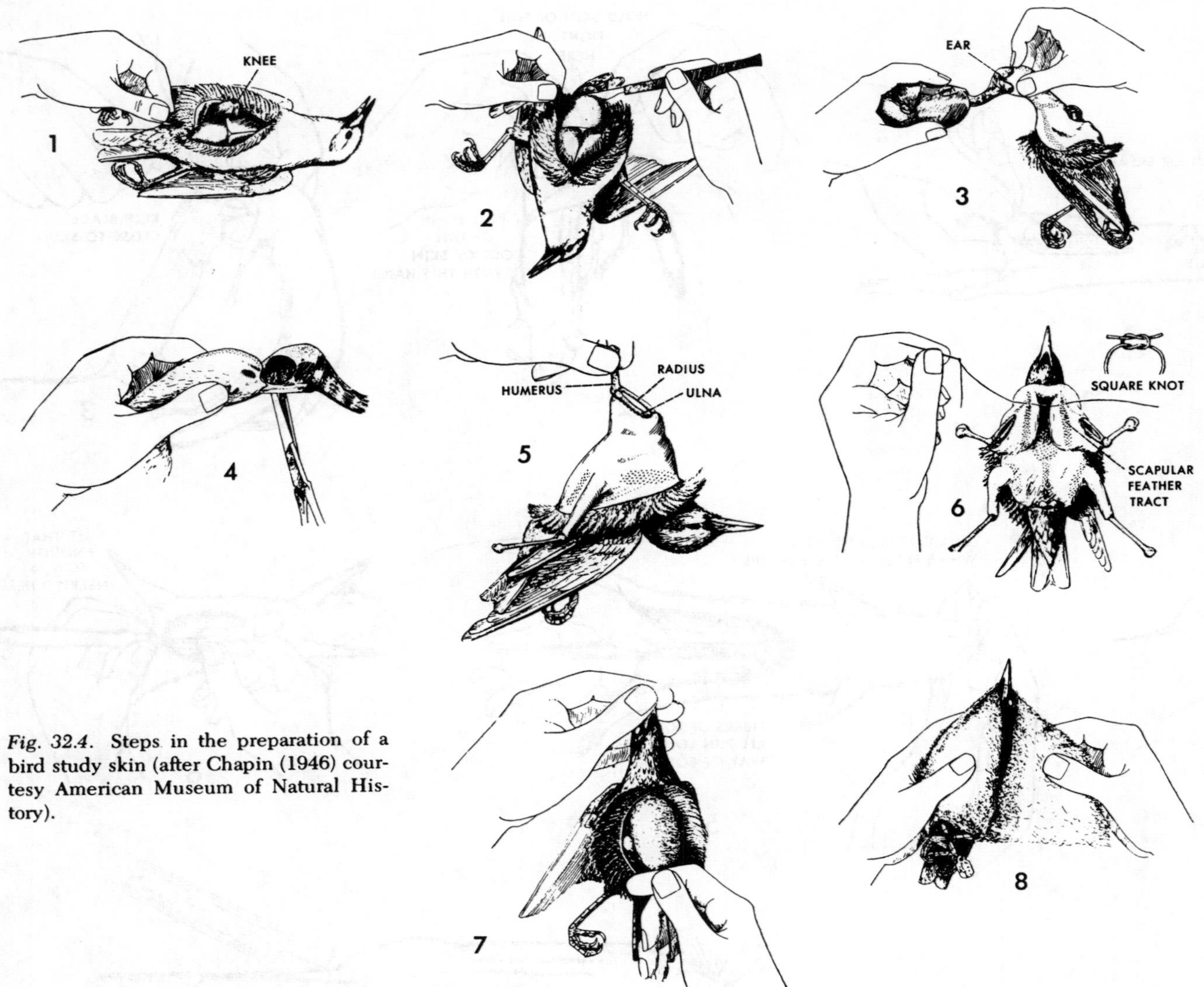

Fig. 32.4. Steps in the preparation of a bird study skin (after Chapin (1946) courtesy American Museum of Natural History).

Pull the skin off the neck and over the head, cutting carefully around the eyes. Leave the lips attached to the mantle and leave the cartilage on the nose. Saw off a portion of the skull with antlers attached. Clean off all flesh and fat, salt liberally, roll up and ship the mantle and antlers to the taxidermist.

If the trophy can be delivered immediately to the taxidermist, case skin the neck (making an encircling cut at the base of the neck at the shoulders) up to the base of the skull. Sever the neck muscles at the base of the skull and twist the head free from the neck vertebrae. The entire head, with antlers attached and the mantle can be turned over to the taxidermist for his immediate attention.

The hide can be removed by cutting along the inside of each leg from the first joint to the mid-belly line. Make an encircling cut around each leg at the first joint and pull the hide from the leg. The skin may be peeled off the body without the use of a knife. This is done by pulling with one hand and using the fist of the other hand to force the hide free from the body. The hide should be thoroughly cleaned of all flesh, fat, and tissue; all blood stains should be wiped off and then sponged with cold or lukewarm water. When possible, the hide should be tacked flat (but not stretched) to the side of a building in the shade and protected from rain. It should then be thoroughly salted and permitted to dry. When dry, it may be removed and rolled up. Do not fold a dry skin as folding will cause it to crack.

PRESERVING GAME MEAT

The primary objectives in all treatment of wild meat to be preserved for table use are: (1) bleed as completely as possible (bleeding is not absolutely essential but it makes longer storage under refrigeration much more satisfactory); (2) cool the carcass as quickly as possible after the kill is made; and (3) clean (remove the viscera) immediately, exercising care to prevent contact of fur, intestinal contents, or other contamination with the meat.

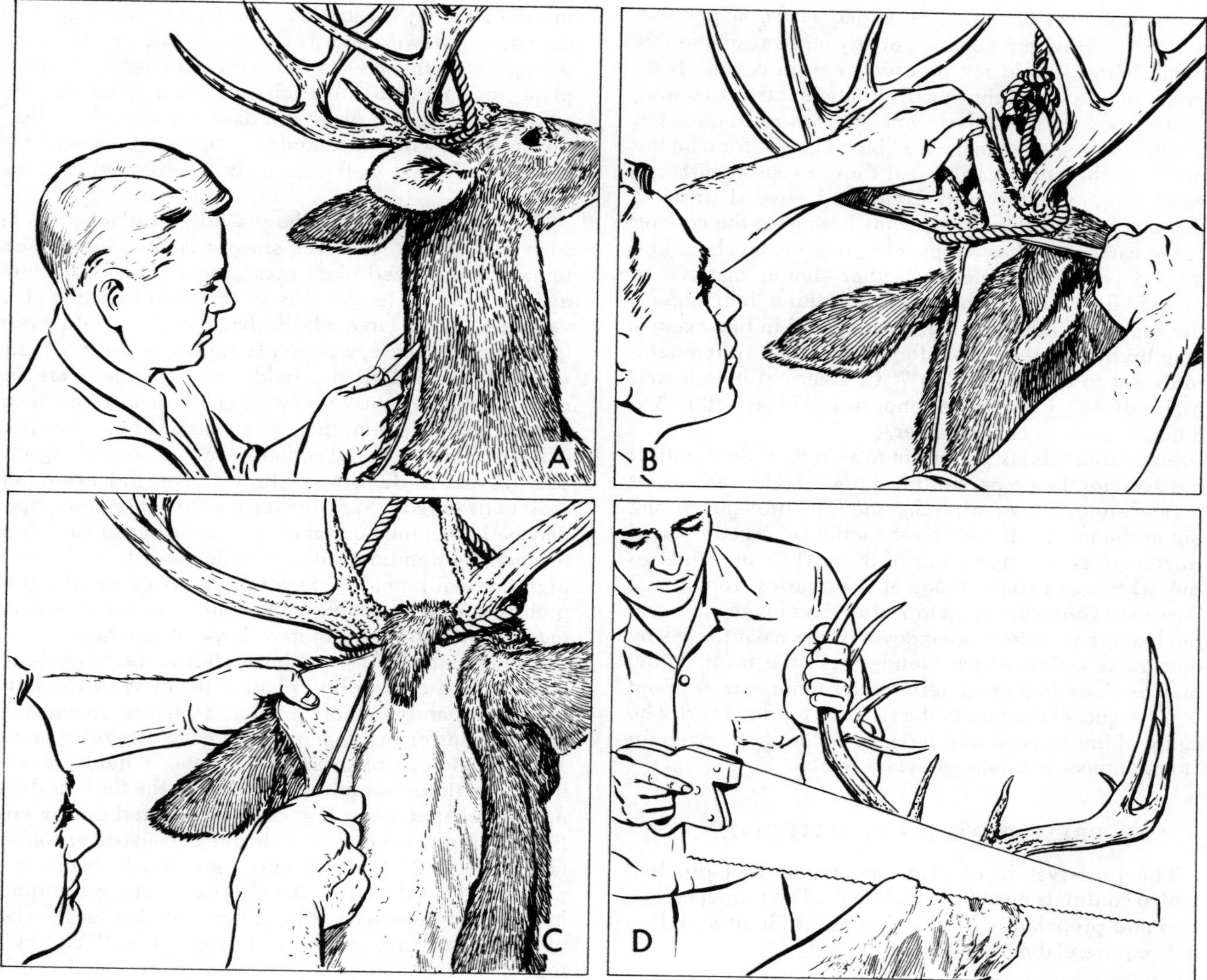

Fig. 32.5. Skinning out a buck deer head for mounting. A—Make a longitudinal cut on the back of the neck from a point midway between the ears to the shoulder. Cut around shoulders. B—Cut from the ears to the base of the antlers, then around the antlers. C—Sever the ears at their base (cartilage to be removed later). Skin out the head, cased, to tip of nose. D—Saw off a portion of the skull with antlers attached.

If the hunter reaches the game (e.g., deer) before it is dead, bleeding should be attempted by severing the jugular veins on either *side* of the neck, making the cuts near the shoulder if the head is to be saved as a trophy. Bleeding should be done with the head as low as, or lower than, the rest of the body. After the animal is bled, the carcass should be shifted so that the head is uphill or, preferably, the carcass should be hung by the head from the branch of a tree. Some individuals immediately cut off the scent-glands (metatarsal glands) from inside the hind legs and sever and remove the testicles of male deer. This is done under the assumption that these organs taint the meat, but some authors have not found the removal of the scent glands to be necessary (Field et al. 1972, 1973 a,b). After placing the carcass with the head higher than the hindquarters, carefully make an incision in the belly immediately below the sternum. Insert the fingers into this opening and press back the viscera so the cut through the hide and belly wall may be extended to the anus. Extreme care should be taken not to cut the rumen, intestines, or the bladder because the contents of these organs will taint the meat. Extend the cut through the midline of the pelvis; a hatchet may be employed to cut through the pelvis if a stout knife is not available. Next, grasp the esophagus and trachea as close to the throat as possible, sever these 2 tubes and permit the viscera to roll downward by its own weight. It may be necessary to make cuts with the knife to free the viscera from the attachments to the body wall. In this way most of the viscera may be removed from the carcass intact, leaving the heart, liver, and lungs attached to the carcass. A deer dressed in this manner is usually referred to as "field dressed"; if the heart, liver, and lungs are removed also, the carcass is referred to as "hog dressed." Some hunters leave the heart and liver attached to the carcass but remove the lungs, slit the throat (after saving the mantle if a trophy is desired) and remove the remainder of the trachea and esophagus.

The body cavity should be wiped as *dry* as possible with dry cloths, grass, leaves, or any other available material. Water should not be used to clean out the body cavity unless the body is badly contaminated. Cleaning of the body cavity with dry materials is recommended because it is desired to have a "blood glaze" form on the inside of the body wall to seal these exposed surfaces. Next, prop open the body cavity with several sticks so that air may circulate freely, thus hastening the cooling of the carcass. If flies are present, the carcass should be draped with cheesecloth or other similar material to prevent flies from reaching and depositing their eggs on the exposed surfaces. A carcass prepared in this manner may be hung out-of-doors for several days in temperatures not to exceed 4° C to 7° C. Deer not eviscerated promptly may begin to decompose and bloat within 5 to 8 hours, even in cool weather.

Many individuals prefer not to skin their deer until it has aged for the proper period of time and is ready to cut up and store. They reason that the hide prevents drying out of the meat. All deer meat should be "aged"—held in storage at a temperature of 3° to 4° C; the time required to age various types of deer varies from 1 to 2 days for a young fawn, up to 7 to 10 days for an old buck. Such aging permits a breakdown of the meat tissues by enzymatic action which "tenderizes" the meat. Aging may be done in a home refrigerator (temperature about 4° C for cuts of deer up to the size of a hindquarter). The aging of the meat should be done before it is frozen for storage; meat will not age when frozen.

PRESERVING PLANT MATERIAL

The preservation of plant specimens is a problem which confronts most field biologists. The proper collection and preparation of plants is not difficult and does not require elaborate equipment.

Terrestrial Vascular Plants

The entire plant should be collected if possible, including stems, leaves, flowers, and underground parts. Specimens with flowers and/or fruits should be obtained since these usually are necessary for identification. Extra flowers (and fruits) for dissection are desirable, especially for few-flowered plants, to avoid sacrificing those of the specimen. If it is impractical to collect the entire plant (e.g., trees, shrubs, large herbs), take representative portions, particularly of leafy stems, flowers and/or fruits. Bark and wood samples often are desirable for woody plant collections. Unless the plants are rare, sufficient material or individuals of smaller plants should be collected to fill at least one folded newspaper sheet about 27.5 × 42.5 cm. A digging tool is needed to obtain underground plant parts. Clean the roots of as much soil debris as possible without causing breakage. Small pruning shears or clippers are desirable for collecting woody plants, although a sharp knife may be used. Coin envelopes are useful for collecting easily detached seeds and fruits.

Accuracy in recording field data is essential. A pocket-sized field notebook, preferably with a hard cover, should be used to record in pencil or water-proof ink the locality, habitat, date, and information such as abundance, flower color (which may fade or alter upon drying), growth habit, scent, and plant size (if entire plant not collected) for each collection. Each species collected at a given place and date is assigned a collection number, which is recorded in the notebook with the collection data, as well as on a tag placed on or with the specimen.

The collections should be placed in a plant press as soon as possible. However, since it is often impractical to carry a full-sized plant press, most plant collections may be handled temporarily in the field by using (1) a vasculum, (2) a large plastic bag, or (3) a field press (portfolio). Of these, a large plastic bag is the most conveniently carried in the field; but specimens are far more subject to damage, as well as to the heating effects of the sun's radiation, than when carried in a vasculum (a light-reflecting metal container, about 50 cm long and 12.5–20 cm in diameter, with a hinged lid extending most of its length). Moistened paper towel or newspaper may be laid in the bottom of the plastic bag or vasculum or wrapped around groups of collections to maintain a high internal humidity. Small plastic bags are useful to protect and keep plants of any one species collection together within a vasculum or large plastic bag.

A temporary field press (portfolio) is the most desirable method of handling plant collections in the field from the standpoint of producing quality specimens, ease of transferring specimens later to a regular press, and precision in recording field data. A field press is bulky and time consuming to handle in the field, and the number of specimens that can be collected during one field outing is limited. A field press consists of folded newspapers (27.5 × 42.5 cm) into which plants are placed after collection, plus alternate felt-paper driers, held tightly between a pair of firm wooden lattice-slat, plywood, or heavy cardboard frames (30 × 45 cm) by a rope or buckled straps. Specimens are arranged within the newspaper sheets as they would be in a plant press. Field data may be written directly on such sheets with a lead pencil, grease pencil, or waterproof felt pen rather than in a field notebook. A canvas or plastic covering for protection against rain, plus carrying handles, are desirable, and shoulder straps may be attached for backpacking.

Plants should be put into a regular plant press for drying as soon as possible. The specimens are carefully spread out within folded newspaper sheets. If a field press was used, the specimen-containing papers can be transferred directly to the regular press, but they should be reopened and the material rearranged if necessary. Only one species should be included in a single specimen-paper. The collection number should be written on the newspaper sheet in lead pencil, grease pencil, or waterproof felt pen.

Plants are arranged so that parts are largely nonoverlapping and all important characters show clearly. Excess foliage or branches may be trimmed, leaving sufficient material to show the branching pattern, leaf arrangement, inflorescence, and flowers. Leaves should be pressed in an unfolded position, with lower and upper surfaces visible. Tall plants may be bent in a V or zig-zag fashion. Before bending herbaceous stems, pinch the tissue to reduce the likelihood of breakage. When grasses and plants with numerous fine springy stems are bent to fit onto a specimen sheet, small paper tabs with center slits may be fitted over the folded corners of a group of such stems to hold them in place. Some overlapping of stems is acceptable for grass and grasslike plants.

Thick, fleshy roots, stems, fruits, and flower heads are split and laid open before pressing; fleshy fruits are preferably sliced to show both longitudinal and transverse sections. Larger flowers may be sectioned longitudinally to show parts when flattened. Very succulent plants, such as many cacti, are difficult to dry and should be split or sliced, sometimes with much of the internal pulpy tissue removed, and/or dipped in boiling water, alcohol, or benzene before pressing. Rolls of paper towel or sponges may be placed beside bulky parts (thick stems, large fruits) to maintain even pressure. Fruits over 1 cm in diameter, large-stemmed succulents, large cones, etc., are normally impossible to press and are preserved in a 3-dimensional state either in boxes or trays if dried or in liquid preservative. Tissue, lens paper or a thin, double layer of foam rubber may be placed below and above very delicate flowers when pressed. To avoid adhesion to the newspaper and possible destruction, place waxed paper on 1 side and white bond paper tabs on the other side of small fleshy fruits and viscid or deliquescent flowers. The paper tabs can be mounted with the specimen later.

Each specimen paper is "sandwiched" between heavy absorbent felt or blotter paper driers, and drier pairs are separated by corrugated cardboard ventilators. The specimen-papers, driers, and ventilators should measure about 30 × 45 cm and may be homemade or purchased from biological supply companies.

As successive specimen sheets are added to the press, care should be taken to keep the layers well aligned and the top level, for stability and equal distribution of pressue, by alternating the position of bulky parts such as roots.

A stack of specimen papers, separated by driers and ventilators and enclosed, top and bottom, by firm, wooden lattice-slat or solid plywood frames (30 × 45 cm) is placed under pressue by 2 or 3 buckled straps passed around the narrow dimensions of the plant press and tightened as much as possible. The plant press should be placed in a dry, warm spot. Retighten the press after a few hours, since the initial rapid loss of moisture may significantly reduce the press bulk and therefore its pressure. If the plants are being dried without artificial heat, open the press after about 24 hours (or in about 6 hours if the plants were wet or very succulent) and replace wet blotters with dry ones. This process is repeated at increasingly longer intervals until the blotters reveal little dampness. Plants should dry within about 1 week. Generally, when the thumb nail will no longer leave an imprint upon the plant tissue, the plants are dry enough to be removed from the press. Rapid moisture removal will minimize discoloration and deterioration (from fungal and bacterial activity) of the plant specimens. Artificial heat will greatly speed drying, but excessive heat may cause scorching or discoloration from a steaming effect. Heat damage usually can be prevented by maintaining air flow through the press. An electric fan-heater which directs warm air through the corrugated ventilators of a press is very effective, especially if the fan is adjusted to continuous high-speed. Plants can be dried in 12 to 24 hours by this method. If plants are being fast-dried with artificial heat, it is especially important that the press straps be tightened frequently, so that adequate pressue is maintained throughout the drying process (Keiser 1974).

Dried plant specimens should be removed from the press but retained within the numbered newspaper sheets during the identification process. Permanent labels should be typed or handwritten with permanent black ink on bond paper and should indicate the scientific name and authority, and collection data including location, habitat, date, other notes, collector's name, and number of the collection. Localities should be as specific as possible, and distances from easily located reference points should be indicated.

Plant specimens are mounted on stiff, high-rag, white, mounting paper, 28 × 44 cm. The label is placed in the lower right-hand corner, and the herbarium designation and accession number are placed in the lower left-hand corner. The specimens are arranged on the sheet in the most revealing and attractive way possible. Plastic glue obtainable from biological supply companies is most often used to attach the specimens, although white binding tape may be used, especially for woody plants. Small envelopes or packets can be affixed to the specimen sheet to hold detached seeds, flowers, fruits, and other parts. Conifer needles often will fall off upon drying, and these are usually put into a large envelope attached to the specimen sheet.

Plants mounted in this manner are known as herbarium specimens and usually are stored in folders on horizontal shelves of metal herbarium cabinets or in tight, wooden or cardboard boxes. Stored herbarium specimens are protected from insect damage with fumigants such as paradichlorobenzene or naphthalene crystals.

Plants or plant parts collected for detailed dissection of flowers or anatomical study of internal tissues may be preserved in AFA.

Bryophytes and Lichens

Bryophytes (mosses and liverworts) and lichens usually are preserved by drying, and usually can be handled similarly to vascular plants. Lichens and bryophytes should never be collected by cutting or scraping them from the substrate surface, but rather taken together with a thin substrate layer. Rock lichens and especially small fragile crustose lichens should be wrapped in tissue paper to keep them intact and secure. Specimens are normally collected in small paper bags or packets on which the collection numbers are written. The specimens may be bagged in habitat groups since it is not usually profitable for a nonexpert to attempt a separation of species in the field. It is preferable to collect mosses in "fruit" (capsular) stage, but limiting collections to these would usually result in missing most of the species present. Field data should include substrate type and microhabitat information such as shading and moisture conditions. The color of lichens in the field, especially of foliose types, should be noted, as it often changes upon drying.

It is not necessary to press lichens and bryophytes to preserve them by drying, but flattening is usually desirable for easier transportation, protection from breakage, and storage. Many specialists prefer that moss collections be dried unpressed in paper bags within larger cloth bags, so that individual species can be more easily separated in the laboratory. Unlike vascular plants, bryophytes and most lichens will regain their flexibility upon remoistening and can then be redried or pressed. Specimens dry and brittle from the field should be moistened before pressing. Bend over some foliose lichens to reveal the underside. A separate plant press is desirable since only minimum pressure is required for moss specimens. The weight of several large books evenly placed on the stack of ventilators and specimen-containing driers is sufficient pressure. Lichens can be more strongly flattened, need to be dried rapidly, and kept absolutely dry during storage.

Lichens and bryophytes are stored in easily opened packets of high quality bond paper (10 × 15 cm) with labels affixed to the upper flap. Crustose lichen specimens taken from rocks should be well wrapped in tissue paper before being placed in packets. The packets are either stored vertically in 10- × 15-cm card file drawers or attached to stiff herbarium sheets and stored horizontally.

Aquatic Plants

Aquatic plants present special problems in pressing related to (1) the flaccidity of the plants, (2) the finely divided or membranous leaves, and (3) the tendency to adhere strongly to the paper upon drying, primarily because of epiphytic diatoms and blue-green algae on surfaces. Before pressing, the plants may be placed in shallow water in a broad pan and manipulated under water to spread the stems and leaves. To avoid collapse of the flaccid plant parts upon removal from the water, a fine-mesh plastic screen is used to lift the plants from the water and transfer them onto white bond paper sheets placed in the folded newspapers of the press. The plants are then covered by a sheet of waxed paper. After drying, the waxed paper can usually be removed easily, and if the plants adhere to the white bond paper sheet, the entire sheet bearing the plant can be mounted. Glue may be added as needed to attach the specimen more firmly. Aquatic mosses may be handled similarly.

The macrophytic algae, including seaweeds and freshwater charophytes, can be preserved either in fluid, such as AFA, or by drying, using the technique described for aquatic vascular plants. Whole mature seaweeds, including the holdfast organs, should be collected, and they must never be kept wet long in a collecting bag or jar as they tend to mold rapidly. Very fleshy seaweeds should be soaked in an alcohol-formalin solution before pressing to prevent molding in the press. All macrophytic algae should be dried under considerable pressure.

The smaller, more delicate algae, whose identification depends much on individual cell characteristics, are normally preserved in fluid. Although AFA may be used, the following preserving-fluid is recommended, mixed in equal proportions to the water in which the algae are growing: iodine 0.5 g, potassium iodide 1.0 g, glacial acetic acid 4 cc, formalin 24 ml, and water 400 ml.

Phytoplankton collections may be concentrated by towing a net of fine bolting silk through the water, or a large volume of water can be left standing after addition of a small amount of formalin, and the bulk of the water poured off when the algae have settled.

Diatoms are identified largely by the markings of their outside silica walls and can be either pickled in preserving-fluid or dried. Identification of blue-green algae often requires chemical tests that cannot be performed on preserved material; therefore some should be dried on paper.

Fungi

Microscopic and macroscopic fungi can be preserved in fluid such as AFA, and most macroscopic fungi can be dried. Liquid preservative destroys the natural color and odor of mushrooms and other agarics that often are important for identification. Thus, unless excellent field notes are taken, drying is preferred. Complete specimens of macroscopic fungi should be collected, including the basal portion below the substrate. The specimens should be wrapped in waxed paper or newspaper to retard moisture loss, or the smaller specimens placed into envelopes or small boxes, and carefully packed in a vasculum, open basket, or box for carrying in the field. Collecting numbers should be affixed to each specimen. Direct contact of the specimens with moisture should be prevented, and they should never be enclosed in plastic bags.

Habitat data, including the kind of substrate or host, is recorded in the field. The specimens should be described fully in regard to color, texture, odor, size, and shape prior to preservation as these characteristics may change considerably upon drying. For mushrooms, describe not only the pileus (cap) top, but the stipe, annulus, gills, and internal flesh. It is necessary to obtain spore prints for the identification of many mushrooms. To make a spore print, (1) place the gill or pore surface flat on a sheet of white paper (cutting a hole in the paper for the stipe), (2) cover with a glass or jar or place in a large plastic bag to prevent air currents from moving the spores, (3) leave unmoved for several hours, (4) remove the spore print, (5) note and record its color when fresh, (6) dry it, and (7) fold and put in an envelope with the specimen.

Proper drying of mushrooms and other macroscopic fungi is critical. Small specimens are easily air-dried, but large, fleshy specimens require rapid drying to avoid decomposition. Rapid drying also helps to retain natural color and odor. Specimens usually are dried 3-dimensionally on screen shelves over an artificial dry heat source. Very large specimens may have to be split or sliced before drying. For efficient storage, macrophytic fungi may also be flattened somewhat in a plant press, but only moderate pressue should be used to avoid undue loss of shape and structure. Dry specimens can be resoftened in a high humidity chamber (but not directly in water) until pliable enough to be dissected.

Parasitic rusts, smuts, and most other pathogens of vascular plants are either collected with the host plant and dealt with as are these when being dried, or preserved in AFA.

Dried fungal specimens are permanently stored in packets, envelopes, or tight paper or tin boxes.

For additional information and techniques the reader is referred especially to Saville (1962), Anon. (1965), Smith (1971), and Knudsen (1972).

Larry Toschik

Appendix

Care of Captive Mammals

Compiled by
JOSEPH A. DAVIS
Brookfield Zoo
Brookfield, Illinois

GENERAL

Asdell, S. A. 1946. Patterns of mammalian reproduction. Comstock Publ. Co., Ithaca, N.Y. 537 p.

Ashbrook, F. G. 1928. Fur-farming for profit. Macmillan Co., New York. 300 p.

Crandall, L. S. 1964. The management of wild mammals in captivity. Univ. of Chicago Press. 769 p.

Davis, J. A. 1961. Red means go! Anim. Kingdom. 64(4):114–118.

Eaton, R. L., (ed.). 1977. The world's cats. Contributions to breeding biology, behavior, and husbandry. Vol. III, No. 3, Carnivore Res. Inst., Burke Museum, Univ. Washington, Seattle. 144 p.

Fowler, M. E. 1978. Restraint and handling of wild and domestic animals. Iowa State Univ. Press, Ames, Iowa. 332 p.

Hediger, H. 1964. Wild animals in captivity. Dover Publ. Inc., New York. 207 p.

Jennison, G. n.d. Table of gestation periods and number of young. A. & C. Black Ltd., London. 8 p.

Karsten, P. 1974. The manual restraint of zoo animals. IZY* 14:189–195.

Livers, T. H. 1973. The use of milk replacers for hand-rearing carnivores. IZY 13:211–213.

Markowitz, H., and V. Stevens, (eds.). 1978. Behavior of captive wild animals. Nelson-Hall Inc., Chicago. 320 p.

Morris, J. G., J. Fujimoto, and S. C. Berry. 1974. The comparative digestibility of a zoo diet fed to 13 species of felid and badger. IZY 14:169–171.

Pinder, N. J., and J. P. Barkham. 1978. An assessment of the contribution of captive breeding to the conservation of rare mammals. Biol. Conserv. 13:187–245.

Rabb, G. B. 1960. Longevity records for mammals at the Chicago Zoological Park. J. Mammal. 41(1):113–114.

Seal, U. S., D. G. Makey, and L. E. Murtfeldt. 1976. ISIS: an animal census system. IZY 16:180–184.

Simon, E. S. 1943. Life span of some wild animals in captivity. J. Bombay Nat. Hist. Soc. 44(1):117–118.

Ullrey, D. E. 1976. Feeding herbivores in the zoo. Amer. Ass. Zool. Parks Aquar. Nat., pp. 141–149.

Zoological Society of London. 1962. Small mammals in captivity. IZY 3:1–35.

Zoological Society of London. 1966. A 'symposium' of articles on the subject of the nutrition of animals in captivity. IZY 6:3–115.

Zoological Society of London. 1976. Principles of zoo animal feeding. IZY 16:1–70.

Zuckerman, S. 1953. The breeding seasons of mammals in captivity. Proc. Zool. Soc. London 122(4):827–950.

MARSUPIALIA

Calaby, J. H., and W. E. Poole. 1971. Keeping kangaroos in captivity. IZY 11:5–12.

Eisenberg, J. F., and E. Maliniak. 1967. Breeding the murine opossum, *Marmosa* sp., in captivity. IZY 7:78–79.

Gasking, W. R. 1965. Breeding kangaroos and wallabies in captivity. IZY 5:106–109.

Tuttle, J. 1973. A simple method of hand-rearing kangaroos. IZY 13:173–174.

Zoological Society of London. 1971. Marsupials in captivity. IZY 11:3–54.

INSECTIVORA

Eisenberg, J., and N. Muckenhirn. 1968. The reproduction and rearing of tenrecoid insectivores in captivity. IZY 8:106–110.

Eisenberg, J. F., and E. Maliniak. 1974. The reproduction of the genus *Microgale* in captivity. IZY 14:108–110.

Hellwing, S. 1973. Husbandry and breeding of white-toothed shrews in the research zoo of the Tel-Aviv University. IZY 13:127–134.

Erinaceidae

Edwards, J. T. G. 1957. The European hedgehog. *in* The UFAW Handbook on the care and management of laboratory animals. The Univ. Fed. for Anim. Welfare, London. 951 p.

Morris, B. 1966. Breeding the European hedgehog in captivity. IZY 6:141–146.

Soricidae

Conaway, C. H. 1958. Maintenance, reproduction and growth of the least shrew in captivity. J. Mammal. 39(4):507–512.

IZY* = International Zoological Yearbook

Crowcroft, P. 1951. Keeping British shrews in captivity. J. Mammal. 32(3):354–355.

Pearson, O. P. 1950. Keeping shrews in captivity. J. Mammal. 31(3):351–352.

Rood, J. P. 1958. Habits of the short-tailed shrew in captivity. J. Mammal. 39(4):499–507.

Rudd, R. L. 1953. Notes on maintenance and behavior of shrews in captivity. J. Mammal. 34(1):118–120.

Talpidae

Henning, W. L. 1952. Methods for keeping the eastern mole in captivity. J. Mammal. 33(3):392–395.

Tupaiidae

Hendrickson, J. R. 1954. Breeding the tree shrew. Nature 174(4434):794–795.

CHIROPTERA

Constantine, D. G. 1952. A program for maintaining the freetail bat in captivity. J. Mammal. 33(3):395–397.

Moshos, S. C. 1961. Bats as laboratory animals. Anat. Rec. 139(3):369–377.

Novick, A. 1960. Successful breeding in captive *Artibeus*. J. Mammal. 41(4):508–509.

Orr, R. T. 1958. Keeping bats in captivity. J. Mammal. 39(3):339–344.

Wimsatt, W. A., and A. Guerriere. 1961. Care and maintenance of the common vampire in captivity. J. Mammal. 42(4):449–454.

PRIMATES

General

Walker, E. P. 1954. The monkey book. Macmillan Co., New York. 153 p.

Prosimians

Basilewsky, G. 1965. Keeping and breeding Madagascan lemurs in captivity. IZY 5:132–137.

Catchpole, H. R., and J. F. Fulton. 1943. The oestrus cycle in *Tarsius:* observations on a captive pair. J. Mammal. 24(1):90–93.

Cook, N. 1939. Notes on captive *Tarsius carbonarius*. J. Mammal. 20(2):173–178.

Lowther, F. De L. 1940. A study of the activities of a pair of *Galago senegalensis moholi* in captivity, including the birth and postnatal development of twins. Zoologica 25(27):433–462.

Phillips, W. W. A. 1931. The food of the Ceylon slender loris *(Loris tardigradus)* in captivity. Spolia Zeylan. 16(2):205–208.

New World

Lindbergh, S. 1976. Natural social structures and feeding procedures in the acclimatisation of South American primates. IZY 16:146–149.

Lorenz, R., and W. A. Mason. 1971. Establishment of a colony of titi monkeys, *Callicebus moloch*. IZY 11:168–175.

Mallinson, J. 1965. Notes on the nutrition, social behaviour and reproduction of Hapalidae in captivity. IZY 5:137–140.

Stevenson, M. F. 1976. Maintenance and breeding of the common marmoset, *Callithrix jacchus*, with notes on hand-rearing. IZY 16:110–116.

Zoological Society of London. 1972. South American primates in captivity. IZY 12:3–68.

Old World

Hollihn, U. 1973. Remarks on the breeding and maintenance of Colobus monkeys, *Colobus guereza*, proboscis monkeys, *Nasalis larvatus*, and douc langurs, *Pygathrix nemaeus*, in zoos. IZY 13:185–188.

Pournelle, G. H. 1962. Observations on captive proboscis monkeys, *Nasalis larvatus*. IZY 3:69–70.

Wackernagel, H. 1977. Feeding of apes and monkeys at Basle Zoo. IZY 17:189–194.

EDENTATA

McCrane, M. 1966. Birth, behaviour and development of a hand-reared two-toed sloth, *Choloepus didactylus*. IZY 6:153–163.

Meritt, D. A., Jr. 1971. The silky anteater, *Cyclopes didactylus*, in captivity. IZY 11:193–195.

Meritt, D. A., Jr. 1976. The La Plata three-banded armadillo, *Tolypeutes matacus*, in captivity. IZY 16:153–156.

LAGOMORPHA

Davison, R. 1974. Adapting the Colorado pika, *Ochotona princeps saxatillis*, to captivity. IZY 14:161–163.

Dice, L. R. 1927. The Colorado pika in captivity. J. Mammal. 8(3):228–231.

Matthews, L. H. 1956. Breeding hares in captivity. Proc. Zool. Soc. London 126:161–163.

Severaid, J. H. 1945. Breeding potential and artificial propagation of the snowshoe hare. J. Wildl. Manage. 9(4):290–295.

RODENTIA

Sciuromorpha

Day, B. N., H. J. Egoscue, and A. M. Woodbury. 1956. Ord Kangaroo rat in captivity. Science 124 (3220): 485–486.

Hill, W. C. O. 1942. Note on the breeding of the Malabar giant squirrel *(Ratufa indica maxima)* in captivity. J. Bombay Nat. Hist. Soc. 43(3):521–522.

Romer, J. D. 1974. Notes on the care and breeding of tree squirrels, *Callosciurus* spp. IZY 14:115–116.

Myomorpha

de Kock, L. L. 1966. Breeding lemmings, *Lemmus lemmus*, for exhibition. IZY 6:164–165.

Egoscue, H. J. 1957. The desert woodrat: a laboratory colony. J. Mammal. 38(4):472–481.

Egoscue, H. J. 1960. Laboratory and field studies of the northern grasshopper mouse. J. Mammal. 41(1):99–110.

Eisenberg, J. F., and E. Maliniak. 1973. Breeding and captive maintenance of the lesser bamboo rat, *Cannomys badius*. IZY 13:204–207.

Poiley, S. M. 1949. Raising captive meadow voles *(Microtus p. pennsylvanicus)*. J. Mammal. 30(3):317–318.

Worth, C. B. 1950. Observations on the behavior and breeding of captive rice rats and wood rats. J. Mammal. 31(4):421–426.

Hystricomorpha

Collins, L. R., and J. F. Eisenberg. 1972. Notes on the behaviour and breeding of pacaranas, *Dinomys branickii*, in captivity. IZY 12:108–114.

Howe, R., and G. C. Clough. 1971. The Bahaman hutia, *Geocapromys ingrahami*, in captivity. IZY 11:89–93.

Maliniak, E., and J. F. Eisenberg. 1971. Breeding spiny rats, *Proechimys semispinosus*, in captivity. IZY 11:93–98.

Oliver, W. L. R. 1977. The hutias Capromyidae of the West Indies. IZY 17:14–20.

Zara, J. L. 1973. Breeding and husbandry of the capybara, *Hydrochoerus hydrochaeris*, at Evansville Zoo. IZY 13:137–139.

CARNIVORA

Canidae

Brambell, M. R. 1974. Breeding fennec foxes, *Fennecus zerda*, at London Zoo. IZY 14:117–118.

Fox, M. W. 1971. Behaviour of wolves, dogs and related canids. Harper and Row, New York. 220 p.

Zoological Society of London. 1968. Canids and felids in captivity. IZY 8:3–96.

Ursidae

Bloxam, Q. 1977. Breeding the spectacled bear, *Tremarctos ornatus*, at Jersey Zoo. IZY 17:158–161.

Fransen, D. R., and S. B. Emerson. 1973. Further notes on hand-raising bears, *Ursus arctos horribilis* and *Ursus arctos middendorffi*, at Los Angeles Zoo. IZY 13:143–145.

Hulley, J. T. 1976. Hand-rearing American black bear cubs at Toronto Zoo. IZY 16:202–205.

Nunley, L. 1977. Successful rearing of polar bears, *Thalarctos maritimus*, at Tulsa Zoo. IZY 17:161–164.

Procyonidae

Poglayen-Neuwall, I. 1973. Preliminary notes on maintenance and behavior of the Central American cacomistle, *Bassariscus sumichrasti*, at Louisville Zoo. IZY 13:207–211.

Mustelidae

Ashbrook, F. G., and K. B. Hanson. 1930. The normal breeding season and gestation period of martens. U S. Dept. Agric. Circ. 107. Washington, D.C. 7 p.

Bassett, C. F. 1957. The martens. *in* UFAW Handbook.

Bissonette, T. H., and E. E. Bailey. 1940. Den and runway system for weasels and other small mammals in the laboratory. Am. Midl. Nat. 24(3):761–763.

Desai, J. H. 1974. Observation on the breeding habits of the Indian smooth otter, *Lutrogale perspicillata*, in captivity. IZY 14:123–124.

Liers, E. E. 1951. Notes on the river otter *(Lutra canadensis)*. J. Mammal. 32(1):1–9.

Wayre, P. 1972. Breeding the Eurasian otter, *Lutra lutra*, at the Norfolk Wildlife Park. IZY 12:116–117.

Wright, P. L. 1942. Delayed implantation in the long-tailed weasel *(Mustela frenata)*, the short-tailed weasel *(M. cicognani)* and the marten *(Martes americana)*. Anat. Rec. 83:341–353.

Wright, P. L. 1948. Breeding habits of captive long-tailed weasels *(Mustela frenata)*. Am. Midl. Nat. 39(2):338–344.

Viverridae

Mallinson, J. J. C. 1973. The reproduction of the African civet, *Viverra civetta*, at Jersey Zoo. IZY 13:147–150.

Wemmer, C. 1971. Birth, development and behavior of a fanaloka, *Fossa fossa*, at the National Zoological Park, Washington, D.C. IZY 11:113–115.

Xanten, W. A., H. Kafka, and D. Olds. 1976. Breeding the binturong, *Arctictis binturong*, at the National Zoological Park, Washington. IZY 16:117–119.

Felidae

Barnes, R. G. 1976. Breeding and hand-rearing of the marbled cat, *Felis marmorata*, at the Los Angeles Zoo. IZY 16:205–208.

Birkenmeier, E., and E. Birkenmeier. 1971. Hand-rearing the leopard cat, *Felis bengalensis borneoensis*. IZY 11:118–121.

Hulley, J. T. 1976. Maintenance and breeding of captive jaguarundis, *Felis yagouroundi*, at Chester Zoo and Toronto. IZY 16:120–122.

Johnstone, P. 1977. Hand-rearing serval, *Felis serval*, at Mole Hall Wildlife Park. IZY 17:218–219.

Koivisto, I., C. Wahlberg, and P. Muuronen. 1977. Breeding the snow leopard, *Panthera uncia*, at Helsinki Zoo, 1967–1976. IZY 17:39–44.

Leyhausen, P. 1966. Breeding the Brazilian ocelot-cat, *Leopardus (=Felis) trigrinus*, in captivity. IZY 6:176–178.

Leyhausen, P., and B. Tonkin. 1966. Breeding the black-footed cat, *Felis nigripes*, in captivity. IZY 6:178–182.

Tennant, M. B., and S. J. Craig. 1977. Breeding cheetahs, *Acinonyx jubatus*, at the Lion Country Safari Parks: a summary. IZY 17:167–169.

Zoological Society of London. 1968. Canids and felids in captivity. IZY 8:3–96.

PINNIPEDIA

Harrison, R. J., L. H. Matthews, and J. M. Roberts. 1952. Reproduction in some Pinnipedia. Trans. Zool. Soc. London 27(5):437–540.

Otten, T., B. Andrews, and D. D. Edwards. 1977. Hand-rearing a California sea lion, *Zalophus californianus*. IZY 17:215–218.

Pournelle, G. H. 1962. Pacific walrus, *Odobenus rosmarus divergens*, at the San Diego Zoo. IZY 3:78–80.

Rigdon, R. H., and G. A. Drager. 1955. Thiamine deficiency in sea lions *(Otaria californiana)* fed only frozen fish. J. Am. Vet. Med. Assoc. 127(944):453–455.

TUBULIDENTATA

Kisling, V. N., Jr., and R. N. Sampsell. 1976. Aardvark diets and milk composition. IZY 16:164–165.

HYRACOIDEA

Mendelssohn, H. 1965. Breeding the Syrian hyrax. IZY 5:116–125.

SIRENIA

Bertram, G. C. L., and C. K. R. Bertram. 1977. The status and husbandry of manatees, *Trichechus* spp. IZY 17:106–108.

UNGULATES

Zoological Society of London. 1965. Ungulates in captivity. IZY 5:1–94.

Perissodactyla

Baker, A. B. 1920. Breeding of the Brazilian tapir. J. Mammal. 1(3):143–144.

Wilson, R. A., and S. Wilson. 1973. Diet of captive tapirs, *Tapirus* spp. IZY 13:213–217.

Young, W. A. 1962. Rearing an American tapir, *Tapirus terrestris*. IZY 3:94–95.

Artiodactyla

Bullermann, R. 1976. Breeding Dall sheep, *Ovis d. dalli*, at Milwaukee Zoo. IZY 16:126–129.

Davidson, A. 1974. Intensive care and re-introduction of neonatal ungulates. IZY 14:183–184.

Dolan, J. M. 1977. The saiga, *Saiga tatarica:* a review as a model for the management of endangered species. IZY 17:25–32.

Müller-Schwarze, D., and C. Müller-Schwarze. 1973. Behavioural development of hand-reared pronghorn, *Antilocapra americana*. IZY 13:217–220.

Romer, J. D. 1974. Milk analysis and weaning in the lesser Malay chevrotian, *Tragulus javanicus*. IZY 14:179–180.

Roots, C. G. 1966. Notes on the breeding of white-lipped peccaries, *Tayassu albirostris*, at Dudley Zoo. IZY 6:198–199.

Walther, F. 1962. The mating behaviour of certain horned animals. IZY 3:70–77.

Wayre, P. 1967. Artificial rearing of roe deer and fallow deer at Norfolk Wildlife Park. IZY 7:168–171.

Appendix

Care of Captive Birds

Compiled by

JOSEPH BELL
Curator, Department of Ornithology
Bronx Zoo
Bronx, New York

GENERAL

Block, M. 1969. Diets for soft-billed birds at Toledo Zoo. IZY 9:195–196.

Dolensek, E., and J. Bell. 1978. Help! A step-by-step manual for the care and treatment of oil-damaged birds. N.Y. Zool. Soc. 38 p.

Hickman, M., and M. Guy. 1973. Care of the wild feathered and furred. Unity Press, Santa Cruz, Calif. 143 p.

Jones, B. T. 1969. Controlling abnormal growth of bills of the American avocet and black-necked stilt, *Recurvirostra americana* and *Himantopus h. mexicanus*. IZY 9:196.

King, J. R., (chairman). 1977. Laboratory animal management: wild birds. Natl. Acad. Sci. Natl. Res. Council. 16 p.

Laughlin, P. A. 1977. Care and treatment of injured birds. Jack-Pine Warbler 55(2):69–75.

Martin, R. D., (ed.). 1975. Breeding endangered species in captivity. Academic Press. 420 p.

Muller, K. A. 1976. Maintaining insectivorous birds in captivity. IZY 16:32–38.

Serventy, D. L., D. S. Farner, and C. A. Nicholls. 1962. Trapping and maintaining shore birds in captivity. Bird-Banding 33(3):123–130.

Suthers, H. B. 1978. Raising altricial birds. N. Am. Bird Bander 3(4):157–159.

Williams, A. S., S. C. Brundage, E. Anderson, J. M. Harris, and D. C. Smith. 1978. Saving oiled birds. Inter. Bird Rescue Center, Berkeley, Calif. 35 p.

Struthionidae (Ostrich)

Dinnes, M. R. 1972. Medical aspects of an ostrich breeding programme, *Struthio camelus*. IZY 12:223–224.

Helfer, T. 1972. Artificial hatching and rearing of ostriches, *Struthio camelus*. IZY 12:132–133.

Rheidae (Rheas)

Bowthorpe, G., and G. Voss. 1968. Breeding the rhea and the emu, *Rhea americana* and *Dromiceius novaelhollandiae*, at Winnipeg Zoo. IZY 8:146–150.

Kruczek, R. 1968. Breeding Darwin's rheas, *Pterocnemia pennata*, at Brookfield Zoo, Chicago. IZY 8:150–153.

Casuariidae (Cassowaries)

Fisher, G. D. 1968. Breeding Australian cassowaries, *Casuarius casuarius*, at Edinburgh Zoo. IZY 8:153–156.

Worrell, E., B. Drake, and R. Krauss. 1975. Breeding the Australian cassowary, *Casuarius casuarius*, at the Australian Reptile Park, Gosford. IZY 15:94–97.

Apterygidae (Kiwis)

Caithness, T. A. 1971. Sexing kiwis, *Apteryx* spp. IZY 11:206–208.

Clayton, L. J. 1972. Breeding and behaviour of the kiwi, *Apteryx australis mantelli*, at Sydney Zoo. IZY 12:134–136.

Hallstrom, Sir E. 1967. Notes on breeding the kiwi, *Apteryx australis*, at Sydney Zoo. IZY 7:176.

Lint, K. C. 1966. Notes on the care and nutrition of Mantell's kiwi, *Apteryx australis mantelli*, at San Diego Zoo. IZY 6:95–96.

Spheniscidae (Penguins)

Best, A. 1967. Care of penguins during transport. IZY 7:23–25.

Davis, D. G. 1967. Keeping penguins in captivity: the penguin paradox. IZY 7:3–11.

Dekker, D. 1967. Keeping and breeding penguins at Amsterdam Zoo. IZY 7:25–27.

Fiennes, R. N. T.-W. 1967. Penguin pathology. IZY 7:11–14.

Lint, K. C. 1967. Care of penguins at San Diego Zoo. IZY 7:37–39.

Sasaki, T. 1967. Breeding and care of Humboldt's penguins, *Spheniscus humboldti*, at Kyoto Zoo. IZY 7:31–32.

Van den Sande, A. P. 1967. Acclimatisation of penguins. IZY 7:15–17.

Diomedeidae (Albatrosses)

Asper, E. D., and J. H. Prescott. 1970. Courtship and nesting of captive black-footed albatrosses, *Diomedea nigripes*. IZY 10:90–92.

Pelecanidae (Pelicans)

Dathe, H. 1961. Breeding the white pelican. IZY 3:95.

Dooley, R. E., and O. Heyland. 1969. Notes on breeding brown pelicans, *Pelecanus o. occidentalis*, at Houston Zoo. IZY 9:120–121.

Greichus, Y. A., A. Greichus, and D. J. Call. 1976. Care and growth of captive white pelicans. Avic. Mag. 82(3):139–142.

Sulidae (Boobies)

Pryor, K., and I. Kang. 1970. The colony of red-footed boobies, *Sula sula rubripes*, at Oahu Sea Life Park. IZY 10:92–95.

Ciconiidae (Storks)

Desai, J. H. 1971. Feeding ecology and nesting of the painted stork, *Ibis leucocephalus*, at Delhi Zoo. IZY 11:208–215.

Piekarz, R. 1965. Breeding white storks, *Ciconia ciconia*, at Warsaw Zoo. IZY 5:126–127.

Threskiornithidae (Ibises)

Mallet, M. 1976. Breeding the Waldrapp ibis, *Geronticus eremita*, at Jersey Zoo. IZY 16:143–145.

Risdon, D. H. S. 1971. Breeding the sacred ibis and the scarlet ibis, *Threskiornis aethiopica* and *Eudocimus ruber*, at the Tropical Bird Gardens, Rode. IZY 11:131–132.

Phoenicopteridae (Flamingos)

Berry, H. H. 1974. Hand-rearing abandoned lesser flamingos, *Phoeniconaias minor*. IZY 14:203–210.

Kear, J. 1974. Notes on keeping flamingos in captivity. IZY 14:142–144.

Kear, J. S., and N. Duplaix-Hall, (eds.). 1975. Flamingos. T. and A. D. Poyser, Ltd. Herfordshire, England. 246 p.

Klos, H.-G. 1969. A brief note on breeding flamingos at West Berlin Zoo. IZY 9:122.

Sprunt, A., and A. Crego-Bourne. 1974. The capture and transport of young Caribbean flamingos. IZY 14:64–66.

Anatidae (Waterfowl)

Humphreys, P. N. 1973. Some veterinary aspects of maintaining waterfowl in captivity. IZY 13:87–94.

Hyde, D. O., (ed.). 1974. Raising wild ducks in captivity. E. P. Dutton, New York 319 p.

Johnstone, S. T. 1973. Nesting places for waterfowl. IZY 13:27–28.

Kear, J. 1966. The food of geese. IZY 6:96–103.

Kear, J. 1973a. Fish for captive waterfowl. IZY 13:94–95.

Kear, J. 1973b. Notes on the nutrition of young waterfowl, with special reference to slipped-wing. IZY 13:97–100.

Kear, J. 1976. The presentation of food to captive waterfowl in relation to their natural behavior. IZY 16:25–32.

Lampson, B. 1973. First breeding of the long-tailed duck, *Clangula hyemalis*, in captivity. IZY 13:70–71.

Louwman, J. W. W., and W. G. van Oyen. 1969. A brief note on breeding the Cape Barren goose, *Cereopsis novaehollandie*, at Wassenaar Zoo. IZY 9:124–125.

Lubbock, M. R. 1973. The propagation and captive management of mergansers and buffleheads. IZY 13:72–77.

Lubbock, M. R. 1974. Capture and transport of waterfowl. IZY 14:61–63.

Marler, C. 1973. Breeding the black spur-winged goose, *Plectropterus gambensis niger*, and the black brant, *Branta bernicla orientalis*, at Flaming Gardens, Olney, IZY 13:58–59.

Murton, R. K., and J. Kear. 1973. The influence of daylight in the breeding of diving ducks. IZY 13:19–23.

Preuss, B. 1973. Breeding the whooper swan, *Cygnus cygnus cygnus*, at Rostock Zoo. IZY 13:41–43.

Ripley, S. D. 1973. Saving the wood duck, *Aix sponsa*, through captive breeding. IZY 13:55–58.

Siegfried, W. R. 1973. Post-embryonic development of the ruddy duck, *Oxyura jamaicensis*, and some other diving ducks. IZY 13:77–87.

Tillery, J. R. 1969. Notes on nesting and hatching behavior of trumpeter swans, *Cygnus c. buccinator*, at Great Bend Zoo. IZY 9:122–124.

Wurdinger, I. 1973. Breeding of bar-headed geese, *Anser indicus*, in captivity. IZY 13:43–47.

Cathartidae (New World Vultures)

Cuneo, F. 1967. Notes on breeding the king vulture, *Sarcoramphus papa*, at Naples Zoo. IZY 7:156–157.

Klos, H.-G. 1966. Hand-rearing a black vulture, *Coragyps atratus*, at West Berlin Zoo. IZY 6:105.

Klos, H.-G. 1973. Hand-rearing Andean condors, *Vultur gryphus*, at West Berlin Zoo. IZY 13:112.

Todd, F. S., and N. B. Gale. 1970. Further notes on the California condor, *Gymnogyps californianus*, at Los Angeles Zoo. IZY 10:15–17.

Accipitridae (Hawks, Eagles, Old World Vultures)

Bouillault, J. 1970. Breeding the griffon vulture, *Gyos fulvus*, at La Fleche Zoo. IZY 10:21–23.

Dathe, H. 1970. Observations on the breeding biology of Steller's sea eagle, *Haliaeetus pelagicus*, at East Berlin Zoo. IZY 10:19–21.

Fiedler, W. 1970. Breeding the white-tailed sea eagle, *Haliaeetus albicilla*, at Vienna Zoo. IZY 10:17–19.

Kawata, K. 1973. Notes on an American golden eagle, *Aquila chrysaetos canadensis*, hatched in captivity. IZY 13:114–115.

Kish, F. 1970. Egg laying and incubation by American golden eagles, *Aquila chrysaetos canadensis*, at Topeka Zoo. IZY 10:26–29.

Kish, F. 1972. First breeding by American golden eagles, *Aquila chrysaetos canadensis*, at Topeka Zoo. IZY 12:136–138.

Mendelssohn, H., and U. Marder. 1970. Problems of reproduction in birds of prey in captivity. IZY 10:6–11.

van Ee, C. A. 1961. Hand-rearing birds of prey. IZY 3:98.

Wayre, P. 1970. Breeding birds of prey and owls in the Norfolk Wildlife Park. IZY 10:5–6.

Wylie, S. R. 1973. Breeding the white-tailed sea eagle, *Haliaeetus albicilla*, at Kansas City Zoo. IZY 13:115–116.

Wylie, S. R. 1976. Breeding the Bateleur eagle, *Terathopius caudatus*, at the St. Louis Zoo. IZY 16:146–147.

Falconidae (Falcons)

Brisbin, I. L., Jr., and C. K. Wagner. 1970. Some health problems associated with the maintenance of American kestrels, *Falco sparverius*, in captivity. IZY 10:29–30.

Meyer-Holzapfel, M. 1970. Breeding kestrels, *Falco tinnunculus*, at Berne Zoo. IZY 10:30–31.

Cracidae (Curassows, Guans, etc.)

Ollson, M. 1976. Captive propagation of curassows Cracidae. IZY 16:147–150.

Turnicidae (Button-quails)

Bell, J., and D. Bruning. 1974. Hand rearing Hemipodes at the New York Zoological Park. IZY 14:196–198.

Gruidae (Cranes)

Archibald, G. W. 1974. Methods for breeding and rearing cranes in captivity. IZY 14:147–155.

Conway, W. G. 1961. Egg replacement by a pair of Sarus cranes, *Grus antigone antigone* L., at New York Zoological Park. IZY 5:129.

Muller-Langenbeck, G. 1971. Notes on hand-rearing a Stanley crane, *Anthropoides paradisea*, at Hanover Zoo. IZY 11:136.

Nakayama, T. 1967. A note on breeding white-necked cranes, *Grus vipio*, at Ueno Zoo, Tokyo. IZY 7:177–178.

Sauey, R. T., and B. Brown. 1977. The captive management of cranes. IZY 17:89–92.

Weber, E. 1974. Breeding the Australian crane, *Grus rubicunda*, at Melbourne Zoo. IZY 14:94–96.

Wylie, S. R. 1970. Observations on the successful breeding and rearing of Sarus cranes, *Grus antigone*, in captivity. IZY 10:99–100.

Zimmerman, D. R. 1978. A technique called cross-fostering may help save the whooping crane. Smithsonian 9(6):52–63.

Rallidae (Rails)

Bowes, T. E. 1974. Breeding the Cayenne wood rail, *Aramides cajanea*. Avic. Mag. 80(2):57–58.

Brown, P. B. 1974. Breeding the Ypecha wood rail at Harwood Bird Garden. Avic. Mag. 80(1):11–13.

Stalheim, P. S. 1975. Breeding behavior of captive yellow rails, *Coturnicops noveboracensis*. Avic. Mag. 81(3):133–141.

Otididae (Bustards)

Gewalt, W. 1962. Breeding the great bustard, *Otis tarda*, in captivity. IZY 4:92–93.

Gewalt, W. 1965. First successful captive breeding of the great bustard, *Otis tarda*, at West Berlin Zoo. IZY 5:129–130.

Recurvirostridae (Avocets, Stilts)

Bell, J., and D. Bruning. 1969. Breeding the European avocet in the New York Zoological Park, *Recurvirostra avosetta*. Avic. Mag. 75(7):251–255.

Goss-Custard, J. D., P. Wilkins, and J. Kear. 1971. Rearing wading birds in captivity. Avic. Mag. 77(1):113–114.

Poulsen, H. 1965. Breeding stilts, *Himantopus* sp., at Copenhagen Zoo. IZY 5:130–131.

Alcidae (Auks)

Conway, W. G., J. Bell, D. Bruning, and E. Dolensek. 1977. Care and breeding of puffins and murres Alcidae at the New York Zoological Park. IZY 17:173–176.

Columbidae (Pigeons, Doves)

Goodwin, D. 1966. Keeping doves and pigeons: some suggestions. Avic. Mag. 72(4):96–106.

Psittacidae (Parrots)

Berry, R. J. 1974. Successful breeding of the St. Vincent parrot, *Amazona guildingii*, at Houston Zoo. IZY 14:96–97.

de Silveira, E. K. P. 1970. Notes on the mating and breeding of macaws, *Ara* spp. and *Anodorhynchus hyacinthinus*, at Brasilia Zoo. IZY 10:100–101.

Dolton, K. W. 1974. Breeding the thick-billed parrot, *Rhynchopsitta pachyrhyncha*. Avic. Mag. 80(2):56.

Dyson, R. F. 1969. Captive hatching and development of a thick-billed parrot, *Rhynchopsitta pachyrhyncha*, at Arizona-Sonora Desert Museum. IZY 9:127–129.

Schmidt, C. R. 1971. Breeding keas, *Nestor notabilis*, at Zurich Zoo. IZY 11:137–140.

Small, R. C. 1975. Nesting and hand-raising of the Hyacinthine macaw, *Anodorhynchus hyancinthinus*. Avic. Mag. 81(2):90–93.

Strigidae (Typical Owls)

Goodman, A., and E. J. Fish. 1973. Breeding behavior of captive striped owls, *Rhinoptynx clamator*. Avic. Mag. 79(5):158–162.

Muller, K. A. 1970. Exhibiting and breeding elf owls, *Micrathene whitneyi*, at Washington National Zoological Park. IZY 10:33–36.

Poulsen, H. 1962. Breeding the snowy owl, *Nyctea scandiaca*, at Copenhagen Zoo. IZY 4:93–94.

Scherzinger, W. 1975. Breeding European owls. Avic. Mag. 81(2):70–73.

Yealland, J. J. 1970. Breeding owls at London Zoo. IZY 10:31–32.

Trochilidae (Hummingbirds)

Lint, K. C. 1966. Hummingbird diets and hummingbird aviary at San Diego Zoo. IZY 6:103–104.

Rongren, B. 1972. On hand-rearing nestling hummingbird chicks; observations on behavior and maturation. Avic. Mag. 78(6):202–205.

Shingler, R. J. P. 1969. Hand-rearing white-breasted hummingbirds, *Amazilia c. chinonopectus*, at Port-of-Spain Zoo. IZY 9:131–132.

Alcedinidae (Kingfishers)

Birkenmeier, E. 1969. Breeding the malachite kingfisher, *Corythornis cristata*, in captivity. IZY 9:132–134.

Weber, E. 1971. Breeding kookaburras, *Decelo novaeguineae*, at Melbourne Zoo. IZY 11:143–144.

Widman, W. F. and H. M. Vorous. 1961. Hatching and rearing of kookaburas at the Washington National Zoological Park, IZY 3:96–97.

Bucerotidae (Hornbills)

Encke, W. 1970. Breeding the red-billed hornbill, *Tockus erythrorhynchus*, at Krefeld Zoo. IZY 10:101–102.

Harvey, P. M. 1973. Breeding the casqued hornbill at "Birdworld." Avic. Mag. 79(1):23–25.

Pipridae (Manakins)

Olney, P. J. 1973. Breeding the blue-backed manakin, *Chiroxiphia pareola*, at London Zoo. Avic. Mag. 79(1):1–3.

Olney, P. J. 1974. First breeding of the blue-backed manakin, *Chiroxiphia pareola*, in captivity. IZY 14:105–106.

Turdidae (Thrushes)

Pinkowski, B. C. 1975. Behavior and breeding of the mountain bluebird in captivity. Avic. Mag. 81(1):15–22.

Drepanidae (Hawaiian Honeycreepers)

Eddinger, C. R. 1971. Hand-rearing Hawaii's endemic honeycreepers. Avic. Mag. 77(4):113–114.

Abbreviations

IZY—International Zoo Yearbook
The Zoological Society of London
Regent's Park
London NW1 4RY

Avic. Mag.—The Journal of the Avicultural Society
Warren & Son, Ltd. (Publisher)
Winchester

APPENDIX TABLE I.

Common and scientific (binomial only) names of North American birds mentioned in text (A.O.U. Committee 1957).

Common Name	Scientific Name	Order	Family
Auk, Great	*Pinguinus impennis*	Charadriiformes	Alcidae
Bittern, American	*Botaurus lentiginosus*	Ciconiiformes	Ardeidae
Blackbird, Brewer's	*Euphagus cyanocephalus*	Passeriformes	Icteridae
Red-winged	*Agelaius phoeniceus*	Passeriformes	Icteridae
Rusty	*Euphagus carolinus*	Passeriformes	Icteridae
Tri-colored	*Agelaius tricolor*	Passeriformes	Icteridae
Yellow-headed	*Xanthocephalus xanthocephalus*	Passeriformes	Icteridae
Bluebird, Eastern	*Sialia sialis*	Passeriformes	Turdidae
Mountain	*Sialia currucoides*	Passeriformes	Turdidae
Western	*Sialia mexicana*	Passeriformes	Turdidae
Bobwhite,	*Colinus virginianus*	Galliformes	Phasianidae
Masked Bobwhite	*Colinus virginianus ridgwayi*	Galliformes	Phasianidae
Brant, Black	*Branta nigricans*	Anseriformes	Anatidae
Bufflehead	*Bucephala albeola*	Anseriformes	Anatidae
Canvasback	*Aythya valisineria*	Anseriformes	Anatidae
Cardinal	*Richmondena cardinalis*	Passeriformes	Fringillidae
Chickadee, Black-capped	*Parus atricapillus*	Passeriformes	Paridae
Chicken, Prairie, Greater	*Tympanuchus cupido*	Galliformes	Tetraonidae
Lesser	*Tympanuchus pallidicinctus*	Galliformes	Tetraonidae
Condor, California	*Gymnogyps californianus*	Falconiformes	Cathartidae
Coot, American	*Fulica americana*	Gruiformes	Rallidae
Cormorant, Double-crested	*Phalacrocorax auritus*	Pelecaniformes	Phalacrocoracidae
Cowbird, Brown-headed	*Molothrus ater*	Passeriformes	Icteridae
Crane, Sandhill	*Grus canadensis*	Gruiformes	Gruidae
Crow, Common	*Corvus brachyrhynchos*	Passeriformes	Corvidae
Cuckoo	*Coccyzus* sp.	Cuculiformes	Cuculidae
Dove, Mourning	*Zenaida macroura*	Columbiformes	Columbidae
Rock (Domestic pigeon)	*Columba livia*	Columbiformes	Columbidae
White-winged	*Zenaida asiatica*	Columbiformes	Columbidae
Duck, Black	*Anas rubripes*	Anseriformes	Anatidae
Black-bellied whistling	*Dendrocygna autumnalis*	Anseriformes	Anatidae
Fulvous whistling	*Dendrocygna bicolor*	Anseriformes	Anatidae
Harlequin	*Histrionicus histrionicus*	Anseriformes	Anatidae
Redhead	*Aythya americana*	Anseriformes	Anatidae
Ring-necked	*Aythya collaris*	Anseriformes	Anatidae
Ruddy	*Oxyura jamaicensis*	Anseriformes	Anatidae
Wood	*Aix sponsa*	Anseriformes	Anatidae
Eagle, Bald	*Haliaeetus leucocephalus*	Falconiformes	Accipitridae
Golden	*Aquila chrysaetos*	Falconiformes	Accipitridae

APPENDIX TABLE I.

(Cont.)

Common Name	Scientific Name	Order	Family
Eider, Common	*Somateria mollisima*	Anseriformes	Anatidae
King	*Somateria spectabilis*	Anseriformes	Anatidae
Spectacled	*Lampronetta fischeri*	Anseriformes	Anatidae
Steller's	*Polysticta stelleri*	Anseriformes	Anatidae
Falcon, Peregrine	*Falco peregrinus*	Falconiformes	Falconidae
Prairie	*Falco mexicanus*	Falconiformes	Falconidae
Finch, House	*Carpodacus mexicanus*	Passeriformes	Fringillidae
Flamingo, American	*Phoenicopterus ruber*	Ciconiiformes	Phoenicopteridae
Flicker, Yellow-shafted	*Colaptes auratus*	Piciformes	Picidae
Flycatcher, Great-crested	*Myiarchus crinitus*	Passeriformes	Tyrannidae
Gadwall	*Anas strepera*	Anseriformes	Anatidae
Gallinule, Common	*Gallinula chloropus*	Gruiformes	Rallidae
Purple	*Porphyrula martinica*	Gruiformes	Rallidae
Goose, Canada	*Branta canadensis*	Anseriformes	Anatidae
Ross'	*Chen rossii*	Anseriformes	Anatidae
Snow	*Chen hyperborea*	Anseriformes	Anatidae
White-fronted	*Anser albifrons*	Anseriformes	Anatidae
Goldeneye, Barrow's	*Bucephala islandica*	Anseriformes	Anatidae
Common	*Bucephala clangula*	Anseriformes	Anatidae
Goshawk	*Accipiter gentilis*	Falconiformes	Accipitridae
Grackle, Common	*Quiscalus quiscula*	Passeriformes	Icteridae
Grouse, Blue	*Dendragapus obscurus*	Galliformes	Tetraonidae
Franklin spruce	*Canachites canadensis franklinii*	Galliformes	Tetraonidae
Ruffed	*Bonasa umbellus*	Galliformes	Tetraonidae
Sage	*Centrocercus urophasianus*	Galliformes	Tetraonidae
Sharp-tailed	*Pedioecetes phasianellus*	Galliformes	Tetraonidae
Gull, California	*Larus californicus*	Charadriiformes	Laridae
Glaucous-winged	*Larus glaucescens*	Charadriiformes	Laridae
Herring	*Larus argentatus*	Charadriiformes	Laridae
Hawk, Ferruginous	*Buteo regalis*	Falconiformes	Accipitridae
Red-tailed	*Buteo jamaicensis*	Falconiformes	Accipitridae
Swainson's	*Buteo swainsoni*	Falconiformes	Accipitridae
Heron, Great blue	*Ardea herodias*	Ciconiiformes	Ardeidae
Jacana	*Jacana spinosa*	Charadriiformes	Jacanidae
Kestrel (Sparrow hawk)	*Falco tinnunculus*	Falconiformes	Falconidae
Kite, Everglade	*Rostrhamus sociabilis*	Falconiformes	Accipitridae
Magpie, Black-billed	*Pica pica*	Passeriformes	Corvidae
Mallard	*Anas platyrhynchos*	Anseriformes	Anatidae
Martin, Purple	*Progne subis*	Passeriformes	Hirundinidae
Merganser	*Mergus merganser*	Anseriformes	Anatidae
Nuthatch, Pygmy	*Sitta pygmaea*	Passeriformes	Sittidae
Osprey	*Pandion haliaetus*	Falconiformes	Accipitridae
Owl, Barn	*Tyto alba*	Strigiformes	Tytonidae
Burrowing	*Athene cunicularia*	Strigiformes	Strigidae
Great gray	*Strix nebulosa*	Strigiformes	Strigidae
Great horned	*Bubo virginianus*	Strigiformes	Strigidae
Saw-whet	*Aegolius acadicus*	Strigiformes	Strigidae
Screech	*Otus asio*	Strigiformes	Strigidae
Snowy	*Nyctea scandiaca*	Strigiformes	Strigidae
Spotted	*Strix occidentalis*	Strigiformes	Strigidae
Partridge, Chukar	*Alectoris chukar graeca*	Galliformes	Phasianidae
Hungarian (Gray)	*Perdix perdix*	Galliformes	Phasianidae
Phalarope, Wilson's	*Steganopus tricolor*	Charadriiformes	Phalaropodidae
Pheasant, Ring-necked	*Phasianus colchicus*	Galliformes	Phasianidae
Phoebe	*Sayornis phoebe*	Passeriformes	Tyrannidae
Pigeon, Band-tailed	*Columba fasciata*	Columbiformes	Columbidae

APPENDIX TABLE I.

(Cont.)

Common Name	Scientific Name	Order	Family
Pintail	*Anas acuta*	Anseriformes	Anatidae
Plover, Upland	*Bartramia longicauda*	Charadriiformes	Scolopacidae
Ptarmigan, Rock	*Lagopus mutus*	Galliformes	Tetraonidae
White-tailed	*Lagopus leucurus*	Galliformes	Tetraonidae
Willow (Red grouse)	*Lagopus lagopus*	Galliformes	Tetraonidae
Quail, California	*Lophortyx californicus*	Galliformes	Phasianidae
Coturnix	*Coturnix coturnix*	Galliformes	Phasianidae
Gambel's	*Lophortyx gambelii*	Galliformes	Phasianidae
Mearn's (Harlequin)	*Cyrtonyx montezumae*	Galliformes	Phasianidae
Mountain	*Oreortyx pictus*	Galliformes	Phasianidae
Scaled	*Callipepla squamata*	Galliformes	Phasianidae
Valley	(see California Quail)		
Rail, Black	*Laterallus jamaicensis*	Gruiformes	Rallidae
Clapper	*Rallus longirostris*	Gruiformes	Rallidae
King	*Rallus elegans*	Gruiformes	Rallidae
Sora	*Porzana carolina*	Gruiformes	Rallidae
Virginia	*Rallus limicola*	Gruiformes	Rallidae
Yellow	*Coturnicops noveboracensus*	Gruiformes	Rallidae
Raven, White-necked	*Corvus cryptoleucus*	Passeriformes	Corvidae
Robin	*Turdus migratorius*	Passeriformes	Turdidae
Sapsucker	*Sphyrapicus* sp.	Piciformes	Picidae
Scaup, Greater	*Aythya marila*	Anseriformes	Anatidae
Lesser	*Aythya affinis*	Anseriformes	Anatidae
Scoter, American	*Oidemia nigra*	Anseriformes	Anatidae
Surf	*Melanitta perspicillata*	Anseriformes	Anatidae
White-winged	*Melanitta deglandi*	Anseriformes	Anatidae
Shoveler	*Anas clypeata*	Anseriformes	Anatidae
Snipe, Common	*Capella gallinago*	Charadriiformes	Scolopacidae
Sparrow, Harris'	*Zonotrichia querula*	Passeriformes	Fringillidae
House	*Passer domesticus*	Passeriformes	Ploceidae
Song	*Melospiza melodia*	Passeriformes	Fringillidae
Tree	*Spizella arborea*	Passeriformes	Fringillidae
White-crowned	*Zonotrichia leucophrys*	Passeriformes	Fringillidae
Starling	*Sturnus vulgaris*	Passeriformes	Sturnidae
Swallow, Barn	*Hirundo rustica*	Passeriformes	Hirundinidae
Tree	*Iridoprocne bicolor*	Passeriformes	Hirundinidae
Violet-green	*Tachycineta thalassina*	Passeriformes	Hirundinidae
Swan, Mute	*Cygnus olor*	Anseriformes	Anatidae
Trumpeter	*Olor buccinator*	Anseriformes	Anatidae
Whistling	*Olor columbianus*	Anseriformes	Anatidae
Teal, Blue-winged	*Anas discors*	Anseriformes	Anatidae
Cinnamon	*Anas cyanoptera*	Anseriformes	Anatidae
Green-winged	*Anas crecca carolinensis*	Charadriiformes	Anatidae
Thrasher, Brown	*Toxostoma rufum*	Passeriformes	Mimidae
Towhee, Rufous-sided	*Pipilo erythrophthalmus*	Passeriformes	Fringillidae
Vulture, Turkey	*Cathartes aura*	Falconiformes	Cathartidae
Woodcock, American	*Philohela minor*	Charadriiformes	Scolopacidae
Woodpecker, Downy	*Dendrocopos pubescens*	Piciformes	Picidae
Golden-fronted	*Centaurus aurifrons*	Piciformes	Picidae
Hairy	*Dendrocopos villosus*	Piciformes	Picidae
Red-bellied	*Melanerpes carolinus*	Piciformes	Picidae
Ivory-billed	*Campephilus principalis*	Piciformes	Picidae
Red-cockaded	*Dendrocopos borealis*	Piciformes	Picidae
Red-headed	*Melanerpes erythrocephalus*	Piciformes	Picidae
Three-toed	*Piciodes* sp.	Piciformes	Picidae
Warbler, Kirtland's	*Dendroica kirtlandii*	Passeriformes	Parulidae
Prothonotary	*Protonotaria citrea*	Passeriformes	Parulidae

APPENDIX TABLE I.

(Cont.)

Common Name	Scientific Name	Order	Family
Wigeon, American (Baldpate)	*Mareca americana*	Anseriformes	Anatidae
Wren, Bewick's	*Thryomanes bewickii*	Passeriformes	Troglodytidae
Carolina	*Thryomanes ludovicianus*	Passeriformes	Troglydytidae
House	*Troglodytes aedon*	Passeriformes	Troglodytidae

APPENDIX TABLE II.

Common and scientific names of North American mammals mentioned in text (Jones et al. 1975).

Common Name	Scientific Name	Order	Family
Antelope, Pronghorn	*Antilocapra americana*	Artiodactyla	Antilocapridae
Armadillo, Nine-banded	*Dasypus novemcinctus*	Edentata	Dasypodidae
Badger	*Taxidea taxus*	Carnivora	Mustelidae
Bat, Gray	*Myotis grisescens*	Chiroptera	Vespertilionidae
Hoary	*Lasiurus cinereus*	Chiroptera	Vespertilionidae
Indiana	*Myotis sodalis*	Chiroptera	Vespertilionidae
Bear, Black	*Ursus americanus*	Carnivora	Ursidae
Brown	*Ursus arctos*	Carnivora	Ursidae
Grizzly	*Ursus arctos*	Carnivora	Ursidae
Polar	*Ursus maritimus*	Carnivora	Ursidae
Beaver	*Castor canadensis*	Rodentia	Castoridae
Mountain	*Aplodontia rufa*	Rodentia	Aplodontidae
Bison (Buffalo)	*Bison bison*	Artiodactyla	Bovidae
Bobcat	*Lynx rufus*	Carnivora	Felidae
Caribou	*Rangifer tarandus*	Artiodactyla	Cervidae
Chipmunk, Eastern	*Tamias striatus*	Rodentia	Sciuridae
Red-tailed	*Eutamias ruficaudus*	Rodentia	Sciuridae
Cottontail, Eastern	*Sylvilagus floridanus*	Lagomorpha	Leporidae
Cougar, (see Lion, Mountain)			
Coyote	*Canis latrans*	Carnivora	Canidae
Deer, Black-tailed (mule deer)	*Odocoileus hemionus*	Artiodactyla	Cervidae
Columbian	*Odocoileus hemionus*	Artiodactyla	Cervidae
Sitka Black-tailed	*Odocoileus hemionus*	Artiodactyla	Cervidae
White-tailed	*Odocoileus virginianus*	Artiodactyla	Cervidae
Elk (Wapiti)	*Cervus elaphus*	Artiodactyla	Cervidae
Ferret, Black-footed	*Mustela nigripes*	Carnivora	Mustelidae
Fisher	*Martes pennanti*	Carnivora	Mustelidae
Fox, Gray	*Urocyon cinereoargenteus*	Carnivora	Canidae
Kit	*Vulpes macrotis*	Carnivora	Canidae
Red	*Vulpes vulpes*	Carnivora	Canidae
Swift	*Vulpes velox*	Carnivora	Canidae
Goat, Mountain	*Oreamnos americanus*	Artiodactyla	Bovidae
Gopher, Pocket	*Geomys, Thomomys* spp.	Rodentia	Geomyidae
Ground Hog (see Woodchuck)			
Ground Squirrel, Arctic	*Spermophilus parryii*	Rodentia	Sciuridae
California	*Spermophilus beecheyi*	Rodentia	Sciuridae
Uinta	*Spermophilus armatus*	Rodentia	Sciuridae
Hare, European	*Lepus europaeus*	Lagomorpha	Leporidae
Snowshoe (Varying)	*Lepus americanus*	Lagomorpha	Leporidae
Jackrabbit, Black-tailed	*Lepus californicus*	Lagomorpha	Leporidae
White-tailed	*Lepus townsendii*	Lagomorpha	Leporidae
Lion, Mountain	*Felis concolor*	Carnivora	Felidae

APPENDIX TABLE II.

(Cont.)

Common Name	Scientific Name	Order	Family
Lynx	*Lynx lynx*	Carnivora	Felidae
Marmot	*Marmota* sp.	Rodentia	Sciuridae
Marten (Pine)	*Martes americana*	Carnivora	Mustelidae
Mink	*Mustela vison*	Carnivora	Mustelidae
Moose	*Alces alces*	Artiodactyla	Cervidae
Mouse, Deer	*Peromyscus maniculatus*	Rodentia	Cricetidae
Grasshopper	*Onychomys* sp.	Rodentia	Cricetidae
House	*Mus musculus*	Rodentia	Muridae
Meadow Jumping	*Zapus hudsonius*	Rodentia	Zapodidae
Pine	*Microtus pinetorum*	Rodentia	Cricetidae
White-footed	*Peromyscus leucopus*	Rodentia	Cricetidae
Muskox	*Ovibos moschatus*	Artiodactyla	Bovidae
Muskrat	*Ondatra zibethicus*	Rodentia	Cricetidae
Nutria	*Myocastor coypus*	Rodentia	Capromyidae
Opossum	*Didelphis virginiana*	Marsupialia	Didelphidae
Otter, River	*Lutra canadensis*	Carnivora	Mustelidae
Peccary, Collared (Javelina)	*Dicotyles tajacu*	Artiodactyla	Tayassuidae
Pig, Wild	*Sus scrofa*	Artiodactyla	Suidae
Pika	*Ochotona* sp.	Lagomorpha	Ochotonidae
Porcupine	*Erethizon dorsatum*	Rodentia	Erethizontidae
Prairie dog, Black-tailed	*Cynomys ludovicianus*	Rodentia	Sciuridae
White-tailed	*Cynomys leucurus*	Rodentia	Sciuridae
Pronghorn (see Antelope)			
Puma (see Mt. Lion)			
Rabbit, Marsh	*Sylvilagus palustris*	Lagomorpha	Leporidae
Swamp	*Sylvilagus aquaticus*	Lagomorpha	Leporidae
Raccoon	*Procyon lotor*	Carnivora	Procyonidae
Rat, Cotton	*Sigmodon* sp.	Rodentia	Cricetidae
Kangaroo	*Dipodomys* sp.	Rodentia	Heteromyidae
Norway	*Rattus norvegicus*	Rodentia	Muridae
Pack	*Neotoma* spp.	Rodentia	Cricetidae
Roof	*Rattus rattus*	Rodentia	Muridae
Wood	*Neotoma* spp.	Rodentia	Cricetidae
Rockchuck	*Marmota flaviventris*	Rodentia	Sciuridae
Seal, Bearded	*Erignathus barbatus*	Pinnepedia	Phocidae
Northern Elephant	*Mirounga angustirostris*	Pinnepedia	Phocidae
Northern fur	*Callorhinus ursinus*	Pinnepedia	Otariidae
Ringed	*Phoca hispida*	Pinnepedia	Phocidae
Sheep, Dall's	*Ovis dalli*	Artiodactyla	Bovidae
Rocky Mountain Bighorn	*Ovis canadensis*	Artiodactyla	Bovidae
Skunk, Spotted	*Spilogale* sp.	Carnivora	Mustelidae
Striped	*Mephitis mephitis*	Carnivora	Mustelidae
Squirrel, Abert's (Tassel-eared)	*Sciurus aberti*	Rodentia	Sciuridae
Flying	*Glaucomys* sp.	Rodentia	Sciuridae
Fox	*Sciurus niger*	Rodentia	Sciuridae
Gray	*Sciurus carolinensis*	Rodentia	Sciuridae
Ground	*Spermophilus* sp.	Rodentia	Sciuridae
Red	*Tamiasciurus hudsonicus*	Rodentia	Sciuridae
Vole, Pine	*Microtus pinetorum*	Rodentia	Cricetidae
Prairie	*Microtus ochrogaster*	Rodentia	Cricetidae
Townsend's	*Microtus towsendii*	Rodentia	Cricetidae
Wapiti (see Elk)			
Weasel, Long-tailed	*Mustela frenata*	Carnivora	Mustelidae
Wolverine	*Gulo gulo*	Carnivora	Mustelidae
Woodchuck	*Marmota monax*	Rodentia	Sciuridae

APPENDIX TABLE III.

Common and scientific names of non-North American mammals mentioned in the text (Walker et al. 1964).

Common Name	Scientific Name	Order	Family
Aoudad	*Ammotragus lervia*	Artiodactyla	Bovidae
Baboon	*Chaeropithecus* sp.	Primates	Cercopithecidae
Boar, European	*Sus scrofa*	Artiodactyla	Suidae
Brush-tailed possum	*Trichosurus vulpecula*	Marsupialia	Phalangeridae
Chimpanzee	*Pan troglodytes*	Primates	Pongidae
Deer, Fallow	*Dama dama*	Artiodactyla	Cervidae
Musk	*Moschus moschiferus*	Artiodactyla	Cervidae
Red	*Cervus elaphus*	Artiodactyla	Cervidae
Roe	*Capreolus capreolus*	Artiodactyla	Cervidae
Eland	*Taurotragus oryx*	Artiodactyla	Bovidae
Elephant, African	*Loxodonta africana*	Proboscidea	Elephantidae
Gazelle, Grant's	*Gazella granti*	Artiodactyla	Bovidae
Thomson's	*Gazella thomsoni*	Artiodactyla	Bovidae
Giraffe	*Giraffa camelopardalis*	Artiodactyla	Giraffidae
Grison	*Galictis cuja*	Carnivora	Mustelidae
Hartebeest	*Alcelaphus* sp.	Artiodactyla	Bovidae
Hippopotamus	*Hippopotamus amphibius*	Artiodactyla	Hippopotamidae
Hyena, Spotted	*Crocuta crocuta*	Carnivora	Hyaenidae
Impala	*Aepyceros melampus*	Artiodactyla	Bovidae
Kangaroo	*Macropus* sp.	Marsupialia	Macropodidae
Kob, Uganda	*Kobus kob*	Artiodactyla	Bovidae
Kudu, Lesser	*Tragelaphus imberbis*	Artiodactyla	Bovidae
Lion	*Panthera leo*	Carnivora	Felidae
Oryx	*Oryx gazella*	Artiodactyla	Bovidae
Rhesus monkey	*Macaca mulatta*	Primates	Cercopithecidae
Rhinoceros, Black	*Diceros bicornis*	Perissodactyla	Rhinocerotidae
Ricefield rat, Phillipine	*Rattus rattus mindanensis*	Rodentia	Muridae
Tiger	*Panthera tigris*	Carnivora	Felidae
Topi	*Damaliscus* sp.	Artiodactyla	Bovidae
Waterbuck	*Kobus defassa*	Artiodactyla	Bovidae
Wart hog	*Phacochoerus aethiopicus*	Artiodactyla	Suidae
Wildebeest	*Connochaetes taurinus*	Artiodactyla	Bovidae
Zebra	*Equus* spp.	Perissodactyla	Equidae

APPENDIX TABLE IV.

Common and scientific names of plants mentioned in text (Scott and Wasser 1979).

COMMON NAME	SCIENTIFIC NAME
Alder, Red	*Alnus rubra*
Alfalfa	*Medicago sativa*
Anise	*Pimpinella* sp.
Arborvitae, Eastern	*Thuja occidentalis*
Asafetida	*Ferula* sp.
Aspen, Bigtooth	*Populus grandidentata*
Aspen, Quaking	*Populus tremuloides*
Balsamroot	*Balsamorhiza* sp.
Basswood	*Tilia americana*
Beech, American	*Fagus grandifolia*
Bentgrass, Redtop	*Agrostis alba*
Bitterbrush, Antelope	*Purshia tridentata*
Bittersweet, American	*Celastrus scandens*
Blackbrush	*Coleogyne* sp.
Blueberry	*Vaccinium* spp.
Bluestem, Big	*Andropogon gerardi*
Little	*Andropogon scoparius*
Bulrush,	*Scirpus* sp.
Bulrush, Alkali	*Scirpus paludosus*
Burnet, Small	*Sanguisorba minor*
Cattail	*Typha* sp.
Cedar, Red	*Juniperus virginiana*
Cherry, Black	*Prunus serotina*
Clover, Alsike	*Trifolium hybridum*
Clover, Bush	*Trifolium* sp.
Rabbitfoot	*Trifolium arvense*

APPENDIX TABLE IV.

(Cont.)

COMMON NAME	SCIENTIFIC NAME	COMMON NAME	SCIENTIFIC NAME
Red	*Trifolium pratense*	Locust, Black	*Robinia pseudoacacia*
Sweet	*Melilotus* sp.	Lupine	*Lupinus* sp.
White	*Trifolium repens*	Magnolia	*Magnolia* sp.
Coontail	*Ceratophyllum* sp.	Mahogany, True Mountain	*Cercocarpus montanus*
Cottonwood	*Populus* spp.	Manzanita	*Arctostaphylos* sp.
Cowparsnip, Common	*Heracleum lanatum*	Maple, Red	*Acer rubrum*
Crownvetch	*Coronilla varia*	Sugar	*Acer saccharum*
Dogwood, Flowering	*Cornus florida*	Milkvetch	*Astragalus* spp.
Red-Osier	*Cornus stolonifera*	Millet, Wild (Common barnyard grass)	*Echinochloa crusgalli*
Douglas-fir	*Pseudotsuga menziesii*	Oak, Live	*Quercus virginiana*
Duckpotato (Arrowhead)	*Sagittaria* sp.	Nuttall	*Quercus nuttallii*
Duckweed	*Lemna* spp.	Pin	*Quercus palustris*
Elder	*Sambucus* sp.	Red (Northern)	*Quercus rubra*
Elm, American	*Ulmus americana*	Willow	*Quercus phellos*
Fir, Balsam	*Abies balsamea*	Olive, Autumn	*Elaeagnus umbellata*
Grape, Wild	*Vitis* sp.	Russian	*Elaeagnus angustifolia*
Grass, Blue	*Poa* sp.	Pea, Siberian	*Caragana arborescens*
Bluebunch Wheat	*Agropyron spicatum*	Penstemon	*Penstemon* sp.
Brome	*Bromus* sp.	Pine, Pinyon	*Pinus edulis*
Canary	*Phalaris* sp.	Ponderosa	*Pinus ponderosa*
Crab	*Digitaria sanguinalis*	White (eastern)	*Pinus strobus*
Crested Wheat	*Agropyron cristatum*	(western)	*Pinus monticola*
Dropseed, Sand	*Sporobolus cryptandrus*	Pondweed	*Potamogeton* sp.
Fescue, Tall	*Festuca arundinacea*	Redroot pigweed (Knot-weed, Smartweed)	*Polygonum* sp.
Foxtail	*Alopecurus* sp.	Reedgrass, Pine	*Calamagrostis rubescens*
Grama, Sideoats	*Bouteloua curtipendula*	Rice, Wild	*Zizania* sp.
Indian	*Sorghastrum* sp.	Rose, Japanese	*Rosa multiflora*
Indian Rice	*Oryzopsis hymenoides*	Rye, Mountain	*Secale montanum*
Intermediate Wheat	*Agropyron intermedium*	Winter	*Secale* sp.
Kentucky Blue	*Poa pratensis*	Sagebrush, Big	*Artemisia tridentata*
Orchard	*Dactylis glomerata*	Saltbush, Fourwing	*Atriplex canescens*
Rice Cut	*Leersia oryzoides*	Sassafras	*Sassafras albidum*
Salt	*Distichlis* sp.	Sedge	*Carex* sp.
Squirreltail, Bottlebrush	*Sitanion hystrix*	Smartweed	*Polygonum* sp.
Sudan	*Sorghum sudanense*	Snowberry	*Symphoricarpos* sp.
Switch	*Panicum virgatum*	Sorghum	*Sorghum* sp.
Western Wheat	*Agropyron smithii*	Spikerush	*Eleocharis* sp.
Wool (Bulrush)	*Scirpus cyperinus*	Strawberry	*Fragaria* sp.
Greenbrier	*Smilax* sp.	Summercypress	*Kochia* sp.
Gum, Black Tupelo	*Nyssa sylvatica*	Thornapple (Hawthorne)	*Crataegus* sp.
Sweet	*Liquidambar styraciflua*	Timothy	*Phleum* sp.
Hackberry	*Celtis occidentalis*	Trefoil, Birdsfoot	*Lotus corniculatus*
Hemlock	*Tsuga* sp.	Valerian	*Valeriana* sp.
Hickory	*Carya* sp.	Walnut, Black	*Juglans nigra*
Holly	*Ilex* sp.	Wildrye, Russian	*Elymus junceus*
Hophornbeam	*Ostrya virginiana*	Willow	*Salix* sp.
Iris, Bulbous	*Iris* sp.	Winterfat	*Eurotia* sp.
Juniper, Rocky Mountain	*Juniperus scopulorum*		
Lespedeza, Korean	*Lespedeza stipulacea*		

APPENDIX TABLE V.

Hatching success of game birds, compiled by D. E. Davis and Sanford D. Schemnitz. Only studies that record at least 50 nests are included, and the reference cited gives only the senior author's name. Investigators are urged to refer to the original publication for additional data. Since data on nesting success vary greatly with time and place, the following list may be considered only approximation of true values. The data listed below have been checked but errors creep into tabulations of this type; the editor will be pleased to be notified of any errors. Asterisk (*) indicates data not given.

			Hatching		Success	
Species	Place	Reference	No. of eggs	Percent of eggs hatching	No. of nests	Percent of successful nests
Canada Goose	Mont.	Atwater, '59	72	29.9	*	*
Canada Goose	Illinois	Kossack, '50	927	56.6	96	*
Canada Goose	Wyo.	Craighead, '49	*	*	88	23.9
Canada Goose	Utah	Williams, '37	410	80.6	95	*
Canada Goose	Calif.	Dow, '43	*	*	170	52.5
Canada Goose	Calif.	Dow, '43	*	*	248	60.0
Canada Goose	Calif.	Naylor, '53	1904	82.6	360	68.5
Canada Goose	Calif.	Miller, '53	810	87.0	201	78.6
Canada Goose	Calif.	Naylor, '54	432	85.2	117	71.0
Canada Goose	Calif.	Collins, '53	*	*	201	17.8
Canada Goose	Mont.	Geis, '56	1221	88.4	383	57.5
Canada Goose	Alaska	Mickelson, '73	*	*	911	68.2
Canada Goose	N.W.T.	MacInnes, '74	*	*	418	88.5
Canada Goose	Alberta	Vermeer, '70	400	83.5	178	41.6
Canada Goose	Alaska	Trainer, '59	*	*	519	76 3
Canada Goose	Wyo.	Dimmick, '68	*	*	134	62.0
Canada Goose	Wash.	Hanson, '71	14796	88.7	3824	70.0
White-fronted Goose	Alaska	Mickelson, '73	*	*	77	84.4
Lesser Snow Goose	N.W.T.	Barry, '66	*	*	14000	88.7
Lesser Snow Goose	Canada	Ryder, '71	*	*	124	86.2
Greater Snow Goose	N.W.T.	Lemieux, '59	*	*	52	67.3
Ross' Goose	N.W.T.	Ryder, '67	351	93.7	*	*
Ross' Goose	N.W.T.	Ryder, '67	230	79.2	*	*
Ross' Goose	Canada	Ryder, '70	1791	88.0	*	*
Ross' Goose	Canada	Hanson, '56	*	*	260	97.7
Emperor Goose	Alaska	Eisenhauer, '72	*	*	152	81.6
Emperor Goose	Alaska	Eisenhauer, '72	*	*	166	90.9
Emperor Goose	Alaska	Mickelson, '73	*	*	81	88.9
Mallard	Utah	Williams, '37	1582	60.0	185	59.0
Mallard	Calif.	Earl, '50	417	49.4	60	52.0
Mallard	Mont.	Girard, '41	1793	71.2	*	*
Mallard	U.S.A.	Kalmbach, '37	*	*	188	55.7
Mallard	Calif.	Miller, '54	1622	91.4	209	85.2
Mallard	Calif.	Hunt, '55	*	*	206	51.5
Mallard	Calif.	Anderson, '56	*	*	510	12.7
Mallard	Calif.	Anderson, '57	616	83.4	161	38.5
Gadwall	N. Dak.	Duebbert, '66	1755	83.6	179	89.9
Gadwall	Calif.	Miller, '54	3834	94.2	381	90.3
Gadwall	Utah	Williams, '37	6000	85.0	660	71.0
Pintail	Calif.	Hunt, '55	*	*	98	39.8
Pintail	Utah	Williams, '37	969	82.0	135	65.0
Pintail	U.S.A.	Kalmbach, '37	*	*	52	48.0
Blue-winged Teal	Iowa	Bennett, '38	*	*	223	57.0
Blue-winged Teal	U.S.A.	Kalmbach, '37	*	*	76	22.4
Blue-winged Teal	Mont.	Girard, '41	888	71.8	107	*
Blue-winged Teal	Minn.	Lee, '64	*	*	257	35.0
Blue-winged Teal	Iowa	Glover, '56	*	*	359	21.45

APPENDIX TABLE V.

(Cont.)

Species	Place	Reference	Hatching: No. of eggs	Hatching: Percent of eggs hatching	Success: No. of nests	Success: Percent of successful nests
Cinnamon Teal	Utah	Williams, '37	2655	84.0	326	62.0
Cinnamon Teal	Calif.	Hunt, '55	*	*	147	55.8
Shoveller	Mont.	Girard, '39	1135	69.7	107	*
Wood Duck	Iowa	Leopold, '51	868	80.0	63	*
Wood Duck	Mass.	McLaughlin, '52	12180	83.5	1427	64.3
Wood Duck	N.H.	Lacaillade, '58	386	91.3	69	60.9
Wood Duck	N.H.	Lee, '54	888	84.6	115	64.3
Florida Duck	Florida	Stieglitz, '68	*	*	93	74.0
Mottled Duck	Texas	Singleton, '53	*	*	108	28.0
Black Duck	Md.	Stotts, '60	1091	94.4	574	38.0
Redhead	Utah	Williams, '37	2651	26.0	212	62.0
Redhead	Iowa	Low, '45	*	*	160	56.2
Redhead	Iowa	Low, '45	827	80.7	122	*
Redhead	Mont.	Lokemoen, '66	57	14.0	138	15.2
Redhead	Calif.	Miller, '54	*	*	60	45.0
Ring-necked Duck	Maine	Mendall, '58	*	*	189	68.3
Lesser Scaup	U.S.A.	Kalmbach, '37	*	*	94	47.8
Greater Scaup	Finland	Hilden, '64	*	*	137	87.0
Bufflehead	B.C.	Erskine, '72	1297	93.0	193	78.8
Barrow's Goldeneye	Iceland	Bengtson, '72	*	*	246	75.0
Common Goldeneye	Finland	Grenquist, '63	1554	50.6	*	*
Common Goldeneye	Minn.	Johnson, '67	*	*	80	62.5
Canvasback	Manitoba	Kiel, '54	*	*	77	77.0
Canvasback	Manitoba	Olson, '64	*	*	131	21.0
Canvasback	Manitoba	Stoudt, '65	*	*	707	45.0
Canvasback	Manitoba	Trauger, '74	*	*	111	2.7
Canvasback	Saskatchewan	Stoudt, '71	*	*	233	65.0
Oldsquaw	Manitoba	Alison, '72	383	80.4	95	59.0
Black Brant	Alaska	Mickelson, '73	211	80.6	821	73.7
Northern Eider	N.W.T.	Cooch, '65	1758	81.8	*	*
Spectacled Eider	Alaska	Dau, '74	*	*	213	73.0
Common Eider	Canada	Guignion, '67	*	*	538	32.0
Common Eider	N.W.T.	Cooch, '65	2043	82.0	*	*
Common Eider	Maine	Choate, '67	*	*	1030	37.7
Common Eider	Maine	Paynter, '51	462	27.6	134	29.1
Red-breasted Merganser	Finland	Hilden, '64	*	*	67	88.0
Hooded Merganser	N. Dak.	Morse, '69	459	92.2	55	80.0
Ruddy Duck	Iowa	Low, '41	546	69.4	71	73.2
Marsh Hawk	N. Dak.	Hammond, '49	303	57.8	60	71.6
Osprey	Md.	Reese, '65	374	48.9	154	60.4
Osprey	N.Y.	Singer, '74	*	*	60	25.0
Screech Owl	Ohio	Van Camp, '75	1949	94.0	511	86.1
Gray Partridge	Mich.	Yeatter, '34	361	76.0	*	*
Gray Partridge	Wisc.	McCabe, '46	1838	84.5	*	*
Hungarian Partridge	England	Lack, '47	57202	90.4	*	*
Hungarian Partridge	England	Middleton, '35	*	*	7251	78.0
Hungarian Partridge	England	Middleton, '35	59825	93.0	4090	*
Hungarian Partridge	Wisc.	McCabe, '46	*	*	435	32.0
Hungarian Partridge	Wisc.	Gates, '73	*	*	69	16.0
Hungarian Partridge	Wash.	Yocom, '43	*	*	68	32.5
Hungarian Partridge	Wash.	Knott, '43	*	*	113	37.1

APPENDIX TABLE V.

(Cont.)

Species	Place	Reference	Hatching		Success	
			No. of eggs	Percent of eggs hatching	No. of nests	Percent of successful nests
Bobwhite Quail	Wisc.	Errington, '33	*	*	53	50.9
Bobwhite Quail	Texas	Parmalee, '55	*	*	59	62.9
Bobwhite Quail	Tenn.	Dimmick, '74	*	*	232	38.8
Bobwhite Quail	Iowa	Klimstra, '50	184	91.8	92	28.3
Bobwhite Quail	Illinois	Klimstra, '57	2086	90.0	264	39.4
California Quail	N.Z.	Williams, '67	343	89.8	59	62.6
California Quail	Calif.	Glading, '38	*	*	83	24.8
Ring-necked Pheasant	Penn.	Randall, '41	*	*	310	20.3
Ring-necked Pheasant	Wash.	Buss, '50	*	*	63	27.0
Ring-necked Pheasant	Oreg.	Eklund, '42	*	*	145	44.8
Ring-necked Pheasant	Iowa	Baskett, '47	*	*	75	36.0
Ring-necked Pheasant	Iowa	Baskett, '47	*	*	140	25.0
Ring-necked Pheasant	Iowa	Baskett, '47	689	82.4	318	23.2
Ring-necked Pheasant	Iowa	Baskett, '47	1319	83.0	533	25.5
Ring-necked Pheasant	Nebr.	Baxter, '73	*	*	1276	13.6
Ring-necked Pheasant	Wisc.	Gates, '75	2901	91.0	2338	30.0
Ring-necked Pheasant	Iowa	Klonglan, '53	*	*	162	17.3
Ring-necked Pheasant	Iowa	Hamerstrom, '36	723	82.3	64	*
Ring-necked Pheasant	Iowa	Hamerstrom, '36	*	*	232	19.0
Ring-necked Pheasant	Iowa	Hamerstrom, '36	*	*	445	23.1
Ring-necked Pheasant	Iowa	Hamerstrom, '36	*	*	139	37.4
Ring-necked Pheasant	Colo.	Yeager, '51	*	*	333	65.0
Ring-necked Pheasant	Minn.	Erickson, '51	*	*	241	28.6
Ring-necked Pheasant	Mich.	English, '41	*	*	193	35.0
Ring-necked Pheasant	Wisc.	Errington, '37	1000	78.9	126	71.3
Ring-necked Pheasant	Minn.	Carlson, '43	*	*	90	30.0
Ring-necked Pheasant	Ohio	Strode, '41	*	*	358	72.0
Ring-necked Pheasant	Wisc.	Buss, '46	*	*	350	29.9
Ring-necked Pheasant	Ont.	Ball, '52	777	73.5	230	32.1
Ring-necked Pheasant	Iowa	Weston, '53	*	*	72	18.0
Sage Grouse	Wyo.	Patterson, '52	*	*	216	38.4
Sage Grouse	Utah	Rasmussen, '38	*	*	98	62.2
Sage Grouse	U.S.A.	Hickey, '55	*	*	533	42.2
Blue Grouse	Alberta	Boag, '66	137	81.8	*	*
Blue Grouse	B.C.	Zwickel, '67a	323	78.0	*	*
Blue Grouse	Alberta	Zwickel, '75	379	95.0	122	56.6
Sharp-tailed Grouse	Utah	Hart, '50	*	*	127	32.3
Sharp-tailed Grouse	Nebr.	Sisson, '76	324	92.0	56	55.0
Sharp-tailed Grouse	Mich. & Wisc.	Ammann, '57	136	88.2	176	40.0
Greater Prairie Chicken	Mich. & Wisc.	Ammann, '57	343	90.9	165	46.0
Ruffed Grouse	N.Y.	Bump, '47	5392	95.6	*	*
Ruffed Grouse	N.Y.	Bump, '47	480	92.0	1431	61.4
Ruffed Grouse	Minn.	Kupa, '66	646	67.0	68	83.0
Rock Ptarmigan	Alaska	Weeden, '64	*	*	101	64.8
Rock Ptarmigan	Alaska	Weeden, '64	393	94.0	86	65.0
Rock Ptarmigan	Scotland	Watson, '65	147	90.0	*	*
Rock Ptarmigan	Alaska	Weeden, '65	393	94.0	86	65.0
Willow Ptarmigan	Scotland	Jenkins, '63	2464	84.0	395	80.3
Willow Ptarmigan	U.S.A.	Hickey, '55	*	*	232	69.0
Clapper Rail	Va.	Stewart, '51	*	*	79	94.0
Clapper Rail	N. Jersey	Kozicky, '49	513	87.3	56	89.3
American Coot	Manitoba	Kiel, '55	1394	99.0	380	97.0

APPENDIX TABLE V.

(Cont.)

Species	Place	Reference	Hatching: No. of eggs	Hatching: Percent of eggs hatching	Success: No. of nests	Success: Percent of successful nests
American Coot	Calif.	Hunt, '55	*	*	163	96.5
American Coot	Iowa	Fredrickson, '69	*	*	161	88.0
Mourning Dove	Georgia	Hopkins, '53	*	*	66	49.0
White-winged Dove	Texas	Kiel, '56	10295	40.2	*	*

APPENDIX TABLE VI.

Clutch size of game and predatory birds, compiled by D. E. Davis and Sanford D. Schemnitz. Only data from investigations including at least 25 complete clutches are included. Reference cites only the senior author. These data have been checked but the editor would be pleased to know of any errors. Refer to the original paper for more details. Asterisk (*) indicates standard deviation not given by author.

Species	Place	Reference	Number of clutches	Mean	Standard deviation
Canada Goose	Calif.	Miller, '53	158	5.13	1.35
Canada Goose	Mont.	Geis, '56	358	5.34	1.31
Canada Goose	Idaho	Steel, '57	189	5.2	*
Canada Goose	Alberta	Vermeer, '70	135	5.53	*
Canada Goose	N.W.T.	MacInnes, '74	430	4.27	*
Canada Goose	Alaska	Mickelson, '73	1038	4.27	*
Canada Goose	Wyo.	Dimmick, '68	114	5.2	*
Canada Goose	Wash.	Hanson, '71	2688	5.5	*
White-fronted Goose	Alaska	Lensink, '69	301	4.75	*
Greater Snow Goose	N.W.T.	Lemieux, '59	118	4.6	*
Lesser Snow Goose	Alaska	Uspenskii, '66	645	3.27	*
Ross' Goose	Canada	Ryder, '70	597	3.7	*
Emperor Goose	Alaska	Eisenhauer, '72	710	4.83	*
Atlantic Brant	Canada	Barry, '62	835	3.9	*
Black Brant	Alaska	Mickelson, '73	58	3.63	*
Black Brant	N.W.T.	Barry, '66	700	3.92	*
Brant	N.W.T.	Barry, '56	203	3.97	1.00
Mallard	Calif.	Hunt, '55	108	8.5	*
Mallard	Calif.	Miller, '54	178	9.2	*
Mallard	Manitoba	Dzubin, '72	111	8.6	*
Mallard	Manitoba	Dzubin, '72	55	7.2	*
Mallard	Vermont & Maine	Coulter, '68	131	9.6	1.85
Black Duck	Vermont & Maine	Coulter, '68	620	9.5	1.56
Black Duck	Md.	Stotts, '60	360	9.1	1.84
American Wigeon	Mont.	Girard, '41	45	9.5	*
Florida Duck	Florida	Stieglitz, '68	78	9.5	*
Pintail	Calif.	Hunt, '55	40	7.2	*
Pintail	Calif.	Miller, '54	41	9.2	*
Pintail	Manitoba	Sowls, '55	45	9.0	*
Blue-winged Teal	Manitoba	Sowls, '55	54	10.6	*
Blue-winged Teal	Minn.	Lee, '64	126	10.3	*
Blue-winged Teal	Iowa	Glover, '56	87	8.0	*
Blue-winged Teal	Manitoba	Dane, '66	145	10.75	*
Cinnamon Teal	Utah	Spencer, '53	104	8.9	*
Cinnamon Teal	Calif.	Miller, '54	32	10.7	*

APPENDIX TABLE VI.

(Cont.)

Species	Place	Reference	Number of clutches	Mean	Standard deviation
Cinnamon Teal	Calif.	Hunt, '55	76	9.3	*
Gadwall	Calif.	Miller, '54	344	11.1	*
Gadwall	N. Dak.	Duebbert, '66	130	9.6	*
Shoveler	Alberta	Keith, '61	585	9.4	*
Shoveler	Calif.	Miller, '54	35	11.1	*
Wood Duck	Mass.	McLaughlin, '52	664	13.6	4.82
Wood Duck	Alabama	Besheārs, '74	232	13.45	*
Wood Duck	N.H.	Lacaillade, '58	42	9.2	*
Wood Duck	N.H.	Lee, '54	74	11.98	*
Redhead	Calif.	Miller, '54	27	13.8	*
Greater Scaup	N.W.T.	Trauger, '75	93	9.0	*
Greater Scaup	N.W.T.	Weller, '69	49	7.8	*
Greater Scaup	Iceland	Bengtson, '71	1409	9.73	*
Lesser Scaup	Saskatchewan	Townsend, '66	94	9.0	*
Bufflehead	B.C.	Erskine, '72	263	8.75	*
Common Goldeneye	Minn.	Moyle, '64	39	10.2	*
Barrow's Goldeneye	Iceland	Bengtson, '71	293	10.37	*
Canvasback	Alberta	Smith, '71	118	7.4	*
Canvasback	Saskatchewan	Stoudt, '71	172	8.2	*
Ruddy Duck	Iowa	Low, '41	71	8.1	*
Ring-necked Duck	Maine	Mendall, '58	423	9.04	1.45
Oldsquaw	Manitoba	Alison, '72	95	6.8	*
Oldsquaw	Iceland	Bengtson, '71	212	7.9	*
White-winged Scoter	Finland	Hilden, '64	187	8.43	*
Black Scoter	Iceland	Bengtson, '71	187	8.7	*
King Eider	Canada	Hanson, '56	53	4.92	*
Northern Eider	N.W.T.	Cooch, '65	1598	3.44	*
Common Eider	N.W.T.	Cooch, '65	188	4.06	*
Common Eider	Canada	Freeman, '70	536	4.5	*
Common Eider	Maine	Gross, '38	110	3.25	1.05
Common Eider	Quebec	Lewis, '39	1131	4.04	1.01
Red-breasted Merganser	Finland	Hilden, '64	144	9.23	*
Red-breasted Merganser	Iceland	Bengtson, '71	158	9.5	*
Hooded Merganser	Oreg.	Morse, '69	55	10.2	*
Common Merganser	Finland	Hilden, '64	35	9.37	*
Marsh Hawk	U.S.A.	Hammond, '49	60	5.05	0.76
Sparrow Hawk	Oreg.	Roest, '57	60	4.73	0.63
Osprey	Md.	Reese, '65	154	2.3	*
Red-tailed Hawk	Alberta	Luttich, '71	68	2.1	*
Screech Owl	Ohio	Van Camp, '75	91	4.43	*
Bobwhite Quail	Tenn.	Dimmick, '74	233	11.9	*
Bobwhite Quail	Illinois	Klimstra, '57	264	13.2	*
Bobwhite Quail	Texas	Parmalee, '55	59	12.9	*
California Quail	New Zealand	Williams, '67	103	13.7	*
Gambel's Quail	Arizona	Gorsuch, '34	42	11.5	*
Scaled Quail	Oklahoma	Schemnitz, '61	39	12.7	*
Greater Prairie Chicken	Wisc.	Hamerstrom, '39	66	12.0	*
Spruce Grouse	Alaska	Ellison, '74	26	7.54	1.48
Spruce Grouse	Nova Scotia	Tufts, '61	39	5.8	*
Sharp-tailed Grouse	Wisc.	Hamerstrom, '39	36	12.1	*
Sharp-tailed Grouse	Utah	Hart, '50	127	11.0	*
Sharp-tailed Grouse	Nebr.	Sisson, '76	28	11.6	*
Sage Grouse	Utah	Rasmussen, '38	161	6.82	*
Sage Grouse	Wyo.	Patterson, '52	154	7.39	*
Blue Grouse	B.C.	Zwickel, '67a	51	6.3	*

APPENDIX TABLE VI.

(Cont.)

Species	Place	Reference	Number of clutches	Mean	Standard deviation
Blue Grouse	Alberta	Zwickel, '75	118	6.37	*
Ruffed Grouse	Minn.	Kupa, '66	99	9.9	*
Ruffed Grouse	N.Y.	Bump, '47	1473	11.5	*
Rock Ptarmigan	Scotland	Watson, '65	148	6.6	*
Rock Ptarmigan	Alaska	Weeden, '64	101	7.0	*
Willow Ptarmigan	Scotland	Jenkins, '63	395	7.1	*
Willow Ptarmigan	Newfoundland	Bergerud, '70b	106	10.2	*
Ring-necked Pheasant	Iowa	Hamerstrom, '36	124	11.2	*
Ring-necked Pheasant	Iowa	Errington, '37	126	11.4	*
Ring-necked Pheasant	Penn.	Randall, '41	157	10.6	3.18
Ring-necked Pheasant	Iowa	Kozicky, '56	60	8.7	*
Ring-necked Pheasant	Wisc.	Gates, '73	574	11.2	4.9
Gray Partridge	Mich.	Yeatter, '34	44	15.7	*
Gray Partridge	Wisc.	McCabe, '46	470	16.4	*
Gray Partridge	Wisc.	Gates, '73	31	14.9	3.9
Gray Partridge	England	Lack, '47	4051	14.6	2.38
Wild Turkey	Missouri	Dalke, '46	25	11.07	*
Wild Turkey	Va.	McDowell, '56	34	12.3	2.4
Clapper Rail	N. Jersey	Kozicky, '49	104	9.97	2.10
Clapper Rail	Va.	Stewart, '51	71	8.38	1.56
Clapper Rail	Calif.	Zucca, '54	27	7.92	*
Virginia Rail	Iowa	Tanner, '54	28	8.1	4.5
Sora Rail	Minn.	Pospichal, '54	29	9.9	*
King Rail	Arkansas	Meanley, '69	67	10.9	*
Common Gallinule	Louisiana	Causey, '68	39	8.33	*
Common Gallinule	Texas	Cottam, '59	142	9.1	*
American Coot	Iowa	Fredrickson, '69	161	9.0	*
American Coot	Iowa	Provost, '47	37	8.84	1.27
American Coot	Manitoba	Kiel, '55	169	9.9	1.3
American Coot	Calif.	Hunt, '55	256	8.7	*
American Woodcock	Maine	Mendall, '43	122	3.96	0.20
Common Snipe	Newfoundland	Tuck, '72	76	3.8	*

APPENDIX TABLE VII.

American Ornithologist Union (1957) numbers and recommended band sizes of North American resident game birds. Adapted from North American Bird Banding Manual. Vol. I (1976). Full numbers represent A.O.U. numbers as listed in the 5th edition of the A.O.U. Check-list (1957). Decimals have been added by the Bird Banding Laboratory to identify hybrids, extra-limital species, and readily identified subspecies.

A.O.U. No.	Species	Band Size	A.O.U. No.	Species	Band Size
288.1	Gray Partridge	3A	294	California Quail	3A
288.2	Chukar	6	295	Gambel's Quail	3A
289	Bobwhite	3B	296	Harlequin Quail	3A
290	Coturnix Quail	3	297	Blue Grouse	5
291	Masked Bobwhite	3A	298	Spruce Grouse	6–5
292	Mountain Quail	4	299	Franklin's Grouse	5
293	Scaled Quail	3A	300	Ruffed Grouse	6–5

APPENDIX TABLE VII.

(Cont.)

A.O.U. No.	Species	Band Size	A.O.U. No.	Species	Band Size
301	Willow Ptarmigan	6–5	308	Sharp-tailed Grouse	6
302	Rock Ptarmigan	5	309	Sage Grouse, female 6, male	7A
304	White-tailed Ptarmigan	4A	309.1	Ring-neck. Pheasant, f. 6, m.	7A
305	Greater Prairie Chicken	6	309.2	Reeves Pheasant, f. 6, m.	7A
305.9	Attwater's Prairie Chicken	6	310	Turkey	9–8
307	Lesser Prairie Chicken	6	311	Chachalaca	5

APPENDIX TABLE VIII.

Gestation periods (copulation to birth) of selected North American mammals. Common and scientific names, except for domestic animals, are from Jones et al. (1975).

Common Name	Scientific Name	Gestation Period	Authority
Badger	*Taxidea taxus*	90 days	Asdell, '46
		9 mo.	Hamlett, '32
Bat, Big Brown	*Eptesicus fuscus*	90 days	Asdell, '46
Bat, Big-eared	*Plecotus rafinesquii*	73 days	Asdell, '64
Bat, Hoary	*Lasiurus cinereus*	90 days	Asdell, '46
Bat, Little Brown	*Myotis lucifugus*	50–60 days*	Asdell, '64
Bat, Red	*Lasiurus borealis*	30 days	Asdell, '46
Bat, Pygmy	*Pipistrellus subflavus*	44 days	Asdell, '46
Bear, Black	*Ursus americanus*	210 days	Asdell, '64
Bear, Grizzly	*Ursus arctos*	195–210 days	Asdell, '64
Beaver	*Castor canadensis*	128 days	Asdell, '64
Bison	*Bison bison*	Approx. 270 days	Asdell, '64
Bobcat	*Lynx rufus*	50 days	Asdell, '64
Caribou	*Rangifer tarandus*	210–240 days	Asdell, '64
Cat, Domestic	*Felis catus*	63 days	Asdell, '64
Chipmunk, Eastern	*Tamias striatus*	31 days	Asdell, '64
Cottontail, Eastern	*Sylvilagus floridanus*	30 days	Asdell, '64
Cow	*Bos taurus*	280 days	Asdell, '64
Coyote	*Canis latrans*	60–65 days	Asdell, '64
Deer, Mule	*Odocoileus hemionus*	199–207 days	Asdell, '64
Deer, White-tailed	*Odocoileus virginianus*	187–198 days	Haugen, '59
		197–222 days	Asdell, '64
Dog, Domestic	*Canis familiaris*	63 days	Asdell, '64
Dog, Prairie, Black-tailed	*Cynomys ludovicianus*	30–35 days	Asdell, '64
Dog, Prairie, Gunnison	*Cynomys gunnisoni*	90 days	Asdell, '46
Dolphin, Common	*Delphinus delphis*	276 days	Asdell, '64
Elk	*Cervus elaphus*	249–262 days	Asdell, '64
Fisher	*Martes pennanti*	338–358 days	Asdell, '64
Fox, Arctic	*Alopex lagopus*	60 days	Asdell, '64
Fox, Gray	*Urocyon cinereoargenteus*	63 days	Asdell, '64
Fox, Red	*Vulpes vulpes*	49–55 days	Asdell, '64
Goat, Domestic	*Capra hircus*	150 days	Asdell, '64
Goat, Rocky Mountain	*Oreamnos americanus*	147 days	Asdell, '64
Gopher, Pocket	*Thomomys talpoides*	40 days	Asdell, '64
Ground Squirrels	*Spermophilus spp.*	(See squirrels, ground)	

APPENDIX TABLE VIII.

(Cont.)

Common Name	Scientific Name	Gestation Period	Authority
Hare, Snowshoe	*Lepus americanus*	38 days	Asdell, '64
Horse	*Equus caballus*	329–345 days	Asdell, '64
Jackrabbit, White-tailed	*Lepus townsendii*	33 days	Asdell, '64
Lynx	*Lynx canadensis*	63–70 days	Asdell, '64
Man	*Homo sapiens*	267 days	Asdell, '64
Marten	*Martes americana*	220–265 days	Asdell, '64
		220–276 days	Asdell, '46
Mink	*Mustela vison*	45–70 days	Asdell, '64
Mole, Eastern	*Scalopus aquaticus*	Approx. 42 days	Asdell, '46
Mole, Hairytail	*Parascalops breweri*	28–42 days	Asdell, '64
Mole, Star-nosed	*Condylura cristata*	Approx. 180 days	Asdell, '46
Moose	*Alces alces*	240–250 days	Asdell, '64
Mouse, Deer	*Peromyscus maniculatus*	24 days	Asdell, '64
Mouse, Grasshopper	*Onychomys leucogaster*	33 days	Asdell, '64
Mouse, Harvest, Western	*Reithrodontomys megalotis*	23 days	Asdell, '64
Mouse, Harvest, Plains	*Reithrodontomys montanus*	21 days	Asdell, '64
Mouse, Meadow	*Microtus pennsylvanicus*	21 days	Asdell, '64
Mouse, House	*Mus musculus*	19 days	Asdell, '46
Mouse, White-footed	*Peromyscus leucopus*	23 days	Asdell, '64
Mouse, Woodland Jumping	*Napaeozapus insignis*	21 days	Asdell, '46
Muskrat	*Ondatra zibethica*	28 days	Asdell, '64
Opossum	*Didelphis virginianus*	12-1/2 days	Asdell, '64
Otter, River	*Lutra canadensis*	288–380 days	Asdell, '64
Otter, Sea	*Enhydra lutris*	240–270 days	Asdell, '64
Pig, Domestic	*Sus scrofa*	112–115 days	Asdell, '64
Porcupine	*Erethizon dorsatum*	112 days	Asdell, '64
Porpoise, Harbor	*Phocoena phocoena*	300–330 days	Asdell, '64
Pronghorn Antelope	*Antilocapra americana*	240 days	Asdell, '64
Rabbit	*Sylvilagus* and *Lepus* (See cottontail, hare, and jackrabbit)		
Rat, Black	*Rattus rattus*	21 days	Asdell, '64
Rat, Cotton	*Sigmodon hispidus*	27 days	Asdell, '64
Rat, Rice	*Oryzomys palustris*	25 days	Asdell, '64
Rat, Eastern Wood	*Neotoma floridana*	30–36 days	Asdell, '46
Rat, Whitethroat Wood	*Neotoma albigula*	30 days	Asdell, '64
Raccoon	*Procyon lotor*	63 days	Asdell, '64
Sea Lion, California	*Zalophus californianus*	Approx. 345 days	Asdell, '64
Seal, Elephant	*Mirounga angustirostris*	340 days	Asdell, '64
Seal, Harbor	*Phoca vitulina*	240–250 days	Fisher, '54
Sheep, Bighorn	*Ovis canadensis*	180 days	Asdell, '64
Sheep, Domestic	*Ovis aries*	150 days	Asdell, '64
Shrew, Short-tailed	*Blarina brevicauda*	17–20 days	Asdell, '64
Shrew, Smoky	*Sorex fumeus*	21 days	Asdell, '64
Squirrel, Flying	*Glaucomys volans*	40 days	Asdell, '64
Squirrel, Fox	*Sciurus niger*	45 days	Asdell, '64

APPENDIX TABLE VIII.

(Cont.)

Common Name	Scientific Name	Gestation Period	Authority
Squirrel, Gray	*Sciurus carolinensis*	44 days	Asdell, '64
Squirrel, Ground, Calif.	*Spermophilus beecheyi*	30 days	Asdell, '64
Squirrel, Ground, Richardson	*Spermophilus richardsonii*	28–32 days	Asdell, '64
Squirrel, Ground, 13-lined	*Spermophilus tridecemlineatus*	28 days	Asdell, '64
Squirrel, Red	*Tamiasciurus hudsonicus*	40 days	Asdell, '64
Skunk, Striped	*Mephitis mephitis*	62 days	Asdell, '64
Walrus	*Odobenus rosmarus*	330 days	Asdell, '46
Weasel, Long-tailed	*Mustela frenata*	205–337 days	Wright, '48
Whale, Sperm	*Physeter catodon*	480 days	Asdell, '64
Wolf, Gray	*Canis lupus*	60–63 days	Asdell, '64
Wolverine	*Gulo luscus*	270(?) days	Wright and Rausch, '55
Woodchuck	*Marmota monax*	31–32 days	Asdell, '64

*Probably delayed implantation.

LITERATURE CITED

Abbott, H. G., and A. W. Coombs. 1964. A photoelectric 35 mm camera device for recording animal behavior. J. Mammal. 45(2):327–330.

Abell, D. H., and F. F. Gilbert. 1974. Nutrient content of fertilized deer browse in Maine. J. Wildl. Manage. 38(3):517–524.

Abelson, P. H. 1965. Translation of scientific literature. Science 149 (3687):929.

Abercrombie, M., C. J. Hickman, and M. L. Johnson. 1973. A dictionary of biology. 6th ed. Penguin Books, Harmondsworth, England. 306 p.

Abler, W. A., D. E. Buckland, R. L. Kirkpatrick, and P. F. Scanlon. 1976. Plasma progestins and puberty in fawns as influenced by energy and protein. J. Wildl. Manage. 40(3): 442–446.

Abramsky, Z. 1978. Small mammal community ecology. Oecologia 34 (2):113–123.

Ackoff, R. L. 1962. Scientific method: optimizing applied research decisions. John Wiley and Sons, New York. 464 p.

Adams, L. 1950. A punch-card system suitable for use with small samples in wildlife management and research. U.S. Fish and Wildl. Serv. Spec. Sci. Rep. (Wildl.) No. 3. 7 p.

Adams, L. 1951. Confidence limits for the Peterson or Lincoln Index used in animal population studies. J. Wildl. Manage. 15(1):13–19.

Adams, L. 1955. A punch-card bibliographic file for vertebrate ecologists. J. Wildl. Manage. 19(4):472–476.

Adams, L. 1957. A way to analyze herbivore food habits by fecal examination. Trans. N. Am. Wildl. Conf. 22:152–159.

Adams, L. 1959. An analysis of a population of snowshoe hares in northwestern Montana. Ecol. Monogr. 29(2):141–170.

Adams, L. 1965. Biotelemetry. BioScience 15(2):155–157.

Adams, L., and S. Hane. 1972. Adrenal gland size as an index of adrenocortical secretion rate in the California ground squirrel. J. Wildl. Dis. 8(1): 19–23.

Adams, L., W. G. O'Regan, and D. J. Dunaway. 1962. Analysis of forage consumption by fecal examination. J. Wildl. Manage. 26(1):108–111.

Adams, L., and S. G. Watkins. 1967. Annuli in tooth cementum indicate age in California ground squirrels. J. Wildl. Manage. 31(4):836–839.

Addy, C. E. (comp.). 1956. Guide to waterfowl banding. U.S. Fish and Wildl. Serv., Laurel, Md. 164 p.

Addy, C. E., and L. G. MacNamara. 1948. Waterfowl management on small areas. Wildl. Manage. Inst., Washington, D.C. 84 p.

Adomaitis, V. A., H. K. Nelson, and F. B. Lee. 1967. The chemical and related technical literature of wildlife conservation. J. Chem. Doc. 7(4):247–250.

Adorjan, A. S., and G. B. Kolenosky. 1969. A manual for the identification of hairs of selected Ontario mammals. Ontario Dept. Lands and For. Res. Rep. (Wildlife) No. 90. 64 p.

Albers, P. H. 1976. Determining population size of territorial red-winged blackbirds. J. Wildl. Manage. 40(4): 761–768.

Aldous, C. M. 1945. A winter study of mule deer in Nevada. J. Wildl. Manage. 9(2):145–151.

Aldous, J. G. 1947. Simple method for cross-indexing a reference file. Science 106 (2744):109.

Aldous, M. C., and F. C. Craighead, Jr. 1958. A marking technique for bighorn sheep. J. Wildl. Manage. 22(4):445–446.

Aldous, S. E. 1936. A cage trap useful in the control of white-necked ravens. U.S.D.A. Bur. Biol. Surv. Wildl. Res. and Mgmt. Leafl. BS–27. Washington, D.C. 5 p.

Aldous, S. E. 1944. A deer browse survey method. J. Mammal. 25(2): 130–136.

Aldrich, J. W., C. S. Robbins, and W. W. Dykstra. 1961. Bird hazard to aircraft. U.S. Fish Wildl. Serv. Wildl. Leafl. No. 429. 10 p.

Alexander, F., and A. K. Chowdhury. 1958. Digestion in the rabbit's stomach. Br. J. Nutr. 12(1):65–73.

Alexander, M. M. 1951. The aging of muskrats on the Montezuma National Wildlife Refuge. J. Wildl. Manage. 15(2):175–186.

Alexander, M. M. 1958. The place of aging in wildlife management. Am. Sci. 46(2):123–137.

Alexander, M. M. 1960. Shrinkage of muskrat skulls in relation to aging. J. Wildl. Manage. 24(3):326–329.

Alford, B. T., R. L. Burkhart, and W. P. Johnson. 1974. Etorphine and diprenorphine as immobilizing and reversing agents in captive and free-ranging mammals. J. Am. Vet. Med. Assoc. 164(7):702–705.

Alison, R. M. 1972. The breeding biology of the oldsquaw (*Clangula hyemalis* Linnaeus) at Churchill Manitoba. Ph.D. Thesis, Univ. of Toronto, Toronto. 129 p.

Allan, J. D. 1975. Components of diversity. Oecologia 18(4):359–367.

Alldredge, A. W., J. F. Lipscomb, and F. W. Whicker. 1974. Forage intake rates of mule deer estimated with fallout cesium-137. J. Wildl. Manage. 38(3):508–516.

Allen, D. L. 1943. Michigan fox squirrel management. Mich. Dept. of Conserv., Game Div. Publ. No. 100, Lansing. 404 p.

Allen, D. L. 1954. Our wildlife legacy. Funk and Wagnalls, New York. 422 p.

Allen, D. L., (ed.) 1956. Pheasants in North America. Stackpole Co., Harrisburg, Pa. 490 p.

Allen, G. M. 1939. A checklist of African mammals. Bull. Mus. Comp. Zool. Harvard. 83:1–763.

Allen, G. R. 1973. The graduate students' guide to theses and dissertations; a practical manual for writing and research. Josey-Bass, Publ., San Francisco. 108 p.

Allen, J. A. 1909. Biographical memoir of Elliott Coues, 1842–1899. p. 397–446 *in* Biographical Memoir. Nat. Acad. of Sci., Washington, D.C. Vol. VI. 472 p.

Allen, L. J., L. H. Harbers, R. R. Schalles, C. E. Owensby, and E. F. Smith. 1976. Range burning and fertilizing related to nutritive value of bluestem grass. J. Range Manage. 29(4):306–308.

Allen, R. W., and M. M. Nice. 1952. A study of the breeding biology of the purple martin *(Progne subis)*. Am. Midl. Nat. 47(3):606–665.

Allen, S. H. 1974. Modified techniques for aging red fox using canine teeth. J. Wildl. Manage. 38(1):152–154.

Allen, S. H., and S. C. Kohn. 1976. Assignment of age-classes in coyotes from canine cementum annuli. J. Wildl. Manage. 40(4):769–797.

Allen, T. J. 1970. Immobilization of white-tailed deer with succinylcholine chloride and hyaluronidase. J. Wildl. Manage. 34(1):207–209.

Allen, W. R., III, and J. M. Collins. 1971. A modified cryostat technique for tooth sectioning. J. Mammal. 52(2):471–472.

Alliston, W. G. 1975. Web-tagged ducklings in pipped eggs. J. Wildl. Manage. 39(3):625–628.

Alt, F. (ed.). 1966. Advances in bioengineering and instrumentation. Plenum Press, New York. 360 p.

Altman, P. L., and D. S. Dittmer. 1961. Blood and other body fluids. Fed. Am. Soc. Exp. Biol., Washington, D.C. 540 p.

Altman, P. L., and D. S. Dittmer. 1962. Growth including reproduction and morphological development. Fed. Am. Soc. Exp. Biol., Washington, D.C. 608 p.

Altman, P. L., (ed.), and D. S. Dittmer. 1966. Environmental biology. Fed. Am. Soc. Exp. Biol., Bethesda, Md. 694 p.

Altman, P. L., and D. S. Dittmer. 1972–1974. Biology data book. 2nd ed. Fed. Am. Soc. Exp. Biol., Bethesda, Md. 3 vol.

Altsheler, B. 1940. Natural history index-guide. 2nd ed. H. W. Wilson Co., New York. 583 p.

Amann, R. P., and J. O. Almquist. 1961. Reproductive capacity of dairy bulls. I. Technique for direct measurement of gonadal and extragonadal sperm reserves. J. Dairy Sci. 44 (8):1537–1543.

Amann, R. P., and J. T. Lambiase, Jr. 1969. The male rabbit. III. Determination of daily sperm production by means of testicular homogenates. J. Anim. Sci. 28(3):369–374.

American National Standards Institute. 1970. The American national standard for the abbreviation of titles of periodicals. Z39.5–1969. 11 p.

American Ornithologists' Union. 1957. Check-list of North American birds. 5th ed. Port City Press Inc., Baltimore, Md. 691 p.

American Public Health Association. 1980. Standard methods for the examination of water and wastewater. Am. Public Health Assoc., Washington, D.C. (in press).

American Radio Relay League. 1974. The ARRL antenna book. Publ. No. 15, Newington, Conn.

American Society of Photogrammetry. 1966. Manual of photogrammetry. 3rd ed. Am. Soc. Photogrammetry, Falls Church, Va. 2 vol. 1199 p.

American Translators Association. 1976. Professional services directory. 3rd ed. Croton-on-Hudson, N.Y. 108 p.

Amidon, E. L. 1978. Computer mapping systems for integrated resource inventories. p. 354–359 *in* H. G. Lund et al. Integrated inventories of renewable natural resources. Proceedings of the workshop: USDA For. Serv., Rocky Mt. For. and Range Exp. Stn. Gen. Tech. Rep. RM-55, Fort Collins, Colo. 482 p.

Ammann, A. P., R. L. Cowan, C. L. Mothershead, and B. R. Baumgardt. 1973. Dry matter and energy intake in relation to digestibility in white-tailed deer. J. Wildl. Manage. 37(2): 195–201.

Ammann, G. A. 1944. Determining the age of pinnated and sharp-tailed grouses. J. Wildl. Manage. 8(2): 170–171.

Ammann, G. A. 1957. The prairie grouse of Michigan. Mich. Dept. Conserv. Tech. Bull. 200 p.

Amos, T. G. 1965. Time lapse photography with synchronized electronic flash for recording insect behaviour. Anim. Behav. 13(4):558–560.

Anas, R. E. 1970. Accuracy in assigning ages to fur seals. J. Wildl. Manage. 34(4):844–852.

Anderka, F. W., and M. I. Dyer. 1967. A design for a minature biopotential radio transmitter. J. Appl. Physiol. 22(6):1147–1148.

Anderson, A. 1963. Patagial tags for waterfowl. J. Wildl. Manage. 27 (2):284–288.

Anderson, A. E., D. E. Medin, and D. C. Bowden. 1972. Indices of carcass fat in a Colorado mule deer population. J. Wildl. Manage. 36 (2):579–594.

Anderson, B. W., and R. D. Ohmart. 1977. Rodent bait additive which repels insects. J. Mammal. 58(2):242.

Anderson, B. W., and R. L. Timken. 1971. Age and sex characteristics of common mergansers. J. Wildl. Manage. 35(2):388–393.

Anderson, C. F. 1961. Anesthetizing deer by arrow. J. Wildl. Manage. 25(2):202–203.

Anderson, D. R., J. L. Laake, B. R. Crain, and K. P. Burnham. 1976. Guidelines for line transect sampling of biological populations. Utah Coop. Wildl. Res. Unit, Logan, Utah. 27 p.

Anderson, D. R., and R. S. Pospahala. 1970. Correction of bias in belt transect studies of immotile objects. J. Wildl. Manage. 34(1):141–146.

Anderson, F., and P. P. De Moor. 1971. A system for radio-tracking monkeys in dense bush and forest. J. Wildl. Manage. 35(4):636–643.

Anderson, H. W. 1966. A simple library filing system for forestry references. Washington Dept. Nat. Resour. Repr. No. 1, Olympia. 27 p.

Anderson, J. 1953. Analysis of a Danish roe-deer population. Dan. Rev. Game Biol. 2:127–155.

Anderson, J. 1961. Biology and management of roe-deer in Denmark. La Terre et la Vie. 108(1):41–53.

Anderson, P. K. 1966. The periodical literature of ecology. BioScience 16(1):794–795.

Anderson, R. K., and F. Hamerstrom. 1967. Hen decoys aid in trapping cock prairie chickens with bownets and noose carpets. J. Wildl. Manage. 31(4):829–832.

Anderson, R. M. 1946. Catalogue of Canadian recent mammals. Natl. Mus. of Canada Bull. No. 102 (Biol. Ser. No. 31), Ottawa. 238 p.

Anderson, R. M. 1965. Methods of collecting and preserving vertebrate animals. 4th ed. rev. Natl. Mus. of Canada Bull. No. 69 (Biol. Ser. No. 18), Ottawa. 199 p.

Anderson, R. R., and F. J. Wobber. 1973. Wetlands mapping in New Jersey. Photogramm. Eng. 39(4): 353–358.

Anderson, S., J. K. Doutt, and J. S. Findley. 1963. Collections of mammals in North America. J. Mammal. 44(4):471–500.

Anderson, S., and J. K. Jones, Jr. 1967. Recent mammals of the world: a synopsis of families. Ronald Press Co., New York. 453 p.

Anderson, S., and R. G. Van Gelder. 1970. The history and status of the literature of mammalogy. BioScience 20 (17):949–957.

Anderson, S. H., and H. H. Shugart, Jr. 1974. Habitat selection of breeding birds in east Tennessee deciduous forest. Ecology 55(4):828–837.

Anderson, T. E. 1969. Identifying, evaluating, and controlling wildlife damage. p. 497–520 *in* R. H. Giles, (ed.). Wildlife management techniques. 3rd ed. The Wildl. Soc., Washington, D.C. 623 p.

Anderson, W. 1956. A waterfowl nesting study on the grasslands, Merced County, California. Calif. Fish and Game 42(2):117–130.

Anderson, W. 1957. A waterfowl nesting study in the Sacramento Valley, California, 1955. Calif. Fish and Game 43(1):71–90.

Anderson, W. H., and F. X. Wallner. 1978. Small format aerial photography: a selected bibliography. Natl. Tech. Inf. Serv. PB279849, Washington, D.C. 14 p.

Andresen, J. W., and J. McCormick. 1962. An evaluation of devices for estimation of tree cover. Broteria Ser. Trimest. Cienc Nat. 31(1):15–30.

Andrewartha, H. G., and L. C. Birch. 1954. The distribution and abundance of animals. The Univ. of Chicago Press, Chicago. 782 p.

Aney, W. W. 1974. Estimating fish and wildlife harvest, a survey of methods used. Proc. Western Assoc. State Game and Fish Commissioners 54:70–99.

Ankney, C. D. 1975. Neckbands contribute to starvation in female lesser snow geese. J. Wildl. Manage. 39(4):825–826.

Anon. 1884–1976. Scientific and learned societies of Great Britain, a handbook compiled from official sources. Allen & Unwin, Ltd., London.

Anon. 1936. More game birds by controlling their enemies. More Game Birds in America-A Foundation, New York. 63 p.

Anon. 1939. Snapping turtle control and utilization. Manage. Bull. No. 1, New York State Conserv. Dept. 16 p.

Anon. 1947. The decoy. Severn Wildfowl Trust 1:52–56.

Anon. 1953. Weasels and their control. U.S. Fish Wildl. Serv. Leafl., Washington, D.C. 1 p.

Anon. 1955. Evaluating and mapping mountain land features for forest management purposes. Wash. Agric. Exp. Stn. Circ. No. 271. 22 p.

Anon. 1957. Extension of BA's program of cooperative abstracting. Biol. Abstr. 31(8):xii.

Anon. 1958. Scientific and learned societies of Great Britain. 59th ed. George Allen and Unwin, London. 215 p.

Anon. 1961–1966. Checklist of conservation organizations and information. IUCN Bull. Supplement nos. 1. Tanganyika, 2. Sweden, 3. German Federal Republic, 4. Canada, 5. France, 6. Venezuela, 7. Kenya, 8. Uganda, 9. Great Britain, 10. Netherlands, 11. Poland, 12. New Zealand, 13. Finland, 14. Transvall Province, 15. Natal Province, 16. Sudan, and 17. Ethiopia.

Anon. 1964. Report: Your views on the conference literature—what BA will do about it. Biol. Abstr. 45(22):xiv.

Anon. 1965. Instructions for collectors, No. 18. Plants. 6th ed. Br. Mus. London. 72 p.

Anon. 1966. Why Biological Abstracts? Biol. Abstr. 47(17):x.

Anon. 1969. Controlling pigeons. U.S. Fish Wildl. Serv. Agric. Exp. Stn. Leafl. No. 205, Purdue Univ., Lafayette, Indiana. 2 p.

Anon. 1971. Manual of veterinary parasitological laboratory techniques. Min. Agric. Fish. and Food. Tech. Bull. No. 18, London. 131 p.

Anon. 1972. Printed leaflet with Rompun. Anim. Health Dept., Div. Baychem Corp. Kansas City, Mo.

Anon. 1976. Current patterns of biological publication. Biol. Abstr. 61(5): xxiv.

Ansell, W. F. H. 1965. Standardisation of field data on mammals. Zool. Afr. 1(1):97–113.

Antelope States Workshop. 1974. Fencing on pronghorn antelope range. Antelope States Workshop Proc. 6:181–183.

Antenucci, J., S. A. Miller, and C. R. Brunori. 1979. Maryland wildlife resources information retrieval system. Trans. N. Am. Wildl. Nat. Resour. Conf. 44:446–456.

Anthony, H. E. 1928. Field book of North American mammals. G. P. Putnam's Sons, New York, London. 625 p.

Anthony, H. E. 1950. The capture and preservation of small mammals for study. Am. Mus. of Nat. Hist. Sci. Guide No. 61. 54 p.

Anthony, R. G., and N. S. Smith. 1974. Comparison of rumen and fecal analysis to describe deer diets. J. Wildl. Manage. 38(3):535–540.

AOAC. 1975. Official methods of analysis of the Association of Official Analytical Chemists. 12th ed. Assoc. Off. Anal. Chem. Washington, D.C. 1094 p.

Applegate, V. C., and H. E. Predmore, Jr. 1947. Age classes and patterns of primeness in a fall collection of muskrat pelts. J. Wildl. Manage. 11(4):324–330.

Arata, A. A. 1959. A quick method of gross analysis of muskrat stomach contents. J. Wildl. Manage. 23(1): 116–117.

Archibald, H. L. 1975. Temporal patterns of spring space use by ruffed grouse. J. Wildl. Manage. 39(3): 472–481.

Arlton, A. V. 1936. An ecological study of the mole. J. Mammal. 17(4):349–371.

Armstrong, D. M. 1972. Distribution of mammals of Colorado. Monogr. No. 3, Mus. Nat. Hist., Univ. Kansas. 415 p.

Armstrong, J. S., and T. S. Overton. 1977. Estimating nonresponse bias in mail surveys. J. Mark. Res. 14(3):396–402.

Armstrong, R. A. 1950. Fetal development of the northern white-tailed deer (*Odocoileus virginianus borealis* Miller). Am. Midl. Nat. 43(3): 650–666.

Arnold, K. A., and D. W. Coon. 1971. A technique modification for color-marking birds. Bird-Banding 42(1): 49–50.

Arnold, K. A., and D. W. Coon. 1972. Modifications of the cannon net foı use with cowbird studies. J. Wildl. Manage. 36(1):153–155.

Aronson, M. H. 1961. Electronic circuitry for instruments and equipment. 4th print. Instruments Publ. Co., Pittsburgh. 312 p.

Arthur, G. C., and D. D. Kennedy. 1972. A permanent site waterfowl trap. J. Wildl. Manage. 36(4):1257–1261.

Arthur, W. J., III, G. S. Hiatt, and A. W. Alldredge. 1978. Response of mule deer to tape recorded fawn distress calls. Wildl. Soc. Bull. 6(3):169–170.

Artmann, J. W. 1971. Capturing sharp-tailed grouse hens by using taped chick distress calls. J. Wildl. Manage. 35(3):557–559.

Artmann, J. W., and L. D. Schroeder. 1976. A technique for sexing woodcock by wing measurement. J. Wildl. Manage. 40(3):572–574.

Arvey, M. D., and W. J. Riemer. 1966. Inland biological field stations of the United States. BioScience 16(4): 249–254.

Asdell, S. A. 1946. Patterns of mammalian reproduction. Comstock Publ. Co., Ithaca, N.Y. 437 p.

Asdell, S. A. 1964. Patterns of mammalian reproduction. 2nd ed. Comstock Publ. Co., Ithaca, N.Y. 670 p.

Ashby, W. C. 1972. Distance measurements in vegetation study. Ecology 53(5):980–981.

Ashcraft, G., and D. Reese. 1957. An improved device for capturing deer. Calif. Fish and Game 43(2):193–199.

Ashley, M. D., and J. Rea. 1975. Seasonal vegetation differences from ERTS imagery. Photogramm. Eng. 41(6):713–719.

Asimov, I. 1972. Biographical encyclopedia of science and technology. Rev. ed. Doubleday Co., Garden City, N.Y. 805 p.

Atkins, H. J. B., (ed.). 1960. Tools of biological research. Blackwell Sci. Publ., Oxford. 175 p.

Atkinson, J. 1971. A handbook for interviewers. Off. of Pop. Censuses and Surv., Soc. Surv. Div., Her Majesty's Stationery Off., London. 170 p.

Atlantic Waterfowl Council. 1972. Techniques handbook of the waterfowl habitat development and management committee—Atlantic Flyway Council. 2nd ed. Atlantic Waterfowl Council, Bethany Beach, Del. 218 p.

Atomic Energy of Canada Ltd. 1960. The AECL radioisotope handbook. Tech. Bull. RP 3, AECL, Ottawa. 64 p.

Atomic Energy of Canada Ltd. 1961. The AECL radioisotope applications handbook. Tech. Bull. RAP-1, AECL, Ottawa. 54 p.

Atwater, M. M. 1959. A study of renesting in Canada geese in Montana. J. Wildl. Manage. 23(1):91–97.

Atwood, E. L. 1956. Validity of mail survey data on bagged waterfowl. J. Wildl. Manage. 20(1):1–16.

Austin, A., and R. Adams. 1978. Aerial color and color infrared survey of marine plant resources. Photogramm. Eng. Remote Sensing 44(4): 469–480.

Austin, D. H., and J. H. Peoples. 1967. Capturing hogs with alpha-chloralose. Proc. Southeastern Assoc. Game and Fish Commissioners 21:201–205.

Avery, M., P. F. Springer, and J. F. Cassel. 1976. The effects of a tall tower on nocturnal bird migration—a portable ceilometer study. Auk 93(2):281–291.

Avery, T. E. 1977. Interpretation of aerial photographs. 3rd ed. Burgess Publ. Co., Minneapolis, Minn. 392 p.

Avicenne, P. 1972. Bibliographical services throughout the world. 1965–69. UNESCO, Paris. 303 p.

Ayars, J. S., P. L. Altman, M. Broadbent, E. J. Huth, D. R. Lincome, and R. V. Ormes. 1972. CBE style manual. 3rd ed. Amer. Inst. of Biol. Sci., Washington, D.C. 297 p.

Ayres, R. U. 1969. Technological forecasting and long range planning. McGraw-Hill Inc., New York. 237 p.

Babakov, G. A. 1961. Estimation of squirrel stocks over large areas. p. 63 *in* Y. A. Isakov, (ed.). Organization and methods of censusing terrestrial vertebrate faunal resources. Moscow Nat. Soc., Inst. Geogr. Acad. Sci., USSR. 104 p.

Bacus, L. C. 1968. The bear foot snare. U.S. Fish Wildl. Serv. Field Training Aid No. 2, Washington, D.C. 14 p.

Baer, C. H., R. E. Severson, and S. B. Linhart 1978. Live capture of coyotes from a helicopter with ketamine hydrochloride. J. Wildl. Manage. 42(2):452–454.

Bailey, A. M., and R. J. Niedrach. 1965. Birds of Colorado. Denver Mus. of Nat. Hist., Denver, Colo. 2 vol. 895 p.

Bailey, J. A. 1967. Sampling deer browse for crude protein. J. Wildl. Manage. 31(3):437–442.

Bailey, J. A. 1968a. A weight-length relationship for evaluating physical condition of cottontails. J. Wildl. Manage. 32(4):835–841.

Bailey, J. A. 1968b. Effects of soil fertilization on the concentration of crude protein in witch-hobble browse. N.Y. Fish and Game J. 15(2):155–164.

Bailey, J. A., W. Elder, and T. D. McKinney, (ed.). 1974. Readings in wildlife conservation. The Wildl. Soc., Washington, D.C. 722 p.

Bailey, J. A., and R. H. McBee. 1964. The magnitude of the rabbit caecal fermentation. Proc. Montana Acad. Sci. 24:35–38.

Bailey, N. T. J. 1951. On estimating the size of mobile populations from recapture data. Biometrika 38(3 and 4):293–306.

Bailey, N. T. J. 1952. Improvements in the interpretation of recapture data. J. Anim. Ecol. 21(1):120–127.

Bailey, R. G. 1976. Ecoregions of the United States (a map). USDA For. Serv., Ogden, Utah. 1 p.

Bailey, R. G. 1978. Descriptions of the ecoregions of the United States. USDA For. Serv. Intermtn. Reg. Ogden, Utah. 77 p.

Bailey, R. W. 1956. Sex determination of adult wild turkeys by means of dropping configuration. J. Wildl. Manage. 20(2):220.

Bailey, T. N. 1971. Immobilization of bobcats, coyotes and badgers with phencyclidine hydrochloride. J. Wildl. Manage. 35(4): 847–849.

Baines, H. 1958. The science of photography. John Wiley and Sons, New York. 319 p.

Baker, M. F., and F. X. Lueth. 1966. Mandibular cavity tissue as a possible indicator of condition in deer. Proc. Southeastern Assoc. Game and Fish Commissioners 20:69–74.

Baker, R. H. 1971. Nutritional strategies of myomorph rodents in North American grasslands. J. Mammal. 52(4):800–805.

Balda, R. P. 1975. Vegetation structure and breeding bird diversity. p. 59–80 *in* Proceedings: A symposium on management of forest and range habitats for nongame birds. USDA For. Serv. Gen. Tech. Rep. WO-1. 343 p.

Baldwin, A. A. 1971. Long range immobilization method. P–R Rep., Proj. W–78–15, Ariz. Game and Fish Dept. 33 p.

Baldwin, S. P., and S. C. Kendeigh. 1927. Attentiveness and inattentiveness in the nesting behavior of the house wren. Auk 44(2):206–216.

Baldwin, W. P. 1947. Trapping wild turkeys in South Carolina. J. Wildl. Manage. 11(1):24–36.

Baldwin, W. P., Jr., and C. O. Handley. 1946. Winter food of bobwhite quail in Virginia. J. Wildl. Manage. 10(2):142–149.

Balgooyen, T. G. 1977. Collecting methods for amphibians and reptiles. USDI Bur. Land Manage. Tech. Note T/N 299. 12 p.

Balham, R. W., and W. H. Elder. 1953. Colored leg bands for waterfowl. J. Wildl. Manage. 17(4): 446–449.

Ball, K. E. 1952. Nesting of the ring-necked pheasant on Pelee Island, Ontario. Can. Field-Nat. 66(3):71–81.

Ballenberghe, V. V., A. W. Erickson, and D. Byman. 1975. Ecology of the timber wolf in northeastern Minnesota. Wildl. Monogr. No. 43. 43 p.

Ballou, H. W. 1968. Guide to microreproduction equipment. 4th ed. Nat. Microfilm Assoc. Annapolis, Maryland.

Baltosser, W. H. 1978. New and modified methods for color-marking hummingbirds. Bird-Banding 49(1): 47–49.

Bamford, J. 1970. Estimating fat reserves in the brush-tailed possum, *Trichosurus vulpecula* Kerr (Marsupialia: Phalangeridae). Aust. J. Zool. 18(4):415–425.

Bandy, P. J., I. McT. Cowan, W. D. Kitts, and A. J. Wood. 1956. A method for the assessment of the nutritional status of wild ungulates. Can. J. Zool. 34(1): 48–52.

Banfield, A. W. F. 1974. The mammals of Canada. Univ. of Toronto Press, Toronto. 438 p.

Banks, E. M., R. J. Brooks, and J. Schnell. 1975. A radiotracking study of home range and activity of the brown lemming *(Lemmus trimucronatus)*. J. Mammal. 56(4):888–901.

Barbour, R. W., and W. H. Davis. 1974. Mammals of Kentucky. Univ. Press of Kentucky, Lexington. 321 p.

Barbour, R. W., C. T. Peterson, D. Rust, H. E. Shadowen, and A. L. Whitt, Jr. 1973. Kentucky birds; a finding guide. Univ. Press of Kentucky, Lexington. 306 p.

Barkalow, F. S., Jr., and R. F. Soots, Jr. 1965. An improved gray squirrel nest box for ecological and management studies. J. Wildl. Manage. 29(4): 679–684.

Barney, R. J. 1972. A 31-day battery-operated recording weather station. USDA For. Serv. Pac. N.W. For. and Range Exp. Stn. Res. Note PNW-185, Portland, Oreg. 7 p.

Barrett, E. C., and L. F. Curtis. 1977. Introduction to environmental remote sensing. John Wiley and Sons Inc., New York. 336 p.

Barrett, M. W. 1979. Evaluation of fertilizer on pronghorn winter range in Alberta. J. Range Manage. 32(1): 55–59.

Barrier, M. J., and F. S. Barkalow, Jr. 1967. A rapid technique for aging gray squirrels in winter pelage. J. Wildl. Manage. 31(4):715–719.

Barron, J. C. 1976. Statistical citations from wildlife and fisheries literature. Wildl. Soc. Bull. 4(3):129–30.

Barry, T. W. 1956. Observations of a nesting colony of American brant. Auk 73(2):193–202.

Barry, T. W. 1962. Effect of late seasons on Atlantic brant reproduction. J. Wildl. Manage 26(1):19–26.

Barry, T. W. 1966. The geese of the Anderson River Delta, Northwest Territories. Ph.D. Thesis. Univ. of Alberta, Edmonton. 181 p.

Bart, J., D. Allee, and M. Richmond. 1979. Using economics in defense of wildlife. Wildl. Soc. Bull. 7(3): 139–144.

Bartholomew, D. J. 1961. A method of allowing for "not-at-home" bias in sample surveys. Appl. Stat. 10(1): 52–59.

Bartholomew, G. A., and T. J. Cade. 1963. The water economy of land birds. Auk 80(4):504–539.

Bartholomew, R. M. 1967. A study of the winter activities of bobwhites through the use of radiotelemetry. Occas. Papers C. C. Adams Cent. Ecol. Studies No. 17. 25 p.

Bartlett, C. O. 1958. A study of some deer and forest relationships in Rondeau Provincial Park. Ontario Dept. Lands For. Wildl. Ser. No. 7. 172 p.

Bartlett, I. H. 1938. White-tails—presenting Michigan's deer problem. Mich. Conserv. 8(2):4–5, 7 to 8(7):8–11.

Bartlett, L. M. 1954. A technique for recording rapid consecutive field observations. Auk 71(4):464.

Bartonek, J. C., and C. W. Dane. 1964. Numbered nasal discs for waterfowl. J. Wildl. Manage. 28(4):688–692.

Basile, J. V., and S. S. Hutchings. 1966. Twig diameter-length-weight relations of bitterbrush. J. Range Manage. 19(1):34–38.

Baskett, T. S. 1947. Nesting and production of the ring-necked pheasant in north-central Iowa. Ecol. Monogr. 17(1):1–30.

Batcheler, C. L. 1971. Estimation of density from a sample of joint point and nearest-neighbor distances. Ecology 52(4):703–709.

Batcheler, C. L. 1975. Development of a distance method for deer census from pellet groups. J. Wildl. Manage. 39(4):641–652.

Batcheler, C. L., and C. M. H. Clarke. 1970. Note on kidney weights and the kidney fat index. N. Z. J. Sci. 13(4):663–668.

Bates, R. S. 1965. Scientific societies in the United States. 3rd ed. M.I.T. Press, Cambridge, Mass. 326 p.

Battelle Memorial Institute. 1963. Directory of selected scientific institutions in the U.S.S.R. Merril Books, Columbus, Ohio. 1 vol. (various paging).

Battelle Pacific Northwest Laboratories and Columbus Laboratories. 1975. Environmental impact monitoring of nuclear power plants. Source book of monitoring methods. Natl. Environ. Stud. Proj., At. Ind. Forum, New York, N.Y. 2 vols.

Batzli, G. O., and F. A. Pitelka. 1971. Condition and diet of cycling populations of the California vole, *Microtus californicus*. J. Mammal. 52 (1):141–163.

Bauer, O. 1963. Improving land for California valley quail. Calif. Dept. Fish and Game, Game Manage. Leafl. 8, Sacramento. 11 p.

Bauer, R. D., A. M. Johnson, and V. B. Scheffer. 1964. Eye lens weight and age in the fur seal. J. Wildl. Manage. 28(2):374–376.

Bauer, R. K., and F. Meissner. 1963. Structures of mail questionnaires: test of alternatives. Public Opin. Q. 27(2):307–311.

Baumgartner, L. L. 1938. Population studies of the fox squirrel in Ohio. Trans. N. Am. Wildl. Conf. 3:685–689.

Baumgartner, L. L. 1940. Trapping, handling and marking fox squirrels. J. Wildl. Manage. 4(4):444–450.

Baumgartner, L. L., and F. C. Bellrose, Jr. 1943. Determination of sex and age in muskrats. J. Wildl. Manage. 7(1):77–81.

Baumgartner, L. L., and A. C. Martin. 1939. Plant histology as an aid in squirrel food-habits studies. J. Wildl. Manage. 3(3):266–268.

Baxter, W. L., and C. W. Wolfe. 1973. Life history and ecology of the ring-necked pheasant in Nebraska. Nebr. Game and Parks Comm., Lincoln. 58 p.

Bayfield, N. G., and R. Hewson. 1975. Automatic monitoring of trail use by mountain hares. J. Wildl. Manage. 39(1):214–216.

Bayoumi, M. A., and A. D. Smith. 1976. Response of big game winter range vegetation to fertilization. J. Range Manage. 29(1):44–48.

Beal, F. E. L. 1895. The crow blackbirds and their food. p. 233–248 *in* Yearbook of agriculture—1894. USDA. Washington, D.C. 608 p.

Beal, F. E. L. 1897. Some common birds in their relation to agriculture. USDA Farmers' Bull. No. 54. 40 p.

Beal, F. E. L. 1911. Food of the woodpeckers of the United States. USDA Biol. Surv. Bull. No. 37. 64 p.

Beal, F. E. L., and S. D. Judd. 1898. Cuckoos and shrikes in their relation to agriculture. USDA Biol. Surv. Bull. No. 9. 26 p.

Beale, D. M. 1962. Growth of the eye lens in relation to age in fox squirrels. J. Wildl. Manage. 26(2):208–211.

Beale, D. M. 1966. A self-collaring device for pronghorn antelope. J. Wildl. Manage. 30(1):209–211.

Beale, D. M., and A. D. Smith. 1967. Immobilization of pronghorn antelopes with succinylcholine chloride. J. Wildl. Manage. 31(4): 840–842.

Beale, D. M., and A. D. Smith. 1973. Mortality of pronghorn antelope fawns in western Utah. J. Wildl. Manage. 37(3):343–352.

Bean, M. J. 1977. The evolution of national wildlife law, prepared for the Council on Environmental Quality. U.S. Gov. Print. Office, Washington, D.C. 485 p.

Bear, G. D. 1971. Seasonal trends in fat levels of pronghorns, *Antilocapra americana*, in Colorado. J. Mammal. 52(3):583–589.

Beardahl, L. E., and V. E. Sylvester. 1974. Spring burning for removal of sagebrush competition in Nevada. Proc. Tall Timbers Fire Ecol. Confer. 14:539–547.

Beasom, S. L., W. Evans, and L. Temple. 1980. The drive net for capturing western big game. J. Wildl. Manage 44(2):478–480.

Beck, C. C. 1972. Chemical restraint of exotic species. J. Zoo Anim. Med. 3:3–66.

Beck, C. C. 1976. Vetalar (ketamine hydrochloride) a unique cataleptoid anesthetic agent for multispecies usage. J. Zoo Anim. Med. 7(3):11–38.

Beck, C. C., and A. J. Dresner. 1972. Vetalar (Ketamine HCL) a cataleptoid anesthetic agent for primate species. Vet. Med. and Small Anim. Clin. 67(10): 1082–1084.

Beck, J. R. 1952. A suggested food rank index. J. Wildl. Manage. 16(3):398.

Beck, T. D., R. B. Gill, and C. E. Braun. 1975. Sex and age determination of sage grouse from wing characteristics. Colo. Div. Game, Fish and Parks. Game Inf. Leafl. No. 49. 4 p.

Beebe, S. P. 1974. Relationships between insectivorous hole-nesting birds and forest management. Yale Univ. Sch. For. Environ. Stud., New Haven, Conn. 49 p. (mimeo.)

Beebe, W. 1926. Pheasants: their lives and homes. New York Zool. Soc. and Doubleday, Doran, N.Y. 309 p.

Beeman, L. E. 1978. Computer-assisted resource management. p. 375–381 *in* H. G. Lund et al. Integrated inventories of renewable natural resources. Proceedings of the workshop: USDA For. Serv., Rocky Mt. For. and Range Exp. Stn. Gen. Tech. Rep. RM–55, Fort Collins, Colo. 482 p.

Beeman, L. E., M. R. Pelton, and L. C. Marcum. 1974. Use of M–99 Etorphine for immobilizing black bears. J. Wildl. Manage. 38(3):568–569.

Beer, J. V., and H. Boyd. 1962. Weights of pink-footed geese in autumn. Bird Study 9(2):91–99.

Beg, M. A., and R. S. Hoffman. 1977. Age determination in the red-tailed chipmunk, *Eutamias ruficaudus*. Murrelet 58(2):26–36.

Behney, W. H. 1936. Nocturnal explorations of the forest deer-mouse. J. Mammal. 17(3):225–230.

Beightol, D. R., and D. E. Samuel. 1973. Sonographic analysis of the American woodcock's peent call. J. Wildl. Manage. 37(4):470–475.

Bekoff, M., (ed.). 1978. Coyotes: biology, behavior and management. Academic Press, New York. 384 p.

Bell, R. H. V. 1971. A grazing ecosystem in the Serengeti. Sci. Am. 225(1):86–93.

Bellrose, F. C. 1976. Ducks, geese and swans of North America. 2nd ed. Stackpole Books, Harrisburg, Pa. 543 p.

Bellrose, F. C., and H. G. Anderson. 1943. Preferential ratings of duck food plants. Ill. Nat. Hist. Surv. Bull. 22(5):417–433.

Bellrose, F. C., and R. Crompton. 1972. Nest houses for wood ducks. Ill. Dept. Conserv., Springfield. 4 p.

Bellrose, F. C., T. G. Scott, A. S. Hawkins, and J. B. Low. 1961. Sex ratios and age ratios in North American ducks. Ill. Nat. Hist. Surv. Bull. 27(6): 391–474.

Belson, W. 1966. The effects of reversing the presentation order of verbal rating scales. J. Advert. Res. 6:30–37.

Belson, W., and J. A. Duncan. 1962. A comparison of check-list and the open response questioning systems. Appl. Stat. 11(2):120–132.

Bendell, J. F., and P. W. Elliott. 1966. Habitat selection in blue grouse. Condor 68(5):431–446.

Bendell, J. F. S., and C. D. Fowle. 1950. Some methods for trapping and marking ruffed grouse. J. Wildl. Manage. 14(4):480–482.

Bengtson, S.-A. 1971. Variations in clutch-size in ducks in relation to the food supply. Ibis 113(4):523–526.

Bengtson, S.-A. 1972. Reproduction and fluctuations in the size of duck populations at Lake Myvatn, Iceland. Oikos 23(1):35–58.

Bennet, E. V. 1961. Aspects of vocalization in red-winged blackbird, *Agelaius phoeniceus* (Linnaeus), as determined by audiospectrographic analysis. Ph.D. Diss. Cornell Univ., Ithaca. 176 p.

Bennett, L. J. 1938. The blue-winged teal, its ecology and management. Collegiate Press, Menasha, Wis. 144 p.

Bennett, L. J., P. F. English, and R. McCain. 1940. A study of deer populations by use of pellet-group counts. J. Wildl. Manage. 4(4):398–403.

Bennett, L. J., and G. O. Hendrickson. 1938. Censusing quail in early fall. J. Wildl. Manage. 2(4):169–171.

Bent, A. C. 1926. Life histories of North American marsh birds. U.S. Natl. Mus. Bull. 135, Gov. Print. Off., Washington, D.C. 490 p.

Bentley, J. R., D. W. Seegrist, and D. A. Blakeman. 1970. A technique for sampling low shrub vegetation by crown volume classes. USDA For. Serv., Pac. S. W. For. and Range Exp. Stn., Res. Note PSW–215, Berkeley, Calif. 11 p.

Bentley, R. G., B. C. Salmon-Drexler, W. J. Bonner, and R. K. Vincent. 1976. A Landsat study of ephemeral and perennial rangeland vegetation and soils. Report of work performed by USDI Bureau Land Management (BLM) for the Natl. Aeronaut. and Space Adm. (NASA), Grant No. S–53966A, Denver Serv. Cent., Denver, Colo. 234 p.

Bently, K. W. 1964. The relief of pain—the search for the ideal analgesic. Endeavour 23(89): 97–101.

Bently, K. W., and D. G. Hardy. 1963. New potent analgesics in the morphine series. J. Chem. Soc. 83:220.

Benton, A. H., and W. E. Werner, Jr. 1974. Field biology and ecology. 3rd ed. McGraw-Hill, New York. 564 p.

Benzinger, T. H., and C. Kitzinger. 1949. Direct calorimetry by means of the gradient principle. Rev. Sci. Instrum. 20(12):849–860.

Berger, D. D., and F. Hamerstrom. 1962. Protecting a trapping station from raptor predation. J. Wildl. Manage. 26(2):203–206

Berger, D. D., and H. C. Mueller. 1959. The bal-chatri: a trap for the birds of prey. Bird-Banding 30(1): 18–26.

Berger, T. J., and J. D. Phillips. 1977. Index to U.S. federal wildlife regulations. Assoc. Syst. Collect., Lawrence, Kansas. 500 p.

Bergerud, A. T. 1963. Aerial winter census of caribou. J. Wildl. Manage. 27(3):438–449.

Bergerud, A. T. 1970a. Eruption of permanent premolars and molars for Newfoundland caribou. J. Wildl. Manage. 34(4):962–963.

Bergerud, A. T. 1970b. Population dynamics of the willow ptarmigan *Lagopus lagopus alleni* L. in Newfoundland 1955 to 1965. Oikos 21(2):299–325.

Bergerud, A. T., and F. Manuel. 1969 Aerial census of moose in central Newfoundland. J. Wildl. Manage. 33(4):910–916.

Bergerud, A. T., and W. E. Mercer. 1966. Census of willow ptarmigan in Newfoundland. J. Wildl. Manage. 30(1):101–113.

Bergerud, A. T., S. S. Peters, and R. McGrath. 1963. Determining sex and age of willow ptarmigan in Newfoundland. J. Wildl. Manage. 27(4): 700–711.

Bergerud, A. T., and H. L. Russell. 1966. Extraction of incisors of Newfoundland caribou. J. Wildl. Manage. 30(4):842–843.

Berryman, J. H. 1971. Predator management: a justifiable tool of wildlife management. Proc. Int. Assoc. Game Fish and Conserv. Commissioners 61:63–70.

Berryman, J. H. 1972. The principles of predator control. J. Wildl. Manage. 36(2):395–400.

Beruldsen, E. T., and A. Morgan. 1934. Grassland research in Australia: notes on botanical analysis of irrigated pastures. Imp. Bur. Plant Genet. Herbage Plants Bull. 14: 33–43.

Beshears, W. W., Jr. 1974. Wood ducks in Alabama. Alabama Dept. Conserv. and Nat. Resour. Spec. Rep. No. 4. 45 p.

Best, A. A. 1971. Rowland Ward's records of big game. 15th ed. Rowland Ward, London. 452 p.

Best, L. B. 1975. Interpretational errors in the "mapping method" as a census technique. Auk 92(3):452–460.

Besterman, T. 1966. A world bibliography of bibliographies, and of bibliographical catalogues, calendars, abstracts, digests, indexes and the like. 4th ed. Societas Bibliographica, Geneva. 5 vol.

Besterman, T. 1971. Biological sciences: a bibliography of bibliographies. Rowman and Littlefield, Totowa, N.J. 471 p.

Bethune, J. E. 1967. Mathematical programming approach to the allocation of resources to publically supported timber management research. Ph.D. Diss. Univ. of Georgia, Athens. 124 p.

Betts, M. M. 1954. Experiments with an artificial nestling. Br. Birds 47(4):229–231.

Betts, M. M. 1956. Further experiments with an artificial nestling gape. Br. Birds 49(6):213–215.

Beveridge, W. I. B. 1957. The art of scientific investigation. W. W. Norton, New York. 178 p.

Beverton, R. J. H., and S. J. Holt. 1957. On the dynamics of exploited fish populations. Fish. Invest. Minist. Agric. Fish. Food (G. B.) Ser. II Salmon Freshwater Fish 19:533 p.

Bhatia, M. 1971. Canadian provincial government publications: bibliography of bibliographies. Univ. of Saskatchewan Libr., Saskatoon. 19 p.

Bidwell, T. C. 1975. College and university sources of remote sensing information. Photogramm. Eng. Remote Sensing 41(10):1273–1284.

Bigler, W. J., and G. I. Hoff. 1974. Anesthesia of raccoons with ketamine hydrochloride. J. Wildl. Manage. 38(2):364–366.

Billingsley, B. B., Jr., and D. H. Arner. 1970. The nutritive value and digestibility of some winter foods of the eastern wild turkey. J. Wildl. Manage. 34(1):176–182.

Biosis. 1979. Serial sources for the BIOSIS data base. Biosciences Information Service of Biol. Abstracts, Philadelphia. 312 p.

Bird, W. M. 1977. Wildlife water basins. U.S. Bur. Land Manage. Tech. Note 298, Denver, Colo. 7 p.

Birney, E. C., and E. D. Fleharty. 1968. Comparative success in the application of aging techniques to a population of winter-trapped mink. Southwestern Nat. 13(3):275–282.

Birney, E. C., R. Jenness, and D. D. Baird. 1975. Eye lens proteins as criteria of age in cotton rats. J. Wildl. Manage. 39(4):718–728.

Bischoff, A. I. 1954. Limitations of the bone marrow technique in determining malnutrition in deer. Proc. Western Assoc. State Game and Fish Commissioners 34:205–210.

Bishop, D. 1959. Science thesis control in Europe and America. Am. Doc. 10(1):51–58.

Bishop, R. A., and C. R. Hungerford. 1965. Seasonal food selection of Arizona Mearns quail. J. Wildl. Manage. 29(4):813–819.

Bissell, H. D., B. Harris, H. Strong, and F. James. 1955. The digestibility of certain natural and artificial foods eaten by deer in California. Calif. Fish and Game. 41(1):57–58.

Biswell, H. H. 1961. Manipulation of chamise brush for deer range improvement. Calif. Fish and Game 47(2):125–144.

Biswell, H. H., and J. H. Gilman. 1961. Brush management in relation to fire and other environmental factors on the Tehama deer winter range. Calif. Fish and Game 47(4):357–389.

Biswell, H. H., R. D. Taber, D. W. Hedrick, and A. M. Schultz. 1952. Management of chamise brushlands for game in the north coast region of California. Calif. Fish and Game 38(4): 453–484.

Black, D. M., (comp.). 1965. Guide to lists of master's theses. Am. Libr. Assoc., Chicago, Ill. 144 p.

Black, H. C. 1958. Black bear research in New York. Trans. N. Am. Wildl. Conf. 23:443–451.

Black, H. C., E. J. Dimock, W. E. Dodge, and W. H. Lawrence. 1969. Survey of animal damage on forest plantations in Oregon and Washington. Trans. N. Am. Wildl. and Nat. Resour. Conf. 34:388–408.

Blackith, R. E. 1958. Nearest-neighbour distance measurements for the estimation of animal populations. Ecology 39(1):147–150.

Blackwelder, R. E. 1963a. Books on zoology (including natural history, physiology, genetics, parasitology, ecology, paleontology, entomology, etc.). Soc. Syst. Zool. Carbondale, Ill. 110 p.

Blackwelder, R. E. 1963b. Classification of the animal kingdom. Southern Illinois Univ. Press, Carbondale, Ill. 94 p.

Blackwelder, R. E. 1972. Guide to the taxonomic literature of vertebrates. Iowa State Univ. Press, Ames, Iowa. 259 p.

Blackwelder, R. E., and R. M. Blackwelder. 1961. Directory of zoological taxonomists of the world. Southern Illinois Univ. Press, Carbondale, Ill. 404 p.

Blagosklonov, K. N. 1977. Attracting birds for forest protection from pests. Lesnoye Khaziaystvo 6:85–86.

Blair, R. M., and E. A. Epps, Jr. 1967. Distribution of protein and phosphorus in spring growth of rusty blackhaw. J. Wildl. Manage. 31(1): 188–190.

Blair, R. M., H. L. Short, and E. A. Epps, Jr. 1977. Seasonal nutrient yield and digestibility of deer forage from a young pine plantation. J. Wildl. Manage. 41(4):667–676.

Blair, W. F. 1941. Techniques for the study of mammal populations. J. Mammal. 22(2):148–157.

Blair, W. F., A. P. Blair, P. Brodkorb, F. R. Cagle, and G. A. Moore. 1968. Vertebrates of the United States. 2nd ed. McGraw-Hill, New York. 616 p.

Blaisdell, J. A., and R. L. Hubbard. 1956. An "outrigger" type deer fence. USDA Calif. For. Range Exp. Stn. Agric. Res. Note 108, Berkeley, Calif. 3 p.

Blake, E. R. 1949. Preserving birds for study. Chicago Nat. Hist. Mus. Fieldiana, Techniques No. 7. 38 p.

Blake, E. R. 1977. Manual of neotropical birds. vol. 1; Spheniscidae (Penguins) to Laridae (Gulls and Allies). Univ. of Chicago Press. 674 p.

Blake, S. F., and A. C. Atwood. 1942 and 1961. Geographic guide to the floras of the world: an annotated list, with special reference to useful plants and common plant names. USDA Misc. Publ. 401 and 797.

Blaker, A. A. 1965. Photography for scientific publication: a handbook. Freeman Co., San Francisco, Calif. 158 p.

Blank, T. H., and J. S. Ash. 1956. Marker for game birds. J. Wildl. Manage. 20(3):328–330.

Blankenship, L. H. 1957. Investigations of the American woodcock in Michigan. Mich. Dept. Conserv., Game Div. Rep. 2123, Lansing. 217 p.

Blaxter, K. L. 1962. The energy metabolism of ruminants. Charles C. Thomas Publ., Springfield, Ill. 332 p.

Blaxter, K. L., (ed.). 1965. Energy metabolism. Proc. 3rd Symp. held in Troon, Scotland, May 1964. Academic Press Inc., New York and London. 450 p.

Bledsoe, B. 1954. Master's theses in science, 1952. Biblio Press, Washington, D.C. 252 p.

Bloemendal, H. 1977. The vertebrate eye lens. Science 197(4299):127–138.

Blohm, R. J., and P. Ward. 1979. Experience with a decoy trap for male gadwalls. Bird-Banding 50(1):45–48.

Blokpoel, H. 1976. Bird hazards to aircraft. Can. Wildl. Serv. and Books Canada Inc., Buffalo, N.Y. 236 p.

Blood, D. A., and A. L. Lovaas. 1966. Measurements and weight relationships in Manitoba elk. J. Wildl. Manage. 30(1):135–140.

Boag, D. A. 1965. Indicators of sex, age, and breeding phenology in blue grouse. J. Wildl. Manage. 29(1): 103–108.

Boag, D. A. 1966. Population attributes of blue grouse in southwestern Alberta. Can. J. Zool. 44(5):799–814.

Boag, D. A. 1972. Effect of radio packages on behavior of captive red grouse. J. Wildl. Manage. 36(2): 511–518.

Boag, D. A., A. Watson, and R. Parr. 1973. Radio-marking versus back-tagging red grouse. J. Wildl. Manage. 37(3): 410–412.

Boag, D. A., A Watson, and R. Parr. 1975. Patagial streamers as markers for red grouse chicks. Bird-Banding 46(3):248.

Boer, A. 1978. Management of deer wintering areas in New Brunswick. Wildl. Soc. Bull. 6(4):200–205.

Boettger, R. W., and M. Smart. 1968. Beaver flowages converted from liabilities to assets. Maine Fish and Game 10(3):5–7.

Boever, W. J., and H. Paluch. 1974. Injectable anesthetics in wild ruminants. Vet. Med. and Small Anim. Clin. 69(5):548–551.

Bogatich, V. 1967. The use of live traps to remove starlings and protect agricultural products in the state of Washington. Proc. Vertebr. Pest Conf. 3:98–99.

Bohl, W. H. 1956. Experiments in locating wild chukar partridges by use of recorded calls. J. Wildl. Manage. 20(1):83–85.

Boise, C. M. 1975. Skull measurements as criteria for aging fishers. N.Y. Fish and Game J. 22(1):32–37.

Boland, D. H. P. 1976. Trophic classification of lakes using Landsat-1 (ERTS-1) multispectral scanner data. USEPA 600/3–76–037. Off. Res. and Dev., Corvallis, Oreg. 245 p.

Bole, B. P., Jr. 1939. The quadrat method of studying small mammal populations. Sci. Publ. of the Cleveland Mus. of Nat. Hist. 5(4):15–77.

Bolen, E. C., J. S. Loven, and B. W. Cain. 1977. A holding sleeve for waterfowl. J. Wildl. Manage 41(4): 789–790.

Bonaccorso, F. J., and N. Smythe. 1972. Punch-marking bats: an alternate to banding. J. Mammal. 53(2): 389–390.

Bonaccorso, F. J., N. Smythe, and S. R. Humphrey. 1976. Improved techniques for marking bats. J. Mammal. 57(1):181–182.

Bonn, G. S., (ed.), 1973. Information resources in the environmental sciences; papers presented at the 18th Allerton Park Institute, November 12–15, 1972. Univ. of Illinois Grad. Sch. of Libr. Sci., Champatgn-Urbana. 238 p.

Bookhout, T. A. 1958. The availability of plant seeds to bobwhite quail in southern Illinois. Ecology 39(4): 671–681.

Bookhout, T. A., and E. M. Harger. 1964. An accurate, inexpensive scale for laboratory use. J. Mammal. 45(2):313.

Boonstra, R., and C. J. Krebs. 1976. The effect of odour on trap response in *Microtus townsendii*. J. Zool. 180(4):467–476.

Booth, E. S. 1950. How to know the mammals. William C. Brown, Dubuque, Iowa. 206 p.

Borhegyi, S. F., and E. A. Dodson. 1961. A bibliography of museums and museum work 1900–1960. Milwaukee Public Mus., Publ. Museology No. 1. 102 p.

Bormann, F. H. 1953. The statistical efficiency of sample plot size and shape in forest ecology. Ecology 34(3):474–487.

Borror, D. J. 1956. Variation in Carolina wren songs. Auk 73(2): 211–229.

Borror, D. J. 1959. Variation in the songs of the rufous-sided towhee. Wilson Bull. 71(1):54–72.

Borror, D. J. 1965. Song variation in Maine song sparrows. Wilson Bull. 77(1):5–37.

Borror, D. J., and C. R. Reese. 1953. The analysis of bird songs by means of a vibralyzer. Wilson Bull. 65(4):271–276.

Borzio, F. 1973. Ketamine hydrochloride as an anesthetic for wildfowl. Vet. Med. Small Anim. Clin. 68(12):1364–1367.

Bothma, J. Du P., J. G. Teer, and C. E. Gates, 1972. Growth and age determination of the cottontail in south Texas. J. Wildl. Manage. 36(4): 1209–1221.

Bottle, R. T., and H. V. Wyatt, (ed.). 1971. The use of biological literature. 2nd ed. Archon Books, Hamden, Conn. 379 p.

Bouffard, S. H., and D. Hein. 1978. Census methods for eastern gray squirrels. J. Wildl. Manage. 42(3): 550–557.

Bourdeau, P. E. 1953. A test of random versus systematic ecological sampling. Ecology 34(3):499–512.

Bourliere, F. 1964. The natural history of mammals. 3rd ed. Alfred A. Knopf, New York. 387 p.

Bourque, B. J., K. Morris, and A. Spiess. 1978. Determining the season of death of mammal teeth from archeological sites: a new sectioning technique. Science 199(4328):530–531.

Bowden, D. C., A. E. Anderson, and D. E. Medin. 1969. Frequency distributions of mule deer fecal group counts. J. Wildl. Manage. 33(4): 895–905.

Bowman, D. E., and A. G. Law. 1964. Effects of temperature and day length on the development of lignin, cellulose, and protein in *Dactylis glomerata* L. and *Bromus inermis* Leyss. Agron. J. 56(2):177–179.

Bowns, J. E. 1976. Field criteria for predator damage assessment. Utah Science 37(1):26–30.

Box, T. W. 1966. Range management theses, 1961–1965. J. Range Mgmt. 19(5):310–313. [Earlier compilations appeared in volumes 14:51–54 for 1961 and 15:57–58 for 1962 of the Journal.]

Box, T. W., and J. Powell. 1965. Brush management techniques for improved forage values in south Texas. Trans. N. Am. Wildl. Nat. Resour. Conf. 30:285–295.

Boyles, D. L., and J. W. Wright. 1977. Photocell system for recording circadian drinking patterns in rodents and primates. Physiol. Behav. 18(4):755–757.

Bradley, O. C., and T. Grahame. 1960. The structure of the fowl. 4th ed. Oliver and Boyd, Edinburgh. 143 p.

Bradley, R. 1977. Making animal sound recordings. Amer. Birds 31(3):279.

Bradt, G. W. 1938. A study of beaver colonies in Michigan. J. Mammal. 19(2):139–162.

Brady, J. R., and M. R. Pelton. 1976. An evaluation of some cottontail rabbit marking techniques. J. Tenn. Acad. Sci. 51(3):89–90.

Brainerd, G. W. 1939. An illustrated field key for the identification of mammal bones. Ohio State Archaeol. Hist. Quart. 48:324–328.

Bramley, P. 1966. Roe deer. Nat. Conserv. Unit of Grouse and Moorland Ecol. Prog. Rep. 12:70–72.

Brand, A. R. 1935. A method for intensive study of bird song. Auk 52(1): 40–52.

Brandborg, S. M. 1955. Life history and management of the mountain goat in Idaho. Idaho Dept. Fish and Game, Wildl. Bull. No. 2, Boise. 142 p.

Brander, R. B. 1968. A radio-package harness for game birds. J. Wildl. Manage. 32(3):630–632.

Bratton, S. P. 1975. The effect of the European wild boar, *Sus scrofa,* on gray beech forest in the Great Smoky Mountains. Ecology 56(6):1356–1366.

Braun, C. E. 1976. Methods for locating, trapping and banding band-tailed pigeons in Colorado. Colo. Div. Wildl. Spec. Rep. No. 39. 20 p.

Braun, C. E., and G. E. Rogers. 1971. The white-tailed ptarmigan in Colorado. Colo. Div. Wildl. Tech. Publ. No. 27. 80 p.

Braun, C. E., R. K. Schmidt, and G. E. Rogers. 1973. Census of Colorado white-tailed ptarmigan with tape-recorded calls. J. Wildl. Manage. 37(1):90–93.

Braun, E. L. 1950. Deciduous forests of eastern North America. Hafner Publ. Co., New York and London. 596 p.

Braun-Blanquet, J. 1928. Pflanzensoziologie. 1st ed. Berlin, Springer-Verlag. 631 p.

Braun-Blanquet, J. 1965. Plant sociology: the study of plant communities. Hafner, London. 439 p.

Bray, O. E., and G. W. Corner. 1972. A tail clip for attaching transmitters to birds. J. Wildl. Manage. 36(2):640–642.

Bray, O. E., R. E. Johnson, and A. L. Kolz. 1975a. A removable car-top antenna system for radio-tracking birds. Bird-Banding 46(1):15–18.

Bray, O. E., K. H. Larsen, and D. F. Mott. 1975b. Winter movements and activities of radio-equipped starlings. J. Wildl. Manage. 39(4):795–801.

Breckenridge, W. J. 1956. Nesting study of wood ducks. J. Wildl. Manage. 20(1):16–21.

Breckenridge, W. J., and J. R. Tester. 1961. Growth, local movements, and hibernation of the Manitoba toad, *Bufo nemiophrys.* Ecology 42(4): 637–646.

Briggs, G. D., R. V. Hendrickson, and B. J. LeBoeuf. 1975. Ketamine immobilization of northern elephant seals. J. Am. Vet. Med. Assoc. 167(7):546–548.

Briggs, R. L. 1977. Mist netting waterfowl. N. Am. Bird Bander 2(2):61–63.

Brillouin, L. 1962. Science and information theory. 2nd ed. Academic Press, New York. 351 p.

Brinker, R. C. 1969. Elementary surveying. 5th ed. Int. Textbook Co., Scranton, Pa. 620 p.

British Library, Lending Division. 1977. Journals in translation. Boston Spa, Yorkshire, England.

British Ornithologists' Union. 1952. Checklist of the birds of Great Britain and Ireland. List Sub-Committee, London. 106 p.

Britten, J., and G. S. Boulger. 1931. Biographical index of deceased British and Irish botanists. 2nd ed. rev. Taylor and Francis Ltd., London. 342 p.

Brocke, R. H. 1972. A live snare for trap-shy snowshoe hares. J. Wildl. Manage. 36(3):988–991.

Brockelman, W. C., and N. K. Kobayashi. 1971. Live capture of free-ranging primates with a blow-gun. J. Wildl. Manage. 35(4):852–855.

Brody, S. 1945. Bioenergetics and growth, with special reference to the efficiency complex in domestic animals. Reinhold Publ. Corp., New York. 1023 p.

Brohn, A., and L. J. Korschgen. 1950. The precipitin test—a useful tool in game law enforcement. Trans. N. Am. Wild. Conf. 15:467–478.

Broley, J. 1950. Identifying nests of the Anatidae of the Canadian prairies. J. Wildl. Manage. 14(4):452–456.

Bronson, F. H., and B. E. Eleftheriou. 1964. Chronic physiological effects of fighting in mice. Gen. Comp. Endocrinol. 4(1):9–14.

Brooks, R. P., and W. E. Dodge. 1978. A night identification collar for beavers. J. Wildl. Manage. 42(2): 448–452.

Brotzman, R. L., and R. H. Giles, Jr. 1966. Electronic data processing of capture-recapture and related ecological data. J. Wildl. Manage. 30(2):286–292.

Brown, D. E. 1977. White-winged dove *(Zenaida asiatica)*. p. 247–272 *in* G. C. Sanderson, (ed.). Management of migratory shore and upland game birds in North America. Int. Assoc. Fish and Wildl. Agencies, Washington, D.C. 358 p.

Brown, D. E., C. L. Cochran, and T. E. Waddell. 1978. Using call-counts to predict hunting success for scaled quail. J. Wildl. Manage. 42(2):281–287.

Brown, D. E., and R. H. Smith. 1976. Predicting hunting success from call counts of mourning and white-winged doves. J. Wildl. Manage. 40(4):743–749.

Brown, E. B., III, W. R. Saatela, and W. D. Schmid. 1969. A compact lightweight live trap for small mammals. J. Mammal. 50(1):154–155.

Brown, E. R., and C. F. Martinsen. 1959. Browse planting for big game. Wash. Game Dept. Biol. Bull. No. 12, Olympia. 63 p.

Brown, G. H. 1952. Illustrated skull key to the recent land mammals of Virginia. Va. Coop. Wildl. Res. Unit Release No. 52–2, Blacksburg. 75 p.

Brown, G. M., Jr., J. Hammack, and M. F. Tillman. 1976. Mallard population dynamics and management models. J. Wildl. Manage. 40(3): 542–555.

Brown, J. H. 1973. Species diversity of seed-eating desert rodents in sand dune habitats. Ecology 54(4):775–787.

Brown, J. H. 1975. Geographical ecology of desert rodents. p. 315–341 *in* M. L. Cody and J. M. Diamond, (eds.). Ecology and evolution of communities. Belknap Press of Harvard Univ. Press. Cambridge, Mass. 545 p.

Brown, J. K. 1976. Estimating shrub biomass from basal stem diameters. Can. J. For. Res. 6(2):153–158.

Brown, L. 1976. Birds of prey: their biology and ecology. Hamlyn Publ. Group Ltd., Middlesex, England. 256 p.

Brown, L. N., and C. H. Conaway. 1961. Dye excretion as a method for determination of small mammal home ranges. Am. Midl. Nat. 66(1):128–137.

Brown, L. N., and R. J. McGuire. 1975. Field ecology of the exotic Mexican red-bellied squirrel in Florida. J. Wildl. Manage. 39(2):405–419.

Brown P., and G. B. Stratton. 1963. World list of scientific periodicals published in the years 1900–1960. 4th ed. Butterworths, London. 3 vol.

Brown, R. L. 1975. Mearns' quail capture method. A final report. W–78–R–15. Arizona Game and Fish Dept. Phoenix. 6 p.

Brown, W. W. 1978. Wetland mapping in New Jersey and New York. Photogramm. Eng. Remote Sensing 44(3):303–314.

Browne, C. A. 1938. Some relationships of soil to plant and animal nutrition—the major elements. p. 777–806 *in* M. A. McCall, (ed.). Soil and men: yearbook of agriculture. Part III. U.S. Gov. Print. Off. Washington, D.C. 1232 p.

Brownie, C., D. R. Anderson, K. P. Burnham, and D. S. Robson. 1978. Statistical inference from hand recovery data: a handbook. U.S. Fish and Wildl. Serv. Resour. Publ. 131. 212 p.

Bruce, J. V., and G. F. Knowlton. 1953. Controlling bats. Utah State Agric. Coll. Ext. Circ. No. 176. 2 p.

Brüggemann, J., D. Giesecke, and K. Walser-Kärst. 1968. Methods for studying microbial digestion in ruminants post mortem with special reference to wild species. J. Wildl. Manage. 32(1):198–207.

Brunetti, O. A. 1965. The use of paper chromatography in wildlife law enforcement. Proc. Western Assoc. of State Game and Fish Commissioners 45:281–284.

Bruns, H. 1960. The economic importance of birds in the forest. Bird Study 7(4):193–208.

Bryan, J. H. D. 1966. A multi-purpose information retrieval system based on edge-notched cards. BioScience 16(6):402–407.

Bryant, M. M. 1943. Area determinations with the modified acreage grid. J. For. 41(10):764–766.

Bryant, M. M., (ed.). 1962. Current American usage. Funk and Wagnalls Co., New York. 290 p.

Buchanan, D. S., A. Nakao, and G. Edwards. 1953. Carbon isotope effects in biological systems. Science 117(3047):541–545.

Buchler, E. R. 1976. A chemiluminescent tag for tracking bats and other small nocturnal animals. J. Mammal. 57(1):173–176.

Buck, W. B., G. D. Osweiler, and G. A. Van Gelder. 1976. Clinical and diagnostic veterinary toxicology. 2nd ed. Kendall/Hunt Publ. Co., Dubuque, Iowa. 380 p.

Buckner, C. H. 1964. Preliminary trials of a camera recording device for the study of small mammals. Can. Field-Nat. 78(2):77–79.

Buech, R. R. 1974. A new live-trap and techniques for winter trapping small mammals. Can. Field-Nat. 88(3): 317–321.

Buechner, H. K. 1950. Life history, ecology, and range use of the prong-horned antelope in Trans-Pecos, Texas. Am. Midl. Nat. 43(2):257–354.

Buechner, H. K., F. C. Craighead, Jr., J. J. Craighead, and C. E. Cote. 1971. Satellites for research on free roaming animals. BioScience 21(24): 1201–1205.

Buell, M. F., and J. E. Cantlon. 1950. A study of two communities of the New Jersey pine barrens and a comparison of methods. Ecology 31(4): 567–586.

Buell, N. E. 1953. Prairie dogs and their control. U.S. Fish Wildl. Serv. Wildl. Leafl. 357, Washington, D.C. 4 p.

Bull, E. L., and R. J. Pedersen. 1978. Two methods of trapping adult pileated woodpeckers at their nest cavities. N. Am. Bird Bander 3(3): 95–99.

Bullard, R. W. 1970. Variation of chemical concentration in surface-coated and tableted grain baits. J. Wildl. Manage. 34(4):925–929.

Bullard, R. W., and S. A. Shumake. 1977. Food-base flavor additive improves bait acceptance by rice field rats. J. Wildl. Manage. 41(2):290–297.

Bump, G. 1950. Wildlife habitat changes in the Connecticut Hill Game Management Area. Cornell Univ. Agric. Exp. Stn. Memoir 289, Ithaca, N.Y. 75 p.

Bump, G., R. W. Darrow, F. C. Edminster, and W. F. Crissey. 1947. The ruffed grouse: life history, propagation, management. N.Y. State Conserv. Dept., Albany. 915 p.

Bunch, T. D., R. W. Meadows, W. C. Foote, L. N. Egbert, and J. J. Spillett. 1976. Identification of ungulate hemoglobins for law enforcement. J. Wildl. Manage. 40(3):517–522.

Bunge, M. A. 1967. Scientific research I: the search for system. Springer-Verlag, N.Y. 536 p.

Bunnell, F. L. 1974. Computer simulation of forest wildlife relations. p. 39–50 *in* H. C. Black, (ed.). Wildlife and forest management in the Pacific northwest. School of Forestry, Oregon State Univ., Corvallis. 236 p.

Bunnell, S. D., J. A. Rensel, J. F. Kimball, Jr., and M. L. Wolfe. 1977. Determination of age and sex of dusky blue grouse. J. Wildl. Manage. 41(4): 662–666.

Burger, G. V. 1969. Response of gray squirrels to nest boxes at Remington Farms, Maryland. J. Wildl. Manage. 33(4):796–801.

Burger, G. V. 1973. Practical wildlife management. Winchester Press, New York. 218 p.

Burger, G. V., R. J. Greenwood, and R. C. Oldenburg. 1970. Alula removal technique for identifying wings of released waterfowl. J. Wildl. Manage. 34(1):137–146.

Burke, C. J., S. M. Byers, and R. A. Montgomery. 1978. A field guide to the aging of wood duck embryos. J. Wildl. Manage. 42(2):432–437.

Burkholder, B. L. 1955. Control of small predators. U.S. Fish Wildl. Serv. Circ. 33. 8 p.

Burleigh, T. D. 1958. Georgia birds. Univ. Oklahoma Press, Norman. 746 p.

Burleigh, T. D. 1972. Birds of Idaho. Caxton Printers, Caldwell, Idaho. 467 p.

Burnham, K. P., and D. R. Anderson. 1979. The composite dynamic method as evidence for age-specific waterfowl mortality. J. Wildl. Manage. 43(2): 356–366.

Burns, M. 1952. The genetics of the dog. Commonwealth Bur. of Anim. Breed. & Genet., Tech. Commun. No. 9, Cunningham and Sons, Edinburgh. 122 p.

Burns, M., and M. N. Fraser. 1966. The genetics of the dog. Oliver and Boyd. 230 p.

Burns, R. W., Jr. 1969. Using the literature on wildlife management. p. 13–45 *in* R. H. Giles, Jr., (ed.). Wildlife management techniques. 3rd ed. rev. Wildl. Soc., Washington, D.C. 623 p.

Burt, W. H. 1954. The mammals of Michigan. rev. ed. Univ. Michigan Press, Ann Arbor. 288 p.

Burt, W. H. 1957. Mammals of the Great Lakes region. Univ. Michigan Press, Ann Arbor. 246 p.

Burt, W. H., and R. P. Grossenheider. 1976. A field guide to the mammals. 3rd. ed. Houghton Mifflin Co., Boston. 289 p.

Burton, M. 1962. Systematic dictionary of mammals of the world. Thomas Y. Crowell, New York. 307 p. Paper edition (1968) titled: University dictionary of mammals of the world.

Buss, I. O. 1946. Wisconsin pheasant populations. Wis. Conserv. Dept. Publ. 326, A–46, Madison. 184 p.

Buss, I. O., and C. V. Swanson. 1950. Some effects of weather on pheasant reproduction in southeastern Washington. Trans. N. Am. Wildl. Conf. 15:364–378.

Bussmann, J. 1933. Experiments with the terragraph on the activities of nesting birds. Bird-Banding 4(1): 33–40.

Butcher, R. L. 1977. Changes in gonadotropins and steroids associated with unilateral ovariectomy of the rat. Endocrinol. 101(3):830–840.

Buttery, R. F. 1978. Modified ecoclass—a Forest Service method for classifying ecosystems. p. 157–168 *in* H. G. Lund et al. Integrated inventories of renewable natural resources. Proceedings of the workshop: USDA For. Serv., Rocky Mt. For. and Range Exp. Stn. Gen. Tech. Rep. RM-55, Fort Collins, Colo. 482 p.

Buttress, F. A. 1966. World list of abbreviations. 3rd ed. Leonard Hill Ltd. London. 186 p.

Byrd, N. A., and H. L. Holbrook. 1974. How to improve forest game habitat. USDA For. Serv., State and Priv. For., S. E. Area For. Manage. Bull., Atlanta, Ga. 4 p.

Cagle, F. R. 1960. Increase of biological serials—a destructive trend? AIBS Bull. 10(1):13–14.

Cahalane, V. H. 1961. Mammals of North America. Macmillan Co., New York. 682 p.

Cain, D. 1971. The Ely chain. USDI Bur. Land Manage., Washington, D.C. 32 p.

Cain, S. A., and G. M. deOliveira Castro. 1959. Manual of vegetation analysis. Harper Bros., New York. 325 p.

Caldwell, J. A. 1963. An investigation of raccoons in northcentral Florida. M. S. Thesis, Univ. Fla., Gainesville. 106 p.

Caldwell, P. J. 1980. Primary shaft measurements in relation to age of sharp-tailed grouse. J. Wildl. Manage. 44(1): 202–204.

Caldwell, P. J., and A. E. Snart. 1974. A photographic index for aging mallard embryos. J. Wildl. Manage. 38(2):298–301.

Calkins, H. A., and J. B. Yule. 1935. The Abney level handbook. U.S. For. Serv., Washington, D.C. 44 p.

Campbell, D. L. 1960. A colored leg strip for marking birds. J. Wildl. Manage. 24(4):431.

Campbell, D. L. 1974. Establishing preferred browse to reduce damage to Douglas fir seedlings by deer and elk. p. 187–192 *in* H. C. Black, (ed.). Wildlife and forest management in the Pacific northwest. Oregon State Univ., Corvallis. 236 p.

Campbell, D. L., and J. Evans. 1975. "Vexar" seedling protectors to reduce wildlife damage to Douglas fir. U.S. Fish Wildl. Serv. Wildl. Leafl. 508, Washington, D.C. 11 p.

Campbell, W. G. 1969. Form and style in thesis writing. 3rd ed. Houghton Mifflin, Inc., Boston. 138 p.

Canfield, R. H. 1941. Application of the line interception method in sampling range vegetation. J. For. 39(4):388–394.

Cannell, C. F., and R. L. Kahn. 1968. Interviewing. p. 526–595 *in* G. Lindzey and E. Aronson, (eds.). The handbook of social psychology, 2nd ed. Addison-Wesley Publ. Co., Reading, Mass. Vol. 2. 819 p.

Cannell, C. F., L. Oksenberg, and J. M. Converse. 1977. Striving for response accuracy: experiments in new interviewing techniques. J. Mark. Res. 14(3):306–315.

Capp, J. C. 1976. Increasing pocket gopher problems in reforestation. Proc. Vertebr. Pest Conf. 7:221–228.

Carlson, C. E. 1943. Unusual pheasant nests from Minnesota. Flicker 15(3):29–31.

Carneggie, D. M., and C. S. Holm. 1977. Remote sensing techniques for monitoring impacts of phosphate mining in southeastern Idaho. p. 251–272 *in* Proc. 2nd William T. Pecora Memorial Symp., Am. Soc. Photogramm. 404 p.

Caroline, M. 1953. Cotton rats. U.S. Fish Wildl. Serv. Washington, D.C. 2 p.

Caron, L., J. Minor, and M. P. Meyer. 1976. Upper Mississippi River underwater feature detection capabilities of water-penetrating aerial photography. Univ. of Minnesota Inst. Agric. For. and Home Econ. Remote Sensing Lab. Res. Rep. 76–1, St. Paul, Minn. 15 p.

Carpenter, J. R. 1938. An ecological glossary. Univ. Oklahoma Press, Norman. 306 p.

Carpenter, J. W., and R. P. Martin. 1969. Capturing prairie dogs for transplanting. J. Wildl. Manage. 33(4):1024.

Carpenter, L. H. 1976a. Nitrogen-herbicide effects on sagebrush deer range. Ph.D. Diss. Colorado State Univ., Ft. Collins. 159 p.

Carpenter, L. H. 1976b. A night-viewing device to monitor activities of wildlife. Colo. Dept. Nat. Res., Div. Wildl. Game Info. Leafl. No. 103. 2 p.

Carpenter, L. H., D. W. Reichert, and F. Wolfe, Jr. 1977. Lighted collars to aid night observations of mule deer. USDA For. Serv., Rocky Mt. For. and Range Exp. Stn. Res. Note RM–338. Ft. Collins, Colo. 4 p.

Carpovich, E. A. 1960. Russian-English biological and medical dictionary. 2nd ed. Tech. Dictionaries, New York. 400 p.

Carr, A. F., Jr. 1939. Notes on escape behavior in the Florida marsh rabbit. J. Mammal. 20(3):322–325.

Carson, J. D. 1961. Epiphyseal cartilage as an age indicator in fox and gray squirrels. J. Wildl. Manage. 25(1):90–93.

Casey, G. A., and W. A. Webster. 1975. Age and sex determination of striped skunks *(Mephitis mephitis)* from Ontario, Manitoba, and Quebec. Can. J. Zool. 53(3):223–226.

Casey, R. S., J. W. Perry, M. M. Berry, and A. Kent, (eds.). 1958. Punched cards: their applications to science and industry. 2nd ed. Reinhold, New York. 697 p.

Casida, L. E. 1960. Research techniques in physiology of reproduction in the female. p. 106–121 *in* Techniques and procedures in animal production research. Am. Soc. of Anim. Sci. 228 p.

Cassady, J. T. 1941. A method of determining range forage utilization by sheep. J. For. 39(8): 667–671.

Caswell, E. B. 1954. A method for sexing blue grouse. J. Wildl. Manage. 18(1):139.

Caswell, H. 1976. The validation problem. p. 313–325 *in* B. C. Patten, (ed.). Systems analysis and simulation in ecology. Academic Press, Inc. N.Y. Vol. 4. 593 p.

Catana, A. J. 1963. The wandering quarter method of estimating population density. Ecology 44(2):349–360.

Caton, J. D. 1877. The antelope and deer of America. Hurd and Houghton, N.Y. 426 p.

Caughley, G. 1974a. Interpretation of age ratios. J. Wildl. Manage. 38 (3):557–562.

Caughley, G. 1974b. Bias in aerial survey. J. Wildl. Manage. 38(4):921–933.

Caughley, G. 1977a. Sampling in aerial survey. J. Wildl. Manage. 41(4): 605–615.

Caughley, G. 1977b. Analysis of vertebrate populations. John Wiley and Sons, London. 234 p.

Caughley, G., and L. C. Birch. 1971. Rate of increase. J. Wildl. Manage. 35(4):658–663.

Caughley, G., and J. Goddard. 1972. Improving the estimates from inaccurate censuses. J. Wildl. Manage. 36(1):135–140.

Caughley, G., R. Sinclair, and D. Scott-Kemmis. 1976. Experiments in aerial survey. J. Wildl. Manage. 40(2):290–300.

Cauley, D. L. 1974. Urban habitat requirements for four wildlife species. p. 143–147 *in* J. H. Noyes and D. R. Progulske, (eds.). Wildlife in an urbanizing environment. Coop. Ext. Serv. Monogr., Univ. Massachusetts, Amherst. 182 p.

Causey, M. K., F. L. Bonner, and J. B. Graves. 1968. Dieldrin residues in the gallinules *Porphyrula martinica* L. and *Gallinula chloropas* L. and its effect on clutch size and hatchability. Bull. Environ. Contam. Toxicol. 3(5):274–283.

Cengel, D. J., J. E. Estep, and R. L. Kirkpatrick. 1978. Pine vole reproduction in relation to food habits and body fat. J. Wildl. Manage. 42(4): 822–833.

Chabreck, R. H., and J. D. Shroer. 1975. Effects of neck collars on the reproduction of snow geese. Bird-Banding 46(4):346–347.

Chambers, R. E., and P. F. English. 1958. Modifications of ruffed grouse traps. J. Wildl. Manage. 22(2):200–202.

Chamrad, A. D., and T. W. Box. 1964. A point frame for sampling rumen contents. J. Wildl. Manage. 28(3): 473–477.

Chandler, A. C. 1916. A study of the structure of feathers, with reference to their taxonomic significance. Univ. Calif. Publ. Zool., Univ. Calif. Press, Berkeley. 13:243–446.

Chapin, J. P. 1946. The preparation of birds for study. Am. Mus. Nat. Hist. Sci. Guide No. 58. 48 p.

Chapman, D. F. 1948. A mathematical study of confidence limits of salmon populations calculated from sample tag ratios. Int. Pac. Salmon Fish. Comm. Bull. 2. 17 p.

Chapman, D. G. 1951. Some properties of the hypergeometric distribution with application to zoological sample censuses. Univ. Calif. Publ. Stat. 1:131–160.

Chapman, F. M. 1912. Color key to North American birds with bibliographical appendix. D. Appleton and Co., New York. 356 p.

Charles-Dominique, P. 1977. Urine marking and territoriality in *Galago alleni* (Waterhouse, 1837–Lorisoidea, Primates)—a field study by radio-telemetry. Z. Tierpsychol. 43:113–138.

Chattin, J. E. 1952. Appraisal of California waterfowl concentrations by aerial photography. Trans. N. Am. Wildl. Conf. 17:421–426.

Cheatum, E. L. 1949a. The use of corpora lutea for determining ovulation incidence and variations in the fertility of white-tailed deer. Cornell Vet. 39(3):282–291.

Cheatum, E. L. 1949b. Bone marrow as an index of malnutrition in deer. New York State Conserv. 3(5):19–22.

Cheatum, E. L., and C. W. Severinghaus. 1950. Variations in fertility of white-tailed deer related to range conditions. Trans. N. Am. Wildl. Conf. 15:170–189.

Chen, G., C. R. Ensor, D. Russell, and B. Bohner. 1959. The pharmacology of 1-(1-Phenyl-cyclohexyl) piperidine-HCL. J. Pharmacol. Exp. Ther. 127(3):241–250.

Chesness, R. A. 1966. Pheasant aging guide. Wildl. Soc. News, No. 103:30.

Chew, R. M. 1961. Water metabolism of desert inhabiting vertebrates. Biol. Rev. 36:1–31.

Chicago University Press. 1969. A manual of style for authors, editors, and copywriters. 12th ed. rev. Univ. of Chicago Press, Ill. 546 p.

Child, K. N. 1973. The cryostat: a tool for the big game biologist. Can. J. Zool. 51(6):663–664.

Choate, E. A. 1973. The dictionary of American bird names. Gambit, Boston. 261 p.

Choate, J. S. 1967. Factors influencing nesting success of eiders in Penobscot Bay, Maine. J. Wildl. Manage. 31(4):769–777.

Christian, J. J. 1963. Endocrine adaptive mechanisms and the physiologic regulation of population growth. p. 189–353 *in* W. V. Mayer and R. C. Van Gelder, (eds.). Physiological mammalogy. Vol. I: Mammalian populations. Academic Press, New York and London. 381 p.

Church, J. M. F., and W. A. Rees. 1976. A computer programmer for primary productivity studies. E. Afr. Wildl. J. 14:169–170.

Chute, F. S., W. A. Fuller, P. R. J. Harding, and T. B. Herman. 1974. Radio tracking of small mammals using a grid of overhead wire antennas. Can. J. Zool. 52(12):1481–1488.

Civil Engineering Department. 1972. The use of remote sensing to obtain data for describing the large river. Interim Rep., Civ. Eng. Res. No. CE–71–72 MMS–32, Colorado State Univ., Fort Collins. 94 p.

Clapp, J. 1962. Museum publications: a classified list and index of books, pamphlets and other monographs, and of special reprints. Scarecrow Press, New York. 2 vol.

Clark, F. H. 1936. The estrous cycle of the deer-mouse, *Peromyscus maniculatus*. Contrib. Lab. Vertebr. Genet., Univ. Michigan. 1:1–7.

Clark, G. L., (ed.). 1961. The encyclopedia of microscopy. Reinhold, New York. 693 p.

Clark, R., D. Smith, and L. Kelso. 1978. Working bibliography of owls of the world, with summaries of current taxonomy and distributional status. Natl. Wildl. Fed. Sci. Tech. Ser. No. 1, Washington, D.C. 319 p.

Clark, R. B., and A. L. Panchen. 1971. Synopsis of animal classification. Chapman and Hall, London. 126 p.

Clark, R. N. 1977. Alternative strategies for studying river recreationists. USDA For. Serv. Gen. Tech. Rep. NC–28. 10 p.

Clark, W. K. 1957. Seasonal foods of the Kodiak bear. Trans. N. Am. Wildl. Conf. 22:145–151.

Clarke, P. F., H. E. Hodgson, and G. W. North. 1978. A guide to obtaining information from the USGS. U.S. Geol. Surv. Circ. 777, Reston, Va. 36 p.

Clements, F. E. 1916. Plant succession: an analysis of the development of vegetation. Carnegie Inst. Publ. 242, Washington, D.C. 512 p.

Clements, F. E. 1928. Plant succession and indicators. H. W. Wilson Co., New York. 453 p.

Clements, J. F. 1974. Birds of the world: a check list. Two Continents Publ. Group, Ltd., New York. 524 p.

Cline, D. R., and R. J. Greenwood. 1972. Effect of certain anesthetic agents on mallard ducks. J. Am. Vet. Med. Assoc. 161(6):624–633.

Cline, D. R., D. B. Siniff, and A. W. Erickson. 1969. Immobilizing and collecting blood from Antarctic seals. J. Wildl. Manage. 33(1):138–144.

Clopper, C. J., and E. S. Pearson. 1934. The use of confidence or fiducial limits illustrated in the case of the binomial. Biometrika. 26(3–4):404–413.

Clore, J. 1976. Commercial pest management of birds in grapes. Proc. Vertebr. Pest Conf. 7:63–67.

Clover, M. R. 1954. A portable deer trap and catch-net. Calif. Fish and Game 40(4):367–373.

Clover, M. R. 1956. Single-gate deer trap. Calif. Fish and Game 42(3): 199–201.

Coblentz, B. E. 1975. Serum cholesterol level changes in George Reserve deer. J. Wildl. Manage. 39 (2):342–345.

Cochran, W. G. 1977. Sampling techniques. 3rd ed. John Wiley and Sons., New York, N.Y. 428 p.

Cochran, W. W. 1972. Long-distance tracking of birds. p. 39–59 *in* S. R. Galler, K. Schmidt-Koenig, G. J. Jacobs, and R. E. Belleville, (eds.). Animal orientation and navigation. NASA SP-262. 606 p.

Cochran, W. W. 1975. Following a migrating peregrine from Wisconsin to Mexico. Hawk Chalk 14(2):28–36.

Cochran, W. W., and R. D. Lord. 1963. A radio-tracking system for wild animals. J. Wildl. Manage. 27(1): 9–24.

Cochran, W. W., G. G. Montgomery, and R. R. Graber. 1967. Migratory flights of *Hylocichla* thrushes in spring: a radiotelemetry study. Living Bird 6:213–225.

Cochran, W. W., D. W. Warner, J. R. Tester, and V. B. Kuechle. 1965. Automatic radio-tracking system for monitoring animal movements. BioScience 15(2):98–100.

Cockrum, E. L. 1952. Mammals of Kansas. Univ. Kansas. Mus. Nat. Hist. Publ. 7(1):1–303.

Cockrum, E. L. 1960. The recent mammals of Arizona: their taxonomy and distribution. Univ. of Arizona Press, Tuscon. 276 p.

Cody, M. L. 1968. On the methods of resource division in grassland bird communities. Am. Nat. 102(924): 107–147.

Cody, M. L. 1974. Competition and the structure of bird communities. Princeton Univ. Press, Princeton, N. J. 318 p.

Coe, R. J., R. L. Downing, and B. S. McGinnes. 1980. Sex and age bias in hunter-killed white-tailed deer. J. Wildl. Manage. 44(1):245–249.

Coffin, D. L. 1953. Manual of veterinary clinical pathology. 3rd ed. Comstock Publ. Assoc. Ithaca, N.Y. 322 p.

Coggins, V. L. 1975. Immobilization of Rocky Mountain elk with M–99. J. Wildl. Manage. 39(4):814–816.

Coil, W. H., and D. K. Wetherbee. 1959. Observations on the cloacal gland of the Eurasian quail *Coturnix coturnix*. Ohio J. Sci. 59(5):268–270.

Cole, G. F. 1959. Key browse survey method. Proc. Western Assoc. State Game and Fish Commissioners 39:181–186.

Coleman, D. C., and R. G. Wiegert. 1967. A simple inexpensive temperature integrator. BioScience 17(7): 481–482.

Collias, N. E. 1963. A spectrographic analysis of the vocal repertoire of the African village weaverbird. Condor 65(6):517–527.

Collias, N., and M. Joos. 1953. The spectrographic analysis of sound signals of the domestic fowl. Behaviour 5:175–188.

Collins, B. D. 1953. A nesting study of the Canada goose at Tule Lake and Lower Klamath National Wildlife Refuges. Proc. Western Assoc. State Game and Fish Commissioners 33:172–176.

Collins, C. T., and R. E. Landry. 1977. Artificial nest burrows for burrowing owls. N. Am. Bird Bander 2(4):151–154.

Collins, H. H., Jr. 1959. Complete field guide to American wildlife: east, central and north. Harper, New York. 683 p.

Colvocoresses, A. P. 1977. Proposed parameters for an operational Landsat. Photogramm. Eng. Remote Sensing 43(9):1139–1145.

Colwell, R. N., (ed.). 1960. Manual of photographic interpretation. Am. Soc. Photogrammetry. Washington, D.C. 868 p.

Coman, B. J., and H. Brunner. 1971. Food-habits analysis using a fiber cross-sectioning technique. J. Wildl. Manage. 35(3):576–579.

Conaway, C. H. 1955. Embryo resorption and placental scar formation in the rat. J. Mammal. 36(4):516–532.

Conley, W. 1978. Population modeling. p. 305–320 *in* J. S. Schmidt and D. L. Gilbert, (eds.). Big game of North America. Stackpole Books. Harrisburg, Pa. 494 p.

Conley, W., and J. D. Nichols. 1978. The use of models in small mammal population studies. p. 14–37 *in* D. P. Snyder, (ed.). Populations of small mammals under natural conditions. Pymatuning Lab. Ecol., Spec. Publ. Ser. Vol. 5, Univ. Pittsburgh. 237 p.

Conley, W., and A. R. Tipton. 1975. A personalized bibliographic retrieval package for natural resource scientists. Mich. State Univ. Agric. Exp. Stn. Res. Rep. 258, East Lansing. 24 p.

Conn, H. J. 1977. Biological stains. 9th ed. Williams & Wilkins Inc., Baltimore. 692 p.

Connolly, G. E., M. L. Dudzinski, and W. M. Longhurst. 1969a. The eye lens as an indicator of age in the black-tailed jack rabbit. J. Wildl. Manage. 33(1):159–164.

Connolly, G. E., M. L. Dudzinski, and W. M. Longhurst. 1969b. An improved age-lens weight regression for black-tailed deer and mule deer. J. Wildl. Manage. 33(3):701–704.

Conover, W. J. 1971. Practical nonparametric statistics. John Wiley and Sons Inc., New York. 462 p.

Considine, D. M., (ed.). 1971. Encyclopedia of instrumentation and control. McGraw-Hill, New York. 788 p.

Cooch, F. G. 1965. The breeding biology and management of the northern eider *(Somateria mollissima borealis)* in the Cape Dorset area, Northwest Territories. Can. Wildl. Serv. Wildl. Manage. Bull. (Ser. 2) No. 10. 68 p.

Cooch, G. 1953. Techniques for mass capture of flightless blue and lesser snow geese. J. Wildl. Manage. 17(4):460–465.

Cook, C. W. 1959. The effect of site on the palatability and nutritive content of seeded wheatgrasses. J. Range Manage. 12(6):289–292.

Cooley, J. H. 1961. Small deer and hare exclosures can be effective. USDA For. Serv. Lake States For. Exp. Stn. Tech. Note 594. 2 p.

Coon, R. A., P. D. Caldwell, and G. L. Storm. 1976. Some characteristics of fall migration of female woodcock. J. Wildl. Manage. 40(1):91–95.

Cooper, C. F. 1957. The variable plot method for estimating shrub density. J. Range Manage. 10(3):111–115.

Cooper, C. F. 1963. An evaluation of variable plot sampling in shrub and herbaceous vegetation. Ecology 44 (3):565–569.

Cooper, J. A. 1978. The history and breeding biology of the Canada geese of Marshy Point, Manitoba. Wildl. Monogr. No. 61. 87 p.

Cooper, J. A., and B. D. J. Batt. 1972. Criteria for aging giant Canada goose embryos. J. Wildl. Manage. 36(4): 1267–1270.

Copelin, F. F. 1963. The lesser prairie chicken in Oklahoma. Okla. Wildl. Cons. Dept. Tech. Bull. No. 6. 58 p.

Copperud, R. H. 1970. American usage: the consensus. Van Nostrand Reinhold. New York. 292 p.

Corbet, G. B. 1966. The terrestrial mammals of western Europe. Dufour Editions, Philadelphia, Pa. 264 p.

Corbet, G. B. 1978. The mammals of the Palearctic: a taxonomic review. Cornell Univ. Press, Ithaca, N.Y. 314 p.

Corbett, R. L., R. L. Marchinton, and C. E. Hill. 1971. Preliminary study of the effects of dogs on radio-equipped deer in a mountainous habitat. Proc. Southeastern Assoc. Game and Fish Commissioners 25:69–77.

Corbin, J. B. 1965. An index of state geological survey publications issued in series. Scarecrow Press, New York. 667 p.

Corner, G. W., and E. W. Pearson. 1972. A miniature 30–MHz collar transmitter for small animals. J. Wildl. Manage. 36(2):657–661.

Cornsweet, T. N. 1963. The design of electric circuits in the behavioral sciences. John Wiley and Sons, New York. 329 p.

Corwin, R., P. H. Heffernan, R. A. Johnston, M. Remy, J. A. Roberts, and D. B. Tyler. 1975. Environmental impact assessment. Freeman Cooper and Co., San Francisco, Calif. 277 p.

Cottam, C. 1936. Economic ornithology and the correlation of laboratory and field methods. USDA Wildl. Res. and Manage. Leafl. B–30, Washington, D.C. 13 p.

Cottam, C., and W. C. Glazener. 1959. Late nesting of water birds in south Texas. Trans. N. Am. Wildl. Conf. 24:382–395.

Cottam, G., and J. T. Curtis. 1956. The use of distance measures in phytosociological sampling. Ecology 37(3):451–460.

Cottam, G., J. T. Curtis, and B. W. Hale. 1953. Some sampling characteristics of a population of randomly dispersed individuals. Ecology 34 (4):741–757.

Coulombre, A. J. 1966. Embryology. BioScience 16(5):368–370.

Coulter, M. W. 1958. A new waterfowl nest trap. Bird-Banding 29(4):236–241.

Coulter, M. W. 1966. Ecology and management of fishers in Maine. Ph.D Thesis. Syracuse Univ. 196 p.

Coulter, M. W., and W. R. Miller. 1968. Nesting biology of black ducks and mallards in northern New England. Vermont Fish and Game Dept. Bull. 68–2, Montpelier. 73 p.

Council of Biology Editors. 1978. CBE style manual. 4th ed. Am. Inst. Biol. Sci., Washington, D.C. 265 p.

Council on Biological Sciences Information. 1970. Information handling in the life sciences. Natl. Res. Counc. Div. Biol. Agric., Washington, D.C. 79 p.

Council on Environmental Quality. 1973. Preparation of environmental impact statements: guidelines. p. 416–439 *in* Council on Environmental Quality. Environmental quality, the fourth annual report of the Council on Environmental Quality. U.S. Gov. Print. Off., Washington, D.C. 499 p.

Council on Environmental Quality. 1978. National Environmental Policy Act—Regulations. Implementation of procedural provisions. Fed. Register 43:55978–56007.

Cowan, I. McT. 1936. Distribution and variation in deer (genus *Odocoileus)* of the Pacific coastal region of North America. Calif. Fish and Game 22(3):155–246.

Cowan, I. McT. 1940. Distribution and variation in the native sheep of North America. Am. Midl. Nat. 24(3):505–580.

Cowan, J. 1959. 'Pre-fab' wire mesh cone gives doves better nest than they can build themselves. Outdoor Calif. 20(1):10–11.

Cowan, R. L., E. W. Hartsook, J. B. Whelan, T. A. Long, and R. S. Wetzel. 1969. A cage for metabolism and radioisotope studies with deer. J. Wildl. Manage. 33(1):204–208.

Cowan, R. L., J. S. Jordan, J. L. Grimes, and J. D. Gill. 1970. Comparative nutritive values of forage species. p. 48–56 *in* Range and wildlife habitat evaluation—a research symposium. USDA For. Serv. Misc. Publ. No. 1147. 220 p.

Cowardin, L. M., and J. E. Ashe. 1965. An automatic camera device for measuring waterfowl use. J. Wildl. Manage. 29(3):636–640.

Cowardin, L. M., V. Carter, F. C. Golet, and E. T. LaRoe. 1977. Classification of wetlands and deepwater habitats of the United States. U.S. Fish Wildl. Serv. 100 p.

Cowardin, L. M., and D. H. Johnson. 1979. Mathematics and mallard management. J. Wildl. Manage. 43(1):18–35.

Cowardin, L. M., and V. I. Myers. 1974. Remote sensing for identification and classification of wetland vegetation. J. Wildl. Manage. 38(2): 308–314.

Cowles, C. J., R. L. Kirkpatrick, and J. O. Newell. 1977. Ovarian follicular changes in gray squirrels as affected by season, age and reproductive state. J. Mammal. 58(1):67–73.

Crabb, W. D. 1941. Civits are rat killers. Farm Sci. Rep. (Iowa Farm Sci.) 2(1):12–13.

Crabb, W. D. 1948. The ecology and management of the prairie spotted skunk in Iowa. Ecol. Monogr. 18(2):201–232.

Craighead, F. C., Jr., and J. J. Craighead. 1949. Nesting Canada geese on the Upper Snake River. J. Wildl. Manage. 13(1):51–64.

Craighead, J. 1976. Studying grizzly habitat by satellite. Natl. Geogr. Mag. 150(1):148–158.

Craighead, J. J., F. C. Craighead, Jr., and H. E. McCutchen. 1970. Age determination of grizzly bears from fourth premolar tooth section. J. Wildl. Manage. 34(2):353–363.

Craighead, J. J., M. G. Hornocker, M. W. Shoesmith, and R. I. Ellis. 1969. A marking technique for elk. J. Wildl. Manage. 33(4):906–909.

Craighead, J. J., M. Hornocker, W. Woodgerd, and F. C. Craighead, Jr. 1960. Trapping, immobilizing, and color-marking grizzly bears. Trans. N. Am. Wildl. Conf. 25:347–363.

Craighead, J. J., and D. S. Stockstad. 1956. A colored neckband for marking birds. J. Wildl. Manage. 20(3): 331–332.

Crampton, E. W., and L. E. Harris. 1969. Applied animal nutrition: the use of feedstuffs in the formulation of livestock rations. 2nd ed. W. H. Freeman, San Francisco. 753 p.

Crandall, D. L. 1958. Ground vegetation patterns of the spruce-fir area of the Great Smoky Mountains National Park. Ecol. Monogr. 28(4): 337–360.

Crase, F. T., C. P. Stone, R. W. DeHaven, and D. F. Mott. 1976. Bird damage to grapes in the United States with emphasis on California. U.S. Fish and Wildl. Serv. Spec. Sci. Rep.—Wildl. 197. 18 p.

Crawford, H. S., Jr. 1960. Effect of aerial 2, 4, 5-T sprays on forage production in west-central Arkansas. J. Range Manage. 13(1):44.

Crawford, H. S., Jr. 1976. Relationships between forest cutting and understory vegetation: an overview of eastern hardwood stands. USDA For. Serv. Res. Pap. NE-349, Northeastern For. Exp. Stn., Upper Darby, Pa. 9 p.

Crawford, H. S., Jr., and A. J. Bjugstad. 1967. Establishing grass range in the southwest Missouri Ozarks. USDA For. Serv. Res. Note NC-22, N. Cent. For. Exp. Stn., St. Paul, Minn. 4 p.

Crawford, R. D. 1978. Tarsal color of American coots in relation to age. Wilson Bull. 90(4):536–543.

Crider, E. D., and J. C. McDaniel. 1967. Alpha-chloralose used to capture Canada geese. J. Wildl. Manage. 31(2):258–264.

Crider, E. D., V. D. Stotts, and J. McDaniel. 1968. Diazepam and alpha-chloralose mixtures to capture waterfowl. Proc. Southeastern Assoc. Game and Fish Commissioners 22:133–141.

Crier, J. K. 1970. Tetracyclines as a fluorescent marker in bones and teeth of rodents. J. Wildl. Manage. 34(4):829–834.

Crispens, C. G., Jr. 1960. Quails and partridges of North America; a bibliography. Univ. Washington Publ. in Biol. 20:1–125.

Crispens, C. G., Jr., and J. K. Doutt. 1970. Studies of the sex chromatin in the white-tailed deer. J. Wildl. Manage. 34(3):642–644.

Crissey, W. F. 1953. The use of a dictating machine to record aerial observations. J. Wildl. Manage. 17(4): 539–540.

Crockford, J. A., F. A. Hayes, J. H. Jenkins, and S. D. Feurt. 1957. Nicotine salicylate for capturing deer. J. Wildl. Manage. 21(2):213–220.

Crockford, J. A., F. A. Hayes, J. H. Jenkins, and S. D. Feurt. 1958. An automatic projectile type syringe. Vet. Med. 53(3):115–119.

Croker, B. H. 1959. A method of estimating the botanical composition of the diet of sheep. N. Z. J. Agric. Res. 2:72–85.

Cronan, J. M., and A. Brooks. 1968. The mammals of Rhode Island. R. I. Dept. Nat. Resour. Wildl. Pam. No. 6. 133 p.

Crook, J. H., and P. Ward. 1968. The quelea problem in Africa. p. 211–229 *in* R. K. Murton and E. N. Wright, (eds). The problems of birds as pests. Instit. of Biol. Symp. No. 17. Academic Press, London and New York. 254 p.

Croon, G. W., D. R. McCullough, C. E. Olson, Jr., and L. M. Queal. 1968. Infrared scanning techniques for big game censusing. J. Wildl. Manage. 32(4):751–759.

Crouch, G. L. 1976. Deer and reforestation in the Pacific northwest. Proc. Vertebr. Pest Conf. 7:298–301.

Crowe, D. M. 1972. The presence of annuli in bobcat tooth cementum layers. J. Wildl. Manage. 36(4): 1330–1332.

Crowe, D. M., and M. D. Strickland. 1975. Dental annulation in the American badger. J. Mammal. 56(1): 269–272.

Crowley, E. T., (ed.), and R. C. Thomas. 1973. Acronyms and initialisms dictionary; a guide to alphabetic designations, contractions, acronyms, initialisms, and similar condensed appellations. 4th ed. Gale Research Co., Detroit, Mich. 635 p.

Crowson, R. A. 1970. Classification and biology. Atherton Press Inc., New York. 350 p.

Croze, H. 1972. A modified photogrammetric technique for assessing age-structures of elephant populations and its use in Kidepo National Park. E. Afr. Wildl. J. 10(2):91–115.

Crump, W. I. 1961. Aerial marking of antelope for migration and distribution studies. Proc. Western Assoc. Game and Fish Commissioners 41:93–98.

Cullison, A. 1975. Feeds and feeding. Reston Publ. Co. Inc., Reston, Va. 486 p.

Cummings, G. E., and O. H. Hewitt. 1964. Capturing waterfowl and marsh birds at night with light and sound. J. Wildl. Manage. 28(1): 120–126.

Cummings, M. W. 1973. Rodents and drip irrigation. Proc. Drip Irrigation Seminar, Agric. Ext. Serv., San Diego, Calif. 4:25–30.

Cunningham, E. R. 1962. A study of the eastern raccoon, *Procyon lotor*, on the Atomic Energy Commission Savannah River Plant. M. S. Thesis. Univ. Georgia, Athens. 55 p.

Cunningham, R. A. 1975. Provisional tree and shrub seed zones for the Great Plains. USDA For. Serv. Res. Pap. RM–150, Rocky Mt. For. Exp. Stn., Ft. Collins, Colo. 15 p.

Cupal, J. J., A. L. Ward, and R. W. Weeks. 1975. A repeater type biotelemetry system for use on wild big game animals. ISA Trans. 14(2):101–108.

Cupal, J. J., R. W. Weeks, and C. Kaltenbach. 1976. A heart rate-activity biotelemetry system for use on wild big game animals. 3rd Int. Symp. Biotelemetry, Pacific Grove, Calif. 4 p.

Curtis, J. T. 1955. A prairie continuum in Wisconsin. Ecology 36(4):558–566.

Curtis, J. T., and R. P. McIntosh. 1951. An upland forest continuum in the prairie-forest border region of Wisconsin. Ecology 32(3):476–496.

Cushing, E. E., Jr., (ed.). 1976. Radioecology and energy resources. Proc. 4th Natl. Symp. Radioecology, Dowden, Hutchinson and Ross Inc., Stroudsburg, Pa. 401 p.

Cushwa, C. T. 1968. Fire: a summary of literature in the United States from the mid 1920's to 1966. USDA For. Serv., Southeastern For. Exp. Stn., Asheville, N. C. 117 p.

Cushwa, C. T., and K. P. Burnham 1974. An inexpensive live trap for snowshoe hares. J. Wildl. Manage. 38(4):939–941.

Cushwa, C. T., R. L. Downing, R. F. Harlow, and D. F. Urbston. 1970. The importance of woody twig ends to deer in the Southeast. USDA For. Serv. Res. Pap. SE-67, Southeastern For. Exp. Stn., Asheville, N.C. 12 p.

Cushwa, C. T., D. R. Patton, W. T. Mason, Jr., and L. J. Slaski. 1978. RUN WILD EAST. A computerized data system for fish and wildlife resources. Trans. Northeast Sect. Wildl. Soc., Fish Wildl. Conf. 35:60–65.

Custer, T. W., and F. A. Pitelka. 1975. Correction factors for digestion rates for prey taken by snow buntings. *(Plectrophenax nivalis).* Condor 77(2):210–212.

Cuthbert, F. J., and W. E. Southern. 1975. A method for marking young gulls for individual identification. Bird-Banding 46(3):252–253.

Cutlip, S. M., and A. H. Center. 1971. Effective public relations. Prentice-Hall, Englewood Cliffs, N.J. 512 p.

Czapowskyj, M. M. 1976. Annotated bibliography on the ecology and reclamation of drastically disturbed areas. USDA For. Serv. Gen. Tech. Rep. NE–21, N.E. For. Exp. Stn., Upper Darby, Pa. 98 p.

Dadd, M. N. 1971. The Zoological Record—current developments. Biol. J. Linnean Soc. 3(3):291–294.

Dagg, A. I. 1972. Research on Canadian mammals. Can. Field-Nat. 86(3): 217–221.

Dagg, A. I. 1974. Mammals of Ontario. Otter Press, Waterloo, Ontario. 160 p.

Dagg, A. I. 1977. Wildlife management in Europe. Otter Press, Waterloo, Ontario, Canada. 324 p.

Dagg, A. I., D. Leach, and G. Sumner-Smith. 1975. Fusion at the distal femoral epiphysis in male and female marten and fisher. Can. J. Zool. 53(11):1514–1518.

Dahlberg, B. L., and R. C. Guettinger. 1956. The white-tailed deer in Wisconsin. Wis. Conserv. Dept. Tech. Wildl. Bull. No. 14. 282 p.

Dahlgren, R. B., M. T. Curtis, and F. R. Henderson. 1964. Lens weights of sharp-tailed grouse. J. Wildl. Manage. 28(4):853–854.

Dahm, P. A. 1957. Uses of radioisotopes in pesticide research. p. 81–146 *in* R. L. Metcalf, (ed.). Advances in pest control research. Vol. 1. Interscience Publ. Inc., New York. 8 vols.

Dale, F. H. 1954. Influence of calcium on the distribution of the pheasant in North America. Trans. N. Am. Wildl. Conf. 19:316–323.

Dale, F. H. 1955. The role of calcium in reproduction of the ring-necked pheasant. J. Wildl. Manage. 19(3): 325–331.

Dale, M. B. 1970. Systems analysis and ecology. Ecology 51(1):2–16.

Dalke, P. D. 1935. Droppings analysis as an indication of pheasant food habits. Proc. Am. Game Conf. 22:387–391.

Dalke, P. D. 1937. The cover map in wildlife management. J. Wildl. Manage. 1(3–4):100–106.

Dalke, P. D. 1941. The use and availability of the more common winter deer browse plants in the Missouri Ozarks. Trans. N. Am. Wildl. Conf. 6:155–160.

Dalke, P. D. 1942. The cottontail rabbits in Connecticut. Conn. Geol. and Nat. Hist. Surv. Bull. 65. 97 p.

Dalke, P. D. 1973. A partial bibliography of Idaho wildlife. Idaho Fish and Game Dept. Wildl. Bull. No. 6, Boise. 132 p.

Dalke, P. D., W. K. Clark, Jr., and L. J. Korschgen. 1942. Food habits trends of the wild turkey in Missouri as determined by dropping analysis. J. Wildl. Manage. 6(3):237–243.

Dalke, P. D., A. S. Leopold, and D. L. Spencer. 1946. The ecology and management of the wild turkey in Missouri. Missouri Conserv. Comm. Tech. Bull. No. 1. 86 p.

Dane, B., C. Walcott, and W. H. Drury. 1959. The form and duration of the display actions of the goldeneye *(Bucephala clangula)*. Behaviour 14:265–281.

Dane, C. W. 1966. Some aspects of breeding biology of the blue-winged teal. Auk 83(3):389–402.

Dane, C. W., and D. H. Johnson. 1975. Age determination of female redhead ducks. J. Wildl. Manage. 39(2):256–263.

Daniel, C., and R. Lamaire. 1974. Evaluating effects of water resource developments on wildlife habitat. Wildl. Soc. Bull. 2(3):114–118.

Daniel, H. A., and H. J. Harper. 1934. The relation between total calcium and phosphorus in mature prairie grass and available plant food in the soil. J. Am. Soc. Agron. 26(12):986–992.

Daniel, W. W. 1975. Nonresponse in sociological surveys: a review of some methods for handling the problem. Sociol. Methods and Res. 3(3): 291–307.

Dansereau, P., P. F. Buell, and R. Dagon. 1966. A universal system for recording vegetation. II. A methodological critique and an experiment. Sarracenia 10:1–64.

Dapson, R. W., and J. M. Irland. 1972. An accurate method of determining age in small mammals. J. Mammal. 53(3):100–106.

Darling, F. F. 1937. A herd of red deer; a study in animal behavior. Oxford Univ. Press, London. 215 p.

Darlington, P. J. 1957. Zoogeography: the geographical distribution of animals. Wiley, New York. 675 p.

Darnell, R. M. 1976. Impacts of construction activities in wetlands of the United States. EPA-600/3-76-045, Off. Res. and Dev., Corvallis, Oreg. 392 p.

Dary, D. A. 1974. The buffalo book; the full saga of the American animal. Sage Books/Swallow Press, Chicago. 374 p.

Dasmann, R. F. 1952. Methods for estimating deer populations from kill data. Calif. Fish and Game 38(2): 225–233.

Dasmann, R. F. 1964. Wildlife biology. John Wiley and Sons, New York. 231 p.

Dasmann, R. F., and R. D. Taber. 1955. A comparison of four deer census methods. Calif. Fish and Game 41(3):225–228.

Dasmann, W. P. 1948. A critical review of range survey methods and their application to deer range management. Calif. Fish and Game 34(4):189–207.

Dau, C. P. 1974. Nesting biology of the spectacled ėider *Somateria fischeri* (Brandt) on the Yukon-Kuskokwim Delta, Alaska. M. S. Thesis. Univ. of Alaska, Fairbanks. 72 p.

Daubenmire, R. 1952. Forest vegetation of northern Idaho and adjacent Washington, and its bearing on concepts of vegetation classification. Ecol. Monogr. 22(4):301–330.

Daubenmire, R. F. 1968. Plant communities: a textbook of plant synecology. Harper and Row, New York. 300 p.

Daubenmire, R. F., and J. B. Daubenmire. 1968. Forest vegetation of eastern Washington and northern Idaho. Wash. Agric. Exp. Stn. Tech. Bull. 60. 104 p.

Dauphine, T. C., Jr. 1971. Physical variables as an index to condition in barren-ground caribou. Trans. Northeast Sect. Wildl. Soc., Fish Wildl. Conf. 28:91–108.

Dauphine, T. C., Jr. 1975. Kidney weight fluctuations affecting the kidney fat index in caribou. J. Wildl. Manage. 39(2):379–386.

Davenport, L. A. 1939. Results of deer feeding experiments at Cusino, Michigan. Trans. N. Am. Wildl. Conf. 4:268–274.

Davenport, L. A., W. Shapton, and W. C. Gower. 1944. A study of the carrying capacity of deer yards as determined by browse plots. Trans. N. Am. Wildl. Conf. 9:144–149.

Davidsohn, I., and J. B. Henry, (eds). 1969. Todd-Sanford clinical diagnosis by laboratory methods. 14th ed. W. B. Saunders Co., Philadelphia. 1308 p.

Davies, P. R. 1973. The use of metomidate, an intramuscular narcotic for birds. Vet. Rec. 92(19):507–509.

Davis, D. E. 1954. A simple method for obtaining attentive data. Auk 71(3): 331–332.

Davis, D. E. 1956. Manual for analysis of rodent populations. Edwards Brothers Inc. Ann Arbor, Mich. 82 p.

Davis, D. E. 1963. Estimating the numbers of game populations. p. 89–188 *in* H. S. Mosby, (ed.). Wildlife investigational techniques. 2nd ed. The Wildl. Soc., Washington, D.C. 419 p.

Davis, D. E. 1964. Evaluation of characters for determining age of woodchucks. J. Wildl. Manage. 28 (1):9–15.

Davis, D. E. 1976. Management of pine voles. Proc. Vertebr. Pest Conf. 7:270–275.

Davis, D. E., and J. T. Emlen, Jr. 1948. The placental scar as a measure of fertility in rats, J. Wildl. Manage. 12(2):162–166.

Davis, D. E., and C. Zippin. 1954. Planning wildlife experiments involving percentages. J. Wildl. Manage. 18(2):170–178.

Davis, H. P., (ed.). 1962. Hunting dogs and their uses. Collier Books, New York. 125 p.

Davis, H. P., (ed.). 1970. The new dog encyclopedia. Stackpole Co., Harrisburg, Pa. 736 p.

Davis, J. A. 1969. Aging and sexing criteria for Ohio ruffed grouse. J. Wildl. Manage. 33(1):628–636.

Davis, J. A. 1977. An ecosystem classification of New York state for natural resource management. N.Y. Fish and Game J. 24(2):129–143.

Davis, J. M. 1966. Uses of airphotos for rural and urban planning. USDA Agric. Handb. No. 315. 39 p.

Davis, J. R. 1959. A preliminary progress report on nest predation as a limiting factor in wild turkey populations. p. 138–145 *in* Proc. 1st Natl. Wild Turkey Manage. Symp. S. E. Sect. of the Wildl. Soc., Memphis, Tenn. 200 p.

Davis, L. I. 1964. Biological acoustics and the use of the sound spectrograph. Southwestern Nat. 9(3):118–145.

Davis, L. S. 1967. Dynamic programming for deer management planning. J. Wildl. Manage. 31(4):667–679.

Davis, R. K. 1964. The value of big game hunting in a private forest. Trans. N. Am. Wildl. Nat. Resour. Conf. 29:393–403.

Davis, R. K., and J. J. Seneca. 1972. Projecting demand for hunting and fishing. A report to the Bureau of Sport Fisheries and Wildlife in fulfillment of contract No. 14–16–0008–541. Nat. Resour. Policy Cent., George Washington Univ., Wash. D.C. 132 p.

Davison, V. E. 1940. A field method of analyzing game bird foods. J. Wildl. Manage. 4(2):105–116.

Davison, V. E. 1962. Taste, not color, draws birds to berries and seeds. Audubon Mag. 64(6):346–350.

Davison, V. E. 1963. Mourning doves' selection of foods. J. Wildl. Manage. 27(3):373–383.

Davison, V. E. 1964. Selection of foods by gray squirrels. J. Wildl. Manage. 28(2):346–352.

Davison, V. E., L. M. Dickerson, K. Graetz, W. W. Neely, and L. Roof. 1955. Measuring the yield and availability of game bird foods. J. Wildl. Manage. 19(2):302–308.

Davison, V. E., and K. E. Graetz. 1957. Managing habitat for white-tailed deer and wild turkeys. Trans. N. Am. Wildl. Conf. 22:412–424.

Davison, V. E., and R. A. Grizzell. 1961a. Choice foods that attract birds in winter in the southeast. Audubon Mag. 63(1):48–54.

Davison, V. E., and R. A. Grizzell. 1961b. Choice food of birds—summer and fall. Audubon Mag. 63(3):162–167, 180.

Davison, V. E., and W. H. Hamor. 1960. A system for classifying plant food of birds. J. Wildl. Manage. 24(3):307–313.

Dawson, W. L. 1923. The birds of California. South Moulton Co., San Diego, Calif. 4 vol.

Dawson, W. R. 1958. Relation of oxygen consumption and evaporative water loss to temperature in the cardinal. Physiol. Zool. 31(1):37–48.

Day, G. I. 1971. Use of oral drugs for capturing game animals. Ariz. Game and Fish Dept. P-R Final Rep., Proj. W–78–15. 13 p.

Day, G. I. 1973. Marking devices for big game animals. Ariz. Game and Fish Dept. Res. Abstr. No. 8. 7 p.

Day, G. I. 1974. Remote injection of drugs. Ariz. Game and Fish Dept., P-R Rep., Proj. W–78–15, 19 p.

Day, G. I., R. F. Dyson, and F. H. Landeen. 1965. A portable resuscitator for use on large game animals. J. Wildl. Manage. 29(3):511–515.

Day, J. 1969. Cap-chur problems and remedies. Ariz. Game and Fish Dept. Res. Abstr. No. 2. 4 p.

Dayton, W. A. 1950. Glossary of botanical terms commonly used in range research. USDA. Misc. Pub. 110. 40 p.

Dealy, J. E. 1960. The densiometer for measurement of crown intercept above a line transect. USDA For. Serv. Res. Note 199. Pac. N. W. For. and Range Exp. Stn. 5 p.

Dealy, J. E. 1966. Bitterbrush nutrition levels under natural and thinned ponderosa pine. USDA For. Serv. Res. Note 33. Pac. N. W. For. and Range Exp. Stn. 5 p.

Dean, R., W. W. Hines, and D. C. Church. 1973. Immobilizing free-ranging and captive deer with phencyclidine hydrochloride. J. Wildl. Manage. 37(1):82–86.

Dearborn, N. 1939. Sections aid in identifying hair. J. Mammal. 20 (3):346–348.

Dearden, B. L., R. E. Pegau, and R. M. Hansen. 1975. Precision of microhistological estimates of ruminant food habits. J. Wildl. Manage. 39(2): 402–407.

DeBenedictis, P. A. 1973. On the correlations between certain diversity indices. Am. Nat. 107(954):295–302.

deCalesta, D. S. 1971. A literature review on cottontail feeding habits. Colorado Div. of Game, Fish and Parks, Spec. Rep. No. 25. 15 p.

deCalesta, D. S., J. G. Nagy, and J. A. Bailey, 1975. Starving and refeeding mule deer. J. Wildl. Manage. 39(4): 663–669.

DeCino, T. J., D. J. Cunningham, and E. W. Schafer. 1966. Toxicity of DRC–1339 to starlings. J. Wildl. Manage. 30(2):249–253.

Dee, N., J. Baker, N. Drobny, K. Duke, I. Whitman, and D. Fahringer. 1973. An environmental evaluation system for water resource planning. Water Resour. Res. 9(3):523–535.

DeGraaf, R. M., (tech. coord.). 1978. Proceedings of the workshop on nongame bird habitat management in the coniferous forests of the western United States. USDA For. Serv. Tech. Rep. 64. Pac. N. W. For. Range Exp. Stn., Portland, Oreg. 100 p.

DeGraaf, R. M., and J. S. Larson. 1972. A technique for the observation of sex chromatin in hair roots. J. Mammal. 53(2):368–371.

DeHaven, R. W., and J. L. Guarino. 1969. A nest-box trap for starlings. Bird-Banding 40(1):49–50.

Deignan, H. G. 1961. Type specimens of birds in the United States National Museum. U.S. Nat. Mus. Bull. No. 221. 718 p.

Deinum, B., A. J. H. Van Es, and P. J. Van Soest. 1968. Climate, nitrogen, and grass. II. The influence of light intensity, temperature, and nitrogen on *in vivo* digestibility of grass and the production of these effects from some chemical procedures. Neth. J. Agric. Sci. 16(3):217–223.

Delacour, J. 1954–1964. The waterfowl of the world. Country Life, Ltd., London. 4 vol.

Delacour, J. 1977. The pheasants of the world. 2nd ed. Spur Publ., Saiga Publ. Co., Ltd., Hindhead, Surrey, England. 395 p.

Dell, J. 1957. Toe clipping varying hares for track identification. N.Y. Fish and Game J. 4(1):61–68.

Dellinger, G. P. 1954. Breeding season, productivity and population trends of raccoon in Missouri. M. A. Thesis. Univ. of Missouri, Columbia. 86 p.

DeLury, D. B. 1951. On the planning of experiments for the estimation of fish populations. J. Fish. Res. Board Can. 8:281–307.

Deming, O. V. 1952. Tooth development of the Nelson bighorn sheep. Calif. Fish and Game 38(4):523–529.

Deming, W. E. 1944. On errors in surveys. Am. Sociol. Rev. 9(4):359–369.

deMoisy, R. G. 1949. Forest surveying. Part 1. The use of steel tape, compass, Abney level, and aneroid barometer in forest surveying and mapping. O.S.C. Coop. Assoc., Corvallis, Oreg. 123 p.

Demong, N. J., and S. T. Emlen. 1975. An optical scope for examining nest contents of tunnel-nesting birds. Wilson Bull. 87(4):550–551.

Denney, R. N. 1958. Sex determination in dressed elk carcasses. Trans. N. Amer. Wildl. Conf. 23:501–513.

Denney, R. N. 1966. Neckbanding techniques with the helicopter. Proc. Western Assoc. Game and Fish Commissioners 46:134–141.

Denney, R. N. 1974. The impact of uncontrolled dogs on wildlife and livestock. Trans N. Am. Wildl. and Nat. Resour. Conf. 39:257–291.

Denny, M. J. S., and T. J. Dawson. 1973. A field technique for studying water metabolism of large marsupials. J. Wildl. Manage. 37(4):574–578.

Deno, R. A. 1937. Uterine macrophages in the mouse and their relation to involution. Am. J. Anat. 60(3):433–471.

DeRoon, A. C., (comp.). 1958. International directory of specialists in plant taxonomy with a census of their current interests. Regnum vegetabile Vol. 13. 266 p.

DesMeules, P., B. R. Simard, and J. M. Brassard. 1971. A technique for the capture of caribou, *Rangifer tarandus,* in winter. Can. Field-Nat. 85(3):221–229.

De Sola, R. 1978. Abbreviations dictionary: new international fifth edition. Elsevier Publ. Co., New York. 654 p.

Devine, T., and T. J. Peterle. 1968. Possible differentiation of natal areas of North American waterfowl by neutron activation analysis. J. Wildl. Manage. 32(2):274–279.

Devlin, J. C., and G. Naismith. 1977. The world of Roger Tory Peterson: an authorized biography. Time Books, New York. 266 p.

DeVries, L. 1976. French-English science and technology dictionary. 4th ed., rev. and enlarged. McGraw-Hill Book Co., New York. 683 p.

DeVries, L. 1978. German-English science dictionary. 4th ed. McGraw-Hill Book Co., New York. 628 p.

DeWeese, L. R., R. E. Pillmore, and M. L. Richmond. 1975. A device for inspecting nest cavities. Bird-Banding 46(2):162–165.

Dewhurst, D. J. 1966. Physical instrumentation in medicine and biology. Pergamon Press, Oxford. 205 p.

deWit, C. T., and J. Goudriaan. 1978. Simulation of ecological processes. 2nd ed. John Wiley and Sons, New York. 174 p.

DeWitt, J. B., and J. V. Derby, Jr. 1955. Changes in nutritive value of browse plants following forest fires. J. Wildl. Manage. 19(1):65–70.

Dewolfe, B. B. 1967. Sound spectrographic analysis of song patterns in Gambel's sparrows *(Zontrichia leucophrys gambelii).* Arctic Inst. N. Am. Grant-in-aid M49, Prog. Rep.

Dhondt, A. A., and E. J. van Outryve. 1971. A simple method for trapping breeding adults in nesting boxes. Bird-Banding 42(2):119–121.

Dice, L. R. 1932. Preparation of scientific specimens of mammals in the field. Univ. Mich. Mus. Zool. Circ. 1, Ann Arbor. 10 p.

Dice, L. R. 1943. The biotic provinces of North America. Univ. Michigan Press, Ann Arbor. 77 p.

Dice, L. R. 1961. Laboratory instruments for measuring the behavior of shy or nocturnal small mammals. J. Mammal. 42(2):159–166.

Dickert, T. G., and K. R. Domeny, (ed.). 1974. Environmental impact assessment: guidelines and commentary. Univ. of California Ext., Berkeley, Calif. 238 p.

Dickman, M. 1968. Some indices of diversity. Ecology 49(6):1191–1193.

Diczfalusy, E., (ed.). 1970. Steroid assay by protein binding. Karolinska Symp. on Res. Methods in Reprod. Endocrinol., Karolinska Inst., Stockholm, Sweden. 366 p.

Diem, K. L. 1954. Use of a deer call as a means of locating deer fawns. J. Wildl. Manage. 18(4):537–538.

Diem, K. L., A. L. Ward, and J. J. Cupal. 1974. Cameras as remote sensors of animal activities. Trans. Int. Congr. Game Biol: 11:503–509.

Dietz, D. R. 1958. Seasonal variation in the nutritive content of five southwestern Colorado deer browse species. M. S. Thesis. Colorado State Univ., Fort Collins. 110 p.

Dietz, D. R., R. H. Udall, and L. E. Yeager. 1962. Chemical composition and digestibility by mule deer of selected forage species, Cache la Poudre range, Colorado. Colo. Game and Fish Dept. Tech. Bull. 14. 89 p.

Dill, H. H., and W. H. Thornsberry. 1950. A cannon-projected net trap for capturing waterfowl. J. Wildl. Manage. 14(2):132–137.

Dillman, D. 1978. Mail and telephone surveys: the total design method. J. Wiley & Sons, New York. 325 p.

Dilworth, T. G., and J. A. McKenzie. 1970. Attempts to identify meat of game animals by starch-gel electrophoresis. J. Wildl. Manage. 34 (4):917–921.

Dimmick, R. W. 1968. Canada geese of Jackson Hole, their ecology and management. Wyoming Game and Fish Comm. Bull. No. 11. 86 p.

Dimmick, R. W. 1974. Populations and reproductive effort among bobwhites in western Tennessee. Proc. Southeastern Assoc. Game and Fish Commissioners 28:594–602.

Dindal, D. L. 1970. Accumulation and excretion of Cl^{36} DDT in mallard and lesser scaup ducks. J. Wildl. Manage. 34(1):74–92.

Dinger, B. E. 1976. Non-radiological effects on terrestrial environs. p. 52–108 *in* R. A. Karam and K. Z. Morgan, (eds.). Environmental impact of nuclear power plants. Pergamon Press Inc., New York. 546 p.

Dirschl, H. J. 1962. Sieve mesh size related to analysis of antelope rumen contents. J. Wildl. Manage. 26(3): 327–328.

Dirschl, H. J. 1969. Foods of lesser scaup and blue-winged teal in the Saskatchewan River Delta. J. Wildl. Manage. 33(1):77–87.

Dixon, J. S. 1934. A study of the life history and food habits of mule deer in California. Calif. Fish and Game 20(3):181–282, 20(4):315–354.

Dobie, J. F. 1961. The voice of the coyote. Univ. Nebraska Press, Lincoln. 386 p.

Doboszynska, T. 1976. A method for collecting and staining vaginal smears from the beaver. Acta Theriol. 21, 22:299–306.

Dodge, W. E., and D. L. Campbell. 1965. Two techniques to reduce captive mortality. J. Mammal. 46(4):707.

Dodge, W. E., and D. P. Snyder. 1960. An automatic camera device for recording wildlife activity. J. Wildl. Manage. 24(3):340–342.

Dolbeer, R. A., C. R. Ingram, and J. L. Seubert. 1976. Modeling as a management tool for assessing the impact of blackbird control measures. Proc. Vert. Pest Conf. 7:35–45.

Domay, F. 1964. Handbuch der deutschen wissenschaftlichen Gesellschaften. Franz Steiner Verlag, Wiesbaden. 751 p.

Dorio, J. C., J. Johnson, and A. H. Grewe. 1978. A simple technique for capturing upland sandpipers. Inland Bird-Banding News 50(2):57–58.

Dorney, R. S. 1966. A new method for sexing ruffed grouse in late summer. J. Wildl. Manage. 30(3):623–625.

Dorney, R. S., and F. V. Holzer. 1957. Spring aging methods for ruffed grouse cocks. J. Wildl. Manage. 21(3):268–274.

Dorney, R. S., and H. M. Mattison. 1956. Trapping techniques for ruffed grouse. J. Wildl. Manage. 20(1):47–50.

Dorney, R. S., D. R. Thompson, J. B. Hale, and R. F. Wendt. 1958. An evaluation of ruffed grouse drumming counts. J. Wildl. Manage. 22(1):35–40.

Doty, H. A., and E. K. Fritzell. 1974. Great horned owls and duck nest platforms. N. D. Outdoors 36(9):19.

Doty, H. A., and R. J. Greenwood. 1974. Improved nasal-saddle marker for mallards. J. Wildl. Manage. 38(4):938–939.

Doty, H. A., and F. B. Lee. 1974. Homing to nest baskets by wild female mallards. J. Wildl. Manage. 38(4): 714–719.

Doude Van Troostwijk, W. J. 1976. Age determination in muskrats. *Ondatra zibethicus* (L.) in the Netherlands. Lutra 18(3):33–43.

Dougherty, R. W., C. H. Mullenax, and M. J. Allison. 1965. Physiological phenomena associated with eructation in ruminants. p. 159–170 *in* R. W. Dougherty, R. S. Allen, W. Burroughs, N. L. Jacobson and A. D. McGilliard, (eds.). Physiology of digestion in the ruminant. Butterworth Inc., Washington, D.C. 480 p.

Douglass, J. F. 1976. Universal index to zoological literature proposed. BioScience 26(9): 528.

Doutt, J. K. 1940. Weighing large mammals in the field. J. Mammal. 21(1):63–65.

Dow, J. S. 1943. A study of nesting Canada geese in Honey Lake Valley, California. Calif. Fish and Game 29(1):3–18.

Dow, S. A. 1952. Antelope ageing studies in Montana. Proc. Western Assoc. State Game and Fish Commissioners 32:220–224.

Dow, S. A., Jr., and P. L. Wright. 1962. Changes in mandibular dentition associated with age in pronghorn antelope. J. Wildl. Manage. 26(1):1–18.

Dowden, P. B., H. A. Jaynes, and V. M. Carolin. 1953. The role of birds in a spruce budworm outbreak in Maine. J. Econ. Entomol. 46(2):307–312.

Downey, J. C. 1966. Insects. BioScience 16(2):134–135.

Downing, R. L. 1959. Significance of ground nesting by mourning doves in northwestern Oklahoma. J. Wildl. Manage. 23(1):117–118.

Downing, R. L. 1971. Comparison of crippling losses of white-tailed deer caused by archery, buckshot, and shotgun slugs. Proc. Southeastern Assoc. Game and Fish Commissioners 25:77–82.

Downing, R. L., and B. S. McGinnes. 1969. Capturing and marking white-tailed deer fawns. J. Wildl. Manage. 33(3):711–714.

Downing, R. L., E. D. Michael, and R. J. Poux, Jr. 1977. Accuracy of sex and age ratio counts of white-tailed deer. J. Wildl. Manage. 41(4):709–714.

Doyle, F. J. 1978. The next decade of satellite remote sensing. Photogramm. Eng. Remote Sensing 44(2): 155–164.

Dozier, H. L. 1942. Identification of sex in live muskrats. J. Wildl. Manage. 6(4):292–293.

Dressler, R. L., and G. W. Wood. 1976. Deer habitat response to irrigation with municipal wastewater. J. Wildl. Manage. 40(4):639–644.

Drewien, R. C., H. M. Reeves, P. F. Springer, and T. L. Kuck. 1967. Back-pack unit for capturing waterfowl and upland game by night-lighting. J. Wildl. Manage. 31(4): 778–783.

Driscoll, R. S. 1963. Sprouting bitterbrush in central Oregon. Ecology 44(4):820–821.

Driver, E. C. 1949. Mammal remains in owl pellets. Am. Midl. Nat. 41(1): 139–142.

Dublin, L. I., A. J. Lotka, and M. Spiegelman. 1949. Length of life, a study of the life table. The Ronald Press Co., New York. 379 p.

Duebbert, H. F. 1966. Island nesting of the gadwall in North Dakota. Wilson Bull. 78(1):12–25.

Duffield, L. F. 1973. Aging and sexing the post-cranial skeleton of bison. Plains Anthropol. 18(60):132–139.

Dukes, H. H. 1977. Dukes' physiology of domestic animals. 9th ed. Comstock Publ., Ithaca, N.Y. 914 p.

Dumbleton, C. W. 1964. Russian-English biological dictionary. Oliver and Boyd, Edinburgh. 512 p.

Duncan, D. A., and L. O. Hylton, Jr. 1970. Effects of fertilization on quality of range forage. p. 57–62 *in* Range and wildlife habitat evaluation—a research symposium. USDA For Serv. Misc. Publ. No. 1147. 220 p.

Dunmire, W. W. 1955. Sex dimorphism in the pelvis of rodents. J. Mammal. 36(3):356–361.

Dunstan, T. C. 1972. A harness for radio-tagging raptorial birds. Inl. Bird-Banding News 44(1):4–8.

Dunstan, T. C. 1973. A tail feather package for radio-tagging raptorial birds. Inl. Bird-Banding News 45 (1):6–10.

Dunstan, T. C., and M. Borth. 1970. Successful reconstruction of active bald eagle nest. Wilson Bull. 82(3):326–327.

Durbin, J., and A. Stuart. 1951. Differences in response rates of experienced and inexperienced interviewers. J. R. Stat. Soc. Ser. A. 114(2): 163–195.

Dusi, J. L. 1949. Methods for the determination of food habits by plant microtechniques and histology and their application to cottontail rabbit food habits. J. Wildl. Manage. 13(3):295–298.

Dusi, J. L. 1952. The food habits of several populations of cottontail rabbits in Ohio. J. Wildl. Manage. 16(2):180–186.

Dwyer, D. D. 1961. Activities and grazing preferences of cows with calves in northern Osage County, Oklahoma. Okla. Agric. Exp. Stn. Bull. B-588, Stillwater. 61 p.

Dwyer, P. D. 1972. Feature, patch and refuge area: some influences on diversity of bird species. Emu 72:149–156.

Dwyer, T. J. 1972. An adjustable radio-package for ducks. Bird-Banding 43(4):282–284.

Dwyer, T. J., and J. V. Dobell. 1979. External determination of age of common snipe. J. Wildl. Manage. 43(3):754–756.

Dzubin, A. 1959. Growth and plumage development of wild-trapped juvenile canvasback *(Aythya valisineria).* J. Wildl. Manage. 23(3):279–290.

Dzubin, A., and J. B. Gollop. 1972. Aspects of mallard breeding ecology in Canadian parkland and grassland. p. 113–152 *in* Population ecology of migratory birds. Bur. Sport Fish. Wildl., Wildl. Res. Rep. 2. 278 p.

Eadie, W. R. 1954. Animal control in field, farm and forest. The Macmillan Co., New York. 257 p.

Eadie, W. R., and W. J. Hamilton, Jr. 1958. Reproduction in the fisher in New York. N.Y. Fish and Game J. 5(1):77–83.

Eakin, M. L. 1958. Checklist of forestry items in a working library. 1958. J. For. 56(8):586–591. (A supplement was prepared by E. M. Johnson in the same journal for 1962 as 60(2):91–93.)

Eardley, A. J. 1951. Structural geology of North America. 2nd ed. Harper and Row, New York. 743 p.

Earl, J. P. 1950. Production of mallards in irrigated land in the Sacramento Valley, California. J. Wildl. Manage. 14(3):332–342.

Eastman Kodak Co. 1971. Kodak data for aerial photography. Rochester, N.Y. 80 p.

Eberhardt, L. L. 1969. Population estimates from recapture frequencies. J. Wildl. Manage. 33(1):28–39.

Eberhardt, L. L. 1977. Relationship between two stock-recruitment curves. J. Fish. Res. Board Can. 34(3):425–428.

Eberhardt, L. L. 1978a. Transect methods for population studies. J. Wildl. Manage. 42(1):1–31.

Eberhardt, L. L. 1978b. Appraising variability in population studies. J. Wildl. Manage. 42(2):207–238.

Eberhardt, L. L., D. G. Chapman, and J. R. Gilbert. 1979. A review of marine mammal census methods. Wildl. Monogr. No. 63. 46 p.

Ebert, D., and D. Francis. 1978. The tree swallow. Virginia Wildl. 39(6): 19.

Eddy, S., and A. C. Hodson. 1961. Taxonomic keys to the common animals of the north central states. Burgess Publ. Co., Minneapolis, Minn. 162 p.

Edminster, F. C. 1954. American game birds of field and forest. Charles Scribner's Sons, New York. 490 p.

Edminster, F. C., and R. M. May. 1951. Shrub plantings for soil conservation and wildlife cover in the Northeast. USDA Circ. No. 887. 68 p.

Edmondson, W. T., (ed.), 1959. Ward and Whipple's freshwater biology. 2nd ed. J. Wiley, New York. 1248 p.

Edmundson, G. C., Jr., and D. R. Cornelius. 1961. Promising grasses for southern California fuel-breaks. USDA For. Serv. Misc. Pap. No. 58, Pac. S. W. For. and Range Exp. Stn., Berkeley. 13 p.

Edwards, A. M., and A. T. Hopwood, (eds.). 1966. Nomenclator zoologicus by S. A. Neave. Volume 6 (Supplement) for the years 1946–1955. Zool. Soc. of London, Regent's Park, London. 329 p.

Edwards, D. K. 1962. Recording animal activity. Science 136(3511): 198–199.

Edwards, E. P. 1974. A coded list of birds of the world. Privately Publ., Sweet Briar, Va. 174 p.

Edwards, M. G. 1961. New use of funnel trap for ruffed grouse broods. J. Wildl. Manage. 25(1):89.

Edwards, P. I., A. H. S. Onions, S. P. Lapage, P. J. P. Whitehead, W. T. Stearn, F. Perring, H. D. W. Eggins, J. L. Cutbill, M. Abbot, T. V. Scrivenor, M. D. Dadd, and R. D. Meikle. 1971. Storage and retrieval of biological information. Biol. J. Linnean Soc. Lond. 3(3):165–299.

Edwards, R. Y., and C. D. Fowle. 1955. The concept of carrying capacity. Trans. N. Am. Wildl. Conf. 20:589–602.

Edwards, W. R., and L. Eberhardt. 1967. Estimating cottontail abundance from livetrapping data. J. Wildl. Manage. 31(1):87–96.

Egler, F. E. 1973. Bibliography of papers by Frank E. Egler concerning right-of-way vegetation management, herbicides and society, candidly annotated by the author: or a contribution of comparative human ethology based on one fellow's folly 1947–1972. Conn. Conserv. Assoc., Bridgewater. 8 p.

Egler, F. E., and S. R. Foote. 1975. The plight of the right-of-way domain, victim of vandalism. Futura Media Serv. Inc., Mount Kisco, N.Y. 2 vols.

Ehrle, E. B., and H. J. Birx. 1970–1971. Organic evolution: selections from the literature. BioScience vol. 20, p. 513–514, 633–634, 730–731, 834–835, 930–931, 1028–1029, 1124–1125, 1321–1322, and vol. 21, p. 94–95, 201, 203. 10 parts.

Eicher, G. J. 1953. Aerial methods of assessing red salmon populations in western Alaska. J. Wildl. Manage. 17(4):521–527.

Einarsen, A. S. 1946. Crude protein determination of deer food as an applied management technique. Trans. N. Am. Wildl. Conf. 11:309–312.

Einarsen, A. S. 1948. The pronghorn antelope and its management. Wildl. Manage. Inst., Washington, D.C. 238 p.

Einarsen, A. S. 1956. Determination of some predatory species by field signs. Oregon State Univ. Monogr. Stud. in Zool. No. 10. 34 p.

Eisenbud, M. 1963. Environmental radiation. McGraw-Hill Book Co. Inc., New York. 430 p.

Eisenhauer, D. I., and D. A. Frazer. 1972. Nesting ecology of the emperor goose (*Philacte canagica* Sewastianov) in the Kokechik Bay region, Alaska. Dept. For. Conserv., Purdue Univ., West Lafayette, Ind. 82 p.

Eklund, C. R. 1942. Ecological and mortality factors affecting the nesting of the Chinese pheasant in the Willamette Valley, Oregon. J. Wildl. Manage. 6(3):225–230.

Eklund, C. R., and F. E. Charlton. 1959. Measuring the temperature of incubating penguin eggs. Am. Sci. 47(1):80–86.

El-Badry, M. A. 1956. A sampling procedure for mailed questionnaires. J. Am. Stat. Assoc. 51(274):209–227.

Elder, W. H. 1950. Measurement of hunting pressure in waterfowl by means of x-ray. Trans. N. Am. Wildl. Conf. 15:490–504.

Elder, W. H. 1952. Failure of placental scars to reveal breeding history in mink. J. Wildl. Manage. 16(1):110.

Elder, W. H. 1955. Fluoroscopic measures of hunting pressure in Europe and North America. Trans. N. Am. Wildl. Conf. 20:298–323.

Elder, W. H., and C. E. Shanks. 1962. Age changes in tooth wear and morphology of the baculum in muskrats. J. Mammal. 43(2):144–150.

Elias, D. J., J. K. Crier, and H. P. Tietjen. 1974. A technique for capturing prairie dogs. Southwestern Nat. 18(4):473–474.

Ellerman, J. R., and T. C. S. Morrison-Scott. 1966. Checklist of palaearctic and Indian mammals, 1758–1946. 2nd ed. Trustees of the British Museum, London. 810 p.

Elliot, D. G. 1897. The gallinaceous game birds of North America. Francis P. Harper, New York. 220 p.

Elliott, H. N. 1953. Wood rats. U.S. Fish Wildl. Serv. Washington, D.C. 2 p.

Ellis, D. H. 1975. First experiments with capturing golden eagles by helicopter. Bird-Banding 46(3):217–219.

Ellis, D. H., and C. H. Ellis. 1975. Color marking golden eagles with human hair dyes. J. Wildl. Manage. 39(2):445–447.

Ellis, J. A., W. R. Edwards, and K. P. Thomas. 1969. Responses of bobwhites to management in Illinois. J. Wildl. Manage. 33(4):749–762.

Ellis, R. J. 1961. Trapping and marking Rio Grande wild turkeys. Proc. Okla. Acad. Sci. 41:202–212.

Ellison, L. N. 1968. Sexing and aging Alaskan spruce grouse by plumage. J. Wildl. Manage. 32(1):12–16.

Ellison, L. N. 1974. Population characteristics of Alaskan spruce grouse. J. Wildl. Manage. 38(3):383–395.

Ellisor, J. E. 1969. Mobility of white-tailed deer in South Texas. J. Wildl. Manage. 33(1):220–222.

Ellisor, J. E., and W. F. Harwell. 1969. Mobility and home range of collared peccary in southern Texas. J. Wildl. Manage. 33(2):425–427.

Emery, D. 1964. Seed propagation of native California plants. St. Barbara Bot. Gard. Leafl. 1(10):81–96.

Emlen, J. T. 1977. Estimating breeding season bird densities from transect counts. Auk 94(3):455–468.

Emlen, J. T., Jr. 1956. A method for describing and comparing avian habitats. Ibis 98(4):565–576.

Emmel, V. E., and E. V. Cowdry. 1964. Laboratory techniques in biology and medicine. 4th ed. Williams and Wilkins Inc., Baltimore. 453 p.

Enderlin, R. W. 1946. Quail trapping techniques. Proc. Western Assoc. Fish and Game Commissioners 26:138–142.

Enders, R. K. 1952. Reproduction in the mink *(Mustela vison)*. Proc. Am. Philos. Soc. 96(6):691–755.

Eng, R. L. 1955. A method for obtaining sage grouse age and sex ratios from wings. J. Wildl. Manage. 19(2): 267–272.

Engle, L. C., and F. B. Clark. 1959. New rodent repellents fail to work on acorns and walnuts. USDA For. Serv. Cent. States, For. Exp. Stn. Note 138, Columbus, Ohio. 2 p.

English, P. F. 1941. Hatchability of pheasant eggs in relation to some known temperatures. J. Wildl. Manage. 5(2):213–215.

Erdos, P. L., and A. J. Morgan. 1970. Professional mail surveys. McGraw-Hill Book Co., New York. 289 p.

Erickson, A. B., D. B. Vessal, C. E. Carlson, and C. T. Rollings. 1951. Minnesota's most important game bird—the pheasant. Flicker 23(3): 23–49.

Erickson, A. W. 1957. Techniques for live-trapping and handling black bears. Trans. N. Am. Wildl. Conf. 22:520–543.

Erickson, J. A., A. E. Anderson, D. E. Medin, and D. C. Bowden. 1970. Estimating ages of mule deer—an evaluation of technique accuracy. J. Wildl. Manage. 34(3):523–531.

Errington, P. L. 1930. The pellet analysis method of raptor food habits study. Condor 32(6):292–296.

Errington, P. L. 1932. Techniques of raptor food habits study. Condor 34(2):75–86.

Errington, P. L. 1933. The nesting and life equation of the Wisconsin bobwhite. Wilson Bull. 45(3):122–132.

Errington, P. L. 1934. Vulnerability of bob-white populations to predation. Ecology 15(2):110–127.

Errington, P. L. 1943. An analysis of mink predation upon muskrat in north-central United States. Iowa State Coll. Agric. Exp. Stn. Res. Bull. 320:794–924.

Errington, P. L. 1963. Muskrat populations. Iowa State Univ. Press, Ames. 665 p.

Errington, P. L., and F. N. Hamerstrom, Jr. 1937. The evaluation of nesting losses and juvenile mortality of the ring-necked pheasant. J. Wildl. Manage. 1(1–2):3–20.

Erskine, A. J. 1971. Growth, and annual cycles in weights, plumages and reproductive organs of goosanders in eastern Canada. Ibis 113(1):42–58.

Erskine, A. J. 1972. Buffleheads. Can. Wildl. Serv. Monogr. Ser. No. 4. 240 p.

Estes, J. E., and L. W. Senger, (eds.). 1974. Remote sensing—techniques for environmental analysis. Hamilton Publ. Co., Santa Barbara, Calif. 340 p.

Etter, S. L., J. E. Warnock, and G. B. Joselyn. 1970. Modified wing molt criteria for estimating the ages of wild juvenile pheasants. J. Wildl. Manage. 34(3):620–626.

Evans, C. D. 1951. A method of color marking young waterfowl. J. Wildl. Manage. 15(1):101–103.

Evans, J. 1970. About nutria and their control. U.S. Fish Wildl. Serv. Resour. Publ. No. 86. 65 p.

Evans, J., J. O. Ellis, R. D. Nass, and A. L. Ward. 1971. Techniques for capturing, handling, and marking nutria. Proc. Southeastern Assoc. Game and Fish Commissioners 25:295–315.

Evans, J., and R. E. Griffith Jr. 1973. A fluorescent tracer and marker for animal studies J. Wildl. Manage. 37(1):73–81.

Evans, K. E., and D. R. Dietz. 1974. Nutritional energetics of sharp-tailed grouse during winter. J. Wildl. Manage. 38(4):622–629.

Evans, M., and J. Kear. 1972. A jacket for holding large birds for banding. J. Wildl. Manage. 36(4):1265–1267.

Evans, R. A., and R. M. Love. 1957. The step-point method of sampling—a practical tool in range research. J. Range Manage. 10(5): 208–212.

Evans, R. R., J. W. Goertz, and C. T. Williams. 1975. Capturing wild turkeys with tribromoethanol. J. Wildl. Manage. 39(3):630–634.

Evans, T. C. 1959. General appraisal of statistical problems and needs. p. 146–151 *in* U.S. Forest Service, Techniques and methods of measuring understory vegetation. Proc. of symposium at Tifton, Ga. S. E. and Southern Forest Exp. Stns., Asheville. 174 p.

Eve, J. H., and F. E. Kellogg. 1977. Management implications of abomasal parasites in southeastern white-tailed deer. J. Wildl. Manage. 41(2):169–177.

Everett, R. L., R. O. Meeuwig, and R. Stevens. 1978. Deer mouse preference for seed of commonly planted species, indigenous weed seed, and sacrifice foods. J. Range Manage. 31(1):70–73.

Ewer, R. F. 1973. The carnivores. Cornell Univ. Press. Ithaca, N.Y. 494 p.

Ewing, G. W. 1974. The laboratory recorder. Plenum Press, New York. 129 p.

Eygenraam, J. A. 1959. On 'the lead' in duck decoys. Trans. Int. Congr. Game Biol. 4:68–77.

Fabos, J. G., and S. J. Caswell. 1977. Composite landscape assessment. Mass. Agric. Exp. Stn. Res. Bull. 637, Amherst. 323 p.

Fager, E. W. 1972. Diversity: a sampling study. Am. Nat. 106(949): 293–310.

Fallon, D. 1965. Eatometer: a device for continuous recording of free-feeding behavior. Science 148 (3672):977–978.

Fankhauser, D. 1964. Plastic adhesive tape for color-marking birds. J. Wildl. Manage. 28(3):594.

Fant, R. J. 1953. A nest-recording device. J. Anim. Ecol. 22(2):323–327.

Fant, R. J. 1957. Criteria for aging pheasant embryos. J. Wildl. Manage. 21(3):324–328.

Farner, D. S., and L. R. Mewaldt. 1953. The recording of diurnal activity patterns in caged birds. Bird-Banding 24(2):55–65.

Farrell, D. J., and A. J. Wood. 1968. The nutrition of the female mink *(Mustela vison)*. I. The metabolic rate of the mink. Can. J. Zool. 46(1):41–45.

Farrell, R. K. 1966. Cryo-branding. Anim. Health Notes, Washington State Univ. 6(1):4–6.

Fashingbauer, B. A. 1962. Expanding plastic collar and aluminum collar for deer. J. Wildl. Manage. 26 (2):211–213.

Faulkner, W. R., and J. W. King. 1970. Manual of clinical laboratory procedures. 2nd ed. The Chemical Rubber Co., Cleveland. 354 p.

Feinberg, E. H. 1973. Foreign journals (letter). BioScience 23(2):74.

Ferguson, H. L., R. W. Ellis, and J. B. Whelan. 1975. Effects of stream channelization on avian diversity and density in Piedmont Virginia. Proc. Southeastern Assoc. Game and Fish Commissioners 29:540–548.

Ferguson, R. B. 1972. Bitterbrush topping: shrub response and cost factors. USDA For. Serv. Res. Pap. INT–125, Intermt. For. Range Exp. Stn., Ogden, Utah. 11 p.

Ferguson, R. B., and J. V. Basile. 1966. Topping stimulates bitterbrush twig growth. J. Wildl. Manage. 30(4): 839–841.

Fernald, M. L. 1950. Gray's manual of botany. 8th ed. Am. Book Co., New York. 1632 p.

Fessenden, G. R. 1949. Preservation of agricultural specimens in plastics. USDA Misc. Publ. 679. 78 p.

Fick, G. W. 1972. Comparison of two light meters for studies of light penetration into herbaceous leaf canopies. Ecology 53(3):526–528.

Ficken, R. W., and M. S. Ficken. 1966. A review of some aspects of avian field ethology. Auk 83(4):637–661.

Field, R. A., F. C. Smith, and W. G. Hepworth. 1972. The pronghorn carcass. Univ. of Wyoming. Agric. Exp. Stn. Bull. No. 575, Laramie. 6 p.

Field, R. A., F. C. Smith, and W. G. Hepworth. 1973a. The mule deer carcass. Univ. of Wyoming Agric. Exp. Stn. Bull. 589, Laramie. 6 p.

Field, R. A., F. C. Smith, and W. G. Hepworth. 1973b. The elk carcass. Univ. Wyoming Agric. Exp. Stn. Bull. 594, Laramie. 8 p.

Filion, F. L. 1974. Methods for increasing returns in mail hunter surveys. Can. Wildl. Serv. Biometrics Sect. Rep. No. 7. 54 p.

Filion, F. L. 1975. Estimating bias due to nonresponse mail surveys. Public Opin. Q. 39(4):482–492.

Filion, F. L. 1976a. Effect of changes in harvest questionnaires on survey estimates. Can. Wildl. Serv. Biometrics Sect. Rep. No. 13. 62 p.

Filion, F. L. 1976b. Exploring and correcting for nonresponse bias using follow-ups of nonrespondents. Pac. Sociol. Rev. 19(3):401–408.

Filion, F. L. 1978a. Increasing the effectiveness of mail surveys. Wildl. Soc. Bull. 6(3):135–141.

Filion, F. L. 1978b. Demographic and socioeconomic characteristics of holders of Canada migratory game bird hunting permits. p. 42–51 *in* H. Boyd. and G. H. Finney, (eds.). Migratory game bird hunters and hunting in Canada. Can. Wildl. Service Report Ser. No. 43. 127 p.

Filion, F. L. 1979. Sources of error in surveys. New surveys–notes on statistical survey activity within the federal government. Stat. Canada 4(3):8–11.

Filion, F. L. 1980. Human dimensions research in wildlife management: elements of a federal strategy. p. 71–74 *in* Canadian wildlife administration. Vol. 6. Ontario Ministry Nat. Resour., Toronto. 90 p.

Findley, J. S., A. H. Harris, D. E. Wilson, and C. Jones. 1975. Mammals of New Mexico. Univ. of New Mexico Press, Albuquerque. 360 p.

Finley, R. B., Jr. 1965. Adverse effects on birds of phosphamidon applied to a Montana forest. J. Wildl. Manage. 29(3):580–591.

Finney, D. J. 1960. An introduction to the theory of experimental design. Univ. of Chicago Press, Chicago, Ill. 223 p.

Fischer, C. A. 1974. A lift-net for capturing male ruffed grouse. J. Wildl. Manage. 38(1):149–151.

Fischer, R. B. 1944. Suggestions for capturing hole-nesting birds. Bird-Banding 15(4):151–156.

Fisher, A. K. 1894. Hawks and owls as related to the farmer. p. 215–232 *in* 1894 Yearbook of agriculture. U.S. Gov. Print. Off., Washington, D.C. 608 p.

Fisher, E. W., and A. E. Perry. 1970. Estimating ages of gray squirrels by lens-weights. J. Wildl. Manage. 34 (4):825–828.

Fisher, H. D. 1954. Delayed implantation in the harbour seal, *Phoca vitulina* L. Nature 173(4410):879–880.

Fisher, R. A., and F. Yates. 1963. Statistical tables for biological, agricultural and medical research. 6th ed. Hafner Publ. Co., New York. 146 p.

Fitch, H. S. 1948. A study of coyote relationships on cattle range. J. Wildl. Manage. 12(1):73–78.

Fitz, G. 1963. How to measure and score big-game trophies: Boone and Crockett official method; Pope and Young archery method. Outdoor Life, New York. 88 p.

Fitzgerald, A. E., and D.C. Waddington. 1979. Comparison of two methods of fecal analysis of herbivore diet. J. Wildl. Manage. 43(2): 468–473.

Fitzgerald, J. P. 1973. Four immobilizing agents used on badgers under field conditions. J. Wildl. Manage. 37(3):418–421.

Fitzner, R. E., and J. N. Fitzner. 1977. A hot melt glue technique for attaching radio-transmitter tail packages to raptorial birds. N. Am. Bird Bander 2(2):56–57.

Fitzwater, W. D., H. L. Dozier, Jr., and H. G. Alford. 1972. EPA compendium of registered pesticides. Volume IV. Rodenticides and mammal, bird, and fish toxicants. Office of Pesticides Programs, U.S. Environ. Protect. Agency, Washington, D.C. 197 p.

Fleharty, E. D., M. E. Krause, and D. P. Stinnett. 1973. Body composition, energy content and lipid cycles of four species of rodents. J. Mammal. 54(2):426–438.

Flerov, K. K. 1960. Musk deer and deer. Fauna of USSR: Mammals, Vol. 1, No. 2. Israel Program for Sci. Transl. Jerusalem. 257 p.

Flood, B. S., M. E. Sangster, R. D. Sparrowe, and T. S. Baskett. 1977. A handbook for habitat evaluation procedures. U.S. Fish and Wildl. Serv. Resour. Publ. No. 132. 77 p.

Floyd, J. F., L. D. Mech, and M. E. Nelson. 1979. An improved method of censusing deer in deciduous-coniferous forests. J. Wildl. Manage. 43(1):258–261.

Floyd, T. J., L. D. Mech, and P. A. Jordan. 1978. Relating wolf scat content to prey consumed. J. Wildl. Manage. 42(3):528–532.

Flux, J. E. C. 1971. Validity of the kidney fat index for estimating the condition of hares: a discussion. N. Z. J. Sci. 14(2):238–244.

Fogarty, M. J. 1969. Capturing snipe with mist nets. Proc. Southeastern Assoc. Game and Fish Commissioners 23:78–84.

Fogl, J. G., and H. S. Mosby. 1978. Aging gray squirrels by cementum annuli in razor-sectioned teeth. J. Wildl. Manage. 42(2):444–448.

Folk, G. E., Jr. 1966. Telemetered physiological measurements of bears in winter dens. 3rd Hibernation Symp., Oliver and Boyd, Edinburgh. 12 p.

Follett, W. 1966. Modern American usage: a guide. Hill and Wang, New York. 462 p.

Follis, T. B., W. C. Foote, and J. J. Spillett. 1972. Observation of genitalia in elk by laparotomy. J. Wildl. Manage. 36(1):171–173.

Follis, T. B., and J. J. Spillett. 1972. A new method for rumen sampling. J. Wildl. Manage. 36(4):1336–1340.

Foote, R. H., 1972. Communication in the biological sciences. p. 376–396 *in* J. A. Behnke, (ed.). Challenging biological problems—directions toward their solution. Oxford Univ. Press, New York. 502 p.

Foote, R. H., (ed.). 1977. Thesaurus of entomology. Entomol. Soc. of Amer., College Park, Maryland. 188 p.

Forbes, E. B., L. F. Marcy, A. L. Voris, and C. E. French. 1941. The digestive capacities of the white-tailed deer. J. Wildl. Manage. 5(1):108–114.

Forbes, R. D., and A. B. Meyer, (eds.). 1955. Forestry handbook. The Ronald Press Co., New York. v.p.

Forbes, R. M., and W. P. Garrigus. 1950. Some relationships between chemical composition, nutritive value, and intake of forages grazed by steers and wethers. J. Anim. Sci. 9(3):354–362.

Forbes, S. A. 1880. The food of birds. Ill. State Lab. Nat. Hist. Bull. 1(3):80–148.

Forbes, T. R. 1941. Instructions for collecting reproductive tracts of wild animals for study. U.S. Fish Wildl Serv. Form 3–1486, Washington, D.C. 3 p. (processed)

Forbush, E. H. 1925–29. Birds of Massachusetts and other New England states. Berwick and Smith Co., Norwood, Mass. 3 vol.

Forman, R. T. T., A. E. Galli, and C. F. Leck. 1976. Forest size and avian diversity in New Jersey woodlots with some land-use implications. Oecologia 26(1):1–8.

Forrester, J. W. 1961. Industrial dynamics. M.I.T. Press. 464 p.

Forsyth, D. J., and T. J. Peterle. 1973. Accumulation of chlorine -36 ring-labeled DDT residues in various tissues of two species of shrew. Arch. of Environ. Contam. and Toxicol. 1(1): 1–17.

Fowler, H. W. 1965. A dictionary of modern English usage. 2nd ed. rev. by Sir Ernest Gowers. Oxford Univ. Press, New York. 725 p.

Fowler, J. A. 1965. An information retrieval system for biological researchers. BioScience 15(6):413–417.

Fowler, M. 1978. Restraint and handling of wild and domestic animals. Iowa State Univ. Press, Ames. 332 p.

Fowler, W. B. 1975. Versatile wind analyser for long unattended runs using C-MOS. J. Phys. E. Sci. Instrum. 8(9):713–714.

Fox, B. J. 1978. A method for determining capture time of small mammals. J. Wildl. Manage. 42(3):672–676.

Fox, G. A., F. W. Anderka. V. Lewin, and W. C. MacKay. 1975. Field assessment of eggshell quality by beta-backscatter. J. Wildl. Manage. 39(3):528–534.

Fox, L. 1959. Photos—are yours good enough? Better Farming Methods 31(12):14–16.

Fox, M. W. 1965. Canine behavior. Charles C. Thomas, Springfield, Ill. 137 p.

Fox, M. W., (ed.). 1975. The wild canids; their systematics, behavioral ecology, and evolution. Van Nostrand Reinhold, New York. 508 p.

Fox, R. R., and D. D. Crary. 1972. A simple technique for the sexing of newborn rabbits. Lab. Anim. Sci. 22(4):556–558.

Francis, R. E. 1978. Current rangeland inventory methods—compatability toward an ecological base? p. 91–109 *in* H. G. Lund et al. Integrated inventories of renewable natural resources. Proceedings of the workshop: USDA For. Serv., Rocky Mt. For. and Range Exp. Stn. Gen. Tech. Rep. RM–55, Fort Collins, Colo. 482 p.

Frandson, R. D. 1974. Anatomy and physiology of farm animals. Lea and Febiger, Philadelphia. 494 p.

Frank, E. J., and E. E. Woehler. 1969. Production of nesting and winter cover for pheasants in Wisconsin. J. Wildl. Manage. 33(4):802–810.

Frankel, S., S. Reitman, and A. C. Sonnenwirth. 1970. Gradwohl's clinical laboratory methods and diagnosis. 7th ed. C. V. Mosby Co., St. Louis. 2 vol.

Franson, J. C., P. A. Dahm, and L. D. Wing. 1975. A method for preparing and sectioning mink *(Mustela vison)* mandibles for age determination. Am. Midl. Nat. 93(2):507–508.

Frantz, S. C. 1972. Fluorescent pigments for studying movements and home ranges of small mammals. J. Mammal. 53(1):218–223.

Franz, J. M. 1961. Biological control of pest insects in Europe. Annu. Rev. Entomol. 6:183–200.

Franzmann, A. W. 1972. Environmental sources of variation of bighorn sheep physiologic values. J. Wildl. Manage. 36(3):924–932.

Fredin, R. A. 1954. Causes of fluctuations in abundance of Connecticut River shad. U.S. Fish Wildl. Serv. Fish. Bull. 88, Washington, D.C. 13 p.

Fredrickson, L. F. and C. G. Trautman. 1978. Use of drugs for capturing and handling pheasants. J. Wildl. Manage. 42(3):690–693.

Fredrickson, L. H. 1968. Measurements of coots related to sex and age. J. Wildl. Manage. 32(2):409–411.

Fredrickson, L. H. 1969. An experimental study of clutch size of the American coot. Auk 86(3):541–550.

Free, J. C., R. M. Hansen, and P. L. Sims. 1970. Estimating dryweights of foodplants in feces of herbivores. J. Range Manage. 23(4):300–302.

Freeman, M. M. R. 1970. Observations on the seasonal behaviour of the Hudson Bay eider *(Somateria mollissima sedentaria).* Can. Field-Nat. 84(2):145–153.

French, C. E., L. C. McEwen, N. D. Magruder, R. H. Ingram, and R. W. Swift. 1956. Nutrient requirements for growth and antler development in the white-tailed deer. J. Wildl. Manage. 20(3):221–232.

Friend, M. 1967. A review of research concerning eye-lens weight as a criterion of age in animals. N.Y. Fish and Game J. 14(2):152–165.

Friend, M. 1968. The lens technique. Trans. N. Am. Wildl. Nat. Resour. Conf. 33:279–298.

Friley, C. E., Jr. 1949. Age determination, by use of the baculum, in the river otter, *Lutra c. canadensis* Schreber. J. Mammal. 30(2):102–110.

Frings, H., and M. Frings. 1957. Recorded calls of the eastern crow as attractants and repellents. J. Wildl. Manage. 21(1):91.

Frings, H., M. Frings, B. Cox, and L. Peissner. 1955. Recorded calls of herring gulls *(Larus argentatus)* as repellents and attractants. Science 121(3140):340–341.

Frings, H., and J. Jumber. 1954. Preliminary studies on the use of a specific sound to repel starlings *(Sturnus vulgaris)* from objectionable roosts. Science 119(3088):318–319.

Frison, G. C., and C. A. Reher. 1970. Age determination of buffalo by teeth eruption & wear. Plains Anthropol. Memoirs 7, Vol. 15, No. 50, Part 2:46–50.

Fry, F. E. J. 1949. Statistics of a lake trout fishery. Biometrics 5(1):27–67.

Fryer, T. B. 1970. Implantable biotelemetry systems. NASA SP–5094, U.S. Gov. Print. Off., Washington, D.C. 113 p.

Fuller, C. H. 1974. Weighting to adjust for survey nonresponse. Public Opin. Q. 38(2):239–246.

Fuller, M. R. 1975. A technique for holding and handling raptors. J. Wildl. Manage. 39(4):824–825.

Furrer, R. K. 1979. Experiences with a new back-tag for open-nesting passerines. J. Wildl. Manage. 43(1): 245–249.

Fyfe, R. W., and H. I. Armbruster. 1977. Raptor research and management in Canada. p. 282–293 *in* R. D. Chancellor, (ed.). World conference on birds of prey, Vienna. 1975. 442 p.

Gabrielson, I. N. 1941. Wildlife conservation. Macmillan, New York. 250 p.

Gabrielson, I. N., and S. G. Jewett. 1940. Birds of Oregon. Oregon State Univ. Monogr., Studies in Zoology No. 2. 650 p.

Gabrielson, I. N., and S. G. Jewett. 1970. Birds of the Pacific Northwest with special reference to Oregon. Dover Books, New York. 650 p. (Reprint of the 1940 edition title: Birds of Oregon, published by the Oregon State Coll., Corvallis.)

Gabrielson, I. N., and F. C. Lincoln. 1959. The birds of Alaska. Stackpole Co., Harrisburg, Pa. 922 p.

Galli, A. E., C. F. Leck, and R. T. T. Forman. 1976. Avian distribution patterns in forest islands of different sizes in central New Jersey. Auk 93(2):356–364.

Galt, H. D., P. R. Ogden, J. H. Ehrenreich, B. Theurer, and S. C. Martin. 1968. Estimating botanical composition of forage samples from fistulated steers by a microscope point method. J. Range Manage. 21(6): 397–401.

Galt, H. D., B. Theurer, J. H. Ehrenreich, W. H. Hale, and S. C. Martin. 1969. Botanical composition of diet of steers grazing a desert grassland range. J. Range Manage. 22(1):14–19.

Gans, C. 1966. An inexpensive arrangement of movie camera and electronic flash as a tool in the study of animal behaviour. Anim. Behav. 14(1):11–12.

Gans, C., and J. J. Bonin. 1963. Acoustic activity recorder for burrowing animals. Science 140(3565):398.

Garcelon, D. K. 1977. An expandable drop-off transmitter collar for young mountain lions. Calif. Fish and Game. 63(3):185–189.

Garfield, E. 1964. Science citation index—a new dimension in indexing. Science 144 (3619):649–654.

Garlough, F. E. 1945. Capturing foxes. U.S. Fish Wildl. Serv. Circ. 8. 11 p.

Garrett, W. N., J. H. Meyer, and G. P. Lofgreen. 1959. The comparative energy requirements of sheep and cattle for maintenance and gain. J. Anim. Sci. 18(2):528–547.

Garrison, G. A., A. J. Bjugstad, D. A. Duncan, M. E. Lewis, and D. R. Smith. 1977. Vegetation and environmental features of forest and range ecosystems. USDA For. Serv. Agric. Handb. No. 475. 68 p.

Gartshore, M. E. 1978. A noose trap for catching nesting birds. N. Am. Bird Bander 3(1):1–2.

Gary, M., R. McAfee, and C. L. Wolf. 1972. Glossary of geology. American Geol. Inst., Washington, D.C. 805 p.

Gasaway, W. C., D. B. Harkness, and R. A. Rausch. 1978. Accuracy of moose age determinations from incisor cementum layers. J. Wildl. Manage. 42(3):558–563.

Gast, J. A. 1963. Rhodamine-B dye for studying movements of animals. Ecology 44(3):611–612.

Gates, F. C. 1949. Field manual of plant ecology. McGraw-Hill Co., New York. 137 p.

Gates, J. M. 1973. Gray partridge ecology in southeast-central Wisconsin. Wis. Dept. Nat. Resour. Tech. Bull. No. 70, Madison. 8 p.

Gates, J. M., and J. B. Hale. 1975. Reproduction of an east central Wisconsin pheasant population. Wis. Dept. Nat. Resour. Tech. Bull. No. 85, Madison. 70 p.

Gates, N. L., J. E. Rich, D. D. Godtel, and C. V. Hulet. 1978. Development and evaluation of anti-coyote electric fencing. J. Range Manage. 31(2): 151–153.

Gaussen, H., P. Legris, M. Viart, and L. Labrone. 1964. International map of the vegetation, Ceylon. Spec. Sheet Surv. Dept. of Ceylon (Sri Lanka).

Gauthreaux, S. A., Jr. 1969. A portable ceilometer technique for studying low-level nocturnal migration. Bird-Banding 40(4):309–320.

Gauthreaux, S. A. 1978. The structure and organization of avian communities in forests. p. 17–37 *in* Proceedings of the workshop management of southern forests for nongame birds. USDA For. Serv. Gen. Tech. Rep. SE–14. 176 p.

Geis, A. D. 1974. Effects of urbanization and type of urban development on bird populations. p. 97–105 *in* J. H. Noyes and D. R. Progulske, (eds.). Wildlife in an urbanizing environment. Coop. Ext. Serv. Monogr., Univ. Massachusetts, Amherst. 182 p.

Geis, A. D. 1976. Effects of building design and quality on nuisance bird problems. Proc. Vertebr. Pest Conf. 7:51–53.

Geis, M. B. 1956. Productivity of Canada geese in the Flathead Valley, Montana, J. Wildl. Manage. 20(4):409–419.

Geist, V. 1966. Validity of horn segment counts in aging bighorn sheep. J. Wildl. Manage. 30(3):634–635.

Geist, V., and F. Walther, (ed.). 1974. The behaviour of ungulates and its relation to management; papers of an international symposium held at the Univ. of Calgary . . . 1971. IUCN Publ., No. 24. 2 vol. 941 p.

Gentry, J. B., M. H. Smith, and R. J. Beyers. 1971. Use of radioactively tagged bait to study movement patterns in small mammal populations. Ann. Zool. Fenn. 8:17–21.

George, H. A. 1963. Planting alkali bulrush for waterfowl food. Calif. Dept. Fish and Game, Game Manage. Leafl. No. 9, Sacramento. 9 p.

George, J. L., and R. T. Mitchell. 1948. Calculations on the extent of spruce budworm control by insectivorous birds. J. For. 46(6):454–455.

Gessaman, J. A. 1972. Bioenergetics of the snowy owl (*Nyctea scandiaca*). Arct. Alp. Res. 4(3):223–238.

Gessaman, J. A., (ed.). 1973. Ecological energetics of homeotherms: a view compatible with ecological modeling. Utah State Univ. Monogr. Ser. Vol. 20. Logan. 155 p.

Getz, L. L., and G. O. Batzli. 1974. A device for preventing disturbance of small mammal live-traps. J. Mammal. 55(2):447–448.

Getz, L. L., and M. L. Prather. 1975. A method to prevent removal of trap bait by insects. J. Mammal. 56(4):955.

Ghiselin, J. 1978a. Environmental reports for nuclear regulatory commission: guidelines thwart sound ecological design. Environ. Manage. 2(2):99–103.

Ghiselin, J. 1978b. Perils of the orderly mind; cost-benefit analysis and other logical pitfalls. Environ. Manage. 2(4):295–300.

Ghiselin, J. 1980. Applied ecology. *in* E. J. Kormondy and J. F. McCormick, (eds.). Handbook of contemporary world developments in ecology. Greenwood Press, Westport, Conn. (in press).

Gibb, J., and P. H. T. Hartley. 1957. Bird foods and feeding habits as subjects for amateur research. Br. Birds. 50(7):278–291.

Gibbs, H. D. 1978. Nutritional quality of mule deer foods, Piceance Basin, Colorado. M. S. Thesis. Colorado State Univ., Fort Collins. 179 p.

Gibson, D. 1957. The ovary as an indicator of reproductive history in the white-tailed deer, *Odocoileus virginianus borealis*. Miller. M. A. Thesis. Univ. of Toronto. 61 p.

Gier, H. T. 1968. Coyotes in Kansas. Kansas State Coll. Bull. 393, Manhattan. 118 p.

Giesen, K. M., and C. E. Braun. 1979. A technique for age determination of juvenile white-tailed ptarmigan. J. Wildl. Manage. 43(2):508–511.

Gifford, C. E., and D. R. Griffin. 1960. Notes on homing and migratory behavior of bats. Ecology 41(2):378–381.

Gilbert, D. L. 1971. Natural resources and public relations. 2nd ed. The Wildl. Soc. Washington, D.C. 320 p.

Gilbert, F. F., and S. L. Stolt. 1970. Variability in aging Maine white-tailed deer by tooth-wear characteristics. J. Wildl. Manage. 34(3):532–535.

Gilbert, P. F., and A. G. Hahn. 1959. The practical use of aerial photographs in game and fish management. Proc. Western Assoc. State Game and Fish Commissioners 39:223–228.

Giles, R. H., (ed.). 1969a. Wildlife management techniques. 3rd ed. The Wildl. Soc., Washington, D.C. 623 p.

Giles, R. H. 1969b. The approach. p. 1–4 *in* R. H. Giles, (ed.). Wildlife management techniques. The Wildl. Soc., Washington, D.C. 623 p.

Giles, R. H., Jr. 1970. The ecology of a small forested watershed treated with the insecticide malathion $-S^{35}$ Wildl. Monogr. No. 24. 81 p.

Giles, R. H., Jr. 1978. Wildlife management. W. H. Freeman & Co., San Francisco. 416 p.

Giles, R. H., Jr. 1979. Modeling decisions on ecological systems. p. 147–159 *in* J. Cairns, Jr., G. P. Patil, and W. E. Waters, (eds.). Environmental biomonitoring, assessment, prediction and management/certain case studies and related quantitative issues. Stat. Ecol. Series. Vol. 11. Int. Coop. Publ. House, Fairland, Md. 433 p.

Giles, R. H., Jr. Validity and feedback. Chapter 18 *in* R. H. Giles, Jr. (ed.) Wildlife management systems (in prep.)

Giles, R. H., Jr. and R. F. Scott. 1969. A systems approach to refuge management. Trans. N. Am. Wildl. Nat. Resour. Conf. 34:103–115.

Gill, J. 1953. Remarks on the analysis of kill-curves of female deer. Proc. Northeast. Wildl. Conf. 9:1–12.

Gill, J. D., and W. H. Healy. 1974. Shrubs and vines for northeastern wildlife. USDA For. Serv. Gen. Tech. Rep. NE–9, N.E. For. Exp. Stn., Upper Darby, Pa. 180 p.

Gill, R. B. 1966. A literature review on the sage grouse. Colorado Dept. of Game, Fish, Parks and Coop. Wildl. Res. Unit. Spec. Rep. No. 6. 39 p.

Gill, T. N., and E. Coues. 1974. Material for a bibliography of North American mammals. (reprinted from 'Report of the United States Geological Survey of Territories, vol. XI, Appendix B, Washington, D.C. 1877'), *in* Contributions to the bibliographical literature of American mammals, part 1. Arno Press, New York. 130 p.

Gilmer, D. S., I. J. Ball, L. M. Cowardin, and J. H. Riechmann. 1974. Effects of radio packages on wild ducks. J. Wildl. Manage. 38(2): 243–252.

Gilmer, D. S., V. B. Kuechle, and I. J. Ball, Jr. 1971. A device for monitoring radio-marked animals. J. Wildl. Manage. 35(4):829–832.

Gimbarzevsky, P. 1978. Land classification as a base for integration of renewable resources inventories. p. 169–177 *in* H. G. Lund et al. Integrated inventories of renewable natural resources. Proceedings of the workshop: USDA For. Serv., Rocky Mt. For. and Range Exp. Stn. Gen. Tech. Rep. RM–55, Fort Collins, Colo. 482 p.

Girard, G. L. 1939. Notes on the life history of the shoveller. Trans. N. Amer. Wildl. Conf. 4:364–371.

Girard, G. L. 1941. The mallard: its management in western Montana. J. Wildl. Manage. 5(3):233–259.

Gist, C. S., and F. W. Whicker. 1971. Radioiodine uptake and retention by the mule deer thyroid. J. Wildl. Manage. 35(3):461–468.

Glading, B. 1938. Studies on the nesting cycle of the California valley quail in 1937. Calif. Fish and Game 24(4):318–340.

Glading, B. 1947. Game watering devices for the arid Southwest. Trans. N. Am. Wildl. Conf. 12:286–292.

Glading, B., H. H. Biswell, and C. F. Smith. 1940. Studies on the food of the California quail in 1937. J. Wildl. Manage. 4(2):128–144.

Glass, B. P. 1973. A key to the skulls of North American mammals. 2nd ed. Okla. State Univ., Stillwater. 54 p.

Gleason, H. A. 1926. The individualistic concept of the plant association. Bull. Torrey Bot. Club 53(1):7–26.

Gleason, H. A. 1939. The individualistic concept of the plant association. Am. Midl. Nat. 21(1):92–110.

Glenn, J. L., R. Straight, and C. C. Snyder. 1972. Ketalar—a new anesthetic for use in snakes. Int. Zoo Yearb. 12(2):224–227.

Glover, F. A. 1956. Nesting and production of the blue-winged teal (*Anas discors* L.) in northwest Iowa. J. Wildl. Manage. 20(1):28–46.

Goddard, J. 1967. The validity of censusing black rhinoceros populations from the air. E. Afr. Wildl. J. 5:18–23.

Godfrey, G. A. 1970. A transmitter harness for small birds. Inl. Bird-Banding News 42(1):3–5.

Godfrey, G. K. 1953. A technique for finding *Microtus* nests. J. Mammal. 34(4):503–505.

Godfrey, G. K. 1954a. Tracing field voles (*Microtus agrestis*) with a Geiger-Muller counter. Ecology 35(1):5–10.

Godfrey, G. K. 1954b. Use of radioactive isotopes in small-mammal ecology. Nature 174(4438):951–952.

Godfrey, G. K. 1955. A field study of the activity of the mole (*Talpa europaea*). Ecology 36(4):678–685.

Godfrey, L. E., (ed.), and H. F. Redman. 1973. Dictionary of report series codes. 2nd ed. Spec. Libr. Assoc., New York. 645 p.

Godfrey, W. E. 1966. The birds of Canada. Natl. Mus. of Canada Bull. No. 203 (Biol. Ser. No. 73). 428 p.

Godin, A. J. 1960. A compilation of diagnostic characteristics used in aging and sexing game birds and mammals. M. S. Thesis. Univ. of Massachusetts, Amherst. 160 p.

Godin, A. J. 1964. A review of the literature on the mountain beaver. U.S. Fish and Wildl. Serv. Spec. Sci. Rep. (Wildl.) No. 78. 52 p.

Godin, A. J. 1977. Wild mammals of New England. Johns Hopkins Univ. Press, Baltimore, Md. 304 p.

Goebel, C. J., and G. Berry. 1976. Selectivity of range grass seeds by local birds. J. Range Manage. 29(5):393–395.

Goforth, W. R., and T. S. Baskett. 1965. Effects of experimental color marking on pairing of captive mourning doves. J. Wildl. Manage. 29(3): 543–553.

Goggins, P. L., D. K. Christie, K. H. Anderson, K. Warner, C. Lombard, O. C. Fenderson, and F. Kircheis. 1971. Planning for Maine fish, wildlife, and marine resources. Maine Dept. Inland Fish. and Wildl., Maine Dept. Sea and Shore Fish., Augusta. 52 p.

Gold, H. J. 1977. Mathematical modeling of biological systems—an introductory guidebook. John Wiley and Sons, N.Y. 357 p.

Golet, F. C., and J. S. Larson. 1974. Classification of freshwater wetlands in the glaciated northeast. U.S. Fish Wildl. Serv. Resour. Publ. 116. 56 p.

Golley, F. B. 1957. An appraisal of ovarian analysis in determining reproductive performance of black-tailed deer. J. Wildl. Manage. 21(1):62–65.

Golley, F. B. 1966. South Carolina mammals, Contr. Charleston Mus. XV. 181 p.

Gollop, J. B. 1956. The use of retrievers in banding flightless young mallards. Trans. N. Am. Wildl. Conf. 21:239–248.

Gollop, J. B., and W. H. Marshall. 1954. A guide to aging duck broods in the field. Miss. Flyway Counc. Tech. Sect. Rep. 9 p. (mimeo.)

Goodall, D. W. 1972. Building and testing ecosystem models. p. 173–194 *in* J. N. R. Jeffers, (ed.). Mathematical models in ecology. Blackwell Sci. Publ. Oxford. 398 p.

Goodman, R. M. 1971. A reliable and accurate implantable temperature telemeter. BioScience 21(8):371–374.

Goodrum, P. D. 1940. A population study of the gray squirrel in eastern Texas. Texas Agric. Exp. Stn. Bull. 591. 34 p.

Goodwin, D. 1977. Pigeons and doves of the world. 2nd ed. Cornell Univ. Press, Ithaca, New York. 446 p.

Goodwin, G. G. 1953. Catalogue of type specimens of recent mammals in the American Museum of Natural History. Bull. Am. Mus. Nat. Hist. Vol. 102, Art. 3. p. 211–411.

Gorsuch, D. M. 1934. Life history of the Gambel quail in Arizona. Univ. of Arizona Bull. 5(4):, Biol. Sci. Bull. No. 2, Tucson. 89 p.

Gotch, A. F. 1979. Mammals—their latin names explained. Blandsford Press, Poole Dorset, England. 271 p.

Gourley, R. S., and F. J. Jannett, Jr. 1975. Pine and montane vole age estimates from eye lens weights. J. Wildl. Manage. 39(3):550–556.

Gower, W. C. 1939. The use of the bursa of Fabricius as an indication of age in game birds. Trans. N. Am. Wildl. Conf. 4:426–430.

Gozmany, L., H. Steinmann, and E. Szily. 1979. Vocabularium nominum animalium Europae septem linguis redactum (Septemlingual dictionary of the names of European animals). Academiai Kiado, Budapest. 2 vol. 1171, 1015 p.

Graber, R. R., and W. W. Cochran. 1959. An audio technique for the study of nocturnal migration of birds. Wilson Bull. 71(3):220–236.

Graber, R. R., and S. L: Wunderle. 1966. Telemetric observations of a robin (*Turdus migratorius*). Auk 83(4):674–677.

Graham, S. A. 1945. Ecological classification of cover types. J. Wildl. Manage. 9(3):182–190.

Gramlich, F. J. 1972. CB caps for pest bird control. Tech. Rel. No. 4–72., Nat. Pest Control Assoc., Elizabeth, N. J. 1 p.

Grange, W. B. 1949. The way to game abundance. Charles Scribner's Sons, New York. 365 p.

Grassland Research Institute. 1961. Research techniques in use at the Grassland Research Institute [Hurley, England] Commonwealth Bureau of Pastures and Field Crops Bull. 45. 166 p.

Grau, G. A., G. C. Sanderson, and J. P. Rogers. 1970. Age determination of raccoons. J. Wildl. Manage. 34(2): 364–372.

Graves, H. B., E. D. Bellis, and W. M. Knuth. 1972. Censusing white-tailed deer by airborne thermal infrared imagery. J. Wildl. Manage. 36(3): 875–884.

Gray, C. W., M. Bush, and C. C. Beck. 1974. Clinical experience using CI-744 in chemical restraint and anesthesia of exotic specimens. J. Zoo Anim. Med. 5(4):12–21.

Gray, P. 1954. The microtomists formulary and guide. Blakiston Co., New York. 794 p.

Gray, P. 1964. Handbook of basic micro-technique. 3rd ed. McGraw-Hill, New York. 302 p.

Gray, P., (ed.). 1970. The encyclopedia of the biological sciences. 2nd ed. Van Nostrand Reinhold Co., New York. 1027 p.

Gray, P. 1973. The encyclopedia of microscopy and microtechnique. Van Nostrand Inc., New York. 638 p.

Gray, P., and L. Langord. 1961. Biological societies. p. 117–142 *in* P. Gray, (ed.). Encyclopedia of the biological sciences. Reinhold Publ. Corp., New York. 1119 p.

Greeley, F. 1953. Sex and age studies in fall shot woodcock *(Philohela minor)* from southern Wisconsin. J. Wildl. Manage. 17(1):29–32.

Greeley, F., R. F. Labisky, and S. H. Mann. 1962. Distribution and abundance of pheasants in Illinois. Illinois Nat. Hist. Surv. Biol. Notes No. 47, Urbana. 16 p.

Green, B. 1978. Estimation of food consumption in the dingo, *Canis familiaris dingo,* by means of ^{22}Na turnover. Ecology 59(2):207–210.

Green, B., and J. D. Dunsmore. 1978. Turnover of tritiated water and ^{22}sodium in captive rabbits *(Oryctolagus cuniculus).* J. Mammal. 59 (1):12–17.

Green, B., and K. Newgrain. 1979. Estimation of milk intake of sucklings by means of ^{22}Na. J. Mammal. 60(3):556–559.

Green, G. W., and D. C. Anderson. 1961. A simple and inexpensive apparatus for photographing events at pre-set intervals. Can. Entomol. 93(9):741–745.

Green, J., and R. B. Janssen. 1975. Minnesota birds: where, when and how many. Univ. of Minnesota Press, Minneapolis. 210 p.

Green, L. R. 1977. Fuelbreaks and other fuel modification for wildland fire control. USDA For. Serv. Agric. Handb. 499, Washington, D.C. 79 p.

Greenewalt, C. H., and F. M. Jones. 1955. Photographic studies of the feeding of nestling house wrens. Am. Sci. 43(4): 541–549.

Greenhall, A. M., and J. L. Paradiso. 1968. Bats and bat banding. U.S. Fish Wildl. Serv. Resour. Publ. 72. 48 p.

Greenhill, A. W., and H. J. Page. 1931. II. The mineral content of intensively treated pasture and a relationship between the nitrogen and phosphorus contents. J. Agric. Sci. 21(2):220–232.

Greenwood, R. J. 1975. An attempt to freeze-brand mallard ducklings. Bird-Banding 46(3):204–206.

Greenwood, R. J. 1977. Evaluation of a nasal marker for ducks. J. Wildl. Manage. 41(3):582–585.

Greenwood, R. J., and W. C. Bair. 1974. Ice on waterfowl markers. Wildl. Soc. Bull. 2(3):130–134.

Greenwood, R. J., and A. B. Sargeant. 1973. Influence of radio packs on captive mallards and blue-winged teal. J. Wildl. Manage. 37(1):3–9.

Greer, J. K. 1965. A cage for small intractable animals. J. Wildl. Manage. 29(4):895–896.

Greer, K. R. 1957. Some osteological characters of known-age ranch minks. J. Mammal. 38(3):319–330.

Greer, K. R. 1968. A compression method indicates fat content of elk (wapiti) femur marrows. J. Wildl. Manage. 32(4):747–751.

Greer, K. R., and R. E. Howe. 1964. Winter weights of northern Yellowstone elk, 1961–1962. Trans. N. Am. Wildl. Conf. 29:237–248.

Greer, K. R., and H. W. Yeager. 1967. Sex and age indications from upper canine teeth of elk (wapiti). J. Wildl. Manage. 31(3):408–417.

Gregory, T. 1927. Random flashlights. J. Mammal. 8(1):45–47.

Greig-Smith, P. 1964. Quantitative plant ecology. 2nd ed. Butterworths Publ. Ltd., London. 265 p.

Grelen, H. E., and E. A. Epps, Jr. 1967. Season of burning affects herbage quality and yield on pine bluestem range. J. Range Manage. 20(1):31–33.

Grenquist, P. 1963. Hatching losses of common goldeneye. Proc. Int. Ornithol. Congr. 13:685–689.

Grenquist, P. 1966. Changes in abundance of some duck and sea-bird populations off the coast of Finland 1949–1963. Finn. Game Res. 27:1–114.

Grice, D., and J. P. Rogers. 1965. The wood duck in Massachusetts. Final Rep. Proj. No. W–19–12. Mass. Div. Fish and Game. 96 p.

Grieb, J. R. 1970. The shortgrass prairie Canada goose population. Wildl. Monogr. No. 22. 49 p.

Grieb, J. R., and M. G. Sheldon. 1956. Radio-controlled firing device for the cannon-net trap. J. Wildl. Manage. 20(3):203–205.

Grier, J. W. 1977. Quadrat sampling of a nesting population of bald eagles. J. Wildl. Manage. 41(3):438–443.

Grier, J. W. 1979. Caution on using productivity or age ratios alone for population inferences. Raptor Research 13(1):20–24.

Griffen, J. 1964. The hunting dogs of America. Doubleday and Co., New York. 311 p.

Griffin, D. R. 1952. Radioactive tagging of animals under natural conditions. Ecology 33(3):329–335.

Griffith, R. E., Jr. 1969. A method for filing black and white photographs. U.S. Fish and Wildl. Serv. Wildl. Leafl. 490. 4 p.

Griffith, R. E., and J. Evans. 1970. Capturing jackrabbits by night-lighting. J. Wildl. Manage. 34(3):637–639.

Griffiths, M., R. Barker, and L. MacLean. 1974. Further observations on the plants eaten by kangaroos and sheep grazing together in a paddock in south-western Queensland. Aust. Wildl. Res. 1:27–43.

Grinnell, J., H. C. Bryant, and T. I. Storer. 1918. The game birds of California. Univ. California Press, Berkeley. 642 p.

Gromme, O. J. 1963. Birds of Wisconsin. Univ. Wisconsin Press, Madison. 219 p.

Gross, A. O. 1938. Eider ducks of Kent's Island. Auk 55(3):387–400.

Gross, J. E., J. E. Roelle, and G. L. Williams. 1973. Program ONEPOP an information processor: a systems modeling and communication project. Colo. Coop. Wildl. Res. Unit Prog. Rep. Ft. Collins. 327 p.

Grumstrup, P. D., and M. P. Meyer. 1977. Applications of large scale 35 mm color and color infrared photography for analysis of fish and wildlife resources on disturbed lands. Univ. of Minnesota Inst. Agric. For. and Home Econ. Remote Sensing Lab Res. Rep. 77–3, St. Paul, Minn. 70 p.

Grzimek, B. 1974–1977. Animal life encyclopedia. Van Nostrand Reinhold, 13 vol.

Grzimek, M., and B. Grzimek. 1960. Flamingo censuses in East Africa by aerial photography. J. Wildl. Manage. 24(2):215–217.

Guarino, J. L. 1968. Evaluation of a colored leg tag for starlings and blackbirds. Bird-Banding 39(1):6–13.

Guarino, J. L. 1975. An overview of problem bird management in agricultural crops. Proc. Great Plains Wildl. Damage Control Workshop 2:130–145.

Guest, L. 1962. A comparison of two-choice and four-choice questions. J. Advert. Res. 2:32–34.

Guignion, D. L. 1967. A nesting study of the common eider *(Somateria mollissima dresseri)* in the St. Lawrence Estuary. M. S. Thesis. Laval Univ., Quebec. 121 p.

Gullion, G. W. 1951. A marker for waterfowl. J. Wildl. Manage. 15(2): 222–223.

Gullion, G. W. 1952. Sex and age determination in the American coot. J. Wildl. Manage. 16(2):191–197.

Gullion, G. W. 1961. A technique for winter trapping of ruffed grouse. J. Wildl. Manage. 25(4):428–430.

Gullion, G. W. 1965. Improvements in methods for trapping and marking ruffed grouse. J. Wildl. Manage. 29(1):109–116.

Gullion, G. W. 1972. Sequence of materials handling for sex and age determination of ruffed grouse and comments concerning tail patterns and colors. Dept. Entomology, Fish, and Wildl. Univ. of Minnesota., St. Paul. 8 p.

Gullion, G. W., R. L. Eng, and J. J. Kupa. 1961. A discussion of three methods for individually marking ruffed grouse. Minn. Agric. Exp. Stn., Sci. J. Ser., Paper No. 4767.

Gunderson, H. L. 1976. Mammalogy. McGraw Hill Book Co., New York, N.Y. 483 p.

Gunderson, H. L., and J. R. Beer. 1953. The mammals of Minnesota. Minnesota Mus. of Nat. Hist. Occas. Paper No. 6. 190 p.

Gurr, E. 1971. Synthetic dyes in biology, medicine and chemistry. Academic Press, New York. 807 p.

Gurr, L. 1955. A pneumatic nest-recording device. Ibis 97(3):584–586.

Guynn, D. C., Jr., W. A. Flick and M. R. Reynolds. 1976. Mathematical modeling and wildlife management: a critical view. Proc. Southeastern Assoc. Fish and Wildlife Agencies 30:569–574.

Guynn, D. E., and P. F. Scanlon. 1973. Crop-gland activity in mourning doves during hunting seasons in Virginia. Proc. Southeastern Assoc. Game and Fish Commissioners 27:36–42.

Gwynne, M. D., and R. H. V. Bell. 1968. Selection of vegetation components by grazing ungulates in the Serengeti National Park. Nature 220 (5165):390–393.

Gysel, L. W. 1956. Measurement of acorn crops. For. Sci. 2(4):305–313.

Gysel, L. W. 1958. Prediction of acorn crops. For. Sci. 4(3):239–245.

Gysel, L. W. 1961. An ecological study of tree cavities and ground burrows in forest stands. J. Wildl. Manage. 25(1):12–20.

Gysel, L. W., and E. M. Davis, Jr. 1956. A simple automatic photographic unit for wildlife research. J. Wildl. Manage. 20(4):451–453.

Haagenrud, H. 1978. Layers in secondary dentine of incisors as age criteria in moose *(Alces alces)*. J. Mammal. 59(4):857–858.

Haas, G. H., and S. R. Amend. 1979. Primary feather molt of adult mourning doves in North and South Carolina. J. Wildl. Manage. 43(1): 202–207.

Hadow, H. H. 1972. Freeze-branding: a permanent marking technique for pigmented mammals. J. Wildl. Manage. 36(2):645–649.

Hadwen, S., and L. J. Palmer. 1922. Reindeer in Alaska. USDA Bull. 1089. 74 p.

Haensch, G., and G. Haberkamp. 1966. Dictionary of agriculture: German, English, French, Spanish. 3rd ed. Elsevier Publ., New York and Amsterdam. 746 p.

Haensch, G., and G. Haberkamp. 1976. Wörtebuch der Biologie; Englisch-Deutsch-Französisch-Spanisch. BLV Verlagsgesellschaft, Munich. 483 p.

Hafenrichter, A. L., J. L. Schwendiman, H. L. Harris, R. S. MacLauchlan, and W. W. Miller. 1968. Grasses and legumes for soil conservation in the Pacific Northwest and Great Basin states. USDA Soil Conserv. Serv. Agric. Handb. 339, Washington, D.C. 69 p.

Hafez, E. S. E. 1962. The behavior of domestic animals. Baillière, Tindall, and Cox Ltd., London. 619 p.

Hagen, H. L. 1953. Nutritive value for deer of some forage plants in the Sierra Nevada. Calif. Fish and Game 39(2):163–175.

Hahn, H. C. 1945. The white-tailed deer in the Edwards Plateau Region of Texas. Texas Game Fish and Oyster Comm., Austin. 50 p.

Haigh, J. C., and H. C. Hopf. 1976. The blowgun in veterinary practice: its uses and preparation. J. Am. Vet. Med. Assoc. 169(9):881–883.

Hailman, J. P. 1969. The continuing problem of fat classes and a "rule-of-thumb" for identifying interval and ratio data. Bird-Banding 40(4): 321–322.

Hairston, N. G. 1959. Species abundance and community organization. Ecology 40(3):404–416.

Hale, J. B. 1949. Aging cottontail rabbits by bone growth. J. Wildl. Manage. 13(2):216–225.

Hale, J. B., R. F. Wendt, and G. C. Halazon. 1954. Sex and age criteria for Wisconsin ruffed grouse. Wis. Conserv. Dept. Tech. Wildl. Bull. No. 9, Madison. 24 p.

Hale, L. J. 1965. Biological laboratory data. 2nd ed. John Wiley and Sons, New York. 147 p.

Hall, C. A. S., and J. W. Day, (eds.). 1977. Ecosystem modeling in theory and practice. John Wiley and Sons. New York. 684 p.

Hall, D. O. 1974. Reducing a maturity bias in estimating populations: an example with cotton rats *(Sigmodon hispidus).* J. Mammal. 55(2):477–480.

Hall, E. R. 1942. Gestation period in the fisher with recommendations for the animal's protection in California. Calif. Fish and Game 28(3):143–147.

Hall, E. R. 1946. Mammals of Nevada. Univ. California Press, Berkeley. 710 p.

Hall, E. R. 1955. Handbook of mammals of Kansas. Univ. Kans. Mus. Nat. Hist. Misc. Publ. No. 7. 303 p.

Hall, E. R. 1962. Collecting and preparing study specimens of vertebrates. Univ. Kans. Mus. Nat. Hist. Misc. Publ. No. 30. 46 p.

Hall, E. R. 1980. The mammals of North America. 2nd ed. Vols. 1 & 2. Wiley Interscience, N.Y. (in press).

Hall, E. R., and K. R. Kelson. 1959. The mammals of North America. Ronald Press, New York. 2 vols. 1083 p.

Hall, T. C., E. B. Taft, W. H. Baker, and J. C. Aub. 1953. A preliminary report on the use of flaxedil to produce paralysis in the white-tailed deer. J. Wildl. Manage. 17(4):516–520.

Hallberg, D. L., F. J. Janza, and G. R. Trapp. 1974. A vehicle-mounted directional antenna system for biotelemetry monitoring. Calif. Fish and Game 60(4):172–177.

Hallisey, D. M., and G. W. Wood. 1976. Prescribed fire in scrub oak habitat in central Pennsylvania. J. Wildl. Manage. 40(3):507–516.

Halloran, A. F. 1961. American bison weights and measurements from the Wichita Mountains Wildlife Refuge. Proc. Okla. Acad. Sci. 41:212–218.

Halloran, A. F., and O. V. Deming. 1956. Water developments for desert bighorn sheep. U.S. Fish Wildl. Serv. Manage. Ser. Leafl. No. 14. 8 p.

Halloran, P. O'C. 1955. A bibliography of references to diseases in wild mammals and birds. Am. J. Vet. Res. 16(61):1–465.

Halls, L. K., and R. Alcaniz. 1968. Browse plants yield best in forest openings. J. Wildl. Manage. 32(1): 185–186.

Halls, L. K., and H. S. Crawford. 1965. Vegetation response to an Ozark woodland spraying. J. Range Manage. 18(6):338–340.

Halstead, B. W. 1972. A golden guide to environmental organizations. Golden Press, New York. 63 p.

Hamerstrom, F. 1963. The use of great horned owls in catching marsh hawks. Proc. Int. Ornithol. Congr. 13:866–869.

Hamerstrom, F., D. D. Berger, and F. N. Hamerstrom, Jr. 1965. The effect of mammals on prairie chickens on booming grounds. J. Wildl. Manage. 29(3):536–542.

Hamerstrom, F., F. N. Hamerstrom, and J. Hart. 1973. Nest boxes: an effective management tool for kestrels. J. Wildl. Manage. 37(3):400–403.

Hamerstrom, F. N., Jr. 1936. A study of the nesting habits of the ring-necked pheasant in northwest Iowa. Iowa State Coll. J. Sci. 10(2):173–203.

Hamerstrom, F. N., Jr. 1939. A study of Wisconsin prairie chicken and sharp-tailed grouse. Wilson Bull. 51(2):105–120.

Hamerstrom, F. N., Jr., and F. L. Camburn. 1950. Weight relationships in the George Reserve deer herd. J. Mammal. 31(1):5–17.

Hamilton, C. L., and H. G. Jepson. 1940. Stockwater developments: wells, springs, and ponds. USDA Farmers' Bull. No. 1859, Washington, D.C. 70 p.

Hamilton, D. A., Jr. 1978. Specifying precision in natural resource inventories. p. 276–281 *in* H. G. Lund et al. Integrated inventories of renewable natural resources. Proceedings of the workshop: USDA For. Serv., Rocky Mt. For. and Range Exp. Stn. Gen. Tech. Rep. RM–55, Fort Collins, Colo. 482 p.

Hamilton, J. W. 1958. Chemical composition of certain native forage plants. Univ. Wyoming Agric. Exp. Stn. Bull. 356. 44 p.

Hamilton, R. 1962. An expansible collar for male white-tailed deer. J. Wildl. Manage. 26(1):114–115.

Hamilton, W. J., Jr. 1933. The weasels of New York. Am. Midl. Nat. 14(4): 289–344.

Hamilton, W. J., Jr., and J. O. Whitaker, Jr. 1979. Mammals of the eastern United States. 2nd ed. Cornell Univ. Press, Ithaca, N.Y. 358 p.

Hamilton, W. J., III. 1962. Evidence concerning the function of nocturnal call notes of migratory birds. Condor 64(5):390–401.

Hamlett, G. W. D. 1932. Observations on the embryology of the badger. Anat. Rec. 53:283–303.

Hammerslough, J. S., and R. G. Bjorklund. 1968. Radio tracking of prematurely dislodged nestling herons. Jack-Pine Warbler 46(2):57–61.

Hammond, M. C. 1961. Waterfowl feeding stations for controlling crop losses. Trans. N. Am. Wildl. Nat. Resour. Conf. 26:67–79.

Hammond, M. C., and C. J. Henry. 1949. Success of marsh hawk nests in North Dakota. Auk 66(3):271–274.

Hamor, W. H. 1970. Guide for evaluating the impact of water and related land resource development projects on fish and wildlife habitat. USDA Soil Conserv. Serv., Lincoln, Nebr. 25 p.

Hampf, F. E. 1964. Site index curves for some forest species in the eastern United States. USDA For. Serv. Div. State and Private For., Upper Darby, Pa. 34 p.

Hancock, J., and H. Elliott. 1978. The herons of the world. Harper and Row Inc., New York. 304 p.

Hanley, T. A., and W. W. Brady. 1977. Seasonal fluctuations in nutrient content of feral burro forages, lower Colorado River Valley, Arizona. J. Range Manage. 30(5):370–373.

Hansen, C. G. 1964. A dye spraying device for marking desert bighorn sheep. J. Wildl. Manage. 28(3): 584–587.

Hansen, M. H., and W. N. Hurwitz. 1946. The problem of non-response in sample surveys. Am. Stat. Assoc. J. 41(236):517–529.

Hansen, R. M., D. G. Peden, and R. W. Rice. 1973. Discerned fragments in feces indicates diet overlap. J. Range Manage. 26(2):103–105.

Hanson, H. C. 1962. Dictionary of ecology. Philosophical Libr., New York. 382 p.

Hanson, H. C. 1967. Characters of age, sex, and sexual maturity in Canada geese. Ill. Nat. Hist. Surv. Biol. Notes No. 49, Urbana. 15 p.

Hanson, H. C., and R. L. Jones. 1968. Use of feather minerals as biological tracers to determine the breeding and molting grounds of wild geese. Ill. Nat. Hist. Surv. Biol. Notes No. 60, Urbana. 8 p.

Hanson, H. C., P. Queneau, and P. Scott. 1956. The geography, birds, and mammals of the Perry River region. Arct. Inst. N. Am. Spec. Publ. 3. 98 p.

Hanson, L. E., and D. R. Progulske. 1973. Movements and cover preferences of pheasants in South Dakota. J. Wildl. Manage. 37(4):454–461.

Hanson, W. C., and L. L. Eberhardt. 1971. A Columbia River Canada goose population, 1950–1970. Wildl. Monogr. No. 28. 61 p.

Hanson, W. R. 1963. Calculation of productivity, survival, and abundance of selected vertebrates from sex and age ratios. Wildl. Monogr. No. 9. 60 p.

Hanson, W. R., and F. Graybill. 1956. Sample size in food habits analysis. J. Wildl. Manage. 20(1):64–68.

Hanssen, A. 1947. The physiology of reproduction in mink *(Mustela vison,* Schreb.) with special reference to delayed implantation. Acta. Zool. 28:1–136.

Harder, J. D. 1968. A literature review on orchard damage by deer. Colo. Div. Game, Fish and Parks, Spec. Rep. No. 12, Ft. Collins. 22 p.

Harder, J. D. 1969. A photoelectric cell system for recording nocturnal activity of mule deer. J. Wildl. Manage. 33(3):704–708.

Harder, J. D., and T. J. Peterle. 1974. Effect of diethylstilbestrol on reproductive performance of white-tailed deer. J. Wildl. Manage. 38(2):183–196.

Harding, P. J. R., F. S. Chute and A. C. Doell. 1976. Increasing battery reliability for radio transmitters. J. Wildl. Manage. 40(2):357–358.

Hardy, J. I., and T. M. Plitt. 1940. An improved method for revealing the surface structure of fur fibers. U.S. Fish Wildl. Serv. Bull. No. 7. 10 p.

Hare, R. C. 1977. How to root cuttings. USDA For. Serv. Southern For. Exp. Stn., New Orleans, La. 6 p.

Harington, C. R. 1968. Denning habits of the polar bear *(Ursus maritimus* Phipps). Can. Wildl. Serv. Rep. Ser. No. 5. 30 p.

Harlow, H. J. 1979. A photocell monitor to measure winter activity of confined badgers. J. Wildl. Manage. 43(4):997–1001.

Harlow, R. F. 1977. A technique for surveying deer forage in the Southeast. Wildl. Soc. Bull. 5(4):185–191.

Harlow, R. F., and R. C. Hooper. 1971. Forages eaten by deer in the Southeast. Proc. Southeastern Assoc. Game and Fish Commissioners 25:18–46.

Harned, B. K., R. W. Cunningham, and E. R. Gill. 1952. An activity analyzer for small animals. Science 116 (3014):369–370.

Harper, D. 1976. Eye in the sky: introduction to remote sensing. Multiscience Publ., Montreal, Canada. 164 p.

Harper, H. T., C. M. Hart, and D. E. Shaffer. 1951. Effects of hunting pressure and game farm stocking on pheasant populations in the Sacramento Valley, California, 1946–1949. Calif. Fish and Game 37(2): 141–176.

Harper, J. A., and W. C. Lightfoot. 1966. Tagging devices for Roosevelt elk and mule deer. J. Wildl. Manage. 30(3):461–466.

Harrington, R., and P. Wilson. 1974. Immobilon-Rompun in deer. Vet. Rec. 94(16):362–363.

Harris, D. 1945. Symptoms of malnutrition in deer. J. Wildl. Manage. 9(4):319–322.

Harris, L. E. 1970. Nutrition research techniques for domestic and wild animals. Vol. I. An international record system and procedures for analyzing samples. Utah State Univ., Logan. 233 p.

Harris, S. W., and M. A. Morse. 1958. The use of mist nets for capturing nesting mourning doves. J. Wildl. Manage. 22(3):306–309.

Harris, S. W., and P. E. K. Shepherd. 1965. Age determination and notes on the breeding age of black brant. J. Wildl. Manage. 29(3):643–645.

Harrison, J. M. 1978. Bird taxidermy. Davis and Charles Press, North Pomfret, Vt. 96 p.

Hart, C. M., O. S. Lee, and J. B. Low. 1950. The sharp-tailed grouse in Utah. Utah State Dept. Fish and Game Publ. No. 3. 79 p.

Hart, E. B. 1973. A simple and effective live trap for pocket gophers. Am. Midl. Nat. 89(1):200–202.

Hartesveldt, R. J. 1951. A simple technique for den-use study. J. Wildl. Manage. 15(1):104–105.

Harthoorn, A. M. 1976. The chemical capture of animals. Bailliere Tindall, London. 416 p.

Hartley, P. H. T. 1948. The assessment of the food of birds. Ibis 90(3):361–381.

Hartmann, H. T., and D. E. Kester. 1975. Plant propagation: principles and practices. 3rd ed. Prentice-Hall Inc., Englewood Cliffs, N.J. 662 p.

Hastings, J. R., and R. M. Turner. 1965. The changing mile. Univ. of Arizona Press, Tucson. 317 p.

Haugen, A. O. 1957. Distinguishing juvenile from adult bobwhite quail. J. Wildl. Manage. 21(1):29–32.

Haugen, A. O. 1959. Breeding record of captive white-tailed deer in Alabama. J. Mamm. 40(1):108–113.

Haugen, A. O. 1964. Visual aids with legible slides. J. Wildl. Manage. 28(1):177–179.

Haugen, A. O., and F. W. Fitch, Jr. 1955. Seasonal availability of certain bush lespedeza and partridge pea seed as determined from ground samples. J. Wildl. Manage. 19(2): 297–301.

Haugen, A. O., M. J. Swenson, M. J. Shult, and S. J. Petersburg. 1976. Immobilization of adult bull bison with etorphine. Proc. Iowa Acad. Sci. 83(2):67–70.

Hausman, L. A. 1920. Structural characteristics of the hair of mammals. Am. Nat. 54(635):496–523.

Hawes, R. A., and R. J. Hudson. 1976. A method of regional landscape evaluation for wildlife. J. Soil and Water Conserv. 31(5):209–211.

Hawkins, R. E., D. C. Autry, and W. D. Klimstra. 1967a. Comparison of methods used to capture white-tailed deer. J. Wildl. Manage. 31(3): 460–464.

Hawkins, R. E., W. D. Klimstra, G. Fooks, and J. Davis. 1967b. Improved collar for white-tailed deer. J. Wildl. Manage. 31(2):356–359.

Hawkins, R. E., W. D. Klimstra, L. W. Lamely, and D. C. Autry. 1970. A new remote capture method for free-ranging deer. J. Mammal. 51(2): 392–394.

Hawkins, R. E., L. D. Martoglio, and G. G. Montgomery. 1968. Cannon-netting deer. J. Wildl. Manage. 32 (1):191–195.

Hawn, L. J., and L. A. Ryel. 1969. Michigan deer harvest estimates: sample surveys versus a complete count. J. Wildl. Manage. 33(4):871–880.

Hay, K. G. 1958. Beaver census methods in the Rocky Mountain region. J. Wildl. Manage. 22(4):395–402.

Hayden, S. S. 1942. The international protection of wildlife: an examination of treaties and other agreements for the preservation of birds and mammals. Columbia Univ. Press, New York. 246 p.

Hayes, F. A., J. H. Jenkins, S. D. Feurt, and J. A. Crockford. 1957. Observations on the use of nicotine for immobilizing semi-wild goats. J. Am. Vet. Med. Assoc. 130(11):479–482.

Hayne, D. W. 1949a. An examination of the strip census method for estimating animal populations. J. Wildl. Manage. 13(2):145–157.

Hayne, D. W. 1949b. Two methods for estimating population from trapping records. J. Mammal. 30(4):399–411.

Hayne, D. W. 1964. Investigation of mail survey reporting by waterfowl hunters. U.S. Fish Wildl. Serv. Unpubl. Rep., Patuxent Wildl. Res. Cent., Laurel, Md. 41 p.

Hayne, D. W. 1969. The use of models in resource management. p. 119–122 *in* L. K. Halls (ed.). White-tailed deer in southern forest habitat. Proc. Symp. U.S. For. Serv. Southern For. Exp. Stn. 130 p.

Hayne, D. W. 1978. Experimental designs and statistical analyses in small mammal population studies. p. 3–10 *in* D. P. Snyder, (ed.). Populations of small mammals under natural conditions. Pymatuning Lab. Ecol., Spec. Publ. Ser. Vol. 5, Univ. Pittsburgh. 237 p.

Hayne, D. W., and J. V. Gwynn. 1977. Percentage does in total kill as a harvest strategy. Trans. 13th Northeast Deer Study Group Meeting. 16 p.

Heady, H. F., and J. Bartolome. 1977. The Vale rangeland rehabilitation program: the desert repaired in southeastern Oregon. USDA For. Serv Resour. Bull. PNW-70, Pac. N. W. For. Range Exp. Stn., Portland, Oreg. 139 p.

Heath, W. B. 1961. A trailing device for small animals designed for field study of the gila monster *(Heloderma suspectum)*. Copeia 1961(4):491–492.

Heberlein, T. A., and R. Baumgartner. 1978. Factors affecting response rates to mailed questionnaires: a quantitative analysis of the published literature. Amer. Sociol. Rev. 43(4):447–462.

Hebert, D. M., and R. J. McFetridge. 1979. Chemical immobilization of North American game mammals. 2nd ed. Alberta Recreation, Parks and Wildl., Fish and Wildl. Div., Edmonton. 250 p.

Heezen, K. L., and J. R. Tester. 1967. Evaluation of radio-tracking by triangulation with special reference to deer movements. J. Wildl. Management. 31(1):124–141.

Heimerdinger, M. A., and R. C. Leberman. 1966. The comparative efficiency of 30 and 36 mm mesh nets. Bird-Banding 37(4):280–285.

Hein, D. 1967. Sources of literature cited in wildlife research papers. J. Wildl. Manage. 31(3):598–599.

Hellmers, H. 1940. A study of monthly variations in the nutritive value of several natural winter deer foods. J. Wildl. Manage. 4(3):315–325.

Hellmers, H. 1964. A simple and efficient file system for reprints. BioScience 14(2):24.

Helm, L. G. 1955. Plastic collars for marking geese. J. Wildl. Manage. 19(2):316–317.

Hemming, J. E. 1969. Cemental deposition, tooth successsion, and horn development as criteria of age in Dall sheep. J. Wildl. Manage. 33(3): 552–558.

Hendee, J. C., and D. R. Potter. 1971. Human behavior and wildlife management: needed research. Trans. N. Am. Wildl. Nat. Resour. Conf. 36: 383–396.

Hendee, J. C., and C. Shoenfeld, (eds.). 1973. Human dimensions in wildlife programs: reports of recent investigations. Wildl. Manage. Inst., Washington, D.C. 193 p.

Hendee, W. R. 1973. Radioactive isotopes in biological research. John Wiley and Sons, Wiley Interscience Publ. Inc., New York. 356 p.

Henderson, F. B., III, and R. J. Ondrejka. 1978. GEOSAT: Geological industry recommendations on remote sensing from space. Photogramm. Eng. Remote Sensing 44(2):165–169.

Henderson, F. R., F. W. Brooks, R. E. Wood, and R. B. Dahlgren. 1967. Sexing of prairie grouse by crown feather patterns. J. Wildl. Manage. 31(4):764–769.

Hendrick, D. J. 1963. The visitometer/a simplified mechanical counter. Passenger Pigeon 25(2):60–68.

Hendricks, W. A. 1949. Adjustment for bias caused by nonresponse in mailed surveys. Agric. Econ. Res. 1(2):52–56.

Henry, D. B., and T. A. Bookhout. 1969. Productivity of beavers in northeastern Ohio. J. Wildl. Manage. 33(4):927–932.

Hensel, R. J., W. A. Troyer, and A. W. Erickson. 1969. Reproduction in the female brown bear. J. Wildl. Manage. 33(2):357–365.

Hepburn, R. L. 1978. A snow penetration gauge for studies of white-tailed deer and other northern mammals. J. Wildl. Manage. 42(3): 663–667.

Hercus, B. H. 1960. Plant cuticle as an aid to determining the diet of grazing animals. Proc. Int. Grassl. Congr. 8:443–447.

Herzfeld, R. P. 1962. Automation in bird photography. Biol. Photogr. Assoc. J. 30(2):53–62.

Herzog, P. W. 1979. Effects of radio-marking on behavior, movements, and survival of spruce grouse. J. Wildl. Manage. 43(2):316–323.

Hespenheide, H. A. 1975. Prey characteristics and predator niche width. p. 158–180 *in* M. L. Cody and J. M. Diamond, (eds.). Ecology and evolution of communities. Belknap Press of Harvard Univ. Press, Cambridge, Mass. 545 p.

Hesselton, W. T. 1970. Deer trapping and tagging in New York State. Trans. Northeast Sect. Wildl. Soc., Fish Wildl. Conf. 27:39–81.

Hesselton, W. T., C. W. Severinghaus, and J. E. Tanck. 1965. Population dynamics of deer at the Seneca Army Depot. N.Y. Fish and Game J. 12(1):17–30.

Hester, A. E. 1963. A plastic wing tag for individual identification of passerine birds. Bird-Banding 34(4): 213–217.

Heusmann, H. W., W. W. Blandin, and R. E. Turner. 1977. Starling-deterrent nesting cylinders in wood duck management. Wildl. Soc. Bull. 5(1):14–18.

Heusmann, H. W., R. G. Burrell, and R. Bellville. 1978. Automatic short term color marker for nesting wood ducks. J. Wildl. Manage. 42(2): 429–430.

Hewitt, O. H., (ed.). 1967. The wild turkey and its management. The Wildl. Soc., Washington, D.C. 589 p.

Heyland, J. D. 1970. Aircraft-supported Canada goose banding operations in Arctic Quebec. Trans. Northeast Sect. Wildl. Soc., Fish Wildl. Conf. 27:187–198.

Heyland, J. D. 1973. Increase the accuracy of your airborne censuses by means of vertical aerial photgraphs. Trans. Northeast Sect. Wildl. Soc., Fish Wildl. Conf. 30:53–75.

Heymer, A. 1978. Ethological dictionary . . . German-English-French. Garland Press, New York and London. 240 p.

Hickey, J. J. 1943. A guide to bird watching. Oxford Univ. Press, New York. 264 p.

Hickey, J. J. 1955. Some American population research on gallinaceous birds. p. 326–396 *in* A. Wolfson, (ed.). Recent studies in avian biology. Univ. Illinois Press, Urbana. 479 p.

Hickman, G. L. 1972. Aerial determination of golden eagle nesting status. J. Wildl. Manage. 36(4):1289–1292.

Hickman, O. E. 1975. Seasonal trends in the nutritive content of important range forage species near Silverlake, Oregon. USDA For. Serv. Res. Pap. PNW-187, Portland, Oreg. 32 p.

Hiehle, J. L. 1961. Improving chamise brushlands for deer and other game. Calif. Fish and Game, Leafl. 4, Sacramento. 27 p.

Hiehle, J. L. 1964. Measurement of browse growth and utilization. Calif. Fish and Game 50(3):148–151.

Higgins, D. A. 1979. Program design and construction. Prentice Hall Inc., Englewood, N. J. 189 p.

Higgins, K. F. 1969. Bursal depths of lesser snow and small Canada geese. J. Wildl. Manage. 33(4):1006–1008.

Higgins, K. F., L. M. Kirsch, and I. J. Ball, Jr. 1969. A cable-chain device for locating duck nests. J. Wildl. Manage. 33(4):1009–1011.

Higgins, K. F., L. M. Kirsch, H. F. Duebbert, A. T. Klett, J. T. Lokemoen, H. W. Miller, and A. D. Kruse. 1977. Construction and operation of cable-chain drag for nest searches. U.S. Fish Wildl. Serv., Wildl. Leafl. 512, Washington, D.C. 14 p.

Higgins, K. F., and L. J. Schoonover. 1969. Aging small Canada geese by neck plumage. J. Wildl. Manage. 33(1):212–214.

Highton, R. 1965. Amphibians and reptiles. BioScience 15(6):442.

Hildebrand, M. 1955. Skeletal differences between deer, sheep, and goats. Calif. Fish and Game 41(4): 327–346.

Hilden, O. 1964. Ecology of duck populations in the island group of Valassaret, Gulf of Bothnia. Ann. Zool. Fenn. 1(3):1–279.

Hilgard, E. R., and R. C. Atkinson. 1967. Remembering and forgetting. p. 314–335 *in* E. R. Hilgard and R. C. Atkinson, (eds.). Introduction to psychology, 4th ed. Harcourt, Brace and World Inc., New York. 686 p.

Hill, C. E. 1966. Mt. Mitchell deer movement. Wildl. N. Carol. 30(11): 20.

Hill, M. O. 1973. Diversity and evenness: a unifying notation and its consequences. Ecology 54(2):427–432.

Hill, R., and W. A. Himwich. 1957. Coding a small reprint collection on the central nervous system. Fed. Proc. 16(3):721–725.

Hillway, T. 1964. Introduction to research. 2nd ed. Houghton Mifflin, Boston, Mass. 308 p.

Himmelsbach, C. J., and G. E. Brociner. 1972. A guide to scientific and technical journals in translation. 2nd ed. Spec. Libr. Assoc., New York. 49 p.

Hintz, J. V., and M. I. Dyer. 1970. Daily rhythm and seasonal change in the summer diet of adult red-winged blackbirds. J. Wildl. Manage. 34(4): 789–799.

Hirst, S. M. 1975. Ungulate-habitat relationships in a South African woodland/savanna ecosystem. Wildl. Monogr. No. 44. 60 p.

Hitchcock, A. S. 1951. Manual of the grasses of the United States. 2nd rev. ed. USDA Misc. Publ. 200. 1051 p.

Hochbaum, H. A. 1942. Sex and age determination of waterfowl by cloacal examination. Trans. N. Am. Wildl. Conf. 7:299–307.

Hocking, R. R. 1976. The analysis and selection of variables in linear regression. Biometrics 32(1):1–49.

Hoekstra, T. W. and P. G. Carr. 1977. Sex determination in white-tailed deer tissues. p. 212–232 *in* Proceedings forensic science: a tool for modern fish and wildlife science. Alberta Recreation, Parks and Wildl., Fish and Wildl. Div., Calgary. 321 p.

Hoff, W., (ed.). 1966. American association of zoological parks and aquariums, 1966 directory. The Assoc., Oglebay Park, Wheeling, W. Va. 108 p.

Hoffman, G. R., and R. R. Alexander. 1976. Forest vegetation of the Bighorn Mountains, Wyoming: a habitat type classification. USDA For. Serv. Rocky Mt. For. and Range Exp. Stn. Res. Pap. RM–170. Ft. Collins, Colo. 38 p.

Hoffmann, R. S., and D. L. Pattie. 1968. A guide to Montana mammals: identification, habitat, distribution and abundance. Univ. of Montana, Missoula. 133 p.

Hoglund, N. H. 1968. A method of trapping and marking willow grouse in winter. Viltrevy Swedish Wildl. 5(3):95–101.

Holbrook, H. L. 1974. A system for wildlife habitat management on southern National Forests. Wildl. Soc. Bull. 2(3):119–123.

Holcomb, L. C., and M. Jaeger. 1978. Growth and calculation of age in mourning dove nestlings. J. Wildl. Manage. 42(4):843–852.

Holliman, D. C. 1977. Purple gallinule *(Porphyrula martinica).* p. 105–109 *in* G. C. Sanderson, (ed.). Management of migratory shore and upland game birds in North America. Int. Assoc. Fish and Wildl. Agencies, Washington, D.C. 358 p.

Holling, C. S. 1966. The strategy of building models of complex ecological systems. p. 195–213 *in* K. E. F. Watt, (ed.). Systems analysis in ecology. Academic Press. N.Y. 450 p.

Holmgren, R. C., and J. V. Basile. 1959. Improving southern Idaho deer winter ranges by artificial revegetation. Idaho Dept. Fish and Game Wildl. Bull. No. 3, Boise. 61 p.

Holyoak, D. 1972. Food of the rook in Britain. Bird Study 19(2):59–68.

Homestead, R., B. Beck, and D. E. Sergeant. 1972. A portable, instantaneous branding device for permanent identification of wildlife. J. Wildl. Manage. 36(3):947–949.

Honess, R. F., and N. M. Frost. 1942. A Wyoming bighorn sheep study. Wyo. Game and Fish Dept. Bull. No. 1, Cheyenne. 127 p.

Hood, S. L., R. A. Monroe, and W. J. Viesek. 1953. Edge-punched cards for scientific literature references. U.S. Atomic Energy Comm. Tech. Inf. Ser. ORO–102. Oak Ridge, Tenn. 19 p.

Hooper, F. F., H. A. Podoliak, and S. F. Snieszko. 1961. Use of radioisotopes in hydrobiology and fish culture. Trans. Am. Fish. Soc. 90(1):49–57.

Hooven, E. F. 1959. Dusky-footed woodrat in young Douglas fir. Oregon For. Res. Cent., Res. Note 41, Corvallis. 24 p.

Hopkins, M. N., and E. P. Odum. 1953. Some aspects of the population ecology of breeding mourning doves in Georgia. J. Wildl. Manage. 17(2): 132–143.

Hopper, R. M., and H. D. Funk. 1970. Reliability of the mallard wing age-determination technique for field use. J. Wildl. Manage. 34(2):333–339.

Hornaday, W. T. 1929. Taxidermy and zoological collecting. Charles Scribner's Sons, New York. 364 p.

Hornocker, M. G., J. J. Craighead, and E. W. Pfeiffer. 1965. Immobilizing mountain lions with succinylcholine chloride and pentabarbital sodium. J. Wildl. Manage. 29(4):880–883.

Hornocker, M. G., and W. V. Wiles. 1972. Immobilizing pumas *(Felis concolor)* with phencyclidine hydrochloride. Int. Zoo Yearb. 12(2): 220–222.

Horton, R. E. 1945. Erosional development of streams and their drainage basins; hydro-physical approach to quantitative geomorphology. Bull. Geol. Soc. Am. 56(3):275–370.

Horvath, J. C. 1974. Economic survey of southeastern wildlife and wildlife-oriented recreation. Trans. N. Am. Wildl. Nat. Resour. Conf. 39:187–194.

Hoskinson, R. L. 1976. The effect of different pilots on aerial telemetry error. J. Wildl. Manage. 40(1):137–139.

Hotchkiss, N. 1967. Underwater and floating-leaved plants of the United States and Canada. U.S. Bureau of Sport Fish. & Wildl. Res. Publ. No. 44. 124 p.

Hough, A. F. 1949. Deer and rabbit browsing and available winter forage in Allegheny hardwood forests. J. Wildl. Manage. 13(1):135–141.

Houston, D. B. 1969. Immobilization of the Shiras moose. J. Wildl. Manage. 33(3):534–537.

Hovind, H. J., and C. E. Rieck. 1970. Basal area and point sampling: interpretation and application. Wis. Dept. Nat. Res. Tech. Bull. 23. 52 p.

Howard, J. A. 1970. Aerial photo-ecology. American Elsevier Publ. Co. Inc., New York. 325 p.

Howard, V. W., and C. T. Engelking. 1974. Bait trials for trapping mule deer. J. Wildl. Manage. 38(4):946–947.

Hower, R. O. 1967. The freeze-dry preservation of biological specimens. Proc. U.S. Natl. Mus. 119 (3549):1–24.

Hubbard, R. L. 1964. A guide to bitterbrush seeding in California. USDA For. Serv., Pac. S.W. For. and Range Exp. Stn., Berkeley. 30 p.

Hubbs, C. L., (ed.). 1958. Zoogeography. Am. Assoc. for the Advancement of Sci. Publ. No. 51. 509 p.

Hudson, K., and A. Nicholls, (eds.). 1975. The directory of world museums. Columbia Univ. Press, New York. 864 p.

Hudson, P., and L. G. Browman. 1959. Embryonic and fetal development of the mule deer. J. Wildl. Manage. 23(3):295–304.

Humason, G. L. 1972. Animal tissue techniques. 3rd ed. W. H. Freeman and Co., San Francisco. 641 p.

Hundley, L. R. 1959. Available nutrients in selected deer-browse species growing on different soils. J. Wildl. Manage. 23(1):81–90.

Hungate, R. E. 1966. The rumen and its microbes. Academic Press, New York and London. 533 p.

Hungerford, D. A., R. G. Snyder, and J. A. Griswold. 1966. Chromosome analysis and sex identification in the management and conservation of birds. J. Wildl. Manage. 30(4):707–712.

Hungerford, K. E. 1957. Evaluating ruffed grouse foods for habitat improvement. Trans. N. Am. Wildl. Conf. 22:380–395.

Hunt, E. G., and A. E. Naylor. 1955. Nesting studies of ducks and coots in Honey Lake Valley. Calif. Fish and Game 41(4):295–314.

Hunt, G. S., and K. J. Dahlka. 1953. Live trapping of diving ducks. J. Wildl. Manage. 17(1):92–95.

Hurlbert, S. H. 1971. The nonconcept of species diversity: a critique and alternative parameters. Ecology 52(4):577–586.

Husband, T. P. 1976. Energy metabolism and body composition of the fox squirrel. J. Wildl. Manage. 40(2):255–263.

Huss, D. L., (chairman). 1974. A glossary of terms used in range management. Am. Soc. of Range Manage., Denver, Colo. 36 p.

Huth, E. J., P. L. Altman, M. W. Burgan, E. H. Feinberg, S. R. Geiger, C. G. Gurtowski, W. H. Klein, and E. Neter. 1978. Council of Biology Editors style manual. 4th ed. Amer. Inst. of Biol. Sci. Arlington, Virginia. 265 p.

Hutnik, R. J., and G. Davis, (eds.). 1973. Ecology and reclamation of devastated land. Gordon and Breach, New York. 2 vols.

Hutton, T. A., R. E. Hatfield, and C. C. Watt. 1976. A method for orienting a mobile radiotracking unit. J. Wildl. Manage. 40(1):192–193.

Imhof, T. A. 1976. Alabama birds. Second (revised) ed. Univ. Alabama Press, University, Alabama. 445 p.

Ingles, L. G. 1965. Mammals of the Pacific states: California, Oregon, and Washington. Stanford Univ. Press, Stanford, Calif. 506 p.

Inglis, J. M., and C. J. Barstow. 1960. A device for measuring the volume of seeds. J. Wildl. Manage. 24(2):221–222.

Innis, G. S. 1979. Spiral approach to ecosystem simulation. p. 211–387 *in* G. S. Innis and R. V. O'Neill, (eds.). Systems analysis of ecosystems. Stat. Ecol. Series. Vol. 9. Int. Coop. Publ. House. Fairland, Md. 402 p.

Institute for Social Research. 1976. Interviewer's manual. Inst. Soc. Res., Surv. Res. Cent., Univ. of Michigan, Ann Arbor, Mich. 143 p.

International Commission on Zoological Nomenclature. 1964. International code of zoological nomenclature, adopted by the 15th International Congress on Zoology. International Trust for Zoological Nomenclature, London. 176 p.

International Federation for Documentation. 1969. Abstracting services. 2nd ed. Int. Fed. Doc., The Hague. 2 Vols.

International Union for the Conservation of Nature and Natural Resources. 1971–1977. United Nations list of national parks and equivalent reserves. 2nd ed. IUCN, Morges, Switzerland.

Interstate Antelope Conference. 1962. Recommended specifications for barbed wire fences (for benefit of livestock and wildlife). Int. Antelope Conf. Trans. 13:100–101.

Interstate Deer Herd Committee. 1950. Fourth progress report on the cooperative study of the Interstate deer herd and its range. Calif. Fish and Game 36(1):27–52.

Ireland, N. O. 1962. Index to scientists of the world from ancient to modern times: biographies and portraits. F. W. Faxon Co., Boston, Mass. 662 p.

Isaacson, I. 1963. Manual for the conservation officer. Legal Publ., Lewiston, Me. 143 p.

Isakov, Y. A. 1961. Organization and methods of censusing terrestrial vertebrate faunal resources; summaries of reports. Israel Program for Sci. Trans., Jerusalem. 104 p.

Iverson, S. L., and B. N. Turner. 1969. Under-snow shelter for small mammal trapping. J. Wildl. Manage. 33(3):722–723.

Jack, H. A. 1945. Biological field stations of the world. Chron. Bot. 9(1):1–73.

Jackson, C. F. 1958. Suggested methods for identifying the meat of the white-tailed deer. N. H. Fish and Game Dept. Tech. Circ. 16. 9 p.

Jackson, C. F. 1962. Use of paper chromatography in identifying meat of game animals. N. H. Fish and Game Dept. Tech. Circ. 19. 15 p.

Jackson, C. H. N. 1948. The analysis of a tsetse-fly population. III. Ann. Eugen. 14:91–108.

Jackson, H. H. T. 1961. Mammals of Wisconsin. Univ. Wisconsin Press, Madison. 504 p.

Jackson, J. A. 1977. A device for capturing tree cavity roosting birds. N. Am. Bird Bander 2(1):14–15.

Jackson, J. A., B. J. Schardien, and G. W. Robinson. 1977. A problem associated with the use of radio transmitters on tree surface foraging birds. Inland Bird Banding News 49(2):50–53.

Jacobs, M. B., M. J. Gerstein, and W. G. Walter. 1957. Dictionary of microbiology. Van Nostrand Inc., Princeton, N. J. 276 p.

Jacobsen, N. K., W. P. Armstrong, and A. N. Moen. 1976. Seasonal variation in succinylcholine immobilization of captive white-tailed deer. J. Wildl. Manage. 40(3):447–453.

Jacobson, H. A., R. L. Kirkpatrick, H. E. Burkhart, and J. E. Davis. 1978a. Hematologic comparisons of shot and live-trapped cottontail rabbits. J. Wildl. Dis. 14(1):82–88.

Jacobson, H. A., R. L. Kirkpatrick, and B. S. McGinnes. 1978b. Disease and physiologic characteristics of two cottontail populations in Virginia. Wildl. Monogr. 60. 53 p.

Jacobson, J. O., E. C. Meslow, and M. F. Andrews. 1970. An improved technique for handling striped skunks in disease investigations. J. Wildl. Dis. 6(4):510–512.

Jaeger, E. C. 1955. A source-book of biological names and terms. 3rd ed. Charles C. Thomas, Springfield, Ill. 317 p.

Jaeger, E. C. 1960. The biologist's handbook of pronunciations. Charles C. Thomas, Springfield, Ill. 317 p.

Jahoda, G. 1970. Information storage and retrieval systems for individual researchers. Wiley-Interscience, New York. 135 p.

Jahoda, G., R. D. Hutchins, and R. R. Galford. 1966. Characteristics and use of personal indexes maintained by scientists and engineers in one university. Am. Doc. 17(2):71–75.

James, T. R., and R. W. Seabloom. 1969. Reproductive biology of the white-tailed jack rabbit in North Dakota. J. Wildl. Manage. 33(3): 558–568.

Jarman, P. J. 1974. The social organization of antelope in relation to their ecology. Behav. 48(3–4):215–267.

Jasik, H., (ed.). 1961. Antenna engineering handbook. McGraw-Hill Book Co., N.Y. 1033 p.

Jeffers, J. N. R., (ed.). 1972. Mathematical models in ecology. Blackwell Sci. Publ., Oxford. 398 p.

Jeffrey, C. 1977. Biological nomenclature. 2nd ed. Crane, Russak Inc., New York. 72 p.

Jenkins, D., and A. Watson. 1962. Fluctuations in a red grouse *(Lagopus scoticus* [Latham] population, 1956–9. p. 96–117 *in* E. D. Le Cren and M. W. Holdgate, (eds.). The exploitation of natural animal populations. Blackwell Sci. Publ., Oxford. 399 p.

Jenkins, D., A. Watson, and G. R. Miller. 1963. Population studies on red grouse, *Lagopus lagopus scoticus* (Lath.) in north-east Scotland. J. Anim. Ecol. 32(3):317–376.

Jenkins, D. W. 1957. Radioisotopes in entomology. p. 195–229 *in* C. L. Comar, (ed.). Atomic energy and agriculture. Am. Assoc. Adv. Sci., Publ. No. 49, Washington, D.C. 450 p.

Jenkins, J. H., S. D. Feurt, F. A. Hayes, and J. A. Crockford. 1955. A preliminary report on a field method using drugs for capturing deer. Proc. Southeastern Assoc. Game and Fish Commissioners 9:41–43.

Jensen, C. H., and G. W. Scotter. 1977. A comparison of twig-length and browsed-twig methods of determining browse utilization. J. Range Manage. 30(1):64–67.

Jensen, G. H., and L. J. Korschgen. 1947. Contents of crops, gizzards, and droppings of bobwhite quail force-fed known kinds and quantities of seeds. J. Wildl. Manage. 11(1):37–43.

Jensen, M. S., and M. P. Meyer. 1976. A remote sensing applications program and operational handbook for the Minnesota Department of Natural Resources and other state agencies. Univ. of Minnesota Inst. Agric. For. and Home Econ. Remote Sensing Lab. Res. Rep. 76–2, St. Paul, Minn. 96 p.

Jewell, D. G. 1978. Building the better bird trap. N. Am. Bird Bander 3(4):156.

Jewell, P. A. 1963. Wildlife research in east and central Africa. Oryx 7: 77–87.

Jewett, S. G., W. P. Taylor, W. T. Shaw, and J. W. Aldrich. 1953. Birds of Washington State. Univ. Washington Press, Seattle. 267 p.

Johansen, H. 1952. Ornithology in Russia. Ibis 94(1):1–48.

Johns, J. E. 1963. A new method of capture utilizing the mist net. Bird-Banding 34(4):209–213.

Johnsgard, P. A. 1973. Grouse and quails of North America. Univ. Nebraska Press, Lincoln. 553 p.

Johnsgard, P. A. 1975a. North American game birds of upland and shoreline. Univ. of Nebraska Press, Lincoln. 183 p.

Johnsgard, P. A. 1975b. Waterfowl of North America. Indiana Univ. Press, Bloomington. 575 p.

Johnsgard, P. A. 1978. Ducks, geese and swans of the world. Univ. Nebraska Press, Lincoln. 404 p.

Johnson, A. S. 1970. Biology of the raccoon in Alabama. Agric. Expt. Stn., Bull. 402, Auburn Univ., Ala. 148 p.

Johnson, E. V., G. L. Mack, and D. Q. Thompson. 1976. The effects of orchard pesticide applications on breeding robins. Wilson Bull. 88(1):16–35.

Johnson, L. L. 1967. The common goldeneye duck and the role of nesting boxes in its management in north-central Minnesota. J. Minn. Acad. Sci. 34(2):110–113.

Johnson, L. L. 1972. An improved capture technique for flightless young goldeneyes. J. Wildl. Manage. 36 (4):1277–1279.

Johnson, M. P., and P. H. Raven. 1970. Natural regulation of plant species diversity. Evol. Biol. 4(5):127–162.

Johnson, P. L., (ed.). 1969. Remote sensing in ecology. Univ. of Georgia Press, Athens. 244 p.

Johnson, R. F., R. O. Woodward, and L. M. Kirsch. 1978. Waterfowl nesting on small man-made islands in prairie wetlands. Wildl. Soc. Bull 6(4):240–243.

Johnson, R. R. 1966. Techniques and procedures for *in vitro* and *in vivo* rumen studies. J. Anim. Sci. 25(3): 855–875.

Johnson, S. R. 1971. A colored leg tag for nestling and adult birds. Bird-Banding 42(2):129–131.

Johnson, W. W. 1969. Dispensing bait with a caulking gun. J. Mammal. 50(1):149.

Johnston, A., and L. M. Bezeau. 1962. Chemical composition of range forage plants of the *Festuca scabrella* association. Can. J. Plant Sci. 42(1): 105–115.

Johnston, A., L. M. Bezeau, and S. Smoliak. 1968. Chemical composition and *in vitro* digestibility of alpine tundra plants. J. Wildl. Manage. 32(4):773–777.

Joint Committtee of the American Society of Agronomy, American Dairy Science Association, American Society of Animal Production, American Society of Range Management. 1962. Pasture and range research techniques. Comstock Publ. Assoc., Ithaca, N.Y. 242 p.

Joint Committee of the American Society of Range Management and the Agricultural Board, Subcommittee on Range Research Methods of the Agricultural Board. 1962. Basic problems and techniques in range research. Nat. Acad. of Sci. Nat. Res. Counc., Publ. No. 890. Washington, D.C. 341 p.

Jolly, G. M. 1965. Explicit estimates from capture-recapture data with both death and immigration-stochastic model. Biometrika 52(1 and 2):225–247.

Jones, F. K. 1965. Techniques and methods used to capture and tag alligators in Florida. Proc. Southeastern Assoc. Game and Fish Commissioners 19:98–101.

Jones, F. L., G. Flittner, and R. Gard. 1954. Report on a survey of bighorn sheep and other game in the Santa Rosa Mountains, Riverside County (California). Calif. Dept. Fish and Game, Sacramento. 26 p. (mimeo.)

Jones, J. K., Jr. 1964. Distribution and taxonomy of mammals of Nebraska. Univ. Kansas Publ. Mus. Nat. Hist. 16(1):1–356.

Jones, J. K., D. C. Carter, and H. H. Genoways. 1975. Revised checklist of North American mammals north of Mexico. Occ. Pap. Texas Tech. Univ. Mus. No. 28:1–14.

Jones, J. K., Jr., and J. A. Homan. 1976. Contribution to a bibliography of recent Texas mammals, 1961–1970. Occ. Pap. Texas Tech. Univ. Mus. No. 41:1–21.

Jones, R. L., R. F. Labisky, and W. L. Anderson. 1968. Selected minerals in soils, plants, and pheasants: an ecosystem approach to understanding pheasant distribution in Illinois. Ill. Nat. Hist. Surv. Biol. Notes 63, Urbana. 8 p.

Jones, W. P. 1976. Writing scientific papers and reports. 7th ed. W. C. Brown Co., Dubuque, Iowa. 336 p.

Jonkel, C. J. 1964. Estimating whole weights of black bears from hog-dressed weights. J. Wildl. Manage. 28(3):581.

Jonkel, C. J., and I. McT. Cowan. 1971. The black bear in the spruce-fir forest. Wildl. Monogr. No. 27. 57 p.

Joselyn, G. B., and G. I. Tate. 1972. Practical aspects of managing roadside cover for nesting pheasants. J. Wildl. Manage. 36(1):1–11.

Joule, J., and G. N. Cameron. 1974. Field estimation of demographic parameters: influence of *Sigmodon hispidus* population structure. J. Mammal. 55(2):309–318.

Judd, S. D. 1903. The economic value of the bobwhite. p. 193–204 *in* 1903 Yearbook of agriculture. U.S. Gov. Print. Off., Washington, D.C. 728 p.

Judd, S. D. 1905a. The bobwhite and other quails of the United States in their economic relations. USDA Biol. Surv. Bull. No. 21. 66 p.

Judd, S. D. 1905b. The grouse and wild turkeys of the United States and their economic value. USDA Biol. Surv. Bull. No. 24. 55 p.

Jumber, J. F., H. O. Hartley, E. L. Kozicky, and A. M. Johnson. 1957. A technique for sampling mourning dove production. J. Wildl. Manage. 21(2):227–229.

June, J. W. 1965. Water development. West. States Sage Grouse Workshop, Walden, Colo. 31 p.

Justice, K. E. 1961. A new method for measuring home ranges of small mammals. J. Mammal. 42(4):462–470.

Kabat, C., I. O. Buss, and R. K. Meyer. 1948. The use of ovulated follicles in determining eggs laid by the ring-necked pheasant. J. Wildl. Manage. 12(4):399–416.

Kabat, C., N. E. Collias, and R. C. Guettinger. 1953. Some winter habits of white-tailed deer and the development of census methods in the Flag Yard of northern Wisconsin. Wis. Cons. Dept. Tech. Wildl. Bull. 7, Madison. 31 p.

Kagarise, C. M. 1978. A simple trap for capturing nesting Wilson's phalarope. Bird-Banding 49(3):281–282.

Kahl, J. 1972. Better homes for feathered fishermen. Outdoor Calif. 33(3):4–6.

Kaiser, F. E., (ed.). 1965. Translators and translations: services and sources in science and technology. 2nd ed. Spec. Libr. Assoc., New York. 214 p.

Kalela, O. 1961. Seasonal change of habitat in the Norwegian lemming, *Lemmus lemmus* (L.). Ann. Acad. Sci. Fenn. Ser. A. IV Biol. 55:1–72.

Kalez, G. B. 1947. Measurement of salmon spawning by means of aerial photography. Pac. Fish. 45(3):49–51.

Kalmbach, E. R. 1934. Field observations in economic ornithology. Wilson Bull. 46(2):73–90.

Kalmbach, E. R. 1937. Crow-waterfowl relationships. USDA Circ. 433. Washington, D.C. 35 p.

Kalmbach, E. R. 1954. The continuing need for food habits research. Wilson Bull. 66(4):276–278.

Kalmbach, E. R., W. L. McAtee, F. R. Courtsal, and R. E. Ivers. 1969. Homes for birds. USDI Fish and Wildl. Serv. Conserv. Bull. 14. 18 p.

Kanuk, L., and C. Berenson. 1975. Mail surveys and response rates: a literature review. J. Mark. Res. 12(4): 440–453.

Karam, R. A., and K. Z. Morgan, (eds.). 1976. Environmental impact of nuclear power plants. Pergamon Press Inc., New York. 546 p.

Karr, J. R. 1968. Habitat and avian diversity on strip-mined land in east-central Illinois. Condor 70(4):348–357.

Karr, J. R. 1979. On the use of mist nets in the study of bird communities. Inl. Bird-Band. News 51(1):1–10.

Karstad, L., J. Spalatin, and R. P. Hanson. 1957. Application of the paper disk technique to the collection of whole blood and serum samples in studies on eastern equine encephalomyelitis. J. Infect. Dis. 101(3):295–299.

Karstad, L., (ed.). 1964. Diseases of Cervidae: a partly annotated bibliography. Wildl. Dis. 43:1–233.

Kavanau, J. L. 1961. Identification of small animals by proximity sensing. Science 134(3491):1694–1696.

Kavanau, J. L. 1963. Continuous automatic monitoring of the activities of small captive animals. Ecology 44(1):95–110.

Kay, R. H. 1964. Experimental biology: measurement and analysis. Reinhold Publ. Corp., New York. 416 p.

Kayser, C. 1961. The physiology of natural hibernation. Pergamon Press, New York. 325 p.

Kazutaka, H., T. D. Siopes, W. O. Wilson, and L. Z. McFarland. 1966. Identification of sex of day-old quail *(Coturnix coturnix japonica)* by cloacal examination. Poult. Sci. 45(3):469–472.

Kearl, W. G. 1965. A survey of big sagebrush control in Wyoming 1952–1964. Univ. of Wyoming Agric. Exp. Stn. Circ. 217, Laramie. 42 p.

Keiser, G. M. 1974. A guide to collecting and preserving plants. USDA For. Serv. Res. Note NE-188, N.E. For. Exp. Stn., Upper Darby, Pa. 6 p.

Keiss, R. E. 1969. Comparison of eruption-wear patterns and cementum annuli as age criteria in elk. J. Wildl. Manage. 33(1):175–180.

Keith, L. B. 1961. A study of waterfowl ecology on small impoundments in southeastern Alberta. Wildl. Monogr. No. 6. 88 p.

Keith, L. B., E. C. Meslow, and O. J. Rongstad. 1968. Techniques for snowshoe hare population studies. J. Wildl. Manage. 32(4):801–812.

Kellert, S. R. 1976. Perceptions of animals in American society. Trans. N. Am. Wildl. Nat. Resour. Conf. 41:533–546.

Kelly, G. 1975. Indexes for aging eastern wild turkeys. p. 205–209 *in* L. K. Halls, (ed.). Proc. 3rd Natl. Wild Turkey Symp., Tex. Chapt. Wildl. Soc., Austin. 227 p.

Kelly, G. M. 1977. Fisher *(Martes pennanti)* biology in the White Mountain National Forest and adjacent areas. Ph.D. Diss. Univ. of Massachusetts, Amherst. 148 p.

Kelsall, J. P., and J. R. Calaprice. 1972. Chemical content of waterfowl plumage as a potential diagnostic tool. J. Wildl. Manage. 36(4):1088–1097.

Kelsall, J. P., T. Mulligan, and L. Lapi. 1975. Chemical examination of feathers by an electron beam. Can. Wildl. Serv. Progr. Note No. 55. 3 p.

Kelsh, H. F. 1940. The slotted-templet method for controlling maps made from aerial photographs. USDA Misc. Publ. 404, Washington, D.C. 29 p.

Kendeigh, S. C. 1952. Parental care and its evolution in birds. Ill. Biol. Monogr. 22:1–356.

Kendeigh, S. C. 1963. New ways of measuring the incubation period of birds. Auk 80(4):453–461.

Kendeigh, S. C., and S. P. Baldwin. 1930. The mechanical recording of the nesting activities of birds. Auk 47(4):471–480.

Kennedy, A. H. 1952. The sexing of beaver. Ont. Dept. Lands and For., Fish and Wildl. Div. 9 p. (mimeo.)

Kennedy, H. E. 1976. Universal index to zoological literature proposed. BioScience 26(9):529.

Kennelly, J. J., and B. E. Johns. 1976. The estrous cycle of coyotes. J. Wildl. Manage. 40(2):272–277.

Kennelly, J. J., B. E. Johns, C. P. Breidenstein, and J. D. Roberts. 1977. Predicting female coyote breeding dates from fetal measurements. J. Wildl. Manage. 41(4):746–750.

Kenneth, J. H., (ed.). 1963. A dictionary of biological terms. 8th ed. Van Nostrand Reinhold Co., New York. 640 p.

Kenyon, K. W., and C. H. Fiscus. 1963. Age determination in the Hawaiian monk seal. J. Mammal. 44(2):280–282.

Keppie, D. M., and P. W. Herzog. 1978. Nest site characteristics and nest success of spruce grouse. J. Wildl. Manage. 42(3):628–632.

Kershaw, K. A. 1964. Quantitative and dynamic ecology. Edward Arnold Publ. Co., London. 183 p.

Kerwin, L. M., and G. J. Mitchell. 1971. The validity of the wear-age technique for Alberta pronghorns. J. Wildl. Manage. 35(4):743–747.

Kessler, F. 1962. Measurement of nest attentiveness in the ring-necked pheasant. Auk 79(4):702–705.

Kessler, F. W. 1964. Avian predation on pheasants wearing differently colored plastic markers. Ohio J. Sci. 64(6):401–402.

Keuffel and Esser Co. n.d. Compensating polar planimeter. Hoboken, N. J.

Keyfitz, N., and W. Flieger. 1971. Population facts and methods of demography. W. H. Freeman and Co., San Francisco. 613 p.

Khramtsov, N. N., and G. A. Timchenko. 1976. Ways of forest production development. Lesnoye Khaziaystvo 9:80–84.

Kibbe, D. P., and R. L. Kirkpatrick. 1971. Systematic evaluation of late summer breeding in juvenile cottontails, *(Sylvilagus floridanus)*. J. Mammal. 52(2):465–467.

Kibler, L. F. 1969. The establishment and maintenance of a bluebird nest-box project. Bird-Banding 40(2):114–129.

Kibrick, E., (ed.). 1962. Bibliographic problems in the natural sciences. Massachusetts Inst. Tech. Libr., Cambridge, Mass. 113 p.

Kiel, W. H., Jr. 1954. Waterfowl breeding population and production in the Newdale-Erickson district of Manitoba—1953. p. 81–85 *in* Waterfowl populations and breeding conditions—summer 1953. U.S. Fish Wildl. Serv. Spec. Sci. Rep., Wildl. 25. 250 p.

Kiel, W. H., Jr. 1955. Nesting studies of the coot in southwestern Manitoba. J. Wildl. Manage. 19(2):189–198.

Kiel, W. H. Jr., and J. T. Harris. 1956. Status of the white-winged dove in Texas. Trans. N. Am. Wildl. Conf. 21:376–388.

Kincaid, S. P. 1975. Bats, biology, and control. Proc. Great Plains Wildl. Damage Control Workshop 2:187–194.

Kindschy, R. R. 1974. Preliminary report on nomad alfalfa seedings. USDI Bur. Land Manage. Spec. Rep., Vale, Oreg. 19 p.

King, D. R. 1975. Estimation of yew and cedar availability and utilization. J. Wildl. Manage. 39(1):101–107.

King, J. G., F. C. Robards, and C. J. Lensink. 1972. Census of the bald eagle breeding population in southeast Alaska. J. Wildl. Manage. 36(4):1292–1295.

King, R. D. 1968. Food habits in relation to the ecology and population dynamics of blue grouse. M. S. Thesis. Univ. British Columbia, Vancouver, B. C. 62 p.

King, T. R., and H. E. McClure. 1944. Chemical composition of some American wild feedstuffs. J. Agric. Res. 69(1):33–46.

Kinne, R. 1960. How to shoot wild life with a camera. Popular Photogr. 46(4):32, 34, 106.

Kinne, R. 1971. The complete book of nature photography. Chilton Book Co., Philadelphia. 192 p.

Kinney, M. R. 1967. The abbreviated citation—a bibliographical problem. Assoc. of Coll. and Res. Libr. Monogr. No. 28. Am. Libr. Assoc., Chicago. 57 p.

Kirby, R. E. 1976. Mapping wetlands on beaver flowages with 35-mm photography. Can. Field-Nat. 90(4): 423–431.

Kirk, T. G. 1978. Library research guide to biology illustrated search strategy and sources. Pierian Press, Ann Arbor, Mich. 79 p.

Kirk, W. G., G. K. Davis, F. G. Martin, E. M. Hodges, and J. F. Easley. 1974. Effect of burning and mowing on composition of pineland three-awn. J. Range Manage. 27(6): 420–424.

Kirkpatrick, C. M. 1944. The bursa of Fabricius in ring-necked pheasants. J. Wildl. Manage. 8(2):118–129.

Kirkpatrick, R. D., and L. K. Sowls. 1962. Age determination of the collared peccary by the tooth-replacement pattern. J. Wildl. Manage. 26(2):214–217.

Kirkpatrick, R. L. 1974. Ovarian follicular and related characteristics of white-tailed deer as influenced by season and age in the Southeast. Proc. Southeastern Assoc. Game and Fish Commissioners 28:587–594.

Kirkpatrick, R. L. 1975. Applicability of basic physiology and nutrition research to practical wildlife management. Proc. Southeastern Assoc. Game and Fish Commissioners 29:476–480.

Kirkpatrick, R. L., D. E. Buckland, W. A. Abler, P. F. Scanlon, J. B. Whelan, and H. E. Burkhart. 1975. Energy and protein influences on blood urea nitrogen of white-tailed deer fawns. J. Wildl. Manage. 39(4):692–698.

Kirkpatrick, R. L., J. L. Coggin, H. S. Mosby and J. O. Newell. 1976a. Parturition times and litter sizes of gray squirrels in Virginia. Proc. Southeastern Assoc. Game and Fish Commissioners 30:541–545.

Kirkpatrick, R. L., J. P. Fontenot, and R. F. Harlow. 1969. Seasonal changes in rumen chemical components as related to forages consumed by white-tailed deer of the Southeast. Trans. N. Am. Wildl. Nat. Resour. Conf. 34:229–238.

Kirkpatrick, R. L., and G. L. Valentine. 1970. Reproduction in captive pine voles, *Microtus pinetorum*. J. Mammal. 51(4):779–785.

Kirkpatrick, R. L., R. W. Vogelsang, R. J. Warren, and P. F. Scanlon. 1976b. Plasma progestin levels of female white-tailed deer during the estrous cycle. Virginia J. Sci. 27(2):46. (Abstr.).

Kirsch, J. B., and K. R. Greer. 1968. Bibliography . . . Wapiti-American elk and European red deer. Montana Fish and Game Dept. Spec. Rep. No. 2, Helena. 147 p.

Kirsch, L. M., and A. D. Kruse. 1973. Prairie fires and wildlife. Proc. Tall Timbers Fire Ecol. Conf. 12:289–303.

Kish, L. 1965. Survey sampling. J. Wiley and Son Inc., New York. 643 p.

Kish, L., and I. Hess. 1959. A "replacement" procedure for reducing the bias of nonresponse. Am. Stat. 13(4):17–19.

Kitchen, H., D. E. Ullrey, L. D. Fay, and W. G. Youatt. 1974. Immobilizing deer with CI–744. Proc. Am. Assoc. Zoo Vet.: 155–156.

Kjellstrom, B. 1975. Be expert with map and compass the "orienteering" handbook. Scribner Co. New York, N.Y. 136 p.

Kjos, C. G., and W. W. Cochran. 1970. Activity of migrant thrushes as determined by radio-telemetry. Wilson Bull. 82(2):225–226.

Klebenow, D. A. 1969. Sage grouse nesting and brood habitat in Idaho. J. Wildl. Manage. 33(3):649–662.

Kleen, V. 1975. What's in the future for cormorants? Ill. Audubon Bull. 175:21–24.

Kleiber, M. 1961. The fire of life: an introduction to animal energetics. John Wiley and Sons, New York. 454 p.

Klein, D. R. 1962. Rumen contents analysis as an index to range quality. Trans. N. Am. Wildl. Nat. Resour. Conf. 27:150–164.

Klein, D. R. 1964. Range-related differences in growth of deer reflected in skeletal ratios. J. Mammal. 45(2): 226–235.

Klement, A. W., Jr. 1965. Natural environmental radio-activity, an annotated bibliography. Fallout Stud. Branch, Div. Biol. and Med. AEC. Wash–1061, Washington, D.C. 125 p.

Klement, A. W., Jr., and V. Schultz. 1962, 1963, 1965, 1966. Terrestrial and freshwater radioecology: a selected bibliography—supplements 1, 2, 3 and 4. USAEC Div. Biol. and Med. TID–3910, Washington, D.C. 79; 95; 115. 128 p.

Klett, E. V. 1965. A portable observation tower. J. Wildl. Manage. 29(1):206–207.

Klevezal, G. A., and S. E. Kleinenberg. 1967. Age determination of mammals from annual layers in teeth and bones. USSR Acad. of Sci. Severtsov Inst. of Anim. Morphol. (Transl. from Russian). Clearing House for Fed. Sci. U.S. Dept. Commer., Springfield, Va. 128 p.

Klevezal, G. A., and M. V. Mina. 1973. Factors determining the pattern of annual layers in dental tissue and bones of mammals. Zh. Obshch. Biol. 34(4):594–604.

Klewe, H-J., and H. P. Kimmich, (eds.). 1978. Biotelemetry IV. Proceedings of the Fourth International Symposium on biotelemetry. Braunschweig, Germany. 291 p.

Klimkiewicz, M. K., and P. D. Jung. 1977. A new banding technique for nesting adult purple martins. N. Am. Bird Bander 2(1):3–6.

Klimstra, W. D. 1950. Bob-white quail nesting and production in southeastern Iowa. Iowa State Coll. J. Sci. 24(4):385–395.

Klimstra, W. D., and E. L. Corder. 1957. Food of the cottontail in southern Illinois. Trans. Ill. State Acad. Sci. 50:247–256.

Klimstra, W. D., and T. G. Scott. 1957. Progress report on bobwhite nesting in southern Illinois. Proc. Southeastern Assoc. Game and Fish Commissioners 11:351–355.

Klinghammer, E., (ed.). 1979. The behavior and ecology of wolves. Garland STPM Press, New York and London. 588 p.

Klonglan, E. D., I. A. Coleman, and E. L. Kozicky. 1956. A pheasant nest activity recording instrument. J. Wildl. Manage. 20(2):173–177.

Klonglan, E. D., and E. L. Kozicky. 1953. Variations in two spring indices of male pheasant populations, Story County, Iowa. Proc. Iowa Acad. Sci. 60:660–664.

Knight, R. R. 1966. Effectiveness of neckbands for marking elk. J. Wildl. Manage. 30(4):845–846.

Knott, N. O., C. P. Ball, and C. F. Yocom. 1943. Nesting of the Hungarian partridge and ring-necked pheasant in Whitman County, Washington. J. Wildl. Manage. 7(3):283–291.

Knowlton, F., P. E. Martin, and J. C. Haug. 1968. A telemetric monitor for determining animal activity. J. Wildl. Manage. 32(4):943–948.

Knowlton, F. F., E. D. Michael, and W. C. Glazener. 1964. A marking technique for field recognition of individual turkeys and deer. J. Wildl. Manage. 28(1):167–170.

Knox, K. L., J. G. Nagy, and R. D. Brown. 1969. Water turnover in mule deer. J. Wildl. Manage. 33 (2):389–393.

Knudsen, J. W. 1966. Biological techniques: collecting, preserving and illustrating plants and animals. Harper and Row, New York. 525 p.

Knudsen, J. W. 1972. Collecting and preserving plants and animals. Harper and Row, New York. 320 p.

Koeppl, J. W. 1979. A simple device for determining degree and aspect of slope. J. Wildl. Manage. 43(1):250.

Koller, D., and M. Negbi. 1961–1966. Germination of seeds of desert plants. Hebrew Univ. Dept. Bot., Jerusalem, Israel. 180 p.

Kolz, A. L. 1975. Mortality sensing wildlife transmitters. Proc. Rocky Mtn. Bioengineer. Symp. 12:57–60.

Kolz, A. L., G. W. Corner, and R. E. Johnson. 1973. A multiple-use wildlife transmitter. U.S. Fish Wildl. Serv. Spec. Sci. Rep. Wildl. 163. 11 p.

Kolz, A. L., G. W. Corner, and H. P. Tietjen. 1972. A radio-frequency beacon transmitter for small mammals. J. Wildl. Manage. 36(1):177–179.

Kolz, A. L., and R. E. Johnson. 1975. An elevating mechanism for mobile receiving antennas. J. Wildl. Manage. 39(4):819–820.

Kolz, A. L., and R. E. Johnson. 1976. Coulometric recorder for timing and counting events in the field. J. Wildl. Manage. 40(2):278–282.

Kolz, A. L., J. W. Lentfer, and H. G. Fallek. 1978. Polar bear tracking via satellite. Rocky Mt. Bioeng. Symp. and Int. ISA Biomed. Sci. Instrum. Symp. 15:137–144.

Komarek, R. 1962. Preface. Proc. Tall Timbers Fire Ecology Confer. 1:v.

Koonz, C. H., and E. J. Strandine. 1945. A rapid and simplified method for revealing the surface pattern of hair. Trans. Am. Microsc. Soc. 64(1):63–64.

Kopischke, E. D. 1966. Selection of calcium-and magnesium-bearing grit by pheasants in Minnesota. J. Wildl. Manage. 30(2):276–279.

Korschgen, L. J. 1948. Late-fall and early-winter food habits of bobwhite quail in Missouri. J. Wildl. Manage. 12(1):46–57.

Korschgen, L. J. 1960. Production of game bird foods in Missouri. J. Wildl. Manage. 24(4):395–401.

Korschgen, L. J. 1962a. Foods of Missouri deer, with some management implications. J. Wildl. Manage. 26(2):164–172.

Korschgen, L. J. 1962b. Food habits of greater prairie chickens in Missouri. Am. Midl. Nat. 68(2):307–318.

Korschgen, L. J. 1966. Foods and nutrition of ruffed grouse in Missouri. J. Wildl. Manage. 30(1):86–100.

Korschgen, L. J. 1973. Principal year-round foods of cottontails in Missouri. Mo. Dept. Conserv., P-R Project W–13–R. 57 p.

Korschgen, L. J., and G. D. Chambers. 1970. Propagation, stocking, and food habits of Reeves pheasants in Missouri. J. Wildl. Manage. 34(2): 274–282.

Korschgen, L. J., W. R. Porath, and O. Torgerson. 1976. Spring and summer foods of deer in Ozark forests. Mo. Dept. Conserv., P-R Project Rep. W–13–R. 55 p.

Kortright, F. H. 1953. The ducks, geese, and swans of North America. Wildl. Manage. Inst., Washington, D.C. 476 p.

Kosin, Ī. L. 1972. The growing importance of Russian as a language of science. BioScience 22(12):723–724.

Koskimies, J. 1954. The use of a barking dog in the hunting of capercaillie and blackgame. Suomen Riista 9:61–63.

Koskimies, J. 1957. Flocking behavior in capercaillie, *Tetrao urogallus* (L.) and blackgame, *Lyrurus tetrix* (L.). Pap. Game Res., Helsinki. 18:1–32.

Kossack, C. W. 1950. Breeding habits of Canada geese under refuge conditions. Am. Midl. Nat. 43(3):627–649.

Kothmann, H. G., and G. W. Litton. 1975. Utilization of man-made roosts by turkeys in West Texas. p. 159–164 *in* L. K. Halls, (ed.). Proc. 3rd Natl. Wild Turkey Symp. Tex. Chapt. Wildl. Soc., Austin. 227 p.

Kozicky, E. L., T. A. Bancroft, and P. G. Homeyer. 1954. An analysis of woodcock singing ground counts, 1948–1952. J. Wildl. Manage. 18(2): 259–266.

Kozicky, E. L., R. J. Jessen, and G. O. Hendrickson. 1956. Estimation of fall quail populations in Iowa. J. Wildl. Manage. 20(2):97–104.

Kozicky, E. L., and F. V. Schmidt. 1949. Nesting habits of the clapper rail in New Jersey. Auk 66(4):355–364.

Kozlik, F. M., A. W. Miller, and W. C. Rienecker. 1959. Color-marking white geese for determining migration routes. Calif. Fish and Game 45(2):69–82.

Krapu, G. L. 1976. Experimental responses of mallards and Canada geese to tribromoethanol. J. Wildl. Manage. 40(1):180–183.

Krapu, G. L., and G. A. Swanson. 1975. Some nutritional aspects of reproduction in prairie nesting pintails. J. Wildl. Manage. 39(1):156–162.

Krebs, J. R., J. C. Ryan, and E. L. Charnov. 1974. Hunting by expectation or optimal foraging? A study of patch use by chickadees. Anim. Behav. 22(4):953–964.

Krefting, L. W. 1951. Construction of the Lake States deer exclosure. USDA For. Serv. Lake States Exp. Stn. Tech. Note 361. 2 p.

Krenz, R. D. 1962. Costs and returns from spraying sagebrush with 2, 4-D. Univ. of Wyoming Agric. Exp. Stn. Bull. 390, Laramie. 31 p.

Kricher, J. C. 1973. Summer bird species diversity in relation to secondary succession on the New Jersey Piedmont. Am. Midl. Nat. 89(1):121–137.

Kristiansson, K., B. Lindkvist, and T. Gustafson. 1977. An altimeter for birds and its use. Ornis Scand. 8:79–86.

Kroeck, D. 1976. Everyone's space handbook. Pilot Rock Inc., Arcata, Calif. 175 p.

Krukoff, B. A., and A. C. Smith. 1937. Notes on the botanical components of curare. Bull. Torrey Bot. Club. 64:401–409.

Krumholz, L. A., (chairman). 1957. Glossary of wildlife terms. J. Wildl. Manage. 21(3):373–376.

Kruzas, A. T., (ed.). 1974. Encyclopedia of information systems and services. 2nd ed. Edwards Bros., Ann Arbor, Mich. 1271 p.

Küchler, A. W. 1964. Potential natural vegetation of the conterminous United States (manual and map). Am. Geogr. Soc. Spec. Publ. 36. New York. 116 p.

Küchler, A. W. 1967. Vegetation mapping. The Ronald Press Co., New York. 472 p.

Kulwich, R., L. Struglia, and P. B. Pearson. 1953. The effect of coprophagy on the excretion of B vitamins by the rabbit. J. Nutr. 49 (4):639–645.

Kupa, J. J. 1966. Ecological studies of the female ruffed grouse *(Bonasa umbellus* L.) at the Cloquet Forest Research Center, Minnesota. Ph.D. Thesis. Univ. of Minnesota. 101 p.

Kuroda, N. 1971. The explanation of the scientific names of the duck tribes of the world. Bull. Biogeograph. Soc. Japan 27(4):19–36.

Kuteev, F. S. 1977. Conference on forest protection. Lesnoye Khaziaystvo 2:94–95.

Kuznetsov, I. V. 1961–1965. Liudi russkoi nauki, ocherki o vydaiushchikhsia deateliakh estestovoznanila i tekhniki. (v.3: Biologiia, meditsina, sel' skhosiaistvennie.) Izd.-vo 'Fiziko-Matematicheskoi Litry", Moscow. 4 v.

LaBeau, D., and G. C. Tarbert, (eds.). 1976. Biographical dictionaries master index; a guide to more than 725,000 listings in over fifty current who's whos and other works of collective biography. Gale Research Co., Detroit, Mich. 3 vol.

Labisky, R. F. 1959. Night-lighting: a technique for capturing birds and mammals. Ill. Nat. Hist. Surv. Biol. Notes No. 40, Urbana. 11 p.

Labisky, R. F. 1968. Nightlighting: its use in capturing pheasants, prairie chickens, bobwhites, and cottontails. Ill. Nat. Hist. Surv. Biol. Notes No. 62, Urbana. 12 p.

Labisky, R. F., S. H. Mann, and R. D. Lord, Jr. 1969. Weights and growth characteristics of pheasant lenses. J. Wildl. Manage. 33(2):270–276.

Lacaillade, H. C., Jr. 1958. Wood duck breeding studies. New Hampshire Job Completion Rep. Proj. No. W–7–R–13, Job No. I-D. 11 p.

Lacher, J. R., and D. D. Lacher. 1964. A mobile cannon net trap. J. Wildl. Manage. 28(3):595–597.

Lack, D. 1947. The significance of clutch-size in the partridge *(Perdix perdix).* J. Animal Ecol. 16(1):19–23.

Lamprey, H. F. 1963. Ecological separation of the large mammal species in the Tarangire Game Reserve, Tanganyika E. Afr. Wildl. J. 1:63–92.

Landin, M. C. 1978. National perspective of colonial waterbirds nesting on dredged material islands. Trans. N. Am. Wildl. Nat. Resour. Conf. 43:89–99.

Lang, L. M., and G. W. Wood. 1976. Manipulation of the Pennsylvania deer herd. Wildl. Soc. Bull. 4(4): 159–165.

Lange, M., and F. B. Hora. 1963. Collins guide to mushrooms and toadstools. Collins, Ltd., London. 257 p.

Langford, W. A., and D. J. Cocheba. 1978. The wildlife valuation problem: a critical review of economic approaches. Can. Wildl. Serv. Fish. and Environ. Can. Occas. Pap. No. 37, Ottawa. 35 p.

Langman, V. A. 1973. A radio-biotelemetry system for monitoring body temperature and activity levels in the zebra finches. Auk 90(2): 375–383.

Lanyon, W. E., and F. B. Gill. 1964. Spectrographic analysis of variation in the songs of a population of blue-winged warblers *(Vermivora pinus).* Am. Mus. Novitates 2176:1–18.

Lapedes, D. N., (ed.). 1977. McGraw-Hill dictionary of the life sciences. McGraw-Hill Book Co., New York. 960 p.

Laramie, H. A., Jr. 1963. A device for control of problem beavers. J. Wildl. Manage. 27(3):471–476.

Laramie, H. A. 1978. Water level control in beaver ponds and culverts. N. H. Fish and Game Dept., Concord. 5 p.

Larimore, R. W. 1957. A marginal-dot system of indexing reference cards. J. Wildl. Manage. 21(1):92–94.

Larsen, T. 1971a. Capturing, handling, and marking polar bears in Svalbard. J. Wildl. Manage. 35(1):27–36.

Larsen, T. 1971b. Sexual dimorphism in the molar rows of the polar bear. J. Wildl. Manage. 35(2):374–377.

Larson, J. S. 1966. Wildlife forage clearings on forest lands—a critical appraisal and research needs. Ph.D. Diss. Va. Polytech. Inst., Blacksburg, Va. 143 p.

Larson, J. S., and S. J. Knapp. 1971. Sexual dimorphism in beaver neutrophils. J. Mammal. 52(1):212–215.

Larson, J. S., and F. C. Van Nostrand. 1968. An evaluation of beaver aging techniques. J. Wildl. Manage. 32 (1):99–103.

Latham, R. M. 1942. Sexing day-old ring-neck pheasant chicks. Pa. Game Comm. Res. Circ. No. 2, Harrisburg. 11 p.

Latham, R. M. 1951. The ecology and economics of predator management. Pa. Game Comm. Rep. II, Harrisburg. 96 p.

Latham, R. M. 1956. Complete book of the wild turkey. Stackpole Co., Harrisburg, Pa. 265 p.

Lauritzen, C. W., and A. A. Thayer. 1966. Rain traps for intercepting and storing water for livestock. USDA Inf. Bull. No. 307, Washington, D.C. 10 p.

LaVal, R. K., R. L. Clawson, M. L. LaVal, and W. Caire. 1977. Foraging behavior and nocturnal activity patterns of Missouri bats, with emphasis on the endangered species *Myotis grisescens* and *Myotis sodalis*. J. Mammal. 58(4):592–599.

Lavigne, D. M., and N. A. Oritsland. 1974. Ultraviolet photography: a new application for remote sensing of mammals. Can. J. Zool. 52(7):939–941.

Lawrence, M. J., and R. W. Brown. 1973. Mammals of Britain: their tracks, trails and signs. Rev. ed. Blanford Press, London. 298 p.

Lawrence, W. H., N. B. Kverno, and H. D. Hartwell. 1961. Guide to wildlife feeding injuries on conifers in the Pacific Northwest. Western For. and Conserv. Assoc. 44 p.

Lawrence, W. H., and C. A. Sherman. 1963. An electronic traffic counter for recording burrow activity of the mountain beaver. J. Mammal. 44 (3):399–405.

Laws, R. M. 1953. A new method of age determination in mammals with special reference to the elephant seal *(Mirounga leonina,* Linn.). Falkland Island Depend. Surv. Sci. Reps. 2: 1–12.

Laws, R. M. 1962. Age determination of pinnipeds with special reference to growth layers in the teeth. Z. Saugetierkd. 27(3):129–146.

Lay, D. W. 1957. Browse quality and the effects of prescribed burning in southern pine forests. J. For. 55(5): 342–347.

Lay, D. W. 1965. Fruit utilization by deer in southern forests. J. Wildl. Manage. 29(2):370–375.

Laycock, G. 1966. The alien animals. Nat. Hist. Press (Am. Mus. of Nat. Hist.), Garden City, N.Y. 240 p.

Laycock, W. A., and D. A. Price. 1970. Environmental influences on nutritional value of forage plants. p. 37–47 *in* Range and wildlife habitat evaluation—a research symposium. USDA For. Serv. Misc. Publ. No. 1147. 220 p.

Leatherwood, S., J. R. Gilbert, and D. G. Chapman. 1978. An evaluation of some techniques for aerial censuses of bottlenosed dolphins. J. Wildl. Manage. 42(2):239–250.

Lechleitner, R. R. 1954. Age criteria in mink, *Mustela vison*. J. Mammal. 35(4):496–503.

Lechleitner, R. R. 1957. The black-tailed jackrabbit on Grey Lodge Refuge, California. Ph.D. Diss. Univ. of California, Berkeley. 179 p.

Leck, C. 1975. The birds of New Jersey their habits and habitats. Rutgers Univ. Press, New Brunswick, N. Jersey. 190 p.

LeCount, A. 1977. Using chest circumference to determine bear weight. Arizona Game and Fish Dept. Wildl. Digest Abstr. 11, Phoenix. 2 p.

LeCroy, M. 1975. Easily built portable blind. Bird-Banding 46(2):166–168.

Lederer, R. J., and R. Crane. 1978. The effects of emetics on wild birds. N. Am. Bird Bander 3(1):3–5.

Ledley, R. S. 1964. High-speed automatic analysis of biomedical pictures. Science 146(3641):216–223.

Lee, A. B. 1950. The microtomist's vade mecum. 11th ed. Blakiston Co., Philadelphia. 753 p.

Lee, F. B. 1960. Minnesota banding and bill-marker studies. Ring 23 (2):232–234.

Lee, F. B., R. L. Jessen, N. J. Ordal, R. I. Benson, J. P. Lindmeier, L. L. Johnson, and J. B. Moyle, (ed.). 1964. Waterfowl in Minnesota. Minn. Dept. Conserv. Tech. Bull. 7. 210 p.

Lee, J. A. 1954. Wood duck research investigations. New Hampshire Job Completion Rep., Proj. No. W-7-R-10, Job No. II-B. 8 p.

Leedy, D. L. 1948. Aerial photographs, their interpretation and suggested uses in wildlife management. J. Wildl. Manage. 12(2):191–210.

Leedy, D. L. 1953. Aerial photo use and interpretation in the fields of wildlife and recreation. Photogramm. Eng. 19(1):127–137.

Leedy, D. L., T. M. Franklin, and E. C. Hekimian. 1975. Highway-wildlife relationships. Final Rep., Natl. Tech. Inf. Serv., Springfield, Va., Vol. 1 and 2. 600 p.

Leege, T. A. 1969. Burning seral brush ranges for big game in northern Idaho. Trans. N. Am. Wildl. Nat. Resour. Conf. 34:429–438.

Leege, T. A., and R. M. Williams. 1967. Beaver productivity in Idaho. J. Wildl. Manage. 31(2):326–332.

Lefebvre, P. W., and J. L. Seubert. 1970. Surfactants as blackbird stressing agents. Proc. Vertebr. Pest Conf. 4:156–161.

Leftwich, A. W. 1973. A dictionary of zoology. 3rd ed. Constable, London. 290 p.

Lehman, D. 1966. Woodcock hunting. Mich. Conserv. 35(4):24–27.

Lehner, P. 1979. The handbook of ethological methods. Garland Press, New York. 403 p.

Lehninger, A. L. 1975. Biochemistry. 2nd ed. Worth Publ. Inc., New York. 1104 p.

Lemieux, L. 1959. The breeding biology of the greater snow goose on Bylot Island, Northwest Territories. Can. Field-Nat. 73(2):117–128.

Lemmon, P. E. 1956. A spherical densiometer for estimating forest overstory density. For. Sci. 2(4):314–320.

Lemmon, P. E. 1957. A new instrument for measuring forest overstory density. J. For. 55(9):667–669.

Lemnell, P. A. 1974. Age determination in red squirrels, *(Sciurus vulgaris)*. Trans. Int. Congr. Game Biol. 11:573–580.

Lenhoff, E. S. 1966. Tools of biology. Macmillan Co., New York. 120 p.

Lensing, J. E., and T. F. Roux. 1975. A capture snare for the smaller mammal predators and scavengers. Madoqua 9(1):57–61.

Lensink, C. J. 1964. Distribution of recoveries from bandings of ducklings. U.S. Fish Wildl. Serv. Spec. Sci. Rep. Wildl. No. 89. 146 p.

Lensink, C. J. 1968. Neckbands as an inhibitor of reproduction in black brant. J. Wildl. Manage. 32(2):418–420.

Lensink, C. J. 1969. The distribution of recoveries from white-fronted geese *(Anser albifrons frontalis)* banded in North America. Bur. Sport Fish and Wildl., preliminary Draft, Bethel, Alaska.

Lentfer, J. W. 1968. A technique for immobilizing and marking polar bears. J. Wildl. Manage. 32(2):317–321.

Leonard, R. M., and E. B. Fish. 1974. An aerial photographic technique for censusing lesser sandhill cranes. Wildl. Soc. Bull. 2(4):191–195.

Leopold, A. 1933. Game management. Charles Scribner's Sons, New York. 481 p.

Leopold, A. S. 1939. Age determination in quail. J. Wildl. Manage. 3(3): 261–265.

Leopold, A. S. 1943. The molts of young wild and domestic turkeys. Condor 45(4):133–145.

Leopold, A. S. 1953. Intestinal morphology of gallinaceous birds in relation to food habits. J. Wildl. Manage. 17(2):197–203.

Leopold, A. S. 1959. Wildlife of Mexico. Univ. California Press, Berkeley. 568 p.

Leopold, A. S. 1977. The California quail. Univ. of California Press, Berkeley, Calif. 281 p.

Leopold, F. 1951. A study of nesting wood ducks in Iowa. Condor 53(5):209–220.

Leopold, L. B., F. E. Clarke, B. B. Hanshaw, and J. R. Balsley. 1971. A procedure for evaluating environmental impact. U.S. Dept. Inter. Geol. Surv. Circ. 645. 13 p.

LeResche, R. E., and R. A. Rausch. 1974. Accuracy and precision of aerial moose censusing. J. Wildl. Manage. 38(2):175–182.

LeResche, R. E., U. S. Seal, P. D. Karns, and A. W. Franzmann. 1974. A review of blood chemistry of moose and other cervidae with emphasis on nutritional assessment. Nat. Can. 101(1–2):263–290.

Leslie, A. S., and A. E. Shipley. 1912. The grouse in health and disease. Smith Elder and Co., London. 472 p.

Leslie, P. H. 1945. On the use of matrices in certain population mathematics. Biometrika 33(3):183–212.

Levi, W. M. 1969. The pigeon. Levi Publ. Co. Inc., Sumter, S. C. 667 p.

Levine, N. D. 1955. A punched card system for filing parasitological bibliography cards. J. Parasitol. 41 (4):343–352.

Levins, R. 1966. The strategy of model building in population biology. Am. Sci. 54(4):421–431.

Levy, E. B., and E. A. Madden. 1933. The point method of pasture analysis. N. Z. J. Agric. 46(5):267–279.

Levy, S. H., J. J. Levy, and R. A. Bishop. 1966. Use of tape recorded female quail calls during the breeding season. J. Wildl. Manage. 30(2): 426–428.

Lewin, V. 1960. Reproduction and development of young in a population of California quail. Ph.D. Diss. Univ. California, Berkeley. 78 p.

Lewis, H. F. 1939. Size of sets of eggs of the American eider. J. Wildl. Manage. 3(1):70–73.

Lewis, J. C. 1962. Preliminary x-ray studies of deer productivity near Crossville, Tennessee. Proc. Southeastern Assoc. Game and Fish Commissioners 16:24–28.

Lewis, J. C. 1977. Sandhill crane *(Grus canadensis)*. p. 5–43 *in* G. C. Sanderson, (ed.). Management of migratory shore and upland game birds in North America. Int. Assoc. Fish and Wildl. Agencies, Washington, D.C. 358 p.

Lewis, N., (ed.). 1978. The new Roget's Thesaurus of the English language in dictionary form. Revised. G. P. Putnam's Sons, New York. 552 p.

Leyhausen, P. 1979. Cat behavior, the predatory and social behavior of domestic and wild cats. Transl. from 3rd. German ed. Garland STPM Press, New York. 340 p.

Lieberman, M., and W. J. McCarty. 1976. The design of a directional, treadle-actuated animal movement recorder. J. Wildl. Manage. 40(1): 190–191.

Liers, E. E. 1951. Notes on the river otter *(Lutra canadensis)*. J. Mammal. 32(1):1–9.

Lincoln, F. C., and S. P. Baldwin. 1929. Manual for bird banders. USDA Misc. Publ. No. 58, Washington, D.C. 112 p.

Linder, R. L., R. B. Dahlgren, and C. R. Elliott. 1971. Primary feather pattern as a sex criterion in the pheasant. J. Wildl. Manage. 35(4): 840–843.

Linduska, J. P. 1947. The ferret as an aid to winter rabbit studies. J. Wildl. Manage. 11(3):252–255.

Lindzey, F. G., and E. C. Meslow. 1976. Winter dormancy in black bears in southwestern Washington. J. Wildl. Manage. 40(3):408–415.

Lindzey, F. G., S. K. Thompson, and J. I. Hodges. 1977. Scent station index of black bear abundance. J. Wildl. Manage. 41(1):151–153.

Linehan, J. T. 1967. Measuring bird damage to corn. Proc. Vertebr. Pest Conf. 3:50–53.

Ling, J. K., D. G. Nicholls, and C. D. B. Thomas. 1967. Immobilization of southern elephant seals with succinylcholine chloride. J. Wildl. Manage. 31(3):468–479.

Linhart, S. B., and J. J. Kennelly. 1967. Fluorescent bone labeling of coyotes with demethylchlortetracycline. J. Wildl. Manage. 31(2):317–321.

Linhart, S. B., and F. F. Knowlton. 1967. Determining age of coyotes by tooth cementum layers. J. Wildl. Manage. 31(2):362–365.

Linhart, S. B., and F. F. Knowlton. 1975. Determining the relative abundance of coyotes by scent station lines. Wildl. Soc. Bull. 3(3): 119–124.

Linsdale, J. M. 1936. The birds of Nevada. Pac. Coast Avifauna No. 23:1–145. (Same as Condor 53(5): 228–249, 1951).

Linsky, A. S. 1975. Stimulating responses to mailed questionnaires: a review. Public Opin. Q. 39(1):82–101.

Linteau, A. 1955. Forest site classification of the northeastern coniferous section, boreal forest region, Quebec. For. Br. Can. Bull. 118.78 p.

Linton, M., and P. S. Gallo, Jr. 1975. The practical statistician: simplified handbook of statistics. Brooks/Cole Publ. Co., Monterey, California. 384 p.

Lintz, J., Jr., and D. S. Simonett, (eds.). 1976. Remote sensing of environment. Addison-Wesley, Reading, Mass. 694 p.

Lion, K. S. 1959. Instrumentation in scientific research. McGraw-Hill Book Co., New York. 324 p.

Lisano, M. E., and J. E. Kennamer. 1977. Seasonal variations in plasma testosterone level in male eastern wild turkeys. J. Wildl. Manage. 41(2):184–188.

Liscinsky, S. A., G. P. Howard, and R. B. Waldeisen. 1969. A new device for injecting powdered drugs. J. Wildl. Manage. 33(4):1037–1038.

Lishak, R. S. 1976. A burrow entrance snare for capturing ground squirrels. J. Wildl. Manage. 40(2):364–365.

Little, A. D., Inc. 1967. Directory of selected research institutes in eastern Europe. Columbia Univ. Press, New York. 445 p.

Litvaitis, J. A., and W. W. Mautz. 1976. Energy utilization of three diets fed to a captive red fox. J. Wildl. Manage. 40(2):365–368.

Liversidge, R. 1970. Identification of grazed grasses using epidermal characters. Proc. Grassld. Soc. Sth. Afr. 5:153–165.

Llewellyn, L. M. 1953. Growth rate of the raccoon fetus. J. Wildl. Manage. 17(3):320–321.

Lloyd, M. 1964. Weighting individuals by reproductive value in calculating species diversity. Am. Nat. 98(900): 190–192.

Lloyd, M., J. H. Zar, and J. R. Karr. 1968. On the calculation of information-theoretical measure of diversity. Am. Midl. Nat. 79(2): 257–272.

Lobdell, C. H. 1972. MAST: a budget allocation system for wildlife management. Ph.D. Thesis. Va. Polytech. Inst. State Univ., Blacksburg. 227 p.

Lobdell, C. H., K. E. Case, and H. S. Mosby. 1972. Evaluation of harvest strategies for a simulated wild turkey population. J. Wildl. Manage. 36(2): 493–497.

Lockard, G. R. 1972. Further studies of dental annuli for aging white-tailed deer. J. Wildl. Manage. 36(1):46–55.

Lofgreen, G. P. 1965. A comparative slaughter technique for determining net energy values with beef cattle. p. 309–317 *in* K. L. Blaxter, (ed.). Energy metabolism. Academic Press, New York and London. 450 p.

Loftin, R. W., and R. D. Bowman. 1978. A device for measuring egg volume. Auk 95(1):190–192.

Logsdon, H. S. 1967. Preliminary results of administering drugs to desert bighorn sheep for capture purposes. Trans. Desert. Bighorn Council. 11:27–52.

Lokemoen, J. T. 1966. Breeding ecology of the redhead duck in western Montana. J. Wildl. Manage. 30(4): 668–681.

Lolley, J. L. 1974. Your library—What's in it for you? John Wiley and Sons, New York. 152 p.

Long, C. A. 1965. The mammals of Wyoming. Univ. Kansas Mus. Nat. Hist. 14(18):493–758.

Longhurst, W. M., M. B. Jones, R. R. Parks, L. W. Neubauer, and M. W. Cummings. 1962. Fences for controlling deer damage. Univ. Calif., Davis. Agric. Exp. Stn. Circ. 514. 15 p.

Longhurst, W. M., A. S. Leopold, and R. F. Dasmann. 1952. A survey of California deer herds, their ranges and management problems. Calif. Dept. Fish and Game Bull. No. 6. 136 p.

Longhurst, W. M., H. K. Oh, M. B. Jones, and R. E. Kepner. 1968. A basis for the palatability of deer forage plants. Trans. N. Am. Wildl. Nat. Resour. Conf. 33:181–192.

Loomis, F. D. 1975. Control of white-tailed deer in field and orchard. Proc. Great Plains Wildl. Damage Control Workshop 2:51–62.

Lord, R. D., Jr. 1957. Estimation of fox populations. Sci. D. Diss. John Hopkins Univ., Baltimore, Md. 87 p.

Lord, R. D., Jr., F. C. Bellrose, and W. W. Cochran. 1962. Radiotelemetry of the respiration of a flying duck. Science 137(3523):39–40.

Lord, R. D., and W. W. Cochran. 1963. Techniques in radiotracking wild animals. p. 149–154 *in* L. E. Slater, (ed.). Bio-telemetry: the use of telemetry in animal behavior and physiology in relation to ecological problems. The Macmillan Co., New York. 372 p.

Loring, J. A. 1946. "Squeaking" animals. Nature Mag. 39(8):430–432.

Lovaas, A. L. 1976. Introduction of prescribed burning to Wind Cave National Park. Wildl. Soc. Bull. 4(2):69–73.

Loveless, C. M., J. D. Coffelt, D. E. Medin, and L. E. Yeager. 1963. A photoelectric-cell device for use in wildlife research. AIBS Bull. 13 (4):55–57.

Loveless, C. M. G. N. Sarconi, J. W. DeGrazio, and C. H. Halvorson. 1966. A simplified data-recording method. J. Wildl. Manage. 30(3): 519–522.

Lovett, J. W., and E. P. Hill. 1977. A transmitter syringe for recovery of immobilized deer. J. Wildl. Manage. 41(2):313–315.

Low, J. B. 1941. Nesting of the ruddy duck in Iowa. Auk 58(4):506–517.

Low, J. B. 1945. Ecology and management of the redhead, *Nyroca americana*, in Iowa. Ecol. Monogr. 15(1):35–69.

Low, J. B., and C. Pierce. 1950. Wild ducks and geese—field to kitchen care. Utah Agric. Ext. Serv. Bull. 206, Logan. 8 p.

Low, S. H. 1935. Methods of trapping shorebirds. Bird-Banding 6(1):16–22.

Low, S. H. 1957. Banding with mist nets. Bird-Banding 28(3):115–128.

Lowe, C. E. 1958. Ecology of the swamp rabbit in Georgia. J. Mammal. 39(1):116–127.

Lowe, C. H., (ed.). 1964. The vertebrates of Arizona. Univ. Arizona Press, Tucson. 259 p.

Lowe, J. I. 1956. Breeding density and productivity of mourning doves on a county-wide basis in Georgia. J. Wildl. Manage. 20(4):428–433.

Lowery, G. H., Jr. 1974a. The mammals of Louisiana and its adjacent waters. Louisiana State Univ. Press, Baton Rouge. 565 p.

Lowery, G. H., Jr. 1974b. Louisiana birds. 3rd ed. Louisiana State Univ. Press, Baton Rouge. 651 p.

Lucas, F. A. 1950. The preparation of rough skeletons. Am. Mus. Nat. History, Sci. Guide No. 59. 20 p.

Ludwick, R. L., J. P. Fontenot, and H. S. Mosby. 1969. Energy metabolism of the eastern gray squirrel. J. Wildl. Manage. 33(3):569–575.

Ludwig, J., and D. E. Davis. 1975. An improved woodchuck trap. J. Wildl. Manage. 39(2):439–442.

Ludwig, J. R., and R. W. Dapson. 1977. Use of insoluble lens proteins to estimate age in white-tailed deer. J. Wildl. Manage. 41(2):327–329.

Lumsden, H. C., V. W. McMullen, and C. L. Hopkinson. 1977. An improvement of fabrication of large plastic leg bands. J. Wildl. Manage. 41(1):148–149.

Luow, J. G., H. H. Williams, and L. A. Maynard. 1949. A new method for the study *in vitro* of rumen digestion. Science 110 (2862):478–480.

Luttich, S. N., L. B. Keith, and J. D. Stephenson. 1971. Population dynamics of the red-tailed hawk *(Buteo jamaicensis)* at Rochester, Alberta. Auk 88(1):75–87.

Lydekker, R. 1898. The deer of all lands: a history of the family Cervidae living and extinct. Rowland Ward, London. 350 p.

Lyon, L. J. 1968a. An evaluation of density sampling methods in a shrub community. J. Range Manage. 21 (1):16–20.

Lyon, L. J. 1968b. Estimating twig production of serviceberry from crown volumes. J. Wildl. Manage. 32(1):115–119.

Lyon, L. J. 1970. Length- and weight-diameter relations of serviceberry twigs. J. Wildl. Manage. 34(2):456–460.

Lysaght, A., (ed.). 1959. Directory of natural history and other field study societies in Great Britain. British Assoc. Adv. Sci., London. 217 p.

MacArthur, R. H., and J. W. MacArthur. 1961. On bird species diversity. Ecology 42(3):594–598.

MacClintock, L., R. F. Whitcomb, and B. L. Whitcomb. 1977. Island biogeography and "habitat islands" of eastern forests. II. Evidence for the value of corridors and minimization of isolation in preservation of biotic diversity. Am. Birds 31(1):6–16.

MacConnell, W. P. 1957. Cover mapping Massachusetts from aerial photographs. Proc. Soc. Am. For., Syracuse, N.Y. p. 159–162.

MacDonald, D., and E. G. Dillman. 1968. Techniques for estimating non-statistical bias in big game harvest surveys. J. Wildl. Manage. 32(1):119–129.

Mace, R. U. 1971. Trapping and transplanting Roosevelt elk to control damage and establish new populations. Proc. Western Assoc. Game and Fish Commissioners 51:464–470.

MacGregor, W. G. 1950. The artificial roost—a new management tool for California quail. Calif. Fish and Game 36(3):316–319.

MacGregor, W. G. 1958. A technique for obtaining food habits material from nestling doves. Calif. Fish and Game 44(1):77–78.

MacInnes, C. D., R. A. Davis, R. N. Jones, B. C. Lieff, and A. J. Pakulak. 1974. Reproductive efficiency of McConnell River small Canada geese. J. Wildl. Manage. 38(4):686–707.

MacInnes, C. D., J. P. Prevett, and H. A. Edney. 1969. A versatile collar for individual identification of geese. J. Wildl. Manage. 33(2):330–335.

Mack, R. N., and D. A. Pyke. 1979. Mapping individual plants with a field-portable digitizer. Ecology 60(3):459–461.

Mackay, R. S. 1970. Bio-medical telemetry. 2nd ed. John Wiley and Sons, New York. 533 p.

Mackworth-Praed, C. W., and C. H. B. Grant. 1957. Birds of eastern and north eastern Africa. 2nd ed. Longmans Green & Co., London. 2 vol.

Mackworth-Praed, C. W., and C. H. B. Grant. 1973. Birds of west central and western Africa. Longman Ltd., London. 2 vol.

MacLennan, J. M., (comp.). 1958. Russian-English bird glossary. Queen's Printer and Controller of Stationery, Ottawa, Canada. 94 p.

Madsen, R. M. 1967. Age determination of wildlife, a bibliography. U.S. Dept. Inter. Libr. Bibliogr. No. 2 Washington, D.C. 111 p.

Magruder, N. D., C. E. French, L. C. McEwen, and R. W. Swift. 1957. Nutritional requirements of white-tailed deer for growth and antler development. II. Pa. Agric. Exp. Stn. Bull. No. 628. 21 p.

Mahoney, R. 1966. Laboratory techniques in zoology. Butterworths, London. 404 p.

Maine Department of Inland Fisheries and Wildlife. 1975. Comprehensive fish and wildlife plan for Maine. Fed. Aid to-Wildl. Restoration Proj. Proposal, Augusta. 88 p.

Maizell, R. E., J. F. Smith, and T. E. R. Singer. 1971. Abstracting scientific and technical literature: an introductory guide and text for scientists, abstractors and management. Wiley-Interscience, New York. 297 p.

Makepeace, L. I. 1956. Rabbits: a subject bibliography. Denver Public Libr., Bibliogr. Cent. for Res., Rocky Mountain Region, Spec. Bibliogr. No. 3. 81 p.

Maki, D. P., and M. Thompson. 1973. Mathematical models and applications. Prentice Hall, Englewood Cliffs, N.J. 492 p.

Malclés, L. N. 1958. Les sources du travail bibliographique spécialisees: sciences exactes et techniques. Tome III. Librarie E. Droz, Geneva. 575 p.

Maltby, L. S. 1977. Techniques used for the capture, handling and marking of brant in the Canadian High Arctic. Can. Wildl. Serv. Progress Notes. No. 72, Ottawa. 6 p.

Mangold, R. E. 1974. Clapper rail studies. Final Rep. Res. on Shore and Upland Migratory Birds in New Jersey. N.J. Div. Fish, Game and Shellfisheries, Trenton. 17 p.

Manly, B. F. J. 1971. A simulation study of Jolly's method for analysing capture-recapture data. Biometrics 27(2):415–424.

Manning, T. H. 1964. Age determination in the polar bear. Can. Wildl. Serv. Occas. Pap. No. 5, Ottawa. 12 p.

Mansell, W. D. 1971. Accessory corpora lutea in ovaries of white-tailed deer. J. Wildl. Manage. 35(2):369–374.

Mansfield, A. W. 1958. The biology of the Atlantic walrus *Odobenus rosmarus rosmarus* (Linnaeus) in the eastern Canadian Arctic. Fish Res. Board Can. Manuscr. Rep. Ser. No. 653. 13 + 146.

Mapston, R. D., and R. S. ZoBell. 1972. Antelope passes their value and use. USDI Bur. Land Manage. Tech. Note D–360, Portland, Oreg. 11 p.

March, G. L., and R. M. F. S. Sadleir. 1970. Studies on the band-tailed pigeon *(Columba fasciata)* in British Columbia. 1. Seasonal changes in gonadal development and crop gland activity. Can. J. Zool. 48(6):1353–1357.

Marchinton, R. L. 1964. Activity cycles and mobility of central Florida deer based on telemetric and observational data. M.S. Thesis. Univ. Florida, Gainesville. 101 p.

Marchinton, R. L., A. S. Johnson, J. R. Sweeney, and J. M. Sweeney. 1970. Legal hunting of white-tailed deer with dogs: biology, sociology and management. Proc. Southeastern Assoc. Game and Fish Commissioners 25:74–89.

Mares, M. A., and D. F. Williams. 1977. Experimental support for food particle size resource allocation in heteromyid rodents. Ecology 58 (5):1186–1190.

Margalef, D. R. 1958. Information theory in ecology. Gen. Syst. 3:36–71.

Marion, W. R., and J. D. Shamis. 1977. An annotated bibliography of bird marking techniques. Bird-Banding 48(1):42–61.

Markowitz, H., and V. Stevens, (eds.). 1978. Behavior of captive wild animals. Nelson-Hall Inc., Chicago. 320 p.

Marks and Clerk. 1971. Bullet for immobilization of animals. Patent Specification, 25 Southamptom Bldg., London. 4 p.

Marlow, B. J. 1956. Chloral hydrate narcosis for the live capture of mammals. C.S.I.R.O. Wildl. Res. 1(1):63–65.

Marples, B. J., and L. Gurr. 1943. A mechanism for recording automatically the nesting habits of birds. Emu 43:67–71.

Marquardt, R. E. 1960a. Smokeless powder cannon with lightweight netting for trapping geese. J. Wildl. Manage. 24(4):425–427.

Marquardt, R. E. 1960b. Investigations into high intensity projectile equipment for net trapping geese. Proc. Oklahoma Acad. Sci. 41:218–223.

Marshall, A. J., (ed.). 1960. Biology and comparative physiology of birds. Academic Press, New York and London. Vol. 1 & 2. 518 p. and 468 p.

Marshall, C. M., J. F. Smith, and A. J. Weber. 1964. A simple technique for removing mandibles of deer without trophy defacement. Proc. Southeastern Assoc. Game and Fish Commissioners 18:137–140.

Marshall, J. T. 1977. Audiospectrograms with pitch scale: a universal "language" for representing bird songs graphically. Auk 94(1):150–152.

Marshall, W. H. 1951. An age determination method for the pine marten. J. Wildl. Manage. 15(3):276–283.

Marshall, W. H., and J. J. Kupa. 1963. Development of radio-telemetry techniques for ruffed grouse studies. Trans. N. Am. Wildl. Nat Resour. Conf. 28:443–456.

Martel, G. F., and R. T. Lackey. 1977. A computerized method for abstracting and evaluating environmental impact statements. Virg. Water Resour. Res. Center. Bull. 105. 93 p.

Martin, A. C. 1946. The comparative internal morphology of seeds. Am. Midl. Nat. 36(3):513–660.

Martin, A. C. 1949. Procedures in wildlife food studies. USDI Wildl. Leafl. No. 325. 10 p.

Martin, A. C. 1960. Food-habits procedures. p. 13:1–13:9 *in* Manual of game investigational techniques. The Wildl. Soc., Washington, D.C.

Martin, A. C., and W. D. Barkley. 1961. Seed identification manual. Univ. of Calif. Press, Berkeley. 221 p.

Martin, A. C., R. H. Gensch, and C. P. Brown. 1946. Alternative methods in upland gamebird food analysis. J. Wildl. Manage. 10(1):8–12.

Martin, A. C., H. S. Zim, and A. L. Nelson. 1951. American wildlife and plants. McGraw-Hill Book Co., New York. 500 p.

Martin, D-J. 1955. Features of plant cuticles. An aid to the analysis of the natural diet of grazing animals, with especial reference to Scottish hill sheep. Proc. Bot. Soc. Edinb. 36: 278–288.

Martin, F. W. 1964. Woodcock age and sex determination from wings. J. Wildl. Manage. 28(2):287–293.

Martin, J. 1977. Computer data base organization. Prentice-Hall Inc. 713 p.

Martin, K. H., R. A. Stehn, and M. E. Richmond. 1976. Reliability of placental scar counts in the prairie vole. J. Wildl. Manage. 40(2):264–271.

Martin, L. M., and J. R. Bider. 1978. A transmitter attachment for blackbirds. J. Wildl. Manage. 42(3):683–685.

Martin, R. L. 1960. Foreign scientific literature in translation. Am. Doc. 11(2):135–150.

Martin, S. G. 1969. A technique for capturing nesting grassland birds with mist nets. Bird-Banding 40(3):233–237.

Martinka, C. J. 1967. Mortality of northern Montana pronghorn in a severe winter. J. Wildl. Manage. 31(1):159–164.

Martinson, R. K., and D. E. Whitesell. 1964. Biases in a mail questionnaire survey of upland game hunters. Trans. N. Am. Wildl. Nat. Resour. Conf. 29:287–294.

Maryland Game and Inland Fish Commission. 1966. Tire nests for squirrels. Annapolis. 6 p.

Maser, C., R. G. Anderson, K. Cromack, Jr., J. T. Williams, and R. E. Martin. 1979a. Dead and down woody material. p. 78–95 *in* J. W. Thomas, (ed.). Wildlife habitats in managed forests—the Blue Mountains of Oregon and Washington. USDA For. Serv. Agric. Handb. No. 553. 512 p.

Maser, C., J. E. Rodiek, and J. W. Thomas. 1979b. Cliffs, talus, and caves. p. 96–103 *in* J. W. Thomas, (ed.). Wildlife habitats in managed forests—the Blue Mountains of Oregon and Washington. USDA For. Serv. Agric. Handb. No. 553. 512 p.

Masters, R. 1978. Deer trapping, marking and telemetry techniques. State Univ. New York Coll. Environ. Sci. For., Adirondack Ecol. Cent. Newcomb, N.Y. 72 p.

Mathiak, H. A. 1938a. A rapid method of cross-sectioning mammalian hairs. J. Wildl. Manage. 2(3): 162–164.

Mathiak, H. A. 1938b. A key to hairs of the mammals of southern Michigan. J. Wildl. Manage. 2(4): 251–268.

Mathiak, H. A. 1965. Pothole blasting for wildlife. Wis. Conserv. Dept. Publ. No. 352, Madison. 31 p.

Mathiak, H. A., and A. F. Linde. 1956. Studies on level ditching for marsh management. Wis. Conserv. Dept. Tech. Wildl. Bull. No. 12, Madison. 48 p.

Mattfeld, G. F. 1973. The effect of snow on the energy expenditure of walking white-tailed deer. Trans. Northeast Sect. Wildl. Soc., Fish Wildl. Conf. 30:327–343.

Mattfeld, G. F., J. E. Wiley, and D. F. Behrend. 1972. Salt versus browse—seasonal baits for deer trapping. J. Wildl. Manage. 36(3):996–998.

Matthiessen, P. 1959. Wildlife in America. Viking Press, New York. 304 p.

Mautz, W. W. 1971. Confinement effects in dry-matter digestibility coefficients displayed by deer. J. Wildl. Manage. 35(2):366–368.

Mautz, W. W. 1978. Sledding on a bushy hillside: the fat cycle in deer. Wildl. Soc. Bull. 6(2):88–90.

Mautz, W. W., R. P. Davison, C. E. Boardman, and H. Silver. 1974. Restraining apparatus for obtaining blood samples from white-tailed deer. J. Wildl. Manage. 38(4):845–847.

Mautz, W. W., and G. A. Petrides. 1971. Food passage rate in white-tailed deer. J. Wildl. Manage. 35(4):723–731.

Mautz, W. W., H. Silver, and H. H. Hayes. 1975. Estimating methane, urine, and heat increment for deer consuming browse. J. Wildl. Manage. 39(1):80–86.

Mautz, W. W., H. Silver, J. B. Holter, H. H. Hayes, and W. E. Urban, Jr. 1976. Digestibility and related nutritional data for seven northern deer browse species. J. Wildl. Manage. 40(4):630–638.

Mayer, W. V. 1952. The hair of California mammals with keys to the dorsal guard hairs of California mammals. Am. Midl. Nat. 48(2):480–512.

Mayer, W. V. 1957. A method for determining the activity of burrowing mammals. J. Mammal. 38(4):531.

Maynard, L. A., and J. K. Loosli. 1969. Animal nutrition. 6th ed. McGraw-Hill Book Co., New York. 613 p.

Maynard Smith, J. 1974. Models in ecology. Cambridge Univ. Press. 146 p.

Mayr, E., and D. Amadon. 1951. A classification of recent birds. Am. Mus. Novit. No. 1496. 42 p.

Mayr, E., E. G. Linsley, and R. L. Usinger. 1953. Methods and principles of systematic zoology. McGraw-Hill Book Co., New York. 328 p.

McAtee, W. L. 1908. Food habits of the grosbeaks. USDA Biol. Surv. Bull. No. 32. 92 p.

McAtee, W. L. 1911. Woodpeckers in relation to trees and wood products. USDA Biol. Surv. Bull. No. 39. 99 p.

McAtee, W. L. 1912. Methods of estimating the contents of bird stomachs. Auk 29(4):449–464.

McAtee, W. L. 1933. Economic ornithology. p. 111–129 *in* Fifty years progress of American ornithology. Am. Ornithol. Union, Lancaster, Pa. 249 p.

McAtee, W. L. 1941. Plants useful in upland wildlife management. USDI Fish Wildl. Serv. Conserv. Bull. 7. 50 p.

McAtee, W. L., (ed.), 1945. The ring-necked pheasant and its management in North America. Am. Wildl. Inst., Washington, D.C. 320 p.

McAtee, W. L., and S. E. Piper. 1936. Excluding birds from reservoirs and fish ponds. USDA Bur. of Biol. Surv. Leafl. No. 120. 6 p.

McCabe, R. A. 1974. Radioactive calcium (Ca^{45}) as a wildlife marker. Trans. Int. Congr. Game Biol. 11:511–524.

McCabe, R. A., and A. S. Hawkins. 1946. The Hungarian partridge in Wisconsin. Am. Midl. Nat. 36(1):1–75.

McCabe, R. A., and G. A. LePage. 1958. Identifying progeny from pheasant hens given radioactive calcium (Ca^{45}). J. Wildl. Manage. 22(2):134–141.

McCaffery, K. R. 1973. Road-kills show trends in Wisconsin deer populations. J. Wildl. Manage. 37(2):212–216.

McCaffery, K. R. 1976. Deer trail counts as an index to population and habitat use. J. Wildl. Manage. 40(2):308–316.

McCaffery, K. R., L. D. Martoglio, and F. L. Johnson. 1974a. Maintaining wildlife openings with picloram pellets. Wildl. Soc. Bull. 2(2):40–45.

McCaffery, K. R., J. Tranetzki, and J. Piechura. 1974b. Summer foods of deer in northern Wisconsin. J. Wildl. Manage. 38(2):215–219.

McCall, J. D. 1954. Portable live trap for ducks, with improved gathering box. J. Wildl. Manage. 18(3):405–407.

McCall, J. D. 1979. The home-range scale; a tool for wildlife habitat assessment. Wildl. Soc. Bull. 7(2): 118–120.

McCloskey, R. J. 1977. Accuracy of criteria used to determine age of fox squirrels. Proc. Iowa Acad. Sci. 84(1):32–34.

M'Closkey, R. T. 1972. Temporal changes in populations and species diversity in a California rodent community. J. Mammal. 53(4):657–676.

McClure, H. E. 1956. Methods of bird netting in Japan applicable to wildlife management problems. Bird-Banding 27(2):67–73.

McCormick, J. A. 1958. Radioisotopes in animal physiology: a selected list of references. USAEC Tech. Inf. Ser. TID-3515, Oak Ridge, Tenn. 118 p.

McCourt, K. H., and D. M. Keppie. 1975. Age determination of juvenile spruce grouse. J. Wildl. Manage. 39(4):790–794.

McCracken, H., and H. Van Cleve. 1947. Trapping: the craft and science of catching fur-bearing animals. Barnes Co., New York. 196 p.

McCulloch, J. S. G., and L. M. Talbot. 1965. Comparisons of weight estimation methods for wild animals and domestic livestock. J. Appl. Ecol. 2(1):59–69.

McCullough, D. R. 1965. Sex characteristics of black-tailed deer hooves. J. Wildl. Manage. 29(1):210–212.

McCullough, D. R. 1975. Modification of the Clover deer trap. Calif. Fish and Game. 61(4):242–244.

McCutchen, H. E. 1969. Age determination of pronghorns by the incisor cementum. J. Wildl. Manage. 33(1): 172–175.

McDonald, I. W., and A. C. I. Warner, (ed.). 1975. Digestion and metabolism in the ruminant. Proc. IV Int. Symp. Ruminant Physiol. Univ. of New England Publ. Unit, Armidale, N.S.W., 2351, Australia. 602 p.

McDonald, P., R. A. Edwards, and J. F. D. Greenhalgh. 1973. Animal nutrition. 2nd ed. Hafner Publ. Co., New York. 479 p.

McDowell, R. D. 1956. Productivity of the wild turkey in Virginia. Virginia Comm. Game and Inland Fish. Tech. Bull. No. 1, Richmond. 44 p.

McDowell, R. D. 1972. Attracting birds. Coll. Nat. Resour. Coop. Ext. Serv. Univ. Connecticut, Storrs. 10 p.

McEwan, E. H. 1970. Energy metabolism of barren ground caribou (*Rangifer tarandus*). Can. J. Zool. 48(2): 391–392.

McEwan, E. H., and A. J. Wood. 1966. Growth and development of the barren ground caribou. I. Heart girth, hind foot length, and body weight relationships. Can. J. Zool. 44(3): 401–411.

McEwen, L. D., and D. R. Dietz. 1965. Shade effects on chemical composition of herbage in the Black Hills. J. Range Manage. 18(4):184–190.

McGilvrey, F. B., and F. M. Uhler. 1971. A starling-deterrent wood duck nest box. J. Wildl. Manage. 35(4):793–797.

McGrady, E., Jr. 1938. The embryology of the opossum. Am. Anat. Mem. 16:233.

McHugh, T. 1972. The time of the buffalo. Alfred A. Knopf Inc., New York. 339 p.

McKinley, D. 1960. A chronology and bibliography of wildlife in Missouri. Univ. Missouri Bull. 61(13):1–128.

McKinley, P., B. Dowell, and W. M. Schleidt. 1976. Wireless microphone for studies of animal vocalizations. Experientia 32:132–133.

McLaughlin, C. L., and D. Grice. 1952. The effectiveness of large scale erection of wood duck boxes as a management procedure. Trans. N. Am. Wildl. Conf. 17:242–259.

McLeod, J. 1974. How to simulate. Simulation 6:vii–x.

McLeod, W. M., D. M. Trotter, and J. W. Lumb. 1964. Avian anatomy. Burgess Publ. Co., Minneapolis, Minn. 143 p.

McMillan, I. 1959. An improved quail roost. Cent. Calif. Sportsman 19 (10):349.

McMillin, J. M., U. S. Seal, K. D. Keenlyne, A. W. Erickson, and J. E. Jones. 1974. Annual testosterone rhythm in the adult white-tailed deer (*Odocoileus virginianus borealis*). Endocrinol. 94(4):1034–1040.

McQuivey, R. P. 1978. The desert bighorn sheep of Nevada. Nev. Dept. Fish and Game Biol. Bull. No. 6, Reno. 81 p.

McVaugh, R., R. Ross, and F. A. Stafleu. 1968. An annotated glossary of botanical nomenclature, with special reference to the international code of botanical nomenclature as adopted by the 10th International Botanical Congress at Edinburgh, 1964. Regnum vegetabile, Vol. 56. 31 p.

Mead, R. A. 1967. Age determination in the spotted skunk. J. Mammal. 48(4):606–616.

Meagher, M. M. 1973. Bison of Yellowstone National Park. U.S. Natl. Park Serv. Sci. Monogr. Ser. No. 1. 161 p.

Meanley, B. 1969. Natural history of the king rail. U. S. Fish Wildl. Serv., N. Am. Fauna. No. 67. 108 p.

Meanley, B. 1971. Blackbirds and the southern rice crop. U. S. Fish Wildl. Serv. Resour. Publ. 100. 64 p.

Mech, L. D. 1967. Telemetry as a technique in the study of predation. J. Wildl. Manage. 31(3):492–496.

Mech, L. D. 1970. The wolf: the ecology and behavior of an endangered species. The Nat. Hist. Press, Garden City, N.Y. 384 p.

Mech, L. D. 1974. Current techniques in the study of elusive wilderness carnivores. Trans. Int. Congr. Game Biol. 11:315–322.

Mechlin, L. M., and C. W. Shaiffer. 1979. Net firing gun for capturing breeding waterfowl. U. S. Fish and Wildl. Serv. N. Prairie Wildl. Res. Center, Jamestown, N. D. 14 p.

Medin, D. E. 1970. Stomach content analyses: collections from wild herbivores and birds. p. 133–145 *in* Range and wildlife habitat evaluation—a research symposium. USDA Misc. Publ. No. 1147. 220 p.

Meeks, R. L. 1968. The accumulation of ^{36}Cl ring-labeled DDT in a freshwater marsh. J. Wildl. Manage. 32(2):376–398.

Meeks, R. L. 1969. The effect of drawdown date on wetland plant succession. J. Wildl. Manage. 33(4):817–821.

Meisel, M. 1924–1929. A bibliography of American natural history: the pioneer century, 1769–1865. The Premier Publ. Co., New York. 3 vol.

Melchior, H. R., and F. A. Iwen. 1965. Trapping, restraining, and marking Arctic ground squirrels for behavioral observations. J. Wildl. Manage. 29(4):671–678.

Mellace, D. R., R. L. Kirkpatrick, and P. F. Scanlon. 1973. Reproductive examination of gray squirrels by laparatomy. Proc. Southeastern Assoc. Game and Fish Commissioners 27:342.

Mendall, H. L. 1938. A technique for banding woodcock. Bird-Banding 9(3):153–155.

Mendall, H. L. 1958. The ring-necked duck in the Northeast. Univ. of Maine Bull. 60(16):1–317.

Mendall, H. L., and C. M. Aldous, 1943. The ecology and management of the American woodcock. Maine Coop. Wildl. Res. Unit, Orono. 201 p.

Meng, H. 1971. The Swedish goshawk trap. J. Wildl. Manage. 35(4):832–835.

Mentis, M. T. 1977. Stocking rates and carrying capacities for ungulates on African rangelands. S. Afr. J. Wildl. Res. 7(2):89–98.

Merchant, J. W., and B. H. Waddell. 1974. The use of high altitude photography and ERTS-1 imagery for wildlife habitat inventory in Kansas. p. 220–231 *in* Proc. Am. Soc. Photogramm. Fall Convention, Washington, D. C.

Merriam, H. 1962. Immobilization technique for Sitka black-tail deer in southeast Alaska. Alaska Dept. Fish and Game Inf. Leafl. No. 18. 6 p.

Merriam, H. G. 1963. Low frequency telemetric monitoring of woodchuck movements. p. 155–171 *in* L. E. Slater, (ed.). Bio-telemetry: the use of telemetry in animal behavior and physiology in relation to ecological problems. The Macmillan Co., New York. 372 p.

Merrill, H. A. 1953. Muskrats. U. S. Fish Wildl. Serv., Washington, D. C. 2 p.

Mess, C. E. K. 1951. Photography. Macmillan Co., New York. 227 p.

Messner, H. E., D. R. Dietz, and E. C. Garrett. 1973. A modification of the slanting deer fence. J. Range Manage. 26(3):233–235.

Metcalfe, C. R. 1960. Anatomy of the monocotyledons. I. Gramineae. Clarendon Press, Oxford. 650 p.

Metcalfe, C. R., and L. Chalk. 1950. Anatomy of the dicotyledons. Clarendon Press, Oxford. Vols. I and II. 1500 p.

Meyer, M. P. 1976. A feasibility study of 35 mm CIR aerial photography applications for monitoring change in 600-foot BLM range resource transects in Montana. Univ. of Minnesota Inst. Agric. For. and Home Econ. Remote Sensing Lab. Res. Rep. 76–6, St. Paul, Minn. 11 p.

Meyer, M. P., R. L. Eng, and F. N. Gjersing. 1974. Waterfowl management using color IR. Photogramm. Eng. 40(2):165–168.

Meyer, M. P., and P. D. Grumstrup. 1978. Operating manual for the Montana 35 mm aerial photography system. 2nd rev. Univ. of Minnesota Inst. Agric. For. and Home Econ. Remote Sensing Lab. Res. Rep 78–1, St. Paul, Minn. 62 p.

Meyer, P. A. 1975. A comparison of direct questioning methods for obtaining dollar values for public recreation and preservation. Environ. Can. Fish. and Mar. Serv. Tech. Rep. Ser. No. PAC/T–75–6, Southern Oper. Branch Pac. Reg. 20 p.

Michener, M. C., and C. Walcott. 1966. Navigation of single homing pigeons: airplane observations by radio tracking. Science 154(3747): 410–413.

Mickelson, P. G. 1973. Breeding biology of cackling geese *(Branta canadensis minima* Ridgway) and associated species on the Yukon-Kuskokwim Delta, Alaska. Ph.D. Thesis. Univ. of Michigan, Ann Arbor. 246 p.

Middleton, A. D. 1935. Factors controlling the population of the partridge *(Perdix perdix)* in Great Britain. Proc. Zool. Soc. London. p. 795–815.

Milchunas, D. G., M. I. Dyer, O. C. Wallmo, and D. E. Johnson. 1978. *In vivo/in vitro* relationships of Colorado mule deer forages. Colorado Div. Wildl. Spec. Rep. No. 43. 44 p.

Millais, J. G. 1897. British deer and their horns. Henry Sotheran and Co., London. 224 p.

Millar, J. B. 1973. Estimation of area and circumference of small wetlands. J. Wildl. Manage. 37(1):30–38.

Millar, J. S., and F. C. Zwickel. 1972. Determination of age, age structure, and mortality of the pika, *Ochotona princeps* (Richardson). Can. J. Zool. 50(2):229–232.

Millard, P. 1968. Directory of technical and scientific translators and services. Archon Books, Hamden, Conn. 136 p.

Miller, A. W., and P. H. Arend. 1960. How to grow watergrass for ducks in California. Calif. Dept. Fish and Game, Game Manage. Leafl. No. 1, Sacramento. 16 p.

Miller, A. W., and B. D. Collins. 1953. A nesting study of Canada geese on Tule Lake and Lower Klamath National Wildlife Refuges, Siskiyou County, California. Calif. Fish and Game 39(3):385–396.

Miller, A. W., and B. D. Collins. 1954. A nesting study of ducks and coots on Tule Lake and Lower Klamath National Wildlife Refuges. Calif. Fish and Game 40(1):17–37.

Miller, C. W. 1942. Principles of photographic reproduction. Macmillan Co., New York. 353 p.

Miller, D. R., C. Maguire, and E. Heiman. 1965. An economical, portable intercommunication system for aerial surveys and reconnaissance. J. Wildl. Manage. 29(4):896–898.

Miller, D. R., and J. D. Robertson. 1967. Results of tagging caribou at Little Duck Lake, Manitoba. J. Wildl. Manage. 31(1):150–159.

Miller, F. L. 1968. Immobilization of free-ranging black-tailed deer with succinylcholine chloride. J. Wildl. Manage. 32(1):195–197.

Miller, F. L. 1974a. Age determination of caribou by annulations in dental cementum. J. Wildl. Manage. 38(1):47–53.

Miller, F. L. 1974b. Biology of the Kaminuriak population of barren-ground caribou. Part II. Can. Wildl. Serv. Rep. Ser. No. 31. 88 p.

Miller, G. 1978. Canadian Wildlife Service studies in Canada's national parks: a bibliography. Can. Wildl. Serv., Edmonton. 179 p.

Miller, G. S., Jr., and R. Kellogg. 1955. List of North American recent mammals. U. S. Natl. Mus. Bull. 205. 954 p.

Miller, H. A., and L. K. Halls. 1969. Fleshy fungi commonly eaten by southern wildlife. USDA For. Serv. Res. Pap. SO–40, Southeastern For. Exp. Stn., New Orleans, La. 28 p.

Miller, H. W. 1957. A modified cannon for use on the projected net trap. Unnumbered pamphlet dist. by Neb. Game, Forestation, and Parks Commission. Bassett. 6 p.

Miller, H. W., and D. H. Johnson. 1978. Interpreting the results of nesting studies. J. Wildl. Manage. 42(3):471–476.

Miller, J. A. 1977. Getting warm. Sci. News 111(3): 42–43.

Miller, W. R. 1962. Automatic activating mechanism for waterfowl nest trap. J. Wildl. Manage. 26(4):402–404.

Milne, L. J., and M. Milne. 1959. Foresight and hindsight on a punch-card bibliography. Am. Doc. 10(1): 78–84.

Mineau, P., and D. Madison. 1977. Radio-tracking of *Peromyscus leucopus*. Can. J. Zool. 55(2):465–468.

Miner, N. R. 1975. Montana golden eagle removal and translocation project. Proc. Great Plains Wildl. Damage Control Workshop 2:155–162.

Mirarchi, R. E. 1978. Crop-gland persistance, parental care and reproductive physiology of the mourning dove in Virginia. Ph.D. Diss. Virginia Polytechnic Inst. and State Univ., Blacksburg. 249 p.

Mirarchi, R. E., P. F. Scanlon, and R. L. Kirkpatrick. 1977a. Annual changes in spermatozoan production and associated organs of white-tailed deer. J. Wildl. Manage. 41(1):92–99.

Mirarchi, R. E., P. F. Scanlon, R. L. Kirkpatrick, and C. B. Schreck. 1977b. Androgen levels and antler development in captive and wild white-tailed deer. J. Wildl. Manage. 41(2):178–183.

Mirov, N. T., and C. J. Kraebel. 1939. Collecting and handling seeds of wild plants. USDA For. Serv. Civ. Conserv. Corps For. Publ. 5, Calif. For. and Range Exp. Stn. 42 p.

Mitchell, G. J. 1971. Measurement, weights, and carcass yields of pronghorns in Alberta. J. Wildl. Manage. 35(1):76–85.

Mitchell, O. G., and R. A. Carsen. 1967. Tooth eruption in the Arctic ground squirrel. J. Mammal. 48(3): 472–474.

Mitchell, R. T. 1963. The floodlight trap/a device for capturing large numbers of blackbirds and starlings at roosts. U.S. Fish and Wildl. Serv. Spec. Sci. Rep. Wildl. No. 77. 14 p.

Mitchell, R. T., and J. T. Linehan. 1967. Protecting corn from blackbirds. U. S. Fish Wild. Serv. Wildl. Leafl. 476. 8 p.

Mittwoch, U. 1963. Sex differences in cells. Sci. Am. 209(1):54–62.

Moen, A. N. 1968a. Energy balance of white-tailed deer in the winter. Trans. N. Am. Wildl. Nat. Resour. Conf. 33:224–236.

Moen, A. N. 1968b. The critical thermal environment: a new look at an old concept. Biol. Sci. 78(11):1041–1043.

Moen, A. N. 1973. Wildlife ecology: an analytical approach. W. H. Freeman and Co., San Francisco. 458 p.

Moen, A. N. 1976. Energy conservation by white-tailed deer in the winter. Ecology 57(1):192–198.

Moessner, K. E. 1963. Why not use blueprints? USDA For. Serv. Intermt. For. Range Exp. Stn. Res. Note INT-4. Ogden, Utah. 2 p.

Moffitt, J. 1942. Apparatus for marking wild animals with colored dyes. J. Wildl. Manage. 6(4):312–318.

Moir, R. J. 1965. The comparative physiology of ruminant-like animals. p. 1–14 *in* R. W. Dougherty, R. S. Allen, W. Burroughs, N. L. Jacobson and A. D. McGilliard, (eds.). Physiology of digestion in the ruminant. Butterworth Inc., Washington, D. C. 480 p.

Monson, R. A., W. B. Stone, and E. Parks. 1973. Aging red foxes *(Vulpes fulva)* by counting the annular cementum rings of their teeth. N. Y. Fish and Game J. 20(1):54–61.

Montgomery, G. G. 1963. Freezing, decomposition, and raccoon lens weights. J. Wildl. Manage. 27(3): 481–483.

Montgomery, G. G. 1964. Tooth eruption in the preweaned raccoons. J. Wildl. Manage. 28(3):582–584.

Montgomery, G. G., W. W. Cochran, and M. E. Sunquist, 1973. Radiolocating arboreal vertebrates in tropical forest. J. Wildl. Manage. 37(3): 426–428.

Montgomery, G. G., and R. E. Hawkins. 1967. Diazepam bait for the capture of whitetail deer. J. Wildl. Manage. 31(3):464–468.

Montgomery, S. J., D. F. Balph, and D. M. Balph. 1971. Age determination of Uinta ground squirrels by teeth annuli. Southwestern Nat. 15(3):400–402.

Moody, D. T. 1970. A method for obtaining food samples from insectivorous birds. Auk 87(3):579.

Moore, A. M., and E. O. Kluth. 1966. A low frequency radiolocation system for monitoring an armadillo population. Proc. Natl. Telem. Conf. 302–304.

Moore, A. W. 1943. The pocket gopher in relation to yellow pine reproduction. J. Mammal. 24(2):271–272.

Moore, J. L. 1970. Bibliography of wildlife theses, 1900–1968. Biol. Inf. Serv., Los Angeles. 579 p.

Moore, J. L. 1972a. A history of bibliographic control of American doctoral dissertations. Spec. Libr. 63(5/6):227–230.

Moore, J. L. 1972b. An analysis of bibliographic control of American doctoral dissertations. Spec. Libr. 63(7): 285–291.

Moore, K. L., (ed.). 1966. The sex chromatin. W. B. Saunders Co., Philadelphia. 474 p.

Moore, T. D., L. E. Spence, and C. E. Dugnolle. 1974. Identification of the dorsal guard hairs of some mammals of Wyoming. Wyoming Game and Fish Dept., Cheyenne. 177 p.

Moore, W. G., and R. L. Marchinton. 1971. Marking behavior and its social function in white-tailed deer. p. 447–456 *in* V. Geist and F. Walther, (eds.). The behavior of ungulates and its relation to management. IUCN Publ. Ser. No. 24, Vol. 1. 511 p.

Morgan, A. H. 1939. Field book of animals in winter. G. P. Putnam's Sons, New York. 528 p.

Morgenweck, R. O., and W. H. Marshall. 1977. Wing marker for American woodcock. Bird-Banding 48(3): 224–227.

Morris, D. 1965. The mammals: a guide to the living species. Harper and Row, New York. 448 p.

Morris, M. J. 1967. An abstract bibliography of statistical methods in grassland research. USDA Misc. Publ. 1030. 222 p.

Morris, P. 1972. A review of mammalian age determination methods. Mammal. Rev. 2(3):69–104.

Morris, W. T. 1967. On the art of modeling. Management Science 13(12): B-707–717.

Morrisey, G. L. 1977. Management by objectives and results for business and industry. 2nd ed. Addison-Wesley Publ. Co., Reading, Mass. 252 p.

Morrison, J. A., C. E. Trainer, and P. L. Wright. 1959. Breeding season in elk as determined from known-age embryos. J. Wildl. Manage. 23(1):27–34.

Morrow, J. L., and D. H. Taylor. 1976. A telemetry system for recording heart rates of unrestrained game birds. J. Wildl. Manage. 40(2):359–360.

Morse, M. A., and D. S. Balser. 1961. Fox calling as a hunting technique. J. Wildl. Manage. 25(2):148–154.

Morse, T. E., J. L. Jakabosky, and V. P. McCrow. 1969. Some aspects of the breeding biology of the hooded merganser. J. Wildl. Manage. 33 (3):596–604.

Morton, M. L. 1965. An apparatus for continuous recording of food intake in caged birds. Ecology 46(6):888–890.

Mosby, H. S. 1955. Live trapping objectionable animals. Va. Poly. Inst. Agric. Ext. Serv. Circ. 667, Blacksburg. 4 p.

Mosby, H. S. 1963a. Wildlife investigational techniques. 2nd ed. The Wildl. Soc., Washington, D.C. 419 p.

Mosby, H. S., (ed.). 1963b. Using wildlife literature. p. 334–341 *in* H. S. Mosby, (ed.). Wildlife investigational techniques. 2nd ed. The Wildl. Soc., Washington, D.C. 419 p.

Mosby, H. S. 1963c. Reporting research results. p. 342–354 *in* H. S. Mosby, (ed.). Wildlife investigational techniques. 2nd ed. The Wildl. Soc., Washington, D.C. 419 p.

Mosby, H. S. 1969. The influence of hunting on the population dynamics of a woodlot gray squirrel population. J. Wildl. Manage. 33(1):59–73.

Mosby, H. S., and C. O. Handley. 1943. The wild turkey in Virginia: its status, life history, and management. Va. Comm. Game and Inland Fish., Richmond. 281 p.

Mosby, H. S., and W. S. Overton. 1950. Fluctuations in the quail population on the Virginia Polytechnic Institute Farms. Trans. N. Am. Wildl. Conf. 15:347–355.

Moseley, L. J., and H. C. Mueller. 1975. A device for color-marking nesting birds. Bird-Banding 46(4): 341–342.

Mossman, A. S. 1960. A color marking technique. J. Wildl. Manage. 24 (1):104.

Mossman, H. W., and K. L. Duke. 1973. Comparative morphology of the mammalian ovary. Univ. of Wisconsin Press, Madison. 461 p.

Mott, D. F. 1975. Cultural and physical methods for managing problem birds. Proc. Great Plains Wildl. Damage Control Workshop 2:147–153.

Mott, J. R., and D. C. Fuller. 1967. Soil survey of Franklin County, Massachusetts. USDA Soil Conserv. Serv., Washington, D.C. 204 p.

Moyer, J. W. 1953. Practical taxidermy: a working guide. Ronald Press Co., New York. 126 p.

Moyle, J. B., (ed.), F. B. Lee, R. L. Jessen, N. J. Ordal, R. I. Benson, J. P. Lindmeier, R. E. Farmes, and M. M. Nelson. 1964. Ducks and land use in Minnesota. Minn. Dept. Conserv. Tech. Bull. 8, St. Paul. 140 p.

Mueggler, W. F. 1966. Herbicide treatment of browse on a big-game winter range in northern Idaho. J. Wildl. Manage. 30(1):141–151.

Mueller-Dombois, D., and H. Ellenberg. 1974. Aims and methods of vegetation ecology. John Wiley and Sons, New York. 547 p.

Munday, B. L., A. Corbould, and G. Goodsall. 1974. Identification of muscle tissue from mammals. J. Wildl. Manage. 38(4):884–886.

Munn, R. E., (ed.). 1975. Environmental impact assessment: principles and procedures. SCOPE workshop on impact studies in the environment. United Nations Environ. Program, Toronto, Canada. 160 p.

Murie, A. 1944. The wolves of Mt. McKinley. U.S. Park Serv. Fauna of the Natl. Parks, Fauna Ser. No. 5. 238 p.

Murie, A. 1948. Cattle on grizzly bear range. J. Wildl. Manage. 12(1):57–72.

Murie, O. J. 1928. Weighing game animals. J. Mammal. 9(1):74–75.

Murie, O. J. 1946. Evaluating duplications in analysis of coyote scats. J. Wildl. Manage. 10(3):275–276.

Murie, O. J. 1951. The elk of North America. Stackpole Co., Harrisburg, Pa. 376 p.

Murie, O. J. 1954. A field guide to animal tracks. Houghton Mifflin Co., Boston, Mass. 374 p.

Murphy, B. E. P. 1964. Application of the property of protein-binding to the assay of minute quantities of hormones and other substances. Nature 201(4920):679–682.

Murphy, B. E. P. 1967. Some studies of the protein-binding of steroids and their application to the routine micro and ultramicro measurement of various steroids in body fluids by competitive protein-binding radioassay. J. Clin. Endocrinol. Metab. 27(7): 973–990.

Murphy, T. M., Jr., and T. T. Fendley. 1973. A new technique for live trapping of nuisance alligators. Proc. Southeastern Assoc. Game and Fish Commissioners 27:308–311.

Murphy, W. F., Jr., P. F. Scanlon, and R. L. Kirkpatrick. 1973. Examination of ovaries in living cottontail rabbits by laparotomy. Proc. Southeastern Assoc. Game and Fish Commissioners 27:343–344.

Murra, K. O. 1962. International scientific organizations: a guide to their library, documentation and information services. Libr. of Congr., Washington, D.C. 794 p.

Murray, B. G., Jr., and F. B. Gill. 1976. Behavioral interactions of blue-winged and golden-winged warblers. Wilson Bull. 88(2):231–254.

Murry, R. E. 1965. Tranquilizing techniques for capturing deer. Proc. Southeastern Assoc. Game and Fish Commissioners 19:4–15.

Murtha, P. A. 1964. The use of aerial photographs in wildlife managment. M.S. Thesis, Cornell Univ., Ithaca, N.Y. 61 p.

Murton, R. K. 1971. Why do some bird species feed in flocks? Ibis 113(4):534–536.

Murton, R. K., N. J. Westwood, and A. J. Isaacson. 1974. A study of wood-pigeon shooting: the exploitation of a natural animal population. J. Appl. Ecol. 11(1):61–81.

Musil, A. F. 1963. Identification of crop and weed seeds. USDA Agric. Handb. No. 219. 171 p.

Musser, G. G., and E. T. Hooper. 1966. Bibliography: mammalogy. BioScience 16(4):291–292.

Myers, G. T., and T. A. Vaughn. 1964. Food habits of the plains pocket gopher in eastern Colorado. J. Mammal. 45(4):588–598.

Myers, H. W., Jr. 1977. Deer fence. Virginia Wildl. 38(7):29–30.

Nagel, W. O. 1960. Make your technical writing useful. Am. Fisheries Soc. and Wildl. Soc. Spec. Publ., McLean, Va. 31 p.

Nagy, J. G., H. W. Steinhoff, and G. M. Ward. 1964. Effects of essential oils of sagebrush on deer rumen microbial function. J. Wildl. Manage. 28(4):785–790.

Nagy, J. G., and R. P. Tengerdy. 1968. II. Antibacterial action of the volatile oils of *Artemisia tridentata* (big sagebrush) on bacteria from the rumen of mule deer. Appl. Microbiol. 16(3):441–444.

Nagy, K. A. 1975. Water and energy budgets of free-living animals: measurement using isotopically labeled water. p. 227–245 *in* N. F. Hadley, (ed.). Environmental physiology of desert organisms. Dowden, Hutchinson and Ross Inc., Stroudsburg, Pa. 283 p.

Nagy, K. A., R. S. Seymour, A. K. Lee, and R. Braithwaite. 1978. Energy and water budgets in free-living *Antechinus stuartii* (Marsupialia: Dasyuridae). J. Mammal. 59(1):60–68.

National Academy of Sciences. 1962. Range research: basic problems and techniques. Natl. Acad. Sci. and Natl. Res. Counc. Publ. 890, Washington, D.C. 341 p.

National Academy of Sciences. 1963. The Eastern European Academies of Sciences: directory. Natl. Acad. of Sci., Natl. Res. Counc. Publ. 1090. Washington, D.C. 148 p.

National Academy of Sciences. 1970. The life sciences; recent progress and application to human affairs, the world of biological research. Requirements for the future. Natl. Acad. of Sci., Washington, D.C. 526 p.

National Academy of Sciences. 1971. Scientific, technical, and related societies of the United States. 9th ed. Natl. Acad. of Sci., Natl. Res. Coun., Washington, D.C. 213 p.

National Agricultural Library. 1971. Directory of information resources in agriculture and biology. U.S. Govt. Print. Off., Washington, D.C. 523 p.

Naylor, A. E. 1953. Production of the Canada goose on Honey Lake Refuge, Lassen County, California. Calif. Fish and Game 39(1):83–95.

Naylor, A. E., and E. G. Hunt. 1954. A nesting study and population survey of Canada geese on the Susan River, Lassen County, California. Calif. Fish and Game 40(1):5–16.

Neal, D. L., and J. L. Neal. 1973. Uses and capabilities of electronic capacitance instruments for estimating standing herbage. Part I: History and development. J. Br. Grassl. Soc. 28(2):81–89.

Nealey, L. D. 1977. Remote sensing/photogrammetry education in the United States and Canada. Photogramm. Eng. Remote Sensing 43(3): 259–284.

Neave, S. A., (ed.). 1939–1940. Nomenclator zoologicus. Zool. Soc. of London, Regent's Park, London. 4 vol.

Neave, S. A. 1950a. Concerning the zoological record. Science 112(2921): 761–762.

Neave, S. A., (ed.). 1950b. Nomenclator zoologicus . . . 1936–45. Zool. Soc. of London, Regent's Park, London, Vol. 5. 308 p.

Needy, J. R. 1966. Filing systems. Natl. Recreation and Park Assoc., Manage Aids Bull. No. 57. 36 p.

Neely, W. W. 1956. How long do duck foods last under water? Trans. N. Am. Wildl. Conf. 21:191–198.

Neff, D. J. 1968. The pellet-group count technique for big game trend, census, and distribution: a review. J. Wildl. Manage. 32(3):597–614.

Nehman, G. I., N. Dee, J. M. Griffin, and B. W. Cost. 1973. Application of the land-use trade-off model to assess land-use capabilities of the Beaufort-Jasper County area. Tech. Rep. Battelle Columbus Labs, Columbus, Ohio. Vol. 2.

Neiland, K. A. 1970. Weight of dried marrow as indicator of fat in caribou femurs. J. Wildl. Manage. 34(4):904–907.

Nellis, C. H. 1968. Some methods for capturing coyotes alive. J. Wildl. Manage. 32(2):402–405.

Nellis, C. H. 1969. Sex and age variation in red squirrel skulls from Missoula County, Montana. Can. Field-Nat. 83(4):324–330.

Nellis, C. H., C. J. Terry, and R. D. Taber. 1974. A conical pitfall trap for small mammals. Northwest Sci. 48 (2):102–104.

Nellis, C. H., S. P. Wetmore, and L. B. Keith. 1978. Age-related characteristics of coyote canines. J. Wildl. Manage. 42(3):680–683.

Nelson, B. A. 1948. Pheasant data from a two-year bag study in South Dakota. J. Wildl. Manage. 12(1): 20–31.

Nelson, D. J., and F. E. Evans, (eds.). 1969. Radioecology. Proc. 2nd Natl. Symp. Conf. 670503, U.S. Dept. Commer. Natl. Tech. Inf. Ser., Springfield, Va. 774 p.

Nelson, D. J., and F. E. Evans, (eds.). 1971. Radio-nuclides in ecosystems. Proc. 3rd Natl. Symp. Radioecology Conf. 710501, U.S. Dept. Commer. Natl. Tech. Inf. Ser., Springfield, Va. 1268 p.

Nelson, H. K., A. T. Klett, and W. G. Burge. 1970. Monitoring migratory bird habitat by remote sensing methods. Trans. N. Am. Wildl. Nat. Resour. Conf. 35:73–84.

Nelson, L., Jr., and F. W. Clark. 1973. Correction for sprung traps in catch/effort calculations of trapping results. J. Mammal. 54(1):295–298.

Nelson, L. K. 1955. A pheasant neck tag. J. Wildl. Manage. 19(3):414–415.

Nelson, M. W., and P. Nelson. 1976. Power lines and birds of prey. Idaho Wildl. Rev. 28(5):3–7.

Nelson, R. C. 1976. Age determination of Canada geese *(Branta canadensis maxima)* by layers in the periosteal zone. M. S. Thesis. Ohio State Univ., Columbus. 43 p.

Nero, R. W., S. G. Sealy, and H. W. R. Copland. 1974. Great gray owls occupy artificial nests. Loon 46 (4):161–165.

Neronov, V. M. 1962. On the possibility of using observations of predatory birds for determining the nature of rodent distribution over a small range. *in* Problems of Ecology. Kievsk. Univ. 4:132.

Nesbit, R. 1959. Use of a mechanical goose caller for management purposes. Wis. Conserv. Bull. 24(4): 23.

Nesbitt, S. A. 1976. A new patagial wing streamer button. Wildl. Soc. Bull. 4(4):188.

Nesbitt, S. A., D. T. Gilbert, and D. B. Barbour. 1978. Red-cockaded woodpecker fall movements in a Florida flatwoods community. Auk 95(1): 145–151.

Nesbitt, W. H., and J. S. Parker. 1977. North American big game. 7th ed. Natl. Rifle Assoc., Washington, D.C. 367 p.

Neter, J., and J. Waksberg. 1964. A study of response errors in expenditures data from household interviews. Am. Stat. Assoc. J. 59 (305):18–55.

Newby, F. E., and V. D. Hawley. 1954. Progress on a marten live-trapping study. Trans. N. Am. Wildl. Conf. 19:452–462.

Newman, D. W., (ed.). 1964. Instrumental methods of experimental biology. Macmillan Co., New York. 560 p.

Newsom, J. D., and J. S. Sullivan, Jr. 1968. Cryo-branding, a marking technique for white-tailed deer. Louisiana Coop. Wildl. Res. Unit, La. State Univ., Baton Rouge. 12 p.

Newton, A. 1893–1896. A dictionary of birds. Adam and Charles Black, London. 1088 p.

Nice, M. M. 1938. The biological significance of bird weights. Bird-Banding 9(1):1–11.

Nicholls, T. H., and D. W. Warner. 1968. A harness for attaching radio transmitters to large owls. Bird-Banding 39(3):209–214.

Nichols, J. D., L. Viehman, R. H. Chabreck, and B. Fenderson. 1976. Simulation of a commercially harvested alligator population in Louisiana. La. Agric. Exp. Stn. Bull. 691. Baton Rouge. 59 p.

Nichols, L. 1978. Mountain goat aerial survey technique evaluation. Fed. Aid Prog. Rep. W–17–9 and W–17–10, Alaska Dept. Fish and Game, Juneau. 31 p.

Nichols, R. G., and M. R. Pelton. 1972. Variations in fat levels of mandibular cavity tissue in white-tailed deer *(Odocoileus virginianus)* in Tennessee. Proc. Southeastern Assoc. Game and Fish Commissioners 26:57–68.

Nichols, R. G., and M. R. Pelton. 1974. Fat in the mandibular cavity as an indicator of condition in deer. Proc. Southeastern Assoc. Game and Fish Commissioners 28:540–548.

Nicholson, A. J. 1941. The homes and social habits of the wood mouse *(Peromyscus leucopus noveboracensis)* in southern Michigan. Am. Midl. Nat. 25(1):196–223.

Nicholson, M. 1957. A dictionary of American-English usage based on Fowler's modern English usage. Oxford Univ. Press, New York. 671 p.

Nicholson, M. 1967. A practical style guide for authors and editors. Holt Inc., New York. 143 p.

Nielson, A. E., and W. M. Shaw. 1967. A helicopter-dart gun technique for capturing moose. Proc. Western Assoc. State Game and Fish Commissioners 47:183–199.

Nixon, C. M. 1964. An improved method of mapping forested areas. J. Wildl. Manage. 28(4):870–871.

Nixon, C. M., M. W. McClain, and R. W. Donohoe. 1975. Effects of hunting and mast crops on a squirrel population. J. Wildl. Manage. 39 (1):1–25.

Nixon, C. M., M. W. McClain, and K. R. Russell. 1970. Deer food habits and range characteristics in Ohio. J. Wildl. Manage. 34(4):870–886.

Nixon, C. M., D. M. Worley, and M. W. McClain. 1968. Food habits of squirrels in southeast Ohio. J. Wildl. Manage. 32(2):294–305.

Noble, R. E., and R. B. Hamilton. 1975. Bird populations in even-aged loblolly pine forests of southeastern Louisiana. Proc. Southeastern Assoc. Game and Fish Commissioners 29:441–450.

Noelle-Neümann, E. 1970. Wanted: rules for wording structured questionnaires. Public Opin. Q. 34 (2):191–201.

Noffsinger, R. E. 1976. Seasonal variation in the natality, mortality, and nutrition of the pine vole in two orchard types. M.S. Thesis. Va. Polytech. Inst. State Univ., Blacksburg. 126 p.

Nolan, V., Jr. 1961. A method of netting birds at open nests in trees. Auk 78(4):643–645.

Nordan, H. C., I. McT. Cowan, and A. J. Wood. 1970. The feed intake and heat production of the young black-tailed deer *(Odocoileus hemionus columbianus)*. Can. J. Zool. 48(2):275–282.

Norman, F. I., and T. L. Riggert. 1977. Nest boxes as nest sites for Australian waterfowl. J. Wildl. Manage. 41(4):643–649.

Northcott, T. H., and D. Slade. 1976. A livetrapping technique for river otters. J. Wildl. Manage. 40(1):163–164.

Northeast Regional Technical Center. 1971. Sources of planting stock and seed of conservation plants used in the Northeast. USDA Soil Conserv. Serv., Upper Darby, Pa. 31 p.

Norton-Griffiths, M. 1974. Reducing counting bias in aerial census by photography. E. Afr. Wildl. J. 12(3):245–248.

Norton-Griffiths, M. 1975. Counting animals. Afr. Wildl. Leadership Found., Nairobi. 110 p.

Novacek, M., and K. Hudec. 1961. Analysis of the food of the starling by remote-control photography. Med. Biol. Illus. 11(3):172–177.

Novak, M. 1977. Determining the average size and composition of beaver families. J. Wildl. Manage. 41(4): 751–754.

Novakowski, N. S. 1965. Cemental deposition as an age criterion in bison, and the relation of incisor wear, eye-lens weight, and dressed bison carcass weight to age. Can. J. Zool. 43(1):173–178.

Novikov, G. A. 1962. Carnivorous mammals of the fauna of the USSR. Keys to the fauna of the USSR. No. 62. Israel Program for Sci. Trans., Jerusalem. 284 p.

Nudds, T. D. 1977. Quantifying the vegetative structure of wildlife cover. Wildl. Soc. Bull. 5(3):113–117.

Numata, M. 1958. Japanese publications in the field of ecology. Ecology 39(3):566–567.

Nusetti, O. A., and M. Aleksiuk. 1975. Regulation of mammalian growth in cold environments: studies of DNA synthesis in *Rattus norvegicus*. J. Mammal. 56(4):770–780.

Oakley, C. 1973. The effects of livestock fencing on antelope. Wyoming Wildl. 37(12):26–29.

Oates, D. W., C. W. Brown, and D. L. Weigel. 1974. Blood and tissue identification of selected birds and mammals. I. Nebr. Game and Parks Comm., Lincoln. 91 p.

Oates, D. W., N. L. Dent, and K. A. Pearson. 1979. Differentiation of white-tailed and mule deer tissue by isoelectric focusing. Wildl. Soc. Bull. 7(2):113–116.

Oates, D. W., and D. L. Weigel. 1976. Blood and tissue identification of selected birds and mammals. II. Nebr. Game and Parks Comm., Lincoln. 118 p.

Oberholser, H. C. 1906. The North American eagles and their economic relations. USDA Biol. Surv. Bull. No. 27. 31 p.

Oberholser, H. C., and E. B. Kincaid, Jr. 1974. The bird life of Texas. (2 vols.) Univ. of Texas Press, Austin. 1057 p.

Odom, R. R. 1977. Sora *(Porzana carolina)*. p. 57–65 *in* G. C. Sanderson, (ed.). Management of migratory shore and upland game birds in North America. Int. Assoc. Fish and Wildl. Agencies, Washington, D.C. 358 p.

Odum, E. P. 1971. Fundamentals of ecology. 3rd ed. W. B. Saunders Co., Philadelphia. 574 p.

Odum, E. P. 1977. The emergence of ecology as a new integrative discipline. Science 195(4284):1289–1293.

Odum, E. P., and C. E. Connell. 1956. Lipid levels in migrating birds. Science 123(3203):892–894.

Odum, H. T., W. M. Kemp, M. Sell, W. Boynton, and M. Lehman. 1977. Energy analysis and the coupling of man and estuaries. Environ. Manage. 1:297–315.

Oelofse, J. 1970. Plastic for game catching. Oryx 10(5):306–308.

O'Farrell, M. J., and G. T. Austin. 1978. A comparison of different trapping configurations with the assessment line technique for density estimations. J. Mammal. 59(4):866–868.

O'Farrell, M. J., D. W. Kaufman, and D. W. Lundahl. 1977. Use of livetrapping with the assessment line method for density estimation. J. Mammal. 58(4):575–582.

O'Gara, B. W. 1978. Sheep depredation by golden eagles in Montana. Proc. Vertebr. Pest Conf. 8:206–213.

Ogilvie, M. A. 1972. Large numbered leg bands for individual identification of swans. J. Wildl. Manage. 36(4):1261–1265.

Ognev, S. I. 1962–1966. Mammals of the USSR and adjacent countries. Israel Program for Sci. Trans., Jerusalem. 7 vol.

Oh, H. K., M. B. Jones, and W. M. Longhurst. 1968. Comparison of rumen microbial inhibition resulting from various essential oils isolated from relatively unpalatable plant species. Appl. Microbiol. 16(1):39–44.

Ohmann, L. F., and R. R. Ream. 1971. Wilderness ecology: a method of sampling and summarizing data for plant community classification. USDA For. Serv. Res. Pap. NC-49, St. Paul, Minn. 14 p.

Oldemeyer, J. L., A. W. Franzmann, A. L. Brundage, P. D. Arneson, and A. Flynn. 1977. Browse quality and the Kenai moose population. J. Wildl. Manage. 41(3):533–542.

Olendorff, R. R., and M. N. Kochert. 1977. Land management for the conservation of birds of prey. p. 291–294 *in* R. D. Chancellor, (ed.). World conference on birds of prey, Vienna. 442 p.

Olendorff, R. R., and J. W. Stoddart. 1974. The potential for management of raptor populations in western grasslands. p. 47–88 *in* F. N. Hamerstrom, B. E. Harrell and R. R. Olendorff, (eds.). Management of raptors. Raptor Res. Rep. No. 2, Raptor Res. Found. Inc., Vermillion, S.D. 146 p.

Oleyar, C. M., and B. S. McGinnes. 1974. Field evaluation of diethylstilbestrol for suppressing reproduction in foxes. J. Wildl. Manage. 38(1):101–106.

Olsen, P. F. 1959. Dental patterns as age indicators in muskrats. J. Wildl. Manage. 23(2):228–231.

Olson, D. P. 1964. A study of canvasback and redhead breeding populations, nesting habitats, and productivity. Ph.D. Thesis. Univ. of Minnesota, Minneapolis. 100 p.

Olson, E. C. 1958. Russian literature in the natural sciences. Libr. Q. 28(4): 295–307.

Olson, K., and J. L. Schmidt. 1974. Discovering wildlife photography. Coop. Ext. Serv., Colo. State Univ., Ft. Collins. 20 p.

Oosting, H. J. 1956. The study of plant communities: an introduction to plant ecology. 2nd ed. W. H. Freeman and Co., San Francisco. 440 p.

Oppenheim, A. N. 1966. Questionnaire design and attitude measurement. Basic Books, New York. 298 p.

Oregon Interagency. n.d. The Oregon interagency guide for conservation and forage plantings. USDA Soil Conserv. Serv., Portland, Oreg. 83 p.

Oregon State Game Commission. 1972. The eagle's lair. Oregon State Game Comm. Bull. 27(4):8.

Oregon State University. 1967. Herbicide and vegetation management. Sch. For., Corvallis. 356 p.

Orsini, M. W. 1962. Technique of preparation, study and photography of benzyl-benzoate cleared material for embryological studies. J. Reprod. Fertil. 3(2):283–287.

Osborn, D. J. 1955. Techniques of sexing beaver, *Castor canadensis*. J. Mammal. 36(1):141–142.

Osgood, D. W., and P. D. Weigl. 1972. Monitoring activity of small mammals by temperature-telemetry. Ecology 53(4):738–740.

Osgood, W. H. 1947. Biographical memoir of Clinton Hart Merriam, 1855–1942. p. 1–57 *in* Biographical Memor. Natl. Acad. of Sci., Washington, D.C. Vol. 24. 380 p.

Oster, G., (ed.). 1955–1964. Physical techniques in biological research. Academic Press, New York. 5 vol.

Osterberg, D. M. 1962. Activity of small mammals as recorded by a photographic device. J. Mammal. 43(2):219–229.

Ostrom, C. E. 1937. Deer and rabbit injury to northern hardwood reproduction. USDA Allegheny For. Exp. Stn. Tech. Note No. 15. 2 p.

Ostrom, C. E. 1942. Frost and rabbits as well as deer destroy tree seedlings. USDA Allegheny For. Exp. Stn. Tech. Note 33. 2 p.

Ostry, M. E., and T. H. Nicholls. 1976. How to identify and control sapsucker injury on trees. USDA For. Serv. Leafl. N. Central For. Exp. Stn., St. Paul, Minn. 5 p.

Otero, J. G., and R. W. Dapson. 1972. Procedures in the biochemical estimation of age of vertebrates. Res. Popul. Ecol. (Kyoto) 13(2):152–160.

Otis, D. L., K. P. Burnham, G. C. White, and D. R. Anderson. 1978. Statistical inference from capture data on closed animal populations. Wildl. Monogr. No. 62. 135 p.

Overman, R. T. 1963. Basic concepts of nuclear chemistry: selected topics in modern chemistry series. Reinhold Publ. Corp., New York. 116 p.

Overman, R. T., and H. M. Clark. 1960. Radioisotope techniques. McGraw-Hill Book Co., New York. 476 p.

Overton, S., and J. Sincock. 1956. Some uses of mark sensing in collecting game management data in the field. Proc. Southeastern Assoc. Game and Fish Commissioners 10:131–134.

Overton, W. S., Jr. 1953. Post season mail survey techniques and procedures. Proc. Southeastern Assoc. Game and Fish Commissioners 7:1–18.

Overton, W. S. 1971. Estimating the numbers of animals in wildlife populations. p. 403–455 *in* R. H. Giles, Jr., (ed.). Wildlife management techniques, 3rd ed. rev. The Wildl. Soc., Washington, D.C. 633 p.

Owaga, M. L. A. 1978. The effect of sieve mesh size on analysis of rumen contents. J. Wildl. Manage. 42(3): 693–697.

Owen, M. 1975a. Cutting and fertilizing grassland for winter goose management. J. Wildl. Manage. 39(1): 163–167.

Owen, M. 1975b. An assessment of fecal analysis technique in waterfowl feeding studies. J. Wildl. Manage. 39(2):271–279.

Owen, M., and R. H. Kerbes. 1971. On the autumn food of barnacle geese at Caerlaverlock National Nature Reserve. Wildfowl 22:114–119.

Owen, R. B., Jr., W. W. Cochran, and F. A. Moore. 1969. An inexpensive, easily attached radio transmitter for recording heart rates of birds. Med. Biol. Eng. 7:565–567.

Owen, R. B., Jr., and J. W. Morgan. 1975. Summer behavior of adult radio-equipped woodcock in central Maine. J. Wildl. Manage. 39(1): 179–182.

Ozoga, J. J., and L. W. Gysel. 1965. A mechanical recorder for measuring deer activity. J. Wildl. Manage. 29(3):632–634.

Ozoga, J. J., and L. J. Verme. 1978. The thymus gland as a nutritional status indicator in deer. J. Wildl. Manage. 42(4):791–798.

Packham, J. C. 1970. Forest animal damage in California. U.S. Fish Wildl. Serv., Sacramento, California. 4 p.

Page, F. J. T. 1959. Field guide to British deer. Mammal Society of the British Isles, Birmingham. 80 p.

Page, I. H. 1965. Why bibliography? Science 149(3679):8.

Page, J. L. 1975. Prescribed burning plan for wildlife habitat improvement. Trans. Inter. Antelope Conf. 16:22 p.

Paine, D. P. 1975. An introduction to aerial photography for natural resource management. Oregon State Univ. Bookstores Inc., Corvallis. 314 p.

Palmer, E. L. 1957. Palmer's fieldbook of mammals. E. P. Dutton, New York. 321 p.

Palmer, T. K. 1970. House finch (Linnet) control in California. Proc. Vertebr. Pest Conf. 4:173–178.

Palmer, T. S. 1912. Chronology and index of the more important events in American game protection, 1776–1911. USDA Biol. Surv. Bull. No. 41. 62 p.

Palmer, W. L. 1959. Sexing live-trapped juvenile ruffed grouse. J. Wildl. Manage. 23(1):111–112.

Palmer, W. L., R. L. Cowan, and A. P. Ammann. 1976. Effect of inoculum source on *in vitro* digestion of deer foods. J. Wildl. Manage. 40(2):301–307.

Palmisano, A. W., and H. H. Dupuie. 1975. An evaluation of steel traps for taking fur animals in coastal Louisiana. Proc. Southeastern Assoc. Game and Fish Commissioners 29:342–347.

Pan, H. P., J. W. Caslick, D. T. Harke, and D. G. Decker. 1965. A simple animal support for convenient weighing. J. Wildl. Manage. 29 (4):890–891.

Papez, N. J., and G. K. Tsukamoto. 1970. The 1969 sheep trapping and transplant program in Nevada. Trans. Desert Bighorn Council 14: 43–50.

Parke, N. G. 1958. Guide to the literature of mathematics and physics including related works on engineering science. 2nd rev. ed. Dover Publ., New York. 436 p.

Parker, H. D., Jr. 1972. Airborne infrared detection of deer. Ph.D. Thesis. Colorado State Univ., Fort Collins, Colo. 186 p.

Parker, J. W. 1972. A mirror and pole device for examining high nests. Bird-Banding 43(3):216–218.

Parker, S. M. 1959. Scientific translations: a guide to sources and services. U.S. Public Health Serv. Publ. No. 514. 19 p.

Parmalee, P. W. 1955. Some factors affecting nesting success of the bobwhite quail in east-central Texas. Amer. Midl. Nat. 53(1):45–55.

Parmelee, D. F., H. A. Stephens, and R. H. Schmidt. 1967. The birds of southeastern Victoria Island and adjacent small islands. Natl. Mus. Can. Bull. No. 222. 229 p.

Parr, D. E., and M. D. Scott. 1978. Analysis of roosting counts as an index to wood duck population size. Wilson Bull. 90(3):423–437.

Parsons, G. R., M. K. Brown, and G. B. Will. 1978. Determining the sex of fisher from the lower canine teeth. N.Y. Fish and Game J. 25(1):42–44.

Parten, M. 1966. Surveys, polls and samples: practical procedures. Cooper Square Publ. Inc., New York. 624 p.

Passmore, M. F., and R. L. Jarvis. 1979. Reliability of determining sex of band-tailed pigeons by plumage characters. Wildl. Soc. Bull. 7(2): 124–125.

Pastore, J. O., (chairman). 1972. Selected materials on the Calvert Cliffs decision, its origin and aftermath. 92nd Congr. of U.S., Joint Comm. on Atomic Energy. 676 p.

Patrick, N. D. 1961. Estimating total weights of black bears from carcass weights. J. Wildl. Manage. 25(1):93.

Patten, B. C., (ed.). 1971. Systems analysis and simulation in ecology. Academic Press, Inc., New York, Vol. I. 607 p.

Patten, B. C., (ed.). 1972. Systems analysis and simulation in ecology. Academic Press, Inc., New York, Vol. II. 592 p.

Patten, B. C., (ed.). 1975. Systems analysis and simulation in ecology. Academic Press, Inc., New York, Vol. III. 601 p.

Patten, B. C., (ed.). 1976. Systems analysis and simulation in ecology. Academic Press, Inc., New York, Vol. IV. 593 p.

Patterson, R. L. 1952. The sage grouse in Wyoming. Sage Books Inc., Denver, Colo. 341 p.

Patton, D. R. 1975. A diversity index for quantifying habitat "edge." Wildl. Soc. Bull. 3(4):171–173.

Patton, D. R. 1978. RUN WILD a storage and retrieval system for wildlife habitat information. USDA For. Serv. Rocky Mt. For. and Range Exp. Stn. Gen. Tech. Rep. RM-51. Ft. Collins, Colo. 8 p.

Patton, D. R., D. W. Beaty, and R. H. Smith. 1973. Solar panels: an energy source for radio transmitters on wildlife. J. Wildl. Manage. 37(2): 236–238.

Patton, D. R., V. E. Scott, and E. L. Boeker. 1972. Construction for an 8-mm time-lapse camera for biological research. USDA For. Serv. Res. Pap. RM-88. Ft. Collins, Colo. 8 p.

Paulik, G. J., and D. S. Robson. 1969. Statistical calculations for change-in-ratio estimators of population parameters. J. Wildl. Manage. 33(1): 1–27.

Paulson, G. L., (ed.). 1974. Environment USA: a guide to agencies, people and resources. Bowker Inc., New York. 451 p.

Paxton, J. 1974. Dictionary of abbreviations. Rowman & Littlefield, Totowa, N.J. 384 p.

Payne, N. F. 1976. Estimating live weight of black bears from chest girth measurements. J. Wildl. Manage. 40(1):167–169.

Payne, S. L. 1951. The art of asking questions. Princeton Univ. Press, Princeton, New York. 249 p.

Paynter, R. A., Jr. 1951. Clutch-size and egg mortality of Kent Island eiders. Ecology 32(3):497–507.

Pearce, J. 1947. Identifying injury by wildlife to trees and shrubs in northeastern forests. U.S. Fish Wildl. Serv. Res. Rep. 13. 29 p.

Pearson, A. H., and G. C. Moore. 1940. Feathers may reveal the age of mourning doves. Ala. Conserv. Mag. 1(1):9–10.

Pearson, A. K., and O. P. Pearson. 1955. Natural history and breeding behavior of the tinamou, *Northoprocta ornata*. Auk. 72(2):113–127.

Pearson, A. M., R. M. Bradley, and R. T. McLaughlin. 1968. Evaluation of phencyclidine hydrochloride and other drugs for immobilizing grizzly and black bears. J. Wildl. Manage. 32(3):532–537.

Pearson, H. A. 1970. Digestibility trials: *in vitro* techniques. p. 85–92 *in* Range and wildlife habitat evaluation—a research symposium. USDA For. Serv. Misc. Publ. No. 1147. 220 p.

Pearson, H. A., J. R. Davis, and G. H. Schubert. 1972. Effects of wildfire on timber and forage production in Arizona. J. Range Manage. 25(4): 250–253.

Pearson, O. P. 1959. A traffic survey of *Microtus-Reithrodontomys* runways. J. Mammal. 40(2):169–180.

Pechanec, J. F., and G. D. Pickford. 1937. A weight method for the determination of range or pasture production. J. Am. Soc. Agron. 29(11): 894–904.

Pechanec, J. F., A. P. Plummer, J. H. Robertson, and A. C. Hull, Jr. 1965. Sagebrush control on rangelands. USDA Agric. Handb. 277. 40 p.

Pechanec, J. F., G. Stewart, and J. P. Blaisdell. 1954. Sagebrush burning, good and bad. Rev. ed. USDA Farmers' Bull. 1948. 34 p.

Peden, D. G., G. M. Van Dyne, R. W. Rice, and R. M. Hansen. 1974. The trophic ecology of *Bison bison* L. on shortgrass plains. J. Appl. Ecol. 11(2):489–498.

Pedersen, R. J. 1977. Summer elk trapping with salt. Wildl. Soc. Bull. 5(2):72–73.

Pedersen, R. J., and J. W. Thomas. 1975. Immobilization of Rocky Mountain elk using powdered succinylcholine chloride. USDA For. Serv. Res. Note PNW–240. 4 p.

Peet, R. K. 1974. The measurement of species diversity. Annu. Rev. Ecol. Syst. 5:285–307.

Pelton, M. R. 1968. A contribution to the biology and management of the cottontail rabbit *(Sylvilagus floridanus mallurus)* in Georgia. Ph.D. Thesis. Univ. Georgia, Athens. 160 p.

Pelton, M. R. 1970. Effects of freezing on weights of cottontail lenses. J. Wildl. Manage. 34(1):205–207.

Pelton, M. R., and L. C. Marcum. 1975. The potential use of radioisotopes for determining densities of black bears and other carnivores. p. 221–236 *in* R. L. Phillips and C. Jonkel, (eds.). Proceedings of the 1975 predator symposium. Montana For. Conserv. Exp. Stn., Univ. Montana, Missoula. 268 p.

Pendleton, R. C. 1952. Some uses of radioisotopes in ecological research. Ph.D. Diss. Univ. of Utah, Salt Lake City. 162 p.

Pendleton, R. C. 1956. Uses of marking animals in ecological studies: labeling animals with radioisotopes. Ecology 37(4):686–689.

Penfound, W. T., and E. L. Rice. 1957. An evaluation of the arms-length rectangle method in forest sampling. Ecology 38(4):660–661.

Pennak, R. W. 1964. Collegiate dictionary of zoology. Ronald Press, New York. 583 p.

Perkins, H. M. 1954. Animal tracks; the standard guide for identification and characteristics. Stackpole, Harrisburg, Pa. 63 p.

Perry, H. R., G. B. Pardue, F. S. Barkalow, and R. J. Monroe. 1977. Factors affecting trap response of the gray squirrel. J. Wildl. Manage. 41 (1):135–143.

Peters, J. L. 1931–1970. Check-list of birds of the world. Harvard Univ. Press, Cambridge.

Peterson, R. L. 1955. North American moose. Univ. of Toronto Press, Toronto. 280 p.

Peterson, R. L. 1966. The mammals of eastern Canada. Oxford Univ. Press, Toronto. 465 p.

Peterson, R. T. 1960. A field guide to the birds of Texas. Houghton Mifflin, Boston, Mass. 304 p.

Peterson, R. T. 1961. A field guide to western birds. 2nd ed. Houghton Mifflin, Boston, Mass. 366 p.

Peterson, R. T., I. J. Ferguson-Lees, and D. I. M. Wallace. 1977. A field guide to the birds of Britain and Europe. 3rd ed. Houghton Mifflin, Boston, Mass. 344 p.

Peterson, S. R., and R. S. Ellarson. 1978. Bursae, reproductive structures, and scapular color in wintering female oldsquaws. Auk 95(1): 115–121.

Petrides, G. A. 1942. Age determination in American gallinaceous game birds. Trans. N. Am. Wildl. Conf. 7:308–328.

Petrides, G. A. 1949. Sex and age determination in the opossum. J. Mammal. 30(4):364–378.

Petrides, G. A. 1950. The determination of sex and age ratios in fur animals. Am. Midl. Nat. 43(2):355–382.

Petrides, G. A. 1951. Notes on age determination in squirrels. J. Mammal. 32(1):111–112.

Petrides, G. A. 1959. Age ratios in raccoons. J. Mammal. 40(2):249.

Petrides, G. A. 1975. Principal foods versus preferred foods and their relations to stocking rate and range condition. Biol. Conserv. 7(3):161–169.

Petrides, G. A., and R. B. Nestler. 1943. Age determination in juvenal bobwhite quail. Am. Midl. Nat. 30 (3):774–782.

Pettingill, O. S., Jr. 1956. A laboratory and field manual of ornithology. 3rd ed. Burgess Publ. Co., Minneapolis, Minn. 379 p.

Pettingill, O. S., Jr. 1970. Ornithology in laboratory and field. 4th ed. Burgess Publ. Co., Minneapolis, Minn. 524 p.

Pettingill, O. S., Jr. 1977. A guide to bird finding. Oxford Univ. Press, New York. 689 p.

Pfister, R. D., B. L. Kovalchik, S. F. Arno, and R. C. Presby. 1977. Forest habitat types of Montana. USDA For. Serv. Gen. Tech. Rep. INT-34, Intermt. For. and Range Exp. Stn., Ogden, Utah. 174 p.

Phillips, A., J. Marshall, and G. Monson. 1964. The birds of Arizona. Univ. of Arizona Press, Tucson 220 p.

Phillips, B. 1978. Hanging a dho-gaza. Inland Bird Band. News 50(6):211–217.

Phillips, J. C. 1930. American game mammals and birds: a catalogue of books, 1582 to 1925. Houghton Mifflin, Boston. 639 p.

Phillips, R. L., and T. H. Nicholls. 1970. A collar for marking big game animals. USDA N. Central For. Exp. Stn. Res. Note NC-103. 4 p.

Phillipson, A. T., (ed.). 1970. Physiology of digestion and metabolism in the ruminant. Proc. III Int. Symp. Ruminant Physiol. Oriel Press Ltd., Newcastle upon Tyne, England, NE 1 8LH. 636 p.

Pielou, E. C. 1966. The measurement of diversity in different types of biological collections. J. Theoret. Biol. 13(1):131–144.

Pielou, E. C. 1967. The use of information theory in the study of the diversity of biological populations. Proc. 5th Berkeley Symp. Math. Stat. Prob. 4:163–177.

Pielou, E. C. 1969. An introduction to mathematical ecology. John Wiley and Sons, New York. 286 p.

Pielou, E. C. 1975. Ecological diversity. John Wiley and Sons, New York. 165 p.

Pielou, E. C. 1977. Mathematical ecology. Wiley-Interscience Publ., New York. 385 p.

Pienaar, U. DEV. 1975a. The drug immobilization of antelope species. p. 35–50 *in* E. Young, (ed.). The capture and care of wild animals. Ralph Curtis Books, Hollywood, Fla. 224 p.

Pienaar, U. DEV. 1975b. The capture and restraint of wild herbivores by mechanical methods. p. 91–99 *in* E. Young, (ed.). The capture and care of wild animals. Ralph Curtis Books, Hollywood, Fla. 224 p.

Pienaar, U. DEV., J. W. van Niekerk, E. Young, P. van Wyk, and N. Fairall. 1966. Neuroleptic narcosis of large wild herbivores in South African national parks with the new potent morphine analogues M–99 and M–183. J. S. Afr. Vet. Med. Assoc. 37(3):277–291.

Pienkowski, E. C. 1965. Predicting transmitter range and life. BioScience 15(2):115–118.

Pimlott, D. H. 1969. The value of diversity. Trans. N. Am. Wildl. Nat. Resour. Conf. 34(2):265–280.

Pinowski, J., T. Tomek, and W. Tomek. 1973. Food selection in the tree sparrow, *Passer m. montanus* (L). Preliminary report. p. 263–273 *in* S. C. Kendeigh and J. Pinowski, (eds.). Productivity, population dynamics and systematics of granivorous birds. PWN-Polish Sci. Publ. Warsaw. 410 p.

Pinto, F. C. 1961. Serological identification of ox, buffalo, goat and deer flesh. Br. Vet. J. 117:540–544.

Pirnie, M. D. 1935. Michigan waterfowl management. Dept. Conserv., Lansing, Mich. 328 p.

Pistey, W. R., and J. F. Wright. 1961. The immobilization of captive wild animals with succinylcholine. II. Can. J. Comp. Med. Vet. Sci. 25(3):59–68.

Plummer, A. P., D. R. Christensen, and S. B. Monsen. 1968. Restoring big-game range in Utah. Utah Div. Fish and Game Publ. 68–3. 183 p.

Plummer, A. P., A. C. Hull, G. Stewart. and J. H. Robertson. 1955. Seeding rangelands in Utah, Nevada, southern Idaho, and western Wyoming. USDA For. Serv. Agric. Handb. No. 71. 73 p.

Plummer, A. P., S. B. Monsen, and D. R. Christensen. 1966. Fourwing saltbush—a shrub for future game ranges. Utah Dept. Fish and Game Publ. No. 66–4, Salt Lake City. 12 p.

Pojar, T. M. 1977. Use of a population model in big game management. Proc. Western Assoc. Game and Fish Commissioners 57:82–92.

Politz, A., and W. Simmons. 1949. An attempt to get the "not at homes" into the sample without callbacks. Am. Stat. Assoc. J. 44(245):9–31.

Polska Akademia Nauk. Komitet Zoologiczny. 1962. Informator zoologiczny: Directory Polish zool. The Academy, Warsaw. 193 p.

Pomeroy, D. E., and M. H. Woodford. 1976. Drug immobilization of marabou storks. J. Wildl. Manage. 40(1):177–179.

Poole, A. J., and V. S. Schantz. 1942. Catalog of the type of specimens of mammals in the United States National Museum, including the Biological Surveys collection. U.S. Nat. Mus. Bull. 178. 705 p.

Poole, R. W. 1974. An introduction to quantitative ecology. McGraw-Hill, New York. 532 p.

Popper, K. 1959. The logic of scientific discovery. Harper and Row, New York. 480 p.

Popper, K. R. 1963. Conjectures and refutations: the growth of scientific knowledge. Harper, New York. 417 p.

Porter, J. R. 1964. The scientific journal—300th anniversary. Bacteriol. Rev. 28(3):211–230.

Pospichal, L. B., and W. H. Marshall. 1954. A field study of sora rail and Virginia rail in central Minnesota. Flicker 26(1):2–32.

Post, G. 1967. Methods of sampling and preserving field specimens for laboratory examination or analysis. Pruett Press Inc., Boulder, Colo. 73 p.

Postovit, J. R., and J. D. Crawford. 1978. Badlands raptor survey. N. D. Outdoors 40(12):6–8.

Postupalsky, S. 1978. Artificial nesting platforms for ospreys and bald eagles. p. 35–45 *in* S. A. Temple, (ed.). Endangered birds: management techniques for preserving threatened species. Univ. Wisconsin Press, Madison. 466 p.

Postupalsky, S., and S. M. Stackpole. 1974. Artificial nesting platforms for ospreys in Michigan. p. 105–117 *in* F. N. Hamerstrom, B. E. Harrell and R. R. Olendorff, (eds.). Management of raptors. Raptor Res. Rep. No. 2, Raptor Res. Found., Vermillion, S.D. 146 p.

Potter, D. R., K. M. Sharpe, J. C. Hendee, and R. N. Clark. 1972. Questionnaires for research: an annotated bibliography on design, construction and use. USDA For. Serv. Res. Pap. PNW–140, Portland, Oreg. 80 p.

Poulton, C. E. 1975. Range resources: inventory, evaluation, and monitoring. p. 1427–1478 *in* R. G. Reeves, (ed.). Manual of remote sensing. Am. Soc. Photogramm., Falls Church, Va. 2 vols. 2142 p.

Prenzlow, E. J. 1965. A literature review on pronghorn behavior. Colo. Dept. of Game, Fish, and Parks; Game Res. Div. and Coop. Wildl. Res. Unit. Spec. Rept. No. 3. 28 p.

Preston, F. W. 1969. Diversity and stability in the biological world. Brookhaven Symp. Biol. 22:1–12.

Preston, R. L., L. H. Breuer, and G. B. Thompson. 1961. Blood urea in cattle as affected by energy, protein and stilbestrol. J. Anim. Sci. 20(4):977. (Abstr.).

Prince, H. H. 1968. Nest sites used by wood ducks and common goldeneyes in New Brunswick. J. Wildl. Manage. 32(3):489–500.

Progulske, D. R. 1957. A collar for identification of big game. J. Wildl. Manage. 21(2):251–252.

Provost, E. E. 1962. Morphological characteristics of the beaver ovary. J. Wildl. Manage. 26(3):272–278.

Provost, M. W. 1947. Nesting of birds in the marshes of northwest Iowa. Am. Midl. Nat. 38(2):485–503.

Prys-Jones, R. P., L. Schifferli, and D. W. MacDonald. 1974. The use of an emetic in obtaining food samples from passerines. Ibis 116(1):90–94.

Pugh, E. 1970. A dictionary of acronyms and abbreviations: some abbreviations in management, technology and information science. 2nd ed. Archon Books, Hamden, Conn. 389 p.

Pugh, G. T. 1963. Guide to research writing. 2nd ed. Houghton Mifflin, Boston, Mass. 56 p.

Puglisi, M. J., S. A. Liscinsky, and R. F. Harlow. 1978. An improved methodology of rumen content analysis for white-tailed deer. J. Wildl. Manage. 42(2):397–403.

Pyrah, D. 1970. Poncho markers for game birds. J. Wildl. Manage. 34(2): 466–467.

Queal, L. M., and B. D. Hlavachick. 1968. A modified marking technique for young ungulates. J. Wildl. Manage. 32(3):628–629.

Quimby, D. C., and J. E. Gaab. 1952. Preliminary report on a study of elk dentition as a means of determining age classes. Proc. Western Assoc. State Game and Fish Commissioners 32:225–227.

Quist, W. J., and R. E. Kirby. 1978. A core sampler for lead/steel shot investigations. Wildl. Soc. Bull. 6(3): 166–169.

Rabchevsky, G. A. 1977. Temporal and dynamic observations from satellites. Photogramm. Eng. Remote Sensing 43(12):1515–1518.

Radford, P. J. 1970. Some considerations governing the choice of a suitable simulation language. p. 87–106. *in* J. G. W. Jones, (ed.). Proc. ARC Symposium on the use of models in agricultural and biological research. Grassland Research Institute. Hurley, Berkshire. 134 p.

Radford, P. J. 1972. The simulation language as an aid to ecological modelling. p. 277–295 *in* J. N. R. Jeffers, (ed.). Mathematical models in ecology. Blackwell Sci. Publ. Oxford. 398 p.

Radiochemical Centre. 1965. Radioactive isotope dilution analysis. RCC review No. 2 UKAEA, Radiochemical Centre, Amersham, England. 12 p.

Radke, W. J., and M. J. Frydendall. 1974. A survey of emetics for use in stomach contents recovery in the house sparrow. Am. Midl. Nat. 92(1):164–172.

Radtke, R., and J. Byelich. 1963. Kirtland's warbler management. Wilson Bull. 75(2):208–215.

Radwan, M. A., and G. L. Crouch. 1974. Plant characteristics related to feeding preference by black-tailed deer. J. Wildl. Manage. 38(1):32–41.

Raim, A. 1978. A radio transmitter attachment for small passerine birds. Bird-Banding 49(4):326–332.

Raitt, R. J., Jr. 1961. Plumage development and molts of California quail. Condor 63(4):294–303.

Ralph, C. J. 1976. Standardization of mist net captures for quantification of avian migration. Bird-Banding. 47(1):44–47.

Ramakka, J. M. 1972. Effects of radiotagging on breeding behavior of male woodcock. J. Wildl. Manage. 36(4):1309–1312.

Ramsey, C. W. 1968. A drop-net deer trap. J. Wildl. Manage. 32(1):187–190.

Randall, P. E. 1941. The life equation of the ringneck pheasant in Pennsylvania. Trans. N. Am. Wildl. Conf. 5:300–320.

Ransom, A. B. 1965. Kidney and marrow fat as indicators of white-tailed deer condition. J. Wildl. Manage. 29(2):397–398.

Raptor Research Foundation. n.d. Suggested practices for raptor protection. Provo, Utah. 3 p.

Rasmussen, D. I., and E. R. Doman, 1943. Census methods and their application in the management of mule deer. Trans. N. Am. Wildl. Conf. 8:369–380.

Rasmussen, D. I., and L. A. Griner. 1938. Life history and management studies of the sage grouse in Utah, with special reference to nesting and feeding habits. Trans. N. Am. Wildl. Conf. 3:852–864.

Rathbone, R. R. 1966. Communicating technical information. Addison-Wesley Publ. Co., Reading, Mass. 104 p.

Rausch, R. A., and A. M. Pearson. 1972. Notes on the wolverine in Alaska and the Yukon Territory. J. Wildl. Manage. 36(2):249–268.

Rawley, E., J. B. Low, and E. O. Greaves. 1950. Venison—its care and cooking. Utah Agric. Ext. Serv. Bull. 200, Logan. 21 p.

Rawson, K. S., and P. H. Hartline. 1964. Telemetry of homing behavior by the deer-mouse, *Peromyscus*. Science 146(3651):1596–1597.

Rearden, J. D. 1951. Identification of waterfowl nest predators. J. Wildl. Manage. 15(4):386–395.

Reddin, M. C., and E. H. Feinberg. 1973. The core literature of biology, its sponsorship and national origin. BioScience 23(6):354–357.

Reddingius, J. 1971. Models as research tools. p. 64–76 *in* P. J. den Boer and G. R. Gradwell, (eds.). Dynamics of populations. Proc. Adv. Study Inst. on 'Dynamics of numbers in populations'. Oosterbeek. Centre for Agricultural Publication and Documentation, Wageningen, The Netherlands. 611 p.

Redfield, J. A. 1974. Demography and genetics in colonizing populations of blue grouse *(Dendragapus obscurus)*. Evolution 27(4):576–592.

Redfield, J. A., and F. C. Zwickel. 1976. Determining the age of young blue grouse: a correction for bias. J. Wildl. Manage. 40(2):349–351.

Reed, D. F. 1971. Giving the deer the steer. Colo. Outdoors 20(5):10–13.

Reed, D. F., T. M. Pojar, and T. N. Woodard. 1973. A video time-lapse system for wildlife surveillance. Colo. Div. Game, Fish, and Parks, Game Inf. Leafl. No. 94. 3 p.

Reed, D. F., T. N. Woodard, and T. M. Pojar. 1975. Behavioral response of mule deer to a highway underpass. J. Wildl. Manage. 39(2):361–367.

Rees, J. W., R. A. Kainer, and R. W. Davis. 1966. Chronology of mineralization and eruption of mandibular teeth in mule deer. J. Wildl. Manage. 30(3):629–631.

Reese, J. 1965. Breeding status of the osprey in central Chesapeake Bay. Maryland Birdlife 21(4):105–108.

Reese, K. P., and J. D. Hair. 1976. Avian species diversity in relation to beaver pond habitats in the piedmont region of South Carolina. Proc. Southeastern Assoc. Fish and Wildl. Agencies 30:437–447.

Reeves, H. M., F. G. Cooch, and R. E. Munro. 1976. Monitoring arctic habitat and goose production by satellite imagery. J. Wildl. Manage. 40(3):532–541.

Reeves, H. M., A. D. Geis, and F. C. Kniffin. 1968. Mourning dove capture and banding. U.S. Fish Wildl. Serv. Spec. Sci. Rep., Wildl. No. 117. 63 p.

Reeves, R. G., (ed.). 1975. Manual of remote sensing. Am. Soc. Photogramm., Falls Church, Va. 2 vols. 2142 p.

Regelin, W. L., J. G. Nagy, and O. C. Wallmo. 1977. Effects of snowdrifts on mountain shrub communities. Trans. Int. Congr. Game Biol. 13:414–419.

Regelin, W. L., O. C. Wallmo, J. G. Nagy, and D. R. Dietz. 1974. Effect of logging on forage values for deer in Colorado. J. For. 72(5):282–285.

Reichard, T. A. 1976. Spring food habits and feeding behavior of fox squirrels and red squirrels. Am. Midl. Nat. 96(2):443–450.

Reichert, R. J., and E. Reichert. 1961. Binoculars and scopes: how to choose, use, and photograph through them. Chilton Co. Book Div., Philadelphia, Pa. 128 p.

Rempel, R. D., and R. C. Bertram. 1975. The Stewart modified corral trap. Calif. Fish and Game 61(4): 237–239.

Reynolds, H. C. 1945. Some aspects of the life history and ecology of the opossum in central Missouri. J. Mammal. 26(4):361–379.

Reynolds, H. G. 1967. Chemical constituents and deer use of some crown sprouts in Arizona chaparral. J. For. 65(12):905–908.

Reynolds, K. C., and K. Edwards. 1977. A short focus telescope for ground cover estimations. Ecology 58(4): 939–941.

Rhodes, L. I. 1972. Success of osprey nest structures at Martin National Wildlife Refuge. J. Wildl. Manage. 36(4):1296–1299.

Rhodes, L. I. 1977. An osprey population aided by nest structures. p. 77–83 *in* J. C. Ogden, (ed.). Transactions of the North American osprey research conference. U.S. Natl. Park Serv. Trans. and Proc. Ser. No. 2. 258 p.

Rice, W. R., and J. D. Harder. 1977. Application of multiple aerial sampling to a mark-recapture census of white-tailed deer. J. Wildl. Manage. 41(2):197–206.

Richens, V. B., and C. G. Madden. 1973. An improved snow study kit. J. Wildl. Manage. 37(1):109–113.

Richter, W. C. 1955. A technique for night identification of animals. J. Wildl. Manage. 19(1):159–160.

Ricker, W. E. 1958. Handbook of computations for biological statistics of fish populations. Fish. Res. Board Can., Bull. No. 119. Ottawa. 300 p.

Ricker, W. E. 1973. Russian-English dictionary for students of fisheries and aquatic biology. Fish. Res. Board Can., Bull. No 183, Ottawa. 428 p.

Ricker, W. E. 1975. Computation and interpretation of biological statistics of fish populations. Fish. Res. Board Can., Bull. No. 191. Ottawa. 382 p.

Rickert, J. E. 1978. A guide to North American bird clubs. Avian Publ. Elizabethtown, Ky. 565 p.

Rickett, H. W., (ed.). 1966–1973. Wild flowers of the United States. McGraw-Hill Book Co., New York. 6 vol. in 14 parts.

Ricklefs, R. E. 1973. Tattooing nestlings for individual recognition. Bird-Banding 44(1):63.

Ridgway, R., and H. Friedmann. 1946. The birds of North and Middle America. U.S. Natl. Mus. Bull. 50, Washington, D.C. Part 10. 484 p.

Riley, C. V. 1963. Revegetation and management of critical sites for wildlife. Trans. N. Am. Wildl. Nat. Resour. Conf. 28:269–283.

Riley, L., and W. Riley. 1979. Guide to the national wildlife refuges. Anchor: Doubleday. 371 p.

Rinaldi, A. M. 1970. Deer and hare forage following strip clearcutting and slash disposal on the Penobscot Experimental Forest, Maine. M. S. Thesis. Univ. Maine, Orono. 81 p.

Riney, T. 1951. Standard terminology for deer teeth. J. Wildl. Manage. 15(1):99–101.

Riney, T. 1955. Evaluating condition of free ranging red deer *(Cervus elaphus)*, with special reference to New Zealand. N.Z. J. Sci. and Technol. Sect. B. 36(5):429–463.

Ripley, S. D. 1977. Rails of the world; a monograph of the family Rallidae. David R. Godine Publ., Boston. 406 p.

Ripley, T. H., and C. J. Perkins. 1965. Estimating ground supplies of seed available to bobwhites. J. Wildl. Manage. 29(1):117–121.

Risser, A. C., Jr. 1971. A technique for performing laparotomy on small birds. Condor 73(3):376–379.

Ritcey, R. W., and R. Y. Edwards. 1956. Trapping and tagging moose on winter range. J. Wildl. Manage. 20(3):324–325.

Roach, B. A. 1974. Scheduling timber cutting for sustained yield of wood products and wildlife. USDA For. Serv. Tech. Rep. NE–14, N.E. For. Exp. Stn., Upper Darby, Pa. 13 p.

Robbins, C. S., B. Bruun, and H. S. Zim. 1966. A guide to field identification: birds of North America. Golden Press, New York. 340 p.

Robbins, C. T., and A. N. Moen. 1975. Composition and digestibility of several deciduous browses in the Northeast. J. Wildl. Manage. 39(2): 337–341.

Robbins, C. T., P. J. Van Soest, W. W. Mautz, and A. N. Moen. 1975. Feed analyses and digestion with reference to white-tailed deer. J. Wildl. Manage. 39(1):67–79.

Robel, R. J. 1965. Differential winter mortality of bobwhites in Kansas. J. Wildl. Manage. 29(2):261–265.

Robel, R. J. 1969. Food habits, weight dynamics, and fat content of bobwhites in relation to food plantings in Kansas. J. Wildl. Manage. 33(2): 237–249.

Robel, R. J., J. N. Briggs, A. D. Dayton, and L. C. Hulbert. 1970. Relationships between visual obstruction measurements and weight of grassland vegetation. J. Range Manage. 23(4):295–297.

Robel, R. J., D. J. Dick, and G. F. Krause. 1969. Regression coefficients used to adjust bobwhite quail whistle count data. J. Wildl. Manage. 33(3):662–668.

Robel, R. J., and P. G. Watt. 1970. Comparison of volumetric and point-analysis procedures to describe deer food habits. J. Wildl. Manage. 34(1):210–213.

Roberts, A. 1940. The birds of South Africa. H. F. and G. Witherby, London. 463 p.

Roberts, A. 1951. The mammals of South Africa. Trustees of "The Mammals of South Africa" Book Fund, Johannesburg, South Africa. 700 p.

Roberts, F. S. 1976. Discrete mathematical models. Prentice-Hall Inc. Englewood Cliffs, New Jersey. 559 p.

Roberts, J. D. 1978. Variation in coyote age determination from annuli in different teeth. J. Wildl. Manage. 42(2): 454–456.

Roberts, R. F. 1977. Big game guzzlers. Rangeman's J. 4(3):80–82.

Roberts, T. S. 1955. A manual for the identification of the birds of Minnesota and neighboring states. Univ. of Minnesota Press, Minneapolis, Minn. p. 459–738.

Roberts-Pichette, P. 1972. Annotated bibliography of permafrost-vegetation-wildlife-landform relationships. Can. For. Serv. For. Manage. Inst., Inf. Rep. FMR-X-43, Ottawa. 350 p.

Robertson, J. H. 1954. A low-cost portable cage for range and pasture plots. J. Range Manage. 7(1):42.

Robinette, W. L. 1966. Mule deer home range and dispersal in Utah. J. Wildl. Manage. 30(2):335–349.

Robinette, W. L., R. B. Ferguson, and J. S. Gashwiler. 1958. Problems involved in the use of deer pellet group counts. Trans. N. Am. Wildl. Conf. 23:411–425.

Robinette, W. L., N. V. Hancock, and D. A. Jones. 1977. The Oak Creek mule deer herd in Utah. Utah Div. Wildl. Resour. Publ. No. 77–15, Salt Lake City. 148 p.

Robinette, W. L., D. A. Jones, J. S. Gashwiler, and C. M. Aldous. 1954. Methods for censusing winter-lost deer. Trans. N. Am. Wildl. Conf. 19:511–525.

Robinette, W. L., D. A. Jones, J. S. Gashwiler, and C. M. Aldous. 1956. Further analysis of methods for censusing winter-lost deer. J. Wildl. Manage. 20(1):75–78.

Robinette, W. L., C. M. Loveless, and D. A. Jones. 1974. Field tests of strip census methods. J. Wildl. Manage. 38(1):81–96.

Robinson, M. W. 1947. An instrument to measure forest crown cover. For. Chron. 23:222–225.

Roby, G. A., and L. R. Green. 1976. Mechanical methods of chaparral modification. USDA For. Serv. Agric. Handb. No. 487, Washington, D.C. 46 p.

Rochelle, J. A., I. Gauditz, K. Oita and J. H. Oh. 1974. New developments in big-game repellents. p. 103–112 *in* H. C. Black, (ed.). Wildlife and forest management in the Pacific Northwest. Oregon State Univ., Corvallis. 236 p.

Rodgers, R. D. 1979. Ratios of primary calamus diameters for determining age of ruffed grouse. Wildl. Soc. Bull. 7(2):125–127.

Roe, F. G. 1951. The North American buffalo: a critical study of the species in its wild state. Univ. Toronto Press, Toronto. 957 p.

Roedel, P. M., (ed.). 1975. Optimum sustainable yield as a concept in fisheries management. Am. Fish. Soc. Spec. Publ. No. 9. Washington, D.C. 89 p.

Roest, A. I. 1957. Notes on the American sparrow hawk. Auk 74(1):1–19.

Roff, D. A. 1973a. On the accuracy of some mark-recapture estimators. Oecologia 12(1):15–34.

Roff, D. A. 1973b. An examination of some statistical tests used in the analysis of mark recapture data. Oecologia 12(1):35–54.

Rogers, D. J., and H. S. Fleming. 1963. Data recording: an inexpensive and efficient method. AIBS Bull. 13(2): 42.

Rogers, J. P. 1964. A decoy trap for male lesser scaups. J. Wildl. Manage. 28(2):408–410.

Rogerson, S. J., E. J. Stevens, and J. G. Hughes. 1976. An improved technique for identification of plant cuticle in animal faeces. N. Z. J. Bot. 14:117–119.

Rohde, W. G. 1977. A selected bibliography: application of Landsat digital multispectral scanner data to agriculture, forestry, and range management. Unpubl. Bibliogr., EROS Data Center Applications Branch, Sioux Falls, S.D. 21 p.

Rohde, W. G., J. K. Lo, and R. A. Pohl. 1978. EROS Data Center Landsat digital enhancement techniques and image availability, 1977. Can. J. Remote Sensing 4(1):63–76.

Rolan, R. G., and H. T. Gier. 1967. Correlation of embryo and placental scar counts of *Peromyscus maniculatus* and *Microtus ochrogaster*. J. Mammal. 48(2):317–319.

Rollman, W. L. 1962. Get it on film. Wis. Conserv. Bull. 26(4):23–24.

Romanov, A. N. 1956. Automatic tagging of wild animals and prospects for its use. Zool. J. Moscow 35:1902.

Roney, E. E., Jr. 1971. Use of the blowgun to immobilize or medicate caged animals. J. Zoo Anim. Med. 2(2):25.

Rongstad, O. J. 1966. A cottontail rabbit lens-growth curve from southern Wisconsin. J. Wildl. Manage. 30(1): 114–121.

Rongstad, O. J. 1969. Gross prenatal development of cottontail rabbits. J. Wildl. Manage. 33(1):164–168.

Roper, L. A., R. L. Schmidt, and R. B. Gill. 1971. Techniques of trapping and handling mule deer in northern Colorado with notes on using automatic data processing for data analysis. Proc. Western Assoc. Game and Fish Commissioners 51:471–477.

Roscoe, D. E., S. W. Nielsen, and T. Becker. 1977. A device for testing waterfowl for lead shot ingestion. Trans. Northeast Sect. Wildl. Soc., Fish Wildl. Conf. 33:45–50.

Rose, G. B. 1973. Energy metabolism of adult cottontail rabbits, *Sylvilagus floridanus*, in simulated field conditions. Am. Midl. Nat. 89(2):473–478.

Roseberry, J. L., and W. D. Klimstra. 1965. A guide to age determination of bob-white quail embryos. Ill. Nat. Hist. Surv. Biol. Notes No. 55, Urbana. 4 p.

Roseberry, J. L., and W. D. Klimstra. 1974. Differential vulnerability during a controlled deer harvest. J. Wildl. Manage. 38(3):499–507.

Rosene, W. 1969. The bobwhite quail; its life and management. Rutgers Univ. Press. 418 p.

Rosenzweig, M. L., and P. W. Sterner. 1970. Population ecology of desert rodent communities: body size and seed-husking as bases for heteromyid coexistence. Ecology 51(2): 217–224.

Rosenzweig, M. L., and J. Winakur. 1969. Population ecology of desert rodent communities: habitats and environmental complexity. Ecology 50(4):558–572.

Rosevear, D. R. 1974. The carnivores of West Africa. British Museum (Natural History), London. 548 p.

Roth, R. R. 1976. Spatial heterogeneity and bird species diversity. Ecology 57(4):773–782.

Rothschild, Lord. 1965. A classification of living animals. 2nd ed. Longmans, Ltd., London. 134 p.

Roughton, R. D. 1975. Xylazine as an immobilizing agent for captive white-tailed deer. J. Am. Vet. Med. Assoc. 167(7):574–576.

Roughton, R. D. 1976. A gun light for night shooting. J. Wildl. Manage. 40(2):362–363.

Roussel, Y. E. 1975. Aerial sexing of antlerless moose by white vulval patch. J. Wildl. Manage. 39(2):450–451.

Roussel, Y. E., and R. Ouellet. 1975. A new criterion for sexing Quebec ruffed grouse. J. Wildl. Manage. 39(2):443–445.

Roussel, Y. E., and R. Patenaude. 1975. Some physiological effects of M–99 etorphine on immobilized free-ranging moose. J. Wildl. Manage. 39(3):634–636.

Rowe, A. L. 1967. Productivity indicators in western larch forests. USDA For. Serv. Intermt. For. and Range Exp. Stn. Res. Note INT–59, Ogden, Utah. 4 p.

Royall, W. C., Jr. 1969. Trapping house sparrows to protect experimental grain crops. U.S. Fish Wildl. Serv. Wildl. Leafl. No. 484, Washington, D.C. 4 p.

Royama, T. 1971. A comparative study of models/or predation and parasitism. Res. Pop. Ecol. Supp. 1. 91 p.

Rubin, J. 1967. International directory of micrographic equipment. Int. Microgr. Congr., Saratoga, California. 519 p.

Ruckel, S. W., P. F. Scanlon, R. L. Kirkpatrick, and M. D. Russell. 1976. Influence of season on reproductive characteristics of woodchucks in Virginia. Proc. Southeastern Assoc. Game and Fish Commissioners 30:386–391.

Rudge, M. R., and R. J. Joblin. 1976. Comparison of some methods of capturing and marking feral goats *(Capra hircus)*. N.Z. J. Zool. 3(1): 51–55.

Ruffner, J. A., and F. E. Blair. 1974. The weather almanac. Gale Research Co., Detroit, Mich. 578 p.

Ruggiero, L. F., and J. B. Whelan. 1976. A comparison of *in vitro* and *in vivo* feed digestibility by white-tailed deer. J. Range Manage. 29 (1):82–83.

Runge, W. 1972. An efficient winter live-trapping technique for white-tailed deer. Saskatchewan Dept. of Nat. Resour. Tech. Bull. 1. 16 p.

Rushmore, F. M. 1969. Sapsucker damage varies with tree species and seasons. USDA For. Serv. Res. Pap. NE-136. Upper Darby, Pa. 19 p.

Russell, K. R. 1979. WILDMIS—A tool for impact assessment and mitigation planning. p. 629–630 *in* G. A. Swanson, (tech. coord.). The mitigation symposium: a national workshop on mitigating losses of fish and wildlife habitats. USDA For. Serv. Rocky Mt. For. Range Exp. Stn. Gen. Tech. Rep. RM–65. Ft. Collins, Colo. 696 p.

Ryder, J. P. 1967. The breeding biology of Ross' goose in the Perry River region, Northwest Territories. Can. Wildl. Serv. Rep. Ser. No. 3. 56 p.

Ryder, J. P. 1970. Timing and spacing of nests and breeding biology of Ross' goose. Ph.D. Thesis. Univ. of Saskatchewan, Saskatoon. 240 p.

Ryder, J. P. 1971. Spring bird phenology at Karrak Lake, Northwest Territories. Can. Field-Nat. 85:181–183.

Saake, N. 1968. Nevada's Canada geese. Nev. Wildl. 2(2):24–25.

Sackman, H. 1975. Delphi critique; expert opinion, forecasting, and group process. D.C. Heath and Co., Lexington, Mass. 142 p.

Sadler, K. C. 1961. Grit selectivity by the female pheasant during egg production. J. Wildl. Manage. 25(3): 339–341.

Sadler, K. C., R. E. Tomlinson, and H. M. Wight. 1970. Progress of primary feather molt of adult mourning doves in Missouri. J. Wildl. Manage. 34(4):783–788.

Sagar, R. G. 1962. Food habit studies on cottontail rabbits. Game Res. Ohio. 1:133–135.

Salt, W. R. 1958. In memoriam: William Rowan. Auk 75(4):387–390.

Salter, S. H. 1966. A note on the recording of egg activity. Anim. Behav. 14(1):41–43.

Salwasser, H., and S. A. Holl. 1979. Estimating fetus age and breeding and fawning periods in the North Kings River deer herd. Calif. Fish and Game 65(3):159–165.

Salyer, J. C. 1955. Improvements in the cannon net trap. U.S. Fish and Wildl. Ser., Branch of Wildl. Res., Wildl. Manage. Ser. No. 12, Washington, D.C. 27 p. (multilith).

Sampson, A. W., A. Chase, and D. W. Hedrick. 1951. California grasslands and range forage grasses. Calif. Agric. Exp. Stn. Bull. 724, Berkeley. 131 p.

Sampson, A. W., and B. S. Jesperson. 1963. California range brushlands and browse plants. Calif. Agric. Exp. Stn. Man. 33, Davis. 162 p.

Sanborn, C. C. 1947. Catalogue of type specimens of mammals in Chicago Natural History Museum. Fieldiana: Zool. 32(4):1–293.

Sanders, O. T., Jr. 1971. Sulfur content of deer hair. M. S. Thesis. Va. Polytech. Inst. and State Univ., Blacksburg. 42 p.

Sanders, O. T., and R. L. Kirkpatrick. 1975. Effects of a polychlorinated biphenyl (PCB) on sleeping times, plasma corticosteroids, and testicular activity of white-footed mice. Environ. Physiol. Biochem. 5(5): 308–313.

Sanders, O. T., and R. L. Kirkpatrick. 1977. Reproductive characteristics and corticoid levels of female white-footed mice fed ad libitum and restricted diets containing a polychlorinated biphenyl. Environ. Res. 13(3):358–363.

Sanderson, G. C. 1950. Methods of measuring productivity in raccoons. J. Wildl. Manage. 14(4):389–402.

Sanderson, G. C. 1961a. Techniques for determining age of raccoons. Ill. Nat. Hist. Surv. Biol. Notes No. 45, Urbana. 16 p.

Sanderson, G. C. 1961b. The lens as an indicator of age in the raccoon. Am. Midl. Nat. 65(2):481–485.

Sanderson, G. C., (ed.). 1977. Management of migratory shore and upland game birds in North America. Int. Assoc. Fish and Wildl. Agencies, Washington, D.C. 358 p.

Sanderson, G. C., R. L. Westemeier, and W. R. Edwards. 1973. Acquisition and management of prairie chicken sanctuaries in Illinois. p. 59–79 *in* W. D. Svedarsky and T. Wolfe, (eds.). The prairie chicken in Minnesota. Univ. Minnesota, Crookston. 102 p.

Sanderson, H. R. 1975. Den-tree management for gray squirrels. Wildl. Soc. Bull. 3(3):125–131.

Sanderson, H. R., and R. L. Hubbard. 1961. Bitterbrush seed spotting on wildfire burns. USDA For. Serv. Res. Note 192, Pac. S. W. For. and Range Exp. Stn., Berkeley. 7 p.

Sanford, F. B. 1958. Planning your research paper. U.S. Fish and Wildl. Serv. Fishery Leafl. No. 447. 32 p.

Sarrazin, J-P. R., and J. R. Bider. 1973. Activity, a neglected parameter in population estimates—the development of a new technique. J. Mammal. 54(2):369–382.

Sarton, G. 1960. Notes on the reviewing of learned books. Science 131(3408):1182–1187.

Sather, J. H. 1950. A light meter for cover-density measurement. J. Wildl. Manage. 14(2):138–143.

Sather, J. H. 1954. The dentition method of aging muskrats. Chicago Acad. Sci. Nat. Hist. Misc. Publ. No. 130. 3 p.

Sauer, B. W., H. A. Gorman, and R. J. Boyd. 1969. A new technique for restraining antlerless mule deer. J. Am. Vet. Med. Assoc. 155(7):1080–1084.

Sauer, P. R. 1966. Determining sex of black bears from the size of the lower canine tooth. N.Y. Fish and Game J. 13(2):140–145.

Sauer, P. R., S. Free, and S. Browne. 1966. Age determination in black bears from canine tooth sections. N.Y. Fish and Game J. 13(2):125–139.

Sauer, W. C. 1976. Control of the Oregon ground squirrel *(Spermophilus beldingi oregonus)*. Proc. Vertebr. Pest Conf. 7:99–109.

Saunders, A. A. 1961. The songs and calls of the wood thrush. Auk 78 (4):595–606.

Saunders, J. K., Jr. 1963. Food habits of the lynx in Newfoundland. J. Wildl. Manage. 27(3):384–390.

Saville, D. B. C. 1962. Collection and care of botanical specimens. Can. Dept. Agric. Publ. 1113 p.

Sawby, S. W., and J. A. Gessaman. 1974. Telemetry of electrocardiograms from free-living birds: a method of electrode placement. Condor 76(4):479–481.

Scanlon, P. F., and D. K. Lenker. 1973. A support device for field laparotomy of white-tailed deer. J. Wildl. Manage. 37(3):423–424.

Scheele, M. 1961. Punch-card methods in research and documentation with special reference to biology. (Transl. from German) Interscience Publ., New York. 274 p.

Scheffer, T. H., and N. Hotchkiss. 1945. Plant-food resources for waterfowl in the Pacific Northwest. Wash. Dept. Game Biol. Bull. No. 7, Olympia, Wash. 39 p.

Scheffer, V. B. 1950. Growth layers on the teeth of pinnipedia, as an indication of age. Science 112(2907):309–311.

Schemnitz, S. D. 1961. Ecology of the scaled quail in the Oklahoma panhandle. Wildl. Monogr. No. 8. 47 p.

Schemnitz, S. D. 1974. Wildlife habitats and management in the boreal forests of northeastern United States and Maritime Canada. Life Sci. and Agric. Exp. Stn. Misc. Rep. 154, Univ. of Maine, Orono. 29 p.

Schilling, C. 1976. Operational aspects of successful ground squirrel control by aerial application of grain bait. Proc. Vertebr. Pest Conf. 7:110–115.

Schindler, D. W. 1976. The impact statement boondoggle. Science 192(4239):509.

Schinner, J. R., and D. L. Cauley. 1974. The ecology of urban raccoons in Cincinnati, Ohio. p. 125–130 *in* J. H. Noyes and D. R. Progulske, (eds.). Wildlife in an urbanizing environment. Coop. Ext. Serv., Univ. Massachusetts, Amherst. 182 p.

Schladweiler, P. 1968. Feeding behavior of incubating ruffed grouse females. J. Wildl. Manage. 32(2): 426–428.

Schladweiler, P., and T. W. Mussehl. 1969. Use of mist-nets for recapturing radio-equipped blue grouse. J. Wildl. Manage 33(2):443–444.

Schlatterer, E. F. 1960. Productivity and movements of a population of sage grouse in southeastern Idaho. M. S. Thesis, Univ. Idaho, Moscow. 87 p.

Schmeckebier, L. F., and R. B. Eastin. 1969. Government publications and their use. 2nd rev. ed. The Brookings Inst., Washington, D.C. 502 p.

Schmid, W. 1967. Sex chromatin in hair roots. Cytogenetics 6(5):342–349.

Schmidt, J. L., and D. L. Gilbert, (eds.). 1978. Big game of North America. Stackpole Books, Harrisburg, Pa. 494 p.

Schmidt-Nielsen, K., and B. Schmidt-Nielsen. 1952. Water metabolism of desert mammals. Physiol. Rev. 32 (2):135–166.

Schnabel, Z. E. 1938. The estimation of the total fish population of a lake. Am. Math. Monthly 45(6):348–352.

Schneegas, E. R., and G. W. Franklin. 1972. The Mineral King deer herd. Calif. Fish and Game 58(2):133–140.

Schneegas, E. R., and S. N. Zufelt. 1965. Rejuvenating decadent bitterbrush. USDA For. Serv. Reg. 5, Inyo Natl. For., Calif. 5 p. (mimeo.)

Schoener, T. W. 1974. Resource partitioning in ecological communities. Science 185(4145):27–39.

Schofield, R. D. 1955. Analysis of muskrat age determination methods and their application in Michigan. J. Wildl. Manage. 19(4):463–466.

Schorger, A. W. 1966a. The wild turkey; its history and domestication. Univ. Oklahoma Press, Norman. 625 p.

Schorger, A. W. 1966b. In memoriam: Paul Lester Errington. Auk 83(1): 52–65.

Schreiber, E. F. 1976. A new method for restraining live birds. Bird-Banding 47(2):165.

Schuerholz, G. 1974. Quantitative evaluation of edge from aerial photographs. J. Wildl. Manage. 38(4): 913–920.

Schultz, R. 1950. A modified Stoddard quail trap. J. Wildl. Manage. 14(2): 243.

Schultz, V. 1961. An annotated bibliography on the use of statistics in ecology—a search of 31 periodicals. U.S. Atomic Energy Commission. Office of Tech. Inf. TID-3908. 315 p.

Schultz, V. 1963. Radionuclides and ionizing radiation in ornithology, a selected bibliography on wild and domestic birds. TID–17762. AEC Div. Tech. Inf., Washington, D.C. 27 p.

Schultz, V. 1969. Ecological techniques utilizing radionuclides and ionizing radiation: a selected bibliography. USAEC Div. Tech. Inf. RLO–2213–1. 252 p.

Schultz, V., L. L. Eberhardt, J. M. Thomas, and M. I. Cochran. 1976. A bibliography of quantitative ecology. Dowden, Hutchinson and Ross Inc., Stroudsburg, Pa. 361 p.

Schultz, V., and A. W. Klement, Jr., (eds.). 1962. Radioecology. Reinhold Publ. Co. and Am. Inst. Biol. Sci., New York. 746 p.

Schultz, V., and A. W. Klement, Jr., (eds.). 1963. Radioecology. Proc. 1st Natl. Symp. Radioecology, Reinhold Publ. Corp., New York. 746 p.

Schultz, V., and F. W. Whicker. 1974. Radiation ecology. Critical Reviews in Environ. Control 5(3):397–421.

Schumacher, F. X., and R. W. Eschmeyer. 1943. The estimate of fish population in lakes or ponds. J. Tenn. Acad. Sci. 18:228–249.

Schuster, J. L. 1965. Estimating browse from twig and stem measurements. J. Range Manage. 18(4): 220–222.

Schwabe, C. W., and L. R. Davis. 1954. Marginal punched cards in veterinary research. Am. J. Vet. Res. 15(57):634–638.

Schwarly, A., J. D. Weaver, N. R. Scott, and T. J. Cade. 1977. Measuring the temperature of eggs during incubation under captive falcons. J. Wildl. Manage. 41(1):12–17.

Schwartz, C. C. 1977. Pronghorn grazing strategies on the shortgrass prairie, Colorado. Ph.D. Diss. Colorado State Univ., Fort Collins. 113 p.

Schwartz, C. C., and J. G. Nagy. 1972. Maintaining rumen fluid for *in vitro* studies. J. Wildl. Manage. 36(4): 1341–1343.

Schwartz, C. C., and J. G. Nagy. 1976. Pronghorn diets relative to forage availability in northeastern Colorado. J. Wildl. Manage. 40(3):469–478.

Schwartz, C. C., J. G. Nagy, and R. W. Rice. 1977. Pronghorn dietary quality relative to forage availability and other ruminants in Colorado. J. Wildl. Manage. 41(2):161–168.

Schwartz, C. W. 1944. The prairie chicken in Missouri. Missouri Conserv. Comm., Jefferson City. 179 p.

Schwartz, C. W., and E. R. Schwartz. 1959. Wild mammals of Missouri. Univ. Missouri Press and Missouri Conserv. Comm., Columbia. 341 p.

Schwartz, M. D. 1977. Environmental law: a guide to information sources. Gale Research Co., Detroit, Michigan. 191 p.

Schwartz, R. J. 1955. The complete dictionary of abbreviations. Thomas Y. Crowell Co., New York. 211 p.

Schwarz, C. F., E. C. Thor, and G. H. Elsner. 1976. Wildland planning glossary. USDA For. Serv. Gen. Tech. Rep. PSW–13. Pac. S.W. For. and Range Exp. Stn., Berkeley, Calif. 252 p.

Schwilling, M. D. 1975. Waterfowl damage control. Proc. Great Plains Wildl. Damage Control Workshop 2:163–169.

Scott, C. 1961. Research on mail surveys. J. Res. Stat. Soc. Ser. A. 124(2):143–195.

Scott, J. P., and J. L. Fuller. 1965. Genetics and the social behavior of the dog. Univ. Chicago Press, Chicago, Ill. 468 p.

Scott, L. 1970. Great horned owls occupy artificial nesting site. Blue Jay 28(3):123.

Scott, M. D., and K. Causey. 1973. Ecology of feral dogs in Alabama. J. Wildl. Manage. 37(3):253–265.

Scott, T. G. 1941. Methods and computations in fecal analysis with reference to the red fox. Iowa State Coll. J. Sci. 15(3):279–285.

Scott, T. G. 1958. Wildlife research. Bull. Ill. Nat. Hist. Surv. 27(2):179–201.

Scott, T. G., and J. A. Ayars. 1969. Writing the scientific report. p. 53–59 *in* R. H. Giles, (ed.). Wildlife management techniques. 3rd ed. The Wildl. Soc., Washington, D.C. 623 p.

Scott, T. G., and C. H. Wasser. 1979. Checklist of North American plants for wildlife biologists. The Wildl. Soc. Washington, D.C. 72 p.

Scott, V. E., K. E. Evans, D. R. Patton, and C. P. Stone. 1977. Cavity-nesting birds of North American forests. U.S. Dept. Agric. Handb. 511, Washington, D.C. 112 p.

Scott, W. B. 1965. Bibliography of J. R. Dymond. Can. Field-Nat. 79(4): 224–229.

Scotter, G. W. 1966. Sieve mesh size as related to volumetric and gravimetric analysis of caribou rumen contents. Can. Field-Nat. 80(4):238–241.

Scotter, G. W. 1967. The winter diet of barren-ground caribou in northern Canada. Can. Field-Nat. 81(1):33–39.

Seal, U. S. 1977. Assessment of habitat condition by measurement of biochemical and endocrine indicators of the nutritional, reproductive, and disease status of free-ranging animal populations. p. 305–329 *in* Proceeding national symposium on classification, inventory and analysis of fish and wildlife habitat. U.S. Fish and Wildl. Serv. Office Biol. Serv. Publ. 78/76. 604 p.

Seal, U. S., A. W. Erickson, and J. G. Mayo. 1970. Drug immobilization of the carnivora. Int. Zoo Yearb. 10: 157–170.

Seal, U. S., and R. L. Hoskinson. 1978. Metabolic indicators of habitat condition and capture stress in pronghorns. J. Wildl. Manage. 42(4):755–763.

Seal, U. S., M. E. Nelson, L. D. Mech, and R. L. Hoskinson. 1978a. Metabolic indicators of habitat differences in four Minnesota deer populations. J. Wildl. Manage. 42(4): 746–754.

Seal, U. S., J. J. Ozoga, A. W. Erickson, and L. J. Verme. 1972. Effects of immobilization on blood analyses of white-tailed deer. J. Wildl. Manage. 36(4):1034–1040.

Seal, U. S., L. J. Verme, and J. J. Ozoga. 1978b. Dietary protein and energy effects on deer fawn metabolic patterns. J. Wildl. Manage. 42(4):776–790.

Seber, G. A. F. 1973. The estimation of animal abundance and related parameters. Hafner Press, New York. 506 p.

Seel, D. C. 1975. A tube for holding birds during examination of molt in the flight feathers. Bird-Banding 46(1):74–75.

Segelquist, C. A. 1966. Sexing white-tailed deer embryos by chromatin. J. Wildl. Manage. 30(2):414–417.

Segelquist, C. A., H. L. Short, F. D. Ward, and R. G. Leonard. 1972. Quality of some winter deer forages in the Arkansas Ozarks. J. Wildl. Manage. 36(1):174–177.

Seidenberg, A. J. 1966. Bibliography: animal ecology. BioScience 16(11): 827–828, 830.

Seidensticker, J., K. M. Tamang, and C. W. Gray. 1974. The use of CI–744 to immobilize free-ranging tigers and leopards. J. Zoo Anim. Med. 5(4):22–25.

Selby, S. M. 1975. Handbook of tables for mathematics. 4th ed. Chem. Rubber Co. Press, Cleveland, Ohio. 1152 p.

Selleck, D. M., and C. M. Hart. 1957. Calculating the percentage of kill from sex and age ratios. Calif. Fish and Game 43(4):309–316.

Selltiz, C., M. Jahoda, M. Deutsch, and S. W. Cook. 1959. Research methods in social relations. Holt, Rinehart and Winston Inc., New York. 622 p.

Selye, H. 1976. Stress in health and disease. Butterworths, Boston and London. 1256 p.

Sen, A. R. 1971. Some recent developments in waterfowl sample survey techniques. J. R. Stat. Soc. Ser. C 20(2):139–147.

Sen, A. R. 1973. Estimation of memory bias in wildlife mail surveys. Proc. Int. Stat. Inst. Bull. 39:401–411.

Sengupta, I. N. 1973. Growth of the biochemical literature. Nature 244 (5411):75–76, 118.

Serventy, D. L., D. S. Farner, and C. A. Nichollas. 1962. Trapping and maintaining shore birds in captivity. Bird-Banding 33(3):123–130.

Seton, E. T. 1937. Lives of game animals. The Literary Guild of America. New York. 8 vol.

Seton, E. T. 1958. Animal tracks and hunter signs. Doubleday, New York. 160 p.

Seubert, J. L. 1948. A technique for nocturnal studies of birds and mammals by the use of infra-red projection and electronic reception. M. S. Thesis. Ohio State Univ., Columbus. 87 p.

Severinghaus, C. W. 1949. Tooth development and wear as criteria of age in white-tailed deer. J. Wildl. Manage. 13(2):195–216.

Severinghaus, C. W. 1955. Deer weights as an index of range conditions on two wilderness areas in the Adirondack region. N.Y. Fish and Game J. 2(2):154–160.

Severinghaus, C. W., and H. F. Maguire. 1955. Use of age composition data for determining sex ratios among adult deer. N.Y. Fish and Game J. 2(2):242–246.

Severinghaus, C. W., H. F. Maguire, R. A. Cookingham and J. E. Tanck. 1950. Variations by age class in the antler beam diameters of white-tailed deer related to range conditions. Trans. N. Am. Wildl. Conf. 15:551–570.

Shackleton, D. M., L. V. Hills, and D. A. Hutton. 1975. Aspects of variation in cranial characters of plains bison *(Bison bison bison* Linnaeus*)* from Elk Island National Park, Alberta. J. Mammal. 56(4):871–887.

Shafer, E. L., Jr. 1963. The twig-count method for measuring hardwood deer browse. J. Wildl. Manage. 27(3):428–437.

Shaiffer, C. W., and G. L. Krapu. 1978. A remote controlled system for capturing nesting waterfowl. J. Wildl. Manage. 42(3):668–669.

Shallenberger, R. J., G. C. Whittow, and R. M. Smith. 1974. Body temperature of the nesting red-footed booby *(Sula sula).* Condor 76(4): 476–481.

Shannon, C. E., and W. Weaver. 1949 The mathematical theory of communication. Univ. Illinois Press, Urbana. 177 p.

Sharma, P. C. 1977. Planning for wildlife conservation: a selected research bibliography. Counc. Plann. Libr. Exchange Bibliogr. No. 1300. 15 p.

Sharp, W. M. 1958a. Aging gray squirrels by use of tail-pelage characteristics. J. Wildl. Manage. 22(1):29–34.

Sharp, W. M. 1958b. Evaluating mast yields in the oaks. Pennsylvania State Univ. Agric. Exp. Stn. Bull. 635. 22 p.

Shaub, B. M. 1951. Photographic records of captured birds. Wilson Bull. 63(4):327–329.

Shaw, S. P. 1971. Wildlife and oak management. p. 84–99 *in* Oak symposium proceedings. USDA For. Serv., N.E. For. Exp. Stn., Upper Darby, Pa. 161 p.

Shaw, S. P., and C. G. Fredine. 1956. Wetlands of the United States; their extent and their value to waterfowl and other wildlife. U.S. Dept. Inter. Fish Wildl. Serv. Circ. 39. 67 p.

Sheatsley, P. B. 1959. The art of interviewing. p. 574–587 *in* C. Selltiz, M. Jahoda, M. Deutsch and S. W. Cook. Research methods in social relations. Holt, Rinehart and Winston Inc., New York. 622 p.

Sheldon, W. G. 1949. Reproductive behavior of foxes in New York State. J. Mammal. 30(3):236–246.

Sheldon, W. G. 1967. The book of the American woodcock. Univ. of Mass. Press, Amherst. 227 p.

Shelford, V. E. 1913. Animal communities in temperate America. Univ. Chicago Press, Chicago. 368 p.

Shelford, V. E. 1945. The relative merits of the life zone and biome concepts. Wilson Bull. 57(4):248–252.

Shelford, V. E. 1963. The ecology of North America. Univ. of Illinois Press, Urbana. 610 p.

Shepherd, R. C. H., I. F. Nolan, and J. W. Edmonds. 1978. A review of methods to capture live wild rabbits in Victoria. J. Wildl. Manage. 42(1): 179–184.

Sheppard, C. W. 1962. Basic principles of the tracer method. John Wiley and Sons, New York. 282 p.

Sheppe, W. 1972. The annual cycle of small mammal populations on a Zambian floodplain. J. Mammal. 53(3):445–460.

Sherborn, C. D. 1940. Where is the ______ collection? Cambridge Univ. Press, Cambridge. 149 p.

Sherwin, C. W., and R. S. Isenson. 1967. Project hindsight—a defense department study of the utility of research. Science 156(3782):1571–1577.

Sherwood, G. A. 1965. Recent modifications in banding equipment for Canada geese. J. Wildl. Manage. 29(3):640–643.

Shields, P. W., and D. A. Duncan. 1966. Fall and winter food of California quail in dry years. Calif. Fish and Game 52(4):275–282.

Shilling, C. W., (ed.). 1964. Atomic energy encyclopedia in the life sciences. W. B. Saunders Co., Philadelphia, Pa. 474 p.

Shomon, J. J., B. L. Ashbaugh, and C. D. Tolman. 1966. Wildlife habitat improvement. Natl. Audubon Soc., New York. 96 p.

Short, H. L., R. M. Blair, and L. Burkart. 1972. Factors affecting nutritive values. p. 311–318 *in* C. M. McKell, J. P. Blaisdell and J. R. Goodin, (eds.). Wildland shrubs—their biology and utilization. USDA For. Serv. Gen. Tech. Rep. INT–1. 494 p.

Short, H. L., R. M. Blair, and C. A. Segelquist. 1974. Fiber composition and forage digestibility by small ruminants. J. Wildl. Manage. 38(2): 197–209.

Short, H. L., D. R. Dietz, and E. E. Remmenga. 1966. Selected nutrients in mule deer browse plants. Ecology 47(2):222–229.

Short, H. L., and A. Harrell. 1969. Nutrient analysis of two browse species. J. Range Manage. 22(1): 40–43.

Short, H. L., D. E. Medin, and A. E. Anderson. 1966. Seasonal variations in volatile fatty acids in the rumen of mule deer. J. Wildl. Manage. 30 (3):466–470.

Short, N. M., P. D. Lowman, Jr., S. C. Freden, and W. A. Finch, Jr. 1976. Mission to earth: Landsat views the earth. NASA SP–360, Washington, D.C. 459 p.

Shryer, J. 1971. A new device for remote injection of liquid drugs. J. Wildl. Manage. 35(1):180–181.

Shtil'mark, F. R. 1963. On the ecology of the Siberian chipmunk *(Eutamias sibericus* Laxm.) in the stonepine forests of western Sayan. Zool. Zh. 42(1):92–101.

Shugart, H. H., T. M. Smith, J. T. Kitchings, and R. L. Kroodsma. 1978. The relationship of nongame birds to southern forest types and successional stages. p. 5–16 *in* Proceedings of the workshop management of southern forests for nongame birds. USDA For. Serv. Gen. Tech. Rep. SE–14. 176 p.

Siegel, S. 1956. Nonparametric statistics for the behavioral sciences. McGraw-Hill, New York. 312 p.

Siegmund, O. H., (ed.). 1979. Merck veterinary manual; a handbook of diagnosis and therapy for the veterinarian. 5th ed. Merck Inc., Rahway, N.J. 1700 p.

Siggins, H. W. 1933. Distribution and rate of fall of conifer seeds. J. Agric. Res. 47(2):119–128.

Sigler, W. F. 1972. Wildlife law enforcement. 2nd ed. Wm. C. Brown Co., Dubuque, Iowa. 360 p.

Siglin, R. J. 1966. Marking mule deer with an automatic tagging device. J. Wildl. Manage. 30(3):631–633.

Silovsky, G. D., H. M. Wight, L. H. Sisson, T. L. Fox, and S. W. Harris. 1968. Methods for determining age of band-tailed pigeons. J. Wildl. Manage. 32(2):421–424.

Silver, H., N. F. Colovos, J. B. Holter, and H. H. Hayes. 1969. Fasting metabolism of white-tailed deer. J. Wildl. Manage. 33(3):490–498.

Silver, J., and A. W. Moore. 1941. Mole control. U.S. Fish Wildl. Serv. Conserv. Bull. 16. 17 p.

Silvy, N. J., J. W. Hardin, and W. D. Klimstra. 1975. Use of a portable net to capture free-ranging deer. Wildl. Soc. Bull. 3(1):27–29.

Silvy, N. J., and R. J. Robel. 1967. Recordings used to help trap booming greater prairie chickens. J. Wildl. Manage 31(2):370–373.

Simkin, D. W. 1965. Reproduction and productivity of moose in northwestern Ontario. J. Wildl. Manage. 29(4): 740–750.

Simmons, N. M. 1971. An inexpensive method of marking large numbers of Dall sheep for movement studies. Trans. N. Am. Wild Sheep Conf. 1:116–126.

Simmons, N. M., and J. L. Phillips. 1966. Modifications of a dye-spraying device for marking desert bighorn sheep. J. Wildl. Manage. 30(1):208–209.

Simon, H. R. 1974. Die Zukunft der Biologischen Bibliographie in Sonderdruck aus Festschrift Fuer Claus Nissen, 1973. Munich. 18 p.

Simpson, E. H. 1949. Measurement of diversity. Nature 163(4148):688.

Simpson, G. G. 1945. The principles of classification and a classification of mammals. Am. Mus. Nat. Hist. Bull. No. 85, New York. 350 p.

Simpson, G. G. 1961. Principles of animal taxonomy. Columbia Univ. Press, New York. 247 p.

Sincock, J. L. 1962. Estimating consumption of food by wintering waterfowl populations. Proc. Southeastern Assoc. Game and Fish Commissioners 16:217–221.

Sincock, J. L., and J. A. Powell. 1957. An ecological study of waterfowl areas in central Florida. Trans. N. Am. Wildl. Conf. 22:220–236.

Singer, F. J. 1974. Status of the osprey, bald eagle and golden eagle in the Adirondacks. N.Y. Fish and Game J. 21(1):18–31.

Singer, F. J., B. B. Ackerman, M. E. Harmon and A. R. Tipton. 1978. Census, trapping and population biology of European wild boar—1978. Management Report Series, Uplands Field Res. Lab. Great Smoky Mountain Natl. Park. 134 p.

Singleton, J. R. 1953. Texas coastal waterfowl survey. Texas Game and Fish Comm. FA Rep. Ser. 11. 128 p.

Singleton, J. R. 1965. Waterfowl habitat management in Texas. Texas Parks and Wildl. Dept. Bull. No. 47, Austin. 68 p.

Siniff, D. B., and R. O. Skoog. 1964. Aerial censusing of caribou using stratified random sampling. J. Wildl. Manage. 28(2):391–401.

Siopes, T. D., and W. O. Wilson. 1973. Determination of the sex of chukar partridge at hatching. J. Wildl. Manage. 37(2):239–240.

Sissenwine, M. P. 1979. Is MSY an adequate foundation for optimum yield? Fisheries 3(6):22–24, 37–38, 40–42.

Sisson, L. 1976. The sharp-tailed grouse in Nebraska. Nebraska Game and Parks Comm. P-R Proj. Rep. W–33–R and W–38–R. 88 p.

Skallerup, H. R. 1957. American state academy of science publications. Univ. Illinois Libr. School Occas. Pap., No. 50. 20 p.

Skeen, J. E. 1974. The relationships of certain rumino-reticular and blood variables to the nutritional status of white-tailed deer. Ph.D. Thesiş. Va. Polytech. Inst. State Univ., Blacksburg. 98 p.

Skellam, J. G. 1972. Some philosophical aspects of mathematical modelling in empirical science with special reference to ecology. p. 13–28 *in* J. N. R. Jeffers, (ed.). Mathematical models in ecology. Blackwell Sci. Publ. Oxford. 398 p.

Skillin, M. E., R. M. Gay, and Other Authorities. 1974. Words into type. 3rd ed. Prentice-Hall Inc., Englewood Cliffs, N.J. 585 p.

Skoss, J. D. 1955. Structure and composition of plant cuticle in relation to environmental factors and permeability. Bot. Gaz. 117(1):55–72.

Skutt, H. R., F. M. Bock, IV, P. Haugstad, J. B. Holter, H. H. Hayes and H. Silver. 1973. Low-power implantable transmitters for telemetry of heart rate and temperature from white-tailed deer. J. Wildl. Manage. 37(3):413–417.

Slade, N. A. 1977. Statistical detection of density dependence from a series of sequential censuses. Ecology 58(5):1094–1102.

Sladen, W. J. L. 1965. Ornithological research in Antarctica. BioScience 15(4):264–268.

Sladen, W. J. L. 1973. Swan research—international protocols for marking. Int. Wildfowl Res. Bur. Publ. 36, p. 71–76.

Slater, L. E., (ed.). 1963. Biotelemetry: the use of telemetry in animal behavior and physiology in relation to ecological problems. Macmillan Co., New York. 372 p.

Sluiter, J. W. 1961. Abrasion of teeth in connection with age in the bat *Myotis myotis*. Proc. Koninki. Nederl. Akademic Van Wetenschappen-Amsterdam, Ser. C 64(3).

Sluiter, J. W., P. F. van Heerdt, and J. J. Bezem. 1956. Population statistics of the bat *Myotis mystacinus*, based on the marking-recapture method. Arch. Neerl. Zool. 12:64–88.

Small, A. 1974. The birds of California. Winchester Press, New York. 310 p.

Smart, C. W., R. H. Giles, Jr., and D. C. Guynn, Jr. 1973. Weight tape for white-tailed deer in Virginia. J. Wildl. Manage. 37(4):553–555.

Smart, J., and G. Taylor. 1953. Bibliography of key works for the identification of the British fauna and flora. 2nd ed. The Systematics Assoc., British Mus. Nat. Hist., London. 126 p.

Smit, P. 1974. History of the life sciences: an annotated bibliography. Hafner Press, New York. 1071 p.

Smith, A. D. 1950. Sagebrush as a winter feed for deer. J. Wildl. Manage. 14(3):285–289.

Smith, A. D. 1952. Digestibility of some native forages for mule deer. J. Wildl. Manage. 16(3):309–312.

Smith, A. D. 1957. Nutritive value of some browse plants in winter. J. Range Manage. 10(4):162–164.

Smith, A. D., and J. C. Malechek. 1974. Nutritional quality of summer diets of pronghorn antelopes in Utah. J. Wildl. Manage. 38(4):792–798.

Smith, A. G. 1971. Ecological factors affecting waterfowl production in the Alberta Parklands. U.S. Fish Wildl. Serv. Res. Publ. No. 98, Washington, D.C. 49 p.

Smith, A. H. 1963. The mushroom hunter's field guide. Rev. ed. Univ. Michigan Press, Ann Arbor. 264 p.

Smith, A. M. 1962. Canadian theses in forestry and related subject fields, 1913–1962. For. Chron. 38(3):376–400.

Smith, C. E., Jr. 1971. Preparing herbarium specimens of vascular plants. USDA Agric. Inf. Bull. No. 348. 29 p.

Smith, D. 1970. Influence of cool and warm temperature and temperature reversal at inflorescence emergence on yield and chemical composition of timothy and brome grass at anthesis. Proc. Int. Grassl. Congr. 11:510–514.

Smith, D. G., and D. A. Spencer. 1976. A simple pole and mirror device. N. Am. Bird Band. 1(4):175.

Smith, D. R., (tech. coord.). 1975. Proceedings of the symposium on management of forest and range habitats for non-game birds. USDA For. Serv. Gen. Tech. Rep. WO–1, Washington, D.C. 343 p.

Smith, G. C., D. W. Kaufman, R. M. Jones, J. B. Gentry, and M. H. Smith. 1971. The relative effectiveness of two types of snap traps. Acta Theriol. 16(8):284–288.

Smith, H. R. 1975. Management of *Peromyscus leucopus* as part of an integrated program to control the gypsy moth. Trans. Northeast Sect. Wildl. Soc., Fish Wildl. Conf. 32:111–129.

Smith, J. N. M., and H. P. A. Sweatman. 1974. Food-searching behavior of titmice in patchy environments. Ecology 55(6):1216–1232.

Smith, N. D., and I. O. Buss. 1963. Age determination and plumage observation of blue grouse. J. Wildl. Manage. 27(4):566–578.

Smith, N. G. 1967. Capturing seabirds with avertin. J. Wildl. Manage. 31(3):479–483.

Smith, N. S. 1970. Appraisal of condition estimation methods for East African ungulates. E. Afr. Wildl. J. 8:123–129.

Smith, N. S., and H. P. Ledger. 1965a. A portable tripod and weighing assembly for large animals. J. Wildl. Manage. 29(1):208–209.

Smith, N. S., and H. P. Ledger. 1965b. A method of predicting liveweight from dissected leg weight. J. Wildl. Manage. 29(3):504–511.

Smith, R. C., and W. M. Reid. 1972. Guide to the literature of the life sciences. 8th ed. Burgess Publ. Co., Minneapolis, Minn. 166 p.

Smith, R. H. 1973. Crab apples for wildlife food. N.Y. Fish and Game J. 20(1):1–24.

Smith, R. L. 1974. Ecology and field biology. 2nd ed. Harper and Row Publ., New York. 850 p.

Smith, T. G., and I. Stirling. 1975. The breeding habitat of the ringed seal *(Phoca hispida)*. The birth lair and associated structures. Can. J. Zool. 53(9):1297–1305.

Smithers, R. H. N. 1973a. Recording data on mammal specimens. National Mus. Monuments Rhodesia, Causeway. 11 p.

Smithers, R. H. N. 1973b. Mammals: the preparation of museum study skins. Natl. Mus. Monuments Rhodesia, Causeway. 12 p.

Smuts, G. L., I. J. Whyte, and T. W. Dearlove. 1977. Advances in the mass capture of lions *(Panthera leo)*. Int. Congr. Game Biol. 13:420–431.

Snedecor, G. W. 1956. Statistical methods, 5th ed. Iowa State Press, Ames. 534 p.

Snider, C. C., and J. M. Asplund. 1974. In vitro digestibility of deer foods from the Missouri Ozarks. J. Wildl. Manage. 38(1):20–31.

Snyder, L. L. 1935. A study of the sharp-tailed grouse. Univ. of Toronto Stud. Biol. Ser. No. 40, Toronto. 66 p.

Society of American Foresters, Committee on Terminology. 1958. Forest terminology; a glossary of technical terms used in forestry. S. A. F., Washington, D.C. 97 p.

Sohn, A. J. 1968. Time-lapse movie camera for recording recreation activity cycles. Proc. Iowa Acad. Sci. 75:184–189.

Soil Conservation Service. 1966. Aerial-photo interpretation in classifying and mapping soils. USDA Agric. Handb. 294. 89 p.

Soil Conservation Society of America. 1952. Soil and water conservation glossary. J. Soil and Water Cons. 7(1):41–52, 7(2):93–104, 7(3):144–156.

Sokal, R. R. 1965. Statistical methods in systematics. Biol. Rev. 40(3): 337–391.

Sokal, R. R., and F. J. Rohlf. 1969. Biometry: the principles and practice of statistics in biological research. W. H. Freeman and Co., San Francisco. 776 p.

Solomon, D. L. 1979. On a paradigm for mathematical modeling. p. 231–250 *in* G. P. Patil and M. L. Rosenzweig, (eds.). Contemporary quantitative ecology and related econometrics. Stat. Ecol. Series. Vol. 12. Int. Coop. Publ. House. Fairland, Md. 689 p.

Solomon, D. L., and C. Walters, (eds.). 1977. Mathematical models in biological discovery. Springer Verlag. New York. 240 p.

Sonenshine, D. E., D. G. Cerretani, G. Enlow, and B. L. Elisberg. 1973. Improved methods for capturing wild flying squirrels. J. Wildl. Manage. 37(4):588–590.

Sooter, C. A. 1946. Muskrats of Tule Lake Refuge, California. J. Wildl. Manage. 10(1):68–70.

Soots, R. F., Jr., and M. C. Landin. 1978. Development and management of avian habitat on dredged material islands. Tech. Rep. DS–78–18. U.S. Army Engin. Waterways Exp. Stn., Vicksburg, Miss. 96 p.

Soper, J. D. 1961. The mammals of Manitoba. Can. Field-Nat. 75(4): 171–219.

Soper, J. D. 1962. In memorium: Rudolph Martin Anderson, 1876–1961. Can. Field-Nat. 76:127–141.

Southern, H. N. 1964. The handbook of British mammals. Blackwell Sci. Publ. Oxford. 465 p.

Southern, H. N., J. S. Watson, and D. Chitty. 1946. Watching nocturnal animals by infra-red radiation. J. Anim. Ecol. 15(2):198–202.

Southern, W. E. 1963. Equipment and techniques for using radiotelemetry in wildlife studies. North Illinois Univ. Dept. Biol. Sci. Rep. No. 3. 33 p. (mimeo.)

Southern, W. E. 1964. Additional observations of winter bald eagle populations: including remarks on biotelemetry techniques and immature plumages. Wilson Bull. 76 (2):121–137.

Southern, W. E. 1971. Evaluation of a plastic wing-marker for gull studies. Bird-Banding 42(2):88–91.

Southwick, E. E. 1973. Remote sensing of body temperature in a captive 25-g bird. Condor 75(4):464–466.

Southwood, T. R. E. 1966. Ecological methods, with particular reference to the study of insect populations. Methuen and Co. Ltd, London. 391 p.

Sowls, L. K. 1948. The Franklin ground squirrel, *Citellus franklini* (Sabine), and its relationship to nesting ducks. J. Mammal. 29(2):113–137.

Sowls, L. K. 1950. Techniques for waterfowl nesting studies. Trans. N. Am. Wildl. Conf. 15:478–487.

Sowls, L. K. 1955. Prairie ducks: a study of their behavior, ecology, and management. Wildl. Manage. Inst., Washington, D.C. and Stackpole Co., Harrisburg, Pa. 193 p.

Sowls, L. K., and P. S. Minnamon. 1963. Glass beads for marking home ranges of mammals. J. Wildl. Manage. 27(2):299–302.

Sowls, L. K., and R. E. Schweinsburg. 1967. An improved propulsion system for short range projection of immobilization darts. J. Wildl. Manage. 31(2):345–346.

Spalding, D. J. 1966. Eruption of permanent canine teeth in the northern sea lion. J. Mammal. 47(1):157–158.

Sparks, D. R., and J. C. Malechek. 1968. Estimating percentage dry weight in diets using a microscopic technique. J. Range Manage. 21 (4):264–265.

Sparrowe, R. D., and P. F. Springer. 1970. Seasonal activity patterns of white-tailed deer in eastern South Dakota. J. Wildl. Manage. 34(2): 420–431.

Special Libraries Association. 1976. How to obtain a translation. Lockheed-California Cent. Libr. Burbank.

Special Reports, Inc. 1973. Who's who in ecology. Vol. 1. Spec. Rep. Inc., New York. 291 p.

Spence, L. E., Jr. 1963. Study of identifying characteristics of mammal hair. Wyoming Game and Fish Comm. P-R Project FW–3–R. 121 p.

Spencer, H. E., Jr. 1953. The cinnamon teal *(Anas cyanoptera* Vieillot*)*: its life history, ecology, and management. M. S. Thesis. Utah State Univ., Logan. 184 p.

Sperry, C. C. 1941. Food habits of the coyote. USDI Wildl. Res. Bull. No. 4. 70 p.

Spillett, J. J., J. B. Low, and D. Sill. 1967. Livestock fences—how they influence pronghorn antelope movements. Utah State Univ. Agric. Exp. Stn. Bull. 470, Logan. 79 p.

Spillett, J. J., and R. S. ZoBell. 1967. Innovations in trapping and handling pronghorn antelopes. J. Wildl. Manage. 31(2):347–351.

Spinner, G. P., and J. S. Bishop. 1950. Chemical analysis of some wildlife foods in Connecticut. J. Wildl. Manage. 14(2):175–180.

Sports Illustrated, (eds.). 1959. Sports Illustrated book of dog training. Lippincott, Philadelphia. 88 p.

Sprungman, O. I. 1951. Photography afield. Stackpole Co., Harrisburg, Pa. 449 p.

Sprunt, A., Jr. 1954. Florida bird life. Coward McCann Inc., New York and Nat. Aud. Soc., New York. 527 p.

Spurr, S. H. 1948. Aerial photographs in forestry. Ronald Press Co., New York. 340 p.

Spurr, S. H. 1960. Photogrammetry and photo-interpretation. Ronald Press Co., New York. 472 p.

Spurr, S. H., and B. V. Barnes. 1973. Forest ecology. 2nd ed. The Ronald Press Co., New York. 571 p.

Squires, W. A. 1968. The mammals of New Brunswick. New Brunswick Mus. Monogr. Ser. No. 5. 57 p.

Stabenfeldt, G. H., and V. M. Shille. 1977. Reproduction in the dog and cat. p. 499–527 *in* H. H. Cole and P. T. Cupps, (eds.). Reproduction in domestic animals. 3rd ed. Academic Press, New York and London. 665 p.

Stacy, R. W. 1960. Biological and medical electronics. McGraw-Hill, New York. 308 p.

Stafford, S. K., and L. E. Williams, Jr. 1968. Data on capturing black bears with alpha-chloralose. Proc. Southeastern Assoc. Game and Fish Commissioners 22:161–165.

Stains, H. J. 1958. Field key to guard hair of middle western furbearers. J. Wildl. Manage. 22(1):95–97.

Stains, H. J. 1959. Use of the calcaneum in studies of taxonomy and food habits. J. Mammal. 40(3):392–401.

Stanka, V. 1958. Institutions of U.S.S.R. active in Arctic research and development. Arctic Inst. N. Am., Washington, D.C. 100 p.

Stasko, A. B., and D. G. Pincock. 1977. Review of underwater biotelemetry, with emphasis on ultrasonic techniques. J. Fish. Res. Board Can. 34(9):1262–1285.

Steedman, H. F. 1960. Section cutting in microscopy. Blackwell, Oxford. 172 p.

Steel, P. E., P. D. Dalke, and E. G. Bizeau. 1957. Canada goose production at Gray's Lake, Idaho, 1949–1951. J. Wildl. Manage. 21(1):38–41.

Steel, R. G. D., and J. H. Torrie. 1960. Principles and procedures of statistics with special reference to the biological sciences. McGraw-Hill Book Co. Inc., New York. 481 p.

Steen, E. B. 1971. Dictionary of biology. Barnes and Noble, Publ., New York. 630 p.

Steere, W. C. 1976. Biological abstracts/BIOSIS; the first fifty years; the evolution of a major science information service. Plenum Press, New York. 233 p.

Steinbach, H. B. 1964. The quest for certainty: Science Citation Index. Science 145(3628):142–143.

Stelfox, J. G., M. C. S. Kingsley, and B. Kloosterman. 1977. Computer-compatible wildlife data forms. Trans. Int. Congr. Game Biol. 13:512–517.

Stelfox, J. G., and J. R. Robertson. 1976. Immobilizing bighorn sheep with succinylcholine chloride and phencyclidine hydrochloride. J. Wildl. Manage. 40(1):174–176.

Stephenson, A. B. 1977. Age determination and morphological variation of Ontario otters. Can. J. Zool. 55(10):1577–1583.

Sterling, K. B. 1974. Last of the naturalists: the career of C. Hart Merriam. Arno Press, New York. 478 p.

Sterner, R. T., and C. P. Breidenstein. 1976. Set of ADVANCED-BASIC programs for literature storage and retrieval with minicomputers. Behav. Res. Methods Instrum. 8(4): 397–398.

Stevenson, J. 1933. Experiments on the digestion of food by birds. Wilson Bull. 45(4):155–167.

Stewart, D. R. M. 1965. The epidermal characters of grasses, with special reference to East African plains species. Bot. Jahrb. 84(182):63–74.

Stewart, D. R. M. 1967. Analysis of plant epidermis in faeces: a technique for studying the food preferences of grazing herbivores. J. Appl. Ecol. 4:83–111.

Stewart, D. R. M. 1970. Survival during digestion of epidermis from plants eaten by ungulates. Rev. Zool. Bot. Afr. 82:343–348.

Stewart, D. R. M., and J. Stewart. 1970. Food preference data by faecal analysis for African plains ungulates. Zool. Afr. 5(1):115–129.

Stewart, G. R., J. M. Siperek, and V. R. Wheeler. 1977. Chemical restraint of black bears. Fourth Int. Bear Conf., Kalispell, Mont. 13 p.

Stewart, P. A. 1954. Combination substratum and automatic trap for nesting mourning doves. Bird-Banding 25(1):6–8.

Stewart, P. A. 1971. An automatic trap for use on bird nesting boxes. Bird-Banding 42(2):121–122.

Stewart, P. A. 1973. Estimating numbers in a roosting congregation of blackbirds and starlings. Auk 90 (2):353–358.

Stewart, R. E. 1951. Clapper rail populations of the Middle Atlantic states. Trans. N. Am. Wildl. Conf. 16:421–430.

Stewart, R. E. 1975. Breeding birds of North Dakota. Tri-College Center for Environmental Studies, Fargo, North Dakota, 295 p.

Stewart, R. E., and H. A. Kantrud. 1971. Classification of natural ponds and lakes in the glaciated prairie region. U.S. Fish Wildl. Serv. Resour. Publ. 92. 57 p.

Stickel, W. H. 1953. Control of snakes. U.S. Fish Wildl. Serv. Wildl. Leafl. 345. Washington, D.C. 8 p.

Stickney, P. F. 1966. Browse utilization based on percentage of twig numbers browsed. J. Wildl. Manage. 30(1):204–206.

Stieglitz, W. O., and C. T. Wilson. 1968. Breeding biology of the Florida duck. J. Wildl. Manage. 32(4):921–934.

Stiles, V. D. 1967. Observations on the behavior of the bobcat *(Lynx rufus rufus)* in the Quabbin reservation. Unpubl. manuscr. Univ. of Mass., Amherst. 80 p.

Stirling, I., and J. F. Bendell. 1966. Census of blue grouse with recorded calls of a female. J. Wildl. Manage. 30(1):184–187.

Stockdale, T. M. 1967. Blackbirds-depredation, research and control in Ohio and the Midwest. Proc. Vertebr. Pest Conf. 3:47–49.

Stoddard, H. L. 1931. The bobwhite quail; its habits, preservation, and increase. Charles Scribner's Sons, New York. 559 p.

Stoddart, L. A. 1941. Chemical composition of *Symphoricarpos rotundifolius* as influenced by soil, site, and date of collection. J. Agric. Res. 63(12):727–739.

Stoddart, L. A., A. D. Smith, and T. W. Box. 1975. Range management. 3rd ed. McGraw-Hill Book Co. New York. 532 p.

Stoddart, L. C. 1970. A telemetric method for detecting jackrabbit mortality. J. Wildl. Manage. 34(3):501–507.

Stokes, A. W. 1954. Population studies of the ring-necked pheasants on Pelee Island, Ontario. Ont. Dept. Lands and For. Wildl. Ser. Tech. Bull. 4. 154 p.

Stokes, J. D., G. E. Delisle, and J. B. McCormick. 1968. Fish and wildlife resource planning guide. California Dept. Fish and Game. 105 p.

Stoll, R. J., Jr., and D. Clay. 1975. Guide to aging wild turkey embryos. Ohio Fish and Wildl. Rep. No. 4, Columbus. 19 p.

Stone, C. P., and D. F. Mott. 1973. Bird damage to ripening field corn in the United States in 1971. U.S. Fish Wildl. Serv. Wildl. Leafl. No. 505. 8 p.

Stone, C. P., D. F. Mott, J. F. Besser, and J. W. DeGrazio. 1972. Bird damage to corn in the United States in 1970. Wilson Bull. 84(1):101–105.

Stone, W. 1933. American ornithological literature. p. 29–49 *in* Fifty years' progress of American ornithology, 1883–1933. Am. Ornithol. Union, Lancaster, Pa. 249 p.

Stone, W. B., A. S. Clauson, D. E. Slingerlands, and B. L. Weber. 1975. Use of Romanowsky stains to prepare tooth sections for aging mammals. N.Y. Fish and Game J. 22(2): 156–158.

Stonehouse, B., (ed.). 1977. Animal marking. Univ. Park Press, Baltimore, Md. 257 p.

Storer, T. I., G. H. Vansell, and B. D. Moses. 1938. Protection of mountain apiaries from bears by use of electric fence. J. Wildl. Manage. 2(4):172–178.

Storm, G. L., R. D. Andrews, R. L. Phillips, R. A. Bishop, D. B. Siniff, and J. R. Tester. 1976. Morphology, reproduction, dispersal, and mortality of midwestern red fox populations. Wildl. Monogr. No. 49. 82 p.

Storm, G. L., and K. P. Dauphin. 1965. A wire ferret for use in studies of foxes and skunks. J. Wildl. Manage. 29(3):625–626.

Storr, G. M. 1961. Microscopic analysis of faeces, a technique for ascertaining the diet of herbivorous mammals. Aust. J. Biol. Sci. 14(1):157–164.

Stott, R. S., and D. P. Olson. 1972. An evaluation of waterfowl surveys on the New Hampshire coastline. J. Wildl. Manage. 36(2):468–477.

Stotts, V. D., and D. E. Davis. 1960. The black duck in the Chesapeake Bay of Maryland: breeding behavior and biology. Chesapeake Sci. 1(3–4):127–154.

Stoudt, J. H. 1965. Project report on habitat requirements of the canvasback during the breeding season. U.S. Fish Wildl. Serv. Proj. A–8. 6 p.

Stoudt, J. H. 1971. Ecological factors affecting waterfowl production in Saskatchewan parklands. Bur. Sport Fish. Wildl. Resour. Publ. 99. 58 p.

Strahler, A. N. 1957. Quantitative analysis of watershed geomorphology. Trans. Am. Geophys. Union 38: 913–920.

Strandberg, C. H. 1967. Aerial discovery manual. John Wiley and Sons Inc., New York. 249 p.

Strange, T. H., E. R. Cunningham, and J. W. Goertz. 1971. Use of nest boxes by wood ducks in Mississippi. J. Wildl. Manage. 35(4):786–793.

Streifer, W. 1974. Realistic models in population ecology. p. 199–266 *in* A. MacFadyen, (ed.). Advances in ecological research. Vol. 8. Acad. Press, New York, 418 p.

Strelkov, A., and K. Yur'yev, (eds.). 1962. Handbook of Soviet zoologists. U.S. Joint Publ. Res. Serv. Transl. No. 13188, Dept. Commerce, Washington, D.C. 443 p.

Strode, D. H., and D. L. Leedy. 1941. Analysis of pheasant reproduction, cover utilization and mortality, Wood County, Ohio. Ohio Wildl. Res. Stn. Release 167, Columbus, 34 p.

Strong, R. M. 1939–1959. A bibliography of birds. Field Mus. Nat. Hist., Chicago. Vol. 25. pts. 1–4.

Strunk, W., Jr., and E. B. White. 1979. The elements of style. Macmillan Publ. Co., New York. 85 p.

Studer, J. J. 1963. Electronic circuits and instrumentation systems. John Wiley and Sons Inc., New York. 423 p.

Stuewer, F. W. 1943. Reproduction of raccoons in Michigan. J. Wildl. Manage. 7(1):60–73.

Stunkard, J. A., and J. C. Miller. 1974. An outline guide to general anesthesia in exotic species. Vet. Med. Small Anim. Clin. 69(9):1181–1186.

Sudman, S. 1967. Reducing the cost of surveys, Aldine Publ. Co., Chicago, Ill. 246 p.

Sudman, S. 1976. Applied sampling. Academic Press, New York. 249 p.

Sudman, S., and N. M. Bradburn. 1974. Response effects in surveys: a review and synthesis. Aldine Publ. Co., Chicago, Ill. 257 p.

Sugden, L. G. 1956. A technique for closing gates on big-game live traps by remote control. J. Wildl. Manage. 20(4):467.

Sugden, L. G. 1976. Waterfowl damage to Canadian grain: current problem and research needs. Can. Wildl. Serv. Occas. Pap. No. 24. 24 p.

Sugden, L. G. and H. L. Poston. 1968. A nasal marker for ducks. J. Wildl. Manage. 32(4):984–986.

Sugden, L. G. and H. L. Poston. 1970. A raft trap for ducks. Bird-Banding 41(2):128–129.

Sullins, G. L., D. O. McKay, and B. J. Verts. 1976. Estimating ages of cottontails by periosteal zonations. Northwest Sci. 50(1):17–22.

Sullivan, E. G., and A. O. Haugen. 1956. Age determination of foxes by x-ray of forefeet. J. Wildl. Manage. 20(2):210–212

Sullivan, J. A., and P. F. Scanlon. 1976. Effects of grouping and fighting on the reproductive tracts of male white-footed mice *(Peromyscus leucopus)*. Res. Popul. Ecol. 17(2): 164–175.

Summerlin, C. T., and J. L. Wolfe. 1973. Social influences on trap response of the cotton rat, *Sigmodon hispidus*. Ecology 54(5):1156–1159.

Sumner, L., and J. S. Dixon. 1953. Birds and mammals of the Sierra Nevada. Univ. California Press, Berkeley. 484 p.

Sundstrom, C. 1968. Water consumption by pronghorn antelope and distribution related to water in Wyoming's Red Desert. Antelope States Workshop Proc. 3:39–46.

Sundstrom, C. 1970. Influence of fencing on antelope in the Red Desert of Wyoming. Trans. Central Mt. and Plains Sect. Wildl. Soc. 4 p.

Sutton, G. M. 1967. Oklahoma birds: their ecology and distribution, with comments on the avifauna of the Southern Great Plains. Univ. of Oklahoma Press, Norman. 674 p.

Svoboda, F. J., and G. W. Gullion. 1974. Techniques for monitoring ruffed grouse food resources. Wildl. Soc. Bull. 2(4):195–197.

Swank, W. G. 1952. Trapping and marking of adult nesting doves. J. Wildl. Manage. 16(1):87–90.

Swank, W. G. 1955. Feather molt as an ageing technique for mourning doves. J. Wildl. Manage. 19(3):412–414.

Swank, W. G. 1956. Protein and phosphorus content of browse plants as an influence on southwestern deer herd levels. Trans. N. Am. Wildl. Conf. 21:141–158.

Swanson, G. 1940. Food habits of the sharp-tailed grouse by analysis of droppings. J. Wildl. Manage. 4(4): 432–436.

Swanson, G. A. 1978a. A simple lightweight core sampler for quantitating waterfowl foods. J. Wildl. Manage. 42(2):426–428.

Swanson, G. A. 1978b. A water column sampler for invertebrates in shallow wetlands. J. Wildl. Manage. 42(3): 670–672.

Swanson, G. A., and J. C. Bartonek. 1970. Bias associated with food analysis in gizzards of blue-winged teal. J. Wildl. Manage. 34(4):739–746.

Swanson, G. A., G. L. Krapu, J. C. Bartonek, J. R. Serie, and D. H. Johnson. 1974. Advantages in mathematically weighting waterfowl food habits data. J. Wildl. Manage. 38 (2):302–307.

Swanson, G. A., V. B. Kuechle, and A. B. Sargeant. 1976. A telemetry technique for monitoring diel waterfowl activity. J. Wildl. Manage. 40(1):187–190.

Swanson, G. A., and A. B. Sargeant. 1972. Observation of nighttime feeding behavior of ducks. J. Wildl. Manage. 36(3):959–961.

Swanson, G. A., and W. H. Thornsberry. 1972. Avian food habits analysis using a modified counter. J. Wildl. Manage. 36(3):949–950.

Swartz, D. 1971. Collegiate dictionary of botany. Ronald Press, New York. 520 p.

Swartzmann, G. L., and G. M. Van Dyne. 1972. An ecologically based simulation-optimization approach to natural resource planning. p. 327–398 *in* R. F. Johnston, P. W. Frank, C. D. Michener., (eds.). Annual Rev. Ecol. System. Annual Review Inc. Palo Alto, Calif. Vol. 3. 520 p.

Sweeney, J. R., R. L. Marchinton, and J. M. Sweeney. 1971. Responses of radio-monitored white-tailed deer chased by hunting dogs. J. Wildl. Manage. 35(4):707–716.

Swick, C. D. 1974. Operational management plan for the coyote. Calif. Dept. Fish and Game, Sacramento.

Swift, D. M., J. E. Ellis, and N. T. Hobbs. 1979. Application of a ruminant energetics model to a study of elk winter range carrying capacity. p. 457–460. *in* Proceedings first conference on scientific research in the National Parks. Natl. Park Serv. Trans. & Proc. Ser. No. 5. 1325 p.

Swift, D. M., and R. K. Steinhorst. 1976. A technique for estimating small mammal population densities using a grid and assessment lines. Acta Theriol. 21:471–480.

Swift, R. W. 1948. Deer select most nutritious forages. J. Wildl. Manage. 12(1):109–110.

Swift, R. W. 1957. The nutritive evaluation of forages. Pennsylvania State Univ. Agric. Exp. Stn. Bull. 615. 34 p.

Sykes, P. W., and R. Chandler. 1974. Use of artificial nest structures by Everglade kites. Wilson Bull. 86 (3):282–284.

Szymczak, M. R., and J. F. Corey. 1976. Construction and use of the Salt Plains duck trap in Colorado. Colo. Div. Wildl. Rep. No. 6. 13 p.

Taber, R. D. 1949. A new marker for game birds. J. Wildl. Manage. 13(2):228–231.

Taber, R. D. 1956a. Deer nutrition and population dynamics in the north coast range of California. Trans. N. Am. Wildl. Conf. 21:159–172.

Taber, R. D. 1956b. Characteristics of the pelvic girdle in relation to sex in black-tailed and white-tailed deer. Calif. Fish and Game 42(1):15–21.

Taber, R. D., and I. McT. Cowan. 1969. Capturing and marking wild animals. p. 277–317 *in* R. H. Giles, (ed.). Wildlife management techniques. 3rd ed. The Wildl. Soc., Washington, D.C. 623 p.

Taber, R. D., and R. F. Dasmann. 1958. The black-tailed deer of the chaparral. Calif. Dept. Fish and Game, Game Bull. No. 8. 163 p.

Taber, R. D., K. L. White, and N. S. Smith. 1959. The annual cycle of condition in the Rattlesnake, Montana, mule deer. Proc. Mont. Acad. Sci. 19:72–79.

Tagg, G. F. 1974. Electrical indicating instruments. Crane, Russak, New York. 227 p.

Takos, M. J. 1947. A semi-quantitative study of muskrat food habits. J. Wildl. Manage. 11(4):331–339.

Talbot, L. M. 1965. A survey of past and present wildlife research in East Africa. E. Afr. Wildl. J. 3:61–85.

Talbot, L. M., and H. F. Lamprey. 1961. Immobilization of free-ranging East African ungulates with succinylcholine chloride. J. Wildl. Manage. 25(3):303–310.

Talbot, L. M., and J. S. G. McCulloch. 1965. Weight estimations for East African mammals from body measurements. J. Wildl. Manage. 29(1): 84–89.

Talbot, L. M., and M. H. Talbot. 1962. A hoisting apparatus for weighing and loading large animals in the field. J. Wildl. Manage. 26(2):217–218.

Talbot, L. M., and M. H. Talbot. 1963. The high biomass of wild ungulates on East African savanna. Trans. N. Am. Wildl. Conf. 28:465–476.

Tanner, W. D., and G. L. Bowers. 1948. A method for trapping male ruffed grouse. J. Wildl. Manage. 12(3):330–331.

Tanner, W. D., and G. O. Hendrickson. 1954. Ecology of the Virginia rail in Clay County, Iowa. Iowa Bird Life 24(4):65–70.

Tansley, A. G. 1920. The classification of vegetation and the concept of development. J. Ecol. 8(1):118–149.

Tansley, A. G., and T. F. Chipp. 1926. Aims and methods in the study of vegetation. Br. Emp. Veg. Comm., Whitefriars Press, London. 383 p.

Taranik, J. V. 1978. Characteristics of the Landsat multispectral data system. U.S. Geol. Surv Open-File Rep. No. 78–187. Reston, Va. 76 p.

Taverner, P. A. 1953. Birds of Canada. Natl. Mus. of Canada and the Musson Book Co., Toronto Book Co., Toronto. 446 p.

Taylor, J. M., and H. Jean. 1964. Rechargeable battery power for a portable photographic recorder. J. Wildl. Manage. 28(2):406–408.

Taylor, W. P., (ed.). 1956. The deer of North America. Stackpole Co., Harrisburg, Pa. and the Wildl. Manage. Inst., Washington, D.C. 668 p.

Teer, J. G. 1964. Predation by long-tailed weasels on eggs of blue-winged teal. J. Wildl. Manage. 28(2):404–406.

Teer, J. G., J. W. Thomas, and E. A. Walker. 1965. Ecology and management of the white-tailed deer in the Llano Basin of Texas. Wildl. Monogr. No. 15. 62 p.

Teicher, M. H., and W. T. Green. 1977. A digital readout vibrational activity monitor for new born animals. Physiol. Behav. 18(4):747–750.

Telberg, I. 1964. Who's who in Soviet science and technology. Telberg Book Co., New York. 301 p.

Telfer, E. S. 1969. Twig weight-diameter relationships for browse species. J. Wildl. Manage. 33(4): 917–921.

Tempelis, C. H., and M. L. Rodrick. 1973. Serologic technique for the identification of animal blood proteins. J. Wildl. Manage. 37(4):584–585.

Temple, S. A. 1972. A portable time-lapse camera for recording wildlife activity. J. Wildl. Manage. 36(3): 944–947.

Tener, J. S. 1954. A preliminary study of the musk-oxen of Fosheim Peninsula, Ellesmere Island, N.W.T. Can. Wildl. Serv., Natl. Parks Branch, Wildl. Manage. Bull. Ser. 1, No. 9, Ottawa. 34 p.

Tennessee Game and Fish Commission. 1972. European hog research project. W–34, final report. 259 p.

Tepper, E. E. 1967. Statistical methods in using mark-recapture data for population estimation. U.S. Dept. of Inter. Libr. Bibliogr. No. 4. 65 p.

Terres, J. K. 1961. Available field check-lists of birds—Canada and the United States. Audubon Mag. 63:44–47, 62, 64, 229, 233, 344.

Tester, J. R., and K. L. Heezen. 1965. Deer response to a drive census determined by radio tracking. BioScience 15(2):100–104.

Tester, J. R., D. W. Warner, and W. W. Cochran. 1964. A radio-tracking system for studying movements of deer. J. Wildl. Manage. 28(1):42–45.

Thibeau, C. E. 1972. Directory of environmental information sources. 2nd ed. Nat. Found. Environ. Control, Boston. 457 p.

Thiessen, A. H., (comp.). 1946. Weather glossary. U.S. Dept. of Commerce, Weather Bureau, Washington, D.C. 299 p.

Thoma, J. A. 1962. Simple and rapid method for the coding of punched cards. Science 137(3526):278–279.

Thomas, D. C. 1977. Metachromatic staining of dental cementum for mammalian age determination. J. Wildl. Manage. 41(2):207–210.

Thomas, D. C., and P. J. Bandy. 1973. Age determination of wild black-tailed deer from dental annulations. J. Wildl. Manage. 37(2):232–235.

Thomas, D. C., and P. J. Bandy. 1975. Accuracy of dental-wear age estimates of black-tailed deer. J. Wildl. Manage. 39(4):674–678.

Thomas, J. W., H. Black, Jr., J. Scherzinger, and R. J. Pedersen. 1979a. Deer and elk. p. 104–127 *in* J. W. Thomas, (ed.). Wildlife habitats in managed forests—the Blue Mountains of Oregon and Washington. USDA For. Serv. Agric. Handb. No. 553. 512 p.

Thomas, J. W., R. M. DeGraaf, and J. C. Mawson. 1977. Determination of habitat requirements for birds in suburban areas. USDA For. Serv. Res. Pap. NE 357. Upper Darby, Pa. 15 p.

Thomas, J. W., C. Maser, and J. E. Rodiek. 1979b. Edge. p. 48–59 *in* J. W. Thomas, (ed.). Wildlife habitats in managed forests—the Blue Mountains of Oregon and Washington. USDA For. Serv. Handb. No. 553, 512 p.

Thomas, J. W., R. J. Miller, H. Black, J. E. Rodiek, and C. Maser. 1976. Guidelines for maintaining and enhancing wildlife habitat in forest management in the Blue Mountains of Oregon and Washington. Trans. N. Am. Wildl. and Nat. Resour. Conf. 41:452–476.

Thomas, J. W., R. M. Robinson, and R. G. Marburger. 1967. Use of diazepam in the capture and handling of cervids. J. Wildl. Manage. 31(4):686–692.

Thomas, K. P. 1969. Sex determination of bobwhites by wing criteria. J. Wildl. Manage. 33(1):215–216.

Thompson, D. R. 1958. Field techniques for sexing and aging game animals. Wis. Conserv. Dept. Spec. Wildl. Rep. No. 1, Madison. 44 p.

Thompson, H. V., and C. J. Armour. 1954. Methods of marking wild rabbits. J. Wildl. Manage. 18(3):411–414.

Thompson, L. 1977. Identification of critical wildlife habitat using an "Impact Risk" mapping technique. p. 421–442 *in* Proceeding national symposium on classification, inventory and analysis of fish and wildlife habitat. U.S. Fish and Wild. Serv. Office Biol. Serv. Publ. 78/76. 604 p.

Thompson, S. 1975. Snake control. Proc. Great Plains Wildl. Damage Control Workshop 2:175–185.

Thomson, *Sir* A. L., (ed.). 1964. A new dictionary of birds. McGraw-Hill, New York. 928 p.

Thomson, W. R. 1975. A photographic technique to quantify lateral cover density. J. South Afr. Wildl. Manage. Assoc. 5:75–78.

Thorley, G. A. 1975. Forest lands: inventory and assessment. p. 1353–1426 *in* R. G. Reeves, (ed.). Manual of remote sensing. Am. Soc. Photogramm., Falls Church, Va. 2 vols. 2142 p.

Thornburn, C. C. 1972. Isotopes and radiation in biology. Halsted Press, John Wiley and Sons Inc., New York. 287 p.

Thornley, J. H. M. 1976. Mathematical models in plant physiology. Academic Press, N.Y. 318 p.

Thornsberry, W. H., and L. M. Cowardin. 1971. A floating bail trap for capturing individual ducks in spring. J. Wildl. Manage. 35(4):837–839.

Thorpe, W. H. 1954. The process of song-learning in the chaffinch as studied by means of the sound spectrograph. Nature 173(4402):465–469.

Thurmon, J. C., D. R. Nelson, and J. O. Mozier. 1972. A preliminary report on the sedative effect of Bay VA 1470 in elk *(Cervus canadensis)*. J. Zoo Anim. Med. 3(4):9–14.

Tiemeier, O. W., and M. L. Plenert. 1964. A comparison of three methods for determining the age of black-tailed jackrabbits. J. Mammal. 45(3): 409–416.

Tietjen, H. P. 1976. Zincphosphide—a control agent for black-tailed prairie dogs. U.S. Fish Wildl. Serv. Wildl. Leafl. No. 509. 4 p.

Tilley, J. M. A., and R. A. Terry. 1963. A two-stage technique for the *in vitro* digestion of forage crops. J. Br. Grassl. Soc. 18(2):104–111.

Tilton, E. M. 1964. A union list of publications in opaque microforms. 2nd ed. Scarecrow Press, New York. 744 p.

Tilton, E. P., (ed.). 1972. The radio amateur's VHF manual. Am. Radio Relay League Publ. No. 23, Newington, Conn. 352 p.

Timm, D. E., and R. G. Bromley. 1976. Driving Canada geese by helicopter. Wildl. Soc. Bull. 4(4):180–181.

Tipton, A. R. 1975. A matrix structure for modeling population dynamics. Ph.D. Thesis. Mich. State Univ., Lansing. 52 p.

Tipton, A. R. 1977. The use of population models in research and management of wild hogs. p. 91–102 *in* G. W. Wood, (ed.). Proceedings of symposium on the research and management of wild hog populations. Belle W. Baruch For. Sci. Inst., Clemson Univ., Georgetown, S.C. 113 p.

Tipton, A. R., and R. T. Lackey. 1978. Use of modeling to assess impacts on fish and wildlife resources. p. 93–96 *in* D. E. Samuel, J. R. Stauffer, C. H. Hocutt, W. T. Mason, Jr., (eds.). Proceedings symposium on surface mining and fish/wildlife needs in eastern United States. Morgantown, W. Va. U.S. Fish and Wildl. Serv. 386 p.

Todd, C. D. 1975. The potentiometer handbook: users guide to cost effective applications. McGraw-Hill, New York. 300 p.

Todd, E. I., and K. W. Kenyon. 1972. Selected bibliography on the sea otter. U.S. Fish Wildl. Serv. Spec. Sci. Rep. No. 149. 40 p.

Todd, J. W., and R. M. Hansen. 1973. Plant fragments in the feces of bighorns as indicators of food habits. J. Wildl. Manage. 37(3):363–366.

Todd, R. L. 1977. Black rail, little black rail, black crake, farallon rail *(Laterallus jamaicensis)*. p. 71–83 *in* G. C. Sanderson, (ed.). Management of migratory shore and upland game birds in North America. Int. Assoc. Fish and Wildl. Agencies, Washington, D.C. 358 p.

Todd, W. E. C. 1928. List of types of birds in the collections of the Carnegie Museum on May 1, 1928. Ann. Carnegie Mus. 18:329–385.

Todd, W. E. C. 1963. Birds of the Labrador Peninsula and adjacent areas. Univ. of Toronto Press, Toronto. 819 p.

Todhunter, E. N. 1970. A guide to nutrition terminology for indexing and retrieval. U.S. Gov. Print. Off., Washington, D.C. 270 p.

Toll, J. E., T. S. Baskett, and C. H. Conaway. 1960. Home range, reproduction, and foods of the swamp rabbit in Missouri. Am. Midl. Nat. 63(2):398–412.

Tomback, D. F. 1975. An emetic technique to investigate food preferences. Auk 92(3):581–583.

Tomlinson, R. E. 1963. A method for drive-trapping dusky grouse. J. Wildl. Manage. 27(4):563–566.

Tomoff, C. S. 1974. Avian species diversity in desert scrub. Ecology 55(2):396–403.

Torgerson, O., and W. H. Pfander. 1971. Cellulose digestibility and chemical composition of Missouri deer foods. J. Wildl. Manage. 35(2): 221–231.

Torre-Bueno, J. R. 1976. Temperature regulation and heat dissipation during flight in birds. J. Exp. Biol. 65(2):471–482.

Townsend, G. H. 1966. A study of waterfowl nesting on the Saskatchewan River delta. Can. Field-Nat. 80(2):74–88.

Trainer, C. E. 1959. The 1959 western Canada goose *(Branta canadensis occidentalis)* study on the Copper River Delta, Alaska. *in* H. A. Hansen, (ed.). U.S. Fish Wildl. Serv. Annu. Waterfowl Rep. 11 p.

Trauger, D. L. 1974. Eye color of female lesser scaup in relation to age. Auk 91(2):243–254.

Trauger, D. L., and R. M. Bromley. 1975. Greater scaup of the West Mirage Islands, Great Slave Lake, Northwest Territories, Unpubl. Manuscr., North. Prairie Wildl. Res. Ctr. Jamestown, ND.

Trauger, D. L., and A. O. Haugen. 1965. Corpora lutea variations of white-tailed deer. J. Wildl. Manage. 29(3):487–492.

Trauger, D. L., and J. H. Stoudt. 1974. Looking out for the canvasback. Part II. Ducks Unlimited 38(4):30–31, 42, 44, 45, 48, 60.

Trautman, C. G. 1950. Criteria for determining the age of juvenile pheasants. South Dakota Pittman-Robertson Quart. Rep. 16:37–75.

Trefethen, J. B. 1964. Wildlife management and conservation, D.C. Heath and Co., Boston. 120 p.

Trefethen, J. B., and L. Miracle, (eds.). 1966. New hunter's encyclopedia. 3rd ed. Stackpole Co., Harrisburg, Pa. 1131 p.

Trelease, S. F. 1975. How to write scientific and technical papers. M.I.T. Press, Cambridge, Mass. 185 p.

Trippensee, R. E. 1941. A new type of bird and mammal marker. J. Wildl. Manage. 5(1):120–124.

Trippensee, R. E. 1948. Wildlife management, Vol. I. McGraw-Hill Book Co., New York. 479 p.

Trippensee, R. E. 1948–1953. Wildlife management. McGraw-Hill, New York. 2 vol.

Trout, L. E., and J. L. Thiessen. 1968. Food habits and condition of mule deer in Owyhee County. Proc. Western Assoc. State Game and Fish Commissioners 48:188–200.

Troyer, W. A., R. J. Hensel, and K. E. Durley. 1962. Live-trapping and handling of brown bears. J. Wildl. Manage. 26(3):330–331.

Tryon, C. A., and D. P. Snyder. 1973. Biology of the eastern chipmunk, *Tamias striatus:* life tables, age distributions, and trends in population numbers. J. Mammal. 54(1):145–168.

Tuck, L. M. 1972. The snipes: a study of the genus *Capella*. Can. Wildl. Serv. Mono. Ser. No. 5. 428 p.

Tueller, P. T., and L. S. Monroe. 1976. Management guidelines for selected deer habitats in Nevada. Agric. Exp. Stn. Publ. No. R104, Reno, Nev. 185 p.

Tufts, R. W. 1961. The birds of Nova Scotia. Nova Scotia Mus., Halifax. 481 p.

Tukey, H. B., Jr. 1966. Leaching of metabolites from above-ground plant parts and its implications. Bull. Torrey Bot. Club 93(6):385–401.

Turabian, K. L. 1973. A manual for writers of term papers, theses, and dissertations. 4th Ed. Univ. of Chicago Press. 216 p.

Turkevich, J. 1963. Soviet men of science; academicians and corresponding members of the Academy of Sciences of the USSR. Van Nostrand Inc., Princeton, N.J. 441 p.

Turkevich, J., and L. B. Turkevich. 1968. Prominent scientists of continental Europe. American Elsevier, New York. 204 p.

Turner, J. C. 1977. Cemental annulations as an age criterion in North American sheep. J. Wildl. Manage. 41(2):211–217.

Turner-Ettlinger, D. M. 1976. Natural history photography. Academic Press, New York. 395 p.

Tuttle, M. D. 1974. An improved trap for bats. J. Mammal. 55(2):475–477.

Tuttle, M. D. 1976. Collecting techniques. Biology of bats of the new world family Phyllostomatidae. Part 1. Mus. Texas Tech Univ. 10:71–88.

Tyson, E. L. 1959. A deer drive vs. track census. Trans. N. Am. Wildl. Conf. 24:457–464.

Uhlig, H. G. 1955. The determination of age of nestling and sub-adult gray squirrels in West Virginia. J. Wildl. Manage. 19(4):479–483.

Uhlig, H. G. 1956. The gray squirrel in West Virginia. W. Va. Conserv. Comm. Div. Game Manage. Bull. No. 3, Charleston. 83 p.

Ullrey, D. E., W. G. Youatt, H. E. Johnson, L. D. Fay, B. E. Brent, and K. E. Kemp. 1967. Digestibility of cedar and jack pine browse for the white-tailed deer. J. Wildl. Manage. 31(3):448–454.

Ullrey, D. E., W. G. Youatt, H. E. Johnson, L. D. Fay, B. E. Brent, and K. E. Kemp. 1968. Digestibility of cedar and balsam fir browse for the white-tailed deer. J. Wildl. Manage. 32(1):162–171.

Ullrey, D. E., W. G. Youatt, H. E. Johnson, L. D. Fay, B. L. Schoepke, and W. T. Magee. 1969. Digestible energy requirements for winter maintenance of Michigan white-tailed does. J. Wildl. Manage. 33(3): 482–490.

Ullrey, D. E., W. G. Youatt, H. E. Johnson, L. D. Fay, B. L. Shoepke, and W. T. Magee. 1970. Digestible and metabolizable energy requirements for winter maintenance of Michigan white-tailed does. J. Wildl. Manage. 34(4):863–869.

Ullrey, D. E., W. G. Youatt, H. E. Johnson, P. K. Ku, and L. D. Fay. 1964. Digestibility of cedar and aspen browse for the white-tailed deer. J. Wildl. Manage. 28(4):791–797.

Underwood, E. J. 1977. Trace elements in human and animal nutrition. 4th ed. Academic Press. New York. 545 p.

United Nations Educational, Scientific and Cultural Organization. 1949+. Scientific institutions and scientists in Latin America. UNESCO Centro de Cooperacion Cientifica para America Latina, Montevideo.

United Nations Educational, Scientific and Cultural Organization. 1953. Directory of institutions engaged in arid zone research. UNESCO, Paris. 110 p.

United Nations Educational, Scientific and Cultural Organization. 1962. Directory of zoological (and entomological) specimen collections of tropical institutions. UNESCO, Paris. 31 p.

United Nations Educational, Scientific and Cultural Organization. 1963. A review of the natural resources of the African continent. UNESCO, Paris. 437 p.

United Nations Educational, Scientific and Cultural Organization. 1965. World guide to science information and documentation services. UNESCO, Paris. 211 p.

United States Bureau of Census. 1967. The current population survey—a report on methodology. Tech. Pap. No. 7, U.S. Gov. Print. Off., Washington, D.C. 91 p.

Uphof, J. C. T. 1959. Dictionary of economic plants. Hafner, New York. 400 p.

Urbston, D. F., C. W. Smart, and P. F. Scanlon. 1976. Relationship between body weight and heart girth in white-tailed deer from South Carolina. Proc. Southeastern Assoc. Game and Fish Commissioners 30:471–473.

Urness, P. J., D. J. Neff, and J. R. Vahle. 1975. Nutrient content of mule deer diets from ponderosa pine range. J. Wildl. Manage. 39(4): 670–673.

USAEC. 1962. Special sources of information on isotopes. 3rd rev. Div. Tech. Inf. TID–4563, Oak Ridge. Tenn. 83 p.

USAEC. 1964. Understanding the atom. Booklets in series: nuclear terms; a brief glossary; fallout from nuclear tests; atoms in agriculture; neutron activation analysis. Div. Tech. Inf., Oak Ridge. Tenn.

U.S. Army Corps of Engineers. 1974. Preparation and coordination of environmental statements. ER 1105–2–507. 30 p.

U.S. Bureau of Land Management. 1964. Water development: range improvements in Nevada for wildlife, livestock, and human use. Reno, Nev. 37 p.

U.S. Bureau of Land Management. 1966. Polyethylene liner for pit reservoir including trough and fencing. Portland Serv. Cent. Tech. Note P 712c. Portland, Oreg. 4 p.

U.S. Bureau of Land Management. 1967. Engineering handbook and construction manual. Washington, D.C.

U.S. Bureau of Land Management. 1974. Proceedings regional fencing workshop. Washington, D.C. 74 p.

U.S. Bureau of Land Management. 1976. Environmental statements. Bur. Land Manage. Manual 1792.

U.S. Central Intelligence Agency. 1974. National environmental policy act implementation procedures. Logistic Instr. 45–16, Fed. Regist. 39:3579–3580.

U.S. Department Agriculture. 1976. How to manage woodlands for birds. USDA For. Serv., N.E. For. Exp. Stn. NE–INF–31–76. 8 p.

U.S. Department Interior. 1966. Focus on the Hudson. Bur. of Outdoor Rec., U.S. Gov. Print. Off. 51 p.

U.S. Fish and Wildlife Service. 1941. Directions for collecting materials for food habits studies. Wildl. Leafl. 193, Washington, D.C. 8 p. (processed)

U.S. Fish and Wildlife Service 1961. Manual for bird banding. Washington, D.C.

U.S. Fish and Wildlife Service. 1975. Directory of national wildlife refuges. U.S. Fish and Wildl. Serv., Washington, D.C. 16 p.

U.S. Fish and Wildlife Service. 1976a. Proceedings of the national wetland classification and inventory workshop, 1975. U.S. Dept. of Inter., Washington, D.C. 358 p.

U.S. Fish and Wildlife Service. 1976b. Habitat evaluation procedures. Div. Ecol. Serv. 30 p.

U.S. Fish and Wildlife Service. 1977a. Mexican wildlife laws. Dept. of the Interior. FS–17. 4 p. (mimeo.)

U.S. Fish and Wildlife Service. 1977b. Improving fish and wildlife benefits in range management. FWS/OBS–77/1, Washington, D.C. 118 p.

U.S. Fish and Wildlife Service. 1978. Terrestrial habitat evaluation criteria—Ecoregion 2410. (unpubl.)

U.S. Fish and Wildlife Service and Canadian Wildlife Service. 1976. North American bird banding manual. Vol. I. Dept. of the Inter., Washington, D.C. (v.p.)

U.S. Fish and Wildlife Service and Canadian Wildlife Service. 1977. North American bird banding manual. Vol. II. USDI, Washington, D.C.

U.S. Forest Service. 1959. Techniques and methods of measuring understory vegetation. Southern Forest Experiment Station and Southeastern Forest Experiment Station, USDA. 174 p.

U.S. Forest Service. 1960. Range improvement standards handbook. Washington, D.C.

U.S. Forest Service. 1963. Range research methods. USDA Misc. Publ. 940. 172 p.

U.S. Forest Service. 1965. Range seeding equipment handbook. Washington, D.C. 150 p.

U.S. Forest Service. 1969. Wildlife habitat improvement handbook. For. Serv. Handb. 2609.11, Washington, D.C. 146 p.

U.S. Forest Service. 1970. Range and wildlife habitat evaluation—a research symposium. USDA For. Serv. Misc. Publ. 1147, Washington, D.C. 220 p.

U.S. Forest Service. 1971. Wildlife habitat management handbook. FSH 2609.23R, Atlanta, Ga. 71 p.

U.S. Forest Service. 1974. Seeds of woody plants in the United States. USDA Agric. Handb. 450. 883 p.

U.S. Forest Service. 1976. Forestry controlled vocabulary: a vocabulary for indexing and retrieving forestry literature. U.S. For. Serv. Tech. Inf. Off., Washington, D.C. [227 p.]

U.S. Forest Service. 1977. Forest Service manual—title 2630.3 (policy). Washington, D.C.

U.S. Geological Survey. 1970. The national atlas of the United States of America. Washington, D.C. 417 p.

U.S. Government Printing Office. 1973. Style manual. 7th ed. Gov. Print. Off., Washington, D.C. 548 p.

Usher, G. 1966. A dictionary of botany. D. Van Nostrand Co., Princeton, N.Y. 404 p.

USHEW. 1970. Radiological health handbook. Rev. ed. USHEW Public Health Serv., Rockville, Md. 458 p.

U.S. Library of Congress. 1913–1940. List of American doctoral dissertations printed in 1912–38. U.S. Gov. Print. Off., Washington, D.C. 26 vols.

U.S. National Marine Fisheries Service. 1975. Guidelines for reviewing and commenting on draft environmental impact statements. Environ. Assess. Div. Instr. Ser. No. 6. 20 p.

U.S. National Park Service. 1976. National register of historic places. U.S. Gov. Print. Off., Washington, D.C. 961 p.

U.S. Nuclear Regulatory Commission. 1976. Preparation of environmental reports for nuclear power stations. USNRC Regul. Guide Ser., Reg. Guide 4.2, Rev. 2.

U.S. Nuclear Regulatory Commission. 1977. Terrestrial environmental studies for nuclear power stations. USNRC Regul. Guide 4.11, Rev. 1. 10 p.

U.S. Office of Water Resources Research. 1971. Water resources thesaurus. 2nd ed. Washington, D.C. 375 p.

Uspenskii, S. M. 1965. Geese of Wrangel Island. Wildfowl Trust Ann. Rep. 16:126–129.

U.S. Rural Electrification Administration. 1972. Powerline contact by eagles and other large birds. REA Bull. 61–10. Washington, D.C. 6 p.

U.S. Soil Conservation Service. 1976. Plant materials study: a search for drought-tolerant plant materials for erosion control, revegetation, and landscaping along California highways. USDA Soil Conserv. Serv. LPMC-1, Davis Calif. 145 p.

Vallentine, J. F. 1971. Range development and improvements. Brigham Young Univ. Press, Provo, Utah. 516 p.

Van Camp, L. F., and C. J. Henny. 1975. The screech owl: its life history and population ecology in northern Ohio. U.S. Fish and Wildl. Serv., N. Am. Fauna No. 71. 65 p.

Van Citters. R. L., and D. L. Franklin. 1966. Telemetry of blood pressure in free-ranging animals via an intravascular gauge. J. Appl. Physiol. 21(5):1633–1636.

Van Citters, R. L., W. S. Kemper, and D. L. Franklin. 1966. Blood pressure responses of wild giraffes studied by radio telemetry. Science 152 (3720):384–386.

Van Dyne, G. M. 1960. A procedure for rapid collection, processing, and analysis of line intercept data. J. Range Manage. 13(5):247–251.

Van Dyne, G. M., and H. F. Heady. 1965. Botanical composition of sheep and cattle diets on a mature annual range. Hilgardia 36(13): 465–492.

Van Gelder, R. G., and S. Anderson. 1967. An information retrieval system for collections of mammals. Curator 10(1):32–42.

Van Nostrand, F. C., and A. B. Stephenson. 1964. Age determination for beavers by tooth development. J. Wildl. Manage. 28(3):430–434.

Van Soest, P. J. 1967. Development of a comprehensive system of feed analyses and its application to forages. J. Anim. Sci. 26(1):119–128.

Van Soest, R. W. M., and W. L. Van Utrecht. 1971. The layered structure of bones of birds as a possible indication of age. Bijdr. Dierkd. 41(1):61–66.

Van Tyne, J. 1952. Principles and practices in collecting and taxonomic work. Auk 69 (1):27–33.

Van Winkle, W., (ed.). 1977. Proceedings of the conference on assessing the effects of power plant induced mortality on fish populations. Pergamon Press. N.Y. 380 p.

Van Winkle, W., S. W. Christensen, and G. Kauffman. 1976. Critique and sensitivity analysis of the compensation function used in the LMS Hudson River striped bass models. Oak Ridge Nat. Lab. Envir. Sciences Div. Publ. No. 944. 100 p.

Varland, K. L. 1976. Techniques for elk immobilization with succinylcholine chloride. Proc. Iowa Acad. Sci. 82(3–4):194–197.

Varner, I. M., R. E. Latimore, D. M. Gauton, E. R. Doman, and D. I. Rasmussen. 1954. Big game range analysis. USDA For. Serv. Intermt. Reg., Ogden, Utah. 54 p.

Varney, J. R., and D. H. Ellis. 1974. Telemetering egg for use in incubation and nesting studies. J. Wildl. Manage. 38(1):142–148.

Vaurie, C. 1964. Russian ornithological literature. Auk 81(2):238–241.

Vaurie, C. 1966. Recent Russian ornithological literature. Auk 83(4): 689–691.

Veaner, A. B. 1971. The evaluation of micro-publications; a handbook for librarians. Am. Libr. Assoc., Chicago. 59 p.

Veatch, J. O., and C. R. Humphrys. 1966. Water and water terminology. Thomas Print. and Publ. Co., Kaukauna, Wis. 375 p.

Verme, L. J. 1962. An automatic tagging device for deer. J. Wildl. Manage. 26(4):387–392.

Verme, L. J. 1965. Swamp conifer deeryards in northern Michigan. J. For. 63(7):523–529.

Verme, L. J., L. D. Fay, and U. V. Mostosky. 1962. Use of x-ray in determining pregnancy in deer. J. Wildl. Manage. 26(4):409–411.

Verme, L. J., and J. C. Holland. 1973. Reagent-dry assay of marrow fat in white-tailed deer. J. Wildl. Manage. 37(1):103–105.

Vermeer, K. 1970. A study of Canada geese, *Branta canadensis*, nesting on islands in southeastern Alberta. Can. J. Zool. 48(2):235–240.

Vernberg, F. J., (comp.). 1963. Field stations of the United States. Am. Zool. 3(3):245–386.

Vesey-Fitzgerald, D. F. 1960. Grazing succession among East African game animals. J. Mammal. 41(2):161–172.

Vestjens, W. J. M., and R. Carrick. 1974. Food of the black-backed magpie, *Gymnorhina t. tibicen* at Canberra. Aust. Wildl. Res., 1:71–83.

Viaud, P., and Y. Le Cain. 1975. An apparatus for recording animal motor activity. Behaviour 52(3–4):313–316.

Vincent, J.-P., and J.-P. Quéré. 1972 Quelques données sur la reproduction et sur la dynamique des populations du rat musqué *Ondatra zibethica* L. dans le nord de la France (Some data on reproduction and population dynamics of the muskrat, *Ondatra zibethica* L. in northern France. Ann. Zool. Ecol. Anim. 4(3): 395–415.

Vindasius, D. 1974. Public participation techniques and methodologies: a resume. Environ. Can. Inland Waters Directorate Soc. Sci. Ser. 12, Ottawa. 30 p.

Vogelsang, R. W. 1977. Blood urea nitrogen, serum cholesterol and progestins as affected by nutritional intake, pregnancy and the estrous cycle in white-tailed deer. M. S. Thesis. Va. Polytech. Inst. State Univ., Blacksburg. 109 p.

Vogelsang, R. W., R. L. Kirkpatrick, and P. F. Scanlon. 1977. Progestin levels as indicators of multiple pregnancy in white-tailed deer. Va. J. Sci. 28(2):69 (Abstr.).

Vogtman, D. B. 1945. Flushing tube for determining food of game birds. J. Wildl. Manage. 9(3):255–257.

Voigt, M. J. 1961. Scientists' approaches to information. ACRL Monogr. 24. Am. Libr. Assoc., Chicago, Ill. 81 p.

Voisey, P. W., and W. Kalbfleisch. 1962. A mechanical treadle for the study of small animal traffic in the field or laboratory. J. Mammal. 43(2):281.

Voth, E. H., and H. C. Black. 1973. A histological technique for determining feeding habits of small herbivores. J. Wildl. Manage. 37(2):223–231.

Wade, D. A. 1973. Control of damage by coyotes and some other carnivores. Colo. State Univ. Coop. Ext. Serv. Bull. 482a, Fort Collins. 16 p.

Wade, D. A. 1976. The use of aircraft in predator control. Proc. Vertebr. Pest Conf. 7:154–160.

Wadkins, L. A. 1948. Dyeing birds for identification. J. Wildl. Manage. 12(4):388–391.

Wadley, F. M. 1954. Limitations of the "zero method" of population counts. Science 119(3098):689–690.

Wagstaffe, R., and J. H. Fidler., (eds.). 1955. The preservation of natural history specimens. Vol. 1. Invertebrates. H. F. and G. Witherby, London. 205 p.

Walker, E. P., F. Warnick, K. I. Lange, H. E. Vible, S. E. Hamlet, M. A. Davis, and P. F. Wright. 1964. Mammals of the world. Johns Hopkins Press, Baltimore, Md. 3 vol.

Walker, P. L., and J. G. H. Cant. 1977. A population survey of kinkajous (*Potos flavus*) in a seasonally dry tropical forest. J. Mammal. 58 (1):100–102.

Wallmo, O. C. 1956. Determination of sex and age of scaled quail. J. Wildl. Manage. 20(2):154–158.

Wallmo, O. C. 1964. Problems in the use of herd classification data. Proc. Ann. Meet. New Mexico-Arizona Sect. The Wildl. Soc. 3:6–18.

Wallmo, O. C., L. H. Carpenter, W. L. Regelin, R. B. Gill, and D. L. Baker. 1977. Evaluation of deer habitat on a nutritional basis. J. Range Manage. 30(2):122–127.

Wallmo, O. C., R. B. Gill, L. H. Carpenter, and D. W. Reichert. 1973. Accuracy of field estimates of deer food habits. J. Wildl. Manage. 37(4):556–562.

Wallmo, O. C., and D. J. Neff. 1970. Direct observation of tamed deer to measure their consumption of natural forage. p. 105–109 *in* Range and wildlife habitat evaluation—a research symposium. USDA For. Serv. Misc. Publ. No. 1147. 220 p.

Walski, T. W., and W. W. Mautz. 1977. Nutritional evaluation of three winter browse species of snowshoe hares. J. Wildl. Manage. 41(1): 144–147.

Walters, C. J., and P. J. Bandy. 1972. Periodic harvest as a method of increasing big game yields. J. Wildl. Manage. 36(1):128–134.

Walters, C. J., R. Hilborn, E. Oguss, R. M. Peterman, and J. M. Stander. 1974. Development of a simulation model of mallard duck populations. Can. Wildl. Serv. Occas. Publ. 20, Ottawa. 35 p.

Walters, C. J., R. Hilborn, and R. Peterman. 1975. Computer simulation of barren ground caribou dynamics. Ecological Modeling. 1(4):303– 315.

Wang, C. H., D. L. Willis, and W. D. Loveland. 1975. Radiotracer methodology in the biological environmental and physical sciences. Prentice-Hall Inc., Englewood Cliffs, N.J. 480 p.

Ward, A. L. 1970. Stomach content and fecal analysis: methods of forage identification. p. 146–158 *in* Range and wildlife habitat evaluation—a research symposium. USDA Misc. Publ. 1147. 220 p.

Ward, A. L. 1971. In vitro digestibility of elk winter forage in southern Wyoming. J. Wildl. Manage. 35 (4):681–688.

Ward, A. L., and J. O. Keith. 1962. Feeding habits of pocket gophers on mountain grasslands, Black Mesa, Colorado. Ecology 43(4):744–749.

Ward, D. R. 1952. Design of laboratories for safe use of radioisotopes. USAEC Tech. Inf. Service AECU-2226, Oak Ridge, Tenn. 48 p.

Warden, R. E., and W. T. Dagodag. 1976. A guide to the preparation and review of environmental impact reports. Security World Publ. Co., Los Angeles. 138 p.

War Department. 1939. Basic field manual. Field service pocketbook: sketching. FM 21–35, U.S. Gov. Print. Off., Washington, D.C.

War Department. 1944. Advanced map and aerial photography reading. FM 21–26, U.S. Gov. Print. Off., Washington, D.C.

Warren, B. H. 1890. Report on the birds of Pennsylvania. With special reference to the food-habits, based on over four thousand stomach examinations. 2nd ed. Off. of Ornithol. State Board Agric., West Chester, Pa. 434 p.

Warren, E. R. 1942. The mammals of Colorado: their habits and distribution. 2nd ed. Univ. Oklahoma Press, Norman. 330 p.

Warren, R. J., and R. L. Kirkpatrick. 1978. Indices of nutritional status in cottontail rabbits fed controlled diets. J. Wildl. Manage. 42(1): 154–158.

Warrick, C. W. 1976. Artificial brush piles. USDI Bur. Land Manage. Tech. Note 290, Denver, Colo. 5 p.

Watson, A. 1965. A population study of ptarmigan *(Lagopus mutus)* in Scotland. J. Anim. Ecol. 34(1): 135–172.

Watt, K. E. F., (ed.). 1966. Systems analysis in ecology. Academic Press, New York. 276 p.

Watt, K. E. F. 1968. Ecology and resource management: a quantitative approach. McGraw-Hill, N.Y. 450 p.

Way, D. S. 1973. Terrain analysis. Dowden, Hutchinson and Ross Inc., Stroudsburg, Pa. 392 p.

Weaver, D. K., and J. A. Kadlec. 1970. A method for trapping breeding adult gulls. Bird-Banding 41(1): 28–31.

Weaver, H. R., and W. L. Haskell. 1968. Age and sex determination of the chukar partridge. J. Wildl. Manage. 32(1):46–50.

Weaver, R. A., F. Vernoy, and B. Craig. 1959. Game water development on the desert. Calif. Fish and Game 45(4):333–342.

Webb, G. J. W., and H. Messel. 1977. Crocodile capture techniques. J. Wildl. Manage. 41(3):572–575.

Webb, J. 1940. Identification of rodents and rabbits by their fecal pellets. Trans. Kansas Acad. Sci. 43:479–481.

Webb, R. 1957. Range studies in Banff National Park, Alberta, 1953. Can. Wildl. Serv. Manage. Bull. No. 1. 24 p.

Webb, W. L. 1943. Trapping and marking white-tailed deer. J. Wildl. Manage. 7(3):346–348.

Weck, J. 1966. Dictionary of forestry in five languages: German, English, French, Spanish, Russian. Elsevier Publ., New York and Amsterdam. 573 p.

Weeden, R. B. 1961. Outer primaries as indicators of age among rock ptarmigan. J. Wildl. Manage. 25 (3):337–339.

Weeden, R. B. 1964. Breeding density, reproductive success, and mortality of rock ptarmigan at Eagle Creek, central Alaska, from 1960–1964. Alaska Dept. Fish and Game, Fed. Aid Wildl. Restoration Proj. W-6-R., Juneau. 13 p.

Weeden, R. B. 1965. Breeding density, reproductive success, and mortality of rock ptarmigan at Eagle Creek, Central Alaska, from 1960 to 1964. Trans. N. Am. Wildl. Conf. 30: 336–348.

Weeden, R. B., and A. Watson. 1967. Determining the age of rock ptarmigan in Alaska and Scotland. J. Wildl. Manage. 31(4):825–826.

Weeks, J. L. 1972. An improved patagial streamer for waterfowl. Bird-Banding 43(2):140–141.

Weigand, J. P. 1977. A technique for sexing live Hungarian partridge in the field. p. 150–153 *in* PERDIX. Part I. Hungarian partridge workshop. Minot, N.D. 233 p.

Weil, B. H., (ed.). 1954. The technical report: its preparation, processing, and use in industry and government. Reinhold Publ. Co., New York. 485 p.

Weiland, E. C. 1964. Methods of tripping traps with a solenoid. Inland Bird-Banding News 36(1): 3–4, 7, 9.

Weissman, A. 1962. Licking behavior of rats on a schedule of food reinforcement. Science 135(3498): 99–101.

Welch, P. S. 1948. Limnological methods. McGraw-Hill Book Co., New York. 381 p.

Weller, M. W. 1956. A simple field candler for waterfowl eggs. J. Wildl. Manage. 20(2):111–113.

Weller, M., and D. V. Derksen. 1972. Use of time-lapse photography to study nesting activities of birds. Auk 89(1):196–200.

Weller, M. W., D. L. Trauger, and G. L. Krapu. 1969. Breeding birds of the West Mirage Islands, Great Slave Lake, N.W.T. Can. Field-Nat. 83(4):344–360.

Wentges, H. 1975. Medicine administration by blowpipe. Vet. Rec. 97(15):281.

Wentworth, B. C., E. M. Pollack, and J. R. Smyth, Jr. 1967. Sexing day-old pheasants by sex-linked down color. J. Wildl. Manage. 31(4):741–745.

Wertz, W. A. 1965. Interpretation of soil surveys for wildlife management. Am. Midl. Nat. 75(1):221–231.

Wesley, D. E., K. L. Knox, and J. G. Nagy. 1970. Energy flux and water kinetics in young pronghorn antelope. J. Wildl. Manage. 34(4): 908–912.

Wesley, D. E., K. L. Knox, and J. G. Nagy. 1973. Energy metabolism of pronghorn antelopes. J. Wildl. Manage. 37(4):563–573.

Wesson, J. A., III, P. F. Scanlon, R. L. Kirkpatrick, and H. S. Mosby. 1979a. Influence of chemical immobilization and physical restraint on packed cell volume, total protein, glucose, and blood urea nitrogen in blood of white-tailed deer. Can. J. Zool. 57(4):756–767.

Wesson, J. A., III, P. F. Scanlon, R. L. Kirkpatrick, and H. S. Mosby. 1979b. Influence of time of blood sampling after death on blood measurements of the white-tailed deer. Can. J. Zool. 57(4):777–780.

Wesson, J. A., III, P. F. Scanlon, R. L. Kirkpatrick, H. S. Mosby, and R. L. Butcher. 1979c. Influence of chemical immobilization and physical restraint on steroid hormone levels in blood of white-tailed deer. Can. J. Zool. 57(4):768–776.

Wesson, J. A., III, P. F. Scanlon, and R. E. Mirarchi. 1974. Immobilization of white-tailed deer with succinylcholine chloride success rate, reactions of deer and some physiological effects. Proc. Southeastern Assoc. Game and Fish Commissioners 28:500–506.

West, G. C., and M. S. Meng. 1968. Seasonal changes in body weight and fat and the relation of fatty acid composition to diet in the willow ptarmigan. Wilson Bull. 80(4): 426–441.

West, N. O., and H. C. Nordan. 1976. Hormonal regulation of reproduction and the antler cycle in the male Columbian black-tailed deer *(Odocoileus hemionus columbianus)*. Part I. Seasonal changes in the histology of the reproductive organs, serum testosterone, sperm production, and the antler cycle. Can. J. Zool. 54(10):1617–1636.

Westemeier, R. L. 1973. Prescribed burning in grassland management for prairie chickens in Illinois. Proc. Tall Timbers Fire Ecol. Conf. 12:317–338.

Westerskov, K. 1950. Methods for determining the age of game bird eggs. J. Wildl. Manage. 14(1):56–67.

Westerskov, K. 1956. Age determination and dating nesting events in the willow ptarmigan. J. Wildl. Manage. 20(3):274–279.

Westfall, C. Z., and R. B. Weeden. 1956. Plastic neck markers for woodcock. J. Wildl. Manage. 20(2): 218–219.

Westoby, M., G. R. Rost, and J. A. Weis. 1976. Problems with estimating herbivore diets by microscopically identifying plant fragments from stomachs. J. Mammal. 57(1):167–172.

Weston, H. G., Jr. 1953. Ring-necked pheasant nesting activities on Birge and Grass Lakes, Emmet County, Iowa, 1953. Iowa Bird Life 23 (2):26–29.

Wetherbee, D. K. 1961. Investigations in the life history of the common corturnix. Am. Midl. Nat. 65(1): 168–186.

Wetmore, A. 1960. A classification for the birds of the world. Smith. Misc. Coll. 139(11):1–37.

Whatley, H. E., M. E. Lisano, and J. E. Kennamer. 1977. Plasma corticosterone level as an indicator of stress in the eastern wild turkey. J. Wildl. Manage. 41(2):189–193.

Wheeler, R. H., and J. C. Lewis. 1972. Trapping techniques for sandhill crane studies in the Platte River Valley. U.S. Fish and Wildl. Serv. Resour. Publ. 107. 19 p.

Whitaker, G. A., E. R. Roach, and R. H. McCuen. 1976. Inventorying habitats and rating their value for wildlife. Proc. Southeastern Assoc. Game and Fish Commissioners 30:590–601.

Whitcomb, B. L., R. F. Whitcomb, and D. Bystrak. 1977. Island biogeography and "habitat islands" of eastern forests. III. Long-term turnover and effects of selective logging on the avifauna of forest fragments. Am. Birds 31(1):17–23.

Whitcomb, R. F. 1977. Island biogeography and "habitat islands" of eastern forest. I. Introduction. Am. Birds 31(1):3–5.

White, C. M. 1967. A device for immobilizing trapped deer. J. Wildl. Manage. 31(4):844–845.

White, G. C. 1979. Computer generated graphics to display biotelemetry data. p. 210–214 *in* F. M. Long, (ed.). Proc. 2nd Inter. Conf. on Wildlife Biotelemetry. Univ. of Wyoming, Laramie. 259 p.

White, J. A., and C. E. Braun. 1978. Age and sex determination of juvenile band-tailed pigeons. J. Wildl. Manage. 42(3):564–569.

Whitehead, G. K. 1964. The deer of Great Britain and Ireland: an account of their history, status and distribution. Routledge and Kegan Paul, London. 597 p.

Whitehouse, S., and D. Steven. 1977. A technique for aerial radio tracking. J. Wildl. Manage. 41(4):771–775.

Whitford, W. G., and M. I. Conley. 1971. Oxygen consumption and water metabolism in a carnivorous mouse. Comp. Biochem. Physiol. 40(3A):797–803.

Whitlock, R. 1974. Deer. Priory Press, London. 80 p.

Whitlock, S. C., and H. J. Miller. 1947. Gunshot wounds in ducks, J. Wildl. Manage. 11(3):279–281.

Whitney, L. F. 1937. How to breed dogs. Orange Judd, New York. 336 p.

Whittaker, R. H. 1965. Dominance and diversity in land plant communities. Science 147 (3655):250–260.

Whittaker, R. H. 1972. Evolution and measurement of species diversity. Taxon 21(2/3):213–251.

Wiant, H. V., and E. D. Michael. 1978. Potential of 3 P sampling in wildlife and range management. p. 304–306 *in* H. G. Lund et al. Integrated inventories of renewable natural resources. Proceedings of the workshop: USDA For. Serv., Rocky Mt. For. and Range Exp. Stn. Gen. Tech. Rep. RM–55, Fort Collins, Colo. 482 p.

Wiegert, R. G. 1975. Simulation models of ecosystems. p. 311–338 *in* R. F. Johnston, P. W. Frank and C. D. Michener, (eds.). Ann Rev. Ecol. System. Annual Review, Inc. Palo Alto, Calif. Vol. 6. 422 p.

Wiener, J. G., and M. H. Smith. 1972. Relative efficiencies of four small mammal traps. J. Mammal. 53 (4):868–873.

Wiens, J. A. 1974. Habitat heterogeneity and avian community structure in North American grasslands. Am. Midl. Nat. 91(1):195–213.

Wiens, J. A., S. G. Martin, W. R. Holthaus, and F. A. Iwen. 1970. Metronome timing in behavioral ecology studies. Ecology 51(2): 350–352.

Wight, H. M. 1930. Michigan's game dog. Amer. For. 36(10):620–623, 637.

Wight, H. M. 1931. Reproduction in the eastern skunk *(Mephitis mephitis nigra)*. J. Mammal. 12(1): 42–47.

Wight, H. M. 1938. Field and laboratory technic in wildlife management. Univ. Michigan Press, Ann Arbor. 107 p.

Wight, H. M. 1956. A field technique for bursal inspection of mourning doves. J. Wildl. Manage. 20(1):94–95.

Wight, H. M., L. H. Blankenship, and R. E. Tomlinson. 1967. Aging mourning doves by outer primary wear. J. Wildl. Manage. 31(4):832–835.

Wilbert, D. E. 1963. Some effects of chemical sagebrush control on elk distribution. J. Range Manage. 16 (2):74–78.

Wilbur, H. M., and J. M. Landwehr. 1974. The estimation of population size with equal and unequal risks of capture. Ecology 55(6):1339–1348.

Wilbur, S. R. 1967. Live-trapping North American upland game birds. USDI Fish and Wildl. Serv. Spec. Sci. Rep., Wildl. No. 106. 37 p.

Wilhm, J. L. 1968. Use of biomass units in Shannon's formula. Ecology 49(1):153–156.

Will, G. B., and E. F. Patric. 1972. A contribution toward a bibliography on wildlife telemetry and radio tracking. New York Dept. of Environ. Conserv. Delmar Wildl. Res. Lab., Delmar. 56 p.

Will, G. C., and G. I. Crawford. 1970. Elevated and floating nest structures for Canada geese. J. Wildl. Manage. 34(3):583–586.

Willard, E. E., and J. L. Schuster. 1973. Chemical composition of six southern Great Plains grasses as related to season and precipitation. J. Range Manage. 26(1):37–38.

Willey, C. H. 1974. Aging black bears from first premolar tooth sections. J. Wildl. Manage. 38(1):97–100.

Williams, C. S. 1934. A simple method for sectioning mammalian hairs for identification purposes. J. Mammal. 15(3):251–252.

Williams, C. S. 1938. Aids to the identification of mole and shrew hairs with general comments on hair structure and hair determination. J. Wildl. Manage. 2(4):239–250.

Williams, C. S., and W. H. Marshall. 1937. Goose nesting studies on Bear River Migratory Waterfowl Refuge. J. Wildl. Manage. 1(3–4):77–86.

Williams, C. S., M. W. Williams, H. A. Baldwin, and R. F. Childs. 1969. A new non-lethal medicated bullet. J. Ariz. Acad. Sci. Program Synop. 5:21.

Williams, G. L. 1972. Soil fertilizers in wildlife management. p. 13–25 *in* L. H. Carpenter and G. L. Williams, (eds.). A literature review on the role of mineral fertilizers in big game range management. Colo. Div. Game, Fish and Parks Spec. Rep. No. 28, Denver. 25 p.

Williams, G. R. 1967. The breeding biology of California quail in New Zealand. Proc. N.Z. Ecol. Soc. 14:88–99 (N.Z. Dept. of Internal Aff. Wildl. Publ. No. 94).

Williams, J. G. 1963. A field guide to the birds of east and central Africa. Houghton Mifflin, Collins Press, London. 288 p.

Williams, L. E., Jr. 1961. Notes on wing molt in the yearling wild turkey. J. Wildl. Manage. 25(4):439–440.

Williams, L. E., Jr. 1966. Capturing wild turkeys with alpha-chloralose. J. Wildl. Manage. 30(1):50–56.

Williams, L. E., Jr. 1967. Preliminary report on methoxymol to capture turkeys. Proc. Southeastern Assoc. Game and Fish Commissioners 21: 189–193.

Williams, L. E., Jr., and R. W. Phillips. 1972. Tests of oral anesthetics to capture mourning doves and bobwhites. J. Wildl. Manage. 36(3):968–971.

Williams, L. E., Jr., and R. W. Phillips. 1973. Capturing sandhill cranes with alpha-chloralose. J. Wildl. Manage. 37(1):94–97.

Williams, M. B. 1977. Needs for the future: radically different types of mathematical models. p. 225–240 *in* D. L. Solomon and C. Walters, (eds.). Mathematical models in biological discovery. Springer-Verlag, New York. 240 p.

Williams, M. W., C. S. Williams, L. A. Meeks, and B. E. Gunning. 1969. Analgesic tolerance to etorphine (M–99) and morphine in the mouse. Proc. Soc. Exptl. Biol. and Med. 131(1):97–100.

Williams, O. 1962. A technique for studying microtine food habits. J. Mammal. 43(3):365–368.

Williams, O. B. 1969. An improved technique for identification of plant fragments in herbivore feces. J. Range Manage. 22(1):51–52.

Williams, T. C. and E. J. Burke. 1973. Solar power for wildlife telemetry transmitters. Am. Birds. 27(4):719–720.

Williams, T. C., J. M. Williams, J. M. Teal, and J. W. Kanwisher. 1974. Homing flights of herring gulls under low visibility conditions. Bird Banding 45(2):106–114.

Williams, T. I., (ed.). 1974. A biographical dictionary of scientists. 2nd ed. John Wiley & Sons, New York. 641 p.

Williamson, K. 1970. Birds and modern forestry. Bird Study 17(2):167–176.

Williamson, V. H. H. 1951. Determination of hairs by impressions. J. Mammal. 22(1):80–84.

Willson, M. F. 1974. Avian community organization and habitat structure. Ecology 55(5):1017–1029.

Wilson, D. E., S. M. Hirst, and R. P. Ellis. 1977. Determination of feeding preferences in wild ruminants from trocar samples. J. Wildl. Manage. 41(1):70–75.

Wilson, E. B., Jr. 1952. An introduction to scientific research. McGraw-Hill, New York. 375 p.

Wilson, K. A., and E. A. Vaughan. 1944. The bobwhite quail in eastern Maryland. Md. Game and Inland Fish Comm., Annapolis. 138 p.

Wilson, L. O., J. Day, J. Helvie, G. Gates, T. L. Hailey, and G. K. Tsukamoto. 1973. Guidelines for capturing and re-establishing desert bighorns. Trans. Desert Bighorn Council. 17:137–154.

Wilson, L. O., and D. Hannans. 1977. Guidelines and recommendations for design and modification of livestock watering developments to facilitate safe use by wildlife. U.S. Bur. of Land Manage. Tech. Note 305, Denver, Colo. 20 p.

Wing, L. W. 1956. Natural history of birds. Ronald Press, New York. 539 p.

Winge, O. 1950. Inheritance in dogs. Comstock Publ. Co. Ithaca, N.Y. 153 p.

Winkler, W. G., and D. B. Adams. 1968. An automatic movie camera for wildlife photography. J. Wildl. Manage. 32(4):949–952.

Winston, F. A. 1954. Status, movement and management of the mourning dove in Florida. Fla. Game and Freshwater Fish Comm. Tech. Bull. No. 2, Tallahassee. 86 p.

Wint, G. B. 1951. Improved method for marking game birds for identification in the field. Oklahoma Agric. and Mech. College Bull. 48, Stillwater. 7 p.

Winter, K. B., and R. F. Honess. 1952. The use of transmission spectra and crystallography of hemoglobin in law enforcement. J. Wildl. Manage. 16(1):111–113.

Winterhelt, S., and E. D. Bailey. 1973. The training and care of the versatile hunting dog. N. Am. Versatile Hunt. Dog Assoc. 105 p.

Wisdom, M. J. 1976. Use of W.S.O. bird computer bank in Wisconsin. Passenger Pigeon 38(4):158–162.

Wishart, W. 1969. Age determination of pheasants by measurement of proximal primaries. J. Wildl. Manage. 33(3):714–717.

Wishart, W. 1977. Aging and sexing sharptail grouse by primary measurements and upper tail coverts. Proc. Prairie Grouse Tech. Counc. Conf. 12:2–3.

Witherby, H. F., F. C. R. Jourdain, N. F. Ticehurst, and B. W. Tucker. 1943. The handbook of British birds. H. F. and G. Witherby, London. 5 vols.

Wobeser, G. A., and F. A. Leighton. 1979. A simple burrow entrance live trap for ground squirrels. J. Wildl. Manage. 43(2):571–572.

Woehler, E. E., and J. M. Gates. 1970. An improved method of sexing ring-necked pheasant chicks. J. Wildl. Manage. 34(1):228–231.

Wolf, G. 1964. Isotopes in biology. Academic Press Inc., New York. 173 p.

Wolff, J. O., and D. F. Holleman. 1978. Use of radioisotope labels to establish genetic relationships in free-ranging small mammals. J. Mammal. 59(4):859–860.

Wolfson, A., D. S. Farner, H. Friedmann, S. C. Kendeigh, E. Mayr, A. H. Miller, and M. M. Nice. 1954. Unpublished theses in ornithology. Auk 71(2):191–197.

Wood, C. A. 1931. An introduction to the literature of vertebrate zoology. Oxford Univ. Press, London. 643 p.

Wood, D. N. 1966. Chemical literature and the foreign-language problem. Chem. in Britain 2(8):346–350.

Wood, J. E., D. E. Davis, and E. V. Komarek. 1958. The distribution of fox populations in relation to vegetation in southern Georgia. Ecology 39(1):160–162.

Wood, M. 1969. A bird-bander's guide to determination of age and sex of selected species. Pennsylvania State Univ., Coll. of Agric., University Park, Pa. 181 p.

Wood, R. A., K. A. Nagy, N. S. MacDonald, S. T. Wakakuwa, R. J. Beckman, and H. Kaaz. 1975. Determination of oxygen-18 in water contained in biological samples by charged particle activation. Anal. Chem. 47(4):646–650.

Woodall, P. F. 1978. Omental fat: a condition index for redbilled teal. J. Wildl. Manage. 42(1):188–190.

Woodcock, W. E. 1976. Aerial reconnaissance and photogrammetry with small cameras. Photogramm. Eng. Remote Sensing 42(4):503–511.

Woodford, F. P. 1968. Scientific writing for graduate students; a manual on the teaching of scientific writing. Rockefeller Univ. Press, New York. 190 p.

Woolf, A. 1970. Immobilization of captive and free-ranging white-tailed deer *(Odocoileus virginianus)* with etorphine hydrochloride. J. Am. Vet. Med. Assoc. 157(5):636–640.

Woolf, A., H. R. Hays, W. B. Allendry, and J. S. Swart. 1973. Immobilization of wild ungulates with etorphine HCL. J. Zoo Anim. Med. 4(4):16–19.

Wooten, W. A. 1955. A trapping technique for band-tailed pigeons. J. Wildl. Manage. 19(3):411–412.

Work, E. A., Jr., and D. S. Gilmer. 1976. Utilization of satellite data for inventorying prairie ponds and lakes. Photogramm. Eng. Remote Sensing 42(5):685–694.

Worrall, V. 1964. Wild mammals and the law, p. 168–173 *in* H. N. Southern, (ed.). The handbook of British mammals. Blackwell Sci. Publ., Oxford. 465 p.

Wrazen, J. A., and G. E. Svendsen. 1979. Sampling stomach contents of live small mammals using intubation. J. Mammal. 60(2):414–415.

Wright, E. G. 1939. Marking birds by imping feathers. J. Wildl. Manage. 3(3):238–239.

Wright, P. L. 1947. The sexual cycle of the male long-tailed weasel *(Mustela frenata)*. J. Mammal. 28(4):343–352.

Wright, P. L. 1948. Breeding habits of captive long-tailed weasels. Am. Midl. Nat. 39(2):338–344.

Wright, P. L. 1966. Observations on the reproductive cycle of the American badger *(Taxidea taxus)*. p. 27–45 *in* I. W. Rowlands, (ed.). Comparative biology of reproduction in mammals. Symp. Zool. Soc. Lond. No. 15, Academic Press, London. 559 p.

Wright, P. L., and M. W. Coulter. 1967. Reproduction and growth in Maine fishers. J. Wildl. Manage. 31(1):70–87.

Wright, P. L., and R. W. Hiatt. 1943. Outer primaries as age determiners in gallinaceous birds. Auk 60(2): 265–266.

Wright, P. L., and R. Rausch. 1955. Reproduction in the wolverine *(Gulo gulo).* J. Mammal. 36(3):346–355.

Wright, V. L. 1978. Causes and effects of biases on waterfowl harvest estimates. J. Wildl. Manage. 42(2): 251–262.

Wyoming Game and Fish Dept. 1977. Handbook of biological techniques. Wyoming Dept. Game and Fish, Cheyenne. 393 p.

Yale Forestry Library. 1962. Dictionary catalog of the Yale forestry library. G. K. Hall, Boston, Mass. 12 vols.

Yang, K. C., C. J. Krebs, and B. L. Keller. 1970. Sequential live-trapping and snap-trapping studies of Microtus populations. J. Mammal. 51 (3):517–526.

Yates, R. F. 1942. Counting the birdhouse visits. Nature Mag. 35(4):192.

Yeager, L. E. 1940. Subjects for filing wildlife literature. J. Wildl. Manage. 4(1):44–54.

Yeager, L. E. 1941. A contribution toward a bibliography on North American fur animals. Ill. Nat. Hist. Surv. Biol. Notes No. 16, Urbana. 209 p.

Yeager, L. E., W. W. Sandfort, and L. J. Lyon. 1951. Some problems of pheasant management on irrigated land. Trans. N. Am. Wildl. Conf. 16:351–367.

Yeatter, R. E. 1934. The Hungarian partridge in the Great Lakes region. Univ. of Michigan Sch. For. and Conserv. Bull. No. 5. 92 p.

Yeatter, R. E. 1948. Bird dogs in sport and conservation. Ill. Nat. Hist. Surv., Circ. 42, Urbana. 64 p.

Yoakum, J. D. 1978. Managing rangelands for the American pronghorn antelope. p. 584–587 *in* D. N. Hyder, (ed.). Proc. First Int. Rangeland Congr. 762 p.

Yocom, C. F. 1943. The Hungarian partridge, *Perdix perdix* Linn. in the Palouse Region, Washington. Ecol. Monogr. 13(2):167–201.

Yocom, C. F., and S. W. Harris. 1965. Plumage descriptions and age data for Canada goose goslings. J. Wildl. Manage. 29(4):874–877.

York, W., and K. Huggins. 1972. Rompun (Bay VA 1470). J. Zoo Anim. Med. 3(4):15–17.

Yoshida, T., and M. Kundatsu. 1964. Studies on caecum digestion. No. 6. Free amino acids in the cecal contents, hard feces, and soft feces of the rabbit. Jap. J. Zootech. Sci. 35:64–69.

Young, S. 1955. Big game exclosures in wildlife management in Utah. Proc. Utah Acad. Sci. 32:65–69.

Young, S. P. 1933. Hints on mountain-lion trapping. Bur. of Biol. Surv. Leafl. No. 94, Washington, D.C. 8 p.

Young, S. P. 1958. The bobcat of North America. Stackpole Co., Harrisburg, Pa., and The Wildl. Manage. Inst., Washington, D.C. 193 p.

Young, S. P., and E. A. Goldman. 1944. The wolves of North America. Am. Wildl. Inst., Washington, D.C. 636 p. (republ. Dover Publ. Inc., New York).

Young, S. P., and E. A. Goldman. 1946. The puma, mysterious American cat. Am. Wildl. Inst., Washington, D.C. 358 p.

Young, S. P., and H. H. T. Jackson. 1951. The clever coyote. Stackpole Co., Harrisburg, Pa., and Wildl. Manage. Inst., Washington, D.C. 411 p.

Youngson, R. W., and B. Mitchell. 1967. Red deer immobilization Isle of Rhum. Nature Conservancy (Kinlock) Rep. 13 p.

Yourdon, E. 1975. Techniques of program structure and design. Prentice Hall, Inc. Englewood, N.J. 364 p.

Ysenbrandt, H. J. B., Th. A. J. Selten, J. J. M. Verschuren, T. Kock, and H. P. Kimmich. 1976. Biotelemetry, literature survey of the past decade. Biotelemetry 3:145–250.

Zach, R., and J. B. Falls. 1976. Bias and mortality in the use of tartar emetic to determine the diet of ovenbirds (Aves: Parulidae). Can. J. Zool. 54(10):1599–1603.

Zarn, M. 1974. Burrowing owl, *Speotyto cunicularia hypugaea.* U.S. Bur. of Land Manage. Endangered Species Rep. No. 11, Denver, Colo. 25 p.

Zarrow, M. X., J. M. Yochim, and J. L. McCarthy. 1964. Experimental endocrinology: a sourcebook of basic techniques. Academic Press, New York and London. 519 p.

Zeleny, L. 1976. The bluebird: how you can help its fight for survival. Indiana Univ. Press, Bloomington. 170 p.

Zeleny, L. 1977. Song of hope for the bluebird. Natl. Geogr. Mag. 151(6): 854–865.

Zepp, R. L., and R. L. Kirkpatrick. 1976. Reproduction in cottontails fed diets containing a PCB. J. Wildl. Manage. 40(3):491–495.

Zippin, C. 1956. An evaluation of the removal method of estimating animal populations. Biometrics 12(2): 163–189.

Zippin, C. 1958. The removal method of population estimation. J. Wildl. Manage. 22(1):82–90.

Zoological Society of London. 1971. List of serials, with title abbreviations pertaining to 1970 literature. Zool. Rec. Suppl. 200 p.

Zucca, J. J. 1954. A study of the California clapper rail. The Wasmann J. Biol. 12:135–153.

Zweifel, F. W. 1961. A handbook of biological illustration. Univ. Chicago Press, Chicago, Ill. 131 p.

Zwickel, F. C. 1975. Nesting parameters of blue grouse and their relevance to populations. Condor 77 (4):423–430.

Zwickel, F. C., and J. F. Bendell. 1967a. Early mortality and the regulation of numbers in blue grouse. Can. J. Zool. 45(5):817–851.

Zwickel, F. C., and J. F. Bendell. 1967b. A snare for capturing blue grouse. J. Wildl. Manage. 31(1): 202–204.

Zwickel, F. C., and A. N. Lance. 1966. Determining the age of young blue grouse. J. Wildl. Manage. 30(4): 712–717.

Zwickel, F. C., and C. F. Martinsen. 1967. Determining age and sex of Franklin spruce grouse by tails alone. J. Wildl. Manage. 31(4):760–763.

Zyznar, E., and P. J. Urness. 1969. Qualitative identification of forage remnants in deer feces. J. Wildl. Manage. 33(3):506–510.

INDEX

B

D

E

F

H

I

J

M

N

O

P

S

T

U

V

W

X

Y

Z